ABRAHAM LINCOLN

Abraham Lincoln
A Life

VOLUME ONE

Michael Burlingame

The Johns Hopkins University Press
Baltimore

© 2008 The Johns Hopkins University Press
All rights reserved. Published 2008
Printed in the United States of America on acid-free paper

Johns Hopkins Paperback edition, 2013
9 8 7 6 5 4 3 2 1

The Johns Hopkins University Press
2715 North Charles Street
Baltimore, Maryland 21218-4363
www.press.jhu.edu

The Library of Congress has cataloged the hardcover edition of this book as follows:

Burlingame, Michael, 1941–
    Abraham Lincoln : a life / Michael Burlingame.
        p. cm.
    Includes bibliographical references and index.
    ISBN-13: 978-0-8018-8993-6 (hardcover: alk. paper)
    ISBN-10: 0-8018-8993-6 (hardcover: alk. paper)
    1. Lincoln, Abraham, 1809–1865.   2. Presidents—United States—
Biography.   I. Title
    E457.B95 2008
    973.7092—dc22
    [B]   2007052919

A catalog record for this book is available from the British Library.

ISBN-13: 978-1-4214-0973-3
ISBN-10: 1-4214-0973-9

*Special discounts are available for bulk purchases of this book. For more information,
please contact Special Sales at 410-516-6936 or specialsales@press.jhu.edu.*

The Johns Hopkins University Press uses environmentally friendly book
materials, including recycled text paper that is composed of at least 30 percent
post-consumer waste, whenever possible.

For Lewis E. Lehrman, Lincolnian extraordinaire

CONTENTS

AUTHOR'S NOTE

Sixteenth president of the United States, the Great Emancipator, and an eloquent spokesman for Union, freedom, and democracy, Abraham Lincoln is one of the most studied and beloved of all Americans. This biography, the first comprehensive one to appear in two-thirds of a century, builds on a foundation of abundant fresh materials—some recently unearthed, others drawn from more traditional sources that historians have underutilized. It offers new interpretations, connecting Lincoln's private and public lives, and incorporates the findings of countless excellent scholarly works on nineteenth-century America published since the appearance of the only comparable multi-volume biography, Carl Sandburg's *Abraham Lincoln: The Prairie Years* (two volumes, 1926), and *Abraham Lincoln: The War Years* (four volumes, 1939). Unlike the ten-volume life-and-times biography of Lincoln that his White House secretaries John G. Nicolay and John Hay published in 1890, this work does not attempt to relate the history of the Civil War. The focus here remains Lincoln himself. Telling the story of Lincoln's life in detail, this narrative aims to avoid a problem that the eminent Civil War historian Allan Nevins identified. "Heavy compression," he warned, could leave a biography of Lincoln "pemmicanized—nutritious but flavorless."[1]

The year after Carl Sandburg's *Abraham Lincoln: The War Years* appeared, he penned a letter that resonates with me. In response to a critic who faulted those volumes for their analytical shallowness, use of dubious sources, lack of documentation, and many factual errors, he wrote of his amazement "that the book got born, considering that many days when completely exhausted I despaired of ever bringing it through in accordance with the original design." By the time he finished, he said, he had spent some $11,000 on the project, "was near a physical wreck, and believed the book would only slowly and across a long future make its way to the audience for whom it was intended."[2]

While I can identify with the sentiments expressed in Sandburg's letter, my approach to Lincoln differs from his. Sandburg was a poet, I am a scholar. Our treatment of the famous letter of condolence to the Widow Bixby, written in 1864, vividly illustrates the difference between those two sensibilities. With a striking command of language, Sandburg described the document thus: "[T]hese were blood-color syllables of a sacred music." I could never craft such a memorable sentence. As a scholar, I was more interested in a question Sandburg skipped over: Did Lincoln actually write the Bixby letter? The answer, as I have tried to show, based on stylistic grounds and on documentary evidence, is No. John Hay, Lincoln's gifted assistant personal secretary, composed it for the president's signature.

Sandburg's biography is long on elegant touches but short on research in unpublished sources. As a result, his biography compares to mine as John Constable's full-size sketches of his 6-foot paintings of English country life compare with the finished canvasses. The subjects—people, horses, cottages, rivers, rainbows, churches, and the like—are all visible in Constable's sketches. But they lack the color, detail, and vividness of the finished works—though both are of the same size. I hope that readers will conclude that this biography, with its fresh information, is more like Constable's finished paintings, offering a portrait of Lincoln in higher resolution and sharper focus, with greater color, texture, and detail.

This biography relies on many sources simply unavailable to Sandburg and others, including the Lincoln Papers at the Library of Congress, which were first opened to public inspection in 1947. Access to that rich collection of 18,000 documents rendered all previous Lincoln biographies obsolete. Manuscript collections of Lincoln's contemporaries have proven exceptionally revealing. In letters, diaries, journals, reminiscences, and other unpublished writings one can glean much new evidence about Lincoln: people would speak with him and then describe their conversations in diaries or letters; they would also comment on him and his policies and doings. Discovering such references in unpublished manuscripts requires much panning of historical gravel; every now and then a nugget appears, and readers will find many of them throughout this book.

Newspapers are another badly neglected source of information about Lincoln. They especially illuminate his early political career, for they not only shed light on his legislative work and political campaigns; they also contain scores of anonymous and pseudonymous contributions, many apparently the handiwork of Lincoln himself. These are particularly helpful because few of his early speeches survive (shorthand reporting was unknown in the 1830s and 1840s).

Other sources of new information include the reminiscences of people who knew Lincoln. Historians tend to view such recollections with skepticism, for memories can dim with time. But the increasing respectability of oral history has changed many scholarly minds. We are fortunate to have the work of Lincoln's law partner and biographer William H. Herndon, who gathered invaluable interview material during his research for a life of Lincoln. Herndon also corresponded with many of Lincoln's friends, family members, colleagues, and neighbors, creating one of the first oral history collections in the country. Without it, we would have little knowledge of Lincoln's early life. Also helpful are interviews that other early biographers, most notably John G. Nicolay and Ida M. Tarbell, conducted in the course of their own research. For decades after the president's assassination, newspapers published recollections of Lincoln's acquaintances. Clipping collections at various repositories as well as searchable on-line historical newspaper archives make those articles readily accessible.

In the year 2000, the Lincoln Legal Papers appeared, reproducing and indexing more than 100,000 documents and illuminating the 5,200 cases that Lincoln handled in two dozen years at the Illinois bar. Only since its appearance can we speak with any authority about Lincoln's career as a lawyer.

Some of the new information I edited and saw into publication in the form of documentary editions of journals, diaries, letters, reminiscences and journalism, of Lincoln's presidential secretaries. It occurred to me that someone could take all this material, combine it with the important findings made by recent historians of mid-nineteenth-century America, and write a fresh cradle-to-grave, detailed, multi-volume biography. A number of senior historians—James M. McPherson, Don E. Fehrenbacher, Richard N. Current, Kenneth M. Stampp, John Niven, Hans L. Trefousse, James A. Rawley, Robert V. Bruce, Douglas L. Wilson, Allen C. Guelzo, William C. Harris, William Hanchett, Philip Shaw Paludan, Mark E. Neely, Gabor S. Boritt, Wayne C. Temple, and Charles B. Strozier, all of whom had made considerable contributions to the Lincoln literature—might have undertaken that challenge. None of them seemed inclined to do so. David Herbert Donald, my mentor at both Princeton and Johns Hopkins in the 1960s, would have been an ideal candidate, but he chose to write a one-volume biography, which appeared in 1995. So, with some trepidation, I decided to try it myself.

Relying on traditional and new-found primary sources like manuscripts, newspapers, reminiscences, and public records, this work also makes full use of the secondary literature that has appeared in the last generation. Historians have ingeniously employed records of election results, legislative roll calls, census returns, and other quantifiable phenomena, and their work helps place Lincoln in his historical context with more precision and clarity than studies based solely on literary sources. The fruits of painstaking efforts by such quantative historians as Kenneth J. Winkle and the late William E. Gienapp thus make signal contributions to this biography.

Some of the interpretations in this biography, and some of the evidence, originally appeared in my *The Inner World of Abraham Lincoln* (1994). Like that volume, *Abraham Lincoln: A Life* offers psychological interpretations as well as fresh evidence. An early student of Lincoln's life plausibly noted that "we can never arrive at an approximately full understanding" of his character until we have made "an extended and intensive study . . . of it from a psychological standpoint."[3] "I do not know," Samuel Eliot Morison wrote to Albert J. Beveridge in the 1920s about Lincoln's bouts of depression, "whether it has occurred to you to call the psychologists and psychiatrists into consultation, but it seems to me they would be more useful advisers than historians."[4] Use of the personality theory and the findings of clinical psychologists does indeed help to illuminate Lincoln's depressions, as well as other patterns in his life that otherwise appear puzzling.

Examining Lincoln's inner life involves speculation, an enterprise that professional historians usually shy away from. But as one Lincoln authority sensibly argued, "the biographer is a person who has by long and arduous concentration upon the particular subject put himself in a unique relation to it. His views ought to be more valuable than the views of other people. Of course, I don't want him to dogmatize ever about anything he can't prove; at the same time I do want him wherever the subject becomes obscure to give me tentatively his own views."[5] Many educated guesses, informed by over twenty years of research on Lincoln, appear in this biography. Each such guess might well begin with a phrase like "in all probability," or "it may well be that," or "it seems likely that." Such warnings, if inserted into the text, would prove wearisome; readers are encouraged to provide such qualifiers silently whenever the narrative explores Lincoln's unconscious motivation.

This caveat should not seem startling. When the practice of history started becoming professional, one of the discipline's leading practitioners, Leopold von Ranke, announced that he sought to describe what occurred in the past "*wie es eigentlich gewesen*" [as it really happened]. Modern historians, more acutely aware of the problems of subjectivity than Ranke was, seek to reconstruct the past "*wie es wahrscheinlich gewesen*" [as it probably happened]. In 1983, the president of the Organization of American Historians observed in his inaugural address that "all historians, whether we admit it or not, work on the basis of what has been called the principle of maximum probability. The educated guess that some attribute to historical-mindedness is really a probability statement."[6]

As central themes this work argues that Lincoln's leadership proved to be the North's secret weapon in winning the Civil War; that Lincoln was an effective leader because he achieved a level of psychological maturity unmatched in the history of American public life; and that such a high level of consciousness was acquired slowly and painfully as he overcame the economic and emotional poverty of his childhood.

Recent scholarship on race enables us to understand Lincoln's views on that subject in context. While some of his early statements grate on modern ears, it should be borne in mind that he belonged to his era. Frontier Illinois, home to many emigrants from south of the Ohio River, was one of the most racist of the free states. Assumptions of black inferiority prevailed among whites not only there but throughout the entire country. Lincoln ultimately became far more idealistic and egalitarian on racial matters than most of his contemporaries, including the popular Democrat Stephen A. Douglas and his numerous admirers.

Lincoln was no reluctant emancipator. He delayed issuing the Emancipation Proclamation because his keen sense of duty, an emotion as strong as his profound hatred of slavery, made him hesitate to violate the oath of office he had taken, an oath that required him to uphold the Constitution. It did not authorize him to do whatever he wanted to do with regard to slavery. The need to keep the support of conservatives and moderates, who were glad to fight for the preservation of the Union but reluctant to fight for black freedom, also constrained him. When in September 1862 he did finally announce his intention to emancipate slaves in the rebellious states, he did so not for short-term political advantage but in spite of the strong possibility that it might harm Republican chances in the upcoming elections. By 1865, the preeminent black leader Frederick Douglass had ample reason to call Lincoln "emphatically the black man's president."[7]

Character is destiny, and Lincoln's remarkable character helped make him not only a successful president but also a model which can be profitably emulated by all. Somehow he managed to be strong-willed without being willful, righteous without being self-righteous, and moral without being moralistic. The importance of his character was recognized during his administration. In December 1863, after Lincoln had issued a momentous proclamation dealing with amnesty and pardon for rebels,

Charles Eliot Norton, a Cambridge intellectual who had once been harshly critical of the president, expressed admiration for that document and its author: "How wise and how admirably timed is his Proclamation. As a state paper its naiveté is wonderful. Lincoln will introduce a new style into state papers; he will make them sincere, and his honesty will compel even politicians to like virtue. I conceive his character to be on the whole the great net gain from the war."[8]

To keep this long book from becoming even longer, I have pared down the manuscript and streamlined the notes. In the original unedited version, which is available online at the website of the Lincoln Studies Center at Knox College in Galesburg, Illinois (www.knox.edu/lincolnstudies), almost every sentence is footnoted; in these printed volumes, only directly quoted material is documented. The text as well as the documentation of the online version is fuller, for much of the material left on the cutting room floor, as it were, is restored in what might be called, in the parlance of filmmakers, a director's cut. That online version will be updated as mistakes are discovered and new information comes to light.

ABRAHAM LINCOLN

1

"I Have Seen a Good Deal of the Back Side
of This World"
Childhood in Kentucky
(1809–1816)

One day in the middle of the Civil War, Abraham Lincoln stole time from his busy schedule to pen some wise paternal advice to a young Union captain who had been squabbling with his superiors. Quoting from *Hamlet*, the president wrote that a father's admonition to his son—"Beware of entrance to a quarrel, but being in, bear it that the opposed may beware of thee"—was good counsel "and yet not the best." Instead, Lincoln enjoined the captain: "Quarrel not at all." The reasons Lincoln gave were practical: "No man resolved to make the most of himself, can spare time for personal contention. Still less can he afford to take all the consequences, including the vitiating of his temper, and the loss of self-control. Yield larger things to which you can show no more than equal right; and yield lesser ones, though clearly your own. Better give your path to a dog, than be bitten by him in contesting for the right. Even killing the dog would not cure the bite."[1] Born into emotional and economic poverty, Lincoln early on "resolved to make the most of himself" and did so, adhering to those precepts.

Ancestry

Like many exceptional children of unexceptional parents, Lincoln was quite curious about his ancestors, especially his grandfathers, neither of whom he knew. He was so intrigued that he planned to conduct genealogical research after he left the presidency. In 1858, when asked about his forebears, he revealed more than a passing acquaintance with his family tree: "I believe the first of our ancestors we know anything about was Samuel Lincoln, who came from Norwich, England, in 1638, and settled in a small Massachusetts place called Hingham, or it might have been Hanghim."[2] (Lincoln loved wordplay.) In two brief autobiographical sketches written for the campaign of 1860, he devoted much space to his lineage. The following year, Lincoln told a Yorkshireman that he planned to visit England, the home of his ancestors.

His father's father was known as Captain Abraham, a rank he attained by 1776 while serving in the Virginia militia. Born in 1744 in Pennsylvania, the future Captain moved with his father, John, and the rest of their family to the Shenandoah

Valley of Virginia around 1766. They settled along Linville Creek in Augusta (later Rockingham) County, where John Lincoln farmed a tract of 600 acres, one-third of which he sold to his son Abraham in 1773. The following year Abraham participated in Lord Dunmore's expedition against the Shawnees, and during the Revolution he joined General Lachlan McIntosh's futile campaign against Fort Detroit.

For unknown reasons, in 1780 the Captain departed with his wife and children on a 250-mile trek to the remote and dangerous Indian hunting grounds of Kentucky while the Revolutionary War still raged and attacks on settlers were common. In 1784 alone, Indians killed more than a hundred migrants traveling the Wilderness Road from Virginia to Kentucky, which was little more than the trail first blazed by Daniel Boone in 1775. Perhaps Grandfather Abraham wished to avoid taxes, or he may have been lured westward by the prospect of easy gains in land speculation. His decision to sell a large farm in western Virginia for paper money showed bad judgment because the soil there was so fertile that German pioneer settlers had made the area highly productive. Captain Abraham's inability to thrive in Virginia suggests that he may have been shiftless.

Captain Abraham died a violent death on the "dark and bloody ground" of frontier Kentucky. As a boy, the future president often heard this harrowing tale, which he called "the legend more strongly than all others imprinted upon my mind and memory."[3] Working his farm one spring day in 1786, the 42-year-old Grandfather Abraham was ambushed by an Indian, who shot him dead before the terrified eyes of his young son, Thomas (father-to-be of the sixteenth president). As the Indian prepared to kidnap the lad, his older brother Mordecai dashed back to the family cabin, grabbed a rifle, aimed at the silver ornament dangling from the Indian's neck, and squeezed the trigger. Luckily for Thomas, his brother's aim was true, and the boy escaped unharmed, at least physically. The Indian may have belonged to a tribe the Captain had battled during his militia service.

Lincoln's opinion of his namesake grandfather is not recorded, but he may well have admired him. Some gifted children with disappointing fathers romanticize their grandfathers, even if they scarcely knew them. In an 1861 speech to New Jersey legislators, Lincoln paid glowing tribute to the soldiers of the Revolution, and Captain Abraham may have been a lifelong source of inspiration to Lincoln as he strove to make the most of himself. In a campaign biography that Lincoln himself read and corrected, William Dean Howells asserted that his subject had "the stubborn notion that because the Lincolns had always been people of excellent sense, he, a Lincoln, might become a person of distinction."[4]

What Lincoln knew about his other grandfather is hard to say. Lincoln once described him as "a Virginia planter or large farmer" who took sexual advantage of a poor, credulous young woman named Lucey Hanks, granddaughter of William Lee, a plantation overseer accused of beating a slave to death. The fruit of that union was Nancy Hanks, mother of the future president. From this aristocratic progenitor, Lincoln believed that he inherited "his power of analysis, his logic, his mental activity, his ambition, and all the qualities that distinguished him from the other members and descendants of the Hanks family."[5]

This grandfather's identity, unknown to history, may well have been known to Lincoln, who was acquainted with several members of the Hanks family, including two great-aunts who had been born in Virginia before or during the Revolution, and also his great-uncle Billy Hanks, father of Lincoln's rail-splitting partner, John Hanks. The Hankses played a long-lasting role in Lincoln's life, caring for his beloved stepmother until her death in 1869. It seems likely that the Hanks family would have shared with Abe what they knew about Nancy Hanks's father.

Lincoln's description of his aristocratic grandsire represents a variation of the "family romance" phenomenon, which causes some children to speculate that they are actually the offspring of more distinguished parents than the ones who raised them. Most people outgrow these fantasies, but some adults—including exceptional people or men with very distant fathers—tend to maintain an unusually strong sense of family romance throughout life. Lincoln fits this category on both counts, for he was truly exceptional and had a distant relationship with his father.

Father Thomas

Lincoln's father, Thomas, was quite undistinguished. As his son later wrote, "by the early death of his father and very narrow circumstances of his mother, even in childhood [Thomas was] a wandering, laboring boy." Born around 1776 in Virginia's Shenandoah Valley, he moved with his parents and four siblings to Kentucky in 1780. Finding most land in the fertile Bluegrass region already taken, the Lincolns pushed on to the hardscrabble terrain between the Cumberland and Green rivers where they established a farm. Later, evidently fearing hostile Indians in that remote locale, they moved to a site on Long Run in Jefferson County. There they lived in a stockade, 18 miles from Louisville.

After Captain Abraham's death, his widow, Bathsheba, and their children resettled in Washington County, where they would be safer. Bathsheba (d. ca. 1833) later stayed with her daughter Nancy, wife of William Brumfield, who owned a large farm near Hardinsburg in Breckinridge County. After Bathsheba's son, Thomas, bought a farm in 1803 on Mill Creek, she and the Brumfields moved in. Three years later, the Brumfields purchased 225 acres a few miles to the north, where they built a log house. Bathsheba, the shrewdest and most intelligent member of the family, prodded both her rather lazy son-in-law and young Thomas, hiring the latter out for good wages.

The documentary record reveals little about Thomas's activities in the decade after his father's death. Under the law of primogeniture, his eldest brother, Mordecai, inherited everything from the paternal estate, which included a few hundred acres in Kentucky. Mordecai may have treated his younger brother unkindly. Emilie Todd Helm, half-sister of Mary Todd Lincoln, "said that the reason why Thomas Lincoln grew up unlettered was that his brother Mordecai, having all the land in his possession . . . turned Thomas out of the house when the latter was 12 years old; so he went out among his relations & the Berrys et al. and there grew up."[6] In 1795, Thomas served in the Kentucky militia for a month, and the following year he worked on a milldam in Hardin County. While laboring there, he lived with his father's cousin, Hananiah Lincoln, a resident of Elizabethtown, 45 miles southwest of Louisville.

Thomas and Hananiah remained in that village only until 1798, when they evidently headed south to Cumberland County. While in that region, Thomas spent time in Tennessee with his prosperous uncle, Isaac Lincoln, whose only child had died quite young. Thomas might have become a surrogate son, but Isaac disapproved of young Tom's indolence and improvidence.

Returning to Kentucky the following year, Thomas shuttled back and forth between Washington and Cumberland counties. In 1802, he moved to Hardin County, where his name appeared on the tax lists for the next fourteen years. In 1803, he purchased a 238-acre farm on Mill Creek where he lived while working in nearby Elizabethtown, a hamlet whose population in 1810 numbered 181. How Thomas could afford to buy that farm is unclear. Perhaps his brother Mordecai shared some of his patrimony with him after Thomas attained his majority, or Thomas may have purchased the Mill Creek property with the savings his mother had set aside from the wages he earned when she hired him out.

Three years after he bought the Mill Creek farm, Thomas journeyed to New Orleans. On June 12, 1806, shortly after returning from Louisiana, he married Nancy Hanks in a ceremony that took place near Poortown in Washington County. Following a brief honeymoon, the newlyweds moved to Elizabethtown, where their first child, Sarah, was born less than eight months after her parents' wedding. A journalist described their residence as "a shed . . . almost bare of household fittings and quite unfit for a human dwelling place."[7] Why the couple did not live on the Mill Creek property is a mystery. Nancy perhaps wished to be closer to her family than to her husband's relatives. She may have been lonely in Elizabethtown, where she had no kin, and perhaps for that reason at the end of 1807 Thomas moved 14 miles to a rock-strewn spread in the "Barrens" on the South Fork of Nolin Creek, known as the Sinking Spring farm. It was near the homestead where Thomas and Betsy Sparrow, who raised Nancy, lived with their foster child, Dennis Hanks, and where Nancy's aunt, Polly Hanks Friend, had settled.

Thomas gambled when he chose that site, for rather than a deed, he purchased a title bond (an assignment of someone's contested right to the land). He would own the property only if others met their financial obligations. Dennis Hanks, a cousin who lived with the Lincolns for three years during Abe's youth, reported that Thomas "couldn't make a living by his trade [of carpentry]; there was scarcely any money in the country. So Tom took up some land—mighty poor land, but the best he could get when he hadn't much to trade for it."[8] Thomas Lincoln may have left Elizabethtown for Nolin Creek because he believed his reputation as a carpenter had been damaged when an influential citizen sued him for shoddy work. The nearest settlement, two and a half miles to the south, was in the vicinity of Hodgen's Mill. On February 12, 1809, in a cabin that an observer called "a miserable habitation," Nancy delivered a baby boy, who was named Abraham after Thomas's father.[9]

The Lincolns remained in Kentucky until 1816, when they removed to Indiana. There Nancy Hanks Lincoln died two years later. Thomas remarried in 1819, and eleven years afterwards he moved to Illinois, where he would remain until his death in 1851. He had known more than his fair share of hardship and sorrow.

Thomas Lincoln shared only a few things in common with his son. Both were able wrestlers as well as good-natured, humorous, and gifted storytellers. A surviving example of Thomas's humor concerns his second wife, who allegedly remarked one day: "We have lived together a long time and you have never yet told me whom you like best, your first wife or me." He responded: "Oh now Sarah, that reminds me of old John Hardin down in Kentucky who had a fine looking pair of horses, and a neighbor coming in one day and looking at them said, 'John, which horse do you like best?' John replied, 'I can't tell, one of them kicks and the other bites and I don't know which is wust.'"[10]

But the qualities that would make Abraham Lincoln famous—his intellectual power, ambition, idealism, eloquence, spirituality, integrity, political wisdom, judgment, leadership—were lacking in Thomas. Henry C. Whitney, to whom Lincoln described his childhood, said that from Thomas Lincoln his son "inherited only 'infancy, ignorance and indigence.'"[11] Few of Thomas's neighbors could remember anything special about him other than that he was "a plain unpretending plodding man," "a good average man," who "attended to his work" and was "among the very commonest of the plain pioneers," "honest and harmless," "illiterate, yet always truthful, conscientious and religious," and "peaceable good."[12] Thomas evidently could read a little but was unable to write anything other than his signature.

Unlike his tall, rangy son, Thomas was thick, weighing between 180 and 200 pounds. He was a bit stoop-shouldered, somewhat clumsy as he walked, and strong. Dennis Hanks found it remarkable that Thomas, though "not a fleshy man," was "built so compact that it was difficult to find or feel a rib in his body."[13] Thomas had dark gray eyes, a low forehead, heavy eyebrows, a sharp chin, and an unusually big Roman nose, which was his most prominent feature. He was indifferent to clothes, and his taste in food was simple—two traits he also shared with his son. "His whole appearance," said one neighbor, "denoted a man of small intel[l]ect and less ambition, and such he was."[14]

If Thomas lacked intellectual power and driving ambition, he impressed people favorably as honest and sociable, slow to take offense, with a lot of common sense. Though he seldom had a cross word for anyone, he did use profanity occasionally. When his young daughter repeated an oath of his, he received a scolding from his wife and never swore again. (One day during his presidency, Lincoln used the expression "by jings" while visiting the telegraph office. When asked about that expression, he apologized to the operators for his profanity, explaining that "by jings is swearing, for my good old mother taught me that anything that had a *by* before it is swearing.")[15] When Lincoln's friend William G. Greene visited Thomas in 1836, he found his manners "Back[w]oodsish" but was "charmed" by his wit and humor and thought him a "mighty hospitable, and a very entertaining host."[16]

For all his humor, Thomas could be taciturn and moody. He often became depressed and withdrew into himself, sometimes wandering out in the barrens for hours on end. Bouts of depression would hardly be surprising in a man who, as a boy, had witnessed his father's murder and then endured wandering, rootless poverty and hard labor. Other losses—recurring financial setbacks and the deaths of his second son in

1813, of his wife in 1818, and of his daughter in 1828—deepened his dejection. He frequently said, "everything that I ever teched either died, got killed or was lost."[17] On other occasions he lamented: "It's the hand of Providence laid upon me."

Thomas's susceptibility to depression may have been in part genetic. His brother Mordecai and his sons were known "as men who at times communed with themselves, absorbed in their own thoughts."[18] Prone to melancholia, depression, and gloomy spells called the "horrors," Mordecai allegedly would "come into his mother's house and sit down for long periods of time without saying a word unless it were to mutter an oath against something or curse somebody." He would sometimes "take up his violin . . . and pace the floor."[19] The "horrors" resembled bouts of *delirium tremens* and may in fact have been the result of heavy drinking, for he reportedly "exercised the privilege (very common in those days) of 'indulging freely' whenever he pleased which happened very often."[20] He also betrayed signs of paranoia, accusing Catholics of stealing his father's land, and over time his hatred of Roman priests intensified.

Many other members of the family had "moody spells."[21] Mary Rowena Lincoln, mother of Thomas's nephew James Lincoln, was reportedly a victim of the "Lincoln hippo [i.e., hypo or depression]." Benjamin Mudd, son of Elizabeth Lincoln Mudd, suffered from what was called "the Lincoln horrors."[22] An uncle of Thomas's confessed to a court that he suffered from "a deranged mind."[23] Another relative in the same area, Mary Jane Lincoln, was committed to the Illinois Hospital for the Insane after a court hearing in which a jury determined "that the disease is with *her* hereditary." She had gone insane in 1854 at the age of 26, was committed to the state asylum in 1867, and died there twenty-one years later.[24]

Thomas Lincoln prospered neither as a carpenter nor a farmer. He learned woodworking from Nancy Hanks's uncle Joseph Hanks Jr. and made his living as a "Cabinet and House Carpenter" until he wed. Thereafter he supplemented his income by farming. His carpentry skills were so rudimentary that people called him a "rough" and "cheap carpenter" who could only "put doors, windows, and floors in log houses" and do a "tolerable" job of joining.[25] He continued laboring as a carpenter after he moved to Indiana, making tables, coffins, doors, and window casings. He worked when jobs came to him, but would not seek them out. Some customers were unhappy with his work. In 1807, Denton Geohegan of Elizabethtown refused to pay Thomas for hewing timbers for his sawmill; some timbers were too short, others too long. (Thomas sued for his fee and won.)

Thomas was even less successful as a farmer, partly because he chose unpromising land to till. The Nolin Creek property—birthplace of the future president—had poor soil except in a few small patches. When in 1811, Thomas abandoned that farm (after the owner took title and refused to lease the property to him), he moved to equally unpromising terrain on Knob Creek, 9 miles away. In 1816, he attempted to make a fresh start in Indiana, and unwisely selected 160 heavily timbered acres. He also built his cabin more than a mile from a reliable water source. He showed similarly bad judgment in Illinois in the 1830s and 1840s.

Even if he had selected land more shrewdly, Thomas lacked the industry, ambition, and intellect to prosper. As Dennis Hanks put it, Thomas "was a man who took the world Easy" and "never thought that gold was God." Hanks's son-in-law was more blunt: Thomas, he declared, "was v[er]y careless about his business, a poor Manager, at time[s] accumulated considerable property which he always managed to make way with about as fast as he made it, & was what is generally called an unlucky Man in business."[26] In 1835, Thomas and four partners leased a mill for a year; when they failed to pay the agreed-upon rent, they were successfully sued.

Several times Thomas took boatloads of pork and other goods down the Mississippi River to New Orleans, usually making little money. In a particularly unfortunate transaction, he was cheated out of the entire load. His son Abraham described that calamity: "Father often told me of the trick that was played upon him by a 'pair of sharpers.' It was [in 1815] the year before we moved from Kentucky to Indiana that father concluded to take a load of pork down to New Orleans. He had a considerable amount of his own, and he bargained with the relatives and neighbors for their pork, so that altogether he had quite a load. He took the pork to the Ohio River on a clumsily constructed flat boat of his own make. Almost as soon as he pushed out into the river a couple of sleek fellows bargained with him for his cargo, and promised to meet him in New Orleans where they arranged to pay him the price agreed upon. He eagerly accepted the offer, transferred the cargo to the strangers and drifted down the river, his head filled with visions of wealth and delight. He thought that he was going to accomplish what he had set out to do without labor or inconvenience. Father waited about New Orleans for several days, but failed to meet his whilom friends. At last it dawned upon him that he had been sold, and all that he could do was to come back home and face the music."[27]

Thomas Lincoln also lost money buying and selling farms, especially in Kentucky, where an archaic surveying system, which permitted claims to be identified by trees, stones, creek bends, and other such imprecise landmarks, produced chaos, leading to innumerable lawsuits. Kentucky law did not require a qualifying examination for surveyors, who reportedly were never correct except by accident. Years later, Lincoln recalled how Kentuckians "used to be troubled with . . . mysterious relics of feudalism, and titles got into such an almighty mess with these pettifoggin' encumbrances turnin' up at every fresh tradin' with the land, and no one knowin' how to get rid of 'em."[28] Because the size of the Mill Creek farm was unclear, Thomas was able to sell it for only £100, though he had paid £118 for it a decade earlier. For $200 he purchased a title bond to the 300-acre Nolin Creek farm and lost it all, including the value of the improvements he had made on the property. He was ejected from the 30-acre Knob Creek farm, which he had leased, not purchased.

Memories of his family's trouble with land titles may have predisposed Lincoln to become a surveyor and a lawyer. As an attorney, he advised young men aspiring to the bar, "Never stir up litigation. A worse man can scarcely be found than one who does this. Who can be more nearly a fiend than he who habitually overhauls the register of deeds in search of defects in titles, whereon to stir up strife, and put money in his pocket?"[29]

Thomas fared just as badly in Indiana. First, he squatted on a 160-acre tract of government land for ten months and then bought it on credit for $320. Thomas probably delayed making a down payment for the same reason that most pioneers did: lack of cash. In 1817 he put down $80, but over the following decade he made no further payments. In 1827 he relinquished half the farm, reducing his debt to $80, which he met by turning over to the government title to 80 acres in a distant county, a property that he had mysteriously acquired four weeks earlier. In 1830 he sold this $160 farm for $125. When a decade later Thomas found himself unable to meet obligations he had assumed for four parcels of Illinois land, his generous son Abraham gave him what amounted to a gift of $200 for a 50-acre tract that had cost Thomas only $50. Shortly thereafter Abraham again rescued his father by paying off a mortgage that Thomas had assumed.

Thomas made scant use of the land he occupied, usually clearing only a few acres for a garden and a corn patch. At Knob Creek, he cultivated only 6 acres along the creek in a strip about 40 feet wide on either side. He worked enough to sustain life, and no more. For the most part, Thomas avoided the market economy, remaining a subsistence farmer. He did, however, grow a little tobacco, which he peddled for 10 cents a pound. On at least one occasion he offered that commodity to satisfy a debt on a horse he had bought on credit. The creditor, impressed that a man would part with his tobacco to pay what he owed, forgave the $10.

According to Thomas's stepson-in-law, John J. Hall, "Thomas Lincoln did not improve with age nor with increasing responsibilities. He was still the same kind and genial 'fellow,' but grew more and more shiftless and good for nothing as the years rolled on." At the rocky Nolin Creek farm, Hall reported, "he did not cultivate the soil nor 'fix up' the old shanty."[30] In Illinois, Tom, along with his stepson, John D. Johnston, and Johnston's five sons, tilled only 40 of their 120 acres. In an area where the average farm was worth $1,600, Tom valued his farm at $100 in the 1850 census, even though he was older than his neighbors, had had time to accumulate more property, and had a large number of family hands to work the land. Thomas ranked behind 79 percent of his neighbors in terms of wealth.[31] George B. Balch, an Illinois neighbor, noted that while most farmers took their crops to market in a wagon, Tom Lincoln used "a basket or a large tray." Balch characterized Thomas as "uneducated, illiterate, and contented with a 'from hand to mouth' living"—in sum, "an excellent spec[imen] of poor white trash," "rough," "lazy," and "worthless." He owned a "few sheep" behind which he "talked an[d] walked slow." Balch added that "[s]everal anecdotes of his ignorance and singularity might be related, but we forbear."[32]

Other neighbors agreed with Balch's assessment of Thomas Lincoln. In Indiana, Nathaniel Grigsby called Thomas "a piddler—always doing but doing nothing great. . . . He wanted few things and Supplied them Easily."[33] William E. Grigsby regarded Thomas as "no account."[34] Robert Mitchell Thompson of Kentucky, whose mother was a cousin of Nancy Hanks, reported that "Thomas Lincoln was always poor" and "was all the time going hunting or roaming around, not satisfied to stay long in any one place."[35] Still others testified that Thomas was "rather indolent and improvident," had an "aversion to work," and was "careless and inert and dull."[36]

William G. Greene spent time at the Lincolns' farm at Goosenest Prairie, in Coles County, Illinois, and observed that Thomas was barely able to eke out a living. Greene found Thomas residing "in a little cabin that cost perhaps $15, and with many evidences of poverty about him." The cabin "looked so small and humble" that Greene "felt embarrassed." It had no stable, no outhouse, and no shrubbery or trees.[37] An early historian of Coles County, who interviewed acquaintances of Thomas Lincoln, called him "one of those easy, honest, commonplace men, who take life as they find it, and, as a consequence, generally find it a life of poverty." He "possessed no faculty whatever of preserving his money, when he made any, hence he always remained poor. He was easily contented, had few wants, and those of a primitive nature. He was a foe to intemperance, strictly honest, and, supposing others the same, often suffered pecuniary losses."[38] Sophie Hanks, who lived in the Lincoln family's Indiana cabin for several years, had a son who attributed Thomas's lack of ambition to frontier isolation: "he was like the other people in that country. None of them worked to get ahead. There wasn't no market for nothing unless you took it across two or three states. The people raised just what they needed."[39]

Thomas preferred hunting to farming. Dennis Hanks recalled, "[w]e all hunted pretty much all the time, Especially so when we got tired of work—which was very often I will assure you."[40] Such behavior was common on the Midwestern frontier. A Northeasterner who moved to central Illinois described the inhabitants there as "destitute of any energy or enterprise," and "their labors and attention being chiefly confined to the hunting of game."[41] In sketches of pioneer life in that same locale, Francis Grierson portrayed a representative farmer, Zack Caverly, who explained, "My ole daddy larnt me te go through this sorrowin' vale like the varmints do—easy en nat'ral like, never gallopin' when ye kin lope, en never lopin' when ye kin lay down. It's a heap easier."[42] Thomas, in short, was a classic Southern backcountry cracker (a term originating in northern Britain). Often of Celtic background, crackers were famously easygoing, improvident, unacquisitive, lazy, and restless. They preferred to spend their days hunting, fishing, and loafing rather then farming. They had little use for education and were often illiterate. Their folkways and culture derived largely from northern England, Scotland, Ireland, Wales, Cornwall, and the Hebrides.

Abraham Lincoln's view of his father's indolence is unrecorded, but he did scold his stepbrother John D. Johnston for that flaw in letters which may reflect his attitude not only toward Johnston but also toward Thomas Lincoln. In 1848, when Johnston asked him for a loan, Lincoln declined, saying: "At the various times when I have helped you a little, you have said to me 'We can get along very well now' but in a very short time I find you in the same difficulty again. Now this can only happen by some defect in your *conduct*. What that defect is, I think I know. You are not *lazy*, and still you *are* an *idler*. I doubt whether since I saw you, you have done a good whole day's work, in any one day. You do not very much dislike to work; and still you do not work much, merely because it does not seem to you that you could get much for it. This habit of uselessly wasting time, is the whole difficulty; and it is vastly important to you, and still more so to your children that you should break this habit." When Johnston, who was "born tired," proposed to leave Illinois for Missouri, Lincoln scolded him in language that could well have applied to his peripatetic father: "such a notion is utterly foolish. What can you do in Missouri, better than here [in Illinois]? Is the land any richer? Can you there, any more than here, raise corn, & wheat & oats, without work? Will any body there, any more than here, do your work for you? If you intend to go to work, there is no better place than right where you are; if you do not intend to go to work, you can not get along any where. Squirming & crawling about from place to place can do no good. You have raised no crop this year, and what you really want is to sell the land, get the money and spend it—part with the land you have, and my life upon it, you will never after, own a spot big enough to bury you in. Half you will get for the land, you spend in moving to Missouri, and the other half you will eat and drink, and wear out, & no foot of land will be bought. Now I feel it is my duty to have no hand in such a piece of foolery."[43]

Thomas Lincoln's indolence, lack of ambition, and disdain for education put him at odds with his smart, enterprising son. Thomas, Abraham said, "grew up, litterally without education" and "never did more in the way of writing than to bunglingly sign his own name."[44] This patronizing language lends credence to the testimony of Dennis Hanks, who called Lincoln "a mother's boy" and doubted "whether Abe loved his father Very well or Not," and concluded "I Don[']t think he Did."[45] The feeling was mutual. According to Augustus H. Chapman, Dennis Hanks's son-in-law, Thomas Lincoln "never showed by his actions that he thought much of his son Abraham when a Boy. [H]e treated him rather unkind" and "always appeared to think much more of his stepson John D Johnston than he did of his own Son Abraham."[46] This preference is not surprising, for Thomas shared much in common with his improvident stepson.

Lincoln's aversion to his father persisted into adulthood. He never once invited Thomas or his wife to Springfield during the entire twenty-four-year span Lincoln lived there. He rarely lent money to his cash-strapped sire. When his law practice took him near his father's home in Coles County, Illinois, Lincoln stayed with Dennis Hanks rather than under the paternal roof. As Thomas lay dying in 1851, his 41-year-old son refused his deathbed appeal for a visit; Lincoln icily enjoined his stepbrother to tell their father "that if we could meet now, it is doubtful whether it would not be more painful than pleasant."[47] After Thomas died, Lincoln failed to attend the funeral, nor did he have a tombstone placed on the grave. Lincoln did not name a son for his father until after Thomas's death. He belittled his father when, referring to one of Thomas's brothers, he told a friend, "I have often said that Uncle Mord had run off with all the talents of the family."[48]

Lincoln's estrangement stemmed not just from Thomas's emotional reserve, painful though that may have been. More deeply wounding was "his father's cold and inhuman treatment of him."[49] Caroline Dall, who spoke with William H. Herndon (Lincoln's law partner and biographer) in 1866 and spent three days examining the biographical materials he had accumulated, said Thomas Lincoln "ill-treated A[braham] to such an extent that he drove him from home."[50] Augustus H. Chapman deplored Thomas's "great barbarity" in dealing with his boy.[51] Dennis Hanks recalled that Thomas would whip young Abe for minor indiscretions. "Sometimes Abe was a little rude," Hanks testified. "When strangers would ride along & up to his father[']s fence Abe always, through pride & to tease his father, would be sure to ask the stranger the first question, for which his father would sometimes knock him a rod." Thomas Lincoln "would pick up a big clod and knock little Abe off the fence, crying: 'Let older people have the first say, will you boy?" Whenever he was "whipped by his father" he "never bawled but dropt a kind of silent unwelcome tear, as evidence of his sensations—or other feelings."[52]

Thomas avoided whipping or scolding his son in front of visitors but would administer punishment after they had left. One day a poor neighbor named Jenkins, who usually went barefoot, called on the Lincolns. Abe greeted him heartily: "Hello, Mr. Jenkins. You are doing better than you used to. You have a new pair of boots." Thomas took his son aside and "gave Abe a little drilling" because his remarks may have wounded Jenkins's feelings. "'Well,' said Abe, 'he's got the boots.'"[53] Lincoln's cousin Sophie Hanks "always said that the worst trouble with Abe was when people was talking—if they said something that wasn't right Abe would up and tell them so. Uncle Tom had a hard time to break him of this."[54] She also recalled how Lincoln "very often would correct his father in talking when his father was telling how anything happened and if he didn[']t tell it jest right or left out any thing, Abe would but[t] in right there and correct it."[55] Thomas would then slap the lad. Abe was physically punished for other kinds of misbehavior, too. He received a beating, for instance, when he released a bear cub from one of Thomas's traps.

Lincoln's father regarded physical strength as sufficient to make a manly man and thought time spent on schooling was wasted. He would "slash" Abe "for neglecting his work by reading."[56] Sometimes he even threw out the boy's books. Five years after Lincoln, at the age of 22, left his father's home, Thomas Lincoln scoffed: "I suppose that Abe is still fooling hisself with eddication. I tried to stop it, but he had got that fool idea in his head, and it can't be got out. Now I hain't got no eddication, but I get along far better than ef I had." Thomas then showed how he kept his accounts by marking a rafter with a piece of coal and proudly declared: "that thar's a heap better'n yer eddication." He added that "if Abe don't fool away all his time on his books, he may make something yet."[57]

Mother Nancy

Lincoln's estrangement from his father is well documented, but little is known about his relationship with his mother, who died when Abe was just 9 years old. In fact, little is known about her at all. She was born in Virginia around 1783 or 1784. Accounts of her appearance differ widely. Her complexion was variously described as "dark," "sandy," "pale," and "exceedingly fair," while her hair was deemed light by some and dark by most. Her eyes were evidently hazel. Though one observer described her as "a heavy built Squatty woman," most people remembered her as taller than average (one estimate placed her at 6 feet). She had "a spare delicate frame," weighed "about 120 pounds," and was "not at all good looking," with a face "Sharp and angular," "high forehead," and "rather Coarse" features that gave her "the appearance of a laboring woman."[58] A minister who interviewed people who knew the Lincolns in Indiana said she was "about five feet ten inches" tall, "bony," "angular," and "lean," with "long arms," large ears, nose, and mouth, small gray-blue eyes, and a big head on a long, stringy neck. Her cheekbones were high and her chest was sunken.[59]

Nancy Hanks was evidently an intelligent, kind woman. Her son called her "intellectual" and "a woman of genius."[60] Dennis Hanks agreed, praising her "quick perception" and good memory.[61] Nathaniel Grigsby said she was noted throughout the family for her strong mind and was "a brilliant woman," far "superior to her husband in Every way."[62] She was notably affectionate and displayed "tenderness—charity & love to the world."[63] Her "cheerful disposition and active habits were a dower" to the pioneers with whom she lived.[64] She also enjoyed a reputation for outdoing all the local women at spinning flax. At camp meetings, the deeply religious Nancy would shout in an attempt to get others to repent.

She was not very sociable, however. She did not talk much, nor did she visit with her neighbors; they, in turn, stopped coming to see her because she did not return their calls. Her lack of sociability may have been linked to her apparent sadness, even depression. Neighbors remembered her "sad appearance" and observed that she was "rather gloomy."[65] Her son Abraham, her relative John Hanks, and Indiana neighbors all commented on her melancholy. A Kentuckian attributed her depression and aloofness to gossip: "People talked about her sometimes, and that depressed her, hurt her."[66] Those hurtful rumors perhaps concerned the unchaste ways of Nancy's mother, Lucey Hanks, who bore Nancy out of wedlock in Virginia and was later charged with fornication in Kentucky. At first, Lucey turned baby Nancy over to her own parents; later the youngster was raised by her childless aunt and uncle, Thomas and Elizabeth Sparrow. She also lived for a time with Richard Berry and his wife Polly Ewing Berry, friends of Thomas Lincoln. Her mother's lack of interest in her may have predisposed Nancy to depression. That she was "base-born" was well known in Indiana and probably common knowledge in Kentucky, too.

Questions were raised about Nancy Hanks's chastity as well as her mother's. Polly Richardson, a neighbor of the Lincolns in both Kentucky and Indiana, told her daughter "that not only was Nancy Hanks an illegitimate child herself but that Nancy was not what she ought to have been," that she was "Loose."[67] Among the people who believed this of Nancy, Judge Alfred M. Brown of Elizabethtown reported that "Rumor says that Nancy Hanks had one child before she married Tho[mas] Lincoln[,] a Son, the father of whom was Isaac Friend."[68] Others called her "of low character," a woman who "did not bear a very virtuous name."[69] William H. Herndon believed that Nancy Hanks "fell in Kentucky about 1805—fell when unmarried—fell afterward."[70] According to Herndon, the "reputation of Mrs. Lincoln is that she was a bold—reckless—daredevil kind of a woman, stepping to the very verge of propriety."[71] Nancy Hanks's wayward behavior may have inspired the story that in a "fair wrestle, she could throw most of the men who ever put her powers to the test." Jack Thomas, clerk of the Grayson County Court, alleged that "he had frequently wrestled with her, and she invariably laid him on his back."[72]

Nancy's courtship with Thomas Lincoln raised some eyebrows. At the time they met she was living in the home of a woman on South Fork Creek, where Thomas Lincoln often came to visit. The young couple would take extensive trips to attend camp meetings and would stay out quite late, scandalizing the neighborhood. Finally, the woman with whom Nancy was staying scolded Thomas for such nocturnal adventures. This reprimand may have prompted Nancy to move temporarily to Washington County and later to marry Tom there, instead of in her adopted home. Other sources, perhaps describing the same woman, testify that Nancy lived with various families in Bourbon County, sewing, weaving, and doing domestic work, and that while there she was courted by Thomas Lincoln, "whose shiftless character caused her friends to think him not worthy of her." A neighbor unrelated to Nancy, "a good kind old lady—a motherly sort of woman," took "a great interest in Nancy" and grew upset because the young woman "got herself 'talked about' from allowing this 'shiftless Linkhorn' to wait on her." The woman persuaded Nancy to go to Washington County with some of her relatives in the Berry family who were attending a camp meeting nearby. She agreed, but if the plan was to get her away from Tom Lincoln, it failed, for he clambered into the wagon and accompanied her.[73]

Some felt that Nancy was not a wanton woman but a victim of idle gossip. Nancy Lincoln Brumfield, Thomas Lincoln's sister, asserted that Nancy Hanks "was more sinned against than sinning." Mrs. Brumfield explained that Nancy visited Elizabethtown when Tom Lincoln was absent, causing tongues to wag. Country folk in that era believed that women should remain at home and work.[74] William H. Herndon observed that "the noblest of women can lose their character quickly in a little village or in a new and sparsely settled country. Everybody knows everybody, and a man's business is the business of the whole community. Such people love to tattle and lie about one another."[75]

Stories about Nancy's unsavory reputation, accurate or not, evidently reached the ears of her son Abe and made him ashamed of her and of her family. Herndon ascribed Lincoln's melancholy in part to his sensitivity about "the origin and chastity of his near and dear relations" and speculated that Lincoln may have felt suicidal because of "the knowledge of his mother's origin."[76] Lincoln "was informed of all this," Herndon believed; "probably it was thrown up to him in Indiana." Herndon reported that "Lincoln remembered the scorn of her neighbors."[77] J. Edward Murr, an Indianan who interviewed several Hoosier acquaintances of the Lincolns, speculated that Abraham "*early* knew that his mother was an illegitimate & this troubled him."[78] Lincoln described his grandmother Lucey as "a halfway prostitute" and acknowledged "that his relations were *lascivious, lecherous,* not to be trusted."[79] Lucey Hanks's sister Nancy had a bastard (Dennis Hanks), and Lucey's daughter Sarah bore six illegitimate children. It was no wonder that in Indiana the Hankses were known as "a peculiar people—not chaste."[80]

Herndon contended that although Lincoln was ashamed of his mother and other Hankses, he did praise her one day around 1850 as the two men were riding in a buggy: "All that I am or hope ever to be I get from my mother—God bless her." Often misinterpreted as a sentimental paean to Nancy Hanks, that statement was in fact a tribute to the genes she passed on to Abraham from her aristocratic father. Lincoln confided to Herndon that his mother was "a bastard," the "daughter of a nobleman—so called of Virginia. My mother's mother was poor and credulous, &c., and she was shamefully taken advantage of by the man. My mother inherited his qualities and I hers." Lincoln asked Herndon: "Did you ever notice that bastards are generally

smarter, shrewder, and more intellectual than others?"[81] Herndon explained that
"[w]hen Lincoln spoke to me as he did, he had reference to his mother's *mind,* nothing
else."[82] In 1887, Herndon wrote that Lincoln believed the "father of Nancy Hanks is
no other than a Virginia planter, large farmer of the highest & best blood of Virginia
& it is just here that Nancy got her good rich blood, tinged with genius. Mr Lincoln
told me that she was a genius & that he got his mind from her." If she had been given
a decent upbringing, Herndon recalled Lincoln telling him, "she must have flourished anywhere, but as it was she was rude & rough. . . . She could not be held to
forms & methods of things; & yet she was a fine woman naturally. It is quite possible
that a knowledge of her origin made her defiant & desperate; she was very sensitive,
sad sometimes—gloomy." Then, Herndon continued, "Lincoln often thought of committing suicide. Why? Did the knowledge of his mother's origin or his own, press the
thought of suicide upon him? Who will weigh the force of such an idea, as illegitimacy on man & woman, especially when that man or woman is very sensitive, such
as Lincoln was?"[83] Whatever the accuracy of Herndon's account, which some scholars
doubt, the great weight of the evidence supports the conclusion that Nancy Hanks
was illegitimate, that her son knew it, and that most likely Lincoln was aware of
his maternal grandfather's identity.

A campaign biographer of Lincoln, John Locke Scripps, reported that his subject
"communicated some facts to me concerning his ancestry which he did not wish to
have published."[84] Scripps was probably alluding to Lincoln's knowledge of his mother's illegitimacy. In the 1890s, eleven Hoosiers who knew Lincoln and several children
of other Indiana acquaintances of Lincoln told J. Edward Murr that Nancy Hanks was
born out of wedlock. Her niece Sophie also asserted that Nancy was illegitimate.

Lincoln may have harbored negative feelings for his mother. At the age of 29, he
made one of the few surviving allusions to her; it was not positive. Describing a
woman whom he had courted, he said that after a long separation, "when I beheld
her, I could not for my life avoid thinking of my mother; and this, not from withered
features, for her skin was too full of fat, to permit its contracting in to wrinkles; but
from her want of teeth, [and] weatherbeaten appearance in general."[85] Lincoln failed
to mark his mother's grave with a stone. In 1844, while campaigning in Indiana, he
told Redmond Grigsby that he would return soon and wanted to have his mother's
gravesite fixed up. But, Grigsby reported, Lincoln "got absorbed in politics and was
never able to get away."[86] In 1860, Lincoln informed Nathaniel Grigsby that he
would return to Indiana and place a monument on his mother's grave. Four years
later, a resident of Spencer County offered to do so if Lincoln would authorize it. A
few weeks before his death, Lincoln allegedly wrote a friend in Gentryville saying
"that in the coming summer, he intended to visit the locality and make provision for
procuring a testimonial of his affection for his mother."[87] Nothing came of these
good intentions.

Little is known about Nancy Hanks Lincoln's treatment of her son. She evidently
dealt out corporal punishment, for when young Abe fell into Knob Creek one summer day and nearly drowned, he feared that his mother might find out and thrash
him. To escape her wrath, he dried his wet garments in the sun.

Nancy Hanks Lincoln, like many of her neighbors, seems to have been an indifferent housekeeper. A woman settler in frontier Illinois attributed the prevalence of squalid cabins to "the incapacity of the mistress of [the] . . . family to appreciate a better condition, or help to create one."[88] The typical Midwestern frontier cabin was described by an English traveler as a "miserable little log-hole."[89] The Lincolns' Sinking Spring abode fit this description. It had a dirt floor and was sparsely furnished, with rough stools serving for chairs. Four legs inserted into a hewed puncheon formed the table. Beds were fashioned from planks placed atop poles which were secured in holes bored in the wall. The dishes were pewter and tin, and the sole cooking utensils were a Dutch oven and a skillet. Only when Thomas Lincoln's second wife, Sarah Bush Johnston, arrived in 1819 did life become less crude for Abe and his sister. Sarah brought a bureau, bed, knives, forks, cooking utensils, and other amenities, as well as a determination to see that a floor was laid, that windows were cut in the walls and covered with greased paper, that the ceiling was painted, and that other improvements were made. If she could persuade Thomas Lincoln to spruce up their abode, it is noteworthy that Nancy failed to do so.

Nancy Hanks Lincoln was content to live in the primitive manner that Thomas favored, never opposing him on any matter. Catering to his simple taste in food, she would walk miles to the nearest mill to have corn ground or to purchase bacon, which, along with cornmeal mush or johnnycake, formed the staple of the family diet.

Nancy may have been casual in her approach to childrearing. A Kentuckian who grew up near Lincoln recalled that in pioneer days "boys were men; their mothers turned them out to go when they got their diapers off and they had to 'root hog or die,' and they got so they could take care of themselves pretty soon. A boy that could not plow when he was eight, was not much of a boy, and all of them had to do it, and they did not whine about it. When they got orders they obeyed them very promptly, and they did not do much talking."[90] Lincoln might have felt neglected, even abandoned, if his mother raised him in this laissez-faire manner. He almost certainly felt abandoned when she died in 1818, leaving 9-year-old Abe with his sister and his unsympathetic father. He may have concluded that his mother did not love him. William Herndon and Jesse Weik, without citing a source, maintained that after Nancy's death and the remarriage of Thomas to Sarah Bush Johnston, "her newly adopted children for the first time, perhaps, realized the benign influence of a mother's love."[91]

Frontier Poverty

Lincoln was ashamed not only of his family background but also of the poverty in which he grew up. When John Locke Scripps interviewed him in 1860, Lincoln expressed reluctance "to communicate the homely facts and incidents of his early life. He seemed to be painfully impressed with the extreme poverty of his early surroundings—the utter absence of all romantic and heroic elements," and even questioned the proposal to have a biography written. "Why Scripps," said Lincoln, "it is a great piece of folly to attempt to make anything out of my early life. It can all be condensed into a single sentence, and that sentence you will find in Gray's Elegy;

'The short and simple annals of the poor.'

That's my life, and that's all you or any one else can make of it."[92] To a close friend Lincoln described "the stinted living" in Kentucky and "pretty pinching times" in Indiana.[93] In 1846 he referred to the "very poor neighbourhood" where he grew up in Indiana.[94] Fourteen years later, he was asked to speak to some homeless and friendless boys in New York. In recounting this event, he recalled his own boyhood: "I thought of the time when I had been pinched by terrible poverty. And so I told them that I had been poor; that I remembered when my toes stuck out through my broken shoes in winter; when my arms were out at the elbows; when I shivered with the cold."[95]

Lincoln did not exaggerate the deprivation he had known as a child. In Kentucky his family's neighbors regarded them as "quite poor," in fact among "the very poorest people."[96] One of those neighbors remembered the Lincoln family living "in abject poverty," characterized Thomas Lincoln as "the poorest man that ever kept house," and maintained that Nancy Hanks Lincoln "was a good woman, whose only fault was that she was very poor."[97] She would walk miles to do laundry at the homes of more prosperous Kentuckians. At the time of Lincoln's birth in 1809, the family lived in "dire poverty," a neighbor recorded.[98] Dennis Hanks, who observed the Lincolns in Kentucky, Indiana, and Illinois, described Thomas as "a Very pore man."[99] Hanks's obituarist said of Hardin County in the early nineteenth century: "It is scarcely possible to exaggerate the rudeness of the society of that time and locality or the primitive character of the people, and there is an overabundance of testimony that the two families [the Lincolns and the Hankses] . . . were below rather than above the average. . . . All the testimony indicates that the families were of the class known as 'poor whites.'"[100] It was the same in Indiana, where one of the Lincolns' sympathetic neighbors, Elizabeth Crawford, invited Abraham's sister Sarah to live in her home. The girl paid for her board by performing housework until she married a year later. When Mrs. Crawford called at the Lincoln home, they had little to offer guests other than raw sweet potatoes, which surprised her. It was not in keeping with the hospitable customs of the frontier. Elizabeth's husband, Josiah Crawford, hired Thomas Lincoln and young Abe to do chores, even though they were "poor help," because he took pity on them.[101]

Others had similar memories of the Lincolns' poverty in Indiana, where they "passed for honest people" but were "very poor."[102] A neighbor there recalled that Lincoln's "folks were awfully poor."[103] Abe was not invited to Elizabeth Ray Grigsby's wedding feast because, unlike other neighbors, he lacked appropriate clothing. At the age of 20, when he tried to buy ready-made shoes on credit, he was mortified when told to come back when he could pay for them. James Grigsby, Sarah Lincoln's brother-in-law, often told his daughter "how poor the [Lincoln] family was."[104] A Hoosier from Rockport called the Lincolns "very poor."[105] A resident of Boonville testified that "the hardships of the [Lincoln] family were extreme."[106] Several other Indianans who had known Lincoln asserted that the "poverty of the Lincolns was extreme." J. Edward Murr claimed that he "could detail a number of incidents touching upon the poverty, not to say the extreme want, of the Lincolns."[107] Murr cited the "extreme poverty of his parents" as a reason why Lincoln could not be considered a typical Kentuckian.[108] Similarly, Joseph D. Armstrong, who during the 1860s and 1870s gathered information about the Lincolns in Indiana, concluded that Thomas "was a very poor man" and that Abe's life "was one of hard labor, and great privation."[109] Lincoln commented wryly on the poverty of his family one evening as his father pronounced the customary blessing over dinner, which that day consisted of a small dish of roasted potatoes. Abe called them "vary poor blessings."[110]

Given the economic and emotional poverty he endured in his early years, it is no wonder that Lincoln, according to his good friend Joseph Gillespie, "felt very strongly that there was more of discomfort than real happiness in human existence under the most favorable circumstances."[111] To an Illinois neighbor Lincoln confided, "I have seen a good deal of the back side of this world."[112]

Old Kentucky Homes

Cut off by a 75-mile-long escarpment misleadingly named Muldraugh Hill, the isolated area of Kentucky where Lincoln spent his first seven years was exceedingly provincial, with few towns, only primitive churches, and virtually no schools. This "Pennyroyal" area got its name because its soil was so poor that nothing but the pennyroyal weed could thrive there. In these backwoods, social life was crude, marred by excessive drinking and savage fighting. Kentuckians fought for the most trivial reasons, if any at all. Often the combatants were merely testing each other's strength, about which they liked to boast. They used their teeth, knees, head, and feet as well as fists as they punched, kicked, scratched, and bit their opponents. They also gouged each other's eyes with thumbs and fingers.

Lincoln was born at Sinking Creek farm, an unpromising homestead of infertile ground, nestled among unproductive ridges. It was "a place for a poet," in the opinion of a leading Kentucky historian, Thomas D. Clark, but not for "a practical farmer who had to grub a living for a growing family from the soil."[113] Others described it as "a sterile tract of land, almost destitute of timber," and "broken bar[r]en land."[114] The neighborhood was thinly settled; the 36-square-mile tax district where the Lincoln farm was located contained 85 taxpayers, 44 slaves, and 392 horses. When Abe was 2, his family moved a few miles northeast to a valley that penetrated Muldraugh's Hill. This Knob Creek spread was not ideal farmland, with its bottomless hollows, deep ravines, and steep, conical hills called "knobs." Remote, small, and subject to flooding, it was much less desirable than the farm they were leaving. Thomas may have been drawn to Knob Creek by its proximity to a ferry and inn, which made it more appealing than the lonely barrens along Nolin Creek. Perhaps he valued the abundance of timber fringing the creek. In any event, the move was uncomplicated; Thomas had two horses and only a few possessions to haul.

Little is known of Lincoln's Kentucky years. One of his earliest memories was of the Knob Creek farm. Reminiscing in 1864, he recalled: "Our farm was composed of three (3) fields. It lay in the valley surrounded by high hills and deep gorges. Sometimes when there came a big rain in the hills the water would come down through the gorges and spread all over the farm. The last thing that I remember doing there was one Saturday afternoon, the other boys planted the corn in what we called the big field; it contained seven (7) acres, and I dropped the pumpkin seeds. I dropped two seeds every other hill and every other row. The next Sunday morning there came a big rain in the hills, it did not rain a drop in the valley, but the water coming down through the gorges washed ground, corn, pumpkin seeds and all clear off the field."[115] This episode may have been memorable to Lincoln because it represented in miniature the futile farming career of his father. Lincoln's only other recorded reminiscence of his Kentucky youth dates from the War of 1812: "I had been fishing one day and caught a little fish which I was taking home. I met a soldier in the road, and, having been always told at home that we must be good to the soldiers, I gave him my fish."[116]

Abe's First Seven Years

Abe had a reputation as a quiet, bashful, polite boy who liked solitude and was "rather noted for Keeping his clothes cleaner longer than any others."[117] He was also described as the "shyest, most reticent, most uncouth and awkward-appearing, homeliest and worse dressed" boy in the neighborhood.[118] He often served as a peacemaker helping settle disagreements. Abe was also regarded as a good wrestler, though he would not fight unless he had to. One day, in the shade of a big tree at the mill, he was attacked without provocation or warning by a bigger boy, who was supported by two friends. Onlookers were astonished when Lincoln whipped each of them in succession and challenged any others who wished to do battle.

Lincoln's pastimes were shaped by his rural surroundings. He liked fishing and hunting with his dog. When the dog would run a rabbit into a hollow tree, Abe used his axe to chop it out. The future president nearly drowned crossing Knob Creek over a footlog; he lost his balance, fell in, and had to be rescued by his friend, Austin Gollaher. Abe and Gollaher improvised their play. Whatever they did, Lincoln delighted in excelling. Lincoln remembered Gollaher and many other Kentuckians fondly. During the Civil War, he asked a resident of the Bluegrass State about the Cessnas, Brownfields, Friends, Ashcrafts, and Kirkpatricks. He expressed a special interest in Gollaher, declaring: "I would rather see Gollaher than any man living." Lincoln then told a scatological story about a prank the two had played as boys.[119]

In Kentucky, Abe briefly attended a school taught by Zachariah Riney, a pious Roman Catholic who was popular with students and respected for his character and education. In later years, Lincoln always spoke of him "in terms of grateful respect" and remembered that Riney made no effort to proselytize his small scholars.[120] On the first day of class, Abe appeared wearing a long, one-piece linsey shirt and, improbably, a sunbonnet. He returned home weeping because his schoolmates teased him. To spare him further humiliation, his mother braided a more masculine straw hat. The windowless, dirt-floored schoolhouse, situated about 3 miles from the Lincolns' cabin, was made of rough logs forming little niches where the youngsters played hide-and-seek.

Later, Abe was a pupil of his neighbor, Caleb Hazel, a young man with a rudimentary education who ran a school 4 or 5 miles from the Lincolns' cabin. Like most other frontier instructors, Hazel taught by subscription, starting up a school when enough parents were willing to pay sufficient sums to make it worthwhile. A friend said Hazel "could perhaps teach spelling reading & indifferent writing & perhaps could Cipher to the rule of three—but had no other qualifications of a teacher except large size & bodily Strength to thrash any boy or youth that came to his School."[121] This last quality was necessary on the frontier, where schoolboys occasionally assaulted their teachers. Thrashings were sometimes administered with switches resembling ox-gads, 5 feet long and quite thick. Once Hazel sent Abe to cut a switch to be used on a classmate, an errand he disliked because, as Gollaher put it, "he never wanted to see anybody punished."[122] Hazel used only a spelling book, and when the more advanced pupils finished it, he would start them over again on one-syllable words. Lincoln went to Hazel more to keep his sister company than to learn much himself, but he did manage to master his letters and a little spelling. Lincoln's brief experience with Caleb Hazel was typical of frontier education at the time—a rough cabin staffed by a scarcely educated teacher using a scant supply of rudimentary books and relying on recitations and liberal doses of harsh physical discipline. Good students were sometimes rewarded with a swig of whiskey or a chaw of tobacco. Years later, Lincoln described the educational system he had known: "There were some schools, so called; but no qualification was ever required of a teacher, beyond *readin, writin, and cipherin,*' to the Rule of Three. If a straggler supposed to understand latin, happened to sojourn in the neighborhood, he was looked upon as a wizzard."[123] "The rule of three" was the means for solving problems involving proportions, where the student was given three numbers in a proportion and asked to calculate the fourth (34 is to 15 as 7 is to X—what is the value of X?)

Lincoln's schooling, at least in the alphabet, may have begun at home. Nancy Hanks Lincoln could not write but was able to read. She often read to her children from the Bible, much to Abe's delight. Her foster parents, Thomas and Elizabeth Sparrow, seemed to care about literacy. They made their other foster child, Dennis Hanks, into the best-educated member of the family; he could write as well as read. It is probably to the Sparrows' credit that Nancy was regarded as better educated than most girls in the area. Her son, as an adult, would demonstrate intimate familiarity with scripture.

It is not clear how literate Abe was when he left Kentucky. Zachariah Riney's daughter said that Abe "learned to read well at the first session" of her father's school.[124] An Indiana playmate and William Makepeace Thayer, who interviewed many of Lincoln's friends, both alleged that Lincoln could read before he turned 8. John Locke Scripps asserted that Lincoln could also write by that age. More modestly, William Dean Howells in his 1860 campaign biography claimed that Lincoln had only "acquired the alphabet and the rudiments of education" while in the Bluegrass State.[125] Dennis Hanks stated flatly, "Abe read no books in Ky."[126]

In backwoods Kentucky, the churches and preachers were as primitive as the schools and teachers. There were three major varieties of religion: "very ignorant Baptists, very noisy Methodists, and very dogmatic Presbyterians."[127] The two Baptist ministers whom the Lincoln family knew best, William Downs and David Elkin, hardly served as models of Christian decorum. The bibulous, disorderly, lazy, and slovenly Downs founded the Little Mount Church only after the Rolling Fork congregation had expelled him. Elkin was hard-drinking, ignorant, impoverished, indolent, and dressed sloppily. Elkin's grandson testified that "when my grandfather went to preaching he did not know but one letter in the alphabet and that was the letter O, and he knew it because it was round."[128]

Nancy and Thomas belonged to Baptist churches in Kentucky and Indiana, and their home library contained a catechism as well as a Bible. According to John Locke Scripps, the pioneers "were glad of an opportunity to hear a sermon, whether delivered by one of their own religious faith or not. Thus it was at least with the father and mother of young Lincoln, who never failed to attend, with their family, upon religious worship." They "gladly received the word, caring less for the doctrinal tenets of the preacher than for the earnestness and zeal with which he enforced practical godliness."[129]

In 1816, Thomas Lincoln decided to relocate to Indiana. His brother Josiah, his second cousins Austin and Davis Lincoln, his friend James Carter, the widow and children of Hananiah Lincoln, and Nancy Hanks's uncle, Joseph Hanks, all lived there. Thomas joined a chain migration from the Rolling Fork of the Salt River in Kentucky to Little Pigeon Creek in southwestern Indiana. Migrants from all over Kentucky poured into Indiana after the War of 1812, when Indian tribes surrendered claims to the southern half of the territory. ("Kentucky had taken Indiana without firing a shot," wags quipped.)[130] The head of the government land office in Vincennes reported that in 1817, the year Thomas Lincoln entered his claim for 160 acres there, "the applications were so numerous that it was impossible to record them as rapidly as they came in."[131]

Troubles besetting Thomas in Kentucky strengthened the lure of Indiana. In February 1816, an ejectment suit filed against him threatened to force him off his rented Knob Creek acres. Having already lost money on his Mill Creek and Sinking Spring farms because of imperfect titles, Thomas at first retained a lawyer to fight the suit but abruptly changed his mind. In May, a court instructed him to ascertain that the road from Muldraugh's Hill through Knob Creek Valley was maintained properly. That order may have helped persuade him to leave. Unusually bad weather later in the year might have also influenced Thomas. Winter came early to Hardin County in 1816, with frost appearing as early as the end of July. By September, ice a quarter inch thick covered the ground. The temperature did not rise above freezing in October, and November was bitterly cold.

Thomas cobbled together a flatboat, loaded it with his tools and barrels of whiskey (his meager capital), left Nancy and the children at Knob Creek, and shoved off for the Ohio River. Before reaching it, his raft capsized, pitching whiskey, tools, and sailor into the Rolling Fork. After salvaging some of his cargo with the help of friendly onlookers, Thomas continued his journey, crossing the Ohio River at Thompson's Ferry. Aided by Francis Posey, who hauled his goods for him in an ox-drawn wagon, Thomas hacked his way through an Indiana forest choked with grapevines and underbrush. The vines were so dense a knife could be driven into the tangle all the way up to the handle. At one point it took several days to chop through just 18 miles of forest. Thomas, whose whole life was a struggle, said "that he never passed through a harder experience than he did going from Thompson's Ferry to Spencer County, Indiana."[132]

Thomas was uncertain where to stake his claim. He was looking for familiar terrain and, like other settlers, wanted to avoid commercial arteries like the Ohio River. A friendly pioneer, William Wood, recommended the site that Thomas chose for his cabin, and promised to guard Thomas's possessions while he fetched his family.

In an 1860 autobiographical sketch, Abraham Lincoln declared that his family's move was "partly on account of slavery; but chiefly on account of the difficulty in land titles in Ky."[133] Some have inferred from this statement that Thomas Lincoln ardently opposed slavery, but that seems unlikely. Lincoln told others that his father moved in order to improve his standard of living. Dennis Hanks scoffed at the idea that Tom left Kentucky because of slavery. "This is untrue," said Hanks. He moved "to better his Condition. . . . Slavery did not operate on him."[134] In 1866, E. R. Burba of Hodgenville reported that "I have never heard that Slavery was any Cause of his leaving Ky—and think quite likely it was Not—for there were very few Slaves in the whole Country round here then."[135] In Kentucky, Thomas had served without apparent qualms on a slave patrol, a kind of informal police headed by a captain empowered to whip slaves found away from their owners without a pass. Lincoln's campaign-year remark—"This removal was partly on account of slavery"—may have been made for political consumption. It may also have referred to Thomas's dislike of a social system that afforded little upward mobility to poor whites like himself. In 1860, John Locke Scripps alleged that Thomas Lincoln "realized in his daily experience and observation how slavery oppresses the poorer classes, making their poverty and social disrepute a permanent condition through the degradation which it affixes to labor."[136] Many such settlers in Indiana, harboring no moral objections to slavery, actively (and successfully) campaigned to keep free blacks from moving into their state.

Before leaving Kentucky, Lincoln and his mother visited the grave of his brother, Thomas, who had died in infancy around 1812. As he crossed the Ohio with his sister and parents, 7-year-old Abraham did not seem like a prodigy destined for greatness. Dennis Hanks thought that "Abe Exhibited no special traits in Ky, Except a good kind—somewhat wild nature."[137] Another Kentuckian remembered him simply as the "gawkiest, dullest looking boy you ever saw," unremarkable except for an exceptionally powerful memory.[138] In that cold autumn the Lincoln family packed up and plunged into the wilderness of southwestern Indiana, seeking a new beginning in "wild and desolate" Hurricane Township.[139]

2

"I Used to Be a Slave"
Boyhood and Adolescence in Indiana
(1816–1830)

In 1817, a British traveler described Indiana as "a vast forest, larger than England, just penetrated in places, by the back-wood settlers, who are half hunters, half farmers."[1] Late in the previous year, Thomas Lincoln, his wife, and their two children entered the Buck Horn Valley of that state, which had just been admitted to the Union.

The family's journey from Kentucky was an arduous one, relentlessly exposing them to the rigors of camping out on cold winter nights. They brought with them little more than clothes, bedding, a Dutch oven, a skillet, and some tinware. The family had lost all their ironware when Thomas's raft overturned on his earlier expedition. Upon reaching their home site they began a new life with just these few household possessions. Their lack of domestic animals and separation by miles from their nearest neighbors added to the uncertainty of their new existence.

Hardships in Frontier Indiana

The Lincolns quickly erected a crude shelter called a "half-faced camp." This temporary expedient commonly thrown up by pioneers had three pole walls and a roof of poles and brush. Where the fourth wall would be, on the southern exposure, a fire was kept burning in cold weather. The Lincolns' pole house had animal skins that covered the open side when the wind howled and the fire was out. It was in this structure, which Dennis Hanks unfondly called "that Darne Little half face Camp," that the family lived for an undetermined time, probably several months.[2] Hanks's distaste for that camp, which he and his foster parents occupied temporarily in 1817, is understandable. It would be relatively comfortable in warm, dry weather, but when winter storms raged and the south wind blew rain and smoke into their faces it proved nearly intolerable. Acquaintances of the Lincolns testified that young Abe lived "amid want, poverty and discomfort that was . . . about on the plane of the slaves he was destined to emancipate," and they described the winter of 1816–1817 as "a veritable childhood Valley Forge of suffering."[3]

Compared to this Little Pigeon Creek neighborhood, Hardin County, Kentucky, seemed a model of settled civilization. Lincoln portrayed it as a "wild region" of "unbroken forest" where "many bears and other wild animals" roamed.[4] Though it was "as unpoetical as any spot of the earth," it inspired him to write poetry thirty years later:

> When first my father settled here,
> 'Twas then the frontier line;
> The panther's scream, filled night with fear
> And bears preyed on the swine.[5]

When the Crawford family first moved to the Little Pigeon Creek area nine years after the Lincolns, through the unchinked spaces in their cabin walls they observed the eyes of wolves reflecting light from the fireplace. Less menacing fauna also abounded near the Lincolns' lean-to, from which 7-year-old Abe shot a wild turkey. He later recalled that event with regret. In an 1860 third person autobiographical sketch, Lincoln wrote: "A few days before the completion of his eighth year, in the absence of his father, a flock of wild turkeys approached the new log-cabin, and A. with a rifle gun, standing inside, shot through a crack, and killed one of them. He has never since pulled a trigger on any larger game."[6]

If game was readily at hand, water was not. Thomas dug holes in his property for badly needed water, only to come up with "a miserable article" that had to be strained.[7] A Yankee douser offered to find water on the farm for a five dollar fee, but the cash-strapped Thomas would not part with that much for "a pig in the polk." With a pet cat tagging along, young Abe often trudged back and forth to fetch clean water from a spring one mile away.[8] It is hard to know why Thomas settled so far from a water source; typically, pioneers made proximity to good water a priority. Perhaps he was one of those who feared that a dread disease called "milk sickness" was likely to be contracted near spring branches.

Little Pigeon Creek's social environment was as primitive as the physical setting. One resident stated in 1866 that the early settlers were quite sociable, kind, and accommodating—"more so than now"—but that "there was more drunkenness and stealing on a small scale, more immorality, less Religion, less well placed Confidence."[9] Pioneer customs, Dennis Hanks recalled, were "very Ruff."[10]

Ignorance and superstition prevailed among the early Hoosiers. They believed that breaking a mirror or carrying a hoe or an ax into a cabin would bring a death in the family within a year's time. The wailing of a dog portended a death the next day. If a dog crossed a hunter's path, it was bad luck unless he locked his little fingers together. Friday was considered an inauspicious day to begin planting or harvesting. If a bird lit on a window or entered the house, it was regarded as a harbinger of woe. Farmers should plant, sow, and fence only if the signs of the moon were propitious. Subterranean crops like potatoes had to be planted in the dark of the moon, unlike tomatoes and beans, which must be planted in the light of the moon. The pioneers hired wizards to restore sick cows to health and thought that a child who was breathed on by a horse would contract whooping cough. Young girls swallowed chicken hearts in the hopes that they would facilitate their quest for true love. Carrying a bag of eggs in one hand and a bag of salt in the other, young men mounted mules facing backward and rode for a mile; if no accident occurred, they concluded that they would have good luck throughout the coming year.

Although Lincoln eventually shed many of the qualities of backwoods Indiana, he remained superstitious throughout life. His law partner, William Herndon, to whom Lincoln once confided, "I feel as if I shall meet with some terrible end," said that a Baptist upbringing "made him [Lincoln] a fatalist" and that a streak of superstition ran through him "like a bluish red vein runs through the whitest marble."[11] When a dog bit one of his children, Lincoln took the boy to Terre Haute, Indiana, to be cured by a "mad stone," which would supposedly drain off any poison when applied to the wound. As a congressman in the late 1840s, he declined to be a member of a party of thirteen people, an act that prompted a friendly colleague to declare sharply that he would rather be dead than be as superstitious as Lincoln. In 1842, Lincoln told his best friend, Joshua Speed, "I always was superstitious."[12] To Henry C. Whitney he confided that as a boy, "I used to wander out in the woods all by myself. It had a fascination for me which had an element of fear in it—superstitious fear. I knew that I was not alone just as well as I know that you are here now. Still I could see nothing and no one, but I heard voices. Once I heard a voice right at my elbow—heard it distinctly and plainly. I turned around, expecting to see some one, of course. No one there, but the voice was there." When Whitney asked what the voice said, Lincoln did not reply: "Deep gloom—a look of pain—settled on his countenance and lasted some minutes."[13]

The most pressing challenge facing the Lincolns in their primitive home was clearing the land. Large for his age, Abe set to work with an axe, and later he remembered that for the next fifteen years he was "almost constantly handling that most useful instrument."[14] He felled trees, chopped them into logs, cleared undergrowth, dug stumps, and grubbed up roots for drying and burning. When not so engaged, he was harrowing, planting, hoeing, plowing, weeding, harvesting, or butchering.

Taking grain to a distant mill provided young Abe a break from that soul-crushing routine. He especially enjoyed watching the mill machinery in action. Even waiting in line at the mill afforded him pleasure. There he would meet other boys, who would joke, tell stories, fight, and wrestle. Lincoln always remembered a bizarre incident that occurred one day at Noah Gordon's mill. Impatient with the mare powering the grindstone, Lincoln hit her with a whip, yelling, "Get up, you lazy old devil!" Just as he uttered the words, "Get up," the horse kicked him unconscious. Upon coming to, he involuntarily completed his injunction: "you lazy old devil!" Lincoln regarded this as a most remarkable event and often discussed it with Herndon.[15]

Once the family had cleared enough land and planted a small crop of corn and vegetables, Thomas built a log cabin, which his family occupied for thirteen years. A windowless, one-story structure measuring 18 by 20 feet, it was high enough to accommodate an overhead bedroom reached by a ladder of pegs stuck into the log walls. There Lincoln and Dennis Hanks slept. Thomas fashioned a few pieces of crude furniture, including a pole bedstead and a slab table and stools. Thirteen people would eventually crowd together in this dismal abode, which afforded little comfort or privacy. (In "one of the best" cabins in southwestern Indiana at this time, William Faux noted that "Males dress and undress before the females, and nothing is thought of it." Faux inferred that "Shame, or rather what is called false shame, or delicacy, does not exist here.")[16]

Death of Nancy Hanks

No sooner had the Lincoln family abandoned the half-faced camp in 1817 than Nancy's aunt and uncle, Thomas and Betsy Sparrow, arrived from Kentucky to occupy it. They brought with them their foster child, Dennis Hanks, bastard son of Mrs. Lincoln's aunt Nancy. Dennis became a kind of surrogate older brother to his second cousin Abe, a decade his junior. The Sparrows had in effect adopted Nancy when she was quite young; she and everyone else in the Little Pigeon Creek area regarded them as her virtual, if not biological, parents. Indeed, young Abraham thought of the Sparrows as his grandparents.

In 1818, within months of the Sparrows' arrival, an epidemic of "milk sickness" swept through southwest Indiana. Cows contracted the malady by eating weeds that contained the toxic substance tremetol; the disease killed not only the cows but also the humans who drank their infected milk. Doctors at that time knew neither the cause of the disease nor a cure for it, which struck down Mrs. Peter Brooner, a neighbor of the Lincolns, and then Thomas and Betsy Sparrow. Nancy Lincoln nursed all three of them as they sickened and died. And then in late September, she, too, contracted the disease.

If Nancy Hanks died the way most victims of milk sickness did, her husband and children in the small cabin must have been horrified as her body was convulsed with nausea, her eyes rolled, and her tongue grew large and turned red. After a few days, as death approached, she probably lay in pain, her legs spread apart, her breath growing short, her skin becoming cool and clammy, and her pulse beating ever more irregularly. Before her final coma, she urged Abe and Sarah to be good to one another and to their father, and to "reverence and worship God."[17] On October 5, 1818, a week after her symptoms first appeared, she died, unattended by a physician.

Young Abe helped his father construct a coffin, a melancholy task that Thomas had performed often that season. Nancy's body was conveyed on a homemade sled to a gravesite near the cabin, where Betsy and Thomas Sparrow were already buried. No tombstone marked her final resting place, and no preacher delivered a funeral sermon until months later, when David Elkin arrived from Kentucky and spoke to a group of about twenty mourners gathered at the grave.

No witnesses described Lincoln's reaction to his mother's death, nor did he say anything directly about its effect on him. Many years later, however, he indirectly revealed something of his emotions when he consoled a young girl whose father had been killed in the Civil War: "It is with deep grief that I learn of the death of your kind and brave Father; and, especially, that it is affecting your young heart beyond what is common in such cases. In this sad world of ours, sorrow comes to all; and, to the young, it comes with bitterest agony, because it takes them unawares." Significantly he added, "I have had experience enough to know what I say."[18]

During the lonely winter following his mother's death, Lincoln cherished hearing the Bible stories she had once told him because they brought back memories of her voice. In January 1861, he spoke of "the sad, if not pitiful condition" of his family after Nancy died.[19] In the late 1840s, Lincoln read William Cowper's poem, "On Receipt of My Mother's Picture" and marked one stanza that may well have reminded him of Nancy Hanks Lincoln:

> Oh that those lips had language! Life has pass'd
> With me but roughly since I heard thee last.
> Those lips are thine—thy own sweet smile I see,
> The same that oft in childhood solaced me.[20]

Lincoln's sister Sarah, who was only 11 when her mother died, assumed the domestic responsibilities of cooking, cleaning, washing, mending clothes, and spinning wool. She was a good-natured, amiable, gentle, intelligent, dark-skinned, heavyset girl. Nathaniel Grigsby remembered her as having an "extraordinary Mind—She was industrious—more so than Abraham—Abe worked almost alone from the head—whilst she labored both." Like her brother, she "could meet & greet a person with the very Kindest greeting in the world—make you Easy at the touch & word."[21] Austin Gollaher, who was quite fond of Sarah, described her as "just as pretty as Abe was homely," with "big brown eyes and curly chestnut hair."[22] But even with the help of kindly neighbors who pitched in, she could hardly replace her mother in the household. The gloom that settled over the cabin after Nancy Hanks Lincoln's death would not lift for more than a year, not until Thomas remarried.

The "profound agony" caused by the loss of his mother left its mark on Abe. Psychologists have found that bereavement in childhood "is one of the most significant factors in the development of depressive illness in later life" and that "a depressive illness in later years is often a reaction to a present loss or bereavement which is associated with a more serious loss or bereavement in childhood."[23] When a parent dies, the quality of the child's relationship with the surviving parent becomes critically important; inadequate care of the child seems to be a central cause of later depression.

In the wake of Nancy's death, Lincoln's unsympathetic father failed to provide Abe with adequate care, and partly as a result, Lincoln would be plagued with depression as an adult. At one point Thomas left his two children with their young cousin Sophie Hanks (who had come to live with the Lincolns around 1818) to fend for themselves while he drifted down the Ohio River to sell pork. He again left the children when he wooed Sarah Bush Johnston in Kentucky, where, according to family tradition, he spent more time than he had intended to. One source alleged that the children, having given him up for dead, became "almost nude for the want of clothes and their stomachs became leathery from the want of food."[24] By the time their new stepmother arrived at the end of 1819, she found Sarah and Abe "wild—ragged and dirty," and thought her stepson "the ugliest chap that ever obstructed my view."[25]

The year and a quarter that separated Nancy Lincoln's death and Sarah Bush Johnston Lincoln's arrival was miserable for both children and left enduring scars. Children often regard the early death of a parent as a deliberate abandonment.

Throughout his life Lincoln feared being abandoned and was inclined to attack those who forsook their party or their principles. He also harbored an abiding wariness of women in general; his mother's death evidently taught him that women are unreliable and untrustworthy.

Stepmother

When Thomas proposed marriage to Sarah Bush Johnston in Kentucky in the fall of 1819, it was the second time he had asked for her hand. They had known each other since childhood. He had had dealings with some of her eight siblings, including her brother Isaac, who had accompanied him to New Orleans in 1806. Sarah had rejected Thomas's first proposal in favor of Daniel Johnston, who passed away a decade after their wedding, leaving her a widow with three young children.

Thomas found 30-year-old Sarah Bush Johnston very attractive. She was handsome, tall, with good posture and a light complexion, and was sprightly, talkative, proud, kind, and charitable. Although her family was "rough, uncouth, [and] uneducated," they occupied rungs far higher on the social and economic ladder than did the Hankses.[26] William Herndon said she "was far above Thomas Lincoln—somewhat cultivated and quite a lady."[27] She impressed people in both Kentucky and Indiana as industrious, strong, healthy, intelligent, and gentle. A tidy housekeeper with good manners and a knack for managing children, she, unlike Thomas's first wife, enjoyed a spotless reputation.

Thomas courted his prospective bride matter-of-factly, blurting out to her one day as she was doing laundry: "Well *Miss* Johns[t]on, I have no wife & you have no husband[.] I came *a* purpose to mary you[.] I *knowed* you from a *gal* & you *knowed* me from a boy—I have no time to loose and if you are willing, let it be done Straight off." She replied that it was "so sudden" and "asked for time to consider, but he said he was not in a mood to fool away time on such an important business as wife hunting." To this she rejoined: "Tommy I know you well & have no objection to marrying you, but I cannot do it straight off as I owe some debts that must first be paid" and "could never think of burdening the man I marry with debt; it would not be right." Thomas promptly settled with her creditors (paying them approximately $3) and showed her the receipts. Meanwhile, her friends and brothers urged her to accept the proposal. She assented, and so they were married on December 2, 1819.[28] Thomas hired his brother-in-law to haul the bride's many household goods, including a bureau, table, spinning wheel, set of chairs, large chest of drawers, cooking utensils, dishes, cutlery, and two beds.

Arriving in Indiana with her three children, Sarah was taken aback by the quasi-ursine condition of the Lincoln cabin and its inhabitants and quickly proceeded to improve both. "I dressed Abe & his sister up—looked more human," she recalled.[29] She scrubbed them until they were "well & clean" and eliminated the lice that had taken up residence in Abe's unruly hair.[30] Appearances mattered to Sarah. When she was a girl, her mother thought her excessively proud because she cared about looking good and keeping up with fashion. When Thomas insisted that she sell some of her furniture because "it was too fine for them to keep," she refused. After replacing the

crude puncheon tables and stools in the Indiana cabin, she swiftly effected other improvements. A floor was laid down, and doors and windows were installed. She
dressed Sarah and Abe in some of the abundant clothing she had brought from Kentucky. In just a few weeks she revolutionized the Lincolns and their house, so that
everything was "snug & comfortable."[31]

Sarah was a good cook, though her culinary skills were wasted on Abe, whom
she described as "a moderate Eater" who obediently "ate what was set before him,
making no complaint: he seemed Careless about this."[32] Her meals were evidently
nutritious, for the boy enjoyed good health. She probably served him the customary
pioneer diet in Indiana, which consisted of cornbread, mush and milk, pork, chickens, quails, squirrels, and wild turkeys. Occasionally, she "used to get some sorghum
and ginger and make some gingerbread. It wasn't often, and it was our biggest treat,"
Lincoln recalled.[33]

Sarah Bush Lincoln tended to Abraham's emotional as well as physical needs.
Augustus H. Chapman reported that she "took an espical liking to young Abe" and
"soon dressed him up in entire new clothes & from that time on he appeared to lead a
new life." She encouraged him to study, for she recognized that he was "a Boy of uncommon natural Talents," which she did all she could to foster.[34] She even moderated
Thomas Lincoln's reluctance to let Abe read. "I induced my husband to permit Abe to
read and study at home as well as at school," she told an interviewer. "At first he
[Thomas] was not easily reconciled to it, but finally he too seemed willing to encourage him to a certain extent."[35]

Abe and his stepmother grew remarkably close. "I can say what scarcely one
woman—a mother—can say in a thousand and it is this—Abe never gave me a cross
word or look and never refused in fact, or Even in appearance, to do any thing I requested him," she remembered. In turn, she "never gave him a cross word." She and
Abe, she thought, were kindred souls: "His mind & mine—what little I had [—]
seemed to run together—move in the same channel." Abe "was dutiful to me
always—he loved me truly I think." She compared him favorably to her own son John:
"Both were good boys, but I must Say . . . that Abe was the best boy I Ever Saw or
Ever Expect to see."[36] He "always wanted to do just as I wanted him."[37]

Lincoln reciprocated the love of his stepmother, whom he called "mama." In 1861,
he told Augustus H. Chapman that "she had been his best Friend in this world & that
no Son could love a Mother more than he loved her." From Lincoln's affectionate tone
Chapman concluded that "few children loved there parents as he loved this Step
Mother."[38] Joshua Speed, Lincoln's closest confidant, recalled that Lincoln's "fondness
for his stepmother and his watchful care over her after the death of his father [in 1851]
deserves notice. He could not bear to have any thing said by any one against her." Near
the end of his life, Lincoln told Speed "of his affection for her and her kindness to
him."[39] To Herndon and others Lincoln said she was "considerate and attentive," a
"kind, tender, loving mother" and a "noble woman" to whom he was "indebted more
than all the world for his kindness—amiability, etc."[40] Curiously, Lincoln seldom visited his stepmother, even after Thomas died. Perhaps he hesitated to return to the paternal cabin lest it remind him of the grim one in Indiana where he had grown up.

Just as Sarah Bush Lincoln seemed to prefer her stepson to her own boy, Thomas Lincoln favored his stepson John D. Johnston over Abe. Remarkably, however, little stepsibling rivalry developed between the two boys. Sarah remembered them quarreling but once, and she thought theirs was an unusually harmonious relationship for stepbrothers. A year younger than Abe, Johnston was a handsome, kind-hearted, generous, hospitable fellow whose major defects were indolence and a quarrelsome streak. His glibness and sociability gave the impression that he was smarter than his shy stepbrother, Abe. Sophie Hanks reported that Abe would stick up for John when he was in the right but "let him get licked" when he was not. She added that John "was not very truthful. Sometimes he would do some devilment. John would not always tell the truth, and Uncle Tom would say, 'Wait till Abe comes, and we'll find out about it.'"[41] In adulthood Johnston became known as "the Beau Brummel of Goose Nest Prairie," who wore the best clothes, even if he could not afford them.[42] He may have had a drinking problem; a ledger showed that Johnston once purchased over 14 gallons of whiskey in four months. After Lincoln had become a successful lawyer and politician, Johnston "would tell with much relish how he once thought Abe a fool, because, instead of spending his evenings sporting with the young folks, he seemed to care for nothing but some old musty books." To Johnston and his contemporaries, such behavior "was clear proof of Abe's insanity. 'But, now,' said he, 'Abe is a great and wise man, and I am a fool still.'"[43] Sarah Bush Lincoln said that "John used to be the smartest when they were little fellows. But Abe passed him. Abe kept getting smarter all the time, and John he went just so far and stopped. I never saw another boy get smarter and smarter like Abe did."[44]

All in all, it is hard to imagine anyone more different from Lincoln than Johnston. Nonetheless, Lincoln spoke of him "in the Most affectionate Manner" and said that he and his stepbrother "were raised together, slept together, and liked each other as well as actual brothers could do."[45] When Abe's sister told him to keep away from the Johnstons or they would ruin him, Abe just laughed and said that John was "all right."[46] In 1848 he wrote to John, "You have always been [kind] to me."[47]

In time, however, Lincoln became impatient with Johnston's laziness, and though he extended himself to help John's children, he was reluctant to subsidize him. For his part, Johnston may have resented Lincoln's lectures on his lack of diligence and may have believed that Lincoln did not do enough for Thomas and Sarah, who lived with Johnston. Dennis Hanks reported that eventually the stepbrothers became "Enimes for awhile on this ground," and added mysteriously, "I Don't want to tell al[l] the thing[s] that I No," for "it would Not Look well in history." Still, Hanks concluded, "I think Abe Dun more for John than he des[er]ved. . . . Abe treated John well."[48]

Lincoln was also friendly with his two stepsisters, Elizabeth and Matilda, who were, respectively, 10 and 8 years old when they came to Indiana. The stepsiblings of the blended Johnston-Lincoln family got along so well, in fact, that two of them, Elizabeth Johnston and Dennis Hanks, became husband and wife. When their daughter Harriet reached school age, Lincoln invited her to live with his family in Springfield and pursue her education there, which she did.

Education

Lincoln's own education continued fitfully in Indiana, where he attended ABC schools for brief stretches. Later in life he laconically referred to his education as "defective" and estimated the aggregate of his time spent in school was less than a year.[49] In 1852, he said the career of his political hero Henry Clay demonstrated that "in this country, one can scarcely be so poor, but that, if he *will*, he *can* acquire sufficient education to get through the world respectably."[50] Lincoln may well have been speaking of himself. Even though there "was absolutely nothing to excite ambition for education" in frontier Indiana, by the age of 21, he said, "somehow, I could read, write, and cipher to the Rule of Three; but that was all."[51] In an 1860 autobiographical sketch written in the third person, he expressed regret at "his want of education," but added that he "does what he can to supply the want."[52]

Lincoln's earliest surviving composition is a bit of doggerel scribbled in an arithmetic notebook:

> Abraham Lincoln
> his hand and pen
> he will be good
> god knows When.[53]

The Indiana school available to young Abe was a low-ceilinged, flea-infested cabin with a floor of split logs, a chimney of poles and clay, and a window of greased paper. Pupils sat on uncomfortable benches without backs but with splinters aplenty. The young scholars usually studied aloud so that the teacher could tell that they were not daydreaming. In such a "blab school," the nineteenth-century Indiana novelist Edward Eggleston "found it impossible to determine in his own mind whether the letters 'b-a-k-e-r' in his spelling book spelled 'lady' or 'shady.'" Eggleston "simply could not force attention upon his mind in the midst of such a din."[54] One Hoosier child "repeated the one word 'heptorpy' from morning to noon and from noon till night in order to make the teacher believe that he was studying his lesson."[55] (Such schooling probably accounts for Lincoln's tendency to read aloud, which irritated his law partner William Herndon. To justify that annoying habit, Lincoln explained: "I catch the idea by 2 senses, for when I read aloud I *hear* what is read and I *see* it; and hence 2 senses get it and I remember it better, if I do not understand it better.")[56]

Frontier teachers, whose ability to administer physical discipline was as important as their scholastic skills, boarded with families in the neighborhood. Preoccupied with enforcing order, making quill pens, and other chores, they hardly had time, even if they had the inclination, to encourage independent thought and understanding. Because instructional technique involved rote memorization, fast learners stagnated while waiting for slower schoolmates to master a lesson. The punishments these teachers dealt out could be harsh, not only for outright misbehavior but also for simply misspelling a word or miscalculating a sum. A wooden switch was always at hand and used liberally, sometimes to the point of inflicting injury or causing the child to vomit from the pain. Lincoln recalled a teacher who slapped a classmate for mispronouncing the names of the biblical figures Shadrach, Meshach, and Abednego. Far from protesting, some parents encouraged the whipping of their children. Perhaps it was well that the school year was short, extending from the close of the fall harvest to the planting season.

Along Little Pigeon Creek, Lincoln's teachers were Andrew Crawford, James Swaney, and Azel Dorsey. Only Dorsey left reminiscences of Lincoln, recalling that the boy came to school in buckskins and a raccoon cap, clutching an old arithmetic book, and was remarkable for his "diligence and eagerness."[57] Lincoln's first Indiana teacher, Crawford, went beyond reading, writing, and arithmetic and tried to instill manners into his backwoods charges. He would have one pupil leave the room and then return, to be formally introduced by another pupil to all the others.

Lincoln, too, tried to civilize his contemporaries by denouncing their mistreatment of animals. On the Midwestern frontier, cruelty to animals was common. At log rollings, men would "round up a chip-munk, a rabbit, or a snake, and make him take refuge in a burning log-heap and watch him squirm and fry."[58] In one of his early bouts of schooling, Lincoln wrote an essay on that subject. As an adolescent, he upbraided John Johnston for smashing the shell of a land turtle against a tree, leaving the suffering animal quivering and defenseless. When his mother urged him to kill a snake, Abe replied: "No, it enjoys living just the same as we do."[59] His stepsister Matilda remembered Abe saying that "an ant[']s life was to it, as sweet as ours to us."[60]

Lincoln's concern for animals persisted into adulthood. One day while traveling in Illinois, dressed more formally than usual, he saw a pig mired down. Reluctant to soil his clothes, he determined to pass the creature by, but his conscience would not allow him to do so. The imploring look in the porcine eyes seemed to say, "*There now! My last hope is gone.*" Moved to pity, Lincoln turned back to rescue the unfortunate beast.[61] He similarly extricated a mud-bound lamb. When he observed a sow attempting to eat one of her piglets, he declared, "By jings! the unnatural old brute shall not devour her own progeny," and clubbed her vigorously.[62] On another occasion he restored two small birds to their nest. When friends derided him for wasting his time, he responded: "Gentlemen, you may laugh, but I could not have slept well to-night, if I had not saved those birds. Their cries would have rung in my ears."[63] In Pontiac, Illinois, where he was abed one stormy night, Lincoln heard a cat mewing outside in the rain. Moved to pity, he was unable to sleep until he opened the door and let the poor feline enter.

Lincoln also chastised his playmates for cruelty to other youngsters. When they tormented James Grigsby, who stuttered badly, Lincoln stepped in. "Abe took me in charge," Grigsby recalled, when "rough boys teased me and made fun of me for stuttering. Abe soon showed them how wrong it was and most of them quit."[64]

Lincoln composed essays on subjects other than cruelty to animals. He showed a piece he wrote on temperance to his neighbor William Wood, who thought it superior to anything he had read in the press. Lincoln's enthusiasm for temperance did not keep him from aiding a poor drunkard sleeping along the roadside one bitterly cold evening. To prevent the fellow from freezing to death, Lincoln carried him to the cabin of Dennis Hanks and stayed the night with him. (Most young Hoosiers showed less compassion. According to Edward Eggleston, Indiana boys who found a drunk would often place a large crate over him and weigh it down with logs "that would make escape difficult when the poor wretch should come to himself. It was a sort of rude punishment for inebriety, and it afforded a frog-killing delight to those who executed justice.")[65] Lincoln's youthful hostility to drink and his kindness to drunks were reflected in a temperance address he delivered many years later. Another lost Lincoln essay, written in 1827 or 1828, dealt with national politics. Wood admired that one, too, and said that it was published. In his twenties, Lincoln often read his first composition, written when he was about 14, to William G. Greene. Lincoln thought highly of that witty piece.

Though his command of spelling was imperfect, Lincoln was far ahead of his schoolmates, whom he often helped out with their spelling. That subject enjoyed pride of place in the frontier curriculum. An Indiana teacher recalled that the "public mind seems impressed with the difficulties of English orthography, and there is a solemn conviction that the chief end of man is to learn to spell." Edward Eggleston noted that often "the pupil does not know the meaning of a single word in the lesson." But that mattered little, for the pioneers believed that words "were made to be spelled, and men were probably created that they might spell them. Hence the necessity for sending a pupil through the spelling-book five times before you allow him to begin to read, or indeed to do anything else." Each school session, morning and afternoon, typically ended with a long spelling class, and Friday afternoons were entirely devoted to spelling matches, viewed as a kind of spectator sport on the frontier. One day, Andrew Crawford asked his charges to spell "defied" and declared that he would keep them in school until they spelled it properly. None of the pupils could meet the challenge until Anna Roby noticed Lincoln at the window with his finger pointing to his eye. She took the hint, changed her guess from "defyed" to "defied," and Crawford finally dismissed the class. Lincoln also assisted his chums with their handwriting.

Spelling became a lifetime preoccupation for Lincoln. Even as president he would unhesitatingly admit when he did not know how to spell a word and ask for guidance. Once when he publicly asked a roomful of visitors how to spell "missile," a government official marveled, "Is there another man in this whole Union who, being President, would have done that? It shows his perfect honesty and simplicity."[66] At a reception in February 1865, Lincoln told Supreme Court Justice David Davis, "I never knew until the other day how to spell the word 'maintenance.' . . . I always thought it was 'm-a-i-n, main, t-a-i-n, tain, a-n-c-e, ance—maintainance,' but I find that it is 'm-a-i-n, main, t-e, te, n-a-n-c-e, nance—maintenance.'" An observer called this scene "a spectacle! The President of a great nation at a formal reception, surrounded by many eminent people, statesmen, ministers, scholars, critics and ultrafashionable people—by all sorts—who honestly and unconcernedly, in the most unconventional way, speaks before all, as it were, of a personal thing illustrative of his own deficiency."[67] In 1864, Lincoln again confessed his weakness as a speller: "When I write an official letter I want to be sure it is correct, and I find I am sometimes puzzled to know how to spell the most common word. . . . I found, about twenty years ago, that I had been spelling one word wrong all my life up to that time. . . . It is *very*. I used always to spell it with two r's—v-e-r-r-y. And then there was another word which I found I had been spelling wrong until I came here to the White House. . . . It is *opportunity*. I had always spelled it, op-*per*-tu-ni-ty."[68] Some fretted that Lincoln's public confessions of lapses in his learning were "a spectacle" coming from an important man, but Joshua Speed marveled that Lincoln "was never ashamed . . . to admit his ignorance upon any subject, or the meaning of any word no matter how ridiculous it might make him appear."[69] Leonard Swett, his close friend on the Illinois legal circuit, admiringly observed that Lincoln "was the only man I have ever known who bridged back from middle age to youth and learned to spell well."[70]

Lincoln's schoolmates did not always appreciate his efforts to enlighten them. Anna Roby remembered one evening remarking that the moon was sinking. "That[']s not so," he replied; "it don't really go down; it Seems So. The Earth turns from west to East and the revolution of the Earth Carries us under, as it were; we do the sinking as you call it. The moon as to us is Comparatively still. The moon[']s sinking is only an Appearance." The skeptical Miss Roby retorted, "Abe—what a fool you are."[71] Astronomy would remain a lifelong interest of Lincoln's, as would mathematics. His passion for math, which led him in his forties to master the first six books of Euclid, was initially stimulated by his teachers, by several textbooks, and by a neighbor, James Blair. His math education enabled Lincoln in his early twenties to master surveying speedily; it also helped him develop a keenly analytical mind.

In contests and games with his schoolmates—broad jumping, footracing, putting the shot, hop-step-and-jumping, slapjack, towel ball, stink base, wrestling, I spy, catapult, bull-pen, and horseshoes—Lincoln shone when he could use his exceptional strength to advantage. He was able to sink an axe deeper into a tree and strike a heavier blow with a maul than anyone in the neighborhood. He could easily carry what three other men would have a hard time lifting. In his early twenties, with the aid of a harness, Lincoln hoisted over a thousand pounds. "How he could chop!" Dennis Hanks exclaimed. "His ax would flash and bite into a sugar tree or sycamore, and down it would come. If you heard him fallin' trees in a clearin' you would say there was three men at work by the way trees fell."[72]

A form of recreation that Lincoln enjoyed little was his father's favorite, hunting. One of his rare hunting expeditions led Lincoln to kill his father's dog. One night Abe and John D. Johnston slipped out to join their friends in search of raccoons, only to have the barking of "Joe," Thomas's house dog, threaten to disclose their nocturnal escapade. To silence the cur, Lincoln and his comrades took it along on their hunt. After they had caught a coon, they sewed its skin around Joe, who promptly ran toward home. En route the dog was attacked and killed by larger canines. Lincoln recounted this odd tale later in life: "Father was much incensed at his death, but as John and I, scantily protected from the morning wind, stood shivering in the doorway, we felt assured little yellow Joe would never be able again to sound the call for another coon hunt."[73] Such a cruel act by a young man so solicitous of animals suggests that Lincoln's hostility toward his father ran deep. This uncharacteristic deed may have been Lincoln's way of retaliating, perhaps unconsciously, against Thomas for having slaughtered young Abe's beloved pet pig.

For all his enjoyment of sports and games, Lincoln possessed a streak of introversion and a fondness for solitude. He disliked crowds and often preferred to be alone. After Nancy Hanks died in 1818, her son matured quickly and had less time for playmates. As one Indiana neighbor recalled, "he seemed to change in appearance and action." He "began to exhibit deep thoughtfulness, and was so often lost in studied reflection we could not help noticing the strange turn in his actions. He disclosed rare timidity and sensitiveness, especially in the presence of men and women, and although cheerful enough in the presence of boys, he did not appear to seek our company as earnestly as before." Another neighbor thought, "Abe was always a man though a boy." He "would say to his play fellows and other boys—Leave off your boyish ways and be more like men."[74]

Lincoln outshone his schoolmates. He arrived at school early, paid close attention to his studies, read and reread his assignments, never wasted time, made swift progress, and always stood at the head of his class. As John Hanks observed, he "*worked his way by toil; to learn was hard for him, but he worked Slowly, but Surely.*"[75] To Anna Roby, Nathaniel Grigsby, and other fellow pupils he often summarized what he had read, using stories and maxims to explain things clearly and simply. He retained that didactic impulse as an adult. It was common for him to read aloud, commenting on a book to a companion. He once discussed Euclid's geometry with a stableman.

Lincoln devoted most of his leisure, such as it was, to study. He quickly got ahead of his classmates and even his instructors. His stepmother recalled: "Abe read all the books he could lay his hands on—and when he came across a passage that Struck him he would write it down on boards if he had no paper & keep it there till he did get paper—then he would re-write it—look at it repeat it—He had a copy book—a kind of scrap book in which he put down all things and this preserved them. He ciphered on boards when he had no paper or no slate and when the board would get too black he would shave it off with a drawing knife and go on again: When he had paper he put his sums down on it"[76] While John D. Johnston attended dances, Abe sat reading by the fire. When working at Josiah Crawford's farm, he read during lunchtime while other hands sat around chatting, smoking, and chewing tobacco. Crawford's wife recollected that "while other boys were out hooking water melons & trifling away their time, he was studying his books . . . he read all our books. . . . We had a broad wooden shovel on which Abe would work out his sums—wipe off and repeat till it got too black for more: then he would scrape and wash off and repeat again and again."[77] On other jobs, too, he always carried a book to peruse during breaks. Sundays he devoted his free time to reading. Walking to and from school, he read aloud at such a decibel level that his voice could be heard for a great distance. In 1828, Lincoln spent a few weeks at the Rockport home of Daniel Grass, whose books he enjoyed. In the evenings he would lie before the fireplace so that he could read, sometimes until midnight or later. When he worked with John Hanks, Lincoln would return to the house at day's end, grab a piece of cornbread, and con a book.

Lincoln allegedly told a friend that "he had got hold of and read through every book he ever heard of in that country for a circuit of about fifty miles," but Elizabeth Crawford recalled that he was more selective. If he picked up a book he thought was not worth his time, "he would close it up and Smile and Say I don[']t think this would pay to read it."[78] Henry C. Whitney agreed that Lincoln was selective and that he would skim parts of the longer books, or skip around through the chapters. Still, Lincoln always liked to have a book at hand for meals (or at least be with someone who could hold an intelligent conversation) and would diligently jot down passages from his reading that particularly struck him.

Reading helped liberate Lincoln from his backwoods environment. In middle age he said that before Johann Gutenberg's great invention, "the great mass of men, at that time, were utterly unconscious, that their *conditions,* or their *minds* were capable of improvement. They not only looked upon the educated few as superior beings; but they supposed themselves to be naturally incapable of rising to equality. To immancipate the mind from this false and under estimate of itself, is the great task which printing came into the world to perform."[79] Print performed exactly that task for Lincoln, emancipating his mind and firing his ambition.

To supplement his meager schooling, young Lincoln educated himself. He practiced writing the letters of the alphabet whenever and however he could, carving letters on slabs of wood, tree trunks, even on the stools and table in his family's cabin. When he did not have charcoal to hand, he wrote in the dust, in sand, or in snow. Dennis Hanks claimed credit for teaching his cousin to write, a boast that may be justified inasmuch as Dennis, ten years older than Abe, could write. As Lincoln's writing skill improved, and it was learned that he was conducting the correspondence for his own family, neighbors came to regard him as "a marvel of learning" and called upon him to write for them, too. John Locke Scripps believed that Lincoln's greatest asset was not so much his skill as a stenographer as it was "his ability to express the wishes and feelings of those for whom he wrote in clear and forcible language."[80] Years later Lincoln told a friend "that the way he learned to write so well & so distinctly & precisely was that many people who Came with them from Ky & different sections after they moved" to Indiana employed him as an amanuensis, which "sharpened" his "perceptions" and taught him "to see other people['s] thoughts and feelings and ideas by writing their friendly confidential letters."[81] He also drafted legal documents, including a contract between his stepbrother and a man who hired Johnston to run a still house. (Lincoln himself worked at that facility in the winter of 1829–1830.)

In addition to writing for his neighbors, Lincoln also read to them. He regularly visited William Wood's house to read newspapers aloud for the edification of the unlettered. He had a knack for making his listeners understand what they heard. When in a puckish mood, he would often invent stories while pretending to read from the paper he was holding.

Sometimes Lincoln memorized items in the press. John Romine recalled that "Abe borrowed a newspaper from me which contained a long editorial about Thomas Jefferson, and read the entire paper by firelight. The next morning he returned the paper, and it seemed to me that he could repeat every word in that editorial, and not only that [—] he could recount all the news items, as well as tell all about the advertisements."[82] J. Rowan Herndon said Lincoln "had the Best memory of any man I Ever Knew," for he "Never forgot any thing he Read."[83]

Young Lincoln admired Lindley Murray's *English Reader*, an anthology of poetry and prose that he called "the greatest and most useful book that could be put in the hands of a child at school."[84] It contained some antislavery sentiments, such as these lines by the eighteenth-century poet, William Cowper:

> I would not have a slave to till my ground,
> To carry me, to fan me while I sleep,
> And tremble when I wake, for all the wealth
> That sinews bought and sold have ever earn'd.
> I had much rather be myself the slave,
> And wear the bonds, than fasten them on him.

(Lincoln would later famously write: "As I would not be a slave, so I would not be a master. This expresses my idea of democracy. Whatever differs from this, to the extent of the difference, is no democracy.")[85]

Lincoln's other schoolbooks included Thomas Dilworth's *New Guide to the English Tongue*, Noah Webster's *American Spelling Book*, and Asa Rhoads's *American Spelling Book*. In addition to his family Bible, Lincoln read volumes borrowed from neighbors, including Josiah Crawford, William Jones, Thomas Turnham, and John Pitcher. Among these works were *The Arabian Nights*, *Aesop's Fables*, *The Kentucky Preceptor*, John Bunyan's *Pilgrim's Progress*, James Barclay's English dictionary, Daniel Defoe's *Robinson Crusoe*, James Riley's *Authentic Narrative of the Loss of the American Brig Commerce*, William Grimshaw's *History of the United States*, a biography of Henry Clay, Mason Weems's life of George Washington, and William Scott's *Lessons in Elocution*. (Curiously, the autobiography of Benjamin Franklin does not seem to have been among the books read by Lincoln, who was to become as famous a representative of the self-made-man ethic as Franklin himself.)

It is not possible to say precisely what Lincoln derived from these volumes. His views on slavery may have been affected by the Scott anthology, which contained Laurence Sterne's indictment of human bondage: "Disguise thyself as thou wilt, still, slavery! still, thou art a bitter draught; and though thousands, in all ages, have been made to drink of thee, thou art no less bitter on that account."[86] Scott also included Cowper's poem, "Cruelty to Brutes Censured," which may have had a special appeal to the young Lincoln. *Robinson Crusoe* perhaps reinforced his sense of irony and fatalism.

In the late 1820s, Lincoln began reading newspapers, especially the New York *Telescope*, the Washington *National Intelligencer*, and the Louisville *Journal*, papers that helped develop his interest in politics. He originally supported Andrew Jackson's Democratic Party but soon switched his allegiance to the National Republicans, whose leader, Henry Clay, would found the Whig Party in the 1830s. Influencing this decision was a prosperous merchant, William Jones, who admired Clay so much that when his hero lost the 1844 presidential election, Jones was unable to attend to business for days. Jones employed young Lincoln in his store and served as a friendly mentor to him. Lincoln hung around the store, where he could read the Louisville *Journal* and discuss politics. In all likelihood, Lincoln's preference for the National Republicans grew from his aversion to the Jeffersonian-Jacksonian celebration of agrarianism and negative government. Eager to escape rural backwardness, he probably associated the Democrats with shiftless frontiersmen like his Democratic father, while the National Republicans represented enterprising lawyers and merchants like Jones.

When Lincoln was about 14 years old, hearing that David Ramsay's biography of the first president offered an account of Washington superior to Mason Weems's, he promptly borrowed a copy of the Ramsay book from Josiah Crawford and read it avidly. Before he could return it, however, the volume inadvertently got soaked by rain that poured into the Lincoln cabin one night. When he told Crawford what had happened and offered to pay for the book, Crawford instead suggested that the lad cut the tops from a field of corn, which he did over the course of three days. Lincoln believed that Crawford, a tightfisted man known for his pettiness in dealing with neighbors, had made an excessive demand, and retaliated by composing satirical verses ridiculing Crawford unmercifully.

Lincoln did not rely solely on the printed word or the classroom for his education; he also queried travelers who stopped at Jones's store. In addition, with Dennis Hanks, Nathaniel Grigsby, and other friends, Lincoln attended political meetings and discussed issues of the day endlessly. Lincoln insisted on thoroughly digesting whatever he read or heard. His stepmother recollected that "Abe, when old folks were at our house, was a silent & attentive observer—never speaking or asking questions till they were gone and then he must understand Every thing—even to the smallest thing—Minutely & Exactly." He "would then repeat it over to himself again & again—sometimes in one form and then in another & when it was fixed in his mind to suit him he became Easy and he never lost that fact or his understanding of it." Occasionally, "he seemed pestered to give Expression to his ideas and got mad almost at one who couldn't Explain plainly what he wanted to convey."[87]

Lincoln never lost this desire to gain a clear understanding of whatever he read or heard. In 1860, he described one of his earliest recollections to a Connecticut clergyman: "I remember how, when a mere child, I used to get irritated when anybody talked to me in a way I could not understand. I don't think I ever got angry at anything else in my life. But that always disturbed my temper, and has ever since. I can remember going to my little bedroom, after hearing the neighbors talk of an evening with my father, and spending no small part of the night walking up and down, and trying to make out what was the exact meaning of some of their, to me, dark sayings. I could not sleep, though I often tried to, when I got on such a hunt after an idea, until I had caught it; and when I thought I had got it, I was not satisfied until I had repeated it over and over, until I had put it in language plain enough, as I thought, for any boy I knew to comprehend. This was a kind of passion with me, and it has stuck by me, for I am never easy now, when I am handling a thought, till I have bounded it north and bounded it south and bounded it east and bounded it west."[88] He rewrote the words of family guests to make his own prose more concise. When visitors came to the cabin, he would patiently listen to them talk. Employing a kind of shorthand, he jotted down their remarks and later went over them repeatedly, striking out extraneous words while retaining the substance and flavor of the conversations.

Religion

It is clear that Lincoln read the Bible, though how diligently he perused it is not recorded. In the 1850s he told an Illinois lawyer that his boyhood library consisted of "66 books of which he was very fond" (i.e., the Bible) and that he "studied it with great care."[89] Lincoln would probably have agreed with the historian who called the Bible "a whole literature, a library," a collection of poems and short stories teaching "history, biography, biology, geography, philosophy, political science, psychology, hygiene, and sociology," as well as "cosmogony, ethics, and theology," and presenting "a worldly panorama" with "particulars so varied that it is hard to think of a domestic or social situation without a biblical example to match and turn to moral ends."[90]

In his mature years Lincoln often referred to the Bible, which he described as "the richest source of pertinent quotations" and "the best gift God has given to man. All the good the Saviour gave to the world was communicated through this book. But for it we could not know right from wrong. All things most desirable for man's welfare, here and hereafter, are to be found portrayed in it."[91] Near the end of the Civil War he told Joshua Speed: "take all of this book [the Bible] upon reason that you can, and the balance on faith, and you will live and die a happier and better man."[92] The Bible, journalist Noah Brooks reported, "was a very familiar study with the President, whole chapters of Isaiah, the New Testament, and the Psalms being fixed in his memory." Lincoln, Brooks added, "would sometimes correct a misquotation of Scripture, giving generally the chapter and verse where it could be found. He liked the Old Testament best, and dwelt on the simple beauty of the historical books."[93] (Of the Psalms, he said: "they are the best, for I find in them something for every day in the week.")[94]

Lincoln often cited the Old Testament. In discussing the relationship between the Declaration of Independence and the Constitution, he alluded to the Book of Proverbs (25:11): "A word fitly spoken is like apples of gold in pictures of silver."[95] While pondering his future, he told a friend he would follow the advice of Moses: "Stand *still* and see the salvation of the Lord"[96] (Exodus 14:13). Responding to Stephen A. Douglas in 1852, he quoted Genesis 5:24: "And Enoch walked with God; and he was not, for God took him."[97] Opening his campaign for the senate in 1858, Lincoln took a text from Ecclesiastes (9:4): "a living dog is better than a dead lion."[98] He made another biblical canine allusion when complaining about press criticism during the Civil War: "Is thy servant a *dog*, that he should do this thing?" (Second Kings 8:13).[99] He also alluded to a passage in Proverbs (30:10) dealing with servants: "Accuse not a servant to his master lest he curse thee and thou be found guilty."[100] In 1861, speaking in Philadelphia, he gave a condensed version of the following passage from the 135th psalm: "If I forget thee, O Jerusalem, let my right hand forget her cunning. If I do not remember thee, let my tongue cleave to the roof of my mouth."[101] When denouncing slavery, Lincoln would repeatedly cite God's injunction to Adam: "In the sweat of thy face shalt thou eat bread" (Genesis 3:19).[102]

Lincoln also liked the New Testament, frequently quoting the words of Jesus:

"Judge not, that ye be not judged." (Matthew 7:1)[103]
"Woe unto the world because of offenses, for it must needs be that offences come; but woe unto that man by whom the offence cometh." (Matthew 18:7)[104]
"Every city or house divided against itself shall not stand." (Matthew 12:25)[105]
"For wheresoever the carcase is, there will the eagles be gathered together." (Matthew 24:28)[106]
"The gates of Hell shall not prevail against it." (Matthew 16:18)[107]
"If they hear not Moses and the prophets, neither will they be persuaded, though one rose from the dead." (Luke 16:31)[108]
"Whatsoever ye would that men should do to you, do ye even so to them." (Matthew 7:12)[109]
"For a good tree bringeth not forth corrupt fruit; neither doth a corrupt tree bring forth good fruit. For every tree is known by his own fruit." (Luke 6:43–44)[110]
"They seek a sign, and no sign shall be given them." (Luke 11:29)[111]
"Out of the abundance of the heart the mouth speaketh." (Matthew 12:34)[112]
"As your Father in Heaven is perfect, be ye also perfect." (Matthew 5:48)[113]

Lincoln's lecture on discoveries and inventions, delivered in the 1850s, contains more than thirty biblical references.

In his youth, Lincoln "didn[']t read the Bible half as much as [is] said," according to Dennis Hanks, who reported that "the Bible puzzled him, especially the miracles. He often asked me in the timber or sittin' around the fireplace nights, to explain scripture."[114] Lincoln's stepmother also testified that "Abe read the bible some, though not as much as [is] said: he sought more congenial books—suitable for his age."[115] (In 1860, Lincoln confessed to a Springfield minister: "I have read my Bible some, though not half as much as I ought.")[116] Sarah Bush Lincoln often entertained guests by having Abe read aloud from the Bible. On one such occasion, Abe evidently resented the assignment and began reading at a furious pace. When Mrs. Lincoln urged him to slow down, he defiantly sped up. In exasperation, she grabbed a broom and chased him out of the cabin, much to his relief. Another time he read aloud from the Book of Isaiah, playfully interpolating passages from Shakespeare.

Lincoln's youthful attitude toward the Bible, as described by his stepmother and Dennis Hanks, may reflect disenchantment with the ignorant preachers and hypocritical churchgoers he observed both in Kentucky and at the Little Pigeon Baptist Church, with which his parents affiliated in 1823 but which Abe did not join. That congregation seethed with personal feuds, quarrels over the proper credentials for those who administered baptism, opposition to benevolent missionary work, and disputes over creeds. The primitive worship, heavy emphasis on arcane doctrinal matters, and ignorant and even drunken preachers probably repelled young Lincoln.

In *The Hoosier Schoolmaster*, the former circuit-riding minister Edward Eggleston portrayed hard-shell Baptist congregations in antebellum Indiana: "Their confession of faith is a caricature of Calvinism, and is expressed by their preachers about as follows: 'Ef you're elected, you'll be saved; ef you a'n't, you'll be damned. God'll take keer of his elect. It's a sin to run Sunday-schools, or temp'rince s'cieties, or to send missionaries. You let God's business alone. What is to be will be, and you can't hender it." These "prodigiously illiterate, and often vicious" fundamentalist parishioners sometimes had ministers who were "notorious drunkards" and who dragged "their sermons out sometimes for three hours at a stretch."[117]

William E. Barton, a clergyman who wrote extensively about Lincoln, described the kind of services young Abe probably attended: "The [Baptist] preachers bellowed and spat and whined, and cultivated an artificial 'holy tone' and denounced the Methodists and blasphemed the Presbyterians and painted a hell whose horror even in the backwoods was an atrocity." Barton speculated plausibly that before Lincoln reached the age of 28 he may not have encountered a Baptist preacher who acknowledged that the earth was round.[118]

After hearing sermons or speeches, Lincoln repeated them nearly verbatim to his friends, mimicking the gestures and accent of the speaker. Often he would return from church, mount a box in the middle of the cabin, and replicate the service. He would do the same outdoors, climbing on a stump and inviting his friends to hear him deliver sermons or political speeches. Because this activity interfered with farmwork, Abe's father frequently scolded him and made him quit. His stepsister Matilda remembered that sometimes she and Lincoln would conduct mock religious services at which she would lead the singing while "Abe would lead in prayer. Among his numerous supplications, he prayed God to put stockings on the chickens' feet in winter."[119]

A strain of irreverence remained with Lincoln all his life. He especially relished humorous stories about ignorant preachers, including one, which involved a Baptist minister in Indiana: "The meeting-house was in the woods and quite a distance from any other house. It was only used once a month. The preacher—an old line Baptist—was dressed in coarse linen pantaloons, and shirt of the same material. The pants, manufactured after the old fashion, with baggy legs and a flap in front, were made to attach to his frame without the aid of suspenders. A single button held his shirt in position, and that was at the collar. He rose up in the pulpit and with a loud voice announced his text thus: 'I am the Christ, whom I shall represent today.' About this time a little blue lizard ran up underneath his baggy pantaloons. The old preacher, not wishing to interrupt the steady flow of his sermon, slapped away on his legs, expecting to arrest the intruder; but his efforts were unavailing, and the little fellow kept on ascending higher and higher. Continuing the sermon, the preacher slyly loosened the central button which graced the waist-band of his pantaloons and with a kick off came that easy-fitting garment. But meanwhile Mr. Lizard had passed the equatorial line of waist-band and was calmly exploring that part of the preacher's anatomy which lay underneath the back of his shirt. Things were now growing interesting, but the sermon was still grinding on. The next movement on the preacher's part was for the collar button, and with one sweep of his arm off came the tow linen shirt. The congregation sat for an instant as if dazed; at length one old lady in the rear of the room rose up and glancing at the excited object in the pulpit, shouted at the top of her voice: 'If you represent Christ then I'm done with the Bible.'"[120]

Lincoln also enjoyed telling the story of a camp meeting where, as the tents were being struck, "a little wizened-faced man ascended the log steps of the pulpit, and clasping his small hands, and rolling his weak eyes upward, squealed out, 'Brethern *and* sistern!'" Because he presented "such a striking contrast to the last speaker," the assembled people paused "to look with wonder upon him." Encouraged by their attention, he resumed: "I rise to norate on toe you on the subject of the baptismal—yes, *the* baptismal! Ahem. There was Noah, he had three sons—ahem—nam*lie*, Shadadarack, Meshisck, *and* Bellteezer! They all went in *toe* the Dannel's den, *and* likewise with them *was* a lion! Ahem." Observing that his auditors were inattentive, the fellow adopted a new tack: "Dear perishing friends, ef you will not hear on toe me on this great subject, I will only say this, that Squire Nobbs has recently lost a little bay mare with a flaxy mane *and* tail amen!"[121]

Even though Lincoln delighted in mimicking backwoods clergymen, something of what they preached became embedded in his psyche, for he remained a Calvinistic fatalist throughout life. He frequently quoted Hamlet's lines, "There's a divinity that shapes our ends,/ Rough-hew them how we will." He also found religious significance in the poetry of Alexander Pope, whose "Essay on Man," he said, "contained all the religious instruction which it was necessary for a man to know."[122] He repeatedly said: "What is to be [will be] and no cares (prayers) of ours Can [arrest] the decree."[123] Lincoln also retained a fondness for the frontier ministers' theatrical style. In 1861 he told the sculptor Leonard Volk, "I don't like to hear cut and dried sermons. No—when I hear a man preach, I like to see him act as if he were fighting bees!"[124]

Relations with the Opposite Sex

Lincoln's great height and sartorial indifference did not endear him to the opposite sex, nor was his physical and social awkwardness very appealing. He was strikingly tall: He reached 6 feet by age 16, and he kept growing until by 21 he attained his full height of 6 feet 4 inches. He was thin, swarthy, and rawboned. Though he was "very careful of his person" and "tolerably neat and clean," his clothes were typically rough and suited to the frontier—tow linen pants in warm weather, buckskin pants in cool weather, flax shirts, linsey-woolsey jackets, short socks, low shoes, and caps fashioned from animal skins. But they fit him poorly; his pants often exposed 6 to 12 inches of shin. This did not bother him, for he cared little about fashion.[125]

Lincoln got along well enough with neighborhood girls, kidding and chatting with them, but they found him "too green and awkward" to care for him romantically.[126] One Indiana maiden recalled that "he was so tall and awkward" and that all "the young girls my age made fun of Abe. They'd laugh at him right before his face, but Abe never 'peared to care. He was so good and he'd just laugh with them. Abe tried to go with some of them, but no sir-ee, they'd give him the mitten every time, just because he was . . . so tall and gawky, and it was mighty awkward I can tell you trying to keep company with a fellow as tall as Abe was."[127] Elizabeth Wood found him "too awkward."[128] Pretty, vain Elizabeth Tuley reported that "he was big and awkward and couldn't dance much." Whenever she was seen with Lincoln, her friends "teased her unmercifully" about "his coat sleeves and pantlegs always being too short."[129] Another young woman who thought him "too big, awkward & ugly" further objected that he "just cared too much for books."[130] Lincoln attended parties but refused to dance. Instead, he would gather several boys together and tell stories, which upset the girls, for they would as a result have trouble rounding up partners for dancing.

For his part, Lincoln returned the girls' indifference. His friend Anna Roby was one of many who noted that Abe "didn't like girls much" and found them "too frivolous."[131] Lincoln's cousin, Sophie Hanks, reported that Abe "didn[']t like the girls company."[132] His stepmother remembered that he "was not very fond of girls."[133] John Hanks said that "I never Could get him in Company with women: he was not a timid man in this particular, but [he] did not seek such company."[134] Some Hoosiers alleged that after Lincoln turned 17 he began to take a romantic interest in the opposite sex, but the evidence tends to support Dennis Hanks, who called Lincoln the "bashfullest boy that ever lived," and John D. Johnston, who said Lincoln "didn't take much truck with the girls" because "he was too busy studying."[135]

Quasi-Slavery as a Rented Laborer

Lincoln was indeed busy, but not always with a book in hand. He worked hard on his father's farm and also for neighbors to whom Thomas rented his boy. Around 1825, Thomas Lincoln found himself in greater financial trouble than usual when a friend defaulted on a loan that he had endorsed. To pay off that note, Thomas removed Abe from school and hired him out to neighbors such as Thomas Turnham, Wesley Hall, William Wood, Silas Richardson, Joseph Gentry, John Dutton, John Jones, and Josiah Crawford. For the next few years, Lincoln was virtually a slave, toiling as a butcher, ferry operator, riverman, store clerk, farmhand, wood chopper, distiller, and sawyer, earning anywhere from 10¢ to 31¢ a day. He handed these meager wages over to Thomas, in compliance with the law stipulating that children were the property of their father and that any money they earned belonged to him. Locked in this bondage, Abraham felt as if he were a chattel on a Southern plantation. "I used to be a slave," he declared in 1856.[136] This painful experience led him to identify with the slaves and to denounce human bondage even when it was politically risky to do so.

Among the people for whom young Lincoln slaved was a neighbor named Carter, who paid him 10¢ a day to cut corn. Josiah Crawford gave him 25¢ daily to split rails, build fences, dig wells, cut pork, clear land, daub his cabin, and perform other farm chores. When Lincoln and Joseph Richardson pulled fodder, they each received 25¢ for a full day's work. In 1827, he spent three months clearing land for John Jones, who compensated the young laborer with corn instead of money. Lincoln received 20¢ a day from James Taylor, who hired him to operate a ferry on Anderson Creek. When not shuttling passengers across that 100-foot-wide expanse of water, Lincoln helped with chores on Taylor's farm, where he lived for several months.

Lincoln's most lucrative work, earning him 31¢ a day, was butchering hogs for Taylor. It was also his nastiest job, involving "Barrells of hot water— blankets— clubs."[137] A hog had to be clubbed, doused in scalding water, and its bristles removed. Then one man held the warm, moist, greasy carcass, as heavy as 200 pounds, nearly perpendicular with its head down; another man ran a gambrel bar through a slit in the animal's hock, over a string pole, and then through the other hock. Holding the hog was a challenge. Lincoln termed this regimen at Taylor's "the roughest work a young man could be made to do."[138] Abe still managed to get in some reading at Taylor's. He would read until midnight, then rise early, make a fire for Mrs. Taylor, put on the water, and straighten up the place.

While working for Taylor, Lincoln built a small boat. One day two gentlemen in a hurry saw the craft and asked Lincoln to row them and their trunks out to a steamer on the Ohio River. He gladly agreed. While boarding the steamboat, the men dumbfounded Lincoln by pitching two silver half-dollars into his vessel. Recounting this episode, he said: "it was a most important incident in my life. I could scarcely credit that I, the poor boy, had earned a dollar in less than a day; that by honest work I had earned a dollar. The world seemed wider and fairer before me; I was a more hopeful and thoughtful boy from that time."[139]

Rowing passengers out onto the Ohio was lucrative, but it soon provoked a ferry owner on the Kentucky shore to sue Lincoln for operating without a license. The presiding justice of the peace, Samuel Pate, ruled for the defense, pointing out that the statute in question covered ferries plying between the southern and northern banks of the Ohio and not ferrymen who merely rowed passengers partway across the river. This episode may have stirred young Lincoln's interest in the law; it might have also predisposed him to read Constable Thomas Turnham's copy of *The Statutes of Indiana* with unusual avidity.

As a ferryman, Lincoln had grown so fond of working on the water that he readily accepted the offer made by a local merchant, James Gentry, to accompany his son Allen on a cargo boat trip to Louisiana. The two young men spent weeks constructing a flatboat for their corn, pork, potatoes, hay, and kraut—all destined for Deep South sugar plantations. In late December 1828, they shoved off from Rockport on a 1,200-mile, seven-week excursion down the Ohio and Mississippi rivers, with Lincoln manning the bow oars and Gentry the tiller. The constantly changing scenery and the boats passing by kept the voyage from becoming monotonous. From the riverbanks, villagers would call out, "Where are you from?" "Where are you bound?" "What are you loaded with?" Gentry and Lincoln slept on the hard deck, which was difficult when storms raged, forcing them to struggle hard to keep their boat from capsizing. On occasion they were pelted by rain for days on end.[140]

As they floated down the Mississippi, Gentry and Lincoln stopped frequently to peddle their cargo. They traded foodstuffs for cotton, tobacco, and sugar. One night, while tied up at a plantation a few miles below Baton Rouge, they were attacked by seven slaves. The blacks, noting that only two young men were aboard the boat, attempted to rob it. Gentry and Lincoln fended them off in a fierce struggle during which both were badly hurt.

After selling all their wares along the banks of the Mississippi, they proceeded to New Orleans. As they strolled about, Lincoln saw something that would leave an indelible impression on him: a slave auction at which scantily clad young women were exhibited on the block and pinched and ogled by prospective buyers. Revolted, Lincoln said: "Allen, that's a disgrace."[141] It was the first time, but not the last, that he would be repelled while observing slavery firsthand.

Lincoln and Gentry probably returned to Illinois via steamboat, perhaps one like the ship Frances Trollope described in her reminiscences of the riverboatmen whom she observed on a voyage up the Mississippi: "We had about two hundred of these men on board, but the part of the vessel occupied by them is so distinct from the cabins, that we never saw them, except when we stopped to take in wood; and then they ran, or rather sprung and vaulted over each other's heads to the shore, whence they all assisted in carrying wood to supply the steam engine; the performance of this duty being a stipulated part of the payment of their passage."[142] When Lincoln reached home, tales of his adventures won him a reputation as a capable boatman and a courageous fighter.

If the trip to New Orleans convinced Lincoln that chattel slavery was disgraceful, it also intensified his desire to escape his own quasi-slavery in Indiana. Soon after his return, Lincoln called on a neighbor, William Wood. When the shy young man found it difficult to get to the point, Wood prompted him: "Abe, what is your Case?"

"Uncle I want you to go to the River—(the Ohio) and give me Some recommendation to some boat."

Citing the law that made children their father's property until they attained their majority, Wood said: "Abe—your age is against you—you are not 21 yet."

"I Know that," protested Lincoln, "but I want a start."

Wood refused, counseling Lincoln to stay with his father until 1830. Reluctantly, Lincoln took that advice.[143]

Lincoln may have been eager to escape his home for some time. An interviewer who spoke with people who knew Lincoln concluded, *"Mr. L does not appear to have cared for home after the death of his mother."*[144] At 13 he worked away from home for the first time, cutting wood with Dennis Hanks and Squire Hall on the banks of the Ohio. Thereafter he frequently absented himself from the paternal cabin. In 1825, at the age of 16, he stayed several months with the Taylors on Anderson Creek. After his sister Sarah wed Aaron Grigsby in the summer of 1826, Lincoln spent much time at their home. In the spring of 1827, he lived with John Jones's family at Dale, returning home only on Saturday nights. That same year Lincoln and John D. Johnston journeyed to Louisville, where they found employment on the Louisville and Portland Canal. In the fall of 1828, while helping Allen Gentry construct their flatboat, Lincoln stayed weeks with the family of Daniel Grass in Rockport. He lived with William Jones when he worked on his farm and at his Gentryville store.

Lincoln heartily disliked farm chores. His employers, neighbors, and family all testified that he "was not industrious as a worker on the farm or at any other Kind of Manu[al] Labor."[145] Lincoln admitted that "his father taught him to work but never learned him to love it."[146]

On the frontier, "laziness" connoted physical, not mental, indolence. A neighbor of the Lincolns in Illinois recalled that Abe "always did take" to "book-readin'" and "on that account we uns uset to think he would n't amount to much. You see, it war n't book-readin' then, it war work, that counted."[147] Another Illinois acquaintance, John Purkapile, declared that "Lincoln was a mighty lazy man. Why, I've seen him under a tree with a book in his hand and too mortal lazy to move when the sun came round."[148] As his stepsister Matilda observed, Lincoln was indeed intellectually industrious, if reluctant to perform farm chores: "Abe was not Energetic Except in one thing—he was active & persistant in learning—read Everything he Could—Ciphered on boards—on the walls."[149] Sarah Bush Lincoln told an interviewer that her stepson "was diligent for Knowledge—wished to Know & if pains & Labor would get it he was sure to get it."[150]

Longing to escape the toilsome world of subsistence farming and make something of himself, Lincoln prophetically told Elizabeth Crawford, "I don't always intend to delve, grub, shuck corn, split rails, and the like."[151] She remembered that "Abe was ambitious, sought to outstrip and override others."[152] His friend Joseph Gentry had a similar recollection: "Abe wa[s]n't fond of work and often told me he never intended to make his living that way—he often said he would get some profession, in fact his whole mind seemed bent on learning and education."[153] Sophie Hanks recalled that her cousin Abe "always had a natural idea that he was going to be something."[154] In 1829, Lincoln wrote this couplet in a friend's copybook:
"Good boys who to their books apply
Will make great men by & by."[155]

When he could, Lincoln lured others into shunning chores with him. He would employ pranks, tricks, stories, and jokes to distract them. One day when he and Dennis Hanks had a job pulling fodder, they procrastinated all morning by playing marbles. At noon, Hanks "reminded Lincoln that they had not pulled any fodder. Lincoln replied that he had rather play marbles any time than pull fodder."[156]

Upon his return from New Orleans, after weeks of freedom as a flatboatman, Lincoln grudgingly resumed the uncompensated toil imposed on him by his father. The contrast to his life on the water seemed to curdle Lincoln's good nature; in 1829 the dark side of his personality emerged as he became testy, belligerent, spiteful, and vindictive. This transformation was especially obvious when he attacked the neighboring Grigsby clan. Although Nathaniel Grigsby was one of his best friends, Abe detested Nathaniel's older brother, Aaron, who had married his sister Sarah in 1826. Lincoln believed that the prosperous Grigsby family mistreated her and looked down on her because she had been "hired help."[157] Joseph C. Richardson remarked on Lincoln's anger at Grigsby: "You may think you have forgiven the fellow who married your sister and abused her, but you never do. You go gunning for him in your sleep."[158]

A year and a half after her wedding, Sarah died in childbirth. Upon hearing the news, Lincoln "sat down on a log and hid his face in his hands while the tears rolled down through his long bony fingers. Those present turned away in pity and left him to his grief."[159] Repeatedly he asked himself: "What have I to live for?" Henry C. Whitney, who thought that "Abraham's inner life was a desert of sorrow," speculated plausibly that Sarah's passing reawakened painful memories of his mother's death.[160] Lincoln and his father blamed Sarah's death on the neglectful conduct of the Grigsby clan. The Grigsbys contended that they had taken good care of her but that the only nearby doctor had been too drunk to tend to her.

Lincoln had another falling out with the Grigsbys when everyone in the neighborhood except his family was invited to celebrate the double wedding of Reuben and Charles Grigsby to Elizabeth Ray and Matilda Hawkins, respectively. "Miffed" and "insulted," Abraham vowed revenge for the slight.[161] With his highly developed knack for mimicry and sarcasm, Lincoln penned a satire in biblical language titled "The Chronicles of Reuben," which described grooms inadvertently bedding down the wrong brides. This burlesque, Nathaniel Grigsby recalled, was so "sharp" and "cutting" that "it hurt us."[162] It became famous in the Buck Horn Valley, where the Chronicles of Reuben were remembered "better than the Bible—better than Watts hymns." Joseph C. Richardson called the Chronicles "the first production that I know of that made us feel that Abe was truly & real[l]y some[one]. This called the attention of the People to Abe intellectually."[163] Lincoln evidently wrote other satirical pieces in Indiana, though none seem to have survived.

Not content with the wounds inflicted on Reuben and Charles, Lincoln wrote a bawdy poem questioning the sexual preference of their brother William:

> I will tell you a Joke about [Josiah?] & Mary
> Tis neither a joke nor a story
> For Reuben & Charles have married 2 Girls
> But Billy has married a boy
> He tried the girls on Every Side
> He had well tried
> None could he get to agree
> All was in vain
> He went home again
> And since that he's married to Natty
>
> so biley and naty agreed very well
> and mamas well pleased at the matc[h]
> the egg it is laid but Natys afraid
> the Shell is So Soft that it never will hatc[h]
> but betsy She Said you Cursed ball head
> my Suiter you never Can be
> besids your low Croch proclaimes you a botch
> and that never Can anser for me.[164]

Thirsting for revenge, William Grigsby challenged Lincoln to a fight, but the larger and stronger Lincoln protested that it would hardly be a fair match. So they hit on a compromise: Grigsby would battle Lincoln's stepbrother, John D. Johnston. As John Gentry recalled it, the fight became a much-anticipated spectacle: "The ring was pitched in Warrick County, a short distance from the old Lincoln homestead. That was for the purpose of evading any investigation by the grand jury. The fight was well advertised. . . . Every township in the county was represented, I reckon. There was a big crowd present. Abe Lincoln was there, and he was mad because he couldn't get anybody to fight him."[165] Johnston and Grigsby pummeled each other until Johnston was seriously hurt. At that point, "Abe burst through, caught Grigsby— threw him off some feet—stood up and swore he was the big buck at the lick." A general melee then broke out.[166]

This uncharacteristically boastful intervention in a fight that he himself caused suggests that Lincoln at age 20 was not entirely a paragon of virtue, despite his reputation as a sociable, cheerful, good-natured, and gentle fellow. The Bolins of Perry County thought that "the young Lincoln of Pigeon Creek, like all his Indiana cronies, was pretty much of a rowdy, and, certainly, was not of a saintly nature."[167] What Henry Whitney aptly called a "reprehensible trait of character" that Lincoln showed in cruelly satirizing the Grigsbys would mar him for years to come; not until midlife did he cease wounding people with his exceptional knack for ridicule.[168]

In other ways Lincoln showed his frontier crudeness. "At times, a highly polished cuss word would escape his lips," his stepmother admitted, and he began to develop a taste for alcohol.[169] In 1858, he told a friend that "he had never taken a drink of any alcoholic beverage in the past twenty years," clearly implying that he stopped drinking in 1838, at the age of 29.[170] Nathaniel Grigsby testified that Lincoln was a *"temperate drinker,"* who drank "his dram as well as all others did, preachers & Christians included."[171] Elizabeth Tuley alleged that at least once Abe "had gotten too much cider of apple-jack . . . and fell in a branch on his face and almost drowned." Her strict father never forgave Lincoln for that one lapse.[172]

In Indiana, Lincoln acquired a lifelong fondness for off-color humor. Dennis Hanks said Lincoln liked to sing "Little Smut[t]y Songs," but Hanks refused to recite their lyrics, for it "would Not Look well in print."[173] J. Rowan Herndon also declined to tell all he knew of Lincoln's anecdotes: "there is many . . . that i could Mention But thay [are] on the vulger order."[174] Lincoln wrote a satire about Charles Harper, who one day encountered Mrs. Noah Gordon as he was riding to the mill with a long bag of wheat. She remarked, "Brother, your bag is too long."

"No," he replied, "it is only too long in the summer."

When Mrs. Gordon told her husband about this ribald remark, he demanded a church trial. Lincoln heard about the proceedings and penned a witty commentary poking fun at the parties involved.[175]

Young Lincoln could be "a kind of forward boy," a "little rude," and "stubborn," according to Dennis Hanks, who also remarked that Lincoln was "a good listener to his Superiors" but "bad to his inferiors" because "he Couldn't Endure Jabber."[176] One day while working on Anderson Creek as a ferryman, he taunted Green B. Taylor about a girl in a nearby town whom Taylor disliked. Exasperated, Taylor hurled a large ear of corn at him. Lincoln then "spanked him good and plenty."[177] Lincoln liked to deflate boastful men. One election day, for example, while en route to the polls, he encountered a braggart named James Larkin, who boasted about his mare's great speed: "Why," said Larkin, "yesterday I run her *five* miles in *four* minutes—and She never drew a *long* breath'" Lincoln replied quietly, "I guess She drew a great many *Short ones*." The consequent laughter enraged Larkin, who "declared he would fight Abe if he wasn't so big. He cussed and jumped around until Abe quietly said, Now Larkin, if you don't shut up I'll throw you in that water."[178]

The Move to Illinois

In 1830, Thomas Lincoln moved his family to a site near the hamlet of Decatur, in Macon County, Illinois, where John Hanks and some of his relatives had settled two years earlier. Hanks's letters extolling the virtues of the Prairie State helped induce Thomas to migrate west. His decision was abrupt; in 1829 he and Abraham had been whipsawing logs for a new cabin in Indiana and had already erected the walls.

Dennis Hanks took the lead in migrating west. He removed his wife, Elizabeth (the elder daughter of Sarah Bush Lincoln), and their four children from Indiana because of an outbreak of the milk sickness. Not wanting to be separated from her daughter and grandchildren, Mrs. Lincoln prevailed upon Thomas to join Dennis and Elizabeth in Illinois. Thomas sold his farm, corn, and pigs to Indiana neighbors, disposed of his wife's lot in Elizabethtown, Kentucky, and from his church obtained a letter of dismission, a kind of recommendation to other Baptist congregations. (Little Pigeon Creek Church records show that a month after that letter was issued, "Nancy Grigsby informed the church that she was not satisfied with Bro. and Sister Lincoln. . . . The church agreed and called back their letter until satisfaction could be attained. . . . The parties convened at Wm. Hoskins and agreed and settled the difficulty." The substance of Mrs. Grigsby's complaint is unknown.)[179]

On March 1, 1830, with his wife, son, stepson, stepdaughters, and their families—eight adults and five children all told—Thomas Lincoln set out for Illinois in a primitive wagon which Abe and his father had constructed almost entirely of wood, with few iron parts. Many neighbors, including James Grigsby, turned out to see them off. Their departure was slightly delayed by Abraham's tardiness. When he finally appeared, Grigsby noticed Thomas, ox whip in hand, looking impatiently at his son. "Watch old Tom flail him," Grigsby said to a friend. But instead of a beating, Thomas gave Abraham the whip and told him to lead the way.[180]

The 225-mile journey took the family past Lickskillett, Loafers Station, Polkberry Creek, the Embarrass River, Polk Patch, Dead Man's Grove, Purgatory Bottom, and Paradise, areas that, judging by their names, no doubt had a story of their own to tell. Problems with the crude wagon wheels—disks of solid wood—forced occasional stops, including one in Vincennes, where Lincoln visited a newspaper office and first beheld a printing press. As they crossed a river coated with a thin layer of ice, they inadvertently left behind Lincoln's dog, which could be heard in the distance howling in despair. Lincoln removed his shoes, rolled up his pants, and waded through the frigid water to rescue the canine. In recounting this story, he said, "I guess that I felt about as glad as the dog."[181] Although the weather was generally mild, the roads were so wet that for long stretches Abe found himself slogging through mud several inches deep. The Kaskaskia River overflowed its banks, almost washing out the corduroy road. Following some debate, the party decided to press on, and for a few miles Abraham led the team through water so high that it threatened to sweep away wagon, oxen, and all.

After two weeks, they finally reached John Hanks's spread on the Sangamon River, 4 miles northwest of Decatur, where they received a hearty welcome. According to Henry C. Whitney, Hanks was "home-spun, matter-of-fact, and dull to a superlative degree, but he was the very soul of generosity, truth, and probity."[182]

As of February 12, 1830, Lincoln was at last legally free to go his own way, but he did not do so. His sense of duty overruled the desire of his heart, and he postponed his self-emancipation in order to help his family as they settled into a new home. Abraham helped Hanks and Thomas Lincoln build a cabin, fence it in, and clear several acres. Conditions there were primitive; deer and wolves roamed about freely, sometimes coming close enough to homes to be visible from doorways and windows. When building cabins for his father and others, Lincoln always served as one of the men to true up corners, a task that required a keen eye and expertise with an ax.

Because he often stayed with the families who hired him as a laborer, Lincoln spent little time in this new cabin. For Macon County sheriff William Warnick, Reuben Brown, William Butler, Charles Hanks, and William Miller, among others, he broke prairie, raised crops, and split rails. One cold day, when Miller's wife (John Hanks's sister Nancy) noticed that Lincoln's pants were worn out, she offered to make him new ones. To his protest that he had no money, she replied that he could chop wood for her instead of paying cash. In both Macon and Sangamon counties, Lincoln and John Hanks cut innumerable cords of wood and divided the profits equally. (Lincoln's later reputation as a rail-splitter was no fanciful invention of political publicists.) Joining them in some of these labors was George Close, who described Lincoln as "the toughest looking man I ever saw," a "poor boy" dressed in "pants made of *flax and tow*, cut tight at the ankle—*his knees were both out.*" Close recalled that they had a "hard time to get work. All a man could do was to keep himself in clothes." Lincoln trudged "5, 6, and 7 miles to his day's work."[183] As a farmhand, he was especially adept with a reap hook, which was "hard, hot, thirsty work."[184] At lunch break, he bolted down his food and spent most of the hour reading.

Henry C. Whitney, to whom Lincoln described his year in Macon County, called that period one of the "three eras of unusual hardship and misery" in Lincoln's "melancholy journey of life." (The other two unusually painful periods, Whitney asserted, were those following the deaths of Nancy Hanks Lincoln in 1818 and his sweetheart Ann Rutledge in 1835.)[185]

Lincoln's introduction to Illinois politics occurred in the summer of 1830 when he was working for William Butler as a plowman at Island Grove, near Springfield. There he heard a speech by Peter Cartwright, a popular Methodist circuit rider campaigning for office. Butler recalled that Lincoln, though "awkward and very shabbily dressed," challenged the speaker for being too dogmatic. "[M]y first special attention was attracted to Lincoln," Butler said, "by the way in which he met the great preacher in his arguments, and the extensive acquaintance he showed with the politics of the State—in fact he quite beat him in the argument."[186]

Later that season, Lincoln put to work the speaking skills he had been cultivating for years as a mimic. He attended a debate in Decatur between two candidates for the state legislature, William L. D. Ewing and John F. Posey. Posey had violated Illinois custom by failing to offer liquid refreshment to the crowd; people on the hard-drinking frontier expected candidates to treat them to alcoholic beverages. When George Close urged Lincoln to abuse Posey, Lincoln responded that he would do so as long as his friends promised not to laugh at him. Frightened when he began speaking, Lincoln quickly warmed up and delivered a respectable speech. Instead of attacking Posey, he spoke well of both candidates and offered a vision of the future of Illinois. After he finished, Ewing complimented Lincoln, calling him "a bright one."[187] Then Posey took Abe aside and "asked him where he had learned So much." When Abe described his program of reading, Posey encouraged him "to persevere."[188]

Thomas Lincoln did not wish to persevere in Illinois. In the summer of 1830 everyone in and around Decatur was attacked by disease-bearing mosquitoes ("gallinippers" in frontier parlance) whose bite transmitted malaria, a debilitating and discouraging disease then variously known as "Illinois shakes," "the ague," or simply "chills and fever." Thomas and his family were seriously afflicted. He and his wife shivered uncontrollably, and their married daughter who came to nurse them was scarcely better off. Miserable, Thomas vowed "that as soon as he got able to travel he would *git out o' thar.*"[189]

Eventually frost killed off the mosquitoes, but relief was short-lived, for a December blizzard dumped 3 feet of snow on central Illinois. Soon thereafter, a freezing rain encrusted the snow with a layer of ice, followed by more snow. Then temperatures plunged below zero and remained there for a fortnight. This season would become immortalized in the annals of Illinois history as "the winter of the deep snow." For two miserable months the Lincolns and their neighbors, ill-prepared for such harsh weather, huddled captive in their cabins while livestock froze and starved outside. Abraham, putting aside his aversion to hunting, braved the cold in search of game. The deer were easy prey because they were caught fast when their sharp hooves broke through the ice crust. To a farmer he encountered, Lincoln reported: "We have used up all of our corn, and now have to go to our neighbors for assistance."[190] One day Lincoln's feet got wet crossing the Sangamon River as he headed for Sheriff Warnick's and became frostbitten as he trudged 2 more miles to his destination. Mrs. Warnick nursed him back to health.

Discouraged by mosquitoes and snowstorms, Thomas Lincoln retreated toward Indiana in the spring of 1831. En route, he stopped at the Coles County home of his sister-in-law, where she and other relatives, including John Sawyer, a good friend of Thomas from Kentucky, persuaded him to settle in their neighborhood. Thomas and his family built a cabin in nearby Buck Grove, where they stayed until 1834, when they moved to Muddy Point, also in Coles County. Three years later they migrated to yet another location in that county, Goosenest Prairie, near Farmington; there Thomas would remain for the rest of his life. His wife Sarah, unhappy with this nomadic existence, told the neighbors "that they moved so often that it reminded her of the children of Israel trying to find the Promised Land." When Thomas suggested yet another move, she flatly refused.[191]

Lincoln did not accompany his family as they headed back to Indiana. In March 1831 his stepmother bundled up his meager possessions, which he slung over his shoulder and he struck out on his own. No longer could Thomas rent him out to neighbors and attach the wages he earned in the abundant sweat of his brow. Though unsure about what he wanted to do, young Lincoln knew for certain that he did not wish to lead the crude life of a subsistence farmer, mired in poverty, superstition, and ignorance. He had had his fill of primitive backwoods agriculture and culture. Later, as a politician, he would not pander to farmers. Despite his enthusiasm for measures promoting economic growth and opportunity, he paid little attention to homestead legislation offering people free farms on government land, which many Republicans considered the best means to end poverty.

In abandoning farm life, Lincoln was hardly unique. Horace Greeley echoed many commentators when he wrote, "[o]ur farmers' sons escape from their fathers' calling whenever they can, because it is made a mindless, monotonous drudgery."[192]

Fleeing that drudgery and what he called "parental tyranny," Lincoln strove to distance himself from the world of his father, who for Abe embodied the indolence, ignorance, and backwardness that he so disliked.[193] Lincoln's adult life clearly represented a flight from the frontier. Once he left the paternal home, Lincoln would never invite Thomas to visit him. Never would he give Thomas the satisfaction of knowing that his name would be carried on by a grandson. Never would Thomas see his grandchildren or his daughter-in-law. Never would Lincoln perform Thomas's work as a farmer and carpenter. Never would he pursue Thomas's favorite forms of recreation, hunting and fishing. As he stepped from the Macon County cabin, Lincoln was free at last, free at last.

3

"Separated from His Father, He Studied
English Grammar"
New Salem
(1831–1834)

In 1848, the 39-year-old Lincoln offered some sage advice to his law partner, William H. Herndon, who had complained that he and other young Whigs were being discriminated against by older Whigs. In denying the allegation, Lincoln urged him to avoid thinking of himself as a victim: "The way for a young man to rise, is to improve himself every way he can, never suspecting that any body wishes to hinder him. Allow me to assure you, that suspicion and jealousy never did help any man in any situation. There may sometimes be ungenerous attempts to keep a young man down; and they will succeed too, if he allows his mind to be diverted from its true channel to brood over the attempted injury. Cast about, and see if this feeling has not injured every person you have ever known to fall into it."[1]

By his own account, Lincoln began his emancipated life "a strange, friendless, uneducated, penniless boy."[2] After escaping from his paternal home, he spent three years preparing himself for a way of life far different from the hardscrabble existence into which he had been born. As he groped his way toward a new identity, he improved himself every way he could.

Frontier Boatman, Humorist, and Jack-of-All-Trades

To earn some pennies, Lincoln accepted an offer from a Kentucky entrepreneur named Denton Offutt to take a flatboat to New Orleans. Offutt was a stocky, talkative, bibulous merchant and speculator constantly on the lookout for quick money. He was also something of a confidence man, peddling a magical expression that would allegedly tame horses when whispered in their ears. Lincoln's friends thought Offutt "gassy" and "rattle brained."[3] A sheriff from whose jail Offutt escaped in 1834 said he tried to pass for the gentleman he was not. When Offutt approached Lincoln, he was trying to recoup losses from a failed pork-packing enterprise by buying corn, beef, and pork cheap and selling them in the South. In February 1831, Offutt proposed to John Hanks, a skilled riverman, that he run a flatboat of goods to New Orleans. Hanks took Offutt to meet his cousin Abraham. "I am seeking employment,"

Lincoln reportedly said. "I have had some experience in boating and boat building, and if you are in want of hands I think I can give you satisfaction."[4] Hanks, Lincoln, and John D. Johnston struck a deal to make the trip south as soon as the snow melted.

In March, the adventuresome trio paddled a canoe from Decatur to Springfield, where they discovered Offutt in the Buckhorn Tavern, dead drunk at midday. After sobering up, Offutt confessed that he had not yet obtained a flatboat, so the first task confronting the three young men would be to build one. They hiked 5 miles north to the mouth of Spring Creek, felled trees, floated the logs to a sawmill near Sangamotown, and, with the help of Charles P. Cabanis, a knowledgeable carpenter, managed to construct a serviceable vessel 80 feet long by 18 feet wide.

During the weeks it took to build the boat, Lincoln impressed the villagers of Sangamotown with both his gawky appearance and his agreeable wit. John E. Roll, who helped with the boat project, described Lincoln as "an awful clumsy looking man," with his "homespun suit . . . cowhide boots, with his trousers strapped down under them," wearing "an old slouch wool hat" and a short coat that exposed several inches of suspenders whenever he bent over.[5] Sometimes Lincoln would strip to the waist for more strenuous work, such as chopping notches and removing the resulting heavy blocks, with his pants rolled to the knees, shirt drenched with sweat, his frizzy hair combed only by his fingers. Caleb Carman, with whom Lincoln boarded, at first regarded him as "a Green horn," and "a fool" because of his "bad Apperance." A brief conversation persuaded Carman that his lodger was, in fact, "a very inte[l]ligent young man" who conversed often about books and politics.[6] When comrades swore at him for refusing to play cards, Lincoln "didn't swear back or even get mad," but rather spent his leisure time reading. Among the books he perused were biographies of George Washington and Francis Marion ("the Swamp Fox").[7]

Lincoln's personality and ability to tell a funny story made him a celebrity in Sangamotown. He was always "verry mer[r]y & full of fun," Caleb Carman remembered.[8] Lincoln struck Clark E. Carr as "the most comical and jocose of human beings, laughing with the same zest at his own jokes as at those of others." Never, said Carr, "have I seen another who provoked so much mirth, and who entered into rollicking fun with such glee." He "could make a cat laugh."[9] Sangamo townsmen would sit on a log as Lincoln regaled them with stories, and when he ended one in an unexpected fashion, they would laugh so hard they fell off. He was also perfectly willing to be the butt of his own jokes. One night at Carman's house, a magician cooked eggs in the hats of several men. When asked for his headgear, Lincoln replied, "Mr the reason why I didn't give you my hat before was out of respect to your Eggs—not care for my hat."[10] His hat became known as "Lincoln's frying pan."[11]

Lincoln's humor was distinctly crude, and his lifelong fondness for off-color stories became legendary. In 1859, when asked, "why do you not write out your stories & put them in a book," Lincoln "drew himself up—fixed his face, as if a thousand dead carcusses . . . were Shooting all their stench into his nostrils, and Said 'Such a book would Stink like a thousand privies.'"[12] In Lincoln's view, clean stories lacked fun. "Very nasty indeed," is how Henry C. Whitney remembered Lincoln's sense of humor.[13] Albert Taylor Bledsoe deemed Lincoln "one of the most obscene men that ever lived."[14] But even those who disapproved sometimes could not help laughing. A New England–born lawyer who practiced with Lincoln in Illinois deplored his racy stories, yet he was frequently reduced to uncontrollable laughter because they were so funny.

Lincoln and his friends were reticent about recording examples of his rough humor. Abner Y. Ellis, for example, told an interviewer, "Modesty and my Veneration for his Memory forbids me to relate" any racy Lincoln stories. Nonetheless, enough of Lincoln's humor has survived to illustrate why his Sangamotown colleagues found him hilarious. Even the reticent Abner Ellis shared this Lincoln joke with William Herndon: "It appears that Shortly after we had pease with England Mr. [Ethan] Allen had occasion to visit England, and while their the English took Great pleasure in teasing him, and trying to Make fun of the Americans and General Washington in particular and one day they got a picture of General Washington, and hung it up in the Back House whare Mr. Allen Could see it and they finally asked Mr A if he saw that picture of his friend in the Back House. Mr Allen said no. but said he thought that it was a very appropriate [place] for an Englishman to Keep it[.] Why they asked. for said Mr. Allen their is Nothing that will Make an Englishman Shit So quick as the Sight of Genl Washington."[15]

Defecation was not the only bodily function that animated Lincoln's jokes; flatulence would serve just as well, especially if the setup was richly detailed and the punch line held the sort of surprise that typified his humor. He told of a "man of audacity, quick witted, self-possessed, & equal to all occasions" who was asked to carve a turkey for a large party. "The men and women surrounded the table & the audacious man being chosen carver whetted his great carving knife with the steel and got down to business & commenced carving the turkey, but he expended too much force & let a fart—a loud fart so that all the people heard it distinctly. As a matter of course it shocked all terribly. A deep silence reigned. However the audacious man was cool & entirely self possessed; he was curiously & keenly watched by those who knew him well, they suspecting that he would recover in the end and acquit himself with glory. The man with a kind of sublime audacity, pulled off his coat, rolled up his sleeves—put his coat deliberately on a chair—spat on his hands—took his position at the head of the table—picked up the carving knife & whetted it again, never cracking a smile nor moving a muscle of his face. It now became a wonder in the minds of all the men & women how the fellow was to get out of his dilemma; he squared himself and said loudly & distinctly—'Now by God I'll see if I can't cut up this turkey without farting.'"[16]

Lincoln also poked fun at drunks. "When I was a little boy," he once said, "I lived in the state of Kentucky, where drunke[n]ness was very co[m]mon on election days. At an election . . . in a village near where I lived, on a day when the weather was inclement and the roads exceedingly muddy, A toper named Bill got brutally drunk and staggered down a narrow alley where he layed himself down in the mud, and remained there until the dusk of the evening, at which time he recovered from his stupor. Finding himself very muddy, [he] immediately started for a pump (a public watering place on the street) to wash himself[.] On his way to the pump another drunken man was leaning over a horse post[;] this, Bill mistook for the pump and at once took hold of the arm of the man for the handle, the use of which set the occupant of the post to throwing up. Bill believing all was right put both hands under and gave himself a thorough washing. He then made his way to the grocery for something to drink. On entering the door one of his comrades exclaimed in a tone of surprise, Why Bill what in the world is the matter[?] Bill said in reply by G-d you ought to have seen me before I was washed."[17]

Lincoln enjoyed telling about a fellow "who had a great veneration for Revolutionary relics. He heard tha[t] an old lady . . . had a dress which she had worn in the Revolutionary War. He made a special visit to this lady and asked her if she could produce the dress as a satisfaction to his love of aged things. She obliged him by opening a drawer and bringing out the article in question. The enthusiastic person took up this dress and delivered an apostrophe to it, 'Were you the dress,' said he, 'that this lady once young and blooming wore in the time of Washington? No doubt when you came home from the dress maker she kissed you as I do now!' At this the relic hunter took the old dress and kissed it heartily. The practical old lady rather resented such foolishness over an old piece of wearing apparel and she said: 'Stranger if you want to kiss something old you had better kiss my ass. It is sixteen years older than that dress.'"[18]

Lincoln's repertoire included bawdy songs, too. He regaled the boys at Sangamotown with such tunes as "Old Old Suckey Blue Skin" and "The Woodpecker Stopping on the Hollow Beach Tree."[19]

Lincoln was not the only member of his family with a penchant for ribaldry. His uncle Mordecai was renowned for his ability to tell smutty stories. Abner Ellis traced Lincoln's "Great passion For dirty Stories" to "his Early training by the Hanks Boys his Cousins."[20]

Lincoln favored stories that illustrated a point and disliked vulgarity for its own sake. William Herndon explained that even though "Lincoln's jokes were vulgar—indecently so," yet he "was not a dirty foul mouthed man by any means." He "was raised among a peculiar people—an ignorant but good people—honest ones. Hence Mr Lincoln preferred jokes to fables or maxims as they, for his people, had the pith-point & force about them to make the point luminous—clear—plain."[21] Leonard Swett reported that if "he told a good story that was. . . . outrageously low and dirty, he never seemed to see that part of it. . . . Almost any man that will tell a vulgar story, has got in a degree a vulgar mind, but it was not so with him."[22] Herndon recalled "a person who so far mistook Mr. Lincoln once as to tell a coarse story without purpose. During its recital Mr. Lincoln's face worked impatiently. When the man had gone he said: 'I had nearly put that fellow out of the office. He disgusts me.'"[23]

In 1864 Lincoln told some White House visitors of a lawyer who "knew more stories and could tell them better than any one I ever knew. He was the life of the bar, and did more than any of us to make the dismal nights in a small county-court town pass off pleasantly." But the man got religion and cleaned up his conversation, and ceased his dirty stories despite the efforts of his friends to draw him out. Finally, under duress, he reluctantly retold one of the bawdy tales for which he had been fa-mous, "and it was a failure. No one laughed." The fellow had omitted expletives and "hard swearing." Lincoln remembered the man explaining, "as I have . . . only told you the plain story, it has failed to amuse you. The question is, gentlemen, *whether the fault is in the story or in you*."[24]

During his stay in Sangamotown, Lincoln made an impression with more than his stories and songs. After the flatboat was finished, the builders fashioned a canoe that two young men commandeered. In the middle of the raging river, the frail vessel capsized, putting the men in grave danger. Lincoln shouted to them to swim to a nearby tree and hang on. He then mounted a log, tied a rope around himself, and handed the end to some anxious spectators. Braving the current, he risked his own safety and brought the men ashore.

In late April 1831, Lincoln, Hanks, Johnston, and Offutt set out for New Orleans with a boatload of bacon, pork, and corn. Years later Lincoln recalled, "I acted both as engineer and engine" on that trip.[25] After only a few miles, the boat ran aground on a milldam at the village of New Salem. Townspeople watched curiously as Lincoln, who made a rather "Singular grotesque appearance," jumped off the boat into the river and took charge.[26] He and his crew transferred the cargo to another vessel to lighten the load. Then Lincoln borrowed an augur to drill a hole in the bow of the flatboat, which hung precariously over the dam. After the water drained out, he plugged the hole, freed the boat, and the journey continued. Struck by Lincoln's ingenuity, Offutt declared that he would have a steamboat built to navigate the Sangamon, and "by thunder, she would have to go" because Lincoln would be the captain.[27]

A few miles below New Salem the boat stopped to load some hogs, which balked when the crew tried to herd them aboard. When corn strewn on the gangplank failed to lure them, Offutt (in Lincoln's words) "conceived the whim that he could sew up their eyes and drive them where he pleased." "I Can't sew the Eyes up," Lincoln ob-jected, so he held the hogs' heads while Offutt stitched their eyes shut.[28] The drastic scheme failed as the blind porkers stayed in the lot and simply went around in circles. Finally, the crew tied them up and hauled them aboard on carts.

Soon after that seriocomic episode, Lincoln nearly abandoned the trip when Johnston and Hanks went on a spree farther down river at Beardstown. Offutt had to track Lincoln down and persuade him to continue. Thereafter, the journey was un-eventful. Occasionally onlookers laughed at the strange craft with its unorthodox sail of plank and cloth.

When they reached New Orleans in May, Lincoln was appalled, as he had been two years earlier, at the sight of slavery. John Hanks alleged that he and Lincoln "Saw Negroes Chained—maltreated—whipt & scourged." Lincoln's "heart bled," though he "Said nothing much" and "was silent from feeling—was Sad—looked bad—felt bad—was thoughtful & abstracted." Hanks maintained that "it was on this trip that he formed his opinions of Slavery; it ran its iron in him then & there—May, 1831. I have heard him say—often & often."[29] To a Lincoln biographer, Herndon reported John Hanks's recollections of the New Orleans episode: "He [Lincoln] saw a slave, a beautiful mulatto girl, sold at auction. She was *felt over, pinched, trotted* around to show to bidders that said article was sound, etc. Lincoln walked away from the sad, inhuman scene with a deep feeling of *unsmotherable* hate. . . . John Hanks, who was two or three times examined by me, told me the above facts about the negro girl. . . . There is no doubt about this."[30] Historians doubt Hanks's assertion, since Lincoln stated that Hanks did not proceed all the way to New Orleans but "had turned back from St. Louis."[31] It is possible that Hanks reported accurately what Lincoln told him at a later time, rather than what he saw with his own eyes. It is also possible that Lincoln's memory was faulty. Herndon alleged that Lincoln often related this story, and it squares with the reminiscences of Allen Gentry's wife about Lincoln's remarks made during his first New Orleans trip. Moreover, Caleb Carman recalled that Lincoln "was opposed to Slavery & said he thought it a curse to the Land."[32]

Throughout this venture, Denton Offutt grew ever more impressed with Lincoln. "Lincoln can do any thing," he marveled. "I really believe he could take the flat-boat back again up the river."[33] Upon Lincoln's return from New Orleans, Offutt hired him to run a store and mill at New Salem. Lincoln readily accepted, delighted to have work that required little physical exertion and paid well. He had dabbled at merchandizing when his family had moved to Illinois; en route he sold needles, pins, pocketknives, eating utensils, and the like, which he had purchased as speculation just before leaving Indiana. Offutt had dreamed up the plan for a New Salem store while returning from Louisiana. Passing through St. Louis, he ordered goods shipped to New Salem and obtained the necessary license.

New Salem

In late July, Lincoln headed for the river village where he was remembered for his ungainly appearance and his exploits on the milldam. Many New Salemites hailed from the Rolling Fork area of Kentucky, near Lincoln's boyhood home on Knob Creek. Among them was the older brother of Lincoln's boyhood chum, Austin Gollaher. New Salem, with its two dozen families, a grain and saw mill, three stores, a saloon ("grocery" in frontier parlance), and a blacksmith shop, was considered an important small town. It served as a trading center for residents of Wolf, Sugar Grove, Concord, Sandridge, Little Grove, Athens, Irish Grove, Indian Point, Rock Creek, Clary's Grove, and other settlements.

New Salem was also a rough and primitive town where violence was commonplace and even religion reflected the crudeness of the frontier. The transplanted Kentuckians, mostly from Barren and Green counties, were hard-shell Baptists who opposed Sunday schools and Bible societies. They devoted Saturdays to shooting matches, card games, horse racing, cock and dog fights, drinking sprees, and fisticuffs. Combatants gouged, bit, kicked, and did anything they could to prevail. On Sunday men were seen with bruised faces, or worse still, missing fingers, eyes, or ears. Womenfolk placed bets on the outcome of fights. Strangers incautious enough to play cards lost their money and then got beaten up. Among the early settlers of Sangamon County, according to Lincoln's friend Milton Hay, "the inherent meanness and vice of the human character frequently manifested itself. Some were given to brawls and violence. Some were malicious, and would vent their malice in slandering a neighbor or injuring his property."[34]

Gander pulling was so popular that a field was set aside for it. A contestant would grease the neck of a gander, lash its feet together, and suspend it from a high tree limb. He would then ride his horse at a fast clip beneath the limb, reach up, grab the gander's head, and try to pull it off. If successful, he won the decapitated bird.

In a frontier hamlet without a jail or whipping post, rowdies had little to fear if they misbehaved. When Baptists would immerse true believers in the Sangamon River, roughnecks would throw logs and animal carcasses from the high bluff, yelling and screaming all the while. From that same bluff the entire community witnessed a fistfight in which a combatant was killed. The Clary's Grove boys were the most notorious bullies in town. "We had hard knuckles and hot blood," said one of their gang members, Thomas S. Edwards. "We could give tough knocks and take em, without ither whining or bearing malice. Ef bad blood was bred at a raising or a shooting-match, it was middlin sure to be spilt afore sundown. . . . We always felt like knocking off somebody's hat, or tramping on somebody's moccasins."[35] In 1833, Edwards was indicted for riot and rape. Sally Marshal alleged that he entered her house one night, threw his coat on the floor, and said "that he would do as he pleased with her . . . he would throw her down there and would fuck her . . . and her Husband should stand and see it."[36]

New Salem's living conditions were as rough as its people. To his family in New Hampshire, Charles James Fox Clarke described the village's cabins, including those of the more prosperous farmers, as "not half so good as your old hogs pen and not any larger."[37] Those dwellings were little better than the half-faced camps of the original pioneers. A staple of the local diet was a form of bread called corn dodgers that were "so hard that you could knock a Texas steer down with a chunk of it, or split an end board forty yards offhand."[38] Writing from central Illinois in 1834, Stephen A. Douglas warned a friend in New York that "persons who have been accustomed to the older and more densely settled States, must expect to experience many inconveniences and perhaps I may add hardships, if they come here."[39] The drudgery of housework and child-rearing made life especially burdensome for women; an English observer called central Illinois "heaven for men and horses, but a very different place for women and oxen."[40] In 1830, a pioneer in nearby Tazewell County confided to a relative: "I pity our women very much." Then he added, "I do not tell them so."[41]

Religious practices in New Salem resembled those Lincoln had witnessed in Indiana. In 1835, Charles James Fox Clarke reported that there were "no settled ministers except in the large towns such as county seats &c. All the preaching we hear is from traveling ministers, such as the free will baptist, iron jacket baptist, Cumberland Presbyterians, Methodists Campbelites &c."[42] To disguise their ignorance, those preachers would often resort to histrionic gestures and high decibel levels.

Drunkenness was common, even among children. Looking back on his early years, Lincoln recalled that "intoxicating liquor [was] recognized by every body, used by every body and repudiated by nobody. It commonly entered into the first draught of the infant, and the last draught of the dying man. From the sideboard of the parson, down to the ragged pocket of the houseless loafer, it was constantly found. Physicians prescribed it in this, that, and the other disease. Government provided it for its soldiers and sailors; and to have a rolling or raising, a husking or hoe-down; any where without it, was *positively insufferable.*"[43] Some New Englanders in the village, led by the pious Dr. John Allen, tried to civilize it by establishing a temperance society. (According to New Salem tradition, Lincoln once said, while pointing to Allen: "There stands the man who, years ago, was instrumental in convincing me of the evils of trafficking in and using ardent spirits. I am glad that I ever saw him. I am glad that I ever heard his testimony on this terrible subject.")[44] When the local schoolmaster joined Allen's group, he was expelled from the Baptist church because the fundamentalist congregants regarded membership in such a society as an unwarranted distraction from God's work. When the same congregation subsequently dismissed a member for drunkenness, a perplexed fellow, brandishing a whiskey flask, asked for clarification: "Brethering, it seems to me that you are not [con]sistent because you have turned out one man for taking the [temperance] pledge and another for getting drunk. Now, brethering, how much of this critter have I got to drink to have good standing among you?"[45] Temperance advocates in New Salem faced ridicule and stiff opposition.

For all its drawbacks, New Salem offered residents a chance to rise based on their talent, ability, and industry. No artificial social barriers stood in anyone's way. As Stephen A. Douglas reported from the region, "no man acknowledges another his superior unless his talents, his principles and his good conduct entitle him to that distinction."[46] Soon after his arrival, Lincoln met the challenge presented by what Dr. Allen called "a notoriously wicked and intemperate place," taking advantage of frontier equality by making friends and allies even of the Clary's Grove boys.[47]

Storekeeper

As he entered New Salem in the summer of 1831, Lincoln thought of himself as "a sort of flo[a]ting Drift wood" swept along by the floods that inundated the region after the "winter of deep snow."[48] Because neither Offutt nor his goods had arrived yet, Lincoln had to postpone his debut as a merchant. He therefore continued as a riverman, piloting a small boat to Beardstown for Dr. David P. Nelson, who was taking his wife and family to Texas. The trip was challenging, for the river had overflowed its banks, and Lincoln sometimes ran far out into the prairie. At Beardstown he awaited the arrival of Offutt's merchandise, which was to be transported to New Salem by a fellow named Potter. When Potter asked how he would recognize Lincoln, Offutt replied: "You can't mistake him; he's as long as a beanpole, and as awkward as he is long."[49]

With nothing much to do after the Beardstown trip, Lincoln, as he put it, "rapidly made acquaintances and friends."[50] The genial personality that won him popularity at Sangamotown did the same in New Salem. One new friend, schoolteacher Mentor Graham, was clerking at the polls on August 1, an election day, when Lincoln entered to vote for the pro–Henry Clay candidate for Congress—an unpopular choice in that heavily Democratic precinct. In need of an assistant, Graham asked the rangy newcomer if he could write. "I can make a few rabbit tracks,"

Lincoln replied.[51] Graham pressed him into service and later testified that Lincoln "performed the duties with great facility—much fairness and honesty & impartially."[52] During lulls, Lincoln delighted his colleagues and voters with jokes and stories. Another townsman, Royal A. Clary, recalled that he "was humorous—witty & good natured & that geniality drew him into our notice So quick."[53] Thanks to those qualities, the penniless newcomer "*had nothing only plenty of friends*," as his companion George Close put it.[54]

In September 1831, Lincoln finally began his career as Offutt's store clerk in a rented log storehouse, dispensing coffee, tea, gunpowder, liquor, tobacco, and other commodities. Offutt hired two assistants for Lincoln, Charles Maltby and William Greene, a 19-year-old Tennessean who, like Lincoln, was a highly entertaining story teller. Greene's main duty at the store was to assess applicants for credit. The three young men slept at the store and took meals at Bowling Green's home, three-quarters of a mile from the village. Greene found his tall colleague "attentive—Kind—generous & accommodating," and recalled that he and Lincoln "slept on the same cott & when one turned over the other had to do likewise."[55]

Lincoln became a popular store clerk. Jesse Baker said that he "drew much attention from the very first. His striking, awkward, and generally peculiar appearance advertised the store round about and drew many customers, who never quit trading there as long as young Abe Lincoln clerked in the establishment. He gave good weight; he was chock full of accommodation, and he wasn't a 'smart Aleck.'"[56]

Lincoln's integrity made him especially appealing to women customers, who trusted him to give an accurate assessment of the wares. Mrs. Hannah Armstrong said she "liked him first rate" because "he was so pleasant and kind."[57] One woman bought a dress for which she paid $2.37. Later that day Lincoln realized he had overcharged her six and a quarter cents, which he refunded to her that very evening. Another woman asked for a pound of tea, which he measured out on a scale inadvertently using the half-pound weight rather than the pound. When he discovered his error, he promptly went to her home and gave her another half-pound of tea. Episodes such as these earned him the sobriquet "Honest Abe."

Although he usually treated his customers kindly, Lincoln could on occasion lose patience with them. He took offense at one Harvey Lee Ross, who asked to see some gloves. Lincoln showed him a pair that he identified as being made of dogskin. When Ross asked how he knew they were dogskin, Lincoln, "rasped" at the challenging tone of the question, replied: "I will tell you how I know they are dogskin gloves. Jack Clary's dog killed Tom Watkins' sheep, and Tom Watkins' boy killed the dog, and old John Mounts tanned the dogskin, and Sally Spears made the gloves, and that is how I know they are dogskin gloves."[58] Lincoln took umbrage at another customer, Charlie Reavis, who used profanity around women in the store. When Reavis ignored warnings to stop, Lincoln accosted him. "I have spoken to you a number of times about swearing in this store in the presence of ladies," he said angrily, "and you have not heeded. Now I am going to rub the lesson in so that you will not forget again." Lincoln grabbed Reavis by the arm, hustled him out of the store, threw him to the ground, and rubbed smartweed in his face.[59]

Lincoln, Maltby, and Greene assumed new responsibilities when Offutt rented the flour and saw mills whose dam had obstructed the flatboat earlier that year. These mills, the only ones within 20 miles of New Salem, brought in a great deal of business. There Lincoln helped unload wheat, measure it out, tie up bags, and collect payments. Offutt also kept Lincoln busy splitting rails and constructing a pen for 1,000 hogs.

Even with all these added duties, Lincoln still had a fair amount of free time. Saturdays were busy, when farmers came to town in large numbers, but the rest of the week was quieter. Lincoln therefore could devote much of his time to the mill while Greene and Maltby minded the store. Most business was transacted between 9 A.M. and 3 P.M. After the store closed, Lincoln would usually devote an hour to wrestling or other physical exercise. With his extremely long legs, he was especially successful in jumping contests.

Lincoln did not spend time gambling, a form of amusement he condemned. When he urged Greene to give it up, his friend protested that he was 90¢ in debt to a demanding creditor and so could not quit until he had won it back. Lincoln offered him a deal: "Billy, if you will promise that you will never gamble again, I'll put up a job that will beat him."

Greene promised to stop "if you will only help me get ahead of him, I swear it."

"Well," said Lincoln, "when he comes into the store again, you bet him one of those seven dollar hats that I can drink out of a full whisky barrel." When the opportunity arose, Greene made the wager, and the men turned to Lincoln. Deceptively strong, and uncommonly clever, the towering Lincoln "squatted down and lifted the one end of the barrel on one knee, then lifted the other end on the other knee, and stooping over, actually succeeded in taking a drink out of the bunghole, which, however, he immediately spat out." Now free of debt, Greene kept his word and gave up gambling.[60]

Like Greene, Denton Offutt also liked to wager, and a bet he made led to one of the formative episodes in Lincoln's young life. Offutt bet rival storekeeper Bill Clary $5 that his lanky clerk could outwrestle any challenger, including Jack Armstrong, leader of the Clary's Grove boys. (Offutt reportedly had won $50 in New Orleans betting that Lincoln could lift 1,000 pounds.) As one of the Clary's Grove boys remembered, he and his cohorts "haw-hawed at this a little, but thought it was some of Dent's 'wind,' for Dent could lie like a peddler. . . . But Jack Armstrong, the pride of our settlement, him that we used to call Salem's Glory, tough as whit-leather, and wiry as a wild-cat, the man that never could be throwed, and we believed never could be throwed, commenced talking back at Dent, saying that his bones was aching with nothing but strength, that he had been laying lazy long enough, and would like a good freshener of a wrestle fust-rate."[61]

Lincoln, who did not share Armstrong's enthusiasm, was quite irritated by Offutt's challenge. He had become popular in New Salem and did not wish to lose the good will of anybody. Moreover, he was by nature a peacemaker, not a fighter. Whenever he and his friend Russell Godbey of New Salem saw a fight taking place, Lincoln would laughingly say: "Lets go and break up the Row."[62] Back in Indiana he had allegedly settled a bitter quarrel between two neighbors over the ownership of a goose. But Lincoln also knew he could not back down from Offutt's challenge to the Clary's Grove boys without being branded a coward.

The day of the match a large crowd gathered near Offutt's store. Though Armstrong was exceptionally strong and a clever wrestler, he found it difficult to cope with Lincoln's great reach and height. As the contest went on, the newcomer was getting the better of it. Just as it seemed that Lincoln would prevail, Bill Clary shouted to his man, "Throw him anyway, Jack."

Breaking the rules of wrestling with a hold permissible only in scuffling, Armstrong instantly threw Lincoln, who angrily "said that if it ever came right, he would give Bill Clary a good licking."[63] At that point a general fight nearly broke out, but Lincoln fearlessly quelled the threat.

John Todd Stuart, Lincoln's friend, mentor and first law partner, called this contest "the turning point in Lincoln's life."[64] His courage, strength, and good-natured acceptance of Armstrong's violation of the rules impressed New Salemites, especially the Clary's Grove boys. They honored him with invitations to referee their horse races, where he further cemented his reputation for fairness. Armstrong became his fast friend and admirer. The popularity he thus gained helped lay the foundation for his political career. As long as Lincoln lived in New Salem, the Clary's Grove boys supported him at election time. (Only later, when he ran for Congress from Springfield, did they vote against him.) In those days, support from the "butcher knife boys" was essential to get a man elected. That Lincoln won such support without sharing their enthusiasm for drinking, gander pulling, and general mayhem was a tribute to his remarkable capacity for making and keeping friends.

Lincoln's essential fairness won him a host of other admirers. A friend who judged a race along with Lincoln declared that he was "the fairest man I ever had to deal with. If Lincoln is in the County when I die I want him to be my adm[inistrato]r, for he is the only man I ever met with that was wholly & purely and unselfishly honest."[65] A cockfight that Lincoln officiated would be immortalized during the Civil War. Babb McNabb's rooster was pitted against Tom Watkins's bird, but when Lincoln threw the two feathered combatants into the ring, McNabb's shunned the challenge. Its furious owner leaped into the pit, seized the bird, and flung him onto a pile of wood, where he raised his head, spread his wing, and crowed lustily. In disgust, McNabb addressed him: "Yes, you little cuss, you are great on dress parade, but you ain't worth a damn in a fight." Lincoln remembered the incident years later and in exasperation he likened General George B. McClellan to McNabb's rooster.[66]

Self-Education

Once established as a promising young man in New Salem, Lincoln began steadily bettering himself, preparing for a career in politics. Most nights, after he and Charles Maltby closed the store, Lincoln would settle into reading and study from 8 o'clock to 11, and then review what he had done.

At first Lincoln concentrated on English grammar, for he did not want to seem like an uneducated bumpkin. In an 1860 autobiographical sketch, written in the third person, he stated: "After he was twenty three, and had separated from his father, he studied English grammar, imperfectly of course, but so as to speak and write as well as he now does."[67] Lincoln began to study grammar soon after he took up his duties as a clerk. The village schoolteacher, Mentor Graham, alleged that Lincoln told him one day that he "had a notion of stud[y]ing grammar." Graham replied: "If you ever Expect to go before the public in any Capacity I think it is the best thing you can do." Eager to begin, Lincoln mused, "If I had a grammar I would Commence now." Curiously, Graham himself did not own such a book, but he thought John Vance did. Lincoln promptly walked several miles to Vance's, borrowed a copy of Samuel Kirkham's *English Grammar in Familiar Lectures,* and "then turned his immediate & almost undivided attention to English grammar."[68] Lincoln found that volume "a puzzler at the start, with its four, five and six headed rules, about as complicated to beginners as the Longer Catechism and the Thirty-nine Articles to young ministers."[69] A New Salemite called Kirkham's dry book "the hardest grammar, I think that anybody ever studied."[70] Night after night, Lincoln labored over the rules and regulations of proper English usage. His assistant, William G. Greene, listened to him recite its rules, correcting him when he made mistakes. Greene recalled that "when he got through with that grammar he knew more grammar than the man who made the book."[71]

Lincoln mastered grammar easily and quickly, obtaining a working knowledge of the subject in a few weeks. Though Greene provided only a little help, his brother Lynn, who had attended Illinois College, spent several days instructing him. Years later, Lincoln told Jonathan Baldwin Turner, who served on the faculty at Illinois College from 1833 to 1848, that his "only instruction in the English language had been from me, through the Green brothers of Tallula, Illinois, while they were students at Illinois College and he was a hired hand working for their mother in the harvest-fields."[72] Another helpmate for Lincoln, Dr. Jason Duncan, modestly stated that "Abraham requested me to assist him in the study of English Grammer, which I consented to do to the extent of my limited ability." Lincoln's rapid progress amazed Duncan: "his application through the winter [of 1831–1832] was assiduous, and untiring, his intuitive faculties were Surprising. [H]e seemed to master the construction of the english language and apply the rules for the same in a most astonishing manner."[73]

In fact, Lincoln never completely overcame his primitive linguistic background. Even in his presidential years his speech betrayed his frontier roots. He began his celebrated 1860 Cooper Union speech by saying, "Mr. Cheerman."[74] As president he said "unly" for "only," "own" for "one," "waal" for "well," "thar" for "there," "was" for "were," "git" for "get," "ye" for "you," "rare" for "rear," and "one on 'em" for "one of them." George Templeton Strong, who recorded some of these Hoosierisms, called the president's grammar "weak" and deemed him "a barbarian, Scythian, yahoo, or gorilla, in respect of outside polish." Strong heard Lincoln say, "me and the Attorney General's very chicken-hearted!"[75] In his antebellum career as a lawyer, he used "ain't" freely, greeting friends in court with a jocular: "Ain't you glad to see me?" or "Ain't you glad I come?"[76] During his famous 1858 debates with Stephen A. Douglas, he one day asked: "Ain't Hitt here?"[77] When a magician at the White House asked for the president's handkerchief, Lincoln replied, "You've got me now, I ain't got any."[78] He said of a supposed relative, "She ain't my cousin, but she thinks she is."[79]

Settled in New Salem, Lincoln became a bookworm. He occasionally indulged in sports and games but never to the neglect of his work or studies. If he had a few minutes of spare time at the store, or, later, at the post office, he would crack open a book. He read walking to dinner at the boardinghouse and strolling about New Salem. When he boarded with the family of the village cooper, Henry Onstot, Lincoln would read after work lying down before the fireplace. When Mrs. Onstot, busy preparing supper, complained that he was in her way, he replied: "Just step over me, Susan." After the meal, he would resume reading.[80]

Now and then Lincoln would walk around reading Kirkham's grammar and would mischievously grab young Robert Rutledge, son of New Salem's innkeeper, hold him under one arm, and nonchalantly continue his ramble, pretending not to notice the lad's yells and kicks. Eventually he would express mock surprise at discovering the youngster's presence.

In New Salem, Lincoln continued devouring newspapers, just as he had done in Indiana. Like many another merchant, he found this habit advantageous in business. He looked forward to the weekly arrival of the St. Louis *Republican* and Louisville *Journal*, two leading newspapers of the West. He particularly relished the *Journal's* politics and wit, subscribing to it even when he lacked the money to buy decent clothes. Lincoln also regularly perused the *Sangamo Journal*, a Whig paper from nearby Springfield, which served as his political bible.

Lincoln especially enjoyed Shakespeare's plays and the poetry of Burns, Cowper, Gray, Pope, and Byron, though he subordinated such pleasure reading to his serious self-improvement studies. In Byron's poems Lincoln evidently responded to the juxtaposition of brooding gloom and rollicking humor. He highly prized Pope's "Essay on Man," especially the following lines:

> All nature is but art unknown to thee;
> All chance, direction, which thou canst not see;
> All discord, harmony not understood;
> All partial evil, universal good;
> And spite of pride, in erring reason's spite,
> One truth is clear, whatever is, is right.[81]

Burns was Lincoln's favorite. After studying hard for two or three hours in the evening, he would relax with a volume of his poems. He especially liked humorous verses like "Tom O'Shanter," "Address to the Dial," "Highland Mary," "Bonny Jeane and Dr. Hornbrook," "Holy Willie's Prayer," and "Epistle to a Young Friend," which he memorized and recited with a Scottish accent. "Burns never touched a sentiment without carrying it to its ultimate expression and leaving nothing further to be said," Lincoln declared.[82] He may well have identified with Burns, a poor farm boy who grew up loathing the drudgery and ignorance of rural life; wrote satirical verse; cherished company, before whom he would tell stories and recite poetry; suffered from depression; and carried a book with him to read whenever he could find time. (Later, as an attorney riding the legal circuit, Lincoln always packed a volume of the Scottish poet in his saddlebags.)

At times, melancholy would overtake Lincoln as he recalled his hardscrabble youth. In such a mood he read "The Cotter's Saturday Night" by Burns, or Thomas Gray's "Elegy Written in a Country Church Yard," or a poem by William Cowper. Lincoln may have detected parallels between New Salem and the settings of Burns's poetry. A New Salemite thought "The Cotter's Saturday Night" would "describe many a prairie Cabin here."[83]

Lincoln also esteemed Edgar Allan Poe's poetry, particularly "The Raven," which he repeated often. He also liked Poe's short stories, notably "The Gold Bug" and "The Facts in the Case of M. Valdemar."

Shakespeare brought Lincoln special pleasure. In New Salem he would sit on the banks of the Sangamon and quote the Bard of Avon with Jack Kelso, a sometime handyman and impractical devotee of poetry. He and Jack were constant companions, frequently seen conversing and arguing. Lincoln may have boarded with Kelso and his wife.

After he left New Salem, Lincoln would regularly carry a copy of Shakespeare's works with him when traveling. He liked above all Shakespeare's political characters Richard III, Hamlet, Macbeth, Julius Caesar, and Coriolanus. His favorite plays were *Hamlet* and *Macbeth*. As president, he told an actor that he had read and reread Shakespeare "perhaps as frequently as any unprofessional reader."[84]

Lincoln had little use for novels; he once told Henry Whitney "that he had never read a novel clear through."[85] But that was not quite the case, for he is known to have read Nathaniel Beverly Tucker's *George Balcombe: A Novel*, published in 1836, and to have recommended it to Abner Y. Ellis. Ellis in turn lent him plays by Edward Bulwer-Lytton, James Kenney, and John M. Morton.

Lincoln's course of self-improvement drew him into the meetings of the Literary and Debating Society in New Salem, presided over by the warm, generous, and sociable James Rutledge. When Lincoln first spoke before the group in the winter of 1831–1832, standing with his hands in his pockets, everyone expected him to tell a funny story. To their amazement, he focused seriously on the question before the society. As he proceeded, he awkwardly gestured to emphasize his points, which were so convincing that they astonished his largely uneducated audience. After the meeting, Rutledge told his wife that "there was more in Abe's head than wit and fun, that he was already a fine speaker; that all he lacked was culture to enable him to reach the high destiny which he Knew was in store for him."[86] As Lincoln gained more experience speaking at these unpretentious meetings, sometimes held in a vacant storeroom, he displayed the logic, intelligence, and spontaneity that would make him the most formidable debater in the New Salem area. David Burner recalled that arguments "seemed to come right out of him without study or long preparation."[87]

Lincoln's skills as a debater may have been honed by Mentor Graham, whose forte as a teacher was elocution. The schoolmaster would have his charges repeat a sentence twenty or more times until they had delivered it properly. Quite possibly he had Lincoln perform such exercises.

No records of Rutledge's debating club survive, but those of some nearby clubs have been preserved. Those organizations usually met once a month, had rules about such things as orderly behavior and strictures against invoking God in argument, and often required that members participate in debate, declamation, composition, criticism, and lecturing. Anonymous papers were solicited and read aloud at meetings, though the bylaws of the Rock Creek Lyceum stipulated that an "anonymous reader shall examine the contents of his box, and on finding any obscene documents by this act be empowered to burn them without further ceremony." Order did not always prevail. At least one of these clubs, the Rock Creek Lyceum, had its meeting broken up by roughnecks. Fittingly, at the time they were debating the question, "Which is the greatest evil which the human family is infested with?" Because of the disruption, however, they adjourned before reaching a verdict.[88] Debate topics from this period in Illinois included what should be done with free blacks if slavery were abolished and whether or not slavery had been beneficial. There were also debates on public works, temperance, banking, public land policy, marriage, and woman's voting and education. During his political career, Lincoln would address many of these issues.

Lincoln's studies progressed well at New Salem, but his career as a clerk did not, primarily because the flighty Offutt neglected the store. In early 1832, the store failed, leaving Lincoln and Maltby unemployed. Such misfortune was common on the frontier. As a resident of central Illinois observed in 1835, "Merchandizing is a tolerably good business, for those who understand it well, and have a sufficient capital to meet all of their engagements. We have but a few such merchants here however, and consequently merchandizing among the Suckers [i.e., Illinoisans] is considered rather a dangerous business."[89]

At this time, Vincent A. Bogue, owner of a store and mill near Springfield, announced that he would cut freight rates in half by bringing a steamboat, *The Talisman*, to Springfield. Farmers could use it to ship their crops cheaply to St. Louis and New Orleans; merchants, mechanics, and professional men also stood to gain. Lincoln and Maltby, out of work after the failure of Offutt's store, saw an opportunity to make New Salem a shipping point for the new steamer. They bought a large log building, which they planned to use for storing and forwarding merchandise and crops. Bogue hired Lincoln and others to clear the channel of the Sangamon. In March the little vessel reached New Salem, where part of its cargo was stored at Lincoln and Maltby's warehouse, and proceeded upriver as far as Portland Landing, a few miles from Springfield.

Just as success seemed within reach, the water level began to drop, forcing the *Talisman*, on which Lincoln served as assistant pilot, to turn back. The boat retreated slowly in the face of stiff prairie winds, making only 3 or 4 miles a day. A sense of *déjà vu* may have overcome Lincoln when the vessel stuck on the same New Salem milldam that had snagged his flatboat a year earlier. By this time, the boat was in sad shape, with the cabin and upper portions severely damaged by trees overhanging the sluggish river. The crew tore away part of the dam and retreated ignominiously to

Beardstown, their mission a failure. After pocketing his $40 fee, Lincoln trudged back to New Salem, where his warehousing business met the same melancholy fate as Offutt's store.

Black Hawk War Service

When Lincoln returned from Beardstown, he found New Salem astir with excitement over brewing trouble. Chief Black Hawk had led 800 members of the so-called British Band of Sauk and Mesquakie (or Fox) tribes across the Mississippi to repossess lands in northern Illinois that they had earlier ceded to the U.S. government. Governor John Reynolds called up the militia. Before the Black Hawk War would end in August, 10,000 state militiamen, aided by one-third of the U.S. regular army, would spend $2 million to chase several hundred Indian warriors from Illinois. Seventy-two whites and 600 to 1,000 Indians were killed.

On April 21, 1832, Lincoln and sixty-seven others from the New Salem area responded to the call-up. Militiamen chose their own officers, and a prosperous sawmill owner, William Kirkpatrick, was confident that he would be elected the company captain. To his intense disappointment, however, the volunteers preferred Lincoln instead. Although Lincoln was reluctant to stand for the office, his friends grabbed him, pushed him forward, and lined up behind him to indicate their choice. Few stood behind Kirkpatrick, who was crushed by the result. Lincoln gleefully exclaimed to William G. Greene, "I'll be damned, Bill, but I've beat him!"[90] This first electoral victory of his life, Lincoln wrote in 1859, was "a success which gave me more pleasure than any I have had since."[91]

Lincoln's unit, the Fourth Illinois Regiment of Mounted Volunteers, part of General Samuel Whiteside's brigade, included some Clary's Grove boys. One of its members described the Fourth as "the hardest set of men he ever saw."[92] The poet William Cullen Bryant portrayed them as "a hard-looking set of men, unkempt and unshaved, wearing shirts of dark calico, and sometimes calico capotes."[93]

Lincoln's toughness, fairness, and native ingenuity made him an effective officer, although not everything went smoothly for him. When he issued his first order as captain, he was told, "Go to the devil, sir!"[94] He may have had some rudimentary militia training in Indiana, but he knew little of military practice and terminology. One day as he was drilling his troops, he wanted them to pass through a gate, but he could not recall the command for having them turn endwise for that purpose. So he improvised, shouting out: "This company is dismissed for two minutes, when it will fall in again on the other side of the gate!"[95]

Lincoln served three brief tours of duty from late April to mid-July, but was disappointed that he saw no combat in the Black Hawk War. He had occasion, however, to witness its horrors. During his first tour, as captain of the Fourth Illinois, he marched west to the Illinois River, then north to the Mississippi, and finally to Rock Island, where he and his men were officially mustered into U.S. service. They proceeded up the Rock River to Dixon's Ferry, then south to Ottawa, where they were disbanded, but not before they had observed casualties. On May 15 Lincoln and his men found the corpses of eleven soldiers, "all scalped some with the heads cut off[,]

Many with their throats cut and otherwise Barbourously Mutilated." These were casualties of the battle at Stillman's Run, where a small band of Indians had routed a much larger militia force.[96] A week later near Ottawa, Lincoln and his men discovered the mutilated bodies of women and children hanging upside down. A member of Lincoln's company reported, "We Saw the Scalps they had taken—scalps of old women & children. . . . The Indians Scalped an old Grand Mother—Scalped her—hung her scalp on a ram rod—that it might be seen & aggravate the whites—They cut one woman open—hung a child that they had murdered in the woman[']s belly that they had gutted—strong men wept at this—hard hearted men Cried."[97] In this charged atmosphere, Lincoln showed courage when his company grew visibly alarmed at a threat posed by a large force of Indians. He was riding a borrowed horse at the time, and though it was more dangerous to march along with his men rather than remain in the saddle, Lincoln sought out the horse's owner, returned it, and took his chances on the ground.

At the end of May, after a month's service, the 1,400-man volunteer army disbanded. Only 300 of them—Lincoln included—reenlisted. For the other 1,100, army life had turned out to be less agreeable than they had anticipated. They insisted on returning home for, they claimed, their enlistment was nearly up, they had to tend their crops and business back home, and they had not enlisted simply to chase Indians across Wisconsin. Moreover, they found their commanding officers inadequate, especially General Sam Whiteside, a legendary hand-to-hand fighter but a failure as a brigade commander. He knew little of tactics and would not take charge of his men.

Lincoln reenlisted because, as he put it, "I was out of work, and there being no danger of more fighting, I could do nothing better."[98] He joined Elijah Isles's company of sixty-one other officers from the original force. (Lincoln was mustered into U.S. service by Lt. Robert Anderson, who in 1861 would command Fort Sumter when it fell to the Confederacy.) The company formed part of a cavalry force charged with protecting the frontier until a new army could be raised. They scouted in northern Illinois, reassuring settlers and menacing Black Hawk as best they could. While undertaking a risky mission to Galena, they paused to bury the victims of yet another massacre.

On June 20, Lincoln volunteered for his final tour as a private in Dr. Jacob Early's Independent Spy Company, a thirty-six-man outfit that primarily conveyed messages and conducted reconnaissance. On one occasion, the men came upon the corpses of several troops killed at Kellogg's Grove and buried them, using their hatchets and hands to dig graves. Lincoln described the scene vividly: "The red light of the morning sun was streaming upon them as they lay, heads towards us, on the ground, and every man had a round red spot on the top of his head, about as big as a dollar, where the redskins had taken his scalp. It was frightful, but it was grotesque, and the red sunlight seemed to paint everything all over."[99] (In 1860, Lincoln's political opponents would belittle Early's unit as useless, claiming that it was held in "general disrepute with men and officers of every other part of the army.")[100]

Military life had its sociable moments for Lincoln and his mates. When not marching, they held footraces, swam, wrestled, played checkers, chess, and cards, and listened to Lincoln as he regaled them with his vast repertoire of stories. They baked bread on ramrods, ate fried meat off of elm bark, and ground coffee in tin cups with their hatchet handles. Of a ration of chickens Lincoln said, "They are much like eating saddle bags," then added, "but I think the stomach can accomplish much to day."[101] Lincoln was elected water bearer, a post he readily accepted in part because it exempted him from less agreeable chores such as cooking or gathering wood. During his three-week stint with the spy battalion, he and John Todd Stuart joined others in search of feminine companionship at Galena. Stuart, who came to know Lincoln well in the Black Hawk War, recollected that they "went to the hoar houses—Gen [James D.] Henry went—his magnetism drew all the women to himself—All went purely for fun—devilment—nothing Else."[102] All in all, Stuart remembered, he and Lincoln "had a first rate time on this campaign—we were well provided—the whole thing was a sort of frolic."[103]

Lincoln's cheerful, agreeable nature stood him in good stead. According to Stuart, "Lincoln had no military qualities whatever except that he was a good clever fellow and kept the esteem and respect of his men. He made a very good Captain."[104] As an officer, Lincoln looked out for his men. When a regular army officer insisted that his own troops must enjoy preferment in rations and pay and then ordered Lincoln to perform an unauthorized act, he reluctantly obeyed. But he protested: "Sir—you forget that we are not under the rules and regulations of the war department at Washington—we are only volunteers under the orders & Regulations of Illinois. Keep in your own sphere & there will be no difficulty, but resistance will hereafter be made to your injust orders & further my men must be Equal in all particulars in rations—arms—camps &c to the regular Army." Acknowledging that Lincoln's complaint was just and realizing that he was determined to have his men treated fairly, the officer thereafter saw to it that the volunteers received the same treatment as the regulars. Lincoln's action endeared him to most of his men.[105]

Lincoln was not popular with everyone, however. His superiors disciplined him for firing his pistol near the camp and for allowing his troops to become drunk. In the first instance, he was arrested for a day, and in the second, he was made to carry a wooden sword for two days. Years later some privates in the company that he commanded disparaged Lincoln's leadership to a Democratic historian and Confederate veteran, John F. Snyder, who reported that they "never spoke in malice of Lincoln, but always in the spirit of ridicule. They regarded him as a joke, an absurdity, and had serious doubts of his courage. Any old woman, they said, would have made a more creditable commander of a company than he did. Profoundly ignorant of military matters, and, from fear of losing his popularity, he made no pretense, or effort, to enforce discipline, or control his men in any way."[106]

In fact, Lincoln occasionally defied his men. One day an old Indian entered the camp, bearing a note signed by Secretary of War Lewis Cass attesting to his good character. Several troops menaced him, swearing that they had volunteered to fight Indians and that they intended to do so now. Lincoln interposed himself between them and the Indian, saying: "Men this must not be done—he must not be shot and killed by us." Even when some accused the man of being a spy, Lincoln would not budge.

"This is cowardly on your part Lincoln," a comrade charged.

"If any man thinks I am a coward let him test it," Lincoln replied, drawing himself up to his full height.

One member of the regiment protested, "Lincoln—you are larger & heavier than we are."

"This you can guard against—Choose your weapons," Lincoln retorted.

That challenge abruptly ended all charges of cowardice. This episode was one of the first times William Greene ever witnessed Lincoln's righteous anger. "He would do justice to all though the heavens fell," Greene noted.[107]

On another occasion Lincoln's sense of fairness cost his troops money. When both his company and that of Lorenzo Dow Thompson of St. Clair wanted the same campsite, Lincoln agreed to wrestle Thompson in order to settle who would get the prize. As he later recalled, he boastfully "told my boys I could throw him, and they could bet what they pleased." Lincoln added: "You see, I had never been thrown. . . . You may think a wrestle, or 'wrastle,' as we called such contests of skill and strength, was a small matter, but I tell you the whole army was out to see it." Thompson had first choice of holds, and when Lincoln felt the strength of the man's grip, he realized he was in for a struggle. After several attempts, Thompson threw him. "My boys yelled out 'a dog fall,' which meant then a drawn battle, but I told my boys it was fair, and then said to Thompson, 'now it's your turn to go down,' as it was my hold then, Indian hug. We took our holds again and after the fiercest struggle of the kind that I ever had, he threw me again, almost as easily at my hold as at his own."[108] Lincoln's men protested, unwilling to lose their bet, but he insisted that "the man actually threw me" and did so fairly.[109] Many years later, Lincoln as president wanted to appoint Thompson to some office, as he explained, "just to show him I didn't bear any malice."[110] Thompson, for his part, esteemed Lincoln highly for his sense of humor and because he was "much of a man."[111]

As a wrestler, Lincoln did better against "the champion of the Southern companies," who, he recalled, "was at least two inches taller and somewhat heavier." But, Lincoln said, "I reckoned that I was the most wiry, and soon after I had tackled him I gave him a hug, lifted him off the ground, and threw him flat on his back. That settled his hash."[112] Lincoln took pride in his wrestling skills. When during his presidency he was told that George Washington had won fame as a wrestler, he said: "If George was loafing around here now, I should be glad to have a tussle with him, and I rather believe that one of the plain people of Illinois would be able to manage the aristocrat of old Virginia."[113]

In 1848, as Lincoln ridiculed Democratic presidential nominee Lewis Cass, he poked fun at his own service record: "in the days of the Black Hawk War, I fought, bled, and came away," he told his fellow Representatives on the floor of the U.S. House. "I was not at Stillman's defeat, but I was about as near it, as Cass was to Hull[']s surrender, and, like him, I saw the place very soon afterwards. It is certain I did not break my sword, for I had none to break; but I bent a musket pretty badly on one occasion. If Gen: Cass went in advance of me in picking huckleberries, I guess I surpassed him in charges upon the wild onions. If he saw any live, fighting Indians, it was more than I did; but I had a good many bloody struggles with the musquetoes; and, although I never fainted from loss of blood, I can truly say I was often very hungry."[114]

Despite this self-mockery, Lincoln felt proud of his role in the Black Hawk War, which proved valuable financially and politically. He earned $175 and 40 acres of public land; gained popularity among both soldiers and civilians by his service in the war; and made friendships that would prove important for his future careers as a politician and lawyer, most notably with John Todd Stuart, John J. Hardin, Edward D. Baker, and Joseph Gillespie. Though he saw no combat, he did get a taste of war, and his selection as captain whetted his appetite for future electoral contests.

Lincoln's military service ended in mid-July when he was mustered out in Wisconsin. With George M. Harrison, he walked rather than rode most of the way home, for their horses had been stolen the night before their departure. At Peoria they bought a canoe, paddled to Havana, sold the boat, and completed their 250-mile journey on foot.

First Bid for Elective Office

Upon returning to New Salem, Lincoln threw himself into the political campaign, which he had decided to enter back in March. After his literary society debut the previous winter, James Rutledge had urged him to run for the legislature. At first Lincoln balked, fearing he had no chance, but Rutledge suggested that "a canvass of the Country would bring him prominently before the people and in time would do him good."[115] Other friends seconded the idea but for a different reason. James Matheny remembered that the idea of Lincoln running for the legislature was "regarded as a joke; the boys wanted some fun; he was so uncouth and awkward, and so illy dressed, that his candidacy afforded a pleasant diversion for them, but it was not expected that it would go any further."[116]

In March Lincoln finally agreed to run and issued a lengthy announcement of his candidacy. John McNamar helped him compose the document and corrected the grammar. Like many other frontier merchants, Lincoln ran as a Whig. But as soon as he announced his intention, the Black Hawk War broke out. By the time it ended, he had only a few weeks to campaign for the legislature.

With the election looming on August 6, Lincoln's chances seemed poor, for he was a little-known Whig in a Democratic district. His formal campaign announcement made his principles clear. He rejected the Jacksonian creed, which *The Democratic Review* summarized in 1838: "As little government as possible; that little emanating from, and controlled by, the people; and uniform in its application to all."[117] Democrats in general believed that the only assertive action that the federal government should undertake was aggressive foreign expansionism. Whigs, on the other hand, favored positive government. A leading Whig spokesman, Horace Greeley of the New York *Tribune*, explained in 1845, "'THE COMMONWEALTH' is the term best expressing the Whig idea of a State or Nation, and our philosophy regards a Government with hope and confidence, as an agency of the community through which vast and beneficent ends may be accomplished," unlike the Democrats, who regard government "with distrust and aversion, as an agency mainly of corruption, oppression, and robbery."[118] The "great fundamental principle" of Whiggery, Greeley declared, was that "government is not merely a machine for making war and punishing felons, but is bound to do all that is fairly within its power to promote the welfare of the people—that its legitimate scope is not merely negative, repressive, defensive, but is also affirmative, creative, constructive, beneficent."[119]

Lincoln shared the Whig vision. He argued that the "legitimate object of government, is 'to do for the people whatever needs to be done, but which they can not, by individual effort, do at all, or do so well, for themselves.' There are many such things—some of them exist independently of the injustice in the world. Making and maintaining roads, bridges, and the like; providing for the helpless young and afflicted; common schools; and disposing of deceased men's property, are instances."[120]

In his 1832 campaign announcement, Lincoln above all championed government support for internal improvements that would enable subsistence farmers to escape rural poverty through participation in the market economy. "That the poorest and most thinly populated countries would be greatly benefited by the opening of good roads, and in the clearing of navigable streams within their limits, is what no person will deny." Lincoln, who knew first-hand about poor and thinly populated places, wanted to spare others the ox-like drudgery that rural isolation had imposed on him and his family. To that end, he recommended affordable projects, primarily to facilitate navigation of the Sangamon River, a subject widely discussed that spring as excitement over the steamboat *Talisman* peaked. Lincoln justly claimed to have some expertise in navigating the Sangamon: "From my peculiar circumstances, it is probable that for the last twelve months I have given as particular attention to the stage of the water in this river, as any other person in the country." For modest sums, he predicted, the river could be straightened and its channel cleared. Desirable as other improvements might be, like canals and railroads, their high cost produced "a heart appalling shock."

Lincoln suggested another technique for liberating people from rural poverty: usury laws. The "baneful and corroding system" of lending money at extortionate interest rates "for the benefit of a few individuals" injured "the general interests of the community" by effectively imposing a heavy tax on borrowers. His implicit message was clear: people could not escape poverty without access to loans at reasonable interest rates. It was a popular issue; in 1833 Illinois legislators outlawed interest rates above 12 percent for loans of a year or longer.

Yet another means for emancipating frontiersmen won Lincoln's approval: public education, which he deemed "the most important subject which we as a people can be engaged in." The kind of superstitious, primitive ignorance that surrounded him in Kentucky and Indiana could be banished by education, which would in turn promote "morality, sobriety, enterprise and industry." Lincoln might have added that, just as he had observed the Sangamon River closely, so too was he intimately familiar with backwoods immorality, drunkenness, indolence, and sloth. He longed to see the day when that kind of world—the world of his father—would disappear.

In the final paragraph of his campaign statement, Lincoln went beyond policy matters to reveal his personal feelings: "Every man is said to have his peculiar ambition. Whether it be true or not, I can say for one that I have no other so great as that of being truly esteemed of my fellow men, by rendering myself worthy of their esteem. How far I shall succeed in gratifying this ambition, is yet to be developed. I am young and unknown to many of you. I was born and have ever remained in the most humble walks of life. I have no wealthy or popular relations to recommend me. My case is thrown exclusively upon the independent voters of this county, and if elected they will have conferred a favor upon me, for which I shall be unremitting in my labors to compensate. But if the good people in their wisdom shall see fit to keep me in the background, I have been too familiar with disappointments to be very much chagrined."[121]

Lincoln's ambition, like that of many other politicians, was clearly rooted in an intense craving for deference and approval. But unlike many power seekers, Lincoln was expansive and generous in his ambition. He desired more than ego-gratifying power and prestige; he wanted everyone to have a chance to escape the soul-crushing poverty and backwardness that he had experienced as a quasi-slave on the frontier. In 1852, he attributed his own views to the recently deceased Henry Clay: "Mr. Clay's predominant sentiment, from first to last, was a deep devotion to the cause of human liberty—a strong sympathy with the oppressed every where, and an ardent wish for their elevation. With him, this was a primary and all controlling passion."[122] That description fits Lincoln as well as it did Clay. From first to last, Lincoln's political goal was to free the oppressed, starting with the kind of frontier people whose conditions he knew first-hand; in time, the scope of his sympathies would broaden.

To forward these principles, Lincoln had to campaign hard in late July and early August. He stumped the huge county, delivering speeches and socializing with the voters. His first campaign address was given at Pappsville, a hamlet 11 miles southwest of New Salem. An auditor remembered that it went something like this: "Fellow citizens, I suppose you all know who I am. I am humble Abraham Lincoln. I have been solicited by many friends to become a candidate for the Legislature. My politics are short and sweet, like the old woman's dance. I am in favor of a national bank. I am in favor of the internal-improvement system and a high protective tariff. These are my sentiments and political principles. If elected I shall be thankful; if not it will be all the same."[123] This speech did not mention public education or usury laws, but it did allude indirectly to the presidential campaign of that year, as Andrew Jackson sought reelection after vetoing the recharter of the Bank of the United States.

Just before this maiden campaign effort, Lincoln quelled a fight. J. Rowan Herndon was whipping Jesse Dodson when Dodson's friends intervened. Lincoln pitched in for Herndon, throwing Dodson's allies about as if they were mere boys. He caught one of them by the neck and seat of his pants and flung him several feet. This decisive action won him many admirers in Pappsville.

Illinois political rallies were usually followed by drinking sprees that inevitably led to fisticuffs, so the fight begun between Herndon and Dodson was not uncommon. During the 1832 canvass in Sangamon County, for example, voters engaged in several fights at groggeries. Gangs from nearby hamlets would gather in Springfield and do battle.

Lincoln poked fun at his own odd appearance. On one occasion he self-depre-catingly observed, "Fellow Citizens: I have been told that some of my opponents have said that it was a disgrace to the County of Sangamon to have such a looking man as I am stuck up for the Legislature. Now, I thought this was a free country. That is the reason that I address you today. Had I known to the contrary I should not have consented to run."[124] On another occasion he said: "Gentlemen I have just re-turned from the Campaign[.] My personal appearance is rather shabby and dark. I am almost as red as those men I have been chasing through the prairies & forests on the Rivers of Illinois."[125]

Lincoln used logical, thoughtful, and engaging speeches to offset the effect of his unprepossessing appearance. Stephen T. Logan, who saw Lincoln address a crowd in Springfield, recalled that he was "very tall and gawky and rough looking," wearing pants that ended 6 inches above his shoe tops. But Logan soon forgot about Lincoln's looks: "after he began speaking I became very much interested in him. He made a very sensible speech. It was the time when [Thomas Hart] Benton was running his theory of a gold circulation. Lincoln was attacking Benton's theory and I thought did it very well. . . . The manner of Mr. Lincoln's speech then was very much the same as his speeches in after life—that is the same peculiar characteristics were apparent then, though of course in after years he evinced both more knowledge and experience. But he had then the same novelty and the same peculiarity in presenting his ideas. He had the same individuality that he kept up through all his life."[126] But his elo-quence did not lead everyone to overlook Lincoln's eccentric outward form. Accord-ing to Henry C. Whitney, "responsible" citizens "could not seriously believe that so ill-dressed and *fresh* a spectacle" as Lincoln "could decently represent this important and populous county."[127]

Lincoln had to overcome more than his looks; campaigning in the 1830s could be grim and tiresome. Local candidates often spoke to audiences of no more than twenty to thirty at social events such as shooting matches or house-raisings. Even smaller audiences would attend evening meetings at log schools illuminated by a few candles. Hard pressed to overcome the deadening effects of such dismal surroundings, candi-dates resorted to the use of wit, humor, and vigorous, colloquial rhetoric and terse arguments.

Lincoln, a political newcomer and long shot, declared that if he were defeated he would try and try again: "when I have been a candidate before you some 5 or 6 times and have been beaten every time I will consider it a disgrace and will be sure never to try it again."[128] And, indeed, in his first try for office he did lose, finishing eighth in a field of thirteen where only the top four vote-getters won legislative seats. It was, he remarked in 1859, "the only time I have been beaten by the people."[129]

Because Sangamon County was huge, Lincoln could not begin to cover it in the short time he had to campaign. On election day, few voters outside New Salem knew who he was. Still, his respectable showing boded well for the future. In New Salem, he did astonishingly well, winning 277 of 300 votes cast even though his candidate for president, Henry Clay, lost that precinct by 115 votes. Lincoln was so popular that several pro-Jackson partisans voted for him because he seemed so honest and worthy. Moreover, he pleased New Salemites who were keen to separate from sprawling Sangamon County and form their own county. Since Lincoln was their local candidate, they counted on him to help achieve that end. Also swelling Lincoln's vote in New Salem was a long-standing enmity between one of his rivals, the Methodist minister Peter Cartwright, and Samuel Hill, the village's leading merchant. Hill, a staunch Democrat, detested Cartwright so much that he not only voted for Lincoln, the Whig, but also worked for him.

Lincoln was quite gratified despite the outcome, for his showing amazed many, including his strongest backers. His skeptical comrades, including James Matheney, discovered that he "knew what he was about and that he had running qualities."[130] And John Todd Stuart believed that Lincoln so impressed everyone with his candor, honesty, and effective speeches that he made friends for future campaigns. "He ran on the square," said Stuart, "and thereby acquired the respect and confidence of everybody."[131]

Frontier Merchant, Postmaster, Surveyor

Two years had to pass before Lincoln could run for office again. In the meantime, though jobless and broke, he resolved to stay in New Salem, where people had been exceptionally kind and where he had many friends. He thought about studying law but feared that his educational background was inadequate for that challenge. He also considered becoming a blacksmith. But before long, Lincoln found himself working at a store once again, this time as a co-owner.

Early in 1832, William Franklin Berry, the son of John M. Berry, a Cumberland Presbyterian minister, bought half-interest in a store from James Herndon. Berry's partner, J. Rowan Herndon, soon sold his half to Lincoln on credit. Shortly after the August election, Berry, Lincoln's junior by two years, and Lincoln opened their emporium with the stock on hand, supplemented by goods, including whiskey, purchased from Henry Inco and James A. Rutledge after their establishment had failed. Some friends wondered why a man of Lincoln's integrity would associate with such a dissolute character as Berry.

Frontier village merchants like Lincoln and Berry were general factotums for everyone and thus came to know what was happening in their neighborhoods. Stores were gathering places, often containing the post office, and usually had a whiskey barrel in a back room with a tin cup dangling from its side.

In January 1833, the new storekeepers bought up the stock of a competitor, Reuben Radford, whose place had been demolished by the Clary's Grove boys, incensed that the clerk had refused to serve them more than two drinks. William G. Greene, who owned the building, bought the surviving merchandise from the agitated Radford for $400. Greene began to fret that he had overpaid, but his friend Lincoln said, "Cheer up, Billy, it's a good thing; we will take an inventory." Not understanding exactly what an inventory was, and fearing that the Clary's Grove boys had committed one, Greene replied: "No more inventories for me."[132] Greene gladly accepted $650 from Lincoln and Berry for the goods and the store, which was a more substantial structure than the one they had.

The little store's stock kept growing. That same month Berry and Lincoln applied for a license to sell liquor by the glass. Daniel Green Burner, who clerked in the store, dispensed drinks for 6¢ apiece. (Burner and several other New Salemites cast doubt on Lincoln's 1858 claim, in the debates with Douglas, that Lincoln "never kept a grocery [saloon] anywhere in the world." Lincoln might have been quibbling; his statement could be interpreted to mean that he never presided over a store where liquor was the main product sold.)[133] Then, in April, the partners bought even more goods from a Beardstown firm. All this expansion left the entrepreneurs, as Lincoln put it, "deeper and deeper in debt," and eventually the business "winked out."[134]

The store failed not just because the partners were overextended but also because Berry was an undisciplined, hard-drinking fellow. He neglected the store and died in 1835, apparently of tuberculosis caused by his dissolute ways. At his funeral, his sin-hating, hard-hearted, prohibitionist father preached a temperance sermon rather than a proper eulogy for his son.

Making matters worse, Lincoln was too soft-hearted to deny anyone credit, no matter how impecunious the applicant might be. Nor could he sue his customers or otherwise pressure them to pay their bills. Moreover, he lacked enthusiasm for the job and was far too likely to interrupt a transaction with a long story. He also erred in letting the bibulous Berry wait on women and in candidly warning their good customers that the whiskey he sold would ruin them and that the tobacco was of poor quality. If he did not know much about some of the goods in the store, he would freely acknowledge his ignorance. He and Berry extended too much credit, bought and sold goods unwisely, failed to keep items properly stocked, and invested so much money in slow-selling merchandise that their stock became an unappealing hodge- podge. In short, they had little aptitude for the business.

When Berry died in 1835, Lincoln's debts amounted to approximately $1,100. "That debt was the greatest obstacle I have ever met in life," he told a friend. "I had no way of speculating, and could not earn money except by labor, and to earn by labor eleven hundred dollars, besides my living, seemed the work of a lifetime." So Lincoln told his creditors that if they "would let me alone, I would give them all I could earn, over my living, as fast as I could earn it." As late as 1860, Lincoln was still being dunned for payment of these New Salem debts. According to Herndon, "the debt galled him and hastened his wrinkles."[135]

While struggling to pay his creditors, Lincoln had few expenses, for his rent was minimal. At first he slept for free in Offutt's store and took his meals with John M. Camron, who charged him $1 per week. Later, Isaac Burner charged him the same fee for room and board. He lodged in the second Lincoln-Berry store even after it folded. When he roomed with James Short, Lincoln paid $2 a week. Meals and laundry were cheap. During his five and a half years in New Salem, Lincoln stayed with Caleb Carman, James Rutledge, the Camron family, and the cooper, Henry Onstot. He also lived with J. Rowan Herndon until that gentleman (perhaps accidentally) shot his wife to death in 1833. Lincoln then moved to the outskirts of the village to Mentor Graham's home for six months.

Graham's hospitality might have been inspired by a singular act of kindness on Lincoln's part. The previous autumn the schoolmaster's family had been very sick, especially his 7-year-old daughter, Ellen, of whom Lincoln was quite fond. Unable to tolerate milk, she needed bread, which Graham could not afford. As Graham later described it, "I was . . . too proud to tell the actual condition we were in. As I walked back to the street [from the mill], my sack on my arm and my head down, thinking over my sad lot, and the disappointment there would be at home, my little girl's wan face uprose before me, and tears gathered in my eyes, falling thick and fast. Just then I had something touch my hand, and looking down, there lay a ten dollar bill. Turning quickly, I saw Lincoln slipping into his office door, glancing furtively toward me."[136]

Lincoln also roomed at the tavern of Nelson Alley, another beneficiary of his generosity. After moving to Springfield in 1837, Lincoln heard that his former landlord, who had once lent him money, was incarcerated in a poorhouse. Lincoln made a personal visit to that facility and arranged for Alley to be released and located in a new home. Throughout his life, Lincoln unfailingly showed his gratitude to those who had helped him in times of need. He rapidly acquired a reputation as an unusually generous, charitable, benevolent young man. One cold winter day he offered to help a barefoot boy who was chopping wood to earn money for shoes. Lincoln sent the lad inside while he did the chopping for him. After completing the job, Lincoln told the boy to purchase the footwear. He also chopped wood and did other chores for widows and orphans. When he saw travelers bogged down, he stopped to help them, despite the taunts of his friends, who said: "Now Lincoln don't make a d—d fool of yourself."[137]

In May 1833, as he struggled to eke out a living, Lincoln was delighted to be named the postmaster of New Salem, a job he would hold until that post office closed three years later. The position had belonged to storekeeper Samuel Hill, who neglected his postal patrons in favor of customers for his merchandise, including liquor. Several New Salem women, indignant that they had to wait while tipplers were served their whiskey, got up a petition to replace Hill with Lincoln. Ossian M. Ross, postmaster at Havana, reviewed the petition, noted that it was signed by leading citizens, and forwarded it with his endorsement to Washington. Also behind the drive to oust Hill was Jason Duncan. Over Lincoln's protests that he had no desire to see Hill fired, Duncan nonetheless preferred charges that led to Hill's resignation and Lincoln's appointment by the Jackson administration. Lincoln's Whiggery did not hurt his chances because, as he explained, the office was "too insignificant, to make his politics an objection."[138] Besides, Lincoln was one of the few people in New Salem who could manage the paperwork. Nelson Alley and Alexander Trent guaranteed the mandatory $500 bond. Lincoln was greatly pleased, not only because he would be able to earn some money but also because he gained access to newspapers he did not subscribe to.

Lincoln's duties were light, for the mail came just twice a week. When picking up their letters and periodicals, customers paid the postmaster (there were no stamps in those days), and sometimes Lincoln advanced the amount due. Of a trusting nature himself, Lincoln was stung when George Spears sent a man for the mail and demanded a receipt for the payment. Lincoln obliged but enclosed a sharply-worded note: "At your request I send you a receipt for the postage on your paper. I am some what surprised at your request. I will however comply with it. The law requires News paper postage to be paid in advance and now that I have waited a full year you choose to wound my feelings by insinuating that unless you get a receipt I will probably make you pay it again."[139] On receiving the receipt and note, Spears immediately rode to New Salem to apologize and explain that it was his messenger he distrusted, not the postmaster.

Another postal customer, who irritated Lincoln repeatedly, became the butt of a retaliatory prank. Johnson Elmore, ignorant but ostentatiously proud, pestered Lincoln several times a day with the question, "Anything for me?" when obviously there would not be. Exasperated but amused, Lincoln drafted a letter to Elmore from a fictitious black woman in Kentucky. The missive discussed possums, dances, corn shuckings, and ended with "Johns—Come & see me and old master won't Kick you out of the Kitchen any more." When Elmore received the fake letter, he could not, in fact, read it (Lincoln knew he was illiterate), but Elmore pretended to do so. Elmore then took the letter to literate friends who told him what it said, prompting him to think they were fooling him. Finally, he brought the document back to postmaster Lincoln. Though it was difficult for him to keep a straight face, Lincoln read the entire letter aloud. Never again was he bothered by the insistent request, "Anything here for me?"[140]

When business took him out of the village, Lincoln delivered letters to homes, using his hat as a mailbag. Storing letters and papers in a hat was not unusual on the frontier, and Lincoln did it for many years.

Lincoln kept his accounts carefully. After the New Salem post office closed in 1836, he had a surplus of about $16, which he took with him when he moved to Springfield the following year. A few months later, a government agent approached Lincoln's friend Anson G. Henry about the outstanding balance. Henry, fearing that the cash-strapped young man might not have it on hand, offered to help Lincoln. But it was unnecessary, for the erstwhile postmaster had in his room all the money—in fact, the very coins—that he had received in New Salem. He turned the funds over to the agent with a simple explanation: "I never make use of money that does not belong to me."[141]

By the middle of 1833, Lincoln's personal finances reached low ebb. The postmaster job paid little, and his debts weighed him down so much that he often had to struggle to pay his modest board bill. He took every odd job he could—serving as an election clerk, splitting rails, tending both the grain mill and the sawmill, clerking in stores (among them Samuel Hill's), and harvesting crops for James Short, who praised him as "the best hand at husking corn on the stalk I ever saw. I used to consider myself very good, but he would gather two loads to my one."[142] All these jobs yielded just enough to make ends meet.

Lincoln's economic situation improved considerably when John Calhoun, the Democratic surveyor of Sangamon County, offered to hire him as an assistant. Business was heavy in the northern part of the county, where New Salem was located, because the voyage of the *Talisman* had prompted most landowners to have their property surveyed for town lots. Frontier wags jested that soon the whole district would be laid out in towns, with no land left for agriculture. The townsite craze lasted from 1832 to 1838. Speculators filed on lands at $1.25 an acre and resold them for higher sums. Town lots became one of the principal exports of Illinois, peddled in the East by slick salesmen. There arose a strong demand for surveyors, whose stakes covered the vacant prairies.

Calhoun and his principal assistant, Thomas M. Neale, knew Lincoln from the Black Hawk War, when they all served in the same regiment. Neale may have recommended Lincoln for the job, and when he replaced Calhoun in 1835, Neale retained Lincoln as an assistant. Friendship trumped politics when Lincoln was offered the job; both Neale and Calhoun were Democrats, as was Pollard Simmons of New Salem, who also endorsed Lincoln. Simmons was devoted to Lincoln, who described Pollard as being "about the best friend I ever had."[143] Lincoln reciprocated by voting for both Calhoun and Neale. But when Simmons jubilantly delivered the actual job offer, Lincoln asked, "Do I have to give up any of my principles for this job? If I have to surrender any thought or principle to get it I wouldn't touch it with a ten foot pole." Assured that he would not have to abandon his Whig convictions, Lincoln gratefully accepted.[144] After he called on Calhoun to accept the offer formally, the chief surveyor's sister-in-law disparaged the new assistant's appearance; Calhoun replied, "he is no common man."[145] Lincoln was ever grateful to Calhoun, whom he held in high esteem and regarded affectionately. A mannerly and agreeable gentleman, Calhoun was unfortunately ruined by alcohol. In later years he would clash with Lincoln in political debates, but the two remained friends despite Calhoun's struggles with whiskey.

Lincoln attacked his surveying duties with characteristic industriousness. He procured a compass and surveyor's chain, and began to study both Robert Gibson's *Treatise on Practical Surveying* and Abel Flint's *System of Geometry and Trigonometry: Together with a Treatise on Surveying*. Both books emphasized higher math, including logarithms, plane geometry, and trigonometry. It is not certain how much time Lincoln spent learning the art of surveying, but it was surely more than six weeks, as some have improbably asserted. He had studied the surveyor's art ever since mastering grammar. Once the latter task was accomplished, he told William Greene, "if that is what they call a science I'll subdue another."[146] He evidently mastered the subject without assistance. Mentor Graham claimed that he taught Lincoln surveying, but that is highly unlikely, for Graham knew little math. (Indeed, Graham's entire claim to be "the man who taught Lincoln" is unfounded. He barely achieved limited certification to teach and was widely regarded as a long-winded classroom tyrant suited only to lower levels of instruction. His former pupils mostly spoke ill of him.)

Having learned the basics, Lincoln set out with his compass, 66-foot chain, marking pins, range poles, plumb bobs, stakes, and ax to pursue his new calling. When a friend told him he needed a horse, Lincoln demurred, saying he "was somewhat of a 'hoss' himself."[147] For a time he borrowed a mount from Jack Armstrong; eventually he bought one, along with a bridle and saddle, on credit.

When he finally recorded his first survey on January 6, 1834, Lincoln's friends and neighbors helped him celebrate his good fortune. A good surveyor and a welcome presence, Lincoln made many friends throughout the sprawling county. The exposure would serve him well in his political future.

Charles Chandler, a Connecticut-born physician who settled on Panther Creek in 1832, had a particular reason to think well of Lincoln. Chandler wanted to buy 80 acres adjacent to his property, and frontier custom dictated that as a settler he had first refusal rights on parcels adjoining his original claim. But another Connecticut newcomer, Henry Laurens Ingalls, coveted the same tract. Once Chandler learned that Ingalls might beat him out for the land, he quickly borrowed some cash, saddled up, and began a desperate dash to the Springfield land office—where Ingalls was also headed. As he rode along, Chandler told his story to some horsemen he had overtaken. One of them was Lincoln, who immediately offered to swap his fresh mount for Chandler's tired one. Chandler declined, estimating that he would beat Ingalls to Springfield anyway, but he was grateful for the offer. "I became a Lincoln man then," he recalled, and when he needed to have that new tract surveyed, he hired the young man from New Salem.[148]

Lincoln quickly gained an enviable reputation as a skillful surveyor. It was important for settlers to register their timber lots, especially to protect them from trespassers and unauthorized pillaging of valuable trees. Lincoln became the preferred expert for determining survey lines in the dense forest. Whenever settlers like Henry McHenry had a disagreement over property boundaries, Lincoln refereed the dispute to the satisfaction of all. McHenry and his neighbors argued over the location of a corner and chose Lincoln to arbitrate the matter. After spending three or four days surveying the area, Lincoln stuck a staff into the ground and announced, "Gentlemen—here *is* the Corner." When the contesting parties dug at that spot, they found the remains of the original survey stake with a lump of charcoal under it, just as the first surveyor had left it.[149]

Between 1834 and 1836, Lincoln surveyed homesites, roads, school sections, and towns, including New Boston, Petersburg, Huron, and Bath. While platting Petersburg, Lincoln changed a line as an act of kindness to Jemima Elmore, widow of a member of the company he had commanded in the Black Hawk War. He calculated that if he ran a street in the usual fashion it would slice a few feet off the end of Mrs. Elmore's house, which was all she owned or was ever likely to own. Lincoln said: "I reckon it won't hurt anything out here if I skew the line a little."[150] Lincoln's work in laying out New Boston earned high praise from Peter Van Bergen, who had invested money to develop the site. "Mr. Lincoln was a good surveyor," Van Bergen said: "he did it all himself, without help from anybody except chainmen &c. and also made a plat of it."[151] The founders of Huron liked his work so much that they allegedly offered him $5,000 to establish a store there.

Surveying on the frontier was rugged work, hard on men, equipment, and clothes alike. Surveyors lived outdoors in all conditions while trying to impose order on a wild, untracked land. Lincoln often went to work in an old, broken straw hat, with no coat or vest, and pants that barely met his boot tops. Elizabeth Abell, in whose home

Lincoln lodged while he was surveying the hills between New Salem and Petersburg, recalled that he would often return at night "ragged and scratch[ed] up with the Bryers." He "would laugh over it and say that was a poore man[']s lot." His trousers often had to be "foxed"—that is, have a buckskin cover sewn on the outside of the leg—to save them from total destruction in the brush. Mrs. Abell foxed Lincoln's trousers for him, as did Hannah Armstrong, whose husband, Jack, was a friend and sometime chainman for Lincoln. She also made Lincoln deerskin breeches and shirts.[152]

Despite his success as a surveyor, Lincoln continued to have financial troubles. The man who sold him a horse on credit, a colorful eccentric named Thomas Watkins, sued Lincoln for payment in April 1834. That same month other creditors, including Peter Van Bergen, also won judgments against him. To satisfy the debts, Lincoln's surveying tools and horse were sold at a sheriff's auction. A friend from Sandridge, James Short, saw that Lincoln was "very much discouraged" and heard him say "he would let the whole thing go by the board." Generously, Short bought Lincoln's possessions for $120 and returned them. Trying to express his gratitude, Lincoln said simply, "Uncle Jimmy, I will do as much for you sometimes."[153] (During the Civil War, Lincoln appointed Short to supervise an Indian agency.)

Election to the State Legislature

While surveying land in Sangamon County, Lincoln also surveyed his political prospects, which seemed encouraging. As a veteran of the Black Hawk War, merchant, humorist, surveyor, handyman, teller of colorful stories, and an honest, helpful friend, he had made himself not only known, but liked and well regarded. He was a Whig with a host of Democratic friends and admirers. The Democrats approached him first in 1834. Because they had supported him for postmaster and surveyor, they had reason to hope Lincoln would join them. During the early and mid-1830s, it was common for ambitious Illinois politicos to affiliate with the Democrats. New Salem Democrats told their party comrades throughout Sangamon County to assist Lincoln or else they would not support their candidates.

It was a Democrat, Justice of the Peace Bowling Green, who persuaded Lincoln to make a second run for the legislature. In March 1834, Green and Lincoln presided over a meeting called to endorse a gubernatorial candidate. Afterward, Green and other Democrats approached Lincoln and offered to remove two of their own nominees in favor of his candidacy. Lincoln immediately recognized that this might hurt the chances of his friend, John Todd Stuart, and informed Stuart of the scheme. Stuart appreciated that Lincoln had "acted fairly and honorably." Confident of his own strength, though, Stuart instructed Lincoln "to go and tell them he would take their votes—that I would risk it."[154]

An important issue in 1834 was a proposal to lop off the New Salem area from Sangamon County (which at that time was over twice the size of Rhode Island) and form a new county. Travel to the county seat, Springfield, imposed hardships on jurors, witnesses, litigants, land filers, and anyone else who had to do public business there. Between New Salem and Springfield lay 20 miles of rough country. In 1832 a resident described how in the spring "our rivers are over-flowed, the channels of all streams are full and traveling in any direction is impeded, and sometimes wholly stopped." A rider would find himself "wading through ponds and quagmires, enjoying the delights of log bridges and causeways, and vainly invoking the name of McAdam, as he plunges deeper and deeper into mire and misfortune."[155] In addition to avoiding the perils of travel to Springfield, voters in New Salem hoped their town would become the seat of the new county.

New Salemites and their neighbors began petitioning for their own separate county in 1830. In the winter of 1832–1833, Hugh Armstrong and Ned Potter obtained 195 signatures on a petition to the legislature calling for a new county; several of Lincoln's friends signed it. Lincoln pledged that he would attempt to get New Salem detached and incorporated into a new county. That pledge won Lincoln nearly unanimous support in the New Salem area, while he secured at least the Whig vote elsewhere in the county.

Lincoln also gained popularity by favoring construction of a canal from Beardstown to the Sangamon River. New Salem had closer ties to Beardstown than Springfield. The canal, Lincoln told the electorate, would prevent spring flooding and allow farmers to transport their produce more cheaply to the Illinois River, 40 miles away. The Illinois was their preferred highway to the world; the Sangamon was mostly unnavigable except in the spring.

Lincoln issued no principled manifestos in 1834 and instead focused heavily on the county separation issue in what he called "more of a hand-shaking campaign than anything else." He stumped extensively, staying with friends like Abner Y. Ellis in Springfield. At Island Grove, when Lincoln approached some thirty men harvesting crops, they declared they would support no man unless he could lend them a hand. Lincoln replied, "well, boys if that is all I am sure of your votes." He grabbed a cradle and easily pitched in; later, every one of the men voted for him. An onlooker, Dr. Richard F. Barrett, observing Lincoln harvesting away, scornfully asked J. Rowan Herndon if the Whig Party could not find a better nominee than that. In response, Herndon urged the doctor to attend a political rally the next day where all the candidates would speak. Barrett did so, later acknowledging to Herndon that Lincoln "knows more than all of them Put together."[156]

Lincoln's personal qualities appealed to the voters, especially his geniality and humor, both of which were highly prized by frontiersmen, and he was gifted in the art of calling on people in their homes. Charles Maltby remembered that Lincoln "made himself pleasant and agreeable with all persons, with the rich or poor, in the stately mansion or log cabin." Dealing with the prosperous, "he was respectful, deferential and sociable," and with the lowly, "affable, agreeable and simple." He talked to the families about their hopes and prospects, about schools, farms, crops, and livestock. People felt "they had met a friend—one near as a brother." He paid attention to the children, gave them candy and nuts, and it was clear that all this "came from the natural impulses of his heart." While other home-visiting candidates tended to talk immediately about politics, Lincoln would propose a tour of the farm while supper was cooking. After the meal he would eventually involve the women and children and regale the family with tales of his own childhood. He was folksy and congenial, and he made people feel he was one of them—clearly, a smarter version of them, but one of them nonetheless.[157]

Lincoln's family-friendly campaign style worked because it was without affectation. Especially appealing to the families was his genuine fondness for children. When he boarded with John Camron, he delighted in playing merry tricks and pranks on his host's many daughters. He would pluck their ears and give them nicknames. In the Camron family, Vienna became "Quinine," Tom he renamed "Tam O'Shanter," Betsy was "Queen Isabella," and Eliza, unaccountably, was dubbed "John."[158] They and the other children of New Salem enjoyed his joking and playfulness as much as he did and loved him for it.

Lincoln also won admirers and votes in the neighboring town of Athens, primarily by saving one of their neighbors from the roughnecks of New Salem. A fierce rivalry had grown up between Athens and New Salem, fueled by raids that residents of one community made on the other; in turn, retaliatory counter-raids were executed. When one of the combatants from Athens incautiously visited New Salem alone, several villagers stuffed him into a sugar hogshead, nailed it shut, and prepared to roll him down the steep 200-foot bluff into the river. Lincoln intervened and talked them out of this potentially fatal plan. Thereafter, the Athens boys voted for him enthusiastically in all his campaigns for the legislature.

A potential threat to Lincoln's electoral chances was his reputation as a religious skeptic. Isaac Snodgrass urged fellow townsmen to vote against him because of his alleged deism. The father of James H. Matheny, Lincoln's close friend, loved Lincoln wholeheartedly but was a strong Methodist and therefore hesitated to vote for him. Lincoln's religious views were in fact unconventional. After discussing with his New Salem friends such iconoclastic works as Constantine de Volney's *The Ruins; or, A Survey of the Revolutions of Empires,* and Thomas Paine's *Age of Reason* and *Common Sense,* Lincoln wrote an essay in a similar vein. When he told his political backer, Samuel Hill, that he intended to publish it, Hill snatched the manuscript from his hands and flung it into the fire. According to Jesse Fell, Lincoln "held opinions utterly at variance with what are usually taught in the Churches," and his views, "would place him entirely outside the Christian pale."[159]

Lincoln lived in a community that took religion seriously. He often discussed religious topics with his friends, many of whom were skeptics. In New Salem, and later in Springfield, his views bordering on atheism shocked many. He pointed out contradictions or logical lapses in the Bible; according to Herndon, Lincoln told him "a thousand times that he did not believe that the Bible, etc., were revelations of God, as the Christian world contends."[160] In many conversations with Edward D. Baker, Lincoln challenged the authenticity of scriptures, unconvinced that they were divinely inspired.

At times, Lincoln appeared saddened by his lack of faith. Albert Taylor Bledsoe, who debated religious issues with Lincoln in Springfield, thought that he "always seemed to deplore his want of faith as a very great infelicity, from which he would be glad to be delivered." The way Lincoln talked about religion, "with an air of such apparent modesty" as well as "gloom and despair," made Bledsoe feel "deep compassion" for his friend.[161] When Samuel Hill's devout wife asked Lincoln, "Do you really believe there isn't any future state?" he replied: "Mrs. Hill, I'm afraid that there isn't. It isn't a pleasant thing to think when we die that is the last of us."[162]

Lincoln found religion as practiced on the frontier unappealing. Detailed doctrinal hairsplitting repelled him, as did the cranky sectarianism that bred enmity and divided communities. In Indiana, Sophie Hanks heard young Lincoln declare "that if he could take the best parts from all the churches, he could make a new church better than any of them."[163] He told a New Salem friend, "I'd like to go to church if I could hear a good sermon. About all one hears is one preacher get up and denounce another or run down the denomination he preaches for."[164] An exception to this rule was Campbellite minister Josephus Hewitt, whose preaching Lincoln admired. Even as late as the Civil War, Lincoln continued to be put off by doctrinal bickering. As he told a congressman, "When any church will inscribe over its altar, as its sole qualification for membership, the Savior's condensed statement of the substance of both law and Gospel, 'Thou shalt love the Lord thy God with all thy heart, and with all thy soul and with all thy mind, and thy neighbor as thyself,' that church will I join with all my heart and all my soul."[165] On good and evil, Lincoln identified with a man who asserted that "when he did good he felt good, when he did bad he felt bad." That, Lincoln said, "is my religion."[166]

Innately tolerant and forbearing, Lincoln was doubtless offended by harsh frontier Calvinism. Because he often spent weekends at George Spears's home, he on occasion probably attended Clary's Grove Baptist Church, which had been founded in Spears's house and was known for punitive discipline of its congregants. John M. Berry, the father of Lincoln's store partner, William F. Berry, was a strapping man with a strong voice and a reputation for rigidity; he denounced his son as a drunk and disowned his daughter for marrying at the age of 14. Not only did he never again speak to her, but when her first-born died, he did not attend the funeral; he limited his formal grieving to a momentary pause in his gardening as his grandchild's funeral procession passed by his farm. Lincoln was probably alienated by such unforgiving, hard-hearted inhumanity in a man purportedly espousing the gospel of a savior who counseled: "Judge not, that ye be not judged."

One of the poems Lincoln memorized, Robert Burns's "Holy Willie's Prayer," satirized the doctrine of predestination:

> O Thou that in the heavens does dwell!
> Who, as it pleases best Thysel',
> Send ane to heaven and ten to hell,
> A' for Thy glory,
> And no for ony gude or ill
> They've done before Thee

That poem, according to James H. Matheny, "was Lincoln's religion."[167] Lincoln poked fun at the doctrine of damnation by telling a story about a Methodist parson who criticized a Universalist minister: "Why, the impertinent fellow declared that all shall be saved, but, my dear Brethren, let us hope for better things."[168]

Despite his unorthodox religious views, in 1834 Lincoln won election to the Illinois Legislature. Democratic crossover votes helped him finish among the top four in a twelve-man contest, even though he was unyielding in his devotion to Whig principles. In the two years since his first try at office, he had become much better known and appreciated. A growing network of loyal friendships, many of them dating from the Black Hawk War, strengthened him. In Lake Fork, for example, when the official Democratic tickets instructing the party faithful whom to vote for disappeared, Lincoln's resourceful friend Hawkins Taylor made up tickets of his own that included Lincoln's name. Although few voters there had heard of Lincoln, Taylor talked him up. "I let each man name whom he pleased for Governor and the other state officers," Taylor remembered, "but not one of them could name four members for the Legislature, and then I would get in Mr. Lincoln's name." According to Taylor, 108 of the 111 men who voted at Lake Fork marked their ballots for Lincoln.[169] Lincoln was overjoyed. Not only was election an honor, but members of the legislature were paid $4 per day, and he told a friend that that was "more than I had ever earned in my life."[170] During his four terms as a legislator, Lincoln received a total salary of $1,762.

By the end of 1834, the piece of human driftwood who had three and a half years earlier washed up on the banks of the Sangamon River at New Salem had been transformed. Though still known as "a mighty Rough man," he had acquired a sense of direction.[171] Having chosen his career as a politician, he would pursue it single-mindedly, distancing himself ever further from the backward, provincial, isolated, ignorant world of Thomas Lincoln.

"A Napoleon of Astuteness and Political Finesse"
Frontier Legislator
(1834–1837)

After leaving his paternal home and settling in New Salem, Lincoln found a surrogate father in Bowling Green, a rotund, easygoing, humorous, jovial "reading man" from North Carolina known as a gifted spinner of yarns. Twenty-two years Lincoln's senior, Green served at various times as justice of the peace, canal commissioner, doorkeeper of the Illinois House of Representatives, judge of elections, county commissioner, sheriff, and candidate for the state senate. In Lincoln's early days in New Salem, he boarded at Green's house, which attracted many visitors, for Green was famously hospitable.

Finding a Surrogate Father

Abner Y. Ellis reported that Lincoln "Loved Mr Green" as "his allmost Second Farther." Green, in turn, "looked on him with pride and pleasur[e]" and "Used to Say that Lincoln Was a Man after his own heart." Green told Ellis "that there Was good Material in Abe and he only Wanted Education." Undertaking to provide that education, Green nurtured his protégé, lending him books, encouraging him to study, and fostering his political career. Though a prominent Democrat, Green urged Lincoln, who opposed the Democrats, to run for the state legislature. Lincoln confided to Ellis "that he owed more to Mr Green for his advancement than any other Man."[1]

Green stimulated Lincoln's interest in the law by inviting him to attend sessions of his court, where Green's directness and informality could lead to humorous moments. When John Ferguson sued Green's poetry-loving friend Jack Kelso for stealing a hog, Green ruled in Kelso's favor, even though he had no proof and witnesses testified that the hog was Ferguson's. Green announced that "the two witnesses we have heard have sworn to a — lie. I know this shoat, and I know it belongs to Jack Kelso. I therefore decide this case in his favor."[2] When Lincoln queried him about the verdict, Green explained that "the first duty of a court is to decide cases justly and in accordance with the truth."[3] Green displayed a similarly casual approach to the niceties of the law when he asked attorney Edward D. Baker if a justice of the peace could preside over slander suits. After Baker replied that only courts of general jurisdiction could hear a slander case, Green expostulated: "Well, think again; you have not read law very well, or very long; try it again; now, have I not jurisdiction; can I not do it?" Once again Baker responded in the negative. After another round of such questioning, Green finally said: "I know I can; for, by Heaven, I have done it."[4]

Lincoln had learned some law from the books Green lent him, which he read in 1832 and 1833. Because few lawyers lived in the New Salem area, the young would-be attorney was often requested to try suits in Green's court. He accepted the challenge but turned down any remuneration. Initially the judge, who enjoyed Lincoln's humor, allowed him to practice for amusement's sake. Green's fat sides would shake as he laughed at the young man's laconic presentation of cases. Soon realizing that Lincoln was more than just a comedian, Green came to respect his intellect.

Green and Lincoln performed a kind of comic duet in one trial. When quizzed by an attorney about the veracity of a bibulous shoemaker named Peter Lukins, Lincoln testified: "he is called lying Pete Lukins." The lawyer then asked Lincoln if he would believe Lukins under oath. Lincoln turned about and said, "ask Esquire Green. He has taken his testimony under oath many times." Green replied: "I never believe anything he says unless somebody else swears the same thing."[5]

Lincoln grew close to Green and his wife, the former Nancy Potter, an unusually maternal, hospitable woman. In 1835, while suffering from depression, Lincoln repaired to the Greens' cabin, where for three weeks they nursed him back to psychological health. When a stroke killed Green in 1842, his widow asked Lincoln to speak at the memorial service. He agreed to do so, but when "he arose he only uttered a few words and commenced choking and sobbing" and acknowledged that "he was unmanned and could not" go on; he therefore "got down and went to Mrs. Green's old family carriage."[6]

Law Student

Even before he began attending Green's court, Lincoln had shown interest in the law. In Indiana he was sued for violating the rights of a Kentucky ferry operator and sat in on trials held before a neighboring judge. He may have actually done some pettifogging before this court, acting as a very junior attorney in minor matters. To Judge John Pitcher of Rockport, Indiana, young Lincoln expressed a desire to study law. During his brief sojourn in Macon County in 1830, Lincoln read law books at the home of Sheriff William Warnick.

Like many other Hoosiers, Lincoln had often attended court sessions in Boonville, where conditions were doubtless primitive. Legal proceedings in a similar community (Fall Creek) were conducted in a double log cabin. While shoeless jurors sat in the woods on a log, their foreman signed indictments on his knee. One Indiana judge quelled a disturbance with his fists, saying: "I don't know what power the law gives me to keep order in this court, but I know very well the power God Almighty gave me."[7]

In New Salem, Lincoln drafted legal documents for his neighbors without charge. He was notably willing to help the poor, including Isaac Burner, for whom he wrote a deed.

Lincoln once pettifogged before Justice of the Peace Samuel Berry, uncle of Lincoln's ill-starred business partner, William F. Berry. The case involved a young woman impregnated by a swain who refused to marry her. Lincoln compared her plight with that of her seducer, likening the young man's honor to a white garment that, if soiled, could be washed clean; but the young woman's honor resembled a glass bottle that, once broken, was gone. Lincoln reportedly won a $100 judgment for his client.

As early as 1832, Lincoln had considered studying law in earnest but hesitated because of his meager education. His trepidation was understandable, for the most widely used legal text, William Blackstone's *Commentaries on the Laws of England,* recommended that the prospective law student should have "formed both his sentiments and style, by perusal and imitation of the purest classical writers, among whom the historians and orators will best deserve his regard"; should be able to "reason with precision, and separate argument from fallacy, by the clear and simple rules of pure unsophisticated logic," and to "steadily pursue truth through any of the most intricate deductions, by the use of mathematical demonstrations"; should have "enlarged his conceptions of nature and art, by a view of the several branches of genuine, experimental philosophy"; should have "impressed on his mind the sound maxims of the law of nature, the best and most authentic foundation of human laws"; and, finally, should have "contemplated those maxims reduced to a practical system in the laws of imperial Rome."[8]

By 1834, however, Lincoln was far less intimidated by the mysteries of Blackstone's *Commentaries,* a copy of which he bought at an auction. This change in attitude could have resulted from his experience in Springfield in April 1833, when he served as a witness in two cases and as a juror in three others. Over half of the members of the bar whom he might have observed in these proceedings had attended neither college nor law school. Even the presiding magistrate was probably unimposing. In 1835, a New York attorney observed Judge Stephen T. Logan of the Sangamon Circuit Court "with his chair tilted back and his heels as high as his head, and in his mouth a veritable corn cob pipe; his hair standing nine ways for Sunday, while his clothing was more like that worn by a woodchopper than anybody else." If Lincoln beheld such a jurist, he may have overcome his self-consciousness about his own appearance.[9] Around that time he told Lynn M. Greene that he "had talked with men who had the reputation of being great men, but could not see that they differed from other men."[10] Perhaps some of those "great men" were Springfield lawyers. Lincoln may also have been encouraged by his experience as a pettifogger before Bowling Green and Samuel Berry.

With his powerfully analytical mind, Lincoln might well have been drawn to lawyers as a class, for they were reputedly the most intelligent members of frontier society. Lawyers also had an advantage over nonlawyers in the political arena, and after his 1834 electoral victory Lincoln's appetite for politics grew stronger. A student who worked with Lincoln observed that he "took up the law as a means of livelihood, but his heart was in politics" and that he "delighted" and "reveled in it [politics], as a fish does in water, as a bird disports itself on the sustaining air."[11] Lincoln's third law partner, William H. Herndon, varied the metaphor, declaring that politics was "his life and newspapers his food," while the law merely served "as a stepping stone to a political life."[12]

Further stimulating Lincoln's ambition to become a lawyer was encouragement from a sophisticated, dignified, college-educated attorney, John Todd Stuart. The tall, slender Stuart was exceptionally handsome and enjoyed a reputation as one of the best jury lawyers in the state. His easygoing, cheerful, good-natured personality and polished, gentlemanly manners won him many friends and favorably impressed numerous jurors. In his law practice he played the role of peacemaker. A Springfield woman who spent much of her youth in Stuart's home deemed him "a type of a gentleman of the olden times, so gentle and courteous—with as fine and gallant a bow for his laundress as for a Duchess."[13]

A Kentuckian like Lincoln, Stuart graduated from Center College in 1826 and studied law with Judge Daniel Breck. Soon thereafter he settled in Springfield, where in 1833 he formed a partnership with Henry E. Dummer. The previous year he had run successfully for the legislature, quickly rising to become a Whig leader in the House of Representatives. There he was known as "Jerry Sly" for his mastery of legislative intrigue. William Herndon thought him "tricky" and a "dodger."[14] Political opponents denounced him as "indolent and inefficient," condemned his "low cunning," and bestowed upon him the sobriquets "sleepy Johnny" and "the Rip Van Winkle of the Junto."[15]

During the Black Hawk War, Stuart came to admire Lincoln so much that he decided to take him under his wing. In a third-person autobiographical sketch, Lincoln wrote that during the election campaign of 1834, "in a private conversation he [John Todd Stuart] encouraged A[braham to] study law. After the election he borrowed books of Stuart, took them home with him, and went at in good earnest."[16] Whenever Lincoln expressed anxiety about the difficulties standing in his way or doubts about entering the legal profession, Stuart reassured him. Without Stuart's mentoring, Lincoln probably would not have become a lawyer. (Years later Stuart predicted that he would be remembered only as "as the man who advised Mr. Lincoln to study law and lent him his law books.")[17]

Although Stuart became Lincoln's mentor, he did not, like Green, play the role of surrogate father. (He was, after all, only a year older than Lincoln.) Jesse W. Fell, who observed the two men during the legislative session of 1834–1835, called them "congenial spirits not only boarding at the same house but rooming and sleeping together. Socially and politically they seemed inseparable." David Davis believed that Lincoln and Stuart "loved one another." Indeed, Fell said, they were "boon companions," though totally different in temperament and appearance. Stuart, who had "all the adornments of a polished gentleman," provided a startling contrast to Lincoln: "rawboned, angular features deeply furrowed, ungraceful, almost uncouth; having little, if any, of the polish so important in society life."[18]

Under Stuart's guidance, Lincoln began his legal studies by wading through Blackstone's *Commentaries*, the work most widely read by aspiring attorneys, though some authorities found it unsuitable for Americans. Lincoln went at his task industriously, claiming to have mastered forty pages of the *Commentaries* on his first day. He recalled, "I began to read those famous works, and I had plenty of time; for, during the long summer days, when the farmers were busy with their crops, my customers were few and far between. The more I read the more intensely interested I became. Never in my whole life was my mind so thoroughly absorbed. I read until I devoured them."[19]

When Lincoln began to "go at" the law "in good earnest" following the 1834 election, he once again "studied with nobody," save Stuart. In those days it was not difficult to become a member of the Illinois bar. "Men in the west are admitted to practice much less qualified than they are in the east," a resident of Champaign County reported. "An ordinary intelligent man with a moderate education can be admitted in about one year."[20] Still, as an autodidact, Lincoln was unusual, for in the 1830s and 1840s most lawyers learned their craft in an attorney's office. By pursuing his studies virtually alone, Lincoln may not have missed much, however. As Joseph Story maintained, "the dry and uninviting drudgery of an office" was "utterly inadequate to lay a just foundation for accurate knowledge in the learning of the law."[21] Josiah Quincy painted an unflattering picture of a typical law office: of "[r]egular instruction there was none; examination as to progress in acquaintance with the law,—none; occasional lectures,—none; oversight as to general attention and conduct,—none."[22]

Lincoln followed a regimen that he would prescribe twenty-four years later to a young man who asked him how to gain "a thorough knowledge of the law." Lincoln replied: "The mode is very simple, though laborious, and tedious. It is only to get the books, and read, and study them carefully. Begin with Blackstone's Commentaries, and after reading it carefully through, say twice, take up Chitty's Pleading, Greenleaf's Evidence, & Story's Equity &c. in succession. Work, work, work, is the main thing."[23] Two years earlier he had indirectly recommended the same course of study to another would-be attorney: "When a man has reached the age that Mr. Widner has, and has already been doing for himself, my judgment is, that he reads the books for himself without an instructer. That is precisely the way I came to the law."[24] In 1855, he told yet another potential law student: "If you are resolutely determined to make a lawyer of yourself, the thing is more than half done already. It is but a small matter whether you read with any body or not. I did not read with any one. Get the books, and read and study them till, you understand them in their principal features; and that is the main thing. It is of no consequence to be in a large town while you are reading. I read at New-Salem, which never had three hundred people living in it. The books, and your capacity for understanding them, are just the same in all places. . . . Always bear in mind that your own resolution to succeed, is more important than any other one thing."[25]

Lincoln, whose "resolution to succeed" was strong indeed, preached what he practiced. In 1860, he urged a young friend who had been rejected by Harvard not to despair: "It is a *certain* truth, that you *can* enter, and graduate in, Harvard University; and having made the attempt, you *must* succeed in it. '*Must*' is the word. I know not how to aid you, save in the assurance of one of mature age, and much severe experience, that you *can* not fail, if you resolutely determine, that you will not. . . . In your temporary failure there is no evidence that you may not yet be a better scholar, and a more successful man in the great struggle of life, than many others, who have entered college more easily."[26]

Some of his neighbors in New Salem were nonplussed by Lincoln's resolute study of law. Before he began preparing himself for a career at the bar, he seemed a rather happy-go-lucky fellow. Parthena Hill told a journalist, "I don't think Mr. Lincoln was overindustrious. . . . He didn't do much. His living and his clothes cost little. He liked company, and would talk to everybody, and entertain them and himself."[27] Others remembered Lincoln in the period before his law studies "as a 'shiftless' young man, who worked at odd jobs," and "a sort of loafer."[28]

But once Lincoln devoted himself to legal studies, he became a different man, much to the consternation of his friends and neighbors. When Russell Godbey initially noticed him with a law book in hand, he asked: "Abe—what are you Studying?" "Studying law," Lincoln replied. Godbey exclaimed: "Great God Almighty!"[29]

So it was that for the first time since his arrival in New Salem, Lincoln became antisocial. In the summer he often sought solitude in the woods in order to read and study undisturbed. Some New Salemites even thought him deranged. Henry McHenry remembered that when Lincoln "began to study law he would go day after day for weeks and sit under an oak tree on [a] hill near Salem, and read—moved round [the] tree to keep in [the] shade—was so absorbed that people said he was crazy. Sometimes [he] did not notice people when he met them."[30] He quit reading poetry to focus on his law tomes. Henry McHenry and others joshed Lincoln because they found it strange that he walked all the way to Springfield for books. When they also teased him about his first name, he began signing letters and documents "A. Lincoln."

Lincoln enjoyed his informal legal training. Many years later, when his son Robert expressed a desire to attend Harvard Law School, Lincoln said: "If you do, you should learn more than I ever did, but you will never have so good a time."[31]

After moving to Springfield in 1837, Lincoln continued to "work, work, work" at mastering the law. Herndon testified that he "was not fond of physical exercise, but his mental application was untiring." Sometimes he would "study twenty-four hours without food or sleep, . . . often walking unconscious, his head on one side, thinking and talking, to himself."[32]

In 1836, Lincoln took some necessary formal steps to become a lawyer. In March he obtained a certificate of good moral character from Stephen T. Logan, and six months later he received his license from the Illinois Supreme Court. After another six months, a clerk of that court officially enrolled him as an attorney. No record survives of the required examination that Lincoln took, but it probably resembled the one administered to John Dean Caton in 1835 by Justice Samuel D. Lockwood of the Illinois Supreme Court. The judge asked Caton what books he had read and how long and with whom he had studied. Then he "inquired of the different forms of action, and the objects of each, some questions about criminal law, and the law of the administration of estates, and especially of the provisions of our statutes on these subjects." The exam lasted no more than half an hour, after which Lockwood told Caton that he would approve his application, though the young man had much to learn if he wanted to become a good lawyer.[33] Lincoln's exact contemporary Gustave Koerner remembered undergoing a similarly casual examination, after which he and another candidate for the bar treated their examiners to a round of brandy toddies. Koerner found this quite a contrast to the bar exam he had taken in his native Germany, where leading jurists grilled him for four hours in Latin.

Freshman Legislator

In December 1834, legislative duties interrupted Lincoln's self-education in the law. Until taking his seat in the General Assembly, he had been indifferent about clothing. He often wore trousers with one leg rolled up and the other down. Overcoming his sartorial insouciance, the freshman legislator decided to purchase new garments. He asked his friend Coleman Smoot: "Smoot, did you vote for me?" When Smoot said yes, Lincoln replied: "Well, you must loan me money to buy suitable clothing for I want to make a decent appearance in the Legislature."[34] Smoot obliged with a generous loan, which Lincoln used to purchase "a very respectable looking suit of jeans," garb that made an ideological as well as a fashion statement. The Whig champion Henry Clay once wore similar apparel to demonstrate support for protective tariffs and encourage the consumption of American-made goods. The outfit was probably inexpensive; much later Lincoln said, "I have very rarely in my life worn a suit of Clothes costing $28."[35]

In the capital city of Vandalia, a primitive village of about 800 souls located 75 miles south of Springfield, Lincoln and three dozen other newcomers joined nineteen returning veterans in the House of Representatives. Three-quarters of the legislators were, like Lincoln, Southern-born. The second-youngest member of that chamber, he belonged to the minority anti-Jackson contingent, which numbered only about eighteen in the lower house; the Democrats were more than twice as numerous. The factions had not yet become formal parties. "It is difficult to catch the hang of parties here," an Illinoisan remarked, "for altho' there is considerable party feeling there is very little party organization."[36] Legislative business was conducted primarily through personal influence. The anti-Jackson forces in Illinois did not officially coalesce to form the Whig Party until 1838.

The Illinois House of Representatives that Lincoln entered was a rudimentary body. Most of his colleagues were farmers, many of them unsophisticated. Representative Alfred W. Cavarly pronounced the word "unique" "you-ni-kue"; when someone asked for a definition, one wag quipped that it was the "female of the unicorn."[37] (A Springfield lobbyist remarked on Cavarly's "very inordinate enlargement of the organ of *self-esteem*. This is shown in the *pomposity* of his delivery and the elevation of his ideas, which are sometimes so '*dape and so profound*,' as Paddy O'Flanagan said of the preacher, '*that the divil a word can you untherstand*.'")[38] Representative Jesse K. Dubois said "imbroligo" instead of "imbroglio," and, as a synonym for it created the neologism "embrigglement."[39] In 1840, David Davis observed, perhaps generously, that the "politicians of the State, of both parties, are of a medium order of intellect." After serving in the General Assembly, Davis commented at the close of one session, "I do not think that the legislature has done much harm. We never inquire, whether it has ever done any good." In 1847, he flatly denounced the General Assembly as "the great source of evil in this State. If there had been none in session for 10 yrs. Ill[inoi]s w[oul]d have been a very prosperous state."[40] An observer of the 1840–1841 House of Representatives said that it "appeared to be composed all of young Men, some of them mere Boys; they forcibly reminded me of a Debating School of Boy Students."[41]

Thomas Ford, governor of Illinois in the 1840s, took a more charitable view of the state's legislators, most of whom were, in his opinion, simply gladhanders. The "great prevailing principle upon which each party acted in selecting candidates for office was, to get popular men," he recalled. "Men who had made themselves agreeable to the people by a continual show of friendship . . . who were loved for their gaiety, cheerfulness, apparent goodness of heart, and agreeable manners." Though unlearned, the members of the General Assembly were, Ford said, "generally shrewd, sensible men, who, from their knowledge of human nature, and tact in managing the masses, are amongst the master spirits of their several counties."[42] Not all legislators were amiable conciliators, however; some hotheads challenged opponents to duels.

The state capitol where Lincoln first served was unprepossessing. A leader of the senate, William Lee Davidson Ewing, called the decade-old building—with its falling plaster, sagging floors, cracked and bulging walls, and crumbling bricks—"manifestly inconvenient for the transaction of public business."[43] The plainness of both the architecture and the furnishings made it resemble a Quaker meetinghouse. Members sat on hard benches instead of cushioned chairs. The speaker of the House of Representatives presided from an armchair resting on a small platform; before him was a primitive desk made by placing a board on some sticks. Built hurriedly on low, wet ground, this statehouse was replaced in 1836 with a more substantial, if no more attractive, edifice.

Some members of the General Assembly thought the capital "the dullest, dreariest place," and the governor complained that "there is no young ladies in Vandalia."[44] The sleepy hamlet, which one of its founders called "a most dull and miserable village" when the General Assembly was not in session, came to life when the legislators arrived.[45] On the opening day of the 1834 session, a Vandalian reported that "last night, all night nearly this town has been a scene of busy, buzzing bargaining, etc. It is said 150 persons, some from the most distant parts of the State [are vying] for the appointments of Sergeant at Arms of the Senate and Doorkeeper of the House of Representatives."[46]

Primitive as it was, Vandalia—with its bookshop, jewelry store, furniture emporium, and other businesses—must have seemed glamorous to the rough young legislator from New Salem. It certainly seemed so to Representative John J. Hardin's wife, who in 1839 wrote from her home in Jacksonville, "I miss the intellectual feasts I enjoyed at Vandalia."[47] A friend of hers wondered: "how can she bear with the dull monotonous town of Jacksonville after leaving the gay scenes of the splendid city of

Vandalia."[48] In 1830, a visitor to the capital marveled that "three meetings of an anti-
quarian and historical society have already taken place, and the whole of their published proceedings are as regular, and as well conducted, and as well printed . . . as if
the seat of society had been at Oxford or Cambridge."[49] In the winter of 1838–1839,
lectures were given at the statehouse by an officer in Napoleon's army and a visitor
from McKendree College, among others; the topics included temperance, phrenol-
ogy, and Prussian education. James Hall, a journalist and litterateur, promoted intellectual life in Vandalia, helping to found schools and lyceums. Parties, dances, and
receptions enlivened society during sessions of the legislature.

Lincoln struck up a close friendship with Senator Orville H. Browning of Quincy
and his wife, Eliza, a charming and witty woman. Years later Senator Browning told
an interviewer: "Lincoln had seen but very little of what might be called society and
was very awkward, and very much embarrassed in the presence of ladies. Mrs. Browning very soon discovered his great merits, and treated him with a certain frank cordiality which put Lincoln entirely at his ease. On this account he became very much
attached to her. He used to come to our room, and spend his evenings with Mrs.
Browning . . . most of his spare time was occupied in this way."[50] In 1839, Lincoln
and three other legislators lightheartedly invited Mrs. Browning to come from her
home in Quincy to the capital, "bringing in your train all ladies in general, who may
be at your command; and all Mrs. Browning's sisters in particular."[51]

In the 1830s, the legislature wielded more power than it would later. As Governor Thomas Ford described it, his office "was feeble, and clothed with but little authority," while the legislators "came fresh from the people, and were clothed with
almost the entire power of government."[52] Voters chose only the governor, lieutenant
governor, senators, and representatives; all other state officers were selected by the
General Assembly. People paid little attention to government, as long as it left them
alone. Politicians "took advantage of this lethargic state of indifference of the people
to advance their own projects, to get offices and special favors from the legislature,
which were all they busied their heads about." Governor Ford decried the "fraud" and
"deceit" that legislators employed in passing special laws and creating offices and jobs,
while ignoring the general welfare. He lamented that the "frequent legislative elections; the running to and fro of the various cliques and factions, before each election;
the anxiety of members for their popularity at home; the settlement of plans to control future elections, to sustain the party in power, on the one side, and to overthrow
it, on the part of the minority, absorb nearly the whole attention of the legislature,
and leave but little disposition or time to be devoted to legitimate legislation."[53]

Others shared Ford's view of the legislature. In 1835, Lincoln's colleague in the
General Assembly, fellow Whig William H. Fithian, complained from Vandalia of
"[t]oo much blowing off steam, for expedition [of] business." Four years later, he lamented: "We have been here now two weeks and as yet so far as I can judge, not one
measure has been adopted for the benefit of the people of Illinois."[54] The Chicago
Democrat condemned Illinois legislators for passing *"most of their time at drinking,
gambling and bawdy houses."*[55] Legislatures throughout the West were held in low esteem. One Hoosier declared: "When I hear of the assembling of a Legislature in one

of these Western States, it reminds me of a cry of fire in a populous city. No one knows when he is safe; no man can tell where the ruin will end."[56] Judge David Davis, appalled by a particularly dangerous criminal standing before his bench, absently sentenced the miscreant to seven years in the Illinois Legislature, where Davis had endured one term.

During the ten-week legislative session in 1834–1835, Lincoln, under the tutelage of John Todd Stuart, remained inconspicuous, quietly observing his colleagues grant petitions for divorce, pass private bills to relieve individual citizens, appeal to Congress for money, declare creeks navigable, lay bills on the table, and listen to committee reports. On roll calls, Lincoln sided with Stuart 101 times but voted against him on 26 occasions. On votes for public officials, Lincoln agreed with Stuart every time save one. Stuart claimed that in 1834 and 1836 "he frequently traded Lincoln off."[57] As he laid plans for a congressional race in 1836, Stuart groomed Lincoln to take over his leadership role in the General Assembly.

Lincoln's first bill sought to limit the jurisdiction of justices of the peace; much amended, it won approval in the House but not the senate. Two weeks into the session he introduced a measure that did pass, authorizing the construction of a toll bridge over Salt Creek. Appreciating his literary skill, colleagues pressed him to draft legislation for them; he also wrote reports for the Committee on Public Accounts and Expenditures.

In addition, Lincoln composed anonymous dispatches about legislative doings for the *Sangamo Journal,* an influential Whig newspaper in Springfield that over the years would publish many of his unsigned articles. Lincoln had easy access to the columns of that paper. As William Herndon recalled, "I frequently wrote the editorials in the Springfield *Journal,* the editor, Simeon Francis, giving to Lincoln and to me the utmost liberty in that direction." Both partners submitted material to the *Journal* up to 1861.[58] James Matheny, who was to be a groomsman at Lincoln's wedding, recalled that when he served as deputy postmaster in Springfield in the mid-1830s, he came to recognize Lincoln's handwriting and estimated that he delivered hundreds of editorials from him to Simeon Francis.

Lincoln's political opponents took note that he was contributing to the *Journal.* The Democratic *Illinois State Register* of Springfield charged that the "writers of the *Journal* have had a *late* acquisition (Lincoln)—a chap rather famous not only for throwing filth, but for *swallowing it afterwards.*"[59] In 1840, the *Register* alleged that the author of a *Journal* article attacking Democrats "is no doubt one of the Junto, whose members deliberate in secret, write in secret, and work in darkness—men who dare not let the light of day in upon their acts."[60] This was doubtless an allusion to Lincoln, a leader of the Whig "Junto" and its most trusted writer.

The partisan press was filled with anonymous attacks and misattributed remarks. In 1841 the *Register* charged that a member of the Junto had contributed pseudonymous articles, signed "Conservative," to the *Journal* and had then tried to ascribe the authorship to Judge Jesse B. Thomas. The *Register* claimed that "the gang who control the *Sangamo Journal* wrote the articles which appear in that paper over the signature of 'A Conservative,' and privately impressed it upon the minds of the friends of the [Martin Van Buren] administration that the Judge [Jesse B. Thomas] was the author. . . . The Junto resorted to this foul stratagem to render the Judge obnoxious to the friends of Van Buren, hoping that thereby he would be driven to become a Federalist [i.e., a Whig]."[61]

Although Lincoln's journalism is not easy to identify with certainty, dozens of pieces from the 1830s seem clearly to be his handiwork, including dispatches from an unnamed Whig member of the legislature. At first, those dispatches simply offered terse accounts of legislative activity; in time, they grew longer and more partisan. One, dated January 23, 1835, sarcastically referred to Whig legislators as "Aristocrats" and reported dissension within the Democratic ranks. Written in Lincoln's characteristic bantering, satirical style, it concluded thus: "The thing was funny, and we Aristocrats enjoyed it 'hugely'."[62]

In the first session of his initial term as a legislator, Lincoln made no formal speeches and only two brief sets of remarks. In one of the latter he humorously commented on the nomination of a surveyor to fill a post that, it turned out, had not been vacated: "if . . . there was no danger of the new surveyor's ousting the old one so long as he persisted not to die," Lincoln said he "would suggest the propriety of letting matters remain as they were, so that if the old surveyor should hereafter conclude to die, there would be a new one ready made without troubling the legislature."[63]

Economic issues dominated the session. The most important bill dealt with the much-discussed proposal to dig a canal from Chicago to La Salle, connecting the Great Lakes with the Illinois River, which fed into the Mississippi. (When completed in 1848, it helped make Chicago a metropolis.) Lincoln, who wished to be known as "the De Witt Clinton of Illinois," voted with the majority to finance that internal improvement with $500,000 in state bonds.[64] (Clinton was the governor of New York when the Erie Canal was built.) The most controversial national issue debated by the legislature involved the Bank of the United States, on which President Andrew Jackson had declared his well-publicized war. Another was the distribution of funds generated by the sale of federal public lands. Lincoln introduced an unsuccessful resolution calling for the U.S. government to remit to the state at least one-fifth of such proceeds collected in Illinois. In fulfillment of his pledge to Hugh Armstrong and Ned Potter, he also submitted a petition of "sundry citizens of the counties of Sangamon, Morgan and Tazewell, praying the organization of a new county out of said counties." The Committee on Petitions reported against it.[65]

That winter of 1834–1835 the General Assembly passed 191 laws, dealing chiefly with roads, corporations, schools, and acts to relieve individuals. A state bank was chartered; the Illinois and Michigan Canal received vital funding; public roads were encouraged; the state was divided into judicial districts; and four colleges were incorporated. Lincoln voted on 131 of the 139 roll calls and was present for at least 59 of the 65 days when the legislature met.

During that session, some observers felt that Lincoln had achieved little. Stuart recalled that Lincoln "was the author of no special or general act" and that he "had no organizing power."[66] John Moses reported that Lincoln "arose in his place and spoke briefly on two or three occasions, without giving any special promise, however, of ability as a debater or speaker. He seemed rather to be feeling his way, and taking the measure of the rising men around him."[67] Lincoln did virtually nothing to implement the three main proposals of his 1832 platform: expanding public education, improving navigation of the Sangamon, and curbing high interest rates. Usher F. Linder said that "if he won any fame at that season I have never heard of it." In 1835, upon meeting Lincoln for the first time, Linder found him "very modest and retiring," "good-natured, easy, unambitious, of plain good sense, and unobtrusive in his manners," resembling "a quiet, unassuming farmer."[68]

Other contemporaries, however, recalled Lincoln's legislative debut more positively. Jesse K. Dubois asserted that before the session ended, "Lincoln was already a prominent man."[69] John Locke Scripps wrote in an 1860 campaign biography (which Lincoln read and corrected) that Lincoln "acquired the confidence of his fellow-members as a man of sound judgment and patriotic purposes, and in this manner he wielded a greater influence in shaping and controlling legislation than many of the noisy declaimers and most frequent speakers of the body."[70]

If Lincoln achieved little renown, he learned a great deal: he had met legislators, lobbyists, judges, and attorneys from around the state and sized them up; had observed a more civilized culture than he had known along Little Pigeon Creek or in New Salem; had paid heed to the shrewd advice of John Todd Stuart; and had seen firsthand how legislation was framed and passed. In addition, he had made friends, in part through his legendary skill at storytelling. Those ten weeks in Vandalia sharpened Lincoln's already keen desire to escape the backwoods world of his father. He wanted to belong to this new realm, peopled with ambitious and talented men, and so he returned to New Salem resolved not only to continue studying law but also to smooth some of his rough edges. Abner Y. Ellis thought that "Lincoln improved rapidly in Mind & Manners after his return from Vandalia his first Session in the Legislature."[71]

Romance

In Illinois, as in Indiana, the bashful Lincoln paid little attention to young women. (In middle age, he admitted that "women are the only things that cannot hurt me that I am afraid of.")[72] When he boarded with John M. Camron, he took no romantic interest in his host's attractive daughters, one of whom described him as "thin as a beanpole and as ugly as a scarecrow!"[73] Between 1831 and 1834, when Daniel Burner and Lincoln both lived in New Salem, Burner never observed him with a girl. Because he could not sing "any more than a crow," Lincoln avoided the singing school, where on weekends young men and women received elementary musical instruction and also courted. When he did attend social occasions where the sexes mingled, he "never danced or cut up."[74] Jason Duncan, who left New Salem in 1833, recalled that Lincoln "was verry reserved toward the opposite sex." Duncan could "not recollect of his ever paying his addresses to any young lady."[75] James Short said that Lincoln "didn't go to see the girls much," for "he cared but little for them," and when he craved companionship, he "would just as lieve the company were all men as to have it a mixture of the sexes."[76] Abner Y. Ellis, who employed Lincoln as a sometime clerk at his store, reported that he was "a verry shy Man of Ladies." One day, Ellis recalled, "while we boarded at this Tavern there came a family Containing an old Lady her Son and Three stilish Daughters from the State of Virginia and stoped their for 2 or 3 weeks and during there stay I do not remember of Mr Lincoln Ever eating at the Same table when they did."[77] A New Salem maiden said that in his mid-twenties, the "homely, very awkward" Lincoln was "a very queer fellow" and "very bashful."[78] One historian speculated that it "was greatly to Lincoln's advantage that he was not a favorite with society women. If he had been, most of his time and energies would have been wasted in agreeable frivolity."[79]

Women who claimed that Lincoln was drawn to them testified that he was socially backward and not a particularly eligible bachelor. Martinette Hardin said he was "so awkward that I was always sorry for him." He "did not seem to know what to say in the company of women."[80] Polly Warnick, whom Lincoln allegedly tried to woo in Macon County, Illinois, had "little interest in a tall gangly youth with an Indiana accent."[81] A woman whose parents had lived in New Salem reported that "Lincoln was not much of a beau, and seemed to prefer the company of the elderly ladies to the young ones."[82]

Those more mature women (in effect surrogate mothers) included Mrs. Bennett Abell, who encouraged Lincoln's ambition. William Butler deemed her "a cultivated woman—very superior to the common run of women about here." While boarding at Bowling Green's, Lincoln came to know the Abells, who lived close by. Mrs. Abell found Lincoln congenial. In time Lincoln boarded with the Abells, where he lived "in a sort of home intimacy." Butler thought it was "from Mrs. Able he first got his ideas of a higher plane of life—that it was she who gave him the notion that he might improve himself by reading &c."[83]

Lincoln's other surrogate mothers included Mary Spears, a woman of uncommon intelligence. He thought that if she had received an education she would have been the equal of any woman. She, in turn, remarked that there was "a great promise—a great possibility in Lincoln."[84] Lincoln called his first landlady in New Salem, Mrs. John M. Camron, "Aunt Polly" and always remembered her affectionately. According to Charles Maltby, "her motherly kindness and counsels to Lincoln reminded him of the advice and instructions of a dear departed mother."[85] Hannah Armstrong, yet another surrogate mother, remembered that he "amused himself by playing with the children, or telling some funny story to the old folks."[86] Lincoln also liked to converse with Sarah Graham, the wife of Mentor Graham, often soliciting her advice about personal matters, including love.

Romantic love finally entered Lincoln's life in the person of Ann Rutledge, the daughter of one of his early New Salem landlords, James Rutledge. Four years younger than Lincoln, she was, by all accounts, attractive, intelligent, and lovable. She weighed approximately 120 pounds, stood 5 feet and 3 inches tall, and had large blue eyes "with a great deal in them." She was smart, moderately educated, pleasant, a good conversationalist, hardworking, and domestically accomplished. Her mother "said she had been noted for three things, her skill with the needle, being a good spinner and a fine cook."[87] She also possessed a kind nature that one observer described as "angelic," and a modesty that left her "without any of the airs of your city Belles."[88] Her cousin, James McGrady Rutledge, called her "a girl whose company people liked . . . seeming to enjoy life, and helping others enjoy it."[89] In the opinion of William G. Greene, her "Character was more than good: it was positively noted throughout the County. She was a woman worthy of Lincoln's love & she was most worthy of his."[90]

Lincoln described Ann as "a handsome girl," "natural & quite intellectual, though not highly Educated," who "would have made a good loving wife."[91] He may have been smitten with her when boarding at her father's tavern in 1831, but she was then engaged to the successful merchant John McNamar (who used the alias McNeil), a partner of Samuel Hill. The women of New Salem considered McNamar "the catch of the village," for he had accumulated between $10,000 and $12,000 by the time he began courting Ann.[92] But Ann's father disapproved of him, perhaps because he was twelve years Ann's senior, unattractive, and cold. (In 1836, McNamar evicted Ann's widowed mother from her home when she fell behind in the rent. After McNamar's death, his widow recollected "that in all the years of their married life, though he was courteous and attentive and a good provider, there was no more poetry or senti-ment in him than in the multiplication table, and that she really never became ac-quainted with him.")[93] Around the time that Lincoln returned from the Black Hawk War, McNamar left New Salem to fetch his family from New York; he did not return for three years. During that period he wrote to Ann so seldom that she believed he had canceled their engagement. Meanwhile, she had moved with her family to Sand-ridge, a few miles from New Salem. It was at this time that Lincoln began to court her, visiting Sandridge often.

Few details of that courtship survive. Parthena Nance Hill recalled that when McNamar stopped writing to his fiancée, "some of the girls lorded it over Ann who sat at home alone while we other young people walked and visited." Lincoln, who thought highly of Ann and "felt sorry for her," began escorting her on evening walks.[94] Mrs. Hill told a friend "that Lincoln was deeply in love with Ann."[95] When visiting her family, Lincoln would cheerfully, if awkwardly, help Ann with household chores. They also studied together, poring over a copy of Kirkham's *Grammar,* which he had given her. In addition, they sang songs from an anthology called "The Mis-souri Harmony." Eventually, according to Ann's sister Nancy, "he declared his love and was accepted for she loved him with a more mature and enduring affection than she had ever felt for McNamar. No one could have seen them together and not be convinced that they loved each other truly."[96]

In early 1835 Abe and Ann evidently became engaged but decided to postpone their wedding for a year because she wished to further her education and Lincoln wanted to prepare for the bar. She also desired to wait until she could honorably break her engagement to McNamar. Ann's brother David urged her to marry Lincoln even before the return of her whilom fiancé, but she declined so that she could personally explain to McNamar her change of heart. While awaiting his return, Ann became sick, probably with typhoid fever. She lingered for several weeks.

Lincoln was distraught. One stormy night he braved the foul weather to walk to Sandridge. En route he stopped at the cabin of Parson John M. Berry, who invited him in. After protesting that he must get to Ann, Lincoln finally accepted Berry's offer to spend the night. Rather than sleep, he paced the floor for hours and decamped early the next morning.

According to her sister Sarah, Ann "had brain fever and was out of [her] head all the time till about two days before she died, when she came to herself and called for Abe." Bowling Green fetched Lincoln. When he arrived "everybody left the room and they talked together." Emerging from that room, Lincoln "stopped at the door and looked back. Both of them were crying."[97] Dr. John Allen, who had been attending Ann, took the devastated Lincoln to his house for the night.

Ann's death on August 25, 1835, crushed Lincoln, leaving him so profoundly grief-stricken that many friends worried that he might lose his mind. Henry McHenry recollected that "after that Event he seemed quite changed, he seemed *Retired*, & loved *Solitude*, he seemed wrap[p]ed in *profound thought, indifferent*, to transpiring Events, had but Little to say, but would take his gun and wander off in the woods by him self, away from the association of even those he most esteemed." His "depression seemed to deepen for some time, so as to give anxiety to his friends in regard to his Mind."[98] William G. Greene testified that "after this sudden death of one whom his soul & heart dearly & lov[e]d," Lincoln's friends were "[c]ompelled to keep watch and ward over Mr Lincoln," for he was "from the sudden shock somewhat temporarily deranged. We watched during storms—fogs—damp gloomy weather Mr Lincoln for fear of an accident. He said 'I can never be reconciled to have the snow—rains & storms to beat on her grave.'"[99] He did not quickly recover. "Long after Anne died," Greene reported, "Abe and I would be alone perhaps in the grocery on a rainy night, and Abe would sit there, his elbows on his knees, his face in his hands, the tears dropping through his fingers."[100]

Elizabeth Abell, who witnessed the depth of Lincoln's grief, recalled that "he was staying with us at the time of her death," which "was a great shock to him and I never seen a man mourn for a companion more than he did for her." The "community said he was crazy" but "he was not crazy," though "he was very disponding a long time."[101] Another surrogate mother, Hannah Armstrong, saw "Lincoln weep like a baby over the death of Ann Rutledge."[102] Nancy Green recollected that Lincoln took Ann's "death verry hard so much so that some thought his mind would become impa[i]red." She reported that her husband, Bowling Green, was so afraid that Lincoln would lose his reason that he "went to Salem after Lincoln [and] brought him to his house and kept him a week or two & succeeded in cheering him up though he was quite molencoly for months."[103] At Green's, Dr. Allen often visited him.

In great despair, Lincoln thought of killing himself. According to John Hill, Lincoln was so "fearfully wrought up upon her death" that Samuel Hill "had to lock him up and keep guard over him for some two weeks . . . for fear he might Commit Suicide. The whole village engaged in trying to quiet him and reconcile him to the loss." Hill remembered that "for a short time his mind wandered."[104] The family of Jack Armstrong was afraid that Lincoln "would go crazy."[105] Henry Sears and his wife recollected that Lincoln "strolled around the neighborhood for the next three or four weeks humming sad songs and writing them with chalk on fences and barns. It was generally feared that the death of Ann Rutledge would drive him insane."[106]

This was not the only time Lincoln considered suicide. He told Mentor Graham "that he felt like Committing Suicide often."[107] To Robert L. Wilson he confided "that although he appeared to enjoy life rapturously, Still he was the victim of terrible melancholly. He Sought company, and indulged in fun and hilarity without restraint." Yet, "when by himself, he told me that he was so overcome with mental depression, that he never dared carry a knife in his pocket."[108] On the third anniversary of Ann's death, an unsigned poem about suicide, perhaps by Lincoln, appeared in the newspaper for which he regularly wrote anonymous pieces.

Decades later, when Isaac Cogdal asked him if he "ran a little wild" after Ann's death, Lincoln replied: "I did really—I run off the track: it was my first. I loved the woman dearly & sacredly . . . . I did honestly—& truly love the girl & think often—often of her now."[109] The depth of Lincoln's sorrow, and the severe depression he suffered after her demise, may have been partly a result of his unresolved grief at the death of his mother and siblings. Ann's death unconsciously reminded him of those old wounds, which began to suppurate once again, causing him to reexperience "the bitter agony" he had endured as a youth. Such intense depression can lead to suicide, even among young and physically healthy people like Lincoln.

While recuperating from the devastating effect of Ann's death, Lincoln neglected his duties at the post office. He often started out for a destination but returned without having reached it; instead he would wander about, absorbed in his thoughts, recognizing no friends or neighbors. Three weeks after Ann died, a New Salem resident complained that the "Post Master (Mr. Lincoln) is very careless about leaving his office open & unlocked during the day—half the time I go in & get my papers &c without any one being there as was the case yesterday."[110]

Years later, when his friend Joshua F. Speed suffered from depression, Lincoln suggested an antidote: "avoid being idle; I would immediately engage in some business, or go to making preparations for it."[111] In the fall of 1835, Lincoln took this cure, throwing himself into the study of law. The previous summer, he had begun to go "at it in good earnest," and a year later he returned to it with even greater enthusiasm. Some friends regarded this ferocious absorption in study as a symptom of a disordered mind. Mentor Graham recalled that Lincoln "was studious—so much so that he somewhat injured his health and Constitution. The Continued thought & study of the man Caused—with the death of one whom he dearly & sincerely loved, a . . . partial & momentary derangement."[112] Lincoln studied so hard and exercised so little that he grew emaciated. Isaac Cogdal told Herndon about "the Crazy spell" following Ann's death, but concluded that "if Mr Lincoln was craz[y] it [was] only technically so—and not radically & substantially so. We used to say—you were Crazy about Ann Rutledge. He was then reading Blackstone—read hard—day & night—terribly hard— . . . was terribly melancholy—moody."[113]

By December 1835, Lincoln managed to pull himself together enough to attend a special session of the legislature, which the governor had called to modify the Illinois and Michigan Canal Act and to reapportion the General Assembly. During his six weeks in Vandalia, he won approval for the incorporation of the Beardstown and Sangamon Canal Company, one of his pet projects. Lincoln bought stock in that corporation and at a public meeting urged others to do so; he even purchased land on the Sangamon a mile from the eastern terminus of the proposed canal, which was never dug. A *Sangamo Journal* article by "Sangamo" (perhaps Lincoln) declared that the project "must be of immense advantage to the country thro' which it will pass, and to the great West generally."[114]

A leading promoter of that enterprise, Francis Arnez, edited the Beardstown *Chronicle,* whose columns in November 1834 contained a slashing attack on Peter Cartwright, a prominent Methodist minister and Jacksonian politico. Though signed "Sam Hill," the piece was actually written by Lincoln, who sent it to Arnez after the *Sangamo Journal* had rejected it. (Arnez agreed to run it only as a paid advertisement.) The irascible, vindictive Hill, known as "the rich man of the village" and "the potentate" with "a peculiar temper" so explosive that he could not drive a carriage team, had been quarreling with the belligerent Cartwright, who lived 6 miles from New Salem in Pleasant Plains. During an earlier squabble with Jack Armstrong, Hill had hired someone to thrash that leader of the Clary's Grove boys. Now he employed Lincoln to attack Cartwright with a pen rather than fists. Lincoln had no special fondness for Cartwright, one of the four candidates who had beaten him out for a legislative seat in 1832. Lincoln's inflammatory 1,500-word philippic, dated September 7, 1834, accused Cartwright of being "a most abondoned hypocrite" and concluded that it was hard to tell whether he "is [a] greater fool or knave" and that "he has but few rivals in either capacity."[115] (The attack was clever but unfair, based on a misreading of Cartwright's writings.) Thus began a pattern of anonymous and pseudonymous journalistic assaults that did Lincoln little credit. (He would quit that ugly practice in 1842, when an offended target of his ridicule challenged him to a duel, an episode discussed in chapter 6.)

Lincoln participated actively in the special session. On December 12, he introduced a debt-relief bill that passed the House but not the senate. He also consistently voted in favor of the Illinois and Michigan Canal, whose supporters finally prevailed on Christmas Eve, when the House by a 29–26 margin authorized the establishment of a Board of Commissioners, empowered it to build the canal, and permitted the governor to borrow up to half a million dollars to fund the effort.

The struggle over the canal pitted northern Illinois against the southern part of the state. Whereas northern Illinois had been settled by ambitious, industrious Yankees who erected mills, churches, schools, villages, and towns, southern Illinois had attracted from the South a more easygoing class of settlers who regarded the Yankees as tightfisted, dishonest, moneygrubbing misers lacking the spirit of generous hospitality. (Lincoln enjoyed quoting a hard-shell Baptist preacher in southern Illinois who declared that the "mercy of God reaches from the Esquimaux of the frozen North to the Hottentot of the sizzling South; from the wandering Arab of Asia to the Injuns of the Western plains; there are some who say that it even extends to the Yankees, but I wouldn't go scarcely that far.")[116] Residents of northern Illinois, in turn, looked on their neighbors to the south as indolent, ignorant primitives, scarcely more advanced than savages.

Legislators from southern Illinois opposed the canal because they feared it might pave the way for Yankees to flood the state. Moreover, their constituents, predominantly Southern subsistence farmers who produced little that anyone might wish to buy, could not understand why the state should undertake such a costly project. Overcoming their resistance was a formidable challenge. A leading champion of the canal, Gurdon Hubbard, doubted that the legislation could have been approved so quickly without Lincoln's invaluable assistance.

During the debates over reapportionment of the General Assembly, Lincoln supported a plan that would have kept the legislature relatively small. When the proposal failed, that body was expanded from fifty-five to ninety-one members. Under the new arrangement, Sangamon County had seven seats rather than four and became the largest delegation in the House of Representatives.

Fortunately for his political career, Lincoln had the prescience to oppose a seemingly minor bill "to improve the breed of cattle," which stipulated that "no bull over one year old shall be permitted to run at large out of an enclosure." Violators would be fined and the proceeds distributed to the farmers with the three best cows, bulls, and heifers within the county. In the Jacksonian "Era of the Common Man," the public regarded this statute as hopelessly elitist and voted its supporters out of office. Less than a year later the General Assembly overwhelmingly repealed the "Little Bull" law.

During the 1835–1836 special session of the General Assembly, Lincoln answered all but 11 of the 130 roll calls. He spent three days writing the report of the Committee on Public Accounts and Expenditures. By supporting the state bank and the canal, he remained true to his Whig principles. His most important contribution was the steadfast encouragement he gave to the Illinois and Michigan Canal, which was begun in 1836 and completed twelve years later.

Sophomore Legislator

In June 1836, two months after the Ninth General Assembly adjourned, Lincoln announced his candidacy for reelection in a campaign statement far more breezy and succinct than the one he had issued four years earlier. He began by paying obeisance to the regnant egalitarianism of the day: "I go for all sharing the privileges of the government, who assist in bearing its burthens." But to that platitudinous opening he added a startling pendant: "Consequently I go for admitting all whites to the right of suffrage, who pay taxes or bear arms, (by no means excluding females.)"[117]

At that time, the exclusion of blacks from the franchise was hardly controversial in Illinois, a state full of Southerners devoted to white supremacy. Indeed, hostility to black voting prevailed throughout the Old Northwest. The Illinois constitution of 1818 limited voting rights to "white male inhabitants" at least 21 years of age. Membership in the militia was open to "free male ablebodied persons, negroes, mulattoes, and Indians excepted." Between 1819 and 1846, the General Assembly outlawed interracial marriage and cohabitation, forbade blacks to testify in court against whites, and denied them the right to attend public schools. In 1848, by a margin of 60,585 to 15,903 (79% to 21%), the Illinois electorate adopted a new constitution banning black suffrage; it voted separately on an article prohibiting black immigration, which passed 50,261 to 21,297 (70% to 30%). With that, Illinois became the only Free State forbidding blacks to settle within its borders. (Oregon and Indiana soon followed its lead.)

Sangamon County was even more negrophobic than the Illinois average (90% voted for the new constitution and 78% against black immigration.) Of the Springfielders voting on black immigration, 84 percent supported the ban, including one-third of those who voted for the Free Soil ticket in 1848. A southern Illinoisan observed that his neighbors born in slaveholding states brought with them "many of the prejudices they imbibed in infancy, and still hold negroes in the utmost contempt; not allowing them to be of the same species of themselves, but look on negers, as they call them, and Indians, as an inferior race of beings, and treat them as such."[118] (American anthropologists like Samuel George Morton, John Bachman, and Louis Agassiz argued that blacks constituted the "lowest grade" of humanity and were "an inferior variety of our species.")[119]

Lincoln's suggestion that women be enfranchised, however, was hardly a campaign cliché. His proto-feminist endorsement of women's suffrage may have been inspired by his participation in debating and literary societies that addressed that question. At a meeting of such an organization in Springfield, he contributed some verses about the sexual double standard:

> Whatever spiteful fools may say,
> Each jealous ranting yelper,
> No woman ever went astray
> Without a man to help her.[120]

Lincoln believed that a "woman had the same right to play with her tail that a man had and no more nor less" and that neither husbands nor wives had a "moral or other right to violate the sacred marriage vow."[121]

Lincoln's support for women's suffrage and his opposition to the sexual double standard reflected his sense of fair play, which constituted the bedrock of his political philosophy. In later years he would never publicly raise the issue of votes for women, but he would speak and act in ways that prefigured the feminist sensibility of generations then unborn. In the late 1850s, he told a youthful female suffragist: "I believe you will vote, my young friend, before you are much older than I."[122] To Herndon, he often predicted that the adoption of women's suffrage was only a matter of time. During his presidency, Lincoln readily spared the lives of soldiers condemned to death by courts martial, but his mercy did not extend to rapists.

Wife-beaters also angered Lincoln, who in 1839 warned a hard-drinking Springfield cobbler to stop abusing his spouse. When this admonition went unheeded, Lincoln and some friends became vigilantes, as one of them later remembered: "The drunken shoemaker had forgotten Lincoln's warning. It was late at night and we dragged the wretch to an open space back of a store building, stripped him of his shirt and tied him to a post. Then we sent for his wife, and arming her with a good stout switch bade her to 'light in.'" She was "a little reluctant at first," but "soon warmed up to her work, and emboldened by our encouraging and sometimes peremptory directions, performed her delicate task lustily and well. When the culprit had been suffi- ciently punished, Lincoln gave the signal 'Enough,' and he was released; we helped him on with his shirt and he shambled ruefully toward his home. For his sake we tried to keep all knowledge of the affair from the public; but the lesson had its effect, for if he ever again molested his wife we never found it out."[123]

Lincoln was generally chivalrous, even avoiding participation in rough gossip about women that many men engaged in. At least once in his New Salem years, how- ever, he did humiliate a young woman with his legendary wit. While he was serving food at a party, "a girl there who thought herself pretty smart" protested that he filled her plate to overflowing. She remarked "quite pert and sharp, 'Well, Mr. Lincoln, I didn't want a cart-load.'" When she returned for more food, he announced in a loud voice: "All right, Miss Liddy, back up your cart and I'll fill it again." The guests all laughed at the embarrassed young woman, who spent the rest of the evening cry- ing.[124]

In the public letter announcing his candidacy for reelection in 1836, Lincoln also promised that as a legislator he would be guided by the wishes of his constituents in- sofar as he knew what those wishes were, and otherwise by "what my own judgment teaches me will best advance their interests."[125] The only policy issue he addressed was internal improvements, which he said should be funded with proceeds from the sale of federal lands rather than by state taxes and borrowing.

In the 1836 campaign, Lincoln joined the Whig leadership and became a virtuoso belittler of Democrats. A legislative colleague from Sangamon County, Robert L. Wilson, "said that Lincoln was by common consent looked up to and relied on as the leading Whig exponent; that he was the best versed and most captivating and tren- chant speaker on their side; that he preserved his temper nearly always, and when extremely provoked, he did not respond with the illogical proposal to fight about it, but used the weapons of sarcasm and ridicule, and always prevailed."[126]

During the campaigns of 1832 and 1834, Lincoln had been reserved and had stumped only in rural areas. But in 1836 he grew bolder and spoke in towns as well as villages, winning the respect of friends and the fear of opponents. His new style made him the leading Whig of the district. On the hustings he almost always kept his tem- per. A week after he declared his candidacy, however, he found it difficult to do so. When Colonel Robert Allen, a prominent Democrat known as a dishonest blowhard, told New Salemites that he could destroy the young politician by revealing informa- tion that he had, but that he would forbear releasing it, Lincoln charged that Allen would be "a traitor to his country's interest" if he refused to make public his suppos- edly damaging facts.[127] Later in the campaign, Lincoln called an anonymous critic "a liar and a scoundrel" and threatened "to give his proboscis a good wringing."[128]

When angry, Lincoln often resorted to ridicule. In July 1836, during a debate at Springfield he was attacked by George Forquer, a Democratic leader derided by Lin- coln in the *Sangamo Journal* as "King George," "the royal George," and "the most unpopular of all the party."[129] Forquer, who had recently converted to the Democratic Party and had subsequently won appointment as register of the Springfield land of- fice, owned a home widely considered the finest in Springfield. Adorning it was a lightning rod, an invention that fascinated Lincoln. In a "slasher-gaff" speech, Forquer said: "This young man will have to be taken down; and I am truly sorry that the task devolves upon me."

Lincoln responded witheringly: "The gentleman commenced his speech by saying that this young man would have to be taken down, alluding to me; I am not so young in years as I am in the tricks and trades of the politician; but live long, or die young, I would rather die now than, like the gentleman[,] change my politics, and simultaneous with the change, receive an office worth $3,000 per year, and then have to erect a lightning-rod over my house, to protect a guilty conscience from an offended God."[130]

In that same canvass, Lincoln attacked other Democratic leaders, most notably Dr. Jacob M. Early, a physician and Methodist minister called "The Fighting Parson," whose skinning by Lincoln became a legend in Sangamon County. At a Springfield meeting, Lincoln, Early, John Calhoun, Richard Quinton, and Ninian W. Edwards addressed a large audience in the courthouse. After Edwards opened the event, the impulsive, hot-tempered Early, widely regarded as an excellent debater, followed. He sharply criticized Ninian Edwards, alleging that Edwards had chided the Democrats for their stand on black suffrage and declared that he "would sooner see his daughter married to a negro than a poor white man."[131] Edwards loudly denied Early's charge. (In fact, Edwards was "naturally and constitutionally an aristocrat" who "hated democracy . . . as the devil is said to hate holy water.")[132]

Provoked by Early's speech, Lincoln challenged him. Lincoln seemed embarrassed and began slowly, but as he went on he relaxed, his squeaky voice settled down, and his words began to pour forth smoothly. He roundly condemned the Democrats and was interrupted several times by outbursts of applause. According to John Locke Scripps's 1860 campaign biography, when Lincoln took his seat, "his reputation was made." He had not only "achieved a signal victory over the acknowledged champion of Democracy, but he had placed himself, by a single effort, in the very front rank of able and eloquent debaters. The surprise of his audience was only equaled by their enthusiasm; and of all the surprised people on that memorable occasion, perhaps no one was more profoundly astonished than Lincoln himself."[133]

Forquer and Early were not the only opponents to feel Lincoln's sting in that campaign. In July, at a Springfield event, Lincoln "skinned" Richard Quinton, and at a meeting in Mechanicsburg he "peeled" another Democrat. Such tactics could be dangerous, for violence was not unknown in Illinois politics. After Usher Linder ridiculed the mayor of Quincy, that official ambushed him with a stout cudgel, landing several blows on the back of his head. Theophilus W. Smith, a state supreme court justice, once pulled a gun on Governor Ninian Edwards, who seized the weapon and broke Judge Smith's jaw with it. At Springfield in 1839, Isaac P. Walker, after being verbally abused by attorney E. G. Ryan, flogged his traducer. Fifteen years later, Paul Selby, editor of the Morgan *Journal*, was caned on the streets of Jacksonville for criticism appearing in that paper.

What Lincoln said as he "peeled" and "skinned" his victims is unrecorded, but he was almost certainly the author of many abusive, insulting, heavy-handed anonymous and pseudonymous attacks on Democrats that appeared in the *Sangamo Journal*. In 1835 and 1836, that Whig paper ran satirical letters ostensibly written by prominent Democrats, making their authors look ridiculous. In all likelihood, Lincoln wrote them, and they shed harsh light on the politics of that time and place.

In February 1836, the *Journal* published two such epistles over the signature "Johnny Blubberhead," a mocking sobriquet for George R. Weber, co-editor of Springfield's Jacksonian newspaper, *The Republican*. Composed in a primitive dialect like that of Lincoln's 1842 pseudonymous "Rebecca" missive (whose authorship Lincoln acknowledged), the first "Blubberhead" letter satirized the convention system and various Democratic leaders. John Calhoun, a leading Democrat, was burlesqued shamelessly. Blubberhead (Weber) reports to Democratic Congressman William L. May: "Since Cal[houn] lost part of his ear against the mantel piece he's been lopsided, and I thinks it hurt his eyedears. He's given greatly to talking to heself; and I heard him talk tother day so I was afeared that somethin was brewen. He said if he took $200 twas nobodys business; he needed it—he'd worked for the party—and he'd be (and then he used an awful word) if he did'nt blow up the whole party if they did'nt do somthin for him." Blubberhead (Weber) recommended firing all the postmasters and outlawing the distribution through the mail of the *Sangamo Journal* as the "way what would make dimocrats of the Van Buren system." He complained that May had allowed another printer, William Walters of Vandalia, to receive government patronage in Illinois: "This aint fair; you promised to give me all the printin and I holds you to your bargain. I would'nt a left the anti-masons if you had'nt promised me." Alluding to charges against May involving theft and lechery, Blubberhead warned him against trying "your old Edwardsville tricks."[134]

May was an easy target for ridicule. A good stump speaker, he served in the Illinois General Assembly in the late 1820s and subsequently in the U.S. House of Representatives (1834–1839). Sandy-haired and powerfully built, May was a politician by profession and a reasonably able attorney. In 1834, though, a Springfield clergyman said that a "greater compound of meanness and stupidity was never mingled" than in May, who had been charged with a burglary a few years earlier. When the accusation appeared in the press, May rallied friends to testify that he had entered the house not to commit a crime but for illicit sexual intercourse. "This," explained the nonplussed minister, "Mr. May published as his defense, and called upon the people to overlook the follies of his youth!"[135]

The second Johnny Blubberhead letter was equally crude. Its author bemoaned the failure of the country to go to war with England in order to enhance Martin Van Buren's electoral prospects. "We is very sorry that England has offered to mediate. Why did'nt you tell Mr. Van Buren not to accept it. If we can get a war agoing, as you say, we can use up all the revenue so that [Henry] Clay's Bill [to distribute revenues from land sales to the states] can't pass—and so as we can have thousands of officers to electioneer for Mr. Van Buren." Blubberhead declared that "I is sorry Mr. Adams has become a dimocrat because as how a good many of our friends thinks it strange; and if they should come to find out that Mr. Van Buren depends altogether on the federals for his election, they will go off from us like shot from a shovel."[136]

Other scandalous letters of this sort, ostensibly by Democrats but doubtless penned by Lincoln, appeared that season in the *Sangamo Journal*. In March "Congressman May" lamented to Weber that since a war with France was not likely, one should be waged on the surplus funds of the federal treasury. "If we help ourselves to those funds, we can elect any man President we please," the author declared. "Do all you can against Clay's Land Bill by talking; but don't publish anything on the subject. Should that bill pass and the surplus funds be divided among the States to make rail roads and canals and pay school-masters, the thing would be out with us."[137]

In another epistolary assault, "William Walters" reportedly urged Congressman May to admit publicly that in 1832 he had written a letter recounting the story of a corrupt bargain involving two Whigs, George Forquer and John Calhoun, who allegedly agreed to switch parties in return for appointment to government offices. In his supposed reply, "May" expressed anxiety that "the people of the West are too independent and highminded to submit to our dictation." But Martin Van Buren, the Democrats' presidential candidate in 1836, assured him that in time they would come around: "He says the people of New York proved somewhat refractory when the harness was first put upon them, and frequently kicked out of the traces, and occasionally broke the heads of their drivers; but by a free use of the whip and spur, holding a tight rein, and making examples of a few of the first offenders, they became so docile and gentle, that he could guide them without reins by the crook of his finger, or wink of the eye." In Washington the system worked well: "Every thing that is determined by our chief is promptly executed, right or wrong. This thing of political honesty, which our opponents stickle so much about, has long since been 'expunged' from the vocabulary of our party." Blubberhead regretted that May's opponent would be John Todd Stuart: "This I have been dreading for a long time. You know he has ever been a thorn in our side, and that all our efforts to break him down, have failed."[138]

Other satirical letters purportedly by Democrats, full of sarcastic humor, focused on voting rights for blacks. Fifteen years earlier Martin Van Buren had endorsed limited suffrage for free blacks in New York. In 1840, Lincoln would openly attack Van Buren for this stand. In 1836 he may have done so publicly, but the meager record of his speeches for that year does not show it. Anonymous and pseudonymous journalism, probably by Lincoln, however, bristles with such assaults, which were not uncommon throughout the country. (There is a grim irony in Lincoln's denunciation of Van Buren's support of limited voting rights for blacks, for in 1865 John Wilkes Booth murdered Lincoln for publicly endorsing that very policy.)

To embarrass Van Buren and his supporters, Whigs in the 1835–1836 special session of the Illinois Legislature introduced a resolution condemning several Democratic policies and slyly included as one of them: "Colored persons ought not to be admitted to the right of suffrage." When, as expected, the Democrats voted against that omnibus resolution, Whigs, including Lincoln, taunted them for implicitly endorsing black voting rights. The *Sangamo Journal* protested that Illinois "is threatened to be overrun with free negroes" and suggested that such undesirables be sent to Van Buren's home state of New York.[139] (In fact, the census of 1835 showed that of the 17,523 people in Sangamon County, only 104 were black.) The editor denounced Van

Buren's running mate, Richard M. Johnson of Kentucky, as "the husband of a negro wench, and the father of a band of mulatoes." (Johnson did have a black mistress who bore him two children.) As election day drew near in 1836, the *Journal* asked: "If Mr. Van Buren be made the president, is it not reasonable to suppose that before his term of service expires, free negro suffrage will prevail throughout the nation? If Col. Johnson be elected, will not every future aspirant to the vice presidency, set about qualifying himself for public favor by marrying a negress? If these men be elected, how long before poor white girls will become the waiting maids of sooty wenches? How long before we shall have a negro president? How long before white men and black men will have passed away, and the whole population of the country become one huge mass of degenerate and stupid mulatoes?"[140]

In January 1836, Lincoln in an anonymous dispatch to the *Sangamo Journal* chastised Democratic legislators for opposing the proposition "that the elective franchise should be kept free from contamination by the admission of colored voters."[141] Four months later, as the political campaign heated up, a letter in the *Sangamo Journal*, also probably by Lincoln, put the following words into the mouth of a Democratic congressman: "if we could only carry our plan into effect to allow free negroes to vote . . . I think our democratic principles would flourish for a long time."[142] In the same issue of the *Sangamo Journal* appeared a letter ostensibly written by a black gentleman named "Sees-Her," but in all likelihood it was composed by Lincoln:

Massa Prenter:

When I was up dare in Springfield the pepul kep axin me, How's the election gwine down in your parts? Now I couldnt den exactly precisely tell how de folks was gwine—but I been asken all around sence, and I gest wants to tell presactly how it is. De gemm'en ob coler all gwine for dat man wat writes de epitaphs of truth and vartue wid a syringe—some to Mr. Katshoun [Calhoun], and skuire the Builder [William Carpenter]. Dis brings me to a write understandin—for to no what make de niggers all vote for dese men.

Now I spose you knows as how you sees dese men goes for Wanjuren [Van Buren], and that dare tudder man wat lub de nigger so. Wanjuren says de nigger all shall vote, and dat oder man in Kentucky state [Richard M. Johnson], is goin to make all the nigger women's children white. Oh hush, ha, he, ho! Youd split your sides laffin to hear Capun [Calhoun] tell how much Wanjuren is goin to do for de nigger—de ways deys goin for him, man—oh, hush! and dat man who used to buse old Jackson so, case as how he was ginst the niggers voting—ah, law! de way he roots for Wanjuren now is sorter singular—he look precisely like a pig off in a Corn Field—wid one ear marked, so he massa know 'em. De way de niggers is goin for him now, oh hush! And skuire, the builder, de ways dey is going to run him ahead em all aint nobodys business—kase as how hese goin to sen all dese poor white folks off to Library [Liberia], and let the free niggers vote—and wen we send all dese tarnal white folks off, we'se goin to send him to Kongress, and den de niggers will be in town! oh, hush!

In grait haist, yours.[143]

The *Journal* also ran a purported Democrat's lament that some party loyalists had grown disenchanted with their legislative ticket of "three preachers and an advocate for the right of suffrage to be extended to negroes."[144] In June another such letter had a Democrat complain: "The people are up in arms about the matter [the Democrats' vote in the legislature on black suffrage]. They say. . . . that they don't like that a free negro should crowd them away from the polls." They were upset because "two of the Van Buren Electoral Ticket . . . voted that . . . free negroes ought to vote at elections."[145] Into the mouth of a Democratic editor whose paper (*The Republican*) had collapsed, an anonymous satirist put these words: "We were the more anxious to keep the Republican agoing, because we wished to defend the conduct of our friends in the Legislature last winter, in regard to their votes in favor of negro suffrage. . . . I do believe if free negroes were allowed to vote here, they [the Democrats] would get every vote."[146] All of these pieces were very probably written by Lincoln.

Lincoln was also likely the author of a July letter by a "Democrat" explaining why one of their candidates, William Carpenter, had dropped out: "at the last session of the Illinois Legislature the squire voted to allow free negroes the right of suffrage." This "Democrat" then asked: "Now if this is an objection against the squire, will it not apply with double force to Mr. Van Buren, our candidate for the Presidency? Did not Mr. Van Buren first bring forward this odious measure in the New York Convention? I say most positively that he did; and for proof of the statement I refer you to the journals of the Convention of 1821, Sept. 19, page 106."[147] Democratic legislative candidates vigorously denied that they favored black suffrage.

This line of attack was unfair, for Van Buren disliked slavery but believed it should be dealt with on the state and local level, not by the federal government. He also supported the abolition of property qualifications for white New Yorkers in 1821 and the retention of such qualifications for blacks. Furthermore, he opposed the abolition of slavery in Washington, D.C. During the 1836 campaign, he publicly declared: "I must go into the presidential chair the inflexible and uncompromising opponent of any attempt on the part of congress to abolish slavery in the District of Columbia, against the wishes of the slave holding states; and also with the determination *equally decided* to resist the slightest interference with the subject in the states where it exists."[148] In private, Van Buren urged important New York friends to attack abolitionists. Nonetheless, the assault on Van Buren's support for limited black suffrage would be repeated vigorously in 1840 and was still being cited in the presidential campaign two decades later.

When not engaged in race-baiting, Lincoln excoriated the Democrats' newly established convention system, which Ebenezer Peck and Stephen A. Douglas had introduced in December 1835. Previously, any Democrat who wished to run for office simply announced his intention and entered the race; now candidates were required to win endorsement at a nominating convention. Lincoln called adherents of this innovation "slaves of the magician [Martin Van Buren]," "eastern trading politicians," and "Hartford Convention federalists from New England," whereas Democrats opposing Peck's innovation were men "born and raised west of the mountains" and "south of the Potomac."[149]

The author of some satirical letters to the *Journal*—all probably by Lincoln—had a Democrat bemoan his party's failure to hold a county caucus to nominate officers: "The people are not yet sufficiently drilled for this purpose."[150] Writing under the name "Spoon River," a correspondent denounced the convention system for assuming "that six men can regulate the affairs of Fulton County better than six hundred; that our old backwoodsmen, squatters, and pioneers have no right to think, and act, for themselves, when with the aid of this machine six men can do it for them, with perfect ease."[151] In a letter ostensibly by the Democratic state printer, William Walters, the author ridiculed Stephen A. Douglas for imposing the convention system on his district.

When U.S. Senator Elias Kent Kane died in 1835, Lincoln poked fun at Democrats like George Forquer who scrambled to replace him: "This news had the magic effect, to produce much of both feigned sorrow and heart-felt rejoicing." Kane's "greatest political friends are glad of it, not that they loved him less, but that they loved his office more."[152] (Forquer denounced the author of this piece as "a monster, devoid of the ordinary susceptibilities of humanity.")[153]

When not ridiculing his political foes, Lincoln praised his friends, including John Todd Stuart. Referring to the passage of the canal bill, he declared that northern Illinois "is under the strongest obligations to the untiring zeal of Mr. Stuart . . . , who has spared no pains in a high minded and honorable way to secure the accomplishment of this great work."[154] Lincoln heralded Archibald Williams as "much the closest reasoner in the Senate" and asserted that it would "be a gratification to any man to hear him tear in tatters the new democracy."[155]

Lincoln assailed members of the "Monster party" for delaying construction of the Illinois and Michigan Canal until they could vest the legislature with the power to appoint canal commissioners.[156] He caustically observed that "there are men hanging on here who are bankrupt in principle, business habits, and every thing else who have the promises of these offices as soon as they shall be made elective."[157] He referred to Democratic supporters of Martin Van Buren as "ruffle-shirted Vannies," whereas supporters of his own favorite candidate for the Whig presidential nomination (Tennessee Senator Hugh Lawson White) he called "the people."[158] (Although White was a Jacksonian, many people in the South and West viewed his candidacy as a protest against the dictation of northern Democrats who had selected Van Buren.)

Lincoln and other Whigs called Democrats "locofocos," a derogatory term originally applied to the most radical faction of the party, which was accused of abandoning Jeffersonian and Jacksonian principles. When opponents denounced that smear tactic, Lincoln responded with a story about a farmer who captured a skunk in his hen house. Reacting to the varmint's protest that he was no polecat, the farmer remarked: "You look like a polecat, . . . act like one, smell like one and you are one, by God, and I'll kill you, innocent & friendly to me as you say you are." The locofocos, Lincoln continued, "'claim to be true democrats, but they are only locofocos—they look like locofocos, . . . act like locofocos,' and turning up his nose and backing away a little . . . as if the smell was about to smother him, 'are locofocos by God.'" Members of the audience "nearly bursted their sides laughing."[159]

In the 1836 campaign, Lincoln emerged as a prominent and effective Whig spokesman. One of his fellow Whig candidates for the legislature, Robert L. Wilson of Athens, recalled that "Lincoln took a leading part," and praised him for "manifesting Skill and tact in offensive and defensive debates, presenting his arguments with great force and ability, and boldly attacking the questions and positions taken by opposing Candidates." Wilson ascribed Lincoln's success to his original style, avoiding "the beaten track of other Speakers, and Thinkers." According to Wilson, Lincoln "appeared to comprehend the whole situation of the Subject, and take hold of its first principles." His "remarkable faculty for concentration" enabled him "to present his subject in such a manner as nothing but conclusions were presented." His "mode of reasoning was purely analytical; his reasons and conclusions were always drawn from analogy." Wilson also praised Lincoln's keen understanding of people and their motives, as well as his prodigious memory for facts and anecdotes, which he applied tellingly to the exact situation at hand. Wilson concluded, "no one ever forgets, after hearing Mr. Lincoln tell a Story, either the argument of the Story, the Story itself, or the author."[160]

One of Lincoln's stiffest political opponents, John Hill (son of the New Salem merchant Samuel Hill), also praised Lincoln for his remarkable eloquence. "The convincing power of Mr. Lincoln's plain conversational method of address," recalled Hill, was "marvelous and almost iresistable, Plain, candid and honest, without the slightest effort at display or oratory." Lincoln carried his auditors "along to unconscious conviction. The benign expression of his face and his earnest interest in the subject, asserted with such simplicity, secured sympathetic absorbtion. All listened in close attention to the end, and when he had finished there pervaded a momentary solemn silence before his audience realised that it was the end." Hill described Lincoln as "the planest man I ever heard." He "was not a speaker but a talker." Such were his "honesty, candor, and fairness" that it "was scarcely possible for an auditor not to believe every word [he] uttered." The same was true of conversation. "He left behind him on all occasions, a feeling one can not express of respect and that accompanied by affection for a good man."[161] Lincoln's fellow attorney and Whig politician Albert Taylor Bledsoe detected in Lincoln's speeches "a homely strength, and a rustic beauty of expression, which are more effective than the oratorical periods of an [Edward] Everett or a [George] Bancroft. His simple, terse, plain, direct English, goes right home to the point."[162]

On August 1, 1836, Lincoln handily won reelection, finishing first in a field of seventeen. In New Salem he ran well ahead of the victorious Whig ticket. (Three months later, Van Buren captured the presidency with the help of Illinois's electoral votes.) Just as he had been in the vanguard during the campaign, so too that winter Lincoln would be a leader of the Whigs in the General Assembly, filling the place vacated by John Todd Stuart, who had run for Congress and lost.

Lincoln was among the few veterans in the enlarged and reapportioned legislature; of the ninety-one members (thirty-six more than its immediate predecessor) less than one-fourth were incumbents. During the 1836–1837 session, Lincoln became prominent as the leader of Whigs in the House. He regularly squelched Democrats with clever stories. In 1839, a Democratic legislator identified ten colleagues, among them Lincoln, who "take up more time than all the members."[163] An Assembly colleague, Robert L. Wilson, thought him "a natural debater" who "was always ready and always got right down to the merits of his case, without any nonsense or circumlocution." As comfortable in the House of Representatives as he was in the houses of New Salem, "he had a quaint and peculiar way, all of his own, of treating a subject, and he frequently startled us by his modes—but he was always right." To Wilson he "seemed to be a born politician." The Whigs "followed his lead, but he followed nobody's lead; he hewed the way for us to follow, and we gladly did so." He combined mastery of the facts with clear thinking and formidable oratorical skill, yet he "excited no envy or jealousy" because of his unpretentious manner and winning wit. His colleagues readily acknowledged that he was "so much greater than the rest of us that we were glad to abridge our intellectual labors by letting him do the general thinking for the crowd." Whig Representatives, Wilson said, "would ride while he would walk, but we recognized him as a master in logic; he was poverty itself when I knew him, but still perfectly independent. He would borrow nothing and never ask favors." (Lincoln seldom asked favors because he believed that "those who receive favors owe a debt of gratitude to the giver and to that extent are obedient and abject slaves.")[164] To Wilson, Lincoln "seemed to glide along in life without any friction or effort."[165]

In fact, Lincoln was not exactly gliding along. Shortly after the General Assembly convened, he wrote from Vandalia to a friend: "my spirits [are] so low, that I feel that I would rather be any place in the world than here. I really can not endure the thought of staying here ten weeks."[166] Aside from his customary melancholy, he may have been downcast because he had nothing to do. The day before Lincoln penned his dispirited letter, a Vandalia newspaper reported that "little business has been done in either the Senate or the House of Representatives thus far" because of "the unfinished situation of the State House. The plastering is new and damp, and it became necessary to the comfort and health of the members to have additional stoves put up."[167]

Downcast or not, Lincoln gathered himself in time to help shape important legislation. He championed the state bank with special vehemence. On January 11, 1837, he defended that institution against an attack by Democrat Usher F. Linder. Sarcastically acknowledging that Linder was his superior in "the faculty of entangling a subject, so that neither himself, nor any other man, can find head or tail to it," Lincoln dismissed his opponent's arguments as "silly" and harshly declared that if Linder were unaware of Illinois's usury statute, "he is too ignorant to be placed at the head of the committee which his resolution proposes." If, on the other hand, he were aware of that usury law (which he did not mention in his flings against the bank), Linder was "too uncandid to merit the respect or confidence of any one." Lincoln went on to denounce "capitalists" who "generally act harmoniously, and in concert, to fleece the people," and politicians, "a set of men who . . . are, taken as a mass, at least one long step removed from honest men." (Lincoln immediately added that "I say this with the greater freedom because, being a politician myself, none can regard it as personal.") He further denounced "that lawless and mobocratic spirit, whether in relation to the bank or any thing else, which is already abroad in the land; and is spreading with rapid and fearful impetuosity, to the ultimate overthrow of every institution, or even moral principle, in which persons and property have hitherto found security."[168]

In this partisan speech, Lincoln did not forthrightly address all the criticisms of the bank. When the legislature incorporated the Bank of Illinois, it anticipated that its stock would be bought primarily by in-state investors. Instead, most shares were purchased by financiers in the East who deviously used the names of Illinois farmers as "owners" of the stock. Linder justly accused the bank commissioners of violating the law. This Lincoln dismissed as a quarrel among selfish capitalists, which was of no concern to the people. In fact, the law had been undermined. Lincoln was also disingenuous in alleging that the bank had met its legal requirement to redeem its notes in specie. This provision of the law was virtually nullified through clever arrangements by which the nine branches of the Bank of Illinois printed notes redeemable only at the issuing branch. To ensure that few such requests for redemption were made, the branches brought their notes into circulation at remote sites.

Though somewhat demagogic, Lincoln's speech rested on the sound notion that economic growth required banks and an elastic money supply. His political opponents, with their agrarian fondness for a metallic currency, failed to understand this fundamental point. Banks, he knew, had a vital role to play in financing the canals and railroads essential for ending rural isolation and backwardness, a goal he cared about passionately. (In fact, the state bank had been revived in the 1830s to finance internal improvements without raising taxes.) In addition, Lincoln wanted to protect the assets earned by ordinary people in the sweat of their brows; he predicted that the destruction of the bank would "annihilate the currency of the State" and thus "render valueless in the hands of our people that reward of their former labors."[169] Banks also allowed the "honest, industrious and virtuous" poor to get ahead through loans. Without internal improvements and banks, argued the *Sangamo Journal,* the poor would forever remain "hewers of wood and drawers of water" for the rich. By making credit difficult to obtain, the Democrats forced the "industrious poor" to accumulate capital on their own before starting a business, a process that might take decades. The Whigs, by making the surplus capital of the rich available through banks, aimed to expand economic opportunity for the poor.[170]

Lincoln's chief goal in the winter of 1836–1837 was to have Springfield chosen as the new state capital. By law, Vandalia's claim to that honor expired in 1839; thereafter, some other town might replace it. A change made sense. In 1819, when Vandalia had been selected, most Illinoisans lived in the southern part of the state, where Vandalia was located. During the 1820s and 1830s, however, more and more settlers flowed into the middle and northern counties, availing themselves of the cheap transportation provided by the Erie Canal, completed in 1825, and by Great Lakes steamboat connections to Chicago, opened in 1832. At the same time, the state's rejection in 1824 of attempts to introduce slavery discouraged some potential immigrants from the South. By 1833, Vandalia seemed inadequate, as one critic put it, because of its "remoteness . . . from the centre, from the most populous districts of the State, and from practicable navigation; its known and striking destitution of any commanding commercial facilities; the unsightly, monotonous appearance, comparative barrenness and flatness of the country immediately surrounding it, rendering it as unhealthy as incommodious, unpleasant, and insusceptible of dense settlement and successful cultivation."[171]

Vandalia did indeed have major shortcomings as the state capital. For two weeks in December 1836, communication with Springfield was entirely cut off because of the condition of the roads. That situation had not improved over the preceding decade. Then a traveler had complained that the "road for three miles east of Vandalia is . . . impassable with wagons, and nearly so on horseback. It is a perfect marsh or swamp, of soft clay, extremely tenacious into which a horse will sink at every step to his knees, and for the whole distance covered with water to the depth of six or eight inches." That same observer, noting that the countryside surrounding Vandalia was "hard and sterile, covered with stunted oaks and apparently unproductive," prophetically remarked, "I think that it can never be a place of much importance."[172]

Yet another drawback of Vandalia was its unhealthy summer climate. A visitor warned that "[b]ilious fever prevailed here, and there were several patients in the hotel where we stayed."[173] In the mid-1820s, that same disease had killed many Vandalians. Five legislators died in the town between 1830 and 1836. A local booster protested that the "trouble was busthead whiskey," which was made too freely available to the lawmakers at Ebenezer Capps's store, a favorite gathering place for members of the General Assembly.[174]

Moreover, critics protested, Vandalia offered inferior lodgings and food. In 1836, Justice Samuel D. Lockwood of the state supreme court complained that "all the accommodations are indifferent."[175] Many years later, John Todd Stuart told an interviewer: "I remember that one of the objections that were urged against keeping the seat of government at Vandalia was that they did not feed us on anything but prairie chickens and venison. A piece of fat pork was a luxury in those days—we had such a longing for something civilized."[176] (One day legislators organizing a deer hunt asked Lincoln to join them. He declined, remarking: "You go get the deer, [the hotel proprietor] Mattox can cook it and I'll eat all you can get.")[177]

Vandalia was also notorious for its lawlessness. In 1837, residents deplored the "frequent recurrence of brawls and drunken frays in our streets" and lamented that "our town has come to the pass, that it is almost dangerous for *one* to walk the streets, unless he is armed with dirks, pistols, &c."[178]

Many towns aspired to become the new state capital, including Springfield, Alton, Decatur, Peoria, and Jacksonville. In an 1834 statewide referendum on relocating the seat of government, Alton had received 7,511 votes, Vandalia 7,148, and Springfield 7,044. Three years later Lincoln led the Springfield forces in the legislature, even though he was the youngest of the nine members from Sangamon County. That delegation, consisting of men whose average height was slightly over 6 feet, was contemptuously labeled by the Springfield *Republican* "the Long Nine," after a type of cheap cigar.[179]

To win support for Springfield, Lincoln and his colleagues did what legislators usually do: they cut deals. As the representative from Morgan County, John J. Hardin, observed in 1836, "members support measures that they would not otherwise vote for, to obtain another member's vote for a friend."[180] To his wife, Hardin described the legislature as a "Den of legislative trading" and renounced politics, saying that a "man has no business here [in Vandalia] unless he will debase himself to bargain & trade for his rights."[181] In 1839, David Davis described to his father-in-law the legislature's "barter, trade & intrigue—'You vote for my measure, & I will vote for yours.'"[182] In the first session of the General Assembly held in the new capital, a journalist reported: "Log rolling is now in most successful operation; and that party which understands the art of *buying* and *selling* votes the best will succeed. In every sense of the word, 'the longest pole will knock off the persimmon.'"[183]

In 1836–1837, the most coveted "persimmons" were roads, canals, railroads, and river improvements, which were universally desired and which the legislature was eager to provide. Illinoisans were, as Governor John Reynolds put it, "perfectly insane" and "*crazed* considerably with the mania" for canals and railroads.[184] That mania was the key to Lincoln's strategy to make Springfield the new capital.

Under Lincoln's direction, the Long Nine promised to support various internal improvements throughout the state in return for endorsement of Springfield's aspirations. Helping Lincoln was his mentor, John Todd Stuart, who lobbied behind the scenes. Since Sangamon County's delegation was the largest in the General Assembly, it had significant leverage when its members voted as a bloc. Governor Thomas Ford noted that the Sangamon delegation was not only large, but also included "some dexterous jugglers and managers in politics," and thus Sangamon County had "a decided preponderance in the log-rolling system of those days."[185]

As legislative business was grinding along in December and January, the Long Nine relentlessly accumulated friends by promising support for internal improvement projects tailored to the needs of each county. It was difficult work, and progress came hard. As Lincoln remarked later, the subject of internal improvements was fraught with difficulty because it was impossible to please everyone: "One man is offended because a road passes over his land, and another is offended because it does not pass over his; one is dissatisfied because the bridge, for which he is taxed, crosses the river on a different road from that which leads from his house to town; another can not bear that the county should be got in debt for these same roads and bridges; while not a few struggle hard to have roads located over their lands, and then stoutly refuse to let them be opened until they are first paid the damages. Even between the different wards, and streets, of towns and cities, we find this same wrangling, and difficulty."[186]

Strong resistance to the internal improvement scheme also came from fiscal conservatives who believed that private funds, not tax dollars, should underwrite river and harbor improvements, railroads, canals, and turnpikes. In addition, some "old fogies were opposed to railroads for the reason that they would be too destructive of timber, believing that the roads were made of split wooden rails laid closely together 'corduroy' fashion!"[187]

On December 13, 1836, a serious threat confronted the Long Nine when John Taylor of Springfield submitted a petition to divide Sangamon County. Taylor and his lieutenant, John Calhoun, had speculated in land that they hoped would become

county seats and thus appreciate in value. In addition, Taylor and others had bought
up acreage at the geographical center of the state, a locale that they named Illiopolis
and hoped to make the capital. Lincoln, not wanting to see the delegation reduced in
size while it was seeking votes for Springfield, adopted delaying tactics, urging that
the question be postponed until Springfield had achieved its goal. When signatures
on a petition favoring division of the county proved fraudulent, the measure failed. In
late January 1837, another attempt to divide the county was made, which was condemned at a mass meeting in Springfield. Soon thereafter Springfield's champions
submitted a remonstrance bearing more signatures than the original petition, thus
killing the proposal.

At one point in the long, tedious process Lincoln succumbed to despair. Jesse K.
Dubois, a fellow legislator who became Lincoln's good friend, recalled that "Lincoln
came to my room one evening and told me that he was whipped—that his career was
ended—that he had traded off everything he could dispose of, and still had not got
strength enough to locate the seat of government at Springfield." Yet, he said, "I
can[']t go home without passing that bill. My folks expect that of me, and that
I can[']t do—and I am finished forever."[188] Robert L. Wilson of the Long Nine also
remembered discouraging moments: "The contest on this Bill was long, and severe;
its enemies laid it on the table twice, once on the table till the fourth day of July and
once indefinitely postponed it." Removing bills from the table "is always attended
with difficulty; but when laid on the table to a day beyond the Session, or when indefinitely postponed, [it] requires a vote of reconsideration, which always is an intense Struggle." But the once-discouraged Lincoln rallied his troops. "In these dark
hours, when our Bill to all appearance was beyond recussitation and all our opponents were jubilant over our defeat, and when friends could see no hope, Mr Lincoln
never for one moment despaired, but collect[ed] his Colleagues to his room for consultation." His "practical common Sense, his thorough knowledge of human nature
then, made him an overmatch for his compeers and for any man that I have ever
known."[189]

On February 17, a motion to table the internal improvements bill passed 39 to 38;
four days later it was taken off the table. A key swing vote was cast by Edward Smith
of Wabash County, an engineer who championed the internal improvements scheme,
which passed the legislature on February 23. Two days later, the council of revision
(consisting of the governor and the state supreme court) refused to approve that bill;
Smith's decision to change his vote may have been influenced by his fear that the
House of Representatives would not override the council's action. He probably struck
a deal with the Long Nine to support the removal of the capital to Springfield in return for the Long Nine's votes to secure final passage of the internal improvements
measure. Opponents of the internal improvements system claimed that its supporters
"found out the price of certain members" and "bought up" enough votes to pass it.[190]
The council's veto was overridden, and the bill to move the capital to Springfield
passed on February 28.

Lincoln provided much of the backbone for the victorious Long Nine. Robert L.
Wilson and another legislator, Henry L. Webb of Alexander County, reported that

on "several occasions their opponents deemed that they had circumvented the movement, and incautious ones crowed lustily over the supposed defeat and discomfiture of Lincoln and his colleagues." Some pessimists "supposed that the measure was lost, but Lincoln was tenacious and resolute." His unexpected flanking movements "would revive their chances." Thus "under his adroit leadership, the bill was carried, although the only political strength in its favor at the start was seven votes in one house and two in the other, with no natural allies, and several delegations of active enemies." The passage of the bill "was felt to be one of the greatest of political triumphs, and its credit was freely ascribed to Lincoln." Wilson said flatly, "had Lincoln not been there, it would have failed."[191]

Lincoln's most important maneuver may have been an amendment he offered on February 24, stipulating that the legislature "reserves the right to repeal this act at any time hereafter."[192] This tautological measure won over the support of four legislators who had previously been in opposition. As amended, the bill was adopted that same day, facilitating Springfield's victory. Helping expedite that choice was another amendment suggested by Lincoln and formally introduced by Alexander P. Dunbar, requiring the town selected as the capital to donate 2 acres of land and pay $50,000 to help cover the cost of a new statehouse. This measure, which virtually eliminated the smaller towns from competition, passed 53–26.

By the time balloting for the removal of the capital took place, Lincoln and his colleagues had cobbled together an alliance of twenty-three legislators who lived in or near Sangamon County; nine who represented counties that would benefit substantially from the internal improvements bill that had just passed; and three who fit neither category. Two of those three unclassifiable representatives were Jesse K. Dubois and Henry L. Webb, friends of Lincoln who wanted to accommodate him. Dubois and Webb were from the southern part of the state, where proposals to shift the capital northward enjoyed little popularity. Dubois explained that he and Webb "defended our vote before our constituents by saying that necessity would ultimately force the seat of government to a central position. But in reality we gave the vote to Lincoln because we liked him and because we wanted to oblige our friend, and because we recognized his authority as our leader."[193] Webb called the legislative triumph of the Long Nine "the master stroke of diplomacy of the Western Hemisphere" and deemed Lincoln "a Napoleon of astuteness and political *finesse.*" According to Henry C. Whitney, Webb "voted for the measure because of his admiration of Lincoln and the inability to resist his importunities. His [original] policy was to leave the capital at Vandalia but [he] yielded to Lincoln."[194]

These thirty-five votes made Springfield the clear front-runner. On the first ballot, Vandalia and Peoria each received only sixteen votes, Alton fifteen, Jacksonville fourteen, and Decatur four. On the second ballot, Springfield picked up nine more votes. On the third, its total again swelled by nine. On the fourth and final ballot, twenty more legislators sided with Springfield, putting it over the top.

The internal improvements bill and the move of the capital to Springfield had lasting implications, not all of them salutary. The strenuous maneuvering to trade votes for each bill earned both praise and blame for years to come.

The improvements bill funded many more projects than the committee drafting it had recommended. It directly benefited forty-four of the state's sixty counties; the other sixteen received cash grants. Representative Richard S. Walker from Morgan County complained "of the bargain and sale that was brought about to make Springfield the successful candidate."[195] In 1838, the leading Whig paper in that county declared that the internal improvement legislation "was carried through the Legislature by bargain and trade. It was a perfect *log-rolling* affair, and was avowed to be such by many of its supporters."[196] In 1844, an editor of that paper, John J. Hardin, told the U.S. House of Representatives during a debate on an internal improvements bill, "I do not wish to enter into a system of log-rolling to carry through this measure. I have seen the evils of that system carried to the extreme in the legislation of my own State; and we are now suffering too severely from its unfortunate results, for me to be willing to see it adopted here."[197] Vandalia's champion, William L. D. Ewing, decried "the foul corruption by which the seat of Government, contrary to justice and the constitution, was removed to Springfield."[198] He contended that the Long Nine "had sold out to the internal improvement men, and had promised their support to every measure that would gain them a vote to the law removing the seat of government."[199]

In July 1838, State Representative Christian B. Blockburger reported witnessing the Long Nine "acting in firm and united phalanx throughout the whole session on this subject. I saw the dangerous influence their numbers enabled them to exert. I saw how votes were swapped off and exchanged, and how quickly the local measures of other members were voted for, when Springfield could receive a vote in return."[200] That same month, a dozen others joined Ewing and Blockberger in deploring the machinations of the Long Nine: "Having staked their all upon this one measure, and having so strong a delegation to act upon the system of log rolling, it was not difficult for them to secure the votes of members who felt but little interested in the subject. Every art, device, and argument that could possibly be used to gain votes were resorted to."[201]

In 1843, a shrewd observer of Sangamon County politics declared that the internal improvements law "and all its sad consequences, are more justly attributed to the 'log rolling' of the 'LONG NINE,'' than any other men or set of men."[202] Lincoln's friend and political ally George T. M. Davis, editor of the Alton *Telegraph*, alleged that Springfield was chosen as the capital by the use of "the basest stratagem and intrigue."[203]

The internal improvements scheme generated patronage opportunities galore. One observer noted that the statute "would never have passed had it not been for the multitude of new offices which it created, and the confident expectation that the friends of the measure [in the legislature] would fill those offices." Soon after the bill's passage, the chairman of the committee which reported it to the legislature received an office under the law worth $3,000 a year. Most of the men appointed to the board of public works were "party leaders who had never been conspicuous for any thing but their blind devotion to the dominant party." None "had the least experience in the important duties assigned them," but because "they had done something for 'the party,'" they "had to be provided for, and if they knew nothing else, they knew that they got good salaries, and that was of course satisfactory."[204] A case in point was Democrat John A. McClernand, who broke with his party to support the measure and as a reward was named treasurer of the Illinois and Michigan Canal.

Lincoln openly acknowledged that he had engaged in log rolling, and his sense of honor demanded that the commitments he and others had made be kept. In 1839, the Vandalia *Free Press*, a Whig newspaper, said: "Lincoln admitted that Sangamon county had received great and important benefits, at the last session of the Legislature, in return for giving support, thro' her delegation to the system of Internal Improvement; and that though not legally bound, she is morally bound, to adhere to that system, through all time to come!"[205] Another Vandalia journal, perhaps describing the same remarks, alleged that one night during the 1838–1839 legislative session, Lincoln and Edward D. Baker clashed over the internal improvements system. After Baker "pronounced himself against the system," Lincoln "replied tartly to his colleague that he for himself and every other Representative of Sangamon county, present and future, should forever support the system of internal improvements because the Sangamon delegation had obtained the seat of Government at Springfield by an understanding with the friends of the system. Mr. L. said he considered the pledges then made as forever binding, not only on him but on Sangamon county itself."[206]

In the joyful celebration following this victory, Lincoln was toasted as "one of Nature[']s Noblemen."[207] Robert L. Wilson "thought that if any man was entitled to that compliment it was he."[208] Orville H. Browning praised the Long Nine: "It was to their judicious management, their ability, their gentlemanly deportment, their unassuming manners, their constant and untiring labor" that Springfield owed its success.[209] Echoing Browning, William Pickering commended Lincoln for his "continuously moral and self-reliant conduct," saying his avoidance of strong language and strong drink, along with his good nature, "formed a striking contrast with the general manners of nearly all by whom he was surrounded."[210] Nor did Lincoln distribute money to win votes. He was given $200 to dispense while promoting the internal improvements project, but only used 75¢, explaining afterwards, "I didn[']t Know how to Spend it."[211]

Helping Lincoln and the other members of the Long Nine in their efforts to round up votes was William Butler, who later told an interviewer: "I was sent down to Vandalia to work in the interest of Springfield. [Peter] Van Bergen was also sent down there with me—though he did no good—but to hear him tell it he did it all. Lincoln and [Usher F.] Linder were the two principal men we relied on in the Legislature to make speeches for us. John T. Stuart was the man we depended upon in caucus. Lincoln was not worth a cent in caucus."[212]

Not all of Lincoln's friends praised him for his work in the legislative session. Several of them foresaw that the internal improvements scheme was far too ambitious for the meager resources of the new state and was therefore doomed to fail. Stephen T. Logan recalled that "I was in Vandalia that winter and had a talk with Lincoln there. I remember that I took him to task for voting for the Internal Improvement scheme. He seemed to acquiesce in the correctness of my views as I presented them to him. But he said he couldn't help himself—he had to vote for it in order to secure the removal here [Springfield] of the seat of government."[213] Usher F. Linder, who later regretted his support for the system, apologetically explained many years later that at the time he, Lincoln, and other enthusiasts "were all young and inexperienced men."[214]

No such misgivings were voiced when the internal improvement bill passed. A dispatch from the capital, probably by Lincoln, described the jubilation: "the huzzas and acclamations of the people were unprecedented.—All Vandalia was illuminated. Bonfires were built, and fire balls were thrown, in every direction."[215] Paying for the system would be simple, according to Representative John Hogan, who predicted that the bonds "would go like hot cakes, and be sought for by the Rothschilds and Baring Brothers," and "that the premium which we would obtain upon them would range from fifty to one hundred per cent.," which by itself "would be sufficient to construct most of the important works, leaving the principal sum to go into our treasury, and leave the people free from taxation for years to come."[216]

Hogan's rosy scenario proved wildly inaccurate. The bargain crafted by Lincoln wound up benefiting Springfield at the expense of Illinois. Governor Thomas Ford called the internal improvements scheme "the most senseless and disastrous policy which ever crippled the energies of a growing country."[217] In 1832, Lincoln had sensibly warned voters about the "heart-appalling" costs of railroads and canals. Four years later he cavalierly ignored his own good counsel and that of friends like Stephen T. Logan, Orville H. Browning, John J. Hardin, Alexander P. Field, and Edwin B. Webb and helped saddle Illinois with a $14 million system of internal improvements that its population of 500,000 could ill afford. Among the approved projects were the laying of 1,300 miles of railroads, deepening the channels of five rivers, constructing a mail route from Vincennes to St. Louis, and awarding $200,000 to compensate the counties through which neither a canal nor a railroad would pass. The interest on the necessary loans exceeded the entire revenue raised by the state in 1836. When the economy collapsed in 1837, any slight chance that the state could pay for the many projects went glimmering. Illinois suspended interest payments on its debt, and for years thereafter its credit rating was poor and its treasury strapped. The state, as Governor Ford noted, "became a stench in the nostrils of the civilized world."[218] In 1843, John Todd Stuart complained: "Our reputation is very much that of a set of swindlers."[219] Illinois did not finally pay off the loans incurred for the internal improvement system until 1880.

When at the same session the General Assembly voted to increase its members' pay from $3 per day to $4, protests deluged the statehouse. One indignant constituent, "a blunt, hard-working yeoman," berated Lincoln, for he "could and would not understand why men should be paid four dollars per day for 'doing nothing but talking and sitting on benches,' while he averaged only about one [dollar] for the hardest kind of work." He asked angrily, "what in the world made you do it?" Lincoln replied: "I reckon the only reason was that we wanted the money."[220]

In addition to passing the internal improvements bill, the statute removing the capital to Springfield, and the pay hike, the legislature continued its routine work of incorporating businesses, schools, and towns; of authorizing roads and declaring streams navigable; and of defining the boundaries of counties. Lincoln participated in these matters, answering all but 17 of the 220 roll calls taken during the first session of the Tenth General Assembly.

Between the time that Lincoln declared his candidacy in 1832 and his triumph as the champion of Springfield's bid to become the state capital, he had become an adept partisan, renowned for logrolling and scourging Democrats, but little more. The day before the General Assembly adjourned, however, he took a step that foreshadowed the statesmanship of his later career.

On March 3, 1837, he and another member of the Long Nine, Dan Stone, filed a protest against anti-abolitionist resolutions that the legislature had adopted six weeks earlier by the lopsided vote of 77–6 in the House and 18–0 in the senate. Lincoln and Stone were part of the tiny minority who opposed the resolutions—less than 7 percent of the entire General Assembly. The overwhelmingly popular resolutions were introduced at the behest of Southern state legislatures outraged by the American Antislavery Society's pamphlets depicting slaveowners as cruel brutes. Equally objectionable was the Society's massive petition drive calling for the abolition of slavery in the District of Columbia. The resolutions passed in Vandalia declared that Illinois legislators "highly disapprove of the formation of abolition societies, and of the doctrines promulgated by them," that "the right of property in slaves is sacred to the slave-holding States by the Federal Government, and that they cannot be deprived of that right without their consent," and that "the General Government cannot abolish slavery in the District of Columbia, against the will of the citizens of said District."[221]

Lincoln wrote a protest against these resolutions and circulated it among his colleagues. None would sign except for Stone, a native of Vermont and a graduate of Middlebury College who was not seeking reelection (he would soon become a judge). Lincoln declared in the document, which he and Stone entered into the journal of the House of Representatives, "that the institution of slavery is founded on both injustice and bad policy."[222] This statement was a precursor of his landmark 1854 Peoria speech attacking the "monstrous injustice of slavery." In 1860, a newspaper widely regarded as his organ explained that "Lincoln could not, and did not vote in favor of the resolutions . . . because the old Calhoun doctrine embraced in the second of the series ['that the right of property in slaves is sacred to the slave-holding states by the Federal Government'] was abhorrent to his ideas of the true meaning of the Constitution."[223]

To proclaim that "slavery is founded on both injustice and bad policy" was a remarkably bold gesture for 1837, when antislavery views enjoyed little popularity in central Illinois—or elsewhere in the nation for that matter. Several months after Lincoln and Stone issued their protest, the quasi-Democratic governor of Illinois, Joseph Duncan, speaking for the clear majority of his constituents, denounced all efforts "to agitate the question of abolishing slavery in this country, for it can never be broached without producing violence and discord," even in the Free States. Duncan added that "if I read my Bible right, which enjoins peace and good-will as the first Christian duties, it must be wicked and sinful to agitate this subject in the manner it has been done by some Abolitionists, especially after our Southern neighbors have repeatedly and earnestly appealed to us not to meddle with it, and assured us their having done so has not only jeopardised their own safety and domestic peace, but in many cases has caused bloodshed and rebellion, which has compelled them, as a measure of prudence and protection, to use more rigidity and severity with their slaves." Furthermore, Duncan argued, abolition without the consent of the Southern states would violate the Constitution. He believed that "it will neither be consistent with sound policy or humanity by a single effort to free all the slaves in the Union, ignorant, vicious, and degraded as they are known to be, and then turn them loose upon the world without their possessing the least qualification for civil government, or knowledge of the value of property, or the use of liberty."[224]

Political leaders outside of Illinois held similar views. Henry Clay, Lincoln's "beau ideal of a statesman," condemned abolitionists as "extremely mischievous" fire-brands who "would see the administration of the Government precipitate the nation into absolute ruin" and "nullify the Constitution." He predicted that "if they are not checked in their progress," the day would come "when the free States will have to decide on the alternative of repudiating them or repudiating the Union."[225] In 1836, Massachusetts Governor Edward Everett urged the state legislature to outlaw aboli-tionists, arguing that "everything that tends to disturb the relations created by this compact [i.e., the Constitution] is at war with its spirit, and whatever by direct and necessary operation is calculated to excite an insurrection among the slaves has been held by highly respectable legal authority an offence against the peace of this Commonwealth."[226] New York Governor William L. Marcy called abolitionists "sin-ister, reckless agitators," then advised his legislature that it might behoove the Free States to provide "for the trial and punishment by their own judicatories, of residents within their limits, guilty of acts therein, which are calculated and intended to excite insurrection and rebellion in a sister state."[227]

Seven months after the Lincoln-Stone protest, Springfield residents publicly con-demned abolitionism. While the Presbyterian synod was meeting there, citizens banded together to disrupt the proposed delivery of an antislavery sermon. Mob vio-lence was averted, but some townspeople met on October 23 and adopted the follow-ing resolutions: "as citizens of a free State and a peaceable community, we deprecate any attempt to sow discord among us, or to create an excitement as to abolition which can be productive of no good result . . . the doctrine of immediate emancipation in this country, (although promulgated by those who profess to be christians,) is at vari-ance with christianity, and its tendency is to breed contention, broils and mobs, and the leaders of those calling themselves abolitionists are designing, ambitious men, and dangerous members of society, and should be shunned by all good citizens."[228] Simeon Francis's newspaper rejoiced "that public opinion in the frontier states is likely to check at once the perfidy of these fanatical men [i.e., the abolitionists]." Westerners "could not be induced to visit upon the South such an accumulation of horrors as is embraced in the meaning of those two words—'universal emancipation.'"[229]

Francis was right: the antislavery movement had difficulty taking root in Illinois. Between 1817 and 1824, some Illinoisans had waged a successful battle against the introduction of slavery into their state constitution, but thereafter enthusiasm for the

antislavery cause dramatically waned. Before 1837 only one county in the state—
Putnam—had an auxiliary of the American Antislavery Society. Attempts to circulate antislavery petitions in 1837 fizzled. In 1841, when the Illinois Antislavery Society
dispatched an agent to spread the abolition gospel, Springfield authorities denied him
permission to speak. Three years later, Ichabod Codding's attempt to deliver an abolitionist lecture in the capital was thwarted by a mob of more than one hundred men
brandishing sticks and boards and blowing horns. They made such a racket that Codding could not be heard. Some of the mob hurled eggs at the speaker while Springfield's police passively observed the commotion and laughed. Simeon Francis
noted that *abolitionist* "is an odious epithet among us; and we do not believe that
there are a dozen men to be found in Sangamon county to whom it can be properly
applied."[230]

As a Morgan County abolitionist noted in 1845, there were many "warm friends
to the slave" in his town. Yet "quite a large portion of western people, who are
anti-slavery in principle and who will subscribe to all the views of the abolitionists
when presented to them in private conversation, still abhor the name *abolitionist*,"
which they associate with "not only all that does belong to it, but every thing that
possibly can be attached to it that is false, such as amalgamation, circulating inflammatory papers among the negroes in order to instigate them to insurrection, and a
desire to do away with slavery by physical force. They also attach to the name all the
views of [William Lloyd] Garrison."[231] An Urbana newspaper observed that *abolition*
is "considered synonymous with treason, . . . disunion, civil war, anarchy and every
horror [of] which an American can conceive."[232]

In such a region at such a time, Lincoln could scarcely expect criticism of slavery,
even that which stopped short of abolitionism, to win him popularity. Yet Lincoln
clearly had come to loathe slavery by 1837. Two decades later he said that "I have always hated slavery, I think as much as any Abolitionist."[233] He had not emphasized
the slavery issue before 1854, he explained, because until then the peculiar institution
seemed to be on the wane. His friend Samuel C. Parks asserted that "Lincoln told the
truth when he said he had 'always hated slavery as much as any Abolitionist' but I do
not know that he deserved a great deal of credit for that for his hatred of oppression &
wrong in all its forms was constitutional—he could not help it."[234] Lincoln expressed
compassion for white men forced to labor like slaves. One day at Beardstown, he observed a steamboat crew "lugging freight on board, working like galley slaves and
being cursed every moment by the brutal mate." To a friend he "freely expressed his
disgust at the tyranny of the mate and his tender sympathy for the white slaves."[235] In
1864, Lincoln publicly declared that "I am naturally anti-slavery. If slavery is not
wrong, nothing is wrong. I can not remember when I did not so think, and feel."[236] In
1858, he said: "The slavery question often bothered me as far back as 1836–1840. I
was troubled and grieved over it."[237] A friend remembered that in 1837, "Lincoln was
talking and men were standing up around him listening to the conversation. . . . One
of them asked him if he was an abolitionist. Mr. Lincoln in reply, reached over and
laid his hand on the shoulder of Mr. [Thomas] Alsopp who was a strong abolitionist
and said, 'I am mighty near one.'"[238] In 1860, Lincoln stated that the protest he and

Stone had issued in 1837 "briefly defined his position on the slavery question; and so far as it goes, it was then the same that it is now."[239]

Lincoln and Stone, while condemning slavery, also criticized abolitionists: "the promulgation of abolition doctrines tends rather to increase than to abate its [slavery's] evils." In this position, they faintly echoed the committee report to which they were objecting. That document asserted that abolitionists had "forged new irons for the black man," "added an hundred fold to the rigors of slavery," "scattered the fire brands of discord and disunion," and "aroused the turbulent passions of the monster mob." The committee could not "conceive how any true friend of the black man can hope to benefit him through the instrumentality of abolition societies."[240] This view that uncompromising abolitionism was detrimental to the true welfare of slaves was common, even among foes of slavery. Elijah P. Lovejoy, the antislavery editor who would die a martyr's death at Alton, Illinois, in 1837, had three years earlier denounced abolitionists as "the worst enemies the poor slaves have" and charged that their efforts were "riveting the chains they seek to break."[241] Henry Clay declared that abolitionists "have done incalculable mischief . . . to the very cause which they have espoused."[242] In 1838, another Whig leader, the future president William Henry Harrison, similarly remarked that the efforts of the abolitionists ("deluded men") would "end with more firmly riveting the chains . . . of those whose cause they advocate."[243] In 1854, the Springfield *Register* claimed that if it had not been for abolitionism, "slavery would have been abolished in Delaware, Maryland, Kentucky, Tennessee, Virginia, and probably in other states. The south by the war made on her rights by the abolitionists, is compelled, by every principle of self respect and local pride, to maintain her position, and she will do it so long as this war is kept up. The abolitionists, instead of aiding the emancipation of the blacks, only perpetuate their bondage."[244]

Abolitionists' tactics and rhetoric could be inflammatory as they pursued what they termed "the duty to rebuke which every inhabitant of the Free States owes to every slaveholder."[245] The leading exemplar of unconditional abolitionism, William Lloyd Garrison, thundered that "every American citizen who retains a human being in involuntary bondage as his property, is . . . a man-stealer." He characterized the "desperadoes from the South, in Congress" as "the meanest of thieves and the worst of robbers" who were not "within the pale of Christianity, of republicanism, of humanity."[246] Garrison called the U.S. Constitution a "covenant with death, and an agreement with hell."[247] To critics of his approach, Garrison said in the famous lead editorial of his newspaper, *The Liberator*, "I am aware that many object to the severity of my language; but is there not cause for severity? I *will be* as harsh as truth, and as uncompromising as justice. On this subject, I do not wish to think, or speak, or write, with moderation."[248]

Such an approach to reform was diametrically opposed to Lincoln's. In a temperance address delivered in 1842, he criticized hectoring crusaders: "It is an old and a true maxim, that a 'drop of honey catches more flies than a gallon of gall.' So with men. If you would win a man to your cause, first convince him that you are his sincere friend." Previous temperance efforts had failed, Lincoln said, because they were led by

"Preachers, Lawyers, and hired agents" whose lack of "approachability" proved "fatal to their success." They "are supposed to have no sympathy of feeling or interest, with those very persons whom it is their object to convince and persuade." They indulged in "[t]oo much denunciation against dram sellers and dram-drinkers," a strategy that was "impolitic, because, it is not much in the nature of man to be driven to any thing; still less to be driven about that which is exclusively his own business; and least of all, where such driving is to be submitted to, at the expense of pecuniary interest, or burning appetite." To expect denunciation to bring about reform "was to expect a reversal of human nature, which is God's decree, and never can be reversed. When the conduct of men is designed to be influenced, persuasion, kind, unassuming persuasion, should ever be adopted." During the Civil War, Lincoln bemoaned what he called the "self-righteousness of the Abolitionists" and "the petulant and vicious fretfulness of many radicals." He doubtless felt the same way about some abolitionists of the 1830s, whose vituperative, intolerant style alienated potential recruits to their worthy cause. In fact, Lincoln may have been trying to persuade abolitionists to exercise more tact. Clearly, the abolition of slavery was on his mind, for in the peroration of this temperance address appeared a seeming non sequitur: "When the victory shall be complete—when there shall be neither a slave nor a drunkard on the earth—how proud the title of that Land, which may truly claim to be the birth-place and cradle of both those revolutions, that shall have ended in that victory."[249]

Lincoln may also have been repelled by the anti-Catholic bigotry of some abolitionists, including Elijah P. Lovejoy, a contentious, sternly puritanical newspaper editor and Presbyterian minister who argued with little evidence that slavery was a papist enterprise. In 1836 he was hounded out of St. Louis, whose numerous Catholics disliked his reference to their church as the "Mother of Abominations" and his warning that Catholicism "was approaching the Fountain of Protestant Liberty" with a "stealthy, cat-like step" and a "hyena grin," seeking to "cast into it the poison of her incantations, more accursed than was ever seethed in the Caldron of Hecate."[250] (One Catholic warned Lovejoy that "should you continue to advance in your dishonest and dishonorable cause of vilifying my religion, I venture to predict your speedy extinction as an Editor in St. Louis.")[251]

Fifteen years after the Lincoln-Stone protest, Lincoln criticized abolitionists who, like Garrison, marched beneath the banner inscribed "No Union with Slaveholders." In a eulogy on Henry Clay, Lincoln criticized Garrisonians: "Those who would shiver into fragments the Union of these States; tear to tatters its now venerated constitution; and even burn the last copy of the Bible, rather than slavery should continue a single hour, . . . have received, and are receiving their just execration." He praised more moderate opponents of slavery, like Clay, and condemned those proslavery apologists who "are beginning to assail and to ridicule" the Declaration of Independence.[252]

The Lincoln-Stone protest further declared that "the Congress of the United States has the power, under the constitution, to abolish slavery in the District of Columbia; but that power ought not to be exercised unless at the request of the people of said District." Lincoln had unsuccessfully tried to amend the original resolution to permit abolition in the District "if the people of said District petition for same." (Twelve years later, as a member of Congress, he would frame legislation to rid the District of slavery with such consent.) Unlike the committee report to which Lincoln and Stone responded, their protest clearly asserted that the Constitution empowered Congress to abolish slavery in the District, a question that was hotly debated at the time and became a litmus test distinguishing the friends of slavery from its foes.

The boldness of the Lincoln-Stone protest is notable but uncharacteristic of Lincoln in his twenties and thirties. When in March 1837 he moved to Springfield from the dying hamlet of New Salem, he was essentially a clever partisan whose promise of future statesmanship would long remain unfulfilled.

"We Must Fight the Devil with Fire"
Slasher-Gaff Politico in Springfield
(1837–1841)

Lincoln began his new life as lawyer and legislator in the "straggling" and "irregular village" of Springfield (population 1,300), which visitors described as "a commonplace, sprawling sort of town, covering about ten times as much ground as it ought" and "a very unattractive, sickly, unenterprising town."[1] Its dirty, dusty, unpaved streets and sidewalks were flanked by log cabins and shabbily constructed frame houses. In 1832, William Cullen Bryant deemed nearby Jacksonville "a horribly ugly village, composed of little shops and dwellings, stuck close together around a dirty square, in the middle of which stands the ugliest of possible brick court-houses," but he thought it outshone Springfield, where "the houses are not so good, a considerable proportion of them being log-cabins, and the whole town having an appearance of dirt and discomfort."[2] A friend of Lincoln recalled that "for many years, it was far from being an inviting city."[3]

The town's mud was notorious. When wet, the black loam of central Illinois became knee-deep "prairie gumbo." A woman from the East declared that nobody "can know the definition of 'Mud' until they come to Springfield. I think scrapers and mats must be fast selling articles here."[4] The family of Elizabeth Capps, who called Springfield "a low, muddy place where it was a common thing for carriages and horses to mire in the mud around the public square," left the city for high and dry Mt. Pulaski.[5] Mud rendered the sidewalks, such as they were, impassable. The streets were even worse; in foul weather they "approached the condition of a quagmire with dangerous sink-holes where the boatmen's phrase 'no bottom' furnished the only description." Not until 1870 was the town square paved, finally making its thoroughfares passable for wagon teams in winter. Garbage and refuse made the muddy streets even more repellant. The streets became "the dumping ground for the community rubbish so that the gutters were filled with manure, discarded clothing and all kinds of trash, threatening the public health with their noxious effluvium." Roaming livestock compounded matters. Throughout the antebellum period, hogs and cattle roamed freely throughout the town.[6] The hogs rubbed against fences and house corners, leaving them filthy.

When the summer sun beat down on privies, sinkholes, stables, abattoirs, and the like, the stench became overwhelming. The numerous ponds around town, which "furnished frog and mosquitoe music for the inhabitants," were always "loathsome to the eye;" in hot weather they became "sickening to the smell."[7] Equally noisome was the market house, which swarmed with green-back flies.

Springfield's business structures were arranged haphazardly and slapped together in the cheapest possible manner. Both its hotels and livery stables were few in number, small, badly managed, and expensive. Its stores were meagerly stocked, and the concert hall was so dirty and shabby that the celebrated soprano Adelina Patti refused to sing there once she had taken the stage and beheld its appearance. The capitol was considered an eyesore, with an interior that impressed one visitor as "the most shabby, forlorn, dirty, dilapidated specimen of a public edifice which we have ever seen."[8]

Other visitors called the city "dull," "inactive," "wanting in public spirit and enterprise," and found "little in and about Springfield to interest or amuse a stranger."[9] Sessions of the legislature provided some diversion, but when the lawmakers departed, the town reverted to its customary dullness. An Ohioan wrote that while he had been to "many a distressing place," Springfield was "the most distressing of all."[10]

Springfield's citizens as well as its streets and buildings failed to please visitors. Hezekiah Morse Wead, a delegate to the 1847 constitutional convention meeting in the city, lamented that during the convention's three-month duration, "no kindness or hospitality or friendship has been extended to these delegates by any of the citizens" save Ninian W. Edwards. "Even the ordinary kindness & civilities of life" were lacking, he confided to his diary.[11] John Hay called Springfield "a city combining the meanness of the North with the barbarism of the South." Shakespeare's Dogberry, Hay quipped, "ought to have been an Illinoisan."[12] A Briton deplored the local manners: "The nasty habit of chewing tobacco, and spitting, not only gives them a dirty look, but makes them disagreeable companions. They eat so fast, and are so silent, and run off so soon when they have finished their meals, that really eating in this country is more like the feeding of a parcel of brutes than men."[13] Brawling and drunkenness were common, especially at election time. In 1839, at least fifteen fights broke out while the polls were open.

Lincoln enjoyed telling a story about Springfield that he had heard from his friend Jesse K. Dubois, the Illinois state auditor. In that capacity, Dubois was once asked by an "itinerant quack preacher" for permission to use the Hall of Representatives for a religious lecture.

When Dubois inquired, "What's it about?" the minister replied, "The Second Coming of Christ."

"Nonsense," retorted the state auditor. "If Christ had been to Springfield once, and got away, he'd be damned clear of coming again."[14]

Settling Down in Springfield

A few weeks after moving from New Salem to the new capital-designate, a gloomy Lincoln confided to a lady friend that "living in Springfield is rather a dull business after all, at least it is so to me. I am quite as lonesome here as [I] ever was anywhere in my life." Beyond the drawbacks of the town itself, he felt embarrassed by his poverty. Calling Springfield a "busy wilderness," he noted that there was "a great deal of flourishing about in carriages here," a form of transportation that he could not afford because of his debts.[15]

Lincoln may have been lonesome for female companionship, but kind male friends helped him settle in. One of them, William Butler, recalled that as he, Lincoln, and two others rode to Springfield from Vandalia after the close of the legislative session in March 1837, they "stopped over night down here at Henderson's Point, and all slept on the floor. We were tired, and the rest slept pretty well." Butler observed, however, "that Lincoln was uneasy, turning over and thinking, and studying, so much so that he kept me awake."

Finally Butler asked: "Lincoln what is the matter with you?"

"Well," came the reply, "I will tell you. All the rest of you have something to look forward to, and all are glad to get home, and will have something to do when you get there. But it isn't so with me. I am going home, Butler, without a thing in the world. I have drawn all my pay I got at Vandalia, and have spent it all. I am in debt— . . . and I have nothing to pay the debt with, and no way to make any money. I don[']t know what to do."

As Butler told an interviewer, he came to Lincoln's assistance: "[W]hen we got to Springfield I went and sold his horse without saying anything to him." Butler paid off his debts and took Lincoln's saddlebags to his home, where Butler's wife washed the clothes they contained. When Lincoln learned that Butler had disposed of his horse, he "was greatly astonished. 'What in the world did you do that for?' he asked."

Lincoln, Butler added, "then went back to get his saddlebags, and they told him they had been taken down to my house. So he came down and asked where they were. I said to him 'I have had them brought down here, and have had your clothes taken out and washed. Now I want you to come down here, and board here and make my house your home.'"

According to Butler, Lincoln "was always careless about his clothes. In all the time he stayed at my house, he never bought a hat or a pair of socks, or a coat. Whenever he needed them, my wife went out and bought them for him, and put them in the drawer where he would find them. When I told him that he couldn't have his clothes, that they were in the wash, he seemed very much mortified. He said he had to go down home to New Salem. I told him that he might take my horse and ride him down there. I also told him that there were his saddlebags, and that there was a clean shirt in them. He took the saddlebags and went and got the horse, and rode down to New Salem, and stayed there about a week. Then he came back and put up the horse."[16]

For the next five years Lincoln took his meals, without charge, at Butler's home, one of the largest in Springfield. Ninian W. Edwards may have prompted Butler to extend this hospitality, for Edwards considered the impoverished newcomer a promising young man who, with a little help, would flourish. In addition, Butler was probably grateful to Lincoln for his recent successful effort to have Springfield named the state's capital.

The Kentucky-born merchant Joshua F. Speed, who became Lincoln's closest friend, proffered equally generous assistance. Speed remembered that Lincoln rode "into town on a borrowed horse, with no earthly goods but a pair of saddle-bags, two or three law books, and some clothing which he had in his saddle-bags. He took an office, and engaged from the only cabinet-maker then in the village, a single bedstead." Lincoln then asked Speed, a silent partner in the general merchandise store, James Bell & Company, how much it would cost to furnish the bed. When the young businessman, nearly five years Lincoln's junior, calculated that mattress, blankets, pillow, sheets, and coverlid would cost $17, Lincoln replied: "It is probably cheap enough: but I want to say that, cheap as it is, I have not the money to pay. But if you will credit me until Christmas, and my experiment here as a lawyer is a success, I will pay you then. If I fail in that I will probably never be able to pay you back at all." (Novice lawyers did not always prosper on the Illinois frontier. One Jacksonville attorney reported in 1835: "Out of the long list of Lawyers that come to this country and settle, there is not one out of an hundred who does *one half* business enough to pay his expenses the first year nor *enough* to pay his expenses for three of the first years.")[17]

Speed recalled that the "tone of his voice was so melancholy that I felt for him. I looked up at him, and I thought . . . that I never saw so gloomy and melancholy a face."

"The contraction of so small a debt seems to affect you so deeply," Speed remarked, "I think I can suggest a plan by which you will be able to attain your end, without incurring any debt. I have a very large room, and a very large double-bed in it; which you are perfectly welcome to share with me if you choose." He explained that "my partner and I have been sleeping in the same bed for some time. He is gone now, and if you wish, you can take his place."

After inspecting the room above the store, Lincoln, "with a face beaming with pleasure," said: "Well, Speed, I'm moved."[18] Between 1837 and 1841, Lincoln bunked with Speed in the room above the store, where Speed's clerks, William H. Herndon and Charles R. Hurst, also slept. There was no partition and hence no privacy. Such sleeping arrangements were common in frontier Illinois.

Neophyte Lawyer

John Todd Stuart, Lincoln's law partner, matched the generosity that Speed and Butler extended to Lincoln. On September 9, 1836, the justices of the Illinois Supreme Court licensed Lincoln to practice law throughout the state. Seven months later he moved to Springfield, where in April the firm of Stuart and Lincoln was formally established in a small, second-floor office on Hoffman's Row, a block of buildings facing the town square. Its meager furniture consisted of a small bed, a buffalo robe, a chair, and a bench. (Stuart's partner during the previous four years, Henry E. Dummer, had moved to another town.)

Most of Stuart and Lincoln's business involved debts in one form or another, though the two men also dealt with various matters in the criminal, common law, and chancery branches of the law. Many of the cases were of small importance, for example, challenging Lincoln to determine who owned a litter of pigs or who was responsible for the death of sheep due to foot rot. Lincoln and Stuart could not make ends meet if they confined their practice to Springfield, so, like most of their colleagues, they rode the First Judicial Circuit, encompassing ten counties. In 1839, when Sangamon County was included in the newly created Eighth Judicial Circuit, Lincoln traveled its nine counties but did the bulk of the firm's work in Sangamon, Tazewell, Logan, and McLean counties.

Tyro though he was, Lincoln handled much of the business of the firm, for politics monopolized Stuart's attention. Defeated in 1836 for Congress, Stuart renewed his quest for that seat the very day after he lost. Lincoln got off to a bad start when Stuart sent him to represent John W. Baddeley, a blunt, English-born merchant of McLean County. When the haughty, aristocratic Baddeley beheld the unprepossessing young attorney, he promptly dismissed him and hired James A. McDougall in his stead.

Lincoln's first law case, *Hawthorn vs. Wooldridge,* which began in 1836, involved a farmer charged with trespass and breach of contract. David Woolridge, Lincoln's client, allegedly "assaulted, struck, beat, bruised and knocked down" James Hawthorn, "plucked, pulled and tore divers quantities of hair" from his head, "with a stick and with his fists gave . . . a great many violent blows and strokes on and about his head, face, back, shoulders, legs, and divers other parts of his body and . . . with great force and violence, struck, shook, pulled, and knocked him . . . down upon the ground, and . . . violently kicked" Hawthorn, "struck him . . . a great many other blows and strokes," "violently thrust his . . . thumbs" into his eyes, "and gouged him . . . to his great pain, distress and injury."[19] The case, involving three separate actions, was argued before a jury, which awarded Hawthorn damages of $36 and costs. The other two actions were settled out of court, with Hawthorn paying the costs of one and Woolridge the other.

No record indicates how the settlement was reached, but Lincoln may well have urged the parties to compromise. Years later he advised lawyers to "[d]iscourage litigation" and to "[p]ersuade your neighbors to compromise whenever you can. Point out to them how the nominal winner is often a real loser—in fees, expenses, and waste of time. As a peace-maker the lawyer has a superior opportunity of being a good man."[20] Most Whig lawyers, including Stuart, shared this view. In his first case Lincoln might have served as such a peacemaker, a role he had often played in his youth. Dennis Hanks recalled, "I've seen him walk into a crowd of jawin' rowdies, and tell some droll yarn, and bust them all up. It was the same when he was a lawyer; all eyes, whenever he riz were on him; there was a suthin' peculiarsome about him."[21]

Lincoln and Stuart usually charged $5 to $10 for their services, dividing those modest fees equally. The only large sum they received was $500 for a sensational murder trial in 1838. The case arose when Henry Truett, quondam register of the Galena land office, cold-bloodedly shot and killed a political opponent, Jacob Early, a doctor and Methodist minister who had criticized Truett's appointment to the land office post. Truett hired Lincoln, Stuart, Stephen T. Logan, Edward D. Baker, and

Cyrus Edwards to defend him; the prosecution team included Stephen A. Douglas. Faced with overwhelming evidence of their client's guilt, Lincoln and his colleagues lamely argued that when Truett pulled a gun on Early, the latter had picked up a chair and was therefore armed when he was shot by Truett, who in fact was merely acting in self-defense. (Witnesses testified that the victim was obviously using the chair as a shield, not a weapon.) Though only in practice for a year, Lincoln was chosen to deliver the closing speech to the jury. No record exists of his words; Logan praised his "short but strong and sensible speech," and Milton Hay recalled that despite "his rawness, awkwardness and uncultivated manner," Lincoln "was expected to make a strong speech in the case, and that expectation was not disappointed."[22] It must have been quite persuasive, for the jury, amazingly, delivered a verdict of not guilty, which doubtless bolstered Lincoln's self-confidence.

If Lincoln had acted as a peacemaker in the Wooldridge case, he played the opposite role in the summer and fall of 1837, waging a vituperative political and legal battle against a pompous attorney, James Adams, who affected fancy dress and enjoyed an unsavory reputation as a lawyer.

The controversy involved both law and politics. Lincoln's close friend, Dr. Anson G. Henry, wanted to unseat Adams as probate justice of the peace, an office Adams had held since the legislature appointed him in 1825. Adams, Lincoln believed, planted a story in the *Illinois Republican*, Springfield's Democratic newspaper, charging that Dr. Henry, as a reward for writing press attacks on Democrats, had won appointment as commissioner to oversee construction of the new state capitol. According to the *Republican*, Henry, "a desperate, reckless adventurer," was "unqualified" and had vastly overpaid a mechanic for demolishing the courthouse to make way for the statehouse and predicted that he would surely overpay contractors for the new building, too.[23] A blistering rebuttal signed "Springfield" (probably by Henry) denounced the "filthy and reckless" attacks in the *Republican*, whose editors (including Stephen A. Douglas, who had recently moved from Jacksonville to serve as register of the Springfield land office and to write for the *Republican*) were "aliens in feeling from the community in which they live."[24]

The newspaper insults led to violence. Henry suspected that Douglas had written the abusive articles and resolved to demand that the editor, George Weber, identify their author. On June 26, 1837, Henry and several friends, armed with canes and pistols, confronted Weber, expecting him to be meek. Douglas, who had come to the office to sound a warning, was sitting there when the committee arrived and threatened violence. Weber punched the spokesman, prompting the delegation to depart.

When Douglas wrote a vivid account of the fracas, Henry's allies resolved to demolish the *Illinois Republican* office. The next evening, while the editor and his staff were out for dinner, a mob led by the inebriated sheriff of Springfield, Garret Elkin, broke down the door and set about wrecking the establishment. Weber and his three brothers, assisted by Jacob M. Early, promptly drove the vandals away.

The following day a mob attacked Weber and his brother John on the street. Sheriff Elkin cudgeled the editor with a weighted whip-stalk, while Doctor Elias H. Merryman assaulted John with his fists. John counterattacked, butted Merryman in the stomach, bowled him over, and began to beat him severely. At that moment Jacob Weber came along and plunged a small knife into the back of Elkin, who fainted from loss of blood. Douglas successfully defended Jacob when he was tried for the stabbing.

Lincoln joined the contest with his pen, spurred on not only by his friendship with Henry but also by a lawsuit against Adams. Lincoln and Stuart had been retained as counsel by Mary Anderson and her son Richard, heirs of the recently deceased Joseph Anderson, who had once employed Adams as an attorney. Joseph Anderson's estate included two parcels of land, one of which was occupied by Adams, who claimed that Anderson had given it to him. Anderson's widow sued, believing that Adams had obtained title fraudulently. Lincoln's investigation of land records convinced him that Adams had forged documents. In six letters to the *Sangamo Journal,* published in June and July and signed "Sampson's Ghost," Lincoln accused Adams of fraud, forgery, and Toryism. ("Sampson" was Andrew Sampson, who had leased land to James Adams with the understanding that Adams would pay the taxes and that Sampson might reclaim the land by compensating Adams for any improvements he made to the property. Adams eventually claimed that he owned the lot in question, though clearly it belonged to Sampson. In the public letters, Lincoln conflated Sampson and Anderson.) Although the Toryism charge was inaccurate—Adams had served in the American army during the War of 1812—Lincoln maintained a generally moderate tone in the Sampson's Ghost letters.

But Lincoln skinned Adams savagely in an unsigned burlesque entitled "A Ghost! A Ghost!" which began with a slightly garbled quotation from one of his favorite plays, *Hamlet:*

"Art thou some spirit or goblin damn'd
Bringst with thee airs from heaven or blasts from hell?"

The "author" of this article is clearly meant to be James Adams, who relates how he had been drinking one night, had fallen off his horse, and was sleeping contentedly on the ground until accosted by a ghost (obviously representing Anderson), who declared in an Irish brogue, which Lincoln employed in jokes and even in formal speeches:

"The rest of the dead is disturbed by the wickedness of the living. I loved my wife and children, and left them my little all. But it is taken away from them—and how can I rest in my grave in pace?"

The ghost offered an autobiographical sketch: "I was born in ould Ireland—swate Ireland;—I kem over to Ameriky—to this blessed land. My wife and little ones came with me here—I bought a few acres—left it in the care of a friend—went farther and died."

When Adams (called "Stranger" in the article) responds, "And what of that? Most men die sometime or other," the ghost accusingly says: "I left my land in the hands of a friend and that friend—Oh! be jiminys! what shall I say? My very grave cannot contain me.—My spirit wanders about seeking rest and finding none. My acres are in the hands of my friend—signed, sealed and delivered!"

Adams: "But, perhaps, this transfer was legal."

Ghost: "By the hill of Hoath, 'tis a lie!"

Adams: "Unless all the proceedings are regular, no transfer can stand, as you well know."

Ghost: "Jiminy's gracious! 'Tis signed with a cross, and I could write my name as well as any can! Oh jiminys! jiminys!"

Adams: "Rather curious, I confess. But did you not make the assignment?"

The ghost, his face radiating "anger, indignation, vengeance," erupted: "Stranger! You lie! How could I assign a judgment before it was obtained? Be Jiminiy Christ it is not so!"[25]

Two weeks later, just before the election, the *Sangamo Journal* ran another story (probably by Lincoln) ridiculing Adams: "The recent noise and excitement made about the wounds and bruises received by Gen. Adams, reminds me of an adventure which happened to me while travelling to this county many years ago. Not far from this place I met a sucker late in the evening returning to his home. 'Good evening friend,' said I. 'How far is it to Springfield?' 'Well, I guess its about five miles.' 'Are you just from there?' 'Well, I am,' and said I, 'What's the news there?' 'Well, there's nothing of any account but a sad accident that happened the other day:—you don't know Gineral Adams?—Well, the Gineral went to stoop down to pick some black-berries and John Taylor's calf gave him a butt right—' 'You don't say so,—and did the Gineral die?' 'No, by G . . . , but the calf did!' "[26]

The same day that this story appeared, Lincoln issued an anonymous handbill reviewing the complicated details of the lawsuit and once again accusing Adams of forgery. When queried, the editor of the *Sangamo Journal,* Simeon Francis, revealed Lincoln's authorship of the handbill. Lincoln's charge seems justified, based on the evidence he marshaled cogently, if intemperately, and also on Adams's long record of ethical lapses. (In 1818, at the age of 25, Adams had been indicted for forging and backdating a deed in New York. Rather than standing trial, he jumped bail and fled the state, leaving behind his wife and young daughter. In 1832, he had unsuccessfully defended an impoverished man accused of murder and then fleeced the man's family of their few worldly goods. In 1838, attempting to discredit a petition drive calling for the division of Sangamon County, Adams obtained a blank copy of the petition and forged the names of free blacks. At Springfield, he engaged in dubious land transac-tions, which Elijah Iles, one of the city's founding fathers and most influential lead-ers, publicly denounced. Adams accused attorney Stephen T. Logan of slander, eventually dropping the charge and paying all court costs. In 1841, he so alienated his fellow Masons in Springfield that their lodge almost dissolved. Two years later, Ad-ams committed bigamy; at that same time, he ran for office in Hancock County, though he was still a resident of Sangamon.)

Lincoln's assaults backfired: Adams won the August election handily, receiving 1,025 votes to Henry's 792. Although Lincoln had built a strong case, the public evidently considered his tactics unfair and regarded Adams as a victim of persecution. The Democrats protested that Adams, "an infirm old man," had been "wantonly slandered," "bitterly persecuted," and "deeply calumniated."[27] The *Sangamo Journal* acknowledged that if "a community can be made to believe, that an individual is persecuted, it is natural for them to sustain him."[28]

Lincoln continued to attack Adams even after the election. On September 6, he published a detailed rejoinder to Adams's defense, which had appeared in the *Illinois Republican* that day. In that document, Lincoln sneered at Adams's alleged misunderstanding of a situation that "the greatest dunce could not but understand." To one of Adams's arguments Lincoln scornfully replied, "Is common sense to be abused with such sophistry?" To Adams's assertion that Lincoln's testimony conflicted with that of the Recorder of Deeds (Benjamin Talbott), Lincoln retorted: "Any man who is not wilfully blind can see at a blush, that there is no discrepancy between Talbott and myself." He called an affidavit by Adams's son-in-law-to-be "most foolish," and deemed Adams himself a "fool." Lincoln concluded that one of the witnesses cited by Adams must be some "black or mulatto boy" because he had observed an important event while in the kitchen of Adams's house. He termed Adams's assertions of fact "false as hell."[29]

On October 7, the *Sangamo Journal* ran a letter by "An Old Settler" (probably Lincoln) accusing Adams of fraud in yet another land transaction. He sententiously declared that Adams "may wince, and screw as other men of the same character usually do, under the lash of Justice and the power of Truth, still he shall not escape."[30] Eleven days later, Lincoln deplored the general's "rascality" and called his defense "foolish," "ludicrous," and "contradictory."[31] Once again, Lincoln had the better argument, but his snide, contemptuous tone undermined his effectiveness.

In 1838, an anonymous piece in the *Sangamo Journal* (probably by Lincoln) once again attacked Adams: "Who is so blind that cannot see the finer marks of forgery in the last [issue of the] Republican? Do we not see evident marks of meanness? But is it surprising that one who has been guilty of defrauding the widow and the orphan—one who has been guilty of repeated acts of baseness—should stop at anything? . . . He stands the living evidence that man is corrupt by nature."[32] When Adams responded to the charges of forgery that had been brought against him in New York, the *Sangamo Journal* published a rejoinder, also probably by Lincoln, alleging that Adams distorted the facts and that he had left New York owing debts still unpaid.

Eventually, the Anderson lawsuit languished, neither dismissed nor pursued, until the death of Adams in 1843, whereupon the court abated the suit. For all the vituperation Lincoln unleashed on their behalf, Anderson's heirs never did receive the land.

Adams was not Lincoln's only target in the 1837 political campaign. On July 1, a special legislative election was held to choose a replacement for Daniel Stone, who had resigned his seat in the General Assembly to accept a judgeship. The Whig candidate, Lincoln's close friend Edward D. Baker, ran against Lincoln's former boss, surveyor John Calhoun. On election eve, an anonymous screed, probably by Lincoln, appeared in the *Sangamo Journal* denouncing Calhoun and other members of Springfield's Democratic "Junto," among them John Taylor and the owners of the *Illinois Republican*. The author accused them of treason against Sangamon County and Springfield because the previous winter they had lobbied to have the county divided up and to have the paper town of Illiopolis chosen as the new state capital. Their motives were selfish; they and their associates owned land in Illiopolis and in villages, including Petersburg, which they hoped would become the seats of new counties created from Sangamon. To enrich themselves, they were making common cause with the spokesmen for Vandalia, who wished to repeal the law designating Springfield as the new state capital.

In the pages of the *Sangamo Journal*, a satirist (probably Lincoln) ridiculed William Walters, co-editor of the *Illinois State Register*, as a "broken down hack."[33] Another scornful letter from the same pen alluded to the split within the Democratic ranks between the old Jacksonians and new converts who were seizing control of the party. In the letter the author has John Calhoun, ostensibly bitter at his electoral defeat in 1834, say: "I thought . . . that I would go to work like an honest man and no longer attempt to obtain a living by locating towns [as county surveyor]."[34]

Special Legislative Session

In July 1837, as the combative Lincoln waged a newspaper war against James Adams and others, Governor Joseph Duncan summoned the legislature to Vandalia for a special session to address the consequences of the financial panic that had struck that spring, drying up the market for Illinois bonds. The state bank was in danger of losing its charter, a development that, in turn, might delay construction of the Illinois and Michigan Canal. In response to this crisis, Duncan recommended that the legislature scrap the internal improvement scheme it had passed earlier that year.

Ignoring this advice, the General Assembly, which met for less than two weeks, first turned its attention to a bill repealing the other major legislation of the last session, the capital removal statute. The champion of repeal, William L. D. Ewing, an able, ambitious, conceited politico, had a reputation for using violence. The short, muscular, impulsive Ewing had several times been indicted (and once convicted) for assault and battery. In 1831, while drunk, he stabbed and badly injured a man who disagreed with him on a minor matter. As receiver of the Vandalia land office, he was found guilty of neglecting his duties. He was also indicted for other misdeeds, among them adultery. In an 1840 quarrel, Ewing threw a chair at a legislator from Chicago, Justin Butterfield. When the two men arranged to fight a duel, only Butterfield's decision to withdraw prevented bloodshed. In his attack on the capital-removal law, Ewing sarcastically denounced "the arrogance of Springfield," maintaining that "its presumption in claiming the seat of government—was not to be endured," and accused the Long Nine of logrolling.

To respond, the Whigs chose Lincoln, who "retorted upon Ewing with great severity; denouncing his insinuations in imputing corruption to him and his colleagues, and paying back with usury all that Ewing had said." Onlookers feared that Lincoln "was digging his own grave; for it was known that Ewing would not quietly pocket any insinuations that would degrade him personally." Ewing then asked the Sangamon County delegation: "Gentlemen, have you no other champion than this coarse and vulgar fellow to bring into the lists against me? Do you suppose that I will condescend to break a lance with your low and obscure colleague?" Usher F. Linder and other observers expected "that a challenge must pass between them," but cooler heads prevailed and no duel took place. (Linder said many years later that "this was the first time that I began to conceive a very high opinion of the talents and personal courage of Abraham Lincoln.")[35] Ewing's bill was referred to a special committee, chaired by Lincoln, who amended it to have Springfield pay the $50,000 it had pledged before work could begin on the statehouse. The measure as amended passed the House but died in senate.

In the brief 1837 session, the General Assembly bristled with hostility toward banks because of the financial panic. As David Davis observed in July: "There are a great many radicals . . . as well as desperate men, a great share of whom by some fortuitous circumstances, are members of the Legislature—and the cry at present—from one end of the State to the other—is—down with the Bank." Davis detected political opportunism at work in this assault.[36] Representative Samuel D. Marshall wryly and correctly predicted that "the bank will not go down. The leaders of the Van Buren party are too much in debt to it to suffer such a result." The Democrats had made threatening noises because they "only wanted the Whigs to take the responsibility so that they might afterwards abuse the Bank again and charge the legalising of the suspension on the Whigs."[37] In fact, Democrats did rally to support the bank. One of them, John Pearson, reflected the views of many colleagues when he said of that institution: "A thing may have been unwise in its creation & yet afterwards prove detrimental to us in its destruction, as some have reasoned in regard to this Bank. . . . If the sudden repeal or even an opposition to this Bank will injure the works the people have begun, why then it is our duty not to oppose it."[38] With the help of such Democrats, Lincoln and his fellow Whigs thwarted attempts to repeal the 1835 charter of the Bank of Illinois. Under that law, if the bank suspended specie payments (redemption of its notes in gold and silver on demand) for more than sixty days, it must disband. The bank did suspend such payments on May 27, 1837, in response to the financial panic. The Whigs managed to persuade the General Assembly to allow the bank to continue its existence temporarily.

Politics, 1838–1840

In the following year's election campaign, the county division issue dominated Sangamon County politics, with the Democrats favoring the proposed change and the Whigs opposing it. Lincoln went to work in the press. Writing from "Lost Townships," an author signing himself "Rusticus"—probably Lincoln—attacked the proposal in the *Sangamo Journal*. On April 15, 1838, Rusticus denounced the editor of Springfield's *Illinois Republican* for catering to land speculators by supporting their attempt to cut up Sangamon "into a litter of counties." Rusticus reported: "I was called on last week, and urged to go for new counties. And what upon earth am I to gain, said I. Why your farm may be made the county seat. It is high and rolling, has a fine view and is in the neighborhood of a large body of timber, and is about in the middle of the proposed new county." Two weeks later Rusticus called the plan to divide Sangamon County into "pea-patch counties" a plot "to benefit certain speculators who own town lots in Allenton, Pulaski and Petersburg" and "to gratify a few men who want offices."[39] In June, Rusticus again inveighed against "dangerous demagogues and speculators," declaring that "[e]very man cannot have a county seat at his door, nor ought he to desire it."[40]

In 1838, Lincoln campaigned not only for his own reelection but also for his law partner, John Todd Stuart, who tried once again to win the congressional seat he had sought two years earlier. The hard times, widely blamed on the Democratic administration in Washington, improved Whig chances and aroused the public to pay more attention than usual to politics. David Davis of Bloomington recalled that no "canvass, in my time, awakened such interest at the start, and retained it to the last. It seemed in my neighborhood, at least, as if every man, woman and twelve-year-old child were enlisted for the fight. Nothing but politics were subjects of conversation and everybody attended political meetings."[41]

Lincoln attacked Stuart's opponent, Stephen A. Douglas, in letters by "A Conservative," which the *Sangamo Journal* ran in January and February 1838. (Democrats opposed to President Van Buren's economic policies referred to themselves as "Conservatives.") In the first missive, Lincoln called Douglas a radical, arguing that ever since the Little Giant had assumed responsibility for the editorials in the *Illinois Republican,* that newspaper had championed "the Utopian scheme of an exclusive specie currency, involving the destruction of all banks—and the dangerous doctrine that all incorporated institutions, and all contracts between the State and its citizens, can be changed or annulled at the pleasure of the Legislature." He also accused Douglas of striking a corrupt bargain to win his nomination. Douglas furiously denied the charges and condemned the "vindictive, fiendish spirit" of "Conservative." With some justice, he protested that "my *private* and *moral,* as well as public and political character [has] been assailed in a manner calculated to destroy my standing as a man and a citizen."[42]

Two weeks later, "Conservative" branded Douglas a "man of expedients" and once again questioned the legitimacy of his nomination. The Democratic convention in Peoria that chose him to run for Congress was, "Conservative" alleged, "gotten up and conducted in such a manner, as to render it both injurious and disgraceful to the party if they attempt to sustain it." Douglas had been register of the Springfield land office, a post coveted by "a certain gentleman [John Calhoun] who resides in Sangamon county, and who has followed a variety of occupations both here and elsewhere, for a living and failed in all." Calhoun, eager to replace Douglas, flattered him with the suggestion that he run for Congress, "telling him that he regretted to see him confined to the dry and laborious occupation of writing answers to the endless and silly enquiries of every applicant about N. W. of S. E. of 23, T. 24 R. 3 W., etc. etc.; that for one whom nature designed for nothing else but to be

'Fixed to one certain spot,
   To draw nutrition, propegate, and rot,'

such a plodding occupation was well enough; but that for one of his towering genius, it was absolutely intolerable. 'You,' continued he, 'may be President of the United states just as well as not. A seat in Congress is not worthy to be your abiding place, though you might with propriety serve one term in the capacity of Representative—not that it would at all become you; but merely in imitation of some king, who being called to the throne from obscurity, lodges for one night in a hovel as he journies to the palace. History gives no account of a man of your age [Douglas was 24] occupying such high ground as you do now. At twenty-four Bonaparte was unheard of; and in fact so it has been with all great men in former times. . . . There is no doubt of a seat in Congress being within your reach. The only question is whether you will conde-scend to occupy it." Thus "flattered out of his senses," "Conservative" alleged, Doug-las arranged matters so that he could win the nomination at Peoria. Operating craftily behind the scenes, he stacked the convention with his supporters and won.[43] (The two lines of poetry quoted in this missive were from Alexander Pope's "Essay on Man," a favorite of Lincoln's.)

The day that this article appeared, Lincoln gave a significant speech to the Young Men's Lyceum in Springfield. Entitled "The Perpetuation of Our Political Institu-tions," it focused primarily on a recent nationwide outbreak of mob violence. In 1835, the country had experienced such a startling increase in mob violence (71 people died in 147 recorded riots that year) that a South Carolina newspaper declared: "Mobs, strikes, riots, abolition movements, insurrections, Lynch clubs seem to be the en-grossing topics of the day."[44] In 1837, Lincoln himself attacked "that lawless and mobocratic spirit . . . abroad in the land."[45] In his Lyceum address Lincoln added his voice to the Illinois Whig chorus denouncing the upsurge in riots and lynching.

In the midst of his ostensibly nonpartisan address, Lincoln struck a blow against Douglas. He alluded to the danger of a coming Caesar, a man "of ambition and tal-ents" who would ruthlessly pursue fame and power, overthrowing democratic institu-tions to achieve his ends. "Many great and good men sufficiently qualified for any task they should undertake, may ever be found, whose ambition would aspire to noth-ing beyond a seat in Congress, a gubernatorial or a presidential chair; *but such belong not to the family of the lion, or the tribe of the eagle.*" Lincoln asked rhetorically if such a person would be content to follow traditional paths to distinction, and then he an-swered, "What! think you these places would satisfy an Alexander, a Caesar, or a Napoleon? Never! Towering genius disdains a beaten path."[46] Clearly, the "towering genius" was Douglas, the man whom the flatterer in "Conservative No. 2" called "a towering genius." (This was probably a slighting reference to Douglas's diminutive stature—5 feet 4 inches—which Lincoln in December 1837 had alluded to: "We have adopted it as part of our policy here, to never speak of Douglass at all. Is'nt that the best mode of treating so small a matter.")[47] Here Lincoln echoed the charges of "Con-servative" from the *Sangamo Journal.* "Conservative" likened Douglas to Bonaparte; Lincoln at the Lyceum warned against men like Napoleon. "Conservative" suggested that Douglas would not be content with a mere seat in Congress; Lincoln denounced any man whose ambition would not be satisfied with such a post. Since the rules of the Lyceum forbade political speeches, Lincoln could not directly attack Douglas, but because his audience was politically aware, he could assume that they had read "Conservative No. 2" earlier in the day and thus understood that Douglas was the target of his remarks about the coming Caesar. It was a clever maneuver to circumvent the ban on partisanship at the Lyceum. (Two decades later Lincoln would again satirize Douglas in an ostensibly nonpolitical address on "Discoveries and Inventions.")

The Lyceum speech could be construed as an attack not only on Douglas but also on the Democratic Party, which Whigs denounced for championing "mobocracy." (A headline in an Illinois Whig paper read: "Mobocracy and Loco-Focoism—One and the Same Thing.")[48]

With some justice, friends criticized this florid address as "highly sophomoric in character" and a prime example of "'spread eagle' and vapid oratory."[49] It illustrated Albert T. Bledsoe's contention that Lincoln, as a young man, was "most wofully given to *sesquipedalian* words, or, in Western phrase, *highfalutin* bombast."[50]

Lincoln may have been imitating the flamboyant oratorical style of Daniel Webster, whom he had heard speak a few months earlier in Springfield. He greatly admired Webster's speeches, which he predicted "will be read for ever."[51] In the Massachusetts statesman's 1825 Bunker Hill address, he reflected on the inability of his generation to achieve the fame of their Revolutionary forefathers: "We can win no laurels in a war for independence. Earlier and worthier hands have gathered them all."[52] Similarly, Lincoln observed that during the Revolutionary era "all that sought celebrity and fame, and distinction, expected to find them in the success of that experiment. . . . This field of glory is harvested, and the crop is already appropriated."

The moral that Lincoln drew from his survey of recent mob violence in Mississippi, Missouri, and Illinois was that "every American, every lover of liberty, every well wisher to his posterity" should "swear by the blood of the Revolution, never to violate in the least particular, the laws of the country; and never to tolerate their violation by others." He portrayed reverence for the law as the "political religion" of the nation.[53] Lincoln echoed an earlier speaker before the Lyceum, his friend Anson G. Henry, who in 1835 had appealed to the young men of Springfield to put down "every symptom of mobocracy and lawless violence by enforcing the laws. The blood of our fathers, let it not have been shed in vain."[54]

Despite its evident banality, Lincoln's address offered beneath the surface a bold commentary on slavery and race, couched so as to give little offense but nevertheless designed to prick the conscience of his audience. In part, the speech was inspired by the recent murder of abolitionist Elijah P. Lovejoy, whom Missouri slaveholders had driven from their state. When Lovejoy transferred operations across the Mississippi River to Alton, Illinois, he encountered an even more unfriendly reception. At a public meeting in 1837, several Alton residents condemned him; soon thereafter mobs twice destroyed his printing presses, dumping them into the river. On November 7, 1837, as he brandished firearms in an attempt to protect yet another press from mob violence, he was killed. His death aroused indignation throughout the North, where he was regarded as a martyr to freedom of expression.

In the Lyceum speech, Lincoln, who several months earlier had denounced slavery as an institution based on "injustice and bad policy," clearly alluded to the murder of Lovejoy in a passage condemning mobs that "throw printing presses into rivers" and "shoot editors." Lincoln's central theme was the danger that mob violence poses to democracy. Although the speech did not mention Lovejoy by name, its application to his murder was obvious. Lincoln's audience might also have been reminded of the Springfield mob that forced the cancellation of an abolitionist sermon the previous October.

If it took courage in the Springfield of 1838 to express sympathy for an abolitionist like Lovejoy, it required even more nerve to speak compassionately of a black man who in April 1836 had stabbed two white men. Lincoln nonetheless did so, referring to a "highly tragic" and "horror-striking scene at St. Louis," where a "mulatto man, by the name of McIntosh, was seized in the street, dragged to the suburbs of the city, chained to a tree, and actually burned to death; and all within a single hour from the time he had been a freeman, attending to his own business, and at peace with the world." (Because the case of McIntosh had been widely publicized by Lovejoy's newspaper, it seems probable that Lincoln was indirectly expressing further sympathy with Lovejoy by calling attention to that atrocity.) Moreover, Lincoln condemned Mississippi mobs for lynching "negroes, suspected of conspiring to raise an insurrection," and "white men, supposed to be leagued with the negroes," and "strangers, from neighboring States, going thither on business."[55]

Thus, within the bombast of the Lyceum address, Lincoln subtly embedded criticism not only of Stephen A. Douglas but also of anti-abolitionists and racial bigotry.

Lincoln continued to attack Douglas. A third installment of the "Conservative" letters submitted to the *Sangamo Journal*, ostensibly written by unhappy Democrats but probably composed by Lincoln, repeated the charge that the Peoria convention which had nominated Douglas was "a mere farce," and denounced the "jugglery" and "secret management" that procured him the nomination.[56]

Lincoln also confronted Douglas in person, both on the stump and in the courtroom. Lincoln and Stuart debated their opponents throughout the campaign. In one encounter, Stuart grew incensed at Douglas's allegations, grabbed his smaller opponent by the neck, and walked about with him; in response Douglas bit Stuart's thumb, scarring it for life. Earlier in the campaign, Douglas, offended by a piece in the *Sangamo Journal*, tried to cane its editor, Simeon Francis, who (as Lincoln described it) caught his would-be assailant "by the hair and jammed him back against a market-cart, where the matter ended by Francis being pulled away from him."[57] In May, when Stuart became ill, Lincoln substituted for him at a debate in Bloomington.

Realizing that the race between his partner and Douglas would be close, Lincoln worked hard and urged other Whigs to follow his example. "If we do our duty we shall succeed in the congressional election," he told a friend, "but if we relax an *iota*, we shall be beaten."[58] His concern proved justified on election day in August, when Stuart narrowly prevailed, receiving 18,254 votes to Douglas's 18,218. Lincoln easily won a third legislative term, running ahead of all the fifteen other candidates, even though some of his old friends in New Salem, Sandridge, and Petersburg voted against him because his party opposed the division of Sangamon County.

When the Eleventh General Assembly convened in December 1838, Lincoln again found himself pitted against William L. D. Ewing, who had run for the legislature that year promising to "be a *thorn* in the side of the 'long nine,' should we again see them" and to "fearlessly expose to the new Legislature the foul corruption by which the seat of Government, contrary to justice and the constitution, was removed to Springfield."[59] As the most prominent Whig, Lincoln was his party's obvious choice for Speaker of the House. Ewing managed to win after several ballots by the vote of 43 to 38, making Lincoln in effect minority leader of the lower chamber. Lincoln might have won if all Whigs had been present and voted for him; as it was, three were absent and two defected to Ewing. Disappointed at his loss, Lincoln declared that Ewing "is not worth a damn."[60] Thus began what one Representative called "a stormy session & a very unpleasant one."[61]

Once organized, the House somewhat desultorily addressed banking questions yet again. Two weeks into the session the Committee on Finance submitted a report written, in all likelihood, by Lincoln. Reflecting the standard Whig position, it condemned President Van Buren's proposal for an independent subtreasury, arguing that a divorce between government and banking was unnecessary and citing the history of "the extraordinary and unprecedented degree of prosperity which accompanied us in our onward march during the period of this union [of banks and government]." The generally dispassionate document criticized the inconsistency of congressional Democrats who between 1831 and 1835 had voted against proposals to separate banking from the government but who now supported Van Buren's plan to do so. The committee expressed concern that the separation of bank and state could lead to the marriage of public funds and executive patronage, an alliance that might corrupt elections. Since the system already in place had worked so well, it should not be abandoned: "Your committee do not wish to be understood as resisting, without inquiry or examination, all changes in the fiscal affairs of the Government," the report said. But, it asked, "what are the grounds, what are the reasons and considerations which render this [proposed] change necessary and proper?"[62]

Proponents of divorce argued that federal funds were insecure in deposit banks, though a recent report by the secretary of the treasury showed that this was not a serious problem. Moreover, Van Buren in his December 1838 annual message praised the conduct of banks. In January, the General Assembly expressed agreement with Lincoln's arguments by instructing Illinois's congressional delegation to vote against the subtreasury plan.

In addition to debating the bank issue on the national level, the legislators addressed state banking concerns, including a resolution condemning the practice of depositing in a Missouri bank the federal taxes collected from Illinois residents. Lincoln at first agreed with the resolution but then moved to table it indefinitely.

Instead of responding to the financial panic and recession by sensibly reducing expenditures for canals and railroads, the General Assembly, with Lincoln's approval, unaccountably appropriated more funds for such purposes. In December, acknowledging that "his own course was identified with the system," Lincoln said that Illinois "had gone too far to recede, even if we were disposed to do so."[63] The following month he reiterated this sentiment in a Finance Committee report: "[W]e are now so far advanced in a general system of internal improvements that, if we would, we cannot retreat from it, without disgrace and great loss."[64] He had pledged to support the system and announced in the General Assembly "that his limbs should be torn asunder before he would violate that pledge."[65]

A year later "A Citizen" (probably Lincoln) defended internal improvements spending in a letter to the *Sangamo Journal*. Illinois legislators had done "that which they thought would be for the future glory and honor of the State." They sought to help farmers create "a ready market for the fruits of their labor" by borrowing money to build roads "whereon the farmer could transport his products to some port of embarkation." An improved transportation network would provide a home market as well as "a cheap and easy conveyance of commodities to foreign markets." The parts of the system in place had "already dispelled the gloom from the face of many a farmer and mechanic." The author warned that to abandon the system would be ill-advised. Should the state manage to get "through it honorably she will get glory." Illinois's "own industry and good management" would pay the debt. The author wished his "fellow citizens to keep constantly in mind that no murmuring or complaining of their's will mend matters." They should not, "like the foolish Israelites, by their murmurings, distract the councils of their State, and put back the work of public improvement, which is fast converting their whole country into a fruitful field." Instead, let them with "contented minds, and cheerful industry," go about making "pork and beef enough in the next thirty years to pay for works fifteen times as costly as those now in progress, if they can find a reasonable market for it."[66]

To meet the costs of the internal improvements system, Lincoln proposed that Illinois buy 20 million acres of public land within the state from the federal government for 25¢ per acre, then sell it for $1.25 per acre. If implemented, the plan would generate enough revenue to pay off the debt. Resolutions endorsing Lincoln's scheme passed the legislature, but Congress ignored them. In 1840, Lincoln urged John Todd Stuart to show them to the influential South Carolina Senator John C. Calhoun, who had proposed a similar plan.

Lincoln also voted to impose a modest tax on land and to change the formula used to compute property taxes. To a dissenting Democrat, Lincoln protested that the old system, which relied almost exclusively upon taxes levied on the property of out-of-state landowners, failed to produce enough revenue. Moreover, it valued all land at either $3 or $4 per acre, allowing owners of valuable property to pay less than their fair share of taxes. Lincoln claimed that the new system "does not increase the tax upon the 'many poor' but upon the '*wealthy few*' by taxing the land that is worth $50 or $100 per acre, in proportion to its value, instead of, as heretofore, no more than that which was worth but $5 per acre." If the wealthy did not like it, there was little reason to worry, for "*they* are not sufficiently numerous to carry the elections."[67]

The Eleventh General Assembly addressed the touchy subject of county divisions. One legislator observed that of all the questions pending, "the most difficult to settle are such as grow out of dispute[s] in relation to county towns and lines of counties that affect such local interest."[68] In 1839, David Davis explained to a Massachusetts relative that there was "a great mania in our State for the creation of new Counties. Speculators who own towns want Counties made for prospective county seats. And then again, the office holding spirit, which is diffused very generally in Illinois, induces the people generally within the limits of the proposed new County, to desire its formation."[69]

Lincoln fought a rear-guard action to prevent the balkanization of Sangamon County. In September 1838, the *Sangamo Journal* had run a letter, probably by Lincoln, accusing division proponents of "selfishness—A desire to make money, or to obtain the little offices in the new counties." The author was particularly harsh in criticizing John Taylor: "Old Sangamon must be cut to pieces to accommodate Col. Taylor. He once endeavored to destroy her through the instrumentality of Illiopolis. He now aims to produce the same result by making use of Petersburg." The letter maintained that Aaron Vandever of Lick Creek wanted a division so that he could win election to the General Assembly, something he could not do in Sangamon County. "In any of the proposed divisions of Sangamon the mass of the people would not be accommodated so far as county business is concerned, as well as they are now."[70]

Despite Lincoln's opposition, it was clear that some kind of division was inevitable. He pragmatically sought to ensure that Sangamon would be carved up into three instead of four new counties, and that Springfield would not be disadvantaged. (If the county were split into four equal sections, Springfield would be isolated in the corner of one.) As a member of the Committee on Counties, Lincoln drafted a bill creating three new counties. When it was reported on January 16, 1839, the House referred it to a special committee (on which Lincoln sat) that amended the bill (all of the amendments being in Lincoln's hand). On February 2, the House debated the measure, with Lincoln arguing against four equal counties. The bill as amended passed, establishing the small new counties of Logan, Dane, and Menard. Sangamon remained large, with five representatives; Lincoln preserved for Sangamon six townships that would have been lost if the county had been divided into four counties of equal size. Thus, as the *Sangamo Journal* noted, "Old Sangamon, though considerably shorn of territory, will still remain among the most extensive and populous counties in the State."[71] In protecting the interests of the county, Lincoln employed the same skills he had used in Springfield's campaign to become the state capital.

At least one of Lincoln's friends criticized him sharply for his stand. In January 1839, William Butler, known as "a quiet, dignified man," accused him of truckling to land speculators.[72] In deference to their friendship, Lincoln judiciously replied: "You were in an ill-humor when you wrote that letter, and, no doubt, intended that I should be thrown into one also; which, however, I respectfully decline being done." Employing the imagery of suicide, as he did surprisingly often, Lincoln declared, "I am willing to pledge myself in black and white to cut my own throat from ear to ear, if, when I meet you, you shall *seriously* say, that you believe me capable of betraying my friends for any price." In closing, Lincoln called himself "[y]our friend in spite of your ill-nature."[73]

Butler had also rebuked the less forbearing Edward D. Baker, who responded heatedly, calling Butler "a fool."[74] Acting as peacemaker, Lincoln explained to Butler that Baker had been "writhing under a severe tooth-ache," hence "at that time was incapable of exercising that patience and reflection which the case required." He counseled that it "is always magnanamous to recant whatever we may have said in passion; and when you and Baker shall have done this, I am sure there will no difficulty be left between you."[75] Lincoln practiced what he preached, exercising over the years an almost superhuman magnanimity.

The General Assembly also addressed the issue of slavery. On January 5, 1839, the Judiciary Committee moved two resolutions, the first condemning the governor of Maine for his refusal to extradite Georgia men who had helped runaway slaves, and the second declaring that citizens of the Free States "ought not to interfere with the property of slaveholding States; which property has been guarantied unto them by the Constitution of the United States, and without which guaranty, the Union, perhaps, would never have been formed."[76] Lincoln initially concurred, but on second thought said he wanted more time for deliberation; finally, he concluded that it was "better to postpone the subject indefinitely."[77]

The subject, however, would not go away; on February 1, it came up again when John Calhoun, in reply to abolitionist petitions, introduced resolutions urging Congress to ignore pleas for the abolition of slavery in both Washington, D.C., and the western territories, and for the prohibition of slave trading among the states. He added that attempts to grant Illinois blacks fundamental rights were "not only unconstitutional, but improper, inexpedient, and unwise."[78] The House defeated Calhoun's motion 44–36, with Lincoln joining the majority.

In March 1839, the General Assembly adjourned. Lincoln had as usual been conscientious, answering 157 of the 181 roll calls and serving on eleven select committees.

The legislature reconvened the following December at the urging of Governor Thomas Carlin. Meeting for the first time in Springfield, the General Assembly had to deliberate in churches, for the statehouse, whose cornerstone had been laid two years earlier, stood unfinished on the public square, surrounded by stagnant pools in which many of the city's free-roaming hogs wallowed. (A wag suggested that wild rice be cultivated there: "It will grow in water from six inches to a foot deep—reproduces well and is a very nutritious article of food. A sufficient quantity could be raised in the State House yard to secure rations for all the State offices.")[79]

Governor Carlin wanted the legislature to modify the internal improvements system, for the state could not pay the interest on the debt needed to support it. As the House of Representatives discussed the governor's proposal in its temporary quarters at the Second Presbyterian Church, Lincoln once again tried to salvage what the Democrats referred to as "Infernal Improvements." He argued "that at least some

portion of our Internal Improvements should be carried on . . . at least one work calculated to yield something towards defraying its expense, should be finished and put
in operation."[80] When he voted for an unsuccessful proposal to have joint-stock companies take over the system, with the state owning some shares, the Springfield
Register sneeringly declared that Lincoln "has blown his pledges to the winds, and
has left the system to shift for itself. What an example of *good faith!*"[81] The jibe was
unfair, for Lincoln voted repeatedly to sustain the system, including the Illinois and
Michigan Canal. When it was proposed that work on the canal be suspended, he
said "we should lose much by stopping the work on the Canal—that a mutual injury
would result to the State by suspending all operations there. . . . The embankments
upon the Canal would be washing away, and the excavations filling up."[82] Although
the legislature did not kill the internal improvements system *de jure*, it did so *de
facto*.

Governor Carlin also recommended an investigation of the state bank. The legislators complied by establishing a special committee, with Lincoln as one of its members. In late December, he reported to John Todd Stuart that the "legislature is in
session, and has suffered the Bank to forfeit it's charter, without *Benefit of Clergy*.
There seems to be but verry little disposition to resuscitate it."[83] A month later, Lincoln had better news for his law partner: "The Bank will be resuscitated with some
trifling modifications."[84] He was right; the following day the investigating committee
defended the bank in a report that Lincoln signed. The General Assembly permitted
that institution to suspend specie payments until the close of the next legislative session.

The removal of the state capital came up yet again, because the citizens of
Springfield, suffering from the economic hard times, had difficulty raising the
$50,000 to help pay for the new statehouse. Some legislators were ready to introduce
a bill relieving the townspeople of that burden, but Lincoln "objected, and, though
fully appreciating the kindly feelings that prompted the proposal, insisted that the
money should and would be paid."[85]

The legislature adjourned on February 1, 1840, after reviving the State Bank,
continuing support for the Illinois and Michigan Canal (but otherwise cutting back
on internal improvements), and incorporating the town of Springfield while leaving
unchanged its new status as state capital. Characteristically, Lincoln had answered
145 of 169 roll calls.

Well before adjournment, Lincoln and other Whigs girded for the presidential
election. Thanks to the hard times caused by the Panic of 1837, they had a good
chance to win. Illinois Whigs had at first opposed the convention system adopted by
the Democrats, believing it to be "a Yankee contrivance, intended to abridge the liberties of the people, by depriving individuals, on their own mere motion, of the privilege of becoming candidates, and depriving each man of the right to vote for a
candidate of his own selection and choice."[86] Eventually, however, defeat at the polls
forced them to reconsider. David Davis told a fellow Whig in 1839: "The longer I live
the more I am convinced that unless the Whigs of this State organize through Conventions they will be beaten at the next General election. Candidates show themselves

as plenty as blackberries."[87] The following year Lincoln and four party colleagues declared that a "disbanded yeomanry cannot successfully meet an organized soldiery."[88] In September 1839, the Whigs of Sangamon County urged their counterparts throughout Illinois to send representatives to a state convention the following month. That conclave chose delegates to the Whig national convention, passed resolutions, adopted a plan for organizing the state, and drafted an address to the people. Lincoln was named one of the five Whig presidential electors and placed on the Whig State Central Committee, which the Democrats derisively called the "Junto." The delegates endorsed the presidential candidacies of both Henry Clay and William Henry Harrison.

Although Lincoln deeply admired Clay, he supported Harrison for expediency's sake. An 1838 editorial in the *Sangamo Journal*, probably by Lincoln, declared (in words which had personal resonance for him) that Harrison's nomination would "proclaim to the world, that poverty shall never arrest virtue and intelligence on their march to distinction." Furthermore, Harrison had earned his country's gratitude for "arduous and valuable services to the community."[89] A May 1839, letter in the *Sangamo Journal*, also probably by Lincoln, argued that Harrison was more electable than Clay. Acknowledging his admiration for Clay, the author nonetheless noted "that the people—the bone and sinew of the country—the main pillar of the republic—I mean the farming and laboring classes" favored Harrison. The author, who signed himself "A Voice from Southern Illinois," added that "the people are for Gen. Harrison, and be it whim or not—they must be humored or the Vannites [Democrats] will take advantage of the deep toned feeling of the public mind in his favor, and a victory which is properly our's will be their's."[90]

In December 1839, delegates to the first Whig national convention agreed with Lincoln, passing over Clay and the other conspicuous leader of the party, Daniel Webster, to nominate the popular, colorless Harrison and send him forth unencumbered by a platform. When a Democratic newspaper sneered at Harrison's simple ways ("Give him a barrel of hard cider and settle a pension of two thousand a year upon him, and our word for it, he will sit the remainder of his days content in a log cabin"), the Whigs made a virtue of them.[91] Instead of principles, he would run on his military record, his humble log-cabin origins, and his fondness for egalitarian hard cider rather than elitist champagne. Some Whig organizers eagerly seized the political low ground, believing that "passion and prejudice, properly aroused and directed, would do about as well as principle in a party contest," and that to "correct the abuses of the [Van Buren] Administration is sufficient motive to vigorous and efficient effort, and in politics, as well as in Philosophy—it is unwise to give more reasons than are necessary."[92] They ridiculed Van Buren as an aristocrat who ate with gold cutlery, wore silk hose and ruffled shirts, scented himself with perfume, and primped before immense mirrors. In a circular signed by the Illinois Whig central committee, including Lincoln, the president was termed effeminate and luxury-loving.[93] Whigs championed Harrison, by contrast, as a true man of the people, content with homespun clothes and log-cabin rusticity.

The campaign insulted the intelligence of many thoughtful people. An Illinois Whig leader, Albert Taylor Bledsoe, declared that observers of the 1840 contest "would have supposed that the whole world had run mad, and rushed into the wild contest on the sublime issues, that log-cabins are the best of all buildings, hard-cider the most delicious of all drinks, and coon-skins the finest of all furs. In no age or country, perhaps, since the dawn of civilization, has humbuggery been exhibited in more gigantic and grotesque forms than in the Harrison campaign of 1840." When Bledsoe expressed "intense mortification that the Whig Party, which had claimed a monopoly of all the intelligence and decency of the country, should descend to the use of such means," Lincoln replied: "It is all right; *we must fight the devil with fire; we must beat the Democrats, or the country will be ruined.*" In response to Bledsoe's protest that ends do not justify means, Lincoln "looked very grave" but "said nothing."[94]

Lincoln was not alone in his evident embarrassment. A British visitor reported that many Whigs "seemed to be a little ashamed of the arts to which their own party had had recourse, in order to enlist the labouring classes in their ranks." Noting that the Democrats had used hickory poles to win support for Andrew Jackson ("Old Hickory") in earlier campaigns, some Whigs rationalized that "one piece of vulgarity and bad taste was justified by another." Thus "neither party had dignity or independence enough to rise superior to such absurdities."[95] A case in point was the New York Whig who reasoned that since his party had been "broken down by the popularity and non-committal character of old Jackson," it was "but fair to turn upon, and prostrate our opponents, with the weapons . . . with which they beat us."[96]

Lincoln took charge of the Harrison campaign in traditionally Democratic Illinois, where "the idea prevailed . . . that all things were fair in politics, love, and war."[97] He predicted the state would turn Whig in 1840. In January, he reported to John Todd Stuart that the "nomination of Harrison takes first rate. You know I am never sanguine; but I believe we will carry the state. The chance for doing so, appears to me 25 per cent better than it did for you to beat Douglass."[98] In the fall and winter of 1839–1840, he helped organize two series of debates with Democrats, the first of which took place in November. They were preceded by informal political discussions in Joshua Speed's store, where one evening Douglas accused the Whigs of committing every imaginable political crime and challenged his opponents to a public debate. The Whig spokesmen were Lincoln, Cyrus Walker, and Edward D. Baker; the Democrats were represented by Douglas, John Calhoun, Josiah Lamborn, and Edmund R. Wiley.

The first debate took place on November 19, with Cyrus Walker making the Whig case and Douglas the Democratic response; Lincoln had the final word. In the course of his remarks, Lincoln called the Democratic editors of the Springfield *Register* "liars" for alleging that he supported John Bennett instead of his old friend Bowling Green for a legislative seat. The *Register* chided Lincoln for the "*assumed clownishness* in his manner which does not become him." According to that paper, he "will sometimes make his language correspond with this *clownish* manner, and he can thus frequently raise a loud laugh among his Whig hearers; but this entire game of buffoonery convinces the *mind* of no man, and is utterly lost on the majority of his audience."[99]

The next night Douglas and Lincoln debated the Bank of the United States. Lincoln evidently did badly. The *Register* ridiculed his efforts and said that even Lincoln's friends thought he had been whipped. One of those friends, Joseph Gillespie, had to agree that against Douglas "Lincoln did not come up to the requirements of the occasion." Gillespie, who said he "never saw any man so much distressed," thought that Lincoln "was conscious of his failure."[100] (Years later, Lincoln told a friend: "I'm one of the thinnest skinned men to any marks of impatience in my audience.")[101]

Later that week, the fiery, hot-tempered, impulsive Edward D. Baker spoke for the Whigs. (One election day, the British-born Baker assaulted a prominent Democrat who had questioned his right to vote. Lincoln said that the bloody-faced Democrat was "the worst whipped man that he had ever seen." In the Illinois General Assembly, Baker threatened to beat a judge who challenged his word.)[102] Baker uttered some harsh words about George R. Weber, co-editor of the *Illinois State Register*, prompting Weber's brother John to yell: "Pull him down!"[103] Relaxing in his office on the second floor of the building where the debate took place, Lincoln heard the commotion below and promptly raced downstairs and beheld Baker confronted by a menacing crowd. Lincoln grabbed a stone pitcher and threatened to smash it on the head of anyone who attacked Baker.

Violence often marred Illinois elections. Around the time of the debates in Springfield, for example, Usher Linder was speaking for the Whig cause in the statehouse and was continuously interrupted by hecklers in the balcony. At the conclusion of his remarks, Lincoln approached Linder, expressing concern for Linder's safety: "Baker and I are apprehensive that you may be attacked by some of those ruffians who insulted you from the galleries, and we have come up to escort you to your hotel. We both think we can do a little fighting, so we want you to walk between us until we get you to your hotel."[104]

In the second round of debates, which attracted an audience of about 500, Lincoln redeemed himself for his earlier failure. According to Gillespie, he "begged to be permitted to try it again and was reluctantly indulged and in the next effort he transcended our highest expectations[.] I never heard & never expect to hear such a triumphant vindication as he then gave of Whig measures or policy."[105] On December 18, Lincoln branded the Democrats' subtreasury plan a "scheme of fraud and corruption."[106] Douglas responded in a manner that caused Lincoln to remark that he "is not now worth talking about."[107]

The day after Christmas, Lincoln gave such a powerful address that it became the Illinois Whig Party's textbook for 1840. He began by candidly admitting that it was "peculiarly embarrassing to me to attempt a continuance of the discussion, on this evening, which has been conducted in this Hall on several preceding ones. It is so, because on each of those evenings, there was a much fuller attendance than now, without any reason for its being so, except the greater interest the community feel in the Speakers who addressed them then, than they do in him who is to do so now. I am, indeed, apprehensive, that the few who have attended, have done so, more to spare me of mortification, than in the hope of being interested in any thing I may be able to say. This circumstance casts a damp upon my spirits, which I am sure I shall be unable to overcome during the evening."

After this painful acknowledgment, Lincoln launched into a sober analysis of President Van Buren's independent subtreasury scheme for government funds, a deflationary plan that, he argued, would create "distress, ruin, bankruptcy and beggary" by removing money from circulation. Hardest hit would be poor people in states with large tracts of public land. "Knowing, as I well do, the difficulty that poor people *now* encounter in procuring homes, I hesitate not to say, that when the price of the public lands shall be doubled or trebled . . . it will be little less than impossible for them to procure those homes at all." Lincoln cited history to support his alternative to the subtreasury, a national bank, which for over forty years had managed to "establish and maintain a sound and uniform state of currency." The Bank of the United States had performed this service cheaply, while the subtreasury would cost more and do less to restore prosperity. In addition, government money was safer in a Bank of the United States than it would be in the hands of government officials like those who had recently embezzled large sums. The Bank was clearly constitutional, Lincoln argued.

As he proceeded, Lincoln abandoned his didactic exposition of economic theory and history and began to scourge the Jackson and Van Buren administrations for their extravagant spending. He went on at length to rebut Douglas's attempt to explain the federal government's unusual expenses in 1838. Lincoln was occasionally abusive: he ridiculed arguments of the opponents of the Bank of the United States as "absurd;" he called Douglas "stupid" and "deserving of the world's contempt;" and he labeled one of Douglas's arguments "*supremely ridiculous.*" Lincoln indulged in some demagoguery, asking of the subtreasury: "was such a system for benefiting the few at the expense of the many, ever before devised?"

Warming to the task, Lincoln became almost hysterical as he savaged the Van Buren administration. "Many free countries have lost their liberty; and *ours may* lose hers; but if she shall, be it my proudest plume, not that I was the *last* to desert, but that I *never* deserted her. I know that the great volcano at Washington, aroused and directed by the evil spirit that reigns there, is belching forth the lava of political corruption, in a current broad and deep, which is sweeping with frightful velocity over the whole length and breadth of the land, bidding fair to leave unscathed no green spot or living thing, while on its bosom are riding like demons on the waves of Hell, the imps of that evil spirit, and fiendishly taunting all those who dare resist its destroying course, with the hopelessness of their effort; and knowing this, I cannot deny that all may be swept way. Broken by it, I, too, may be; bow to it I never will. The *probability* that we may fall in the struggle *ought not* to deter us from the support of a cause we believe to be just; it *shall not* deter me. If ever I feel the soul within me elevate and expand to those dimensions not wholly unworthy of its Almighty Architect, it is when I contemplate the cause of my country, deserted by all the world beside, and I standing up boldly and alone and hurling defiance at her victorious oppressors. Here, without contemplating consequences, before High Heaven, and in the face of the world, I swear eternal fidelity to the just cause, as I deem it, of the land of my life, my liberty and my love."[108]

Although such rhetorical bombast marred this speech, Lincoln made some legitimate economic points. The independent treasury scheme would have been deflationary, though not as badly as Lincoln predicted. Moreover, he sensibly praised the useful regulatory function that the Bank of the United States had served, something like the role that the Federal Reserve System would play at a later time.

Joshua Speed, recalling that Lincoln gave this address "without manuscript or notes," marveled at his powers of concentration: "He had a wonderful faculty in that way. He might be writing an important document, be interrupted in the midst of a sentence, turn his attention to other matters entirely foreign to the subject on which he was engaged, and take up his pen and begin where he left off without reading the previous part of the sentence. He could grasp, exhaust, and quit any subject with more facility than any man I have ever seen or heard of."[109] (Responding to Speed's observation "that his mind was a wonder," Lincoln modestly remarked, "you are mistaken—I am slow to learn and slow to forget that which I have learned—My mind is like a piece of steel, very hard to scratch any thing on it and almost impossible after you get it there to rub it out.")[110] A Democrat who heard the speech remarked that Lincoln "surprised me by his ability and by his apparent logical frankness. . . . His statements were clear, and his arguments must have given great satisfaction to the party he represented. He asserted his propositions with firmness and supported them in the most effective manner."[111] Even the *Register* praised Lincoln's effort as "in the main, temperate, and argumentative" and mercifully free of "coarse invective, unfounded ridicule, and personal abuse." The Democratic editor said it was "pleasant to find a man among them [the Whigs] who occasionally is able to . . . deal in sober reason."[112] The speech was widely published in the Whig press and issued as a campaign document in pamphlet form.

Lincoln stumped for Harrison throughout Illinois. In March, Lincoln campaigned as he made his rounds on the legal circuit. With Edward D. Baker, he spoke in Jacksonville, where Douglas and the bibulous, combative Josiah Lamborn, a representative of the darker side of frontier politics, made their replies. Noted for "bitter and unmeasured" denunciations of Whigs, the tall, slender Lamborn had a peculiar tawny complexion and a crippling deformity that had evidently made him vengeful and acerbic.[113] Lamborn's undoubted brilliance was overshadowed by his lack of scruples and his drinking habits. He became an alcoholic, abandoned his family, and as attorney general of Illinois accepted bribes.

Lincoln spent much time in the southern part of the state, known as "Egypt," chief stronghold of the Democratic Party. Lincoln's speaking style, accent, and folksy approach to politics seemed more suitable to this area than to the northern part of the state. He canvassed Egypt most intensively after the August elections, in which the Democrats won the legislature and two of the state's three congressional seats. He was joined by his friend Edward D. Baker, former governor Joseph Duncan, and Alexander P. Field, the fiercely partisan Illinois secretary of state, a "tall, perfectly formed" man "with erect, soldierly bearing, and the polished manners of a born courtier" whose "otherwise handsome features were marred by a nodular, potato-like nose."[114] Field told a friend that the Whigs "lost the legislature in consequence of the Great Majorities against us in the southern part of the State. That part of the State has not been properly attended to or their Majorities certainly would have been greatly reduced. Baker (Ed) Lincoln Gov Duncan & myself are going to spend all our time in the Southern Counties discuss[ing] the principles of our party in every neighborhood: and challenge these men [Democratic leaders] to a fair discussion of this administration[,] organize our friends, [and] circulate documents amongst them."[115] The Democratic press sarcastically remarked, "Missionaries Field and Lincoln have again been sent forth . . . by the 'Junto' of Springfield, to make a last effort in bringing the ignorant and heathenish Democrats of Illinois from out of their blinded and self-destructive errors and threaten them with the anathema of the Holy Federal Church if they do not open their eyes."[116]

Illness compounded the hardships of campaigning in such a primitive region. As Baker and Lincoln stumped Egypt, they found themselves "shaking with the ague one day, and addressing the people the next." In the absence of railroads and stage lines, they had to ride on horseback with their clothes jammed into saddlebags. They covered vast distances through swamp and over prairie, all the while enduring miserable accommodations. But "no matter how tired, jaded and worn the speaker might be, he was obliged to respond to the call of the waiting and eager audiences."[117]

Lincoln's oratorical skills proved a valuable weapon in the Whig arsenal, for many Westerners seldom read newspapers and thus obtained political information solely from stump speakers. John Hay observed that it was difficult for city-dwellers "to form any adequate conception of the intense affection and eager interest that a . . . jolly, eloquent, and discreet partisan leader excites among his constituency of the backwoods." His triumphs occur in "rural school-houses and groves," where his "wit is rewarded by hearty laughter, and his eloquence by yells of approbation." In regions with few sources of entertainment, "a popular orator, who can make men laugh and cry, becomes entwined with their sluggish, emotional natures, and a speech is to them not an incident of an evening, but the event of a week."[118]

Baker's style differed from Lincoln's. An opponent recalled that Lincoln "did not possess the poetry and pathos of Baker or Linder, but he had an earnestness which denoted the strength of his inward convictions and the warmth of his heart."[119] Harman G. Reynolds, a prominent Mason in Springfield, recollected hearing Lincoln during this campaign: "The very first impression made upon us was that he could be implicitly trusted, and he had not spoken five minutes until we felt certain that he was a man of power." Reynolds was especially struck by "the rich and musical intonation of his voice, his honest utterances, and naïve, homebred way of thinking and speaking, so unlike other men."[120]

Connoisseurs of political speaking gave Lincoln good marks, despite some reservations about his appearance. Gustave Koerner reported that at a Belleville rally in April, the other orators "outshone Lincoln in melody of voice and graceful delivery," but that he was the strongest "in argument." Lincoln's "appearance was not very prepossessing," for his "exceedingly tall and very angular form made his movements rather awkward," and his features, especially his high cheekbones, were unpleasant to behold, said Koerner. "His complexion had no roseate hue of health, but was then rather bilious, and, when not speaking, his face seemed to be overshadowed by melancholy thoughts." Koerner observed Lincoln carefully and detected "a good deal of intellect in him, while his looks were genial and kind," but doubted that he "had much reserve will-power."[121] Earlier that month, Lincoln won a more positive notice in a Whig newspaper, the Alton *Telegraph,* which reported that his "highly argumentative and logical" speech in that city "was enlivened by numerous anecdotes" and "was received with unbounded applause." The *Telegraph* also noted that at Carlinville on April 6, Lincoln spoke "with great power and eloquence."[122]

Negrophobia loomed large in the campaign. The few extant examples of Lincoln's speeches show that he indulged in the same race-baiting that he had so freely employed four years earlier. For their part, the Democrats labeled Harrison an "Abolitionist of the first water" and a hypocrite who would "make slaves of White men" while making "free men of black slaves."[123] A Democratic campaign paper in Springfield denounced Lincoln and his fellow Whigs for seeking to deliver the federal government "into the hands of a set of fanatics, who boldly proclaim that they would sacrifice their country, its liberties, its honor, and its glory, TO MAKE THE NEGRO THE EQUAL OF THE WHITE MAN!" and alleged that wherever "an abolitionist is found, he is loud and warm in support of Harrison. There are some three hundred abolitionists, it is said, in the county of Sangamon, every one of whom is for Harrison."[124] In Springfield, Democrats attacked the Whigs for soliciting aid from "that separate, distinct, and fanatical party, called Abolitionists."[125]

Responding in kind, Lincoln and other Whigs reiterated their earlier charges about Van Buren's support for black suffrage in 1821. At Carlinville on April 6, Lincoln reportedly showed that the Democratic presidential nominee was "clothed with the sable furs of Guinea," that his "breath smells rank with devotion to the cause of Africa's sons," and that his "very trail might be followed by scattered bunches of *Nigger wool.*"[126] In a debate with Douglas, he said "that if his opponent tacked the wool upon Harrison's head he would pull it off." Douglas "retorted that he would begin just where the other gentleman left off, and that he would stick to the wool question."[127] In another debate with Douglas, Lincoln praised the Bank of the United States, denounced the president's subtreasury plan, told "many highly amusing anecdotes which convulsed the house with laughter," and "reviewed the political course of Mr. Van Buren, and especially his votes in the New York Convention in allowing Free Negroes the right of suffrage."[128] When Douglas accused the Whig presidential candidate of dodging the issue of abolitionism, Lincoln protested that the document cited by his opponent was not genuine.

In a March 1840 debate with Douglas at Jacksonville, Lincoln ambushed the Little Giant on the abolition issue. While preparing for that event, Lincoln had his "head-strong and revengeful" friend Dr. William H. Fithian, a skilled practitioner of political dirty tricks, write to Van Buren asking if William M. Holland's biography of the president accurately described Van Buren's support for black suffrage in 1821.[129] Van Buren confirmed Holland's account. In a debate with Douglas, Lincoln asserted that Van Buren "had voted for Negro Suffrage under certain limitations." When Douglas denied it, Lincoln read aloud from Holland's life of the president. Douglas called it a forgery, whereupon Lincoln produced Van Buren's letter to Fithian. Douglas angrily seized the volume, damned it, and flung it out into the audience.[130] At Pontiac, Illinois, Douglas had misquoted Holland's biography of Van Buren. When Lincoln reached Bloomington, he asked David Davis to obtain a copy of that volume. Davis did so, and the next day Lincoln confronted Douglas with it.

In justifying his tactics, Lincoln told James Matheny that Douglas "was always calling the Whigs Federalists—Tories—Aristocrats" and alleging that "Whigs are opposed to liberty—Justice & Progress. This is a loose assertion I suppose to Catch votes. I don't like to *catch votes by* cheating men out of their judgment, but in reference to the whigs being opposed to Liberty &c let me Say that that remains to be seen & demonstrated in the future. The brave don't boast. A barking dog don't bite."[131]

In April, Lincoln once again used Holland's life of Van Buren to prove that the president had "advocated and supported Abolition principles, and opposed in the New York Convention the right of universal suffrage." Addressing a Whig rally in heavily Democratic Belleville, he charged that "Van Buren had always opposed the interests of the West—was in feeling and principle an Aristocrat—had no claims upon the people on the score of Democracy, and was unworthy of their confidence and support." Lincoln analyzed Van Buren's rise to power "in a manner which drew forth bursts of applause and peals of laughter from the assemblage."[132]

Lincoln's Whig friends also emphasized the race issue. The *Sangamo Journal* denounced Van Buren's "love for free negroes," manifested not only in his previous support for black suffrage, but also in his tolerance for courtroom testimony by blacks. In 1839, at the court martial of a naval officer, two free blacks who had witnessed the alleged crime testified against the officer, who was convicted and cashiered. Calling this a "monstrous and high-handed proceeding," the *Journal* protested Van Buren's refusal to declare a mistrial. The *Journal* declared that this would lead to a day when black testimony, even from slaves, would place whites at the mercy of blacks. Not stopping there, the editor predicted that Van Buren's approval of the court martial verdict would lead to black suffrage and "one step more—too horrid to be contemplated—and that amalgamation."[133]

Lincoln's oratory in 1840, like that of other Harrison campaigners, tended to pander to popular taste. In an unusually perceptive commentary on the young Lincoln, John M. Scott, an attorney who eventually became chief justice of the Illinois State Supreme Court, described one of Lincoln's speeches during that campaign. The young legislator, "already regarded as one of the ablest of the Whig speakers in that campaign," stood in a wagon to address his audience. There was something "in him that attracted and held public attention," Scott recalled. "Even then he was the subject of popular regard because of his candid and simple mode of discussing and illustrating political questions." In 1840, the dominant economic issues "were not such questions as enlisted and engaged his best thoughts—they did not take hold of his great nature and had no tendency to develop it." Occasionally "he discussed the questions of the time in a logical way, but much time was devoted to telling stories to illustrate some phase of his argument, but more often the telling of these stories was resorted to for the purpose of rendering his opponents ridiculous." That "was a style of speaking much appreciated at that early day." In such oratory, Lincoln "had no equals in the state." A story he told was "not one it would be seemly to publish, but rendered as it was in his inimitable way it contained nothing that was offensive to a refined taste." Scott noted Lincoln's gift for telling off-color stories in a way that "they gave no offense even to refined and cultured people." That day Lincoln's story was met "with loud bursts of laughter and applause." It placed "the opposing party and its speakers in a most ludicrous position," and it "gave him a most favorable hearing for the arguments he later made in support of the measures he was sustaining." In that period, Lincoln's mastery of humor was very effective and made him a popular speaker. Acknowledging that it was "not a fair mode of treating an adversary," Scott explained that "it is a mode of attack greatly relished by popular assemblies" because "most people like to see their opponents discomfited by being made the butt of a well told story."[134]

As Scott observed, insult and ridicule were common in frontier politics, but Lincoln deployed them so mercilessly that they constituted a form of cruelty that reflected his primitive background. Not until midlife would Lincoln change his ways and earn a justified reputation for infinite forbearance and goodwill. If, as president, he could declare that he had "not willingly planted a thorn in any man's bosom," during his youth and early adulthood he positively delighted in planting such thorns.[135]

In a celebrated event at Springfield on July 20, for example, Lincoln excoriated Judge Jesse B. Thomas, who had been accused of writing anonymous letters for the press. In fact, Lincoln and his fellow Whigs were the authors of those letters, for which Thomas chided them in a speech. Lincoln's riposte was merciless. He "began by saying, that he was a humble member of 'the Long Nine,' so that he could not swell himself up to the great dimensions of his learned and eloquent adversary. The effort to do so would, he feared, be attended with the fate of the frog in the fable, which tried to swell itself to the size of the ox. But he could do this—he could prick a few pin-holes in his adversary, and cut him down to his natural size." Then he proceeded to describe "with minute accuracy, the political career of Judge Thomas, and his various somersaults." He told how "a new light had struck the learned Judge, and with what wonderful agility he went right over." As he delivered his "absolutely overwhelming and withering" remarks, Lincoln was "terrific in denunciation," mimicking Thomas's gestures and accent. The distraught Thomas "began to blubber like a baby, and withdrew from the assembly. He cried all the rest of the day."[136] The Democratic *Illinois State Register* chided Lincoln for his "rude assault upon the private character" of Thomas, declaring that even fellow Whigs were disavowing what became celebrated in the annals of Illinois politics as "the skinning of Thomas."[137] The next day a remorseful Lincoln apologized to Thomas.

Lincoln also skinned Colonel Dick Taylor, a Democratic candidate for the state senate whose assaults on Whig elitism nettled him. The "showy, bombastic" Taylor was "a talkative, noisy fellow" and "a consummate fop" who "never appeared in public without a ruffled shirt, a blue coat and brass buttons, and a gold-headed cane."[138]

When Taylor denounced Whigs as aristocrats, Lincoln "replied that whilst Col. Taylor had his stores over the county, and was riding in a fine carriage, wore his kid gloves and had a gold headed cane, he [Lincoln] was a poor boy hired on a flat boat at eight dollars a month, and had only one pair of breeches and they were of buckskin." He explained to the audience, "if you know the nature of buckskin when wet and dried by the sun they would shrink and mine kept shrinking until they left for several inches my legs bare between the top of my Socks and the lower part of my breeches—and whilst I was growing taller they were becoming shorter: and so much tighter, that they left a blue streak around my leg which you can see to this day—If you call this aristocracy I plead guilty to the charge."[139] Lincoln then unbuttoned Taylor's vest and out cascaded his ruffled shirt "like a pile of Entrails," causing the crowd to "burst forth in a furious & uproarious laughter."[140]

Occasionally Lincoln's attacks backfired. At Belleville, he sought to illustrate the economic distress brought about by the Panic of 1837 and Democratic policies. As an example, he noted that just that day he had seen a fine horse sold by a constable for the unusually low price of $27. At that, the constable, who was in the audience, cried out that the horse had only one eye. The "nonplussed" Lincoln "seemed rather depressed and was less happy in his remarks than usual."[141] A Democrat gleefully exclaimed: "How very fortunate for the Whigs that Mr. Lincoln saw the sale of the *one-eyed* horse that day! He was thus enabled to prove that Mr. Van Buren caused it, together with all the other ills of life that us poor mortals 'are heir to.'"[142] At Waterloo, down in Egypt, opposition speaker Adam Snyder scolded Lincoln for his low-road tactics and warned him "that if his mission was to convert the lost and benighted, other weapons must be used."[143] In Salem, Lincoln reportedly "was completely done up, even his anecdotes failed to command attention." When an ally "told him he was wasting his time," he replied: "it is a fact, but my friends at home think I am not doing my duty unless I am out, so I may as well stay."[144]

On the whole, though, Lincoln did well on the stump. In late May, the Quincy *Whig* reported that the Democrats "have not been able to start a man that can hold a candle to him in political debate,—All of their crack nags that have entered the lists against him, have come off the field crippled or broken down."[145] In a debate with John A. McClernand at Shawneetown on September 5, he impressed the crowd with "the novelty of his attacks, ludicrous comparisons and fund of anecdote."[146] He also won credit for eschewing criticism of Van Buren's purportedly sybaritic style of living, a staple of Whig campaign strategy originated by Whig Congressman Charles Ogle of Pennsylvania. According to a letter in the Democratic *Illinois State Register*, at Shawneetown, Lincoln "emphatically declared that the Ogle mode of demagoguing is a small and contemptible affair" and "stated that he never alluded to the furniture of the President's house himself, and that he knew it was a mere trick to gull the people—and his only justification for his party was that Mr. [John Quincy] Adams was denounced on the same ground."[147]

Shortly thereafter at Equality, Lincoln delivered a speech that sent the Whig faithful into ecstasies. He likened Democrat Josiah Lamborn's switch from Whig to Democrat to the adventures of a slave in Kentucky who had been sent by his master to deliver two puppies to a neighbor. En route, the slave stopped at a dramshop for refreshment, leaving outside the covered basket containing the dogs. While he was imbibing, two jokers replaced the pups with piglets. Upon arrival at his destination, the slave was astounded to see that the canines had become porcine. Returning to his master, the slave once again paused at the dramshop, where the pranksters removed the pigs and restored the pups to the basket. When explaining to his master how the dogs had been transformed into pigs, the slave was startled to observe that the pigs were once again pups. The nonplussed slave expostulated: "I isn't drunk, but dem dar puppies can be pigs or puppies just when dey please!" Just so, Lincoln said, Lamborn could be a Whig or a Democrat "just when he pleased."[148]

Lincoln could adapt his style to the situation. When he visited Mt. Carmel in early September, he delivered a "dignified and eloquent" address before a mixed audience in the afternoon and a more informal one to an all-male group that evening, when "he seemed to let himself down to their level, pouring forth a current of witticisms and anecdotes which aroused the wildest bursts of applause."[149] A Democratic paper reported that in Mt. Vernon later that month, as Lincoln again debated McClernand, he spoke with "much urbanity and suavity of manner" and "was listened to with attention." He showed that he was "well calculated for a public debater," for "he seldom loses his temper, and always replies jocosely and in good humor," so much so that "the evident marks of disapprobation which greet many of his assertions, do not discompose him, and he is therefore hard to foil."[150]

On his swing through Egypt, Lincoln debated Isaac P. Walker, a toplofty, highly partisan, sarcastic, unpleasant Democrat. They clashed in Albion, where Walker had once lived. In his silk hat and black broadcloth suit, Walker looked far more distinguished than Lincoln, who wore blue jeans. But Lincoln's wit offset his poor appearance and allowed him to prevail. In order to deprive his opponent of any advantage that his former residence in Albion might confer, Lincoln began by quoting from Byron's poem "Lara":

> He, their unhoped but unforgotten lord,
> The long self-exiled chieftain, is restored:
> There be bright faces in the busy hall,
> Bowls on the board, and banners on the wall.
> He comes at last, in sudden loneliness,
> And when they know not, when they need not guess,
> They more might marvel, when the greetings o'er,
> Not that he came, but *why he came not before.*

An onlooker remarked that "Lincoln's sallies on 'why he came not before' had taken the wind out of his opponent's sails completely."[151]

In late October, a Jacksonian legislator, Dr. William G. Anderson, repeatedly interrupted Lincoln's speech at Lawrenceville, charging that the speaker was "falsifying the acts and record of the Democratic party."[152] Lincoln must have replied heatedly, for Anderson declared that Lincoln's attack on him "imported insult" and ominously demanded an explanation. A duel seemed likely, but Lincoln disarmed that threat with a conciliatory reply: "I entertain no unkind feeling to you, and none of any sort upon the subject, except a sincere regret that I permitted myself to get into such an altercation."[153]

What Lincoln said in his many other speeches may be inferred from contributions in the *Sangamo Journal* and *The Old Soldier,* a campaign paper that he helped edit. Many of the opinion letters signed "A Looker-on," "An Old Jackson Man," and the like, were evidently Lincoln's handiwork.

In November 1839, "A Looker-on" excoriated Democrats for attacking the Illinois state bank, calling them "would-be dictators" whose charges were mere "absurdities." The author, who claimed to have been in Vandalia in 1835 when the General Assembly chartered the bank, pointed out that leading Democrats had championed that institution. Similarly, in 1837 Democrats had procured the suspension of the requirement that the bank redeem its notes in specie. So, "A Looker-on" concluded, as the bank "is their own dog, they may whip it, and, I trust, the Whigs will only stand by and see it well done."[154]

Several articles by "An Old Jackson Man" roundly condemned the Van Buren administration for extravagance and corruption. Democrats had denounced John Quincy Adams for spending $12 million to $15 million annually, he pointed out, but Van Buren had expended over $40 million. Under Van Buren, "republican simplicity and economy" had been lost. He also alleged that Van Buren had bribed newspaper editors with patronage and had abandoned the one-term principle, which Democrats had championed in the 1820s. The Democratic Party in Illinois abused the patronage power, "An Old Jackson Man" charged: "Look at the list of Van Buren Conventions held throughout the State, in all of them you find the Registers and Receivers of Land Offices the prominent members of all such conventions, dictating to the people who they shall vote for almost every office, while the small fry, composing the main body of these dictatorial assemblies, is principally composed of post masters, office-holders and office seekers." The Van Buren administration tolerated corrupt officials like William L. D. Ewing, who, when he stepped down as receiver of pubic monies at Vandalia, "was found a defaulter and judgment obtained against him, for about fifteen thousand dollars," but the Democrats nonetheless ran him for the state senate, the U.S. senate, and made him acting governor and speaker of the Illinois House of Representatives. The author also denounced the Van Buren administration's proposal for a 200,000-man militia, which, he alleged, amounted to "a proposition to raise a standing army," a "new engine of patronage and power." This "Old Jackson Man" issued a warning: "Give to an ambitious and unprincipled President—the sub-treasury—the control of the national funds;—and to his army of office holders and office hunters, two hundred thousand trained militia men—twenty-five thousand men in each military division—twelve thousand five hundred men in actual pay and active service in each division,—the whole body looking to the President for appointment and promotion, the whole under his direction and control;—give him these, and you will afterwards scarce dare to refuse any thing his rapacity may demand."[155]

In a similar vein, "Son of an Old Ranger" attacked Van Buren's record in the War of 1812: while Harrison "was camped in the field or ranging our frontiers, fighting our

battles, defending our women and children from the murderous tomahawk and scalp-
ing knife, and adding new lusture to the American name with his splendid victories,"
at the same time Van Buren "was in the New York Legislature, voting for Rufus King,
the federal anti-war candidate for Senator."[156] When a Democratic campaign paper
alleged that Harrison had not behaved heroically at the Battle of Raisin River, a
"Kentucky Volunteer" (probably Lincoln) replied: "I have no doubt the writer of the
above lines had rather be considered a knave than a fool, and therefore, I shall
pitch him on to the first horn of the dilemma, and treat it as a base attempt to deceive
the people."[157]

In a public debate at Petersburg, Lincoln attacked Archer Herndon, who had accused Lincoln of being "an interloper." Lincoln replied that "when he had been a
candidate as often as Herndon he would quit."[158] Herndon was also assailed in the
press. A letter by "A Citizen" (probably Lincoln) chastised him for supporting Van
Buren in 1840 after having opposed him four years earlier. Condemning this apostasy, "Citizen" sneered: "If any man does deserve office at the hands of Van Buren,
you surely do. To sustain him, you have sacrificed all—character, reputation, conscience, and the good opinion of tried friends." This citizen did not eschew strong
language; he called Herndon a "traitor" and scorned his "truckling and fawning—a
bowing and scraping to the powers that be—which, in the absence of any other testimony than your own professions of honesty, furnishes us with the best key to your
motives."[159] The combative Herndon heatedly rejected such charges made by members of what he called "the British-Negro-Indian-Sympathy-and-Anti-Republican-
Blood-hound party."[160]

A writer (probably Lincoln) pretending to be Herndon asked Van Buren: "We
know you honestly consider the negroes, particularly the fat sleek ones, superior to
poor white folks; but why, in the name of *Guinea* itself, can you not suppress even your
honest sentiments until after the election?"[161]

In November, Harrison swamped Van Buren, carrying nineteen of the twenty-six
states. The president did manage to eke out a victory in Illinois, capturing 51 percent
of the votes to Harrison's 49 percent. Hard times, Van Buren's bland personality, and
the vogue for egalitarianism combined to doom the incumbent. His victory in Illinois, the only free state he carried other than New Hampshire, apparently owed
much to immigrants who worked on the Illinois and Michigan Canal. David Davis,
a Whig friend of Lincoln who narrowly lost a bid for the state senate, complained that
"if the *Irish* did not vote more than *3 times* we could easily carry the State." Davis
added that the "Irish vote along the line of the canal increased (at the late election)
most wonderfully, and in nearly every other county of the State, the Whig vote has
enlarged greatly."[162]

Like Davis, Lincoln was angered by such irregularities. On election day, when he
heard that an Illinois railroad contractor had brought a construction gang to take over
the polls, Lincoln told him menacingly: "you will spoil & blow if you live much longer." That night Lincoln confided to Joshua Speed, "I intended to Knock him down
& go aw[a]y and leave him a-kicking."[163] On a similar occasion in Springfield, Lincoln stymied a group of Democrats who had threatened to seize the polls and prevent

their opponents from voting. Armed with an ax handle, he scared off the obstruction-ists. When the legislature convened soon after the November elections, Lincoln pro-posed an investigation of electoral fraud.

Despite the result in Illinois, Lincoln was jubilant over Harrison's victory. (In Springfield, Harrison won 63 percent of the vote, slightly more than the 59 percent that Whig presidential candidates usually received there.) At a raucous celebration, Lincoln "made a great deal of sport with his speeches, witty sayings and stories." He "even played leap-frog."[164]

In 1840, Lincoln sought a fourth legislative term, though in March he told Stuart that "I think it is probable I shall not be permitted to be a candidate."[165] Many Sanga-mon County Whigs outside the capital had resisted the convention system and objected to the "Springfield Junto" that supported it. The "Junto" had further alien-ated voters by opposing the division of the county. Thomas J. Nance, a Democrat in Rock Creek near New Salem, criticized the Junto to a resident of the capital: "Most of our citizens are becoming acquainted with the officious meddling of a few men. . . . this disposition to misrepresent all our reasonable askings will have one good effect—this is to convince us that we must unite to repel their dictating edicts."[166] At a meeting in South Fork, voters declared that they "disapprove of the dictative course pursued by the Springfield Junto of lawyers and office holders." They threatened to "do all we can to put the Junto down."[167] In 1839, the "Junto" had also antagonized some Whigs by selecting John Bennett of Petersburg, rather than Bowling Green, as a candidate for the General Assembly.

Despite all this, the Sangamon County Whigs did nominate Lincoln at their convention that March, though they rejected all other Springfield residents save Ed-ward D. Baker, whom they chose to run for state senate. (Why Lincoln did not re-ceive that honor is unclear.) Lincoln reported that Ninian W. Edwards "was verry much hurt at not being nominated" and added that for his own part he "was much, verry much, wounded myself at his [Edwards's] being left out. The fact is, the country delegates made the nominations as they pleased; and they *pleased* to make them all from the country, except Baker & me, whom they supposed necessary to make stump speeches."[168] (Lincoln was better known for his oratory than his organizational skills. Anson G. Henry complained that when it came to such tasks as compiling lists of important Whigs who should receive government documents, "You need not expect Stewart [John Todd Stuart], Baker or Lincoln to do this kind of work. I am the only working man of *this Sort* in Springfield. I have all my life beat the bush for others to catch the bird.")[169] On election day in August, Lincoln retained his seat in the Gen-eral Assembly, coming in fifth in a field of ten, with 1,844 votes. The leading candi-date received only 15 more votes than Lincoln, while the sixth-place finisher lagged 578 votes behind him.

In August, shortly after election day, the General Assembly began a session marred by special bitterness occasioned by an impending change in the partisan bal-ance. The Democrats, aware that this session represented "the last apple they will have" because of the Whigs' triumph in the national election, were "determined to extract every drop of juice while they have the chance."[170] Whig Senator William

H. Fithian likened the Democrats to "the Indian who was badly wounded and knew that he must die [and therefore was] determined to do as much mischief before he did expire as he possibly could."[171] One Illinois Whig editor deplored the rampant partisanship of most lawmakers: "Elected at a time of high party excitement, and with an eye single to his blind devotion and subserviency to that party, . . . the Representative too frequently enters upon the discharge of his duties . . . governed and controlled only by the most sordid views, selfish motives, and basest passions, to which the asperity of party feeling can give birth."[172]

Governor Thomas Carlin summoned the legislature to a special session beginning on November 23, two weeks before the constitutionally stipulated date for the regular session, in order to grapple with the mounting state debt. It seemed unlikely that Illinois could meet the interest payments due on January 1. Because the new capitol was still not quite ready for occupancy, the legislators met in Springfield churches. Once again, William L. D. Ewing defeated Lincoln for Speaker of the House. After some vigorous but futile attempts to have Vandalia restored as the state capital, the General Assembly then prepared to convene its regular session on December 7.

The Democrats tried to seize the moment for some mischief. Since a recent law provided that the Bank of Illinois would have to resume specie payments at the end of the "next session" of the legislature, Democrats argued that the Bank must meet that burdensome requirement as of December 5 when the special session closed. The Whigs, hoping to have the regular session combined with the special session and thus postpone the bank's day of reckoning, boycotted the legislature, thereby preventing the necessary two-thirds quorum for adjournment *sine die*. When the representatives gathered on December 5, the Whigs stayed away, except for Lincoln, Joseph Gillespie, and Asahel Gridley, who were to observe the proceedings and demand roll call votes. The frustrated Democrats, eager to hurt the state bank by adjourning, instructed the sergeant-at-arms to round up absent Whigs. When that tactic failed, the Democrats managed to bring in enough of their own previously absent members to create a quorum. Lincoln and his two Whig colleagues angrily bolted for the door, which was locked. Because the sergeant-at-arms had received no instruction to unlock the door, he refused to do so. Lincoln then opened a window and stepped through, followed by Gillespie and Gridley. When the sergeant-at-arms was instructed to pursue, he exclaimed: "My God! gentlemen, do you know what you ask? Think of the length of Abe's legs, and then tell me how I am to catch him."[173]

This unconventional departure through the church's first-floor window drew laughter from the Democratic members, who derisively shouted: "He who fights and runs away, lives to fight another day."[174] The *Register* sneered at the "gymnastic performance of Mr. Lincoln and his flying brethren" and recommended that the statehouse be raised "in order to have the House set in the *third story!* so as to prevent members from *jumping out of the windows!*" That way, "Mr. Lincoln will in future have *to climb down the spout!*"[175] One observer reported that after the House adjourned, "Such a clapping of hands and stamping you never heard—on the whole I must say I consider the conduct of both parties disgraceful in the extreme."[176] Years later, Lincoln was ridiculed as "a long-legged varment" who was "great at *jumping*" and who "earned his membership in the junto by jumping out of the windows of the State House to save the bank."[177]

Lincoln found this episode very embarrassing. According to Gillespie, he "always regretted that he entered into the arrangement as he deprecated everything that Savored of the revolutionary."[178] In later years, whenever the matter came up, he would change the subject.

When the regular session began on December 7, 1840, the House of Representatives, finally meeting for the first time in the new capitol, wrangled over the debt crisis. Lincoln managed, after much cajoling, to persuade his colleagues to raise the general land tax and to issue special bonds to cover the pending interest obligations. Lincoln's "interest bonds" scheme was criticized as "a mere gull trap, set for the purpose of catching money holders & sharpers."[179] The tax hike, however, yielded insufficient revenue to solve the problem, and in July 1841 the state defaulted on its interest payments, causing the price of Illinois bonds to plunge. A Democratic state senator complained that the "very men who voted for the rail Road system, men who indebted the State millions, are afraid to vote one cent of taxes on their constituents to sustain the tottering credit of the State."[180] In 1842, the state took in revenues of less than $100,000, while interest payments approached $800,000.

A struggle over the Whig-dominated supreme court convulsed the legislature. The justices had angered Democrats by overruling Governor Carlin's decision to remove Alexander P. Field, a partisan Whig, from his post as secretary of state. When the court also seemed likely to weaken the Democrats' electoral base by denying aliens the right to vote (most of the state's 10,000 foreign-born voters were Democrats), the General Assembly entertained a motion to pack the supreme bench by adding five justices, a proposal that became "the Lion measure of the session."[181] The ensuing debate was, in the words of a state senator, "vehement & exciting, partaking much of party abuse & personal crimination."[182] In the midst of the heated exchanges, a member of the lower house reported that the "very Genius of Disorganization is holding the reins whilst Old Nick whips the horses. Every thing is done by party votes."[183] Beholding the spectacle from Washington, John Todd Stuart lamented: "I have often been ashamed of my State or rather of its Loco Legislators. They are a laughing stock."[184] Lincoln's friend, Senator William H. Fithian, thought that he had previously seen "the business of the people . . . carelessly and tardily attended to by their Representatives," but now he felt "compelled to say, I have never until this session, fully realized the length and breadth of the unparalleled embarrassments of the people of Illinois."[185]

Although the main battleground of this war was in the House, Lincoln scarcely took part; he had prepared remarks that he could not deliver because speaker Ewing allowed the Democrats to cut off debate. On February 1, when the bill cleared the House by a 45–43 vote, the *Sangamo Journal* published a letter by a member of that body (probably Lincoln) indignantly protesting that the "Judiciary of Illinois is to be assailed, and the constitution in its spirit, if not in the letter, violated, and the members who would have raised a voice in its defence, are to be gagged into silence!" Hyperbolically comparing the proceedings to the Alien and Sedition Acts of 1798, the author denounced Ewing and his "alarming" parliamentary rulings. He asserted that "it is sufficiently revolting to the feelings of freemen, to be gagged into silence under any circumstances," but "if this gag law can be enforced, in relation to a particular measure before that measure is before the House, then any thing like freedom of debate may be cut off, and the members literally gagged into silence."[186]

When Ewing rejected this protest as "gratuitous and unfounded," the aggrieved legislator replied in a statesmanlike fashion, remarking that he "had not been induced by any unkind feelings towards the speaker" and that there was "no reason we should wound each other's feelings, or that those civilities and kindnesses which mark the character and intercourse between gentlemen, should be violated and endangered." He maintained that the "official conduct, or decisions of public officers is public property, and are fair and legitimate subjects of criticism, so that facts are correctly stated, and inferences fairly drawn. In my own much more humble sphere, I freely concede the right of investigating my public conduct, and if dealt ingenuously with, will not be found to complain."[187]

Lincoln was not so conciliatory in late February, when he and thirty-four other Whig Representatives denounced the court-packing statute as "a party measure for party purposes," which manifested "supreme contempt for the popular will," undermined "the independence of the Judiciary, the surest shield of public welfare and private right," and set a "precedent for still more flagrant violations of right and justice."[188] In April, a satirical communication in the *Sangamo Journal,* probably by Lincoln, suggested that the judiciary bill passed only because a member (Ebenezer Peck) was bought off with an appointment as clerk of the state supreme court. Another such communication, also probably by Lincoln, ridiculed Stephen A. Douglas for his inconsistency as an opponent of "life offices" who nevertheless accepted such a post as a supreme court judge.

In the 1840–1841 session, Lincoln once again fought on behalf of the Illinois and Michigan Canal, moving that the state increase the land tax and issue bonds to complete the project. A Democrat from Montgomery County countered with one of Lincoln's own favorite tactics, the funny story with a concealed barb. He compared Lincoln to an Arkansas toper who had passed out and, when all other means to revive him failed, regained consciousness at his wife's suggestion that a brandy toddy might be the best medicine. Upon hearing the words "brandy toddy," the bibulous gentleman sat up, saying "that is the stuff!" Lincoln seemed to think the more debt that the state assumed, the better. Lincoln responded in kind. His critic's actions during the legislative session, he quipped, called to mind an old Indiana bachelor who "was very famous for seeing *big bugaboos* in every thing." One day while hunting with his brother, this gentleman fired repeatedly at a treetop. His sibling, who saw no target, asked what he was trying to shoot. When told that it was a squirrel, the brother, "believing that there was some humbug about the matter, examined his person, and found on one of his eye lashes a *big louse* crawling about. It is just so with the gentleman from Montgomery. He imagined he could see squirrels every day, when they were nothing but *lice*."[189] Lincoln's remarks "convulsed the whole house," forcing a halt to all business. The Speaker banged his gavel to no avail. Legislators of both parties laughed, "screamed and yelled," "thumped upon the floor with their canes," "clapped their hands," "threw up their hats," "shouted and twisted themselves into all sorts of contortions, until their sides ached and the tears rolled down their cheeks." One spasm succeeded another until the Representatives "seemed to be perfectly exhausted."[190] Much as they admired Lincoln's wit, the legislators rejected his argument that "to prosecute the work now was in fact the most economical plan that could be adopted: to stop it, would involve the State in much more debt and ruin."[191]

Lincoln clashed with another Democrat, John A. McClernand, over the state bank. From southern Illinois, McClernand was a devoted foe of all banks. Vain and overbearing, he was an effective if unscrupulous speaker, always ready for a political fight. His knowledge of the classics, his grandiloquent manner, and his smooth delivery led people to call him "The Grecian Orator."[192] According to Gustave Koerner, McClernand "was bold in his assertions, denunciatory of his opponents, perfectly fearless, an experienced public speaker, never trying to persuade but to subdue."[193]

McClernand and Lincoln held an especially heated debate over the question of whether the state bank should be the fiscal agent for Illinois. Lincoln, with asperity, accused Democrats of underhanded dealing. He declared that there was "a manifest disposition on the part of some of the Van Buren men to prop up the Bank, and it is perfectly apparent that the party are prepared to detach a fraction of themselves to go with the Whigs in sustaining the Bank—their usual policy—and then throw the odium of Suspension upon the Whigs." Lincoln "said that he was tired of this business. If there was to be this continual warfare against the Institutions of the State, the sooner it was brought to an end the better. If the great body of the [Democratic] party would act upon conservative principles, he was willing to go with them, but this scheme of detaching a fragment from their party to help the Whigs pass a measure and then turn around and kick and cuff us for it, he had seen practiced long enough."[194] Lincoln's attempt to protect the interests of the bank proved futile, for it was compelled to shut its doors the following year.

With his departure from the General Assembly, Lincoln found himself out of office for the first time in seven years. He had chosen not to seek reelection, for he wished to obtain the Whig nomination for Congress. The apprentice phase of his political career was thus over.

Since entering the legislature in 1834, he had gained stature. In December 1840, a member of "the lobby"—a kind of mock legislature that met in the capitol after the General Assembly sessions adjourned for the day—called him "emphatically a man of *high standing*," a "self-made man, and one of the ablest, whether as a lawyer or legislator, in the State. As a speaker he is characterized by a sincerity, frankness, and evident honesty, calculated to win the attention and gain the confidence of the hearer."[195] (Thomas J. Henderson, who recalled hearing Lincoln during this session of the General Assembly, was less favorably impressed, saying that he "was awkward in manner, when speaking, with a swaying motion of body and a swinging of his long arms that were somewhat ungraceful." Henderson "heard members laughing and talking about appointing a committee to hold his coat tails when he was speaking and keep him still.")[196] A few months later, the Fulton *Telegraph* said: "we think the great talents, sacrifices and high standing of Mr. Lincoln should bring our friends to the decision of taking him up as a candidate for Governor."[197]

Lincoln had little interest in that post, for Whigs stood no chance of winning statewide office. In July 1841, a western Illinois newspaper reported that "since his return from the circuit [in mid-June], Lincoln declines being considered as a candidate for Governor."[198] Five months later, the *Sangamo Journal* announced that "since Mr. Lincoln returned from the circuit, he has expressed his wishes not to be a candidate for Governor."[199] An item in that same paper the following year finally scotched the proposal: "We do not believe that he desires the nomination. He has already made great sacrifices in sustaining his party principles; and before his political friends ask him to make additional sacrifices, the subject should be well considered. The office of Governor, which would of necessity interfere with the practice of his profession, would poorly compensate him for the loss of four years of the best portion of his life."[200] (Some Whigs also objected that Springfield should not have both the party's only congressional seat and the governorship.)

In 1840, Lincoln's ambition had grown more intense, fueled by his new status as a presidential elector, Whig campaign manager, chief stump speaker and organizer, as well as Whig floor leader in the state House of Representatives. William H. Herndon believed that "Lincoln as Early as 1830 be[g]an to dream of a destiny—I think it grew & developed & bloom[ed] with beauty &c in the year *1840 Exactly*. Mr Lincoln in that year was appointed general Elector from the State—Mr Lincoln told me that his ideas of [becoming] something—burst on him in 1840."[201]

Lincoln now felt ready to advance from the state to the national legislature. In the General Assembly he had learned how to build coalitions, how to persuade his colleagues to do his bidding, and how to roll logs. According to Lyman Trumbull, a colleague in the Illinois House of Representatives, Lincoln was viewed "by his political friends as among their shrewdest and ablest leaders, and by his political adversaries as a formidable opponent." Trumbull, who was critical of Lincoln, nonetheless acknowledged that among the highly talented men who served in the legislature in 1840–1841, "he stood in the front rank."[202]

But for all Lincoln's growing sense of strength and competence, there was, as Samuel C. Parks noted about the Lincoln of 1841, "nothing to indicate the future reformer, either in religion, or morals, or politics."[203] His greatness as a moral statesman in years to come would have been hard to predict based on his legislative record, which showed him to be likable and clever, but little more. He understood the nuts and bolts of lawmaking and excelled at ridiculing Democrats. In his leadership role, however, he curiously had little to do with framing legislation. Of the 1,647 bills passed during Lincoln's four terms, he directly introduced only 10; another 21 had been brought forward by committees on which he served. Lincoln offered only eight resolutions and fourteen petitions. It is no wonder that fellow Whig leaders observed that during his years in the legislature, Lincoln "never gave any special evidence of that masterly ability for which he was afterward distinguished."[204] By the age of 32, Lincoln had proved himself to be an ambitious, gifted partisan but exhibited few signs of true statesmanship.

"It Would Just Kill Me
to Marry Mary Todd"
Courtship and Marriage
(1840–1842)

In 1842, Lincoln wed Mary Todd, a woman who was to make his domestic life "a burning, scorching hell," as "terrible as death and as gloomy as the grave," according to one who knew him very well.[1]

Courting Mary Owens

Lincoln's courtship of Mary Todd is poorly documented, but indirect light is shed on it by his earlier, well-recorded romance with Mary S. Owens. Born in Kentucky a few months before Lincoln, Mary Owens received a good education at the home of her wealthy father, a planter in Green County. She was older, bigger, and better-educated than Ann Rutledge. Raised in a relatively sophisticated society, she dressed more elegantly than women in and about New Salem. Her clothes may have been more attractive than Ann Rutledge's, but her features and figure were not. Standing 5 feet, 5 inches tall, she was plump, weighing between 150 and 180 pounds, and considered "not pretty," "matronly," "strong nervous & muscular," with a "massive, angular, square, prominent, and broad" forehead, "fair skin, deep blue eyes," and "dark curling hair." Though emphatically less comely than Ann Rutledge, Mary Owens was more intellectually gifted and accomplished. Caleb Carman remembered her as "Sharp— Shrewd and intellectual," and brighter than Ann. Others deemed her "verry Talented," "smart, sharp," "quick & strong minded," "very intellectual," a "good conversationalist," as well as "a splendid reader." She reportedly "loved wit & humor," had an "Excellent disposition," was "jovial," "social," "good natured," "gay and lively," "light-hearted and cheery," as well as "kind and considerate." In her dealings with men, she showed "a little dash of coquetry."[2]

She was also spunky and unconventional, as her 1835 correspondence with Thomas J. Nance reveals: "You are well aware Thomas, that in writing you this letter, I am transgressing the circumscribed limits, laid down by tyrannical custom, for our sex." Social disapproval did not intimidate her: "if I am condemned by the cold, unfeeling and fastidious of either Sex, I care not, for I trust, my Heart, has learned to rise superior to those groveling feelings, dictated by bosoms, that are callous to every refined emotion."[3]

In the fall of 1833, Mary Owens spent a month in New Salem with her sister, Mrs. Bennett Abell, who was eager to have Lincoln as a brother-in-law. Lincoln found Mary Owens intelligent and "agreeable."[4] She in turn recalled that they "were congenial spirits" who saw "eye to eye" on political matters. Three years later, Lincoln accepted Betsy Abell's startling proposition that she bring her sister Mary back from Kentucky for him to wed.[5] (Mrs. Abell, according to a friend, "was a great talker, and sometimes said more than she ought.")[6] Lincoln agreed, and Mary returned to New Salem for a year and a half, to be courted by Lincoln.

After the relationship ended, Lincoln wryly told his close friend Eliza Browning, wife of fellow Whig legislator Orville H. Browning, that he had seen "no good objection to plodding life through hand in hand with her." But the courtship did not go well. When Mary returned to New Salem in 1836, Lincoln found her less attractive than he had remembered. "I knew she was over-size," he confided to Mrs. Browning, "but she now appeared a fair match for Falstaff." In addition, she looked old: "when I beheld her, I could not for my life avoid thinking of my mother; and this, not from withered features, for her skin was too full of fat, to permit its contracting in to wrinkles; but from her want of teeth, weather-beaten appearance in general, and from a kind of notion that ran in my head, that *nothing* could have commenced at the size of infancy, and reached her present bulk in less than thirtyfive or forty years; and, in short, I was not [at] all pleased with her." He tried to convince himself "that the mind was much more to be valued than the person." Despite his reservations, Lincoln felt honor-bound to follow through on his pledge: "I had told her sister that I would take her for better or for worse; and I made a point of honor and conscience in all things, to stick to my word, especially if others had been induced to act on it, which in this case, I doubted not they had, for I was now fairly convinced, that no other man on earth would have her." Understandably he hesitated before marrying such a woman. "Through life I have been in no bondage, either real or immaginary from the thraldom of which I so much desired to be free," he told Mrs. Browning. He "really dreaded" the prospect of wedding Mary Owens.

After procrastinating as long as possible, he finally proposed. To his surprise, she turned him down. "I verry unexpectedly found myself mortified . . . . in a hundred different ways," he wrote. "My vanity was deeply wounded by the reflection, that I had so long been too stupid to discover her intentions, and at the same time never doubting that I understood them perfectly; and also, that she whom I had taught myself to believe no body else would have, had actually rejected me with all my fancied greatness." Ruefully he conceded that other men "have been made fools of by the girls; but this can never be with truth said of me. I most emphatically, in this instance, made a fool of myself." He resolved "never again to think of marrying," for "I can never be satisfied with any one who would be block-head enough to have me."[7]

This account of the courtship is misleading, for Lincoln's correspondence with Mary Owens indicates that he had become quite fond of her and backed away only after she wounded him repeatedly. A letter he wrote her in December 1836 from

Vandalia suggests he really was in love. In this missive, Lincoln complained of "the mortification of looking in the Post Office for your letter and not finding it." He scolded her: "You see, I am mad about that *old letter* yet. I don[']t like verry well to risk you again. I'll try you once more any how." The prospect of spending ten weeks with the legislature in Vandalia was intolerable, he lamented, for he missed her. "Write back as soon as you get this, and if possible say something that will please me, for really I have not [been] pleased since I left you."[8] Such language, hardly that of an indifferent suitor, tends to confirm Parthena Hill's statement that "Lincoln thought a great deal" of Mary Owens.[9]

The romance ended largely because of the couple's incompatibility. With good reason she thought his manners oafish. As she explained, "Mr. Lincoln was deficient in those little links which make up the great chain of woman[']s happiness, at least it was so in my case; not that I believed it proceeded from a lack of goodness of heart, but his training had been different from mine, hence there was not that congeniality which would have otherwise existed."[10] Lincoln had behaved in ways that she understandably considered thoughtless and insensitive. One day while riding with other New Salem young women and their swains, they came to a creek, which all the men save Lincoln gallantly helped their companions cross. Mary Owens chided her escort: "You are a nice fellow! I suppose you did not care whether my neck was broken or not." With a laugh, Lincoln replied that he reckoned she was plenty smart "enough to care for herself."[11]

A similar incident provoked her to tell Lincoln that she thought he was not promising husband material. One day he accompanied her and Mrs. Bowling Green on a walk. As they climbed a steep hill, he offered no help to Nancy Green, who was struggling to carry her youngster, "a great big fat child—heavy & crossly disposed." After reaching their destination, "Miss Owens Said to Lincoln—laughingly—You would not make a good husband Abe." She chided Lincoln: "You've walked for more than a mile with us—a great, strong fellow like you, and let that woman carry a baby that weighs nearly forty pounds, and never so much as lifted your finger to help her." Lincoln replied: "Why, she never asked me."

"Oh, she didn't! And you hadn't politeness enough to offer to help her, but must wait to be asked."

"Why, I never thought of it. I always supposed she would be afraid to let a fellow like me touch the baby for fear he might break it or something. I'd carry a bushel of them for you, Mary."

"Yes, *now*."

"*Any* time."

"If I *asked* you?"

"Well, I reckon you could ask me if you wanted them carried."

"I just tell you what it is, Abe Lincoln, any man fit to be a husband would have offered to carry that child when he could see its mother was nearly tired to death."

"And I didn't offer?"

"No, you didn't."

"And so I'm not fit to be a husband?"

"That's just the fact."

Lincoln laughed the incident off, but it was a turning point in their relationship, which thereafter began to cool.[12]

Soon after this contretemps, Lincoln spent a few weeks on a surveying expedition; when he returned to New Salem, he asked one of the Abells' sons if Mary Owens was at their home. When the lad said she was, Lincoln asked him to tell her that he would visit later that day. But she had made plans to dine with her cousin, Mentor Graham. When she heard that Lincoln would call, she regarded the occasion as an opportunity to test his devotion: "She thought a moment and Said to herself if I can draw Lincoln up there to Grahams it will all be right. . . . She wanted to make L bend." (She reportedly was a strong-minded woman who "loved Power & conquest.")[13] When Lincoln dropped by the Abells' home to see Mary Owens, Betsy Abell informed him that she was at Mentor Graham's, a mile and a half distant. Lincoln asked if Mary had known he was coming to call. When Mrs. Abell said no, one of her children corrected her, insisting that young Samuel had informed her. His feelings hurt, Lincoln returned to New Salem without stopping at Graham's.

According to one of Mary's relatives, Lincoln "thought that as he was Extremely poor and Miss Owens very rich that it was a fling on him on that account. This was at that time Abe[']s tender spot."[14] His hypersensitivity regarding the differences in their social class appeared in a letter he wrote to Mary in May 1837, shortly after he had moved to Springfield. They had considered the possibility of her joining him there, evidently as Mrs. Abraham Lincoln. He discouraged her, saying "I am afraid you would not be satisfied. There is a great deal of flourishing about in carriages here, which it would be your doom to see without shareing in it. You would have to be poor without the means of hiding your poverty." For this reason he believed that they should not wed. "Whatever woman may cast her lot with mine, should any ever do so, it is my intention to do all in my power to make her happy and contented; and there is nothing I can immagine, that would make me more unhappy than to fail in the effort. I know I should be much happier with you than the way I am, provided I saw no signs of discontent in you." He urged her to consider the prospect carefully before deciding. "My opinion is that you had better not do it. You have not been accustomed to hardship, and it may be more severe than you now immagine." But, he hastened to add, "I am willing to abide [by] your decision."[15]

Three months later, in his final surviving letter to Mary Owens, Lincoln discussed the prospect of marriage lukewarmly: "I want in all cases to do right, and most particularly so, in all cases with women. I want . . . more than any thing else, to do right with you, and if I *knew* it would be doing right, as I rather suspect it would, to let you alone, I would do it. And for the purpose of making the matter as plain as possible, I now say, that you can now drop the subject, dismiss your thoughts (if you ever had any) from me forever, and leave this letter unanswered, without calling forth one accusing murmur from me. And I will even go further, and say, that if it will add any thing to your comfort, or peace of mind, to do so, it is my sincere wish that you should. Do not understand by this, that I wish to cut your acquaintance. I mean no such thing. What I do wish is, that our further acquaintance shall depend upon yourself. If such further acquaintance would contribute nothing to your happiness, I am sure it would not to mine. If you feel yourself in any degree bound to me, I am now willing to release you, provided you wish it; while, on the other hand, I am willing, and even anxious to bind you faster, if I can be convinced that it will, in any considerable degree, add to your happiness."[16]

Unsurprisingly she rejected his proposal, returned to Kentucky, and eventually married her brother-in-law. A few months after her departure, Lincoln remarked to Betsy Abell: "Tell your Sister, that I think she was a great fool, because she did not stay here and marry me."[17]

The Mary Owens courtship reveals an aspect of Lincoln's character that helps explain his intense political ambition, namely a deep-seated inferiority complex. Some political psychologists maintain that such ambition is often rooted in "an intense and ungratified craving for deference." Many aspiring politicos like Lincoln expect power "to overcome low estimates of the self."[18] The compensatory psychological benefits of political power and fame strongly appeal to those with damaged self-esteem, especially "the 'provincial' or the 'small-town boy' or the 'country boy'" who wants "to succeed against the stigma of rusticity."[19] Lincoln is a good example of such a "provincial." As noted earlier, in his 1860 conversations with John Locke Scripps, he "seemed to be painfully impressed with the extreme poverty of his early surroundings—the utter absence of all romantic and heroic elements."[20] In the autobiography he prepared for Scripps, he virtually apologized for his humble origins, calling Thomas Lincoln "a wandering laboring boy" who "grew up litterally without education." In that sketch, Lincoln said of his meager schooling: "He regrets his want of education, and does what he can to supply the want."[21] For the *Dictionary of Congress,* Lincoln described his education as "defective."[22] As an attorney, he felt inferior to his better-educated colleagues. His second law partner, Stephen T. Logan, recalled "an occasion when he had got very much discouraged." In a Danville court, Edward D. Baker "had got very much the advantage of him," and he "came and complained to me that Baker had got so much the start of him that he despaired of getting even with him in acquirements and skill."[23] In 1861, Lincoln told an alumnus of Rutgers College that he "always regretted the want of a college education. Those who have it should thank God for it."[24] The positive reception his speeches received in the East in early 1860 astonished him. To a Connecticut minister who praised his address in Norwich, Lincoln said: "Certainly, I have had a most wonderful success, for a man of my limited education." He was especially struck by the lavish praise of a Yale professor of rhetoric.[25]

Lincoln's ancestry also embarrassed him. In 1859, he wrote that his parents were both born in Virginia of "undistinguished families—second families, perhaps I should say."[26] When leading citizens of Logan County, Illinois, proposed to name their county seat after him, Lincoln replied: "I don't believe I'd do that; I never knew anything named Lincoln that amounted to anything."[27] While he expressed some reservations about the Lincoln side of the family, he was especially ashamed of his mother's family. As he told voters during his first political campaign: "I was born and have ever remained in the most humble walks of life." A decade later he referred to himself at 22 as "a strange, friendless, uneducated, penniless boy."[28]

Psychologist G. Stanley Hall speculated that Lincoln's ambition was rooted in his feelings about his appearance: "His height, long limbs, rough exterior, and frequent feeling of awkwardness must have very early made him realize that to succeed in life he must cultivate intrinsic mental and moral traits, which it is so hard for a handsome man or women to excel in. Hence he compensated by trying to develop intellectual distinction."[29] In his initial political campaign, Lincoln declared candidly: "I have no other [ambition] so great as that of being truly esteemed of my fellow citizens."[30] That thirst for admiration lasted a lifetime; only political success would slake it and permit relief from a nagging, deep-seated sense of inferiority.

Emotional as well as material and educational poverty seems to have plagued the young Lincoln. Neither parent met his most basic psychological needs. Nancy Hanks Lincoln may have provided her young son with love and support during his first nine years, but he evidently viewed her death as an act of abandonment. In later life, he seldom mentioned her; one of the few times he did so, in his letter to Eliza Browning about his love life, it was in unflattering terms. His father offered little nurturance. Perhaps the best thing Thomas Lincoln ever did for his son was to marry Sarah Bush Johnston, but by the time she arrived in Indiana, the boy's psyche had endured many assaults. Suffering from emotional malnutrition, Lincoln thought himself unloved and unlovable. To compensate, he sought in public life a surrogate form of the love and acceptance he had not known at home; by winning elections he would prove to himself that he was lovable.[31]

Lincoln's conduct toward Mary Owens may have been affected by his distrust of women, stemming from the death of his mother. The "bitter agony" that Lincoln experienced as a 9-year-old in Indiana seems to have crippled his capacity for trusting and loving women lest they abandon him as his mother had done. Throughout life he harbored irrational fears of abandonment. When Joshua Speed married, Lincoln plaintively told the newlyweds, "I feel som[e]what jealous of both of you now; you will be so exclusively concerned for one another, that I shall be forgotten entirely."[32] In 1858, after his defeat by Stephen A. Douglas, Lincoln remarked to a friend: "I expect everybody to desert me."[33] In 1839, as already noted, he concluded a speech on banking with a strange peroration, envisioning himself abandoned in his defense of the right, alone, boldly hurling defiance at his country's enemies. In politics, his greatest anger was directed at former allies who had abandoned his party.

Courting Mary Todd

The Mary Owens affair also reveals Lincoln's extraordinary passivity in dealing with women and his scrupulous determination to carry out promises, even bad ones. These traits resurfaced when he became involved with the temperamental, headstrong, volatile Mary Todd. Two years after Mary Owens disappeared from Lincoln's life, he met Miss Todd, another well-educated Kentuckian from a prosperous family and the cousin of his law partner John Todd Stuart. Evidently, she believed that if her much-admired cousin had chosen Lincoln as a partner, the young attorney must also be an admirable fellow. Mary was short, plump, and, though not pretty, had striking blue eyes and a fine complexion. Friends recalled that she was "impulsive & made no attempt to conceal her feeling, indeed it would have been an impossibility had she desired to do so, for her face was an index to every passing emotion." She had "an unusual gift of sarcasm" and "now and then indulged in sarcastic, witty remarks, that cut like a Damascus blade."[34]

While in Springfield to visit her eldest sister, Elizabeth, who had married Ninian W. Edwards—son of the former governor—Mary Todd met eligible bachelors aplenty at the Edwards home, a social center for the city's elite. Illinois was a promising hunting ground for a woman in search of a husband. A surfeit of unmarried men so longed for mates that a transplanted Kentuckian, John J. Hardin, urged young women from his native state to migrate northward if they wanted to be married. In 1840, Sangamon County had 24 percent more men than women. Catherine Bergen Jones of Springfield recalled that "nearly every young man in town would ask a young lady to take his arm in the evenings and promenade in a long procession down the muddy paths. Girls were in the minority and even those in their early teens were in demand."[35]

In the capital's social whirl during legislative sessions, Mary Todd was a belle. Young men liked her wit and older men her cultivation. She was "the very creature of excitement," a Springfielder reported in 1840; she "never enjoys herself more than when in society and surrounded by a company of merry friends."[36] One such friend was Joshua Speed, who brought Lincoln along to events at the Edwards home. Lincoln began seeing Mary in the winter of 1839–1840. According to a relative of Ninian Edwards, Lincoln admired her "naturally fine mind and cultivated tastes," for she was "a great reader and possessed of a remarkably retentive memory," was "quick at repartee and when the occasion seemed to require it was sarcastic and severe." Her "brilliant conversation, often embellished with apt quotations," made her "much sought after by the young people of the town."[37]

Initially, her sister Elizabeth encouraged the romance, for she realized that Lincoln was a man on the way up and that Mary should therefore wed him. In time, however, she came to recognize his social deficiencies, which she described to an interviewer: "L. Could not hold a lengthy Conversation with a lady—was not sufficiently Educated & intelligent in the female line to do so—He was charmed with Mary's wit and fascinated with her quick sagacity—her will—her nature—and Culture—I have happened in the room where they were sitting often & often and Mary led the Conversation—Lincoln would listen & gaze on her as if drawn by some Superior power, irresistably So: he listened—never Scarcely Said a word." Mrs. Edwards withdrew her earlier support for Lincoln and prophetically told her sister that they were not "Suitable to Each other." Mary "was quick, lively, gay—frivolous it may be, Social and loved glitter Show & pomp & power."[38]

Elizabeth Edwards, like others in Springfield, realized that Lincoln was "a mighty rough man," "uncouth," "moody," "dull in society," "careless of his personal appearance," "awkward and shy."[39] He avoided church, he once confessed to Mary Owens, because "I am conscious I should not know how to behave myself."[40] Herndon recalled that "Lincoln had poor judgment of the fitness and appropriateness of things. He would wade into a ballroom and speak aloud to some friend: 'How clean these women look!'"[41] At Springfield social gatherings, young ladies avoided Lincoln. "We girls," Catherine Bergen Jones recollected, "maneuvered so as to shift on each other the two awkward, diffident young lawyers, Abraham Lincoln and Samuel H. Treat. We preferred the jovial Robert Allen, Stephen A. Douglas, William Black, or the Jones brothers, John Albert and Edward, for our escorts."[42] The girls may have shunned Lincoln in part because of his ineptitude on the dance floor. When asked why he did not dance, he explained that "my feet weren't made that way."[43] At a party in Jacksonville, Lincoln reportedly approached Mary Todd, saying: "I want to dance with you in the worst way." Afterward she told him: "Mr. Lincoln I think you have literally fulfilled your request—you have danced the worst way possible."[44]

Early on, Mary became aware of Lincoln's gaucheries, which irritated her. When she teased him about a social indiscretion, he found it hard to understand why she cared so much about something so unimportant. Her cousin, Stephen T. Logan, warned Mary that Lincoln "is much too rugged for your little white hands to attempt to polish."[45]

(Mary never reconciled herself to Lincoln's lack of polish, even after years of marriage. A Springfield resident, who called Mrs. Lincoln "haughty," said "it hurt her that Lincoln was so plain and dressed so plain."[46] Her half-sister Emilie reported that "she complained because L. would open [the] front door instead of having [a] servant do so and because L. would eat butter with his knife she raised 'merry war.'"[47] (When a friend remarked, "Mary if I had a husband with a mind like yours [has,] I wouldn[']t care what he did," she admitted: "It is very foolish. It is a small thing to complain of.")[48] It maddened her when he answered the door in his shirtsleeves and told callers that he would "trot [the] woman folks out."[49] As president, whenever he read in his stocking feet, Mary Lincoln would order a servant to fetch his slippers. Extremely clothes-conscious, she criticized him for having shirt cuffs too frayed for a man in his exalted station. She asked Ward Hill Lamon to show her husband how to remove his hat properly, but despite the best efforts of Lamon and Secretary of State William Henry Seward, the president never mastered that social grace.)

Just how Lincoln courted Mary Todd is unclear.[50] When in Springfield, he regularly spent Sundays at the Edwards home. Ninian Edwards recalled that "Mr. Lincoln and Mr Speed were frequently at our house—seemed to enjoy themselves in their conversation beneath the dense shade of our forest trees."[51] But Lincoln could not have visited that home often in the winter and spring of 1840, for politics and his law practice frequently took him out of town. He would not have seen much of Mary Todd in the summer, which she spent with relatives in Missouri. When she returned, Lincoln was busily campaigning throughout southern Illinois. He did not mention her in any of the surviving letters he wrote in 1840, nor does her correspondence or that of their friends refer to any romance between them that year. Joshua Speed said that they courted through the mails that fall: "In 1840 Lincoln went into the Southern part of the State as Elector Canvasser debator Speaker—Here first wrote his *Mary*— She darted after him—wrote him."[52]

Others confirmed Speed's suggestion that Mary Todd took the initiative in the courtship. In 1875, Orville H. Browning told an interviewer: "I always thought then and ever since that in her affair with Mr Lincoln, Mary Todd did most of the court-ing." Browning added that "Miss Todd was thoroughly in earnest [in] her endeavors to get Mr. Lincoln" and stated flatly that there "is no doubt of her exceeding anxiety to marry him." Browning reported that in "those times I was at Mr. Edwards' a great deal, and Miss Todd used to sit down with me, and talk to me sometimes till mid-night, about this affair of hers with Mr. Lincoln."[53] William Butler's sister-in-law, Sarah Rickard, thought that Mary Todd "certainly made most of the plans and did the courting" and "would have him [Lincoln], whether or no." Rickard alleged that "it was the talk of Springfield that Mary Todd would marry him in spite of himself."[54] Herndon believed that "Miss Todd wanted L. terribly and worked, played her cards, through Mrs. [Simeon] Francis's hands."[55] In pursuing her quarry, "she read much & committed much to memory to make herself agreeable," according to Mrs. Benjamin S. Edwards.[56]

Despite their differences and their failure to spend much time together, Lincoln and Mary evidently became engaged some time in the fall of 1840. Lincoln's matri-monial impulsiveness recalls his abrupt acceptance of Betsy Abell's 1836 proposition that he wed Mary Owens.

Why they decided to marry is difficult to understand, for they were, as Elizabeth Edwards and many others noted, quite different. Howard M. Powel, a Springfield neighbor, recalled that "Mr. and Mrs. Lincoln were not a congenial couple; their tastes were so different that when a boy I often wondered why they were married."[57] William Herndon concluded that she was "the exact reverse" of her husband in "figure and physical proportions, in education, bearing, temperament, history—in everything."[58] Mary Lincoln herself referred to "our opposite natures."[59]

Their backgrounds could hardly have been more dissimilar. Almost ten years after Lincoln was born in the Kentucky backwoods, Eliza Parker Todd, descendant of friends of George Washington, and Robert S. Todd, son of the eminent General Levi Todd, had their fourth child—a daughter they named Mary. The Todds lived in a very different Kentucky from the one inhabited by Thomas Lincoln, occupying as they did a prominent social position in Lexington, self-identified as "the Athens of the West." In contrast to young Abe's all-too-brief formal schooling, Mary Todd was sent to Lexington's best private schools, among them Madame Victorie Char-lotte Leclere Mentelle's Academy, where French was spoken exclusively; there she studied social graces such as conversation, dancing, and letter writing. Soon after Lincoln's sister died bearing a child to a frontiersman in Indiana, Mary Todd's sister Elizabeth wed the son of Illinois's governor. When Lincoln left his father's cabin for New Salem, Mary Todd visited the stately mansion of Henry Clay to show off her new pony.

Abraham Lincoln and Mary Todd did share one important childhood experience: the premature death of their mothers. Mary was 6 when Eliza Parker Todd succumbed to a postbirth bacterial infection; Lincoln was 9 when milk sickness cut short Nancy Hanks's life. From these painful losses, both children sustained debilitating psychological wounds that contributed to the marital problems they would face later.

Mary Todd called her privileged childhood "desolate" not only because of the actual death of her mother but also because of the metaphorical death of her father.[60] With the passing of his first wife, Robert Smith Todd paid little attention to Mary and her siblings. A scant few weeks after his wife's burial, he traveled to nearby Frankfort and courted young Elizabeth Humphreys, whom he wed a year later and with whom he would sire nine half-siblings for Mary over the next fifteen years. Mary evidently felt betrayed, abandoned, and rejected by her "impetuous, high-strung, sensitive" father.[61] Deep-seated anger at him and his second wife apparently smoldered in her unconscious.

According to Elizabeth Todd, Mary "left her home in Kentucky to avoid living under the same roof with a stepmother."[62] Mary's siblings shared her disaffection. Younger brother George "complained bitterly" about Betsy Humphreys' "settled hostility" and alleged that he had been forced to leave "his father's house in consequence of the malignant & continued attempts on the part of his stepmother to poison the mind of his father toward him." George claimed that his father was "mortified that his last child by his first wife should be obliged, like all his other first children, to abandon his house by the relentless persecution of a stepmother."[63] All of Eliza Parker Todd's daughters quit Lexington when of age. After Elizabeth married Ninian W. Edwards and settled in Springfield, she brought over her sisters one-by-one, introduced them to society, and gave them weddings. Robert and Betsy Todd rarely visited these offspring, who seldom returned to Kentucky. Exacerbating family tensions was the hostility of Eliza Todd's formidable mother toward her son-in-law and his second wife.[64]

Mary Todd had legitimate grievances against her stepmother. She confided to a friend that her "early home was truly at a *boarding* school," Madame Mentelle's Academy.[65] Since Mary was willful and mischievous, she frequently clashed with her prim and proper young stepmother. At the age of 10, Mary had a row with Betsy Todd when the youngster awkwardly deployed willow branches to transform her narrow frock into a hoop skirt. Upon seeing the clumsy result, her stepmother declared, "What a fright you are," and ordered Mary and her niece, Elizabeth, to "take those things off, & then go to Sunday school." Elizabeth remembered that "we went to our room chagrined and angry. Mary burst into tears, and gave the first exhibition of temper I had ever seen or known her to make. She thought we were badly treated, and expressed herself freely on the subject."[66]

As an adult, Mary continued to have difficulties with her stepmother. In the late 1840s, while Lincoln attended Congress, his wife and their two young boys, Robert and Eddie, stayed with the Todds in Lexington. One day Eddie Lincoln brought in a kitten, much to his stepgrandmother's dismay. Mrs. Lincoln reported the sequel to her husband: "in the midst of his happiness Ma [Betsy Todd] came in, she you must know dislikes the whole cat race, I thought in a very unfeeling manner, she ordered the servant near, to throw it out, which, of course, was done, Ed—screaming & protesting loudly against the proceeding, she never appeared to mind his screams, which were long & loud, I assure you." Significantly she added: "Tis unusual for her *now a days*, to do any thing quite so striking, *she* is very obliging & accommodating, but if she thought any of us, were on her hands again, I believe she would be *worse* than ever."[67] Mary Lincoln underscored *now a days*, implying that such unfeeling treatment of children was common earlier. Betsy Todd's indifference to Eddie's sensibilities may well have reminded Mary of similar episodes in her own childhood.

Mary Todd may also have disliked Betsy Humphreys Todd for bearing nine rivals for paternal favor. During the Civil War, all but one of these half-siblings supported the Southern cause, and Mary did not conceal her hostility toward them.[68] In 1862, she shocked a confidante by expressing the hope that her brothers in Confederate uniform would be captured or slain. "They would kill my husband if they could, and destroy our Government—the dearest of all things to us," she declared, shortly after her half-brother Samuel had died at the battle of Shiloh.[69] When her half-brother Alexander was killed in 1863, she said "it is but natural that I should feel for one so nearly related to me," but Alexander had "made his choice long ago. He decided against my husband, and through him against me. He has been fighting against us; and since he chose to be our deadly enemy, I see no special reason why I should bitterly mourn his death."[70] When the press condemned her sadistic half-brother David, chief of Richmond's prisons during the war, she told a reporter that "by no word or act of hers should he escape punishment for his treason against her husband's government."[71]

Although such evidence of Mary Todd's attitude toward her family is not conclusive, it does suggest that she harbored a rage she was unable to vent directly. It also suggests that she might seek a surrogate father; indeed, she may have married Lincoln in part because she saw in him a benevolent paterfamilias who would indulge her and fill the void created in her life when Robert Smith Todd began a second family. More than a foot taller and nearly ten years Mary's senior, he radiated the quality of being old. During Lincoln's early years in Springfield, one observer said that the lanky attorney called to mind "the pictures I formerly saw of old Father Jupiter, bending down from the clouds, to see what was going on below," especially when Lincoln conversed with young women at parties: just "as an agreeable smile of satisfaction graced the countenance of the old heathen god, as he perceived the incense rising up—so the face of L[incoln] was occasionally distorted into a grin as he succeeded in eliciting applause from some of the fair votaries by whom he was surrounded."[72] Among such "fair votaries" was Mary Todd, a young woman likely to be attracted to a man resembling Father Jupiter, a man who would take care of her like a kind father.

Mary Todd's youthful qualities may have appealed to Lincoln. A woman in Washington during the Civil War believed that the president saw in his wife, "despite her foibles and sometimes her puerileness, just what he needed." Those foibles included "natural want of tact," "deficiency in the sense of the fitness of things," "blundering outspokenness," and "impolitic disregard of diplomatic considerations."[73] That very puerileness was perhaps what attracted him to her; with his deep paternal streak, he enjoyed children and child surrogates. Mary Todd fit that role well; as Helen Nicolay put it, Lincoln's "attitude toward his wife had something of the paternal in it, almost as though she were a child, under his protection."[74] Thus, when Lincoln proposed to Mary Todd, he did so because, in all likelihood, he believed she wanted him to do so and because he desired a "child-wife."

Mary certainly needed a great deal of protection, or at least looking after, for she had mental problems, including manic depression. Orville H. Browning, who thought her "demented," recalled that she "was a girl of much vivacity in conversation, but was subject to . . . spells of mental depression. . . . As we used familiarly to state it she was always 'either in the garret or cellar.'"[75] A childhood friend, Margaret Stuart, testified that Mary in her Kentucky years was "very highly strung, nervous, impulsive, excitable, having an emotional temperament much like an April day, sunning all over with laughter one moment, the next crying as though her heart would break."[76] Manic depression is not the only diagnosis that seems to fit Mary Lincoln's condition; she exhibited many symptoms associated with narcissism and with borderline personality disorder.[77] In later life, after Lincoln's death, her instability grew very marked. Her nephew, Albert Stevenson Edwards, believed that she "was insane from the time of her husband['s] death until her own death."[78] In 1875, an Illinois court adjudged her insane and had her confined in a mental hospital.[79] But even before the tragedy of the assassination, David Davis, alluding to her conduct as First Lady during the Civil War, called her a "natural born thief" for whom "stealing was a sort of insanity."[80] In fact, he thought she was "deranged" as far back as the 1840s.[81]

Psychiatric problems ran throughout Mary's family. Dr. George R. C. Todd, youngest of her biological siblings, was especially troubled.[82] A fellow physician in South Carolina who knew him well said that Dr. Todd referred to himself as the "black sheep" of the family, that he did "not get along with people," and that he was "very egotistical, and extremely jealous of his professional reputation. Very peculiar and eccentric. Drank whiskey to excess." Dr. Todd's lawyer recalled that he was "inclined to be abrupt almost to brusqueness in his manner to those whom he did not like." He "took no pains to conceal his dislike for those who had incurred his displeasure," and he "refused to consort with his own contemporaries to any great extent." He was "given to moods of deep melancholy."[83] Like his sister Mary, he had an explosive temper that bordered on madness. He was described by a Union prisoner-of-war as "the most vicious wretch I ever knew" because he cruelly mistreated enemy patients. During the Civil War, he would, in "raving fits of madness," assault sick and wounded Yankees under his care. When a young Union lieutenant from Kentucky irritated him, Dr. Todd "pulled him off the bunk to the floor and kicked him in the most brutal manner." Upon the death of the prisoner the next day, Dr. Todd declared: "I am G-d d-d glad of it. I meant to kill the son of a b-h before he left here."[84] During the Gettysburg campaign, he infuriated Northerners by looting private homes. He told dubious tales about his role in divvying up the last of the Confederate treasury in 1865, and he also claimed, most improbably, that he had visited the White House early in the war and aroused the president's suspicions about his loyalty. When ordered arrested, he said, he outwitted his pursuers and escaped.

Other siblings betrayed signs of mental instability. Mary's eccentric, heavily tattooed half-brother David, who ran away from home at the age of 14, also mistreated Union prisoners.[85] Stationed briefly at Libby Prison in Richmond as a captain in the Confederate army, David Todd was known as one of the most brutal officers in that grim facility. He slashed a POW with his saber and kicked the corpses of the Union dead, calling them damned abolitionists. In 1871, David died, supposedly of wounds sustained at Vicksburg, but some friends maintained that "he had been shot in a whore house brawl before he went to War— . . . and that this old wound had more to do with his early demise than the Yankee Minie [bullet]."[86] Mary's brother Levi, two years her senior, was described by his wife as an improvident drunkard with a "Cruel and inhuman manner." He alienated family and acquaintances and died friendless in 1865.[87] Mary's "pugnacious, loud voiced" sister Ann, if not actually unbalanced, was "the most quick tempered and vituperative" of Robert Todd's daughters. She was "usually in a temper."[88] Mary called Ann a woman who "possesses such a miserable disposition & so false a tongue" that "no one respects" her. Ann's "tongue for so many years, has been considered 'no slander'—and as a child & young girl, [she] could not be outdone in falsehood. . . . I grieve for those, who have to come in contact with her malice, yet even *that*, is so well understood, [that] the object of *her wrath*, generally rises, with good people, in proportion to her *vindictiveness*."[89] (When shown this assessment of her character, Ann replied with some justice: "Mary was writing about herself.")[90]

Mary's niece Julia, daughter of Elizabeth Edwards, was mentally unstable. "Insanity," Elizabeth said in 1875, "appeared . . . in the case of my own daughter, at the early age of thirteen,—for six months, she was so decidedly flighty, as to be closely guarded." At "no time has she ever been natural in her demeanor. God pity those who are the victims—and who are the anxious sufferers in such terrible afflictions!"[91] Born in 1837, the beautiful Julia at the age of 18 wed Edward Lewis Baker, co-owner of the Springfield *Illinois State Journal*. A good friend of Julia's, Ada Bailhache, wife of Edward Baker's business partner, recalled that "Mrs Baker was a wayward girl and very attractive woman to the great sorrow of her family and friends. There was a scandal connected with her about 1872, and Mr Baker was sent as Consul to the Argentine Republic where they remained until Mr Baker's death [in 1897]. . . . He was probably not molested in courtesy to [the] memory of Lincoln, as it was better for them not to return." The "blow to her mother and father, was one they never recovered from."[92] Because Julia was unable to manage her own affairs, a court in the 1870s appointed a trustee for her.[93] Mary Lincoln referred to her niece as a "poor, silly" creature and expressed sympathy for Elizabeth Edwards: "How unfortunate a Mother, must consider herself, to *so rear*, a child—Naturally weak."[94] When she visited Washington in 1864, Julia Baker scandalized polite society with her bizarre, risqué behavior.

Another niece of Mary Todd, Elizabeth Edwards Clover (Julia Baker's sister), inherited much of her famous aunt's wardrobe, which she regularly wore, even though the large silk skirts, lace shawls, and tiny carriage parasols had long since passed out of style. As a Springfield matron recalled, no one "thought anything of it" because "the Todds had always been eccentric."[95] Mary's sister Elodie told her fiancé, "I am a *Todd,* and some of these days you may be unfortunate enough to find out what they are." She confessed to him that "I cannot govern my temper or tongue" and that "I am one of the most unforgiving creatures you ever knew."[96] The daughter of Mary Todd Lincoln's nephew, Albert S. Edwards (Julia Baker's brother), died in the Norbury Sanitarium, a "Private Residential Home for the Treatment of Nervous and Mental Disorders."[97] In 1906, Mary Lincoln's son Robert wrote from Georgia that "I have been down here for nearly two months trying to recover from a nervous breakdown."[98]

In late 1840, Lincoln broke his engagement to Mary Todd. According to a friend, he had concluded that they "were not congenial, and were incompatible" and "ought not to marry."[99] He may well have doubted his ability to satisfy her intense emotional neediness. After his death, she stated that, despite his "deep feeling" and his "amiable nature," Lincoln was "*not,* a demonstrative Man, when he felt most deeply, he expressed, the least."[100] Elizabeth Edwards called Lincoln "a cold man" with "no affection,"[101] and her husband concurred, saying: "Lincoln was not a warm hearted man."[102] Herndon declared that Lincoln "ought never to have married," for he "had no quality for a husband. He was abstracted, cool, never loved, and could not from his very nature."[103] Henry C. Whitney agreed, stating that "so great & peculiar a man as Lincoln could not make any woman happy," for "he was too much allied to his intellect to get down to the plane of the domestic relations."[104]

Another powerful consideration gave Lincoln pause as he contemplated marrying Mary Todd: in the autumn of 1840 he fell in love with Matilda Edwards, a beautiful 18-year-old cousin of Ninian Edwards who had come to Springfield from Alton and stayed with Mary Todd at the Edwards home.[105] Like many other young women, she visited the capital during legislative sessions to attend the numerous parties given then. A "legislative winter was as eagerly looked forward to by the ladies of the State as the politicians because it promised a season of constant gaiety and entertainment. An invitation to spend such a time in Springfield was a coveted honor. The pretty girls from all over the State flocked [t]here under the care of fathers, uncles, brothers, cousins, any relation, however remote who could be induced to bring them."[106]

The "very bright" Matilda Edwards was "something of a coquette" and "a most fascinating and handsome girl, tall, graceful, and rather reserved," who "moved at ease among the social and refined classes at Alton."[107] Her "gentle temper, her conciliatory manners, and the sweetness of her heart made her dear to all who knew her."[108] Lincoln was among the many young men who held her dear. In the winter of 1840–1841, she and Mary Todd "seemed to form the grand centre of attraction. Swarms of strangers who had little else to engage their attention hovered around them, to catch a *passing smile.*"[109] (She received twenty-two offers of marriage before wedding Newton D. Strong in 1843.) In January 1841, Jane D. Bell reported that Lincoln had declared "if he had it in his power he would not have one feature in her face altered, he thinks she is so perfect." Mrs. Bell added that Lincoln and Joshua

Speed "spent the most of their time at [the] Edwards [home] this winter" and that "Lincoln could never bear to leave Miss Edwards's side in company" because "he fell desperately in love with her."[110] Yet he was too shy to approach the young beauty, who informed Elizabeth Edwards that Lincoln "never mentioned Such a Subject to me: he never even Stooped to pay me a Compliment."[111] After becoming enamored of Matilda Edwards, Lincoln confided to John J. Hardin "that he thought he did not love" Mary Todd "as he should and that he would do her a great wrong if he married her."[112] To Mrs. William Butler, Lincoln declared, "it would just kill me to marry Mary Todd."[113]

And so Lincoln felt compelled to break his engagement, but just how he did so is unclear. Alluding to Matilda Edwards, Joshua Speed recalled that "Lincoln—seeing another girl—& finding he did not love [the woman who eventually became] his wife wrote a letter saying he did not love her." When Speed was shown that document, he "tried to persuade Lincoln to burn it up," whereupon Lincoln said: "Speed I always Knew you were an obstinate man. If you won't deliver it I will get Some one to do it." Speed replied: "I Shall not deliver it nor give it to you to be delivered: Words are forgotten—Misunderstood—passed by—not noticed in a private Conversation—but once put your words in writing and they Stand as a living & eternal Monument against you. If you think you have *will* & Manhood Enough to go and see her and Speak to her what you say in that letter, you may do that." Acting on Speed's advice, Lincoln visited Mary Todd and, again according to Speed, "told her that he did not love her—She rose—and Said 'The deciever shall be decieved wo is me.'; alluding to a young man She fooled." Speed reported that "Lincoln drew her down on his Knee—Kissed her—& parted—He going one way & She another—Lincoln did Love Miss [Matilda] Edwards—'Mary' Saw it—told Lincoln the reason of his Change of mind—heart & soul—released him."[114]

It is not known what Mary Todd said to Lincoln when he asked to be released. She admitted after his death that, during their courtship, "I doubtless trespassed, many times & oft, upon his great tenderness & amiability of character."[115] Perhaps she deliberately manipulated his conscience to win him back. Her sister Elizabeth recalled that the "world had it that Mr L backed out, and this placed Mary in a peculiar Situation & to set herself right and to free Mr Lincoln's mind She wrote a letter to Mr L Stating that She would release him from his Engagements," with the understanding "that She would hold the question an open one—that is that She had not Changed her mind, but felt as always."[116] She thus left him the option of renewing the engagement if he so desired. She clearly hoped he would do so.

Under these circumstances, it is little wonder that, as Ninian Edwards put it, Lincoln "in his Conflicts of duty—honor & his love went as Crazy as a *Loon*."[117] On January 21, 1841, Martinette Hardin McKee told her brother: "We have been very much distressed, on Mr Lincoln's account; hearing that he had two Cat fits and a Duck fit."[118] A week later, Jane D. Bell reported that Lincoln "is in rather a bad way. . . . The doctors say he came within an inch of being a perfect lunatic for life. He was perfectly crazy for some time, not able to attend to his business at all. They say he does not look like the same person."[119]

In fact, Lincoln went "crazy for a week or so" and was nursed back to health at the Butlers' home, where his friend Orville H. Browning was staying. Browning said his friend "was so much affected as to talk incoherently, and to be delirious to the extent of not knowing what he was doing." This "aberration of mind resulted entirely from the situation he . . . got himself into—he was engaged to Miss Todd, and in love with Miss Edwards, and his conscience troubled him dreadfully for the supposed injustice he had done, and the supposed violation of his word which he had committed."[120] Many friends, including James H. Matheny, feared that Lincoln might kill himself.[121] According to Speed, they "had to remove razors from his room—take away all Knives and other such dangerous things—&c—it was terrible."[122] Lincoln declared that he "would be more than willing" to die, but, he said, "I have an irrepressible desire to live till I can be assured that the world is a little better for my having lived in it."[123]

Before those friends were able to confiscate potentially lethal objects, a fellow legislator, Hiram W. Thornton, recalled encountering Lincoln "sitting on a box behind a woodshed. One leg was resting upon the other in a flexed position and he was whetting a knife on the bootleg." When Thornton asked what he was doing, Lincoln replied: "I am just getting this knife sharp enough to do what I want to do with it." Thornton then took the knife and spoke with his colleague, who "emphasized that he was no good and he had better be out of the world than in it."[124]

In despair, Lincoln turned to his physician-friend, Anson G. Henry, who may have helped persuade Mary Todd to release him from the engagement. From January 13 to 18 Lincoln spent several hours each day with Henry. It is not known what Dr. Henry prescribed as a treatment, but if he followed the customary procedures of that time he would have subjected Lincoln to a painful regimen of bleeding, leeching, the application of heated cups to the temples, mustard rubs, foul-tasting medicines, and cold-water baths.

On January 20, Lincoln confessed to John T. Stuart: "I have, within the last few days, been making a most discreditable exhibition of myself in the way of hypochondriaism [i.e., depression] and thereby got an impression that Dr. Henry is necessary to my existence." Three days later he elaborated: "I am now the most miserable man living. If what I feel were equally distributed to the whole human family, there would not be one cheerful face on the earth. Whether I shall ever be better I can not tell; I awfully forebode I shall not. To remain as I am is impossible; I must die or be better, it appears to me."[125] He also wrote to Dr. Daniel Drake of Cincinnati describing his symptoms and asking advice. That well-known physician replied that he could make no recommendation without a personal interview.

In the General Assembly that January, Lincoln behaved oddly. With unwonted testiness, he lashed out at a fellow legislator who had chided him about his "jump" from the church window the previous month. Lincoln "said that as to jumping, he should jump when he pleased and no one should hinder him."[126] Soon thereafter on the floor of the House of Representatives, he alluded to his lack of appeal to the opposite sex: "if any woman, old or young, ever thought there was any peculiar charm in this distinguished specimen . . . I have, as yet, been so unfortunate as not to have discovered it."[127] Shortly after making these remarks, he stopped attending sessions of the General Assembly, just when his leadership was needed to combat the Democrats' court-packing scheme, which barely passed the House. He answered no roll calls on January 13, 14, 15, 16, 18, or 20. On January 19, he voted on one roll call but missed the other five. On January 21, he resumed casting votes regularly. Such absenteeism was unusual for Lincoln, who in four legislative terms missed only 180 of 1,334 roll calls; over half of those absences occurred during this session.

On January 24, Lincoln appeared to James C. Conkling to be "reduced and emaciated," with barely enough strength "to speak above a whisper." Conkling sympathized with him: "Poor L! How are the mighty fallen! . . . His case at present is truly deplorable but what prospect there may be for ultimate relief I cannot pretend to say. I doubt not but he can declare 'That loving is a painful thrill, And not to love more painful still' but would not like to intimate that he has experienced 'That surely 'tis the worst of pain To love and not be loved again.'"[128] In the midst of this period of depression, John Todd Stuart's wife observed Lincoln at the capitol "with his feet braced against one of the pillars. His face looked like Bunyan's figure, 'Giant Despair.'"[129]

By late January, Lincoln seemed to have recovered. On January 26, Mrs. John J. Hardin told her husband: "I am glad to hear Lincoln has got over his cat fits[.] [W]e have concluded it was a very unsatisfactory way of terminating his romance[.] [H]e ought to have died or gone crazy[.] [W]e are very much disappointed indeed."[130]

In March, after the legislature had adjourned, Turner R. King saw Lincoln in Springfield "hanging about—moody—silent." King believed that the "question in his mind was 'Have I incurred any obligation to marry that woman.'"[131] Although he had broken the engagement, Lincoln was still tormented by the thought that he really should have wed Mary Todd, not because he loved her, but because his tyrannical conscience nagged him unmercifully. James C. Conkling reported that Lincoln, the "poor hapless simple swain who loved most true but was not loved again," would probably "now endeavor to drown his cares among the intricacies and perplexities of the law."[132]

New Law Partner

Conkling was right. The following month, Lincoln amicably ended his partnership with John Todd Stuart and joined forces with Stephen T. Logan, a better lawyer and worse politician than Stuart. Logan, displeased with the ethical obtuseness of his partner, Edward D. Baker, sought to replace him. He had observed young Lincoln in three cases where they opposed each other; Lincoln won all three. At that same time Lincoln may have felt the need for more rigorous legal training than could be provided by Stuart, who, as a congressman, perforce spent much time in Washington. If so, Lincoln could hardly have picked a better mentor than Logan, a Kentuckian nine years his senior. Stuart, who regarded Logan as the ablest attorney in Sangamon County, said that the "rapidity of his intellectual perceptions were like flashes of lightning."[133] In 1843, the *Sangamo Journal* declared that Logan "is regarded as perhaps the best lawyer in the State, and has undoubtedly a fine logical mind. His voice is not pleasant, but he has a most happy faculty of elucidating, and simplifying the most obstinate questions."[134] John Hay thought him "one of the finest examples of the purely legal mind that the West has ever produced."[135] Supreme Court justices John McLean and David Davis, as well as leading attorneys such as Gustave Koerner, Usher F. Linder, Elihu B. Washburne, Isaac N. Arnold, and Benjamin S. Edwards all concurred.

Logan had a brilliant mind but an unimpressive appearance. In 1843, an observer called him "the very personification of carelessness."[136] Gustave Koerner, who sat in the General Assembly with Logan, described him as "the most slovenly man, not only in the Legislature, but in the city of Springfield." Although he was rich and owned a magnificent estate, he dressed shabbily, never wearing a necktie. In cold weather his headgear was a fur cap, which in the summer he replaced with a cheap straw hat. Completing his wardrobe were rough, coarse brogans, baggy pants, and coat. Hezekiah Morse Wead reported that when Logan "rises to speak, his mouth is filled with tobacco which he rolls over and stows away inside of his cheek, and spits forth as he get[s] excited in small punches from his filthy mouth."[137] People were astonished that such an eminent lawyer would dress so shabbily and have traces of tobacco juice streaking his face.

Wead, a fellow delegate to the 1847 Illinois constitutional convention, voiced some other negative feelings people had about Logan. Wead confided to his diary that Logan was clever and skillful but given to "sophistry." Shallow, even devious, he was "always specious, frequently ingenious and sometimes powerful, but his great forte is in making a skillful use of men's prejudices. . . . Sometimes he approaches a subject boldly, probes it to the bottom and handles it like a man of intellect, but such instances are rare, and only occur where the subject itself is not deep or obscure. He has always, an argument calculated to draw the mind from deep and useful investigation—he plays around the true question, raising collateral issues, and deceiving men with straws and chaff, while the grain is not seen. . . . His mind is limited to a certain sphere, but in that limit he is superior. Quick of apprehension, possessing a happy faculty of compassion, and great knowledge of the prejudices of men, he is calculated to exercise & does exercise a great influence: but with all his influence and all his tact he is utterly unable to comprehend the strength of a powerful intellect or the superiority of a mind which towers immensely above his own."[138]

Logan also lacked a winning personality, for he had a volatile temper and was notoriously tightfisted. Herndon called him "a little shriveled-up man," who was "cold, ungenerous, snappy, [and] irritable" and who died "without a warm friend in the world."[139]

Logan and Lincoln became close friends personally and politically despite their different values. Logan cared a great deal about money and made lots of it, while Lincoln did not care about it and made comparatively little. Logan revered the law while Lincoln regarded a legal career as simply the means to facilitate a political career.

In Logan's view, Lincoln had not systematically studied law under Stuart, who was, he said, "never a reader of law; he always depended more on the management of

his case." Consequently, Lincoln's approach was piecemeal and lacked deep understanding. Despite a few years of successful practice, "Lincoln's knowledge of the law
was very small when I took him in," Logan maintained. "He would work hard and
learn all there was in a case he had in hand" and thereby "got to be a pretty good
lawyer though his general knowledge of law was never very formidable." After joining
forces with Logan, Lincoln "turned in to try to know more and studied to learn how
to prepare his cases."[140] (To William H. Herndon, Lincoln explained: "As I am constituted I don't love to read generally, and as I do not love to read I feel no interest in
what is thus read. I don't, & can't remember such reading. When I have a particular
case in hand I have that motive, and feel an interest in the case.")[141]

For three years Lincoln worked with Logan, who taught his young partner a
great deal. The older man also shared Lincoln's natural inclination to act as a peacemaker, for Logan discouraged litigation and tried to resolve controversies amicably.

Logan may have influenced Lincoln's approach to jury trials. Joseph Wallace
found it "entertaining and instructive" to watch Logan argue a case to a jury: "Resting
one foot on a chair, he commences with a few commonplace remarks uttered in a clear
conversational tone." Then he "lays hold of the leading facts and strong points of his
case, states them with singular perspicuity and force, dwells on them at length, and
presents them from every standpoint favorable to his client." As "he warms to his
work," his "small frame involuntarily assumes a more erect and impressive attitude;
his gestures become more rapid; his shrill voice is pitched to a higher key; his gray
eyes glow with animation; every muscle is at play, and every energy of his nature
aroused, while words, sentences, arguments, illustrations, appeals, flow in torrents
from his lips."[142]

Such performances inspired Lincoln, who said "that it was his highest ambition
to become as good a lawyer as Logan."[143] He described Logan as "the best *nisi prius*
[i.e., trial] lawyer he ever saw," one who could "make a nice distinction in the law, or
upon the facts, more palpable to the common understanding, than any lawyer he ever
knew."[144] Lincoln wrote that Logan was "almost a father to me"; he felt for Logan a
reverent affection that he never felt for his biological father.[145]

Under Logan's tutelage, Lincoln expanded his legal horizons to include practice
in the Federal Courts and the Illinois Supreme Court, both of which had transferred
operations to Springfield from Vandalia in 1839. Of the 411 Supreme Court cases that
Lincoln appeared in during his twenty-four-year legal career, a substantial number
were tried during his brief partnership with Logan. In response to the hard times following the Panic of 1837, Congress enacted a short-lived bankruptcy law in 1841 to
relieve debtors, many of whom enlisted the services of Logan and Lincoln. They
handled seventy-seven such cases, more than any other firm in Springfield and the
fourth largest number of any firm in the state.

Logan stopped riding the circuit when he joined forces with Lincoln, who trav-
eled not only the Eighth Judicial Circuit but also many other counties, among them
Coles, where his stepmother and father resided. He ventured as far east as Clark
County along the Indiana border and as far west as Madison County on the Missis-

sippi River. At first, Logan and Lincoln occupied an office across from Hoffman's Row; in 1843, they moved to the Tinsley building on the southeast corner of the public square. Of the roughly 850 cases they were involved in, 70 percent related to debt collection.

In the winter and spring of 1841, Lincoln avoided Mary Todd, much to her distress. He may even have considered leaving the country; on March 5, John Todd Stuart recommended him for the post of chargé d'affaires at Bogotá, Colombia. In June, Mary lamented to a friend that Lincoln "deems me unworthy of notice, as I have not met *him* in the gay world for months." She consoled herself with the knowledge "that others were as seldom gladdened by his presence as my humble self." Yet, she confessed, "I would that the case were different, that he would once more resume his Station in Society, that 'Richard should be himself again,' much, much happiness would it afford me."[146] According to her cousin Martinette Hardin, Mary Todd wanted Lincoln back because she had "made up her mind that he should marry her at the cost of her pride to show us all that she was not defeated."[147]

While ignoring Mary Todd, Lincoln sometime in 1841 briefly courted Sarah Rickard, the sister of Mrs. William Butler (née Elizabeth Rickard). He had often seen Sarah at the Butlers' house, where he boarded between 1837 and 1842. She was only 12 years old when they first met; four years later he seriously paid her court and proposed marriage, remarking that since she was named Sarah, she was destined to marry Abraham. She rejected the offer because, as she later explained, "his peculiar manner and his General deportment would not be likely to fascinate a young girl just entering the society world."[148] The fatherly qualities that appealed to Mary Todd were lost on Sarah, who thought of him as a big brother, not a potential mate.[149]

In the summer of 1841, Lincoln spent six weeks in Kentucky with Joshua Speed at his family's stately home, Farmington, near Louisville. There his spirits revived as he enjoyed the Speeds' gracious hospitality, the luxurious appointments of a house far grander than any he had lived in, the companionship of his closest friend, the maternal warmth of Speed's mother, the playfulness of Speed's older half-sister Mary, and the intellectual stimulation provided by Speed's brother, James. Years later James recalled: "I saw him daily; he sat in my office, read my books, and talked with me about his life, his reading, his studies, his aspirations." Lincoln impressed everybody at Farmington "with his intelligent, vigorous mind, strong in grasp, and original" and showed himself to be "earnest, frank, manly, and sincere in every thought and expression. The artificial was all wanting."[150] (In 1864, Lincoln would appoint James Speed attorney general of the United States.)

An example of the qualities that endeared Lincoln to the Speed family was his conduct at dinner one evening at which mint jelly was served to accompany the mutton. Unfamiliar with that condiment, he helped himself to all of it. When another container of jelly was brought out, he noticed that each of the other diners took only a small amount. Without embarrassment he said with a quiet laugh, "I seem to have taken more than my share."[151]

When it came time to leave, Speed's mother gave Lincoln an Oxford Bible, which she called "the best cure for the 'Blues.'"[152] In late October 1841, Joshua Speed reported that since Lincoln's return to Springfield, "he has been eminently successful in his practice" and "is in fine spirits and good health."[153] Three months later, Lincoln cheerfully told Speed that he recently had "been quite clear of hypo."[154]

Lincoln soon found an opportunity to return the Speeds' kindness, for just as he was recovering from his romantic misadventures with Mary Todd, Joshua Speed, who was highly susceptible to Cupid's arrows, found himself tormented by an affair of the heart. He had fallen in love with a young neighbor, Fanny Henning, and impulsively proposed to her. When she accepted, however, instead of joy, Speed endured "immense suffering" because he doubted that he really loved her.[155] Now Lincoln played counselor and emotional nursemaid to Speed, reversing their earlier roles, writing him several letters that reveal as much about their author as they do about their recipient. He assured Speed that his anxiety was groundless, rhetorically asking his doubt-torn friend: "How came you to court her? Was it because you thought she desired it; and that you had given her reason to expect it? If it was for that, why did not the same reason make you court Ann Todd [cousin of Mary Todd], and at least twenty others of whom you can think, & to whom it would apply with greater force than to her? Did you court her for her wealth? Why, you knew she had none. But you say you reasoned yourself into it. What do you mean by that? Was it not, that you found yourself unable to reason yourself out of it? Did you not think, and partly form the purpose, of courting her the first time you ever saw or heard of her? What had reason to do with it, at that early stage? There was nothing at that time for reason to work upon. Whether she was moral, aimiable, sensible, or even of good character, you did not, nor could not then know; except perhaps you might infer the last from the company you found her in. All you then did or could know of her, was her personal appearance and deportment; and these, if they impress at all, impress the heart and not the head. Say candidly, were not those heavenly black eyes, the whole basis of all your early reasoning on the subject?"[156]

This document suggests indirectly that Lincoln had several doubts about wedding Mary Todd: that he persuaded himself that he loved her because she wanted and expected him to do so; that he feared he was interested in her wealth and social status; and that he had allowed his head to rule his heart.

When Speed reported that he was deeply concerned about his fiancée's health, Lincoln poignantly referred to his own experience as he tried to comfort his friend: "Why, Speed, if you did not love her, although you might not wish her death, you would most calmly be resigned to it. Perhaps this point is no longer a question with you, and my pertenacious dwelling upon it, is a rude intrusion upon your feelings. If so, you must pardon me." Alluding to his own doubts about Mary Todd, he added: "You know the Hell I have suffered on that point, and how tender I am upon it."[157]

On February 15, 1842, despite his misgivings, Speed married Fanny Henning, prompting Lincoln to write yet another revealing letter: "I do fondly hope . . . that you will never again need any comfort from abroad. But should I be mistaken in this . . . still let me urge you, as I have ever done, to remember in the dep[t]h and even the agony of despondency, that verry shortly you are to feel well again. I am now fully convinced, that you love her as ardently as you are capable of loving. Your ever being happy in her presence, and your intense anxiety about her health, if there were nothing else, would place this beyond all dispute in my mind. I incline to think it probable, that your nerves will fail you occasionally for a while; but once you get them fairly graded now, that trouble is over forever. I think if I were you, in case my mind were not exactly right, I would avoid being *idle;* I would immediately engage in some business, or go to making preparations for it, which would be the same thing."[158] Lincoln seemed to be trying to persuade himself not to take seriously his doubts about Mary Todd, and if he should perchance succumb to them, he should immediately busy himself with some project.

As the day of Speed's wedding approached, Lincoln became agitated. When Speed wrote him shortly after the ceremony, Lincoln opened the envelope, as he reported, "with intense anxiety and trepidation—so much, that although it turned out better than I expected, I have hardly yet, at the distance of ten hours, become calm." With relief he told Speed, "our *forebodings,* for which you and I are rather peculiar, are all the worst sort of nonsense." Speed confided his fear that the Elysium of which he had dreamed "is never to be realized." Lincoln reassured him that "it is the peculiar misfortune of both you and me, to dream dreams of Elysium far exceeding all that any thing earthly can realize. Far short of your dreams as you may be, no woman could do more to realize them, than that same black-eyed Fanny. If you could but contemplate her through my immagination, it would appear ridiculous to you, that any one should for a moment think of being unhappy with her. My old Father used to have a saying that 'If you make a bad bargain, *hug* it the tighter'; and it occurs to me, that if the bargain you have just closed can possibly be called a bad one, it is certainly the most *pleasant one* for applying that maxim to."[159] Here Lincoln seemed to be telling himself that he should not be disappointed if Mary Todd did not measure up to his unreasonable ideal and that he should marry her even if the engagement was a "bad bargain."

In March 1842, when Speed informed Lincoln that he was much happier than he had anticipated, Lincoln rejoiced with him but confessed that his own pleasure in the newlyweds' bliss was diminished by his guilty conscience, which continued to torment him about Mary Todd. Referring cryptically to "that fatal first of Jany. '41," he asserted that since that time, "it seems to me, I should have been entirely happy, but for the never-absent idea, that there is *one* still unhappy whom I have contributed to make so. That still kills my soul. I can not but reproach myself, for even wishing to be happy while she is otherwise."[160]

In July, Lincoln again confided to Speed misgivings about breaking his engagement to Mary Todd. He said he could not follow Speed's (unidentified) advice yet: "I must regain my confidence in my own ability to keep my resolves when they are made. In that ability, you know, I once prided myself as the only, or at least the chief, gem of my character; that gem I lost—how, and when, you too well know. I have not yet regained it; and until I do, I can not trust myself in any matter of much importance." With characteristic fatalism and passivity in matters of the heart, he declared that his own course was now to obey the injunction of Moses: "Stand *still* and see the salvation of the Lord."[161]

Near-Duel

While awaiting a sign from the Almighty, Lincoln accepted a challenge to fight a duel, an act that he later called "the meanest thing he ever did in his life."[162] In August and September 1842, the *Sangamo Journal* ran three letters signed by "Aunt Rebecca" of "Lost Townships" ridiculing the Democratic leader James Shields. An impetuous, hot-tempered, 36-year-old native of Ireland, Shields was a lawyer with a reputation as an exceptionally vain and ambitious egotist. His behavior at times scandalized polite society. In 1849, he wrote a letter to his opponent for a U.S. senate seat, Judge Sidney Breese, threatening to kill him. In court one day he smashed another attorney over the head with a legal tome, exclaiming: "If you have no law in your head I'll bate some into it."[163]

In August 1842, Shields, the state auditor, announced that his office would no longer accept in payment of taxes any notes issued by Illinois's state bank. Written the day after this order was published, the second "Rebecca" letter, which Lincoln was to acknowledge as his handiwork, ridiculed Shields as a "conceity dunce" and "a fool as well as a liar" with whom "truth is out of the question, and as for getting a good bright passable lie out of him, you might as well try to strike fire from a cake of tallow." The letter also poked fun at Shields's manliness and vanity, having him say to a group of young women: "Dear girls, *it is distressing*, but I cannot marry you all. Too well I know how much you suffer; but do, do, remember, it is not my fault that I am so handsome and *so* interesting."[164]

Enraged, Shields demanded the author's identity. When Lincoln confessed, the feisty Irishman insisted on a retraction and an apology, alleging that "I have become the object of slander, vituperation and personal abuse, which were I capable of submitting to, I would prove myself worthy of the whole of it."[165] Indeed, he had become such a laughingstock in Springfield that people on the street teased him about it. His law partner, Gustave Koerner, thought that nobody "of the least spirit could have taken those insults without seeking satisfaction, even by arms, if necessary." Shields, Koerner explained, "was a young man who had his reputation for honesty at stake; and to have in addition his personal features and peculiar habits ridiculed in a small but select society in which he daily moved was more than even a saint could have borne."[166]

For guidance, Lincoln turned to his friend, Dr. Elias Merryman, who had once fought a duel and had, as a surgeon, witnessed several others. (Merryman "boasted in his peculiar way that he had killed a white man, a negro and an Indian by virtue of his diploma.")[167] Lincoln told Merryman that "he was wholly opposed to duelling, and would do any thing to avoid it that might not degrade him in the estimation of himself and friends; but, if such *degradation* or a *fight* were the only alternative, he would fight."[168] The notoriously combative Merryman, known as "the bully of Springfield," rather than bringing a cool head to the situation, relished the prospect of a duel between Lincoln and Shields.[169] Acting on Merryman's advice, Lincoln formally replied to Shields that "there is in this so much assumption of facts, and so much menace as to consequences, that I cannot submit to answer that note."[170] When Shields responded with a more temperate and specific letter of complaint, Lincoln again refused to answer until the auditor withdrew his first note. Frustrated by such maneuvers, Shields without further ado issued a challenge.

Perplexed, Lincoln consulted his fellow Whig leader, Albert Taylor Bledsoe, who recalled that Lincoln came to his office one night "with somewhat more than the usual gloom seated on his melancholy face" and said: "That fool letter which I wrote for the Sangamo *Journal* has made Shields mad, and he has challenged me. I have accepted the challenge, and, *without thinking*, I have chosen Dr. Merryman for my second. I believe he would rather see a fight than not; if I have to fight, I will fight; but I don't care about fighting just to gratify Dr. Merryman. Now, if you will come in, and make Dr. Merryman do right (for I know you have more influence with him than any other man), the whole difficulty may be settled." When Bledsoe asked about Merryman's role, Lincoln replied: "the friend of Shields says that if I will explain or apologize he will withdraw the challenge, and the quarrel can be settled honorably to both parties. But Dr. Merryman says, if Shields will first withdraw the challenge, then I will explain or apologize, and the quarrel may be settled honorably to both parties. And there they have come to a deadlock. Now I don't see, if both things have to be done, that it makes much difference which is done first. It seems to me that Dr. Merryman is disposed to stand upon niceties, and I don't think he ought to stand upon niceties in a case of life and death."[171]

Bledsoe recommended to Lincoln, who had the choice of weapons, that he select cavalry broadswords. "I know Shields well," Bledsoe said, "and his courage is not of the truest stamp; there is altogether too much of bluster and bravado about the man . . . ; he is trying to make you back out, and you can make him back out very easily . . . if you will choose broadswords." Bledsoe assured Lincoln that Shields "will never fight you in the world. You are at least seven inches taller than Shields, and your arms are three or four inches longer than his; so that you could cut him down before he could get near enough to touch you. I know you will never do this; because he will never fight you with broadswords. He will show the white feather first."[172] (Shields was approximately 5 feet 8 inches tall; Lincoln was 6 feet 4 inches.)

Following Bledsoe's advice, Lincoln stipulated that the weapons be broadswords "of the largest size" and that the field of honor be divided into two contiguous rectangular zones, each 10 feet wide and 6 feet deep, which the combatants would occupy during the fight. Separating the two zones would be a plank set on edge, which neither duelist could cross over. When Shields's second protested that broadswords were "[b]arbarous weapons for the nineteenth century" and insisted that the duelists use pistols or rifles, Lincoln's second replied: "they are barbarous; so is dueling, for that matter. It is just as well to have the whole thing of a piece."[173]

Lincoln explained his choice of broadswords to Usher F. Linder: "I did not want to kill Shields, and felt sure that I could disarm him . . . ; and furthermore, I didn't want the d–d fellow to kill me, which I rather think he would have done if we had selected pistols."[174] With a broadsword, Lincoln declared, "I could have split him in two."[175] (Lincoln's clever tactic seemed to violate the spirit of the code of honor, which dictated that participants should be equally matched.) Lincoln may have received coaching from Bledsoe, who had learned the broadsword drill at West Point, or from Dr. Merryman, an accomplished swordsman, or from Major Thomas Duncan, a brother-in-law of his friend Josiah M. Lucas.

Because dueling was illegal in Illinois, the affair of honor, scheduled for September 22, was to take place on Missouri soil across the Mississippi River from Alton. (Known as Bloody Island, it had been the scene of earlier duels.) En route to that location, Lincoln and Dr. Merryman stopped at White Hall, where Merryman's friend Elijah Lott, the local postmaster, learned of the impending duel. Eager to avert bloodshed, Lott notified John J. Hardin, who was attending court in nearby Carrollton. Hardin immediately left for Alton, accompanied by Dr. Revel W. English, a Democratic legislator.

On his way to Alton, Lincoln cracked a joke. The situation reminded him, he said, of a Kentuckian who volunteered for service in the War of 1812. As he was about to leave home, his sweetheart presented him a bullet pouch and belt with the embroidered motto: "Victory or Death." In expressing his gratitude, the young man said: "Isn't that rather too strong? Suppose you put 'Victory or Be Crippled.'"[176] When Lincoln and his entourage (Merryman, Bledsoe, and Bledsoe's father, Moses O. Bledsoe) arrived and unloaded a bundle of huge broadswords, onlookers became curious and began speculating. After breakfast at the hotel, Lincoln and Shields, with their seconds and surgeons, boarded a ferry.

Word spread quickly, drawing hundreds of excited residents to the hotel galleries, the streets, and the riverbank. Many clambered aboard the ferry, including the town constable and some would-be peacemakers, among them Lincoln's friends William Butler and John J. Hardin as well as Dr. English and two Altonians, Samuel Buckmaster, director of the state penitentiary, and Dr. Thomas M. Hope, editor of the *Democratic Union* (who five years later would fight a duel himself). The dueling parties sat at opposite ends of the boat.

After the ferry reached Bloody Island, seconds prepared the field of honor while Lincoln remained silent, looking quite sober. He slowly removed from its scabbard a saber resembling a fence-rail (cavalry sabers were 3 1/2 feet in length and weighed nearly 5 pounds), and like a man testing a knife or scythe he had just ground, lightly ran his thumb along the edge. He then arose, lifted the sword high and sliced a twig from an overhanging willow tree.

Meanwhile, the peacemakers sought a compromise. Hardin and English urged both Merriman and Whiteside to submit the matter to four men of their choice who would examine the case and make a recommendation. The leading role was taken by the brusque, loud-voiced Dr. Hope. After vainly begging Shields to compromise, Hope grew angry and declared that the auditor "was bringing the Democratic party of Illinois into ridicule and contempt by his folly." Impatiently, he blurted out: "Jimmy, you — little whippersnapper, if you don't settle this I will take you across my knee and spank you."[177]

That seemed to break the deadlock. Shields's seconds thereupon agreed to withdraw his notes, and in return Lincoln acknowledged: "I did write the 'Lost Township' letter which appeared in the Journal of the 2nd. Inst but had no participation, in any form, in any other article alluding to you. I wrote that, wholly for political effect. I had no intention of injuring your personal or private character, or standing as a man or a gentleman; and I did not then think, and do not now think that that article could produce or has produced that effect against you, and had I anticipated such an effect I would have forborne to write it. And I will add, that your conduct towards me, so far as I knew, had always been gentlemanly; and that I had no personal pique against you, and no cause for any."[178]

All participants in the near-duel took the ferry back to Alton, where a crowd awaited them. A humorist on the boat draped a sheet over a log, making it look like a human body, and fanned it vigorously as if caring for an injured duelist. Shields and Lincoln debarked together, pleasantly conversing as if nothing had happened.

Not surprisingly, the Democratic press lashed out at Lincoln, derisively calling him "Aunt Becca," rebuking him for his "most unwarrantable and unprovoked attack" on Shields, sneering at him for imagining that "an Irishman would run at the sight of a broad *sword*," and ridiculing him as a "valiant man, who once attempted to frighten an Irishman with a broad sword, and who, when he found that impracticable procured his friends to manage 'an amicable settlement.'"[179] The editor of the Shawnee-town *Illinois Republican*, Samuel D. Marshall, was less indignant: "We are gratified to learn that the duel which was to have taken place between our friends Shields and Lincoln did not come off, and that the whole affair was arranged satisfactorily to the parties, without bloodshed. They are both gentlemen of undoubted personal and moral courage, and we feel highly gratified that the matter has terminated thus happily."[180] When the Chicago *Democrat* demanded that Shields and Lincoln be punished, Marshall protested that "the evils of dueling like those of Intemperance must be cured by public opinion and not by the Legislature." Marshall contended that if "Lincoln had refused to fight Mr. Shields no one would have gone further in denouncing him as a coward than the Editor of the *Democrat*," John Wentworth, who "now seeks to impose an infamous punishment on him for doing the very thing he would have abused him most unmercifully for not doing." Marshall declared that once "public opinion makes the refusal to accept as honorable as the offer of a challenge, then come on with your laws but not till then." But as things stood, with "the present most repugnant and incomprehensible state of public opinion upon this subject," Marshall would "deem a conviction for this offence highly disgraceful to the State. So long as public opinion countenances fighting let men fight in 'peace.'" If dueling is to be outlawed, "let the man who sends a challenge be punished alone."[181]

Although Lincoln may have derived some solace from Marshall's words, he was probably startled when a Whig editor, George T. M. Davis, attacked him in the *Alton Telegraph and Democratic Review* for getting involved in a near-duel. Davis scolded the would-be combatants, pointing out that they were lawyers, legislators, and leaders of their communities who had nonetheless blatantly violated the law. Dueling, Davis insisted, "is the calmest, most deliberate and malicious species of murder—a relict of the most cruel barbarism that ever disgraced the darkest periods of the world—and one which every principle of religion, virtue and good order, loudly demands should be put a stop to."[182] Another Whig paper, the Jacksonville *Illinoisan*, chastised Lincoln, Shields, and other potential duelists in Springfield, warning that if they passed through Jacksonville en route to their appointed fields of honor, those "vaunted knights of chivalry" would "be unceremoniously arrested and taken to the first hog-hole and there cooled off."[183] In late September, a Chicagoan sarcastically told Lyman Trumbull that "We are very busy here, indeed too much so to fight duels; but there are a number of gentlemen practicing cut and thrust to prepare themselves for a Winter Campaign in Springfield."[184]

The affair embarrassed Lincoln terribly. The following year the Whig Party rejected his bid for a congressional nomination in part because, as he put it, he "had talked about fighting a duel."[185] After a participant in the near-duel later attempted to discuss it with him, Lincoln said that he "seems anxious to revive the memory of an affair that I am trying to forget."[186] Shortly before his death, he replied abruptly to a question about the Shields affair: "if you desire my friendship you will never mention the circumstance again!"[187] Mary Lincoln told a friend that Lincoln "was always so ashamed" of the near-duel that they agreed never to allude to it.[188] Whenever his colleague at the bar, Henry C. Whitney, tried to get him to talk about the matter, "he always parried the subject, as if he was ashamed of it."[189] In 1858, when Herndon reported to him that people in the East were eager to hear about the Shields affair, Lincoln "regretfully" observed: "If all the good things I have ever done are remembered as long and well as my scrape with Shields, it is plain I shall not soon be forgotten."[190] His embarrassment prompted Lincoln to stop writing abusive anonymous and pseudonymous letters, though he continued to ridicule political opponents in speeches.

Marriage

Five days after helping Lincoln reconcile his differences with Shields, John J. Hardin assisted him in effecting another reconciliation, this time with Mary Todd. Hardin and his wife, who fancied herself a matchmaker, invited Lincoln and Mary to attend the wedding of Hardin's sister Martinette at their home in Jacksonville on September 27. When the young people who were assembled at the Hardins' went for a ride, they left Mary behind because she had no escort. As she sadly watched their carriage depart, she was astonished to see Lincoln ride up. According to the wife of John Todd Stuart, Mary "went down & he said he had come for her to join the party." Off they went and soon were reconciled. Thereafter they met clandestinely at the house of Simeon Francis.[191]

Sarah Rickard recalled a different version of the event: "I sat next to Mr. Lincoln at the wedding dinner. . . . Mary Todd sat just across. Of course, rather than bring constraint upon the company, they spoke to each other, and that was the beginning of the reconciliation."[192] They renewed courting secretly because, as Mary later explained, "the world—woman & man were uncertain & slippery and [we thought] that it was best to keep the secret Courtship from all Eyes & Ears."[193]

A week after that reunion with Mary in Jacksonville, Lincoln asked Joshua Speed a pointed question: "Are you now in *feeling* as well as *judgement*, glad you are married as you are?" He acknowledged that such a query would be "impudent" coming from anyone but himself, but he was sure Speed would pardon him. "Please answer it quickly as I feel impatient to know."[194] Lincoln believed he could not wed Mary Todd unless Speed had found happiness in matrimony. In reply, Speed advised him "not to hesitate or longer doubt that happiness would be the result of his marriage to Miss Todd," and assured Lincoln that he found contentment once "he and Miss Henning had finally made up and determined to risk their happiness in each other's keeping."[195]

Taking this advice, Lincoln wed Mary Todd on November 4 with virtually no advance notice. That morning, the bride-to-be announced to her sister that "she and Mr. Lincoln would get married that night."[196] Similarly, Lincoln informed Charles Dresser, an Episcopal minister, "I want to get hitched tonight."[197] The abruptness startled Elizabeth Edwards, who told an interviewer that the "marriage of Mr L & Mary was quick & sudden—one or two hours notice."[198] The license was issued on the day of the ceremony. Three years earlier, Mrs. Edwards had given her sister Frances an elaborate wedding—"one of the grand affairs of its time"—and counted on providing one for Mary.[199] Such grand events were common among Springfield aristocrats like the Edwardses and Todds.

When Lincoln also told Ninian Edwards of their plans to wed that evening at Dresser's home, he responded: "That will never do. Mary Todd is my ward. If the marriage is going to take place, it must be at my house."[200] His wife Elizabeth also insisted that the ceremony take place in their home, admonishing Mary: "Do not forget that you are a Todd. But, Mary, if you insist on being married today, we will make merry, and have the wedding here this evening. I will not permit you to be married out of my house."[201] She added angrily: "Mary Todd even a free negro would give her family time to bake a ginger cake."[202] Instead they would be compelled to send into town for gingerbread and beer instead of more appropriate fare. Mary, who resented the patronizing attitude of her sister and brother-in-law toward Lincoln as a man of humble origins, replied: "Well, that will be good enough for plebeians I suppose."[203] Those cakes, still warm, arrived just before the ceremony.

A handful of people, including the two groomsmen, James H. Matheny and Beverly Powell, and the two bridesmaids, Julia Jayne and Ann Rodney, gathered in the Edwards home that evening, where the Reverend Dr. Charles N. Dresser performed the ceremony. Matheny recalled that at first "there was more or less stiffness about the affair due, no doubt, to the sudden change of plans and resulting 'town talk,' and I could not help noticing a certain amount of whispering and elevation of eyebrows on the part of a few of the guests, as if preparing each other for something dramatic or unlooked-for to happen." That "something" was provided by the rotund, crude State Supreme Court Justice Thomas C. Browne, known as "the Falstaff of the bench," who habitually blurted out whatever was on his mind. Unfamiliar with the Episcopal service, Browne was nonplussed when the groom turned to the bride and said "with this ring I thee endow with all my goods and chattels, lands and tenements." At that point the judge blurted out: "Lord Jesus Christ, God Almighty, Lincoln, the Statute fixes all that." Startled and amused by this outburst, Parson Dresser paused to stifle the impulse to burst out laughing; after a minute or so he managed to regain his composure and pronounce the couple man and wife.[204]

In commenting on his marriage a week after the ceremony, Lincoln told Samuel D. Marshall: "Nothing new here, except my marrying, which to me, is matter of profound wonder."[205] A newspaper in Winchester found it noteworthy that the duelist of September had become the bridegroom of November: "Linco[l]n, who was to have been flayed alive by the sword of Shields, has given up the notion of dueling, and taken up one no less fatal to bachelors than the sword is to animal existence—in short, he is *married!* 'Grim visaged war hath smoothed his wrinkled front,' and now 'he capers nimbly in a ladys' [chamber]."[206]

After the ceremony, the newlyweds did not take a honeymoon but moved into a no-frills hostelry, the Globe Tavern, a large, ugly frame structure that Lincoln thought "very well kept" and economical, with room and board costing a mere $4 per week.[207] The Globe's proprietor was miserly with candles, and his brief menu consisted primarily of sour buckwheat cakes and corn cakes. Nonetheless, John Todd Stuart and his bride had lived there immediately after their wedding, and Mary's sister Frances and her husband, William Wallace, had spent the early years of their married life at the Globe.

From the outset, people wondered why Lincoln and Mary Todd wed. A guest at the Lincolns' wedding, Mrs. Benjamin S. Edwards, later wrote, "I have often doubted that it was really a love affair." Instead, Mrs. Edwards saw the marriage as a match "made up" by "mutual friends."[208] Ida Tarbell, who queried many friends and relatives of the Lincolns, stated that Abraham and Mary "were utterly unsuited for sympathetic companionship. I doubt if Mary Todd had the faintest conception of the meaning of the words."[209] Eleanor Gridley, who also interviewed people who had known the Lincolns, concluded that Mary Todd did not love Lincoln. Mrs. Gridley asked a biographer of Mrs. Lincoln rhetorically, "if she loved him, would she have often annoyed him, confused him and later when her husband became the most distinguished man of the Commonwealth would she have embarrassed and humiliated him, which she often did? No, rather, if she loved she would have been considerate, thoughtful, careful lest she add another burden to his troubled soul."[210] Yet another woman who interviewed friends and neighbors of the Lincolns in Springfield—including one of Mary's bridesmaids—concluded that the "question whether Lincoln loved her, even when he married her, cannot be answered."[211]

In later years, each of the Lincolns spoke offhandedly about the possibility of the other's dying. Once Mary said that if he were to die, "his spirit will never find me living outside the boundaries of a slave State."[212] In 1857, she told her half-sister Emilie that "I often laugh & tell Mr. L[incoln] that I am determined my next Husband *shall be rich*."[213] For his part, in 1860, Lincoln told an audience in Bloomington: "I think very much of the people, as an old friend said he thought of woman. He said when he lost his first wife, who had been a great help to him in his business, he thought he was ruined—that he could never find another to fill her place. At length, however, he married another, who he found did quite as well as the first, and that his opinion now was that any woman would do well who was well done by."[214] An editor wondered what Mrs. Lincoln would "say of her husband's opinion, that her loss can be so easily and satisfactorily replaced."[215]

Close friends thought that honor and obligation, not love, impelled Lincoln to marry. Herndon asserted that "Lincoln knew that he did not love the girl: he had promised to wed her: he knew what would eventually come of it and it was a conflict between sacrificing his *honor* and sacrificing his *domestic peace:* he chose the latter—saved his honor and threw away domestic happiness."[216] In Joshua Speed's opinion, "Lincoln Married her for honor."[217] According to Orville H. Browning, Lincoln "undoubtedly felt that he had made [a mistake] in having engaged himself to Miss Todd. But having done so, he felt himself in honor bound to act in perfect good faith towards her—and that good faith compelled him to fulfil[l] his engagement with her, if she persisted in claiming the fulfillment of his word." Browning said he "always doubted whether, had circumstances left him entirely free to act upon his own impulses, he would have voluntarily made proposals of marriage to Miss Todd."[218] Mrs. William Butler "advised him if he had given his promise to marry Miss Todd he must in honor keep his word unless she released him."[219]

Others pointed to the purely practical advantage of the marriage for both parties. John Todd Stuart agreed that little love was involved; he told Herndon the marriage "was a policy Match all around."[220] Herndon himself called it a "political match." She wanted Lincoln because he was "a rising man," while he wanted "her family power."[221] It is possible that Lincoln thought he could enhance his political career through a marriage alliance with the more aristocratic Whig element, but such a calculating approach to wedlock seems out of character for Lincoln, who was engaged to Ann Rutledge and later proposed to Sarah Rickard, neither of whom belonged to well-connected Illinois society. A few months after his nuptials, he was defeated for the Whig congressional nomination partly because of his reputation "as the candidate of pride, wealth, and aristocratic family distinction," a reputation that accompanied his new status as an in-law of the Todd family.[222]

On his wedding day, Lincoln, appearing and acting "as if he was going to the Slaughter," said to one of his groomsmen, James Matheny, "I shall have to marry that girl." Matheny reported that Lincoln "often" confided "directly & indirectly" that "he was driven into the marriage."[223] While dressing for the ceremony, he was asked where he was headed. "I guess I am going to hell," came the reply.[224]

All this, coupled with the fact that Mary gave birth slightly less than nine months after the wedding, tends to confirm Wayne C. Temple's hypothesis that she seduced Lincoln the night before and made him feel obliged to wed her immediately in order to preserve her honor.[225] She could not, of course, have known if she were pregnant, but she might have been, and this knowledge could have constrained a man with an exceptionally tender conscience and highly developed sense of honor to marry her, despite strong misgivings. Lincoln's willingness to do so would have been fortified if, as James Matheny alleged, Mary Todd "told L. that he was in honor bound to marry her."[226] This explanation is plausible, if not provable. It helps explain why the wedding took place on such short notice; why Lincoln looked like an animal en route to the slaughter; why he said he was "going to hell"; why he married someone whom he did not love; why Orville H. Browning believed that Lincoln was not "entirely free to act upon his own impulses"; why Herndon claimed that Lincoln "self-sacrificed himself rather than to be charged with dishonor"; and why Lincoln told Matheny that he "had to marry that girl" and that he "was driven into the marriage."[227]

Other considerations make it seem likely that Mary Todd seduced Lincoln in order to trap him into matrimony. It would not have been out of character, for her ethical sense was underdeveloped. Two decades after her wedding, as First Lady of the United States, she accepted bribes, padded expense accounts and payrolls, appropriated wages from White House servants, tried to raid the stationery fund, helped peddle cotton trading permits and pardons, disguised personal expenses in government bills, and engaged in other illegal activities.[228] Moreover, she was 23 years old, rapidly approaching the much-dreaded state of old-maidhood. (In the 1830s and 1840s, women in Sangamon County on average married at 19 and men at 27.) The historian Frank H. Hodder speculated that she "hung on to Lincoln because she knew mighty well that unless she captured some green-horn she would never marry at all."[229] To be sure, she was courted by the lovesick Edwin Bathurst ("Bat") Webb, a courtly, "rather aristocratic" Virginia-born legislator. In early 1842, Webb confided to a friend: "I wish I was married to some quiet sensible body who would love me a little & my children a great deal. I would enter into [a] compact to stay at home & obey orders the balance of my days."[230] But Webb's small children were, in Mary Todd's view, "two *sweet little objections*."[231] His age presented another problem (he was sixteen years her senior).

Neither Lincoln nor Mary Todd seems to have been undersexed. William Herndon considered her "the most sensual woman" he ever knew.[232] William Jayne, brother of Mary Todd's bridesmaid Julia Jayne, recalled that in the early 1840s, Mary was "a woman of . . . strong passions" who was "capable of making herself quite attractive to young gentlemen."[233] Her niece called her "an incorrigible flirt."[234] A Springfield neighbor of the Lincolns remembered that she "dared me once or twice to Kiss her."[235]

Similarly, despite his social awkwardness with girls in his youth, Lincoln was "a Man of strong passion for woman," according to his good friend David Davis, who said that Lincoln's "Conscience Kept him from seduction" and "saved many a woman."[236] Herndon recollected that Lincoln was "a man of terribly strong passions for woman" and "could scarcely keep his hands off them." Lincoln once confessed to Herndon that in the mid-1830s he had succumbed to "a devilish passion" for a girl in Beardstown.[237] Well after his wedding, Lincoln while on the circuit made improper advances to a young woman sleeping in a bed near his. Lincoln told Milton Hay, James H. Matheny, and Herndon that while spending the night at the home of a friend, he was awakened by the foot of his host's grown daughter, which inadvertently "fell on Lincoln's pillow. This put the *devil* into Lincoln at once, thinking that the girl did this of a purpose. Lincoln reached up his hand and put it where it ought not to be. The girl awoke, got up, and went to her mother's bed and told what had happened."

Fortunately for Lincoln, who hurriedly departed the next morning, the mother urged her daughter to keep quiet.[238]

Lincoln told a similar tale to James Short: while surveying in Sangamon County, "he was put to bed in the same room with two girls, the head of his bed being next to the foot of the girls' bed. In the night he commenced tickling the feet of one of the girls with his fingers. As she seemed to enjoy it as much as he did he then tickled a little higher up; and as he would tickle higher the girl would shove down lower and the higher he tickled the lower she moved." Lincoln "would tell the story with evident enjoyment" but "never told how the thing ended."[239] Lincoln said repeatedly "about sexual contact, 'It is the harp of a thousand strings.'" A colleague at the bar, Oliver L. Davis, thought that Lincoln's "mind ran on sexual [matters?]."[240] He liked sexual jokes and stories; in 1859, he asked the newlywed Christopher Columbus Brown, "why is a woman like a barrel?" When Brown admitted his ignorance, Lincoln replied: "You have to raise the hoops before you put the head in."[241] That same year he delivered a lecture on "Discoveries and Inventions" in which he speculated about the first human invention, the fig-leaf apron, remarking with a sly sexual innuendo that "it is very probable she [Eve] took the leading part; he [Adam], perhaps, doing no more than to stand by and thread the needle."[242]

In early adulthood, Lincoln may have patronized prostitutes. As already noted, during the Black Hawk War he and other militiamen visited a whorehouse in Galena. Herndon told Caroline Dall that "Up to the time of Anne Rutledge's death Lincoln was a pure perfectly chaste man. Afterwards in his misery—he fell into the habits of his neighborhood."[243] Herndon alleged that from 1837 to 1842, Lincoln and Joshua Speed, "a lady's man," were "quite *familiar*—to go no further [—] with the women."[244] On at least one occasion Lincoln shared Speed's taste in fancy women—in fact, the very same woman. Speed said that around 1839 or 1840, he "was keeping a pretty woman" in Springfield, and Lincoln, "desirous to have *a little*," asked his bunkmate, "do you know where I can get *some*." Speed replied, "Yes I do, & if you will wait a moment or so I'll send you to the place with a note. You cant get it without a note or by my appearance." Armed with the note from Speed, Lincoln "went to see the girl—handed her the note after a short 'how do you do &c,'. Lincoln told his business and the girl, after some protestations, agreed to satisfy him. Things went on right—Lincoln and the girl stript off and went to bed. Before any thing was done Lincoln said to the girl—'How much do you charge'. 'Five dollars, Mr. Lincoln'. Mr. Lincoln said—'I've only got $3.' Well said the girl—'I'll trust you, Mr Lincoln, for $2.' Lincoln thought a moment or so and said—'I do not wish to go on credit—I'm poor & I don't know where my next dollar will come from and I cannot afford to Cheat you.' Lincoln after some words of encouragement from the girl got up out of bed,—buttoned up his pants and offered the girl the $3.00, which she would not take, saying—Mr Lincoln—'You are the most Conscientious man I ever saw.'"[245]

In New Salem, improbable rumors circulated about Lincoln's sexual adventures. He reportedly sired a daughter with Mrs. Bennett Abell. It was also whispered that Jason Duncan's wife bore Lincoln's child. Similar stories were spread about Lincoln and another of his surrogate mothers, Hannah Armstrong, though that was treated as a joke. Hannah's husband used to tease Lincoln about the supposed child Abe had with Mrs. Armstrong. Later, people joshed the widowed Hannah Armstrong about her alleged trysts with Lincoln. She recalled that early in 1861, as she was about to visit him in Springfield, "the boys got up a story on me that I went to get to sleep with Abe &c—." She replied "that it was not every woman who had the good fortune & high honor of sleeping with a President."[246]

Lincoln had a voyeuristic streak. A New Salem farmer named Joe Watkins kept a stud horse, and "Lincoln requested him that when ever a mare come he would be sure to let him know *it,* as he wanted to *see it.* Watkins did so, and Lincoln always attended."[247]

As a married man, Lincoln continued to show signs of a robust sexuality, though Herndon said he "was true as steel to his wife, during his whole marriage life."[248] Schuyler Colfax, speaker of the U.S. House of Representatives during the Civil War, recalled that he and Lincoln "often went to Ford's opera house to regale ourselves of an evening, for we felt the strain on mind and body was often intolerable." They found "real relaxation" in watching "those southern girls with their well rounded forms, lustrous hair and sparkling voices. We thought it a veritable treat to see them dance and hear their song."[249] Also at Ford's Theatre, Lincoln and his assistant personal secretary John Hay one night "occupied [a] private box" where both men "carried on a hefty flirtation with the Monk Girls in the flies."[250] At a White House reception, Lincoln shook hands with a beautiful woman as she passed through the receiving line; when she prepared to leave, he offered to shake her hand once more. When she remarked that he had already done so, he smilingly replied: "Yes, but madame, you are so good looking that I would like to shake hands with you again."[251]

As president, Lincoln allegedly told a friend: "I believe there is even a system of female brokerage in offices here in Washington, for I am constantly beset by women of all sorts, high and low, pretty and ugly, modest and the other sort. Here, yesterday, a very handsome young lady called; she would not take a denial, was admitted, and went straight to work soliciting a certain office for somebody supposed to be her husband. She pled her cause dexterously, eloquently, and at times was almost successful by her importunate entreaties. By degrees she came closer and closer to me as I sat in my chair, until really her face was so near my own that I thought she wanted me to kiss her; when my indignation came to my relief, and drawing myself back and straightening myself up, I gave her the proper sort of a look and said: 'Mrs.—, you are very pretty, and it's very tempting, BUT I WON'T.'"[252]

Thus it seems reasonable to conclude that if Mary Todd did try to seduce Lincoln in November 1842, she was in all likelihood successful. Twenty-three years later, she clearly indicated that she thought her husband was seducible. On March 26, 1865, while the Lincolns were visiting General Grant's headquarters at City Point, Virginia, Mrs. Lincoln and Mrs. Grant traveled to the front, escorted by Grant's aide Adam Badeau. That officer, to make conversation on the long carriage ride, speculated that a battle would soon occur, for officers' wives had been ordered to the rear; the only exception had been Mrs. Charles Griffin, to whom the president had issued a special permit. Mrs. Lincoln bristled at the news: "What do you mean by that, sir? . . . Do you mean to say that she saw the President alone? Do you know that I never allow the President to see any woman alone?"[253]

It is possible that Lincoln knew that Mary Todd would make his life miserable when he married her, but Herndon believed that she changed dramatically after the wedding. Before marriage, he asserted, she was "rather pleasant—polite—civil—rather graceful in her movements—intelligent, [and] witty." Indeed, she could be "affable and even charming in her manners." But "after she got married she became soured—got gross—became material—avaricious—insolent—mean—insulting—imperious; and a she wolf." Herndon thought that the wolf "was in her when young and unmarried, but she unchained it . . . when she got married. Discretion when young kept the wolf back for a while, but when there was no more necessity for chaining it was unchained to growl—snap & bite at all."[254] Herndon frequently saw her in "spells of frenzy."[255]

Abundant evidence supports Herndon's characterization of Mary Lincoln as a "tigress," a "she-wolf," and the "*female wild cat of the age.*"[256] (When she was First Lady during the Civil War, the two main presidential secretaries referred to her as "the Hell-Cat" and "Her Satanic Majesty," and the presidential physician, Dr. Robert K. Stone, thought her "a perfect devil." The commissioner of public buildings, who had frequent contact with her, likened Mary Lincoln to a hyena.)[257] James Matheny declared that "*Ferocity*—describes Mrs L's conduct to L."[258] A Springfield neighbor, James Gourley, reported that the Lincolns "got along tolerably well, unless Mrs. L got the devil in her." According to Gourley, she "was gifted with an unusually high temper" that "invariably got the better of her." If "she became excited or troublesome, as she sometimes did when Mr. Lincoln was at home, . . . he would apparently pay no attention to her. Frequently he would laugh at her, which is a risky thing to do in the face of an infuriated wife; but generally, if her impatience continued, he would pick up one of the children and deliberately leave home as if to take a walk. After he had gone, the storm usually subsided, but sometimes it would break out again when he returned."[259] A carpenter who worked on the Lincolns' house, Page Eaton, recalled that Mary "was rather quick-tempered" and "used to fret and scold about a great deal."[260] Peter Van Bergen once heard her "yelling & screaming at L. as if in hysterics."[261]

Women as well as men found Mary Lincoln bad-tempered and even violent. Her half-sister Emilie said that sometimes she "would get into a temper when things did not go just right."[262] Harriet Hanks noted that she had an "ungovernable temper," which Mrs. John A. Logan characterized as "really a species of madness."[263] Martinette Hardin and her friends did not much like her cousin Mary Todd because "she had such a bad temper."[264] A woman who interviewed Mary Lincoln's "personal and intimate friends" said they depicted her as a person "of violent temper, ungovernable and willful beyond all reason and when her will was defied she indulged in a series of outrageous tantrums, which so tormented her patient husband that he was well nigh distracted."[265] Another woman who spoke with Springfield friends of the Lincolns reported that "Mrs. Lincoln was sharp and shrewish with an uncontrolled temper," and "every one I met could give me some example of it." One instance concerned a young man who danced with Mary Todd in 1839. When she used a French phrase, he replied: "I don't understand dog Latin." She lashed out, saying: "Strange for a puppy not to understand his native language."[266] A woman who lived in Springfield in the 1850s recalled that Mary Lincoln had "attacks of what we called in those days, hysteria."[267] Neither Mrs. James Leaton, wife of Springfield's Methodist minister, nor Mrs. Noah Matheny "regarded Mrs. Lincoln very highly—that is her temper and disposition generally was not at all commendable."[268]

Mary Lincoln abused her husband physically as well as verbally. When a farmer peddling apples door-to-door approached Lincoln, "Mrs. Lincoln came out and demanded of her husband why he was purchasing apples and set upon him with such violence that he feared Lincoln was in actual physical danger from his wife."[269] Lincoln got a taste of her temper shortly after their wedding. One morning at the Globe Tavern she arrived late for breakfast, as usual, inconveniencing the other guests. Boardinghouse etiquette dictated that in the morning, no one could eat until all guests were seated at the table. Lincoln, evidently irritated and embarrassed, gently chided her as she entered the room. She instantly sprang up, threw a cup of hot coffee at him, and fled in hysterics.[270] Lincoln "sat there in humiliation and silence" while Mrs. Jacob Early helped clean him up.[271] A similar event took place at dinner one night in December 1860. Thurlow Weed witnessed her outburst when Lincoln "cracked a joke which displeased Mrs. Lincoln because she erroneously imagined it to be at her expense. Quicker than a flash she picked up a cup of hot tea and flung it clear across the table at Mr. Lincoln's head, then jumped up in great fury and rushed out of the room."[272]

Now and then Mary Lincoln physically injured her husband. One day when Lincoln, absorbed in his newspaper, permitted the fire in the parlor to die down and then ignored several requests to add some fuel, Mary struck him with a piece of firewood, declaring: "I'll make you hear me this time." The next day he appeared in court with a bandaged nose.[273] On another occasion Jesse K. Dubois accompanied Lincoln to the house on Eighth Street by way of the butcher shop, where Lincoln picked up meat intended for some visitors from Kentucky. When Mary unwrapped the meat, she was so upset at her husband's choice that she became enraged, "abused L[incoln] outrageously" and hit him in the face. He wiped off the blood and returned to the office with Dubois.[274] As the Civil War drew to a close, a White House steward observed Mary Lincoln assault her husband: she allegedly "Struck him hard—damned him—cursed him."[275]

Mary Lincoln also attacked her husband with cleaning implements, cutlery, and vegetables. The daughter of Springfield's Methodist minister in the late 1850s heard her mother say that the Lincolns "were very unhappy in their domestic life" and that Mary Lincoln "was seen frequently to drive him from the house with a broomstick."[276] One day in the mid-1850s, a knife-wielding Mary Lincoln chased her husband through their yard. When he realized that they were being observed, he suddenly wheeled about, grabbed his wife, and marched her back, saying: "There d—n it, now Stay in the house and don't disgrace us before the Eyes of the world."[277] One day Lincoln fled the house as his wife vented her anger with "very poorly pitched potatoes."[278] Other neighbors occasionally saw "the front door of the Lincoln home . . . fly open and papers, books, [and] small articles would literally be hurled out."[279] On another occasion, as Lincoln prepared to depart Springfield for a nearby town, his "wife ran him out [of the house] half dressed" and followed him with [a] broom." Lincoln told the serving girl "not to get scared" but to bring him some clothing, which he donned and then "went up town through [the] woodhouse & alley."[280] Thus Turner R. King, a political ally of Lincoln, had good reason to characterize Mary Lincoln as "a hellion—a she devil" who "vexed—& harrowed the soul out of that good man" and "drove him from home &c—often & often."[281] Similarly, in 1862 Herndon was fully justified in exclaiming: "Poor Lincoln! He is domestically a desolate man—has been for years to my own knowledge" because of his marriage to "a very curious—excentric—*wicked* woman."[282]

The hired help also felt Mary Lincoln's wrath. She frequently struck servants and had trouble keeping them because of her tyrannical ways. One day when a servant displeased Mrs. Lincoln, she had the girl's trunk thrown into the middle of the street. Similarly, she ordered a servant boy, Phillip Dinkel, "to get out, and threw his suit case out the window after him." On another occasion, she hired a servant girl to help the two she already had, then fired all three within a day.[283] After being hit by Mary, one servant complained to her uncle, a miller named Jacob Tiger. When Tiger asked Mary Lincoln for an explanation, she struck him with a broom. Tiger then demanded satisfaction of Lincoln, who mournfully replied, "can't you endure this one wrong done you by a mad woman without much complaint for old friendship's sake while I have had to bear it without complaint and without a murmur for lo these last fifteen years[?]"[284]

Mary behaved similarly toward her sons, though she sometimes repented afterward. Neighbors recalled that she was "turbulent—loud—always yelling at children" and "was prone to excitability and rather impulsive, saying many things that were sharp and caustic, and which she afterward usually regretted."[285] She lashed out corporally as well as verbally. One day she brought home a new clock, which she told her sons not to touch. According to Mrs. Benjamin S. Edwards, a "short time afterward she went into the room and found that two of them had taken the clock to pieces. She whipped them."[286] Describing the conduct of his wayward young son Robert, Lincoln in 1846 told Joshua Speed that "by the time I reached the house, his mother had found him, and had him whip[p]ed."[287] She did not always rely on others to punish the lad; in fact, a servant in the house recalled that Mary Lincoln "would whip Bob a good deal."[288] She once "held a private-strapping party" with her youngest son, Tad, after he had fallen into a mud puddle.[289] Elizabeth Edwards said her sister Mary had a "high temper and after her outburst[s] normally was penitent. If she punished [the] children [she] would seek to make amends by presents and affectionate treatment."[290]

Occasionally Lincoln would intervene to protect his children from their mother's wrath. One summer afternoon she accused a son of stealing 10¢, flew into a rage when he denied it, and beat his legs with a switch. The punishment ceased as Lincoln entered the room, where the boy cringed in fright as his mother stood over him. When Lincoln asked what had happened, she replied incoherently. Lincoln solved the crisis by having the boy empty his pockets, then turned to his wife and said tenderly, "Mary! Mary!"[291]

Now and then these roles were reversed: Lincoln would use corporal punishment, and his wife would object. Once he found young Robert and his friends putting on a play with dogs. The boys fastened a rope around one canine's neck, tossed the rope over a beam, and tugged hard to make the beast rise up. When the animal-loving Lincoln beheld the scene, he grabbed a barrel stave "and immediately began plying it indiscriminately on the persons of such boys as were within reach." Mary Lincoln reportedly "was very angry, and reproached her husband in language that was not at all adapted to Sunday School."[292] Harriet Hanks Chapman observed Lincoln as he "undertook to correct his Child" corporally. His wife, "determined that he Should not," tried to take from him whatever implement he was using to administer discipline, but "in this She failed," whereupon she "tried tongue lashing but met with the Same fate, for Mr Lincoln corrected his Child as a Father ought to do, in the face of his Wife[']s anger and that too without even Changing his Countenance, or making enny reply to his wife."[293]

Mary Lincoln continued to practice harsh discipline during her husband's presidency. One day during the Civil War, Tad mutilated a new pair of copper-toed shoes which he disliked because they reminded him of the so-called Copperheads (Democratic opponents of his father's administration). According to the White House steward, when Mrs. Lincoln "was about to whip him, he rushed to his father's office and complained that, because it was against his principles to patronize 'the copperheads,' even with his toes, he was about to suffer. The President caught him in his arms and said, 'I guess I must exercise my Executive clemency a little, and pardon you, my patriotic boy; you shall not be whipped for this offence. Go and explain your case to your mother as it now stands.'"[294] Mary Pinkerton, who as a young girl frequently visited the White House to play with the Lincoln children, recalled how Tad would sometimes tease her and pull her hair. When she complained to the president, he "would dry my tears and tell Tad he should be ashamed for teasing such a little girl—and then maybe for a whole hour Tad and I would be good friends again." But, she noted, things were "different when Mrs. Lincoln was the judge. She had a terrible temper—and when I would go to her with my stories about Tad, she would punish him severely." Although the president "was always so kind and gentle," his wife "was often short-tempered and bitter-tongued."[295]

Throughout his marriage Lincoln would flee the house in search of peace and quiet. Herndon recalled that Lincoln, after marital squabbles, often came to their office early, accompanied by his young son Robert. There Lincoln, "full of sadness," would sit quietly. Realizing that he "was driven from home, by a club—knife or tongue," Herndon discreetly left so that his melancholy partner could regain his composure.[296] One morning, after Lincoln and Robert finished breakfast at a restaurant, the father remarked: "Well, Robby, this ain't so very bad after all, is it? If ma don't conclude to let us come back we will board here all summer."[297] (Turner R. King alleged that sometimes Mary Lincoln refused to cook for her husband.) Herndon said that Lincoln once lived in the office "for three days at a time on cracker[s] & cheese."[298] To enable him to sleep over at the office "on nights of domestic discord," Lincoln purchased a couch 6 and 1/2 feet long.[299]

At times Lincoln sought refuge with a fellow lawyer. A visitor to a Springfield attorney one morning observed a tall gentleman silently enter the office and proceed to the back room. After lunch, the lawyer said, "Why, Mr. Lincoln, I had forgotten your coming in here. I did n't remember that you were in the back room, or I would have asked you to go home to dinner with me. Folks away?" Lincoln "looked very serious. 'No, folks are not away, I'm away.'" The attorney later explained to a friend that "this has happened before. Sometimes Mr. Lincoln's home is not very agreeable, though he has never been known to speak of it, but I know that he takes it very much to heart and that it breaks him up when anything occurs. He has his own office near here with a partner and clerks, but he has come in to find a quiet place. I supposed when he went in that he had come to consult some law book that I had in the other room, but he has probably sat silently there all this time."[300]

According to Josiah P. Kent, a neighbor of the Lincolns, it "was never difficult to locate" Mary Todd Lincoln. "It mattered not who was present when she fell into a rage, for nothing would restrain her. . . . Her voice was shrill and at times so penetrating, especially when summoning the children or railing at some one whose actions had awakened her temper, she could easily be heard over the neighborhood." Whenever she exploded, Kent thought it was "little wonder that Mr. Lincoln would suddenly think of an engagement he had downtown, grasp his hat, and start for his office."

Mrs. Lincoln alienated tradesmen as well as her husband and their neighbors. When she accused the iceman of "swindling her in weight," that gentleman "got mad—cursed—and vowed she should never get ice again." After he "refused to come in her part of town," Mary Lincoln offered Kent 25¢ if it would induce him to sell her ice once again. On another occasion, she offered Kent a quarter to drive her in the family carriage while Lincoln was away. She evidently gave the money to her son Bob to pay Kent, who alleged that he had not received any cash from the boy. She then "became angry and shouted 'Don[']t you tell me Bob didn't pay you.'"[301]

Dinner parties at the Lincoln home frequently ended with Mary berating her husband. Herndon, who thought the "suppers were very fine indeed," reported that she would invite members of the Springfield elite, while Lincoln would "choose a few of his boon companions to make things lively" and swap stories with them. After the guests had departed, the hostess "would be as mad as a disturbed hornet" and "lecture L[incoln] all night, till he got up out of bed in despair and went whistling through the streets & alleys till day &c. &c. It would take a ream of paper to write it all out just as it did often happen."[302] Mary Lincoln's nephew, Albert S. Edwards, confirmed part of Herndon's story when he told a journalist: "I can remember that when I was a boy the trouble Mr. Lincoln used to cause at social gatherings. He would get a crowd around him in the gentlemen's room and start a conversation, with the result that the ladies would be left alone downstairs, and would have to send some one to break up Mr. Lincoln's party, in order to get the gentlemen downstairs."[303]

Sometimes to avoid his wife Lincoln would depart Springfield altogether. According to Anna Eastman Johnson, a neighbor during the 1850s, one evening Lincoln, carrying "a prodigious carpet-bag," appealed to her father: "Mary is having one of her spells, and I think I had better leave her for a few days. I didn't want to bother her, and I thought as you and I are about the same size, you might be kind enough to let me take one of your clean shirts! I have found that when Mrs. Lincoln gets one of these nervous spells, it is better for me to go away for a day or two."[304] A couple in a nearby house recalled "that they always knew when Mrs. Lincoln was having a tantrum, for Mr. Lincoln would appear at their home with a small desk and say, 'May I leave these papers with you? Mrs. Lincoln is not well today.'"[305] Lincoln's stepnephew John J. Hall alleged that during the summer of 1846 or 1847 his uncle Abraham visited Coles County evidently to escape his wife.[306] One evening Abner Y. Ellis, postmaster of Springfield, swapped stories with Lincoln at the post office until nearly midnight. Finally, Lincoln sighed, "Well I hate to go home." When Ellis invited him to stay at his house, he accepted.[307]

Even church did not soften Mary's temper. According to Herndon, while she attended worship services, Lincoln would watch after their children. Once, upon emerging from church, she observed Lincoln conversing with a friend; indignantly she screamed at him and chased him home. On another occasion, she yelled at him on the street when he failed to notice that one of their boys had fallen from the wagon he had absentmindedly been pulling.

Such episodes took place both indoors and out of doors. One day while Mary Lincoln was running errands, her husband stayed home to supervise a carpenter. When that craftsman summoned Lincoln to ask for advice, Mary returned home to discover her youngest son howling. The carpenter reported that she "had rather a hasty temper and at once she sought her husband and berated him soundly for letting the child sit on the floor and cry." Lincoln replied, "Why, Mary, he's just been there a minute," and picked up the lad and cuddled him.[308] It is little wonder that some observers likened the Lincolns' marriage to that of Socrates and Xanthippe.[309]

When in widowhood Mary Lincoln applied for a pension, many witnesses testified before a congressional committee that she "had been a curse to her husband."[310] Sarah Corneau, a neighbor of the Lincolns, said that her family and others living near the house at Eighth and Jackson Streets thought "the most wonderful thing" about the tall lawyer "was the patience and forbearance which Lincoln seemed to have with his wife, who . . . had locally established the name of being almost a shrew."[311] Mrs. Charlotte Rodrigues DeSouza, who made dresses for Mary Lincoln, described her as a nervous, highly strung woman who sometimes tried the unusually mild and gentle temperament of her husband.[312] Jane King, a playmate of Tad Lincoln, felt "actual hatred" for Mary Lincoln, whom she considered a "horrid woman."[313] A journalist stationed in Springfield in 1860 later wrote that the "curse of Lincoln's life" was his "unhappy mad wife."[314]

In Springfield, men like William Herndon and Milton Hay understandably called Lincoln "woman whipt," "woman cowed," and "hen pecked."[315] Ordinarily Lincoln submitted to spousal tirades quietly, believing that "it is better at times to let a woman have her way."[316] Mary Lincoln regularly shouted at her husband when she needed firewood. According to a historian of Springfield, from "the kitchen door would issue the loud exclamation of 'Fire! Fire! Fire!' The neighborhood understood that there was need for wood in the kitchen and his [Lincoln's] acknowledgment was contained in the simple, mild reply, 'Yes Mary, yes Mary.'"[317] On a train trip, Mary Lincoln was, according to a fellow passenger, "almost hysterical about the baggage and fairly forced Mr. Lincoln to walk back three-quarters of a mile . . . to see that it was safe—which he did uncomplainingly."[318]

Mary Lincoln took a dim view of her in-laws. When Eleanor Gridley interviewed neighbors, friends, and relations of Lincoln, she "found verified evidence that Mrs. Lincoln would neither permit her children to see the old stepmother, of whom Mr. Lincoln was fond, nor allow her to visit them at her home. But, Mr. Lincoln never spoke disparagingly of his wife. 'Mary is so busy,' or 'she cannot be parted from her children for a day.' None of them, however, believed his excuses, but forgave him for the act."[319] According to Herndon, "Mrs. Lincoln held the Hanks tribe in contempt and the Lincoln family generally—the old folks—Thomas Lincoln & his good old wife. Mrs. Lincoln was terribly aristocratic and as haughty & as imperious as she was autocratic: she was as cold as a chunk of ice. Thomas Lincoln and his good old wife were never in this city [Springfield]."[320] Mary Lincoln "refused furiously" her husband's request to let the adolescent son of his stepbrother, John D. Johnston, live at their home and attend Springfield schools.[321]

Mary was scarcely more kind to some of her own kin. Dr. Albert A. North of Springfield once hired a relative of hers to conduct some business for him. When the young man arrived in the Illinois capital, he called to pay his respects to Mrs. Lincoln, who "told the young gentleman in coarse, cruel, and brutish language that she did not wish her poor relatives to pile themselves on her and eat her up." He then "tried to explain to her that out of respect he had called to see her, said he had plenty of money and had a good position and did not need her charity and did not deserve her coarse, savage, and brutal language; he quickly left the house, deeply mortified, leaving Mrs. Lincoln in one of her haughty, imperious, and angry states." After Lincoln apologized and offered to help the young man out, he allegedly called Lincoln "one of the noblest of men" and his wife "a savage."[322] Another relative who offended Mary Lincoln was the daughter of her cousin Dr. Lyman Beecher Todd. According to Harriet Hanks Chapman, who was living with the Lincolns at the time, Mrs. Lincoln excluded the young woman when inviting guests to a party because Miss Todd "had intimated that Robert L. . . . was a sweet child but not good looking."[323]

Mary Lincoln was angry at her husband in part because he made comparatively little money. Charles Arnold, a Springfield neighbor of the Lincolns, said Elizabeth Edwards "was the social leader of Springfield and she gave fine parties. Mrs. Lincoln was poor and she resented the way people passed her by. She was hurt and envious."[324] In 1857 Mary Lincoln complained to her half-sister Emilie that when in New York she saw passenger steamers about to sail for Europe, "I felt in my heart, inclined to sigh, that poverty was my portion, how I long to go to Europe."[325] J. G. McCoy recalled that Mary Lincoln "was ambitious to shine in a social way, beyond Mr. Lincoln's inclination or financial ability to sustain, and was given to scolding and complaining of Mr. Lincoln in a manner and to a[n] extent exceedingly unpleasant to him."[326] William T. Baker described her as "a woman whose tastes and desires demanded larger finances than Mr. Lincoln could arrange for" and was therefore "dissatisfied with the progress that Mr. Lincoln was making."[327]

Preston H. Bailhache, a physician in practice with Mary Lincoln's brother-in-law, recalled that she "was very desirous of having a carriage to take herself and packages home, but was unable to persuade Mr. Lincoln to purchase one." Intent on shaming him, she one day called at his office and informed him that she had arranged for a vehicle to carry him home. Giving no signs of surprise, he calmly descended the stairs and beheld "an old fashioned one-horse dray," to which Mrs. Lincoln pointed and said, "There is your carriage." He smiled and clambered aboard, urging her to follow his lead. She did not appreciate the joke and refused his offer. Lincoln then instructed the driver to convey him to Eighth and Jackson.[328]

Lincoln gladly ceded control of the household to his spouse. He once said, "I myself manage all important matters. In little things I have got along through life by letting my wife run her end of the machine pretty much in her own way."[329] When a workman hesitated to chop down a shade tree before their house, Lincoln asked: "Have you seen Mrs. L?" Told that it was her idea, he exclaimed: "Then in God's name cut it down clean to the roots!"[330] One day Mary Lincoln "casually observed at the breakfast table that she was without a cook." Although she had not specifically requested him to hire one, Lincoln did so anyway, only to have her reject the person he chose. After several such incidents, Lincoln quietly bowed out of household affairs and, probably with some relief, let her have her way.[331]

Mary Lincoln was not well regarded as a cook or hostess. She had been raised in a house full of servants who prepared all the meals. A slave called Aunt Chaney, "well trained by Mrs. Todd's mother," was "an autocrat in the kitchen, resenting any intrusion into her domain."[332] Dennis Hanks's daughter Harriet, who spent a year and a half in the Lincoln home during the mid-1840s, recalled that the family table "was usually set vary Sparingly. Mrs. Lincoln was vary *economical* So much so that *by Some She* might have been pronounced Stingy."[333] Elizabeth Edwards said that her sister Mary "loved fine clothes and was so close or economical at the kitchen [so] that she might have money for luxuries" and was "economical, even requiring Robert to wash dishes."[334] According to Herndon, "Mrs. Lincoln was a very stingy woman" whose "table at home generally was economized to the smallest amount." On top of Mary's unpredictable temper, the likelihood of a disappointing meal made Lincoln reluctant to ask friends to his home. David Davis told Herndon "that Lincoln never invited him to his house," and Herndon "heard many others of Lincoln's best friends say the same thing." For his own part, however, Lincoln did not mind that she "set a poor table," for, as Herndon put it, he "ate mechanically" and "filled up and this is all: he never complained of bad food nor praised the good."[335]

Mary Lincoln could be as tightfisted as her husband was generous. Herndon maintained that Lincoln could "never say 'No' to any one who puts up a poor mouth, but will hand out the last dollar he has, sometimes when he needs it himself, and needs it badly."[336] The Lincolns quarreled about the wages of servants, including a young woman who wanted a raise from $1.25 per week to $1.50. Mary refused, telling the girl to leave if she could not accept the smaller salary. Lincoln very much wanted the servant to stay, so when he failed to persuade Mary, he tried to make a clandestine deal with the girl to feign accepting the $1.25 on the condition that he would surreptitiously make up the difference. Mary overheard this and barged in, exclaiming, "What are you doing—I heard Some Conversation—Couldn't understand it—I'm not going to be deceived—Miss[,] you Can leave[,] and as for you Mr L[,] I'd be ashamed of myself."[337] Lincoln himself hired Margaret Ryan, promising her a 75¢ bonus and instructing her "not to fuss with Mrs. L."[338]

Another domestic dustup occurred when young John F. Mendosa and his father were selling blackberries to Mrs. Lincoln, who balked at the asking price of 15¢ per pint. She "started to run them down because they were so small" and refused to pay more than 10¢. When Lincoln observed this haggling, he gave the lad a quarter for a pint, much to his spouse's dismay. According to Mendosa, she "scolded Mr. Lincoln for taking them. Mr. Lincoln spoke up and told me to tell father that it was cheap enough, that he had earned every cent of it, and more too."[339]

Sometimes Lincoln used guile to cope with his wife's penuriousness. A young man once asked him to contribute to the fund drive of the local fire department. "Well," replied he, "I'll go home to supper and ask Mrs. Lincoln what she has to say. After supper she will be in good humor, and I will ask her if we shall give fifty dollars. She will say, 'Abe, when will you learn some sense? Twenty dollars is enough.' Come around in the morning and get your money." This approach worked.[340]

Always able to laugh at himself, Lincoln relished jokes about henpecked husbands. He probably identified with the hapless Mr. Jones whom he described as "one of your meek men" with "the reputation of being badly henpecked." A few days after Mrs. Jones "was seen switching him out of the house," a friend told him that a "man who will stand quietly and take a switching from his wife, deserves to be horsewhipped." Jones responded, "why, it didn't *hurt* me any; and you've no idea what a *power* of *good* it did Sarah Ann!"[341]

Lincoln was "much amused" when Henry C. Whitney read him a story about two fellows who met after a long separation.

"Where have you been, Jim?"

"Oh! It was so quiet at home, I 'listed and have been in the war since I saw you—and where have you been?"

"Oh! Susie made so much war on me at home that I went out timbering in the woods to get a little peace."[342]

During the Civil War, when asked if Clement L. Vallandigham, a banished Democratic critic of the administration, should be captured and tried if he returned from exile, Lincoln responded: "Perhaps the best way to treat him would be to do as the man did who had been annoyed with a very troublesome wife, and who had been relieved by her absconding, and who by no means desired her return, and who therefore advertised *one cent reward* for her return."[343] Lincoln told Chauncey Depew the story of a farmer who consulted him about obtaining a divorce after he and his wife had quarreled over the color to paint their new house. His client explained, "I wanted it painted white like our neighbors', but my wife preferred brown. Our disputes finally became quarrels. She has broken crockery, throwing it at my head, and poured scalding tea down my back, and I want a divorce." Lincoln urged the couple to compromise their differences for the sake of their children. A month later the farmer reported that he and his wife had reached a compromise: "we are going to paint the house brown."[344] Lincoln was fond of quoting from his favorite poet, Robert Burns, these lines: "Sic a wife as Willie had, / I would no gie a button for her."[345]

Milton Hay pitied Lincoln. In 1862 he said of the president: "Poor man! I think some woman ought to talk kindly to him, and I suppose he has got to go from home to hear it."[346] Lincoln regarded that home with understandable misgivings. When he came back to Eighth Street from work, he usually entered the kitchen, inquired about his wife's mood, and only then passed through the front door.[347]

Herndon alleged that Lincoln usually paid his wife no heed when she was enraged but that occasionally he would flare up. Remorsefully, Lincoln admitted to Herndon one Monday that the previous day, when Mary "had annoyed him to the point of exasperation," he "lost his habitual self-control." She "was in a tirade so fierce" that he grabbed her, "pushed her through the door," and exclaimed: "If you can't stop this abuse, damn you, get out." Lincoln told Herndon "that he was deeply sorry for this act. He was not accustomed to lose his temper. . . . Lincoln thought it possible that some people on their way to church had seen the incident, and he was greatly depressed that he had permitted himself to do and say what he had done and said."[348]

Mary Lincoln may have suffered from what a Springfield neighbor called "monthly derangements" (which later came to be known as premenstrual stress). Frederick I. Dean, whose family lived directly across Eighth Street from the Lincolns, said that as a boy he "noticed strange vagaries on the part of Mrs. Lincoln." He informed a historian that from overheard conversations he got the idea that the vagaries were regular, brief, and stemmed from "a functional derangement common alone to women." Shortly after Lincoln's assassination, when Dean spoke to William Herndon about these matters, the attorney "said they corresponded exactly with his own ideas, and exactly in line with what Mr Lincoln had frequently himself told him, with broken tearful voice."[349]

Mary Lincoln suffered from many anxieties. She panicked at the first sign of a thunderstorm, prompting Lincoln to leave his office "to quiet her fears and comfort her until the storm was over."[350] When he was out of town, she would become frightened and turn to neighbors for relief. James Gourley recalled one such occasion: "Mrs Lincoln had a bad girl [servant] living with her: the boys & men used to Come to her house in L[incoln']s absence and scare her: She was crying & wailing one night—Called me and said—'Mr Gourly—Come—do Come & Stay with me all night—you can Sleep in the bed with Bob and I.'"[351] While her husband was away, she hired neighborhood boys to spend the night in her house. Fred I. Dean recalled that Mrs. Lincoln "had me, young as I was, to sleep in the house, with some of the other neighbors' boys."[352] After Robert Todd Lincoln went off to boarding school in

1859, Josiah Kent stayed with Mary Lincoln in her spouse's absence. "I spent many a night at the house, sleeping usually in the same room which Robert had occupied," Kent recollected.[353] While on similar duty in the early 1850s, Howard M. Powel noticed that "Mrs. Lincoln was very nervous and subsequently easily scared." One night "some miscreant came and made a hideous noise against the weatherboarding of the house and Mrs. Lincoln promptly fainted."[354]

Another Springfield neighbor, Elizabeth A. Capps, reported that "Mrs. Lincoln was a bright woman, well educated, but so nervous and crazy acting she was the laughingstock of the neighborhood."[355] Mrs. Capps recalled a day that neighbors came running to Mary's cries of "fire!" only to find fat burning in a pan. On another occasion Mary screamed "Murder!" because an old, bearded umbrella repair peddler was loitering on the back porch waiting for her. On departing, the umbrella man mumbled, "I wouldn't have such a fool for my wife!"[356] A Springfield man heard a peddler one day describe how he had "knocked at Mrs. Lincoln's door, as at any door, and had stepped in when she answered the knock and had started to open his pack." Mary Lincoln began "to scream and carry on" and repeatedly yelled "for him 'to leave, to leave, to leave.'" The peddler sought out Lincoln and told him: "If you have any influence over your wife in God's world, go home and teach her some sense."[357] To her neighbor John B. Weber, Mary Lincoln once screamed: "Keep this little dog from biting me." Weber described the canine as "a little thing" that was "too small and good natured to do anything."[358]

For all the misery she caused Lincoln, creating what his law partner aptly called "a domestic hell on earth," Mary Todd proved a useful goad to his ambition.[359] John Todd Stuart told an interviewer that she "made him Presdt." She "had the fire—will and ambition—Lincoln[']s talent & his wife[']s Ambition did the deed." Stuart heard Joshua Speed say that "Lincoln needed driving—(well he got that.)"[360] Mary Lincoln's friend James Bradwell thought that she "made Mr. L. by constantly pushing him on in his ambition."[361] Charles Arnold, who lived across the street from the Lincolns, declared that she was "very ambitious for her husband" and "kept nagging her husband on."[362] Her sister Elizabeth testified that "Mrs. Lincoln was an ambitious woman—the most ambitious woman I ever saw—spurred up Mr. Lincoln, pushed him along and upward—made him struggle and seize his opportunities."[363] A law student in the Lincoln and Herndon office stated that "there is no doubt that she was constantly spurring him on for she was very ambitious."[364] Herndon less charitably likened her to a toothache that "kept one awake night and day."[365]

During her courtship, Mary allegedly described "the man of her choice, mentioning his unprepossessing appearance and awkwardness, and with a merry appreciation of the humor of the prediction, again said: 'But I mean to make him the President of the United States all the same. You will see that, as I always told you, I will yet be the President's wife.'"[366] In the late 1840s, she predicted to Ward Hill Lamon that Lincoln "is to be President of the United States some day; if I had not thought so I never would have married him, for you can see he is not pretty."[367]

Mary Lincoln's ambition for her husband became a byword in central Illinois. In 1856, when friends urged Lincoln to seek the gubernatorial nomination, Democratic Congressman Thomas L. Harris of Petersburg remarked that he "never will be dunce enough to run for governor—(unless his wife makes him.)"[368] She "made no effort to conceal her belief that her gifted husband would some day be President." Over his objections, she would at social gatherings "talk confidently of his future, predicting his nomination and election."[369]

In another way Mary Lincoln indirectly stoked her husband's ambition. According to Milton Hay, she made "his home tolerably disagreeable and hence he took to politics and public matters for occupation. If his domestic life had been entirely happy, I dare say he would have stayed at home and not busied himself with distant concerns."[370] Joshua Speed believed that with a kindly wife "Lincoln would have been a devoted husband and a very—*very* domestic man."[371] An unidentified close friend of Lincoln's maintained that his domestic misery "operated largely in his favor; for he was thereby kept out in the world of business and politics. Instead of spending his evenings at home, reading the papers and warming his toes at his own fireside, he was constantly out with the common people, was mingling with the politicians, discussing public questions with the farmers who thronged the offices in the court-house and state house, and exchanging views with the loungers who surrounded the stove of winter evenings in the village store. The result of this continuous contact with the world was, that he was more thoroughly known than any other man in his community. His wife, therefore, was one of the unintentional means of his promotion." If Lincoln had married Ann Rutledge or some other woman more agreeable than Mary Todd, "the country would never have had Abraham Lincoln for its President."[372] Herndon agreed, insisting that Lincoln "was by nature a domestic man, a lover of home and children."[373]

Lincoln's friend and political ally Carl Schurz, who spent time with Mary Lincoln during the Civil War, summed up the feelings of many when he wrote: "it was no secret to those who knew the family well, that his domestic life was full of trials. The erratic temper of his wife not seldom put the gentleness of his nature to the severest tests; and these troubles and struggles, which accompanied him through all the vicissitudes of his life from the modest home in Springfield to the White House at Washington, adding untold private heartburnings to his public cares, and sometimes precipitating upon him incredible embarrassments in the discharge of his public duties, form one of the most pathetic features of his career."[374] In an interview, Schurz put it even more strongly, calling the marriage "the greatest tragedy of Mr. Lincoln's existence."[375]

7

"I Have Got the Preacher by the Balls"
Pursuing a Seat in Congress
(1843–1847)

In 1843, Mary Lincoln, eager to get to Washington, urged her husband to run for Congress. He required little goading, for his ambition was strong. Because voters in the Sangamon region had sent a Whig, John Todd Stuart, to Congress in the two previous elections, whoever secured that party's nomination would probably win. But Lincoln faced formidable challengers for that nomination, notably his friends Edward D. Baker and John J. Hardin.

Political Rivals

Charming, magnetic, and strikingly handsome, the English-born Baker was a renowned orator who could also impress with his abilities to sing, dance, play the piano, and compose poetry. Like Lincoln, Baker had grown up in poverty. His ambition was so intense that when he discovered that his English birth made him ineligible for the presidency, he allegedly wept as he criticized his parents: "In justice to me they might have come to America a few years earlier." Impulsive, eager for glory, Baker won many friends—among them Lincoln—with his personal warmth, commanding presence, generosity, and *joie de vivre*. He was especially popular with young men, who loved and followed him unquestioningly.

With the possible exception of Lincoln, Baker was the best Whig speaker in central Illinois. The "snarling silver trumpet of his voice" was clear and well-modulated, and his fluency and enthusiasm fascinated audiences. Whether on the stump or in front of a jury, Baker's good-natured friendliness, impetuous delivery, and quick wit proved irresistible.[1]

Not everyone admired Baker, however; many found him shallow, lacking in principle, and careless in business. Charles H. Ray spoke dismissively of his "frothy, ginger beer oratory," and Herndon recalled that Baker's "style and matter were not absolutely original—nor deep—nor exact—not what the world calls philosophic."[2] Other critics objected to Baker's lack of "moral worth & stability of character."[3] John J. Crittenden thought his "moral weight is not as great as it should be."[4] Baker's law partner, Stephen

T. Logan, characterized him as "a brilliant man but very negligent" and complained that "I could not trust him in money matters. He got me into some scrapes by collecting and using money."[5] (At the time of his death early in the Civil War, Baker had failed to account for $10,000 that he had been given to raise a regiment.) Another law partner, Isaac Jones Wistar, recalled that Baker had squandered "his large fees as fast as received, and in spite of his great earnings, was most generally penniless." (After his untimely death in 1861, his family was left destitute.) There was, said Wistar, "absolutely no trace of order or system" about his "ill-regulated and erratic character." Relying on his prodigious memory, Baker kept financial records and case dockets in his hat or secreted about his person.[6] In many ways, he seemed a perpetual adolescent.

Baker was also hopelessly vain. Some contemporaries criticized the "excessive protuberance of the organ of self esteem upon Mr. B's cranium."[7] Nothing made him happier than hearing people liken him to Napoleon I. Mary Lincoln's cousin, Elizabeth Grimsley, told a friend in 1861, "I cannot bear that man. He seems to have such a supreme contempt for lesser intellects, that it quite lowers his own in my estimation."[8] In 1849, Baker's aggressive pursuit of a cabinet position was regarded as a joke indicative of his unrealistic estimate of his own talent. David Davis admired Baker's "genius & talents of a high order" but thought him "a queer fellow—the most restless man in the world, and of unbounded ambition."[9]

Despite his faults, Baker inspired in Lincoln a deep affection. He loved him as if he were his brother. In 1846, he named his second son Edward Baker Lincoln. Together Lincoln and Baker practiced law, championed the Whig Party, and debated religion.

Lincoln's other rival for the congressional nomination, John J. Hardin, was a third cousin to Mary Lincoln and very popular with the transplanted Kentucky Whigs of the district. An able man with a quick, retentive mind, Hardin lacked Baker's fluency as an orator. Though he tended to stammer and hesitate, his fierce sarcasm and cutting wit made him a formidable opponent. The wife of Governor Joseph Duncan described him as a "plain blunt man when his indignation was aroused [—] woe to the man who . . . felt the heavy strokes of his 'meat-axe oratory.'"[10]

Born in Kentucky a year after Lincoln, Hardin imbibed politics from his father, Martin D. Hardin, a U.S. senator, secretary of state of Kentucky, and a leading attorney so fierce that he was said to resemble "a kitchen knife whetted on a brick."[11] After graduating from Transylvania University in Lexington, Hardin studied law with the chief justice of the Kentucky Supreme Court. In 1830, he moved to Jacksonville, Illinois, where he quickly achieved eminence. During the Black Hawk War he became a major general of the state militia, and in 1836 he won a seat in the General Assembly, to which he was reelected in 1838 and 1840. Colleagues in the legislature deemed him "clever," "firm," "fearless," and "smart."[12] Lincoln characterized the intensely ambitious Hardin as "our best Whig," a "man of desperate energy and perseverance" who "never backs out" and who was "talented, energetic, usually generous and magnanimous."[13] Much as he admired Hardin, Lincoln may have resented his jeering taunts about Lincoln's celebrated exit through a window in an attempt to block a legislative quorum.

During the winter of 1842–1843, Lincoln began his quest for the congressional nomination, to be decided at a convention in May. On February 14, Lincoln told a Whig leader in Beardstown, "if you should hear any one say that Lincoln don't want to go to Congress, I wish you as a personal friend of mine, would tell him you have reason to believe he is mistaken. The truth is, I would like to go very much."[14] Two weeks thereafter, at a meeting of Whigs in Springfield, Lincoln drew up the party platform, opposing direct federal taxes and endorsing a protective tariff, a national bank, distribution to the states of proceeds from federal land sales, and the convention system of choosing candidates.

Three days later there appeared a circular, written by Lincoln, elaborating on the various planks. Here he indulged in mild demagoguery, implausibly arguing that a protective tariff would burden "the wealthy and luxurious few, while the substantial laboring many . . . go entirely free." Only those "whose pride, whose abundance of means, prompt them to spurn the manufactures of our own country, and to strut in British cloaks, and coats, and pantaloons, may have to pay a few cents more on the yard for the cloth that makes them." Sarcastically, Lincoln remarked: "A terrible evil, truly, to the Illinois farmer, who never wore, nor never expects to wear, a single yard of British goods in his whole life." The tariff was far preferable to a system of direct federal taxation, under which "the land must be literally covered with assessors and collectors, going forth like swarms of Egyptian locusts, devouring every blade of grass and every other green thing." All citizens would thus "be perpetually haunted and harassed by the tax-gatherer." Lincoln ridiculed opponents of Henry Clay's plan to distribute the proceeds of federal land sales: "Many silly reasons are given, as is usual in cases where a single good one is not to be found." Lincoln's intense hostility toward Whig deserters erupted in the circular's denunciation of John Reynolds, William L. D. Ewing, and Richard M. Young, all of whom had been helped by the Whigs and who then became "perseveringly vindictive in their assaults upon all our men and measures."

Whigs must adopt the convention system, Lincoln argued, for "while our opponents use it, it is madness in us not to defend ourselves with it." Nominating conventions created party harmony and united the faithful behind one candidate. "If two friends aspire to the same office, it is certain that both cannot succeed. Would it not, then, be much less painful to have the question decided by mutual friends some time before, than to snarl and quarrel until the day of the election, and then both be beaten by the common enemy?" To illustrate the point, Lincoln employed a scriptural aphorism that he would famously use in 1858: "he whose wisdom surpasses that of all philosophers has declared that 'a house divided against itself cannot stand.'"[15]

During the first three weeks of March, supporters of Baker and Lincoln battled so strenuously for the endorsement of the Sangamon County Whigs that a Democratic paper remarked, "If we are to believe either of the two factions it would be difficult to decide which is the bigger rascal."[16] Baker ultimately outworked and outmaneuvered Lincoln to win the endorsement in Springfield on March 20. When the convention met, it appeared that Baker commanded an overwhelming majority. Asked to withdraw because Baker's lead was so great, Lincoln graciously acquiesced that morning. But it turned out that his rival's lead was much smaller than he had thought. If Lincoln had fought throughout the afternoon, he might have been nominated. Evidently overconfident, Lincoln had failed to match Baker's relentless energy. The outcome mortified him and angered his wife, who roundly berated him for not working hard enough to win.

Some of Baker's supporters criticized Lincoln for his ties to the aristocratic Edwards and Todd families, which prompted Lincoln to remark laughingly: "Well that sounds strange to me for I do not remember of but *one* [member of those families] *that ever came to See Me and While he Was in town he Was accused of Stealing a Jews Harp.*" Publicly Lincoln may have made light of his opponent's tactics, but privately he confided bitterly to a friend his astonishment that he could be portrayed as an elitist.

Lincoln cited other considerations that worked against him. "Baker is a Campbellite," he noted, "and therefore, as I sup[p]ose, with few acceptions got all that church." (Campbellites, followers of Alexander Campbell, were also known as Reformed Baptists and later as Disciples of Christ.) Mary Todd had relatives in the Presbyterian and Episcopal churches, "and therefore whereever it would tell, I was set down as either the one or the other." In addition, Lincoln complained, it was said that "no christian ought to go for me, because I belonged to no church, [and] was suspected of being a deist." Moreover, with some Whigs his reputation suffered because of the notorious "duel" with Shields.[17] Stung by the perception that he was a hotheaded, aristocratic nonbeliever, he emphatically assured James Matheny: "I am now and always shall be the same Abe Lincoln that I always was."[18]

Lincoln's views on temperance may also have injured his candidacy. In the year leading up to the Springfield Whig convention, the temperance movement swept through the capital. The local chapter of the Washington Temperance Society (a precursor of Alcoholics Anonymous), founded in 1841 after proselytes from Alton had stirred up interest, had attracted over 350 members by year's end. Lincoln had addressed the society at a meeting held in a church, and, noting that several of the society's reformed drunkards were deemed too uncouth for the polite worshippers there, Lincoln chided self-righteous, "uncharitable," "cold-blooded," and "feelingless" reformers who held that drunkards "should be shunned by all the good and virtuous" as "utterly incorrigible. . . . moral pestilences." Drunkards, he maintained, were people whose heads and hearts "will bear an advantageous comparison with those of any other class." Indeed, Lincoln declared, there "seems ever to have been a proneness in the brilliant, and the warm-blooded, to fall into this vice. The demon of intemperance ever seems to have delighted in sucking the blood of genius and of generosity." So he appealed to his Christian audience for forbearance: "If they believe, as they profess, that Omnipotence condescended to take on himself the form of sinful man, and, as such, die an ignominious death for their sake, surely they will not refuse submission to the infinitely lesser condescension, for the temporal, and perhaps eternal salvation, of a large, erring, and unfortunate class of their own fellow creatures."[19] This last sentence offended many in attendance, who interpreted it as a criticism of their piety. Insulted and outraged Christians complained: "It's a shame that he should be permitted to abuse us so in the house of the Lord."[20]

(When defending some female temperance activists who been found guilty of demolishing barrels of liquor, Lincoln told the judge: "it might be well to offset the money damages with the damage which might have resulted if the destroyed liquor had been used for beverage purposes." The women were fined 1¢.)[21]

Over his protest, the Sangamon County Whigs chose Lincoln as a delegate to the congressional district convention, where he was obliged to vote for Baker. Though he lamented that "I shall be 'fixed' a good deal like a fellow who is made groomsman to a man that has cut him out, and is marrying his own dear 'gal,'" Lincoln derived some solace from the action of the Menard County convention, which endorsed his candidacy.[22] "It is truly gratifying to me to learn that while the people of Sangamon have cast me off, my old friends of Menard [New Salem was located in recently created Menard County] who have known me longest and best of any, still retain their confidence in me," he told Martin S. Morris.[23] When Baker tried to get Menard's two delegates to vote for him, Lincoln protested: "This is all wrong. Upon the same rule, why might not I fly from the decision against me in Sangamon and get up instructions to their delegation to go for me? . . . I would as soon put my head in the fire as to attempt it." He felt honor-bound not to hinder Baker's nomination. "I should despise myself were I to attempt it," he declared to Morris.[24]

Baker had ample reason to woo the Menard County delegates, for John J. Hardin was emerging as a formidable rival at the district level. When the district convention assembled at Pekin on May 1, Baker and Hardin were virtually deadlocked, with seventeen delegates favoring Hardin and sixteen leaning toward Baker. Lincoln, the foremost advocate of Baker's candidacy, appealed to a Menard County delegate, George U. Miles: "Other Counties have gone for me & are instructed for me if I'm a candidate—I[']ll be nominated the 1st ballot—My honor is out with Baker. I'd Suffer my right arm to be cut off before I'd violate it. It is impossible for me to run. I, after the Nominations, will get up & decline and I want you to go for Baker. Menard—your two votes—will settle the question. Baker will be nominated." Miles refused, explaining that he and the other delegate from Menard County were "instructed to go for Hardin after you, and [I] will suffer my right arm Cut off before I'll violate my instructions."[25]

In fairness, Baker should have received the Menard County votes and hence the nomination. A week before the convention, John Bennett of Petersburg reported that two formal meetings and several informal ones, including militia musters, had been held at which Menard County Whigs expressed their preference. All things considered, Bennett said, "I suppose Baker has a majority."[26] Miles and his colleague had been instructed to vote for Hardin at a meeting that attracted few voters, but later at a much more heavily attended gathering they received instructions to support Baker by an eighty-vote majority.[27] A prominent Democrat in Petersburg, Thomas L. Harris, asserted that he significantly helped Hardin secure the nomination.

Failing to win over the Menard delegates, Lincoln sought to assist Baker through other means. Immediately following Hardin's nomination, Lincoln asked James Monroe Ruggles, the secretary of the convention, if he would favor a resolution supporting Baker for the following congressional term. When Ruggles answered affirmatively, Lincoln said: "You prepare the resolution—I will support it—and I think we can pass it."[28] That resolution caused a stir, especially among Hardin's supporters. Introduced by Lincoln and moved by Ruggles, it said: "*Resolved*, That this convention, as individuals, recommend E. D. Baker as a suitable person to be voted for by the whigs of this district, for Representative to Congress, at the election in 1844, subject to the decision of a District Convention, should the whigs of the district think proper to hold one." Following a heated discussion, it passed by a vote of nineteen to fourteen. This Pekin agreement seemed to establish a principle of one-term congressmen who would cede the seat to a successor in regular rotation, with Lincoln as the obvious heir-apparent to Baker. Such arrangements were not uncommon in the politics of the time.

In mid-May, Lincoln told Joshua Speed that he would cheerfully abide by the results of the Pekin convention: "we shall have no split or trouble about the matter; all will be harmony."[29] Lincoln's friend Simeon Francis urged Hardin to "banish every thought from your mind that there is dissatisfaction with your nomination."[30] Playfully, Lincoln challenged Hardin to a contest: if Sangamon County delivered a majority for Hardin more than double the majority he won in his home county of Morgan, then the Morgan County Whigs would have to throw a barbecue for their counterparts in Sangamon. To help make sure that he won his bet, Lincoln campaigned for Hardin extensively throughout Sangamon County. But despite what he said to Speed, Lincoln apparently begrudged Hardin the nomination. He may also have felt that Hardin's triumph over Baker was unfair. (Hardin's reputation for integrity was not spotless; some questioned his honesty.) On election day Lincoln did not vote for Hardin, who won the district handily; instead, he cast ballots for justice of the peace and constable, refusing to express any preference for congressional or county office candidates. Such uncharacteristically spiteful behavior suggests the intensity of his disappointment. That disappointment was shared by his wife, who wept copiously on the day that Hardin left Illinois to take his seat in Congress.

Domestic Life

Mary Lincoln perhaps derived some consolation both from the house she and her husband bought in 1844 and from their growing family. After beginning their married life in the Globe Tavern, the Lincolns briefly moved into a small house on Fourth Street. On January 16, 1844, Charles Dresser (the minister who had performed their wedding ceremony) sold them a one-and-a-half-story, five-room cottage at Eighth and Jackson Streets, where they spent the next seventeen years. Lincoln gave Dresser $1,200 in cash and real estate worth $300. In May, Dresser handed over the deed to Lincoln, whose family moved in shortly thereafter. The house, conveniently located a few blocks from Lincoln's office, had been built in 1839.

The Lincolns' marriage had gotten off to a shaky start in the Globe. She regularly complained about her husband's failure to come to bed on time; when she retired for the night, he often excused himself to fill a water pitcher, and while downstairs doing so, he would sit on the porch and relate stories to anyone who cared to listen. She would cough to signal that she wanted him to return to their room; sometimes he ignored her coughing till after midnight. She would occasionally retaliate by enter-taining gentlemen callers in their room with the door locked, hoping to annoy her neglectful spouse.

Mary Lincoln had been unpopular at the Globe, where the women boarders liked to hold small get-togethers in their rooms. Never wishing to invite her to join them, they would creep upstairs to the designated meeting site, fearful that she might guess where they were headed. They were especially careful to tread lightly as they passed her door, for they did not wish to arouse her anger.

Life at the boardinghouse worsened after August 1, 1843, when Robert Todd Lincoln was born. (That day Lincoln jestingly told a friend that he had worried that the infant "might have one of my long legs and one of Mary's short ones, and he'd have a terrible time getting through the world.")[31] Baby Robert wailed loudly, much to the dismay of the other boarders, who threatened to leave the Globe if the Lincolns remained. The delicate Robert suffered from a respiratory problem known as "sum-mer complaint." Mrs. Albert Taylor Bledsoe, who was then staying at the Globe, did not like Mary Lincoln but nevertheless each day for several weeks she helped wash and dress baby Robert. Mrs. Bledsoe's 6-year-old daughter Sophia, who was fond of infants, also helped care for him. She delighted in carrying the rather heavy Robert about, frequently taking him to a vacant lot next to the Globe and placing him on the ground, where he lay peacefully in the tall grass. In later years Sophia Bledsoe "won-dered how Mrs. Lincoln could have trusted a particularly small six-year-old with this charge" and expressed amazement that "at that early age I missed doing him any damage."[32]

Lincoln would occasionally help out with the infant. One day as baby Robert was shrieking, Lincoln picked him up and carried him around the room while Mary sat by, quietly crying. The proprietress of the Globe assured the couple that their child merely had colic and was in no danger. "Does it do any good to pack him round this way?" Lincoln asked. When told it did not, he looked over at Mary and said "in a manner as though he expected her to protest": "If it don't do him any good, I'm damned if I don't put him down."[33] Mary Lincoln often asked her husband to care for Robert, whom he would wheel about in a baby carriage. When a neighbor criticized him, remarking "that is a pretty business for you to be engaged in, when you ought to be down to your law office," he replied simply: "I promised."[34]

Lincoln performed other domestic chores. His wife, having grown up in a pros-perous home with slaves to tend children, cook, and clean, felt that such duties were beneath her. According to a neighbor, she "was quite disposed to make a servant girl" of Lincoln, compelling him "to get up and get the breakfast and then dress the chil-dren, after which she would join the family at the table, or lie abed an hour or two longer as she might choose."[35] Another Sangamon County resident testified that "Lincoln would start for his office in the morning and she'd go to the door and holler: 'Come back here now and dress those children or they won't be tended today. I'm not going to break my back dressing up those children while you loaf at the office talking politics all the day.'"[36] In 1860, a visitor to the Lincoln home heard her cry out, "Abraham! Abraham! come and put this child to bed!"[37]

While washing dishes one day in the mid-1840s, she was heard to sigh: "What would my poor father say if he found me doing this kind of work."[38] When Robert was old enough, she delegated dishwashing to him. In addition, she had her husband do the breakfast dishes and sometimes, wielding a piece of stove wood, drove him out of their house to fetch some breakfast meat. Page Eaton remembered that Lincoln "always used to do his own marketing . . . and before he went to Washington I used to see him at the baker's and butcher's every morning with his basket on his arm."[39] Lincoln would rise early to buy fresh bread from Jim Hall. The day after his election as president in 1860, Lincoln, accompanied by a black boy, called as usual on Hall and said: "I am not ashamed to carry a loaf of bread home under my arm, but my wife says it is not dignified for a president-elect to carry bread under his arm through the streets, so, hereafter, this boy will come in my place."[40] (At that same time she also thought it undignified for her husband to milk their cow. A servant recollected that in the winter of 1860–1861, Lincoln insisted on performing that duty "because he did not think I ought to expose myself. His wife, however, used to object to his doing the milking.")[41]

Mary Lincoln found herself overwhelmed by the demands of motherhood as she gave birth to three more sons (Edward in 1846; William in 1850; and Thomas, better known as Tad, in 1853). Her cousin, Elizabeth Todd Grimsley, recalled that Mary was "always over-anxious and worried about the boys and withal was not a skillful nurse" and "was totally unfitted for caring for them" when they became sick.[42] If anything untoward happened to her children, she became hysterical. One day in 1844 she overreacted to the illness of young Robert and sent the maid to fetch a doctor, shouting after her, "Charity! Charity! run for your life and I'll give you fifty dollars when you get back." Mrs. Frederick S. Dean, who lived across the street from the Lincoln home, took pity on the distracted newcomer and gently quieted her down when her hysterics threatened to disturb the neighborhood. Another neighbor, Elizabeth Lushbaugh Capps, recalled that it was not unusual "to see her standing out on their terrace in front of the house, waving her arms and screaming, 'Bobbie's lost! Bobbie's lost!' when perhaps he was just over in our house. This was almost an every day occurrence." Mrs. Capps remembered a time "when Robert could just barely walk Mrs. Lincoln came out in front as usual, screaming, 'Bobbie will die! Bobbie will die!' My father ran over to see what had happened. Bobbie was found sitting out near the back door by a lime box and had a little lime in his mouth. Father took him, washed his mouth out and that's all there was to it." Mary Lincoln's frequent outbursts so frightened the neighborhood children that they feared her; rather than playing with Bob at his house, they would invite him to their homes.[43]

Lincoln developed an immunity to his wife's alarmist cries of distress. One summer day on the courthouse square, while he was regaling friends with a story, young Robert rushed up exclaiming that his mother insisted that Lincoln come home and rescue young Tad, who had fallen into the cistern. To the surprise of his cronies, Lincoln refused, noting that Tad had done this before.

The Lincolns' unpretentious house at Eighth and Jackson Streets was modestly furnished. Lincoln was not a fastidious homeowner. Illinois Congressman William

A. Richardson recalled that "his fences were always in need of repair, his gate wanted a hinge, the grass in his yard needed cutting, and the scene around his home betrayed a reckless indifference to appearances."[44] In November 1860, a visitor observed broken panes of glass by the front door and broken blinds on the side of the house.

Mary Lincoln wanted to expand the upstairs of the house into a full second story. Lincoln, who opposed the idea, allegedly had conspired with local carpenters to have an inflated estimate of the cost prepared so that he could reasonably claim that it was too expensive. In 1856, while he was on the circuit, Mary had the job done anyway. The contractors she hired agreed to complete the work in the few weeks that he would be absent. Upon his return, he pretended not to recognize his home, asking his neighbor Abner Wilkinson, "Wilkie can you tell me where old Abe Lincoln lived around these parts?"[45] The neighbors, anxious to see how Lincoln would react, observed his conduct with amusement. His wife, however, was not amused. "Come in, you old fool," she ordered. "Don't you know your own house when you see it?"[46] After scolding her for spending too much, Lincoln teased: "Mary, you remind me of the story of the fellow who went to California and left one baby at home and when he returned three years later, found three. The fellow looked at his wife and then at the children and said, 'Well, Lizzie, for a little woman and without help, you have raised thunder amazingly.'"[47] (Mary Lincoln may have paid for the improvements herself, for two years earlier she had sold an 80-acre lot that her father had bequeathed her and realized a profit of $1,200. The expansion cost $1,300.)

Some residents of Springfield were puzzled by this remodeling job. Mrs. John Todd Stuart, who did not care for Mary Lincoln, told her daughter that far from needing space, "Mary seldom ever uses what she has."[48] In fact, the expansion added so much space that the Lincolns took in a boarder, Stephen Smith, the brother of Mary's brother-in-law, Clark M. Smith. He slept at the Lincoln home but ate elsewhere. According to the woman whom Stephen Smith later married, the Lincolns had a boarder "because Mr. Lincoln, riding the circuit at that time, was away from home a great deal and Mrs. Lincoln was afraid to be alone."[49]

Mary Lincoln had decided on the addition soon after a successful tailor acquired an impressive house in their neighborhood; she was displeased that a mere tailor should have a more handsome residence than one of the city's more eminent lawyers. John E. Roll, who had helped remodel the house in 1849, reported that "Mrs. Lincoln decided their means justified a more pretentious house."[50] In the 1840s, a house with a two-story back was a status symbol that she "was consumed with a desire" to have.[51] The alteration did make the house stand out, dwarfing adjacent homes. Mary Lincoln's nephew termed it "one of the more pretentious residences of Springfield."[52] An architectural historian classified the remodeled house as "purely transitional," blending "both the Greek Revival and the succeeding Parvenu" styles.[53]

Whereas nearly every house in Springfield was landscaped carefully with trees, shrubbery, and neat flower gardens, the Lincolns did little to improve the appearance of their yard. Mary Lincoln's sister Frances said that neither of the Lincolns "loved the beautiful—I have planted flowers in their front yard myself to hide nakedness—ugliness &c. &c. have done it often—and often—Mrs L never planted trees—Roses—never made a garden, at least not more than once or twice."[54] James Gourley, who lived next door to the Lincolns for many years, remembered that "Lincoln was a poor landscape gardener and his yard was graced by very little shrubbery. He once decided to plant some rosebushes in the yard, and called my attention to them, but in a short time he had forgotten all about them." Lincoln, Gourley added, "never planted any vines or trees of any kind; in fact seemed to take little, if any, interest in things of that kind. Finally, however, yielding to my oft-repeated suggestion, he undertook to cultivate a garden in the yard in back of his house; but one season's experience in caring for his flowers and vegetables sufficed to cure him of all desire for another."[55] The house's bare appearance moved one observer to criticize its "almost unbecoming absence of taste and refinement."[56]

Lincoln avoided this house as much as possible because, according to William Herndon, "his home was Hell" and "absence from home was his Heaven."[57] So much did he enjoy life on the circuit each spring and fall that he rejected a job offer from a Chicago firm that paid much more than he could earn in Springfield. Rather than return home on weekends like the other circuit riders, he stayed over in the little county seats by himself, even though, as one of them put it, "nothing could be duller than remaining on the Sabbath in a country inn of that time after adjournment of court. Good cheer had expended its force during court week, and blank dullness succeeded." Nevertheless, Lincoln "would entertain the few lingering roustabouts of the barroom with as great zest, apparently, as he had previously entertained the court and bar, and then would hitch up his horse . . . and, solitary and alone, ride off to the next term in course."[58] David Davis and the other attorneys "soon learned to account for his strange disinclination to go home." Lincoln "never had much to say about home, and," Davis recalled, "we never felt free to comment on it. Most of us had pleasant, inviting homes, and as we struck out for them I'm sure each one of us down in our hearts had a mingled feeling of pity and sympathy for him."[59] To Davis and others it was obvious that Lincoln "was not domestically happy."[60] Herndon remembered that "while all other lawyers, every Saturday night after court hours, would start for home to see wife & babies," Lincoln "would see us start home and know that we were bound to see good wife and the children. Lincoln, poor soul, would grow terribly sad at the sight, as much as to say—'I have no wife and no home.' None of us on starting home would say to Lincoln—'Come, Lincoln, let's go home,' for we knew the terrors of home to him."[61]

In addition to being the only lawyer on the circuit to avoid his home on the weekends, Lincoln was one of the few who attended every circuit court. In 1860, his good friend Leonard Swett asserted that "for perhaps five years Lincoln and myself have been the only ones [i.e., lawyers] who have habitually passed over the whole circuit."[62]

Unlike David Davis, Richard Yates, and other attorneys and politicians who wrote home regularly, Lincoln seldom corresponded with his wife. (Herndon said his partner "hated" to write letters.)[63] Nor did she write often to him. In 1850, Davis reported that Lincoln had not received word from Mary since he left Springfield seven weeks earlier. Two years thereafter, Davis said that Lincoln, while on the circuit, had not heard from home in six weeks. Adeline Rossiter Judd, wife of Norman B. Judd, once asked Lincoln, then traveling the circuit, about his spouse. When he replied that he had received no word from her since he had started out three weeks earlier, Mrs. Judd rhetorically asked, "But Mr. Lincoln, aren't you married?"

"No, no," he protested, "if there was anything the matter Mary would write."

Mrs. Judd, who received letters from her husband every day when they were separated, was dumbfounded.[64]

The tone of the few surviving letters between the Lincolns is notably cool compared with the loving warmth expressed by other couples in their circle—the Judds, the Lyman Trumbulls, the David Davises, the Jesse W. Fells, the Richard Yateses, the John M. Palmers, the Stephen T. Logans, the Joseph Duncans, the Orville H. Brownings, and the John Todd Stuarts. Trumbull wrote to his beloved spouse every other day when they were apart. Palmer told his mate: "Men are charged with indifference to their wives and perhaps it is true of many but I declare to you that all my thoughts and feelings and love is far more ardent towards you than they were on the night when I first called you my own dear wife."[65] Richard Yates told his wife: "Caty I am desperately in love with you."[66] When away from his "Dearest Eliza," Orville H. Browning wrote her twice weekly. In 1844 he declared to her: "oh, how I wish you were with me. . . . No man on earth owes more to the devotion of a wife, and I hope God will give me the means to repay it in kindness and affection."[67] His letters from the circuit contained what she called "Such beautiful poetry, Such Sighing, and Loveing, dearing, and all that kind of thing."[68] Writing from Washington in 1841, Jesse W. Fell exclaimed to his wife: "How often, and with what absorbing interest have I thought of thee, since we parted. How frequently have I wandered in imagination to the 'Far,' 'far West,' and then fancied myself one of a little group, with my wife and boy by my side. . . . How often, and how fondly have I wished that my person could keep pace with my imagination, that I could again behold you, that I could once more be surrounded by those objects, the nearest and dearest in life, my wife and boy."[69] In 1860, David Davis assured his spouse that "All the honors of the world pale before my undying love for you."[70] Nothing of this sort appears in Lincoln's letters to his wife. Those letters, among other things, cast doubt on Mary Lincoln's claim that "my darling husband . . . worshipped me so greatly, that often he said, that I was his weakness."[71]

Lincoln's habit of staying away from home began early in the marriage. In the first year, when Mary was pregnant, he was gone nearly ten weeks. (David Davis's wife "was a little critical of Lincoln, whom she adored, for staying out on the circuit when Mary was expecting.")[72] Although he suffered from homesickness while on the circuit in early 1843, as the years went by he remained away more and more until finally he was absent from Springfield more than four months a year. In 1854, David Davis said that "Mr. Lincoln is so much engaged here [on the circuit] that he will not find time to go home—so that before he gets home again he will have been absent six (6) weeks."[73] Robert Todd Lincoln recalled that during his childhood and early youth, his father "was almost constantly away from home."[74] In 1858, Lincoln wrote that "I am [away] from home perhaps more than half my time."[75] Two years later, a Springfield

minister informed a colleague that Lincoln was frequently absent on the Sabbath because "for the last three or four years he has been away from home much of the time
and engaged in very exhausting labors."[76] Even when not on the road, Lincoln rarely
passed the evening at his house. According to Herndon, he frequently left home
between seven and eight A.M. and returned at midnight or even later.

To a neighbor Mrs. Lincoln complained "that if her husband had Staid at home
as he ought to, that She could love him better."[77] If their separations were painful to
her, it is hard to understand why she regularly absented herself from Washington during Lincoln's term in Congress (1847–1849) and during his presidency, when she left
him for months at a time.

Presidential Politicking

In 1844, Lincoln campaigned passionately for the Whig presidential standard-bearer,
Henry Clay, whom he said he "almost worshipped."[78] Lincoln could easily identify
with Clay, for, as he observed at Clay's death in 1852, the Kentucky statesman
had—like Lincoln—been born to "undistinguished parents" in "an obscure district,"
had only a "comparatively limited" formal education, and "added something to his
education during the greater part of his whole life." His political philosophy, as Lincoln interpreted it, reflected Lincoln's own views. Clay's eloquence, Lincoln thought,
manifested itself not in "elegant arrangement of words and sentences" but rather (like
Lincoln's) in a "deeply earnest and impassioned tone, and manner, which can proceed
only from great sincerity and a thorough conviction." Like Lincoln, Clay believed that
"the world's best hope depended on the continued Union of these States." Like Lincoln, Clay "loved his country partly because it was his own country, but mostly because it was a free country" and "burned with a zeal for its advancement, prosperity
and glory, because he saw in such, the advancement, prosperity and glory of human
liberty, human right and human nature." Like Lincoln, Clay "desired the prosperity
of his countrymen partly because they were his countrymen, but chiefly to show to
the world that freemen could be prosperous." Like Lincoln, Clay was "in principle
and in feeling, opposed to slavery."[79] (Few other eulogists of Clay mentioned his antislavery views.)

Whigs entertained high hopes for Clay's success in 1844. A Baltimorean reported
as early as February that the "enthusiasm of 1840 is returning. The Whigs look forward to the approaching contest," for they had faith in "the justness of their cause—and
in its righteousness read their claim to certain success."[80]

Throughout the campaign Lincoln and his fellow Whigs concentrated on the
tariff issue while Democrats focused on expansionism in Texas and Oregon. The tariff
of 1842—the chief accomplishment of the Whig-dominated Twenty-Seventh
Congress—had been designed to restore prosperity, encourage foreign investment,
improve the balance of trade, and enhance government revenues. Because most of
these goals had been achieved, Whigs decided to emphasize the tariff issue in the
presidential campaign. In May, Lincoln did speak once about Texas, endorsing the
Whig argument "that Annexation at this time upon the terms agreed upon by John
Tyler was altogether inexpedient."[81]

During the winter of 1843–1844, Lincoln joined Edward D. Baker, Stephen T. Logan, and John Todd Stuart speaking nightly throughout Sangamon County. Such extensive campaigning was necessary because, as David Davis explained to his brother-in-law in Massachusetts, Illinoisans "get their information by public speaking, and it is well that they do. Otherwise, they would have none, for newspaper taking is not a trait in Western character."[82] Several times during the spring, Lincoln debated John Calhoun, the Democratic congressional nominee in the Seventh District. Lincoln called Calhoun "the ablest Democrat in the State" and insisted "that Calhoun gave him more trouble in his debates than Douglas ever did, because he was more captivating in his manner and a more learned man."[83] (David Davis described Calhoun as "a social, companionable man, wholly destitute of moral principle, & reckless in pecuniary matters—of talents of a high order.")[84]

In late March, Lincoln and Calhoun held a protracted debate at Springfield during which Lincoln "proved conclusively that the English are now flooding this country with tracts & money to break down the present Whig tariff [of 1842]." Calhoun, who was fair and courteous, complained that the tariff "did not tax silk & wool high enough" and "that it was done to 'benefit the *rich* to the injury of the poor man.'"[85] James Gourley, who heard that debate, said "Calhoun was an able man—No mistake—one of the ablest men that ever made Stump Speeches in Ills—He came nearer of whipping Lincoln in debate than Douglas did."[86] John B. Weber, who also attended the debate in Springfield, marveled at the way "Lincoln used to stagger me with his tariff speeches: he so arranged his facts—his arguments—his logic that it approached me from such a peculiar angle that they struck me forcibly."[87] In Tazewell County, where neither Whigs nor Democrats showed much excitement, the audience listened to the two men "calmly and quietly," for they were "determined to decide this contest as they honestly believe it should be decided—upon the measures, acts and principles of the two parties."[88] In April, a partisan Democratic observer said that Lincoln presented "all the stereotyped slanders upon Mr. Van Buren" which were "ably and successfully rebutted and exposed by Mr. Calhoun, in the course of the recent discussion."[89]

Milton Hay believed that debating with Calhoun advanced Lincoln's political education. During the 1830s and 1840s, Calhoun was the best intellect on the Democratic side, and though he lacked Stephen A. Douglas's oratorical power, he surpassed the Little Giant in elucidating the issues logically. Calhoun was especially talented at informal discussions, just the sort of debate in which he and Lincoln often clashed. "Like Lincoln he could fairly state his opponents side of the question, and argue with fairness and preserve his temper." Better educated than Lincoln, Calhoun had devoted himself singlemindedly to the study of politics. "Frequent contact and conflict with such an opponent," Hay speculated, "habituated the sententious, precise and guarded statement of political propositions for which Mr Lincoln became so remarkable."[90]

In the spring and fall, Lincoln stumped Illinois, often with Calhoun as a sparring partner; when not debating face-to-face, one of them would speak and the other would do so the next day at the same location. An admiring Jesse W. Fell recalled

that in "these elaborate speeches," Lincoln "evinced a thorough mastery of the principles of political economy which underlie the tariff question, and presented arguments in favor of the protective policy with a power and conclusiveness rarely equaled,
and at the same time in a manner so lucid and familiar and so well interspersed with
happy illustrations and apposite anecdotes, as to secure the delighted attention of
his auditory."[91]

Contemporary press summaries of Lincoln's oratory are sketchy, but evidence
supports David Davis's 1844 assertion that Lincoln was "the best Stump Speaker in
the State." He "shows the want of early education," Davis acknowledged, "but he has
great powers as a speaker."[92] In February, Lincoln defended national and state banks
in addition to the tariff. On March 1, he tried to persuade farmers in Sugar Creek
that a high protective tariff "made every thing they bought cheaper."[93] In mid-March,
he and Edward D. Baker debated Calhoun and Alfred W. Cavarly in Jacksonville.
Later that month, at a debate with those two Democrats in Springfield, he "promised
to forfeit his 'ears' and his 'legs' if he did not demonstrate, that protected articles have
been cheaper since the late Tariff [of 1842] than before."[94] On April 6, Lincoln spoke
for two hours to the Clay Club of Peoria; Calhoun replied a week later. After the
Democratic leader's four-hour speech, Lincoln reportedly "overwhelmed Calhoun
and his friends by his argument, ridicule and good natured sarcasm."[95]

In that city two months later, Lincoln delivered a pro-tariff speech to the Whig
state convention. Initially, he made a poor impression, fumbling for the right words
and speaking in a tremulous voice. But he grew more confident as he went along. As
one auditor recalled, he "straightened up, his countenance brightened, his language
became free and animated, as, during this time he had illustrated his arguments by
two or three well-told stories." Eventually, "he became eloquent, carrying the swaying
crowd at his will" with his "closeness and soundness of logic," his "numerous facts,"
and his "elaborate and powerful arguments."[96]

That summer in Peoria, Lincoln debated William L. May, who insisted that
Lincoln not refer to May's erratic political history. (May had been a Whig in his native Kentucky, switched to the Democratic Party when he moved to Illinois, and
then resumed his Whig loyalty, only to return to the Democrats in 1844. President
Jackson appointed him receiver of public moneys for the United States Land Office
in Springfield; in 1841 he became mayor of that city.) Poking fun at the Whigs' tall
liberty pole, which had a decayed section that was replaced, May "ridiculed the
whole concern," declaring that "the pole was hollow at the butt end." Lincoln replied
that the hollow spot "was where the Col. had crawled out of the Whig party! He
proposed to stop up the hole so that he couldn't get back again!" The audience
howled at the jest and laughed even harder when May lost his composure and "fell
'to cursing like a very drab.'" May threatened to resort to the code duello, but calmed
down when Lincoln apologized, "saying that he was in the predicament of the fellow
who knocked his daddy down, and explained his ungracious conduct by the remark
that the old man stood so fair he had to hit him."[97]

Because, as Lincoln explained in 1860, it "was not fashionable here [in Illinois] in
those days [the 1840s] to report one's public speeches," it is hard to know precisely

what facts and arguments he used in his Whig campaign addresses.[98] But a revealing article in the *Sangamo Journal* by one "Lancaster," probably a Lincoln pseudonym, may shed light on his thinking. Protective tariffs did not unfairly burden "the poor farmer," Lancaster argued, because all "manufactured articles were sold as low and many lower after [the enactment of the 1842 tariff] than they were before." Prices stayed down because manufacturers "were encouraged to start their factories believing they could find a sale for their goods," and the increased number of firms heightened competition, thus preventing "any extortion in prices." Lancaster insisted that "*These facts prove that our revenue is paid entirely by the foreign manufacturers;* except perhaps occasionally some of our Fops and Dandies may be inclined to show off with a London Coat, a Paris pair of boots, or ornament his table with a set of *English knives and forks,* or his parlour with an European carpet." Echoing Lincoln's 1843 Whig Party circular, Lancaster noted that farmers and working men "do not indulge in those luxuries." American manufacturers "can furnish an article good enough for us, and if our office holders want to ape the Paris or London fashions, and are willing to give their custom to the foreign manufacture, and pay the duty themselves, it is certainly democratic to grant them the liberty." American manufacturers of broadcloth would benefit from a 35 percent tariff, but farmers would also benefit from that protection, for the manufacturers paid for wool and lard oil, which the farmers produced, and paid wages to workers, who spent three-quarters of their income on goods produced by farmers. Lancaster concluded that an "examination into the business of cotton goods, boots, shoes, cordage, iron, lead, and in fact most all articles coming under the denomination of manufactures will exhibit the fact that nine tenths of all the protection goes indirectly into the pocket of the farmer."[99]

The rising tide of immigration was beginning to roil parts of the country in 1844, foreshadowing the growth of the nativist movement that would peak a decade later. When the Democrats tried to blame the Whigs for bloody anti-Catholic riots in Philadelphia, Lincoln and his party forcefully denied that there was any "hostility of the Whig party in general of *foreigners and Catholics.*" At a Springfield public meeting in June, the Whigs adopted resolutions, presented by Lincoln, condemning the riots and asserting that "in admitting the foreigner to the rights of citizenship, he should be put to some reasonable test of his fidelity to our country and institutions; and that he should first dwell among us a reasonable time to become generally acquainted with the nature of those institutions; and that, consistent with those requisites, naturalization laws, should be so framed, as to render admission to citizenship under them, as convenient, cheap, and expeditious as possible." Moreover, "we will now, and at all times, oppose as best we may, all attempts to either destroy the naturalization laws or to so alter them, as to render admission under them, less convenient, less cheap, or less expeditious than it now is." In addition, they resolved that "the guarantee of the rights of conscience, as found in our Constitution, is most sacred and inviolable, and one that belongs no less to the Catholic, than to the Protestant; and that all attempts to abridge or interfere with these rights, either of Catholic or Protestant, directly or indirectly, have our decided disapprobation, and shall ever have our most effective opposition."[100]

At this meeting Lincoln gave a speech in which he "expressed the kindest, and most benevolent feelings towards foreigners" and "alleged that the whigs were as much the friends of foreigners as democrats." A Democratic paper chided him for "stating that the Catholics demanded the exclusion of the Bible from the public schools," when in fact "all they wanted was the privilege . . . of introducing and using their own translation."[101] Ebenezer Peck responded by summoning a Democratic meeting at which, according to a Whig account, he "presented statements, declarations, and, as he said, quotations, which, the evening after were proved to be *falsehoods* and *forgeries* by Mr. Lincoln."[102] In the 1850s, Lincoln would once again denounce xenophobia and religious bigotry.

By October, Lincoln acknowledged that Clay would probably lose in Illinois. In August the Democrats had won substantial majorities in the General Assembly, and the state's Whig press conceded victory to the Democratic presidential nominee, James K. Polk. So Lincoln crossed the Wabash River and spoke several times in southwestern Indiana. At Bruceville, Democrats disrupted his meeting, but nothing daunted, Lincoln waited for the uproar to subside, then finished his speech. After hearing Lincoln's address in Rockport, his former employer, William Jones, admiringly reported that Lincoln "knows what he is talking about. He makes his arguments as plain as the nose on your face. You can't miss the point. They are as outstanding as his jokes are funny."[103] James C. Veatch remarked that Lincoln's "plain, argumentative" tariff speech did "honor to himself and the whig cause."[104] Later Veatch recalled that, once again, Lincoln had begun poorly; his "appearance was awkward, his voice high and squeaky, and he had none of that extreme dignity which clothed the State orators I had heard." But soon Veatch "was struck by his manner of statement" as he discussed the shopworn tariff issue, placing "things in a new light" so that "dry facts became interesting." Veatch reported that by the time Lincoln finished it was "the most remarkable speech that I had ever heard." (Veatch would play a key role in helping Lincoln win the Republican nomination for the presidency sixteen years later.)[105]

That November, Clay received only 105 electoral votes to Polk's 170; Polk won 49.6 percent of the popular votes to Clay's 48.1 percent. In Illinois, where enthusiasm for the annexation of Texas and for the American claim to all of the Oregon Territory was especially strong, the expansionist Polk swamped Clay, 54 percent to 42 percent. Lincoln was "not only disappointed but disgusted," and regarded Clay's defeat "as a great public calamity and a keen personal sorrow."[106] Other Illinois Whig leaders reacted similarly. David Davis declared: "Clay's defeat has weaned me from politics. I shall quit the Legislature and attend to my own private business. There is precious little use for any Whig in Illinois to be wasting his time and efforts. This State cannot be redeemed. I should as leave think of seeing one rise from the dead."[107]

Along with many of his party colleagues, Lincoln blamed the outcome on New York antislavery Whigs who had voted for the Liberty Party candidate, James G. Birney, thus ensuring that Polk would carry the Empire State and, with it, the nation. (In New York, Birney received 15,814 votes, constituting 1.05% of the total; had one-third of Birney's votes gone to Clay, the Kentuckian would have won.) In 1845,

Lincoln told a Liberty Party supporter that if the "whig abolitionists of New York had voted with us last fall, Mr. Clay would now be president, whig principles in the ascendent, and Texas not annexed; whereas by the division [of the Liberty and Whig forces], all that either had at stake in the contest, was lost." An antislavery Whig had declared to Lincoln that he could not vote for the slaveholder Clay, because people of conscience "are not to do *evil* that *good* may come." Plaintively Lincoln asked: "If by your votes you could have prevented the *extension,* &c. of slavery, would it not have been *good* and not *evil* so to have used your votes, even though it involved the casting of them for a slaveholder? By the *fruit* the tree is to be known. An *evil* tree can not bring forth *good* fruit. If the fruit of electing Mr. Clay would have been to prevent the extension of slavery, could the act of electing have been *evil?*"[108]

Lincoln's analysis of the Liberty Party's role in the 1844 election, accurate as far as it went, was somewhat misleading. The antislavery Whigs of New York objected to Clay's wavering on the annexation of Texas, which he had opposed in April; four months later he seemed to recant. His waffling probably cost him New York, but it may well have gained him Tennessee, where he prevailed by a scant 267 votes. If he had won New York at the cost of losing Tennessee, Clay would still have been defeated. The most important element in Polk's victory was the dramatic increase in the Democratic vote between 1840 and 1844, largely attributable to enthusiasm for the annexation of Texas among Southerners and Westerners, and to disaffection with Whiggery among Northern Catholics and immigrants who resented the party's flirtation with nativists (like the American Republicans, also known as the Native Americans) and its choice of the militantly Protestant Theodore Frelinghuysen as Clay's running mate.

Third Law Partnership

A month after the election, Lincoln amicably ended his partnership with Stephen T. Logan, who wanted to take into the firm his 20-year-old son David, recently admitted to the bar. Political considerations may also have played a role, for Logan aspired to Congress and hesitated to run as long as he was still in partnership with Lincoln. John W. Bunn believed that the two men disagreed over fees and the proper way to deal with cases. Logan, said Bunn, "was very keen after the money," while "Mr. Lincoln didn't seem to care for money at all."[109]

To replace Logan, Lincoln selected an inexperienced, erratic, impulsive attorney nearly ten years his junior, William H. Herndon. Years later Herndon described himself in 1844 as "a young, undisciplined, uneducated, wild man."[110] During an election campaign, Lincoln spotted him in Springfield urging a crowd of young men to vote for Whig candidates. By that time Herndon had come to hate the Democrats' proslavery inclinations. Lincoln halted, called Herndon over, asked his name, and said: "So you are a good Whig, eh? How would you like to study law with me?" Thereafter Lincoln regularly discussed politics with Herndon and took him into the Logan-Lincoln law office to prepare for the bar. After a year and a half, Lincoln went a step further, asking his apprentice: "Billy do you want to enter into partnership with me in the law business?" Herndon, who thought Lincoln was

joking, replied: "Mr Lincoln this is something unexpected by me—it is an unde-
served honor; and yet I say I will gladly & thankfully accept the kind and generous
offer." He then broke down crying, for, as he later said, "I thought I was in
Heaven."[111]

This curious choice puzzled Lincoln's friends and biographers, and even Herndon himself. Asked why Lincoln chose him, Herndon replied, "I don't know and no
one else does."[112] Residents of Springfield offered several different explanations. According to John W. Bunn, either John Todd Stuart or Joshua Speed had recommended
Herndon to Lincoln, who accepted the suggestion "largely out of pity" for the young
man. Herndon's proslavery father, Archer G. Herndon, enraged by the antislavery
enthusiasm his son had acquired at Illinois College, withdrew him from school and
for all intents and purposes abandoned him.[113]

Another Springfielder reported that "Lincoln took Herndon as a partner to save
him from ruin, drink & women."[114] That hypothesis seems confirmed by Herndon's
acknowledgment that Lincoln "picked me out of the gutter and made a man of me. I
was a drunkard till he took me in hand and kept me straight."[115] Lincoln's sense of
pity may have been aroused by Herndon's relative poverty and by the shabby treatment he had suffered at the hands of his father, conditions to which Lincoln could
easily relate. He may also have chosen Herndon because, unlike Logan or Stuart, the
younger man would not be a political rival.

Lincoln viewed Herndon as a surrogate son, a role for which the young man was
well suited. Lincoln, Herndon said, was "truly paternal in every sense of the word"
and was "the best friend I ever had or expect ever to have except my wife & mother."[116]
Estranged from his hard-drinking, proslavery sire, Herndon went to live at the
Springfield store of Joshua Speed, where Lincoln also roomed. In time, Herndon
became a temperance zealot, perhaps as a gesture of rebellion against his father. Later
he spoke of Lincoln as though he were a surrogate father, calling him "the great big
man of our firm" and himself "the little one," and remarking that the "little one
looked naturally up to the big one."[117] Herndon recalled that Lincoln "moved me by a
shrug of the shoulder—by a nod of the head—by a flash of the eye and by the quiver
of the whole man."[118]

Lincoln looked after Herndon as if he were his own son. Once, when the junior
partner lay ill for three months, some of Lincoln's friends urged him to end the partnership. Lincoln "exclaimed vehemently: 'Desert Billy! No, never! If he is sick all the
rest of his days, I will stand by him.'"[119] Herndon, perhaps recalling this episode, said
that at one point he "had become so dissipated that some of Lincoln's friends thought
proper to advise a separation, but Lincoln, with great dignity, declined their counsel,
and the manner of the act so moved Herndon as to sober him and endeared him to
Lincoln forever."[120] Lincoln stood by Herndon for sixteen years, dividing fees equally
with him. Only after the election of 1860 did the partnership end. The firm of Lincoln and Herndon would handle approximately 3,400 cases, of which half involved
debt collection, and would argue on average fifteen cases annually before the Illinois
Supreme Court. At first, Herndon was, as he later recalled, "inclined to lawyers[']
tricks false pleas—and so on. Lincoln strictly forbade it."[121]

Election to Congress

Lincoln quietly launched a campaign for the 1846 congressional nomination eight months before the district convention was to assemble. On the circuit, he had been practicing law in five of the district's counties—Sangamon, Logan, Menard, Tazewell, and Woodford—which together would have sixteen delegates at the nominating convention to be held at Petersburg on May 1. Lincoln counted on the eleven votes of Menard, Sangamon, and Logan, where he was especially well known and popular. If he could then add the six delegates from the district represented by Senator Robert S. Boal (comprising Tazewell, Woodford, and Marshall counties), he would have a majority. In the autumn of 1845 while in Lacon, he called on Boal, who said "it had always been his understanding since the Pekin convention" that Lincoln would be the nominee in 1846.[122]

If Baker and Hardin would abide by the Pekin understanding of 1843, Lincoln seemed to have the nomination sewed up. In keeping with its terms, Hardin had stepped down in 1844 in favor of Baker, who won the seat. But Hardin was not so accommodating in 1846; despite the Pekin agreement, he intended to run for Congress once again. In September 1845, Lincoln called at his home in Jacksonville, where he reported Baker's plans and asked about Hardin's. Hardin equivocated. Two months later Lincoln reported that "Baker is certainly off the track, and I fear Hardin intends to be on it."[123] To preempt Hardin, who delayed announcing his candidacy, Lincoln obtained pledges from Whigs as he traveled the legal circuit that fall. He also urged leading Whig editors not to support Hardin. In response, the *Tazewell Whig* of Pekin, the *Beardstown Gazette*, the *Illinois Gazette* of Lacon, and the *Sangamo Journal* backed Lincoln's candidacy; in the Seventh District, only one Whig paper—the *Morgan Journal* (in Hardin's hometown of Jacksonville)—was opposed.

When some Whig leaders urged Hardin to seek the gubernatorial nomination instead, he replied that he would prefer another term in Congress to the governorship, though he would not actively campaign for it. When Hardin accused Allen Ford, editor of the *Illinois Gazette* of Lacon, of trying to sidetrack his bid for Congress by raising the gubernatorial option, Ford explained that he "would gladly see" him reelected to the U.S. House "were it not that the impression has prevailed" that Hardin had, in keeping with the Pekin agreement, yielded to Baker in 1844 and would do the same for Lincoln in 1846.[124] In response to a similar charge by Hardin, Lincoln denied it, pointing out that he had gone to the office of the *Sangamo Journal* "and told them it was my wish that they should not fall in with the nomination for Governor."[125] Hardin was reluctant to run for governor because no Whig stood much chance of winning statewide office in solidly Democratic Illinois.

As Lincoln maneuvered for the congressional nomination, his political correspondence became so heavy that he enlisted the help of Gibson W. Harris, an aspiring law student clerking in the Lincoln-Herndon office. To Harris, Lincoln dictated letters to politicos throughout the district. When the young man suggested using a printed circular letter, Lincoln demurred, contending that such a document "would not have nearly the same effect; a written one had the stamp of personality, was more flattering to the recipient, and would tell altogether more in assuring his good-will, if not his support." So Harris spent many days laboriously writing out more letters, each custom-tailored to the recipient.[126]

In February, Lincoln did some politicking throughout the northern half of the district. Among the counties he targeted was Putnam, where hostility to slavery was strong, thanks in part to the efforts of the noted abolitionist Benjamin Lundy, who had settled there in 1838 and published his newspaper, *The Genius of Universal Emancipation*. When two Free Soilers, Thomas Alsop and Franklin King, asked Lincoln about slavery, they were, as King recalled, "so well pleased with what he said on the subject that we advised that our anti-slavery friend[s] throughout the district should cast their vote for Mr. Lincoln: which was genirally done."[127] (It is not known what Lincoln told them, but in October 1845, he had written an Ohio antislavery leader that he opposed the expansion of the peculiar institution into the western territories: "we should never knowingly lend ourselves directly or indirectly, to prevent that slavery from dying a natural death—to find new places for it to live in, when it can no longer exist in the old.")[128] King, Alsop, and their friends significantly helped Lincoln win the district. Once in Congress, Lincoln had King's brother appointed register of the Springfield land office, much to the dismay of William Butler and some other Whigs. (The Liberty Party's congressional candidate, Elihu Walcott, won only 2% of the vote in 1846.)

Lincoln effectively argued that the Pekin understanding should be interpreted to mean that Hardin should not be nominated because he had already served his term in Congress. On January 7, 1846, Lincoln explained to Dr. Robert S. Boal that he would gladly have given way to Hardin if neither of them had been in Congress or if they both had been; but "to yield to Hardin under present circumstances, seems to me as nothing else than yielding to one who would gladly sacrifice me altogether." Lincoln declared that "turn about is fair play" and asked for "a fair shake."[129] Boal agreed, and when Hardin tried to enlist his support, the good doctor replied that while he admired and liked the former congressman, "I do not see how we can avoid adopting the maxim that 'turn about is fair play' so far as the 7th District at least is concerned, and whether right or wrong, this is my *only reason* for favoring the pretensions of Mr Lincoln."[130] Similarly, the *Tazewell Whig*, edited by Benjamin F. James, chairman of the Whig District Central Committee, declared in December 1845, "we unhesitatingly say that the motto of 'turn about is fair play' should be recognized in the future nomination for representative."[131] The following February, James's paper said: "We conceive it due to Mr. Lincoln, that the people of this district should pay a substantial tribute to his worth, energy and patriotic exertions in behalf of Whig principles."[132]

This "fair play" argument prevailed. Ira J. Fenn, a resident of Lacon, informed Hardin that some of Lincoln's backers "are endeavoring to impress upon the mind of the People that it is Lincoln[']s right to have the office next Term" because "the doctrine of 'taking turns' was established by the Pekin Convention, that it has so far been acted on, that it is now Lincolns turn, that Hardin has had his turn, that it is due to Lincoln on account of his great services to the Whig party, on account of his talent & worth, that he is poor & Hardin is Rich, That This is the only Whig district, in short that this is the only crumb that a Whig politician can obtain in the State, and that no one deserves [it] more than Lincoln." Though Fenn himself rejected the rotation-in-office principle, he told Hardin: "I shall not be surprised if the new doctrine should get a pretty good hold of the public mind. Its preachers make it appear plausible."[133] On January 12, P. N. Thompson of Pekin reported to Hardin that Lincoln had assiduously gathered pledges from prominent Whigs and that nobody "supposed here, until your letter was published, that you had any desire to again represent us in Congress." Although Hardin might have made headway against Lincoln because of all his "ardent friends," Thompson said that now the dominant sentiment was "'Hardin is a good fellow and did us and himself great credit and honor by his course in Congress, Lincoln is also a good fellow and has worked hard and faithfully for the Party, if he desires to go to Congress let him go this time, *turn about is fair play.*' This latter remark I hear made in the store daily." Thompson also noted that Lincoln's exhaustive travels on the circuit made him very widely known, and "from this fact would have an advantage over you."[134] The following month, John H. Morrison of Tremont told Hardin that "Lincoln spins a good yarn, is what we call a clever fellow, has mixed much with our Citizens; and has done much in sustaining Whig principles in Illinois," and "our people think that it is Abraham's turn now."[135]

Discouraged by such reports, Hardin tried to sow animosity between Lincoln and Baker by misrepresenting to each man what the other had said. In the autumn of 1845, Baker called on Hardin, who alleged that Lincoln had reported that Baker would not seek the nomination at all. This was in fact not what Baker had told Lincoln, nor was it what Lincoln reported to Hardin. (Baker had promised not to oppose Lincoln but said he would resist any attempt by Hardin to seek another term. There was so much hostility between Hardin and Baker that in February 1846, when Hardin volunteered his services to the military, he did so through Stephen A. Douglas rather than Baker, for, he told Douglas, "the manner in which he [Baker] has recently acted towards me in endeavoring to prevent my renomination to Congress, would prevent me from making the request of him.")[136]

Angered by Lincoln's purported statement to Hardin, Baker wrote Lincoln urging him to drop out of the race. Similarly, Hardin managed to hurt Lincoln's relations with Baker by alleging that Baker informed him that Lincoln could defeat Hardin but that Baker could not. Eventually, Lincoln persuaded Baker that Hardin had erred in summarizing his remarks. Baker withdrew after Lincoln expressed reluctance to abandon his dream of a congressional seat.

Desperate to counter the turn-about-is-fair-play argument, Hardin proposed that the convention system be scrapped in favor of a preferential primary election. Lincoln, sensing that the "movement is intended to injure me," urged Whig editors to take "strong ground for the old system, under which Hardin & Baker were nominated."[137] On January 19, 1846, Lincoln calmly and firmly told Hardin that the primary scheme was unfair: "I have always been in the habit of acceding to almost any proposal that a friend would make; and I am truly sorry I can not in this." He tactfully declared his satisfaction "with the old system under which such good men [as Baker and Hardin] have triumphed."[138] In reply, Hardin denounced the convention system as "anti-republican," criticized Lincoln for trying to derail his congressional candidacy by having him nominated for governor, and belittled the Pekin agreement for its assumption that "the District is a horse which each candidate may mount and ride a two mile heat without consulting any body but the grooms & Jockeys." He implied that he had never agreed to the Pekin compromise in the first place. Hardin's contention seemed disingenuous, for he announced shortly after winning the congressional race in 1843 that he would not seek reelection. In 1844 he kept his word and did not challenge Baker for the nomination.

Refusing to be provoked, Lincoln on February 7 gently criticized Hardin's assumption "that the District is a horse which, the first jockey that can mount him, may whip and spur round and round, till jockey, or horse, or both, fall dead on the track." He insisted that his qualifications for the congressional seat were substantial: "If I am not, (in services done the party and in capacity to serve in future) near enough your equal, when added to the fact of your having had a turn, to entitle me to the nomination, I scorn it on any and all other grounds." Lincoln concluded with a mild protest: "After, by way of imputations upon me, you have used the terms 'management' 'manoevering' and 'combination' quite freely, you, in your closing paragraph say: 'For it is mortifying to discover that those with whom I have long acted & from whom I expected a different course, have considered it all fair to prevent my nomination to congress.' Feeling as I do, the utter injustice of these imputations, it is somewhat difficult to be patient under them—yet I content myself with saying that if there is cause for mortification any where, it is in the readiness with which you believe, and make such charges, against one with whom you truly say you have long acted; and in whose conduct, you have heretofore marked nothing as dishonorable. I believe you do not mean to be unjust, or ungenerous; and I therefore am slow to believe that you will not yet think *better* and think *differently* of this matter."[139]

Though nettled by Hardin's failure to abide by the Pekin accord, Lincoln insisted that "nothing be said" against him.[140] When Gibson Harris proposed that he respond in kind to Hardin's tactics, Lincoln said, "Gibson, I *want* to be nominated. I should like very much to go to Congress; but unless I can get there by fair means I shall not go. If it depends on some other course, I will stay at home."[141] Lincoln's scrupulousness was followed by his supporters in the press, including the *Sangamo Journal*, which later explained that "we cautiously avoided saying any thing in our paper, that might touch the feelings of either party."[142] One "H" protested in the *Tazewell Whig* that the "friends of Messrs. Lincoln and Baker have a right to complain of a want of good faith on the part of Mr. Hardin and his friends," and Allen N. Ford emphatically denied Hardin's interpretation of the Pekin convention resolution: "If the principle of rotation in office is not only recognized in that resolution [passed in Pekin in 1843] but by Gen. H. himself . . . then we confess our incapacity to comprehend the import of language or action."[143]

On January 31, the Whigs of Athens named Lincoln as their choice for Congress. Two weeks later, on the eve of other precinct meetings, Hardin, despairing of his prospects, withdrew from the race. He had failed to act as promptly and work as energetically as had Lincoln. Hardin's announcement bluntly addressed the Pekin convention agreement: "I deem it an act of justice to myself to state, that this report [that he had agreed to step aside after one term and let Baker and Lincoln have their turns] is utterly without foundation. I never made any bargain, or had any understanding directly or indirectly with Mr. Baker, or any other person, respecting either the last or any future canvass for Congress. Neither Mr. Baker, or any other voter of the District knew I would not be a candidate for re-election, until I stated that fact publicly after my election."[144] Along with his withdrawal statement, Hardin revealed his scheme for a preferential primary to replace the convention, but he did not provide a copy of Lincoln's reply.

As this statement indicates, there is some doubt about the exact terms of the Pekin understanding. Stephen T. Logan thought that "there was no agreement—no understanding between Hardin—Baker—Lincoln & Logan about rotation in office."[145] But James H. Matheny testified that though there may have been no formal pact, "there was a Kind of implied understanding that Hardin—Baker—Lincoln should rotate in Congress."[146] Whatever the case might have been, in 1846 many Seventh District Whigs believed that there had been an agreement of some sort whereby Hardin would serve one term in Congress, then Baker, then Lincoln. As the *Sangamo Journal* observed, Hardin's contention "is strictly true," but "the doings of the Pekin Convention did seem to point that way; and the General's voluntary declination, as to the canvass of '44 was, by many, construed into an acquiescence on his part. These things had led many of his most devoted friends to not expect him to be a candidate at this time."[147]

Though bitter, Hardin graciously refused to run as an independent candidate or otherwise injure Lincoln's chances. He publicly declared that "if I had cause for personal complaint, I would rather suffer real or supposed wrong, than be the means of producing dissension amongst my political friends."[148] Lincoln, fearful of Whig defections, did his best to salve the wounded feelings of Hardin and his followers. By May 1, when the Whig District Convention assembled in Petersburg, Lincoln's nomination was a foregone conclusion.

Lincoln may well have feared that Hardin might thwart his future aspirations. David Davis, for one, believed Hardin could have "controlled the politics & the affairs of the State."[149] In 1847, however, Hardin was killed in the Mexican War, thus clearing the political field for Lincoln. Baker, who could also have posed a threat to Lincoln's political future, moved to Galena, Illinois, in 1848, and soon thereafter to California.

In late May, the Democrats of the Seventh District nominated the well-known Methodist circuit-riding preacher, Peter Cartwright, to run against Lincoln. (Earlier, when it seemed that John Calhoun might be the Democratic candidate, articles in the *Sangamo Journal* attacked Calhoun fiercely. The editor of the *Illinois State Register* accused Lincoln of penning those "bitter, unjust, and malignant" pieces.)[150] Almost a quarter-century older than Lincoln, the colorful, energetic, ambitious Cartwright was an imposing man and a formidable foe. He was approximately 6 feet tall, strongly built, with a head of curly black hair above a round, clean-shaven face and piercing eyes. A contemporary said his "countenance . . . could blaze with mirth, flash with contempt, frown with wrath or darken with defiance. His intellectual faculties corresponded with his superb physical organism, and his perceptions were quick, clear, and usually correct. But giving intensity to his entire being was that indomitable energy characterizing those 'born to rule,' and securing to such a recognition of their position as 'leaders.'"[151] Around his home near Pleasant Plains, the combative Cartwright was known as something of a bully. T. G. Onstot, a friend of the preacher, reported that he was "warlike" and "much like a boy with a chip on his shoulder." But he had winning qualities too, Onstot recalled, among them "great conversational powers, coupled with keen wit." A "man of great force of character," he "generally carried his point" as a preacher and a politician. Onstot said that Cartwright "could interest a crowd as well as any man I ever knew."[152]

Little is known about the Lincoln–Cartwright campaign, for the press virtually ignored it. Herndon described it as "an energetic canvass of three months . . . during which Lincoln kept his forces well in hand. He was active and alert, speaking everywhere, and abandoning his share of business in the law office entirely."[153] James Gourley recalled that Lincoln made a speech in Petersburg "against Peter Cartwright in his Congression[al] race—1846[.] He skinned Peter & Erastus Wright—the abolitionist."[154] The only extant newspaper report of an appearance by Lincoln merely noted that at Lacon, he "gave us a good speech" on the tariff. "In a most logical, argumentative effort, he demonstrated the necessity of a discriminating tariff, and the excellence of that adopted by the whig congress of 1842; and also that the consumer does not usually pay the tariff, but the manufacturer and importer." Lincoln concluded "with some general observations on the Mexican war, annexation of Texas, and the Oregon question."[155]

Those observations may have resembled what Lincoln told Williamson Durely in 1845: "I never was much interested in the Texas question. I never could see much good to come of annexation; inasmuch, as they were already a free republican people on our own model; on the other hand, I never could very clearly see how the annexation would augment the evil of slavery. It always seemed to me that slaves would be taken there in about equal numbers, with or without annexation." But insofar as the annexation of Texas might strengthen slavery, he was opposed to it: "It is possibly true, to some extent, that with annexation, some slaves may be sent to Texas and continued in slavery, that otherwise might have been liberated. To whatever extent this may be true, I think annexation an evil."[156] Curiously, Lincoln ignored the objection that if Texas were admitted to the Union as a slave state, the proslavery forces would gain power in Congress and the electoral college.

It has been alleged that Lincoln initially supported the Mexican War in 1846 before changing his mind and criticizing it in 1847. In later years, the *Illinois State Register* claimed that "Lincoln went through the district and . . . at all times vowed his purpose to support a vigorous prosecution of the war."[157] Since the *Register* was trying to portray Lincoln, then a candidate for higher office, as a hypocrite, its account of his 1846 campaign is suspect. Direct evidence of Lincoln's attitude toward the war is skimpy. The press reported that he, along with Governor Thomas Ford, Dr. Elias Merryman, David L. Gregg, and David B. Campbell, spoke to a group of cadets and militia members in Springfield on May 30, 1846. The brief newspaper account merely says that the speeches "were in the right spirit—warm, thrilling, effective," and gave no details as to who said what.[158] In all likelihood, Lincoln was agnostic about the war rather than a strong supporter. In January 1848, he asserted that when hostilities broke out, "it was my opinion that all those who, because of knowing too *little*, or because of knowing too *much*, could not conscientiously approve the conduct of the President, in the beginning of it, should, nevertheless, as good citizens and patriots, remain silent on that point, at least till the war should be ended."[159] He later opined that "the principal motive" for the president's decision to provoke the war "was to divert public attention from the surrender of 'Fifty-four, forty, or fight' to Great Britain, on the Oregon boundary question."[160]

What Lincoln thought about the Oregon question is unknown. Democrats taunted him about his silence on the issue; in May 1846, the *Illinois State Register* asked, "Is Lincoln for 54 40 [i.e., all of the Oregon Territory], or is he for 'compromising' away our Oregon territory to England . . . ? This, the People ought to know, before they vote next August. No shuffling, Mr. Lincoln! Come out, square!"[161] Albert J. Beveridge, noting that the *Sangamo Journal* enthusiastically supported the claim that the United States was entitled to all of the Oregon Territory, inferred that Lincoln did too, for his views and the *Journal*'s usually coincided. But in the summer of 1846, the *Illinois State Register* complained that while "the Oregon question was pending the Journal expressed no opinion in regard to it, for the reason that it had not the courage to go with its party, against the 54 40 claim of our government. Since the question has been settled, it denounces Mr. Polk for subscribing to the proposition for which every whig Senator voted."[162] In the spring of 1845, several mass meetings about the Oregon question were held at Springfield and addressed by many leading political figures of central Illinois, but not Lincoln. Like his opponents Stephen A. Douglas and John Calhoun, Lincoln's Whig allies Edward D. Baker and John J. Hardin were outspoken champions of expelling the British from the lower half of the Oregon Territory, which was jointly occupied by Great Britain and the United States. Lincoln probably shared the views of most congressional Whigs, who urged a peaceful compromise with the British rather than the belligerent "Fifty-four forty or fight" stance favored by many senate Democrats.

Lincoln campaigned relentlessly, going around the district over and over. He spoke extensively during the 1846 campaign in Tazewell County, where Shelby Cullom's family lived. Cullom's father Richard drove Lincoln to his meetings throughout the county. In his stump speech, Lincoln would say: "Fellow citizens: Maj. Cullom has been everywhere with me, and has heard this speech time and again. The only way I can deceive him with it is to go down to the other end and give it to him backward."[163]

Because of his campaigning and his extensive legal practice, Lincoln was well known throughout the district. In 1847, a Boston journalist described a stagecoach ride he shared with Lincoln from Chicago to Springfield. Once they reached the Seventh Congressional District, Lincoln "knew, or appeared to know, every body we met, the name of the tenant of every farm-house, and the owner of every plot of ground. Such a shaking of hands—such a how d'ye do—such a greeting of different kinds, as we saw, was never seen before; it seemed as if he knew every thing, and he had a kind word, a smile and a bow for every body on the road, even to the horses, and the cattle, and the swine."[164]

Lincoln spent little money on his election. Prominent Whigs collected a $200 campaign fund, of which the candidate used less than a dollar. "I did not need the money," Lincoln said as he returned the balance of the cash. "I made the canvass on my own horse; my entertainment, being at the houses of friends, cost me nothing; and my only outlay was seventy-five cents for a barrel of cider which some farm-hands insisted I should treat them to."[165]

Eighteen years later Lincoln described the 1846 campaign as the least acrimonious of his political career: "It is a little singular that I who am not a vindictive man, should have always been before the people for election in canvasses marked for their bitterness: always but once: When I came to Congress it was a quiet time: But always besides that the contests in which I have been prominent have been marked with great rancor."[166] The canvass, however, was not without its ugly side. Cartwright avoided meeting Lincoln in public discussion and instead launched a whispering campaign denouncing his opponent as an infidel. Robert Boal of Lacon recollected that "Cartwright *sneaked* through this part of the district, after Lincoln, and grossly misrepresented him."[167] As a result, many pious Christian Whigs were reluctant to vote for Lincoln.

Such attacks angered Lincoln. When the president of Illinois College wished him success, Lincoln replied, "I do not know. We are dealing with men that would just as soon lie as not."[168] At Postville, where Cartwright had accused Lincoln of being a "skeptic," the Whig candidate responded by reading to his audience a passage from the Illinois constitution stipulating that "no religious test shall ever be required as a qualification to any office or public trust under this state." Lincoln then added: "Brother Cartwright may be well posted in theology but he is not informed as to the constitution of his own state which he has several times sworn to maintain."[169]

Lincoln decided to meet the charge of atheism head-on. On July 31 he issued a handbill protesting that he was no "open scoffer at Christianity." He acknowledged that he was "not a member of any Christian church" but asserted that he had "never denied the truth of the Scriptures" and had "never spoken with intentional disrespect of religion in general, or of any denomination of Christians in particular." At one time, he admitted, he "was inclined to believe in what . . . is called the 'Doctrine of Necessity'—that is, that the human mind is impelled to action, or held in rest by some power, over which the mind itself has no control." He had even defended this proposition in private discussions—never publicly—but had given up doing so five years earlier. That doctrine, he asserted, was "held by several of the Christian denominations." He declared that "I do not think I could myself, be brought to support a man for office, whom I knew to be an open enemy of, and scoffer at, religion." No man, he said, "has the right thus to insult the feelings, and injure the morals, of the community in which he may live. If, then, I was guilty of such conduct, I should blame no man who should condemn me for it; but I do blame those, whoever they may be, who falsely put such a charge in circulation against me."[170]

Some residents of the Seventh District found Lincoln's "lawyer like declaration" less than forthcoming. One said of it that in "war, politics and religion, a ruse is admissible."[171] The criticism has some merit, for in this document Lincoln seemed to make two different claims: that he never believed in infidel doctrines, and that he never publicly espoused them. If the former were true, the latter would be superfluous; if the former were untrue, the latter would be irrelevant. Moreover, his reference to the doctrine of necessity was a dodge, for he was accused of infidelity, not fatalism.

In addition, Lincoln's assertion that he had "never denied the truth of the Scriptures" is belied by the testimony of friends, as is the implication that he was skeptical only in his early years. After moving to Springfield in 1837, Lincoln continued expressing the irreverent views he had proclaimed in New Salem. John Todd Stuart recalled that "he was an avowed and open Infidel—Sometimes bordered on atheism. . . . Lincoln went further against Christian beliefs—& doctrines & principles than any man I ever heard: he shocked me. . . . Lincoln always denied that Jesus was . . . the son of God."[172] James Matheny also said he was "shocked" by Lincoln's views on religion. Lincoln, he said, "was an infidel—have heard Lincoln call Christ a bastard. . . . Lincoln attacked the Bible & new Testament on two grounds—1st From the inherent or apparent contradiction under its lids & 2dly From the grounds of Reason—sometimes he ridiculed the Bible & New Testament—sometimes seemed to Scoff at it." Though Matheny knew Lincoln well from 1834 to 1860, he "never heard that Lincoln changed his views."[173] Lincoln told his unbelieving protégé William Herndon "a thousand times that he did not believe that the Bible, etc., were revelations of God, as the Christian world contends."[174] Lincoln often discussed Christianity with Edward D. Baker; the former challenged the authenticity of the scriptures, while the latter defended them. Lincoln was never "ribald or blasphemous in the slightest degree." Their "controversy was candid and sincere: Lincoln seemed unable to . . . bring his mind to the belief that they [scriptures] were inspired."[175]

In Springfield, Lincoln also debated religion with Albert Taylor Bledsoe, a Whig leader and attorney. In 1842–1843, while both men boarded at the Globe Tavern, "Lincoln was always throwing out his Infidelity to Bledsoe, ridiculing Christianity, and especially the divinity of Christ."[176] From "various conversations with him on the subject of religion," Bledsoe recalled that Lincoln "always seemed to deplore his want of faith as a very great infelicity, from which he would be glad to be delivered." Lincoln spoke about this subject "with an air of such apparent modesty, that his gloom and despair, seeming to border on a state of insanity," aroused in Bledsoe "no other feeling than one of deep compassion."[177]

Lincoln's 1846 handbill may seem to have been a clever attorney's ingenious exercise in obfuscation, but it was more than that. The "doctrine of necessity," as Lincoln understood it, was a kind of determinism akin to that of Jeremy Bentham and of later depth psychologists who maintained that acts and thoughts are dictated by forces beyond the control of the rational, conscious individual. Lincoln believed that no act was unselfish. For example, when he aided birds or animals in distress, he was not behaving altruistically; he selfishly wished to avoid the pain that his hypersensitive conscience would cause him if he did not so act. At the opposite end of the moral spectrum, unkind and ungenerous acts were often committed not out of malice or evil, but because their perpetrators were in the grip of unconscious forces and "knew not what they did." This belief inclined Lincoln to be unusually charitable, forbearing, nonjudgmental, compassionate, and forgiving, especially in his later years. Yet Lincoln found determinism hard to square with the fundamental principles of law and morality. He told his good friend Joseph Gillespie "that he could not avoid believing in predestination although he considered it a very unprofitable field of speculation because it was hard to reconcile that belief with responsibility for one[']s act[s]."[178]

Cartwright's tactics availed him little in those localities where he and Lincoln were well known, but in the northern part of the district the whispering campaign proved effective. Shortly after the election, *The Illinois Gazette* of Lacon declared that "Mr. Lincoln is right in supposing that Mr. Cartwright circulated the story [about Lincoln's infidelity] in this county, and also that he, Mr. L., lost some votes thereby. It appears the Rev. gentleman circulated the same story in other parts of the District." The *Gazette*'s editor, Allen Ford, denounced such reveling "in the filth of defamation and falsehood."[179]

Though he lost Woodford and Marshall counties, Lincoln won the district's other nine as he captured 56 percent of the vote, topping Hardin's 53 percent in 1843 and Baker's 52 percent in 1844. His success was part of a national trend, which saw Whigs triumphant in 53.6 percent of congressional contests, a substantial improvement over the party's showing in 1844 and 1845. The turnout in the Seventh District in 1846 was somewhat lower than it had been in 1843 and 1844, perhaps because the outcome was a foregone conclusion and also because many voters were serving in the Mexican War, which had broken out three months earlier. The *Illinois State Register* blamed Cartwright's defeat on "General Apathy," noting that the traditionally large Whig majority in the district "has served to dispirit the democrats and deter them from exertion."[180]

Many Democrats probably supported Lincoln, for in the Seventh District the Whig nominee for governor received only 426 more votes than his Democratic opponent, while Lincoln won 1,511 more votes than Cartwright. Some of the men who voted for both Lincoln and the Democratic gubernatorial candidate may have objected to Cartwright's profession. During the campaign, "an aspiring Democrat said to Mr. Lincoln, 'Such is my utter aversion to the meddling of preachers in politics, that I will vote for you Even at the risk of losing cast with my party, if you think the contest doubtful.'" Lincoln responded: "I would like your vote, but I fully appreciate your position, and will give you my honest opinion on the morning of Election day." When that day arrived, Lincoln confidently told this Democrat: "I am now satisfied that I have got the preacher by the [balls], and you had better keep out of the ring."[181]

Other opponents of the Whig Party may have voted for Lincoln because they admired (in the words of a Springfield Democrat) "his commanding talents and deserving popularity."[182]

Lincoln felt little elation upon achieving the goal that he had long sought; he confided to Joshua Speed that his election "to Congress, though I am very grateful to our friends for having done it, has not pleased me as much as I expected."[183] Such a letdown is not unusual among the compulsively ambitious, for the attainment of power satisfies only temporarily the hunger for approval rooted in a damaged sense of self-worth. Another reason for the lack of euphoria on Lincoln's part may have been the peculiar congressional timetable stipulating that the Thirtieth Congress would not meet until December 1847. Wishing to avoid conflict with fellow Whigs, Lincoln did not try to fill the unexpired term of his friend Edward D. Baker, who in January 1847 quit his seat to participate in the Mexican War.

Poet

While waiting for his congressional term to begin, Lincoln indulged his poetical muse, writing verses inspired by his 1844 campaign swing through Indiana. The sight of old haunts which he had not visited for fourteen years prompted him to compose what he called "poetry, or doggerel" about his youth.[184] In 1846 and 1847 he submitted to attorney Andrew Johnston a few poems, some of which Johnston published anonymously in the Quincy *Whig*. (Lincoln did not want his authorship revealed, for, as he told Johnston, "I have not sufficient hope of the verses attracting any favorable notice to tempt me to risk being ridiculed for having written them.")[185] Their most striking feature is morbidity, reflecting Lincoln's obsession with death, rooted in his childhood experiences of loss.

To attorney Johnston he sent not only his own verses but also a copy of his favorite poem, William Knox's "Mortality." "I would give all I am worth, and go into debt, to be able to write so fine a piece as I think that is," he told Johnston.[186] Lincoln said that Knox's verses "sounded to him as much like true poetry as any thing that he had ever heard."[187] Gibson W. Harris heard Lincoln recite the poem often in his law office, and Lawrence Weldon observed him one night on the legal circuit sitting before the dying embers in a fireplace quoting Knox's poem. Lincoln discovered the poem in a newspaper in 1845, shortly after his campaign trip to Indiana. The memories awakened by his return to Indiana made him susceptible to the appeal of Knox's dirgelike quatrains:

> Oh why should the spirit of mortal be proud!
> Like a swift flying meteor—a fast flying cloud—
> A flash of lightning—a break of the wave,
> He passeth from life to his rest in the grave.
>
> The leaves of the Oak, and the Willow shall fade,
> Be scattered around, and together be laid.
> And the young and the old, and the low and the high,
> Shall moulder to dust, and together shall lie.

The third stanza may have been particularly meaningful to Lincoln:

> The infant a mother attended and loved—
> The mother that infant's affection who proved
> The husband that mother and infant who blest,
> Each—all are away to their dwellings of rest.

This might well have brought back images of Nancy Hanks, her aunt and uncle, and his infant brother, all of whom died in Lincoln's youth. The fourth stanza perhaps conjured up memories of Ann Rutledge and of his sister:

> The maid on whose brow, on whose cheek, on whose eye
> Shone beauty and pleasure—her triumphs are by;
> And alike from the memory of the living erased
> And the memory of mortals, who loved her and praised—

The remaining ten stanzas continue in a similar vein but without such obvious reference to Lincoln's life.

Lincoln's own 1846 poem, "My Childhood Home I See Again," is similarly obsessed with "loved ones lost." The first canto clearly deals with Lincoln's own family and friends.

> My childhood-home I see again,
>   And gladden with the view;
> And still as mem'ries crowd my brain,
>   There's sadness in it too.
>
> O memory! thou mid-way world
>   'Twixt Earth and Paradise,
> Where things decayed, and loved ones lost
>   In dreamy shadows rise.
>
> And freed from all that's gross or vile,
>   Seem hallowed, pure, and bright,
> Like scenes in some enchanted isle,
>   All bathed in liquid light.
>
> As distant mountains please the eye,
>   When twilight chases day—
> As bugle-tones, that, passing by,
>   In distance die away—
>
> As leaving some grand water-fall
>   We ling'ring, list its roar,
> So memory will hallow all
>   We've known, but know no more.
>
> Now twenty years have passed away,
>   Since here I bid farewell

To woods, and fields, and scenes of play
  And school-mates loved so well.

Where many were, how few remain
  Of old familiar things!
But seeing these to mind again
  The lost and absent brings.

The friends I left that parting day—
  How changed, as time has sped!
Young childhood grown, strong manhood grey,
  And half of all are dead.

I hear the lone survivors tell
  How nought from death could save,
Till every sound appears a knell,
  And every spot a grave.

I range the fields with pensive tread,
  And pace the hollow rooms;
And feel (companions of the dead)
  I'm living in the tombs.[188]

These verses call to mind Isaac Watts's hymn, "The Shortness of Life, and the Goodness of God," which Lincoln copied into his commonplace book of 1824–1826:

Time what an em[p]ty vaper [']tis and days how swift they are
swift as an indian arr[ow] fly on like a shooting star
the presant moment Just [is here] then slides away in h[as]te
that we can never say they['re ours] but [only say] th[ey]'re past.[189]

Lincoln was fond of "The Inquiry" by Charles Mackay, which treated death and the afterlife:

Tell me, ye winged winds
That round my pathway roar,
Do ye not know some spot
Where mortals weep no more?
Some lone and pleasant vale
Some valley in the West,
Where, free from toil and pain,
The weary soul may rest?
The loud wind dwindled to a whisper low,
And sighed for pity as it answered, No.

Tell me, thou mighty deep,
Whose billows round me play,
Knows't thou some favored spot,

> Some island far away,
> Where weary man may find
> The bliss for which he sighs;
> Where sorrow never lives
> And friendship never dies?
> The loud waves rolling in perpetual flow
> Stopped for awhile and sighed to answer, No.
>
> And thou, serenest moon,
> That with such holy face
> Dost look upon the earth
> Asleep in Night's embrace—
> Tell me, in all thy round
> Hast thou not seen some spot
> Where miserable man
> Might find a happier lot?
> Behind a cloud the moon withdrew in woe,
> And a voice sweet but sad responded, No.
>
> Tell me, my secret soul,
> Oh, tell me, Hope and Faith,
> Is there no resting-place
> From sorrow, sin, and death?
> Is there no happy spot
> Where mortals may be blessed,
> Where grief may find a balm
> And weariness a rest?
> Faith, Hope, and Love, best boon to mortals given,
> Waved their bright wings and whispered,
>
> Yes, in Heaven.[190]

One of Lincoln's favorite speeches from Shakespeare was Richard II's lament, which John Hay heard him read in Springfield and Washington:

> For heaven's sake, let us sit upon the ground,
> And tell sad stories of the death of kings:—
> How some have been deposed, some slain in war,
> Some haunted by the ghosts they have deposed;
> Some poisoned by their wives, some sleeping killed;
> All murdered:—For within the hollow crown
> That rounds the mortal temples of a king
> Keeps Death his court; and there the antic sits,
> Scoffing his state, and grinning at his pomp,—
> Allowing him a breath, a little scene
> To monarchize, be feared, and kill with looks;

Infusing him with self and vain conceit,—
As if this flesh, which walls about our life,
Were brass impregnable,—and humored thus,
Comes at the last, and with a little pin
Bores through his castle walls and—farewell, King!

Lincoln was fascinated by this speech. He was also fond of sad songs. As a boy in Indiana, he used to sing "John Anderson's Lamentation," which contained the line "In yonder cold graveyard, her body doth lie."[191] As a fledgling attorney, he was heard singing lugubrious pieces like "Mary's Dream," "Lord Ullin's Daughter," and "The Soldier's Dream." His favorite song was a ballad titled "Twenty Years Ago," which he sang often in Illinois and later in the White House. The verses that most affected him were these:

I've wandered to the village, Tom; I've sat beneath the tree
Upon the schoolhouse play-ground, that sheltered you and me:
But none were left to greet me, Tom, and few were left to know
Who played with us upon the Green, some twenty years ago.

Near by the spring, upon the elm you know I cut your name,—
Your sweetheart's just beneath it Tom; and you did mine the same.
Some heartless wretch has peeled the bark,—t'was dying sure but slow,
Just as *she* died whose name you cut, some twenty years ago.

My lids have long been dry, Tom, but tears came to my eyes;
I thought of her I loved so well, those early broken ties:
I visited the old churchyard, and took some flowers to strew
Upon the graves of those we loved, some twenty years ago.[192]

Lincoln especially admired Oliver Wendell Holmes's "The Last Leaf," which also dealt with the death of loved ones. He was fondest of this stanza:

The mossy marbles rest
On lips that he has pressed
  In their bloom;
And the names he loved to hear
Have been carved for many a year
  On the tomb.

Of these verses he said: "For pure pathos, in my judgment, there is nothing finer than those six lines in the English language!"[193] When Lincoln recited that stanza, his eyes would tear up. Holmes's lines doubtless called to Lincoln's mind the graves of his mother, sister, and Ann Rutledge.

In his copy of Byron's poetry, Lincoln turned down the page containing these sorrowful verses:

The spell is broke, the charm is flown!
Thus is it with life's fitful fever!

> We madly smile when we should groan;
> Delirium is our best deceiver.
> Each lucid interval of thought
> Recalls the woes of Nature's charter,
> And he that acts as wise men ought,
> But lives, as saints have died, a martyr.[194]

Lincoln also liked to quote from Thomas Moore's "The Fire-Worshippers":

> Oh, ever thus, from childhood's hour,
> I've seen my fondest hopes decay;
> I never lov'd a tree or flow'r
> But 't was the first to fade away.
> I never nurs'd a dear gazelle,
> To glad me with its soft black eye,
> But when it came to know me well,
> And love me, it was sure to die![195]

Lincoln's own poetry and his literary taste indicate that his predisposition to depression was rooted in the death of loved ones in his early years.

Another psychological concern appears in a poem he composed after his 1844 visit to southwestern Indiana: fear of insanity. His schoolmate Matthew Gentry, three years older than Lincoln, had at the age of 19 gone berserk and tried to kill his parents. Thereafter he was locked up as a madman. Lincoln's verses reveal the horror he felt as he observed Gentry:

> But here's an object more of dread
>   Than aught the grave contains—
> A human form with reason fled,
>   While wretched life remains. . . .
>
> When terror spread, and neighbors ran
>   Your dangerous strength to bind,
> And soon, a howling, crazy man
>   Your limbs were fast confined;
>
> How then you strove and shrieked aloud,
>   Your bones and sinews bared;
> And fiendish on the gazing crowd,
>   With burning eyeballs glared—
>
> And begged, and swore, and wept, and prayed,
>   With maniac laught[er] joined—
> How fearful were these signs displayed
>   By pangs that killed thy mind!
>
> And when at length tho' drear and long,
>   Time soothed thy fiercer woes,

How plaintively thy mournful song
   Upon the still night rose.

I've heard it oft, as if I dreamed,
   Far distant, sweet and lone—
The funeral dirge, it ever seemed
   Of reason dead and gone.

To drink it's strains, I've stole away,
   All stealthily and still,
Ere yet the rising God of day
   Had streaked the Eastern hill.

Air held his breath; trees, with the spell,
   Seemed sorrowing angels round,
Whose swelling tears in dew-drops fell
   Upon the listening ground.

But this is past; and nought remains,
   That raised thee o'er the brute;
Thy piercing shrieks, and soothing strains,
   Are like, forever mute.

Now fare thee well—more thou the *cause*,
   Than *subject* now of woe.
All mental pangs, by time's kind laws,
   Hast lost the power to know.

O death! Thou awe-inspiring prince,
   That keepst the world in fear;
Why dost thou tear more blest ones hence,
   And leave him ling'ring here?[196]

Lincoln's reaction to Gentry's insanity suggests that he may have feared that he might lose his own mind. In the opinion of his neighbors, he had gone crazy at least twice—following the death of Ann Rutledge in 1835 and after breaking his engagement to Mary Todd in 1841. Perhaps he feared that such an attack would recur. He may also have feared that his wife was insane. She behaved irrationally, starting early in their marriage. According to William Herndon, Lincoln "held his wife partly insane for years."[197] During his presidency, he told the superintendent of the Old Capitol prison that the "caprices of Mrs. Lincoln, I am satisfied, are the result of partial insanity."[198]

Economic Issues

As he prepared to take his seat in Congress, Lincoln wrote memoranda on the tariff issue. The most striking passage, foreshadowing his mature antislavery pronouncements, begins with a biblical quotation that he would cite frequently in the 1850s and

1860s: "In the sweat of thy face shalt thou eat bread."[199] He argued that since "most good things are produced by labour, it follows that [all] such things of right belong to those whose labour has produced them. But it has so happened in all ages of the world, that *some* have laboured, and *others* have, without labour, enjoyed a large proportion of the fruits. This is wrong, and should not continue. To [secure] to each labourer the whole product of his labour, or as nearly as possible, is a most worthy object of any good government."[200] Lincoln used this principle in 1847 to justify protective tariffs, and he would later cite it while attacking slavery. In 1858, for example, he described the proslavery argument as "the same old serpent that says you work and I eat, you toil and I will enjoy the fruits of it." He declared that "each individual is naturally entitled to do as he pleases with himself and the fruit of his labor."[201]

In applying this principle to the issue of protectionism, Lincoln drew a distinction between *useful* and *useless* labor. The latter included transporting goods from abroad when they could be produced as cheaply at home. Curiously, as he had done in his earlier discussions of the tariff, Lincoln continued to ignore the powerful "infant industries" rationale. Nor did he emphasize the argument made by many other Whigs, that without high tariffs, an unfavorable balance of trade would damage the United States as specie was drained overseas, leading to a credit shortage and consequent economic stagnation.

On July 6, 1847, Lincoln made his maiden speech before a national audience. As a delegate to the Harbor and River Convention in Chicago, he had a chance to speak on federal support of internal improvements. Ten thousand people attended this convention, where delegates from the North and West remonstrated against President Polk's veto of a river and harbor appropriations bill, an action that Westerners interpreted as a pro-Southern blow to their region's interests. When news of the veto reached Chicago, ships there lowered flags to half-mast, and a sandbar at the harbor's entrance was christened "Mount Polk." Snags in rivers became known as "Polk stalks." At the convention, a New York Democrat, David Dudley Field, spoke in favor of a strict construction of the Constitution and supported only limited river and harbor improvements. Horace Greeley wrote that Lincoln responded "briefly and happily" to Field.[202] When Lincoln rose amid vigorous applause to speak, a Pennsylvanian asked a delegate who he was. "Oh," came the reply, "that is Abe Lincoln of Springfield, the ablest and wittiest stump speaker on the Whig side in the State of Illinois."[203]

Some Whigs, not sympathizing with Field's argument, had tried to silence him with shouts of derision.[204] Ever the peacemaker, Lincoln urged the delegates to consider themselves "a band of brothers" and not interrupt each other: "I hope there will be no more interruption—no hisses—no jibes." Responding to Field's argument, Lincoln respectfully pointed out that the New Yorker had ignored a central issue: "Who is to decide differences of opinion on constitutional questions? What tribunal? How shall we make it out? The gentleman from Pennsylvania (the Hon. Andrew Stewart) says Congress must decide. If Congress has not the power, who has? Is it not, at least, for Congress to remedy the objection [that the Constitution did not authorize Congress to appropriate funds for internal improvements], and settle this great question.

If there is any other tribunal, where is it to be found? My friend from Pennsylvania, Mr. Benton and myself, are much alike on that subject."[205]

Lincoln ignored the landmark 1803 Supreme Court ruling in *Marbury vs. Madison* that the Court itself was the ultimate arbiter of constitutional disputes. A decade later he would at much greater length question the Court's power to declare acts of Congress unconstitutional.

Lincoln's Old-Man Archetype

In Chicago, the 38-year-old Lincoln first became known as "Old Abe." Elihu B. Washburne of Galena recalled that one day "several of us sat on the sidewalk under the balcony of the Sherman House, and among the number [was] the accomplished scholar and unrivaled orator, [S.] Lisle Smith. He suddenly interrupted the conversation by exclaiming, 'There is Lincoln on the other side of the street. Just look at "Old Abe,"' and from that time we all called him 'Old Abe.'"

Washburne thought Smith's remark peculiar: "Old Abe, as applied to him, seems strange enough, as he was then a young man."[206] Washburne's puzzlement was understandable because even as Lincoln grew older he did not show obvious signs of aging. At 50, he was described as "so exceedingly 'well preserved' that he would not be taken for more than thirty eight."[207] The following year a journalist reported from Springfield that "Mr. Lincoln's age, I believe, is fifty-one, but he certainly has no appearance of being so old. His hair is black, hardly touched with gray, and his eye is brighter than that of many of his juniors."[208] Another journalist at that time wrote that "the popular sobriquet, 'Honest *Old* Abe,' is inappropriate and somewhat lacking in truth. . . . Why should a man be called old when he is in the very prime of life? . . . No one who looks upon his animated features, upon his determined eye, or listens to his hearty, fascinating conversation, would call that man old."[209] A friend who had known him for more than two decades said in 1860, the "term 'old' is hardly as applicable as the epithet *honest*, for he is in the full vigor of life, with a powerful constitution, and no symptoms of decay, mental or physical."[210]

Nonetheless, others sensed what S. Lisle Smith did. A friend from Lincoln's youthful days in Indiana reported that "Abe was always a man though a boy."[211] The journalist George Harris Monroe said that when Lincoln was 39, "he had the aspect of one considerably older than his real age."[212] Gibson W. Harris recollected that "'Honest Old Abe' was a colloquialism familiar to all Springfield before he was thirty-seven," and that Lincoln deemed himself old "when in his late thirties."[213] At 39, Lincoln declared to Herndon: "I suppose I am now one of the old men."[214] Reportedly he once said, "I . . . have been kept so crowded with the work of living that I felt myself comparatively an old man before I was forty."[215] In 1854, Lincoln told a friend that people began calling him "old" before he had turned 30.[216]

Why he should be deemed old when he betrayed few physical signs of aging cries out for explanation. The Swiss psychologist Carl Jung maintained that everyone is dominated by an archetypal figure, a condition unrelated to the experiences of childhood. Lincoln's archetype seems to have been the Old Man, combining the qualities of the Wise Elder and the Great Father. Regardless of physical appearance, the mature

Lincoln seemed to radiate the positive qualities of being old. Accordingly, many Illinoisans regarded him with filial reverence. In early 1861, when Lincoln visited his stepmother, one resident remembered that the people of Charleston greeted him with special warmth and that "[o]ld men and women talked to Mr. Lincoln with the confidence and assurance of loving children in a great family reunion."[217] A train conductor in Illinois recollected how people in railroad restaurants "tried to get as near Lincoln as possible when he was eating, because he was such good company, but we always looked at him with a kind of wonder. We couldn't exactly make him out. . . . [T]here was something about him that made plain folks feel toward him a good deal as a child feels toward his father."[218] That "something" was Lincoln's Old Man archetype. During his presidency, it would play a vital role in sustaining Union morale, for many Northerners trusted him as one would trust a benevolent, wise father.

Defending a Slaveowner

Lincoln had not dealt with the slavery issue during his congressional campaign, but he confronted it in the fall of 1847 when a Kentucky slaveholder, Robert Matson, employed his legal services to help recover a slave family. Matson cultivated a farm in Coles County, Illinois, with slaves imported from Kentucky, where he also owned a farm. At first, when he began this pattern, after each harvest he would return them across the Ohio River, and the following spring he would import a new gang from Kentucky; this procedure was legal in Illinois, where the law only forbade a slaveholder from domiciling bondsmen. Matson nonetheless permanently retained a slave in Illinois named Anthony Bryant as an overseer, thus technically freeing him. Bryant, however, did nothing to assert his free status until the spring of 1847, when his wife, Jane, and their children, who had arrived in Illinois two years earlier, seemed in danger of being permanently separated from him. (In 1845, Matson evidently feared that if he returned the slaves to Kentucky, his creditors would seize them.) Matson's hot-tempered, jealous housekeeper-mistress, known as "a vicious negro hater," suspected that he was sexually involved with Jane Bryant and demanded that she and her children be sold.[219] To thwart that possibility, Anthony Bryant enlisted the help of two local abolitionists, Hiram Rutherford, a Pennsylvania-born physician, and Gideon Ashmore, a hotel-keeper known as "a wide-awake business man" whom "nothing pleased so well as a stiff legal fight." A "strong anti-slavery man," Ashmore sheltered Jane Bryant and her offspring at his hotel.[220] Matson sued for possession of his slaves, who at the direction of a justice of the peace were temporarily jailed in Charleston.

Soon thereafter, Lincoln arrived in Coles County, where he had suits pending in the circuit court. There he was approached by Usher F. Linder, an attorney for Matson, who wanted to sue Rutherford and Ashmore for damages. That conversation turned out to be important, for subsequently Dr. Rutherford asked Lincoln to serve as his lawyer. Rutherford told Lincoln of the situation, emphasized that they had seen eye-to-eye on public issues, and requested that he defend him in court. Rutherford remembered that as he related the case to Lincoln, "a peculiarly troubled look came over his face now and then, his eyes appeared to be fixed in the distance beyond me and he shook his head several times as if debating with himself some question of grave import." Lincoln responded "with apparent reluctance" that he must refuse for "he had already been counseled with in Matson's interest and was therefore under professional obligations to represent the latter unless released." Rutherford was angry with Lincoln, who tried his best to explain that "as a lawyer, he must represent and be faithful to those who counsel with and employ him." Lincoln then went to Linder and obtained a release. When, however, he informed Rutherford that he was now free to represent him in court, his offer was spurned. Later, the hot-tempered Rutherford, whose pride was offended, admitted to an interviewer, "I was a little hasty."[221] So it was that Lincoln came to represent a slaveowner in court. Had Rutherford been less petulant, Lincoln would have represented the blacks and their protectors.

However reluctant Lincoln may have been to act on Matson's behalf, he argued his client's case forcefully. According to Orlando Ficklin, co-counsel along with Charles Constable for the Bryants, Lincoln presented "his opponents' points and arguments with such amplitude and seeming fairness and such liberality of concession of their force and strength that it increased in his adversaries their confidence of success." But then with "trenchant blows" and "cold logic" he subtly wove together and presented evidence favoring his client's case. Ficklin recalled that the "fact that General Matson had at such a time when he placed a slave on his Illinois farm, publicly declared that he was not placed there for permanent settlement, and that no counter statement had ever been made publicly or privately by him, constituted the web and woof of the argument of Mr. Lincoln, and these facts were plausible, ingeniously and forcibly presented to the court, so as to give them all the effect and significance to which they were entitled and more."[222]

A local historian of Charleston, who evidently interviewed participants in the case, reported Lincoln's argument in the case differently. "His main contention was that the question of the right of the negroes to their freedom could only be determined by a regular habeas corpus proceedings, and not by a mere motion, as was then attempted. His argument was masterful along that line, but it was very clear that he was carefully and adroitly shunning the vital question at issue in the case." Judge William Wilson, chief justice of the Illinois Supreme Court, asked him: "your objection is simply to the form of the action by which, or in which this question should be tried, is it not?"

"Yes, sir."

"Now, if this case was being tried on issue joined in a habeas corpus, and it appeared there, as it does here, that this slave owner had brought this mother and her children voluntarily, from the state of Kentucky, and had settled them down on his farm in this state, do you think, as a matter of law, that they did not thereby become free?"

A hush fell over the packed courtroom as Lincoln prepared to address the substance rather than the form of the case. He answered: "No, sir, I am not prepared to deny that they did."[223]

Lincoln winced when opposing counsel Charles Constable quoted from John Philpot Curran's well-known speech about slavery: "I speak in the spirit of the British law, which makes liberty commensurate with and inseparable from British soil;

which proclaims even to the stranger and sojourner the moment he sets his foot upon British earth, that the ground on which he treads is holy and consecrated by the genius of universal emancipation."[224] Constable's co-counsel, Orlando Ficklin, gave an impassioned speech citing the Northwest Ordinance of 1787 and the Illinois Constitution of 1818. After the trial, Lincoln complimented him: "Ficklin do you know that I think that latter part of your speech was as eloquent as I ever listened to?"[225]

Lincoln's case was weak, for Jane Bryant had been in Illinois for two years and was clearly not just a seasonal worker. His client therefore lost. In the court's decision, Judge Wilson ruled that: "Neither the place of residence, nor the declared intentions of Matson, countervail the fact that he voluntarily domiciled his servants here for two years or upwards. Even if, from some contingency, they had remained but a day, the circumstance of his having transferred their domicil from Kentucky, and fixed it in Illinois, would have produced the same result." Thus, "by bringing Jane and her children into the State of Illinois, and domiciling them here," Matson "had forfeited all claim to their services, and entitled them to be discharged therefrom."[226] With the aid of Dr. Rutherford, the Bryant family was able to immigrate to Liberia, where they were observed the following year living "truly in a deplorable condition."[227]

Lincoln's agreement to represent Matson has been called "one of the greatest enigmas of his career," the "most profound mystery ever to confound Lincoln specialists," and "one of the strangest episodes in Lincoln's career at the bar."[228] Six years earlier, in the case of *Bailey vs. Cromwell*, he and John Todd Stuart had successfully defended a black woman who sued for her freedom. They convinced the Illinois Supreme Court that the sale of the woman, who had been purchased in Illinois, was invalid, for she was free under the provisions of both the Northwest Ordinance of 1787 and the Illinois State Constitution. It was just the argument that Ficklin used in the Matson case.

In representing Matson, however, Lincoln demonstrated his acceptance of the advice of Judge George Sharswood, a well-known mid-nineteenth-century American commentator on legal ethics who urged lawyers to refrain from passing judgment on clients. Sharswood believed that an attorney "is not morally responsible for the act of the party in maintaining an unjust cause, nor for the error of the court, if they fall into error, in deciding it in his favor." A lawyer "who refuses his professional assistance because in his judgment the case is unjust and indefensible, usurps the functions of both judge and jury."[229] In 1844, the eminent jurist David Dudley Field observed that in the United States it was assumed that "a lawyer is not at liberty to refuse any one his services."[230] So, despite his antislavery convictions, Lincoln accepted the Matson case in keeping with what became known in England as the "cab-rank" rule—stipulating that lawyers must accept the first client who hails them—and with the prevailing Whig view that lawyers should try to settle disputes in an orderly fashion through the courts, trusting in the law and the judges to assure that justice was done. As a colleague at the bar said of Lincoln, he "was like the rest of us and took the defense of anyone who had a chance with the law."[231]

Another case pitting Lincoln's humanitarian principles against his professional obligations involved antislavery editor Paul Selby, with whom Lincoln worked in 1856 to launch the Illinois Republican Party. Three years earlier, Col. James Dunlap, a rich Democrat who took offense at editorials Selby had published in his newspaper, the *Morgan Journal*, caned Selby in the Jacksonville public square. Dunlap hired Lincoln, who hardly sympathized with his principles or conduct, to take his side in court against Selby.

Ideological neutrality characterized Lincoln's law practice in general, not just in slave-related cases. In malpractice suits he would represent doctors and patients alike; railroads being sued by boat owners whose vessels crashed into their bridges, as well as boat owners suing railroads for obstructing navigation with their bridges; and stock subscribers reneging on their pledges and corporations suing such stock subscribers. At least three times he was defeated because of a precedent that he had helped to establish earlier. On the stump Lincoln defended the Whig economic program favoring banks, corporations, and internal improvements like railroads, but in court he showed no hesitancy in representing clients suing those banks, corporations, and railroads.

Like other members of the bar, Lincoln could ill-afford to be finicky about clients; there were simply too many lawyers and too few clients. David Davis lamented in 1844 that the "law is not profitable."[232] Five years later Davis told Lincoln that the "practice of Law in Illinois at present promises you but poor remuneration, for the Labor—Except in the large commercial places in the State, the practice will always be poor."[233] Davis recalled that when he moved to central Illinois in the 1830s, he had expected to find few attorneys; instead he discovered that the state "was full of able lawyers."[234] An Ohio lawyer complained in 1844 that "great fortunes are not acquired at the bar, and few become rich. . . . The same industry, learning and abilities, applied to any other employment of life, would yield a much greater return." The legal profession "has a large number of members in proportion to the business," and that number was growing rapidly as the "farmer abandons his plough, the tailor his thimble, the clerk his desk, and without study or education, they rush into a profession which is, in their view, the avenue to fame and fortune."[235]

A few lawyers did view slave cases from a principled position and not, as Lincoln did, neutrally, as just another piece of necessary business. Known as the "Attorney General for Runaway Negroes," Ohio's Salmon P. Chase often represented blacks fleeing from bondage and never defended a slaveholder. He became a leader of the more radical political antislavery forces. On the other hand, in 1860 a leading Massachusetts abolitionist, future wartime governor John A. Andrew, defended the owner of a slave ship whose vessel was being threatened with forfeiture.

Some attorneys who were not dedicated opponents of slavery, like Lincoln's friend Orville H. Browning, represented fugitive slaves. According to John W. Bunn, Lincoln avoided fugitive slave cases "because of his unwillingness to be a party to a violation of the Fugitive Slave Law, arguing that the way to overcome the difficulty was to repeal the law."[236]

Journey to Washington

In October 1847, Congressman-elect Lincoln rented his Springfield house to Cornelius Ludlum and, with Mary and the children, set out to assume his new post in Washington. On their circuitous journey the family passed the first night in a St. Louis hotel where Joshua Speed, evidently traveling with them, was also a guest. They proceeded by boat to Frankfort, where they caught a train for Lexington, intending to spend three weeks with the Todds.

On the last leg of their trip, 4-year-old Robert and his 18-month-old brother Eddie irritated their fellow passengers, including Joseph Humphreys, nephew of Mary Lincoln's stepmother. Young Humphreys, arriving at his aunt's home before the Lincolns, exclaimed: "I was never so glad to get off a train in my life. There were two lively youngsters on board who kept the whole train in a turmoil, and their long-legged father, instead of spanking the brats, looked pleased as Punch and aided and abetted the older one in mischief."[237]

As this anecdote suggests, Lincoln was notoriously indulgent to his sons. William Herndon observed that Lincoln was "so blinded to his children's faults" that if "they s[hi]t in Lincoln's hat and rubbed it on his boots, he would have laughed and thought it smart. . . . He worshipped his children and *what* they worshipped; . . . disliked what the[y] hated, which was everything that did not bend to their . . . whims." Herndon complained that when the boys came to the office with their father, they "would take down the books—empty ash buckets—coal ashes—inkstands—papers—gold pens—letters etc., etc. in a pile and then dance on the pile."[238] Many Springfield residents shared Herndon's view that Lincoln "was too kind, too tender & too gentle to his children: he had no domestic government—administration or order." Herndon added that Lincoln "was liberal—generous—affectionate to his children, loving them with his whole heart, . . . as loving & tender as a nursing mother."[239] Mary Lincoln recalled her husband's statement about childrearing: "It [is my] pleasure that my children are free—happy & unrestrained by parental tyranny. Love is the chain whereby to Lock a child to its parents."[240] A Springfield neighbor remembered having a meal at the Lincoln house: "Mr. Lincoln was carving the chicken, and the first thing he did was to cut off the drumstick and gave it to Tad . . . , and then he said, smiling at the rest of the company, 'Children have first place here, you know.'"[241]

The visit with Mary's family went smoothly in part because Robert Smith Todd was fond of his son-in-law, whom he had met at Springfield in 1843. That visit pleased Mary because her father and husband came to like each other. She and Lincoln pledged to take the first convenient opportunity to visit Lexington. To help the newlyweds out, Todd gave them 80 acres of land near Springfield, provided annual gifts for the remaining six years of his life (totaling over $1,100), and assigned to them notes of various Illinois merchants who owed him money. Lincoln, who in 1843 told Joshua Speed that he could not come to Kentucky because of "poverty," doubtless appreciated these funds.[242]

In 1844, Robert Smith Todd offered to assist Lincoln politically. He explained to Ninian W. Edwards: "Mr. Lincoln I discover is using his influence & talents for the Whig Cause. . . . I can use influence here if Mr Clay is elected (of which there can *be no* doubt) to procure some appointment for him, which will keep him out of Congress until his Situation in a monied point of view, will enable him to take a stand in Congress, creditable both to himself and Country. *Such as District Attorney or Judge.*"[243] Todd confided to Edwards that "I feel more than grateful that my daughters all have married gentlemen whom I respect and esteem, and I should be pleased if it could ever be in my power to give them a more substantial evidence of my feelings than in mere words or professions. . . . I will be satisfied if they discharge all their duties and make as good wives as I think they have good husbands."[244]

Arriving at the Todd house shortly after the irate Joseph Humphreys, the Lincolns were warmly received. During this vacation, Lincoln spent much time reading periodicals like *Niles Register* and a poetry anthology, including William Cullen Bryant's "Thanatopsis," which he committed to memory. In that volume, titled *Elegant Extracts, or Useful and Entertaining Passages from the Best English Authors and Translations*, Lincoln marked with a pencil some verses, including Pope's couplet: "Know then thyself, presume not God to scan; / The Proper study of Mankind is man."

He scribbled marginalia next to these lines from "The Grave," by John Blair:

> The last end
> Of the good man is peace. How calm his exit.
> Night dews fall not more gently to the ground,
> Nor weary, worn-out winds expire so soft

Lincoln might have been thinking of his wife when he marked this passage from "Love of Fame":

> A dearth of words, a woman need not fear;
> But 'tis a task indeed to learn to *hear*.
> Doubly like Echo sound is her delight,
> And the last word is her eternal right.
> Is't not enough plagues, wars and famines rise
> To lash our crimes, but must our wives be wise? [245]

Lincoln was so impressed with Cowper's poem "Charity," dealing with slavery and the slave trade, that "he bracketed and even turned down the page upon which it appeared." He marked the following verses:

> Oh that the voice of clamor & debate
> That pleads for peace 'til it disturbs the State
> Were hushed in favor of thy generous plea,
> The poor thy clients, and heaven's smile thy fee.[246]

From the same poem he also made notations beside these lines:

> But Ah! What wish can prosper, or what prayer
> For merchants rich in cargoes of despair,
> Who drive a loathsome traffic, gauge and span,
> And buy the muscles and the bones of man?

The tender ties of father, husband, friend,
All bonds of nature in that moment end;
And each endures, while yet he draws breath,
A stroke as fatal as the scythe of death.[247]

During this visit Lincoln had ample opportunity to observe the cruelties of slavery. In Lexington newspapers, he may well have read advertisements like this one placed by a slave dealer: "Those who have slaves rendered unfit for labor by Yaws, Scrofula, Chronic Diarrhea, Negro Consumption, Rheumatism &c, and who wish to dispose of them on reasonable terms will address J. King, No. 29 Camp St., New Orleans."[248] His in-laws may have explained to Lincoln that in Louisiana, some plantations of absentee owners were run by overseers who deliberately worked to death such diseased slaves, whom they bought cheap. The future president may also have heard tales about the notoriously ill-tempered Caroline A. Turner, who savagely mistreated her slaves, killing half a dozen before one strangled her to death.

In Lexington, Lincoln could observe slavery as well as read and hear about it. He doubtless saw the public square, with its slave auction block and whipping post, where some blacks were openly flogged. Lincoln may have seen coffles file by the Todd house, for Lexington was the state's principal slave market. The noisome holding pens of a slave dealer practically abutted the home of Mary Lincoln's grandmother, the redoubtable Elizabeth R. Parker. Lincoln perhaps witnessed auctions there or at the public square, where one was held in mid-November, when a man sold five of his slaves to satisfy a judgment obtained against him by Robert Smith Todd.

From his wife's older relatives, Lincoln probably heard stories about his own kin, including his great-uncle, Thomas Lincoln, who had settled a few miles outside Lexington and prospered until his marriage to a physically abusive wife ended in divorce. (Lincoln may have derived some comfort from the knowledge that he was not the only man in the family with a violent spouse.)

On November 13, Lincoln heard Henry Clay launch his fourth attempt to win the presidency with a speech about James K. Polk's actions precipitating the war with Mexico, a conflict still officially underway at the time. "This is no war of defence," Clay charged, "but one unnecessary and of offensive aggression. It is Mexico that is defending her fire-sides, her castles and her altars, not we." Plaintively he asked: "Must we blindly continue the conflict, without any visible object, or any prospect of a definite termination?" He declared that all nations "look upon us, in the prosecution of the present war, as being actuated by a spirit of rapacity, and an inordinate desire for territorial aggrandizement." He emphatically opposed the extension of slavery into any territory acquired from Mexico: "I have ever regarded slavery as a great evil, a wrong, for the present, I fear, an irremediable wrong to its unfortunate victims. I should rejoice if not a single slave breathed the air or was within the limits of our country."[249]

With these words ringing in his ears, Lincoln soon left Kentucky to take his seat in Congress, where he would denounce President Polk's Mexican War policy and try to abolish slavery in the District of Columbia. Accompanying him was a wife who aspired "to loom largely" in the nation's capital.[250]

8

"A Strong but Judicious Enemy to Slavery"
Congressman Lincoln
(1847–1849)

Lincoln's entire public service on the national level before his election as president was a single term in the U.S. House. Although he had little chance to distinguish himself there, his experience proved a useful education in dealing with Congress and patronage.

Washington, D.C.

Arriving in Washington on December 2, 1847, the Lincolns found themselves in a small, dark, dingy train depot, widely considered a disgrace to both the city and the railroad company. As they emerged from this unfortunate structure, they beheld an "an ill-contrived, ill-arranged, rambling, scrambling village" of approximately 40,000 souls.[1]

Europeans expressed scorn for the capital, which reminded an Englishwoman "of a vast plantation with houses purposely kept far apart to give them room to grow and spread."[2] Eminent British novelists were especially critical. Charles Dickens described it as "the head-quarters of tobacco-tinctured saliva," a "City of Magnificent Intentions," with "spacious avenues, that begin in nothing, and lead nowhere; streets, miles-long, that only want houses, roads, and inhabitants; public buildings that need but a public to be complete."[3] Anthony Trollope wrote in 1862: "Of all places that I know it is the most ungainly," the "most unsatisfactory," and "the most presumptuous in its pretensions. There is a map of Washington accurately laid down; and taking that map with him in his journeyings a man may lose himself in the streets . . . as one does . . . in the deserts of the Holy Land, between Emmaus and Arimathea." Trollope lamented that "no one knows where the places are, or is sure of their existence, and then between their presumed localities the country is wild, trackless, unbridged, uninhabited and desolate." Trollope described a walk along one of the city's main thoroughfares, Massachusetts Avenue: "Tucking your trousers up to your knees, you will wade through the bogs, you will lose yourself among rude hillocks, you will be out of the reach of humanity."[4]

Yet another Briton, Alexander MacKay, thought that "at best, Washington is but a small town, a fourth-rate community."[5] The Chevalier de Bacourt disparaged the "miserable, desolate look" of "the so-called city of Washington," which in his view was "neither city nor village" but rather "a collection of houses put anywhere and everywhere with no regularity."[6]

Some Americans were also taken aback by their capital. A Bostonian protested that Washington "covers too much ground to generate a cheerful spirit, for vastness is repellant to the social pleasure of unceremonious visiting." Moreover, it lacked "the native aristocracy of wealth or talent to be found in the commercial cities."[7] In 1854, Mark Twain praised the city's public buildings but not their setting. To him, they looked like "so many palaces in a Hottentot village."[8] Carl Schurz described Washington as "a strange-looking city. Imagine a broad street lined on both sides with hotels and shops, then wide stretches of open country and again streets interrupted by vacant lots; groups of houses scattered about in apparent disorder, with here and there a marble palace which contains one of the Government Departments. This strange jumble leaves the spectator in doubt whether all this grandeur is in a state of development or is already approaching decay."[9] He thought that the capital "had throughout a slouchy, unenterprising, unprogressive appearance." The "departments of State, of War, and of the Navy were quartered in small, very insignificant-looking houses which might have been the dwellings of some well-to-do shopkeepers who did not care for show. There was not one solidly built-up street in the whole city—scarcely a block without gaps of dreary emptiness." Few residences "had the appearance of refined, elegant, and comfortable homes. The streets, ill-paved, if paved at all, were constantly covered with mud or dust." Along those streets "geese, chickens, pigs, and cows had still a scarcely disputed right of way."[10] (One day in 1858, while strolling about the city, a senator was sent sprawling to the pavement by "a great, dirty pig.")[11]

Despite its roaming livestock, noisome sewer system, and unpaved, unlit, garbage-strewn streets, Washington appeared splendid to some small-town Midwesterners. In 1849, an Illinoisan praised the capital as "a great city." The "public buildings are superb," he gushed, adding that "there is many now under the course of erection that will throw those built a few years ago entirely in the shade as regards architecture." He called the view from the west portico of the Capitol "one of the finest that I have ever beheld," for as "far as the eye can reach is but one mass of buildings while away to the right is the *beautiful* residences of *oppulent citizens* with their *parks* and *yards* beautifully embellished, whilst to the left rolls the majestic *potomac* its waters covered with vessels conveying merchandise."[12] Even the bumpy main thoroughfare, Pennsylvania Avenue, with its uneven, carriage-rattling cobblestones, impressed Lincoln's Illinois friend Jesse W. Fell, who described it in 1841: "Casting my eyes into the spacious avenue that fronts the room in which I am writing and what a buisey scene is ther[e] presented.—Thousands of persons of every age and sex—of every character and complexion—and from almost every part of the world—constitute the living, moving mass. Some brought here on business—some sent here by the sovereign people—some in search of office—some for pleasure—some for mischief—and all of them busily intent on the prosecution of their respective objects, make up this great, bustling bab[b]le."[13]

Another Midwesterner, however—Ohio Senator Benjamin F. Wade—found the city objectionable because of its large black population. An antislavery Radical who was to denounce Lincoln during the Civil War for his tardiness in issuing the Emancipation Proclamation, Wade observed upon arriving at the capital in 1851: "On the whole, this is a mean God forsaken Nigger rid[d]en place. The Niggers are certainly the most intelligent part of the population but the Nigger smell I cannot bear, yet it is in on and about every thing you see." Wade lamented that the food was "cooked by Niggers, until I can smell & taste the Nigger."[14]

For the political elite, life in Washington combined "magnificence and squalor." In 1851, Mary Elizabeth Wilson Sherwood reported that dinner parties there were "handsome and very social, the talk delightful," but she deplored the conduct of congressmen from the Southwest who "got fearfully drunk at dinners."[15] Decades later, Mrs. Sherwood exclaimed: "How primitive Washington was in those days!" The "small, straggling city, with very muddy streets," she wrote, was "cold and dreary in winter then; the houses were insufficiently heated, the hotels abominable." But in a capital noted for "the proud prominence of intellect over material prosperity," she found that "high thinking" helped offset "plain living."[16]

Washington was a town full of men, for the wives of most members of Congress did not accompany their spouses. Those footloose lawmakers were, as a journalist noted, "exposed to many strong temptations" and hence were "too often corrupted by evil example and impure association."[17] A British visitor grew disenchanted with the "coarse, unattractive surface" of Washington society, where "the social sway of women" was limited.[18]

Like the capital of Illinois, Washington was exciting only when the legislature was in session. Upon the adjournment of Congress, the city reverted to its customary, dull monotony.

For a few days, the newly arrived Lincolns resided at The Indian Queen, a shabby hotel, unimpressive even by the low standards of Pennsylvania Avenue. Soon thereafter, like most members of the Thirtieth Congress, they settled at one of the city's numerous boardinghouses. They chose Mrs. Ann Sprigg's, located on a site where the Library of Congress was later built. It formed part of Carroll Row, across from the Capitol. That structure was surmounted by a wooden dome and lacked the wings it would eventually acquire.

Theodore Dwight Weld, a prominent abolitionist who roomed at Mrs. Sprigg's in 1842, depicted it thus: "The iron railing around the Capitol Park comes within fifty feet of our door. Our dining room overlooks the whole Capitol Park which is one mile around and filled with shade trees and shrubbery. I have a pleasant room on the second floor with a good bed, plenty of covering, a bureau, table, chairs, closets and clothes press, a good fire place, and plenty of dry wood to burn in it. We have about twenty boarders, mostly members of Congress." Weld explained that his Virginia-bred landlady was "*not* a slaveholder, but hires slaves. She has eight servants all colored, 3 men, one boy and 4 women. All are free but 3 which she hires and these are buying themselves."[19]

The Lincolns admired Mrs. Sprigg. During the Civil War, Lincoln called her "a most worthy and deserving lady," and even the sharp-tongued Mary said she "found her a most estimable lady."[20]

Eight of Lincoln's fellow congressmen lived at Mrs. Sprigg's, known informally as "the Abolition house."[21] Among them was Joshua R. Giddings of Ohio, the most radical antislavery Representative, whose sobriquets included "the [General] Blucher of abolitionism" and "the Lion of Ashtabula, [Ohio]." Giddings was 6 feet 2 inches tall, courageous, self-assured, impossible to intimidate, and ever prepared to battle for righteousness; he declared that in Congress "I allways make the fir fly."[22] In 1846, he taunted a Georgia Representative who threatened him with a pistol and a sword-cane: "Come on! The people of Ohio don't send cowards here!"[23] Upon Congressman John Quincy Adams's death in February 1848, Giddings assumed leadership of the antislavery forces in the House. Another of Lincoln's messmates opposed to slavery was John Dickey of Pennsylvania, who struck a fellow boarder as "a very offensive man in manner and conversation" and "seemed to take special pleasure in ventilating his opinions and provoking unpleasant discussions."[24]

The other boarders were drawn to Lincoln. The journalist Nathan Sargent, who served (appropriately enough) as sergeant-at-arms of the U.S. House, recalled that the Illinois Whig was "genial and liked," "fond of fun and humor," and "ever ready to match another's story by one of his own."[25] Representative James Pollock of Pennsylvania found Lincoln "full of good humor, ready wit and with an unlimited fund of anecdote, which he would relate with a zest and manner that never failed to bring down the 'Mess', and restore harmony & smiles, when the peace of our little community was threatened by a too earnest or heated controversy on some of the exciting questions of the hour."[26]

Pollock, a puritanical "old fogy" Whig who in 1854 was elected governor of Pennsylvania as the candidate of the nativist Know–Nothing Party, angrily participated in one of those heated controversies. In January 1849, Pollock criticized a bill concerning the admission to the Union of California and New Mexico, causing an exceptionally heated row. When he denounced Giddings as an irresponsible agitator, the Ohioan replied that he would not tolerate such criticism of his motives "by a miserable Doughface who had not mind enough to form an opinion nor courage enough to avow it." Enraged by this insult, Pollock leaped up from the table and confronted Giddings, who also rose. Pollock quickly calmed down.[27]

When such intemperate debates on slavery occurred at mealtime, Lincoln defused the tension with amusing anecdotes. Although he had strong feelings about slavery, he was careful to express them in such as way as to offend no one, even proslavery colleagues. When he was preparing to share an anecdote, he would set down his utensils, put his elbows on the table, cup his face in his hands, and preface his remarks with "That reminds me." His fellow diners keenly relished the prospect of a hilarious recitation. They liked him not only for his humor but also for his amiability, kindness, and unpretentious manners.[28]

Lincoln often relaxed with messmates or other congressmen at a nearby bowling alley. Although he was quite awkward at the sport, he enjoyed it and played with gusto. Whenever it was known he was at the alley, people would make a point to drop by to listen to his stories, many of which were off-color. He modestly tried to make it appear that he had gotten his material from others, although his auditors suspected he was misleading them on that score.

Popularity

Lincoln's humor won him friends all over Capitol Hill. Around Christmas of 1847, he began to frequent the small post office of the House of Representatives, where members often gathered to swap yarns. After diffidently remaining silent for a while, he eventually started to tell stories and quickly outstripped all competitors. His repertoire was so vast that he never repeated a story but, as a reporter put it, delivered one after another "like the successive charges in a magazine gun, and always pertinently adapted to some passing event." His tales of the Black Hawk War were especially popular with newspaper correspondents, who were bored by congressional pomposity.[29]

In Washington he picked up several new stories, some of them quite obscene. Representative William M. Cocke of Tennessee remembered that whenever he "saw a knot of Congressmen together laughing I knew that they were surrounding Lincoln and listening to his filthy stories."[30] Moses Hampton of Pennsylvania recalled two such off-color tales, one involving an "old Virginian stropping his razor on a certain *member* of a young negro's body" and the other about "the old woman[']s *fish*" which "get[s] *larger*, the more it is handled."[31]

Colleagues in the House admired not only Lincoln's humor but also his character and personality. In May 1848, a Washington correspondent reported that "no member of whom I have any knowledge, possesses in a higher degree the respect and confidence of the House" than Lincoln—heady praise for a newcomer.[32] A few months later, another journalist called Lincoln a "universal favorite here—an entirely self-made man, and of singular and striking personal appearance."[33] His colleagues praised his warmth, generosity, magnanimity, and practical common sense.

Lincoln was especially grateful for the treatment he received from the renowned educational reformer and antislavery militant, Horace Mann. In 1865, Lincoln told Mann's sister-in-law that he "was *very kind to me*" and "it was something to me at that time to have him so—for he was a distinguished man in his way—and *I* was nobody."[34] Among those members whom Lincoln especially liked was Daniel M. Barringer of North Carolina, with whom he shared a desk and many meals.

In addition to his character and humor, Lincoln's oratorical prowess won him respect. Charles H. Brainard, a Washington-based publisher who saw Lincoln often during his congressional term, reported that whenever the Illinois Whig "addressed the House, he commanded the individual attention of all present." If occasionally his speeches "lacked rhetorical grace and finish, they had directness and precision, and never failed to carry conviction to every candid mind, while his sallies of wit and humor, and his quick repartee whenever he was interrupted by questions from his political opponents, would be followed by peals of laughter from all parts of the hall."[35]

This was no small accomplishment in a chamber whose notoriously poor acoustics made it difficult to hear speakers. The 60-foot-high domed ceiling, modeled on the Pantheon at Rome, created a distracting echo. Almost every member had difficulty hearing and making himself heard. To be audible, a speaker had to strain to the utmost. Frequently, reporters for the *Congressional Globe,* unable to make out what was said on the floor, noted that the remarks of an honorable gentleman were inaudible. In 1844, John J. Hardin complained that of "all the places to speak or to try & do any business, the Hall of the House is the worst I ever saw. I would prefer speaking in a pig pen with 500 hogs squealing . . . or talk to a mob when a fight is going on, or endeavor to speak to a set of men at a muster when the studs are exhibiting—than to try to fix the attention of the House. Not one man in fifty can make himself heard on acc[oun]t of the construction of the Hall, & no one but J Q Adams is even listened to by the House, unless there is a quarrel going on or the prospect of a row is brewing. Last week the scenes in the House would have disgraced the meanest western grocery. Bullying & Billingsgate are the only order of the day."[36]

Although the House's acoustics were poor, the 95-foot-long chamber was, as Charles Dickens observed a "beautiful and spacious hall, of semicircular shape, supported by handsome pillars." Dickens also reported that the chamber was "handsomely carpeted" but deplored the "state to which these carpets are reduced by the universal disregard of the spittoon with which every honourable [i.e., Representative] is accommodated." The "extraordinary improvements on the pattern which are squirted and dabbled upon it in every direction, do not admit of being described," Dickens added.[37] Statues of Liberty and History, as well as full-length portraits of Washington and Lafayette, decorated the hall. Crimson drapery festooned the spaces between the twenty-six massive marble columns. Light was provided by an unreliable gas system, which one member in 1849 described disapprovingly: "our gas has just gone out for the second time, giving us a very bright stink but the darkest possible light."[38] That Representative also found the Capitol bewildering, "a series of blind, gloomy and crooked labyrinths, through which a stranger threads his devious way with difficulty."[39]

Unlike her husband, Mary Lincoln enjoyed little popularity, and by April 1848, she had returned to her father's home in Lexington. She may have been lonely, for there were few congressional wives with whom to socialize. (In 1845, only 72 of the 221 members of the House were accompanied by family members.) At the boarding-house, Mary Lincoln seldom appeared save at mealtime. Some boarders at Mrs. Sprigg's, like those in the Globe Tavern five years earlier, found her disagreeable. On April 16, 1848, Lincoln wrote her saying that all the guests "or rather, all with whom you were on decided good terms—send their love to you. The others say nothing." Lincoln had mixed feelings about his wife's absence. "In this troublesome world," he told her, "we are never quite satisfied. When you were here, I thought you hindered me some in attending to business; but now, having nothing but business—no variety—it has grown exceedingly tasteless to me. I hate to sit down and direct documents, and I hate to stay in this old room by myself."[40]

Such loneliness afflicted other congressmen, including Joshua Giddings, who complained to his spouse in June 1848: "last Sunday I was home with wife children & friends[;] now here [I am] solitary and alone in the midst of so many thousands surrounded with heated walls and almost burning pavements. I am homesick."[41] In 1854, Richard Yates, representing Lincoln's district, lamented to Mrs. Yates: "You speak of being lonely but I do assure you that you cannot feel near as lonely as I do. Sometimes a feeling of loneliness comes over me which is nearly insupportable. The days are weeks and the weeks months."[42]

Life of a Freshman Representative

Like many of his colleagues, Lincoln found routine congressional work unrewarding. In 1844, John J. Hardin told a law partner: "Having a seat in Congress is not the thing it is cracked up to be." Almost nothing "about life in Washington [is] desirable. There is a vast deal of . . . drudgery to do, in reading & writing letters on business which no lawyer would attend to, & which would not pay him if he did. Still they must be answered. The Hours of eating here destroy all business habits, & the Hours of the House destroy a man's health."[43]

Representatives usually spent their mornings answering correspondence, visiting government offices on behalf of constituents, attending committee meetings, and conning newspapers. House sessions customarily ran from noon till early evening, at which time caucuses were often held. Committee work could be tedious, as Isaac Holmes of South Carolina noted when he remarked that the Commerce Committee spent two-thirds of its time "with the consideration of such subjects as bounties on codfish, while the vastly more important subjects were greatly neglected."[44]

As a lowly freshman, Lincoln occupied an undesirable seat at the back of the House chamber in what was known as the "Cherokee Strip" on the Whig side of the aisle. He also was assigned to unimportant committees (those on Expenditures in the War Department and on Post Offices and Post Roads). The chairman of the latter said that "no man on that Committee worked more industriously than he [Lincoln] did."[45]

The House teemed with activity. The Representatives' desks made the lower chamber a convenient place for them to take care of their correspondence and other business, much to the annoyance of colleagues who were addressing them. Even more annoying was the cacophony created by members clapping their hands to summon ubiquitous page boys for various chores, like delivering messages, or fetching water, newspapers, and envelopes. A Representative's wife likened the "confusion and noise of the House of Representatives" to "a hundred swarms of bees."[46] In 1849, a Kentuckian reported that the House "is but a continued scene of dissension, distraction, disorder, and uproar. No speech is listened to while the floor is occupied—the *honorable* members are skipping to and fro, laughing, talking, whispering, cursing one another, slapping their hands together, rapping on the desk for the messenger boys, &c.,—altogether making a bedlam that outlives the pit of a theatre or tap room. It is impossible to hear a speech in the galleries."[47] From those galleries, Horace Greeley noted, a visitor could "look down on the noisy Bedlam," which would "give him large opportunities for headache, meagre ones for edification."[48]

To many Representatives, their colleagues' inattention made little difference, for speeches were designed for home consumption, while the real business of the House was transacted in committees and private consultations. In the first several months of 1848, the desultory debates in the House lacked interest and relevance. Whenever a dull speaker took the floor, "a forest of newspapers" appeared, as members caught up on their reading.[49] In early February 1848, a Massachusetts Representative reported that he and his colleagues "have not done much business" and complained that "there does not appear to be a disposition to do so."[50] Small wonder that Lincoln's immediate predecessors disparaged the House: "The most stupid place generally I was ever in," said John J. Hardin, while Edward Baker lamented that the "House is dull and so are many of its members."[51]

Much time was wasted on private bills, which formed "rather a tedious and stupid subject of debate."[52] Most of the claims that Congress investigated were not acted upon, for a legislative body was ill-suited to function as a court of claims.

The House Whig leadership in Lincoln's term lacked distinction, though the octogenarian John Quincy Adams was still serving. But "Old Man Eloquent" was well beyond his prime. The majority leaders, Samuel Vinton of Ohio (chairman of the Ways and Means Committee) and Truman Smith of Connecticut (de facto national party chairman since 1842), enjoyed a reputation for above-average sagacity, but the shrewd, savvy, well-informed Smith lacked oratorical skills and, like the conservative Vinton, was no match for Adams in his heyday. Nor was House speaker Robert C. Winthrop, a mild-mannered, touchy, hyper-dignified Boston Brahmin who reportedly was "so timid that when he had bid a friend good-night he would call him aside and ask him not to say anything about it."[53]

Speeches

Much as Lincoln enjoyed the popularity that his humor and personality won him, he aspired to do more than merely ingratiate himself with his colleagues, a slight majority of whom were Whigs. (Lincoln was also in the occupational majority: three-quarters of the Representatives were lawyers.) On December 13, 1847, Lincoln told his law partner: "As you are all so anxious for me to distinguish myself, I have concluded to do so, before long."[54]

Lincoln hoped to accomplish this goal with a memorable speech. Speechmaking was vitally important to new members, whose maiden efforts always attracted close critical attention. As one journalist noted, a "young Representative is anxious to show to the world in general, and to his constituents in particular, that he is somebody. . . . To make one set speech, at least, is therefore the great idea of his Congressional life." He longed "to make a spectacle of himself for one brief hour," preferably early in the session, to "show his constituents that he is ever on hand, prompt in attention to their great interests."[55] Lincoln decided to make his mark with a speech on the Mexican War, which many Whig members condemned.

Lincoln's brief initial speech, given on January 5, did not prove to be his magnum opus. It dealt with a government mail contract and was not a conspicuous success. He presented his argument in the form of a legal pleading. Congressman Joseph Root of

Ohio said of it: "This whole matter was treated by the gentleman from Illinois precisely as if the House were sitting as a court of equity, having before them the railroad company, the Post Office Department, and such of the good people of the United State[s] as were interested in the expedition of this mail; and he seemed to consider that the only question was, what is right between the parties?"[56] As a Democratic journalist put it, Lincoln labored under a common misapprehension among freshman members of the House, who falsely assumed "that if they were only in that body they would say this, or do that, and then it would be settled."[57] He was interrupted at the beginning of his remarks and admonished that he must not reveal in debate what had taken place in committee deliberations.

Lincoln's party, which had been critical of the Mexican War since it began in May 1846, intended to make President James K. Polk's conduct of hostilities a centerpiece of the presidential campaign. Those plans were scotched in February 1848 when a peace treaty arrived in Washington and won senate ratification the following month. Attention then shifted to the president's justification for going to war in the first place.

On December 22, 1847, Lincoln introduced a series of resolutions asking Polk to supply information about the commencement of the war. In his annual message earlier that month, the president had insisted that the conflict began as a result of Mexican soldiers "invading the territory of the State of Texas, striking the first blow, and shedding the blood of our citizens on our own soil."[58] In eight legalistic interrogatories, which became known as "spot resolutions," Lincoln clearly intimated that the soil where blood was initially spilled was not American and that in the spring of 1846 Polk had dispatched troops to Mexico in order to provoke an attack. Lincoln was particularly graphic in inquiring if "the People of that settlement [where hostilities began], did, or did not, flee from the approach of the United States Army, leaving unprotected their homes and their growing crops, *before* the blood was shed."[59] Polk ignored these interrogatories.

Lincoln ran a risk in questioning the legitimacy of the war, for as his colleague James Dixon of Connecticut said in making a similar point: "I know full well, that if a man says he does not believe the region on this side of the Rio Grande is American soil, he will instantly be denounced as a traitor."[60] This bold gesture by Illinois's lone Whig Representative prompted a Baltimore journalist to remark that Lincoln's questions "stick to the *spot* in Mexico, where the first blood of the war was shed, with all the tightness that characterized the fabled shirt of the fabled Nessus! Evidently there is music in that very tall Mr. Lincoln."[61] Back in Illinois, Whig journals also applauded Lincoln's resolutions as "direct to the point" and "based on facts which cannot be successfully controverted."[62]

Democratic newspapers sneered at Lincoln's "pathetic lamentation over the fate of those Mexicans," a statement that strongly contrasted with "his cold indifference in regard to our own slaughtered citizens."[63] The *Illinois Globe* of Charleston claimed that Lincoln's spot resolutions "show conclusively, that the littleness of the pettifoging lawyer has not been merged into the greatness of the statesman."[64] Lincoln's indirect attack on Polk reminded the editor of the Ottawa *Free Trader* of a "hen-roost robbing coon."[65] Charles Lanphier, editor of the *Illinois State Register*, told a Democratic congressman: "Our long legged friend from the 7th dist. has very properly damned himself 'by resolution.' . . . He may well exclaim 'out damned *spot*,' for Cain's mark is on him. Give him hell."[66] Lanphier's newspaper did just that, declaring that Lincoln's resolutions encouraged "moral traitors" to hope that they could "make a respectable fight against the defenders of the country's honor."[67] The Chicago *Times* claimed that Lincoln "made himself ridiculous and odious . . . in giving aid and comfort to the Mexican enemy."[68]

On January 3, 1848, Lincoln provoked further Democratic criticism by voting for Representative George Ashmun's amendment asserting that the Mexican War had been "unnecessarily and unconstitutionally begun by the President."[69] Pointing out that 1,000 young men from Illinois's Seventh District were fighting in Mexico, the Springfield *Register* asked rhetorically: "What will these gallant heroes say when they learn that their representative has declared in the national councils that the cause in which they suffered and braved everything, was 'unconstitutional,' 'unnecessary,' and consequently infamous and wicked?"[70]

Nine days later Lincoln delivered his major hour-long speech on the war, making explicit what had been implicit in his spot resolutions. He would have remained quiet, he said, if Polk had not stated in his annual message that the Mexican government was solely responsible for provoking the war. Moreover, the president had asserted that Congress implicitly endorsed his interpretation of the war's origin by voting to supply troops in the field. Lincoln, who always voted for such supplies, could not let these pronouncements go unchallenged. In addition, he said, he was moved to speak out because earlier in the session Illinois Democratic Congressman William A. Richardson had introduced resolutions echoing Polk's self-serving version of history.

Lincoln disputed that version. Calling the president's discussion of the issue in his recent message "from beginning to end, the sheerest deception," he denied Polk's assumption that either the Nueces River or the Rio Grande formed the southern boundary of Texas. (In Lincoln's opinion, that boundary was located in the "stupendous deserts" between the two.)[71] After systematically reviewing Polk's address, he declared that he found it "incomprehensible" that "any man, with an honest purpose only, of proving the truth, could ever have *thought*, of introducing" such flimsy evidence to support his argument. Lincoln made a strong case, for the Rio Grande had not been widely regarded as the southern boundary of Texas; therefore, the territory between the Rio Grande and the Nueces, 150 miles to the north, was at best disputed land, if not actually Mexico's. Before 1846, such leaders as Andrew Jackson, John Quincy Adams, John C. Calhoun, and Thomas Hart Benton had acknowledged this basic fact.

Lincoln urged Polk to respond to the interrogatories he had propounded earlier: "Let him answer with *facts*, and not with arguments. Let him remember he sits where Washington sat, and so remembering, let him answer, as Washington would answer." If the president could "show that the soil was ours, where the first blood of the war was shed—that it was not within an inhabited country, or, if within such, that the inhabitants had submitted themselves to the civil authority of Texas, or of the United

States, . . . then I am with him for his justification." But if Polk could not prove his case, "then I shall be fully convinced, of what I more than suspect already, that he is deeply conscious of being in the wrong—that he feels the blood of this war, like the blood of Abel, is crying to Heaven against him." Lincoln maintained that the chief executive had deliberately provoked a war while "trusting to escape scrutiny, by fixing the public gaze upon the exceeding brightness of military glory that attractive rainbow, that rises in showers of blood—that serpent's eye, that charms to destroy."

Lincoln then shifted his focus from the origin of the war to the present situation, which saw American forces controlling much of Mexico. Should the United States seize all of that country's territory? Any of it? Should the war be continued? Having "plunged into" war, Polk, according to Lincoln, "has swept *on* and *on*, till, disappointed in his calculation of the ease with which Mexico might be subdued, he now finds himself, he knows not where." The president's discussion of the war in his annual message, Lincoln said, resembled "the half insane mumbling of a fever-dream." In describing the various rationales for the war and the different peace terms that might be acceptable, Polk showed that his "mind, tasked beyond it's power, is running hither and thither, like some tortured creature, on a burning surface, finding no position, on which it can settle down, and be at ease." The president, in sum, "is a bewildered, confounded, and miserably perplexed man."

In treating the history of Texas, Lincoln uttered words that would return to haunt him thirteen years later when some Southern states left the Union: "Any people anywhere, being inclined and having the power, have the *right* to rise up, and shake off the existing government, and form a new one that suits them better. This is a most valuable,—a most sacred right—a right, which we hope and believe, is to liberate the world. Nor is this right confined to cases in which the whole people of an existing government, may choose to exercise it. Any portion of such people that *can, may* revolutionize, and make their *own*, of so much of the ter[r]itory as they inhabit. More than this, a *majority* of any portion of such people may revolutionize, putting down a *minority*, intermingled with, or near about them, who may oppose their movement."[72] In this rather gratuitous passage, Lincoln may have been trying to curry favor with Southern Whigs resentful of Northern congressmen, like John Quincy Adams, who had denied the legitimacy of the Texas revolution of 1836. At that time Lincoln was cooperating with several Southern Whig congressmen in an attempt to help General Zachary Taylor of Louisiana win their party's presidential nomination.

A fellow member of the Illinois delegation, Democrat John A. McClernand, recalled that Lincoln "was earnest and spoke with greater rapidity than I ever had heard him speak before. I attributed it to the fact that he had only an hour allotted to him and wanted to say as much as possible in that time. His deficiency in gesticulation was fully made up by the deep earnestness of his manner."[73]

Just before delivering his remarks, Lincoln confided to Whig Congressman Richard W. Thompson of Indiana that he was nervous. "It was not surprising that he felt this way," Thompson explained, "considering the forum upon which he was for the first time appearing, where those who have gained reputation are few, compared with the multitude who have lost it. The occasion was an embarrassing one to him, and was made more so by the fact that he was gazed at by so many eyes, and watched by adversaries who would have rejoiced at his failure. He was not even personally known to all the members. His appearance was not attractive."[74] Describing some brief remarks that he had delivered a week before his address on the Mexican War, Lincoln told Herndon: "I find speaking here and elsewhere about the same thing. I was about as badly scared, and no worse, as I am when I speak in court."[75] (In 1856, Lincoln confided to Henry C. Whitney: "When I have to speak, I always feel nervous till I get well into it. . . . I hide it as well as I can.")[76] While reminiscing about this speech, Lincoln said that "he felt like the boy whose teacher asked him why he didn't spell better. The boy replied: 'Cause I hain't just got the hang of the school house. But I'll get on better later.'"[77]

Reaction to the speech was predictably partisan. William Schouler, a Massachusetts Whig leader, reported that the "tall, raw-boned, thin and spare" Lincoln "speaks with rapidity and uses a good deal of gesture, some of which is quite new and original. He was listened to, however, with great attention, and made a sound, sensible and manly speech."[78] According to Congressman Thompson, Lincoln scored a success, rising "above the common Congressional level. . . . I heard no other criticism of his speech than what came from himself—for, unlike many I have known, he placed a modest estimate upon his own abilities. His friends were satisfied—more than that, they were delighted."[79] The Baltimore *American* deemed it "a very able speech."[80] An Illinois Whig newspaper reported that the address "is spoken of as an able effort, and at once places him in the front rank of the best speakers in the House."[81]

Lincoln's opponents were less pleased. As he had doubtless anticipated, Democrats—including colleagues in the House—took exception to his arguments. Representative John Jameson of Missouri expressed astonishment that the congressman from a district that had sent into battle such heroes as John J. Hardin, Edward D. Baker, and James Shields could "get up here and declare that this war is unconstitutional and unjust, and thereby put so many of his brave constituents in the wrong, . . . committing moral if not legal murder." Lincoln, Jameson speculated, must have been responding to pressure from "the party screw."[82] John L. Robinson of Indiana called Lincoln a hypocrite for supporting the presidential candidacy of General Taylor while denouncing Polk for starting the war. Taylor, according to Robinson, was more responsible for the outbreak of hostilities than was the president. The Hoosier congressman also scolded Lincoln for not informing his constituents during the 1846 election campaign that he regarded the war as "unnecessary and unconstitutional."[83] Willard P. Hall of Missouri denounced congressional war critics (not mentioning Lincoln specifically): "Who does not know that the speeches of honorable members of Congress have been published in Mexican newspapers, and read at the head of Mexican armies, to incite them to attack our troops? Who does not know that the people of Mexico have read and thought over these productions until they believe there is a Mexican party in this country, and Mexican Representatives on this floor?"[84] Howell Cobb of Georgia, who maintained that Corpus Christi was the spot where the war began, taunted Lincoln and other Whigs: "You are stickling about the commencement of this war; tell me how it was that you sat quietly, without opening your mouths in complaint, and allowed the army of the United States to plant themselves on the western border of the Nueces, thus commencing the war, as you now claim?"[85] A New York *Evening Post* correspondent dismissively remarked that Lincoln sang the "usual burden of whig songs" in "various keys."[86]

The shrillest criticism came from the Illinois Democrats. In Sangamon County they met to condemn Lincoln for supporting "the schemes of . . . apologists and defenders of Mexico, and revilers of their own country."[87] A mass meeting in Clark County denounced Lincoln for his resolutions "against his own country" and urged that they "be long remembered by his constituents."[88] In Morgan County, a similar gathering condemned Lincoln as the "Benedict Arnold of our district" who would "be known here only as the Ranchero Spotty of one term."[89] Democratic newspapers took up the cry, including the Springfield *Register,* the Peoria *Democratic Press,* and the Peoria *Free Press.* The Belleville *Advocate* was typical of the rest when it claimed that Lincoln "is against his country in her struggle with a foreign and unprincipled government."[90]

Lincoln was doubtless unsurprised by Democratic criticism; he may have been nonplussed, however, when William Herndon, a strong Whig, found fault with his partner's support of the Ashmun amendment and his denunciation of Polk. In response, Lincoln emphatically declared: "I will stake my life, that if you had been in my place, you would have voted just as I did [on the Ashmun amendment]." Rhetorically, he asked: "Would you have voted what you felt you knew to be a lie? I know you would not. Would you have gone out of the House—skulked the vote? I expect not." William A. Richardson's resolutions made "the direct question of the justice of the war; so that no man can be silent if he would. You are compelled to speak; and your only alternative is to tell the *truth* or tell a *lie.* I can not doubt which you would do."[91] (To Usher F. Linder, Lincoln stressed the point even more forcefully, arguing that congressional Whigs "are compelled to *speak* and their only option is whether they will, when they do speak, tell the *truth,* or tell a foul, villainous, and bloody falsehood.")[92]

Herndon's contention, as Lincoln paraphrased it, was "that if it shall become *necessary, to repel invasion,* the President may, without violation of the Constitution, cross the line, and *invade* the ter[r]itory of another country; and that whether such *necessity* exists in any given case, the President is to be the *sole* judge." After denying the relevance of such an argument to the case against Polk, Lincoln declared, "Allow the President to invade a neighboring nation, whenever *he* shall deem it necessary to repel an invasion, and you allow him to do so, *whenever he may choose to say* he deems it necessary for such purpose—and you allow him to make war at pleasure. Study to see if you can fix *any limit* to his power in this respect, after you have given him so much as you propose." Lincoln cited a hypothetical case: "If, to-day, he should choose to say he thinks it necessary to invade Canada, to prevent the British from invading us, how could you stop him? You may say to him, 'I see no probability of the British invading us' but he will say to you 'be silent; I see it, if you don[']t.'" Lincoln contended that Herndon's interpretation differed from that of the Founding Fathers: "The provision of the Constitution giving the war-making power to Congress, was dictated, as

I understand it, by the following reasons. Kings had always been involving and impoverishing their people in wars, pretending generally, if not always, that the good of the people was the object." But the framers of the Constitution believed that such an abuse of power was "the most oppressive of all Kingly oppressions" and they therefore made sure that "*no one man* should hold the power of bringing this oppression upon us." But Herndon's "view destroyed the whole matter, and places our President where kings have always stood."[93]

To an Illinois Baptist minister who defended Polk's conduct in bringing on the war, Lincoln stressed that the U.S. Army in proceeding to the Rio Grande at the president's order, before hostilities had commenced, had "marched into a peaceful Mexican settlement, and frightened its inhabitants away from their homes and their growing crops." If those actions seemed inconsequential to the clergyman, Lincoln asked, "Would you venture to so consider them, had they been committed by any nation on earth, against the humblest of our people? I know you would not. Then I ask, is the precept 'Whatsoever ye would that men should do to you, do ye even so to them' obsolete?—of no force?—of no application?"[94]

As these letters suggest, Lincoln was truly outraged by Polk's conduct. The main arguments of Lincoln's speech echoed those he had heard Clay espouse in November 1847, arguments made by many other Whigs. The Chicago *Journal* sarcastically exclaimed: "Oh! Most righteous war! An American army in the midst of the 19th century, robbing a weak and defenceless nation of her territory to subsist upon."[95] Lincoln shared the *Journal*'s indignation and excoriated Polk not only for partisan reasons (though the speech was to some extent a characteristically Lincolnian attack on Democrats, replete with personal ridicule) but also to express his anger at what he perceived to be gross unfairness. Herndon, who warned Lincoln that he was committing political suicide by criticizing the way in which the war was provoked, later said that "his sense of justice and his courage made him speak . . . as to the War with Mexico."[96] The Polk administration had, in Lincoln's view, played the bully, and he hated bullies. The passion behind Lincoln's invective was striking, for it was among the bitterest antiwar speeches delivered in the House up to that time.

Six months after denouncing Polk, Lincoln again turned his attention to the origins of the Mexican War. In the midst of a humorous speech ridiculing the 1848 Democratic presidential nominee, he suddenly abandoned his satirical tone and indignantly rebuked House Democrats: "The marching an army into the midst of a peaceful Mexican settlement, frightening the inhabitants away, leaving their growing crops, and other property to destruction, to *you* may appear a perfectly amiable, peaceful, unprovoking procedure; but it does not appear so to *us*. So to call such an act, to us appears no other than a naked, impudent absurdity."[97] The passion in these sentences, so different from the rest of the speech, illustrates the depth of Lincoln's anger.

In addition, Lincoln may have denounced Polk's action because he came to realize that the war might expand the realm of slavery. Most Midwesterners who opposed the war did so because of their antislavery convictions. One historian speculated plausibly that "underneath the whole pile of political froth, Lincoln had a deep, underlying motive in displaying hostility to the Mexican war and that motive was his desire to thwart the expansion of slavery. He had not felt the bearing the war had upon slavery when he was back in Springfield; but in Washington it loomed large to him and gave him quite a different perspective."[98]

Herndon wrongly alleged that misgivings about Lincoln's antiwar stand were widespread among Illinois Whigs. It is true that Caleb Birchall, a Springfield bookseller who in 1842 had been a member of the executive committee of the Henry Clay Club, said that Lincoln had "rendered himself very unpopular."[99] But virtually all criticism of Lincoln's "spot resolutions" and his subsequent speech came from Democrats. No Whig journal criticized his stand on the war, and the party named him to serve as an assistant presidential elector in 1848. Despite his pledge to step down after one term, some Whigs favored his renomination. In April 1848, Allen Ford of the Lacon *Illinois Gazette* editorialized that Lincoln "has ably and faithfully discharged his duties; and if he has at no time intimated a willingness or desire to retire at the expiration of the term for which he was elected, we are not sure but that the interests of the district would be quite as well promoted by his re-nomination and reelection for another term."[100] Lincoln was not averse, as he told Herndon: "It is very pleasant to learn from you that there are some who desire that I should be reelected. . . . I made the declaration that I would not be a candidate again, more from a wish . . . to keep peace among our friends, and to keep the district from going to the enemy, than for any cause personal to myself. . . . [I]f it should so happen that nobody else wishes to be elected I could not refuse the people the right of sending me again."[101] (There was no disgrace in serving only one term. In the 1840s and 1850s, the average length of service for a U.S. Representative was three years.)

But Stephen T. Logan did want to run, and the Whig nominating convention chose him. Samuel C. Parks said that just before the Whig convention met, he—with Lincoln's full knowledge—"canvassed the members of the convention and was compelled to report that, with the exception of himself and a certain other delegate from Christian county, he found no one who was favorable to Lincoln's re-nomination." Parks explained that the reason was not the Mexican War issue or Lincoln's vow not to run again. Rather, it was "his failure to secure any substantial political patronage for the 'faithful' of his party in the district."[102] This objection was not entirely reasonable. The Democrats controlled the White House, and Lincoln could exercise little influence in patronage decisions. Years later, while president, he remarked to an importunate Democratic Representative: "That reminds me of my own experience as an old Whig member of Congress. I was always in the opposition, and I had no troubles of this kind at all. It was the easiest thing imaginable to be an opposition member—no running to the Departments and the White House."[103]

In August 1848, Stephen T. Logan lost the Seventh District congressional seat to his Democratic opponent, Major Thomas L. Harris, a hero of the Mexican War, by less than one percentage point (49.8% to 49.1%, 7,201 votes to 7,095). Losing this hitherto safe district was, David Davis lamented, "a terrible blow to the Whigs everywhere in the State."[104] Some Democratic observers, along with Herndon, saw in

Logan's defeat a repudiation of Lincoln's antiwar stance. Logan himself attributed it in part to "Lincoln's unpopularity."[105]

Lincoln did not concur in that judgment. He told William Schouler that "a good many Whigs, without good cause, as I think, were unwilling to go for Logan, and some of them so wrote me before the election. On the other hand Harris was a Major of the war, and fought at Cerro Gordo, where several Whigs of the district fought with him."[106] Complicating matters was the Liberty Party candidate, who won 166 votes (1% of the total), most of which would probably have gone to Logan if there had been a two-man race. Moreover, Logan and other Whigs were guilty of complacency. Logan "told his friends at and around Delevan that his Election was sure—That they need not go to the polls."[107] The *Illinois State Journal* blamed Logan's defeat in part on "the inactivity of the whigs" and also on a German-language handbill circulated by the Democrats falsely alleging that Logan was a nativist bigot.[108]

The greatest handicap the Whigs labored under was Logan's off-putting personality. As one observer noted, the "suavity and affability so needful in winning popularity with the masses were wanting in his character, and he was too frank and unbending to be always popular with either the people or the politicians."[109] In fact, the voters regarded the Whig candidate as "a cold—avaricious and little mean man."[110] This unfortunate reputation was enhanced by Logan's response to a Democratic charge that he had paid only 50¢ to help finance the return of a soldier's body from Mexico; indignantly the wealthy Logan protested that he had contributed $3. Such tightfistedness did not sit well with some Whigs, who thought him "too selfish" and "cold and parsimonious."[111] Logan was also intellectually arrogant and domineering. Hezekiah Morse Wead, a fellow delegate to the 1847 Illinois constitutional convention, noted that Logan "is above all other men proud of his abilities & he gratifies that pride by the constant exercise of his powers. . . . Submission to his opinions is in his opinion, a duty due from other men, and that submission he intends to exact." Logan, he concluded, "is what might safely be called a 'smart' man, but he is very far from being a great one."[112]

The victorious Major Harris believed that Logan, who "raised no enthusiasm and no sympathy," failed to capitalize on strong Whig sentiment in the district.[113] Harris's triumph, James Shields exulted, was all the sweeter because it was "so unexpected and so extraordinary."[114] A Whig candidate more politically astute and personally appealing than Logan probably would have won. In November the Whig presidential nominee, Zachary Taylor, outpolled his Democratic opponent by 1,481 votes in the Seventh District.

Two years later, while his party was suffering a setback nationally, the handsome, energetic, likable, hard-working Whig congressional candidate Richard Yates successfully challenged Harris, winning by a margin of 754 ballots, capturing 53 percent of the vote. The charming, impulsive, handsome, sociable Yates was far more prepossessing than Logan. He radiated sincerity and enthusiasm. John Hay reported that "Yates is the people's darling. They like his pleasant voice and his genial eyes as much as they do his honor and his eloquence."[115] Yates was an exceptionally effective campaigner; as Nathan Morse Knapp put it, he "would tie the star-spangled banner over his opponent's head, cork up his a[sshol]e with a newspaper copy of the Declaration of Independence, make a fourth of July speech in his ears, and leave before he could get discombobulated enough to see the track upon which the gallant Dick had departed!"[116] Democrats complained that his addresses were "of the Fourth of July order, appealing to the friends, 'the noble friends' of his boyhood—pointing to the imaginary stars and stripes of his visions, reminding us of Bunker Hill, Concord and Lexington . . . and generally letting off at the crowd a series of sentimental fire works."[117]

When Logan ran for a seat on the Illinois State Supreme Court in 1855, he was "worse beaten than any other man ever was since elections were invented," Lincoln remarked.[118] (Logan lost 31,535 to 21,932—59% to 41%—to the little-known Onias C. Skinner of Quincy.) The previous year, on the other hand, Lincoln had run for the General Assembly and won the largest number of votes cast for any legislative candidate in Sangamon County. If he had truly alienated voters with his Mexican War stand, he would not have been so popular in 1854.

Illinois Whigs other than Logan fared badly in the August 1848 elections. The party saw its share of the state House of Representatives decline from 33 percent to 31 percent, and Whig congressional nominees received 30,000 fewer votes than their Democratic opponents. In neighboring Missouri and Indiana, Whig candidates suffered similarly discouraging results.

President-Making

The presidential election of 1848 dominated the long first session of Lincoln's congressional term. Both houses devoted so much attention to the subject that one journalist sniffed: "The time will come when the people will send men to Congress to do the business of the people—leaving to the people the liberty of making their Presidents."[119]

No sooner had Lincoln arrived in Washington in December 1847 than he was accosted by "the great Kentucky Kingmaker," Senator John J. Crittenden, champion of Zachary Taylor's candidacy. The influential Democratic leader, Duff Green, a boarder at Mrs. Sprigg's, told Lincoln that Taylor would have the support not only of Whigs but also of Calhounites like himself. (Green's nephew was Ninian W. Edwards, husband of Mary Lincoln's sister Elizabeth.) Lincoln agreed with these veteran politicians. Fearing realistically that his "beau ideal of a statesman"—the septuagenarian Henry Clay, a three-time loser in presidential contests—was unelectable, Lincoln had already decided to support Taylor, a hero of the Mexican War. The traditional Whig issues—banks, tariffs, and internal improvements—had lost their popular appeal, as had Clay, who after his defeat in 1844 forswore another presidential race. But the Great Compromiser changed his mind and came to Washington in January 1848 to enlist support for yet another White House bid. A speech he gave at that time swayed many, including a congressman who said: "Mr. Clay speaks more charmingly than any other man—his voice is like the breaking of eggs into good wine—his power over a great audience is unequalled, and the enthusiasm of the people at the sound of his voice is like the shout of the morning stars."[120]

The Sage of Ashland was still eloquent, but his time was past. As early as the spring of 1847, after Taylor's electrifying victory at Buena Vista in February over Santa Anna's much larger army—following on the heels of his earlier triumphs at Palo Alto, Resaca de la Palma, and Monterrey—Whig leaders had realized that the modest, unassuming, successful general was their most eligible standard-bearer, a kind of modern-day Cincinnatus-cum-George-Washington. A Whig Representative from Georgia declared: "We go for success. The people have shown, in all cases, their partiality for military men whenever they have been placed before them. All the civil merits of waggon bills and mill boys cannot give the eclat of a single victory on the battlefield."[121] In June 1847 Representative George Ashmun of Massachusetts observed that the "Taylor fever has been spreading far & wide" and predicted that attempts to resist it would fail.[122] The following January, another Bay State congressman lamented the rise of "military democracy," complaining that "Our candidates, unless the war spirit is soon checked, will be taken from the Generals in the field."[123] But even in Massachusetts many Whigs were ready to embrace Taylor because he seemed likely to win. A journalist in Boston thought that "this fighting and voting every four years and getting beat is not what it is cracked up to be," and urged his party to "*Nominate the man who will beat;* that is the one. If Taylor is the man, put him through."[124]

Some Illinois Whigs had caught the Taylor fever in the spring of 1848. In March, Silas Noble of Dixon announced that he was "for any Whig we can beat the Loco's with. I would rather beat them with Henry [Clay] than any other man but if we cannot beat them with him let us try Old Rough & Ready."[125] John J. Hardin acknowledged that "Clay has more devoted friends than any other man in the nation; but owing to the prominent & decided part he has taken on all subjects for 40 years past, he has an amount of personal opposition accumulated against him, which (although wholly unjust) makes it very easy to excite prejudice against him."[126]

On August 30, 1847, Whig Party leaders attending a state constitutional convention gathered at the Springfield home of Ninian W. Edwards to discuss the presidential election. According to one delegate, James W. Singleton, Lincoln explained that the purpose of the meeting was to choose "some other man than Henry Clay as the standard bearer of the Whig party." Lincoln put forward Taylor's name and urged "the necessity of immediate action," for "if the Whigs did not take Taylor for their candidate," then "the Democrats would!" (As late as March 1848, Democrats still contemplated drafting the apolitical general.) Lincoln reportedly asserted that "the Whig party had fought long enough for *principle,* and should change its motto to *success!*" After resolutions were adopted "in accordance with the views expressed by Mr. Lincoln," Clay stalwarts Singleton and Charles Constable "immediately left the house." Lincoln, Singleton claimed, "even went so far as to try to prevent me from taking a seat in the Philadelphia Convention [of the national Whig Party], and urged me to surrender my seat to Dr. [Elias] Zabriskie—Zabriskie then being a citizen of New Jersey, and not Illinois, because Zabriskie was for Taylor, and I was for Henry Clay, for the Presidency."[127]

In Congress, Lincoln struck up a pro-Taylor partnership with the tiny, frail sickly, brilliant Alexander H. Stephens of Georgia. Stephens was eager to nominate the slaveholding general in order to protect Southern interests, which seemed omi-nously threatened by the introduction of the 1846 Wilmot Proviso prohibiting slavery in any territory acquired from Mexico. (It passed the House but failed in the senate.) As enthusiastic backers of the Hero of Buena Vista, they formed the first Congres-sional Taylor Club, dominated by Southerners. Calling themselves "the Young Indi-ans," they corresponded with Whigs in all regions as they organized the Taylor movement.

Stephens admired Lincoln, who, he recollected, "was careful as to his manners, awkward in his speech, but was possessed of a very strong, clear and vigorous mind." Lincoln "always attracted and riveted attention of the House when he spoke," for "his manner of speech as well as thought was original." Lincoln "had no model. He was a man of strong convictions and was what [Thomas] Carlyle would have called an ear-nest man."[128] In turn, Lincoln thought highly of the charming, kind, fiercely indi-vidualistic Stephens. Of all the Southern Whigs, Lincoln's favorite was Stephens. On February 2, 1848, Lincoln reported to Herndon that the Georgia Representative, "a little slim, pale-faced, consumptive man, with a voice like [Stephen T.] Logan's has just concluded the very best speech, of an hour's length, I ever heard. My old, with-ered, dry eyes, are full of tears yet."[129] (In that speech, Stephens declared that "the principle of waging war against a neighboring people to compel them to sell their country, is not only dishonorable, but disgraceful and infamous.")[130]

In December and January, Lincoln worked behind the scenes with Stephens and other Young Indians to promote Taylor's candidacy. On February 9, Lincoln publicly declared that he, like many other Whig leaders in Illinois, was "decidedly in favor of General Taylor as the Whig candidate for the next Presidency."[131] He supported Old Rough and Ready "because I am satisfied we can elect him, that he would give us a whig administration, and that we can not elect any other whig." With Taylor heading the ticket, Lincoln predicted that the Whigs would gain one more House seat in Il-linois and probably win the state's electoral votes. To an Illinoisan who feared that Clay supporters could not be induced to back Taylor, Lincoln explained that he sided with Taylor "not because I think he would make a better president than Clay, but because I think he would make a better one than [Democrats like] Polk, or [Lewis] Cass, or [James] Buchanan, or any such creatures, one of whom is sure to be elected, if he is not."[132] Clay, Lincoln believed, stood "no chance at all." Even if the Kentucky statesman managed to gain New York, which he had narrowly lost in 1844, he would fail to carry Tennessee as well as the new states of Florida, Texas, Iowa, and Wiscon-sin in 1848. Another alternative to Taylor, the colorless, chilly Supreme Court Justice John McLean, was "not 'a winning card'" in Lincoln's opinion.[133]

Some Whigs objected to Taylor because his views on public affairs were quite unknown. In late January, congressional Whigs decisively rejected the Young Indi-ans' attempt to secure an endorsement for their man. At the same time, newspapers published letters by Taylor in which he refused to be trammeled by any party's prin-ciples or nomination. Such statements injured Taylor's standing among Whigs. Par-ticularly damaging was an April letter appearing in the Richmond *Whig* that reaffirmed Taylor's status as a no-party candidate. Caleb B. Smith of Indiana reported that 75 percent of his fellow Northern Whig congressmen thought "that Genl. Taylor cannot be run with the least prospect of success in the North, if he shall adhere to his present position of declining to give his opinions. The idea of running him as a 'No Party candidate' is out of the question."[134] Senator Willie Mangum of North Carolina and others like him believed that Taylor was too stand-offish and insufficiently committed to Whig principles.

To meet these objections, Lincoln proposed that Taylor announce his intention to endorse a national bank if Congress were to pass a bill establishing one; recommend a higher protective tariff; pledge not to abuse his veto power; and seek to acquire no territory from Mexico "so far South, as to enlarge and agrivate the distracting question of slavery."[135] Other Young Indians offered similar advice. In April, Taylor responded by issuing a statement identifying himself as a Whig, denouncing wars of conquest, and proclaiming his willingness to sign Whig economic measures into law if they were passed by Congress.

When Usher F. Linder expressed concern that Whig criticism of the Mexican War might injure Taylor's chances, Lincoln denied that he had opposed the war per se, for he—unlike some antiwar congressmen—always voted in favor of supplies for the troops. His criticism of Polk did not constitute opposition to the war. To Linder's contention that attacks on the president rob "Taylor and Scott of more than half their laurels," Lincoln replied that over forty congressmen backed Taylor and all had voted for the Ashmun amendment. Linder had asked, "have we as a party, ever gained any thing, by falling in company with abolitionists?" Lincoln pointed to the election of 1840, when abolitionists joined forces with the Whigs to elect Harrison. Moreover, Lincoln argued, critics of Polk were not necessarily abolitionists; in fact, thirty-seven Whig Representatives from Slave States had voted for the Ashmun amendment.[136]

Linder's observation about abolitionists was curious, for radical opponents of slavery displayed little enthusiasm for Taylor. In 1847, Joshua R. Giddings declared that the Whigs "who have got up this movement in favor of Gen. Taylor, knowing him to be in favor of extending slavery, are men of desperate political fortunes, who have become anxious to share in the spoils of office; they are men who would sell their party, their country and their God for an ephemeral success, or to enable them to bask in the sunshine of executive favor."[137] Another Ohio congressman acidly remarked of Taylor's candidacy: "To kill women and children and hurry men unprepared to eternity because they refuse to give us their land now free in order that we may cover it with slaves, are certainly high qualifications, for the highest office in the gift of a free nation of professing Christians."[138] Taylor's ownership of a Louisiana plantation worked by scores of slaves hardly endeared him to opponents of the peculiar institution like Horace Greeley, who insisted that Whigs "cannot, with any decency, support Gen. Taylor. His no-party letters; his well understood hostility to the Wilmot Proviso; his unqualified devotion to slavery; his destitution of qualifications and principles, place him 'at an immeasurable distance' from the Presidency. . . . If we nominate Taylor, we may elect him, but we destroy the Whig party. The off-set to Abolitionism will ruin us."[139]

Most Whigs, however, agreed not with Greeley but with former Congressman Edward McGaughey of Indiana, who believed that the party "must have the aid of gunpowder—the fortress of Locofocoism can not be taken without it."[140] In June, the Whig national convention assembled at Philadelphia, with Lincoln in attendance, and chose Taylor to run against the bland Michigan Senator Lewis Cass, whom the Democrats had nominated the previous month. The Whigs' failure to adopt a platform led one disillusioned Michigan editor to satirize the party's principles in nonsense verse:

> Sound the hewgag, strike the tonjon
> Beat the Fuzguzzy, wake the gonquong
> Let the loud Hosanna ring
> Bum tum fuzzelgum dingo bim.[141]

A Pennsylvania Whig declared that instead of a formal platform, all the party needed to do was quote Taylor's famous battlefield order: "A little more grape, Captain Bragg."[142]

Although many Northern Whigs were outraged by the nomination of a slaveholder who had never been a true backer of the party or its principles, Lincoln reported on June 12 that such disaffected elements "are fast falling in" and predicted that "we shall have a most overwhelming, glorious, triumph." He took heart from the fact that "all the odds and ends are with us—Barnburners [Free Soil Democrats in New York], Native Americans, [John] Tyler men, disappointed office seeking locofocos, and the Lord knows what." He gloated that "Taylor's nomination takes the locos on the blind side. It turns the war thunder against them. The war is now to them, the gallows of Haman, which they built for us, and on which they are doomed to be hanged themselves."[143] Even Horace Greeley ultimately supported Taylor in order to defeat "that pot-bellied, mutton-headed, cucumber Cass!"[144]

En route back to Washington from Philadelphia, Lincoln stopped in Wilmington, Delaware, where he attacked Polk's "high-handed and despotic exercise of the veto power" in "utter disregard of the will of the people," and impugned his motives for provoking war with Mexico.[145] Lincoln, like many other Whigs, charged that Polk started the war with Mexico to distract public attention from his failure to gain all of the Oregon Territory from Great Britain despite his belligerent campaign rhetoric about "fifty-four forty or fight." Ten days later, on the floor of the House, Lincoln denounced Polk's veto of an internal improvements bill and Cass's hostility to federal support for such legislation. Although that subject had been debated early in the session, Lincoln may have refrained from speaking on traditional Whig economic policies until Taylor, whose views on those matters were sketchy, was safely nominated. Lincoln also probably realized that with the earlier ratification of a treaty ending the Mexican War, criticism of the administration's conduct in provoking that conflict would no longer yield political dividends. A New York *Tribune* correspondent called it "a very sensible speech," showing that Lincoln not only "understood the subject" but even "succeeded in making the House understand it."[146]

On July 27, Lincoln treated the House to a partisan stump speech on the presidential question. Prompted by criticism of Taylor's pledge to use the veto power sparingly, it commanded the attention of his colleagues and gallery onlookers. Lincoln praised the general's willingness to defer to Congress, for that accorded with the "principle of allowing the people to do as they please with their own business." He admitted that he did not know if Taylor would join him in supporting the Wilmot Proviso. (Lincoln voted for the proviso or its equivalent at least five times during his congressional term.) As "a Western free state man, with a constituency I believe to be, and with personal feelings I know to be, against the extension of slavery," Lincoln hoped and trusted that Taylor would sign a bill containing the controversial proviso. (He was right about his constituency; in 1849 the Illinois General Assembly voted to instruct the state's congressional delegation to support measures excluding slavery from all territory gained from Mexico.) Lincoln may have learned that in May, Taylor had privately given assurances that he would not veto Wilmot's measure. Since Cass would definitely support the expansion of slavery and veto the proviso, it was better to vote for a candidate who might not do so. Moreover, under a Cass administration, the country would probably embark on "a course of policy, leading to new wars, new acquisitions of ter[r]itory and still further extensions of slavery."

With his customary sarcasm and ridicule, Lincoln poked fun at Congressman Alfred Iverson of Georgia, who a day earlier had delivered a slashing speech after which, Lincoln said, "I was struck blind, and found myself feeling with my fingers for an assurance of my continued physical existence. A little of the bone was left, and I gradually revived." Responding to Iverson's claim that the Whigs had "deserted all our principles, and taken shelter under Gen: Taylor's military coat-tail," Lincoln accused the Democrats of having used "the ample military coat tail" of Andrew Jackson: "Like a horde of hungry ticks you have stuck to the tail of the Hermitage lion to the end of his life; and you are still sticking to it, and drawing a loathsome sustenance from it, after he is dead. A fellow once advertised that he had made a discovery by which he could make a new man out of an old one, and have enough of the stuff left to make a little yellow dog. Just such a discovery has Gen: Jackson's popularity been to you. You have not only twice made President of him out of it, but you have had enough of the stuff left to make Presidents of several comparatively small men since; and it is your chief reliance now to make still another." Lincoln then lampooned Cass's military record, comparing it wryly to his own experience in the Black Hawk War.

Lincoln scornfully summarized Cass's waffling course on the Wilmot Proviso: "When the question was raised in 1846, he was in a blustering hurry to take ground for it. He sought to be in advance, and to avoid the uninteresting position of a mere follower; but soon he began to see glimpses of the great democratic ox-gad waving in his face, and to hear, indistinctly, a voice saying 'Back' 'Back sir' 'Back a little'. He shakes his head, and bats his eyes, and blunders back." Lincoln also belittled Cass's government financial accounts, which allegedly showed that the Michigander "not only did the labor of several men at the same *time;* but that he often did it at several *places,* many hundreds of miles apart, at the same time." He went on to mock Cass's "wonderful eating capacities," which enabled him to consume "ten rations a day in Michigan, ten rations a day here in Washington, and near five dollars worth a day on the road between the two places!" Everyone, Lincoln remarked, has "heard of the animal standing in doubt between two stacks of hay, and starving to death. The like of that would never happen to Gen: Cass; place the stacks a thousand miles apart, he would stand stock still midway between them, and eat them both at once; and the green grass along the line would be apt to suffer some too at the same time."

After excoriating Polk's conduct in bringing on the Mexican War, Lincoln alluded to the divisions within the New York Democratic Party, which reminded him of what "a drunken fellow once said when he heard the reading of an indictment for hog-stealing: The clerk read on till he got to, and through the words 'did steal, take, and carry away, ten boars, ten sows, ten shoats, and ten pigs' at which he exclaimed 'Well, by golly, that is the most equally divided gang of hogs, I ever did hear of.'" Lincoln concluded by remarking, "If there is any *other* gang of hogs more equally divided than the democrats of New-York are about this time, I have not heard of it."[147]

Throughout the final half-hour of his idiosyncratic speech, Lincoln was so genial and humorous that his colleagues laughed uproariously several times. With comic gestures, he delivered his remarks while strolling up and down the aisle. Whig newspapers called the speech "excellent and humorous" and praised Lincoln as "a very able, acute, uncouth, honest upright man, and a tremendous wag withal!"[148] He was in fact the leading Whig wag in Congress. Democrats also complimented him. When an Eastern Representative asked an Ohioan, "how did you like the lanky Illinoisan's speech? Very able, wasn't it?" the Buckeye replied: "the speech was pretty good, but I hope he won't charge mileage on his travels while delivering it."[149] Senator Hannibal Hamlin of Maine, while observing Lincoln give this speech, asked who he was. "Abe Lincoln, the best story teller in the House," he was told.[150]

After Congress adjourned on August 14, Lincoln remained in Washington for nearly a month, helping the Whig Executive Committee of Congress organize the national campaign. He corresponded with several party leaders, who reported encouraging news, and sent out thousands of copies of speeches by himself and other Whigs. Like a benign mentor, he urged young Whigs in Sangamon County to take an active role in the campaign and not passively look for instructions from their elders. "You must not wait to be brought forward by the older men," he told William Herndon. "For instance do you suppose that I should ever have got into notice if I had waited to be hunted up and pushed forward by older men. You young men get together and form a Rough & Ready club, and have regular meetings and speeches." When Herndon complained that the older Whigs were discriminating against the younger ones, Lincoln responded with paternal wisdom, urging him not to wallow in jealousy, suspicion, or a feeling of victimhood: "The way for a young man to rise, is to improve himself every way he can, never suspecting that any body wishes to hinder him. Allow me to assure you, that suspicion and jealousy never did help any man in any situation. There may sometimes be ungenerous attempts to keep a young man down; and they will succeed too, if he allows his mind to be diverted from its true channel to brood over the attempted injury. Cast about, and see if this feeling has not injured every person you have ever known to fall into it."[151]

Stumping for Taylor

Lincoln stumped vigorously for Taylor. In late August and early September, he spoke in Washington and nearby Maryland. In September, he spent eleven days in Massachusetts. Remarking on Lincoln's appearance in New England, the Chicago *Democrat* sneered, "Who would have thought it that Massachusetts would ever become so doubtful that it would be necessary to send to Illinois for aid? Well, Illinois has no use for her Whigs."[152] In fact, because Lincoln believed that Taylor had little chance of winning the Prairie State, he felt free to canvass New England rather than returning home.

Lincoln was needed in Massachusetts, where dissatisfaction with Taylor ran especially deep. Joshua Giddings had spoken against the general that summer to large and enthusiastic crowds in the state, and it seemed that Whig defections in November might prove serious. One young Bay State Whig bitterly complained that Southerners "have trampled on the rights and just claims of the North sufficiently long and have fairly shit upon all our Northern statesmen and are now trying to rub it in."[153] "Conscience Whigs" like Charles Sumner, Henry Wilson, Charles Allen, and Anson Burlingame denounced Taylor and his "Cotton Whig" allies. Wilson, who in 1847 had said that the "free state Whigs must dictate the policy of the Party or the Party had better be defeated and broken up," stormed out of the Philadelphia convention, declaring: "I will go home; and, so help me God, I will do all I can to defeat" Taylor. At that convention, which Horace Greeley called the "slaughterhouse of Whig principles," Charles Allen announced that the party "is here and this day dissolved."[154]

In August, Wilson, Allen, Sumner, and other antislavery militants met at Buffalo, where they formed the Free Soil Party, selected as their presidential candidate Martin Van Buren (who in November would win 14% of the Northern popular ballots but no electoral votes), adopted a vigorous antislavery platform, and chose as their motto "Free Soil, Free Speech, Free Labor, and Free Men." To some Boston Whigs these bolters seemed like "a set of Chinese bonzes, in gowns and pigtails, attempting to introduce the idolatrous worship of Foh-Even."[155] The new party's gubernatorial candidate predicted that Van Buren would siphon off 25,000 Massachusetts votes from Taylor. Although they had no expectation that Van Buren could win, some Free Soilers hoped that his candidacy would throw the election into the House of Representatives. Just as Joshua Giddings had four years earlier campaigned to convince antislavery Whigs not to vote for the Liberty Party's James Birney, so now Lincoln sought to persuade antislavery Whigs not to support the Free Soiler Van Buren.

Searching for help, Massachusetts Whigs looked west. Some suggested that Ohio's Senator Thomas Corwin should be invited, but he was busy campaigning back home. Lincoln may have been invited in lieu of Corwin. Like the Ohioan, Lincoln was hostile to slavery and a good Whig and had also made a notable speech criticizing Polk's war policy. Lincoln's attack on the president had won the approval of Massachusetts Whigs, including a Hingham resident who in March told his congressman:

"Our attention has been arrested in this quarter by the able speech of Hon. Mr. Lincoln of Illinois."[156]

On September 13 the Massachusetts state Whig convention took place in Worcester, where Lincoln arrived two days earlier, evidently invited by his friend, Congressman Charles Hudson. The chairman of the Whig City Committee, Alexander H. Bullock, sought out Lincoln, explained the political situation in detail, and asked him to speak the next night as a substitute for the scheduled Whig orator, who had backed out at the last moment. The Illinoisan agreed, suggesting that a tariff speech might be suitable. Bullock urged that Lincoln instead address the Whig cause in general and that he do so discreetly lest he offend potential Free Soilers.

Taking this advice, Lincoln repeated the congressional stump speech he had delivered in July, to which he appended a special plea to antislavery Whigs. Some of them found Van Buren suspect because of his tendency to accommodate slaveholders, his reputation as a clever political operator, and his espousal of negative government. Like other Whig campaigners, Lincoln argued that a vote for Van Buren was in effect a vote for Cass. For opponents of slavery to "unite with those [Democrats] who annexed the new territory to prevent the extension of slavery in that territory" seemed to Lincoln "to be in the highest degree absurd and ridiculous." He criticized purists who intended to "do their duty and leave the consequences to God," and he chastised the delegates to the Buffalo Free Soil convention for their silence about the Mexican War.[157] The Free Soil platform, he said, "embraces a few general declarations in regard to other topics [than slavery], but they are so general" that they called to mind "the pantaloons offered at auction by a Yankee pedlar," who described them as "large enough for any man and small enough for any boy." He also asserted that Taylor would be a better Whig president than Clay, for "Taylor's ground and the Whig ground is that the people ought to do as they please in regard to all questions of domestic policy," whereas Clay "was and is always ready to give his opinions and preferences, and thus would present motives for others to prostitute themselves to gain favor with him, if in power." The Whig failure to adopt a platform, Lincoln argued, was "preferable and far more useful to the great majority of the country than the variegated and impracticable 'platforms' that it had become the fashion . . . to adopt."[158]

As usual, Lincoln made little impression at first. His awkward appearance and soft delivery did not bode well. But soon his humorous stories and anecdotes, eloquent passages, and sarcastic put-downs of Cass, Van Buren, and other Democrats elicited warm applause and loud cries of "Go on! go on!"[159] The pro-Whig Boston *Atlas* called his address "one of the best speeches ever heard in Worcester" and claimed that it had caused "several Whigs who had gone off on the 'Free Soil' sizzle" to return to the party fold.[160]

Thanks to his ingratiating Western style, which many Massachusetts Whigs found refreshing, Lincoln received invitations to speak from Boston, Taunton, New Bedford, Dedham, Dorchester, Cambridge, Chelsea, and Lowell, all of which he accepted. In New Bedford a Quaker diarist found Lincoln's speech "pretty sound" but "not tasteful," perhaps because, as a local Whig paper noted, it was "enlivened by frequent flashes of genuine, racy, western wit."[161] In Boston, Lincoln compared Van

Buren "to a man having a gun which went off at both ends" and thus "would kill the object in view and those who supported him at the same time."[162] A Lowell resident testified that Lincoln "pointed his arguments with amusing illustrations and funny stories, which he seemed to enjoy as he told them, for he joined in a comical way in the laugh they occasioned, shaking his sides, which peculiar manner seemed to add to the good humor of the audience. He had a voice of more than average compass, clear and penetrating, pronouncing many of his words in a manner not usual to New England."[163]

From Boston to Dedham, Lincoln rode with George Harris Monroe, a young journalist who recalled that the silent, reserved Illinois congressman "was as sober a man in point of expression as ever I saw." Once arrived, he continued to seem ill-at-ease, having little to say to the many people he met. They wondered if they had made a mistake by inviting him. Their doubts grew as he began speaking rather stiffly. Soon, however, he relaxed, rolling up his sleeves, loosening his tie, and captivating the audience with his casual manner and pungent humor. Monroe admired "the homely way he made his points," with "no attempt at eloquence or finish of style." The speech, Monroe thought, "was not a great one, but it was a marvel of cleverness."[164] Lincoln concentrated on Van Buren and said "very little against Cass except he was worth a million and a half dollars."[165]

In Taunton, the "Lone Star of Illinois," as Lincoln was called, began his address leaning against a wall and speaking indifferently. As time passed, he warmed up and won over his audience with a barrage of "argument and anecdote, wit and wisdom, hymns and prophecies, platforms and syllogisms," which a Whig paper said flew out "like wild game before the fierce hunter of the prairie."[166]

Free Soil editors were less enthusiastic. One of them ridiculed Lincoln's defense of Whig vagueness on the issues: "This distinguished sucker went against all political platforms, and thus consoled the whigs for the loss of theirs. He told them that the whig party always went against executive influence, (which, for a party always out of power is not very wonderful,) and it would be inconsistent with this if their candidate should seek to influence them by expressing his opinions."[167] Another judged Lincoln to be "far inferior as a reasoner to others who hold the same views, but then he was more unscrupulous, more facetious, and with his sneers he mixed up a good deal of humor. His awkward gesticulations, the ludicrous management of his voice, and the comical expression of his countenance, all conspired to make his hearers laugh at the mere anticipation of the joke before it appeared." The editor criticized Lincoln's "recklessness and audacity" in misrepresenting the Free Soilers' case. Lincoln quoted a Lowell Free Soiler who satirized the Whig argument thus: "General Taylor is a slaveholder, therefore we go for him to prevent the extension of slavery." A more appropriate syllogism, Lincoln countered, would be: "Gen. Taylor is a slaveholder, but he will do more to prevent the extension of slavery than any other man whom it is possible to elect." He then sarcastically summarized the Free Soil argument in yet another syllogism: "We can't go for Gen. Taylor because he is not a Whig. Van Buren is not a whig; therefore we go for him." Lincoln criticized Van Buren for favoring the Mexican War and Texas annexation, though in fact the former president had opposed both.[168]

In Boston, Lincoln shared the platform with William Henry Seward, who declared that "all Whigs agree—that Slavery shall not be extended into any Territory now free—and they are doubtless willing to go one step further—that it shall be abolished where it now exists under the immediate protection of the General Government [i.e., in Washington, D.C.]"[169] Lincoln then followed with what Seward described as "a rambling story-telling speech, putting the audience in good humor, but avoiding any extended discussion of the slavery question."[170] The following day, Lincoln "with a thoughtful air" told the New York senator: "I have been thinking about what you said in your speech. I reckon you are right. We have got to deal with this slavery question, and got to give much more attention to it hereafter than we have been doing."[171] In 1860, Lincoln reminisced with Seward: "Twelve years ago you told me that this cause would be successful, and ever since I have believed that it would be."[172]

(Seward was not the only U.S. senator whose antislavery speeches impressed Lincoln. One day in the capitol he listened intently to Hannibal Hamlin of Maine denouncing human bondage; the Illinois Representative nodded enthusiastically whenever the Pine State senator scored a telling point. When they met as president-elect and vice-president-elect in 1860, Lincoln told Hamlin: "I have just been recalling the time when, in '48, I went to the Senate to hear you speak. Your subject was not new, but the ideas were sound. You were talking about slavery, and I now take occasion to thank you for so well expressing what were my own sentiments at that time.")[173]

Edward Lillie Pierce, an antislavery radical, asserted that during Lincoln's Massachusetts campaign swing, he "did not rise at any time above partisanship, and he gave no sign of the great future which awaited him as a political antagonist, a master of language, and a leader of men."[174] That was true of Lincoln's political career in general during the 1830s and 1840s.

In late September, while returning to Illinois, Lincoln stopped in Albany to visit Thurlow Weed, an influential Whig journalist and political operative who introduced him to the Whig vice-presidential candidate, Millard Fillmore. Then, as he sailed from Buffalo to Chicago, Lincoln observed a steamboat aground on a Detroit river sandbar. The sight inspired him to devise plans for a boat with an apparatus like water wings allowing it to float over such obstacles. After the November elections he worked on his idea, for which he obtained a patent.

Lincoln spent the latter part of October extensively canvassing his district in Illinois, where he continued urging Free Soilers to vote for Taylor. At Lacon on November 1, he "scored with the most scathing language, that 'consistency' of the Abolitionists, which, while they professed great horror at the proposed extension of slave territory, they [had in 1844] aided in the election of Mr. Polk; for which, and its disastrous consequences, they were responsible, as they held the balance of power."[175] Lincoln defended Taylor's purported egotism, "saying that in order to do what Taylor had done a man had to be somewhat egotistical."[176]

On election day, Taylor made such a strong showing in the lower South and Pennsylvania that he was able to defeat Cass (who lost New York thanks to the defection of antislavery Democrats to Van Buren) by a margin of 45 percent to 42 percent in the popular vote and 163 to 127 in the electoral college. Taylor carried Massachusetts with 61,070 votes to Van Buren's 38,058 and Cass's 35,281. The Hero of Buena Vista also won the Seventh District of Illinois by a majority of 1,481 but lost statewide to Cass, 45 percent to 42 percent, even though he received 7,009 more ballots than Clay had in 1844 and 18,550 more votes than Whigs had gotten in congressional contests the previous August. Taylor captured nearly 60 percent of the vote in Springfield.

Dealing with the Slavery Issue

Upon returning to Washington in December for the brief second session of the Thirtieth Congress, slated to expire in March 1849, Lincoln participated in a fierce legislative struggle over slavery. Both major parties, sobered by the electoral showing of the Free Soilers, hoped to neutralize those upstarts somehow.

The slavery debates had actually begun in earnest during the first session, in 1848, and Lincoln's awareness of the issue increased significantly before his term ended. As Massachusetts Senator Henry Wilson recalled, "the subject of slavery in the abstract was a topic of frequent discussion in the XXXth Congress. Its sinfulness, its wrongs, its deleterious influences, its power over the government and the people, were perhaps more fully discussed in that than in any previous Congress."[177] In fact, slavery was by far the most frequently discussed topic in that congress. Lincoln paid special attention to the subject in the second session, as he had told William Henry Seward he would.

During the previous session, Lincoln had done little about it other than voting with the antislavery bloc. He may have avoided speaking on the slavery issue for fear of endangering party unity in a presidential election year. Joshua R. Giddings, the leading antislavery member of Congress, helped shape Lincoln's views. A fellow Representative from Illinois, Orlando B. Ficklin, recalled that Lincoln "was thrown in a mess [rooming house] with Joshua R. Giddings. In this company his views crystallized, and when he came out from such association he was fixed in his views on emancipation."[178] Early in his congressional career, on December 21, 1847, Lincoln had supported Giddings's motion to refer an antislavery petition from District of Columbia residents to the Judiciary Committee. It was a divisive vote; Illinois Congressman John Wentworth reported that "I have never known a reference of a petition to cause such an excitement before."[179] A motion to table was defeated 98–97, with Speaker Winthrop casting a tie-breaking vote. A week later, Lincoln voted for a motion by Caleb B. Smith of Indiana similar to Giddings'. Two days thereafter, he opposed tabling a petition "praying that the public lands may be appropriated in aid of the extinction of slavery."[180]

In the summer of 1848, the debate over slavery in the territories grew intense, posing the gravest threat to national unity since the South Carolina nullification crisis of 1832–1833. In late June, Congressman Wentworth told a friend: "we are just now in an awful state of excitement. A dissolution of the Union is threatened on every side. . . . Here is the *battle* ground; & it appears that, what is to be done for free principles, must be done within a few weeks. Some kind of a compromise will pass the Senate. Then comes the House, where a desperate fight will be made."[181]

As Wentworth predicted, a compromise was proposed in the senate by John M. Clayton of Delaware, who urged the establishment of territorial governments in Oregon, California, and New Mexico. While retaining the antislavery statutes passed by the unofficial provisional government of Oregon, Clayton's bill would have kept the legislatures of the other two territories from adopting laws relating to slavery, thus leaving the question to the Southern-dominated U.S. Supreme Court. Clayton and many other Southern Whigs had hoped thereby to avoid a direct vote on the controversial Wilmot Proviso. Southern Whigs in the lower chamber viewed the Clayton Compromise as a threat to Taylor's presidential hopes. Northern Whigs suspected that this legislation might facilitate the expansion of slavery; they also feared that it might help support Texas's claim to much of New Mexico, thus increasing substantially the area of a slave state. Antislavery militants denounced the compromise as a sellout to the South. "The fate of millions & millions is to be voted upon," observed Massachusetts Representative Horace Mann, a Conscience Whig; as the House was polled, the customary bedlam in the chamber died down, and "it was still as a church. Every man wanted to know how every other man voted."[182] By a margin of 112–97, the House tabled Clayton's bill, thus killing it.

Then the lower chamber passed a bill of its own, establishing a territorial government for Oregon with the proviso that Thomas Jefferson's antislavery Northwest Ordinance should be applied there. Lincoln supported the measure, which passed 128–71. A week later, he joined the majority in rejecting President Polk's recommendation to extend the 1820 Missouri Compromise line to the West Coast, widely regarded as a measure favorable to slavery expansion because most of the Mexican Cession lay south of that line.

By the time Congress adjourned in mid-August, Oregon had finally become a territory, one without slavery. The attempt to fasten the peculiar institution on California and New Mexico had been thwarted, and those territories remained unorganized. A journalist called these developments "the only signal defeat the slave power has ever experienced under this government."[183] An antislavery congressman exulted over the "great triumph," which he considered "one of the most glorious things that has happened this century."[184]

On only three occasions during the long first session of the Thirtieth Congress did Lincoln vote against Giddings and other antislavery militants. In April 1848, he sided with a 130–42 majority in tabling Conscience Whig John G. Palfrey's resolutions calling for an investigation of riots following the attempt of many Washington slaves to escape. Twenty other Northern Whigs, among them five from New England, joined Lincoln; thirty-six, including twelve from New England, supported the resolution. An antislavery congressman from Massachusetts explained that "we were all glad that the subject of Mr. Palfrey's resolutions had their quietus" because "if the matter had been sent to a committee, it would have been found, that there was really no sufficient cause, for the interference of the House, on the grounds he presented. It would seem, therefore, like a failure on our side & a triumph on theirs. But, as the whole matter of those resolutions was laid on the table, it was a kind of drawn game,—the opponents [i.e., proslavery forces], indeed, having an advantage, but not such an advantage as they would otherwise have gained."[185]

The following month, Lincoln was the only Northern Whig opposing Amos Tuck's motion to suspend the rules to permit the introduction of a resolution directing relevant committees to report a bill outlawing slavery and the slave trade in Washington. The motion lost by a 90–54 margin. It is difficult to understand Lincoln's vote, for he was no friend of either slavery or the slave trade in the capital, as his actions during the second session of the Thirtieth Congress would show dramatically. In the July and August debates over slavery in the territories, Lincoln voted with the Giddings bloc on thirteen of fourteen roll calls. He broke with them to join the 104–69 majority favoring the suspension of the rules to permit consideration of a joint resolution declaring it expedient to establish civil government in New Mexico, Oregon, and California. Nine other Northern Whigs voted to suspend the rules, including Joseph Root, a witty, sharp-tongued, militant opponent of slavery from the Western Reserve of Ohio. Lincoln also differed with the Giddings–Palfrey–Tuck–Mann forces (known as "Ultraists") on the presidential question; they preferred John McLean to Taylor.

Lincoln's antislavery voting record in the first session served as a prelude to his more dramatic action in the second session.

Though doing little about the peculiar institution in 1848, other than voting with the antislavery forces, Lincoln that year expanded his knowledge of slavery through firsthand observation, as he had done in Kentucky the previous autumn. In the late 1840s, Washington was a predominantly Southern town. John Randolph of Virginia called it "a depot for a systematic slave market—an assemblage of prisons where the unfortunate beings, reluctant, no doubt, to be torn from their connections, and the affections of their lives, were incarcerated and chained down, and thence driven in fetters like beasts, to be paid for like cattle."[186] In 1854, with obvious distaste, Lincoln spoke about Washington's slave pens: "in view from the windows of the capitol, a sort of negro-livery stable, where droves of negroes were collected, temporarily kept, and finally taken to Southern markets, precisely like droves of horses, had been openly maintained for fifty years."[187] Lincoln was alluding to the Georgia Pen, also known as Robey's Pen, which an observer called a "a wretched hovel, 'right against' the Capitol," encircled "by a wooden paling fourteen or fifteen feet in height," where "all colors, except white . . . both sexes, and all ages, are confined, exposed indiscriminately to all the contamination which may be expected in such society and under such seclusion."[188]

Lincoln observed slavery up close when, in January 1848, slave traders seized a black waiter at Mrs. Sprigg's boardinghouse and, before the horrified eyes of his wife, clapped him in irons and dragged him off to a slave prison. The unfortunate victim had been buying his freedom for $300, all but approximately $60 of which he had paid by the time he was abducted. In response, Giddings introduced a resolution (supported by Lincoln) calling for an investigation of the matter and for the repeal of slave trading in the District. The following month, Lincoln opposed tabling a resolution nearly identical to the Wilmot Proviso.

In April 1848, over seventy slaves in the District of Columbia boldly tried to escape aboard the schooner *Pearl*, which had been chartered by an abolitionist sympathizer, Daniel Drayton. Betrayed by a black man, the fugitives, after traveling 140 miles, were overtaken, imprisoned, promptly sold, and removed farther south. The capital was in a frenzy of excitement as hundreds of incensed whites marched on the office of an antislavery newspaper, *The National Era,* demanding that its editor, Gamaliel Bailey, leave the District. When Bailey refused, the mob began to stone the building, but the police, assisted by leading citizens who feared that the capital might be moved to another city, restored order before significant damage was done or blood was shed. When Joshua Giddings went to the District jail to assure Drayton and Sayers that they would receive legal counsel, a mob threatened the congressman's life. Doubtless this episode reminded Lincoln and many others of the fatal attack on Elijah Lovejoy's newspaper office in Alton, Illinois, a decade earlier.

In the House, Giddings and John G. Palfrey introduced resolutions of inquiry, which touched off an angry debate marred by fierce rhetoric and a menacing tone. An antislavery congressman reported that "we have had threats, insults, the invocation of mob-rule & lynch law, &, indeed, all the whole Southern armory has been exhausted upon us. Their orators . . . begin as tho' they were calling up a herd of slaves from a distant cotton-field" and "gesticulate, as tho' they had the lash in hand, & were cutting into the flesh, before & behind."[189] One such Southerner, Andrew Johnson, who in 1865 would become president, tauntingly asked Palfrey if he wanted his daughter to marry a black man. In the upper chamber, Henry S. Foote of Mississippi invited New Hampshire Senator John P. Hale, a leading antislavery spokesman, to visit his state and promised that his constituents, with the assistance of their senator, would lynch him.

Lincoln had been a silent observer of these episodes and debates during the first session, which forced him to think about the peculiar institution more seriously than he had done since 1837. Then he had condemned slavery as an institution "based on injustice and bad policy."

In the second session of the Thirtieth Congress, Lincoln acted on his increased sensitivity to the slavery issue. Early in that session, Palfrey of Massachusetts, one of the handful of antislavery militants in the House, asked leave to submit a bill abolishing slavery in Washington, D.C. Because it contained no provision for compensating owners, Lincoln voted against it; he was one of only six Northern Whigs to do so. That same day he voted twice to support a motion by Joseph Root instructing the committee on territories to propose legislation excluding slavery from California and New Mexico. An effort to table lost 106–80; the resolution then passed 108–80. Palfrey called the latter vote "very encouraging."[190] On December 18, Lincoln again voted in favor of Root's measure. That day Giddings introduced legislation to allow District residents, including blacks, to express their opinion on abolishing the peculiar institution; it was tabled by a vote of 106–79, with Lincoln and nine other Northern Whigs siding with the majority. A Whig journalist complained that Giddings, Palfrey, and their allies "come nearly every day with a number of sixpenny propositions, which have had the effect to exasperate and madden the Southern members."[191]

On December 21, when Daniel Gott of New York submitted a resolution calling for the abolition of the slave trade in the District, Lincoln, for unclear reasons, joined three other Northern Whigs in an unsuccessful bid to table it. Giddings condemned this vote by Lincoln and others as "direct support of the slave trade."[192] But Lincoln, like some fellow Whigs, thought the resolution's preamble—which stated that slave trading in the District was "contrary to natural justice" and "notoriously a reproach to our country throughout Christendom and a serious hindrance to the progress of republican liberty among the nations of the earth"—was too abrasive.[193] Resolutions like Gott's had been offered many times, but without such a controversial preamble, which Whig Congressman Caleb B. Smith, an opponent of slavery, criticized for its tendency to "inflame or excite the people of the South" and "hold them up to the odium of the country."[194] Horace Greeley, who wrote the preamble and persuaded Gott to adopt it, insisted that the same forces would have opposed the measure even if the preamble had not been included. Perhaps Lincoln opposed Gott's resolution not only because he objected to the inflammatory preamble but also because he himself was preparing a stronger measure. Later that day, when Gott's resolution was adopted 98–87, Lincoln and two other Northern Whigs voted with the minority.

The voting took place amid great excitement, for it represented the first congressional action limiting the domestic slave trade. This dramatic gesture struck fear into the hearts of Southern senators and Representatives, who warned that their region might withdraw from the Union if the Free States did not back down. Senators John C. Calhoun of South Carolina and Henry Foote of Mississippi (the would-be lyncher of Senator Hale) organized a caucus of Southern members of Congress to respond to what they considered Northern acts threatening the interests of their section. A Boston journalist astutely observed that scoffers at Southern truculence "have no idea of the deep, and hidden, and giant-like under-current of emotion that is flowing through the hearts of many Southrons."[195] Representatives from below the Mason-Dixon line had been complaining during the debates on slavery that they felt "wounded and offended at the style of language so often indulged in by gentlemen on this floor, who treat the question as men of a single idea, denouncing the institution and those who live in its midst."[196] That undercurrent would eventually lead to a war that cost 620,000 men their lives.

Intimidated by the prospect of disunion, the House on January 10 voted (with Lincoln and fifteen other Northern Whigs in the 119–81 majority) to reconsider the Gott resolution, thus effectively consigning it to oblivion. These votes on Gott's resolution caused Horace Greeley to term Lincoln "one of the very mildest type of Wilmot Proviso Whigs from the free States" and Indiana Congressmen George W. Julian to deem him "a moderate Wilmot Proviso man" whose "anti-slavery education had scarcely begun."[197]

But in fact Lincoln's antislavery education was well advanced, as he demonstrated the very day that he voted to reconsider the Gott resolution: he announced he would offer a substitute for that measure, a bill more advanced than the New Yorker's resolution, calling for the abolition of slavery itself—not just slave trading—in the District of Columbia. (Twelve years earlier, as a state legislator, he had unsuccessfully tried to help facilitate the abolition of slavery in the District.) He evidently agreed with William Lloyd Garrison that the "abolition of the slave traffic . . . is impractical while slavery exists. There is no reason why slave-trading should be prohibited if slave-holding is justified and allowed."[198] Lincoln proposed that, starting in 1850, all children born to slave mothers in the District were to be free; that their mothers' owners would be responsible for supporting and educating those children; that the children in return "would owe reasonable service, as apprentices, to such owners . . . until they respectively arrive at the age of __ years when they shall be entirely free"; that if owners emancipated slaves in the District, Congress would compensate them at full market value (to be determined by a board consisting of the president and his secretaries of state and the treasury); and that fugitive slaves reaching the District would be extradited by municipal authorities. (Lincoln was evidently trying to mollify those who feared that abolition would make Washington a mecca for runaways.) The bill was to take effect only if a majority of the voters of the District approved it. Lincoln announced "that he was authorized to say, that about fifteen of the leading citizens of the District of Columbia to whom this proposition had been submitted, there was not one but who approved of the adoption of such a proposition."[199]

When colleagues shouted out, "Who are they?" "Give us their names!" Lincoln did not reply. Two were Joseph Gales, co-editor of the *National Intelligencer*, and his partner William S. Seaton, the mayor of Washington. A day earlier, Giddings and Lincoln had called on Seaton. Years later Lincoln told an interviewer: "I visited Mayor Seaton, and others whom I thought best acquainted with the sentiments of the people, to ascertain if a bill such as I proposed would be endorsed by them. . . . Being informed that it would meet with their hearty approbation I gave notice in congress that I should introduce a Bill. Subsequently I learned that many leading southern members of Congress, had been to see the Mayor, and the others who favored my Bill and had drawn them over to their way of thinking. Finding that I was abandoned by my former backers and having little personal influence, I *dropped* the matter knowing it was useless to prosecute the business at that time."[200] Lincoln's measure suffered the fate of earlier such proposals. Between 1805 and 1862, none ever reached a vote.

As president, Lincoln would introduce a scheme for gradual, compensated emancipation, with a provision offering federal assistance to freed slaves wishing to leave the country; no such clause appeared in his 1849 measure. A plan for colonization might have rendered his statute more palatable to whites. One Washington correspondent believed that if a gradual, compensated emancipation bill were accompanied by "a law prohibiting free blacks from settling here, every [white] man in the district will hold up both hands in favor of the measure. A more lazy, dirty, impudent set of rascals never breathed than the free blacks who infest Washington."[201]

Some Southerners condemned Lincoln as an abolitionist. At the opposite end of the political spectrum, the antislavery purist Wendell Phillips regarded Lincoln's proposal to end slavery in the District as "one of the poorest and most confused specimens of pro-slavery compromise."[202] Joshua Giddings, however, praised Lincoln's bill, which he had helped draft. On January 8, 1849, the Ohio antislavery militant recorded in his diary: "Mr. [John] Dickey of P[ennsylvani]a and Mr. Lincoln of Illinois were busy preparing resolutions to abolish slavery in the D C this morning. I had a conversation with them and advised them to draw up a bill for that purpose and push it through. They hesitated and finally accepted my proposition. . . . Mr. Lincoln called on me this evening and read his bill and asked my opinion which I freely gave." Three days later, Giddings confided to his diary that "our whole mess remained in the dining-room after tea, and conversed upon the subject of Mr. Lincoln's bill to abolish slavery. It was approved by all; I believe it as good a bill as we could get at this time, and am willing to pay for slaves in order to save them from the Southern market."[203]

Giddings's judgment was echoed by *The National Era*, whose abolitionist editor, Gamaliel Bailey, said two weeks before Lincoln announced his plan: "we should like to see a bill [emancipating slaves in the capital] prepared, submitting the question to the [legally] qualified [i.e., adult white male] voters of the District, with the distinct information that a liberal appropriation would be made to aid in the act of emancipation. Such a bill, we doubt not, would pass Congress, and we have just as little doubt as to the decision of the citizens of this District under it." A measure of that sort "would be giving to thousands of citizens, unrepresented in any legislative body, an opportunity to do a high act of justice, with some grace; and would also result in the *emancipation*, not *transfer*, of the victims of Slavery. Pass an act of abolition, without such provision as we have suggested, and before it could take effect, almost every slave in the District would be sold to the South."[204]

Some abolitionists objected to compensating slaveholders, but others (including Elihu Burritt, Gerrit Smith, and Abel Stevens) did not. In Washington the leading abolitionists and most active conductors on the local underground railroad—William L. Chaplin and Jacob Bigelow—originally opposed compensation but eventually endorsed it. In 1848, Chaplin called upon antislavery forces to spurn "all that class of cute philosophers, who raise doubt about *buying people out of bondage*" and to "reject the dogma, that money is lost which is paid for slaves. Every dollar thus paid is a most effective sermon to the conscience of the guilty." Five years later, Bigelow wrote that "On the subject of paying for slaves, to secure their freedom, I acknowledge that I once *theorised* against it; but was, long ago very summarily cured of my theory, when I came to practice upon it."[205] Some leading antislavery politicians, among them William Henry Seward and Salmon P. Chase, also supported compensation for Washington slaveowners. (Like Lincoln, Seward favored compensated emancipation in the District of Columbia only if a majority of voters there approved it.)

Horace Greeley decried Lincoln's provision to require that the electorate of the District vote on emancipation: "it seemed to me much like submitting to a vote of the inmates of a penitentiary a proposition to double the length of their respective terms of imprisonment."[206] But in fact many citizens of the District had long opposed slavery and slave trading in their midst. In 1828, nearly 600 Washingtonians had petitioned Congress to abolish slavery there. Moreover, because Congress controlled the District, and because no senators or Representatives were elected by its residents, some argued that it would be unjust to deny the voters there a say in the matter; the electorate of a state (or its representatives) had to be consulted if slavery were to be abolished within its borders. Congress might technically have the power to abolish slavery in the District without such a referendum, but it would be unwise to do so, said the Baltimore *Sun,* citing Shakespeare: "it is well to have a giant's strength, but tyrannous to use it like a giant. We submit, however, that to abolish slavery in the District without the consent of a majority of the white population would be a wanton exercise of that absolutism with which Congress has been vested in its legislative relation to the people of the District. . . . For our part, we believe it would be greatly conducive to the peace of the nation on this subject, if slavery was abolished there by their own consent and free will."[207] The Georgetown *Advocate,* a pro-Taylor journal, agreed that compensated emancipation in Washington, D.C., would face few objections. A congressman in late 1847 reported that there was evidently "a very large party in the District favorable to the *gradual* abolition of slavery in the District, and a small party in favor of the *immediate* abolition. A majority of Congress is disposed to leave this matter to the voters of the District."[208] In 1854, Lincoln himself said that six years earlier "I heard no one express a doubt that a system of gradual emancipation, with compensation to owners, would meet the approbation of a large majority of the white people of the District."[209] In 1850, Illinois Congressman (and future governor) William Bissell, referring to the possible abolition of slavery in Washington, reported from the capital that "it is well understood here that if the question was submitted to the people of the *District* a large majority would vote in favour of it."[210]

In offering compensation to slaveowners, Lincoln had majority opinion on his side. When Lincoln announced that he planned to submit such a bill, a correspondent for the pro-Taylor Boston *Atlas* noted that it was "believed that there is a large majority of the House in favor of some such proposition" and "that the sooner some step of the kind is taken, the better it will be for the peace and union of the country." It was universally agreed, said the paper, that "whatever action may be had in the premises, *compensation* must follow. This may be the ground of compromise that will continue. We must take men and the laws as they are, not as one would have them, and regulate our legislation on those principles of justice and expediency, which so marked and honored the national councils of our fathers."[211] A New York *Herald* reporter who opposed slavery declared that it would be "dishonorable in the extreme" to "free at once all slaves, without compensating their owners."[212] House Speaker Robert C. Winthrop believed that "compensation must go hand in hand with emancipation. It is this view which takes away the idea of selfishness from Northern philanthropy. If we admit that we are to unite with the South in bearing the burdens & defraying the cost of Abolition, we make it a matter of joint interest in regard to which our voices may fairly be heard." The only way to persuade slaveowners to accept emancipation would be to offer compensation, he argued. "Those who oppose such a course, however philanthropic they may be in theory, are practically riveting the bonds which they desire to break."[213]

In framing his bill, Lincoln may have been influenced by Great Britain's abolition of West Indian slavery in 1834. Parliament had appropriated £20,000,000 to compensate the owners of 800,000 liberated bondsmen. Similarly, Congress during the Revolutionary War had offered to compensate slaveowners whose bondsmen served in the army and thus gained their freedom. Lincoln might also have considered the example set by Pennsylvania, whose legislature abolished slavery gradually, liberating children born to slave mothers after a specified date once those children had attained their majority. New Jersey and New York had followed Pennsylvania's lead.

In 1860, Wendell Phillips triggered a lively debate by denouncing Lincoln as "the slave hound of Illinois" because his 1849 emancipation bill included a fugitive slave clause.[214] In a public letter to Phillips, Joshua Giddings defended Lincoln: "his conversing with the people of the District, the preparation of his bill, the avowal of his intention to present it, were important." Such actions placed him among "those who were laboring in the cause of humanity. He avowed his intention to strike down slavery and the slave trade in the District; to strike from our statute book the act by which freemen were transformed into slaves; to speak, and act, and vote for the right," and "cast aside the shackles of party, and took his stand upon principle." Chiding Phillips, Giddings added: "You speak of that act with great severity of condemnation. I view it as one of high moral excellence, marking the heroism of the man. He was the only member among the Whigs proper [as opposed to the handful of antislavery Ultraists] of that session, who broke the silence on the subject of those crimes."[215]

Sydney Howard Gay, managing editor of the New York *Tribune* and a militant opponent of slavery, also challenged his old friend Phillips. In August 1860, William Herndon, probably speaking for Lincoln, told Gay: "Your reply to Wendell Phillips's article in the Liberator was correct." Gay, Herndon said, was "familiar—too familiar—with legislative business not to know that . . . no one man can possibly get his own ideas put into any statute—any law, or any Constitution." Passing bills involved "concession—compromise." When "Lincoln was in Congress this State of affairs Existed: he was then a strong Anti-Slavery man and is now the same. This I know, though he wishes and will act under the Constitution: he is radical in heart, but in action he must Conform to Law & Constitution as Construed in good old times." Herndon, a conspicuous admirer of Phillips, concluded: "Lincoln, in reference to the Bill about which Mr. Phillips wrote his articles, was actuated by Anti-Slavery sentiments alone. . . . In doing this he had to consult his friends' feelings and ideas or he could do nothing; and so his bill was drawn up with a reference to all the aforesaid Conditions—conflicting sentiments & ideas." Lincoln "wanted the slave trade in the District of Columbia cut up by the roots and slavery gradually abolished."[216]

Echoing Herndon, a New York *Tribune* correspondent in the fall of 1849 described Lincoln as "conspicuous in the last Congress—especially during the last session, when he attempted to frame and put through a bill for the gradual Abolition of Slavery in the District of Columbia. He is a strong but judicious enemy to Slavery, and his efforts are usually very practical, if not always successful."[217] Eleven years later, Joshua Giddings declared that while he and Lincoln were in Congress "they became intimately acquainted—boarding at the same house, and sitting opposite each other at meals; that he thought he knew the heart of Abraham Lincoln as well as any living man, and speaking from that knowledge, he believed that every beat of 'honest

Abe's' heart was a throb of sincerity and truth—in a word, that he is that noblest work of God—an honest man. He believed Lincoln's loyalty to republican principles, and to the cause of freedom and humanity, was unquestionable and beyond suspicion."[218]

Throughout the winter of 1848–1849, antislavery forces battled various schemes to finesse the Wilmot Proviso. When Whig Congressman William B. Preston of Virginia, following the lead of Illinois Senator Stephen A. Douglas, proposed the admission of the Mexican Cession as a single state, calling this expedient "the only door" through which a compromise acceptable to both North and South could pass, Northern Whigs balked, demanding that the Wilmot Proviso be applied to that territory. An attempt to omit it was defeated, pleasing antislavery congressmen like Horace Mann, who exclaimed "Glorious!!"[219] On February 27, the House killed Preston's bill.

Another attempt to circumvent the Wilmot Proviso was made late in the session when Wisconsin Senator Isaac P. Walker proposed to abrogate the laws of Mexico, including statutes dealing with slavery, in the Mexican Cession and allow the president to frame appropriate rules for that territory. Though it passed in the senate, it died by a vote of 114–100 in the House. The next day (the final one of the session), supporters of that measure tried to railroad it through, provoking such a heated debate that fisticuffs broke out in both houses, causing blood to flow freely. A congressman reported that some colleagues "were fiercely exasperated & had the north been as ferocious as the south, or the whigs as violent as the Democrats, it is probable there would have been a general melée."[220] A Kentuckian described the mayhem in the lower chamber more vividly: "Imagine 230 tom cats fastened in a room, from which escape is impossible, with tin cans tied to their tails—raging and screaming, and fighting, and flying about from 6 P.M. to 6 A.M., twelve hours—and you will have some idea of the last jubilee in the House. About ten o'clock, [Richard K]. Meade of Virginia, and Giddings of Ohio, had a fight—Meade drunk. About 3 A.M., Sunday morning, [Jacob] Thompson of Mississippi, and [Orlando B.] Ficklin of Illinois, had a knock down—both drunk. Many members were drunk, as I was assured by one of their own body—as eyes and ears informed me."[221] Observed an Alabamian: "The whole matter . . . was disgraceful to the Congress of the United States."[222]

A relieved Giddings reported that "we weathered the most dangerous point on the last night of the late session. Our barque will now glide along I think in smooth water."[223] Thus California and New Mexico remained unorganized as Taylor was inaugurated, which suited the antislavery forces, who felt that the "best thing that can be done in regard to the territories, this session, is to do nothing."[224] Giddings thought the March 3 vote "a fatal blow to the institution [of slavery], from which it never recovered. And its downfall may be dated from that eventful night."[225]

That winter congressmen also wrangled over the claim of the heirs of Antonio Pacheco, who sought compensation for a slave who had been taken away from him twelve years earlier. The army had seized Pacheco's bondsman Lewis to serve in the Seminole wars; when the Indians captured Lewis, the military considered him to have gone over to the enemy. Hence at the end of the conflict Lewis was sent west with his captors. In debating this claim, Giddings and his allies insisted that humans could not be considered property and hence Pacheco's claim should be denied. Lincoln voted regularly with the Giddings bloc on that claim, which ultimately failed to win approval.

Patronage Scramble

In the wake of Taylor's victory, Lincoln was, as a constituent wrote, "harast to deth by applicants for the various offices."[226] Aggressive Whigs besieged members of Congress, clamoring for government jobs, including such posts as diplomats, customs collectors, postmasters, judges, attorneys, marshals, census takers, clerks, and land office registers and receivers. Lincoln could easily identify with John J. Crittenden, who in March reported: "I have never witnessed a greater or more widespread cupidity for office. It has absolutely sickened me."[227] Lincoln may well have exclaimed "amen!" when a constituent said, "You must find it irksome and troublesome attending to the numerous calls for office in our State." He doubtless would have endorsed the sentiment expressed by David Davis, who in 1853 declared: "If men would use half the industry & energy, in any other calling, that they do, in running down an office, they would get rich."[228]

Lincoln conscientiously tended to the requests of office seekers, just as he had dutifully answered constituents' mail and regularly voted on the floor of the House. (He missed only one quorum call and 13 of 456 roll calls during his term). But as a lame-duck freshman, he wielded little influence. "Not one man recommended by me has yet been appointed to any thing, little or big, except a few who had no opposition," he acknowledged in May 1849.[229] Many Illinois Whigs were indignant at the shabby treatment his recommendations received from the Taylor administration. Although he later would say during his own presidency that "he did not regard it as just to the public to pay the debts of personal friendship with offices that belonged to the people," Lincoln tried to procure jobs for some close personal and political friends, including Anson G. Henry, Jesse K. Dubois, and Simeon Francis.[230] For Henry he won an Indian agency, and for Dubois, the receivership of public monies in Palestine, Illinois, but he failed to secure a position for Francis, who wanted to move to Oregon.

Patronage distribution created bitterness. When Lincoln obtained the pension agency in Springfield for his brother-in-law, Dr. William Wallace, a defeated rival complained that "Mrs Lincoln said to some one the other day—that she was now so happy—that she had got Mr. L. to give the Pension Agency to the Doctor & now all of their family difficulties was made up—so you see I was offered up as a sacrifice—a sort of burnt offering—to heal family broils."[231] (Wallace had apparently been refusing to speak to Lincoln.) Lincoln turned down the request of George W. Rives, a Whig activist in Paris, Illinois, for a job in Minnesota because Anson Henry had applied for a job in that same territory. Later, when told that Rives had openly abused him for this decision, Lincoln grew irritated. In December 1849, Rives once again asked for a recommendation; Lincoln answered with some asperity that his "feelings were wounded" by allegations that Rives had criticized him. But after giving Rives a mild scolding, Lincoln magnanimously endorsed him anyway. In the 1850s, Rives became an enthusiastic supporter of Lincoln, whom he called "one of the best men God ever made."[232]

Lincoln's characteristic diffidence handicapped him in patronage struggles. As a would-be Indiana postmaster observed in February 1849, "a modest man stands no chance now a days, either with the ladies, or as a successful applicant for the smiles of Government."[233] In writing recommendations, Lincoln would mildly and reasonably acknowledge that incumbents were able men who had opposed the Whigs and simply suggest the names of replacements if vacancies should occur. When endorsing one James T. B. Stapp, for example, he praised him as "better qualified" than other applicants but admitted that "a large majority of the whigs of the District" preferred someone else.[234]

With more supplicants than jobs to satisfy them, Lincoln had to make choices, some of which were not popular back home. Dr. Richard F. Barrett, with whom Lincoln had served on the Illinois Whig Central Committee in 1840, talked with many Springfield party faithful who "all agree that men older in service and of more weight and strength of character could have been selected for office."[235] Among the most controversial appointees recommended by Lincoln was Turner R. King as register of the Springfield land office. King was "a kind of worthless man" in William Herndon's estimation.[236] Scandalized by the appointment, Dr. Barrett told Thomas Ewing: "I think Mr. Lincoln has been imposed upon by King, and his friends." Barrett claimed that King, whom he had known for years, had become "a *free drinker, card player, bankrupt*, and *loafer*, and for months and years has done little or nothing for an honest livelihood," and was therefore "wholly undeserving the patronage of the Government."[237] William Butler, who wanted the post that went to King, lodged similar complaints. In April, Lincoln informed Philo Thompson, King's principal sponsor, that a "tirade is still kept up against me here [in Springfield] for recommending" King and urged Thompson to gather 200 to 300 signatures on a petition favoring King.[238] In response, Thompson assured Lincoln that King was a "*warm active whig*" and sent a petition stating that while "King may sometimes drink spirits, or throw a Card for amusement," he was not "an Abolitionist, a Drunkard and a Gambler" in "any true sense."[239] After receiving this document, Lincoln informed Ewing that there was "*no mistake about King's being a good man*" and charged his friend William Butler with acting "in bad faith" by launching a "totally outrageous" assault on King.[240]

Political calculation may have been behind Lincoln's conduct in this matter. Lincoln favored King over his old friend William Butler because King resided in Tazewell County in the northern part of the Seventh Congressional District. King could help win it for Whigs like Lincoln. Moreover, King's brother and business partner, Franklin, had influence with militant antislavery forces. Whatever the reason behind the appointment, Lincoln had made an enemy of Butler, who for the next decade opposed his political aspirations. That opposition would help thwart Lincoln's bid to secure a political appointment for himself.

Would-Be Bureaucrat

At first, Lincoln had not planned to ask for an office at all, because, as he explained to Joshua Speed, "there is nothing about me which would authorize me to think of a first class office; and a second class one would not compensate me for being snarled at by others who want it for themselves." He could, he said, "have the Genl. Land office [a position in the Department of Interior] almost by common consent," but he did not wish to antagonize other Illinoisans who sought that lucrative post, which paid $3,000 a year.[241] (The governor of Illinois earned $1,000 annually, and an Illinois Supreme Court justice $1,200.) In due course, however, Lincoln did become a candidate for that job and thereby found himself embroiled in a complicated and often mean-spirited struggle.

The General Land Office was considered one of the more important government bureaus, whose commissioner supervised several dozen clerks. Illinois residents thought their state was entitled to that commissionership, for Ohio had controlled it for a decade, then Indiana for eight years, and Illinois (in the persons of James Shields and Richard M. Young) had done so for merely five years. It seemed only fair that a Sucker should be commissioner for a few more years, after which another western state could have a turn.

Initially, Lincoln backed Cyrus Edwards for the job, based on recommendations by several Whigs, including William Thomas, Nathaniel Pope, and Lincoln's old friend Joseph Gillespie. Although some Illinois party members were unenthusiastic about Edwards, when the governor and the legislature of Kentucky also endorsed him and appealed for Lincoln's help in February, Lincoln agreed to press his candidacy.

While Lincoln threw his weight behind Edwards, the only other Whig congressman from Illinois, Edward D. Baker, who had moved to Galena in 1848 and promptly won election to the House, supported Col. James L. D. (Don) Morrison, a haughty, demagogic, egotistical Whig state senator from St. Clair County and a Mexican War veteran. Morrison's opponents charged that he would face a conflict of interest if he became commissioner, for he had purchased some ancient French claims to land near Peoria that would be extremely valuable if sustained. His ethical sense was so feeble that when he predicted to Governor John Reynolds that he would be rich some day, the Old Ranger replied: "I guess you will be, Don, if you can manage to keep out of the penitentiary that long."[242]

In response to Baker, Elihu B. Washburne of Galena, who probably would have won that district's congressional seat if Baker had not intervened, acted for many who resented Baker's pushiness. He came out against Morrison and backed Martin P. Sweet. Joining Washburne were influential Whigs like S. Lisle Smith and Justin Butterfield of Chicago. Thus a three-way contest developed, pitting Edwards, Morrison, and Sweet against one another.

Lincoln, meanwhile, feared that a candidate from some other state might win the commissionership. In February, he told Joshua Speed that former Congressman Edward W. McGaughery of Indiana was lobbying for the job "and being personally known, he will be hard to beat by any one who is not."[243] (Cyrus Edwards's main problem was that he was unknown in Washington.) Also in the hunt were aspirants from Alabama, Iowa, Florida, and Mississippi. To head off these interlopers, Lincoln and Baker agreed to support either Edwards or Morrison, who were to decide between them which one would drop out of the running. (Sweet had earlier withdrawn his candidacy.) On April 19, Lincoln told Edwards: "what I can do for you I shall do, but I can do nothing till all negotiation between you and Don is at an end, because of my pledge to Baker. Still they know at the Department I am for you."[244]

On April 6, fear that Illinois was not promoting a strong enough candidate led Anson G. Henry and four other Illinois Whig leaders to urge Lincoln to seek the commissionership himself, lest an out-of-stater win it. Illinois Whigs had already lost the chief justiceship of the Minnesota Territory by failing to unite on a candidate.

Apparently, Lincoln had thought about applying even before Cyrus Edwards asked his help. Weeks earlier, when David Davis urged him to do so, Lincoln replied: "I do not much doubt that I could take the Land-office if I would. It also would make me more money than I can otherwise make. Still, when I remember that taking the office would be a final surrender of the law [practice], and that every man in the state, who wants it himself, would be snarling at me about it, I shrink from it."[245] Lincoln told Justin Butterfield "that he did not want the office of Commissioner of the land office and . . . could not afford to abandon his profession for a temporary appointment."[246] Denying that Lincoln's legal career would suffer if he were to accept the commissionership, Davis reminded his friend that he would make little money at the bar unless he moved to a large city.

On April 7, Lincoln, who had returned to Springfield a week earlier, cautiously replied to Anson G. Henry and other Whig chieftains, saying that "if the office can be secured to Illinois by my consent to accept it, and not otherwise, I give that consent." Lincoln insisted that he "must not only be chaste but above suspicion." If offered the job, he insisted, "I must be permitted to say 'Give it to Mr. Edwards, or, if so agreed by them, to Col. Morrison, and I decline it; if not, I accept.'" He added that "if at any time, previous to an appointment being made, I shall learn that Mr. Edwards & Col. Morrison have agreed, I shall at once carry out my stipulation with Col. Baker."[247] Edwards said that he did not wish to burden his friends or to play the role of dog-in-the-manger and wanted Lincoln to feel "entirely untrammelled" to do what he thought best in order to defeat Baker's candidate, whoever that might be.[248]

A few days later, yet another formidable candidate entered the contest, Justin Butterfield, an able, witty attorney from Chicago. A native of New Hampshire, the 59-year-old Butterfield had practiced law in New York before moving to Illinois. In 1841, President John Tyler named him U.S. district attorney in Chicago, a post he held until 1844. Lincoln enjoyed telling how Butterfield "was asked at the beginning of the Mexican War if he were not opposed to it; he said 'no, I opposed one War [the War of 1812]. That was enough for me. I am now perpetually in favor of war, pestilence and famine."[249] Others, however, disliked Butterfield's offensive sarcasm. In 1839, he came near fighting a duel with William L. D. Ewing.

Butterfield had lobbied the Taylor administration for the job of Treasury Department solicitor, but when he saw his chances fading, he turned his attention to the

General Land Office post. On April 12, Josiah M. Lucas, an Illinois Whig journalist serving as a clerk in that agency, alerted his longtime friend Lincoln that "Butterfield is trying his best for the place, although not here in person, he is operating through friends," among them Interior Secretary Thomas Ewing, Congressman Truman Smith, and Senator Daniel Webster.[250] In May, the outgoing commissioner of the General Land Office, Richard M. Young (whom Butterfield denounced as "the most treacherous whining sniveling creature that ever existed"), had reported similar developments to Lincoln and urged him to "lay modesty aside and strike for yourself—From what I can learn Mr. B[utterfield] of C[hicago]—contrary to what he said to me when you was here, and after having lost the Solicitorship of the Treasury, is now playing a strong game for the Land office. Some think he will succeed—now can[']t you prevent, by urging the claims of one A. Lincoln—who I am sure would be more acceptable here than any Whig in Illinois? What say you—Whatever you do, it will be well for it to be done quickly—and I am very sure that you can succeed better with this man Lincoln, than any person else."[251] On May 13, William H. Henderson, a former colleague of Lincoln's in the Illinois Legislature, made a similar appeal from Washington: "you should come on here without delay" for "your success would be better secured by your presence. It is said that the President is for you, & perhaps a majority of the Cabinet, and that Mr. Ewing is warmly in favour of Friend Butterfield of Chicago." Five days later Henderson was more importunate: "Your friends require your immediate presence[;] delay is fatal."[252]

Butterfield complained that "Lincoln appears to think that he has an absolute right to the support of all the members of the Cabinet who served with him in Congress [i.e., Postmaster General Jacob Collamer and Navy Secretary William B. Preston]. A sentiment of this kind will not go down with the People, who will never subscribe to the doctrine that one election to Congress confers a right to a *continual* claim to future offices." He also argued that a majority of Illinois's delegates to the 1848 Whig national convention favored his candidacy; that he was the choice of "an overwhelming Majority of the Whigs of the Northern part of the State which contains the only Whig congressional district in the State and is entitled as a matter of right and Justice to this office"; and that his own "qualifications for the office are paramount to Mr Lincoln."[253] Butterfield accused Lincoln's friends of conducting "a foul plot to defeat me by falsehood fraud and misrepresentation."[254] He was particularly suspicious of Edward D. Baker, whose opposition had "its origin in personal malice and hostility because I ridiculed his attempts to force himself upon the President for a Cabinet appointment."[255]

Like some other Whigs, Lincoln did not believe that Butterfield had earned a patronage reward. Butterfield had supported Clay for the presidency in 1848 and did little for the party during the campaign. Butterfield's appointment, predicted Thomas Mather, "would be odious in the extreme" to most Illinois Whigs.[256] Lincoln called Butterfield his "personal friend" who was "qualified to do the duties of the office," but insisted that "of the quite one hundred Illinoisans, equally well qualified, I do not know one with less claims to it." Heatedly, he declared that it would "mortify me deeply if Gen. Taylor[']s administration shall trample all my wishes in the dust."[257] To Secretary of the Navy William B. Preston, Lincoln complained: "In 1840 we fought a fierce and laborious battle in Illinois, many of us spending almost the entire year in the contest. The general victory came, and with it, the appointment of a set of drones, including this same Butterfield, who had never spent a dollar or lifted a finger in the fight." Eight years later Butterfield was similarly inactive. "Yet, when the election is secured by other men's labor, and even against his effort, he is the first man on hand for the best office that our state lays any claim to. Shall this thing be?" Employing imagery that he would later use when denouncing slavery, Lincoln predicted that Illinois "whigs will throw down their arms, and fight no more, if the fruit of their labor is thus disposed of."[258] Lincoln, who hated to see some people enjoy the fruit of others' labor, urged Duff Green to use his influence to defeat Butterfield by supporting Morrison, Edwards, or himself. He implored Joseph Gillespie to write to Crittenden or Taylor. To Indiana Congressmen Elisha Embree and Richard W. Thompson he predicted that the appointment of Butterfield would be "an egregious political blunder" and solicited them to lobby Taylor; both responded positively.[259]

Butterfield's chances looked good, however, because the president granted cabinet members control over appointments in their departments, and Secretary of the Interior Thomas Ewing insisted on the Chicago attorney. Just as the final decision was about to be made, Anson G. Henry prevailed on Taylor to postpone the matter for three weeks. "I told him Butterfield[']s appointment would ruin us in Ills.," Henry confided to a friend. Secretary William B. Preston informed Henry that "Lincoln is the only man in Illinois that can beat Butterfield, but that he can do it if he comes on, & his friends back him up."[260] Other Illinois Whig leaders, including Josiah M. Lucas and Nathaniel G. Wilcox, implored Taylor to put off the decision until Lincoln could reach Washington. Lucas urged Lincoln to press his claims in the capital: "Things are moved here by *personal importunity. . . . you* possess an influence *here*."[261] According to Lucas, Taylor and Postmaster General Jacob Collamer preferred Lincoln to Butterfield. "Pocket your *modesty*, as the preacher did his religion," Lucas counseled.[262] On May 21, Lucas spoke with Taylor, who "expressed great partiality for Lincoln" and was "astonished" to learn from letters Lucas showed him that Butterfield was not the choice of most Illinois Whigs. According to Lucas, Ewing, Caleb B. Smith, and Truman Smith had misled the president. Taylor said he would delay his decision until he heard more from the people of the Prairie State.[263]

A week later, however, immediately after calling on Taylor, Duff Green's son reported to Lincoln that the president "declined to depart from the rule he has established, to wit, to read no letters and listen to no explanations on the subject of appointments unless presented to him through the Secretaries of the respective departments. He requested me to file your letter with the secretary of the Interior, but as you desire it to be confidential I do not think proper to do so, without hearing further from you." Green added that the "understanding in the Land Office, among the Clerks here, is that the appointment of Butterfield has been determined on, and that it is to take effect on the 1st June."[264]

In response to this news, Lincoln implored Illinois friends as well as congressional colleagues to write on his behalf. Friendly newspaper editors like Allen Ford of
the Lacon *Illinois Gazette* endorsed his candidacy. "It is beyond all doubt the almost
unanimous desire of the friends of the administration in this state" that Lincoln
should win the commissionership, Ford asserted.[265]

Casting a wider net than Lincoln, Butterfield secured endorsements from the
legislatures of Iowa, Michigan, and Wisconsin; from many bar associations; and from
northern Illinois, his home base. He also attacked Lincoln downstate, especially in
Springfield, where he circulated two petitions. The first, Butterfield claimed, was
"signed by the clerk of the circuit court, clerk of the county court, Judge of Probate
and Sheriff of the county, being all the Whig county officers elected by the People,
and also signed by the leading Whigs of the county. They offered to provide for me in
addition the petition of a Majority of all the Whig voters in the county if I desired
it."[266] The other petition contained the signatures of twenty-eight "Whig mechanics
of the City of Springfield" who declared that they were "dissatisfied with the course
of Abraham Lincoln as a member of Congress" and supported Butterfield's application.[267]

It is hard to know what to make of these petitions. According to Butterfield, they
proved that "Lincoln's boasted 'overwhelming majority' like Falstaff's men 'in Buck-
ram' . . . have vanished into thin air." But Anson G. Henry alleged that nearly all the
signatures on one of them had been obtained under false pretenses. "I have the first
man yet to see who does not regret having signed it," he told Lincoln on June 11.[268]
Butterfield sneered that Stephen T. Logan and Lincoln were asking those who had
signed this petition "in the most pathetic manner to retract, but I am informed they
have all refused with the exception of one or two against whom they prevailed by
threats and menaces."[269] Lincoln was suffering from the spite of disappointed patronage seekers. The first petition had been circulated by William Butler, and the second
by Caleb Birchall, who resented Lincoln's support of a rival aspirant for the Springfield postmastership.

More may have been at work than the disaffection of unsuccessful place hunters.
Herndon recalled that "Lincoln was not at all times *the* popular man in Sangamon
County" because "he was not a social man, not being 'hail fellow well met,'" and also
because "he was a man of his own ideas—had the courage of his convictions and the
valor of their expression." Often "abstracted and absent minded," Lincoln would pass
friends on the street without greeting them. Herndon believed that "this was taken
for *coldness—dignity—pride*" by some people who "misjudged and disliked" him for
his seeming aloofness.[270] Envy may also have poisoned the minds of some. "Lincoln
outstript his contemporaries & companions and they feel a terrible jealousy against
the man who overheaded—outstript them," according to Herndon.[271] Moreover, he
was not a joiner; his name did not appear on the membership rolls of the Masons, the
militia, the churches, or other community groups.

Butterfield believed that Lincoln was plotting to cheat him out of the commissionership by circulating petitions and taking them to Washington "on the very eve of
the appointment and obtain the appointment by a coup de main, before I should have

any opportunity to expose the misrepresentations contained in his petitions." He claimed that petitions favoring Lincoln had been signed by farmers ignorant of their content. "What these petitions contain no one knows," Butterfield told a friend on June 7, "but you know that 99 out of 100 will sign such petitions without even reading them or caring what they contain—how much reliance is to be placed on such petitions?" By contrast, Butterfield boasted, "I have circulated petitions only among professional men and leading and intelligent whigs who are presumed to know something about the nature of the office and the qualifications requisite to fill it."[272] Butterfield also complained that friends of Lincoln had falsely told cabinet members that Butterfield had suffered a stroke that had injured his mind. To counteract this charge, Butterfield obtained statements from physicians, a druggist, and Chicago's mayor.

To prevent Lincoln's planned visit to Washington, Butterfield proposed that neither of them travel to the capital. Lincoln demurred, telling Butterfield's emissary "that if he were at liberty to consult his own feelings, he would cheerfully accede to your proposition, and remain at home, but he had so far committed himself to his friends that he could not now accede to it."[273]

And so in the second week of June, both Lincoln and Butterfield hastened to Washington. En route, Lincoln chatted with a good-natured Kentucky gentleman who offered him a plug of tobacco, a cigar, and a glass of brandy. Lincoln politely declined each in turn, explaining that he did not chew, smoke, or drink. The Kentuckian, who had become fond of Lincoln, said: "See here, my jolly companion, I have gone through the world a great deal and have had much experience with men and women of all classes, and in all climes, and I have noticed one thing." When Lincoln eagerly asked what that observation might be, the Kentuckian replied: "those who have no vices have d—d few virtues." Lincoln laughed heartily and enjoyed repeating the story.[274]

Arriving in Washington, Lincoln was greeted by Nathaniel G. Wilcox, who informed him that Taylor planned to name Butterfield because he came from northern Illinois. In Wilcox's room, Lincoln wrote an appeal to the president, arguing that both he and Butterfield were equally qualified and that "if it appears that I am preferred by the Whigs of Illinois," he should be appointed, for the Prairie State deserved recognition and other Midwestern states had already received their fair share of patronage. He further maintained that central Illinois had been neglected in the allotment of offices; the marshal, Benjamin Bond, came from the south (Clinton County) and the district attorney, Archibald Williams, from the west (Quincy)—both residents of towns over a hundred miles from Springfield. Plaintively, he asked Taylor: "I am from the center. Is the center nothing?—that center which alone has given you a Whig representative? On the score of locality, I admit the claim of the North is no worse, and I deny that it is any better than that of the center."[275]

Butterfield claimed that Chicago in particular and northern Illinois in general deserved special consideration. To David Hunter he wrote on June 4: "the South and Middle Sections of the State have monopolized all the important offices . . . while the Northern part of the State which contains the only whig Congressional District in the State has had nothing; now you know that there is more intelligence and enterprise, more Whigs and more of the materials for making Whigs in the North part of the State than there is in all the rest of the State besides—it contains . . . the only Whig Congressional District."[276] Butterfield's supporters made the same argument. The loss of the Seventh Congressional District seat by Stephen T. Logan in 1848 strengthened the hand of the northern Illinois Whigs.

In early June, Nathaniel G. Wilcox and Josiah M. Lucas called on Taylor to plead Lincoln's case, arguing that he was the choice of three-fourths of the people of Illinois ("as against Butterfield, forty-nine fiftieths"), that he "was a western man" who "emigrated to Illinois when but a youth—he has grown up with her, and is loved by her people—a self made man, and now stands at the head of the bar in his state."[277] The president replied somewhat heatedly: "I had always intended to give the Commis[s]-ionership of the General Land Office to Illinois. I have already given two appointments to that State—the Marshal to the Southern part, and the District Attorney to the center; and I think the commissionership should go to the north."[278] Whigs in northern Illinois also pointed out that the two previous commissioners of the General Land Office had been from central part of their state.

These arguments helped Butterfield to win the contest, much to the delight of the Chicago *Journal*, which praised the appointment as "a tribute alike to the Northern portion of our own State, and to her devoted Whigs."[279] Upon learning the bad news, Lincoln returned to his room and lay down in a fit of depression. He later declared: "I hardly ever felt so bad at any failure in my life."[280] The following day, when Lincoln called on Ewing to retrieve his papers, the secretary told him that if Lincoln had applied for the commissionership when the administration first came to power, instead of maintaining his support of Cyrus Edwards, he would have won it. To placate Edwards, Lincoln asked the secretary to give him a letter stating those facts. Ewing did so, but Edwards was not mollified. Believing that Lincoln had acted in bad faith, Edwards broke off their friendship.

To Edwards's confidant and protégé Joseph Gillespie, Lincoln lamented: "The better part of one's life consists of his friendships; and, of these, mine with Mr. Edwards was one of the most cherished." He claimed that he had "not been false to it." At any time before June 2, he was ready to step aside for Edwards; only after that date, when he was reliably informed that Edwards had withdrawn and that he and Butterfield were the sole Illinoisans in the running, did he decide "to be an applicant, *unconditionally*."[281] If Lincoln had acted in 1849 as he did in 1843, when he declared that his "honor is out with Baker" and that he would "Suffer my right arm to be cut off before I'd violate it," he may well have preserved his friendship with Edwards. In 1850, Lincoln unsuccessfully tried to repair the damaged relationship by offering to support Edwards "cheerfully and heartily" to replace Butterfield, who was reportedly about to resign.[282] Only in 1860 did Edwards finally agree to "bury the hatchet."[283]

Two weeks after his defeat, Lincoln had recovered his good spirits. On July 9, he informed David Davis that "I am less dissatisfied than I should have been, had I known less of the particulars." With characteristic magnanimity, he added: "I hope my good friends every where will approve the appointment of Mr. B[utterfield] in so far as they can, and be silent when they can not."[284] Four days later, he told Gillespie: "I am not greatly dissatisfied. I wish the office had been so bestowed as to encourage our friends in future contests."[285]

Sorting out the affair afterwards, Elihu B. Washburne, who worked on Butterfield's behalf, believed Lincoln was viewed as "a mere catspaw of Baker." The "appointment of Lincoln would have been considered a triumph of Baker, and as such would have inspired contempt," Washburne said.[286] He also felt that Whigs in northern Illinois deserved the commissionership. Lincoln himself believed that Secretary Ewing's support of Butterfield was decisive. Ewing evidently found Butterfield more highly qualified than Lincoln and believed that he was the best land lawyer in Illinois. Even after Ewing had determined to name Butterfield, Taylor could have overruled his secretary of the interior, as he did in some other cases; but the president chose not to do so. Lincoln may also have lacked sufficient status to gain the appointment. In 1850, when Nathaniel G. Wilcox recommended him for the post of secretary of the interior during the cabinet shakeup following Taylor's death, Democratic Congressman William A. Richardson of Illinois replied that Orville H. Browning was the only Whig from central Illinois who stood a chance of winning that post. Butterfield had more connections in Washington than did Lincoln; among them were Daniel Webster and a justice of the Supreme Court, who was unfamiliar with Lincoln.

Lincoln was not the only one with disappointed hopes. Taylor and his cabinet generally bungled patronage distribution, awarding places in a slapdash manner. Ewing allegedly fired able Whigs and appointed bibulous Democrats in their place.

Lincoln's boldness in framing an antislavery bill may also have hurt his chances. Years later Joshua Giddings observed that instead of cautiously avoiding the explosive slavery issue, Lincoln "saw a few members standing aloof from the Democratic and Whig organizations, working by every honorable means to call the attention of the House and country to the crimes of slavery. They were called 'agitators,' and the line of demarcation, which separated them from other members, was well defined." Giddings implied that Lincoln may have injured his standing with the Taylor administration by aligning himself with such agitators.[287]

In fact, many Taylor Whigs hoping to win posts in the new administration avoided the slavery issue during the second session of the Thirtieth Congress lest they offend the slaveholding president-elect. In December 1848, Gamaliel Bailey scorned those cautious Whig Representatives who shied away from the slavery issue: "There be many expectants among Congressmen of comfortable appointments at home or abroad. Why compel these gentlemen to make their mark on obnoxious questions, where to vote *nay* you would ruin them with their constituents and to vote *yea* might endanger their standing with the Powers that are to be. 'Lie low—and keep dark' is a safe policy. Let there be no agitation. Let the ordinary party issues have free course, and suppress all vexed questions."[288] Caleb B. Smith, for example, had emphatically opposed slavery in the first session of the Thirtieth Congress but lost his enthusiasm in the second session, evidently for fear that he might jeopardize his chances for a cabinet appointment. On January 10, after voting to reconsider the Gott resolution,

Smith refused to answer when Giddings asked if he wished slavery in Washington to continue.

Ewing may have employed underhanded tactics while championing Butterfield. In 1850, protests accusing Butterfield of being inefficient and behaving in an "ungentlemanly and uncouth" manner led to an examination of his original appointment.[289] In the course of that inquiry, a congressional committee sought to discover whether some of Lincoln's letters of recommendation had been fraudulently removed before the president made his decision. The committee learned that in fact letters endorsing Lincoln had somehow been suppressed. While it could not be proven beyond cavil that Ewing had ordered someone to tamper with Lincoln's file, the suspicion arose that he had done so. In August 1850, the Washington correspondent of the New York *Herald* reported that there was "much opposition making its appearance here, just now, to the continuance in office of Mr. Commissioner Butterfield. . . . The manner in which he received his appointment, by means of the . . . suppression of the brief of the recommendations of his principal competitor, the Hon. Abraham Lincoln, . . . by a clerk in the Interior Department, is much talked of here and commented upon."[290]

There was good reason to suspect foul play. On July 8, when Lincoln inspected the sealed file of his endorsements that Ewing had given him two weeks earlier, he was surprised to find that two of the most important documents—letters from Indiana Congressmen Richard W. Thompson and Elisha Embree—were missing. A summary of the letters indicates that Thompson "first recommended Butterfield supposing Lincoln would not accept—prefers Lincoln" and that Embree was "against Butterfield—prefers Lincoln." Indignantly, Lincoln asked Ewing to explain the absence of the missives that may have spelled the difference between victory and defeat. He told the secretary: "I relied upon, and valued, them more than any other two letters I had, because of the high standing of the writers, because of their location within the Public Land states, and because they did (what few other members of Congress could) speak of my character and standing *at home*." On June 21, Postmaster General Collamer had told Lincoln "that Mr. B[utterfield] appeared to be better recommended from the Public Land states" than he was. "I felt sure he was mistaken," Lincoln informed Ewing. "If these letters were not before the cabinet, the judge [Collamer] was nearer right than I supposed. *With* them, I had the State of Indiana clearly; *without* them Mr. B. had it. The letter of Mr. Thompson was a recantation from Mr. B. to me; so that without it, I not only lost him, but he stood in full life, recommending Mr. B."[291]

Lincoln decided against making a public protest about the letters, even though Ewing's response did not satisfy him. In 1850, Lincoln said privately that he could have revealed the "piece of villainy" that denied him the commissionership and filled him "with indignation." But, he added, "my high regard for some of the members of the late cabinet; my great devotion to Gen: Taylor personally; and, above all, my fidelity to the great whig cause, have induced me to be silent." Much as he would like to "confound the guilty," he feared that such a public exposure of the story "might also injure some who are innocent," "disparage a good cause," and "reflect no credit upon me."[292]

Lincoln did, however, criticize Taylor's passivity. By the summer of 1849, the president was thought to be ruled by his cabinet. In a letter that foreshadowed his own presidential style of active leadership and echoed the complaints of other prominent Whigs, Lincoln told Secretary of State Clayton that Taylor appeared to defer excessively to his cabinet in the distribution of patronage. Such conduct, Lincoln warned, "is fixing for the President the unjust and ruinous character of being a mere man of straw." Recalling that Taylor during the Mexican War had overruled a council of war's unanimous recommendation against fighting a battle, Lincoln declared that this story, whether true or not, "gives him more popularity than ten thousand submissions." The public, Lincoln advised, "must be brought to understand, that they are the *President's* appointments. He must occasionally say, or seem to say, 'by the Eternal,' 'I take the responsibility.' Those phrases were the 'Samson's locks' of Gen. Jackson, and we dare not disregard the lessons of experience."[293]

In 1850, after Taylor's untimely death, Lincoln praised his "sober and steady judgment," his "dogged incapacity to understand that defeat was possible," his lack of tyrannical instincts as well as of "*excitement*" and "*fear*," his aversion to "*sudden* and *startling* quarrels," his magnanimity, his solicitude for his troops, and "his unostentatious, self-sacrificing, long enduring devotion to his *duty*." These very qualities were to distinguish Lincoln himself as president.[294] Some thought Lincoln's dogged pursuit of a patronage job resulted from the pressure of economic necessity. A Massachusetts congressman said that at "the close of Mr. Lincoln's term in Congress, the Administration of Gen. Taylor was just coming into power. He had lost some of his . . . business because of his being in Congress, and he felt like abandoning the practice of the law. For this reason he wanted Gen. Taylor to appoint him Comer. of the Genl. Land Office."[295] His good friend, Representative Richard W. Thompson, with whom he discussed these matters, saw the same motive at work. As the remarks he made to David Davis in February 1849 indicate, Lincoln feared that his law practice had suffered during his sojourn in Washington. While stumping Maryland in September 1848, Lincoln's fellow campaigner, William Pickney Whyte, played a trick on him at their hotel. As Whyte later recalled, in the morning "I arose first and assuming a woe begone tone I said, Abe, you should see your horse." Lincoln sprang from bed exclaiming in alarm, "My Lord, he isn't dead is he?" In fact, his mount was perfectly healthy; Lincoln had panicked, Whyte explained, because he "was very poor."[296]

More importantly, perhaps, Lincoln may have had little desire to return to provincial Springfield after consorting with leading lawyers and politicians in sophisticated Washington. Parties and soirees for 300 to 900 guests were a regular occurrence at the capital. A congressional chaplain of the mid-1840s observed that almost "every man in Congress has made himself noteworthy at home by some gift or accomplishment; he can play the fiddle well, tell a good story, manage a caucus, make an effective speech, indite striking paragraphs, laugh loud and long, listen complaisantly while others talk, talk fluently and copiously himself, or has a pretty and clever wife. These gifts and graces are, of course, brought to the Federal Capital, and invested in the joint-stock company of social life."[297] Lincoln's own strong ambition had been fortified by his two years in Washington, where conversation was brilliant and he could hobnob with eminent men of impeccable manners and great wit.

Lincoln's congressional colleagues included the redoubtable John Quincy Adams, who in February 1848 suffered a stroke on the floor of the House and died shortly thereafter. Lincoln, who may have witnessed the former president's collapse, was named to a committee charged with arranging the funeral. One of the giants of the senate, Daniel Webster of Massachusetts, now and then invited Lincoln to his Saturday breakfasts, where the Illinoisan's humor and geniality charmed the senator's other guests. (On March 4, 1849, Lincoln told John Cook, son of the deceased U.S. Senator Daniel Cook: "I want you to go with me to the Senate Chamber. I want to introduce you to one of the greatest men of the Nation and a warm personal friend of your father," Daniel Webster.)[298]

Lincoln's reaction to Webster's hospitality may well have resembled his reaction to a dinner given by Governor Levi Lincoln which he attended at Worcester in September 1848. Thirteen years later, he said: "I had been chosen to Congress then from the wild West, and with hayseed in my hair I went to Massachusetts, the most cultured State in the Union, to take a few lessons in deportment." Lincoln added "that the dinner at Governor Lincoln's by reason of its elaborate hospitality and social brilliancy was different in kind from any function he had ever attended before. He remarked upon the beauty of the china, the fineness of the silverware and the richness of all the table appointments, and spoke of the company of distinguished and thoroughly educated men whom he met there in the animated, free and intimate conversation inspired by such an accomplished host as Governor Lincoln."[299] Lincoln probably observed something like this at Washington. In any event, he clearly wished to be reelected. Mary Lincoln shared her husband's desire to remain in the glamorous capital.

Others were as disappointed at Lincoln's defeat as he was. The treatment he received at the hands of Secretary Ewing and the Taylor administration angered many active Illinois Whigs. David Davis called it "outrageous" and expressed wonderment "that the voice of Members of Congress from a State is not taken about appointments."[300] That summer, the chief justice of the Illinois Supreme Court, William Wilson, reported "great indignation on the part of the Whigs of this State at the course pursued in the appointment of Butterfield over Lincoln & that it would take but little to call forth a public expression against Mr Ewing."[301] In the fall, Usher F. Linder, speaking in the Illinois House of Representatives, called Ewing "*universally odious*," a man who "*stinks in the nostrils of the nation*," a "lump of ice, an unfeeling, unsympathizing aristocrat, a rough, imperious, uncouth, and unamiable" fellow, "unsuited to wield the immense patronage placed in his hands, from the fact that he . . . could disregard the almost unanimous wish of the people—the whig people of Illinois, and overlook the claims of such men as Lincoln, Edwards and Morrison, and appoint a man [Butterfield] . . . who could not, as against any one of his competitors, have obtained one twentieth of the votes of Illinois."[302] In attacking the secretary publicly, Linder voiced the private feelings of many, including Elihu B. Washburn, who fumed, "Ewing *must go out*."[303]

Some Whigs regretted Linder's indiscretion; among them was Lincoln, who asserted publicly that if he had known that such a speech was to be given, he would have tried to stop it. He magnanimously praised Butterfield and Ewing, saying of Butterfield that when he became commissioner, "I expected him to be a faithful and able officer, and nothing has since come to my knowledge disappointing that expectation." Of Ewing he added: "I believe him, too, to be an able and faithful officer."[304]

(As it turned out, criticism dogged Butterfield until a paralytic stroke forced him to resign in 1852. Despite his claims of robust health, during his tenure he frequently left Washington because of illness. He also engaged in wholesale nepotism. An anonymous, undated memorandum in the Interior Department files excoriated him for hiring at least nine close relatives while dismissing such people as Lincoln's friends Josiah M. Lucas and William H. Henderson.)

To restore peace and forestall other attacks on Butterfield's appointment, the administration tried to appease Lincoln by offering him the secretaryship of the Oregon Territory, which he promptly declined, urging that it be given instead to his friend Simeon Francis. Soon thereafter, as Lincoln attended court in Bloomington with John Todd Stuart, a special messenger arrived with an offer to appoint him governor of Oregon at a salary of $3,000 a year. Truly tempted, Lincoln asked Stuart if he should accept. His former law partner said he "thought it was a good thing: that he could go out there and in all likelihood come back from there as a Senator when the State was admitted." Lincoln, according to Stuart, "finally made up his mind that he would accept the place if Mary would consent to go." But she had no wish to live in a remote frontier and would not consent. Joshua Speed later told Stuart "that Lincoln wrote to him that if he [Speed] would go along, he would give him any appointment out there which he might be able to control. Lincoln evidently thought that if Speed and Speed's wife were to go along, it would be an inducement for Mary to change her mind. . . . But Speed thought he could not go, and so the matter didn't come to anything."[305] During her husband's presidency, Mary Lincoln liked to remind him that she had kept him from "throwing himself away" by accepting the governorship of Oregon.[306]

And so Lincoln returned to Springfield. Not long after his defeat by Butterfield, he told a friend: "I have a little property and owe no debts; it is perhaps well that I did not get this appointment. I will go home and resume my practice, at which I can make a living—and perhaps some day the people may have use for me."[307]

This setback may have been a blessing in disguise. Richard W. Thompson believed that Lincoln's failure to win the commissionership of the General Land Office was "most fortunate both for him and the country." If he had been successful, Thompson speculated, he would have stayed on in Washington, "separated from the people of Illinois," sinking "down into the grooves of a routine office, so that he would never have reached the eminence he afterwards achieved as a lawyer, or have become President of the United States."[308]

Five years would pass before he again sought public office. During that political hiatus he underwent a painful introspective ordeal from which he emerged a different man. At the age of 40, he was an accomplished partisan politician of limited scope;

by 45, he had somehow transformed himself into the statesman that the world would come to revere. Signs of that statesmanship had appeared in his congressional term (when he denounced the president's conduct in provoking the Mexican War and when he framed an emancipation bill for the District of Columbia) and during his tenure as an Illinois legislator (when he declared that slavery was based on "injustice and bad policy.") But only after he had passed through a fiery psychological trial at midlife was he to fulfill the promise foreshadowed in those gestures.

"I Was Losing Interest in Politics and Went to the Practice of the Law with Greater Earnestness Than Ever Before"
Midlife Crisis
(1849–1854)

A colleague at the bar maintained that Lincoln's life between 1849 and 1854, although outwardly "uneventful and even unimportant," was really a time "in which by thought and much study he prepared himself for his great life work."[1] Indeed, Lincoln did mature remarkably during those years, passing through a highly successsful midlife crisis. Semiretired from public life (he campaigned sporadically and desultorily for others but ran for no office himself), the slasher-gaff politico who reveled in sarcasm and excelled at ridicule somehow developed into a statesman, a principled champion of the antislavery cause who rose far above the narrow partisanship of his earlier years. To be sure, the 1837 Lincoln-Stone protest and his 1849 proposed statute abolishing slavery in the District of Columbia showed Lincoln's interest in the slavery issue but only as a minor matter in his political consciousness. Believing "that God will settle it, and settle it right, and that he will, in some inscrutable way, restrict the spread of so great an evil," he had concluded that "it is our duty to wait."[2]

From 1849 until 1854, Lincoln focused assiduously on his legal career. He later wrote that at that time, "I was losing interest in politics" and "went to the practice of the law with greater earnestness than ever before." By 1854 the legal profession, he said, "had almost superseded the thought of politics" in his mind.[3]

Looking back on his legal career, Lincoln considered that it had two distinct stages, separated by his term in Congress. Before serving in the House of Representatives, he handled petty cases of debt collection, property damage, land titles, negligence, trespassing livestock, divorce, and slander, from which he earned little money, even though he and his partners had an extensive practice. To make ends meet, Lincoln and other lawyers in Springfield traveled the circuit during the spring and fall, when rural counties held court. In the winter and summer, the attorneys would remain in Springfield, appearing before the Illinois State Supreme Court, the Sangamon County Court, and the Federal District Court, as well as justices of the peace.

When Lincoln returned from Washington, Illinois was changing rapidly. In 1848, the adoption of a new state constitution, the completion of the Illinois and

Michigan Canal, the launching of a rail line connecting Chicago with Galena, and the arrival of a presidential message via the telegraph for the first time all heralded the end of the frontier era. During the 1850s, the state's rail network expanded rapidly (from 111 miles to 2,790) and its population doubled (from 851,470 to 1,711,951). Urban areas in particular grew swiftly. In 1850, Chicago had a population of 29,963; by the end of the decade, that figure had soared to 109,260. Springfield's population increased twofold in that same period (from 4,533 to 9,320). Railroads slashed the travel time between those cities from 3 days to 12 hours. The 705-mile Illinois Central Railroad system, begun in 1851, was the world's longest when completed five years later.

Illinois's transformation changed the lives of the state's lawyers. Because they now found more and more business in their own towns, they no longer had to spend weeks and months traveling from one county seat to another in quest of clients; by the end of the decade, only Lincoln continued attending courts throughout the circuit. Simultaneously, night sessions became more common, reducing the opportunities for convivial gatherings after dark. Rather than petty cases tried under the common law, more and more commercial causes filled the dockets, especially those involving railroads. Attorneys increasingly found themselves working for out-of-state corporations. The law became less a means of resolving local disputes and promoting community harmony than an impersonal mechanism for dealing with the booming industrial and commercial revolutions. Lincoln found the new climate more profitable but less congenial than the old one.

Law Practice

Lincoln must surely have experienced a letdown when he exchanged the glamorous world of Washington for his unprepossessing law practice in provincial Springfield. Henry C. Whitney thought that "no lawyer's office could have been more unkempt, untidy and uninviting."[4] It contained only a plain, small desk and table, a couch, a rusty antique stove, a bookcase, and a few wooden chairs. The floors were so seldom cleaned that plants took root in the accumulated dirt. (As a congressman, Lincoln had distributed seeds to his farmer constituents; the contents of some of the packets he had brought home from Washington leaked out and sprouted in the office.) Little light penetrated the filthy windows, and the upper and center panels of the office door leading to the hallway were missing. In the crude bookcase were copies of Blackstone, Kent's *Commentaries*, Chitty's *Pleadings*, and a small number of other volumes. (There were few books because Lincoln and Herndon regularly used the well-stocked law library at the nearby capitol.) Outside hung a cheap, weather-beaten sign by the staircase leading to the office.

In these crude surroundings Lincoln spent many monotonous hours dealing with what he called "the drudgery of the law."[5] As an Ohio attorney noted in 1849, the "business of a lawyer's office, generally has as little interest as a merchant's counting room. Declarations, pleas or demurrers, bills or answers in chancery, petitions in dower or partition, conveyances, depositions, the collection of notes, engross the time of an attorney."[6] Much of Lincoln's fabled yarn-spinning was done outside his office.

As Gibson W. Harris, who studied there from 1845 to 1847, put it, an "attorney's 'den'
is about the last place for genial humor; for, except to a peculiarly constituted mind,
the law is a dry and uninteresting study."[7]

Some of the office drudgery fell to Harris, but most of it was performed by Herndon, who in 1857 described Lincoln as a "*hoss*" and added that "I am the runt of the
firm and no 'hoss.'"[8] As the runt, he said he "'*toted books*,' and '*hunted up authorities*'
for Lincoln," who "detested the mechanical work of the office."[9] Herndon claimed
that he "made out his best briefs in the largest law cases and . . . Lincoln would argue
his case from those briefs and get the credit for them" while the junior partner "was
the power behind them."[10] Herndon drafted pleadings and other papers for cases in
the district courts, while Lincoln wrote them for supreme court cases. In addition to
composing wills, mortgages, contracts, deeds, and other documents requiring no litigation, Herndon managed the office. Lincoln did most of the interviewing and litigation, as well as zealously drumming up business for the firm.

The Lincoln-Herndon partnership, formed in 1844 and lasting until Lincoln
departed Springfield as president-elect in 1861, was harmonious. The two men, according to Herndon, "never had a cross word—a quarrel nor any misunderstandings—
however small." He asserted that when Lincoln "did attach himself to man or woman
he was warmly wrapt in the man or woman—nothing but demonstrations of dishonesty or vice could shake him."[11] When other lawyers tried to supplant Herndon, Lincoln rebuffed their overtures. Herndon's fondness for liquor often landed him in
trouble and embarrassed his partner, but Lincoln characteristically overlooked this
foible. Herndon acknowledged that "in his treatment of me Mr. Lincoln was the most
generous, forbearing, and charitable man I ever knew. Often though I yielded to
temptation he invariably refrained from joining in the popular denunciation which,
though not unmerited, was so frequently heaped upon me. He never chided, never
censured, never criticized my conduct."[12]

The tolerant, humane, even-handed treatment Lincoln accorded his junior partner also characterized his approach to clients and their disputes. He often sought to
resolve matters at a personal level, out of court. His motto was "it is better to get along
peaceably if possible" rather than litigate.[13] When John Foutch asked him to sue a
livestock dealer who had reneged on an agreement to sell him some cattle, Lincoln
told him he had a strong case and then asked how old he was. Discovering that the
potential client had just turned 21, Lincoln urged him to drop the matter: "If you start
out and win this suit, you will be running to me for a lawsuit every time any little
disagreement comes up. John, don't have it. John, you go home." Foutch took the advice.[14]

Lincoln would question potential clients closely, trying to divine their motives. If
after patiently considering the facts, he thought the case was fair and winnable, he
would say: "My friend you are in the right—[I] can so demonstrate it to the minds of
the jury—send home the conviction to the mind of the court [of] its legality and its
justice. I have no reasonable doubt of this, but I advise you as a good man to go to
your neighbor and say to him what you have done and ask him kindly but firmly to do
justice & right. Then if he will not do it I'll make him."[15] He would also advise such

clients, "Don't give me your strong points; they will take care of themselves. Tell me your weak points, and after that I can advise what is best to be done."[16]

If potential clients were merely carrying on a community quarrel, or had a weak case, or were acting out of avarice, hate, ill-will, or malice, Lincoln would tell them frankly, "My friend you are in the wrong—You have no justice and no equity with you—I would advise you to drop the matter."[17] One day he earnestly told a young man that "there is no reasonable doubt but that I can gain your case for you; I can set a Whole neighborhood at loggerheads; I can distress a widowed Mother and her six fatherless children, and thereby get for you six hundred Dollars which you seem to have a legal claim to; but which rightfully belongs, it appears to me, as much to the woman and her children as it does to you. You must remember that some things that are legally right are not morally right. I shall not take your case—but I will give you a little advice for which I will charge you nothing. You seem to be a sprightly, energetic man, I would advise you to try your hand at making six hundred dollars in some other way."[18]

If a potential client's case seemed just but difficult to prove, Lincoln would tell him, "My friend—you are in the right but I don't think your evidences are sufficiently strong, always allowing a little for exaggerations, when so made—to drive conviction home to the minds of the jury: I advise you to compromise; and if you can't get this and can't find other and further proofs, I advise you to drop the case."[19] He often told would-be clients, "You have no case; better settle."[20]

About one-third of Lincoln's cases were dismissed, most of them doubtless because of such counsel. Like many other antebellum attorneys, Lincoln viewed the role of peacemaker as the lawyer's principal function. Characteristically, he told a client in Menard County: "I understand Mr. Hickox will go, or send to Petersburg tomorrow, for the purpose of meeting you to settle the difficulty about the wheat. I sincerely hope you will settle it. I think you *can* if you *will*, for I have always found Mr. Hickox a fair man in his dealings. If you settle, I will charge nothing for what I have done, and thank you to boot. By settling, you will most likely get your money sooner; and with much less trouble & expense."[21] He offered similar advice to a man in Canton: "I do not think there is the least use of doing any more with the law suit. I not only do not think you are sure to gain it, but I do think you are sure to lose it. Therefore the sooner it ends the better."[22] When a student in his office asked why he did not charge clients whose cases were settled out of court, he replied: "They won't care to pay me; they don't think I have earned a fee unless I take the case into court and make a speech or two."[23]

Lincoln displayed his ingenuity as a peacemaker, as well as his generous nature, when he was asked to sue an eccentric attorney, John D. Urquhart, for a piddling sum. Lawyers in Springfield helped support this unfortunate, who often borrowed money without repaying it. A newcomer to town named Smith, unaware of the informal charity that kept Urquhart afloat, stormed into Lincoln's office insisting that he bring suit against that poor soul for a debt of $2.50. Failing to dissuade the indignant Smith, Lincoln agreed to sue Urquhart but insisted on a $10 fee, which was promptly given. With this cash in hand, he called on Urquhart, gave him $5, and brought suit against him for $2.50. The defendant confessed judgment and paid the $2.50. "I couldn't see any other way of making things satisfactory to Mr. Smith and all concerned," Lincoln explained.[24] When another client who wished to sue for a trivial sum rejected advice to drop the matter, saying he wanted to "show the blamed rascal up," Lincoln replied: "My friend, if you are going into the business of showing up every rascal you meet, you will have no time to do anything else the rest of your life."[25]

Slander and Libel Cases

Lincoln was especially active in promoting social harmony in dealing with slander cases, when parties were accused of such offenses as theft, perjury, larceny, forgery, fraud, murder, drunkenness, and operating a whorehouse. He often mediated these suits, sometimes persuading a defendant to admit guilt if the plaintiff agreed to remit the monetary settlement, minus court costs. On other occasions he convinced his client to acknowledge the plaintiff's good character and reputation or got the plaintiff to drop charges.

Slander was traditionally a common law offense; in addition, the Illinois Legislature had made it punishable by fines up to $1,000. The statute specifically deemed actionable false accusations of adultery and fornication, and several of Lincoln's eighty-nine slander cases involved such charges. In one, it was alleged that "Mrs. Beatty and Dr. Sullivan were seen together in Beatty's stable, one morning, very early, in the very act."[26] In another, a woman accused a man of boasting that he had known her carnally and claiming that she "has been fucked more times than I've got fingers and toes for damned if it aint so big I can almost poke my fist in[.]"[27] Charles Cantrall and his wife alleged that she had been slandered by John Primm, who reportedly stated that "William King *screwed* Charles Cantrall's wife twice while he was gone, and before that he crawled in bed with her and her husband and screwed her."[28] James Ellison, a minister, was accused of having sexual relations with a woman whom he kept in the woods for a time until his wife discovered the secret and ended the affair. One of Lincoln's clients denounced a woman as "a base whore" and "a nasty stinking strumpet" and said he could "prove it by the Nances. They have rode her in the corner of the fence many a time."[29]

Bestiality was alleged in a few of Lincoln's slander suits. Newton Galloway declared that William Torrence "caught my old sow and fucked her as long as he could" and "knocked up my old sow and it [is] now bellying down and will soon have some young bills."[30] Another client of Lincoln's supposedly "did have sexual intercourse with or carnal knowledge of a cow," and yet another reputedly "has been caught frigging a bitch."[31]

Racial prejudice exacerbated some cases. One of Lincoln's clients was accused of "open & shameful criminal intercourse & base prostitution" with a black man and "raising a family of illegitimate children by said negro."[32] Another client, William Dungey, alleged that Joseph Spencer had wrongfully accused him of being a black man. In presenting this case to the jury, Lincoln was, as one of the opposing counsel recalled, "both entertaining and effective. A dramatic and powerful stroke was his direct reference to Spencer's accusation that Dungey was a 'nigger.' It had a curious touch of the ludicrous by his pronunciation of a word which, instead of detracting, seemed to add to the effect. I hear him now as he said: 'Gentlemen of the jury, my client is not a negro, though it is no crime to be a negro. His skin may not be as white as ours, but I say he is not a negro, though he may be a Moor.'" On Spencer's defense team was Clifton H. Moore, a resident of the town where the case was being tried.[33]

The most celebrated example of Lincoln's mediation in a slander suit was the case involving a Catholic priest, Charles Chiniquy, proprietor of the community of St. Ann's in Kankakee County. (After the Civil War, Chiniquy would achieve notoriety by charging that Jesuits had plotted Lincoln's assassination.) In 1855, he was sued for calling the proprietor of a nearby settlement a perjurer. As the trial date approached, both sides girded for a desperate fight, as did the communities where the parties lived. Because feeling ran so high, a change of venue was ordered, and the trial took place in Champaign County. Many partisans of the principals flocked there, filling the hotels. The first time the case was tried, it was dismissed when a juror was excused because his child became deathly ill. A second trial ended in a hung jury. Lincoln, who detested that sort of litigation, so dreaded the prospect of yet another trial that he strove mightily to effect a compromise and was ultimately successful.

Lincoln also tried libel cases. In 1851 he represented his Whig friend and colleague, William H. Fithian, who successfully sued George W. Casseday for claiming that Fithian had shamefully abandoned his wife's corpse. The court awarded Fithian damages of $547.90. Thereafter Casseday declared on his personal property tax schedule that among his possessions was the "character of Dr. Fithian, $547.90, which I bought and paid for."[34]

Divorce Cases

Lincoln also tried to promote social harmony in handling divorces, which he found disagreeable. Toward the end of his life he said: "I learned a great many years ago, that in a fight between man and wife, a third party should never get between the woman's skillet and the man's ax-helve."[35] He and his partners participated in 145 divorce actions, 88 in Sangamon County alone; these constituted 40 percent of all such cases heard there between 1837 and 1860. Females brought nearly two-thirds of them. Desertion was the most common complaint alleged by women; few charged their husbands with bigamy, impotence, or felonious conviction. Adultery was alleged more or less equally between the sexes. Lincoln's willingness to take on so many cases illustrates his solicitude for women, for usually male defendants would not contest a divorce. His motive could hardly have been mercenary, for there was little money to be made in these divorce cases. Deserter-husbands were hard to find and to dun for fees, whereas most women who filed for divorce did not have to pay lawyers' fees and court costs.

Lincoln's concern for women's feelings was manifested in the 1838 case of *Samuel Rogers vs. Polly Rogers*. As counsel for the husband, Lincoln urged him not to persist in alleging adultery in the complaint (which he had done originally) because the divorce could easily be won on grounds of desertion. When the court saddled Rogers with heavy alimony payments, he appealed the decision, arguing that his complaint "was muted" simply because of "tenderness to the said defendants [i.e., his wife's] character."[36]

Lincoln's tender feelings for women were especially noticeable in a Tazewell County divorce case. His client was an attractive and cultivated woman, unfortunately married to a highly disagreeable, mean-spirited man in no way her equal. Lincoln convinced the jury that the husband had insulted her in the most vile fashion and created no end of strife, but he could not prove the acts of personal violence necessary under the divorce statute. One observer noted that Lincoln "did the best he could & appealed to the jury to have compassion on the woman & not bind her to such a man & such a life as awaited her, as the wife of such a man." The jury shared Lincoln's view of the matter but, lacking evidence of physical abuse, it felt compelled to find for the husband. One holdout, however, dug in his heels, saying to his fellow jurors: "I am going to lie down to sleep, & when you get ready to give a verdict for that woman, wake me up, for before I will give a verdict against her, I will lie here until I rot, & the pis-mires carry me out of the Keyhole."[37]

Lincoln did not always side with women in such cases. He unsuccessfully represented an odious man in a precedent-setting custody case which saw Illinois courts move away from the common law tradition that children were the property of their fathers. Ann Cowls had divorced her husband, Thomas Cowls, who, she charged, was "negligent of the education and moral welfare of the children, and addicted to excessive and frequent intoxications, and . . . in the habit of quarreling with [the woman he was living with] in the presence of the children, and driving her from home." Moreover, he "habitually uses profane, indecent, immoral, and vulgar language as well in the presence of the children as elsewhere, and is in other respects wholly disqualified from educating the children in a respectable and moral manner." After the divorce, in keeping with common law tradition, Thomas Cowls had retained custody of their children. Ann Cowls subsequently alleged that her former husband was living "in a state of fornication" with "a woman of notoriously bad character" who was "unqualified in any manner for the proper care of and education" of children. In awarding her custody, the Illinois Supreme Court ignored Lincoln's arguments and stressed the best-interests-of-the-child doctrine, which was to influence subsequent cases of child welfare in Illinois. In so ruling, the court characterized Lincoln's client unflatteringly: "Here we have grouped together into one disgusting and revolting picture, those features of a father's character who has become unworthy of the charge of his own offspring."[38]

This sort of action led Gibson Harris to conclude that in a law office "the tendency to believe in total depravity is depressingly strong, such is the somber light in which human nature frequently shows itself in the confidings of client to counsel."[39]

Trial Lawyer

Herndon believed that Lincoln was a better appellate than circuit court attorney. Trial lawyers, Herndon argued, must have "quickness—sharpness—versatility of mind—a mind that can move and leap here and there as occasions & contingencies quickly demand and quickly form accurate judgments. Technical, quick, analytic—sagacious—cunning minds—cold, heartless—conscienceless men succeed in the circuit courts in bad cases and good alike." Lincoln, in his partner's view, did not fit that description, but his was a minority opinion.[40] Indeed, most of Lincoln's colleagues at the bar considered him an adept trial lawyer, especially before a jury. Usher Linder thought Lincoln's "greatest forte was as a lawyer—and I don[']t know whether he was strongest before the Judge or the Jury—I certainly never asked to have him against me."[41] Isaac N. Arnold considered Lincoln "the strongest jury-lawyer we ever had in Illinois," for he could "compel a witness to tell the truth when he meant to lie. He could make a jury laugh, and, generally, weep, at his pleasure." A "quick and accurate reader of character," Lincoln "understood, almost intuitively, the jury, witnesses, parties, and judges, and how best to address, convince, and influence them. He had a power of conciliating and impressing every one in his favor. . . . He excelled all I ever heard in the statement of his case. However complicated, he would disentangle it, and present the turning point in a way so simple and clear that all could understand. Indeed, his statement often rendered argument unnecessary, and often the Court would stop him and say, 'If that is the case, we will hear the other side.' He had, in the highest possible degree, the art of persuasion and the power of conviction. His illustrations were often quaint and homely, and always clear and apt, and generally conclusive. He never misstated evidence, but stated clearly, and met fairly and squarely his opponent's case. His wit and humor, and inexhaustible stores of anecdote, always to the point, added immensely to his power as a jury-advocate."[42]

Hiram W. Beckwith, who observed Lincoln practice in Danville, agreed with Arnold. Beckwith called Lincoln "an admirable tactician, ready for the surprises and turns of a trial, and quick to change his line of attack or defense as emergency required. He was an adept, both as aggressor and at retort, in the badinage and sparrings of counsel that spice the course of a trial." He rarely lost his temper, even in rancorous proceedings, and he seemed to enjoy the combat. To avoid boring the jurymen, he made few notes during a trial. "Notes are a bother, taking time to make, and more to hunt them up afterward," he told Beckwith. "Lawyers who do so soon get the habit of referring to them so much that it confused and tired the jury." For the same reason, Lincoln would not read to jurors from statutes or quote authorities; rather, he would turn to opposing counsel or to the bench and say to the jury, "These gentlemen will allow, or the Judge, if need be, will tell you, that the law of the case is thus or so," and would summarize the relevant statute in clear, simple language.

According to Beckwith, Lincoln "relied on his well-trained memory that recorded and indexed every passing detail," and skillfully kept the jury focused on the main issues. Lincoln was not, Beckwith recounted, "emotional and dramatic" like some colleagues on the circuit; he lacked "grace, music; nor were his thoughts set to words . . . in harmonic measure." His "shrill voice, in its higher tones, his stooping form, and long arms swinging about" made a poor first impression. "But all this either eluded notice, or was quickly forgot in the spell that radiated [from] his wonderful face and in the force of the words that came from his earnest lips." His presentation even interested and entertained onlookers in court. Beckwith disagreed with those who maintained that Lincoln "in his earlier career was a mere 'case lawyer.'" To the contrary, "few, if any, practitioners were better, if as well, grounded in the elementary principles of the law. His knowledge of these, as well as the very reason for them, was so well mastered that he seemed to apply them to individual 'cases' as if by intuition." A mere "case lawyer," said Beckwith, "would have had little chance . . . with Mr. Lincoln."[43]

Peers admired Lincoln's way with a jury trial. Henry C. Whitney thought that only Stephen T. Logan outshone Lincoln on the circuit. Whitney recalled that Lincoln offered "clear statements of his facts and points, and argued his cases with great force and frequently with aggressiveness and pugnacity." In the "rough-and-tumble practice on the circuit, where advocacy was relied on rather than exact knowledge or application of legal principles," Lincoln was "especially effective."[44] Orlando B. Ficklin, an attorney in Charleston, recalled that Lincoln "had a fashion of pointing at the jury with his long bony forefinger of his right hand. There seemed to be something magnetic always about that finger," which appeared to ask, "Don't you see?"[45] According to Leonard Swett, Lincoln as a trial lawyer "had few equals and no superiors. He was as hard a man to beat in a closely contested case as I have ever met. . . . He was wise as a serpent in the trial of a case, but I tell you I have got too many scars from his blows to certify that he was harmless as a dove."[46] James S. Ewing of Bloomington, who often heard Lincoln in court, marveled at his personal touch: "By the time the jury was selected, each member of it felt that the great lawyer was his friend and was relying upon him as a juror to see that no injustice was done."[47] From the bench, Judge John M. Scott thought not only that Lincoln knew the law "and had that knowledge ready for use at all times," but also that he "knew right and justice and knew how to make their application to the affairs of every day life." "Few lawyers," he added, "ever had the influence with a jury, Mr. Lincoln had." Especially remarkable was his "talent for examining witnesses—with him it was a rare gift. It was a power to compel a witness to disclose the whole truth."

Lack of egotism, a quality at the core of Lincoln's personality, won over many juries, colleagues, and judges. Judge Scott noted, "No lawyer on the circuit was more unassuming than was Mr. Lincoln. He arrogated to himself no superiority over any one—not even the most obscure member of the bar." He "had the happy and unusual faculty of making the jury believe that *they*—and not *he*—were trying the case. In that mode of presenting a case he had few if any equals. An attorney makes a grave mistake if he puts too much of *himself* into his argument before the jury or before the court. Mr. Lincoln kept himself in the background."[48]

In his law-practice, Lincoln employed his legendary talent as a storyteller with great effect; colleagues loved him for it. As a young attorney, he would often drop by the court clerk's office to socialize with fellow lawyers. It was "always a great treat," Milton Hay remembered, "when Lincoln got amongst us—we would always be sure to have some of those stories of his for which he had already got a reputation."[49] (Hay read law at Lincoln's office at night and helped him by copying briefs and declarations. A cheerful, tobacco-chewing, imposing figure with a forehead like Daniel Webster's, Hay became a leading member of the Illinois bar.) Lincoln also used his stories in court. With many lawyers, Judge Scott observed, relying on anecdote "would be a most dangerous experiment but it never failed with Mr. Lincoln. When he chose to do so, he could place the opposite party and his counsel too for that matter in a most ridiculous attitude by relating in his inimitable way a pertinent story. That often gave him a great advantage with the jury." Scott cited the example of a case involving crops damaged by the defendant's hogs: "The right of action under the law of Illinois as it was then depended on . . . whether the plaintiff's fence was sufficient to turn ordinary stock. There was some little conflict in the evidence on that question but the weight of the testimony was decidedly in favor of plaintiff." Appearing for the defendant, Lincoln conceded the damage to the crops and focused instead on the fence. He "told a little story about a *fence* that was so *crooked* that when a hog went through an opening in it, invariably it came out on the same side from whence it started. His description of the confused look of the hog after several times going through the fence and still finding itself on the side from where it had started was a humorous specimen of the best story telling. The effect was to make plaintiff's case appear ridiculous and while Mr. Lincoln did not attempt to apply the story to the case, the jury seemed to think it had some kind of application to the fence in controversy—otherwise he would not have told it and shortly returned a verdict for defendant. Few men could have made so much out of so little a story."

Lincoln's delivery of a story would often be more effective than its substance. "He always seemed to have an apt story on hand for use on all occasions," Scott recalled. "If he had no story in stock he could formulate one instantly so pertinent it would seem he had brought it into service on many previous occasions. . . . That is a talent akin to the power to construct a parable—a talent that few men possess."[50] Lincoln once employed a story to defend a client accused of assault and battery. The fellow had been insulted and bodily attacked by the plaintiff, who was trounced after initiating hostilities. Lincoln "told the jury that his client was in the fix of a man who, in going along the highway with a pitchfork on his shoulder, was attacked by a fierce dog that ran out at him from a farmer's door-yard. In parrying off the brute with the fork, its prongs stuck into the brute and killed him.

"'What made you kill my dog?' said the farmer.

"'What made him try to bite me?'

"'But why did you not go at him with the other end of your pitchfork?'

"'Why did he not come after me with his other end?'

"At this Mr. Lincoln whirled about in his long arms an imaginary dog and pushed its tail end toward the jury. Thus was the defensive plea of 'son assault demesne'—loosely, that 'the other fellow brought on the fight,' quickly told, and in a way that the dullest mind would grasp and retain."[51] (This story appeared in a 1739 compilation, *Joe Miller's Jests*, a copy of which Lincoln received from Judge Samuel Treat, who said that the Springfield attorney "evidently learned its entire contents, for he found Lincoln narrating the stories contained therein around the circuit, but very much embellished and changed, evidently by Lincoln himself.")[52]

Lincoln told another story when replying to an opposing counsel who had offered two arguments that canceled each other out. Lincoln said this reminded him of "the cooper who, having trouble in closing up a barrel, put a boy inside to hold the head in place. The plan worked so well that the cooper drove on the hoops and finished the job, forgetting all about the boy or how he was to be gotten out."[53]

Lincoln also enjoyed relating an account of a client accused of stealing pigs. Offering no defense, he simply instructed Lincoln to argue the case on general principles and not to worry. Despite abundant evidence of his guilt, the man was acquitted by the jury. Puzzled, Lincoln asked for an explanation. Admitting that he had stolen the porkers, the client revealed that he had sold the pigs at cut-rate prices to members of the jury, who feared that if they delivered a guilty verdict, they would have to return the pigs to the rightful owner.

Lincoln was most inclined to employ humor when he and his client stood on shaky ground. An example was his defense of a wealthy, pro-Southern colonel who had cow-whipped an antislavery editor on the streets of Jacksonville. The editor brought suit for $10,000 and hired a lawyer who in court melodramatically described the disgrace that his client had suffered. The jurors were so profoundly affected by this tearful presentation that Lincoln's client seemed to have no chance of exoneration. When his turn to speak came, Lincoln took his feet from the table on which he had placed them, slowly rose from his seat, and lifted up and partly straightened out his great length of legs and body, and removed his coat. As he did so, he gazed intently at a piece of paper on the table. He picked it up and silently continued to examine it. After a while, he burst out laughing. Everyone in the courtroom grinned as he laid the paper down, removed his tie, then laughed once again. This produced tittering among the spectators. Continuing to disrobe, he took off his vest, again inspected the paper, and broke out in laughter once more. At this point everyone in court roared with glee. When he finally addressed the court, Lincoln apologized for his undignified behavior and pointed out that the claim for damages as originally written asked for $1,000. He speculated that the editor had changed his mind and decided that the injury to his dignity was worth $10,000. This argument undid the effect of the plaintiff's attorney and led the jury to award damages of only $300.

A juryman before whom Lincoln conducted a case recalled that he "knew nearly every juror, and when he made his speech he talked to the jurors, one at a time, like an old friend who wanted to reason it out with them and make it as easy as possible for them to find the truth." Lincoln was usually terse and undogmatic before juries. He was careful to say "This is the way it seems to me," rather than "This is the way it is."[54]

Herndon reported that when Lincoln stood before a jury he "was awkward, angular, ungainly, odd and, being a very sensitive man, I think that it added to his awkwardness. . . . Sometimes his hands, for a short while, would hang by his side. . . . He used his head a great deal in speaking, throwing or jerking or moving it now here and now there, now in this position and now in that, in order to be more emphatic, to drive the idea home." He "never beat the air, never sawed space with his hands, never acted for stage effect; was cool, careful, earnest, sincere, truthful, fair, self-possessed,

not insulting, not dictatorial; was pleasing, good-natured; had great strong naturalness of look, pose, and act." As he proceeded, Lincoln "gently and gradually warmed
up; his shrill, squeaking, piping voice became harmonious, melodious, musical, if you
please, with face somewhat aglow; his form dilated, swelled out, and *he rose up a splendid form*, erect, straight, dignified."[55]

As a general tactic, Lincoln shrewdly conceded much to opposing counsel. Attorney James C. Robinson recalled that he "had the manner of treating his antagonist
with such perfect fairness, as to make the jury and bystanders think that he could not
be induced to take advantage of him—a manner which was the hell-firedest lie that
was ever acted, because the very fairness he assumed was an ambuscade to cover up a
battery, with which to destroy the opposing counsel, and so skillfully laid, too, that
after it had done its work, only occasionally would the defeated party, and almost
never would the uninitiated, discover the deception." Lincoln, said Robinson, "possessed this power to a degree beyond that of any lawyer I ever knew and he used it to
such an extent that it was his very strongest weapon in the trial of a case."

Robinson gave a generalized example of Lincoln's technique: "If he were defending a case, after the jury were empanelled, he would give the very closest attention to
the opening statement by the plaintiff's attorney—indeed, as if he had never heard of
the case before." Then he would sincerely praise his learned opponent, marvel at what
new things he had just learned, and, almost apologetically, concede what seemed to
be most of the main points of the case. But the barb would be hidden in his concession of those points "if the facts are as he stated them," and in allowing that he would
"presume" his opponent "will be able to fully prove that fact."

If opposing counsel "was not thoroughly alert to the situation, or did not know
Lincoln's tactics, he was inclined to overlook the fact that the admissions, so regretfully made by Lincoln, were only as to facts which were the most easily susceptible of
proof, that the doubtful points were always carefully guarded with an 'if' and he
would frequently think that he had a 'walk-over.' Lincoln's client, under the same
impression, would frequently writhe in his chair, as he heard his lawyer seemingly
confess judgment in favor of the other side. The jury would settle back in their chairs,
thoroughly convinced that here was a lawyer who would not deny facts, who would
not take an unfair advantage, who wanted his case tried with fairness and honesty to
both sides, who simply wanted justice done, regardless of who won or who lost the
case, and they were at once disposed to look with special favor upon any move he
might make during the trial."

At this point, Lincoln's opponent would be in trouble, according to Robinson.
"If, seeing his case so nearly conceded and so mildly contested, he was lulled into inactivity during the trial and failed to close every loophole of escape for the defendant,
his awakening to discover the fatality of his omission, of that one of the points which
Lincoln had so meekly held in reserve was the controlling element in the case, came
after the evidence was closed and too late to retrieve." Lawyers familiar with Lincoln
"were not deceived in this way," Robinson said, "but the average juror could never see
anything but his exceeding fairness and innocence in a trial—an innocence like that
of a coal of fire in a bag of flax."[56]

Most testimony about Lincoln's prowess before juries is reminiscent and therefore may be tainted by the desire to place the martyr-president in an unduly favorable light. But contemporary evidence supports the positive image painted by Herndon, Beckwith, Arnold, Davis, Swett, and others. In 1859, an editor in northern Illinois reported that "Lincoln tries a suit well. By his genial spirit he keeps the Court, the jury and the opposite counsel in good humor, and sometimes by a comical remark, or a clever joke, upsets the dignity of the court. He never makes a big fight over a small or immaterial point, but frankly admits much, though never enough to damage his case. In this he differs much from little lawyers, who adhere with unyielding pertinacity to trifles, and make their greatest efforts at nothing."[57]

Nine years earlier, a newspaper in Danville described Lincoln as "rough, uncouth and unattractive," yet possessing "an energy that rather courts opposition than defies it" and "a mind deeply imbued by study, and with the love of legal philosophy. . . . All the force of a great intellect, all the force of a thoroughly informed understanding, all the might of a determined spirit, are constantly at work. Grasping with ease the points [that seem] to others so intricate, his style of reasoning is profound, his deductions are logical, his investigations are acute." When examining witnesses, "he displays a masterly ingenuity and a legal tact that baffles concealment and defies deceit. And in addressing a jury, there is no false glitter, no sickly sentimentalism to be discovered." He eschewed "a rhetorical display of sublime nothings. Seizing upon the minutest points, he weaves them into his argument with an ingenuity really astonishing. Bold, forcible and energetic, he forces conviction upon the mind, and by his clearness and conciseness, stamps it there, not to be erased." Lincoln "may have his equal," the paper concluded, but "it would be no easy task to find his superior."[58]

Lincoln, however, had difficulty persuading juries when he was not sure his client was in the right. Judge David Davis, before whom he tried innumerable cases, considered Lincoln "a good Circuit Court lawyer" in general, especially "if he thought he was right."[59] On the other hand, Stephen T. Logan believed Lincoln "couldn't fight in a bad case."[60] Samuel C. Parks stated that "when he [Lincoln] thought he was wrong he was the weakest lawyer I ever saw." Parks cited the case of an accused larcenist defended by Lincoln, Parks, and William H. Young. "Lincoln was satisfied by the evidence that he was guilty & ought to be convicted," Parks related. "He called Young & myself aside & Said 'If you can say any thing for the man do it—I can[']t —if I attempt it the Jury will see that I think he is guilty & convict him of course.'" Without a word, Young and Parks submitted the case to the jury, which was unable to agree on a verdict. Lincoln's action spared the client a prison sentence, Parks believed. On another occasion, Lincoln represented a clever fellow in a civil suit and made a solid argument in his defense. When opposing counsel produced clear evidence refuting that defense, Lincoln absented himself; Judge Davis sent a man to fetch him from his hotel. There he said to the court official, "Tell the Judge that I can't come—*my hands are dirty & I came over to clean them.*'" When he received this news, Davis dismissed the suit, merely remarking: "Honest Abe."[61] While defending an accused murderer, Lincoln told his co-counsel, Leonard Swett, that their client was probably not innocent and recommended that they have him plead guilty to manslaughter and hope that the judge would give him the minimum sentence. Swett disagreed, whereupon Lincoln withdrew, saying: "I cannot argue this case, because our witnesses have been lying, and I don't believe them."[62] Joseph Gillespie insisted that it "was not in his [Lincoln's] nature to assume or attempt to bolster up a false position. He would abandon his case first." Gillespie instanced an 1839 debt case from which Lincoln withdrew and his "less fastidious" replacement won the case.[63] More often, Whitney recollected, instead of withdrawing from a trial when he became convinced that his client was untruthful, Lincoln "would simply do what he honestly could for success, and no more."[64]

In the long run, extensive experience before juries eventually made Lincoln somewhat cynical about them. In 1863 he wrote that "a jury can scarcely be empannelled, that will not have at least one member, more ready to hang the panel than to hang the traitor."[65]

Life on the Circuit

When Lincoln first began riding the Eighth Judicial Circuit in 1839, it was larger than the state of Rhode Island. (As the population grew, the circuit expanded and then shrank.) Jury trials took place in unprepossessing courtrooms that were vacant ten months a year. When roads became passable in the spring, and again when the summer heat abated in the fall, lawyers teamed up with the state's attorney and the presiding judge, mounted horses or clambered into buggies, and began the 500-mile, three-month trek through the circuit's many county seats, located mostly in primitive hamlets scattered throughout central Illinois. In each of these villages, the cavalcade would spend anywhere from three days to two weeks, depending on the volume of business. The judge and his entourage reminded one attorney "of a big schoolmaster with a lot of little boys at his heels."[66] Most lawyers covered only part of the circuit, generally the counties near their homes; Lincoln worked all of it.

Lincoln's old, odd-looking horse, decrepit buggy, and ill-fitting garments combined to give him an unusual appearance. His brown, high-crowned hat lacked nap, his trousers were too short, and his coat and vest seemed to flap like garments on a scarecrow. Around his shoulders he draped a shawl. He carried a carpetbag and a faded green umbrella, missing the knob and tied with a rope around its middle to keep it closed. His threadbare, untidy appearance led some to criticize his wife. Like other circuit riders, Lincoln used his hat as a briefcase, tucking all kinds of papers into the inside band. On windy days his headgear would sometimes blow off, scattering important documents about the streets.

The antebellum circuit courts were casual. Occasionally, drunks would shatter courtroom decorum; judges would have the offending parties jailed till they sobered up. The informality of court proceedings was illustrated by an incident in Champaign County. There, as Lincoln was addressing a jury, he lost a button from his suspenders. He paused, inspected the damage, and said to the jury: "Excuse me, gentlemen, for a moment while I fix my tackling." He ambled over to a woodbox near the stove, selected a large splinter, whittled it to a sharp point with his pocketknife, used it to repair his suspenders, then told the jurors: "Now, gentlemen, I am ready to go on."[67]

From 1848 to 1862, Lincoln's good friend David Davis presided over the Eighth Circuit, succeeding Samuel H. Treat. Born in Maryland in 1815, Davis attended Kenyon College and Yale law school before settling in Bloomington, Illinois. There he quickly acquired a reputation as an outstanding business lawyer. A faithful Whig, he was only modestly successful in politics; he did manage to win a seat in the General Assembly for one term and election as a delegate to the 1847 Constitutional Convention. Both his body and his personality were large. He weighed around 300 pounds and had a forceful character and executive talent. Ambitious, vain, fun-loving, industrious, and genial, he eagerly acquired friends and money.

Davis's traits as a jurist were inseparable from his personality. The judge reminded one friend of "a greyhound [who] takes the scent. He never relied on his knowledge of authorities, and never allowed his legal lore to smother his common-sense perception of equity and justice."[68] He ignored technicalities in pursuit of equity. On the bench he usually set a genial tone that put attorneys at ease. Occasionally, however, he could erupt in anger. His affability, conversational skills, and love of good stories made him popular with lawyers and residents of the circuit alike.

An example of Davis's tendency to take the law into his own hands occurred one day in Bloomington, where the docket was full of debt claims cases. To the assembled attorneys and clients eager to make collections, Davis announced: "this court is loaded with cases arising out of the [financial] panic. I know these men, they will pay as soon as they can. Court is adjourned to the next term."[69] To one journalist Davis seemed like a man "perfectly cut out for a Judge" because he was "completely at his ease in the seat of justice. With the greatest unconcern he goes through his duties, and succeeds in keeping a swarm of lawyers within the bounds of reason; and that, too, without losing his temper—a marvelous performance for a Judge."[70]

After court adjourned for the day, Davis would usually gather the attorneys in his room for a merry evening of storytelling and scintillating conversation. Efficiently and willingly, he promoted harmony among the lawyers on the circuit, authoritatively settling minor disputes. His manners and sense of propriety were exemplary, and he could be a good friend as well as an outspoken enemy. His strong acquisitive streak and keen business sense made him rich.

Davis's principal weakness was vanity, making him unusually susceptible to flatterers. If he took an interest in a young man, he demanded "unremitting and persistent adulation and servitude."[71] But while he insisted on deference from some, he gave it to others, above all to Lincoln. In dealing with his flock of them, Davis strove to be impartial, never intending to display favoritism to any lawyer. But as one of the riders of the Eighth Circuit put it, "such was the marked deference he showed to Mr. Lincoln that Lincoln threw the rest of us into the shade."[72] Such partiality did not manifest itself in the judicial record, however; of the eighty-seven cases Lincoln tried before the judge without a jury, he won only forty.

Sessions of the circuit court enlivened the dull life of rural Illinois, in effect providing farmers with the equivalent of entertainment that city-dwellers enjoyed in theaters, opera houses, lecture halls, and concert auditoriums. "The courthouse was the center of interest for the mass of people who were generally uncultured and

ignorant," Herndon recounted. "When court commenced people flocked to the
county seat to see and to hear and to learn. Eloquence was in demand," for "the people
loved to hear *talk—talk*. The lawyers knew this and it stimulated them—made them
ambitious to succeed and conquer." Most of them were "young and ambitious, struggling each in his way to acquire glory." They resembled stars of the stage, with loyal
fans. "If a young lawyer made a fine speech and tickled the crowd—was eloquent and
gained his case he got the hearty applause of the people & glory too. His fame was
fixed at once."[73] Court sessions also took the place of newspapers, bringing the locals
up to date on the wider world.

In 1859, a journalist described the scene in Urbana when court was in session:
"during the past week, nearly every resident of the county has been in our beautiful
city—Courting. The streets have been literally thronged with every imaginable specimen of the genus homo. Lawyers, judges, clients, honorables, prisoners of all *bars,*
and so forth, besides others, have been in attendance at our Circuit Court. Some
think, perhaps, that they have not received justice, while others believe they have a
little too much of it. Altogether they have had a lively time."[74]

Arriving in town, the dust-covered lawyers would immediately be accosted by
potential clients needing help in preparing pleas, filing demurrers, drawing chancery
bills, or defending themselves from litigious neighbors or officers of the law. Amid
this confusion, the legal crew had to be quick-witted and flexible. Sometimes they
would find themselves enlisted to try a case on very short notice, even as the jury was
being empaneled.

Generally, circuit lawyers would arrive on Sunday in order to be ready for the
opening of court at noon the next day. Monday afternoons were usually consumed in
summoning and swearing in the grand and petit jurors and having the grand jury
consider indictments. In election years, the afternoon and evening of the first court
day would be devoted to political speeches by the attorneys. The sheriff chose jurors,
who were often the same men from one term to the next. Some of them were David
Davis's friends, whose intelligence and integrity guaranteed that their verdicts would
hold up on appeal. Cases in default, where one party failed to appear, were quickly
disposed of, and testimony was taken in *ex parte* cases, like uncontested divorces.
Around 4 P.M. the court adjourned, to reassemble Tuesday morning. For the rest of
the day, lawyers would amuse themselves by taking walks, playing cards, writing
verses for each other's amusement, drinking whiskey, fighting, wrestling, racing on
foot and on horses, and even holding dances. Occasionally, a humorous mock trial
would be conducted at which an attorney would be indicted for a ludicrous "crime."
When convicted, he would have to accept the absurd punishment good-naturedly.
Egalitarianism prevailed, for the sociable attorneys put on no airs in their dealing
with colleagues or townspeople.

Killing time could be difficult when there were few clients. Reminiscing about
his early experiences on the circuit, Lincoln said that in Urbana "I listened to a French
street peddler's antics . . . half a day once, simply because I had not one particle of
business."[75] He also recalled a time when, in a country town during a court session, a
rustic was startled to find several attorneys lounging about the courthouse. Upon ask-

ing if they all had business there, he was told: "No, they have not come to court because they have any business here, but because they have no business anywhere else."[76]

On Tuesday mornings the attorneys buckled down to work, which was often boring and tedious. An Urbana newspaper lamented that the court dealt with such unimportant matters as "a dog suit, a wood-stealing Irishman, [and] a half-crazy horse thief."[77] The editor of the *Vermilion County Press* similarly complained that the Danville court was swamped by minor cases involving liquor law violations whose "wearying, troublesome littleness drags out the time of the court, and prevents application to cases of more importance."[78]

In the early years of the circuit, most cases involved assault and battery, unpaid debts, minor squabbles, slander, horse trades, petty larceny, and occasionally manslaughter. In the 1830s and 1840s Illinois was lightly populated, society relatively uncomplicated, land plentiful, employment widespread, and litigation quite simple, requiring little sophistication on the part of the lawyers. Cases originating in debt often generated other actions. Creditors would say of debtors who failed to repay loans, "I'll take it out of his hide." During the ensuing combat, spectators would comment freely on the contestants, spawning slander suits. Occasionally, someone would for convenience dismantle a neighbor's fence and fail to put it back up, leading to fisticuffs that might eventuate in a murder trial. Henry C. Whitney thought it "strange to contemplate that in those . . . primitive days, Mr. Lincoln's whole attention should have been engrossed in petty controversies or acrimonious disputes between neighbors about trifles; that he should have puzzled his great mind in attempting to decipher who was the owner of a litter of pigs, or which party was to blame for the loss of a flock of sheep, by foot rot; or whether some irascible spirit was justified in avowing that his enemy had committed perjury; yet I have known him to give as earnest attention to such matters, as, later, he gave to affairs of state."[79]

Such cases yielded little financial reward. Cash-strapped pioneers would usually pay a little and write IOUs for the remainder or else give some livestock in lieu of money. In 1840, David Davis complained that after several weeks on the circuit with "considerable business to do," he had "realized in money but little from it. The practice of the Law in Illinois nowadays, is not a very easy business, and withal not very profitable. I am satisfied that no professional man ought ever to locate himself in a country purely agricultural. It is only where manufacturing or commercial business is done, that a lawyer can expect always to have plenty to do."[80] Four years later Davis noted that practicing law in Illinois did not provide "much profit or personal comfort."[81]

Personal comfort was scarce indeed for circuit lawyers in the 1830s and 1840s. They traversed the prairies on horseback or in homemade conveyances over muddy roads that were little better than trails. Often the mud became so thick that wagons bogged down, forcing the passengers to use fence-rails as pries to help the horses pull them out of the muck. Unbridged streams had to be swum. Once when the caravan of lawyers and judges approached a shallow creek, Lincoln puckishly warned that it was deep and advised his colleagues to strip off their clothes and ride their horses across it.

Shivering in the cold air, they complied and rode into the water, which barely reached their mounts' fetlocks. Lincoln enjoyed his prank hugely and remarked, "I don't think a bridge across the stream would interfere with navigation!"[82]

Accommodations were also primitive. Gibson W. Harris complained about the "wretched," "cheerless and uncomfortable" taverns, where the "food, though commonly of good material, was often badly cooked and poorly served." Travelers could not even count on protection from the elements; sometimes they found miniature snowbanks on their beds. The rooms seldom contained more than a bug-filled bed, a chair or two, and a spittoon. Guests washed up outdoors in tin basins and counted themselves lucky to have soap. Towels were so scarce that anyone who slept in would have a hard time finding a dry one. When taverns were unavailable, lawyers would stay at a farmer's home. The host usually declared that his guest's company was compensation enough; the attorney would often pay indirectly, surreptitiously slipping a quarter to one of the household's children. Two attorneys often had to sleep in the same bed, and there would be as many as eight staying in one room. Lincoln frequently shared a bed with Usher Linder or Leonard Swett. Many beds were not long enough, the morning coffee was usually burnt, and the breakfast indifferent.

Most accounts of life on the circuit are reminiscent, but Judge David Davis wrote numerous letters describing it vividly. In 1848, he complained: "This thing of traveling in Illinois, and being eaten up by bed bugs and mosquitoes . . . is not what it is cracked up to be." In 1851, he reported to his beloved wife that the "tavern at [Mt.] Pulaski [population 350] is *perhaps* the hardest place you ever saw. A new landlord by the name of Cass, just married—every thing dirty & the eating *Horrible.* Judge Robbins, Lincoln, Stuart & every body else from Springfield [were there]. The old woman looked as we would suppose the witch of Endor looked. She had a grown daughter, who waited on the table—table greasy—table cloth greasy—floor greasy and every thing else ditto. . . . Waiting among greasy things. Think of it. I wonder if she ever washed herself. I guess the dirt must be half an inch thick all over her." From Clinton, Pekin, Metamora, Paris, Charleston, and other towns Davis reported "plenty of bedbugs," "sand a foot deep," "the place horribly dusty." He called one hostelry "the meanest tavern you ever saw" with floors that "don[']t look to have been scoured for a quarter of a century." The food on the road was "wretched. . . . This Kentucky cooking, just as the middling classes in Kentucky know how to prepare, is hardly fit for the stomach of a horse."

Weather could be a torment. When the oppressive summertime heat lasted into the fall, Davis observed that "Holding Courts in such weather has exhausted lawyers, jurors, witnesses & Judge too. If such weather continues, . . . the prospect in Pekin will be anything but agreeable. Mosquitoes prevail there, and a body will have to be in a constant state of warfare." Rain made life miserable. One day in 1852, Davis told his wife how he and his companions waited for a ferry to convey them over the Sangamon River: "Could not cross. For 2 hours staid in rain, waiting for Ferryman. Swam the horses, took the buggy over straddle a canoe." Davis informed his brother-in-law that "[b]ad roads, broken bridges, swimming of horses, & constant wettings, are the main incidents in Western travel."[83] Especially bothersome were the slews, "miniature swamps, miry and sticky, and extremely difficult to cross with teams and wagons."[84]

Unlike his colleagues, Lincoln bore these hardships without complaining. Herndon recalled that his partner cared little about food: "he sat down and ate as it were involuntarily, saying nothing." He was a *most perfect gentleman* to his hosts and their families and servants. "Others would growl—complain—become distressed, and distress others—with the complaints and whine about what they had to eat—how they slept—and on what and how long—and how disturbed by fleas, bed bugs or what not."[85] Only rarely Lincoln would voice displeasure with the food. He once remarked wryly, "Well—in the absence of anything to Eat I will jump into this Cabbage."[86] Allegedly he told a waiter, "if this is coffee, then please bring me some tea, but if this is tea, please bring me some coffee."[87]

Lincoln complained so little because he loved life on the circuit. He turned down an offer to become a partner with the Chicago attorney Grant Goodrich because, he explained, "he tended to Consumption—That if he went to Chicago that he would have to sit down and Study hard—That it would Kill him—That he would rather go around the Circuit . . . than to sit down & die in Chicago." David Davis believed that "Mr Lincoln was happy—as happy as *he* could be, when on this Circuit—and happy no other place. This was his place of Enjoyment. As a general rule when all the lawyers of a Saturday Evening would go home and see their families & friends at home Lincoln would refuse to go home."[88] Even after railroads connecting Springfield with most of the county seats were completed in the mid-1850s, Lincoln seldom returned home on weekends.

Lincoln was also one of the very few attorneys who traveled the entire circuit each spring and fall. While most of them stayed close to home, attending only circuit courts in counties adjacent to their own, Lincoln, Swett, Lamon, and Davis covered it all, becoming in essence a family. "We journeyed together along the road," said Swett, "slept in the same cabin or small hotel at night, breakfasted, dined, and supped together every day, and lived as intimately and in a manner as friendly as it is possible for men to live."[89]

Despite bad food, dirty hostelries, and other irritants, life on the circuit had its charms. "If the business on our circuit was meagre, the good cheer and conviviality were exuberant," Whitney remembered; "and if we did not make much money, our wants 'were few and our pleasures simple,' and our life on the circuit was like a holiday."[90]

Lincoln's intelligence, geniality, and humor made him exceptionally popular on the circuit. As Usher Linder recalled, everywhere he went "he brought sunshine. All men hailed him as an addition to their circle."[91] A resident of a county seat on the Eighth Circuit remembered that whenever Lincoln arrived for a court session, "as he alighted and stretched out both his long arms to shake hands with those nearest to him, and to those who approached—his homely face, handsome in its broad and shunshiny smile, his voice touching in its kindly and cheerful accents—everyone in his presence felt lighter in heart and became joyous. He brought light with him."[92]

Often at night the attorneys and village men would gather in the courtroom and double over in laughter as Lincoln related jokes and stories from his inexhaustible supply. In 1883, Herndon reported that "Judges—Jurors—Witnesses—Lawyers—merchants—&c. &c have laughed at these jokes &c in the night till every muscle—nerve and cell of the body in the morning was sore at the whooping & hurrahing exercise. Such was Lincoln's past-time & glory on the circuit: it was his *Heaven* and his home his *Hell*. No human being can describe these nightly revels. Such amusements—such sports & tricks would not be tolerated now in any American society, & yet for *us* on the circuit at that time in those places it drove away the Devil for awhile."[93]

Back in Springfield, Lincoln also convulsed visitors to his law office. In 1846, Gibson W. Harris told a sick friend: "I wish you co[uld] be in the office about two hours, to hear Lincoln tell his tales and anecdotes, of which he has any amount[.] I think you would laugh yourself well in that length of time. I sometimes have to hold my sides at times, so convulsed with laughter, as to be almost unable to keep my seat. I have seen a dozen or more, with their hands on their sides[,] their heads thrown back, their mouths open, and the tears coursing down their cheeks, laughing as if they would die, at some of Lincoln's jokes."[94] Lincoln's puns were ingenious. One evening he asked Judge John Dean Caton, "if it is true, as has been stated, that all three of you [supreme court] judges came from Oneida county, New York?" When informed that it was so, Lincoln replied: "*I could never understand before why this was a One-i-dea court.*"[95]

Lincoln loved to tell about a minor case he tried in 1858 at Bloomington. The young opposing counsel, exceptionally fearful of losing, took special pains to avoid defeat. The presentation to the jury lasted well into the night, and the anxious fellow could scarcely sleep. The next morning he arrived early at the courthouse, where he learned to his chagrin that he had lost. When Lincoln asked him about his case, he sadly replied: "It's gone to h—l."

"Oh well," said Lincoln, "then you'll see it again."[96]

Lincoln also relished describing an episode that took place during his 1858 campaign against Stephen A. Douglas. After giving a speech in a small town, a local physician of the Democratic persuasion asked him if he could reply. Upon acceding to this request, Lincoln was approached by a lame man who advised him not to respond: "He and I live here. I am enough for him; let me answer him."

When the doctor finished, the lame man limped to the speaker's stand and offered such a sharp riposte to the doctor's remarks that he leaped up and shouted in rage: "That's a lie."

The spectators anticipated a fight, but to their surprise the speaker calmly replied, "Doctor, I'll take anything from you but your pills."

More angry than ever, the physician retorted: "I thank you. I am not a pill peddler. I have quit practicing medicine."

The lame man smilingly observed, "Ah, you have, have you? Well, then, the country is safer than I thought it was."[97]

Sometimes Lincoln joked with David Davis. One day Lincoln hastened into court as the judge was quietly wrapping up business and announced that "he desired to make a single motion of great importance to his case at that particular stage of the proceedings, which accounted for his somewhat hurried entrance into the room and anxiety to get the attention of the judge." Approaching the bench, Lincoln said: "May it please your Honor, I am like the Irish sailor, and beg your Honor to excuse me for this hurried interruption."

"On condition," replied the judge, "that you explain your analogy to the Celtic sailor."

"Well," said Lincoln, "an Irish sailor was overtaken at sea by a heavy storm, and he thought he would pray but didn't know how, so he went down on his knees and said: 'Oh, Lord, you know as well as meself that it's seldom I bodder ye, but if ye will only hear and save me this time, bedad it will be a long time before I bodder ye again.'"[98]

Lincoln liked to describe the misadventures of John Moore, a bibulous Illinois state treasurer who, after drinking to excess one Saturday night, tried to drive home in his cart drawn by two steers. As he passed through a wooded grove, one of the wheels hit an obstacle, dislodging the yoke ring and freeing the steers, which ran off. Moore, who had fallen asleep, awoke the next morning, surveyed the scene, and declared: "If my name is John Moore, I've lost a pair of steers; if my name ain't John Moore, I've found a cart."[99]

Lincoln could amaze as well as amuse his colleagues. When working with a team, he was affable and polite but secretive and headstrong. Once Swett and Whitney sat in the back of a courtroom "utterly astonished at the cruel mode in which he applied the knife to all of the fine-spun theories we had crammed the jury with."[100] Swett "never knew him in trying a law-suit to ask the advice of any lawyer he was associated with," nor could Gibson W. Harris recall "a single circumstance tending to show that he was influenced in his judgment or his conduct by any of his associates."[101]

If colleagues resented Lincoln's treatment, they did not show it. He made good friends in the fellowship of the circuit, for, as David Davis put it, it was "impossible for a body of intelligent gentlemen to associate together, day by day, six months of the year, without becoming attached to each other and without mutual benefit." Although there was "a generous rivalry," it "evoked no envious spirit. It was an era of good feeling, and friendships were formed which lasted for life."[102] Lincoln grew fond of many of his colleagues, including Usher Linder, Archibald Williams, Kirby Benedict, Edwin B. ("Bat") Webb, Judge Davis, Leonard Swett, and Ward Hill Lamon.

Linder, a fellow Kentuckian, rivaled Lincoln as a storyteller. A Democrat as a young man, Linder switched over to the Whigs for more than a decade and finally returned to his earlier loyalty, becoming a close ally of Stephen A. Douglas. In 1864, Linder wrote Lincoln saying: "I am constrained to beleeve friend Lincoln that you have ever cherished the kindest feelings for me, as I know I have for you, and although we have been often thrown in opposition to each other I think there has never been any thing said by either that has left a pang behind."[103] Lincoln regarded Usher's talent as a speaker highly. Once when they were jointly defending an accused criminal, Linder recommended that they employ delaying tactics to protect their client's interest. Judge Davis had ruled that the case must be concluded by that night. After dinner, Lincoln began a judicial filibuster but found he could not hold forth longer than an hour. Linder stepped in and spoke for three hours on innumerable topics, including a 45-minute disquisition on the prosecuting attorney's whiskers. Lincoln "said he never envied a man so much as he did Linder on that occasion. He thought he was inimitable in his capacity to talk interestingly about everything and nothing, by the hour."[104] In 1856, when Linder's teenage son shot and wounded another young man, Lincoln volunteered to represent him gratis, an offer that brought tears to the eyes of the distraught father. During the Civil War, the same fellow joined the Confederate army, was captured, and then released from prison camp at Lincoln's request. Lincoln's friendship continued even though Linder was not the easiest man to like. Linder could be violent; in 1859, he pummeled a fellow attorney in open court.

Archibald Williams, a Quincy attorney, called Linder "a loathsome drunkard regardless alike of truth and decency."[105] Lincoln admired Williams, whom he first met while they served together in the General Assembly. Lincoln deemed him "the most natural and most learned" as well as the "strongest-minded and clearest headed" lawyer of his acquaintance, and later appointed him U.S. district judge for Kansas.[106] Like Stephen T. Logan, Williams dressed shabbily, so much so that once a clerk at a hotel where he was staying accosted him, mistakenly thinking he was a derelict, and asked: "Pardon me, sir, but are you a guest of this hotel?" In reply, Williams exploded, "Hell, no! I am one of its victims. I am paying five dollars a day!"[107] The tall, angular, and awkward Williams resembled Lincoln, according to Linder, who said "for homeliness of face and feature," Williams "surpassed Mr. Lincoln."[108]

Kirby Benedict, a quick-witted, impetuous, kind, and amiable Democratic lawyer in Decatur, was another favorite of Lincoln's. Linder knew "from Lincoln's own lips that he enjoyed Benedict's society hugely." As president, Lincoln declined to remove Benedict from the chief justiceship of the New Mexico Territory, a post to which Franklin Pierce had appointed him. Justifying his decision, Lincoln explained "that he had enjoyed too many happy hours in his society, and he was too good and glorious a fellow for him to lay violent hands upon; that he could not find it in his heart to do so, and he wouldn't."[109] Told that the judge had a drinking problem, Lincoln replied: "I know Benedict. We have been friends for thirty years. He may imbibe to excess, but Benedict drunk knows more law than all the others on the bench in New Mexico sober. I shall not disturb him."[110]

Benedict's drinking habits were not unusual on the Eighth Circuit. A Danville editor observed that the Illinois bar "has great legal talent, but it has also the most *drunken* lawyers of any bar on the face of the earth."[111] The state's attorney for the circuit, David B. Campbell, was often too intoxicated to perform his duties. When Usher Linder thrice appeared at court inebriated, Judge Davis threatened to ban him from practice in the circuit.

Edwin B. ("Bat") Webb, an affable, courteous attorney with highly polished manners, was devoted to Lincoln, who reciprocated the feeling. A leading Whig in southern Illinois, Webb was known as an exceptionally hospitable host and a paragon of integrity. He and Lincoln served together in the legislature and campaigned for

Whig presidential candidates in the 1840s. Lincoln was among those in the General Assembly who admired Webb's common sense, amiability, and command of parliamentary procedure.

Though Lincoln had many good friends, few of them were truly close. One of those few was David Davis. Gustave Koerner recalled that the judge "loved and admired Lincoln," who in turn was "more intimate with him than with any other man."[112] Their friendship flourished despite their many differences in appearance, temperament, values, and social background. Davis was 5 inches shorter and a hundred pounds heavier than Lincoln and had an assertive personality while Lincoln's was more passive. Lincoln was indifferent to money and lived modestly; Davis was a shrewd investor who became rich. Lincoln's sartorial insouciance was legendary; Davis was something of a Beau Brummel. Davis had attended college and law school; Lincoln had spent less than twelve months in frontier blab schools. The two did share some things in common: they were devoted to the Whig Party; each had rock-ribbed integrity; and they both were excellent storytellers and exceedingly affable.

Judge John M. Scott believed that together the "quiet and most deliberate" Lincoln and the "vehemently impulsive, resolute and forceful" Davis "were greater because of their close association and had the benefit of each other[']s peculiar qualities." Lincoln "planned and looked far into the future to discover what the end of a proposed measure would be," while "Davis with his abrupt energy and impulsive purpose to overcome all opposition, carried into effect much of what Lincoln devised." Neither of them "would ever have occupied the exalted positions they did, had it not been for the helpful influence each exerted for the other. Lincoln knew Davis' great powers and that a close alliance with him was necessary to him in developing his own plans and purposes." Davis possessed "much ability to organize political forces and nothing afforded more gratification than to exercise his powers in that direction on behalf of Mr. Lincoln in whom he then saw or thought he saw evidences of his coming greatness." Whereas "Lincoln knew better what ought to be done in political matters," Davis "knew better how to do it."[113]

Davis, Lincoln, and Leonard Swett were known as "the great triumvirate" on the circuit. Swett, one of the foremost criminal lawyers of his era, enjoyed immense popularity, for he was charming, magnetic, eloquent, generous, unselfish, entertaining, and a devoted friend. When trying a jury case, Lincoln preferred him as his partner to all others, seeming "to lean on him, and to say in effect, 'I am all right now that Swett is with me.'"[114]

The only thing like a formal partnership Lincoln had outside Springfield was with Ward Hill Lamon, a tall, stout, hard-drinking, humorous, earthy Virginian, who practiced in Danville. Friends described him as "chivalrous, courageous, generous," and "a reckless, dashing, pleasant, social, good looking fellow, an admirable singer, free with money and fond of comic stories," a "brave man" and "a fine boxer" quite "proud of his Herculean frame." A reporter thought him "the most jolly moral philosopher of the day," although, being no student, he probably never read a book from cover to cover.[115] In Vermilion County, at the extreme eastern end of the circuit, Lincoln teamed up with Lamon, eighteen years his junior, on more than 150 occasions.

Lamon drummed up business and Lincoln tried the cases. Their quasi-partnership lasted from 1852 to 1857, when Lamon won election as prosecutor of the Seventeenth Judicial Circuit and moved to Bloomington. Each day after court adjourned, Lamon entertained Lincoln and the other attorneys, supplying a pitcher of liquor to slake their thirst. When he had drunk enough to loosen up, Lamon could be persuaded to sing songs like "The Blue-Tailed Fly," "Cousin Sally Downard," and some off-color ditties. During his presidency, Lincoln appointed Lamon marshal of the District of Columbia and used him as a bodyguard and troubleshooter.

One day during a break in a trial, Lamon tore the seat of his pants in an informal wrestling match. He returned to the courthouse without having a chance to repair the damage, cutting a comical figure before the jury. As a joke, one attorney circulated a subscription to raise money to buy him a new pair of pants. Most of his colleagues signed it and pledged absurd amounts to the fund, but when the document reached Lincoln he wrote his name and the following message: "I can contribute nothing to the end in view."[116]

Another humorous incident involved a client who served as conservator for his deranged, well-to-do sister. He hired Lamon and Lincoln to block an attempt by a bounder to wed the young woman for her money and remove the conservator. Winning the case, the attorneys received $250, an amount set by Lamon. When Lincoln discovered the size of the fee, he told his partner: "this is all wrong. The service was not worth that sum. Give him back at least half of it." Reluctantly Lamon complied. Judge Davis, observing this transaction disapprovingly, blared out a rebuke heard by all present: "Lincoln, I have been watching you and Lamon. You are impoverishing this bar by your picayune charges of fees, and the lawyers have reason to complain of you. You are now almost as poor as Lazarus, and if you don't make people pay you more for your services you will die as poor as Job's turkey!" When a leading member of the bar applauded this pronouncement, Lincoln retorted: "That money comes out of the pocket of a poor, demented girl, and I would rather starve than swindle her in this manner." Lincoln did not want his firm to be known as "Catch 'em and Cheat 'em." That evening Davis summoned him before his moot tribunal, known as "The Ogmathorial Court." (Davis coined the neologism.) He was convicted and slapped with a fine, which he paid good-naturedly.[117]

Income from Law Practice

This was not an isolated instance, for Lincoln charged notoriously low fees. After successfully representing a client in a complicated slander suit, he asked for $25. "We were astonished," recalled opposing counsel, "and had he said one hundred dollars it would have been what we expected. The judgment [$600] was a large one for those days: he had attended the case at two terms of court, had been engaged for two days in a hotly-contested suit, and his client's adversary was going to pay the bill."[118] In 1856, he wrote a client saying: "I have just received yours of the 16th, with check on Flagg & Savage for twenty-five dollars. You must think I am a high-priced man. You are too liberal with your money. Fifteen dollars is enough for the job. I send you a receipt for fifteen dollars, and return to you a ten-dollar bill."[119] When Lincoln

charged the Chicago banking firm of George Smith and Company a mere $25 for
trying and winning their case, the head of the firm thanked John W. Bunn for recommending Lincoln, saying: "We asked you to get the best lawyer in Springfield and
it certainly looks as if you had secured one of the cheapest."[120] After offering advice to
a young man about collecting a debt, Lincoln refused to accept any money for the
consultation. When the client insisted on giving him at least a present as compensation, Lincoln replied: "when you go down stairs just stop at the stationers, and send
me up a bottle of ink."[121] For collecting $2,000 on behalf of a client who had lent that
sum to a deadbeat, Lincoln charged a fee of only $2.

In notes he wrote for a law lecture, Lincoln stressed that the "matter of fees is
important, far beyond the mere question of bread and butter involved. Properly attended to, fuller justice is done to both lawyer and client. An exorbitant fee should
never be claimed. As a general rule never take your whole fee in advance, nor any
more than a small retainer. When fully paid beforehand, you are more than a common mortal if you can feel the same interest in the case, as if something was still in
prospect for you, as well as for your client. And when you lack interest in the case the
job will very likely lack skill and diligence in the performance. Settle the amount of
fee and take a note in advance. Then you will feel that you are working for something, and you are sure to do your work faithfully and well. Never sell a fee note—at
least not before the consideration service is performed. It leads to negligence and
dishonesty—negligence by losing interest in the case, and dishonesty in refusing to
refund when you have allowed the consideration to fail."[122] In the 1860 presidential
contest, Lincoln's small fees were cited as evidence of his admirable character.

It is impossible to determine with precision just how much Lincoln earned from
the practice of law, but a fee book that he kept while in partnership with John Todd
Stuart and another one kept by Herndon for the years 1845–1847 shed some light on
the matter. They indicate that most cases yielded $10 for circuit and supreme court
work and $20 for cases in the U.S. courts. With Stuart and Herndon, Lincoln split
fees evenly; with Logan, he received one-third of the fees. In partnership with Stuart
from 1837 to 1841, he averaged about $1,000 annually; with Logan as a partner, his
income rose approximately 50 percent. By the late 1850s, he earned roughly $4,000 to
$5,000 a year. Compared with other lawyers in Springfield, Lincoln was not espe-
cially prosperous. According to the census of 1860, he ranked twelfth of the seventeen attorneys in terms of assets. (Of the 414 Springfield households listed in the
census, the Lincolns ranked 127th.) The five lawyers who owned less than he did—
including Herndon—were much younger, averaging 32; Lincoln was then 51 years
of age.

Although Lincoln seemed relatively insouciant in setting fees, he was not careless
about collecting them. After winning a case for a client, Lincoln wrote him: "as the
Dutch justice said when he married folks, 'Now, vere ish my hundred tollars.'"[123] At
least half a dozen times he sued for unpaid fees.

On the circuit after his return from Congress, Lincoln read widely, carrying
books with him, among them Euclid's geometry, the Bible, Shakespeare, and volumes of poetry by Burns, Poe, and others. After dinner he would often fetch a candle

and read well into the night. In 1860, he wrote that during the past decade he had "studied and nearly mastered the Six-books of Euclid."[124] Herndon, who often slept in the same bed with Lincoln while on the circuit, marveled at his partner's ability to focus: "How he could maintain his mental equilibrium or concentrate his thoughts on an abstract mathematical proposition, while Davis, Logan, Swett, Edwards, and I so industriously and volubly filled the air with our interminable snoring was a problem none of us could ever solve."[125] Lincoln's fascination with geometry led him to address the ancient problem of squaring the circle. Equipping himself with paper, compass, ruler, pencils, and bottles of ink of different colors, for two days he labored to the point of exhaustion on the insoluble puzzle.

Lincoln was unusually inquisitive, eager to learn about a wide variety of subjects. On the circuit, he would quiz drivers, blacksmiths, and others, pumping them for information. If he spied a new agricultural implement on the street, he would examine it carefully to determine its function and understand how it worked. Lincoln was a teacher manqué, eager to share what he learned. One day in Clinton, he grew so excited when one of Euclid's propositions suddenly became clear to him that he grabbed a hostler and explained the demonstration to him.

Appellate Lawyer

For all his acknowledged skill as a jury-trial lawyer, Lincoln was even more successful on the appellate level. For cases in the federal courts and the Illinois Supreme Court, he had time enough to prepare extensively and master the facts and law. Henry C. Whitney called Lincoln "an uneven lawyer" whose "best results were achieved as a result of long and continuous reflection; the various elements of a case did not group themselves in apt and proper position and order in his mind on first impression; hence he was not as self-reliant in a new case as in one he had fully discussed and decided in his own mind, and his first impressions in a case were not his best ones."[126]

Lawyers from afar regularly asked Lincoln to handle cases on appeal to the Illinois Supreme Court. Most of Lincoln's appearances before that tribunal were in Springfield, though now and then he would travel to Ottawa when it met there. In the 1840s he averaged about forty supreme court cases annually until the fall of 1847, when he left Illinois to serve in Congress. In the 1850s, he had fewer cases, but they involved higher stakes. Of the 5,173 documented cases that he and his partners participated in, 411 were tried in the Illinois Supreme Court. All of them were civil rather than criminal, primarily involving the ownership of horses and other animals.

The most lucrative cases concerned iron horses. Lincoln represented various railroads, including the Illinois Central, the Alton and Chicago, and the Tonica and Petersburg. On behalf of individuals, he sued the Alton and Chicago, the Illinois River, the Northern Cross, and the Chicago, Burlington, and Quincy lines. The only corporation that gave him a regular retainer was the Illinois Central, which he represented in several dozen cases. Most of them involved simple questions and were tried in lower courts. As part of his retainer agreement, he pledged not to represent anyone suing the Illinois Central. In 1854, when a farmer asked him to bring suit against that railroad, Lincoln refused because, he explained to the corporation's general solicitor, "as I had sold myself out to you, I turned him over to Stuart."[127] On another occasion, he reversed that sequence when a farmer whose cow had been killed by a train asked him to sue a railroad. Upon learning of this potential suit, the company tried to hire Lincoln; he turned down the offer and represented the farmer, who won a liberal settlement. Approximately 4 percent of Lincoln's total case load involved railroads.

Lawyers and courts in antebellum Illinois blazed trails, for there were few precedents to guide them. The General Assembly had given legal status to the English common law, but it was not clear what elements of that corpus were relevant to frontier America. Attorneys and judges, as Herndon noted, "had to think deeply."[128]

The challenge was especially marked in railroad cases, where no common law existed to guide courts. Lincoln helped establish important precedents in this area. One notable example dealt with stock subscribers who reneged on their pledges. To raise capital, railroad corporations issued stock that many Illinoisans, eager to have the tracks pass near or through their property, agreed to purchase. In time, some subscribers changed their minds and refused to pay. In *Barrett vs. Alton and Sangamon Railroad Company* (1851), one of Lincoln's first railroad cases, James A. Barrett maintained that when he agreed to buy shares of the company's stock, the rail line was projected to cross his property; later, when the company changed the route (but not the termini), Barrett understandably lost his enthusiasm and declined to honor his pledge. Lincoln, representing the railroad in the circuit and the supreme courts, won at both levels. His principal argument was that *"[l]egislation* and *adjudication* must follow, and conform to, the progress of society."[129]

Six years later, however, Lincoln found himself on the other side of the argument when he represented Charles Sprague, who reneged on his pledge to purchase $50,000 worth of stock in the Illinois River Railroad. Finding against Sprague, the court observed that it had "nowhere met with a more satisfactory exposition of the general principle of the law, governing the respective rights of corporations and individual stockholders therein, as connected with the subject, than in the case of *Barret vs. The Alton and Sangamon Railroad Company*."[130] In 1859, Lincoln met with a similar defeat when the supreme court ruled that his client, Daniel Earp, must honor a pledge to buy stock in the Terre Haute and Alton Railroad Company. The court again cited the Barrett case, saying that if what it had ruled there "has not shown satisfactory reasons for the rule of law which we hold on this subject, we despair of doing so now."[131] Thus was Lincoln twice hoist with his own petard.

Lincoln helped set another precedent in the 1857 case of *Illinois Central Railroad Company vs. Morrison and Crabtree,* which dealt with the obligations of common carriers to insure their freight. The plaintiffs alleged that the railroad company had been grossly negligent in transporting 400 head of their cattle; some of the livestock had died in transit, and many others lost a great deal of weight. Lincoln, along with Henry C. Whitney and O. B. Ficklin, successfully defended the corporation before the supreme court, which agreed with Lincoln's argument that the common law (which held the carrier strictly liable for goods lost or damaged in its care) had to be modified to take into account the dramatic changes wrought by railroads. Carriers could limit their liability and in effect cease to act as insurers by reducing their rates in return for the shipper's agreement to waive the right to sue.

The most lucrative case Lincoln tried, *Illinois Central Railroad vs. McLean County, Illinois and Parke*, better known as the McLean County tax case, involved the power of counties to tax the corporation. In 1851, the General Assembly had granted the railroad a charter stipulating that its property would be exempt from taxation; in return, it would pay the state a percentage of its gross receipts. Some counties regarded the state's action as an unconstitutional usurpation of their authority to tax. In the summer of 1853, Champaign County officials discussed the matter with Lincoln, who was subsequently approached by the corporation, which was already being taxed by McLean County. Since Champaign County had made the first overture, he told the clerk of its circuit court: "The question, in its magnitude, to the Co[mpany] on the one hand, and the counties in which the Co[mpany] has land, on the other, is the largest law question that can now be gotten up in the State; and therefore in justice to myself, I can not afford, if I can help it, to miss a fee altogether." Indeed, the stakes were high for both the counties and the corporation; the former anticipated a large tax windfall and the latter dreaded the prospect of having to pay property taxes in each of the two dozen countries through which its rails passed, above and beyond its levy to the state government. If the county would compensate him at a level roughly equivalent what the corporation would, then Lincoln would feel obliged to work for it. The judge of the Champaign County Court urged that "no time is to be lost in securing the services of Mr. Lincoln," but nothing came of his initiative.[132] In October Lincoln therefore accepted the offer of the corporation, which gave him a $200 retainer.

In cooperation with Mason Brayman, another Springfield attorney working for the railroad, and with James F. Joy of Detroit, general counsel of the Illinois Central, Lincoln filed suit to block McLean County's attempt to tax the corporation. The county agreed to have the case dismissed by the circuit court in order to appeal it to the supreme court expeditiously. There in 1856, Lincoln and his colleagues prevailed after arguing the case twice. Lincoln cited the landmark 1819 U.S. Supreme Court case of *McCulloch vs. Maryland* and two dozen others. It ranks as one of the most persuasive and complex briefs he ever penned.

In 1859 and 1860, Lincoln argued another important tax case, *The People vs. Illinois Central Railroad*, which involved an attempt by State Auditor Jesse K. Dubois, Lincoln's close friend, to sue the company for underpayment of taxes. Dubois ignored Lincoln's advice not to bring suit. Lincoln, in his final case before the supreme court, successfully defended the corporation, arguing that the state had assessed the company's property incorrectly. The court ruled that taxes should be levied on the actual, not prospective, value of property. An Illinois Central official later said this "was a case of considerable importance and it was largely due to the efforts of Mr. Lincoln that judgment was rendered in favor of the company."[133]

Although David Davis regularly ignored technicalities, Lincoln did not. In 1849, he represented a client who had guaranteed an appeal bond that the original debtor failed to pay. In the Illinois Supreme Court, Lincoln argued that the guarantor need not honor the bond because of a minor discrepancy between the wording of the bond and the original judgment, which the debtor had appealed. Both documents indicated that the debtor owed $909.41, but Lincoln maintained that the bond was invalid because the original judgment against his client specified that he must pay $909.41 plus $7.50¾ costs, whereas the appeal bond, guaranteeing that the debt would be paid if the appeal failed, stipulated that the debtor must pay $841.54 in debt and $58.87 in damages (total $909.41) plus costs (amount unspecified). The court sensibly ruled that because the difference in wording was so minor and the amount owed was exactly the same in both documents, the guarantor of the bond must pay up.

In the 1857 murder case of *The People vs. Bantzhouse*, Lincoln took advantage of a newly appointed state's attorney, James B. White, who failed to note that homicide cases must be tried within two consecutive terms of a court. As counsel for the accused, Lincoln moved for a continuance and a change of venue. When White did not object, Lincoln successfully asked for dismissal on the grounds that the speedy trial rule had been violated.

Of the many cases Lincoln handled in his twenty-four years at the bar, none was more important than *Hurd vs. The Rock Island Bridge Company*, better known as the *Effie Afton* case, tried in September 1857 before the U.S. Circuit Court in Chicago, Justice John McLean presiding. The previous year a river-packet, the *Effie Afton*, had crashed into a pier of the first railroad bridge thrown across the Mississippi River (linking Davenport, Iowa, and Rock Island, Illinois). Both the ship and the draw span of the bridge caught fire and were destroyed. Alleging that the bridge materially obstructed navigation, the ship's owner, Jacob S. Hurd, sued the bridge company for $50,000. The case became a *cause célèbre*, pitting the river towns, principally St. Louis, against rail hubs, notably Chicago. The future of western railroads was jeopardized by the suit, which might lead to the prohibition of all bridge construction over the Mississippi.

Norman B. Judd, a leading railroad attorney who was engaged by the bridge company, suggested that it also hire Lincoln, whom he described as "one of the best men to state a case forcibly and convincingly that I ever heard, and his personality will appeal to any judge or jury hereabouts." The Springfield attorney, said Judd, was the only man "who can without doubt win that case."[134] Lincoln spent months in preparation, carefully inspecting the bridge site and the relevant documents. (His job was made easier by his experience arguing an earlier case involving similar circumstances, *Columbus Insurance Co. vs. Peoria Bridge Company*, in which he represented insurers who had paid for damage sustained by a canal boat that had struck the pier of a bridge over the Illinois River. Unlike the *Effie Afton* case, he pleaded on behalf of the boat owners.)

In his closing speech to the jury (preserved thanks to the shorthand reporting of Robert R. Hitt, who would cover Lincoln's debates with Stephen A. Douglas the following year), Lincoln demonstrated a formidable command of the details of the case. He argued that "the current of travel" flowing east and west had as much right to protection as that flowing north and south; that a substantial amount of traffic crossed the bridge; that the rail line, unlike the river, was an all-weather highway for commerce; that the pilot of the ship had not exercised reasonable skill and care; that one of the ship's two paddle wheels had stopped working as it passed through the draw; and that it was unreasonable to expect railroad companies to dig tunnels beneath the Mississippi or to erect suspension bridges high above it. An observer recollected that "Lincoln's examination of witnesses was very full and no point escaped his notice. I thought he carried it almost to prolixity, but when he came to his argument I changed my opinion. He went over all the details with great minuteness, until court, jury, and spectators were wrought up to the crucial points. Then drawing himself up to his full height, he delivered a peroration that thrilled the court-room and, to the minds of most persons, settled the case."[135]

A fellow attorney called this case "the one in which his [Lincoln's] powers were exhibited to the most advantage."[136] Another said, "I have always considered it as one of the ablest efforts I ever heard from Mr. Lincoln at the bar. His illustrations were apt and forcible, his statements clear and logical, and his reasons in favor of the policy (and necessarily the right) to bridge the river, and thereby encourage the settlement and building up of the vast area of fertile country to the west of it, were broad and statesmanlike."[137] After splitting nine to three in favor of the bridge company, the jury was dismissed. In 1862 the case ended when the U.S. Supreme Court overturned a lower court order to remove a portion of the bridge.

In 1857, the firm of Lincoln and Herndon tried another celebrated railroad case, *St. Louis and Chicago Railroad vs. Dalby,* which has been hailed as "probably the most far-reaching case" Lincoln ever had before the supreme court.[138] In fact, Herndon, not Lincoln, represented the client in both the circuit and the supreme courts.

Another area where the common law remained silent was the liability of municipalities for negligence. Lincoln helped establish an important precedent in the 1853 case of *Browning vs. City of Springfield,* which involved his friend and colleague at the bar, Orville H. Browning. While walking the streets of the capital one day, Browning fell and broke his leg. Alleging that the city had failed to keep its streets in proper repair, he hired Lincoln to sue for damages. After losing in the circuit court, he won before the supreme court, which ruled that in the absence of common law provisions to cover the case, a set of guidelines should be followed "based upon sound sense in accordance with strict morality, and keeping pace with the progress of improvements of the age."[139]

Lincoln practiced extensively in the federal courts in Illinois once he was admitted to do so in 1842. About 7 percent of his total case load consisted of trials at the federal level, where he, not Herndon, did virtually all the litigating. The federal courts handled disputes among citizens of different states. Residents of other states trying to collect sums larger than $500 from Illinoisans would often hire Lincoln to bring suit in federal courts. It is impossible to determine the extent of his practice there because the Chicago fire of 1871 consumed most of the Illinois federal records prior to 1855. The surviving documents indicate that Lincoln was involved in 332 federal cases, in addition to the 72 bankruptcy actions he and Logan handled in the brief period when the federal bankruptcy law was in effect (1842–1843). Many of those cases, like most of the ones Lincoln dealt with in the state court system, involved debt collection. In 1841, David Davis reported that in Illinois "the great business of lawyers is the collection of debts—and there being always more of every thing else than of money here, the business is not a very easy one; hence clients are continually writing—to keep up a running correspondence with whom—occupies about half of one's time."[140] Debt litigation comprised 55 percent of Lincoln's total case load. (The rest consisted of matters pertaining to inheritance, 15 percent; foreclosing on mortgages, 7 percent; divorce, 3 percent; slander, 2 percent; and medicine, less than 1 percent.)

The sums involved in federal cases were often large and therefore yielded handsome fees. In 1859, Lincoln received $1,500 for his work in *Beaver vs. Taylor & Gilbert*, where he successfully argued that his clients deserved title to acreage in southern Illinois. That same year, he billed Nicolas H. Ridgely $500 for a real estate matter. Another major case, the last that Lincoln tried in federal court, also involved a real estate dispute. In Chicago, a large tract of alluvial land had been formed when the federal government ordered a channel dug across two parcels of lakefront land owned by different parties. This misnamed "Sandbar case" (*Johnston vs. Jones and Marsh*) dragged on for years. At the fourth trial of the matter, lasting eleven days in the early spring of 1860, Lincoln successfully defended his client's claim and received a $350 fee. One of Lincoln's co-counsel, Van H. Higgins, said after the trial that "he had no idea before of what a great lawyer he [Lincoln] was."[141]

In federal court, Lincoln and his partners were involved in two dozen patent cases, including *Parker vs. Hoyt*, an 1850 action he successfully argued in Chicago involving infringement of a patented waterwheel. Lincoln thought of his triumph as one of the high points of his legal career. He was especially interested in the issues involved, for he had long ago worked at a sawmill where he learned much about waterwheels. His co-counsel, Grant Goodrich, said Lincoln "had a great deal of Mechanical genius, could understand readily the principles & mechanical action of machinery, & had the power, in his clear, simple illustrations & Style to make the jury comprehend them."[142]

In 1855, another patent case took Lincoln to Cincinnati for a major trial that would affect his future. The McCormick Reaper Company sued the John H. Manny Company of Rockford, Illinois, for infringing its patent. Because the case was originally scheduled to be tried in Illinois before Judge Thomas Drummond, Manny hired Lincoln as associate counsel, paying him a retainer of $1,000 to keep McCormick from employing him. Lincoln's name was suggested because he knew Judge Drummond and because the firm wanted to have local talent on the legal team. But the lead attorney for Manny, George Harding of Philadelphia, was unenthusiastic about Lincoln; his choice for co-counsel was Pittsburgh attorney Edwin M. Stanton. Reluctantly, Harding dispatched an associate, Peter Watson, to consult with Lincoln. When Watson knocked on the door of the house at Eighth and Jackson Streets, Mary Lincoln poked her head out of a window and asked, "Who is there?"

Watson explained that he had come from Philadelphia to see her husband.

"Business or politics?" she queried.

"When told it was business, she (Mrs. Lincoln) indicated her satisfaction by the modified tone in which she shouted, 'Abe, here is a man wants to see you on business.'"

Dressed casually, Lincoln opened the door and invited Watson into the parlor, which his guest found unprepossessing. As Harding related, "Watson was satisfied that he not the associate we wanted, but, after some conversation, concluded that Lincoln had qualities which might be rather effective in that community, that it would be unwise to incur his hostility by turning him down after consulting him, and paid him a retainer (at which he seemed much surprised), arranged for quite a substantial fee to be paid at the close of the litigation, and left him under the impression that he was to make an argument and should prepare himself for it."

When Watson reported back to Harding, however, they agreed that Lincoln would not in fact help present the argument but that Stanton would be hired to do so. Lincoln would be sidetracked, but he was not informed of this altered plan. When the trial was moved from Chicago to Cincinnati, to suit the convenience of Justice John McLean, who was to preside instead of Drummond, the need for Lincoln's services as local talent disappeared. Instead of letting him go, Harding and Watson allowed him to proceed writing his brief. As Lincoln worked away, he looked forward to jousting with some of the finest legal minds in the country.

When he arrived in the Queen City, Lincoln was surprised to discover that he would not help present the argument. The sophisticated Stanton and Harding, for their part, were taken aback when they first beheld their unprepossessing co-counsel, whose clothes fit him badly. After being introduced, Lincoln suggested that they proceed to the court "in a gang." Stanton pulled Harding aside and said, "Let that fellow go with his gang. We'll walk up together." And so they did, snubbing Lincoln. At the courthouse, Stanton emphatically announced that only he and Harding would be arguing their client's case.[143]

Throughout the trial, Harding and Stanton continued to ignore their associate. When Lincoln asked Watson to present Harding with a copy of the argument he had laboriously prepared, the Philadelphia attorney returned it unopened. Harding remembered that "in all his experience he had never seen one man insult another more grossly, and that too without reason, than Stanton insulted Lincoln on that occasion." Stanton "conducted himself toward Lincoln in such a way that it was evident that he, Stanton, thought Lincoln was of no importance, and deserved no consideration whatever from himself, and he refused to talk with him, and told Harding that it was shameful that such a low-down country lawyer should be sent to associate with them." Stanton "refused to walk with Lincoln or to be seen on the street with him." In court, Stanton "refused to talk with, or say anything to Lincoln, but utterly ignored him, even refusing to take from Lincoln's hands one of the models used in the case."[144] Stanton, who referred to Lincoln as a "giraffe" and a "long-armed baboon," once rudely jerked him by the coattails and told him to step aside as lawyers examined the reapers on display.[145] Thereafter, Stanton "did not attempt to conceal his unkind feelings" toward Lincoln until he was appointed secretary of war in 1862.[146] (Later Stanton said, "What a mistake I made about that man when I met him in Cincinnati.")[147]

Understandably, Lincoln felt so badly treated and so humiliated, and was so deeply disappointed, that he told Ralph Emerson, an officer of the Manny Company who had suggested that Lincoln be hired, that he planned to quit. Only persistent lobbying by Emerson and Watson persuaded him to stay on. As Lincoln closely observed the proceedings, he looked depressed but was fascinated by the dueling high-powered attorneys. He sat directly behind Harding as the Philadelphian held forth, following each step of the argument.

As he left town, Lincoln told his hostess, "You have made my stay here most agreeable, and I am a thousand times obliged to you; but in reply to your request for me to come again I must say to you I never expect to be in Cincinnati again. I have nothing against the city, but things have so happened here as to make it undesirable for me ever to return here."[148]

When Lincoln received a check for his services, he returned it, insisting that since he had not made the argument he deserved no more than he had been given as a retainer. The check was once again sent to Springfield with the explanation that Lincoln had prepared a case and was entitled to a fee as though he had delivered it. Eventually Lincoln accepted both the argument and the money.

Murder Cases

Although 95 percent of the documented cases that Lincoln and his partners handled were civil, they participated in several trials for murder and assault with intent to murder. One of the more controversial murder cases was that of Isaac Wyant, who attacked his neighbor Ason Rusk with a knife. In self-defense, Rusk shot his assailant in the arm, which was subsequently amputated. In 1855, thirsting for revenge, Wyant shot Rusk to death in cold blood. Lincoln helped prosecute the case. (He substituted as prosecutor sometimes when the state's attorney was absent; at other times he was hired by interested parties to assist the prosecutor, who was often young and inexperienced.) Leonard Swett defended Wyant with the novel insanity plea and won despite Lincoln's best efforts. Later, when informed by authorities at the state insane asylum that Wyant was truly deranged, Lincoln expressed regret for having prosecuted him so vigorously. Lincoln helped prosecute another murder case, *The People vs. Denton and Denton.* The defendants, James and George W. Denton, accused of murdering their brother-in-law with axes, were found not guilty.

One murder case held such a special fascination for Lincoln that he published a long account of it anonymously. James H. Matheny called it "the most remarkable trial that ever took place in Springfield."[149] Lincoln, Logan, and Baker defended Archibald and William Trailor, who were charged with the murder of Archibald Fisher. A coerced confession from a brother of the accused men, along with suspicious circumstantial evidence, seemed to establish their guilt. Some residents of Springfield were in the mood to lynch the alleged felons. After the prosecution presented what seemed an airtight case, Lincoln called only one witness, who testified that Fisher was alive and staying with him, sound in body if not in mind. He suffered from amnesia and could not recall where he had been recently. The case was dismissed.

According to Governor Thomas Ford, "in all cases of murder arising from heat of blood or in [a] fight it was impossible to convict. The juries were willing enough to convict an assassin or one who murdered by taking a dishonorable advantage, but otherwise if there was a conflict and nothing unfair in it."[150] That proved untrue in the case of William Fraim, a client of Lincoln's who was convicted of stabbing to death an opponent in a drunken brawl. He was hanged after Lincoln had exhausted all legal remedies.

In 1859, Lincoln represented Melissa Goings, a 77-year-old woman accused of murdering her husband; she claimed she had acted in self-defense. During a recess in the trial, she fled Illinois, eventually winding up on the Pacific coast. When the court bailiff charged that Lincoln had suggested she flee, he replied: "I didn't run her off. She wanted to know where she could get a good drink of water, and I told her there was mighty good water in Tennessee."[151]

In another murder case in 1859, Lincoln's client, Thomas Patterson, was found guilty of manslaughter in the death of Samuel DeHaven. The deceased, while drunk, had tried to buy a hatchet on credit at Patterson's store. When Patterson refused him, the enraged DeHaven picked up a spade and approached the storekeeper, who flung a 2-pound lead weight at Dehaven, killing him. Lincoln and Leonard Swett were unable to persuade the jury that the well-to-do Patterson acted in self-defense. According to Henry C. Whitney, who was also part of the defense team, Lincoln made "a very poor" closing speech. Whitney personally thought that Patterson, whom he characterized as "a worthless doggery keeper," was guilty of murder.[152] Lincoln seems to have shared Whitney's feelings about their client, and that doubt undermined his advocacy. Swett argued so effectively that it seemed as if Patterson would be acquitted. But the next day Lincoln undid all the good that Swett had done, and Patterson was convicted and sentenced to three years in jail. Feeling responsible for the outcome, Lincoln successfully appealed to the governor for a pardon, and Patterson was released after spending one year in the penitentiary.

In his best-known murder case, the "Almanac Trial," Lincoln defended William "Duff" Armstrong, 24-year-old son of his good friends from New Salem days, Hannah and Jack Armstrong. In September 1857, the defendant was accused of killing James Preston "Pres" Metzker, a 28-year-old father of three. Along with several other young men, including Armstrong, Metzker had been drinking on the outskirts of a camp meeting near Hiawatha in Mason County. Around 10 P.M., the inebriated Armstrong lay down to sleep not far from the impromptu bars that were a common feature at camp meetings. Suddenly the much taller and stronger Metzker, also intoxicated, awoke him and picked a fight. After they battled, Metzker similarly provoked 27-year-old James Norris. Not long thereafter, Armstrong and Norris attacked him. The latter clubbed Metzker from behind, fracturing his skull. Armstrong was accused of hitting Metzker in the eye with a kind of blackjack called a slungshot. Somehow Metzker managed to mount his horse and ride home, where he died three days later.

Norris and Armstrong were arrested, jailed in nearby Havana, and indicted for murder. Armstrong's family hired the local firm of Dilworth & Campbell, which successfully moved for a change of venue. Unfortunately for Norris, his court-appointed attorney failed to do the same; in November he was swiftly tried, convicted of manslaughter, and sentenced to eight years at hard labor. It seemed likely that Armstrong

would meet a similar fate when tried in Beardstown that same month. Public sentiment ran strongly against Armstrong, whose rather wild behavior, including quarrels
with schoolmates, was well known and exaggerated. The possibility of a lynching
hung heavy in the air. Compounding the Armstrongs' woes, Jack suddenly died in
November, leaving Hannah a poor widow.

One of the Clary's Grove gang, Thomas S. Edwards, sought out Lincoln. "I set
down and told him all about the boy's fix and the widder's trouble, and asked what
could be done. He set there a minute, pushing his gold specks up into his hair, looking kind o' serious at the floor. I imagined that, like the balance of the lawyers, he was
thinking about his fee." Edwards assured Lincoln that he would be paid. The attorney then "looked up, smiling quietly, a way he has got, more with his eyes than his
mouth, and says: 'You Ed'ards! you ought to know me better than to think I'd take a
fee from any of Jack Armstrong's blood.' Then he laid his hand on my shoulder in his
old fashion, and says: 'Why, bless your soul, I've danced that boy on my knee a hundred times in the long winter nights by his father's fire, down in old Howard. I
wouldn't be worthy to take your hand, Tom, if I turned on him now. Go back and tell
old Hannah to keep up a good heart, and we will see what can be done.'"[153]

In November, while in Beardstown representing a client, Lincoln called on Armstrong's lawyer, Caleb J. Dilworth of Havana, who filled him in on the facts of the
case. To Dilworth's delight, Lincoln volunteered to help defend the lad. That night
they interviewed some witnesses. When the prosecution won a continuance, Lincoln
had more time to prepare his defense. He visited Hannah at her home in Mason
County, traversed the scene of the crime, inspected records of the Norris trial, unsuccessfully requested that Armstrong be released on bail, and interviewed witnesses.

One of those witnesses, Nelson Watkins, had been drinking with the others on
the fatal night. He owned the homemade slungshot that Armstrong had allegedly
used to strike and kill Metzker; it had been discovered near the scene of the crime.
Armstrong denied ever having had possession of it. Shortly after the trial, Watkins
told juror John T. Brady "that Mr. Lincoln . . . questioned him about the sling shot,
and asked how it happened to be lost, and then found near the spot where Metzker
was killed." Watkins somewhat implausibly stated that he had gone to sleep under a
wagon and had placed the weapon on its frame; the next morning he had forgotten
about it, and it evidently fell off the wagon as it passed near the crime scene. Watkins
then confided to Brady that "he told Mr. Lincoln that he (Lincoln) did not want to
use him (Watkins) as a witness, as he knew too much, and he began to tell Lincoln
what he knew, and Mr. Lincoln would not allow him to tell him anything and said
to Watkins: 'All I want to know is this: Did you make that sling-shot? and did Duff
Armstrong ever have it in his possession?' Watkins said he replied: 'On cross-
examination they may make me tell things I do not want to tell.'" Lincoln assured
him that he would not be questioned about any subject other than the alleged murder weapon. Watkins further confided to Brady "that Duff Armstrong killed Metzker by striking him in the eye with an old fashioned wagon hammer and that he saw
him do it."[154] It is not clear how Lincoln could guarantee that Watkins would not be
asked damaging questions on cross-examination.

Armstrong's trial began in Beardstown on May 7, 1858. Taking charge of the jury selection for the defense, Lincoln exercised great care. From the first pool of potential jurors only four were chosen, so a second pool of fifty was brought in. Although Lincoln did not know the potential jurors personally, he sought to empanel young men on the assumption that they would be more sympathetic to Armstrong than older men would be. The dozen men finally chosen ranged in age from 24 to 38.

Lincoln's folksy approach to the trial was apparent when he examined the witness William Killian. Lincoln began by asking his name. "William Killian," was the reply. "Bill Killian?" Lincoln repeated in a familiar way; "tell me, are you a son of old Jake Killian?" "Yes sir," answered the witness. "Well," said Lincoln, somewhat aside, "you are a smart boy if you take after your dad."[155]

Killian and another witness, William A. Douglas, testified that although Armstrong had behaved like a rowdy on occasion, he never did anything vicious. Lincoln summoned other witnesses who stated that Armstrong and Norris had not colluded and that Armstrong used only his fists against Metzker.

Lincoln called an expert witness, Dr. Charles E. Parker, who stated that both of Metzker's skull injuries could have been caused by the blow Norris had administered to the back of the victim's head. Nelson Watkins swore that he owned the slungshot and that Armstrong had never possessed it. Then Charles Allen, the prosecution's chief witness, took the stand. According to jury foreman Milton Logan, the questioning went something like this:

Q. Did you see Armstrong strike Metzker?

A. Yes.

Q. About how far were you from where the affair took place?

A. About 40 feet. I was standing on a knoll or hill looking down at them.

Q. Was it a light night?

A. Yes, it was.

Q. Any moon that night?

A. Yes, the moon was shining almost as bright as day.

Q. About how high was the moon?

A. About where the sun would be at 10 o'clock in the day.

Q. Are you certain there was a moon that night?

A. Yes, sir; I am certain.

Q. You are sure you are not mistaken about the moon shining as brightly as you represent?

A. No, sir; I am not mistaken.

Q. Did you see Armstrong strike Metzker by the light of the moon and did you see Metzker fall?

A. I did.

Q. What did Armstrong strike him with?

A. With a slungshot.

Q. Where did he strike Metzker?

A. On the side of the head.

Q. About what time did you say this happened?

A. About 11 o'clock at night.[156]

Another juror remembered that "Lincoln was very particular to have him [Allen] repeat himself a dozen or more times during the trial about where the moon was located" and "was very careful not to cross Mr. Allen in anything, and when Allen lacked words to express himself, Lincoln loaned them to him."[157] The prosecutor, who had gone over the same ground eliciting the same testimony, felt confident that he would win.

But then Lincoln sprang a trap, producing an 1857 almanac showing that the moon, instead of being high overhead at 11 P.M., when Metzker was attacked, was low on the horizon and due to set within an hour. This flummoxed Allen and led the prosecutor to object strenuously. Judge James Harriott examined the volume, as did the prosecutor and the jurymen. This shattered Allen's credibility, which was not strong to begin with. (According to a local attorney, "Allen's general reputation in the vicinity of Oakford for truth and veracity was exceedingly bad." Thompson McNeeley, a noted criminal lawyer in Petersburg who served as a U.S. Representative, often told friends "that Allen would swear to anything in a trial and would work on either side of the case very nicely.")[158]

Lincoln's closing speech was, by all accounts, a tour de force. It is not known just what he said, but it probably incorporated points Lincoln made in these suggestions for instructing the jury: "That if they have any reasonable doubt as to whether Metzker came to his death by the blow on the eye or the blow on the back of the head, they are to find the defendant not guilty, unless they further believe from the evidence, beyond all reasonable doubt, that Armstrong and Norris acted in concert against Metzker, and that Norris struck the blow on the back of the head. That if they believe from the evidence that Norris killed Metzker, they are to acquit Armstrong unless they also believe from the evidence, beyond a reasonable doubt, that Armstrong acted in concert with Norris in the killing or purpose to kill or hurt Metzker."[159]

Because of the sultry heat on that summer day, Lincoln removed his coat, tie, and vest; as he proceeded, one suspender slid from his shoulder. Juror John T. Brady recalled that "this 'backwoodsy' appearance" made Lincoln "about as homely, awkward appearing [a] person as could be imagined; but all this was forgotten in listening to his fiery eloquence, his masterly argument, his tender and pathetic pleading for the life of the son of his old benefactor."[160] Another juror recollected that Lincoln began by "saying he appeared before us without any expectation of reward; that the prisoner's mother, Hannah Armstrong, had washed and mended his worn shirts and clothes and done for him when he was too poor to pay her, and that he stood there to but partially try and pay the debt of gratitude he owed her. He carried us with him as if by storm and before he had finished speaking there were many wet eyes in the room."[161] (Duff said that Lincoln "did his best talking when he told the jury what true friends my father and mother had been to him in the early days, when he was a poor young man at New Salem. He told how he used to go out to Jack Armstrong's and stay for days; how kind mother was to him, and how, many a time, he had rocked me to sleep in the old cradle.")[162] An observer reported that "in words of thrilling pathos Lincoln appealed to the jurors as fathers of sons who might become fatherless, and as husbands of wives who might be widowed, to yield to no previous impressions, no ill founded prejudice, but to do his client justice."[163] Juror Brady recollected that "[t]ears were plentifully shed by every one present; the mother of Duff Armstrong . . . wore a huge sun-bonnet, her face was scarcely visible, but her feelings were plainly shown by her sobs."[164] The assistant prosecutor thought that Lincoln's story of his New Salem days was "told so pathetically that the jury forgot the guilt of the boy." Lincoln wept, for his "sympathies were fully enlisted in favor of the young man, and his terrible sincerity could not help but arouse the same passion in the jury. I have said it a hundred times, that it was Lincoln's *speech* that saved that criminal from the Gallows."[165] Lincoln's co-counsel, William Walker, maintained that the concluding fifteen-minute segment of that speech "was as eloquent as I Ever heard, and Such [was] the power, & earnestness with which he Spoke, that jury & all, Sat as if Entranced, & when he was through found relief in a gush of tears. I have never Seen Such mastery Exhibited over the feelings and Emotions of men, as on that occasion."[166] The judge, on the other hand, thought that the "Almanac may have cut a figure—but it was Doct Parkers testimony confirming Lincolns theory—the Court Saw this—"[167]

But, curiously, when the jury withdrew, nine of its members voted to find Armstrong guilty. As the deliberations went on, however, the effect of Lincoln's speech and the damaged credibility of the chief prosecution witness eventually led to a unanimous verdict of not guilty. One juror said that he and his colleagues "thought Allen was telling the truth. I know that he impressed me that way, but his evidence with reference to the moon was so far from the facts that it destroyed his evidence with the jury."[168]

Lincoln was not in court when the jury announced its verdict. Upon his return, the jurors shook his hand as if they were old friends. Hannah Armstrong, who had withdrawn to await the verdict, was overjoyed. When informed of the good news, she hurried to thank the jury, the court, and Lincoln. "We were all affected," she recalled, "and tears streamed down Lincoln's Eyes." He told her, "I pray to God . . . that this lesson may prove in the End a good lesson to him and to all."[169] He instructed Duff to return home "and be a good boy, and don't get into any more scrapes. That is all I ask of you."[170] Soon thereafter Lincoln helped Hannah Armstrong fend off attempts to take from her the land she had inherited from her husband.

Mentor

In dealing with his fellow attorneys, Lincoln was unfailingly courteous to all, especially to junior members of the bar. Gibson W. Harris recalled that Lincoln's "courtesy to young practitioners was little less than proverbial, and it was never more gracious than when he was the opposing counsel. He had a happy knack of setting them at ease and encouraging them to put forth their best efforts. In consequence they all liked him."[171] Lincoln did not seek popularity with young attorneys but he won their affection, and they came to him often.

In 1851, tyro attorney James Haines was startled when Lincoln, his co-counsel on a case, urged him to make the initial speech in defense of their client. Nervous, Haines suggested that Lincoln take the lead. Tactfully, the older man placed his hand on Haines's shoulder and said: "No, I want you to open the case, and when you are doing it talk to the jury as though your client's fate depends on every word you utter. Forget that you have any one to fall back upon, and you will do justice to yourself and your client." That, Haines recalled, was "a fair sample of the way he treated younger members of the bar."[172] Lewis H. Waters received similar treatment. Though much older than Waters, Lincoln insisted that the young man act as lead counsel on their case and wrote out instructions that he urged Waters to copy and submit to the court as his own handiwork. When attorney Joe Blackburn was starting out as a nervous, 19-year-old, he began his presentation in such a confused fashion that he was tempted to let the case go by default. But Lincoln, who had been paying close attention, rose and made Blackburn's point for him so effectively that the judge granted his demurrer. When the opposing counsel complained about this meddling, Lincoln replied "that he claimed the privilege of giving a young lawyer a boost when struggling with his first case, especially if he was pitted against an experienced practitioner."[173] Similarly, James H. Hosmer, in the midst of his first important case, floundered badly in a sea of details. Lincoln approached him saying: "Young man, I have handled cases like this in the past. Let us see if I can't help you out." Guided by the veteran attorney, young Hosmer won his case.[174]

"I remember with what confidence I always went to him," recollected Lawrence Weldon. One time when he approached Lincoln with a paper he could not understand, the older man said: "Wait until I fix this plug for my 'gallus,' and I will pitch into it like a dog at a root."[175] No other lawyer was so willing to assist junior colleagues at the bar.

Lincoln's solicitude for young attorneys was doubtless shaped by his own experience as an aspiring lawyer, when John Todd Stuart had been so kind to him. Jonathan Birch speculated plausibly that "somehow—probably because of the recollection of his own early struggles—his heart seemed especially filled with sympathy and concern for the young man whose footsteps took him in the direction of the law." Memories of his law studies led Lincoln to visit young men poring over Blackstone, Chitty, et al. He would greet them cheerfully, peruse their volumes, test their knowledge, and play games with them.

Lincoln occasionally tested their knowledge formally, in the capacity of a bar examiner. He began examining Jonathan Birch by asking what books he had read. When the young man complied, Lincoln said: "Well, that is more than I had read before I was admitted to practice." He then told how he had once argued a case against a college-educated attorney whose erudition impressed the judge and other attorneys, but not the jurors. "And they," said Lincoln with a laugh, "were the fellows I was aiming at." He resumed the exam, rapidly posing questions that taxed Birch's memory but not his knowledge of the law. Lincoln abruptly ended the exam, wrote out a recommendation for a license, and offered some advice about future study which, Birch recalled, "was about the first thing that had been said to indicate that the entire proceeding was, after all, an examination to test the applicant's ability to practice law."[176]

Like Herndon, these young men were surrogate sons to Lincoln, whose paternal streak ran deep. Gibson W. Harris recollected that he "took undisguised pleasure in fathering many of us younger persons, including some already in their thirties."[177] Congressman R. R. Hitt, who covered Lincoln as a shorthand reporter in the 1850s, confided to his journal that "he treated me with the utmost kindness, almost like a father."[178] In 1860, the influential newspaperman Joseph Medill told Lincoln, his senior by fourteen years, "I have spoken to you with all the sincerity and truthfulness of a son writing to his father."[179] Though especially solicitous of these younger men, Lincoln was also kind to jurors, bailiffs, sheriffs, deputies, and all officers of the court.

Anger

Lincoln usually appeared relaxed and unruffled in court. One day in a significant railroad case which Whitney was arguing with his help, opposing counsel scored so many points that Whitney expressed some unease to his partner. "All that is *very* easily answered," Lincoln remarked, and when he addressed those points, he blew them away "as easily as a beer-drinker blows off the froth from his foaming tankard."[180]

For all Lincoln's equanimity, though, he could erupt in terrible anger as he did in the 1843 case of *Regnier vs. Cabot and Taylor,* for example. Lincoln's client, Eliza Cabot, sued Francis Regnier, charging that he had publicly declared that one Elijah Taylor "has Rogered her" and that he "has got skin there [from Eliza Cabot] as much as he wanted." When Lincoln took the floor, he bitterly denounced Regnier for slandering a friendless school teacher. His tirade was, a colleague recalled, "as bitter a Philippic as was ever uttered." Cabot won a judgment of $1,600.[181] Seven years later, defending an orphan girl who had been seduced and abandoned, Lincoln reacted to defamatory testimony against his client by pouring upon the witness "a torrent of invective and denunciation of such severity as rarely ever falls from the lips of an advocate at the bar." Turning to his client, he abruptly shifted gears, becoming mild and tender as he spoke on her behalf.[182]

In a similar case, Lincoln tore into slanderers during his closing speech in *Dunn vs. Carle,* an adultery case involving a married man. When the defendant went to great lengths to obtain testimony that the woman had sex with other men, Lincoln, believing that his testimony as well as that of his witnesses was untrue, attacked them mercilessly and won a crushing victory. Lincoln ridiculed one witness, S. H. Busey, who intimated that he was a ladies' man: "there is Busey—he pretends to be a great heart smasher—does wonderful things with the girls—but I'll venture that he never entered his flesh but once & that is when he fell down & stuck his finger in his [anus]."[183]

Lincoln ridiculed another witness who identified himself as J. Parker Green. To discredit him, Lincoln asked: "Why J. Parker Green? . . . What did the J. stand for? . . . John? . . . Well, why did n't the witness call himself John P. Green? . . . That was his name, was n't it? . . . Well, what was the reason he did not wish to be known by his right name? . . . Did J. Parker Green have anything to conceal; and if not, why did J. Parker Green part his name in that way?" Green became an object of scorn, helping Lincoln to win his case.[184] (During the Civil War, when an Iowa congressman recommended for office a man named H. Clay Caldwell, Lincoln said he would not appoint anyone who "parted his name in the middle." He relented when it was explained that Caldwell employed only the initials H. C. when signing his name.)[185]

Lincoln's indignation knew no bounds in the case of Rebecca Thomas, the poor widow of a Revolutionary War veteran. In Lincoln's view, her agent, Erastus Wright, had charged too much for winning a pension. Lincoln took the case gratis. The notes for his speech to the jury read: "No contract.—Not professional services.—Unreasonable charge.—Money retained by Def't not given by Pl'ff.—Revolutionary War.—Describe Valley Forge privations.—Ice—Soldier's bleeding feet.—Pl'ffs husband.—Soldier leaving home for army. Skin Def't.—Close." In speaking of this trial, David Davis recollected that when Lincoln "attacked Meanness & littleness—vice & fraud—he was most powerful—was merciless in his Castigation."[186] According to Herndon, when his partner recounted how Wright had taken advantage of the widow, he "rose up to about 9 f[ee]t high—grew warm—then eloquent," attacking "as with a thunderbolt the miscreant who had robbed one that helped the world to liberty." Herndon recalled never seeing Lincoln "so wrought up."[187] (Lincoln acted as pension attorney for several other clients in addition to Mrs. Thomas, but not gratis.) In *Todd vs. Ware*, Lincoln again excoriated the same Wright, accusing him of lying. While discussing the endorsements on some promissory notes, Lincoln said of Wright: "he manifestly prevaricates—manifestly attempts to cheat his conscience and his God, with the mere literal import of his language, while [which?] he substantially and intentionally falsifies to the court."[188] For good measure, Lincoln also skinned Wright in the 1846 congressional campaign.

Lying witnesses also provoked Lincoln's wrath. As Herndon put it, "woe be to him, if Mr. Lincoln took the notion in his head that the man was swearing to a wilful lie. Whips of scorpions in a man's conscience could be no worse. To flee from Mr. Lincoln and conscience was impossible in the witness. In this condition I have seen the witness on the stand turn pale—& tremble, great big drops of sweat—drops of agony stood out all over the man's face."[189] One day a physician offering expert testimony made some implausible claims, prompting Lincoln to ask him how much money he was receiving for his participation in the trial. The large amount astonished the jurors. Lincoln then "rose, turned, and, stretching out his long right arm and forefinger, . . . cried in a shrill voice, overflowing with the hottest indignation: 'Gentlemen of the jury, big fee, big swear.'"[190]

Disgruntled clients could tax Lincoln's goodwill. When Henry C. Whitney asked him to deal with a particularly difficult client, Lincoln replied: "Let him howl."[191] Once a client spurned his advice, saying: "I will be d[amne]d if I do." Lincoln responded: "I will be d[amne]d if I attend to your suit, if you don't."[192] In 1853, Lincoln snapped at a client who sulked and complained about the verdict in a fraud suit, which awarded him some money. Lincoln grew angry and cried out, "You old fool, you'll keep on until you won't get a cent."[193]

Unscrupulous lawyers could also expect to feel the sting of Lincoln's wrathful denunciation. In 1847 at Tremont, Lincoln argued on behalf of an elderly gentleman who had sold oxen to two young men named Snow, taking their note in payment. When he tried to collect from them, they refused to pay, saying they were minors when the note was written and therefore could not, under the law, be held accountable for contracts they had signed. Lincoln, believing that the lads had swindled the old man on the advice of their counsel, slowly rose and said: "Gentlemen of the jury, are you willing to allow these boys to begin life with this shame and disgrace attached to their character? If you are, *I* am not." He then quoted Iago's speech about reputation from *Othello* ("Good name in man or woman. . . .") Then, unbending to his full height and gazing at the Snow brothers with compassion, he pointed at the opposing counsel and said: "*Gentlemen of the Jury,* these poor, innocent boys would never have attempted this low villainy, had it not been for the advice of these lawyers." Since they were now over 21, the brothers should either pay what they owed or return the oxen. After re-buking practitioners who so disgraced the legal profession, he concluded: "And now, gentlemen, you have it in *your* power to set these boys right before the world." The jury found for the old man.[194]

According to Leonard Swett, any attorney "who took Lincoln for a simple-minded man would very soon wake upon on his back, in a ditch." When lawyers "went at him to joust him from his position and take away his weapons," Lincoln "arose like a lion wakened from his lair. His stooping form straightened, his angular features acquired force and expression, his eye flashed, all his powers of logic, sarcasm, and ridicule were aroused, and rejecting all compromise, he fought it out on that line until he was routed or until he carried the day."[195] One day when attorney Amzi McWilliams shouted "No! No!! No!!!" at a client of Lincoln's, he shouted back "Oh! Yes! Yes!! Yes!!!" while staring "daggers at McWilliams, who quailed under Lincoln's determined look."[196] When Usher Linder interrupted Lincoln repeatedly as he was presenting his client's case and the judge refused to stop the disruptions, Lincoln grew exasperated, shook his fist at his opponent, and declared angrily: "I did not bother you in your plea, and if the court cannot protect me I can protect myself. Now, sir, we'll have no more of this."[197]

Lincoln once grew irritated when an attorney for the other side challenged poten-tial jurors by asking if they were acquainted with Lincoln, who in turn asked mem-bers of the jury pool if they knew the other attorney. When the judge admonished him, saying: "Now, Mr. Lincoln, you are wasting time. The mere fact that a juror knows your opponent does not disqualify him."

"No, your Honor," Lincoln replied. "But I am afraid some of the gentlemen may *not* know him, which would place me at a disadvantage."[198]

One day opposing counsel used a Latin quotation and asked Lincoln: "That is so, is it not?" Lincoln drolly replied, to the delight of the judge and the consternation of his opponent: "If that's Latin you had better call another witness."[199]

In court, Lincoln occasionally deflated other lawyers with his remarkable gift for puns and barbed anecdotes. When opposing counsel once claimed that "he could bring a man to prove an alibi," Lincoln replied: "I have no doubt you can bring a man to prove a lie by."[200] Lincoln once skewered a glib young lawyer who patronized him during a trial. Exasperated, he likened his opponent to "an old mud scow that used to run on the Sangamon river" whose "engine was a rather weak affair and when they blew the whistle the wheels would stop." To the jurors Lincoln said that his opposite number "was in a somewhat similar condition, that when he was using his tongue so vigorously, his brain failed to work."[201]

More gently Lincoln poked fun at Stephen T. Logan, one of the few men more careless about his attire than Lincoln himself. On the brink of a courtroom defeat to his former partner, Lincoln resorted to ridicule as he addressed the jury: "My learned friend [Logan] has made an able speech to you. He has analyzed the testimony with his accustomed acuteness and skill, and laid down to you the law with his usual ability and confidence. And I am not going to assert, positively, that he is mistaken, either as to the law or the evidence. It would not become me to do so, for he is an older and better lawyer than I am. Nevertheless I may properly make a suggestion to you, gentlemen of the jury. And now I ask you, and each of you, to look, closely and attentively, at my friend, the counsel on the other side, as he sits there before you,—look at him all over, but especially at the upper part of him, and then tell me if it may not be possible that a lawyer who is so unmindful of the proprieties of this place as to come into the presence of his Honor and into your presence, gentlemen of the jury, with his standing collar on wrong-end-to, may not possibly be mistaken in his opinion of the law?" This query elicited uproarious laugher when it was observed that indeed Logan had fastened his collar so that its two points were "sticking out behind, like horns."[202]

Lincoln generally maintained good relationships with colleagues like Logan because he respected their skills and readily acknowledged his own weaknesses. Despite his gentle teasing of Logan, Lincoln had such respect for him that he would direct potential clients his way. In the early 1850s, when an Ohio lawyer asked him to sell some land in Illinois owned by a minor, Lincoln in vain looked through Joseph Story's *Conflict of Laws,* acknowledged his ignorance of the relevant statute, and said, "I cannot give you an opinion without further examination; you are in a hurry to return home and I will give you the best advice that I can." He led his guest to the door and pointed to a nearby building, saying: "That is the office of ex-Judge Logan; go to him; if there is a man in Illinois who can give you an opinion at once, he is the man; I am not."[203] On another occasion he told a potential client to seek out John Todd Stuart, explaining that "he's a better lawyer than I am."[204] As Joseph Gillespie said of Lincoln's humility: "It required no effort on his part to admit another man's superiority."[205]

Judge, Lobbyist

Though he was intensely ambitious, Lincoln did not aspire to become a judge or a state's attorney. Occasionally, however, he did serve as a temporary judge on the circuit. In antebellum Illinois, lawyers could substitute for judges who were unavoidably absent. When David Davis needed someone to pinch-hit for him, he usually chose Lincoln, who presided only if lawyers for both sides approved. (They often did so, for the arrangement eliminated delays, to the relief of clients and witnesses.) On the bench Lincoln showed his usual tact. Once when some lawyers used various technicalities in a case where they had little ground to stand on, he patiently allowed them to go on for a full day before finally handing down a decision against them, written so carefully that there could be no appeal. "But how are we to get this up to the Supreme Court?" they asked. "Well, you've all been so smart about this case," Lincoln replied coolly, "that you can find out for yourselves how to carry it up."[206]

As a judge, Lincoln did not play favorites. In April 1858 at Urbana, his friend Henry C. Whitney and other attorneys were trying to postpone action on a creditor's note. Whitney claimed that he had in a timely fashion submitted a demurrer to the court clerk, who could not find it. Lincoln, after listening to heated arguments about the supposed filing, denied Whitney, saying: "Demurrer overruled if there ever was one," implying that he did not believe Whitney and thought he was merely trying to delay matters.[207]

To a newly-named judge who asked how to conduct himself on the bench, Lincoln replied: "There is no mystery in this matter . . . ; when you have a case between neighbors before you, listen well to all the evidence, stripping yourself of all prejudice, if any you have, and throwing away if you can all technical law knowledge, hear the lawyers make their arguments as patiently as you can, and after the evidence and the lawyers' arguments are through, then stop one moment and ask yourself: What is justice in this case? and let that sense of justice be your decision. Law is nothing else but the best reason of wise men applied for ages to the transactions and business of mankind."[208] This approach to the law also characterized his approach to governing, as he repeatedly showed during his presidency.

Lincoln was ideally situated to be a lobbyist, for he lived in Springfield, had served four terms in the legislature, and had a large circle of politically well-connected friends. There is some evidence that he engaged in lobbying. In 1853, he received $25 from the commissioners of the Illinois and Michigan Canal for opposing legislation compensating a mill owner for alleged damage done to his business by the canal. That same year he told John A. Rockwell that he had managed to get his coal mining charter passed by the senate but failed to do so in the House for want of time. He would, if desired, try to get it passed at the next session. The following year he lobbied against the Atlantic and Mississippi Railroad, which had long been trying to win legislative approval to construct a line with a terminus at what became known as East St. Louis. Lincoln may have been acting at the behest of the Illinois Central, which did not welcome competition.

Reputation

Not everyone entertained a high opinion of Lincoln's legal ability. Some, like Dr. Allen B. Clough, thought him a lightweight jokester. Clough observed him before the court in Champaign County and said in 1860: "I have seen and heard 'Old Abe' at the legal bar, (*and other kinds*) in this county during every term of the Circuit Court since the Spring of /57, and I never saw him do a good thing yet in his profession, and I have seen him whipped several times by young lawyers of no pretensions. . . . He has great clownish wit, ready for a joke on any occasion[, a] good memory, therefore he readily copies from others,—has a large base of brain but small perceptive faculties."[209] Others simply belittled him. William Herndon's brother Elliott, an attorney in Springfield and a fervent Democrat, thought Lincoln "had no mind [not] possessed by the most ordinary of [men]. . . . I never [knew him to] thoroughly understand any [thing in law]."[210] Another Democratic attorney in Springfield, George Edmonds, who became the first territorial judge of Utah, singled out "lack of application" as Lincoln's greatest fault as a lawyer. He "was a lazy man" who "absolutely refused to put more than the minimum of time on any case that he might be interested in. He used to come into the state library at Springfield, and we would see him try to study the cases and make notes of precedents, and so on but he couldn't keep at it long at one time. He would slam down the books and come over to tell us funny stories." But, Edmonds admitted, that did not "mean that he slighted his work. He didn't need to study so much as the rest of us, because he could grasp the essentials of the argument in an instant. Things that other lawyers could not see through without great diffi-culty were perfectly clear to him at once. Still, he was not a great lawyer."[211]

Even his friends acknowledged that Lincoln was "not what might be called an industrious lawyer."[212] The admiring Gibson W. Harris reported that "as a formal student Lincoln struck me as actually lazy." Days of slack business found him with feet on a table reading Burns or Byron, not law. After an hour or so, he would "stretch himself at full length on the office lounge, his feet projecting over the end of it, hands under his head and eyes closed, and in this attitude would digest the mental food he had just taken."[213] Herndon similarly recalled that "Lincoln never read much law—and never did I see him read a law book through and no one else ever did." When he arrived at the office around 9 A.M., Herndon said, "the very first thing he did was to pick up some newspaper, if I had not hidden them, and read them aloud, much to my discomfort: he would spread himself out on the sofa—one leg on a chair—another on the table or stove." Now and then Lincoln "would read something in the papers and that would suggest to him an idea and he would say—['] that puts me in mind of a story that I heard down in Egypt in Ills;['] and then he would tell the story and that story would suggest another and so on. Nothing was done that morning. Declarations—pleas—briefs & demurrers were flung to the winds."[214] (Lincoln also wrote aloud, as it were. "I write by ear," he told Gibson W. Harris. "When I have got my thoughts on paper, I read it aloud, and if it sounds all right I just let it pass.")[215]

Occasionally, lack of application caught up with Lincoln. Defending his father-in-law, Robert Todd, in a debt matter, he called a witness whose testimony badly hurt Todd's case. If Lincoln had properly prepared the witness, or had not called him at all, Todd might not have lost. Three years later, in the case of *Rogers vs. Dickey,* Lincoln fumbled a case before the supreme court because he did not in-clude in his original pleading important cases that he later cited in his request for reconsideration. He could have prevailed if he had earlier called attention to the precedents included in the appeal.

Unlike other lawyers, Lincoln kept no commonplace book of reported court decisions and did not read supreme court decisions. Instead, when seeking authorities and precedents, he relied heavily on digests and treatises that summarized cases.

Lincoln could "go off 'half-cocked'" at times. In 1856, while he and Whitney were trying an important land case in Champaign County, Whitney worried that they would lose because Henry Dickerson was to testify against their client. Lincoln said: "we'll beat that easy enough for Henry Dickerson has served a term in the Penitentiary." Whitney was amazed, for Dickerson was a highly respected citizen who had never seen the inside of a jail.[216] Whitney also recalled with astonishment that Lincoln did not realize that a suit on a foreign judgment could not be defended as if it were a suit brought in Illinois. Lincoln blundered, too, while arguing a case before the state supreme court. He read from a reported case that contained passages supporting his case. But inadvertently he read too far and provided the court with a good precedent against his client. Hesitating, he remarked half-humorously, "There! there! may it please the Court; I reckon I've scratched up a snake."[217]

"I have seen him lose cases of the plainest justice, which the most inexperienced member of the bar would have gained without effort," reported Herndon, who concluded that his partner, for all his skills before a jury, "was a 2d rate lawyer. A *great* lawyer is one who is the master of the whole law—and who is ever ready to attend in a *masterly* way all cases that come before him right or wrong—good or bad—ready or not ready, except ever ready through his legal love and his own sagacity." Rhetorically, he exclaimed, "What—make a *great* lawyer of a man who never read law much!" David Davis stated that Lincoln "could hardly be called very learned" and that "*he read law books but little,* except when the cause in hand made it necessary."[218]

In the January 1860 term of the Illinois Supreme Court, the firm of Lincoln and Herndon suffered an embarrassing series of reverses, losing nine of ten cases, largely because of incompetence. Since Lincoln was preoccupied with his Cooper Institute speech and other matters related to the impending presidential campaign, it is likely that he had little to do with these cases.

More than once Lincoln had occasion to apologize for running a sloppy office and for negligence in details. In his notoriously untidy office, papers were easily mislaid. Atop a package of letters, newspapers, pamphlets, and other miscellaneous documents, he affixed a label stating, "When you can't find *it* any where else look into this."[219] In 1850, he confessed to a client: "I am ashamed of not sooner answering your letter, herewith returned; and, my only appologies are, first, that I have been very busy in the U.S. court; and second, that when I received the letter I put it in my old hat, and buying a new one the next day, the old one was set aside, and so, the letter lost sight of for a time."[220] Four years later he sent a similar apology to Milton K. Alexander: "It pains me to have to say that I forgot to attend to your business when I was in Clinton, at Court in May last. Your best way would be to address me a letter at Clinton, about the time I go there to court in the fall (Oct. 16th. I think) and then it will be fresh, & I will not forget or neglect it."[221]

Examples of negligence appear sporadically throughout Lincoln's career. In 1846, for example, he filed an affidavit concerning the case of *Chancey vs. Jackson* in which he said that he received a letter from R. J. Hamilton asking him to attend to that case; that he "considered himself engaged to do so, and in good faith intended to do the same; that having considerable other, and earlier business in said court, he lost sight of the case; and the judgment therein, as it seems, was reversed for want of a joinder in error." Lincoln added that he "had no actual knowledge of a rule being taken in the case for joinder in error, or of the reversal for want of joinder, until this morning." He "believes that appellee, through said Hamilton, relied for attention to the case, exclusively on the affiant, and therefore had no other attorney nor attendants."[222] That same year the New York attorney William M. Evarts asked Cyrus Edwards "to see Lincoln and ask him why he does not remit the $125.00 he collected as dividend on stock of the Alton Fire Insurance Co. for my client. . . . I know he has collected it but I cannot find out from him why he does not remit it."[223] In 1838, Lincoln apologized to Levi Davis, saying that the firm of Lincoln and Stuart "received yours of the 2nd. inst. by due course of mail, and have only to offer in excuse for not answering it sooner, that we have been in a great state of confusion here ever since the receipt of your letter. . . . We beg your pardon for our neglect in this business." Then he added lamely, "if it had been important to you or your client we would have done better."[224]

But in general, Lincoln was conscientious. Preparing for trial, he anticipated what opposing counsel might do. He told a friend that "he habitually studied the opposite side of every disputed question, of every law case, of every political issue, more exhaustively, if possible, than his own side. He said that the result had been, that in all his long practice at the bar he had never once been surprised in court by the strength of his adversary's case—often finding it much weaker than he had feared."[225]

It is difficult to describe Lincoln's stature as a lawyer with any precision. We cannot, for example, compare the number of cases won and lost because of incomplete statistics. Even where such numbers can be generated, as in Lincoln's appearances before the Illinois Supreme Court, the won–lost yardstick is misleading, for it fails to account for the degree of difficulty involved in each case. Some apparent losses may have been victories in substance. If, for example, Lincoln's client were sued for $1,000 and the jury found for the plaintiff but awarded damages of only $1, the defendant, though technically a loser, would probably have been more than satisfied with his attorney.

The true test of Lincoln's ability would be to assess cases on their merits, judging how well he did compared to what most lawyers would have done. Such judgments are necessarily subjective and hard to make in hindsight. Even with the abundant documentary evidence that has been unearthed concerning Lincoln's career at the bar, the challenge is still formidable. Those documents, though numerous, shed little light on the substance of his arguments before juries.

Lawrence Weldon thought that Lincoln "could not perhaps be called a great lawyer, measured by the extent of his acquirement of legal knowledge. He was not an encyclopedia of cases, but . . . in the clear perception of legal principles, with natural

capacity to apply them, he had very great ability."[226] A juror in an 1859 case argued by Lincoln said that he "is not a great lawyer but a good one." His opposing counsel, Norman Purple, "in intricate questions, is too much for him. But when Purple makes a point, which cannot be logically overturned, Lincoln avoids it by a good-natured turn, though outside the issue. Lincoln's chief characteristics are candor, good nature, and shrewdness. He is a gentleman throughout. I wish I could add—the scholar. He possesses a noble heart, an elevated mind, and the true elements of politeness."[227]

Henry C. Whitney said of Lincoln's record on the circuit that he "was not more than ordinarily successful for a first-class lawyer."[228] He "did not stand at the head of the bar, except as a jury lawyer," another contemporary observer and admirer of Lincoln acknowledged. "Before the Court he was inferior, both in argument and influence, . . . to such men as Judge [Joel] Manning, Judge Purple, and Mr. [Elihu N.] Powell."[229] He certainly did not belong to the tribe of legal giants like Reverdy Johnson, Daniel Webster, David Dudley Field, and other attorneys celebrated for their profound learning and ability to affect history in actions before the U.S. Supreme Court. (Lincoln did present one case, a highly technical one, before that tribunal.) Informants for the nation's leading credit-rating agency described him in 1856 as "a G[oo]d man & to be relied on," and two years later as "prompt efficient and skillful."[230] In sum, Lincoln was a highly capable but not outstanding lawyer.

Lincoln offered characteristically modest estimates of his own stature as an attorney. In 1860, while discussing the political antecedents of a Pennsylvania leader, he remarked: "I suppose we could say of General Cameron, without offence, that he is 'not Democrat enough to hurt him.' I remember that people used to say, without disturbing my self-respect, that I was not lawyer enough to hurt me."[231] Likening himself to swine scavenging acorns in a forest, he said: "I'm only a *mast-fed* lawyer."[232] According to a resident of one of the towns in which Lincoln practiced on the circuit, he was "aware of his inferiority as a lawyer" and always ready to acknowledge it "with a smile or a good natured remark," which endeared him to his colleagues.[233]

It is hard to assess the importance of Lincoln's legal career in shaping his political life. Certainly, his widespread practice on the Eighth Circuit helped acquaint him with many voters, and that experience enhanced his uncanny ability to read public opinion. The friends he made on the circuit (among them David Davis, Leonard Swett, and John Todd Stuart) lent invaluable assistance in promoting his political fortunes. Lincoln's work as a legal draftsman doubtless contributed to his ability to write terse, precise prose and to think through such difficult legal subjects as emancipation and *habeas corpus*. His knowledge of human nature was deepened by widespread contact with all sorts of people in court and out, and his powers of persuasion were strengthened. He honed his God-given talent as a logician during his twenty-four years at the bar. In his practice, he settled innumerable disputes, a task he performed regularly in the White House. In all these ways, Lincoln's legal career helped prepare him for greatness as president.

But that greatness rested largely on his moral vision, which was little fostered by an adversarial legal system in which he acted as a hired gun. Such a system can easily produce a kind of ethical agnosticism. Fortunately for the nation, it did not do so in Lincoln's case.

Political Dabbling

From 1849 to 1854, Lincoln retained some interest in politics, though nothing like what he had shown in the previous seventeen years or the subsequent eleven. In June 1850, he refused to sign a call for a rally in support of the fateful compromise measures pending in Congress. In 1852, however, he did inject some political content into his eulogy on Henry Clay. After quoting the Great Compromiser's eloquent defense of the American Colonization Society, Lincoln offered his own biting commentary on slavery: "Pharaoh's country was cursed with plagues, and his hosts were drowned in the Red Sea for striving to retain a captive people who had already served them more than four hundred years."[234] (This concern about divine punishment for the sin of slavery was to reappear in one of his greatest state papers, the second inaugural address.)

During the presidential campaign of 1852, Lincoln spoke occasionally on behalf of the Whig standard-bearer, Winfield Scott, for whom he served as an elector. As Lincoln observed in his 1860 autobiographical sketch, however, "he did something in the way of canvassing, but owing to the hopelessness of the cause in Illinois, he did less than in previous presidential canvasses."[235] The speech that he did give still reflected the immaturity of the pre-1854 Lincoln. In it he resorted to the ridicule and sarcasm that had long been his stock-in-trade. His remarks were prompted by Stephen A. Douglas, who had attacked Scott while praising the Democratic presidential nominee, Franklin Pierce of New Hampshire. Responding to the Little Giant, Lincoln engaged in a lawyerlike quibble over the meaning of the word "with," denounced "the utter absurdity" of Douglas's arguments, and compared Pierce to a Springfield militia leader who rode at the head of his men "with a pine wood sword, about nine feet long, and a paste-board cocked hat, from front to rear about the length of an ox yoke, and very much the shape of one turned bottom upwards; and with spurs having rowls as large as the bottom of a teacup, and shanks a foot and a half long." Lincoln pictured the Democratic nominee complying with the rules of the Springfield militia, which stipulated that "no man is to wear more than five pounds of cod-fish for epaulets, or more than thirty yards of bologna sausages for a sash." Scott should fear, said Lincoln, that some day he would be attacked by Pierce "holding a huge roll of candy in one hand for a spy-glass; with B U T labelled on some appropriate part of his person; and with Abrams' long pine sword cutting in the air at imaginary cannon balls, and calling out, 'boys there's a game of ball for you,' and over all streaming the flag, with the motto, 'We'll fight till we faint, and I'll treat when it's over.'" He also criticized Pierce for expressing hostility to the Fugitive Slave Act of 1850 and likened him to a mulatto.[236]

Midlife Crisis

This minor address was notable as the last such crude partisan speech that Lincoln would ever deliver. Between 1849 and 1854, while sitting on the political sidelines and

devoting himself outwardly to the practice of law, Lincoln inwardly was undergoing a
profound transformation, successfully wrestling with the challenges of midlife. Little
documentation of his inner life survives; he kept no diary, seldom wrote revealing
personal letters, and confided few of his innermost thoughts to anyone. Yet he was
clearly trying to come to grips with the questions that many men address, consciously
or unconsciously, as they pass from the first half of life to the second half during their
early forties: What do I really want from life? Is the structure of my life so far truly
satisfactory? What kind of legacy do I wish to leave? Have I paid too much attention
to the demands of the outer world and conformed too much to its pressures? What do
I hope to accomplish with the rest of my days? What do I really care about most?
What are my basic beliefs? How have I failed to live up to the dream I formed many
years ago? How can I realistically modify that dream? Have I suppressed parts of my
personality that now need to be developed? How shall I deal with the uglier aspects of
my personality? How have I behaved in a destructive fashion, and how have I in turn
been affected by the destructiveness of others? Have I chosen the right career and the
right spouse?

Introspection of this sort is often triggered by a sense of failure, which Lincoln
painfully experienced. In 1857, a Democratic newspaper contemptuously observed that
"Lincoln is undoubtedly the most unfortunate politician that has ever attempted to rise
in Illinois. In everything he undertakes, politically, he seems doomed to failure. He has
been prostrated often enough in his political schemes to have crushed the life out of any
ordinary man."[237] As a political ally noted, Lincoln had plenty of setbacks to brood over:
"He went into the Black Hawk war as a captain, and . . . came out a private. He rode to
the hostile frontier on horseback, and trudged home on foot. His store 'winked out.' His
surveyor's compass and chain, with which he was earning a scanty living, were sold for
debt. He was defeated in his first campaign for the legislature—defeated in his first attempt as a candidate for Congress. Four times he was defeated as a candidate for Presidential Elector, because the Whigs of Illinois were yet in a hopeless minority. He was
defeated in his application to be appointed Commissioner of the General Land
Office."[238] It was painful for Lincoln to reflect on these setbacks, for he was "keenly
sensitive to his failures," and any allusion to them made him "miserable," according to
Herndon.[239] In his mid-forties he lamented, "With *me*, the race of ambition has been a
failure—a flat failure."[240] In reflecting on his legal career, he said: "I am not an accomplished lawyer. I find quite as much material for a lecture, in those points wherein I have
failed, as in those wherein I have been moderately successful."[241] In 1855, he remarked
"with much feeling" that "men are greedy to publish the success of [their] efforts, but
meanly shy as to publishing the failures of men. Men are ruined by this one sided practice of concealment of blunders and failures."[242]

Lincoln worried about his legacy. In 1851, he told Herndon: "How hard—oh
how more than hard, it is to die and leave one's Country no better for the life of him
that lived and died her child."[243] Joshua Speed recalled Lincoln uttering a similar
lament: "He said to me he had done nothing to make any human being remember
that he had lived—and that to connect his name with the events transpiring in his
day & generation and so impress himself upon them, as to link his name to some-

thing that would redound to the interest of his fellow man was what he desired to live for."[244]

Lincoln's obsession with death, which dated back to his youth, became even more marked in his early forties. A heightened awareness of mortality is common among men at that stage of life. In Lincoln's case it became especially acute in 1850 when his second son, three-year-old Eddie, died after an illness of fifty-two days. Lincoln told a friend that if he "had twenty children he could never cease to sorrow for that one."[245] A poem, perhaps by Lincoln, appeared in the *Illinois State Journal* a week after the boy's death. Titled "Little Eddie," it read:

> Those midnight stars are sadly dimmed,
> That late so brilliantly shone,
> And the crimson tinge from cheek and lip,
> With the heart's warm life has flown -
> The angel of Death was hovering nigh,
> And the lovely boy was called to die.
>
> The silken waves of his glossy hair
> Lie still over his marble brow,
> And the pallid lip and pearly cheek
> The presence of Death avow.
> Pure little bud in kindness given,
> In mercy taken to bloom in heaven.
>
> Happier far is the angel child
> With the harp and the crown of gold,
> Who warbles now at the Savior's feet
> The glories to us untold.
> Eddie, meet blossom of heavenly love,
> Dwells in the spirit-world above.
>
> Angel Boy—fare thee well, farewell
> Sweet Eddie, We bid thee adieu!
> Affection's wail cannot reach thee now
> Deep though it be, and true.
> Bright is the home to him now given
> For "of such is the Kingdom of Heaven."

The lad's funeral was conducted by the Rev. Dr. James Smith, who frequently visited the grieving parents and provided what Lincoln gratefully called "loving and sympathetic ministrations."[246] Smith gave them a copy of his 676-page book, *The Christian's Defense,* which (according to Smith) Lincoln found convincing. Mary Lincoln said her husband's "heart, was directed towards religion" following Eddie's death.[247] Soon after the funeral, the Lincolns rented a pew in the First Presbyterian Church, where Smith served as pastor.

The following year, Lincoln's father passed away. As Thomas lay dying near Charleston, a day's journey from Springfield, Lincoln rejected his deathbed appeal for a visit. Coldly, Lincoln wrote his stepbrother, John D. Johnston, to tell their father "that if we could meet now, it is doubtful whether it would not be more painful than pleasant."[248] Lincoln neither attended Thomas's funeral nor arranged for a tombstone to mark his grave.

In some men, the painful questioning that often occurs at midlife can lead to despair; in others, it produces stagnation. But it can also be a creative, if turbulent, period during which inner psychological growth takes place and leads to profound maturity. Out of the crucible of midlife introspection can emerge an awareness of one's own identity and uniqueness that breeds self-confidence and inspires confidence in others. A hallmark of such psychological progress is an ability to overcome egotism, to avoid taking things personally, to accept one's shortcomings and those of others with equanimity, to let go of things appropriate for youth and accept gladly the advantages and disadvantages of age. People able to meet these challenges successfully radiate a kind of psychological wholeness and rootedness that commands respect.

Lincoln was such a person after his period of retreat from politics. As he came to be more fully himself, Lincoln resembled the archetypal Kentuckian described by Ralph Waldo Emerson in a lecture that the future president heard and remembered. The Sage of Concord said that men from the Bluegrass State proclaim by their manners: "Here I am; if you don't like me, the worse for you."[249] During the final eleven years of his life, Lincoln impressed people with what Herndon called "that peculiar nature . . . which distinguishes one person from another, as much to say 'I am myself and not you.'"[250] Joshua Speed, his closest friend, said: "If I was asked what it was that threw such charm around him, I would say it was his perfect naturalness. He could act no part but his own. He copied no one either in manner or style."[251] Lincoln "had no affectation in any thing," Speed reported. "True to nature[,] true to himself, he was true to every body and every thing about and around him—When he was ignorant on any subject no matter how simple it might make him appear he was always willing to acknowledge it—His whole aim in life was to be true to himself & being true to himself he could be false to no one."[252] In 1859, a perceptive friend noted that what Lincoln "does and says is all his own. What Seward and others do you feel that you have read in books or speeches, or that it is a sort of deduction from what the world is full of. But what Lincoln does you feel to be something newly mined out—something above the ordinary."[253] John W. Forney, an influential newspaper editor who saw Lincoln often during his presidency, recalled that he "was a man of the most intense individuality, so that his capacity to stand alone, and, in a measure, outside of others, was one of the hidden forces of his character."[254] Admiral David Dixon Porter, who knew Lincoln in the Civil War, thought he "had an originality about him which was peculiarly his own."[255] John Littlefield recalled that Lincoln "was a very modest man in his demeanor, and yet gave you an impression of strong individuality. In his freedom of intercourse with people he would seem to put himself of a par with everybody; and yet there was within him a sort of reserved power, a quiet dignity which prevented people from presuming on him, notwithstanding he had thrown down the social bars. A person of less individuality would have been trifled with."[256]

Lincoln's highly evolved sense of his own identity lent him what some called "psychic radiance." His good friend and political ally Joseph Gillespie observed him in 1858 as residents of Highland, Illinois, flocked around him: "there was some magnetic influence at work, that was perfectly inexplicable, which brought him and the masses into a mysterious correspondence with each other." As time passed, Gillespie recalled, that "relation increased and was intensified to such an extent that afterwards at Springfield I witnessed a manifestation of regard for Mr. Lincoln, such as I did not suppose was possible."[257] Like others, Henry C. Whitney was hard put to identify Lincoln's special quality. Though Lincoln was "awkward and ungainly," Whitney said, "there nevertheless was in his *tout ensemble* an indefinable *something* that commanded respect."[258]

Some thought Lincoln's magnetism stemmed from his distinctive voice. An Illinois congressman remembered that Lincoln "personally won men to him, and those who came in contact with him felt the spell and submitted to its thralldom, led by the invisible chords of his marvelous power.... As well might the hasheesh-eater attempt to analyze its seductive influence as for those who felt the spell of Lincoln's voice and presence, to say where and what it was."[259] In 1859 a Wisconsinite marveled at Lincoln's voice, which "had something peculiarly winning about it, some quality which I can't describe, but which seemed to thrill every fiber of one's body."[260]

In 1863, Jane Grey Swisshelm, a Radical critic of Lincoln's administration, called on him in Washington "with a feeling of scorn for the man who had tried to save the Union and slavery." But quickly she was "startled to find a chill of awe pass over me as my eyes rested upon him. It was as if I had suddenly passed a turn in a road and come into full view of the Matterhorn.... I have always been sensitive to the atmosphere of those I met, but have never found that of any one impress me as did that of Mr. Lincoln, and I know no word save 'grandeur' which expresses the quality of that atmosphere."[261] That same sense of grandeur impressed an Illinois railroad conductor, who often observed leading politicians on his train. He considered Lincoln "the most folksy of them. He put on no airs. He did not hold himself distant from any man." Yet "there was something about him which we plain people couldn't explain that made us stand a little in awe of him.... You could get near him in a sort of neighborly way, as though you had always known him, but there was something tremendous between you and him all the time."[262]

The modesty that accompanied Lincoln's grandeur was genuine. Like most people who have truly come to grips with their own dark side—and Lincoln had a cruel streak that had marred his conduct toward political opponents in earlier years—he cherished no exalted self-image. "I am very sure," he told a friend one day in the White House, "that if I do not go away from here a wiser man, I shall go away a better man, for having learned here what a very poor sort of a man I am."[263] To a delegation of clergy who called at the Executive Mansion, he declared, "I may not be a great man—(straightening up to his full height) I know I am not a great man."[264] This lack of egotism, a hallmark of psychological maturity, impressed many observers. It is an especially noteworthy quality in a politician, for seekers of political preferment often have exceptionally needy egos.

Thus in 1854, when Lincoln reentered the political world wholeheartedly, he was a changed man. No more would he ridicule and belittle his opponents. No more would he travel the political low road of narrow partisanship. Summoned by a grave national crisis, the partisan politico was about to emerge from his semiretirement as a true statesman.

10

"Aroused as He Had Never Been Before"
Reentering Politics
(1854–1855)

For Lincoln, 1854 was an *annus mirabilis*. As he later said of himself, by that year the practice of law "had almost superseded the thought of politics in his mind, when the repeal of the Missouri compromise aroused him as he had never been before."[1] He and hordes of other Northerners were outraged by the Kansas-Nebraska Act, which threw open to slavery millions of acres in the West that had long been set aside for freedom. That legislation, introduced in January 1854 by Stephen A. Douglas, allowed settlers in the central plains territories to decide for themselves if slavery should exist there. The statute, which its author said rested on the principle of "popular sovereignty," raised "a hell of a storm" as Douglas predicted it would because it repealed the 1820 Missouri Compromise forbidding slavery in the northern portion of the Louisiana Purchase (encompassing what would become the states of Kansas, Nebraska, Iowa, Minnesota, North Dakota, South Dakota, Colorado, Wyoming, and Montana.)[2]

Indignation swept the Free States, where voters had been relatively indifferent to the slavery issue since the Compromise of 1850. "There is a North, thank God," exclaimed a New England abolitionist in March 1854. "We have found out where even the people of N[ew] Hampshire had a heart and soul, stored away in a secret place under their waistcoats. We thought they had no such articles about them."[3] Antislavery Democrats in Congress denounced Douglas's bill "as a gross violation of a sacred pledge, as a criminal betrayal of precious rights, as part and parcel of an atrocious plot" to transform free territory into "a dreary region of despotism, inhabited by masters and slaves," and condemned Douglas for sacrificing the peace of the nation to gratify his insatiable ambition.[4] "We are in the midst of a Revolution," declared the New York *Tribune*. "The attempted passage of this measure is the first great effort of Slavery to take American freedom directly by the throat. . . . Should success attend the movement, it is tantamount to a civil Revolution, and an open Declaration of War between Freedom and Slavery on the North American Continent, to be ceaselessly waged till one or the other party finally and absolutely triumphs."[5] New York Senator William Henry Seward reported from Washington that protests against the

Kansas-Nebraska bill from Northern legislatures, clergymen, and citizens' assemblies were "coming down upon us as if a steady but strong North wind was rattling through the country."[6] In February 1854, Charles Henry Ray, editor of a paper in northern Illinois, told a friend: "I am up to my neck in Nebraska. Great God! how I hate and despise the movers of that infamous scheme, and I have but just begun to hate them, and to fight it."[7] Such hatred was so widespread that when Douglas returned to Illinois, he said of his trip: "I could travel from Boston to Chicago by the light of my own [burning] effigy at night."[8]

Whigs in Illinois, Lincoln observed, "were thunderstruck and stunned; and we reeled and fell in utter confusion." But quickly they arose in a fighting mood, each one "grasping whatever he could first reach—a scythe—a pitchfork—a chopping axe, or a butcher's cleaver."[9] Lincoln's weapon of choice was the pen, which he used to write editorials condemning the Kansas-Nebraska Act and urging voters to elect opponents of that measure. When some of his fellow Whigs who shared his anger at the "encroachments of slavery" seemed unwilling to take action against them, Lincoln reportedly said "if we hold these opinions in regard to the outrages upon the black man why should we fear to avow them and say what we think and do what we can in behalf of right and justice?"[10] Similarly, upon learning of the passage of the Kansas-Nebraska Act he told his friend and fellow Whig leader T. Lyle Dickey that the nation could not continue to exist half-slave and half-free.

Lincoln did not, however, call at this time for the establishment of a new party. In an editorial that he may well have written, the *Illinois State Journal* predicted in July 1854: "there will be, in our opinion, no large third party. There always have been but two large permanent parties in the country; and when the Nebraska matter is disposed of, the members of the free soil party will fall into the ranks of one of the parties."[11] Similarly, Lincoln's political ally David Davis urged Massachusetts Senator Julius Rockwell to "save the Whig party. I don[']t fancy its being abolitionized— although no one can be more opposed to [the] admission [of] Nebraska than I am."[12] Throughout the Free States, Whigs in 1854 hoped to reunite the party's northern and southern wings for the next presidential contest. Only in 1856 would Lincoln and other antislavery Whigs in the Prairie State help form a new party to combat the expansion of slavery and thus fulfill the prophecy of the New York *Tribune* that the "passage of the Nebraska bill will arouse and consolidate the most gigantic, determined and overwhelming party for freedom that the world ever saw."[13]

Northern Racism

Diving once again into the political waters, Lincoln found himself swimming in a sea of Negrophobia. Illinois Democrats blatantly attacked Lincoln and other opponents of Douglas's legislation as "nigger worshippers," "nigger agitators," and "nigger-stealers."[14] In September 1854, the Quincy *Herald* alleged that the "abolitionists of Chicago partake too largely of the instincts of the nigger himself to be 'ashamed' of anything they do."[15] The *Herald* claimed that there "are hundreds of abolitionists that wouldn't hesitate a minute . . . to marry nigger women."[16] The *Herald* was joined by other race-baiting Illinois Democratic journals, including the Springfield *Register*, the Morris *Gazette,* and the *Pike County Union.* Douglas's own organ, the Chicago *Times,* attacked those who opposed the Kansas-Nebraska Act for allegedly promoting miscegenation at the 1847 constitutional convention, where they had voted "to legalize in this State this identical intercourse between negroes and white women, and to place such intercourse, filthy and repulsive as it is, upon the same equal footing as marriages between our white citizens."[17] In western Illinois, a newspaper made the same allegation against a Whig congressional candidate: "He voted [in 1847] *against* a proposition preventing the intermarriage of whites with blacks; which was equivalent to voting that whites and niggers might intermarry."[18]

Illinoisans were among the most bigoted of all Northerners. The constitutional convention of 1847 had endorsed a ban on black migration into the Prairie State, a provision that voters overwhelming approved the following year. In debates on that provision, anti-black sentiment was freely expressed. George Lemon of Marion, for example, doubted that blacks "were altogether human beings. If any gentleman thought they were, he would ask him to look at a negro's foot! (Laughter) What was his leg doing in the middle of it? If that was not sufficient, let him go and examine their nose; (roars of laughter) then look at their lips. Why, their sculls were three inches thicker than white people's."[19] Lemon's remarks captured the feelings of many Illinoisans who were vehemently opposed to the presence of blacks in their state.

The Chicago *Times* asserted that there "is in the great masses of the people a natural and proper loathing of the negro, which forbids contact with him as with a leper," and proudly boasted that the Prairie State "wisely kept her soil for white men alone . . . inhibited the negro from coming within her limits for settlement . . . denied to the negro an equal participation in the right to settlement . . . and declared that Illinois should never be cursed with slavery, and that her people should not be crowded and inconvenienced by an inferior and deteriorated race."[20] An antislavery journalist noted that the black man in Illinois "has no rights, except the right of being taxed; he has no privileges, except the privilege of paying. His children are booted out of public schools, while no provision is made for their separate education; his testimony is not received in a Court of justice; his accounts, though he may be an honest hard-working mechanic, are worth nothing in evidence; his friends, if they remove hither from any other State, though perchance just redeemed from the thrall of chattel Slavery, are liable to be thrust into prison and thence sold into bondage."[21] The editors of the *Illinois State Journal* acknowledged that they shared "in common with nineteen-twentieths of our people, a prejudice against the nigger."[22] The militantly antislavery Chicago *Tribune* explained that many Illinoisans resisted abolition because they feared "that if the slaves were liberated, they would become roaming, vicious vagrants; that they would overrun the North, and subsist by mendicancy and vagrancy; and that from the day they were made free, they would cease to work."[23] The Chicago *Herald* referred to blacks as members of a "poor, ignorant and imbecile race" and applauded a Milwaukee theater proprietor who expelled a black from the audience. "We utterly despise that spirit that would debase our own race to a social equality with the inferior races," the *Herald* proclaimed. When a slave ship was captured, the *Herald* regretted that abolitionists did not peer into the hold "to see a couple of thousand of those naked, musky, greasy cannibals at one of their usual feasts of raw beef and dead negroes."[24] Democrats in Illinois and Ohio decorated wagons carrying young white women with banners reading: "Fathers protect us from Negro Equality."[25]

Such antiblack sentiment, though especially vehement in Illinois, was far from unique in the Old Northwest. In 1858, Indiana Congressman George W. Julian referred to his state and Illinois as "outlying provinces of the empire of slavery" and lamented that Hoosiers "hate the negro with a perfect, if not a supreme hatred."[26] Another Indiana congressman declared that his constituents had three strong "antipathies": "abolitionism, free-niggerism, and slavery."[27] In 1851, an overwhelming majority of Indiana voters (108,513 to 20,951) approved a constitutional clause forbidding blacks to settle in their state. Their counterparts in Wisconsin rejected black suffrage by a margin of 40,915 to 23,074. A Republican senator from the Badger State, Timothy O. Howe, viewed blacks "in the main . . . as so much animal life," while the editor of a Republican newspaper in Grant County summarized the party's creed bluntly: "No slaveholders and no niggers in the territories—white men must own and forever occupy the great west."[28] In Ohio, the Republican-dominated legislature forbade blacks to join the state militia, prompting a Democratic journal to observe: "Black Republicans regard the nigger as good enough to make political capital with but consider his skin too black, nose too flat and heel too long to be permitted to unite with them in a corn stalk muster."[29] A prominent Ohio Republican newspaper said "it is really desirable that the negro should be expelled."[30] Ohio Senator Ben Wade, an antislavery Radical, supported colonization of blacks in order "to hear no more about negro equality or anything of that kind. . . . we shall be . . . glad to rid ourselves of these people."[31] In Missouri, antislavery partisans held similar views because, as some St. Louis workingmen declared, they wanted "White Men for Our City, and Our City for White Men!"[32]

Elsewhere in the North opponents of slavery expansion demonstrated little fondness for blacks. The editor of the New York *Tribune* declared: "we make no pretensions to special interest in or liking for the African Race. We love Liberty, Equality, Justice, Humanity—we maintain the right of every man to himself and his own limbs and muscles; for in so doing we maintain and secure our own rights; but we do not like negroes, and heartily wish no individual of that race had ever been brought to America. We hope the day will come when the whole negro race in this country, being fully at liberty, will gradually, peacefully, freely, draw off and form a community by themselves."[33] The editor of that paper, Horace Greeley, criticized free blacks in New York, maintaining that they "have great faults," being "vicious," "indolent," "dissipated," "generally ignorant," and "groveling in their tastes and appetites."[34] An 1855 *Tribune* editorial calling for equal suffrage for all races noted: "As a class, the Blacks are indolent, improvident, servile, and licentious; and their inveterate habit of appealing to White benevolence or compassion whenever they realize a want or encounter a difficulty, is eminently baneful and enervating."[35] The *Tribune* in 1857 observed that "the children of the emancipated slaves of our own State, who have now enjoyed some thirty years of comparative freedom, ought to be more industrious, energetic, thrifty, [and] independent, than a majority of them are," that "they have not done so well as might fairly have been expected of them," and that "the cause of Emancipation throughout the world is thereby embarrassed and retarded." According to the *Tribune*, in "their private conversation, no men are more frank in acknowledgment and reproof of negro sloth and vice than Abolitionists."[36]

A case in point was the eminent antislavery divine, Theodore Parker of Boston, who in 1857 told a friend: "There are inferior races which have always borne the same ignoble relation to the rest of men, and *always will*. For two generations, what a change there will be in the condition and character of the Irish in New England! But in twenty generations, the negroes will stand just where they are now; that is, if they have not disappeared. In Massachusetts there are no laws now to keep the black man from any pursuit, any office, that he will: but there has never been a rich negro in New England; not a man with ten thousand dollars, perhaps none with five thousand dollars; none eminent in any thing except the calling of a waiter."[37] Parker told a Massachusetts antislavery convention that the "African is the most docile and pliant of all the races of men; none has so little ferocity. . . . No race is so strong in the affectional instinct which attaches man to man by tender ties; none so easy, indolent, confiding, so little warlike."[38] In a commentary on John Brown's 1859 raid at Harper's Ferry, which he backed, Parker wrote that the "Anglo-Saxon with common sense does not like this Africanization of America; he wishes the superior race to multiply rather than the inferior."[39] Another Unitarian minister, William Ellery Channing, lamented that antislavery societies "ought never to have permitted our colored brethren to unite with us in our associations!"[40] A black preacher observed that some abolitionists, no matter how much they might hate slavery, nonetheless "hate a man who wears a colored skin worse."[41]

One of Parker's most enthusiastic fans, Lincoln's partner William Herndon, wrote to a congressman in 1859: "I see you have got the nigger up in the House 'a—ready.' Can you kick him out when you want him gone? Niggers are great institutions, are they not? My *colored brethren* here say—'Why—Good *Lord-a-massy* Billy—de nigger am de great object of the American Gobernment—dey am always de talk—Can't legislate for mail bags: but that de nigger am in the threads—in de whole bag massa—What am you going—you white folks—to do with the darkey?'" Herndon added: "'The Niggers' (as they themselves say) are America's great home-made institution."[42] A correspondent for the abolitionist paper that first published *Uncle Tom's Cabin* declared that "the real evil of the Negro race" is "that they are so fit for slavery as they are."[43]

The New York *Journal of Commerce* articulated a common theme of antiblack prejudice when it declared that "the negroes held in slavery in the United States, are much better off, physically and morally, than their ignorant and degraded brothers in Africa." On that continent the typical native "is an habitual drunkard, a thief, a liar, revengeful, licentious, groveling in his habits, almost destitute of natural affection, [and] unprogressive in character." Any student of ethnology "knows that a superior and an inferior race cannot continue to occupy the same territory on terms of equality. Either the inferior race will be enslaved, and in that condition increase and multiply, if treated with reasonable kindness,—or, in the attempt to compete with the superior race, be ultimately wiped out of existence by their greater skill and strength."[44]

Ethnologists like Louis Agassiz did in fact preach the doctrine of black racial inferiority. That eminent professor of zoology and geology at Harvard opposed both slavery and social equality for blacks, whom he described as "indolent, playful, sensual, imitative, subservient, good-natured, versatile, unsteady in their purpose, devoted and affectionate." They were "entitled to their freedom, to the regulation of their own destiny, to the enjoyment of their life, of their earnings, of their family circle. But with all this nowhere do they appear to have been capable of rising, by themselves, to the level of the civilized communities of the whites, and therefore I hold that they are incapable of living on a footing of social equality with the whites in one and the same community without becoming an element of social disorder."[45]

At Illinois College, an abolitionist hotbed, Professor Jonathan Baldwin Turner offered a similar ethnological analysis in *The Three Great Races of Men* (1861). Turner described whites as polar people and blacks as equatorial people. The "great mission" of the former "is to analyze and to conquer," while that of the latter was "to enjoy and adore . . . as one is a being of intellect, of the head—the other of sentiment, of the heart." If they lived with whites, blacks were bound to be subordinate. "The two races cannot dwell together . . . *first* because God never designed that they should . . . and *second*, because each race is still essentially barbarian in the only line where the other has begun to be civilized—the one in the head, the other in the heart." Turner recommended that blacks be colonized to Haiti or other tropical lands south of the United States.[46]

Julian Sturtevant, president of Illinois College, supported emancipation but held that colonization was not necessary because blacks, unable to compete with whites, would die out once they were freed. Other leading opponents of slavery—including the Reverend Mr. James Freeman Clarke, Moncure Conway, Theodore Tilton, and Samuel Gridley Howe—all thought blacks were intellectually inferior to whites. The eminent author and Radical Republican, Bayard Taylor, called blacks "the lowest type of humanity known on the face of the earth."[47]

If Negrophobia was strong among antislavery Northerners, it was much more rampant among Democrats who, according to Ohio Republican leader Salmon P. Chase, wanted "simply to talk about the universal nigger question, as they call it. All that they seem to say is 'nigger, nigger, nigger.'"[48] In 1858, a leading newspaper of New England, the Springfield (Massachusetts) *Republican,* observed that for Northern Democrats "Negrophobia is . . . pretty much all that is left for stump uses"; hence, their campaign documents are "all about niggers—nothing but niggers."[49]

To combat their opponents' demagoguery, Republicans and other opponents of slavery expansion had to insist that they truly championed the interests of whites. The New York *Times* defended Republicans, arguing that they had insisted "always and everywhere, that they aimed at the good of the *white men* of the country, and had nothing to do with negroes." In 1858, that paper spoke for many when it disavowed any "abstract love of the negro." Republicans, said the *Times,* had "uniformly and most emphatically repudiated the idea that they had anything whatever to do with negroes or negro rights."[50] The New York *Tribune* protested against "the silly lie that ours is a 'negro party'—that 'it has no idea but "nigger! nigger!"'—that it cares nothing or

The first known photograph of Lincoln, ca. 1846. When this image first appeared in published form in 1895, the noted geologist and author John Wesley Powell expressed his delight. Lincoln's pictures, he said, "have never quite pleased me, and I now know why. I remember Lincoln as I saw him when I was a boy; after he became a public man I saw him but few times. This portrait is Lincoln as I knew him best: his sad, dreamy eye, his pensive smile, his sad and delicate face, his pyramidal shoulders, are the characteristics which I best remember; amid I can never think of him as wrinkled with care, so plainly shown in his later portraits. This is the Lincoln of Springfield, Decatur, Jacksonville, and Bloomington." Robert Todd Lincoln later stated that this "daguerreotype was on the walls of a room in my father's house from my earliest recollection," along with one of his mother. Daguerreotype probably by Nicholas H. Shepherd, Springfield. Abraham Lincoln Presidential Library and Museum, Springfield, Illinois.

Mary Todd Lincoln, probably also taken by Nicholas H. Shepherd in about 1846 and likely the companion mentioned by Robert Todd Lincoln. Library of Congress.

Alexander Hesler took this photograph in Chicago in February 1857. Lincoln called the likeness "a very true one; though my wife, and many others, do not. My impression is that their objection arises from the disordered condition of the hair." (The photographer had mussed Lincoln's hair to make him look more natural.) After Lincoln won the Republican presidential nomination in 1860, his supporters rushed a lithograph of the photo into print. Lincoln then enjoyed telling friends that newsboys hawking it on city streets cried out: "Ere's yer last picter of Old Abe! He'll look better when he gets his *hair* combed!" Abraham Lincoln Presidential Library and Museum, Springfield, Illinois.

Lincoln as he appeared on the eve of the debates with Stephen A. Douglas in 1858. The photographer, T. Painter Pearson, offered his subject a mirror so that he could tidy up. Lincoln allegedly replied: "It would not be much of a likeness if I fixed it up any." Library of Congress.

Ambrotype dated May 7, 1858, the day Lincoln won the Duff Armstrong case. After the acquittal, 22-year-old Abraham M. Byers stopped Lincoln on the street and asked him to pose in his studio. At first Lincoln protested, insisting that his white linen suit was too dirty, but eventually he yielded, leading to one of the few images showing him looking directly into the camera. Abraham Lincoln Presidential Library and Museum, Springfield, Illinois.

Mathew Brady took this photo in New York on February 23, 1860, the day Lincoln delivered his Cooper Union speech. The artist-photographer George H. Story scheduled and attended the session. Afterward, Lincoln allegedly said that Brady and the Cooper Union speech made him president. The sculptor Truman H. Bartlett observed that "Lincoln's tall & well made body, vivified by his kind & undemonstrative nature" enabled him "to stand with perfect ease, unconscious & dignified force, making this portrait one of unique distinction." Bartlett thought this image of Lincoln "the only portrait of him in existence which while including the larger part of Lincoln's body produces on the observer the extraordinary effect so often described by the one word, 'presence.'" Abraham Lincoln Presidential Library and Museum, Springfield, Illinois.

Alexander Hesler took this photograph in Chicago on June 3, 1860, less than three weeks after the Chicago Convention. "That looks better and expresses me better than any I have ever seen," Lincoln allegedly said; "if it pleases the people I am satisfied." That year a journalist wrote that Lincoln was 51 years of age, "but he certainly has no appearance of being so old. His hair is black, hardly touched with gray, and his eye is brighter than that of many of his juniors." Illinois State Historical Society, Springfield, Illinois.

The house in Springfield, where the Lincolns lived from 1844 to 1861 and the only one they ever owned. Charles Dresser, the Episcopalian minister who presided at the Lincolns' wedding in 1842, sold it to them. The photograph, taken by John Adams Whipple [in 1860], shows Lincoln and his son Willie behind the front fence. Mary's sister Frances said that neither of the Lincolns "loved the beautiful—I have planted flowers in their front yard myself to hide nakedness—ugliness &c. &c. have done it often—and often—Mrs L never planted trees—Roses—never made a garden, at least not more than once or twice." Abraham Lincoln Presidential Library and Museum, Springfield, Illinois.

thinks nothing of the interests and welfare of White Men."[51] The *Tribune's* editor maintained that the Republican Party "contemplates primarily the interest of Free White Labor, for which it struggles to secure the unoccupied territory of the Union."[52] Iowa Senator James Harlan declared that the "policy of the Republican party invites the Anglo-Saxon . . . and others of Caucasian blood, by its proposed preemption and homestead laws, to enter and occupy [the territories], and by the exclusion of slavery it will practically exclude the negro and kindred races."[53] A leader of Virginia's antislavery movement chastised Democrats for their monomaniacal preoccupation with race: "It is niggers, niggers, niggers, first and always. . . . Tariff and everything else must be made to suit their niggers. Our interest . . . is the White man[']s interest. I am proud to say that I belong to the white man[']s party [i.e., the Republicans]."[54]

In Illinois, Macon County Republicans proclaimed that "the industry, virtue and patriotism of the free white laboring classes is the great bulwark of our political freedom" and "our cause is that of the white man, and our object the encouragement and prosperity of free white labor, and the spread of free society."[55] A Republican leader in Galena insisted that his "party is really and truly the white man's party."[56] The Springfield *Illinois State Journal* agreed, asserting that the Republican Party was "preeminently the white man's party. It defends the cause of free labor and honorable industry against the encroachments of slave labor. It repels the modern Democratic dogma, that slavery should not only be nationalized but should be made dependent, not upon color, but condition."[57] A constituent wrote to an Illinois Republican congressman: "No matter whether we are opposed to the extension of slavery from our humanity and love of right and justice, or from hatred of niggers (of the latter class are many Illinois Republicans) we are terribly in earnest in our opposition to the extension of that institution."[58] According to the Chicago *Tribune,* the "doctrine of the Abolition party is, to let the African race alone, neither marry nor cohabit with them; to give them their freedom; treat them as human beings; pay them for their work; separate the whites from adulterous communication with them, and preserve the purity of the Caucasian blood from African admixture."[59]

Some Republicans responded to the Democrats' race-baiting in kind. When the Democratic Rushville *Times* advised Republicans to "be consistent! Just agree to sleep with Fred Douglass and marry your daughters to specimens of the thick-lip-gentry and be done with it," *The Free Press* of Pittsfield reminded the *Times* "that its co-laborers of the South live among niggers, work among niggers, eat among niggers, drink among niggers and sleep with niggers. That they never get out of sight of a nigger, and their constant intercourse with niggers corrupts even their manners and language, and leads them to acquire *nigger antics, nigger pronunciation, and nigger language.* . . . The Anti-Nebraska men are laboring to keep Kansas and her white people free from the foul contamination with niggers; their purpose is to keep niggers out of Kansas."[60]

Attacking the Kansas-Nebraska Act

Lincoln eschewed such racial arguments in his attacks on the Kansas-Nebraska Act. He applauded Senator William Henry Seward's high-minded speech against that legislation in mid-February. The following month the *Illinois State Journal* ran an editorial, probably by Lincoln, that expressed themes he would stress in formal speeches later that year. It condemned the Democratic *Illinois State Register* for supporting Douglas's bill. "If he [George Walker, co-publisher of the *Register*] can find any 'principle' in the constitution that allows George Walker, white man, to enslave George Walker, black man, then he has some ground for 'conscience sake' to stand upon." But there was no such constitutional justification for allowing slavery to expand into the northern portion of the Louisiana Purchase. "If the principle of free government means anything, the black man *must* stand on the same footing of 'governing himself' as the white. . . . The Register with one blow would annul the grandest principle of free government and give to ten thousand slaveholders from the south, the privilege of setting up slave pens in Nebraska, thus widening the foulest curse, and fostering the most 'insidious enemy' that holds in the bosom of our Republic."[61]

Throughout 1854, the *Journal* continued publishing editorials, in all likelihood by Lincoln, assailing the Kansas-Nebraska Act. One of them 'that virtually all authorities agree was Lincoln's handiwork' ridiculed the fourteenth section of that law, which stated that it was "the true intent and meaning of this act not to legislate slavery into any territory or State, not to exclude it therefrom, but to leave the people thereof perfectly free to form and regulate their domestic institutions in their own way." Sarcastically, Lincoln proposed an analogy to expose the illogic of that assertion: "Abraham Lincoln has a fine meadow, containing beautiful springs of water, and well fenced, which John Calhoun had agreed with Abraham (originally owning the land in common) should be his, and the agreement had been consummated in the most solemn manner, regarded by both as sacred." In time Calhoun had "become owner of an extensive herd of cattle," which, because of a drought, was starving. Thereupon Calhoun, "with a longing eye on Lincoln's meadow," dismantles his neighbor's fence.

"'You rascal,' says Lincoln, 'what have you done? What do you do this for?'

"'Oh,' replies Calhoun, 'everything is right. I have taken down your fence; but nothing more. It is my true intent and meaning not to drive my cattle into your meadow, nor to exclude them therefrom, but to leave them perfectly free to form their own notions of the feed, and to direct their movements in their own way!'

"Now would not the man who committed this outrage be deemed both a knave and a fool,—a knave in removing the restrictive fence, which he had solemnly pledged himself to sustain;—and a fool in supposing that there could be one man found in the country to believe that he had not pulled down the fence for the purpose of opening the meadow for his cattle?"[62]

While this barb was aimed at his former surveying boss, Democrat John Calhoun, Lincoln understandably focused attention most closely on Stephen A. Douglas. From 1854 to 1860, Lincoln and Douglas engaged in an ongoing political and moral contest, of which their celebrated debates in 1858 formed only a part.

Douglas proved a formidable, immensely popular opponent, as Lincoln acknowledged. From 1852, when both Henry Clay and Daniel Webster died, until 1860, Douglas loomed larger than any other American politician, presidents included. Pugnacious, arrogant, vituperative, and ferociously ambitious, he was, as a Southerner who served with him in the U.S. House recalled, "distinctly a man of large faculties."[63] He had a knack for genially convincing everyone he met that he was their good and true friend, interested in what they were interested in, and caring about what they cared about. They in turn felt drawn to him and disposed to support him. A journalist who accompanied Douglas on a campaign swing reported that he "can talk religion with the priests as well as politics with the statesman." At train stations where they stopped, "more regularly than the conductor, Mr. Douglas is on the platform with a good-bye to the leaving, and a welcome to the departing traveler—a shake of the hand with one man that stands at the depot and the touch of the hat to another. He knows everybody; can tell the question that affects each locality; calls the name of every farm-owner on the way."[64] Douglas's overflowing energy and uncommon industriousness led people to call him "a steam engine in britches."[65] With his "hail-fellow-well-met" manner he could be exceptionally persuasive, and he radiated a magnetism that won him countless followers. Though short (5 feet 4 inches), his broad shoulders, muscular frame, huge head, bright eyes, and firm mouth gave him a most imposing presence.

Lincoln referred to him as Judge Douglas, for he had served briefly on the Illinois Supreme Court, where he scandalized older members of the bar with his lack of dignity. At lunch he would occasionally sit in a fellow attorney's lap and ramble on about politics and the past. He constantly gave the impression that he was electioneering. Douglas's suave and hearty manner made him popular with colleagues in Congress. "Many a time have I watched him," said John W. Forney, editor of the Philadelphia *Press,* "leading in the keen encounters of the bright intellects around the festive board. To see him threading the glittering crowd with a pleasant smile or a kind word for every body, one would have taken him for a trained courtier." But, Forney observed, "he was more at home in the close and exciting thicket of men." There he was truly in his element. "To call each one by name, sometimes by his Christian name; to stand in the centre of a listening throng, while he told some Western story or defended some public measure; to exchange jokes with a political adversary; or, ascending the rostrum, to hold thousands spell-bound for hours, as he poured forth torrents of characteristic eloquence—these were traits that raised up for him hosts who were ready to fight for him." Under his banner "[e]minent men did not hesitate to take their stand," and "[ri]per scholars than himself, older if not better statesmen, frankly acknowledged his leadership and faithfully followed his fortunes."[66] Forney's colleague John Russell Young praised Douglas as "a man of great nature," the "most buoyant of Americans, full of life and aggressiveness and animal vigor, a man of the multitude," the "most gifted, the most popular, the most strenuous of Democratic statesmen, the most accomplished debater in America, quick, apt, ready, irrepressible."[67]

Carl Schurz, who observed Douglas debating in the senate in 1854, recalled that his sentences "went straight to the mark like bullets, and sometimes like cannon-balls, tearing and crashing." It was hard, Schurz thought, "to surpass his clearness and force of statement when his position was right; or his skill at twisting logic or in darkening the subject with extraneous, unessential matter, when he was wrong; or his defiant tenacity when he was driven to defend himself, or his keen and crafty alertness to turn his defense into attack, so that, even when overwhelmed with adverse argument, he would issue from the fray with the air of the conqueror."[68]

With equal justice, Douglas's detractors called him egotistical, belligerent, scornful, quarrelsome, demagogic, unscrupulous, shifty, brash, haughty, impudent, vituperative, intensely partisan, vindictive, humorless, coarse, vulgar, profane, and morally obtuse. Young deplored Douglas's "insane yearning for immediate success" and his willingness to truckle to Southern slaveholders. "He believed in the rowdy virtue of American politics, and had much of the rowdy in his nature."[69] Horace White thought him "patriotic beyond a doubt," but "color blind to moral principles in politics, and if not stone blind to the evils of slavery was deaf and dumb to any expression concerning them."[70] Even the Little Giant's friends lacked "confidence in his moral principle."[71]

In debate, Douglas could be abusive. According to Schurz, the senator was "utterly unsparing" of "the feelings of his opponents. He "would nag and nettle them with disdainful words of challenge, and insult them with such names as 'dastards' and 'traitors.' Nothing could equal the contemptuous scorn, the insolent curl of his lip with which, in the debates to which I listened, he denounced the anti-slavery men in Congress as 'the Abolition confederates,' and at a subsequent time, after the formation of the Republican party, as 'Black Republicans.'" Worse still, "he would, with utter unscrupulousness, malign his opponents' motives, distort their sayings, and attribute to them all sorts of iniquitous deeds or purposes of which he must have known them to be quite guiltless." His "style of attack was sometimes so exasperatingly offensive, that it required, on the part of the anti-slavery men in the Senate, a very high degree of self-control to abstain from retaliating." Schurz never saw "a more formidable parliamentary pugilist" in whom "there was something . . . which very strongly smacked of the bar-room. He was the idol of the rough element of his party, and his convivial association with that element left its unmistakable imprint upon his habits and his deportment." Douglas "would sometimes offend the dignity of the Senate by his astonishing conduct. Once, at a night session of the Senate I saw him, after a boisterous speech, throw himself upon the lap of a brother senator and loll there, talking and laughing, for ten or fifteen minutes, with his arm around the neck of his friend, who seemed to be painfully embarrassed, but could or would not shake him off."[72]

A journalist observed Douglas attack senatorial rivals in an 1854 speech that had no trace of dignity. He abused colleagues so mercilessly that a fight seemed likely to break out. His language and tone were "wholly alien to that body, and disgraceful alike to it and to him that it was indulged in."[73] In 1856 the Little Giant rebuked Charles Sumner, asking: "Is his object to provoke some of us to kick him as we would a dog in the street, that he may get sympathy upon the just chastisement?"[74] (Two days later South Carolina Congressman Preston Brooks, wielding a heavy cane, cudgeled Sumner into insensibility on the senate floor.) Such conduct earned Douglas the reputation of "a bully who only insults peaceable men."[75] Douglas taunted New York Senator William Henry Seward, saying: "Ah, you can't crawl behind that free nigger 'dodge.'" According to a reporter covering the senate, Douglas "always uses the word 'nigger' and not 'negro' as it appears in his printed speeches." (Seward told the Little Giant, "no man who spells Negro with two gs will ever be elected President of the United States.") That journalist informed his readers that only "those who know Douglas, or who heard him, can be aware of his low 'Short Boy' style of speaking. His sneering tone and vulgar grimaces must be heard and seen rather than described."[76] In 1858, another journalist, E. L. Godkin, termed Douglas "a model demagogue," who "is vulgar in his habits and vulgar in his appearance, 'takes his drink,' chews his quid, and discharges his saliva with as much constancy and energy as the least pretentious of his constituents."[77] Commenting on the premature death of President Zachary Taylor, Douglas tastelessly remarked: "It was the hand of Providence that saved us from our first and only military administration. Taylor was gathered to his fathers."[78]

In 1844, John Quincy Adams described Douglas giving a vehement speech in the House of Representatives. Defending a committee report, the Illinoisan "raved out his hour in abusive invectives upon the members who had pointed out its slanders, and upon the Whig party." Douglas's "face was convulsed, his gesticulation frantic, and he lashed himself into such a heat that if his body had been made of combustible matter it would have burnt out. In the midst of his roaring, to save himself from choking, he stripped off and cast away his cravat, unbuttoned his waistcoat, and had the air and aspect of a half-naked pugilist." Adams, known as Old Man Eloquent, wrote in astonishment: "this man comes from a judicial bench, and passes for an eloquent orator!"[79]

Douglas's combativeness led other observers to compare him to a boxer. In 1860, a Massachusetts journalist described him as "a chunky man" who "looks like a prize fighter." Indeed, he possessed "excellent prize fighting qualities. Pluck, quickness and strength; adroitness in shifting his positions, avoiding his adversary's blows, and hitting him in unexpected places in return." Douglas's "strong point is his will to have his own way." Withal, he was "a plucky, hard, unscrupulous, conscienceless fellow."[80] The Springfield, Massachusetts, *Republican* maintained that Douglas's "main power lies in his appeals to the passions and the lower instincts of the mob," especially its racial prejudices.[81]

Douglas's greatest asset was his prowess in debate. Congressman Isaac N. Arnold called him the U.S. senate's "leading debater" in the 1850s: "He had been accustomed to meet for years in Congress the trained leaders of the nation, and never, either in single combat, or taking the fire of a whole party, had he been discomfited." He "was bold, defiant, confident, aggressive; fertile in resources, terrible in denunciation, familiar with political history, practiced in all controversial discussion, of indomitable physical and moral courage, and unquestionably the most formidable man in the nation on the stump."[82] According to Arnold, the Little Giant "had a wonderful faculty of extracting from his associates, from experts, and others, by conversation, all they knew of a subject he was to discuss, and then making it so thoroughly his, that all seemed to have originated with himself."[83] A fellow senator, William Pitt Fessenden of Maine, credited Douglas with Houdini-like qualities: "You may drop him in the middle of a morass, from which escape seems impossible, and before your back is turned he will have built a corduroy road across it, and be out again and at you harder than ever."[84]

Like Fessenden, Lincoln found it virtually "impossible to get the advantage" of Douglas, for "even if he is worsted, he so bears himself that the people are bewildered and uncertain as to who has the better of it."[85] In 1854, Lincoln said of Douglas's debating style: "It was a great trick among some public speakers to hurl a naked absurdity at his audience, with such confidence that they should be puzzled to know if the speaker didn't see some point of great magnitude in it which entirely escaped their observation. A neatly varnished sophism would be readily penetrated, but a great, rough *non sequitur* was sometimes twice as dangerous as a well polished fallacy."[86]

After witnessing Douglas clash with senatorial opponents, Harriet Beecher Stowe made a similar observation: "His chief forte in debating is his power of mystifying the point. With the most off-hand assured airs in the world, and a certain appearance of honest superiority, like one who has a regard for you and wishes to set you right on one or two little matters, he proceeds to set up some point which is *not* that in question, but only a family connection of it, and this point he attacks with the very best of logic and language; he charges upon it horse and foot, runs it down, tramples it in the dust, and thus turns upon you with—'Sir, there's your argument! didn't I tell you so? you see it's all stuff,' and if you have allowed yourself to be so dazzled by his quickness as to forget that the routed point is not after all the one in question, you suppose all is over with it." In addition, Mrs. Stowe said, "he contrives to mingle up so many stinging allusions to so many piquant personalities, so many fillips upon sore and sensitive places, that by the time he has done his mystification a dozen others are ready and burning to spring on their feet to repel some direct or indirect attack, all equally wide of the point. His speeches, instead of being like an arrow sent at a mark, resemble rather a bomb which hits nothing in particular, but bursts and send[s] red-hot nails in every direction." Mrs. Stowe thought it "a merciful providence that with all his alertness and adroitness, all his quick-sighted keenness, Douglas is not witty—*that* might have made him too irresistible a demagogue for the liberties of our laughter-loving people, to whose weaknesses he is altogether too well adapted now." The Republicans, she concluded, "have pitted against them a leader infinite in resources, artful, adroit, and wholly unscrupulous."[87]

Douglas treated the 1854 Illinois legislative and congressional campaigns as a referendum on the Kansas-Nebraska Act and on his leadership. In January he had accurately predicted that Northerners would assail him "without stint or moderation. Every opprobrious epithet will be applied to me. I shall be, probably, hung in effigy in many places."[88] To vindicate himself, he returned from Washington late in the summer to speak on behalf of Democratic candidates, especially Thomas L. Harris, challenger to Lincoln's friend Congressman Richard Yates. When Yates announced his intention of retiring, Lincoln urged him to seek reelection. Yates recalled Lincoln's statement that "though he could not promise me success in a district so largely against us, yet he hoped for the sake of the principle, I would run, and if I would, he would take the stump in my behalf. I remember his earnestness, and so deeply did he implore me that the question was one worthy of our noblest efforts whether in victory or defeat, that I consented."[89] When political leaders asked if he would like to run for Yates's seat, Lincoln "seemed gratified by the compliment" but refused, saying: "No;

Yates has been a true and faithful Representative, and should be returned."[90] Lincoln took to the hustings in August shortly after the announcement of Yates's candidacy. The following month, a Chicago editor reported that "*Lincoln* tells me that Yates is on 'praying ground' in his District. Lincoln canvasses it with & for him."[91]

Lincoln was no longer the fierce Whig partisan of old but rather a principled opponent of slavery expansion. As Yates's campaign manager, he tried to marshal support for the incumbent congressman, reaching across party lines to seek the help of anti-Nebraska Democrat John M. Palmer. "You know how anxious I am that this Nebraska measure shall be rebuked and condemned every where," Lincoln wrote Palmer on September 7. He added that if the Democrats had nominated Palmer instead of Thomas L. Harris, Lincoln would not have opposed him: "I should have been quiet, happy that Nebraska was to be rebuked at all events. I still should have voted for the whig candidate; but I should have made no speeches, written no letters; and you would have been elected by at least a thousand majority."[92]

To counter rumors that Yates was a nativist bigot, Lincoln drafted a letter for him to circulate. Yates ignored the advice and later acknowledged that his failure to heed it probably cost him the election. Antiforeign, anti-Catholic sentiment was sweeping the North, in some states becoming the dominant theme in 1854. Supporters of this movement, called Native Americans or Know-Nothings, adopted the slogan, "Americans must rule America." They believed that Catholicism was incompatible with America's democratic, individualistic values; that Catholics wielded disproportionate power; that established political parties and professional politicians were corrupt and unresponsive to the popular will; that slavery and liquor were evil; and that immigrants were the source of crime, corruption, pauperism, wage reductions, voter fraud, and the defeat of antislavery candidates.

Know-Nothings in Springfield approached Lincoln, asking if they could run him for the state legislature. A party leader, Richard H. Ballinger, and two colleagues visited Lincoln's law office, where he received them kindly but flatly turned them down, stating "that he had belonged to the old Whig party and must continue to do so until a better one arose to take its place. He could not become identified with the American party—they might vote for him if they wanted to; so might the Democrats; yet he was not in sentiment with this new party." Lincoln asked "who the native Americans were. 'Do they not,' he said, 'wear the breech-clout and carry the tomahawk? We pushed them from their homes and now turn upon others not fortunate enough to come over as early as we or our forefathers. Gentlemen of the committee, your party is wrong in principle.'" He added humorously: "When this Know-nothing party first came up, I had an Irishman, Patrick by name, hoeing in my garden. One morning I was there with him, and he said, 'Mr. Lincoln, what about the Know-nothings?' I explained that they would possibly carry a few elections and disappear, and I asked Pat why he was not born in this country. 'Faith, Mr. Lincoln,' he replied, 'I wanted to be, but my mother wouldn't let me.'"[93]

In September, Lincoln debated John Calhoun, who alleged that the Whigs and Know-Nothings were acting in concert. Lincoln disparaged Know-Nothingism and even "doubted its existence."[94] (The following year he condemned the Know-Nothings in an eloquent private letter to his old friend Joshua Speed, who had asked where Lincoln stood politically now that the Whigs were defunct. "I am not a Know Nothing," he declared. "That is certain. How could I be? How can any one who abhors the oppression of negroes, be in favor of degrading classes of white people? Our progress in degeneracy appears to me to be pretty rapid. As a nation, we began by declaring that '*all men are created equal*.' We now practically read it 'all men are created equal, except negroes, *and foreigners, and catholics*.' When it comes to this I should prefer emigrating to some country where they make no pretence of loving liberty—to Russia, for instance, where despotism can be taken pure, and without the base alloy of hypocracy."[95] Lincoln "avowed that if the K[now] N[othing] movement was successful, that he could be no longer of any use to his fellow men in politics.")[96]

One day when Lincoln was out of town, Springfield Whigs nominated him for the General Assembly, much to his surprise and his wife's dismay. Upon reading a press account indicating that he was being put forward for the state House of Representatives, she rushed to the newspaper's offices and ordered her husband's name stricken from the list of candidates. Later, when William Jayne called seeking permission to reinstate Lincoln's name, he found the potential candidate "the saddest man I Ever Saw—the gloomiest." Lincoln, nearly in tears, paced the floor, resisting Jayne's blandishments by saying, "No—I can't—you don't Know all. I Say you don't begin to Know one half and that's Enough."[97] Henry C. Whitney explained that it "was Mrs. Lincoln's opposition which so much disturbed him. She insisted in her imperious way that he must now go to the United States Senate, and that it was a degradation to run him for the Legislature."[98] But despite his wife's objections, Lincoln remained on the ballot, explaining to a friend: "I only allowed myself to be elected, because it was supposed my doing so would help Yates."[99]

The First Great Speech

For the campaign Lincoln prepared a long, masterful speech arraigning Douglas, the Kansas-Nebraska Act, and slavery with a passionate eloquence that heralded the emergence of a new Lincoln. Like a butterfly hatching from a caterpillar's chrysalis, the partisan warrior of the 1830s and 1840s was transformed into a statesman. Abandoning his earlier "slasher-gaff" style, he began to speak with authority as a principled, articulate, high-minded champion of the antislavery cause. He dissected Douglas's popular sovereignty doctrine with surgical precision, forceful logic, and deep moral conviction.

Lincoln had planned to debate Douglas, just as he had done on earlier occasions. In September, the Little Giant was to speak in Bloomington, where a leading Whig, Jesse W. Fell, proposed that he share time with Lincoln. "No, I won't do it!" Douglas exclaimed. "I come to Chicago, and there I am met by an old line abolitionist; I come down to the center of the State, and I am met by an old line Whig; I go to the south end of the State, and I am met by an anti-administration Democrat. I can't hold the abolitionist responsible for what the Whig says; I can't hold the Whig responsible for what the abolitionist says; and I can't hold either responsible for what the Democrat says. It looks like dogging a man over the State. This is my meeting; the people have come to hear me, and I want to talk to them."[100] Fear of Lincoln's ability as a debater may have led Douglas to reject Fell's suggestion. In October the Little Giant called Lincoln "the most difficult and dangerous opponent that I have ever met" in debate.[101] Lincoln saw the logic of Douglas's position. That evening he replied to the speech that the Little Giant gave in the afternoon. Lincoln's remarks prefigured the memorable address he would deliver at Springfield and Peoria a few days later (discussed below).

While in Bloomington, Lincoln attended a reception at Douglas's hotel suite, where the Little Giant offered liquor to his callers. When Lincoln declined, Douglas asked:

"What, do you belong to a temperance society?"

"No, I don't belong to any temperance society, but I am temperate in this that I don't drink anything."[102]

Douglas may have been taunting Lincoln with a subtle allusion to the temperance movement, which had fielded candidates for public office. Although he had spoken on behalf of temperance in 1842, Lincoln did not participate in the Illinois anti-alcohol crusade of the mid-1850s.

In October, Lincoln responded to Douglas in Springfield, where thousands of Illinoisans had flocked to attend the State Fair. There the Little Giant defended his record and asserted that the defection of anti-Nebraska Democrats could not defeat his party: "I tell you the time has not yet come when a handful of traitors in our camp can turn the great State of Illinois, with all her glorious history and traditions, into a negro-worshipping, negro-equality community."[103] Sitting directly before Douglas, Lincoln listened with close attention, obviously planning to offer a rejoinder. At the close of the speech, Lincoln announced to the crowd that a leading Anti-Nebraska Democrat, Lyman Trumbull, might reply to it the following day, but in case Trumbull could not do so, he himself would.

When John W. Bunn opined that it would be hard to respond to the Little Giant's speech, Lincoln replied: "No, it won't. Douglas lied; he lied three times and I'll prove it!"[104] The next afternoon, in Trumbull's absence, he did so before an unusually large crowd at the statehouse. He repeated this address twelve days later in Peoria and wrote it out for publication. It became known as the Peoria Speech, though he delivered virtually the same remarks earlier at Springfield.

Lincoln had prepared his remarks with special care, conducting research in the state library. Among the books that influenced his thinking was Leonard Bacon's *Slavery Discussed in Occasional Essays from 1833 to 1846*, in which the author, a Congregational minister, declared that "if those laws of the southern states, by virtue of which slavery exists there, and is what it is, are not wrong—nothing is wrong."[105] (In 1864, Lincoln would famously write that "[i]f slavery is not wrong, nothing is wrong.")[106]

Lincoln gave a preliminary version of the speech in Winchester as well as Bloomington. A member of the Winchester audience recalled that "he made a few gestures, more with his head than he did with his hands or arms." In discussing the way in which the three-fifths provision of the Constitution diminished the political rights of Free State voters, he said: "Talk about equal rights, I would like some man to take a pointer dog, and nose around, and snuff about, and see if he can find my rights in such a condition." He illustrated this image by mimicking "with his head and face the acts of a dog doing that." Richard Yates said of Lincoln's effort in Winchester: "I have heard this winter all the big men in Congress talk on this question, but Lincoln's is the strongest speech I ever heard on the subject."[107] Winchester and Bloomington were just a warm-up for Springfield and Peoria.

In this Springfield-Peoria speech, his first oratorical masterpiece, Lincoln presented a comprehensive analysis and denunciation of slavery and its apologists. Before getting to the substance of his address, he graciously "said that he should not assail the motives and not impeach the honesty of any man who voted for the Nebraska Bill, much less, his distinguished friend, Judge Douglas." He gave Douglas "credit for honesty of intention and true patriotism—referring whatever of wrong he might happen to find among his actions, entirely to a mistaken sense of duty." He invited the Little Giant to point out any mistakes he might make in recounting the history of the slavery controversy; Douglas consented to do so.

Lincoln offered some bantering comments about Douglas and the Know-Nothings. He found nothing unusual in Douglas's attacks on the nativists, for he already had 95 percent of the foreign-born voters on his side, and no one could blame him for trying to win over the remaining 5 percent. (Douglas looked "grim as Mont Blanc" at this point.) Lincoln also addressed the Little Giant's claim that the Whig Party had died. Pointing to the election returns in New England and Iowa, he observed that the Democratic Party was "in a very bad way."[108]

After these preliminaries, Lincoln traced the course of the slavery issue in American politics, showing how the Kansas-Nebraska Act was "wrong in its direct effect, letting slavery into Kansas and Nebraska—and wrong in its prospective principle, allowing it to spread to every other part of the wide world, where men can be found inclined to take it." Douglas often interrupted this historical survey to challenge Lincoln's accuracy, as he had been invited to do. When Lincoln suggested that the senator was not the true author of the Nebraska bill—that in 1848 Democratic presidential candidate Lewis Cass had put forward the theory of popular sovereignty—the crowd laughed and applauded. Incensed, Douglas rose, shook his hair, and "looking much like a roused lion," said "in his peculiarly heavy voice which he uses with so much effect when he wishes to be impressive, 'No, Sir! I will tell you what was the origin of the Nebraska bill. It was this, Sir! God created man, and placed before him both good and evil, and left him free to choose for himself. That was the origin of the Nebraska bill." Lincoln, who "looked the picture of good nature and patience," smilingly replied: "I think it is a great honor to Judge Douglas that he *was the first man to discover that fact.*" The audience once again burst out laughing, to the Little Giant's evident discomfiture.[109]

Lincoln quoted from an 1849 speech in which Douglas lauded the Compromise of 1820: "The Missouri Compromise had been in practical operation for about a quarter of a century, and had received the sanction and approbation of men of all parties in

every section of the Union. It had allayed all sectional jealousies and irritations growing out of this vexed question, and harmonized and tranquilized the whole country.
All the evidences of public opinion at that day, seemed to indicate that this Compromise had been canonized in the hearts of the American people, as a sacred thing
which no ruthless hand would ever be reckless enough to disturb."

Lincoln said of Douglas's 1849 speech: "It is powerful and eloquent; the language
is choice and rich. I wish I was such a master of language as my friend, the Judge."

Douglas interjected: "A first-rate speech." (Renewed applause.)

In dealing with the 36° 30' line established in the Missouri Compromise, Lincoln
was asked by Douglas: "And you voted against extending that line, Mr. Lincoln?"
(Laughter)

"Yes, sir, because I was in favor of running that line much further south. (Great
applause.)" Turning to the Wilmot Proviso, Lincoln recounted that "the Judge introduced me to a particular friend of his, one Davy Wilmot, of Pennsylvania. (Laughter.)"

"I thought you would be fit associates (great laughter)," quipped Douglas, to
which Lincoln replied: "Well, in the end it proved we were, and I hope to convince
this audience that we may be so yet. (Uproarious applause.)"[110]

After sketching the historical background of the current crisis, Lincoln displayed
intense moral conviction as he excoriated Douglas's popular sovereignty doctrine.
The senator had nothing to say about the morality of slavery, proclaiming that: "I do
not know of any tribunal on earth that can decide the question of the morality of
slavery or any other institution. I deal with slavery as a political question involving
questions of public policy."[111] (Douglas did not always eschew moral argument in
politics. When attacking nativism, he said: "To proscribe a man in this country on
account of his birthplace or religious faith is subversive of all our ideas and principles
of civil and religious freedom. It is revolting to our sense of justice and right.")[112] With
unwonted vehemence, Lincoln denounced Douglas's neutrality on such a burning
moral issue: "This *declared* indifference, but as I must think, covert *real* zeal for the
spread of slavery, I can not but hate." *Hate* was a word Lincoln rarely used, but he repeated it in this address: "I hate it because of the monstrous injustice of slavery itself.
I hate it because it deprives our republican example of its just influence in the
world—enables the enemies of free institutions, with plausibility, to taunt us as
hypocrites—causes the real friends of freedom to doubt our sincerity, and especially because it forces so many really good men amongst ourselves into an open
war with the very fundamental principles of civil liberty—criticising the Declaration of Independence, and insisting that there is no right principle of action but
self-interest."

(Lincoln found slavery "monstrous" because, among other things, it represented
the systematic theft of the fruits of hard labor, a kind of institutionalized robbery. In
1860, Lincoln remarked, "I always thought that the man who made the corn should
eat the corn."[113] Thirteen years earlier, when first introduced to Ward Hill Lamon, he
teased the younger man, a native of Virginia, about white Southerners' aversion to hard
work. When Lamon protested, Lincoln sarcastically replied, "Oh, yes; you Virginians

shed barrels of perspiration while standing off at a distance and superintending the work your slaves do for you. It is different with us. Here it is every fellow for himself, or he doesn't get there."[114] For the rest of his life, Lincoln was to stress this theme again and again, most memorably in his second inaugural address.)

Lincoln then balanced his repeated use of the word *hate* with a conciliatory gesture toward slaveholders. "I think I have no prejudice against the Southern people," he said. "They are just what we would be in their situation. If slavery did not now exist amongst them, they would not introduce it. If it did now exist amongst us, we should not instantly give it up." He acknowledged that "some southern men do free their slaves, go north, and become tip-top abolitionists; while some northern ones go south, and become most cruel slave-masters." Whenever Southerners assert that "they are no more responsible for the origin of slavery, than we; I acknowledge that fact. When it is said that the institution exists; and that it is very difficult to get rid of it, in any satisfactory way, I can understand and appreciate the saying."

Lincoln confessed that he saw no easy solution to the problem of slavery. "If all earthly power were given me, I should not know what to do, as to the existing institution." His "first impulse would be to free all the slaves, and send them to Liberia,—to their own native land." Yet that was impractical: "whatever of high hope, (as I think there is) there may be in this, in the long run, its sudden execution is impossible." Should all such slaves "landed there in a day, they would all perish in the next ten days." Moreover, "there are not surplus shipping and surplus money enough in the world to carry them there in many times ten days."

If colonization was not feasible, what alternatives remained? "Free them all, and keep them among us as underlings?" It was not clear "that this betters their condition." Still, Lincoln said, "I think I would not hold one in slavery." What else could be done? "Free them, and make them politically and socially, our equals?" Lincoln confessed that "[m]y own feelings will not admit of this; and if mine would, we well know that those of the great mass of white people will not." In a democracy, he added, a "universal feeling, whether well or ill-founded, can not be safely disregarded. We can not, then, make them equals." Here he did not say that blacks *were not* the equals of whites; rather he implied that while they might be equal to whites in many respects, white prejudice would prevent blacks from being *made* equals, that is to say, given equal rights by a government responsive to the wishes of the overwhelmingly white electorate.

In dealing with the controversial Fugitive Slave Act of 1850, which outraged many Northerners, Lincoln conceded that when white Southerners "remind us of their constitutional rights, I acknowledge them, not grudgingly, but fully, and fairly; and I would give them any legislation for the reclaiming of their fugitives, which should not, in its stringency, be more likely to carry a free man into slavery, than our ordinary criminal laws are to hang an innocent one."

(While publicly supporting the Fugitive Slave Act, Lincoln privately denounced it as "very obnoxious" and exclaimed that it was "ungodly! no doubt it is ungodly!"[115] A conductor on the underground railroad told a fellow abolitionist that Lincoln "was often a contributor to the funds needed for the protection of the fugitives."[116] In 1843,

Luther Ransom, a prominent Springfield abolitionist, reportedly said that Lincoln "always helps me when I call upon him for a man that is arrested as a runaway."[117] In 1855, Lincoln told his best friend, Joshua Speed, while discussing captured runaway slaves: "I hate to see the poor creatures hunted down, and caught, and carried back to their stripes, and unrewarded toils."[118] Five years later, when a leading abolitionist was jailed for resisting the Fugitive Slave Act, Lincoln recommended that the Republican Party pay his fines. As a lawyer, Lincoln avoided cases dealing with runaways because he was unwilling "to be a party to a violation of the Fugitive Slave Law, arguing that the way to overcome the difficulty was to repeal the law."[119] In 1857, Lincoln responded positively to the appeal of a free black woman whose son faced enslavement in New Orleans. The incautious young man had worked on a steamboat and was seized in the Crescent City because he lacked free papers. Lincoln asked his old friend Alexander P. Field, then practicing law in New Orleans, to represent the accused, a native of Springfield, and offered to pay all costs. With William Herndon, he also called on Illinois Governor William Bissell, who alleged that he had no power to help rescue the unfortunate fellow. According to Herndon, Lincoln "exclaimed with some emphasis: 'By God, Governor, I'll make the ground in this country too hot for the foot of a slave, whether you have the legal power to secure the release of this boy or not.'"[120] Thwarted at first by technical complications, Lincoln eventually raised money to procure the young man's freedom. As president, he similarly tried to cut through red tape to save a young slave by offering to pay the owner up to $500 for his freedom.)

After conceding that the Fugitive Slave Act should be faithfully enforced, Lincoln insisted that "all this, to my judgment, furnishes no more excuse for permitting slavery to go into our own free territory, than it would for reviving the African slave trade by law." To Lincoln's mind, the statute "which forbids the bringing of slaves *from* Africa; and that which has so long forbid[den] the taking [of] them *to* Nebraska, can hardly be distinguished on any moral principle."

Lincoln indignantly rejected Douglas's justifications for repealing the Missouri Compromise, dismissing as an "absurdity" the contention that votes for the Wilmot Proviso showed that the Missouri Compromise had been abandoned in principle by supporters of that measure. Neither did the Compromise of 1850 vitiate the Missouri Compromise, for the former "had no more direct reference to Nebraska than it had to the territories of the moon." Douglas's contention that the original Nebraska bill, which he introduced on January 4 and which contained no reference to the Missouri Compromise, was no different from the revised version he submitted several days later, which repealed the Missouri Compromise, prompted a scornful response from Lincoln: "It is as if one should argue than white and black are not different." It was therefore obvious, Lincoln concluded, that "the public never demanded the repeal of the Missouri compromise."

More importantly, the abrogation of the Missouri Compromise was "manifestly unjust." The South and North had each made concessions in 1820; now the South wanted to renege on its end of the bargain while enjoying the benefits of the North's concession. To illustrate this point, Lincoln employed one of his favorite images, a man unfairly taking food from another man who deserved it: "It is as if two starving men had divided their only loaf; the one had hastily swallowed his half, and then grabbed the other half just as he was putting it to his mouth!"

Lincoln dismissed as an "inferior matter," a "palliation," and a "*lullaby*" the contention of Douglas and many others that slavery would never spread into Kansas and Nebraska even if popular sovereignty were applied there. Lincoln pointed out that over 860,000 slaves—fully 25 percent of the nation's unfree population—lived north of the Missouri Compromise line (in Delaware, Maryland, Missouri, Virginia, Kentucky, and the District of Columbia). Moreover, in western Missouri, abutting Kansas, slavery flourished. The best way to keep Kansas free was to prevent the peculiar institution from entering it in the first place. By allowing slaves to be brought into that territory as soon as it was thrown open to settlement, Douglas guaranteed that slavery would fasten itself on Kansas in perpetuity. "To get slaves into the country simultaneously with the whites, in the incipient stages of settlement, is the precise stake played for, and won in this Nebraska measure," Lincoln maintained. Slavery never sank deep roots in Illinois, he said, because the Northwest Ordinance of 1787 had specifically banned the peculiar institution there. But neighboring Missouri, having no such ban, became a slave state.

If Kansas and Nebraska were thrown open to slavery, it would encourage the outlawed African slave trade by increasing the demand for slaves, Lincoln predicted. Thus Douglas's bill "does, in fact, make slaves of freemen by causing them to be brought from Africa, and sold into bondage." That argument was somewhat strained.

More solid was Lincoln's fundamental point, which distinguished his position from Douglas's: that blacks were fully human and thus entitled to certain basic rights. The popular sovereignty doctrine—resting on the assumption that if settlers in Kansas and Nebraska were allowed to take their swine with them, they should also be allowed to take their slaves—was, Lincoln contended, "perfectly logical" only "if there is no difference between hogs and negroes." Lincoln flatly refused "to deny the humanity of the negro" and argued that white Southerners showed by their actions, if not their words, that they agreed with him. In both the North and the South there lived few "natural tyrants," he said; most people in both sections "have human sympathies" that made them hostile to slavery. White Southerners revealed their own anti-slavery feelings in many ways. In 1820, Southern senators and Representatives joined with Northerners to declare African slave traders pirates subject to the death penalty. Addressing the citizens of the South, Lincoln asked: "Why did you do this? If you did not feel that it was wrong, why did you join in providing that men should be hung for it? The practice was no more than bringing wild negroes from Africa, to sell to such as would buy them. But you never thought of hanging men for catching and selling wild horses, wild buffaloes or wild bears." Why did respectable white Southerners "utterly despise" slave dealers, refusing to socialize with them, befriend them, or even touch them, Lincoln asked. "You do not so treat the man who deals in corn, cattle or tobacco." The existence in the United States of more than 430,000 free blacks, worth more than $200 million if enslaved, further showed that white Southerners realized that slaves were human beings, not mere chattel. "How comes this vast amount of property to be running about without owners?" The freedmen were slaves liberated by their masters or descendants of slaves who had been so liberated. What induced their owners to free them? "In all these cases," Lincoln concluded, "it is your sense of justice, and human sympathy, continually telling you, that the poor negro has some natural right to himself—that those who deny it, and make mere merchandise of him, deserve kickings, contempt and death." Rhetorically, he queried white Southerners: "why will you ask us to deny the humanity of the slave? and estimate him only as the equal of the hog? Why ask us to do what you will not do yourselves?" They were good questions.

If blacks were human and not chattel, then Douglas's argument that the Missouri Compromise violated "the sacred right of self government" was false. Lincoln agreed with the Little Giant's basic premise: "The doctrine of self government is right—absolutely and eternally right," but whether that doctrine was relevant in the current debate over Kansas and Nebraska depended "upon whether a negro is *not* or *is* a man. If he is *not* a man, why in that case, he who *is* a man may, as a matter of self-government, do just as he pleases with him. But if the negro *is* a man, is it not to that extent, a total destruction of self-government, to say that he too shall not govern *himself*?" Like an Old Testament prophet, Lincoln declared: "When the white man governs himself that is self-government; but when he governs himself, and also governs *another* man, that is *more* than self-government—that is despotism. If the negro is a *man*, why then my ancient faith teaches me that 'all men are created equal;' and that there can be no moral right in connection with one man's making a slave of another." To Douglas's contemptuous assertion that antislavery forces argued that the "white people of Nebraska are good enough to govern themselves, *but they are not good enough to govern a few miserable negroes*,"[121] Lincoln replied: "no man is good enough to govern another man, *without that other's consent*. I say this is the leading principle—the sheet anchor of American republicanism." After quoting the Declaration of Independence, Lincoln called the relationship between master and slave a "total violation" of its central principle: "The master not only governs the slave without his consent; but he governs him by a set of rules altogether different from those which he prescribes for himself. Allow ALL the governed an equal voice in the government, and that, and that only is self-government."

Lincoln explained that he was not advocating equal political rights for blacks, but rather was "combating what is set up as [a] MORAL argument" for permitting slaves "to be taken where they have never yet been—arguing against the EXTENSION of a bad thing, which where it already exists, we must of necessity, manage as best we can."

Douglas was wrong, said Lincoln, in asserting that the extension of slavery into Kansas and Nebraska concerned only settlers in those territories: "The whole nation is interested that the best use shall be made of these territories. We want them for the homes of free white people. This they cannot be, to any considerable extent, if slavery shall be planted within them." Here Lincoln was not making the argument espoused by some Free Soilers, that they wanted slavery kept out of the territories because they disliked blacks and had no desire to live near them. Instead, Lincoln emphasized something that his own family had acted on four decades earlier: "Slave States are places for poor white people to remove FROM; not to remove TO. New free States are the places for poor people to go to and better their condition." Lincoln objected not to the presence of blacks but to the presence of slaveowners and their hierarchical social system.

(In asserting that Republicans wanted the territories to become "homes of free white people," Lincoln was adopting what the Chicago *Tribune* called "a narrow method" for attacking slavery. It was necessary to appeal to white self-interest because, said the *Tribune*, "it is far easier to convince the multitude that Slavery is a baleful evil to them than to possess them with the idea that it is a cruel wrong to the enslaved. . . . [S]o inveterate are the prejudices of color; so deep rooted . . . is the conviction that the African is a being of an inferior order; so intolerant is the Caucasian of African assertion of equality; so low, under the depressing influence of 'the institution,' has the national morality descended, that this method, narrow and incomplete as it is, holds out the only promise of success.")[122]

Northern whites also had a stake in the outcome of the debate over slavery expansion, Lincoln averred, because of "constitutional relations between the slave and free States, which are degrading to the latter." Free State residents did not wish to help catch runaway slaves, as the Fugitive Slave Act of 1850 mandated. It was, Lincoln said, "a sort of dirty, disagreeable job, which I believe, as a general rule the slave-holders will not perform for one another." Northern whites also did not want more Slave States because the Constitution's three-fifths clause permitted those states to have representation of their unfree population in the U.S. House and in the electoral college. Offering an argument which had been made repeatedly since 1789, Lincoln protested that it was grossly unfair for South Carolina, where 274,567 whites lived, to have the same number of Representatives in Congress as Maine, with a white population of over 580,000. The three-fifths rule, Lincoln calculated, gave the Slave States twenty more Representatives in the House and votes in the electoral college than they would have had in the absence of such a rule. Without those extra congressmen, the Kansas-Nebraska Act, which passed the House by a seven-vote margin, might never have been adopted.

Lincoln pledged to obey the Constitution's fugitive slave clause and three-fifths rule "fairly, fully, and firmly," but he balked at letting the settlers of Kansas and Nebraska—"a mere handful of men, bent only on temporary self-interest"—decide whether the nation should add more Slave States: "when I am told I must leave it altogether to OTHER PEOPLE to say whether new partners are to be bred up and brought into the firm, on the same degrading terms against me, I respectfully demur." Lincoln insisted "that whether I shall be a whole man, or only, the half of one, in comparison with others, is a question in which I am somewhat concerned; and one which no other man can have a sacred right of deciding for me." Scornfully he dismissed "this mighty argument, of self government. Go, sacred thing! Go in peace."

To those claiming that opposition to the Kansas-Nebraska Act posed a threat to the Union, Lincoln forcefully replied that it was Douglas and his supporters who imperiled national unity by needlessly reviving the slavery controversy, which had been defused by the Compromise of 1850. "It could not but be expected by its author, that it would be looked upon as a measure for the extension of slavery, aggravated by a gross breach of faith." Speaking again with the moral passion of a biblical prophet like Amos or Hosea, Lincoln declared that "Slavery is founded in the selfishness of man's nature—opposition to it, in his love of justice. These principles are an eternal antagonism; and when brought into collision so fiercely, as slavery extension brings them, shocks, and throes, and convulsions must ceaselessly follow." Supporters of slavery might repeal the Missouri Compromise, the Declaration of Independence, and "all past history," but "you still can not repeal human nature." Paraphrasing Jesus, he said: "It still will be the abundance of man's heart, that slavery extension is wrong; and out of the abundance of his heart, his mouth will continue to speak." Lincoln agreed that the Union was indeed worth preserving: "Much as I hate slavery, I would consent to the extension of it rather than see the Union dissolved, just as I would consent to any GREAT evil, to avoid a GREATER one." (By 1861, he would change his mind on this question.) But the Kansas-Nebraska Act did endanger the Union, he insisted; quoting *Hamlet,* he added that it "hath no relish of salvation in it."

Lincoln pointed out a basic flaw in the popular sovereignty argument: its failure to specify at what point in the development of a territory its settlers could forbid slavery. "Is it to be decided by the first dozen settlers who arrive there? or is it to await the arrival of a hundred?" And just who would be empowered to take action against the peculiar institution; was it the territorial legislature, or the people in a referendum?

To those Whigs who opposed the Kansas-Nebraska Act but who hesitated to demand the restoration of the Missouri Compromise lest they be seen as pro-abolitionist, Lincoln counseled: "Stand with anybody that stands RIGHT. Stand with him while he is right and PART with him when he goes wrong. Stand WITH the abolitionist in restoring the Missouri Compromise; and stand AGAINST him when he attempts to repeal the fugitive slave law. In the latter case you stand with the southern disunionist. What of that? you are still right. In both cases you oppose the dangerous extremes." That, he said, "is good old whig ground. To desert such ground, because of any company, is to be less than a whig—less than a man—less than an American."

Scouting Douglas's attempt to enlist the Founding Fathers as supporters of popular sovereignty, Lincoln quite rightly pointed out that the "argument of 'Necessity' was the only argument they ever admitted in favor of slavery; and so far, and so far only as it carried them, did they ever go. They found the institution existing among us, which they could not help; and they cast blame upon the British King for having permitted its introduction." In 1787, they forbade slavery from expanding from the original states into the Old Northwest. In writing the Constitution, "they forbore to so much as mention the word 'slave,' or 'slavery,' in the whole instrument." So "the thing is hid away, in the constitution, just as an afflicted man hides away a wen or a cancer, which he dares not cut out at once, lest he bleed to death; with the promise, nevertheless, that the cutting may begin at the end of a given time." The early Congresses followed suit, prohibiting the exportation of slaves in 1794; outlawing the importation of slaves into the Mississippi Territory in 1798; forbidding U.S. citizens from participation in the slave trade between foreign countries in 1800; restraining the internal slave trade in 1803; banning the importation of slaves in 1807; and declaring the African slave trade to be piracy in 1820. So the Founders showed "hostility to the PRINCIPLE" of slavery "and toleration, ONLY BY NECESSITY."

But, Lincoln argued, Douglas was forsaking the Founding Fathers by placing slavery "on the high road to extension and perpetuity; and, with a pat on its back, says to it, 'Go, and God speed you.'" Warming to his task, Lincoln deplored this betrayal of the Framers' vision: "Near eighty years ago we began by declaring that all men are created equal; but now from that beginning we have run down to the other declaration, that for SOME men to enslave OTHERS is a 'sacred right of self-government.' These principles can not stand together. They are as opposite as God and mammon." He was especially incensed at Indiana Senator John Pettit who, in supporting the Kansas-Nebraska bill, referred to the Declaration of Independence as "a self-evident lie." None of his colleagues in the Douglas camp rebuked Pettit for that statement. Passionately, Lincoln remarked that if such words had been spoken "to the men who captured Andre, the man who said it, would probably have been hung sooner than Andre was. If it had been said in old Independence Hall, seventy-eight years ago, the very door-keeper would have throttled the man, and thrust him into the street." ("The applause that followed was continued for some minutes.")[123] The new cynicism about the Declaration was "a sad evidence that, feeling prosperity we forget [about] right—that liberty, as a principle, we have ceased to revere."

In his heartfelt peroration, Lincoln urged North and South alike to reconsider their views: "In our greedy chase to make profit of the negro, let us beware, lest we 'cancel and tear to pieces' even the white man's charter of freedom. Our republican robe is soiled, and trailed in the dust. Let us repurify it. Let us turn and wash it white, in the spirit, if not the blood, of the Revolution. Let us turn slavery from its claims of 'moral right,' back upon its existing legal rights, and its arguments of 'necessity.' Let us return it to the position our fathers gave it; and there let it rest in peace. Let us re-adopt the Declaration of Independence, and with it, the practices, and policy, which harmonize with it. Let north and south—let all Americans—let all lovers of liberty everywhere—join in the great and good work. If we do this, we shall not only have saved the union; but we shall have so saved it, as to make, and to keep it, forever worthy of the saving; we shall have so saved it, that the succeeding millions of free happy people, the world over, shall rise up, and call us blessed, to the latest generations."[124]

This statesmanlike speech, delivered with the utmost conviction, "attracted a more marked attention," Lincoln observed, than had his earlier addresses and was published in the *Illinois State Journal*.[125] Significantly, Lincoln devoted little attention to nativism, temperance, or any issue other than slavery. The Springfield *Register* thought it noteworthy that "Lincoln spoke of Judge Douglas in a less denunciatory manner than is the custom on such occasions."[126] He had come a long way since the 1830s and 1840s, when he heaped ridicule on James Adams, Dick Quinton, George Forquer, James Shields, Peter Cartwright, Lewis Cass, James K. Polk, Dick Taylor, Jesse B. Thomas, and other Democrats.

Horace White recalled the occasion in Springfield vividly: "It was a warmish day in early October, and Mr. Lincoln was in his shirt sleeves when he stepped on the platform." Although "awkward, he was not in the least embarrassed," starting off in a "slow and hesitating manner, but without any mistakes of language, dates, or facts." It became immediately clear that "he had mastered his subject, that he knew what he was going to say, and that he knew he was right." Lincoln's "thin, high-pitched falsetto voice of much carrying power . . . could be heard a long distance in spite of the bustle and tumult of the crowd." Betraying his backwoods upbringing, Lincoln spoke with "the accent and pronunciation peculiar to his native State, Kentucky." In time, as "he warmed up with his subject, his angularity disappeared," and he took on an air "of unconscious majesty." While progressing through his three-hour oration, "his words began to come faster and his face to light up with the rays of genius and his body to move in unison with his thoughts." Lincoln's gestures, "made with his body and head rather than with his arms," were "the natural expression of the man, and so perfectly adapted to what he was saying that anything different from it would have been quite inconceivable." He presented "not a graceful figure, yet not an ungraceful one": a "tall, angular form with the long, angular arms, at times bent nearly double with excitement, like a large flail animating two smaller ones, the mobile face wet with perspiration which he discharged in drops as he threw his head this way and that like a projectile." Now and then "his manner was very impassioned, and he seemed transfigured with his subject." Sweat "would stream from his face, and each particular hair would stand on end." At that point "the inspiration that possessed him took possession of his hearers also. His speaking went to the heart because it came from the heart." The crowd "felt that he believed every word he said, and that, like Martin Luther, he would go to the stake rather than abate one jot or tittle of it." At "such transfigured moments as these," when his words resembled "electrical discharges of high tension," Lincoln seemed to White like an "ancient Hebrew prophet."[127]

In his dispatch to the Chicago *Journal*, White described Lincoln as "a mammoth" who "had this day delivered a speech, the greatest ever listened to in the state of Illinois, unless himself has made a greater." Douglas "never in his life received so terrible a back fall. For vigor of thought, strength of expression, comprehensiveness of scope, keenness of argument—extent of research, and candor of presentation, the speech of Mr. Lincoln has rarely been equaled in the annals of American eloquence."[128] White considered Lincoln's address "one of the world's masterpieces of argumentative power and moral grandeur, which left Douglas's edifice of 'Popular Sovereignty' a heap of ruins."[129]

Herndon agreed, calling Lincoln's speech "the profoundest, in our opinion, that he has made in his whole life." Lincoln, according to Herndon, "quivered with emotion" as he "attacked the Nebraska bill with unusual warmth and energy" as well as "scorn and mockery." He "felt upon his soul the truths burn which he uttered," and the audience, "as still as death," sensed "that he was true to his own soul" and "approved the glorious triumph of truth by loud and continued huzzahs. Women waved their white handkerchiefs in token of woman's silent but heartfelt assent." At certain passages his feelings "swelled within and came near stifling utterance," most notably "when he said that the Declaration of Independence taught us that 'all men are born free and equal'—that by the laws of nature and nature's God, 'all were free'—that the Nebraska law chained men, free and equal, and 'that there was as much difference between the glorious truths of the immortal Declaration of Independence and the Nebraska bill, as there was between God and Mammon.' These are his own words. They were spoken with emphasis, feeling, and true eloquence,—eloquent, because true, and because he felt, and felt deeply, what he said."[130]

Immediately after Lincoln finished, Douglas "took the stand actually quivering," complained that "he had been grossly assailed though in a perfectly courteous manner," that Lincoln had handled him "without mercy or gloves," and argued that Lincoln and other critics aimed "to agitate until the people of the South would, from fear of their slaves, set them free."[131]

Democrats attacked the speech for alleging that "the white man had no right to pass laws for the government of the black man without the nigger's consent." The Springfield *Register* sneered at it as an act of lèse-majesté: "Endowed by heaven with a talent to hoodwink the blind, and with a facility of speech well calculated to deceive the ignorant, he vainly imagines himself a *great man*, and as such, endeavored to cope with such men."[132]

The Springfield-Peoria address greatly enhanced Lincoln's stature in Illinois. "Hitherto he had been appreciated chiefly in his own Congressional District," as one Douglas adherent put it. But at the capital, "men of influence from every county of the State, substantial men and politicians, who had gathered together at the holding of the Fair, had heard him. On that day he opened the outer gate of the path that he followed to the Presidency."[133]

This oratorical masterpiece was, as Ward Hill Lamon's ghost-written biography of Lincoln maintained, "almost perfectly adapted to produce conviction upon a doubting mind. It ought to be carefully read by every one who desires to know Mr. Lincoln's power as a debater, after his intellect was matured and ripened by years of hard experience."[134] It contained the seeds of his later powerful arguments against slavery.

After Lincoln finished his memorable address in Springfield, two dozen of the state's most militant opponents of slavery met at the capitol, praised the speech, and formed what they styled the Republican Party of Illinois. Although Lincoln did not attend that conclave, the delegates elected him to the party's twelve-member state central committee, an act that Democrats cited as proof positive of Lincoln's radical abolitionism.

On October 16, Lincoln delivered substantially the same speech in Peoria that he had given at Springfield, adding a response to Douglas's most recent criticism of the October 4 address. Lincoln began by saying he "could appreciate an argument, and, at times, believed he could make one, but when one denied the settled and plainest facts of history, you could not argue with him; the only thing you could do would be to stop his mouth with a corn cob."[135] In fact, Douglas had made some egregious historical errors, asserting that Illinois had been admitted to the Union as a Slave State and that the Constitution had mandated the end of the African slave trade. But Lincoln was more concerned with Douglas's moral arguments than his factual errors. The senator had maintained that the U.S. government was made by white men for white men. Lincoln thought this comment showed "that the Judge has no very vivid impression that the negro is a human; and consequently has no idea that there can be any moral question in legislating about him." In Douglas's opinion, Lincoln continued, "the question of whether a new country shall be slave or free, is a matter of as utter indifference, as it is whether his neighbor shall plant his farm with tobacco, or stock it with horned cattle." Lincoln objected that "whether this view is right or wrong, it is very certain that the great mass of mankind take a totally different view." By 1854, most people around the world had come to "consider slavery a great moral wrong; and their feelings against it, is not evanescent, but eternal. It lies at the very foundation of their sense of justice; and it cannot be trifled with. It is a great and durable element of popular action, and, I think, no statesman can safely disregard it."[136]

A Democratic newspaper in Peoria attacked Lincoln for virtually sanctioning miscegenation. In arguing "that no people were good enough to legislate for another people without that other's consent; or in other words:—the people of Nebraska are not competent to legislate for the negro without the negro's consent," Lincoln had denied the legitimacy of Illinois's constitutional provision forbidding whites and blacks to marry. After all, the paper asserted, that prohibition was made "without consulting the feelings of the negroes." So if Lincoln is correct, "our laws 'with adequate penalties, preventing the intermarriage of whites with blacks' and that 'no colored person shall ever, under any pretext, be allowed to hold any office of honor or profit in this state,' ARE ALL WRONG, because each of these provisions have been adopted without the consent of the negro."[137]

The Peoria *Republican* took a more favorable view of "Lincoln's truly able and masterly speech." The editors said they had "never heard the subjects treated of so eloquently handled, nor have we often seen a speaker acquit himself with greater apparent ease and self-possession."[138]

After replying to Douglas at Springfield and Peoria, Lincoln planned to continue the pattern, starting at Lacon on October 17. The senator, however, had become hoarse and canceled his Lacon appointment. Lincoln, not wishing to take advantage of his rival's indisposition, also called off his appearance there. Douglas recovered sufficiently to speak in Princeton on October 18 but the following day temporarily retired from the campaign trail to recruit his health; before election day he managed to give a few mores speeches. Meanwhile, Lincoln fulfilled engagements in Urbana, Chicago, and Quincy.

Lincoln was, according to Herndon, "thoroughly displeased" by Douglas's appearance at Princeton two days after he declined to renew their debate at Lacon because he was allegedly too unwell. Understandably, this action tended to confirm Lincoln's belief that Douglas lacked political scruples. Four years later, Lincoln would have much more evidence of Douglas's unethical nature.[139]

As Lincoln was leaving Urbana in an ancient omnibus, a new friend, the young attorney Henry C. Whitney, criticized him for making the "most execrable music" on a harmonica. He replied: "This is my band; Douglas had a brass band with him in Peoria, but this will do me." Whitney recalled that Lincoln's "attire and physical habits were on a plane with those of an ordinary farmer." His hat lacked any nap, his coat seemed ten years old, his boots were unshined, his valise "was well worn and dilapidated," and his umbrella "was substantial, but of a faded green, well worn, the knob gone, and the name 'A. Lincoln' cut out of white muslin, and sewed in the inside."[140]

Senate Bid

In November, Democrats lost badly throughout the Free States, including Illinois. "Never before have the democracy of Illinois been so completely vanquished," observed the Joliet *Signal*.[141] Opponents of the Kansas-Nebraska Act dominated both the legislature and the congressional delegation, gratifying antislavery journals like the New York *Tribune*, which deemed the election a referendum on Douglas: "No Senator of the United States ever before received such a withering repudiation."[142] Douglas's Illinois colleague in the senate, James Shields, ascribed the defeat in their state to the Little Giant's dictatorial insistence that all Democratic candidates support the unpopular Kansas-Nebraska Act. Many voters, Shields reported, thought that Douglas had become the tool of Missouri Senator David Rice Atchison, who wanted Kansas, located on Missouri's western border, to become a Slave State. Democrat John M. Palmer deeply resented the high-handed tactics of the Little Giant, whom he called "this miniature negro driver, this small sample of a Carolina overseer who speaks to us as if we were slaves."[143]

Despite the Democrats' poor showing, Yates lost his bid for reelection, largely because he was labeled a Know-Nothing. The foreign-born overwhelmingly supported his opponent, Thomas L. Harris. Those same voters had already been alienated by the temperance crusade conducted in part by Whigs. Ironically, Yates was also hurt by rumors that he was a drunkard. In September, Lincoln reported that the congressman's "enemies are getting up a charge against him, that while he passes for a temperate man, he is in the habit of drinking secretly," a charge which Lincoln dismissed even though, as it turned out, Yates did in fact have a drinking problem.[144] (Half a dozen delegates reported that Yates was drunk at the 1860 convention which nominated him for governor.) Democrats denounced Yates as a friend to blacks. As the Springfield *Register* said, "those who are in favor of repealing all laws making distinctions between whites and blacks, and are willing to let the negroes vote, sit on juries and give evidence in court against the white man, and that whites and blacks marry indiscriminately, just let them vote for Mr. Yates." Illinois Democrats had concentrated their utmost efforts on defeating Yates. Douglas had issued orders to "beat the d[amne]d little pup." In October it was reported that "the Douglasites would willingly lose every other of the nine Districts to see Thomas L. Harris elected."[145] The Democratic legislature had recently redrawn Yates's district, lopping off northern counties where Whigs predominated and adding southern counties with more Democratic voters. Yates was further damaged by his failure to deliver on all his patronage promises.

If Yates bemoaned his defeat, Lincoln regretted his own victory in the legislative contest, for, as he soon learned, it rendered him ineligible for the U.S. senate seat that he hoped to gain when the newly elected General Assembly, with a slim majority of anti-Nebraska members, convened in January.

It is uncertain just when the prospect of the senatorship first tickled Lincoln's ambition, but as election day approached, it seemed clear that he might attain such a high office. On September 27, he wrote to George Gage, a candidate for the General Assembly, about the senatorship. Gage replied: "I have strong hopes we shall elect a Senator the ensueing session & that you will succede[.] Rest assured you have my best wishes[.] I shall try and render you all the assistance I can."[146] Around this time Lincoln read aloud to Henry C. Whitney passages from Byron's "Childe Harold," reciting the following canto "earnestly, if not, indeed, reverently":

> He who ascends to mountain tops, shall find
> Those loftiest peaks most wrapt in clouds and snow;
> He who surpasses or subdues mankind
> Must look down on the hate of those below;
> Though high above the sun of glory glow,
> And far beneath the Earth and Ocean spread,
> Round him are icy rocks, and loudly blow
> Contending tempests on his naked head,
> And thus reward the toils which to those summits led.

Whitney believed that Lincoln had "a premonition that he was destined to ascend to the mountain tops of human achievement."[147] In political terms, that mountain top was a U.S. senate seat. In 1859, he told Norman B. Judd: "I would rather have a full term in the Senate than in the Presidency."[148] A year later, Lincoln said: "I would rather have a full term in the Senate—a place in which I would feel more consciously able to discharge the duties required, and where there was more chance to make [a] reputation, and less danger of losing it—than four years in the Presidency."[149]

Invitations to speak outside his congressional district may have stoked Lincoln's senatorial ambition. Horace White, urging Lincoln to campaign in Chicago, told him: "the Whigs are bound to elect a U.S. Senator in place of [James] Shields. Chicago has five votes in the Legislature and influences a great many more in Northern Illinois. Part of our Representatives in the next Assembly will be Whigs, part Free-Soilers & part Anti-Nebraska Democrats. These Democrats might bolt at the nomination of a Whig for the Senate. . . . The idea is to have you go to Chicago and make a speech. You will have a crowd of from Eight to ten or fifteen thousand and the result will be that the people will demand of their Representatives to elect a Whig Senator. What might be doubtful otherwise will thus be rendered certain."[150]

At the same time, Richard L. Wilson, editor of the Chicago *Journal*, told Lincoln that "the defeat of *Shields* is certain."[151] Neither Wilson nor White specifically alluded to Lincoln's own candidacy, but William H. Randolph of Macomb did. In his appeal for Lincoln to stump in western Illinois, Randolph said: "Your name is also spoke[n] of as a candidate for U S Senator[.] Can we not reasonably hope to elect a thorough anti Nebraska Legislature[?] If so we hope for your election to that place[.]"[152] Abraham Jonas of Quincy, imploring Lincoln to canvass his locale, dropped a hint that he might thereby win support for a senate bid: "I trust you may be able to pay us the visit and thereby create a debt of gratitude on the part of the Whigs here, which they may at some time, have it in their power, to repay with pleasure and with interest."[153]

Lincoln, Herndon recalled, was "ambitious to reach the United States Senate, and warmly encouraged in his aspirations by his wife," campaigned for the post with "his characteristic activity and vigilance. During the anxious moments that intervened between the general election [in November] and the assembling of the Legislature [in January] he slept, like Napoleon, with one eye open."[154] And he kept relentlessly busy pursuing the goal.

Three days after the November election, Lincoln began writing a torrent of letters asking support for his senate bid. On November 10 he appealed to Charles Hoyt of Aurora: "You used to express a good deal of partiality for me; and if you are still so, now is the time. Some friends here are really for me, for the U.S. Senate; and I should be very grateful if you could make a mark for me among your members."[155] That same day he told Jonathan Y. Scammon of Chicago that some "partial friends here are for me for the U.S. Senate; and it would be very foolish, and very false, for me to deny that I would be pleased with an election to that Honorable body. If you know nothing, and feel nothing to the contrary, please make a mark for me with the members."[156] The following day he asked Jacob Harding of Paris to visit his legislator and "make a mark with him for me," for "I really have some chance."[157] Later that month he appealed to Thomas J. Henderson of Toulon: "It has come round that a whig may, by possibility, be elected to the U.S. Senate; and I want the chance of being the man. You are a member of the Legislature, and have a vote to give. Think it over, and see whether you can do better than to go for me."[158] The following month he told Joseph Gillespie that "I have really got it into my head to try to be United States Senator; and if I could have your support my chances would be reasonably good."[159]

In late November, belatedly realizing that his status as a member-elect of the General Assembly might render him ineligible for the senate, Lincoln formally declined election as a state Representative. Although this step helped pave the way for his elevation to the senate, it was risky, for anti-Nebraska forces enjoyed only a slim majority in the legislature and were divided by old party animosities. In the special election called to replace Lincoln, the Democratic candidate, Jonathan McDaniel, surprisingly defeated Republican Norman Broadwell. McDaniel's supporters conducted a "still hunt," eschewing an overt campaign and waiting on election day to vote until the last minute. This tactic lulled the Whigs into complacency. Although Yates had received 2,166 votes the previous month in Sangamon County, Broadwell won only 984. Lincoln had paid little attention to the Broadwell-McDaniel contest, in part perhaps because Broadwell favored Yates for the senate. Shields gloated over the unexpected result, telling Charles Lanphier, editor of the Springfield *Register*: "Nobly done. You are a glorious set of Democrats. You turned the tables upon the Whigs. They made a maneuver to crush us, and were blown up by a mine while making the maneuver. This is the best Christmas joke of the season."[160] Lincoln offered that same journalist a different gloss on the election: "It reminds me of Montecue Morris, a private in Baker's regiment in the Mexican War. Some of the soldiers had purchased a barrel of cider and were retailing it, at good profit, for twenty cents a glass. Montecue, whose tent was backed up to the cider barrel tent, tapped the other end of the barrel, through his tent, and began retailing the cider at ten cents a glass. He sold considerable before he was detected. That's the way we were served by the American vote and, while it's funny, it hurts."[161]

It hurt more than Lincoln may at first have realized. The anti-Nebraska forces in the legislature were understandably angry at Lincoln and other Sangamon County Whigs for losing that seat. David Davis told Lincoln that voters would say "Damn Springfield—the Whigs have behaved so shamefully, that they ought to be punished & Lincoln should not be elected."[162] The Aurora *Guardian* objected to Lincoln's resignation from the legislature: "This fact, together with his over-weaning anxiety to obtain the place, will stand, and *ought to do*, against him seriously."[163] The *Rock River Democrat* concurred, saying that Lincoln "overreached himself that time, and may do so again before a Senator is chosen."[164]

Broadwell's defeat especially disenchanted the abolitionists. On December 29, an antislavery editor reported from Springfield that "I find here a strong feeling against Lincoln among those who should properly be his friends. . . . The election of that Nebraska man in the county of Sangamon to fill the vacancy occasioned by Abe's resignation has done more than any thing else to damage him with the Abolitionists. That has put the seal to their discontent."[165] Lincoln also alienated antislavery Radicals by failing to make common cause with them when they gathered in Springfield to form the Illinois Republican Party. At that meeting, held on October 4 and 5, they elected Lincoln, without his knowledge, to their central committee. (When some delegates objected that Lincoln was too conservative on the slavery issue, the antislavery firebrand Owen Lovejoy vigorously defended him.) The following month Lincoln declined that honor, saying: "I have been perplexed some to understand why my name was placed on that committee. I was not consulted on the subject; nor was I apprized of the appointment, until I discovered it by accident two or three weeks afterwards. I supposed my opposition to the principle of slavery is as strong as that of any member of the Republican party; but I had also supposed that the *extent* to which I feel authorized to carry that opposition, practically, was not at all satisfactory to that party. The leading men who organized that party, were present, on the 4th. of Oct. at the discussion between Douglas and myself at Springfield, and had full oppertunity to not misunderstand my position."[166]

On November 30, Zebina Eastman, an abolitionist from Chicago, declared in his newspaper *The Free West*: "We could not advise the republicans to support for this station [U.S. senator], Lincoln, or any of the moderate men of his stamp. He is only a Whig, and the people's movement is no whig triumph. All of whiggery that survived has been crushed out in the recent Congressional election." Eastman preferred Owen Lovejoy, Ichabod Codding, Richard Yates, and William Bissell to Lincoln.[167] When criticized by the Chicago *Press and Tribune*, Eastman replied: "Our opposition is based upon short comings on the Republican basis. He is reported to be a Compromise Whig, and having a full attachment to that mummy of a party, which has done us no good in this State, but has brought upon us all the calamities and defeats of the Republican movement. He dares not oppose the fugitive slave law—and he would not pledge himself not to go against the admission of any more Slave States. If these cannot be gotten from him, of what service would he be in the Senate, when the Slavery question comes up? The Senator to be elected from this State, must be prepared to vote against the admission of Kansas or Nebraska as Slave States, or else we have only been fighting in the past election over the shell disgorged of the oyster."[168] (A Democratic editor in Joliet sneered at Eastman's attack on Lincoln: "The Free West, . . . having received for the cause of abolition and nigger equality all the aid and comfort from the whigs that it demanded, now turns about and attempts to kick them out of the abolition ranks.")[169] Other antislavery militants favored Yates if an abolitionist like Codding or Lovejoy could not win.

To help combat such opposition, Lincoln enlisted the aid of Congressman Elihu B. Washburne of Galena, a former Whig who had volunteered to do all he could to secure Lincoln's election. The ambitious, obstinate, strong-willed, and belligerent Washburne was a simple, earnest fellow, not intellectually gifted but with a deep streak of common sense. In December, Lincoln told him: "I have not ventured to write all the members [of the legislature] in your district, lest some of them should be offended by the indelicacy of the thing—that is, coming from a total stranger. Could you not drop some of them a line?" As time passed, Lincoln grew ever more concerned about his lack of support in northern Illinois. On December 14 he told Washburne that "there must be something wrong about U.S. Senator, at Chicago. My most intimate friends there do not answer my letters; and I can not get a word from them." He asked the Galena congressman to "pump" John Wentworth, a leading anti-Nebraska Democrat from Chicago, to discover what was amiss.[170]

Washburne jumped in to help, writing not only to legislators but also to Eastman, urging him to reconsider. The abolitionist editor would not yield and retorted that many anti-Nebraska Democrats "have a repugnance at voting for Lincoln," who "did not give entire satisfaction to the Republicans in his speech in Chicago. Did not take high ground enough."[171] Washburne received similar word from Anson Miller of Rockford, who reported that he had "spoken with our Senator and Representatives as to Lincoln for U.S. Senator. They are not committed but one thinks L is not enough Anti Slavery. He wishes him—L—to take the ground of 'no further extension of slavery'—'no more slave territory.' Better write Lincoln and suggest to him the absolute importance of taking high ground in the slavery question. Without this he cannot get the vote of the Northern members."[172]

In response, Washburne implored Eastman, whom he considered "easy to manage," to be flexible and magnanimous: "I feel the greatest interest about the Senator. I am afraid our friends will be so impracticable that we may lose the fruits of our splendid victory. We must be yielding and liberal all round. I mentioned Lincoln, not because he had been a whig, but because he is a man of splendid talents, of great probity of character, and because he threw himself into the late fight on the *republican platform* and made the greatest speech in reply to Douglas ever heard in the State. *I know he is with us in sentiment*, and in such times as these, when we want big men and true men in the Senate, it seems cruel to strike him down. I thought, also he could combine more strength than any other man in the State. He has great personal popularity, and the entire confidence of all men of all parties. In the election for the legislature the whigs, it must be confessed, have been very liberal to the old democrats and free-soilers who came into the republican movement. I hope the same liberal spirit may continue to guide the new party.—I can say to you, that in the event of the success of Lincoln [neither] you, nor your friends will have any cause to complain. He will not only carry out our views fully in the Senate, but he will be with us in our views and feelings."[173]

Eastman bypassed Lincoln and consulted with the more vocally antislavery Herndon, who assured him that his partner was "all right."[174] Herndon later recalled that the "Anti-Slavery men of Chicago—the whole north of this State, knew me early as an abolitionist. Hence trusted me—Sent down a committee to see me and enquired—'Can Mr Lincoln be trusted'?" Herndon responded emphatically: "I pledge you my personal honor that at the proper time he *shall* be with us."[175] Herndon was persuasive. Later, Eastman told him that he had visited Springfield "to learn from some thing nearer than public report, and public life, what were Mr. Lincoln[']s particular feelings and scruples in regard to the colored people of the United States. I wanted to know if he was their friend—if he was their friend, we knew he was a politician that could be trusted. You Satisfied me."[176]

With Eastman in the fold, Lincoln managed to convert another antislavery journalist, Charles Henry Ray, editor of the Galena *Jeffersonian*, who at first opposed his candidacy. In December, Ray told Washburne: "I cannot well go in for Lincoln or any one of his tribe. I have little faith in the strength of their anti-slavery sentiments, and as the slavery question is the only one likely to be discussed for years yet, let us have some one whose opposition to the institution admits of no question." Ray confessed that "I am afraid of 'Abe.' He is Southern by birth, Southern in his associations and Southern, if I mistake not, in his sympathies. I have thought that he would not come squarely up to the mark in a hand to hand fight with Southern influence and dictation. His wife, you know, is a Todd, of a pro-Slavery family, and so are all his kin. My candidate must be like Caesar's wife—not only not suspected, but above suspicion." Ray also hesitated because he did not want to alienate anti-Nebraska Democrats by supporting a Whig. But, he added, "I *do* desire to lend a helping hand to check-mate the rascals who are making our government the convenient tool of the slave power; and if I can best do so by going for Lincoln, why, I am on hand."[177]

Over the next three weeks Ray grew to appreciate Lincoln, in part because of Washburne's lobbying. According to Washburne, Ray "*is in reality for the man who will be of the most service to him.* He looks for an overthrow of the powers that be, and he wants friends in that contingency."[178] In January, the Galena congressman reported to Lincoln that Ray, who had won election as clerk of the Illinois State senate at the beginning of the month, "wants a position in the House next Congress and I am going to write him if you are elected, we will all take hold and help. I think he can do something with some of the Anti-Nebraska Democrats. He also wants the Legislature to do something for him in connection with the census. All these matters can be worked in."[179] (Ray won appointment as a trustee of the Illinois and Michigan Canal at Lincoln's request.) On January 12, Ray confided to Washburne: "I have made up my mind—this is private—that our best course is to go in strong for Lincoln when the day comes, and I shall so advise our friends of the Anti-Nebraska party, and shall labor to that end."[180]

Ray may have been influenced by a talk Lincoln gave on January 4 to the Springfield chapter of the American Colonization Society in which he reviewed the history of the African slave trade and efforts to abolish it. He also introduced resolutions calling for the legislature to instruct the Illinois congressional delegation to restore the Missouri Compromise, to work to prevent the admission of Kansas or Nebraska as slave states, to "use their utmost endeavors to prevent domestic slavery ever being established in any country, or place, where it does not now legally exist," to resist "to their utmost, the now threatened attempt to divide California, in order to erect one portion thereof into a slave-state," and to oppose "the now threatened attempt to revive the African slave-trade."[181]

In addition to Washburne, another U.S. Representative from northern Illinois, Jesse O. Norton of Joliet, helped Lincoln woo legislators from that region. In December, Norton reported to Lincoln from Washington: "I have written to an influential Whig in Oswego (Kendall Co). to have your interests looked to in connexion with their Delegate. I have also written to my friend Strunk of Kankakee. I have also written a kind but pointed letter to Eastman of the Free West. I hope he will see the impropriety of his course." Norton believed "that one of the main things to be done, is to keep down all bickerings in the newspapers, as leading almost certainly to heart burnings & a schism." A month later the congressman urged Lincoln to accommodate antislavery militants: "it seems to me that, you might, by some concessions, such as could be made by you without any sacrifice of principle, bring the whole free soil element to your support. I speak of those who have hitherto been distinctive 'Free Soilers.' Are you bound to stand by *every thing* in the Compromise measures of 1850? Could'nt you concede to them a modification of the Fugitive Slave act? With this & such positions as you can assume in relation to the prohibition of Slavery in the Territories & the admission of additional Slave States, I cannot see why these men cannot unite upon you to a man."[182]

Lincoln took Norton's advice, telling legislators that he would not pledge to vote against the Fugitive Slave Act, but he would vote to strip that law "of its obnoxious features."[183] Lincoln had already publicly declared that any legislation for the return of runaways "should not, in its stringency, be more likely to carry a free man into slavery than our ordinary criminal laws are to hang an innocent one." This was a clear reference to the procedural problems and evidentiary bias against alleged runaways found in the Fugitive Slave Act.

In gaining the support of antislavery legislators from northern Illinois, Lincoln received enthusiastic and invaluable help from his old congressional messmate, Joshua Giddings of Ohio. The day after Christmas, Washburne informed Lincoln that "I have this moment had a long talk with Giddings and he is your strongest possible friend and says he would walk clear to Illinois to elect you. He will do anything in the world to aid you, and he will to-day write his views fully on the whole subject to Owen Lovejoy, in order that he may present them to all the freesoilers in the Legislature. He will advise them most strongly to go for you *en masse.*" Giddings was as good as his word, writing to Lovejoy twice and showing the letters to other Illinoisans.[184]

David Davis weighed in for Lincoln, too. Lobbying General Assembly members, Davis persuaded some antislavery militants to support the Springfield attorney. Other Eighth Circuit lawyers, including Leonard Swett and T. Lyle Dickey, also worked on Lincoln's behalf. But a few Radicals, like Abraham Smith of Bureau County, remained obdurate. Smith told Lincoln bluntly: "I don[']t like Lincoln personally—have much reason to dislike thee."[185] (The previous year, Lincoln had represented a client who successfully sued Smith for libel. The abolitionist probably also objected to Lincoln because of the Matson case, in which he defended a slave owner.)

The same regional rivalry that had thwarted Lincoln's bid for the commissionership of the General Land Office five years earlier continued to be a stumbling block for him. In December, Washburne advised him that an influential voter in Winnebago County complained "that the Springfield influence has always been against us in the north, and that if you should be elected the north would be overlooked for the center and the South part of the State."[186] Astounded by this objection, Lincoln assured Washburne that for "a Senator to be the impartial representative of his whole State, is so plain a duty, that I pledge myself to the observance of it without hesitation; but not without some mortification that any one should suspect me of an inclination to the contrary." Citing his record in the General Assembly, where he had supported the Illinois and Michigan Canal (a pet project of northern Illinois) and other measures of interest to that part of the state, Lincoln protested that he would be "surprized if it can be pointed out that in any instance, the North sought our aid, and failed to get it." Similarly, while in Congress he had offered his "feeble service" to promote the interests of northern Illinois. "As a Senator, I should claim no right, as I should feel no inclination, to give the central portion of the state any preference over the North, or any other portion of it."[187]

By the time the legislature convened in early January, Lincoln's hard work lining up the antislavery members had paid dividends; Washburne, Norton, Giddings, Ray, Davis, and others had overcome the objections of most abolitionists. Lincoln later told Norton: "Through the untiring efforts of friends, among whom yourself and Washburne were chief, I finally surmounted the difficulty with the extreme Anti-Slavery men, and got all their votes, Lovejoy's included."[188] To help win the vote of abolitionist Senator Wait Talcott, who represented Winnebago and neighboring counties in the North, Washburne suggested that Talcott hire Lincoln to represent him in a major patent infringement case. Lincoln appealed directly to Talcott and won his support.

As the General Assembly gathered, Lincoln was understandably confident of his prospects for the senatorship. Of the 100 members of the legislature, a majority opposed the Kansas-Nebraska Act. In the House of Representatives, Lincoln estimated that the Whigs and anti-Nebraska Democrats outnumbered the Democrats forty-four to thirty-one; their majority in the senate was only thirteen to twelve.

The chief business before the legislature was choosing a U.S. senator, a high-stakes contest that both sides desperately sought to win. As Washburne put it, the "whole country is looking to the election of Senator in our State, and should the Anti-Nebraska men fail to elect, a shout of triumph would go up from the Nebraskaites that would make us all hang our heads."[189] The Democracy justly feared that if an anti-Nebraska candidate won the senatorship, the nation would interpret it as a repudiation of Douglas and popular sovereignty. Lincoln reported in December that a leader of the regular Democrats had written to a legislator saying in effect that the anti-Nebraska forces "have a clear majority of at least nine, on joint ballot. They *outnumber* us, but we must *outmanage* them. Douglas must be sustained. We must elect the Speaker; and we must elect a Nebraska U S. Senator, or elect none at all." Lincoln speculated that all pro-Nebraska members of the General Assembly received similar letters.[190] From Washington, Yates informed Lincoln: "There is the greatest anxiety here as to the election of a Senator from our State—The peculiar connection of Douglas with the State & the Nebraska question causes that election to be looked to with more interest than that of any other State."[191]

Upon convening, the General Assembly filled all its offices save one with Democrats. By a vote of 40–24, Thomas J. Turner, an ardent prohibitionist and militant abolitionist, became speaker of the house. George T. Brown and Charles H. Ray were chosen secretary of the senate and enrolling and engrossing clerk, respectively. Only one Whig was elected in either chamber. "I do not say that the whigs have any pledges in return for this liberality," a journalist observed, "but as all their efforts, hopes, and energies are concentrated upon the great object of securing the election of Senator . . . there can be no question but they will expect favors in return."[192]

Many Whigs besides Lincoln—including Cyrus Edwards, Joseph Gillespie, Don Morrison, Richard Yates, and Archibald Williams—hoped to win election to the senate as a result of such anticipated magnanimity. On January 6, Lincoln informed Washburne that other contenders' prospects were poor, for he himself was the front-runner with twenty-six committals; no one else had more than ten. Lincoln began to make personal appeals to legislators once they assembled in Springfield. One recalled that when Lincoln approached them, his "manner was agreeable and unassuming; he was not forward in pressing his case upon the attention of members." Yet before the conversation ended, the topic of the senatorship would arise, and Lincoln would say, in essence: "Gentlemen, this is rather a delicate subject for me to talk upon; but I must confess that I would be glad of your support for the office, if you shall conclude that I am the proper person for it."[193]

The Democrats anticipated that if the incumbent, James Shields, were unable to prevail, the legislature would adjourn without choosing his successor, thus leaving the seat vacant temporarily. Shields had injured his reelection chances by supporting the Kansas-Nebraska Act despite his opposition to it in principle. Anti-Nebraska Democrats like William H. Bissell and Lyman Trumbull were regarded as possibilities, though Bissell's poor health seemed to disqualify him. Lincoln worried that pro-Nebraska Democrats, realizing that Shields's prospects were hopeless, might unite behind Bissell, but that fear proved illusory. Douglas insisted that the party "stand by Shields to the last and make no compromises." If the Irishman were to lose, then the Democrats could denounce their opponents as nativist bigots who opposed Shields simply because he had been born abroad.[194]

By refusing to meet with the House, the senate Democrats delayed the vote. On January 12, the ever-optimistic Shields said of the anti-Nebraskaites: "A fusionist party cannot hold together long. Time kills it. Delay has killed them."[195] As the days passed, however, less optimistic Democrats grew concerned. On January 17, James W. Sheahan, editor of Douglas's organ (the Chicago *Times*), wrote in alarm to Charles Lanphier at Springfield: "I think that all hope of electing Shields is gone: that the postponement of the election is a hazardous matter." Anti-Nebraskaites "will let no means be untried to get a man. I think therefore that too long trifling with Shields' name will not bring a vote to us, but will close some men against us, in which case they may slip over to the opposition. A new man should be talked of at once; and before the election, let a caucus be held, at which *Shields' declination* should be read by some one." But who should that new man be? Sheahan thought Governor Joel Matteson the most electable.

Matteson, who discreetly opposed the Kansas-Nebraska Act, had managed to ingratiate himself with both factions of the Democratic Party. By 1854, he had become one of the most popular and trusted politicos of Illinois, for he entertained lavishly and avoided controversy timidly. Even the Whigs harbored few negative feelings for him. But if the popular Matteson were to become a senate candidate, the Democrats had to move quickly, for another aspirant, the vain, wealthy William B. Ogden of Chicago was busily bribing legislators to support his candidacy. "*Ogden has bought up some of the doubtful men*," Sheahan reported, "& unless our man goes to work, he will find the market empty. Hopes ought to be held out to Matteson that Shields will not be in the way."[196]

Though unannounced as a candidate for the senate seat, Matteson, also a wealthy man, was quietly bribing legislators himself. Elected governor in 1852, he would soon become celebrated for his corruption. As he was about to leave office in 1856, he fraudulently redeemed $388,528 worth of twenty-year-old canal scrip for new state bonds. The scrip had already been redeemed once but had not been canceled; Matteson knowingly enriched himself at the expense of the state. When the General Assembly investigated this scheme in 1859, it became known as the Great Canal Scrip Fraud, one of the worst political scandals in nineteenth-century Illinois. An anti-Nebraska Democrat, George T. Allen, who called pro-Nebraska Democrats "a den of thieves, drunkards gamblers and blackguards," told Lyman Trumbull in 1866 that "the Democratic, or Nebraska, members of the Legislature employed every means to buy my vote for Matteson" during the senatorial election eleven years earlier.[197] Evidently aware of such bribery attempts, the Quincy *Whig* rejoiced that the Nebraskaites had failed to "buy or bully a sufficient number of members to reverse" the people's "plainly expressed will."[198] The Chicago *Democrat* declared that "it is time our Legislature was composed of other than marketable material."[199]

Matteson worked industriously to line up votes. The first legislator he approached was John Strunk, a Kankakee Whig who at the beginning of the legislative session had told Lincoln that he "would walk a hundred miles" to elect him. In February 1855, Lincoln reported that "Strunk was pledged to me, which Matteson knew, but he succeeded in persuading him that I stood no chance of an election, and in getting a pledge from him to go for him as second choice."[200] Strunk was a good friend of the governor. Matteson then got anti-Nebraska Democrats E. O. Hills, Gavion D. A. Parks, David Strawn, Henry S. Baker, A. H. Trapp, and Frederick S. Day to follow suit, even though he was assuring other legislators that he would support Douglas through fair weather and foul. With these seven votes in hand, Matteson then assured the pro-Nebraska Democrats that he could win if he had their support after they had cast a few ballots for other candidates. Matteson's appeal led them to abandon Shields in his favor. Meanwhile, Democrats had gained control of the state senate with the defection of Whig Don Morrison and anti-Nebraska Democrat Uri Osgood, who was allegedly "bought outright."[201] The senate then refused to hold a joint session with the House to elect a senator until Matteson had lined up the necessary votes. And so it was not until February 8 that the joint session took place.

Although Matteson tried to operate behind the scenes, rumors began circulating about his candidacy. In late January, John Todd Stuart's wife Mary Stuart reported from Springfield that the "senatorial election has not yet come on, but it is believed now that Gov. Matteson has a better chance of success than any other, of the numerous candidates."[202] Richard J. Oglesby heard reports that Lincoln's "chance is growing small by degrees."[203] The anti-Nebraska Democrat John M. Palmer told his wife: "I think Gov. Matteson will be elected Senator. The chances are that both wings of the democracy will unite on him." The logic behind choosing Matteson was, Palmer explained, simple: "He is anti Slavery in all his antecedents and is a decided anti-Douglas man which is the real point involved in the controversy. The great end we have in view is the organization of the Democratic party on the basis of the personal independence of its Members. Shields goes now which will be a warning that Douglas cannot disregard. He will see the handwriting upon the wall."[204]

On February 8, the statehouse galleries and lobby were packed as the voting began. Lincoln received forty-five votes on the initial ballot, a mere five short of victory. (Because one senator persistently abstained, only fifty votes were required to win.) Those five votes could have been provided by Norman B. Judd, Burton C. Cook, Henry Baker, George T. Allen, and John M. Palmer, anti-Nebraska Democrats all. But adamant in their refusal to vote for a Whig, they united behind Lyman Trumbull, an antislavery Democrat from Alton who had just won a seat in the U.S. House. (Baker and Allen lived in Madison County, part of Trumbull's district.) Those five liked Trumbull personally and regarded his election to the senate as essential to unite the opponents of Douglas's popular sovereignty dogma, for it would lure thousands of Democrats, who would balk at the choice of Lincoln, to support the Anti-Nebraska Party.

In 1844, Trumbull had been passed over for the senate in part because of his condescending manner and aloof personality. Indeed, he enjoyed an unenviable reputation "as the most cold-blooded man who had ever appeared in public life in Illinois."[205] Thomas Ford, who said Trumbull was "devoured by ambition for office," thought him "remarkable for a small, lean face, giving promise of narrow, cramped views, great prejudices and industry in finding fault with others."[206] In 1846, Gustave Koerner described Trumbull as the "most unscrupulous fellow on earth." Referring to Trumbull's unsuccessful bid for a seat in Congress, Koerner declared that the "slanders, contrivances, intrigues & conspiracies resorted to by him in this last canvass would fill a volume."[207] Born and raised in Connecticut, Trumbull came to Illinois in his early twenties, practiced law, entered politics, and earned respect, if not affection, for his powerful intellect, exceptional industry, skill as a debater, and mastery of constitutional law. But by opposing the Kansas-Nebraska Act, he alienated the pro-Nebraska Democrats, who regarded him as a combination of Judas and Benedict Arnold.

Lincoln understood that Trumbull's supporters would be hard to woo. In mid-January he confided to Yates: "I may start with 20 or 25 votes, but I think I can, in a few ballots, get up to 48. . . . But how I am to get the three additional votes I do not yet see." He predicted that the contest could degenerate into "a general scramble," in which case anyone, including Trumbull, might win.[208]

Although it was speculated that Trumbull could have as many as eighteen votes on the initial ballot, he actually received only five, while Lincoln's closest competitor, Shields, had forty-one. Over the next five ballots, Lincoln's vote decreased, Shields's held steady, and Trumbull's grew. When it became clear that Lincoln could not win, Stephen T. Logan moved for adjournment till the morning, but the anti-Nebraska Democrats teamed up with their estranged party colleagues to defeat the motion. The seventh ballot created great excitement as the pro-Nebraska Democrats suddenly switched from Shields to Matteson, who received forty-four votes. On the eighth ballot the governor picked up two more while Lincoln's total dwindled to twenty-seven and Trumbull's swelled to eighteen. The following ballot showed Lincoln with fifteen, Trumbull with thirty-five, and Matteson with forty-seven. Sensing that the governor was about to win, some Nebraskaites grew nervous and declared that they preferred Lincoln or Lovejoy to the turncoat Trumbull. Jokingly, Lovejoy told them, "Boys, if you want me elected, you have got no time to lose, for it will be too late after another ballot."[209]

Lincoln feared that Matteson would win on the next ballot. The governor, however, was hoist with his own petard, for Shields's supporters deeply resented Matteson's failure to back the incumbent. If a Democratic caucus had been held in a timely fashion, they believed, Shields would have won or, at the very least, the election of a senator would have been postponed; but to enhance his own prospects, Matteson had scotched the proposal for a caucus. Some of Shields's angrier friends determined that Matteson would not gain by that move, and though they did not vote against the governor, they kept the anti-Nebraska forces apprised of Matteson's maneuvers, including his "loan of money to certain Whigs and free soilers who were to vote for him." They also reported that "certain men were voting for Judge Trumbull as a democrat a few times until both Shields and Lincoln could be dropped and Matteson brought into the field." Some "Matteson men in disguise," who "had been into all sorts of railroad and State fund speculation" with the governor, were ready "to desert Judge Trumbull whenever their votes could elect Gov. Matteson."[210] Tipped off by the disgruntled Shields men, Lincoln and his allies threw their support to Trumbull, who won on the tenth ballot, receiving fifty-one votes to Matteson's forty-seven.

Lincoln feared that some of Trumbull's supporters might well defect to Matteson unless, as he put it, "they should be kept on T[rumbull's side] by seeing my remaining men coming on to him. I accordingly gave the intimation which my friends acted upon, electing T[rumbull on] that ballot." It was, he said, an impulsive decision, made in the "*heat* of battle." Lincoln explained that "few, if any, of my remaining 15 men would have gone over from me without my direction; and I gave the direction, simultaneously with forming the resolution to do it."[211]

Some of Lincoln's fifteen die-hard supporters, notably Stephen T. Logan, wept bitterly at their man's appeal to switch to Trumbull. One senator (George W. Waters) refused to vote for him, going instead for Archibald Williams. The rest reluctantly cast ballots for Trumbull, but Logan went along only after Lincoln begged him to do so. Logan had worked hard all winter for his former partner and understandably thought Judd, Palmer, et al. were acting most ungenerously.

Jubilation reigned among the anti-Nebraska forces at Trumbull's election. A tremendous roar rang out in the lobby of Representatives Hall, which overflowed with well-wishers. The New York *Tribune* hailed the "glorious result" as "a fitting finale to the Repeal of the Missouri Compromise by Douglas & Co."[212] Zebina Eastman crowed that of "all the candidates named for the station, the successful one was the most obnoxious to the aspiring leader [Douglas], and whose election is the most mortifying to him personally and politically."[213] Similarly, the Chicago *Tribune*, which called Trumbull "a man of more real talent and power than Abram Lincoln," thought that "a more decisive and emphatic rebuke to Stephen A. Douglas could not have been administered."[214]

If Matteson and his friends did resort to bribery, which seems highly probable, then it is easy to understand why Lincoln rejoiced at thwarting the governor's scheme. "I regret my defeat moderately," he told Washburne, "but I am not nervous about it. I could have headed off every combination and been elected, had it not been for Matteson's double game—and his defeat now gives me more pleasure than my own gives me pain." Lincoln was not gloating or being vindictive; he was genuinely offended by Matteson's tactics and regarded his defeat as a triumph for antislavery principles and a rebuke to Democrats who had supported the Kansas-Nebraska Act. "On the whole," he mused to Washburne, "it is perhaps as well for our general cause that Trumbull is elected. The Neb[raska] men confess that they hate it worse than any thing that could have happened. It is a great consolation to see them worse whipped than I am. I tell them it is their own fault—that they had abundant opertunity to choose between him & me, which they declined, and instead forced it on me to decide between him & Matteson."[215]

Lincoln correctly gauged the level of discomfort in the Douglas camp. Trumbull reported that the pro-Nebraska Democrats "are exhibiting towards me a great deal of ill natured & malignant feeling."[216] The editor of the Chicago *Times* told Douglas that Trumbull's election constituted "the severest blow we could have received."[217] The Chicago *Democratic Press* echoed that sentiment: "no other man could have been elected to the Senate whose presence there would be regarded by Mr. Douglas as a more signal rebuke."[218]

Though pleased that he had delivered a blow to the Douglas forces, Lincoln acknowledged that it "was rather hard for the 44 to have to surrender to the 5—and a less good humored man than I, perhaps would not have consented to it—and it would not have been done without my consent. I could not, however, let the whole political result go to ruin, on a point merely personal to myself."[219]

Despite the stoic tone of Lincoln's letters, his failure to win the senate seat plunged him into depression. As Herndon noted, Lincoln "thirsted for public notice and hungered—longed for approbation and when he did not get that notice or that approbation—was not thoroughly appreciated [—] he writhed under it."[220] Elihu B. Washburne thought "no event in Mr. Lincoln's entire political career . . . brought to him so much disappointment and chagrin as his defeat for United States Senator in 1855."[221] Shortly after the election, Joseph C. Howell reported that "Lincoln like his friends feels very much hurt."[222] When Samuel C. Parks, a pro-Lincoln legislator, tried to console him by saying he would surely be elected senator in 1858, he predicted that "the taste for the senatorship would get out of his mouth" by then.[223] Joseph Gillespie, another legislator active on Lincoln's behalf, accompanied him home after the defeat and later recalled, "I never saw him so dejected. He said the fates seemed to be against him and he thought he would never strive for office again[.] He could bear defeat inflicted by his enemies with a pretty good grace; but it was hard to be wounded in the house of his friends."[224] One of those friends was John M. Palmer, an antislavery Democrat who had already offended his party by opposing the Kansas-Nebraska Act and said he therefore must vote for a Democrat for the senate. He recollected that Lincoln "felt hurt and was a little angry."[225]

However dejected he may have been, Lincoln, at a party in honor of the senator-elect, cheerfully responded to a query about his disappointment by saying he was "not *too* disappointed to congratulate my friend Trumbull."[226] (Later, he praised Trumbull as "a peculiar man; peculiar for his rigid honesty, his high-toned independence, & his unswerving devotion to principle. A more conscientious man can not be found. He can not be bought; he can not be bribed; he can not be frightened out of what he knows to be right. I wish we had more such men as Lyman Trumbull than we have in public office.")[227] Recovering his good spirits, Lincoln told Samuel C. Parks he believed "that his defeat was the best thing that ever happened to him."[228] To young Shelby Cullom, who offered condolences, he replied: "my boy, don't worry; it will all come right in the end."[229] When asked if he were bitter about Judd's failure to support him, Lincoln replied: "I can't harbor enmity to any one; it's not my nature."[230] Lincoln's magnanimity would eventually pay dividends, for the short, chunky, red-faced Judd was to play a key role in promoting his political fortunes.

Not all of Lincoln's friends were as forgiving as he was. "There was a great deal of dissatisfaction throughout the State at the result of the election," Parks reported. Because the Whigs "constituted a vast majority of the Anti Nebraska Party," they understandably "thought they were entitled to the senate and that Mr. Lincoln by his contest with Mr. Douglas had earned it."[231] James Matheny denounced the Democrats who had refused to support Lincoln and called Trumbull "mean, low lived, [and] sneaking."[232] David Davis swore that if he had been in Lincoln's place, he would not have capitulated. To a friend Davis wrote that he was unhappy with the election of Trumbull, who, he said, "has been a Democrat all his life—dyed in the wool—as ultra as he could be." Davis thought Lincoln "ought to have been elected. . . . I had spent a good deal of time at Springfield getting things arranged for Lincoln, and it was supposed that his election was certain. I was necessarily absent the day of the election, & have been since glad of it, for I reckon that Trumbull's election is better than that the matter should have passed over. But if I had been there, there were ten members of the Legislature, who would have fully appreciated the fact that 46 men should not yield their preference to 5."[233] Stephen T. Logan, "overcome with grief and emotion," declared in the legislature that antislavery men who refused to vote for Lincoln had exhausted his patience: "A feather was light—but it was the last feather that broke the camel's back. They have laid on us that last feather, and my back is broke."[234] (Abraham Smith, a conductor on the underground railroad, claimed that his opposition to Lincoln may have been the "feather that turned the scale.")[235] Joseph Gillespie angrily complained to Lincoln: "I am tired of being dragooned by some half dozen men who are determined either to rule or ruin. I am out of all temper with and have no faith in the honesty of men who insist that ten whigs shall go with one Democrat because they cannot in conscience vote for a Whig." Gillespie was "well satisfied with Trumbull[,] yet his five particular friends who would rather see the Country go to the Devil than vote for a whig are not at all to my taste[.] I have made up my mind that henceforth I can be as reckless as they are."[236]

In reacting indignantly to Trumbull's victory, no one outdid Mary Lincoln, who denounced his "cold, selfish treachery." She even turned on her old friend and bridesmaid Julia Jayne, now Mrs. Lyman Trumbull, calling her "ungainly," "cold," "unsympathizing," and "unpopular."[237] Shortly after the election, she snubbed Julia Trumbull as the two women emerged from a church service; when Mrs. Trumbull tried to catch her eye, Mary Lincoln looked away. Julia persuaded her mother to invite Mrs. Lincoln to a party, but the invitation was declined. When the two politicians' wives met by chance, Mary Lincoln was singularly ungracious. Julia reported that "I have shaken hands with Mary, her lips moved but her voice was not audible[.] I think she was embarrassed."[238]

During the 1860 campaign, Republican leaders eager to smooth relations between Lincoln and Trumbull enlisted Mrs. Norman B. Judd's aid in an attempt to heal the breach. At Springfield Mrs. Judd found neither Mary Lincoln nor Julia Trumbull willing to take the first step; eventually, after much cajolery, Mrs. Trumbull consented. But as she prepared to call on her former friend, she balked when Adeline Judd innocently observed, "You are doing a great service to the cause & the country by this act." Flinging down her bonnet, Julia Trumbull declared that she would not be reconciled simply for political reasons. Undaunted, Mrs. Judd then turned to Mary Lincoln, who in time agreed to invite Mrs. Trumbull for a ride. At the Trumbull home, Mary Lincoln refused to accompany Adeline Judd to the door. "Why didn't Mrs. Lincoln come in?" asked a miffed Julia Trumbull. "I told her not to," replied Mrs. Judd. "I thought it was better."

Despite this inauspicious start, the two former enemies spoke as they rode by the courthouse, where Lincoln, Trumbull, Judd, and others observed them. Judd blanched as one of the men whispered, "How did she do it?"

In August 1860, Judd told Mrs. Trumbull that "a systematic effort has been made for political purposes to poison Mary[']s mind" against her, that John A. McClernand and another Democrat (unnamed) "instigated their wives to do it," that Mrs. McClernand probably "was unconscious of it," that "Mary had been told a great many things & advised if she had any self respect to keep away" from Julia Trumbull, that "Mary fully understood this attempt now & felt how unjust she had been" to Mrs. Trumbull and was "very happy to be again upon the old terms" with her former bridesmaid.

The rapprochement was short-lived, for relatives and politicians soon persuaded Mary Lincoln that the peace overture had been part of a plot to make former Democrats gain the upper hand over erstwhile Whigs in the Republican coalition. When invited to a party at the Trumbulls' home, Mrs. Lincoln developed a convenient headache.

Early in the Lincoln administration at a presidential reception, Mrs. Trumbull paused in the receiving line to chat with the First Lady, who instructed the usher, "Tell that woman to go on." "Will you allow me to be insulted in this way in your house?" Julia Trumbull asked the president.[239]

Shortly after her husband's assassination, Mary Lincoln complained that Mrs. Trumbull "has not yet honored me with a call, should she ever deign, she would not be received—She is indeed 'a whited Sepulchre.'"[240]

Judd, one of the five anti-Nebraska Democrats whose obstinacy spoiled Lincoln's chances, appreciated that "Lincoln never joined in that clamor" against them. "He had the good sense to see that our course was the result of political sagacity," Judd explained. "If we had voted for him, we should simply have been denounced by our own papers as renegades who had deserted the democrats and gone over to the Whigs." But as events unfolded, "that charge couldn't be maintained a moment against us." To the contrary, "we could maintain our entire consistency as anti-Nebraska Democrats, and that enabled us to carry over a fraction of the Democratic party sufficiently large to give us control of the State."[241]

Some of Lincoln's admirers reconciled themselves to his defeat after Trumbull attacked Douglas in the senate. In 1857, John H. Bryant of Princeton, brother of the poet and antislavery leader William Cullen Bryant, told Trumbull that "I often hear it said, that the Legislature when they elected you, did the best thing they could have done, that you had met your adversary [Douglas] . . . with more adroitness and skill, than probably any other man could have done. For Mr Lincoln I know the people have great respect, and great confidence in his ability and integrity. Still the feeling here is, that you have filled the place, at this particular time, better than he could have done."[242]

Disappointing though his defeat was to both him and his spouse, Lincoln could derive satisfaction for having laid the foundation for the Illinois Republican Party, which would mature into a full-blown organization by 1856. By magnanimously throwing his support to Trumbull, Lincoln had helped cement the coalition of former Whigs and former Democrats. He might also have taken heart from John M. Palmer's pledge that he and his Democratic friends would "stand by him in the next fight . . . against Douglas."[243] Lincoln's statesmanlike reaction to his loss illustrated the truth of Richard J. Oglesby's observation that he "submit[t]ed to adversity and injustice with as much real patience as any Man I Ever knew—because he had an abiding belief that all would yet come out right or that the right would appear and Justice finally be awarded to him."[244] And so it would.

"Unite with Us, and Help Us to Triumph"
Building the Illinois Republican Party
(1855–1857)

"You enquire where I now stand," Lincoln wrote to Joshua Speed in the summer of 1855. "This is a disputed point. I think I am a Whig; but others say there are no whigs, and that I am an abolitionist." That was not the case, he insisted, for "I now do no more than oppose the *extension* of slavery."[1] To unite all who shared this goal became Lincoln's quest. As he helped build a new antislavery party to replace the defunct Whig organization, he little imagined that he would soon become its standard-bearer. In this party endeavor, he displayed the statesmanlike qualities that would character-ize his presidency: eloquence, shrewdness, industry, patience, selflessness, diplomacy, commitment to principle, willingness to shoulder responsibility, and a preternatural sense of timing. While many joined the Republican ranks out of hostility to the South, the tolerant Lincoln played down sectional antagonism and focused on the evils of the peculiar institution itself.

Difficulty in Forming a New Party

Of all the obstacles Lincoln faced in rallying Illinoisans against the extension of slav-ery, none was more formidable than the upsurge of nativism and prohibitionism. In June 1855, the prohibitionist distraction faded after voters in the Prairie State soundly defeated a measure outlawing the sale of liquor. The nativist movement, however, proved more durable.

In 1855, the Know-Nothings of Illinois united to form a branch of the American Party, which denounced Catholicism, immigrants, and the expansion of slavery. Their bigotry alienated many other antislavery advocates, making it difficult to keep the successful anti-Nebraska coalition intact. Antagonizing the foreign-born, who constituted 20 percent of Illinois's population, would be politically ruinous, but so, too, would be any move that offended the nativists. David Davis, who shared Lin-coln's views, complained that the "intelligent and right-minded and useful portion of the Whig party in this state will not join the K[now] N[othing]s. They cannot affili-ate with them at all, believing their policy to be mean, narrow, and selfish, and hence the State will go for Douglass. The liquor vote goes for the Democrats, and the foreign vote, by the present course of things, is forced to go for them. But for the combined force of these two elements, the Democracy would have been by this time—owing to their devotion to slavery—past any chance of doing harm."[2]

In the summer and fall of 1855, abolitionists Owen Lovejoy, Joshua R. Giddings, Ichabod Codding, and Zebina Eastman campaigned throughout Illinois trying to enlist support for their cause and lay the groundwork for a Republican victory in the 1856 presidential election. The Joliet *Signal* sneered at this effort to promote what it called "a nigger-stealing, stinking, putrid abolition party," and Whig papers expressed skepticism about the endeavor.[3] In Quincy at the end of July, the proselytizers managed to convince some western Illinois Whigs, Free Soilers, and anti-Nebraska Democrats to band together on a platform opposing the extension of slavery.

When Lovejoy proposed that a state antislavery convention meet in Springfield that autumn, Lincoln replied that although he was ready to endorse the principles of the Quincy meeting, the time was not yet ripe for a new party. "Not even *you* are more anxious to prevent the extension of slavery than I," he told Lovejoy; "and yet the political atmosphere is such, just now, that I fear to do any thing, lest I do wrong." The main problem was that the Know-Nothing organization had "not yet entirely crumbled to pieces," and until the antislavery forces could win over elements of it, "there is not sufficient materials to successfully combat the Nebraska democracy with." As long as nativists "cling to a hope of success under their own organization," they were unlikely to abandon it. "I fear an open push by us now, may offend them, and tend to prevent our ever getting them." In central Illinois the Know-Nothings were, Lincoln said, some of his "old political and personal friends," among them Joseph Gillespie of Edwardsville. Lincoln "hoped their organization would die out without the painful necessity of my taking an open stand against them." Of course he deplored their principles: "Indeed I do not perceive how any one professing to be sensitive to the wrongs of the negroes, can join in a league to degrade a class of white men." He was not squeamish about combining with "any body who stands right," but the Know-Nothings stood wrong.[4]

In 1855, Lincoln, like many others, still nursed a hope that the Whig Party might continue as a viable organization. In the presidential election of 1848, it had won 43 percent of the popular vote, and four years later its share of the vote had declined only slightly to 42 percent. Moreover, Whigs held four of Illinois's nine seats in the U.S. House of Representatives.

Lyman Trumbull concurred with Lincoln about the wisdom of forming a new party, telling Lovejoy that it was "very questionable" whether "it would be advisable at this time to call a State Convention of all those opposed to the repeal of the Missouri Compromise, irrespective of party." In the Alton area "there is so much party feeling, so great aversion to what is called *fusion,* that very few democrats would be likely to unite in a Convention composed of all parties. If a convention of the Democracy, opposed equally to the spread of slavery, to abolition & Know Nothingism, could be called, we could, I think, get a respectable representation from this part of the State, and such a movement would probably damage the Nebraska democracy more than anything else which could be done; but I do not presume any considerable portion of the North would unite in a Convention of this kind." To carry Illinois, "we must keep out of the pro-slavery party a large number of those who are democrats." To accomplish that objective required overcoming "old party associations, & side issues, such as Know Nothingism & the Temperance question."[5] Discouraged by Lincoln and Trumbull, Lovejoy and his allies postponed plans for a statewide convention.

Joshua Giddings also tried to enlist Lincoln's support for a new antislavery party. In September, the Ohio congressman invited Lincoln to meet with him, Archibald Williams, and Richard Yates, saying: "You my dear sir may now by your own personal efforts give direction to those movements which are to determine the next Presidential election."[6] Because he had to be in Cincinnati on business at that time, Lincoln could not accept his friend's invitation.

Lincoln's doubts about launching a new party in 1855 were as great as his skepticism about nonviolent abolition. Writing to Kentucky attorney George Robertson, who during the congressional debates over the Missouri Compromise in 1820 had predicted the peaceable elimination of slavery, Lincoln said: "Since then we have had thirty six years of experience" which "demonstrated, I think, that there is no peaceful extinction of slavery in prospect for us." Lincoln pointed to the unsuccessful 1849 effort made by Kentuckians, led by Henry Clay, to abolish slavery gradually. Their defeat, "together with a thousand other signs, extinguishes that hope utterly," Lincoln declared. He bemoaned the decline of American virtue since 1776, when the nation "called the maxim that 'all men are created equal' a self evident truth." Now, he said, "we have grown so fat, and have lost all dread of being slaves ourselves, we have become so greedy to be *masters* that we call the same maxim 'a self-evident lie.'" Sarcastically, he observed: "The fourth of July has not quite dwindled away; it is still a great day—for *burning fire crackers*!!!" The idealism of the Revolutionary era, which had prompted several states to abolish slavery, "has itself become extinct," he lamented.

Lincoln's compassion for the slaves shone through his assessment of their current plight: "So far as peaceful, voluntary emancipation is concerned," Lincoln wrote to Robertson, "the condition of the negro slave in America, scarcely less terrible to the contemplation of a free mind, is now as fixed, and hopeless of change for the better, as that of the lost souls of the finally impenitent." He predicted that the "Autocrat of all the Russias will resign his crown, and proclaim his subjects free republicans sooner than will our American masters voluntarily give up their slaves." Foreshadowing a speech that would make him famous three years later, Lincoln told Robertson: "Our political problem now is 'Can we, as a nation, continue together *permanently— forever*—half slave, and half free?' The problem is too mighty for me. May God, in his mercy, superintend the solution."[7]

To another Kentuckian, Joshua Speed, Lincoln also unbosomed himself on the vexed question of slavery. Speed had criticized Northerners for agitating the slavery issue, which, he maintained, concerned Southerners alone; the people of the North should mind their own business. In response, Lincoln argued that Speed ought to applaud the restraint shown by him and other Free State residents who were willing to honor constitutional provisions regarding fugitive slaves and states rights. With heartfelt emotion, Lincoln reminded Speed of a journey they had taken years earlier: "In 1841 you and I had together a tedious low-water trip, on a Steam Boat from Louisville to St. Louis. You may remember, as I well do, that from Louisville to the mouth of the Ohio there were, on board, ten or a dozen slaves, shackled together with irons. That sight was a continual torment to me; and I see something like it every time I touch the Ohio, or any other slave-border. It is hardly fair for you to assume, that I have no interest in a thing which has, and continually exercises, the power of making me miserable. You ought rather to appreciate how much the great body of the Northern people do crucify their feelings, in order to maintain their loyalty to the constitution and the Union."

Passing from old memories to current affairs, Lincoln expressed outrage at events in Kansas, where proslavery forces, led by Missourians, ran roughshod over Free Soilers, stealing elections by fraud and violence, expelling antislavery legislators, and passing statutes that forbade criticism of slavery and imposed the death penalty on anyone assisting runaway slaves. When Speed declared that if he were president he would support the death penalty for the so-called Missouri border ruffians, Lincoln replied that there was little hope for a "*fair* decision of the slavery question in Kansas" because the Kansas-Nebraska Act was not really a statute: "I look upon that enactment not as a *law,* but as *violence* from the beginning. It was *conceived* in violence, *passed* in violence, is maintained in violence, and is being executed in violence." Sarcastically he predicted that Kansas would enter the Union as a Slave State, even though most settlers there opposed slavery: "By every principle of law, ever held by any court, North or South, every negro taken to Kansas is free; yet in utter disregard of this—in the spirit of violence merely—that beautiful Legislature [in Kansas] gravely passes a law to hang men who shall venture to inform a negro of his legal rights."

The friends of slavery would prevail in Congress, Lincoln predicted, because Northern politicians were corruptible. With asperity perhaps rooted in his defeat for the senate a few months earlier, he told Speed: "Standing as a unit among yourselves, you [slaveholders] can, directly, and indirectly, bribe enough of our men to carry the day—as you could on an open proposition to establish monarchy." Scornfully he referred to the Democratic party's iron discipline: "Get hold of some man in the North, whose position and ability is such, that he can make the support of your measure—whatever it may be—a *democratic party necessity,* and the thing is done." Reluctant as he was to deny anyone "the enjoyment of property *acquired,* or *located,* in good faith," Lincoln could not "admit that *good faith,* in taking a negro to Kansas, to be held in slavery, is a *possibility* with any man." No sensible person could "misunderstand the outrageous character of this whole Kansas business."

In response to Speed's professed willingness to dissolve the Union if the rights of slaveholders were violated, Lincoln said that he would not back secession if the tables were turned and Kansas were admitted as a Slave State. To be sure, Speed had expressed the hope that Kansas would be admitted as a Free State; but, Lincoln rejoined, slaveholders' deeds belied their words. "All decent slave-holders *talk* that way; and I do not doubt their candor. But they never *vote* that way." In private correspondence or conversation, "you will express your preference that Kansas shall be free," but "you would vote for no man for Congress who would say the same thing publicly." Echoing his 1854 Peoria address, Lincoln told his old friend that "slave-breeders and slave traders, are a small, odious and detested class, among you; and yet in politics, they dictate the course of all of you, and are as completely your masters, as you are the masters of your own negroes." Though dubious about the prospects for a free Kansas, Lincoln said he would work for that cause: "In my humble sphere, I shall advocate the restoration of the Missouri Compromise, so long as Kansas remains a territory; and when, by all these foul means, it seeks to come into the Union as a Slave-state, I shall oppose it."[8]

In the fall of 1855, Lincoln stumped Illinois to carry out that pledge. As he had done the previous year, he followed Douglas around the state, responding to the Little Giant's attempts to reunite the Democratic Party and vindicate his record. No account of Lincoln's speeches has survived. He probably made arguments similar to the ones contained in his 1854 addresses and in his subsequent letters to Robertson and Speed. Lincoln's efforts won the approval of Samuel Hitt, who told David Davis: "I am glad Lincoln is at Douglass' heels. D's friends here are using every possible means to build him up, and, lamentable to tell, they make some head way."[9] In December, Davis reported that "Lincoln made a few very able speeches this fall and was to answer Douglas at Danville, when he [Douglas] was taken sick." The senator had come down with bronchitis and underwent throat surgery in December. He had worn himself out campaigning not only in Illinois but in several other states as he positioned himself for yet another presidential run.

During the campaign, Lincoln was also thinking about the 1856 election and how to promote the antislavery cause. He probably shared the pessimistic view of David Davis, who noted that election results in New York and Massachusetts gave "such an impetus to this Know Nothing movement throughout the free states, & so frittered away & weakened the opposition to the democracy, that the next Presidential race will certainly be spoiled."[10] (In New York and Massachusetts, Know-Nothing candidates for secretary of state and governor, respectively, won. Rufus Choate expressed the disgust that many Northerners, including Lincoln, felt at the nativists' triumph: "Any thing more low, obscene, feculent, the manifold leavings of history have not cast up. We shall come to the worship of onions, cats and things vermiculate.")[11]

To lay plans for combating the Know-Nothing threat, Lincoln met in January 1856 with Ebenezer Peck, Lyman Trumbull, Jackson Grimshaw, Joseph Gillespie, C. D. Hay, and Gustave Koerner, among others. It was agreed that the antislavery Whigs and Democrats would have to work together, but they were not sure how to respond to the possibility that the Know-Nothings might field their own candidates for office. The antislavery men, who realized that a former Democrat stood a much better chance of winning than an ex-Whig, favored William H. Bissell for governor.

Launching the New Party: The Decatur Editors' Convention

Shortly after the 1855 elections, a group of antislavery newspapermen launched another attempt to unify the friends of freedom. In November, Paul Selby of the Jacksonville *Morgan Journal* proposed that editors of anti-Nebraska journals convene to lay the foundation for a new party. When the Winchester *Chronicle* seconded the idea, young John G. Nicolay, editor of the *Pike County Free Press*, provisionally endorsed the suggestion not only because such a convention would "be the most direct means of bringing about a triumphant victory in our next State election" but also because "it will tend to bring about a proper appreciation and recognition of the power and influence of the Political Press." To be effective, "all ultraism would have to be avoided, and conservative principles adopted as a basis of union."[12] Other editors also feared "too much *ultraism*."[13]

Soon after the *Pike County Free Press*'s endorsed the formation of a new party, more than twenty papers followed suit. When George T. Brown of the Alton *Courier* and John T. Morton of the Quincy *Whig* suggested that the meeting be held on February 22 at Decatur, centrally located and well-served by trains, Nicolay protested that it "will scarcely leave time to make the necessary arrangements. We have plenty of time before us, and it is not worth while to act in too much haste."[14] Despite Nicolay's objections, however, the recommendation for time and place was accepted. On January 10 a call signed by five papers appeared in the Decatur *Illinois Chronicle*, whose editor, William J. Usrey, predicted an attendance of fifty to seventy-five. But when a severe snowstorm hit central Illinois, only twelve hardy journalists managed to reach Decatur for the event.

Lincoln participated in the meeting as an informal guest. He had grown more optimistic about the chances for successful fusion because hostility to slavery and to the South was mounting throughout the North, largely in response to the outrages in Kansas. One conservative Northern paper declared that after "fighting the battle of the South for twelve long years, defending its political rights, domestic institutions, social character, manners and habits on all occasions, recent occurrences have convinced us that the time has come for the North, with its superior numbers, intelligence, wealth and power, to take a stand, firm and fixed as its granite hills, against the threatening, bullying, brow-beating, skull-breaking spirit of the South—a spirit that tramples on Compromise; violates the sacred freedom of parliamentary debate; and murders the settlers upon our common soil for simply opposing, by voice and vote, the fastening of slavery upon a free and virgin Territory. . . . However mischievous and detestable the sentiments promulgated by [the Republicans] may be, they have never resorted to bullets and bludgeons to carry their points, or to silence their opponents."[15]

Republicans meeting in Decatur rejoiced at the swift decline of prohibitionist strength and had new confidence that they could defuse the nativist threat. According to Charles H. Ray of the Chicago *Tribune*, who would play a leading role at the editors' conference, Republicans might win the support of the 20,000 antislavery Germans in Illinois by assuring them "that the party does not contemplate any change of the naturalization laws." Ray predicted that with such a plank "in our temperate platform and [William] Bissell thereupon we can whip Douglas and Nebraska clean out of the state."[16] Ray nonetheless feared that the Democrats were scheming with the Know-Nothings to have Bissell nominated by the nativists before the Republican state convention, thus tainting him in the eyes of the Germans. "I am still of the opinion that K Nism will damage us," Ray wrote in early May. If the Republicans repudiated nativism, "we get the German, English, Protestant Irish, Scotch and Scandinavian vote—in all about 30,000—more than double the K N strength, which in its palmiest days was not over 25,000 and is not now 15,000."[17]

In Decatur, Lincoln helped draft a platform containing an antinativist plank. One editor, German-born George Schneider of the Chicago *Staats-zeitung*, who came to Decatur "with his war paint on," had prepared a declaration sharply condemning Know-Nothingism.[18] Because it provoked strong opposition, Schneider turned in desperation to Lincoln, who, after reading it, told the editors: "The resolution introduced by Mr. Schneider is nothing new. It is already contained in the Declaration of Independence and you cannot form a new party on proscriptive principles." Lincoln's intervention, according to Schneider, "saved the resolution" and "helped to establish the new party on the most liberal democratic basis."[19]

Schneider's memory may have been faulty, for the resolution adopted was clearly a compromise. On the one hand, it roundly condemned prejudice in the appointment of men to office: "in regard to office we hold merit, not birth place to be the test, deeming the rule of Thos. Jefferson—is he honest? is he capable?—the only true rule." In dealing with immigration, the resolution declared that "we shall maintain the Naturalization laws as they are, believing as we do, that we should welcome the exiles and emigrants from the Old World, to homes of enterprise and of freedom in the New." On the other hand, the resolution reached out to the Know-Nothings, who opposed public funding of Catholic schools: "while we are in favor of the widest tolerance upon all matters of religious faith, we will repel all attacks upon our Common School System, or upon any of our Institutions of an educational character, or our civil polity by the adherents of any religious body whatever." Lincoln, with his strong desire to wean away the Know-Nothings, may have added the passage about schools.

Lincoln composed the "States Rights Plank" which read: "Resolved, That the conditions which are demanded under pleas of 'rights' as being essential to the security of Slavery throughout its expanded and expanding area, are inconsistent with freedom, an invasion of our rights, oppressive and unjust, and must be resisted."[20] The preamble and the other resolutions called for the restoration of the Missouri Compromise and endorsed the principle that slavery was local (and hence the exception) and freedom national (and hence the rule). But they also affirmed that the Fugitive Slave Act must be obeyed and that the federal government was not authorized to tamper with slavery in the states where it existed.[21]

After adopting this declaration of principles and naming a central committee (which included Herndon), the editors called for a state convention of antislavery forces to meet in Bloomington on May 29. It is likely that Herndon's selection was made at the behest of Lincoln, who evidently wanted him to serve as his agent in building the party. (Selby recalled that when the committee was chosen, some of the members "were suggested by Mr. Lincoln, while the others received his approval.")[22] Throughout the winter and spring, Herndon conducted an active political correspondence, wrote editorials, delivered speeches on behalf of the cause, and helped with preparations for the Bloomington Convention. By having Herndon act as his surrogate, Lincoln probably sought to preserve his reputation as a Moderate.

The editors did not formally endorse a gubernatorial candidate, though some wanted to run Lincoln. He, however, had been trying, along with other antislavery leaders, to woo the popular antislavery Democrat and Mexican War hero, William H. Bissell, who seemed the most electable of all the anti-Nebraska leaders. In 1850 as a congressman, Bissell had achieved national renown by accepting Jefferson Davis's challenge to a duel; the Illinoisan specified that the weapons should be army muskets charged with ball and buckshot, to be used at close range. An eloquent speaker, Bissell suffered from poor health, which made his availability problematic. (Lamed by syphilis contracted in Mexico, he would die in 1860 at the age of 49.)

At the dinner following the editors' convention, Lincoln announced his support for Bissell. When toasted as "our next candidate for the U.S. Senate," he replied that "he was very much in the position of the man who was attacked by a robber, demanding his money, when he answered, 'my dear fellow, I have no money, but if you will go with me to the light, I will give you my note.'" Lincoln added: "if you will let me off, I will give you my note." The editors would not let him off, so, after apologizing for his presence, he spoke for half an hour. He "stated that he believed he was a sort of interloper there and was reminded of the incident of a man not possessed of features the ladies would call handsome, while riding on horseback through the woods met an equestrienne. He reined his horse to one side of the bridle path and stopped, waiting for the woman to pass. She also checked her horse to a stop and looked him over in a curious sort of a way, finally broke out with,

"Well, for land sake, you are the homeliest man I ever saw."

"Yes, madam, but I can't help it."

"No, I suppose not, she said, but you might stay at home."

Lincoln said "that he felt as though he might have stayed at home on that occasion."[23]

Turning serious, Lincoln referred to the proposition some of the editors had made that he run for governor. "If I should be chosen," he remarked, "the Democrats would say it was nothing more than an attempt to resurrect the dead body of the old Whig party. I would secure the vote of that party and no more, and our defeat will follow as a matter of course. But I can suggest a name that will secure not only the old Whig vote, but enough Anti-Nebraska Democrats to give us the victory. That man is Colonel William H. Bissell."[24]

The editors' convention had in effect launched the Republican Party of Illinois. Under Lincoln's leadership, it steered a moderate course to avoid alienating potential allies, especially conservative Whigs and Know-Nothings; at the same time, it forcefully condemned the expansion of slavery. The editors shied away from the name "Republican," which, as antislavery Congressman John Wentworth of Chicago observed, meant to many voters "a sort of Maine Law, Free Love, Spiritual Medium &c. &c. concern."[25] Indeed, the New York *Herald* charged that "Socialism in its worst form, including the most advanced theories of women's rights, the division of land, free love and the exaltation of the desires of the individual over the rights of the family, and the forced equality of all men in phalansteries, or similar organizations, are a part of the logical chain of ideas that flow from the anti-slavery theory which forms the soul of black republicanism."[26] In some states, when anti-slavery forces banded together, they called themselves "the People's Party" or "the Opposition" rather than Republicans. Understandably, then, the *Illinois State Journal* declared that the editors' platform was "neither 'Know Nothing' nor 'Republican.'"[27]

First Republican Convention

The gubernatorial nomination would be formally considered at the convention summoned for May 29, 1856 at Bloomington. Three weeks before that date, the anti-Nebraska forces in Sangamon County issued a call for a convention to choose delegates. Because Lincoln was at that time on the circuit, Herndon, who was busily promoting the convention, took the liberty of signing his partner's name to the call. (Herndon's claim that he propelled a reluctant Lincoln to throw himself into the movement to establish the Republican Party is improbable. John M. Scott rightly observed that the Bloomington Convention came about "mainly through his [Lincoln's] management and by his advice.")[28]

Moderation was the watchword that spring. As Herndon told Lyman Trumbull, "We intend to get the best men in our State to attend the convention in Bloomington, and where we hope to be conservative—not hunkerish—firm—conciliatory—united, putting every man's individual opinions on other questions out of sight, sinking them in the greater one of Slavery Extension" and to "frame some broad, liberal, conciliatory, firm, resolutions or platform."[29] E. B. Washburne urged Richard Yates to help recruit delegates for the Bloomington Convention: "If we will all wheel in under that Anti-Nebraska Convention Call, and go to work to get delegations from all the counties, we can have a convention, which in point of character and ability will be without a parallel in the state[']s history."[30]

Most important, the anti-Nebraska forces needed to select the right gubernatorial candidate. As Lincoln had suggested at Decatur, William Bissell was the obvious choice. In January the colonel had indicated a willingness to run, saying that although his health was shaky and he would prefer to serve as a private in the ranks rather than a leader, he would do whatever the party thought best. By early May, he had changed his mind. As he explained to Trumbull, he began to fear the anti-Nebraska organization was not being formed for success: "The Convention at Bloomington is too likely to be composed of the same persons, and very few others, that composed the Decatur Convention. And nominations by such a convention are but the surest modes of killing off the nominees." Instead of these Whig editors leading the way, he said, "the anti Nebraska Democrats ought to have rallied, and taken the control and direction of this Bloomington Convention—made it, and its candidates, their own." Bissell concluded, "my present inclination is to decline a nomination, should one be tendered me."[31]

Bissell's reluctance placed the entire movement in jeopardy. No record of Lincoln's direct attempts to reassure him survives, but through Herndon he indirectly conveyed the optimism needed to dispel Bissell's gloom. Two weeks after Bissell had expressed his reluctance to run for the governorship, Herndon told Trumbull of an upbeat discussion he had just had with his partner: "Lincoln & myself had a long talk in reference to affairs, and I have never seen him so sanguine of success, as in this Election—*he is warm*. I gathered this from him,—recollect he has been round our Judicial Circuit—, that the people are warm and full of feeling on this question—this great & mighty issue. They have moved more since Bissell wrote you than in the past year—never saw so much '*dogged determination*' to fight it out;—that Democrats are coming to us daily— . . . and if you will look over our papers you will see that Lincoln is correct. He says this—that some few corrupt old line whigs who are gaping for office in and about towns, are going with the nigger driving gentlemen [i.e., Democrats], but that the whigs & Democrats in the country are all right on the question, and are becoming more so every day—riper and riper they grow for Freedom the longer the time is extended."[32]

Prospects brightened four days later when Bissell reversed course, informing George T. Brown, a leading organizer of the Bloomington Convention, that he would in fact accept the gubernatorial nomination, even though his health was so impaired that he could not campaign vigorously. Brown, who would preside at the opening of the conclave at Bloomington, had worked hard to ensure that the tone of "the proceedings will be conservative."[33] On May 27, Lincoln probably felt relieved as he boarded a train in Danville, where he had been attending court, and headed off to Bloomington; there, if Brown's efforts proved effective, if Bissell honored his most recent pledge, and if the delegates ratified a moderate platform like the one hammered out at the editors' conference in February, victory seemed entirely possible. While in Danville, Lincoln had also been able to recruit several young lawyers and editors to accompany him to Bloomington.

En route to the convention, Lincoln and Henry C. Whitney strolled about Decatur during a layover. Upon reaching the courthouse, Lincoln grew reminiscent, describing his experiences in Macon and Sangamon counties during the 1830s, the Hanks family, and the difficulties he had to overcome in his early life. Later that afternoon, seated on a tree trunk in a brush thicket, he expressed to his colleagues, including Joseph O. Cunningham, "his hopes and fears of the results of the coming convention, and of his earnest wish that the old Whig element from Southern Illinois might be well represented there."[34] He did not, Cunningham recalled, "attempt to conceal fears and misgivings entertained by him as to the outcome of the gathering. He was well assured that the radical element of the northern counties would be there in force, and feared the effect upon the conservative element of the central and southern parts of the State."[35] The next day, as his train rolled northward toward Bloomington, Lincoln anxiously inquired of fellow passengers if they were delegates from southern Illinois, 'where antislavery sentiment was scarce.' He was jubilant upon discovering two trainmates from Egypt who would attend the convention. Arriving in Bloomington the next day, Lincoln eagerly sought out Whig friends from Egypt, among them Jesse K. Dubois. Lincoln's goal was to persuade Dubois and other Conservatives to unite with the abolitionists of northern Illinois and the Moderates of the central part of the state.

Energetically but discreetly, holding no official position other than the chairman of the nominations committee, Lincoln was the master spirit of the convention, managing through some political alchemy to convince former enemies to set aside their differences and cooperate for the greater good. Chicago delegate John Locke Scripps thought that "no other man exerted so wide and salutary an influence in harmonizing differences, in softening and obliterating prejudices, and bringing into a cordial union those who for years had been bitterly hostile to each other."[36] Whitney "never saw him more busily engaged, more energetically at work, or with his mind and heart so thoroughly enlisted." Although Lincoln "was in a state of enthusiasm and suppressed excitement throughout this convention," he "kept his mental balance, and was not swerved a hair's breadth from perfect equipoise in speech or action." (Whitney was in a good position to observe Lincoln, for he stayed with him at David Davis's house during the convention.)[37]

In promoting moderation at the convention, Lincoln had help from T. Lyle Dickey and Archibald Williams, who were also staying at the Davis home. Those three, said Whitney, "did more than all others combined in shaping the moderate and conservative" platform.[38] In particular, they helped craft the main slavery plank in the platform, which said: "*Resolved*, That we hold, in accordance with the opinions and practices of all the great statesmen of all parties, for the first sixty years of the administration of the government, that, under the constitution, congress possesses full power to prohibit slavery in the territories; and that while we maintain all constitutional rights of the south, we also hold that justice, humanity, the principles of freedom as expressed in our Declaration of Independence, and our national constitution and the purity and perpetuity of our government, require that that power should be exerted to prevent the extension of slavery into territories heretofore free."[39] In justifying this stance to radical Anti-Nebraska Democrats, Lincoln said: "Your party is so mad at Douglas for wrecking his party that it will gulp down anything; but our party [Whig] is fresh from Kentucky and must not be forced to radical measures; the Abolitionists will go with us anyway, and your wing of the Democratic party the same, but the Whigs hold the balance of power and will be hard to manage, anyway. Why I had a hard time to hold Dubois when he found Lovejoy and Codding here; he insisted on going home at once."[40]

Intervening to settle more disputes between Radicals and Conservatives, Lincoln offered advice on the other platform planks, which were based on the document adopted at the Decatur editors' conference. They denounced the violence in Kansas, called for the restoration of the Missouri Compromise, urged the admission of Kansas as a Free State, professed devotion to the Union, pledged to "support the constitution of the United States in all its provisions," criticized nativist bigotry ("we will proscribe no one, by legislation or otherwise, on account of religious opinions, or in consequence of place of birth"), and attacked the administration of Governor Matteson.[41] The platform was adopted unanimously.

The convention chose a slate of presidential electors, headed by Lincoln and Frederick Hecker, a German-born antislavery leader who persuaded many of his fellow countrymen to support the Republican Party. Lincoln was also named a delegate to the Republican national convention, scheduled to meet in June at Philadelphia.

Uniting the delegates was their indignation at events in Kansas, where on May 21 pro-slavery militia sacked the Free Soil town of Lawrence, and in Washington, where on May 22 Congressman Preston Brooks of South Carolina cudgeled abolitionist Senator Charles Sumner of Massachusetts into insensibility at the Capitol. Earlier in May another Southern-born Democratic congressman, Philemon T. Herbert of California, shot and killed an Irish waiter in a Washington hotel dining room. Those violent acts enraged the North. In the subsequent election campaign, Republicans aroused the Free States with their appeal to remember "bleeding Kansas and bleeding Sumner." Fueling the anger in Bloomington were refugees from Kansas, including Governor Andrew H. Reeder, who on the night of May 28 described to a crowd the violence he had observed in that territory before being compelled to flee for his life. The people who heard Reeder speak called for Lincoln, who briefly compared the abrogation of the Missouri Compromise to the destruction of a fence, thus allowing one man's cattle to eat the crops belonging to his neighbor. Lincoln also spoke of the outrages in Kansas, including the destruction of newspaper offices and the dismissal of government employees for political reasons.

The next day another fugitive from Kansas, James S. Emery of Lawrence, portrayed the outrages he had witnessed in that territory. After Emery described the sacking of Lawrence he watched Lincoln stride to the podium with a giraffe-like gait. His hair was tousled, his clothes were not neat, and his shoulders were stooped. But the delegates, so arrested by Lincoln's intensely serious look, scarcely noticed his appearance. Emery recalled that he "at once held his big audience and handled it like the master he was before the people pleading in a great and just cause."[42]

Incredibly, Lincoln's remarks on that occasion have not survived, and this oration, believed to be one of his masterpieces, has become known as the "lost speech." Reporters were allegedly so carried away by it that they dropped their pencils and listened spellbound. Although many journalists were present, only two brief newspaper accounts of the speech's substance are extant. According to the Alton *Courier*, edited by George T. Brown, Lincoln "enumerated the pressing reasons of the present movement," said he "was here ready to fuse with anyone who would unite with him to oppose [the] slave power," and referred to "the bugbear [of] disunion which was so vaguely threatened." Apropos of Southern threats to secede, he said: "It was to be remembered that the *Union must be preserved in the purity of its principles as well as in the integrity of its territorial parts*." He quoted from Daniel Webster's famous reply to Robert Hayne in 1830: "Liberty and Union, now and forever, one and inseparable." Lincoln also rejected Douglas's contention that his doctrine of popular sovereignty squared with the teachings of Henry Clay, and maintained that a "sentiment in favor of white slavery now prevailed in all the slave state papers" except for a few Border States.[43]

Lincoln was doubtless referring to the Richmond *Enquirer*, which he saw regularly. That journal ran several inflammatory editorials declaring, among other things:

"Slavery is the natural and normal condition of the laboring man, whether
white or black."

"Make the laboring man the slave of one man, instead of the slave of
society, and he would be far better off."

"Two hundred years of labor have made laborers a pauper banditti. Free
society has failed, and that which is not free must be substituted."

"We do not adopt the theory that Ham was the ancestor of the negro race.
The Jewish slaves were not negroes; and to confine the jurisdiction of
slavery to that race would be to weaken its scriptural authority, for we
read of no negro slavery in ancient times. Slavery, black or white, is
necessary."[44]

The only other contemporary account of Lincoln's remarks appeared in the Belleville *Advocate*, edited by Nathaniel Niles, a delegate to the convention: "Abraham
Lincoln by his wonderful eloquence electrified the audience of two thousand men . . .
and excelled himself. Men who had heard him often said he never spoke as well
before. . . . He paid his respects to those 'National Whigs,' as they call themselves,
who are all the time stepping about to the *music of the Union*! He had no doubt but
that the music of an overseer's lash upon a mulatto girl's back would make some of
them dance a Virginia hornpipe. 'Let them step,' said he, 'let them dance to the music
of the Union, while we, my old Whig friends, stand fast by Principle and Freedom
and the Union, together.'"[45]

In a dispatch written that day, John Locke Scripps described the delivery and
reception of Lincoln's speech: "For an hour and a half he held the assemblage spell
bound by the power of his argument, the intense irony of his invective, and the deep
earnestness and fervid brilliancy of his eloquence. When he concluded, the audience
sprang to their feet and cheer after cheer told how deeply their hearts had been
touched, and their souls warmed."[46] The Bloomington *Pantagraph* said of Lincoln's
words: "Several most heart-stirring and powerful speeches were made during the
Convention; but without being invidious, we must say that Mr. Lincoln, on Thursday
evening, surpassed all others—even himself. His points were unanswerable, and the
force and power of his appeals, irresistible."[47]

Reminiscent accounts tend to confirm the meager press reports. Thomas J. Henderson recalled that at one point, Lincoln, "after repelling with great power and earnestness the charge of disunion made against the Anti-Nebraska party," stood up "as
if on tip-toe, his tall form erect, his long arms extended, his face fairly radiant with
the flush of excitement, and, as if addressing those preferring the charge of disunionism, he slowly, but earnestly and impressively, said: 'We do not intend to dissolve the
Union, nor do we intend to let you dissolve it.'" Then, Henderson said, "everybody
present rose as one man to their feet, and there was a universal burst of applause . . .
such as I have never seen on any other occasion. It was amid the wildest excitement
and enthusiasm, continued for several minutes before Mr. Lincoln resumed his
speech."[48] Others remembered Lincoln uttering a slightly different version of that
rousing sentence, obviously a reply to Southern leaders who threatened disunion if an

antislavery candidate won the White House: "We say to our Southern brethren: 'We won't go out of the Union, and you shan't!'"[49]

Judge John M. Scott of Bloomington recollected that as Lincoln began speaking, there was "an expression on his face of intense emotion seldom if ever seen upon any one before. It was the emotion of a great soul. Even in stature he appeared greater. A sudden stillness settled over that body of thoughtful men as Mr. Lincoln commenced to speak. Every one wanted to hear what he had to say." After his customary slow beginning and careful choice of words, Lincoln steadily "increased in power and strength of utterance until every word that fell from his lips had a fullness of meaning not before so fully appreciated. The scene in that old hall was one of impressive grandeur. Every man, the venerable as well as the young and the strong, stood upon his feet. In a brief moment every one in that . . . assembly came to feel as one man, to think as one man and to purpose and resolve as one man." It was, Scott believed, "the speech of his life in the estimation of many who heard it. . . . It was a triumph that comes to but few speakers. It was an effect that could only be produced by the truest eloquence."[50] Other eyewitness testimony confirms Scott's awestruck account.

The failure of newspapers to report the content of Lincoln's remarks may have resulted from a deliberate political decision. It appears that the speech was not fully written out. Lincoln told the crowd the night before that he had prepared a speech, but he may have meant that he had assembled some notes or an outline. According to Joseph Medill, "Lincoln did not write out even a memorandum of his Bloomington speech beforehand," but he carefully prepared it nonetheless. "He intended days before to make it, and conned it over in his mind in outline and gathered his facts, and arranged his arguments in regular order and trusted to the inspiration of the occasion to furnish him the diction with which to clothe the skeleton of his great oration." After the address, "Mr. Lincoln was strongly urged by party friends to write out his speech, to be used as a campaign document for the Fremont Presidential contest of that year; but he declared that 'it would be impossible for him to recall the language he used on that occasion, as he had spoken under some excitement.'" Beyond that excuse of faulty memory, however, Medill believed "that, after Mr. Lincoln cooled down, he was rather pleased that his speech had not been reported, as it was too radical in expression on the slavery question for the digestion of Central and Southern Illinois at that time, and that he preferred to let it stand as a remembrance in the minds of his audience."[51]

In 1908, Eugene F. Baldwin, a Peoria editor and publisher, agreed that "the great mass of the leaders felt that Lincoln made too radical a speech and they did not want it produced for fear it would damage the party. Lincoln himself said he had put his foot into it and asked the reporters to simply report the meeting and not attempt to record his words and they agreed to it."[52] Some biographers have endorsed this conclusion, which seems plausible, though no hard evidence supports it. It is also possible that reporters were indeed so caught up in the excitement that they stopped writing in order to listen. That had happened before when Edward Bates delivered a stirring address at the Chicago River and Harbor Convention in 1847.

Returning to Springfield, Lincoln was accosted on the train by a delegate who declared: "I never swear, but that was the damndest best speech I ever heard."[53]

On June 10, before a crowd at the Springfield courthouse, Lincoln hailed the work of the convention. The Democratic *Register* sneered: "his niggerism has as dark a hue as that of [William Lloyd] Garrison or Fred Douglass."[54]

The 1856 Campaign

With Bissell heading their state ticket, anti-Nebraskaites had reason to be optimistic. "Since the nomination of Bissell we are in good trim in Illinois," Lincoln reported. "If we can save pretty nearly all the whigs, we shall elect him, I think, by a very large majority."[55] But saving the old-line Whigs would not be easy; Archibald Williams described such a Whig as "a gentleman who takes his toddy regularly, and votes the Democratic ticket occasionally."[56]

Nationally, the Democrats reacted to the public revulsion against the Kansas-Nebraska Act and the turmoil in Kansas by rejecting both incumbent president Franklin Pierce and Stephen A. Douglas. Instead, they chose as their standard-bearer James Buchanan of Pennsylvania, who had recently been in London as U.S. minister to the Court of St. James and thus was untainted by the Kansas-Nebraska Act and its consequences. This move alarmed Lincoln, who observed that "a good many whigs, of conservative feelings, and slight pro-slavery proclivities, withal, are inclining to go for him, and will do it, unless the Anti-Nebraska nomination be such as to divert them."

Lincoln, who had worked so hard to ensure that Illinois's Republicans avoided taking a radical antislavery stance, hoped the Republican national convention, meeting in mid-June at Philadelphia, would follow suit. His favorite candidate was John McLean, whose nomination, he said, "would save every whig, except such as have already gone over hook and line." The mainstream Whigs might, however, flee to Buchanan if the Republicans chose a Radical like Salmon P. Chase of Ohio, Nathaniel P. Banks of Massachusetts, William Henry Seward of New York, Frank P. Blair of Missouri, or John C. Frémont of California. Blair and Frémont might be acceptable to Illinois Whigs for vice-president, but not president. To former Democrat Lyman Trumbull, Lincoln pointed out that 90 percent of the anti-Nebraska votes came from "old whigs." Rhetorically he asked: "In setting stakes, is it safe to totally disregard them? Can we possibly win, if we do so?" Alluding to his own defeat at Trumbull's hands, he noted: "So far they have been disregarded. I need not point out the instances." Lincoln assured Trumbull that he was "*in*, and shall go for any one nominated unless he be '*platformed*' expressly, or impliedly, on some ground which I may think wrong."[57] Lincoln's view was shared by his friend Orville H. Browning, who told Trumbull: "McLean, in my opinion, would be stronger in this state than any one whose name has been suggested. We have many, very many, tender footed whigs, who are frightened by ugly names, that could not be carried for Freemont, but who would readily unite with us upon McLean."[58]

Though chosen a delegate to the Republican national convention, Lincoln did not attend. At Bloomington he had declined the honor "on account of his poverty and business engagements," but when Jesse W. Fell offered to pay his expenses, Lincoln said he might be able to go after all. At the last minute, however, Lincoln wired Fell that he could not accept, so Fell's brother Kersey went as his replacement. At the same time, Lincoln, who was on the circuit, urged Trumbull to attend. On June 15, the senator replied that he had hesitated to go "but your letter just received decides the question. I will go . . . and do what I can to have a conservative man nominated and conservative measures adopted."[59] Lincoln wrote to Elihu B. Washburne endorsing McLean; delegates at the convention used that letter to bolster the Ohioan's candidacy.

At Philadelphia the Republicans did not choose a conservative candidate. To Lincoln's dismay, John C. Frémont, a former Democrat known as "the Pathfinder" for his celebrated explorations in the West, secured the presidential nomination. William L. Dayton of New Jersey was selected as his running mate.

Though chagrined by the nomination of Frémont, Lincoln doubtless found some consolation in the 110 votes he himself received for vice-president. The Illinois delegation had supported McLean for president; when that Ohioan lost, a leading Prairie State delegate, Congressman William B. Archer, resolved to nominate Lincoln for the second spot on the ticket. Working well into the night with Nathaniel Green Wilcox and Martin P. Sweet, Archer lined up support for Lincoln. At the Illinois caucus, Trumbull declared that they should pick "a man of decided Whig antecedents" for vice-president. When Wilcox suggested Lincoln, Trumbull said he had named a "very good man." No one, however, seconded the motion. Several hours later, well into the night, Wilcox met with Archer and others, including two delegates from Indiana, Caleb B. Smith and Schuyler Colfax. Upon learning that Easterners were uniting on Dayton, Wilcox again suggested to Archer that they back Lincoln. Archer responded positively and summoned the other Illinois delegates, who resolved to present Lincoln's name to the convention. Archer, Wilcox, William Ross, and others lobbied throughout the night, calling on Daniel S. Dickinson and Thurlow Weed of New York, Thaddeus Stevens of Pennsylvania, and Chauncey F. Cleveland of Connecticut. Archer asked a fellow congressman, John Allison of Pennsylvania, to nominate Lincoln.

The next day Allison complied, describing Lincoln as a "prince of good fellows, and an Old-Line Whig." Seconding the nomination, Archer declared that he "had been acquainted with the man who had been named for 30 years. He was born in gallant Kentucky, and was now in the prime of life . . . and enjoying remarkable good health. And, besides, the speaker knew him to be as pure a patriot as ever lived. He would give the Convention to understand, that with him on the ticket, there was no danger of Northern Illinois. Illinois was safe with him, and he believed she was safe without him. With him, however, she was doubly safe."[60] Suddenly an Ohio delegate interrupted Archer, shouting out: "Will he fight?" To the amusement of the delegates, Archer, "a grey-haired old gent, slightly bent with age," then "jumped straight from the floor, as high as the Secretaries' table, and cried out, shrill and wild, 'Yes.'" The delegates were "convulsed, and a tremendous yell of approbation substantially inserted a fighting plank in the platform." According to the journalist Murat Halstead,

Archer "slightly spoiled the effect of his vaulting performance, adding: 'Why, he's from Kentucky, and all Kentuckians will fight.' There was a peculiar restlessness and heavy breathing through the multitude, showing that they were strong in the faith that men born north of the Ohio could fight as well as those who had suffered the accident of birth on the other side of that stream."[61]

Also seconding Lincoln's nomination was John M. Palmer, who said: "I have known him long, and I know he is a good man and a hard worker in the field, although I never heard him—for when he was on the stump, I dodged. He is my first choice . . . . We can lick Buchanan any way, but I think we can do it a little easier if we have Lincoln on the ticket with John C. Fremont."[62] Representative John Van Dyke of New Jersey, who had served with Lincoln in the Thirtieth Congress, added his voice to the modest chorus of praise: "I knew Abraham Lincoln in Congress well, and for months I sat by his side. I knew him all through, and knew him to be a first-rate man in every respect."[63]

These gratifying accolades came too late; Dayton won on the second ballot, largely because of his conservative Whig background, because his state was doubtful, because he had supported McLean, because he was not a Know-Nothing, and because he had ingratiated himself with the antislavery forces by endorsing an amendment to the Fugitive Slave Act providing jury trials for accused runaways. Wilcox thought that if the entire Illinois delegation had worked for Lincoln from the start, and if the convention had delayed selecting a vice-presidential candidate for a few hours, Lincoln would have won.

Lincoln did not actively encourage friends to promote his vice-presidential candidacy. He had earlier told O. B. Ficklin, who suggested that he might be suitable for that honor: "There is one office I am not fitted for—the office of vice-president." Ficklin "knew he referred to his lack of grace and elegant manners, so desirable in a presiding officer [of the U.S. Senate]. He had no thought of becoming President—the Senate was his aim."[64]

Word that he had been seriously considered for the vice-presidency may have changed Lincoln's mind. Jesse W. Weik wrote that this "tribute to his genius and ability" reportedly "afforded him more real gratification than any other which came to him during the years of his political activity."[65] When the news arrived of his near-nomination for vice-president, Lincoln modestly shrugged it off, saying the candidate being discussed was probably Levi Lincoln of Massachusetts. After friends showed him that indeed he was the one who almost won the vice-presidential nomination, he remained seemingly unmoved, but according to James H. Matheny, it may have inspired him to think of running for the presidency, and Henry C. Whitney believed that "from that time Lincoln trimmed his sails to catch the breeze which might waft him to the White House."[66]

Lincoln probably was flattered by notices in the Republican press. The Chicago Democrat said: "We are glad Mr. Lincoln got so many votes for Vice President. There is no political Maine Lawism [a reference to prohibition] or Know-Nothingism about him and a better Fremont man does not live."[67] The Ottawa Republican was even more complimentary: "we would have supported Mr. Lincoln for the second office in the gift of the people though we hope some day to vote for him for the first. He is among the men who endure."[68]

Hobbled by Frémont's nomination, Illinois's fledgling Republicans also faced a dilemma in the Third Congressional District, where on July 2 an uncompromising abolitionist, Owen Lovejoy, defeated Leonard Swett's bid to run for a U.S. House seat. Lovejoy, whose brother Elijah had been murdered in 1837 by an anti-abolitionist mob in Alton, seemed too radical for mainstream voters. A Congregationalist minister, he fiercely opposed slavery. Short, stout, "with a face of flint, a mouth of decision, and in every way and motion, bearing the mark of a radical, suggestive, and indomitable man," he was "quick and peremptory, and not over courteous in his bearing, looking like one more ready to demand his rights, and to enforce them, than to ask favors."[69] Alarmed conservatives bolted and looked for another candidate. On July 16 they chose T. Lyle Dickey to challenge Lovejoy and his Democratic opponent, threatening to split the antislavery vote.

Although Lincoln did not directly urge his good friend Dickey to withdraw, he did so indirectly through David Davis. To Davis he explained on July 7: "When I heard that Swett was beaten, and Lovejoy nominated, it turned me blind. I was, by invitation, on my way to Princeton [where Lovejoy lived]; and I really thought of turning back. However, on reaching that region, and seeing the people there—their great enthusiasm for Lovejoy—considering the activity they will carry into the contest with him—and their great disappointment, if he should now be torn from them, I really think it best to let the matter stand." Acknowledging that it "is not my business to advise in the case," he nonetheless told Davis to show his letter to others, including Ashahel Gridley, who had denounced Lovejoy as a "nigger thief."[70] Two days after the Bloomington conclave, Davis, echoing Lincoln's arguments, informed Dickey that even though the "nomination of Lovejoy deadens enthusiasm, dispirits and causes all people who really love the Union of the States to pause," the sentiment in favor of him was strong throughout the district because "the outrages in Kansas, and the general conduct of the Administration, with the attack on Mr. Sumner, have made Abolitionists of those who never dreamed they were drifting into it." The many Whigs objecting to Lovejoy's nomination, among them Davis, who despised him, still preferred the preacher, as an opponent of slavery expansion, to a Democrat who did not oppose it. Others felt that Lovejoy had won the nomination fairly, that the process should be honored, and that they had agreed to fuse and must abide by the decision of the fusion convention. Lovejoy's "views and opinions are becoming the views and opinions of a majority of the people," Davis observed; if Dickey ran, he would surely lose.[71] In mid-September Dickey reluctantly agreed to withdraw. Seven weeks later, Lovejoy won by more than 6,000 votes.

Lincoln's own congressional district also caused him distress, for Yates declined to run for the seat he had lost two years earlier. In July, Lincoln met with Yates, Trumbull, James Matheny, and other Republican leaders in an attempt to persuade John M. Palmer to run, and former Whigs to support him if he did. When Palmer refused, the Republicans settled on little-known John Williams as their sacrificial lamb in the congressional race.

Lincoln threw himself into the presidential campaign, delivering over fifty speeches around Illinois in an unusually bitter and violent campaign. His principal concern was to woo disaffected Whigs, a class well represented by his old friend Joseph Gillespie, who still resented the anti-Nebraska Democrats who had voted against Lincoln for senator the previous year. Gillespie was tempted to support the American Party ticket, headed by former Whig president Millard Fillmore. In June, Gillespie told Lincoln that when he saw the results of the Bloomington Convention, he had entertained the hope that conservatives would band together to defeat the forces of Douglas and Pierce. But when he learned that a leading anti-Nebraska Democratic paper in Alton endorsed James Buchanan for president, he concluded that the Democrats who had participated in the Bloomington Convention were betraying the cause. Therefore, he would vote for a true conservative like Fillmore even if the former president stood little chance of winning, for "it would be more creditable to be fighting under that banner than to triumph in such company as I fear some of the wire workers at Bloomington are."[72]

Lincoln heard from others to the same effect. A southern Illinoisan told him that "as Mr. Fillmore was Elicted to the vice presidency as a Whig [in 1848], many of the Whigs in this Section of our County Still adhere to him Not Considering by Whom he was Nominated, hence the Difficulty here to Git all the Whigs here to drop him."[73]

To enlist antislavery Whigs, Lincoln had to confront the charge of abolitionism and fears of disunion. John M. Palmer reported that in southern Illinois "the *dog howl* of Abolitionism-Black Republicanism" had frightened many old Whigs. In addition, others "feel that they are called specially to the patriotic duty of 'saving the Union' which can only be done by throwing their votes away on Fillmore."[74] Lincoln learned that his friend Edwin B. Webb "*is really right, & wants to have Richardson & Douglass defeated,* but stands opposed to Abolitionism, & *is afraid of separating the Union, through any means, & fancies the Republican Movements* are likely to do it." Webb was reportedly "a good Soul, a right minded man . . . , but timidly afraid of doing mischief to the integrity & perpetuity of the Union."[75] From Springfield, Benjamin S. Edwards reported that Frémont's nomination was "particularly unfortunate," for in central Illinois "a great many are startled . . . by the cry of abolitionist—and will shrink from the support of a man of so little reputation as F[remont], & one whom they are persuaded was forced on the public by abolitionists. Nor is he liked by the Whigs, who though willing to support a democrat in opposition to Buchanan, are not yet prepared to support unhesitatingly a man whose antecedents have so little to recommend him." Edwards told Lyman Trumbull that Illinois Republicans faced an uphill fight: "You need . . . vindication against the charges of abolition, and opposition to the Union which however unfounded they may be are yet made, and must be met."[76]

Lincoln responded to the challenge energetically. With Herndon, he stumped extensively, particularly in southern Illinois, where his services were in demand. This was disagreeable, discouraging labor. Frequently, crowds failed to turn out because there were simply too few Republicans in the area. In rural counties, Republican processions, headed by a few frantic marshals leading a brass band and a carriage full of local dignitaries, often looked pitiful when the shy farmers would not fall in behind them. The result was a poor excuse for a parade. Among the many annoyances speakers had to endure were odiferous petroleum torches, glee clubs singing banal campaign songs nasally, loud brass bands playing indoors, and tedious party adherents who boasted endlessly of their service to the cause.

Lincoln began to canvass the state in July with a speech at Lovejoy's hometown of Princeton; he proceeded to Dixon, Sterling, Chicago, Galena, and Oregon City. No full text of his many other Illinois addresses that year has survived, but in an extant draft fragment of his Galena speech, he refuted the charge of sectionalism leveled against the Republicans, a charge he called "the most difficult objection we have to meet." Lincoln briefly summarized the "naked issue" that divided the Democrats from his party: *"Shall slavery be allowed to extend into U.S. territories, now legally free?"* Appealing to fair-minded voters, he asked "how is *one* side of this question, more *sectional*, than the other?" If the parties were, like most other institutions, divided along sectional lines, how should the problem be solved? The answer was simple, he declared: one side must yield. Republicans "boldly say, let all who really think slavery ought to spread into free territory, openly go over against us." But why, he asked, should anyone who opposed slavery vote Democratic? "Do they really think the *right* ought to yield to the *wrong*? Are they afraid to stand by the *right*? Do they fear that the constitution is too weak to sustain them in the right? Do they really think that by right surrendering to wrong, the hopes of our constitution, our Union, and our liberties, can possibly be bettered?"

To those who objected that Frémont and Dayton were both from Free States, Lincoln pointed out that the Constitution stipulated that the president and vice-president must come from different states, not different sections. Although it had become customary for one of the standard-bearers to be a resident of a Free State and his running mate from a Slave State, it was not mandatory. He conceded that Frémont would probably receive all of his electoral votes from Free States, but Lincoln pointed out that Buchanan expected to win mainly with the votes of Slave States, with some help north of the Mason-Dixon line. Why, Lincoln asked, was this the case? "It is not because one *side* of the question dividing them, is more sectional than the *other*; nor because of any difference in the mental or moral structure of the people North and South. It is because, in that question, the people of the South have an immediate palpable and immensely great pecuniary interest; while, with the people of the North, it is merely an abstract question of moral right, with only *slight*, and *remote* pecuniary interest added." The value of Southern slaves would double if slavery were allowed to expand; it would be reduced if slavery were hemmed in. This consideration "unites the Southern people, as one man. But it can not be demonstrated that the *North* will gain a dollar by restricting it." It was a pity, Lincoln observed, that moral principle constituted "a looser bond, than pecuniary interest." He excoriated Northern Democratic presidential aspirants for selling out to the South. Scornfully, he noted that the party lash and personal ambition led them to auction off their principles and abandon "their own honest impulses, and sense of right."[77]

At Princeton, young Clark E. Carr attended Lincoln's speech and found it disappointing. "From what I had heard of Mr. Lincoln I expected to be interested in his speech—to be greatly moved and charmed by his eloquence," Carr wrote. But there "was not a brilliant utterance, no flight of oratory, no well-rounded periods, no rhetorical climax, simply a plain, homely talk, rather an apology than otherwise for being a Republican. He took great pains to make the audience understand that, while he abhorred slavery, to be a Republican did not by any means imply an effort to overthrow slavery, but simply to prevent its extension into new territory. He gave a history of the Missouri Compromise . . . and made a lawyer's argument to prove that it was constitutional, and that there was no justification for its repeal. Among other things, he declared himself not to be opposed to the Fugitive Slave law. He used such homely illustrations as that the thing was 'as plain as the nose on a man's face,' 'like rain running off from a duck's back,' and 'the longest pole gets the persimmons.' He did not attempt to conceal the fact that he had always been a high-tariff Whig, but he handled that matter gingerly, so as not to drive away the Free Soil Democrats who were inclined to come into the new Republican party."[78]

Journalist Noah Brooks, who heard Lincoln speak at Dixon, assessed him differently. His "irresistible force of logic," "clinching power of argument," and "manly disregard of everything like sophistry or clap-trap" impressed not only Republicans like Brooks but also rock-ribbed Democrats "who had withstood the arguments and truths of scores of able men." Those Democrats "were forced to confess that their reason was held captive while they listened to the plain, straight-forward and sledge-hammer logic of the speaker." Brooks remembered that when Lincoln first stood on the platform, "almost everyone was disappointed" by his personal appearance; but once he started to explain "the reasonableness of what was asked by the North, and the madness and folly of the demand of the South that all governmental power and legislative action should be subservient to the interests of her own peculiar institutions, his manner and appearance were entirely lost and forgotten in the magic of his eloquence and in the fund of irresistible argument which he poured forth." Lincoln's "manner, never tedious or harsh, became instinct with life, energy and electric vivacity. Every motion was graceful, every inflection of his voice melodious, and, when dropping for the moment, argument, he good-naturedly appealed to his fellow-republicans to admit certain alleged charges, and then went on to show how, notwithstanding all this, the platform and principles of the party were untouched and uninjured, his consummate shrewdness and long-headed, astute perceptions of the truth never failed to touch the audience with a sudden shock of pleasure and surprise, which brought forth spontaneous bursts of applause from friends and opponents."

When "an unusually impertinent and persistent" heckler interrupted him, Lincoln wearily replied: "Look here, my friend, you are only making a fool of yourself by exposing yourself to the ridicule which I have thus far succeeded in bringing upon you every time you have interrupted me. You ought to know that men whose business it is to speak in public, make it a part of their business to have something always ready for just such fellows as you are. You see you stand no show against a man who has met, a hundred times, just such flings as you seem to fancy are original with yourself; so you may as well, to use a popular expression, 'dry up' at once.'"[79]

Lincoln also defeated hecklers in Vandalia. When a Democratic physician interrupted him, calling Frémont a "wooly head," Lincoln retorted: "What . . . has Fremont said, that you call him a wooly head? I ask you, sir?"

The doctor offered no response.

"You can make this charge, and yet, when called upon to justify it, your lips are *sealed*," Lincoln said.

As the doctor consulted with friends, Lincoln remarked, "That's right, gentlemen, take counsel together, and give me your answer."

Finally, the heckler said that Fremont "found the wooly horse [i.e., supported abolitionism] and ate dogs."

"*That* ain[']t true—but if it was, how does it prove that Fremont is a *wooly head*—how?" Lincoln queried.

The doctor, "wearing the expression of a man standing on a bed of live coals, did not get off any answer." Lincoln closed the colloquy saying, "You're *treed,* my friend."[80]

In early August, Lincoln swung throughout southeastern Illinois. At Grand View he was accompanied by Henry P. H. Bromwell, who recalled that Lincoln "made one of the most masterly speeches of his life, and his jovial spirit seemed to fill the assembly" even though the room contained more than a hundred Fillmore and Buchanan supporters and only half a dozen Republicans.[81] In nearby Shelbyville, Lincoln and Democrat Anthony Thornton, an "aristocrat in mien, deportment, and bearing, commensurately financed, elegantly attired and possessing unusual ability with energy to use it," were to debate on August 9. Thornton recollected that because "it was my meeting and as a matter of courtesy, I consented that Mr. Lincoln should open the discussion. He commenced at two o'clock and spoke until nearly five. He knew he was addressing people who sympathized with the South, and he made a most ingenious and plausible speech. He, however, spoke so very long that I became apprehensive as to any effort I might make to a wearied crowd. I began my reply by telling one of Mr. Lincoln's stories and thus obtained the attention of the crowd and made a short speech."[82] The Democratic press ridiculed Lincoln's address as "prosy and dull in the extreme—all about 'freedom,' 'liberty' and niggers."[83] With characteristic modesty, Lincoln said that since there were only sixteen registered Republicans in Shelby County, "however poorly I may defend my cause, I can hardly harm it, if I do it no good."[84]

Later that month Lincoln spoke in Kalamazoo, Michigan. Alluding to Stephen A. Douglas's reluctance to specify just how and when the people of Kansas could, under his popular sovereignty doctrine, prohibit slavery, Lincoln sarcastically referred to the Little Giant as "a great man—at keeping from answering questions he don't want to answer." Cogently Lincoln argued that once slavery managed to take root in Kansas, attempts to expel it would fail: "suppose that there are ten men who go into Kansas to settle. Nine of these are opposed to slavery. One has ten slaves. The slaveholder is a good man in other respects; he is a good neighbor, and being a wealthy man, he is enabled to do the others many neighborly kindnesses. They like the man, though they don't like the system by which he holds his fellow-men in bondage. And here let me say, that in intellectual and physical structure, our Southern brethren do not differ from us. They are, like us, subject to passions, and it is only their odious institution of slavery, that makes the breach between us. These ten men of whom I was speaking, live together three or four years; they intermarry; their family ties are strengthened. And who wonders that in time, the people learn to look upon slavery with complacency? This is the way in which slavery is planted, and gains so firm a foothold. I think this is a strong card that the Nebraska party have played, and won upon, in this game."

Here, as elsewhere, Lincoln urged all opponents of the peculiar institution to abjure Fillmore, even though he was not an avowed friend of slavery or the Kansas-Nebraska Act. To those who denied that Northerners had any stake in the slavery expansion debate, Lincoln pointed out that they had an obvious interest in preserving the territories "for the homes of free white people." Northerners also had an interest in keeping the principle of freedom alive, for the nation prospered and grew strong because it was free and "every man can make himself."

Lincoln protested against the Richmond *Enquirer*'s assertion that "slaves are far better off than Freemen." In response he exclaimed: "What a mistaken view do these men have of Northern laborers! They think that men are always to remain laborers here—but there is no such class. The man who labored for another last year, this year labors for himself, and next year he will hire others to labor for him."

Regarding Southern threats to secede if Frémont were to win, Lincoln asked: "How is the dissolution of the Union to be consummated? . . . Who will divide it? Is it those who make the charge" that the Republicans threaten the existence of the Union? "Are they themselves the persons who wish to see this result? A majority will never dissolve the Union. Can a minority do it?"

Lincoln denied that Frémont and his party were abolitionists. "I know of no word in the language that has been used so much as that one 'abolitionist,' having no definition." Anticipating his famous "House Divided" speech of 1858, Lincoln argued that the federal government must be "put on a new track. Slavery is to be made a ruling element in our government. The question can be avoided in but two ways. By the one, we must submit, and allow slavery to triumph, or, by the other, we must triumph over the black demon. We have chosen the latter manner. If you of the North wish to get rid of this question, you must decide between these two ways—submit and vote for Buchanan, submit and vote that slavery is a just and good thing and immediately get rid of the question; or unite with us, and help us to triumph. We would all like to have the question done away with, but we cannot submit."

Lincoln movingly appealed to Democrats to honor the principles they had espoused before the introduction of the Kansas-Nebraska Act. Their party, he said, "has ever prided itself, that it was the friend of individual, universal freedom." Now, to support Douglas's handiwork, Democrats have abandoned their idealism. In closing, he implored Democrats to "come forward. Throw off these things, and come to the rescue of this great principle of equality." He would not exclude former Whigs from his exhortation: "to all who love these great and true principles" he beckoned: "Come, and keep coming! Strike, and strike again! So sure as God lives, the victory shall be yours."[85]

According to a Democratic paper, Lincoln's "very fair and argumentative address" proved "far too conservative and Union loving in his sentiments to suit his audience," which frowned when he "proclaimed that the southern men had hearts, consciences and intellects like those around him."[86]

Returning to Illinois, Lincoln repeated his warning about the inevitable conflict between slavery and freedom. At Bloomington in September, he addressed a large crowd: "It is my sincere belief that this government can not last always part slave and part free.—Either Slavery will be abolished—or it must become equally lawful everywhere—or this Union will be dissolved. There is natural incompatibility between the institutions incident to Slave-holding States—so irreconcilable in their character, that they can not co-exist perpetually under the same Government." When T. Lyle Dickey warned him that preaching such a doctrine would hasten the outbreak of a bloody civil war, Lincoln reluctantly agreed to stop.[87]

Lincoln also spoke in Petersburg, where the local Democratic journal labeled him the "great high-priest of abolitionism," the "depot master of the underground railroad," and "the *post mortem* candidate for the vice presidency of the abolition political cock-boat."[88] In Jacksonville, the opposition press was more charitable, calling Lincoln "a fine speaker" and "certainly the ablest black republican that has taken the stump at this place."[89] Another observer praised Lincoln's speech in Jacksonville, where he "held a great audience in breathless attention for some three hours, in sunshine & rain with their umbrellas over their heads, still shouting 'go on'—while he was demolishing the Bucchaneers & Filmorites right & left so effectively that not a soul of them have dared to peep since except to say '*I am for Fremont.*'"[90]

In August, Lincoln and Herndon felt optimistic about the outcome of the election. "We are gaining on the nigger Democracy every day," Herndon informed Lyman Trumbull.[91] Lincoln told the senator that "we shall ultimately get all the Fillmore men, who are real[l]y anti-slavery extension—the rest will probably go to Buchanan, where they rightfully belong." A "great difficulty" in persuading antislavery Fillmore supporters to back Fremont "is that they suppose Fillmore as good as Fremont" on slavery expansion "and it is a delicate point to argue them out of it," for "they are so ready to think you are *abusing* Mr. Fillmore."[92]

The Fillmore men proved very difficult to convert. In July, George T. Brown observed that the "Fillmorites are making a good deal of stir. Jo Gillespie is moving heaven and Earth."[93] The following month Richard Yates reported from Jacksonville that "the Fi[l]more diversion is large in this section of the State—splitting the Anti-Nebraska vote *right* in the *middle*. We have *slight* hopes of making it right yet, but *very slight*. If it's leaders were true to their professions we would soon get them back, but with some of them I fear that a fondness for the 'peculiar institution' is a dominant motive."[94] In September, Lincoln heard from Yates that in central Illinois "there are five times as many *proslavery* whigs as we have estimated."[95] Lincoln appealed in vain to those erstwhile allies. At a Springfield meeting in September, he "received as many curses as blessings from the crowd," which contained "insolent" Democrats, "surly" Know-Nothings, and others who were "cold and suspicious."[96] In late September Herndon told Wendell Phillips, "Had we a few months longer to go on I think we would carry this State for Fremont. Were the Republicans and the Americans to join, we could easily, now—at this moment, carry the State for Freemont."[97] But the American Party adherents would not fuse with the Republicans.

Lincoln, who guessed that Buchanan would receive about 85,000 votes, Frémont 78,000, and Fillmore 21,000, urged an old friend, John Bennett of Petersburg, to reconsider his support for the ex-president: "Every vote taken from Fremont and given to Fillmore, is just so much in favor of Buchanan. The Buchanan men see this; and hence their great anxiety in favor of the Fillmore movement. They know where the shoe pinches. They now greatly prefer having a man of your character go for Fillmore than for Buchanan, because they expect several to go with you, who would go for Fremont, if you were to go directly for Buchanan."[98]

On September 8 Lincoln wrote a form letter to the supporters of the American Party's candidate arguing that Fillmore could only win if the election were thrown into the House of Representatives, where the former president might prevail as a compromise candidate. But that would never happen if Buchanan carried Illinois, whose electoral votes, when combined with those of the South and of the Democratic standard-bearer's home state of Pennsylvania, would assure his election. Therefore, Fillmore backers in Illinois should vote for Frémont because Fillmore had no chance of carrying the state. "This is as plain as the adding up of the weights of three small hogs," Lincoln declared.[99] He sent this letter, marked "confidential," to many "good, steady Fillmore men" throughout the state.[100]

In Bloomington on September 16, Lincoln ridiculed Douglas's popular sovereignty scheme, which "reminded him of the man who went into a restaurant and called for a ginger cake which was handed to him but spying the sign 'Sweet Cider for sale' he handed the cake back and said he would take a glass of cider in its place." After drinking the cider he started to leave, whereupon "the keeper called to him to come back and pay for his cider." The customer replied: "Cider? Why I gave you the cake for the cider."

"Well then pay me for the cake."

"Pay you for the cake. I didn't have the cake."

"'Well,' replied the keeper scratching his head, 'that is so but it seems to me I am cheated some way in the deal.'"

"And so," said Lincoln, "somebody, the North or South, is bound to be cheated by Mr. Douglass' theory of squatter sovereignty."[101]

In mid-September Lincoln spent another week stumping southern Illinois. The unpopularity of the Frémont-Dayton ticket in Egypt meant "my efforts are more needed" there than elsewhere, he lamented.[102] The challenge was daunting. Old Whigs leaning toward Frémont were dissuaded by Edward Bates of Missouri, who was especially effective in Morgan, Sangamon, and Madison counties, where the outcome of the election hung in the balance.

The following month Lincoln addressed a rally in Ottawa, where he was introduced as "Our next United States Senator."[103] In Belleville, the largest city in Egypt and home to many German Americans, including Lieutenant-Governor Gustave Koerner, Lincoln "referred to the Germans and the noble position taken by them in just and dignified terms. When he called down the blessings of the Almighty on their heads, a thrill of sympathy and pleasure ran through his whole audience."[104] Koerner, who introduced Lincoln to the crowd, recalled that he "spoke in an almost conversational tone, but with such earnestness and such deep feeling upon the questions of the day that he struck the hearts of all his hearers." Saying that he had found "the Germans more enthusiastic for the cause of freedom than all other nationalities," Lincoln "almost with tears in his eyes, broke out in the words: 'God bless the Dutch!' Everybody felt that he said this in the simplicity of his heart, using the familiar name of Dutch as the Americans do when amongst themselves. A smart politician would not have failed to say 'Germans.' But no one took offense."[105]

Soon thereafter a campaign encounter with another German won Lincoln a life-long devotee. In Pittsfield to deliver a speech, he called at the office of the *Pike County Free Press* to get some materials printed. The paper was edited by a young journalist, John G. Nicolay, who had helped arrange a political rally for Lincoln. Later that evening, as a member of the Republican committee, Nicolay was introduced to the speaker; that introduction changed his life. The young man became an enthusiastic admirer even before hearing the magnetic speech, which further strengthened his devotion to Lincoln. Four years later he would become Lincoln's chief personal secretary.

Nicolay's fellow Germans struggled to balance their hatred of slavery with their revulsion against nativism. Traditionally Democrats, they despised the Kansas-Nebraska Act but loved its author, Douglas, for his opposition to the Know-Nothings. The Republicans' choice of William Bissell sat well with the Germans, however. A leading Democrat had predicted in April that the "only danger we have to fear is that the Republicans will nominate Bissle, in which event our German vote may be endangered—We cannot persuade them that Bissle is not a Democrat and with a Catholic wife Know-Nothingism won't take a good hold upon him."[106] To woo Illinois Germans, Lincoln urged the widespread dissemination of antislavery German newspapers and helped raise funds for the relief of Friedrich Hecker, a prominent German campaigner whose house had burned down in August.

All the while the Democrats strove to pin the nativist label on the Republicans. In September, Lincoln heard rumors that Chicago Germans were deserting the party; "scared a little," he anxiously asked Charles H. Ray if there were any truth in such reports.[107] Despite this threat, the Republicans captured over half the German vote in November.

The Democratic press also denounced Frémont supporters as "nigger-worshippers." An account in the Joliet *Signal* of a Republican rally there on October 8 sarcastically observed that it "was a wonderful day for the niggers and nigger-worshippers of this county. Our city was literally filled with enthusiastic Fremonters."[108] The following week the Springfield *Register* declared: "Black republicanism not only teaches the doctrines of amalgamation with negroes, but it sets its negro advocates up to preach a dissolution of the confederacy. Can white men, who love their country, participate in this unholy work?"[109] Another Democratic paper described the Republican program thus: "Down with the Foreigners and Up with the Darkies. . . . Imagine a big, burly, thick-lipped African crowding Gen. Shields away from the polls on election day! That is the practical working of the Fusion policy."[110] Democrats sang racist ditties like the following:

> Come Democrats and listen,
> And I will sing you a song.
> 'Tis all about the nigger-worshippers
> And it will not take me long.
> Fremont is on their platform,
> And their principles endorse,
> To worship niggers night and morn,
> And ride the Wooly Horse.[111]

The Democrats' tactics worked. Buchanan carried Illinois handily, winning 105,528 votes to Frémont's 96,278 and Fillmore's 37,531. Frémont received 74 percent of the vote in northern Illinois, 37 percent in the central part of the state, and 23 percent in Egypt (mostly from Germans living near St. Louis). Nationwide the Democratic nominee garnered 174 electoral votes to Frémont's 114 and Fillmore's 8; in the popular vote Buchanan won 45 percent of the ballots cast, Frémont 33 percent, and Fillmore 21 percent. Like Republicans throughout the North, the Frémonters of Illinois had failed to gain the support of either the conservative Whigs, who feared disunion, or the Know-Nothings, who believed the false charge that Frémont was a Catholic as well as the allegation that he was too radical on the slavery issue.

Bissell, a moderate opponent of slavery who could not plausibly be accused of nativism, did far better than Frémont among the 1852 Scott voters, especially in southern and central Illinois. He won the governor's race with 111,466 votes (47%) to his opponent's 106,769 (45%). "This is glory enough for Ill[inoi]s," Herndon crowed. "We Fremont men feel as if victory perched on our banner."[112] Despite this triumph, a conscience-stricken Bissell hesitated to take the oath of office, for in 1850 he had accepted Jefferson Davis's challenge to a duel and was, he thought, ineligible to serve as governor because Illinois law disqualified from office-holding anyone who had issued or accepted a challenge to duel. Lincoln and other party leaders persuaded him to overcome his scruples and assume the governorship.

Lincoln accurately ascribed Buchanan's success to lack of cooperation among his opponents and to the Democrats' race-baiting. Republicans, Lincoln told his political allies, "were without party history, party pride, or party idols," and were merely "a collection of individuals, but recently in political hostility, one to another; and thus subject to all that distrust, and suspicion, and jealousy could do." The Democrats enjoyed a significant advantage, for their ranks contained "old party and personal friends, jibing, and jeering, and framing deceitful arguments against us" while dodging the real issue. "We were constantly charged with seeking an amalgamation of the white and black races; and thousands turned from us, not believing the charge (no one believed it) but *fearing* to face it themselves."[113]

Taking a longer view, Lincoln hailed the election result as a milestone on the road to equal rights. "Our government rests in public opinion," he told Republican banqueters in December. "Public opinion, on any subject, always has a *'central idea,'* from which all its minor thoughts radiate. That 'central idea' in our political public opinion, at the beginning was, and until recently has continued to be, 'the equality of men.' And although it was always submitted patiently to whatever of inequality there seemed to be as matter of actual necessity, its constant working has been a steady progress towards the practical equality of all men." Reiterating a theme he had stressed at the Bloomington convention six months earlier, Lincoln called the presidential contest "a struggle, by one party, to discard that central idea, and to substitute for it the opposite idea that slavery is right, in the abstract, the workings of which, as a central idea, may be the perpetuity of human slavery, and its extension to all countries and colors." To promote the ideal of equality, the solid majority who opposed Buchanan must unite. Warming to his theme, Lincoln said, "Let every one who really believes, and is resolved, that free society is not, *and shall not be,* a failure, and who can conscientiously declare that in the past contest he has done only what he thought best—let every such one have charity to believe that every other one can say as much. Thus let bygones be bygones. Let past differences, as nothing be; and with steady eye on the real issue, let us reinaugurate the good old 'central ideas' of the Republic. We *can* do it. The human heart is with us—God is with us. We shall again be able not to declare, that 'all States as States, are equal,' nor yet that 'all citizens as citizens are equal,' but to renew the broader, better declaration, including both these and much more, that 'all *men* are created equal.'"[114]

This eloquent address helped clinch Lincoln's reputation as the leader of Illinois's Republicans. A correspondent of the *Illinois State Journal* declared: "There is no man upon whom they would so gladly confer the highest honors within their gift, and I trust an opportunity may not long be wanting which will enable them to place him in a station that seems to be by universal consent conceded to him, and which he is so admirably qualified by nature to adorn."[115]

To Noah Brooks, Lincoln expressed guarded hopes for the future. While "the Free Soil party is bound to win, in the long run," it was not certain that its victory was imminent. "Everything depends on the course of the Democracy. There's a big anti-slavery element in the Democratic party, and if we could get hold of that, we might possibly elect our man in 1860. But it's doubtful—*very* doubtful. Perhaps we shall be able to fetch it by 1864; perhaps not."[116] Lincoln's pessimism seemed justified in April 1857, when Republicans lost the Springfield municipal elections. "We quarreled over Temperance," Herndon explained; "we ran some K[now] N[othing]s, and the Dutch to a man united against this proceeding: we are whipped badly. . . . We have learned a good lesson—do better next time."[117]

Newspapers would play a central role in building up the party. Anticipating the 1860 election, Lincoln and Frank Blair laid plans to have the *Missouri Democrat* of St. Louis, which had a large circulation in southern Illinois, become a Republican paper that year. The Louisville *Journal* would follow suit, as would an unnamed Virginia newspaper. All this was to seem coincidental and thus make the Republican Party appear strong and growing stronger. Lincoln also helped found the Republican Club of Springfield, organized by the photographer John G. Stewart, a friend of Robert Lincoln and a veteran of the Frémont campaign.

Throughout the winter of 1856–1857, Lincoln continued to help strengthen the Republican Party in Illinois, often attending caucuses of legislators. When in doubt about how to deal with the Democrats, Norman B. Judd would say, "I will go round and bring in Old Abe tomorrow night." Lincoln regularly obliged, amazing the lawmakers with his shrewd analysis of their opponents' thinking and offering much-appreciated advice about legislative strategy, particularly in combating a reapportionment law that would have ruined the Republicans' electoral prospects.[118]

Collecting a $5,000 Fee

Much as he wanted to help the Republican cause, in 1857 Lincoln was forced by economic necessity to devote most of his energy to practicing law. "I lost nearly all the working part of last year, giving my time to the canvass," he wrote in August, "and I am altogether too poor to lose two years together."[119] To replenish his coffers, he sued the Illinois Central Railroad for $5,000 as a fee for services in the case of *Illinois Central Railroad vs. McLean County, Illinois and Parke.* Accounts of Lincoln's efforts to collect his fee, the largest of his career, differ. According to Herndon, when Lincoln submitted a bill for $2,000, a company official expostulated: "Why, *sir*, Daniel Webster would not have charged that much."[120] (Mason Brayman, who hired Lincoln to argue the case, testified that he offered a fee of $1,250, and when Lincoln presented his bill, he was told: "Why that is as much as a first-class city lawyer would charge.")[121] Smarting from this rebuff, Lincoln returned to Springfield, en route stopping in Bloomington, where he consulted prominent attorneys. They told him that he should have asked for $5,000 and urged him to sue for that amount. Lincoln did so and won.

Sources connected with the Illinois Central present a different account: they maintain that the suit was a mere formality and that the company had all along intended to pay Lincoln his fee. Documents in the company files indicate that Lincoln submitted his bill to John M. Douglas, an acquaintance of his who served as solicitor for the company. Douglas referred the matter to the head of the company's law department, Ebenezer Lane, who in turn passed it along to the president, William H. Osborn. In the summer of 1856, Osborn asked James F. Joy his opinion of Lincoln's bill. Joy's reply is not extant, but he later recalled telling Lincoln that his fee was excessive. The egotistical Joy held Lincoln in contempt, regarding him as a run-of-the-mill provincial attorney. (For his role in the case, Joy had received only $1,200 above and beyond his regular salary. "I think there would have been no difficulty with

Mr. Lincoln's bill if I had charged as, perhaps, I ought to have done, five thousand dollars," Joy later mused.)[122] In response, Lincoln "said that he had done good work; that the amount in litigation far exceeded the fee many thousand times over, and that he thought he ought to get a good fee."[123] Joy recollected that the Illinois Central leaders said to Lincoln (in effect): "Bring suit against the company for the amount demanded and no attempt will be made to defend against it. If by the testimony of other lawyers it shall appear to be a fair charge and there shall be a judgment for the amount, then we shall be justified in paying it."[124]

This reminiscence may be inaccurate, for less than a month after filing suit for his fee, Lincoln told some potential clients: "I have been in the regular retainer of the [Illinois Central] Co[mpany] for two or three years; but I expect they do not wish to retain me any longer. . . . I am going to Chicago . . . on the 21st inst. and I will then ascertain whether they discharge me; & if they do, as I expect, I will attend to your business."[125] There may have been some bad blood between Lincoln and Joy; Charles L. Capen, an eminent attorney who investigated the handling of the fee, reported that "the whole trouble was with Mr. James F. Joy . . . whom Mr. Lincoln afterward despised."[126] In 1855, Joy had rudely questioned a modest bill Lincoln submitted for services to the company. (Seven years later, John M. Douglas, a friend of Judge Thomas Drummond, who aspired to a seat on the U.S. Supreme Court, thought it best not to have Joy lobby President Lincoln on the judge's behalf. Douglas said "it would do no good for Joy to see Lincoln but possibly [do] harm growing out of past relations.")[127]

The case was slated for trial at Bloomington on June 18, 1857; Lincoln was prepared to fight hard for his fee, suggesting that the suit was not a friendly one. In notes for his plea, he alleged that he, not Joy, had "made the point & argument on which the case turned," and asked: "Are or [are] not the *amount* of *labor*, the *doubtfulness* and *difficulty* of the *question*, the *degree* of *success* in the *result*; and the *amount* of pecuniary interest *involved*, not merely in the particular case, but covered by the principle decided, and thereby *secured* to the client, all proper elements, by the custom of the profession to consider in determining what is a reasonable fee in a given case[?]" He concluded that "$5000 is not an unreasonable fee in this case."[128] To buttress his argument, he supplied a deposition signed by attorneys Norman B. Judd, Grant Goodrich, Orville H. Browning, Archibald Williams, Norman H. Purple, and Stephen T. Logan, all of whom agreed that the amount asked was reasonable. Gustave Koerner told him that he would have been justified in asking twice as much. On the day of the trial, John M. Douglas, the company attorney, did not appear, leading the judge to award Lincoln his fee by default. Mortified by his failure to be in court when the case was tried, Douglas asked that it be retried, evidently so that he could save face; he did not want his superiors to see that the company had lost by default. Lincoln, gracious beyond what could reasonably have been expected, decided to forego his victory, agreeing with opposing counsel to have a perfunctory second trial with a predetermined outcome. On June 25, the court, after a very brief trial, again awarded Lincoln his requested fee. The railroad could have appealed but instead consented to give Lincoln his $5,000. (Douglas did not admire Lincoln. In 1860 he told George B. McClellan that Lincoln "is not a bold man. He has not nerve to differ with his party and its leaders.")[129]

Why Illinois Central executives required Lincoln to sue them is unclear. Joy's explanation that it was "a friendly suit" is contradicted by Lincoln's notes for a brief and by his fear of losing his retainer with the company. Perhaps officials of the Illinois Central, which was in desperate financial straits, suspected that the corporate directors in New York would object to such a large sum. At that time, shareholders in Great Britain were sending agents to inspect the company's books, and they may have balked at a $5,000 fee. In any event, their behavior did little credit to the company's managers.

Though it may not be obvious why the Illinois Central wanted Lincoln to sue for his fee, the company's motive for settling is: its executives wished Lincoln to represent them in another tax suit that the state of Illinois threatened to file. To prosecute the case, Lincoln's friend, State Auditor Jesse K. Dubois, sought to hire Lincoln, who would probably have accepted if he had not been on retainer to the Illinois Central. He declined, however, and in December 1857 urged Dubois to abandon his plan. Henry C. Whitney, who represented the Illinois Central in Champaign County, told officials of the company that "we could not afford to have Lincoln as our enemy, instead of an ally."[130] The Illinois Central's chief attorney explained to its president: "We can now look back & in some degree estimate the narrow escape we have made." Having Lincoln as opposing counsel would have been a serious setback, the attorney explained, because he knew all about "the obscurity of those sections of our charter, relating to taxation, which, unexplained by the History of the Charter," would harm the railroad's position. In addition, Lincoln was "not only the most prominent [member] of his political party, but the acknowledged special adviser of the Bissel[l] Administration."[131]

A year later, Stephen A. Douglas, referring to the $5,000 fee, accused Lincoln of "taking the side of the company against the people."[132] Lincoln replied that because the McLean County tax case "was worth half a million dollars" to the Illinois Central, he thought a fee of $5,000 reasonable, while the company "wanted to pay me about $500." That, Lincoln said, constituted "the whole truth about the fee; and what tendency it has to prove that I received any of the people's money, or that I am on very cozy terms with the Railroad Company, I do not comprehend."[133] (It has been suggested that Lincoln's fee in this case enabled him to run against Douglas for the senate in 1858, but that contention does not withstand scrutiny. He split the money evenly with Herndon and then lent his share to Norman B. Judd, who did not repay it until 1865.)

The charge that Lincoln was a railroad lawyer siding with corporations against the people is misguided. Although he did represent the Illinois Central and other railroads successfully on many occasions, he often brought suit against them. Like most other lawyers of his time and place, he was prepared to represent virtually any client against any foe. The major exception was the Illinois Central, whose retainer prevented him from suing it on behalf of others. He worked steadily for that company from 1852 to 1860, handling forty-seven documented cases, but those cases constituted a tiny percentage of his business. (It is impossible to determine with precision what portion of Lincoln's income derived from various clients.) Aside from the large fee he wrested from it in the McLean County tax case, he received modest sums; his annual retainer was $250, and his fee for trying most cases was $10.

Whatever he did receive from the Illinois Central he was grateful to get. He told Herndon: "Billy, it seems to me that it will be bad taste on your part to keep on saying the severe things I have heard from you about railroads and other corporations. The truth is, instead of criticizing them, you and I ought to thank God for letting this one fall into our hands." Henry C. Whitney, also hired by the Illinois Central, told an interviewer: "I had authority to employ additional counsel whenever I chose to do so, and in Judge Davis's circuit I frequently applied to Lincoln when I needed aid. I never found him unwilling to appear in behalf of a great 'soulless corporation.'"[134] According to Whitney, Lincoln said during the trial of a case in which he represented the railroad corporation: "Counsel avers that his client has a *soul*. This is possible, of course; but from the way he has testified under oath in this case, to gain, or hope to gain, a few paltry dollars he would sell; nay, has already sold, his little soul very low. But our client is but a conventional name for thousands of widows and orphans whose husbands' and parents' hard earnings are represented by this defendant, and who possess souls which they would not swear away as the plaintiff has done for ten million times as much as is at stake here."[135]

In July 1857, Lincoln and his family traveled to New York, evidently to collect the $5000 fee awarded to him. (Company officials refused to pay, so Lincoln on August 1 had the sheriff of McLean County issue an execution on the corporation, which only then agreed to comply with the court order.) He later recalled that he spent his time in New York "visiting with his wife the various 'lions' of the city."[136] Mary Lincoln reported to her half-sister Emilie in September: "This summer has strangely & rapidly passed away—some portion of it, was spent most pleasantly in travelling east, we visited Niagara, Canada, New York & other points of interest." She added that "when I saw the large steamers at the New York landing, ready for their European voyage, I felt in my heart, inclined to sigh, that poverty was my portion, how I long to go to Europe. I often laugh & tell Mr. L- that I am determined my next Husband *shall be rich*."[137]

This trip to Niagara was the family's second; the first had occurred nine years earlier, when Lincoln returned home from his Massachusetts campaign swing. The majesty of the falls inspired him to meditate on "the indefinite past." He marveled that when "Columbus first sought this continent—when Christ suffered on the cross—when Moses led Israel through the Red-Sea—nay, even, when Adam first came from the hand of his Maker—then as now, Niagara was roaring here." Mastodons and mammoths, "now so long dead, that fragments of their monstrous bones, alone testify, that they ever lived, have gazed on Niagara. In that long—long time, never still for a single moment. Never dried, never froze, never slept, never rested."[138]

Attacking the Dred Scott Decision

As 1857 dawned, the tide of political unrest seemed to be ebbing. On New Year's day, the *Illinois State Journal* announced that the mood "throughout our Republic is buoyant and encouraging. The prospect before the nation is well calculated at once to induce gratitude to Divine Providence."[139] Most importantly, the violence in Kansas had finally been quelled, thereby cooling off both Southern disunionism and Northern antislavery zeal. Then the U.S. Supreme Court abruptly shattered the calm.

On March 6, 1857, that tribunal handed down its decision in the case of *Dred Scott vs. Sandford,* ruling that Congress could not prohibit slavery from entering the western territories and that blacks, both slave and free, were not American citizens. The Chicago *Tribune* spoke for millions when it called the majority opinion of Chief Justice Roger B. Taney and six colleagues "[s]udden, unexpected and shocking to the sensibilities and aspirations of lovers of freedom and humanity," reversing "the current of progressive ideas and christian humanity," and bidding fair to reintroduce "the iniquitous despotism and legalized inhumanity of barbarian ages."[140]

In June at Springfield, Lincoln denounced the court in one of his most eloquent speeches, prompted by Stephan A. Douglas's address there two weeks earlier. The Little Giant had declared that the "history of the times clearly shows that our fathers did not regard the African race as any kin to them, and determined so to lay the foundations of society and government that they should never be of kin to their posterity. (Immense applause.)" But, Douglas added, "when you confer upon the African race the privileges of citizenship, and put them on an equality with white men at the polls, in the jury box, on the bench, in the executive chair, and in the councils of the nation, upon what principle will you deny their equality at the festive board and in the domestic circle?" He also denounced Republican criticism of the Dred Scott decision, declaring that anyone who "resists the final decision of the highest judicial tribunal aims a deadly blow to our whole republican system of government" and is "an Amalgamationst."[141] (In 1856, Douglas had declared during a senate debate: "We do not believe in the equality of the negro, socially or politically, with the white man. Our people are a white people; our State is a white State; and we mean to preserve the race pure, without any mixture with the negro.")[142]

In reply, Lincoln stated that the Republicans "offer no *resistance*" to the Dred Scott decision, for the court might change its mind. (Lincoln had first-hand knowledge of such a reversal, for in the one case that he argued before that august tribunal—*Lewis vs. Lewis* in 1849—the court overruled a decision it had issued ten years earlier.) He conceded that it would be "revolutionary" not to "acquiesce in it as a precedent," if—and only if—it "had been made by the unanimous concurrence of the judges, and without any apparent partisan bias, and in accordance with legal public expectation, and with the steady practice of the departments throughout our history, and had been in no part, based on assumed historical facts which are not really true; or, if wanting in some of these, it had been before the court more than once, and had there been affirmed and re-affirmed through a course of years." But because the decision satisfied none of those requirements, it was "not resistance," "not factious," "not even disrespectful" to regard it "as not having yet quite established a settled doctrine."

Curiously, Lincoln did not make the common Republican argument, raised by dissenting justices in the case, that the decision regarding congressional power to prohibit slavery in the territories was *obiter dictum,* an incidental observation lacking the force of law.

Heatedly, Lincoln challenged Taney's suggestion that the condition of American blacks had improved since the adoption of the Constitution. Pointing out that in 1857 fewer states allowed blacks to vote or masters to manumit their slaves than had done so seventy years earlier, Lincoln eloquently and compassionately described the plight of the black man in America: "All the powers of earth seem rapidly combining against him. Mammon is after him; ambition follows, and philosophy follows, and the Theology of the day is fast joining the cry. They have him in his prison house; they have searched his person, and left no prying instrument with him. One after another they have closed the heavy iron doors upon him, and now they have him, as it were, bolted in with a lock of a hundred keys, which can never be unlocked without the concurrence of every key; the keys in the hands of a hundred different men, and they scattered to a hundred different and distant places; and they stand musing as to what invention, in all the dominions of mind and matter, can be produced to make the impossibility of his escape more complete than it is. It is grossly incorrect to say or assume, that the public estimate of the negro is more favorable now than it was at the origin of the government."

Lincoln protested vehemently against Douglas's racial demagoguery. Conceding that there was "a natural disgust in the minds of nearly all white people, to the idea of an indiscriminate amalgamation of the white and black races," Lincoln scornfully observed that Douglas "evidently is basing his chief hope, upon the chances of being able to appropriate the benefit of this disgust to himself. If he can, by much drumming and repeating, fasten the odium of that idea upon his adversaries, he thinks he can struggle through the storm. He therefore clings to this hope, as a drowning man to the last plank. He makes an occasion for lugging it in from the opposition to the Dred Scott decision. He finds the Republicans insisting that the Declaration of Independence includes ALL men, black as well as white; and forthwith he boldly denies that it includes negroes at all, and proceeds to argue gravely that all who contend it does, do so only because they want to vote, and eat, and sleep, and marry with negroes!" Bosh! said Lincoln. "I protest against that counterfeit logic which concludes that, because I do not want a black woman for a *slave* I must necessarily want her for a *wife*. I need not have her for either, I can just leave her alone. In some respects she certainly is not my equal; but in her natural right to eat the bread she earns with her own hands without asking leave of any one else, she is my equal, and the equal of all others."

Cleverly, Lincoln showed that Douglas's complaint about the Republicans' desire to promote racial mixing was better directed at whites in the South, where the mulatto population of 405,751 dwarfed the mulatto population of the North (56,649). These figures demonstrated that "slavery is the greatest source of amalgamation." If Douglas were sincere in his desire to prevent racial amalgamation, he should oppose the expansion of the peculiar institution.

Lincoln was especially indignant at the way that Douglas made "a mere wreck—mangled ruin" out of the Declaration of Independence, which "contemplated the progressive improvement in the condition of all men everywhere," by insisting that it "referred to the white race alone, and not to the African." The authors of that "glorious" document, Lincoln observed, "intended to include *all* men," black as well as white, "but they did not intend to declare all men equal *in all respects*. They did not mean to say all were equal in color, size, intellect, moral developments, or social capacity. They defined with tolerable distinctness, in what respects they did consider all men created equal—equal in 'certain inalienable rights, among which are life, liberty, and the pursuit of happiness.'" They "did not mean to assert the obvious untruth, that all were then actually enjoying that equality, nor yet, that they were about to confer it immediately upon them." Rather they "meant to set up a standard maxim for free society, which should be familiar to all, and revered by all; constantly looked to, constantly labored for, and even though never perfectly attained, constantly approximated, and thereby constantly spreading and deepening its influence, and augmenting the happiness and value of life to all people of all colors everywhere." The Declaration's statement about equality was intended to be "a stumbling block to those who in after times might seek to turn a free people back into the hateful paths of despotism." Its authors "knew the proneness of prosperity to breed tyrants, and they meant when such should re-appear in this fair land and commence their vocation they should find left for them at least one hard nut to crack."

Lincoln chided Douglas for his inconsistent application of the popular sovereignty doctrine. Whereas the Little Giant opposed federal intervention in the Kansas Territory to forbid slavery, he supported federal intervention in the Utah Territory to control Mormon settlers. This double standard "is only additional proof . . . that that doctrine was a mere deceitful pretense for the benefit of slavery."

In closing, Lincoln passionately drew a distinction between the two parties: "The Republicans inculcate, with whatever of ability they can, that the negro is a man; that his bondage is cruelly wrong; and that the field of his oppression ought not to be enlarged. The Democrats deny his manhood; deny, or dwarf to insignificance, the wrong of his bondage; so far as possible, crush all sympathy for him, and cultivate and excite hatred and disgust against him; compliment themselves as Union-savers for doing so; and call the indefinite outspreading of his bondage 'a sacred right of self-government.'" Economic self-interest helped explain the Democrats' views, Lincoln argued: "The plainest print cannot be read through a gold eagle [coin]; and it will be ever hard to find many men who will send a slave to Liberia, and pay his passage while they can send him to a new country, Kansas, for instance, and sell him for fifteen hundred dollars."[143]

Curiously, Lincoln dwelt at much greater length on the Supreme Court's denial of black citizenship than on the overthrow of the Missouri Compromise. Politically, it would have been safer to focus on the latter rather than the former, given the intense Negrophobia of the Illinois electorate. Moreover, he did not attempt to show how the decision might affect Douglas's popular sovereignty doctrine; that task he postponed for a year. Given the weak reasoning of the court's majority opinion and concurring opinions, the vigorous dissents of Justices Benjamin R. Curtis and John McLean, and the significance of the slavery issue in American life, Lincoln was justified in maintaining that *Dred Scott* did not definitively settle the question of slavery in the territories.

The *Southern Illinoisan* called Lincoln's speech an "able and masterly refutation of Douglas' slanders."[144] In the Chicago *Tribune*, Herndon praised it for containing "no rant—no fustian—no bombast." Instead, "there was something in it of more force and power than these; the heart felt, and he gave utterance to the heart inspiration, clothed in the eternal maxims of purest reason."[145] Herndon told friends in Massachusetts that "Lincoln 'bursted Douglas wide open' as we say [in the] west" with his "gentlemanly—strong—powerful and conclusive speech," which contrasted sharply with the Little Giant's "low, gutter, rabble-rousing" effort.[146] Gustave Koerner, however, found Lincoln's remarks "too much on the old conservative order." Lincoln, he said, was "an excellent man, but no match to such impudent Jesuits & sophists as Douglas."[147]

The speech attracted attention outside Illinois. The New York *Times* ran excerpts, though it incorrectly identified the site where it was given as Indianapolis.[148] The New York *Tribune* published a synopsis submitted by an Illinoisan who declared that "there is not a man in this State whose opinions on political subjects command more universal respect by all classes of men, than his."[149]

A striking feature of this speech was Lincoln's compassionate description of the plight of blacks. Usually he shied away from expressing concern for the suffering of the slaves, probably because Illinois voters would be unresponsive to such antislavery appeals. But when Julian M. Sturtevant commented to him that St. Louis opponents of slavery seemed to care only for the well-being of whites, Lincoln replied: "I must take into account the rights of the poor negro."[150]

A Democratic paper, in commenting on Lincoln's address, sneered at him as a failure in whatever he turned his hand to. He probably would not have disagreed, at least not strenuously. Around that time he wrote a private memo comparing his lack of success with Douglas's string of accomplishments: "Twenty-two years ago Judge Douglas and I first became acquainted. We were both young then; he a trifle younger than I. Even then, we were both ambitious; I, perhaps, quite as much so as he. With *me*, the race of ambition has been a failure—a flat failure; with *him* it has been one of splendid success. His name fills the nation; and is not unknown, even, in foreign lands. I affect no contempt for the high eminence he has reached. So reached, that the oppressed of my species, might have shared with me in the elevation, I would rather stand on that eminence, than wear the richest crown that ever pressed a monarch's brow."[151]

In 1858, the comparatively obscure Lincoln would challenge the internationally famous Douglas in what became known as the Lincoln-Douglas debates, not the Douglas-Lincoln debates. They would raise Lincoln to national prominence and fatally injure the Little Giant's chances to win the presidency. In time, most people would remember Douglas only as Lincoln's debate opponent, while the name of Lincoln would "fill the nation" and reverberate around the world.

"A House Divided"
Lincoln vs. Douglas
(1857–1858)

Throughout 1857 and the first half of 1858, Lincoln devoted himself to his law practice. When asked to speak publicly on behalf of the Republicans, he replied in May 1858: "It is too early, considering that when I once begin making political speeches I shall have no respite till November. The *labor* of that I might endure, but I really can not spare the time from my business."[1]

Lecture on "Discoveries and Inventions"

He did, however, carve out time to deliver a lecture on "Discoveries and Inventions." In 1855, Lincoln and some friends, including Henry C. Whitney, had read and discussed historian George Bancroft's recent oration on "The Necessity, the Reality, and the Promise of the Progress of the Human Race," which celebrated mankind's progress in the nineteenth century as "unequaled in its discoveries and its deeds."[2] Lincoln remarked "that he had for some time been contemplating the writing of a lecture on *man* . . . from his earliest primeval state to his present high development" and "detailed at length the views and opinions he designed to incorporate in his lecture."[3]

(Mrs. Norman B. Judd provided another version of the lecture's origin. In 1856, Lincoln told her that one evening he and fellow lawyers on the circuit were discussing the date at which the brass age began. He recalled that Tubal Cain, the son of Lemach, worked in brass and that his brother Jubal made harps and organs. Checking his recollection in the Bible, he ransacked the Old Testament and compiled a list of the discoveries and inventions mentioned there. Shortly afterward, he accepted an invitation to address the Young Men's Literary Society in Bloomington; he used those Old Testament notes, as well as some research in an encyclopedia, to create his lecture.)

Lincoln's lecture, "Discoveries and Inventions," like his 1838 Lyceum address, was ostensibly nonpolitical but in fact contained a thinly disguised put-down of Stephen A. Douglas. At the time, the Little Giant was championing a program of bumptious, expansionistic nationalism known as "Young America," a title that distinguished it from "old fogy" Whigs and senior Democratic leaders. The term applied to a faction of the Democratic Party eager to revive the jingoistic spirit of Manifest Destiny that had prevailed in the mid-1840s; to promote the expansion of the United States southward and westward; to emulate the contemporary Young Germany and Young Italy movements; to express sympathy for gallant, unsuccessful European revolutionaries, especially the Hungarians, whose bid for independence had been squashed by Russian troops in 1848; and to repudiate the stuffy conservatism of superannuated officeholders like Lewis Cass. Douglas was widely regarded as Young America's chief spokesman. In his lecture, Lincoln discussed "Young America" as if it were a person—Douglas—rather than a movement or a slogan. "Some think him conceited, and arrogant," Lincoln remarked, adding that Young America (i.e., Douglas) had reason "to entertain a rather extensive opinion of himself." Lincoln poked fun at Young America for coveting Cuba (a favorite hobby of Douglas's) and other territory: "He owns a large part of the world, by right of possessing it; and all the rest by right of *wanting* it, and *intending* to have it." Citing a passage from Joseph Addison's play, *Cato*, Lincoln playfully remarked: "As Plato had for the immortality of the soul, so Young America has 'a pleasing hope—a fond desire—a longing after' ter[r]itory." Young America also lusted after political office (in Douglas's case, the presidency): "He has a great passion—a perfect rage—for the '*new*'; particularly new men for office." Mocking Douglas's popular sovereignty doctrine as well as his expansionism, Lincoln said: "He is a great friend of humanity; and his desire for land is not selfish, but merely an impulse to extend the area of freedom." Lincoln alluded to Douglas's well-known fondness for liquor and cigars: "His horror is for all that is old, particularly 'Old Fogy'; and if there be any thing old which he can endure, it is only old whiskey and old tobacco."

Turning from political satire, Lincoln became serious, asserting that "the discovery of America, and the introduction of Patent-laws" ranked among the most significant of all modern developments. He extolled not only patents like the one he himself held but the cast of mind that produced them: "To be fruitful in invention, it is indispensable to have a *habit* of observation and reflection." He deemed written language "the great invention of the world" and called printing "the *better* half of writing." The ignorance of the Dark Ages he considered "slavery of the mind," which Gutenberg's printing press abolished, creating a "habit of freedom of thought." Such imagery came easily to a man who had emancipated himself from rural ignorance and backwardness through the written and printed word and who strove to end chattel slavery.[4]

The lecture failed to impress. At Pontiac an auditor reported that "the people generally were disappointed in his lecture as it was on no particular subject and not well connected. He was, I thought, decidedly inferior to many a lecturer I have heard."[5] In Jacksonville, where the audience was small, he refused to accept an honorarium, asking only for enough money to cover expenses. When a mere forty people showed up to hear him in Bloomington, Lincoln canceled the event. Later he referred to this lecture as "rather a poor one."[6]

Herndon agreed, calling "Discoveries and Inventions" a "lifeless thing." He thought that Lincoln, for all his skill as a political speaker, "had not the fire, taste, reading, eloquence, etc., which would make him a lecturer."[7] Although Lincoln did compose a fragment of a talk, probably written in the late 1850s, to be delivered to law students, he never again attempted a formal nonpolitical lecture.

Douglas's Bid for Republican Support

While devoting himself to law and his lecture, Lincoln also followed closely the high political drama unfolding in Washington, where Douglas had declared war on the Buchanan administration. During the autumn of 1857, pro-slavery Kansans, though a distinct minority of the territory's population, had managed to dominate the constitutional convention in the town of Lecompton, largely because Free Soilers, regarding the election for delegates as fraudulent, had shunned the polls. When the territory applied for statehood under a pro-slavery constitution passed at Lecompton, Buchanan in a special message on December 8 urged Congress to accept this outcome and admit Kansas, even though most fair-minded observers regarded the constitution as woefully unrepresentative of majority opinion among the settlers. Northerners were outraged by what they considered yet another example of Southerners' high-handed, arbitrary behavior and contempt for fair play. Douglas, suffering from hurt pride, very fearful that if he supported the Lecompton Constitution he would doom his chances for reelection in 1858, resentful of Buchanan for ignoring his patronage requests, and incensed by the administration's support for a clear miscarriage of popular sovereignty, immediately denounced the president's message. "By God sir, I made Mr. James Buchanan, and by God sir, I will unmake him!" he exclaimed. Buchanan warned him to beware of the melancholy fate of senators who had opposed President Andrew Jackson, saying: "Mr. Douglas, I desire you to remember that no Democrat ever yet differed from an administration of his own choice without being crushed." Douglas replied: "Mr. President, I wish you to remember that General Jackson is dead, sir."[8]

The Little Giant's impulsive revolt, an uncharacteristic act for such a pragmatic champion of Democratic unity, cheered his party colleagues back home. "Your position takes the wind clean out of the B[lack] Republican leaders. Their only hope is that you will yet waver," a constituent wrote.[9] Another declared: "You have adopted the only course that could save the Northern Democracy from annihilation at the next election."[10] Even some Illinois Republicans applauded his stand and considered backing him for reelection.

Observing the "'*rumpus*' among the democracy over the Kansas constitution," Lincoln was reminded of a case he had tried involving two contentious old farmers who had come to blows. Lincoln was hired to defend the winner of the fight, who was sued by the loser for assault and battery. When a witness for the plaintiff sought to exaggerate the fight's importance, Lincoln asked him how much ground the pugilists had covered.

"About an acre, stranger," replied the witness.

"Well, now, witness," said Lincoln, "just tell me, *wasn't that just about the smallest crop of a fight off of an acre of ground that ever you heard of?*"

"That's so, stranger; *I'll be gol darned if it wasn't!*"

After this exchange, the jury fined Lincoln's client 10 cents.[11]

Lincoln counseled his allies to "stand clear" of the fight, for "both the President and Douglas are wrong," and Republicans "should not espouse the cause of either, because they may consider the other a little the farther wrong of the two." He told Lyman Trumbull that Douglas was attempting "to draw off some Republicans on this dodge" and had made "some impression on one or two."[12] Trumbull doubted that the controversy would "amount to much, except perhaps to help us a little with the people."[13]

But in fact, Douglas's rebellion shook the political world. Many Republicans in the East regarded his bolt as providential, splitting the Democrats and smoothing the way for a Republican victory in 1860. Douglas met with Horace Greeley, editor of the influential New York *Tribune,* who believed that the senator might well join the Republican Party. Greeley therefore urged Illinoisans to support the Little Giant's reelection bid. Lauding Douglas's "fidelity and courage," Greeley told his many readers that the senator's "course has not been merely right—it has been conspicuously, courageously, eminently so."[14] Though privately Greeley called the Little Giant "a low and dangerous demagogue" with "enormous self-conceit," the *Tribune* editor was convinced that Douglas could not be beaten.[15] Greeley wrote to John O. Johnson, secretary of the Illinois Republican State Central Committee, urging him to back Douglas. Johnson, speaking for a party that had been formed largely to oppose Douglas and his popular sovereignty doctrine, replied that "we shall without a doubt send one of the *best republicans, ablest statesmen,* and *truest men,* which can be found in [the] West, to fill the place which Mr Douglas now occupies. On the contrary, if an attempt is made to any extent, to get up sympathy for Mr Douglas, in his present position, it will *inevitably result in our defeat.*"[16]

Other leading papers in the East, including the Boston *Atlas and Daily Bee,* the Albany *Evening Journal,* the Hartford *Courant,* as well as the *Atlantic Monthly,* seconded Greeley's motion that Republicans support Douglas. "The general recognition of the principle of popular sovereignty is all that is needed to restore peace to the country, and to allay the agitation of the Slavery question," declared the New York *Times.*[17] The Springfield, Massachusetts, *Republican* praised Douglas as "the man who leads the battle against the administration and the slave power," chastised Illinois Republicans for opposing him, and called "ridiculous" the "sensitiveness" and "ill-temper" they displayed in protesting against "eastern politicians" for supporting the senator's reelection bid. They regarded Lincoln as "a man of less intellectual ability and political power" than Douglas.[18] Even the Washington *National Era,* the antislavery periodical that had first serialized Harriet Beecher Stowe's bestselling novel, *Uncle Tom's Cabin,* endorsed the Little Giant.

Prominent New England Republicans like Henry Wilson, Truman Smith, Nathaniel P. Banks, and Anson Burlingame sided with Greeley. On the floor of the House of Representatives, Massachusetts Congressman Burlingame called Douglas "gallant and gifted" and urged voters to stand by him and his Democratic allies "without distinction of party."[19] (In December 1858, Burlingame would express gratitude to Douglas Democrats for helping him win reelection.)

Along with Greeley's editorials, Burlingame's speech—the first pro-Douglas public feeler by a Republican congressman—infuriated his party colleagues in Illinois. Contemptuously Lincoln referred to the Massachusetts congressman as "Sister Burlingame." "There seems to be a considerable notion pervading the brains of political wet nurses at the East," observed the Chicago *Press and Tribune* in response to Burlingame, "that the barbarians of Illinois cannot take care of themselves." Caustically the paper remarked that "Mr. Burlingame would look well on the stump with a Douglas orator whose every other sentence contained a whisky-inspired jeer at the 'Black Republicans.' . . . If the Republicans of Illinois should now sink all party differences and reelect Mr. Douglas, their party would be so disintegrated that the State would be lost to freedom in 1860, or if saved, saved only because he (Douglas) allowed it to be saved. The Republican party would be wholly at his mercy."[20]

Lincoln, the obvious candidate to challenge the Little Giant for his senate seat, indignantly asked Lyman Trumbull, "What does the New-York Tribune mean by it's constant eulogising, and admiring, and magnifying [of] Douglas? Does it, in this, speak the sentiments of the republicans at Washington? Have they concluded that the republican cause, generally, can be best promoted by sacraficing us here in Illinois?" Bitterly he added, "If so we would like to know it soon; it will save us a great deal of labor to surrender at once."[21]

Trumbull wondered how the Republicans ought to respond to the Little Giant's revolt. "Should Douglas be driven out of the African democracy, as I think he will be, what are we to do with him? You know the 'man who won the elephant' found it difficult to dispose of him."[22] He told Lincoln: "I do not feel just now either like embracing Douglas, or assailing him. As far as he goes I believe him to be right, though his course now is utterly inconsistent with what it was a year ago."[23] Trumbull added that he had "seen the difficulty which the laudation of Douglas by Republicans was likely to occasion us in Ill[inoi]s" and had "remonstrated with some of our friends about it; but his course was so unexpected to many & was looked upon as such a God send that they could not refrain from giving him more credit than he deserves." Some Republicans in Washington "act like fools in running after and flattering Douglas. He encourages it and invites such men as Wilson, Seward, Burlingame, [Marcus J.] Parrott, &c., to come & confer with him & they seem wonderfully pleased to go."[24] Republican Senator James Dixon of Connecticut wanted to establish yet another new party, with Douglas at its head, to overthrow the Southern-dominated Democracy. The Little Giant encouraged such courtship, telling Senator Henry Wilson "that he hoped '*the Republicans would do as little as possible about Candidates for Eighteen sixty. Let the Charleston convention* [of the national Democratic Party] *be held, and when they have made their ticket we will all combine and crush it into powder.*'"[25] Alluding to these politicos (especially Seward), Chicago mayor John Wentworth, known as Long John because he was 6'9" tall, warned Lincoln: "you are sold for the Senate by men who are drinking the wine of Douglass at Washington."[26]

Douglas later denied consorting with the Republicans, though abundant evidence suggests that he did. Several times he informed prominent Republicans that he had severed his ties with the Democrats, that he had "checked his baggage through," that "he had crossed the Rubicon and burned his boats," that "hereafter he should be found in the opposition to the South." On a map he pointed out how his plan to have the Pacific Railroad run southwest from the Missouri River would facilitate the influx of so many settlers that slavery could never take hold along its route. He also assured Republicans that the Kansas-Nebraska Act was essentially an antislavery statute.[27] Anson Burlingame, Schuyler Colfax, and Frank Blair often met with Douglas at his house to hold private conversations during which the senator inveighed against Southern high-handedness. Colfax described at length a three-hour interview he and Burlingame had with Douglas on December 14, 1857. Blair also acknowledged that those meetings took place. The Little Giant asked Pennsylvania Congressman John Covode to request Trumbull to win the backing of Illinois Republicans for his reelection.

Evidently speaking for his law partner, William Herndon protested to Congressman Elihu B. Washburne about rumors "that Illinois was to be chaffered for, and *huckstered* off without our consent, and against our will:—that we were to get *Treason* and the *Traitor* as the consideration for the sale—that Douglas was to be elevated to the Senate again over the heads of long-pure and well tried Republicans." In tones reminiscent of Lincoln's heated complaint about John J. Hardin's attempt to cheat him out of the nomination for the U.S. House a decade earlier, Herndon insisted that Illinoisans "want to govern ourselves 'in our own way.' We want the man *that* we want, and have him, and *him alone. . . .* We in Illinois know pretty well who the pimps of traf[f]ic are. N[ew] York—Massachusetts—may sell their own men just as they please, but *Illinois is not for sale*. We are not willing to be sacrificed for a *fiction*." If the Republicans of Illinois were to run Douglas as their candidate for the senate, "the masses would drag us from power and grind us to powder." The Little Giant's "abuse of us as Whigs—as Republicans—as men in society, and as individuals, has been so slanderous—dirty—low—long, and *continuous,* that we cannot soon forgive, and *can never forget*." If Douglas were to embrace the antislavery cause, "then it is sufficient time to ask us in Illinois to give up the great & honorable, and grab—raise the mean and undivine."[28]

In addition to wooing members of Congress, Douglas sent an emissary to ask the editor of the Chicago *Press and Tribune,* Charles H. Ray, if he would support the Little Giant for reelection as a Republican. "We are almost confounded here by his anomalous position," Ray told Trumbull, "and know not how to treat him and his overtures to the Republican party."[29] In January, O. M. Hatch, the tall, lean, and affable secretary of state of Illinois, noted that party leaders "concluded to *Keep cool* for the present, and see what might be developed in Congress."[30] Congressman Elihu B. Washburne allegedly visited Ray at the behest of Horace Greeley seeking support for Douglas. After some discussion, Ray and other editors rejected Greeley's overture. Ray urged Trumbull to "tell our friends in the House [presumably including Washburne], who may be more zealous than discreet, that we in Illinois have not delegated our powers to them, and that we may not ratify bargains that they make—in a word, that among the inducements which they hold out to the 'distinguished Senator' to ensure the continuance of his fight with the Administration, they must not hold up the Senatorship as the prize of his defection. I take it, that it is a foregone conclusion that Abm. Lincoln will be the next Republican candidate for Mr. Douglas' seat, and that he will occupy it if we have a majority, or, that we must make up our minds to a fight."[31]

It is not clear if Washburne actually lobbied on behalf of the Little Giant. According to a correspondent of Long John Wentworth, he did. When Lincoln mentioned this rumor to the Galena congressman, he emphatically denied it, though he did tell Herndon in April: "I have said, God speed him [Douglas]. I am rejoiced to see him laboring so manfully in a direction to make some amends for the injury he has brought upon the country. He is doing a grand service for the republican party, and for one, while he pursues his present course, I shall not lay a straw in his path. He is fighting this Lecompton swindle in all its phases, with boldness and determination. If things go on, as it now seems inevitable, if he be not with us, a vast number of his followers will be, and hence I cannot see the wisdom of abusing him, or them, as matters stand now. I have no fears that the republican party is to be swallowed by them. I say leave open wide the doors and invite all to come on to our platform and greet them with kind words. Our party is not so large but what it will hold a few more."[32]

Both Herndon and his partner ignored insinuations that Washburne was flirting with Douglas. Lincoln speculated to the congressman that the rumor was probably based on "some misconstruction, coupled with a high degree of sensitiveness," and assured him: "I am satisfied you have done no wrong."[33]

Lincoln could not, however, share Washburne's enthusiasm for Douglas. To Lincoln it appeared obvious that the Little Giant, though opposing Buchanan on a matter of fact (i.e., whether the Lecompton Constitution truly reflected the views of most Kansans), continued to side with the president on matters of general policy. In May, Lincoln told a friend: "there remains all the difference there ever was between Judge Douglas & the Republicans—*they* insisting the Congress *shall*, and *he* insisting that congress *shall not*, keep slavery out of the Ter[r]itories *before & up to the time* they form State constitutions." By making common cause to fight the Lecompton Constitution, neither the Illinois senator nor the Republicans "conceded anything which was ever in dispute between them."[34]

Four months earlier the Springfield *Journal* had run an editorial, which Lincoln may well have written, questioning Douglas's sincerity. During the 1856–1857 session of Congress, the Little Giant had seemed unconcerned about fair play in Kansas: "if he did not cheer on the Border Ruffians in their work of devastation and plunder, we all know how he reviled and defamed the Free State men and Republicans, not only as the authors of these outrages, but as seeking to prolong the troubles in Kansas." Republicans "most cheerfully give him all due credit for his recent condemnation of the Lecompton Constitution; but we demand to know why he did not lift up his voice in defense of popular sovereignty in Kansas, when Lawrence, Leavenworth and Osawatomie were ravaged, when he *knew*, or ought to have known, that till the present time there has been scarcely an office-holder in the whole Territory who was not notorious, during all the troubles there, as connected with the bandits who robbed and murdered the people, fleeing from their burning homes. He *knows* that Mr. Buchanan, instead of handling these men as pirates and outlaws, has appointed them to office in the midst of a people they have pillaged."[35]

While some of Lincoln's friends dismissed Douglas's rebellion as an election-year gimmick, others were truly tempted to ally with anti-Lecompton Democrats. Pascal P. Enos told Henry Wilson that although he supported Lincoln for the senate, he did not feel bound to oppose Douglas "under all circumstances."[36] In March, Ozias M. Hatch and Jesse K. Dubois asked Lincoln about overtures being made by Douglas's allies. In reply, Lincoln urged them to resist the senator's siren song: "we must never sell old friends to buy old enemies. Let us have a State convention, in which we can have a full consultation; and till which, let us all stand firm, making no committals as to strange and new combinations."[37]

In December 1857, Lincoln prepared a speech angrily warning Republicans not to flock to Douglas's banner, no matter how much they might admire his attacks on the Buchanan administration. He scorned the demagoguery of the Little Giant, whom he called "the most dangerous enemy of liberty, because the most insidious one."[38] He was especially incensed at Douglas's remarks in June 1857, when the Little Giant charged that whoever believed that blacks were included in the Declaration of Independence's assertion that "all men are created equal" must necessarily "license him [the black man] to marry a white woman." According to Douglas, the Founding Fathers "had witnessed the sad and melancholy results of the mixture of the races in Mexico, South America and Central America, where the Spanish, from motives of policy, had admitted the negro and other inferior races to citizenship, and consequently to political and social amalgamation. The demoralization and degradation which prevailed in the Spanish and French colonies, where no distinction on account of color or race was tolerated, operated as a warning to our Revolutionary fathers to preserve the purity of the white race." The Founders understood "the great natural law which declares that amalgamation between superior and inferior races brings their posterity down to the lower level of the inferior, but never elevates them to the high level of the superior race."[39]

(In the 1858 campaign, Douglas would assert that the "experience of the world in all ages proves that the negro is incapable of self-government in all climes," prompting a Republican paper to ask "what the experience of the world has to say on the subject of French, or German, or Russian, or Irish, or Italian capacity for self-government?"[40] In that campaign, Douglas was also to argue that all presidents from the time of Washington had implicitly endorsed the proposition that blacks were not citizens by refusing to grant them passports.)

Lincoln also condemned a resolution (allegedly written by Douglas) endorsed by Morgan County Democrats, who declared their opposition "to placing negroes on an equality with white men, by allowing them to vote and hold office, and serve on juries, and testify in the courts against white men, *and marry white women*, as advocated by those who claim that the declaration of Independence asserts that white men and negroes were created equal by the Almighty."[41] Lincoln further deplored the Little Giant's allegation of November 1857, that "Black Republicans . . . will allow the blacks to push us from our sidewalk and elbow us out of car seats *and stink us out of our places of worship.*"[42]

Douglas's indifference to the evils of slavery, which contrasted starkly with the Republican view that the peculiar institution was "not only morally wrong, but a 'deadly poison' in a government like ours, professedly based on the equality of men," aroused Lincoln's ire. Republicans, he advised, should not "oppose any measure merely because Judge Douglas proposes it." Indeed, they ought to join him in assaulting the Lecompton Constitution, which "should be throttled and killed as hastily and as heartily as a rabid dog." But the "combined charge of Nebraskaism, and Dred Scottism must be repulsed, and rolled back. The deceitful cloak of 'self-government' wherewith 'the sum of all villanies' [i.e., slavery] seeks to protect and adorn itself, must be torn from it's hateful carcass."[43]

Most Illinois Republicans agreed that Douglas was hardly a fit champion of their cause, no matter how vehemently he combated the Lecompton Constitution. The Chicago *Press and Tribune* said that in battling the Lecompton fraud Douglas was simply "an efficient co-worker, and we shall treat him accordingly." The Little Giant "has recanted none of his political heresies, nor has he given evidence of any intention of doing so. . . . [I]t is asking too much of the freemen of Illinois . . . to support a man for the Senate who, if not avowedly a champion of slavery expansion, gives all his influence to it, and against the personal and political rights of free white people who depend upon their own honest industry for a livelihood."[44] State Auditor Jesse K. Dubois remarked: "It is asking too much for human nature . . . to now surrender to Judge Douglas after having driven him by force of Public opinion to do what he has done to quietly let him step foremost in our ranks now and make us all take back seats."[45] The *Illinois State Journal* spoke bluntly: Republicans "intend to stand firmly by their own colors and let the Douglas men 'skin their own skunks.'"[46]

Many of the party faithful believed that Lincoln had earned the senatorial nomination. They regarded him as their most capable leader and felt that it was only fair to reward the magnanimity he had shown by bowing to Trumbull in the 1855 senate contest. The Clinton *Central Transcript,* observing that a "penitent prostitute may be received into the church but she should not lead the choir," speculated that if the Republicans had no champion like Lincoln, a few might "lend a hand in again electing Judge Douglas." But Lincoln deserved the party's allegiance, and Republicans "do not feel like sacrificing the gallant Lincoln upon the shrine of the man who turned traitor upon treason, even though his future should be indorsed by Greeley & Co."[47] An editor in Dixon agreed: "We want no such ominous wooden horses run into our camp. All eyes are turned toward Mr. Lincoln as . . . the unanimous choice of the people."[48] Charles Henry Ray urged Republicans to shun Douglas, insisting that "Abe Lincoln cannot be overlooked—should not be."[49] Gustave Koerner recommended that Republicans make the Douglasites "understand, that *Lincoln* is our man" and that "we will try every means to elect men favorable to him."[50] A Chicago Republican told Greeley, "We all think more highly of Douglas than we did a year ago, but still we hope to be pardoned for preferring one of the 'truest and most effective advocates of Republican principles' [i.e., Lincoln] to the Little Giant."[51] Heatedly John M. Palmer protested against the "Wall Street Operation" by which "Lincoln to whom we are under great obligations and all of our men . . . are to be kicked to one side and we are to throw up our caps for Judge Douglass and he very coolly tells us all the time that we are abolitionists and Negro Worshippers and that he accepts our votes as a favor to us."[52] In support of his candidacy, Long John Wentworth's paper said: "Lincoln has worked hard and had nothing."[53]

Democrats tried to sow dissention and to alarm voters by alleging that despite his public praise for Lincoln, Wentworth was secretly maneuvering to win the nomination himself. "Under no possible circumstances will Wentworth allow Lincoln to be chosen," declared Douglas's organ, the Chicago *Times*, whose editor reported that Wentworth "openly declares that Lincoln can never get elected."[54] The *Illinois State Register* warned that "the Chicago autocrat of black republicanism will have complete control of a majority of the next legislature, and if that party should have a majority . . . he will control the nominations of its caucus."[55] In truth, though Wentworth may have harbored senatorial ambitions, he realized that his chances were poor, for his abrasive, arrogant personality had alienated many Republicans as well as former allies in the Democratic Party. He therefore did nothing to promote his own candidacy. Lincoln bemoaned the "everlasting croaking about Wentworth" in the Democratic press, which sought to frighten men into supporting Democratic candidates for the legislature because the Republicans might choose Wentworth senator. When Democrats also alleged that Lincoln had gained Wentworth's support by agreeing to back Long John for governor, Lincoln denied it. "I am not directly or indirectly committed to any one" for governor, he told Charles L. Wilson. "I have had many free conversations with John Wentworth; but he never dropped a remark that led me to suspect that he wishes to be Governor. Indeed, it is due to truth to say that while he has uniformly expressed himself for me, he has never hinted at any condition."[56]

In addition to these challenges at home, Lincoln and the Illinois Republicans had to contend with the Eastern Republicans' persistent enthusiasm for Douglas. Norman B. Judd, Wentworth, Herndon, and others kept praising Lincoln to their friends in the East. Alluding to Seward, Herndon asked Theodore Parker to "tell *him* to keep his fingers out of our fight—keep his wishes to himself, if he is for Douglas."[57] In March, Herndon visited Washington, New England, and the Middle Atlantic states, ostensibly as a mere sightseer, but in reality acting as his partner's eyes and ears. (As president, Lincoln would dispatch his personal secretaries and many others on such missions.) Lincoln, though he professed a liking for Greeley, was personally "dejected" by the influential editor's support of Douglas, saying (in substance), that the man "is not doing me, an old Republican and a tried antislavery man, right. He is talking up Douglas, an untrue and an untried man, a dodger, a wriggler, a tool of the South once and now a snapper at it—hope he will bite 'em good—but I don't feel that it is exactly right to pull me down in order to elevate Douglas. . . . I wish that someone would put a flea in Greeley's ear—see Trumbull, Sumner, Wilson, Seward, Parker, Garrison, Phillips, and others, and try and turn the currents in the right directions. These men ought to trust the tried and true men."[58]

Taking the hint, Herndon packed his bags and headed for Washington. There he met with Douglas, who told him: "Give Mr. Lincoln my regards when you return, and tell him I have crossed the river and burned my boat." He added "that he and the Republicans would be together soon." From Trumbull, Herndon learned that some

Eastern Republicans were scheming to betray their Illinois counterparts by supporting Douglas's reelection bid. Rumor had it that Greeley, Seward, Weed, Henry Wilson, and Douglas had struck a bargain whereby the Little Giant pledged to support
Seward for president in 1860 if the editor of the *Tribune* would back Douglas's reelection in 1858. Evidently, the Little Giant in the winter of 1857 had agreed to help defeat
the Lecompton Constitution in return for Greeley's promise to back him and other
anti-Lecompton Democrats for reelection.

In New York, Herndon called on Greeley, who, he reported, "evidently wants
Douglas sustained and sent back to the Senate." Greeley "talked bitterly—somewhat
so—against the papers in Ill[inoi]s—and said they were fools." When Herndon referred to the Little Giant as one who had "abused and betrayed" the North, Greeley
replied: "Forget the past and sustain the *righteous*." The "Republican standard is too
high," the editor declared; "we want something practical." The party platform, in his
view, was "too abstract" and "ought to be *lowered*—'slid down.'"[59]

After returning home, Herndon informed Greeley that Illinois Republicans
could not possibly support Douglas. Three months later, Herndon scoffed at Greeley's belief that Douglas might join the Republicans: "Did Douglas ever give an inch
in his whole political life?" he asked. "He is the most imperious and selfish man in
America. He is the greatest liar in the world."[60] Herndon doubtless wrote in consultation with Lincoln, who did not directly communicate with Greeley in 1858.

Seward's role in Illinois politics is not clear. Privately, he lauded Douglas and
other anti-Lecompton Democrats: "God forbid that I should consent to see freedom
wounded, because my own lead or even my own agency in saving it should be rejected.
I will cheerfully cooperate with these new defenders of this sacred cause in Kansas,
and I will award them all due praise . . . for their large share of merit in its deliverance."[61]
Yet when publicly accused of supporting Douglas, Seward through his allies vehemently denied it. In the summer, Seward urged his Illinois friend Samuel L. Baker to
visit the prominent Whig John Bell of Tennessee and get him to endorse Lincoln.
Baker reported to Lincoln that "Seward & Weed both assured me they would do all
they could to help us with money & otherwise."[62] In December 1858, Douglas, in conversation with Charles Henry Ray, spoke freely about his cooperation with Seward;
Ray was convinced that the two men had struck a bargain the previous year.

Warned that Seward's allies in Illinois might balk if Lincoln's candidacy were
regarded as an anti-Seward gesture, Lincoln scouted reports that Seward or Greeley
actually conspired with Douglas. On June 1, Lincoln told Charles L. Wilson that
Greeley might prefer Douglas over himself, but "I do not believe it is so, because of
any secret arrangement with Douglas." Rather, it was "because he thinks Douglas'
superior position, reputation, experience, and *ability*, if you please, would more than
compensate for his lack of a pure republican position, and therefore, his re-election
[would] do the general cause of republicanism, more good, than would the election of
any one of our better undistinguished pure republicans." Lincoln extended this assessment to include Seward, speculating that the New Yorker "feels about as Greeley
does; but, not being a newspaper editor, his feeling, in this respect, is not much
manifested." He assured Wilson that neither he nor his friends had "been setting

stakes against Gov. Seward. No combination has been made *with* me, or *proposed* to me, in relation to the next Presidential candidate."[63]

Although he did not write to Greeley, Lincoln actively corresponded with Illinois Republicans, promoting unity and giving advice about increasing the party's strength in the legislature, which would choose a senator early in 1859. Perhaps at Lincoln's bidding, his friend Jesse K. Dubois urged Republicans in northern Illinois to support a moderate platform, lest they drive off potential supporters in Egypt. Lincoln implored Wentworth's enemies in Chicago to stop criticizing the mayor, warning that "the unrelenting warfare made upon him, is injuring our cause."[64]

Lincoln denied that former Democrats like Wentworth were more likely than former Whigs to desert the Republican Party and support Douglas. There were, after all, some notable examples of pro-Douglas Whigs, among them President Jonathan Blanchard of Knox College, Buckner S. Morris, James W. Singleton, Usher F. Linder, Anthony Thornton, T. Lyle Dickey, and Edwin B. Webb, as well as Cyrus, Ninian, and Benjamin S. Edwards. Even Lincoln's old friend Anson G. Henry supported the Little Giant, and John Todd Stuart declared that he sided with Douglas on the slavery issue, though out of friendship for his former partner he would neither campaign for the senator nor vote for legislators in November. In February, Simeon Francis wrote Douglas a fan letter.

Lincoln's modesty in promoting his own candidacy disappointed Norman B. Judd, chairman of the state Republican Party, who declared on April 19: "If Lincoln expects to be Senator he must make a personal canvass for it in the center of the State. So I advised him two months ago—but I do not hear of any fruits."[65] Some northern Illinois Republicans had begun to argue that since Trumbull of Belleville was already in the senate, it would be fitting if a Northerner like W. B. Ogden or Elihu B. Washburne rather than Lincoln should be the party's candidate to replace Douglas. When Boone County Republicans asked if he wanted a formal endorsement for senator, Lincoln declined: "I suppose it is hardly necessary that any expression of preference for U.S. Senator, should be given at the county, or other local conventions and meetings. When the Republicans of the whole State get together at the State convention, the thing will then be thought of, and something will or will not be done, according as the united judgment may dictate."[66]

On April 21, fear that Douglas might seduce Illinois Republicans all but evaporated at the Democratic state convention in Springfield. There the delegates endorsed the party's 1856 platform calling for popular sovereignty, berated Republicans harshly, and failed to denounce the Buchanan administration for supporting the Lecompton Constitution and for dismissing pro-Douglas government employees. This action alienated antislavery men who could have been won over by the Little Giant. Republicans rejoiced at the "hard blows, and withering strokes" that the pro-Buchanan and pro-Douglas factions administered to one another. "Oh what a sight!" Herndon exclaimed. "Plunderers of the People now at bloody war with each other over the spoils." Douglas "cut his own throat with his own hands," Herndon observed; "he cut himself loose from the Southern Democracy, and ... tore loose from, all Republican sympathy."[67] The disaffected pro-administration delegates, constituting roughly one-tenth of the total and calling themselves National Democrats, bolted the convention and resolved to hold a conclave of their own in June. Sneered at by their detractors as Buchaneers and Danites, they received patronage from the administration as it removed many of Douglas's supporters from office.

The evening of the Democrats' turbulent convention, Lincoln met in Springfield with two dozen leading Republicans to discuss strategy. Everyone in attendance was optimistic about the party's chances and made it clear that they had no intention of supporting Douglas. They expressed great indignation at the course of Anson Burlingame and deplored the wavering of some Illinois congressmen, including Washburne. When some voiced concern that ex-Democrats in their party would desert Lincoln, George T. Brown reassured them that he had spoken with several Democrats-turned-Republican, all of whom vowed their determination to back Lincoln. Brown added that Trumbull's election in 1855 made it morally imperative that he and other former Democrats in the party support Lincoln. Anxiety over Washburne's reported apostasy was dissipated by State Representative Cyrenius B. Denio and Charles H. Ray, to whom the Galena congressman scoffed at rumors that he supported Douglas's reelection. Lincoln was quite disturbed by the controversy over Washburne and assured Ray that he had given no credence to the rumors. He maintained that both Wentworth and Washburne were dependable.

Lincoln rejoiced that the badly divided Democrats left Springfield on April 21 "in not a very encouraged state of mind," while the Republicans with whom he had conferred "parted in high spirits. They think if we do not triumph the fault will be our own, and so I really think."[68] The following day the Republicans agreed to hold their convention on June 16 at Springfield. As Herndon explained, "*Probably,* had not Douglas called *his* convention, or had he not taken the Cincinnati platform as the groundwork of his future course, then it is likely that a kind of compromise would have taken place, *but now and on his present grounds—never.*"[69]

Lincoln denied that he and his colleagues were plotting to make common cause with the pro-Buchanan National Democrats in order to defeat Douglas. "Of course the Republicans do not try to keep the common enemy from dividing; but, so far as I *know,* or *believe,* they will not unite with either branch of the division," he said, adding that "it is difficult for me to see, on what ground they could unite; but it is useless to spend words, there is simply nothing of it. It is a trick of our enemies to try to excite all sorts of suspicions and jealousies amongst us."[70] The following month, Lincoln declared that "if being rather pleased to see a division in the ranks of the democracy, and not doing anything to prevent it" is proof of a conspiracy, then the accusation was valid. "But if it be intended to charge that there is any alliance by which there is to be any concession of principle on either side, or furnishing of the sinews, or partition of offices, or swopping of votes, to any extent; or the doing of anything, great or small, on the one side, for a consideration, express or implied, on the other, no such thing is true."[71]

In fact, Republicans did work behind the scenes to promote discord in the Democratic ranks. Herndon freely acknowledged that the "Ill[inoi]s State Journal, and each and every Republican, is trying to create the split" between the Douglas and Buchanan forces; "we want to make it wider and deeper—hotter and more impassable. Political hatred—deep seated opposition is what is so much desired, and if we can do this between the worshipers of Buck & Dug we will effect it."[72] Lincoln was kept ignorant of such machinations. Herndon reported to Trumbull that his partner "does not know the details of how we get along. I do, but he does not. That kind of thing does not suit his tastes, nor does it suit me, yet I am compelled to do it—do it because I cannot get rid of it."[73] Since his father and brother staunchly supported Buchanan, Herndon was unusually well placed to learn the doings of the National Democrats.

Preserving Republican Unity

A threat to Republican unity emerged in early June when disgruntled Conservatives schemed to defeat Congressman Owen Lovejoy, whom the *Illinois State Register* called a "notorious nigger worshipping abolitionist."[74] Spearheaded by some of Lincoln's close friends—including David Davis, Leonard Swett, T. Lyle Dickey, and Ward Hill Lamon—the anti-Lovejoy movement attracted conservatives like Josh Whitmore, who declared: "I am not only mad, but tired of this Nigger Worshipping. If Lovejoy is to be the nominee, I am ready to vote for a Douglas Democrat."[75] Lincoln, who received appeals from abolitionists to thwart the plot, warned Lovejoy that "[y]our danger *has been* that [the] democracy would wheedle some republican to run against you without a nomination, relying mainly on democratic votes. I have seen the strong men who could make the most trouble in that way, and find that they view the thing in the proper light, and will not consent to be so used." But, he added, "they have been urgently tempted by the enemy; and I think it is still the point for you to guard most vigilantly."[76] When Lovejoy's renomination seemed inevitable, Lincoln counseled Ward Hill Lamon not to support an independent candidate, for such a move would "result in nothing but disaster all round," assuring a Democratic victory, injuring Lincoln's chances for a senate seat, and destroying the reputation of the bolters' nominee.[77] In response to an attack on David Davis, who was accused of advising friends not to vote for Lovejoy, Lincoln wrote a pseudonymous letter to the Chicago *Press and Tribune* defending the judge: "Davis expects Lovejoy to be nominated, and intends to vote for him, and has so stated without hesitation or reserve." Furthermore, Davis disapproved of "a scheme concocted by certain influential persons, to bring out a stump candidate without a nomination, for the purpose of ensuring Lovejoy's defeat."[78] In thanking Lincoln, Davis explained that a bolt would probably have occurred if delegates had not feared that it would harm Lincoln's senatorial prospects. When chastised for supporting an abolitionist who hurt the party's chances statewide, Lincoln replied: "It is the people, and not me, who want Lovejoy. The people have not consulted me on the subject. If I had opposed Lovejoy, I doubtless should have repelled voters from among our own friends, and gained none from Douglas' friends."[79] Lincoln was right about Lovejoy's popularity; in November, he won reelection by the lopsided vote of 22,373 to 14,998, a more decisive victory than he had achieved in 1856.

Lovejoy's candidacy drove T. Lyle Dickey from both the Republican Party and Lincoln, with whom he had been close since the 1830s. Born and raised in Kentucky, Dickey had been a devoted Henry Clay Whig with an abhorrence of abolitionism.

When in August he announced his defection to the Democrats, Republicans expressed regret. Clifton H. Moore told Lincoln that Dickey "is to[o] good a man to loose" but added that he "will do us less harm" as "an open enemy" than he would "in pretending to be a republican & go growling about trying to sour every body."[80] Four years earlier, Dickey had told Lincoln, "I love you and want you to be a U.S. Senator"; now he denounced Lincoln for abandoning Henry Clay Whiggery.[81]

As the date for the Republican state convention approached, Lincoln grew optimistic. "I think our prospects gradually, and steadily, grow better," he told Washburne on May 15. "There is still some effort to make trouble out of 'Americanism.' If that were out of the way, for all the rest, I believe we should be 'out of the woods.'"[82] Less sanguine Republicans feared that many of Illinois's 37,351 Fillmore voters might make common cause with Douglas on a "Union-saving" platform.

Douglas remained a difficult and dangerous foe. Lincoln worried about his attempts to woo Republicans while holding on to Democrats by playing down his differences with the Buchanan administration. When in April the Little Giant refused to support the English bill (a Democratic compromise measure designed to heal the breach created during the fight over the Lecompton Constitution), Lincoln noted with satisfaction that many Illinois Democrats were "annoyed" and "begin to think there is a 'negro in the fence,'—that Douglas really wants to have a fuss with the President;—that sticks in their throats."[83] To Lincoln, Joseph Medill expressed "great alarm at the prospect [in the] North [of Illinois] of Republicans going over to Douglas, on the idea that Douglas is going to assume steep free-soil ground, and furiously assail the administration on the stump when he comes home." Lincoln inferred that there "certainly is a double game being played some how." The pro-Buchanan National Democrats were slated to hold a convention at Springfield in the second week of June. "Possibly," Lincoln mused, "even *probably*—Douglas is temporarily deceiving the President in order to crush out the 8th of June convention here." But he predicted the Little Giant's attempt to please both factions would fail: "Unless he plays his double game more successfully than we have often seen done, he can not carry many republicans North, without at the same time losing a larger number of his old friends South."[84]

To defeat Douglas's "double game" Lincoln had to convince his party colleagues that the senator was hardly a true believer in their principles. Republican leaders in Washington were still urging their Illinois counterparts to back Douglas. (On the eve of the state convention, Lincoln received word that his friend from the Thirtieth Congress, Representative Richard W. Thompson of Indiana, and his messmate at Mrs. Sprigg's boardinghouse, journalist Nathan K. Sargent, wanted Lincoln to step aside in favor of the Little Giant.) In private correspondence and anonymous journalism, Lincoln had for months been arguing against fusion with Douglas; at the Republican state convention, he seized the opportunity to make his case in what would become one of his most famous speeches.

Nomination for the Senate

On June 16, Republican delegates crowded into the Hall of Representatives in Springfield, where they speedily adopted a platform similar to the one passed at the 1856

Bloomington Convention and nominated candidates for the two state offices to be contested that fall. In the midst of their deliberations, the Chicago delegation unfurled a banner reading "Cook County for Abraham Lincoln," which was greeted with loud shouts. When it was suggested that the text be amended to read: "Illinois for Abraham Lincoln," the motion received a deafening barrage of hurrahs. Later that day, Charles L. Wilson, editor of the Chicago *Journal,* unexpectedly offered a resolution which won unanimous, enthusiastic approval: "Resolved that Abraham Lincoln is the first and only choice of the Republicans of Illinois for the United States Senate, as the successor to Stephen A. Douglas."[85] Wilson sought to counter the Democrats' whispering campaign alleging that if the Republicans won the legislature, they would send John Wentworth to the senate.

A journalist reported that "[u]nanimity is a weak word to express the universal and intense feeling of the convention. *Lincoln!* LINCOLN!! LINCOLN!!! was the cry everywhere, whenever the senatorship was alluded to. Delegates from Chicago and from Cairo, from the Wabash and the Illinois, from the north, the center, and the south, were alike fierce with enthusiasm, whenever that loved name was breathed."[86] This was an extraordinary development, for state parties did not usually endorse a candidate for senate before the election of the legislature, which would decide who would fill that post. But so intensely did the Republicans of Illinois resent Horace Greeley, Anson Burlingame, and other Easterners who urged them to support Douglas that, in many counties, they had passed resolutions endorsing Lincoln for the senate. The Chicago *Press and Tribune* declared: "We assure our eastern contemporaries who have been so sorely troubled with fear that the Republicans of Illinois could not take care of their own affairs, that this action, where not spontaneous, has been provoked by their interference, though it is the result of no arrangement or concert. It is the natural and expected remonstrance against outside intermeddling."[87]

That evening Lincoln addressed the delegates, uncharacteristically reading from a manuscript. He had been working steadily on his speech for over a week, taking great pains trying to make it accurate. He delivered it slowly and carefully, fully aware that his auditors might be startled by his arguments. Lincoln aimed to show that Douglas's rebellion against Buchanan, which rendered the Little Giant so attractive to many opponents of slavery, was superficial and that the senator and the president fundamentally agreed on basic principles and had cooperated, either by design or coincidence, in promoting the interests of the slaveholding South.

Lincoln began with a paraphrase of what he considered "the very best speech that was ever delivered," Daniel Webster's second reply to Senator Robert Y. Hayne in 1830.[88] "If we could first know *where,* we are, and *whither* we are tending, we could then better judge *what* to do, and *how* to do it." (Webster had begun his famous address thus: "When the mariner has been tossed for many days in thick weather, and on an unknown sea, he naturally avails himself of the first pause in the storm, the earliest glance of the sun, to take his latitude, and ascertain how far the elements have driven him from his true course. Let us imitate this prudence, and, before we float farther on the waves of this debate, refer to the point from which we departed, that we may at least be able to conjecture where we now are.")[89]

Since the introduction of the Kansas-Nebraska Act, a measure "with the *avowed* object, and *confident* promise, of putting an end to slavery agitation," that agitation "has not only, *not ceased*, but has *constantly augmented*." Such agitation, Lincoln predicted, "*will* not cease, until a *crisis* shall have been reached, and passed." That was inevitable, he said, because "[a] house divided against itself cannot stand," as Jesus had long ago warned. "I believe this government cannot endure, permanently half *slave* and half *free*. I do not expect the Union to be dissolved—I do not expect the house to *fall*—but I *do* expect it will cease to be divided. It will become *all* one thing, or *all* the other. Either the *opponents* of slavery, will arrest the further spread of it, and place it where the public mind shall rest in the belief that it is in course of ultimate extinction; or its *advocates* will push it forward, till it shall become alike lawful in *all* the States, *old* as well as new—*North* as well as *South*."

After prophesying the future, Lincoln analyzed the past, arguing that a conspiracy to expand slavery had been actively pursued over the past four years. In 1854, the Kansas-Nebraska Act "opened all the national territory to slavery; and was the first point gained." The "popular sovereignty" justification for this momentous change Lincoln scornfully defined as the belief that "if any *one* man, choose to enslave *another*, no *third* man shall be allowed to object." The election of James Buchanan in 1856 was the second point gained, for it seemingly endorsed the popular sovereignty doctrine, as did the final annual message of President Franklin Pierce in December 1856. A third point gained by the proslavery forces was the Dred Scott decision in 1857. Lincoln thought it noteworthy that when Douglas was asked if "the people of a territory can constitutionally exclude slavery from their limits," the Little Giant had replied, "That is a question for the Supreme Court." Equally noteworthy was Buchanan's inaugural address calling on all Americans to abide by whatever decision the court might reach in the case of Dred Scott. Two days later (a suspiciously short time), the justices handed down their controversial decision, ruling not only that blacks were excluded from citizenship and that Congress could not prohibit slavery from entering the territories, but in addition that "whether the holding a negro in actual slavery in a free State, makes him free, as against the holder, the United States courts will not decide, but will leave to be decided by the courts of any slave State the negro may be forced into by the master." This last point, Lincoln said, was "made, not to be pressed *immediately*; but, if acquiesced in for a while, and apparently *indorsed* by the people at an election, *then* to sustain the logical conclusion that what Dred Scott's master might lawfully do with Dred Scott, in the free State of Illinois, every other master may lawfully do with any other *one*, or one *thousand* slaves, in Illinois, or in any other free State."

The behavior of Douglas, Pierce, Buchanan, and the Supreme Court (presided over by Roger B. Taney) aroused Lincoln's suspicion. "These things *look* like the cautious *patting* and *petting* a spirited horse, preparatory to mounting him, when it is dreaded that he may give the rider a fall," he said. Switching the metaphor, he continued: "We can not absolutely *know* that all these exact adaptations are the result of preconcert." Nevertheless, "when we see a lot of framed timbers, different portions of which we know have been gotten out at different times and places and by different workmen—Stephen [Douglas], Franklin [Pierce], Roger [B. Taney], and James [Buchanan], for instance—and when we see these timbers joined together, and see they exactly make the frame of a house or a mill, all the tenons and mortices exactly fitting, and all the lengths and proportions of the different pieces exactly adapted to their respective places, and not a piece too many or too few—not omitting even scaffolding—or, if a single piece be lacking, we can see the place in the frame exactly fitted and prepared to yet bring such piece in—in *such* a case, we find it impossible to not *believe* that Stephen and Franklin and Roger and James all understood one another from the beginning, and all worked upon a common *plan* or *draft* drawn up before the first lick was struck."

Lincoln pointedly asked why the Kansas-Nebraska Act's provision regarding the people of a *state* as well as of a territory was "lugged into this merely *territorial* law" and why the justices of the Supreme Court had failed to "declare whether or not the . . . Constitution permits a *State,* or the people of a State, to exclude it." These anomalies and this recent history convinced Lincoln that "we may, ere long, see . . . another Supreme Court decision, declaring that the Constitution of the United States does not permit a *state* to exclude slavery from its limits." Illinoisans "shall *lie down* pleasantly dreaming that the people of *Missouri* are on the verge of making their State *free*; and we shall *awake* to the *reality*, instead, that the *Supreme* Court has made *Illinois* a *slave* State," Lincoln predicted, "unless the power of the present political dynasty shall be met and overthrown."

Reaching the central point of his address, Lincoln maintained that to achieve the overthrow of the slave power, its opponents must resist the overtures of the Douglasites. Relentlessly he argued that the Little Giant was not "the aptest instrument" to thwart the slavery expansionists; the senator and his followers wanted to give the impression that he sought to keep slavery from expanding, but in fact there was little reason to believe it. Douglas's resistance to the Lecompton Constitution, though admirable, did not prove the point, for the quarrel with Buchanan was about a matter of fact, not principle. Lincoln noted that Douglas's supporters "remind us that *he* is a very *great* man, and that the largest of *us* are very small ones." Conceding the point, Lincoln quoted from Ecclesiastes: "a *living dog* is better than a *dead* lion" and maintained that even though the Little Giant was not exactly a deceased lion, he was "a *caged* and *toothless* one." (Democrats used this unfortunate metaphor to ridicule Lincoln throughout the campaign, comparing him to "a puppy-dog fighting a lion.")[90] How, Lincoln asked, could Douglas "oppose the advances of slavery? He don't *care* anything about it," and his "avowed *mission is impressing* the 'public heart' to *care* nothing about it." Nor would Douglas necessarily resist calls for reopening the African slave trade. "For years he has labored to prove it a *sacred right* of white men to take negro slaves into the new territories. Can he possibly show that it is *less* a sacred right to *buy* them where they can be bought cheapest? And, unquestionably they can be bought *cheaper in Africa* than in *Virginia*."

On the issue most dear to Republicans—prohibiting the expansion of slavery— "clearly, he [Douglas] is not *now* with us—he does not *pretend* to be—he does not *promise* to *ever* be." The Republican cause "must be entrusted to, and conducted by its own undoubted friends—those whose hands are free, whose hearts are in the work—who *do care* for the result." He reminded his party colleagues that though they were a combination of "*strange, discordant,* and even, *hostile* elements," they had successfully "fought the battle through, under the constant hot fire of a disciplined, proud, and pampered enemy" who was now "*wavering,* dissevered and belligerent." (Here again Lincoln borrowed from Webster's second reply to Hayne, in which the Massachusetts orator alluded to "States dissevered, discordant, belligerent.")[91] This was no time to falter. Optimistically, he predicted that "sooner or later the victory is *sure* to come."[92]

Lincoln had worried about the nation becoming all slave as far back as 1849, when antislavery forces were trounced at the Kentucky constitutional convention. He told Joseph Gillespie that he had asked a Kentuckian why the peculiar institution had such a powerful grip on a state with relatively few slaveowners. The reply was revealing: "you might have any amount of land, money in your pocket or bank stock and while travelling around no body would be any the wiser but if you had a darkey trudging at your heels every body would see him & know that you owned slaves—It is the most glittering ostentatious & displaying property in the world and now says he if a young man goes courting the only inquiry is how many negroes he or she owns and not what other property they may have. The love for Slave property was swallowing up every other mercenary passion. Its ownership betokened not only the possession of wealth but indicated the gentleman of leisure who was above and scorned labour." According to Gillespie, "These things Mr Lincoln regarded as highly seductive to the thoughtless and giddy headed young men who looked upon work as vulgar and ungentlemanly. Mr Lincoln was really excited and said with great earnestness that this spirit ought to be met and if possible checked. That slavery was a great & crying injustice an enormous national crime and that we could not expect to escape punishment for it." He also predicted that a few years hence "we will be ready to accept the institution in Illinois and the whole country will adopt it."[93]

Lincoln's "House Divided" speech was hardly the first public expression of the thesis that either slavery or freedom would inevitably triumph. Lincoln explicitly denied that he was "entitled to the enviable or unenviable distinction of having first expressed that idea. The same idea was expressed by the Richmond *Enquirer* in 1856."[94] He was "forcibly attracted" to an editorial by George Fitzhugh which appeared in that paper on May 6, 1856: "Social forms so widely differing as those of domestic slavery, and (attempted) universal liberty, cannot long co-exist in the Great Republic of Christendom. They cannot be equally adapted to the wants and interests of society. The one form or the other, must be very wrong, very ill suited, to promote the quiet, the peace, the happiness, the morality, the religion and general well-being of the community. Disunion will not allay excitement and investigation,—much less beget lasting peace. The war between the two systems rages every where; and will continue to rage till the one conquers and the other is exterminated.—If with disunion, we could have 'the all and end all there,' the inducements would be strong to attempt it."[95] The Richmond paper also declared that "[t]wo opposite and conflicting forms of society cannot, among civilized men, co-exist and endure. The one must give way and cease to exist, the other become universal. If free society be unnatural, immoral, un-christian, it must fall, and give way to a *slave society—a social system old as the world, universal as man.*"[96] The Richmond *Whig* insisted that "far from believing that slavery must die, we have long held the opinion that it is the normal and only humane rela-tion which labor can sustain toward capital."[97]

Nor was there any novelty in the speculation that Illinois might welcome slavery. Dumas J. Van Deren, editor of the Matoon *National Gazette,* declared in 1857: "We candidly and firmly believe today that if Illinois were a slave state, the best men of Kentucky, Virginia, Tennessee, and even states farther South, would be here as soon as they could remove their families, and the prairies of Illinois would be made to smile as a lovely garden."[98] From the South came comments like those in the Jackson *Mississippian*: "Establish slavery in Illinois and it would give us the key to the great West. The South should not content herself with maintaining her ground; she should progress. She should expand her institutions wherever soil, climate, and production are adapted to them."[99]

For decades, abolitionists had been making Lincoln's point about the incompati-bility of slavery and freedom. In 1835, William Goodell predicted that one or the other "must prevail to the destruction of the other. The laborers at the south will be free, or the laborers at the north will lose their freedom."[100] The following year, James G. Birney insisted that if "slavery live at the South, liberty must die at the North. There is no middle ground."[101] Eleven years later, a New Hampshire Free Soiler edi-torialized: "*Slavery* or freedom must *triumph*" for "unless justice is a phantom and all liberty a lie they cannot live and flourish in the same land together."[102]

In the fateful year 1854, several militant opponents of slavery stressed that argu-ment. Frederick Douglass told a Chicago audience that "liberty and slavery cannot dwell in the United States in peaceful relations. . . . [O]ne or the other of these must go to the wall. The South must either give up slavery, or the North must give up lib-erty. The two interests are hostile, and irreconcilable. The just demands of liberty are inconsistent with the overgrown exactions of the slave power."[103] Henry Ward Beecher declared that "the two great principles must come into collision and fight till one or the other is dead. It is like a battle between a vulture and an eagle. Slavery is a vulture, of base talons and polluted beak; and liberty is . . . an eagle. They must fight till there is a declaration of victory on one side or the other."[104] Benjamin F. Wade told the sen-ate, "Slavery must now become general, or it must cease to be at all."[105] Theodore Parker, whom Lincoln admired, analyzed the political situation of the country in similar fashion: "These two Ideas [freedom and slavery] are now fairly on foot. They are hostile; they are both mutually invasive and destructive. They are in exact opposi-tion to each other, . . . and one will overcome the other."[106] The New York *Tribune* asserted that the "permanence of the Union is predictable only upon one of two con-ditions, either the South must put an end to slavery or the North must adopt it."[107]

In 1857, Lincoln's law partner predicted that there would soon be "[u]niversal free-dom for all the race, or universal despotism for *white and black*."[108] The previous year, James S. Pike, the New York *Tribune*'s Washington correspondent and a radical op-ponent of slavery, made the same point, calling "the longer continuance of the existing political Union . . . a political impossibility," unless the North and South agreed "to go back to the position of the founders of the Government, and regard Slavery as an exceptional institution, and administer the Government in the interest of universal Freedom."[109] (A Maine Republican told Pike, "your opinion is by no means a heretical or unusual one but is shared by nearly all of the intelligent thinkers in the country who are opposed to slavery.")[110] Five months after Lincoln delivered his "House Divided" speech, a leading Republican spokesman, William Henry Seward, made the same point when he famously described the "collision" between North and South as "an irrepressible conflict between opposing and enduring forces, and it means that the United States must and will, sooner or later, become either entirely a slave-holding nation or entirely a free-labor nation."[111]

Northerners and Southerners alike had used the quotation from Jesus about "a house divided" long before Lincoln cited it. In 1847, Daniel Webster said: "If a house be divided against itself, it will fall, and crush every body in it."[112] In 1806, a Maryland critic of slavery, John Parrish, observed that "[a] house divided against itself cannot stand; neither can a government or constitution: this is coincident with the present Chief Magistrate's [Jefferson's] opinion in his Notes on the State of Virginia."[113] In 1852, the Boston abolitionist Edmund Quincy wrote: "It was said more than eighteen hundred years ago that a house divided against itself cannot stand, and the truth of the saying is written on every page of history." Quincy predicted that slavery would either be abolished or it would "at last make a fissure that will shatter into heaps the proud structure upon the heads of those that put their trust into it."[114] Theodore Parker, sermonizing about slavery, said that there "can be no national welfare without national Unity of Action. . . . Without that a nation is a 'house divided against itself.'"[115] In 1850, a Southern secessionist declared that the American "system of government rests on '*the broad basis of the people*,'" who "are not homogenious, they do not assimilate, they are opposed in interests, at variance in opinions—*they are at war*, inevitable, unavoidable war. . . . The cement is broken, the house is divided against itself. It MUST FALL."[116] Five years later, the American Anti-Slavery Society adopt- ed the following resolution: "a Church or Government which accords the same rights and privileges to Slavery as to Liberty, is a house divided against itself, which cannot stand."[117]

Lincoln's other prediction—regarding a second Dred Scott decision—was not far-fetched. The Bloomington *Pantagraph* had mentioned such a possibility less than a week after the Supreme Court ruled in the first one. Lincoln was probably alluding to *Lemmon vs. the People*, which had begun in New York in 1852 and dealt with the right of slaveholders to take their slaves with them into Free States. In 1841, the New York Legislature adopted a law stipulating that "no person imported, introduced or brought into this State," could be held in bondage. In October 1857, the Lemmon case was argued before the New York Supreme Court, which upheld the statute by a 5–3 vote. While the case was being considered by the state's court of appeals, opponents of slavery feared that it would eventually reach the U.S. Supreme Court, where Taney and his colleagues might overrule New York's statute and pave the way for nationalizing slavery. The case was pending in 1858 and not argued before the New York

Court of Appeals until 1860. In 1854, Harriet Beecher Stowe had warned that the Taney court might decide the case in such a way that "it may be declared lawful for slave property to be held in the northern free States. Should this come to pass, it is no more improbable that there may be, four years hence, slave depots in New York City, than it was four years ago, that the South would propose a repeal of the 'Missouri Compromise.'"[118] Theodore Parker predicted that the court would rule in the Lemmon case "that a Master *may* take his Slaves in transit through a free State, & keep them in it a reasonable time, subject not only to his own caprice, but defiant of the Laws of that State."[119] In 1858, Lyman Trumbull echoed that warning: "There is now a case pending, known as the 'Lemmon Case,' and when the country gets prepared to receive the decision, you will probably hear again from the Supreme Court of the United States, the doctrine announced, that under the Constitution Slavery goes into all the States of the Union."[120]

Earlier that year several senators—including Henry Wilson of Massachusetts, James Harlan of Iowa, Zachariah Chandler of Michigan, and William Pitt Fessenden of Maine—had warned of a new Dred Scott decision forbidding states to outlaw slavery. The organ of the Buchanan administration declared that Southerners had a right to take slaves into Free States. In February 1858, the California Supreme Court determined that the slave Archy Lee was to remain the property of his owner, who had moved to Sacramento from Mississippi in 1857.

Many others before Lincoln charged that a conspiracy was afoot to nationalize slavery; among them were the New York *Tribune*, Congressman David Wilmot, Senators Benjamin F. Wade and William Pitt Fessenden, and the Independent Democrats who had issued the famous denunciation of the Kansas-Nebraska bill when it was first introduced. In all likelihood, Lincoln sincerely believed his allegation of conspiracy. In a draft of a speech written during the 1858 campaign, he declared: "I claim no extraordinary exemption from personal ambition. That I like preferment as well as the average of men may be admitted. But I protest I have not entered upon this hard contest solely, or even chiefly, for a mere personal object. I clearly see, as I think, a powerful plot to make slavery universal and perpetual in this nation. The effort to carry that plot through will be persistent and long continued, extending far beyond the senatorial term for which Judge Douglas and I are just now struggling. I enter upon the contest to contribute my humble and temporary mite in opposition to that effort." The evidence to prove a conspiracy was, he admitted, "circumstantial only," but the "string of incontestable facts" appeared to him "inconsistent with every hypothesis, save that of the existence of such conspiracy. . . . Judge Douglas can so explain them if any one can. From warp to woof his handiwork is everywhere woven in."[121]

Unbeknownst to Lincoln, there was solid evidence of collusion between Buchanan and the U.S. Supreme Court. In February 1857, only the five Southern justices favored overturning the Missouri Compromise. Worried that such a split decision might not sit well with Northerners, Buchanan urged his friend, Justice Robert C. Grier of Pennsylvania, to side with his colleagues from below the Mason-Dixon line. Grier complied and let Buchanan know that the court would decide the case soon after his inauguration. Buchanan, who may well have seen a draft of Chief Justice Roger B. Taney's majority opinion, prepared his inaugural address accordingly, urging the public to abide by whatever decision the court might reach.

The Republican press in Illinois hailed Lincoln's speech as "able, logical, and most eloquent."[122] In Vermont, the Burlington *Free Press* praised its "sound doctrine, lucid statements, clear distinctions, and apt illustrations."[123] William Herndon called Lincoln's "quite compact—nervous—eloquent" speech "the best executive expression of the ideas of political Republicanism, as at present organized, that I have seen."[124] At the opposite end of the ideological spectrum, the New Orleans *Delta* reported that "[s]omebody named Lincoln, who in the eyes of his friends is an unshorn Sampson of Free-soilism, ... made a speech in which he hit the 'Little Giant' some terrible blows."[125] Horace Greeley's New York *Tribune* ran the text of the speech, which it deemed "admirable," "compact," "forcible," "concise," "able," and "caustic." Lincoln, said the *Tribune*, "never fails to make a good speech, . . . and this is one of his best efforts."[126] (The speech did not change Greeley's mind about Douglas, however. In July, he still privately chided Illinois Republicans for opposing the senator's reelection: "You have repelled Douglas, who might have been conciliated, and attached to our own side, whatever he may *now* find it necessary to say, or do, and, instead of helping us in other states, you have thrown a load upon us that may probably break us down.")[127] In 1860, Thurlow Weed's newspaper said that this speech "called back the Republicans to their original creed," thus preventing a "great calamity," namely, accepting Douglas and popular sovereignty. "This great speech . . . marked Abraham Lincoln as no ordinary man. Thoughtful men saw in its author a statesman who had the sagacity to discover the peril that awaited the Republican party if it dallied with the specious theory of Stephen A. Douglas."[128]

Douglas's supporters took heart from the "House Divided" speech because it seemed too radical for Illinois. "I had thought until recently that the Little Giant was dead in Illinois—until I saw the speech Mr Lincoln made to the Republican Convention in Springfield," remarked a Democrat in Bloomington. "I do not believe that there is any Western State that can upon a fair canvass be brought to endorse the sentiments of that Springfield Speech. It is abolition and disunion so absolutely expressed that it should be made to burn Mr Lincoln as long as he lives."[129] The Democratic press reviled the speech as an incitement to civil war and a call for abolition.

Lincoln was probably unsurprised by such attacks; before he delivered it, his political confidants had warned that the speech was too extreme and advised him to tone it down. He rejected their advice. When Samuel C. Parks suggested that he modify one passage before publishing it, Lincoln asked: "Isn't it true?"

"Certainly it is true, but it is premature. The people are not prepared for it, and Douglas will beat us with it all over the state."

"I think that the time has come to say it, and I will let it go as it is."[130]

After the election, some friends told Lincoln that his defeat was due to the radicalism of the speech. "Well Gentlemen, you may think that Speech was a mistake, but I never have believed it was, and you will see the day when you will consider it was the wisest thing I ever said."[131] Lincoln told Horace White that "all of his wise friends had objected to that 'house' paragraph, but he thought the people were much nearer to the belief than the politicians generally supposed." Therefore, "while he was willing to assume all the risks incident to the use of that phrase, he did not consider the risk great."[132]

The warnings were valid, however. A few days after the speech John Locke Scripps told Lincoln that its opening lines were too "ultra" for some of his Kentucky-born friends "who want to be Republicans, but who are *afraid* we are not sufficiently conservative, who are also somewhat afraid of our name, but who hate 'Locofoism' most cordially." Those Kentuckians interpreted the "House Divided" segment of the speech as "an implied pledge on behalf of the Republican party to make war upon the institution in the States where it now exists. They do not perceive that you refer to a moral tendency, but insist that your meaning goes to a political warfar[e] under legal forms against slavery in the States."[133] In reply, Lincoln insisted that his address was not an abolitionist document: "I am much mortified that any part of it should be construed so differently from any thing intended by me," he told Scripps. "The language, 'place it [slavery] where the public mind shall rest in the belief that it is in course of ultimate extinction,' I used deliberately, not dreaming then, nor believing now, that it asserts, or intimates, any power or purpose, to interfere with slavery in the States where it exists." Emphatically he declared that "whether the clause used by me, will bear such construction or not, I never so intended it."[134] The charge of "ultraism" would dog Lincoln throughout the campaign as he tried to woo conservative former Whigs.

The Senate Campaign Begins

Douglas and his allies tried to discredit Lincoln by asserting that as a congressman he had opposed funding supplies for the troops during the Mexican War. The Chicago *Times*, Douglas's organ, made the outrageous claim that Lincoln swore an oath to "refuse to vote one dollar to feed, clothe, or minister to the wants of the sick and dying volunteers from my own State, who are suffering in Mexico. Let them die like dogs! Let them die for want of medicine! Let the fever-parched lips of my Illinois neighbors crack in painful agony—not one drop of cooling liquid shall soothe them if I can help it."[135] Other Democratic papers joined in the attack, calling Lincoln "a friend of the 'greasers'" and an "apologist of Mexico" who "pandered to [the] greasers' profit and advantage" and whose "tory demagogism" and "mountebank antics" provided "'aid and comfort' to a foreign enemy during a bloody war."[136]

Joseph Medill warned Lincoln that "thousands of our party are old Democrats, and you know their sentiments on this Mexican War supply question. It ruined [Ohio Senator Thomas] Corwin. The game of the *Times* is to make a *personal issue* . . . and not a party fight." Henry C. Whitney told Lincoln that the *Times*'s allegation was "the most potent & dangerous weapon that can be used against you in the rural districts" and urged that Lincoln not "lose ground by inattention to these apparently trifling but really formidable matters:—the fight is one effectually between you & Douglas as if you were in the field for a popular vote." In Egypt, Democrats reportedly exhumed "the Skeletons of all those who died on the plains of Mexico and attempted to prove by the use of Volcanic thunder—ignoring sound arguments—that they all died at the hands of *Abe Lincoln*."[137]

Lincoln swiftly provided Medill an account of his congressional votes on Mexican War appropriations, which he had always supported, and protested that the Chicago *Times*, "in its' blind rage to assail me," had ascribed to him a vote that had been cast by another Illinois congressman, John Henry, before Lincoln had taken his seat in the House. Scornfully, he observed: "I scarcely think any one is quite vile enough to make such a charge in such terms, without some slight belief in the truth of it."[138] Medill's paper denounced "the intense meanness which prompted the *Times* to falsify his position, and the intenser meanness which induces it not to retract its calumnies."[139] Other Republican papers called the allegation "a blistering and cowardly misrepresentation," a "self-evident lie," and an example of "the kind of ammunition with which these Black Democrats are compelled to fight."[140] To their credit, the Democratic *Illinois State Register* acknowledged that the *Times*'s charge was erroneous, and the Matoon *Gazette*, which had originated the allegation, apologetically retracted it. In the end, Lincoln said later, the *Times*'s abusive tactics had "helped him amazingly."[141] This was not the last dirty trick that Douglas and his organ would play on Lincoln, for the Little Giant and his editor-friend James W. Sheahan would prove to be unscrupulous opponents, willing to make false charges, garble Lincoln's words, resort to bribery, and engage in shameless demagoguery.

Each candidate ran scared. A week after his nomination, Lincoln predicted that the Republican nominees for statewide office (Newton Bateman for superintendent of public instruction and James Miller for state treasurer) "will be elected without much difficulty," but he guessed that "with the advantages they [the Democrats] have of us, we shall be very hard run to carry the Legislature," which would choose the next senator.[142] In July, Herndon reported that his partner meticulously calculated Republican prospects in each county and was "gloomy—rather uncertain, about his own success."[143] In assessing Douglas's strengths, Lincoln said "that he was a very strong logician; that he had very little humor or imagination, but where he had right on his side very few could make a stronger argument; that he was an exceedingly good judge of human nature, knew the people of the state thoroughly and just how to appeal to the[ir] prejudices and was a very powerful opponent, both on and off the stump."[144] Douglas reciprocated the sentiment. Upon hearing of Lincoln's nomination, he told a friend: "I shall have my hands full. He is the strong man of his party—full of wit, facts, dates, and the best stump speaker, with his droll ways and dry jokes, in the West. He is as honest as he is shrewd; and if I beat him, my victory will be hardly won."[145] More profanely, the Little Giant later said: "Of all the G-d d—d Whig rascals of Springfield Abe Lincoln is the most honest."[146]

On July 9 Douglas opened his reelection campaign with a speech before a crowd of several thousand Chicagoans. He began by complimenting Lincoln, describing him as "a kind, amiable, and intelligent gentleman, a good citizen and an honorable opponent." In general, the tone of this address was so conciliatory that the Chicago *Press and Tribune* hoped that the senator "will conduct the canvass before him with

proper regard for the decencies which he has so far repeatedly violated, and for fairness that he never observed."[147] In that speech, Douglas denounced Lincoln's "House
Divided" address for advocating "boldly and clearly a war of sections, a war of the
North against the South, of the free states against the slave states—a war of
extermination—to be continued relentlessly until the one or the other shall be subdued." The Little Giant argued that Lincoln's policy of "uniformity" would lead to
despotism, for if people did not have the right to decide for themselves whether to allow slavery in their midst, they were no longer free. The true safeguard of liberty,
Douglas asserted, was "diversity," not "uniformity."

Turning to the race issue, which he was to emphasize heavily throughout the
campaign, Douglas attacked Lincoln's criticism of the Dred Scott decision. In a characteristic appeal to the intense Negrophobia of Illinoisans, Douglas flatly declared:
"this government was made by the white man, for the benefit of the white man, to be
administered by white men, in such manner as they should determine. . . . I am opposed to negro equality. I repeat that this nation is a white people—a people composed of European descendants—a people that have established this government for
themselves and their posterity, and I am in favor of preserving not only the purity of
the blood, but the purity of the government from any mixture or amalgamation with
inferior races. I have seen the effects of this mixture of superior and inferior races—this
amalgamation of white men and Indians and negroes; we have seen it in Mexico, in
Central America, in South America, and in all the Spanish-American states, and its
result has been degeneration, demoralization, and degradation below the capacity for
self-government. I am opposed to taking any step that recognizes the negro man or
the Indian as the equal of the white man. I am opposed to giving him a voice in the
administration of the government." (A Cherokee protested to Douglas that his tribe
and others in the West were "vastly superior, in every respect, to any portion of the
Negro race" and urged the Little Giant "to draw the necessary distinction between
Indians and negroes.")[148] Among those inferior races were the Chinese, Douglas implied: "I do not acknowledge that the Cooley must necessarily be put upon an equality
with the white race." The senator closed with a salvo against the "unholy, unnatural"
alliance between the Republicans and the pro-Buchanan Democrats.[149]

The Chicago *Press and Tribune* cited this speech as proof that Illinois Republicans had been justified in rejecting their Eastern counterparts' advice to embrace
Douglas. In his Chicago address, the senator had "avowed and re-affirmed his old
and most odious doctrines—his adhesion to the dogma that a majority may enslave a
minority, and that Slavery goes by virtue of the Constitution wherever that Constitution goes." If the Little Giant had acknowledged "that Freedom was a little better
than Slavery for the new Territories," he would have been applauded vigorously; as it
was, many auditors "went home disappointed—many of them grieved." The *Press and
Tribune* also denounced Douglas for badly misrepresenting the "House Divided"
speech. Angrily, it observed that "Mr. Lincoln *believes* that there is now a struggle,
and that it will continue till a certain result is reached; but Mr. Douglas *says* that Mr.
Lincoln *calls upon* the participants in the struggle to throw down the slow weapon of
the ballot box and *precipitate the result by the sword!*" Such garbling was "childish," a

"low prevarication." The paper condemned Douglas's espousal of the "monstrous" doctrine that the United States, in order to remain a free country, must have "diversity" (i.e., tolerate Slave States in its midst).[150]

Lincoln, who sat through Douglas's speech, reported that the Little Giant sought "to make it appear that he is having a triumphal entry into, and march through the country; but it is all as bombastic and hollow as Napoleon's bulletins sent back from his campaign in Russia." A majority of the crowd, he estimated, consisted of Republicans, some of whom called for him to respond to Douglas, but since the hour was late, it was arranged that he would speak the following night.[151]

The Chicago *Press and Tribune* asserted that "the Douglas meeting was the product of three weeks hard drumming and coaxing, aided by cannon and clap-trap, fuss and feathers, and profusion of pyrotechnics and costly parade," complete with "hired claquers" and fireworks.[152] Alluding to Douglas's cannon, Lincoln (who condemned such hoopla) said: "There is a passage, I think, in the Book of the Koran, which reads: 'To him that bloweth not his own horn—to such a man it is forever decreed that . . . his horn shall not be blowe-ed!' "[153] Republicans throughout Illinois shared Lincoln's scorn for his opponent's triumphal style, with its elaborate processions, brass bands, flag-bedecked trains, militia escorts, booming artillery, banner-festooned wagons, and gaudy pageantry.

The next day, before an audience almost as large as Douglas's (and, by Lincoln's reckoning, five times as enthusiastic), the challenger responded to the Little Giant in a speech that seemed to a Democratic journalist "a talk" that made "no attempt at oratory."[154] With gentle mockery he dismissed the charge of Republican collusion with the Buchaneers. More bitingly, he maintained that "popular sovereignty" had become a meaningless concept, for thanks to the Dred Scott decision, inhabitants of a territory could only vote to exclude slavery at the very final stage of territorial settlement, when a constitution was to be adopted and application for statehood was to be submitted. According to the Supreme Court, Lincoln noted, "if any one man chooses to take slaves into a territory, all the rest of the people have no right to keep them out." Thus, for all intents and purposes, popular sovereignty was a dead letter, and Douglas was hypocritical in proclaiming his devotion both to it and to the Dred Scott decision, which negated it. Lincoln asked: "how much is left of this vast matter of Squatter Sovereignty I should like to know?" A member of the audience answered: "it has all gone." (Lincoln would return to this point in a debate the following month at Freeport.)

Douglas's willingness to support the right of people in a territory to frame a constitution in accord with their own wishes was nothing new, for, as Lincoln maintained, no one had ever denied it. Sarcastically he predicted that his opponent "will claim in a little while, that he is the inventor of the idea that the people should govern themselves; that nobody ever thought of such a thing until he brought it forward."

Should Douglas be credited with defeating the Lecompton Constitution? In the senate, twenty Republicans and only three Democrats voted against it; in the House, over ninety Republicans and only twenty-two Democrats voted against it. "Now who was it that did the work?" Lincoln asked rhetorically. (Douglas's boast that he and his colleagues had won the victory reminded a Republican of three English tailors who sent a petition to Parliament beginning: "We, the men of England.")[155]

Lincoln protested against Douglas's misinterpretation of his "House Divided" speech. "I am not [a] master of language," he confessed. "I have not a fine education; I am not capable of entering into a disquisition upon dialectics," but he insisted that the senator had distorted his meaning. (Two years later, Lincoln analyzed his strengths and weaknesses as an orator: "I am not much of a rouser as a public speaker. I do not and cannot put on frills and fancy touches. If there is anything that I can accomplish, it is that I can state the question and demonstrate the strength of our position by plain, logical argument.")[156] Obviously, the nation had existed half slave and half free for more than eight decades, but it had done so only because people expected that the peculiar institution would ultimately die out; the Kansas-Nebraska Act had demolished that expectation. Boldly Lincoln declared, "I have always hated slavery, I think as much as any Abolitionist. . . . I have always hated it, but I have always been quiet about it until this new era of the introduction of the Nebraska Bill began. I always believed that everybody was against it, and that it was in the course of ultimate extinction." The Constitution, he argued plausibly, was framed and adopted by men who "intended and expected the ultimate extinction" of slavery.

In refuting Douglas's "uniformity charge," Lincoln stated his belief that "each individual is naturally entitled to do as he pleases with himself and the fruit of his labor, so far as it in no wise interferes with any other man's rights." But he drew a distinction between laws like the Indiana statute regulating the cultivation of cranberries and laws establishing slavery; only a man who saw nothing morally wrong with human bondage could equate the two. Douglas, Lincoln charged, "looks upon all this matter of slavery as an exceedingly little thing—this matter of keeping one-sixth of the population of the whole nation in a state of oppression and tyranny unequalled in the world." But slavery, Lincoln insisted, should not be regarded "as something on a par with the question of whether a man shall pasture his land with cattle, or plant it with tobacco." Douglas might demur, but "there is a vast portion of the American people that do *not* look upon that matter [slavery] as being this very little thing." Rather, they "look upon it as a vast moral evil." As Lincoln scornfully argued, it was "nonsense" to assert that anyone who wished to keep slavery from expanding necessarily therefore wanted to force all states to have identical laws regarding cranberries.

By insisting that the Dred Scott decision must, like all Supreme Court rulings, be supported unconditionally, Douglas was being hypocritical, for the Little Giant and his party had endorsed Andrew Jackson's defiance of the court's well-known contention, made in the 1819 case of *McCulloch vs. Maryland,* that Congress had the power to charter a national bank. Lincoln appealed to his audience to honor the Declaration of Independence and to recall what had been achieved under the blessings of liberty. He pointed out that Americans were not united by blood but rather by a devotion to the principles of the Declaration. Germans, Irish, French, and Scandinavians who had immigrated since 1783 could find no ancestors among those who had made the Revolution, but they felt deeply attached to the United States "when they look through that old Declaration of Independence [and] they find that those old men say that 'We hold these truths to be self-evident, that all men are created equal,' and then they feel that that moral sentiment taught in that day evidences their relation to those men, that it is the father of all moral principle in them, and that they have a right to claim it as though they were blood of the blood, and flesh of the flesh of the men who wrote that Declaration and so they are."

This Revolutionary-era idealism, Lincoln said, contrasted sharply with Douglas's contention that inferior races should not be allowed to enjoy the rights accorded to the superior race. This reasoning he likened to "the arguments that kings have made for enslaving the people in all ages of the world." Monarchs "always bestrode the necks of the people, not that they wanted to do it, but because the people were better off for being ridden. That is their argument, and this argument of the Judge is the same old serpent that says you work and I eat, you toil and I will enjoy the fruits of it. Turn it whatever way you will—whether it come from the mouth of a King, an excuse for enslaving the people of his country, or from the mouth of men of one race as a reason for enslaving the men of another race, it is all the same old serpent."

To understand the purpose of the Declaration, Lincoln urged his audience to bear in mind a statement by Jesus: "As your Father in Heaven is perfect, be ye also perfect." Christ, he said, "set that up as a standard," and so the Declaration should be regarded. "So I say in relation to the principle that all men are created equal, let it be as nearly reached as we can. If we cannot give freedom to every creature, let us do nothing that will impose slavery upon any other creature."

Lincoln pleaded with Republicans not to forget Douglas's racist demagoguery; they should remember, he insisted, "all the hard names that Judge Douglas has called them by—all his repeated charges of their inclination to marry with and hug negroes." Emphatically, he declared: "I protest, now and forever, against that counterfeit logic which presumes that because I do not want a negro woman for a slave, I do necessarily want her for a wife. My understanding is that I need not have her for either, but as God made us separate, we can leave one another alone and do one another much good thereby. There are white men enough to marry all the white women, and enough black men to marry all the black women, and in God's name let them be so married. The Judge regales us with the terrible enormities that take place by the mixture of races; that the inferior race bears the superior down. Why, Judge, if we do not let them get together in the Territories they won't mix there." Eloquently he concluded, "let us discard all this quibbling about this man and the other man—this race and that race and the other race being inferior, and therefore they must be placed in an inferior position. . . . Let us discard all these things, and unite as one people throughout this land, until we shall once more stand up declaring that all men are created equal."[157]

This remarkable address, with its soaring rhetoric and heartfelt idealism, was published in the New York *Times,* which deemed it "an able speech"; in the New York *Tribune,* which hailed it as "admirable and thoroughly Republican"; in the Bangor, Maine, *Courier,* which praised its "plain, candid, common sense exposition of Republican doctrine"; and in the New York *Herald,* which referred to Lincoln as Douglas's "nigger worshipping competitor" espousing the "most repulsive disunion nigger equality principles and doctrines."[158] The abolitionist Chicago *Congregational Herald* detected in Lincoln "a champion" who was willing to "stand by the Declaration of Independence and fight for *human* rights, for *man as man,* irrespective of country, race, creed, or other accidental circumstances."[159] A leading abolitionist in eastern Illinois, Abraham Smith, congratulated Lincoln: "while some republicans—good men & true—but *cautious* will say thou hast taken too high ground . . . I am rejoiced that by thy speeches at Springfield & Chicago thou art fairly mounted on the eternal invulnerable bulwark of *truth*."[160]

"The war is begun," remarked the Chicago *Journal*. "The first fire has been exchanged," and "the Little Giant is wounded in several vital parts. In sound, manly argument, Lincoln is too much for him."[161] The Chicago *Press and Tribune* observed that even though Lincoln's speech was "an unstudied and unpremeditated effort," a product of "hurried and imperfect preparation," it offered "a clear comprehensive and overwhelming refutation of the sophistries and charletanisms" of Douglas's remarks the night before.[162] An editor of that paper told Lincoln, "Your peroration to the spirit of Liberty was capital."[163]

Douglas and other Democrats repeatedly quoted that peroration (which the Chicago *Times* found "disgusting"), along with the opening paragraph of the "House Divided" speech, to illustrate Lincoln's radicalism on the race issue. The *Illinois State Register* alleged that in his Chicago address, "Lincoln takes bold and unqualified ground with Lovejoy and ultra abolitionism. . . . Old Whigs can see in it the 'contemptible abolitionism' in which Mr. Lincoln desires to engulf his old whig friends."[164] The Chicago *Times,* which likened the challenger to the abolitionist Theodore Parker, regarded Lincoln's Chicago speech as a "vain attempt to escape from awkward positions in which he had placed himself by his Springfield address." In it the *Times* saw an appeal for slaves to rise up and kill their masters.[165] The Boston *Courier* called it "inelegant, discursive, and laborious."[166] The Madison, Wisconsin, *Argus* detected in the speech only a "few sickly attempts at irony, a plentiful supply of cant, and one or two faint quibbles."[167]

Thanks to Douglas's prominence, the attention of the nation focused on the Illinois senate race. Sharing the Little Giant's spotlight, Lincoln began to emerge as a national figure. A Cincinnatian told Lincoln that the campaign "is assuming national importance in the eyes of the people of all sections of the Country."[168] From upstate New York, Charles Henry Ray informed him, "you are like Byron, who woke up one morning and found himself famous. In my journey here from Chicago, and even here—one of the most out-of-the-way, rural districts in the State, among a slow-going and conservative people, who are further from railroads than any man can be in Illinois—I have found hundreds of anxious enquirers burning to know all about the newly raised-up opponent of Douglas."[169]

Some Republicans chided Lincoln for not attacking Douglas more vigorously. One admirer of Lincoln's address called it "a first rate *defensive Speech*" but urged its author "to *assail* & *keep assailing*."[170] Similarly, Norman B. Judd told Lyman Trumbull, "Lincoln has commenced it gallantly. The only trouble will be that (as I told him) he will allow Douglass to put him on the defensive."[171]

When the two candidates spoke in Springfield a week later, the contrast between them was highlighted by their mode of transportation to the capital and by their appearance. Fashionably attired in the so-called plantation style, with a ruffled shirt, dark blue coat with shiny buttons, light-colored trousers, well-polished shoes, and a wide brimmed hat, Douglas was the glass of fashion in his well-tailored broadcloth and linen garments. Traveling in imperial fashion, he and his wife, along with a large entourage, rode in the private rail coach maintained by the Illinois Central. Accompanying it was a platform car outfitted with a small cannon called "Popular Sovereignty," which heralded the Little Giant's approach.

On that same train Lincoln traveled alone as a regular passenger, toting an ancient carpetbag and a bulging umbrella. He wore an ill-fitting coat, vest and trousers, all of black alpaca. On his head sat a too-large, battered, napless stovepipe hat. The outfit made him resemble a preacher. Later in the campaign, while garbed in a similar ensemble, he met Carl Schurz, a young German-American Republican leader from Wisconsin, who wrote that he had seen "several public men of rough appearance; but none whose looks seemed quite so uncouth, not to say grotesque, as Lincoln's."[172]

Like all lawyers working for the railroad, Lincoln had a free pass, which he used to campaign simply, and usually alone. The Chicago *Press and Tribune* noted the sharp contrast in styles between Douglas and Lincoln. The Republican challenger "goes from one appointment to another without parade or ostentation. He charters no palatial cars with a bar-room and hotel aboard. He has no cannon and powder monkeys before him to announce his coming or departure."[173] Occasionally, Lincoln would even ride on freight trains. One day sitting in the caboose of such a train which was shunted onto a siding while Douglas's special train, decorated with flags and banners, whizzed by, Lincoln jocularly remarked: "Boys, the gentleman in that car evidently smelt no royalty in our carriage."[174]

En route to the capital, Douglas stopped in Bloomington, where he once again praised Lincoln as "a kind-hearted, amiable gentleman, a right good fellow, a worthy citizen, of eminent ability as a lawyer, and, I have no doubt, sufficient ability to make a good Senator." But he also attacked his rival as a miscegenationist. "Why, he would permit them [i.e., blacks] to marry, would he not? And if he gives them that right, I suppose he will let them marry whom they please, provided they marry their equals. If the divine law declares that the white man is the equal of the negro woman, that they are on a perfect equality, I suppose he admits the right of the negro woman to marry the white man." He asserted that the "only hope that Mr. Lincoln has of defeating me for the Senate rests in the fact that I was faithful to my principles and that he may be able in consequence of that fact to form a coalition with Lecompton men who wish to defeat me for that fidelity."[175] When he finished, the crowd called for Lincoln, who refused to give a speech, saying: "This meeting was called by the friends of Judge Douglas, and it would be improper of me to address it."[176]

In Springfield on the afternoon of July 17, Douglas repeated his Chicago speech, placing special emphasis on Lincoln's belief that the Declaration of Independence's assertion that "all men are created equal" covered blacks. To the crowd's amusement, Douglas sneered: "He thinks that the negro is his brother. I do not think that the negro is any kin of mine at all." The signers of the Declaration "did not intend to in-clude the Indian or the negro in that declaration." Warming to his white supremacy theme, Douglas went on: "I am opposed to Indian equality. I am opposed to putting the coolies, now importing into this country, on an equality with us, or putting the Chinese or any other inferior race on an equality with us." Douglas predicted that Lincoln would work to eliminate the Illinois black code forbidding African Ameri-cans to settle in the state. "When he lets down the bars and the floods shall have turned in upon us and covered our prairies thick with them till they shall be as dark and black as night in mid-day," Lincoln would advocate giving them the same citi-zenship rights as whites. The Little Giant then went into graphic and extensive detail about the indignities of "nigger equality" and race-mixing—hordes of blacks invading the state, holding office, becoming judges, and—horror of horrors, marrying with whites. "We must preserve the purity of the race not only in our politics but in our domestic relations," he thundered.[177] (The word "nigger" appears in the account pub-lished by the Indianapolis *Indiana State Sentinel*, which supported Douglas, but not in the Chicago *Times*. This difference lends credence to the claim that Douglas regu-larly used the word "nigger" instead of "negro," though the *Congressional Globe* and his organ, the Chicago *Times*, sanitized his language.) To this racist appeal, the Chicago *Journal* protested that "the subject of ethnology is not a question in the current poli-tics . . . and has nothing whatever to do with the principles for which the Republican party are contending."[178]

In response, that evening at the statehouse Lincoln renewed his attack on the popular sovereignty doctrine as "the most errant humbug that has ever been at-tempted on an intelligent community." He also responded to Douglas's interpretation of the Declaration of Independence. Did the senator mean to amend that document to read that all "Europeans are created equal?" What about Russians in Asia? "I ex-pect ere long he will introduce another amendment to his definition. He is not at all particular. He is satisfied with any thing which does not endanger the nationalizing of slavery. It may draw white men down, but it must not lift negroes up. Who shall say, 'I am the superior, and you are the inferior?'"

Lincoln acknowledged that the Declaration of Independence should not be con-strued literally. "I do not understand the Declaration to mean that all men were created equal in all respects," he conceded, offering a bizarre example of one respect in which the races were unequal. Blacks, he said, "are not our equal in color." His meaning is obscure; what is a superior color? Perhaps he was being satirical. In any event, when he repeated it, he did so with a strong qualifier: "Certainly the negro is not our equal in color—perhaps not in many other respects; still, in the right to put into his mouth the bread that his own hands have earned, he is the equal of every other man, white or black. In pointing out that more has been given you, you can not be justified in taking away the little which has been given him. All I ask for the negro is that if you do not like him, leave him alone. If God gave him but little, that little let him enjoy." Note-worthy here is Lincoln's agnosticism about black inferiority, above and beyond the dubious category of color; the black *may* be inferior to the white in other respects as well, but he did not identify them. Nor did Lincoln say that God gave black people little; he insisted only that *if* God gave them little, they should be allowed to enjoy that little undisturbed.[179] This carefully hedged treatment of the racial inferiority argument differed sharply from Douglas's unqualified racism. A Democrat objected that Lincoln's speech—especially his query "Who shall say, 'I am the superior, and you are the inferior?'" and his observation that blacks are "not our equal in color—perhaps not in many other respects"—belied his protestations about black inferiority: "Mr. Lincoln *may* not be in favor of 'negro equality' but he cannot follow up his declarations on this subject and land short of so odious a doctrine."[180] It was a telling point, for Lincoln's remarks did imply that blacks might not be inferior to whites.

Many believed that Lincoln's speech effectively countered Douglas's racial demagoguery. One auditor reported that Lincoln "was particularly clear and forcible," delivering an address "full of solid argument, full of caustic criticism, full of pointed illustrations."[181] The *Illinois State Journal* declared that it was "a most masterly answer to all the quirks, quibbles, sophistries, misrepresentations and falsehoods of Mr. Douglas."[182] A correspondent for the Alton *Courier* called it "splendid . . . the best speech which has yet been made."[183] When urged to have one of his orations issued as a pamphlet, Lincoln chose this one, for, he said, it appeared "to be the most 'taking' speech I have made."[184] It even removed the scales from the eyes of the Louisville *Journal*, which remarked: "We had supposed him [Lincoln] to be an impracticable abolitionist or something near it from the representation of his views made by Douglas in his Chicago speech; but after reading the speeches of Lincoln at Chicago and Springfield, we find he has been most grossly misrepresented by Douglas."[185] Another Louisville paper, the *Democrat*, grudgingly observed that "Lincoln is able, and does full justice to the bad cause he advocates."[186]

Not all Republicans were pleased. One complained to Lincoln: "You are *too easy* on the Scamp! You should, you *must* be *severer* on him . . . . just throw aside a little, or sufficient, of your over-abundance of 'the milk of human kindness.'"[187] Horace Greeley complained that, although Lincoln's "House Divided" speech "was in the right key," his "Chicago speech was bad; and I fear the new Springfield speech is worse. If he dare not stand on broad Republican ground, he cannot stand at all."[188] Democrats, of course, disliked the speech and harped on Douglas's themes. The Springfield *Register* objected that in Lincoln's "peevish, fretful and feeble" Springfield address, "no allusion is made to the interests of the *white man*" and that all the "great questions" of the day "sink, in his mind, into insignificance compared with the interest of the *negro*."[189]

Attempting to sort out his thoughts about race, Lincoln wrote a memorandum, probably in 1858, appealing to religious sentiment in a discussion of the alleged inferiority of blacks. "Suppose it is true," he mused, "that the negro is inferior to the white, in the gifts of nature; is it not the exact reverse [of] justice that the white should, for that reason, take from the negro, any part of the little which has been given him? 'Give to him that is needy' is the christian rule of charity; but 'Take from him that is needy' is the rule of slavery."

For religious defenders of slavery, like the Rev. Dr. Frederick A. Ross, Lincoln had withering contempt. The "sum of pro-slavery theology," Lincoln wrote, "seems to be this: 'Slavery is not universally *right*, nor yet universally *wrong*; it is better for *some* people to be slaves; and, in such cases, it is the Will of God that they be such." Acknowledging that "there is no contending against the Will of God," he insisted that "there is some difficulty in ascertaining, and applying it, to particular cases." Suppose, for example, that Dr. Ross, a Presbyterian divine who had published a defense of slavery in 1857, "has a slave named Sambo, and the question is 'Is it the Will of God that Sambo shall remain a slave, or be set free?'" God "gives no audable [*sic*] answer to the question, and his revelation—the Bible—gives none. . . . No one thinks of asking Sambo's opinion on it." Ultimately, then, Dr. Ross himself must decide the question. "And while he consider[s] it, he sits in the shade, with gloves on his hands, and subsists on the bread that Sambo is earning in the burning sun. If he decides that God Wills Sambo to continue a slave, he thereby retains his own comfortable position; but if he decides that God will's Sambo to be free, he thereby has to walk out of the shade, throw off his gloves, and delve for his own bread." So Dr. Ross can hardly be expected to exercise "that perfect impartiality, which has ever been considered most favorable to correct decisions." In commenting on this example, Lincoln displayed some passion. "But, slavery is good for some people!!! As a *good* thing, slavery is strikingly peculiar, in this, that it is the only good thing which no man ever seeks the good of, *for himself*. Nonsense! Wolves devouring lambs, not because it is good for their own greedy maws, but because it [is] good for the lambs!!!"[190]

(In 1860, Lincoln would evince equal scorn for the proposition that slavery was "a *necessity* imposed upon us by the negro race." In a letter he never sent, he contemptuously wrote: "That the going many thousand miles, seizing a set of savages, bringing them here, and making slaves of them, is a *necessity* imposed on *us* by *them*, involves a species of logic to which my mind will scarcely assent.")[191]

The two candidates focused on central Illinois, where legislative races would be the most hotly contested. In the thick of the struggle, Douglas sometimes lost his composure. At Beardstown on August 11, he assailed Lyman Trumbull for alleging that Douglas's opposition to the Lecompton Constitution was hypocritical. The Little Giant reportedly "raved like a maniac," "tore his hair," and "shook his fists" while branding his senatorial colleague an "infamous liar" and a "miserable, craven-hearted wretch" who would "rather have both ears cut off than to use that language in my presence, where I could call him to account."

Douglas also said, without evident irony, that while he wished "to discuss principles alone, without any indulgence in personalities," his rival had stooped to personal attacks. He had treated Lincoln "with marked respect and kindness," and in return, he claimed, he had received abuse: his opponent had charged him with conspiring to nationalize slavery and then criticized him for not responding. Haughtily Douglas explained, "I did not suppose that there was a man in America so degraded in his own soul, as to believe that such a charge could be true against the Supreme Court and two Presidents." He went on to call the allegation "an infamous lie" and an "assault upon my private and public character." He charged that Lincoln made personal attacks in order to shift attention from his own radicalism. "Lincoln has been told by his abolition supporters that he made a great blunder in his speech at Springfield, that he should not have avowed the abolition doctrines as broadly, as rankly, as undisguisedly as he did, and that I was getting the advantage of him on the defense of his own issues," Douglas said. "He is determined now to change the discussion, if possible, from the principle involved to a personal contest. I confess that I have no taste for personal contests before public audiences." He then proceeded to ridicule Lincoln's "exploits with broad-swords, on his trip to Missouri with Gen. Shields."

Douglas further alleged that in 1851 the Illinois Legislature had passed the following resolution: "The people of each State and each *Territory* should be left by Congress to legislate for themselves, subject to no limitation whatever." Two days later a Republican charged Douglas "with *deliberately falsifying the record.* There is no such resolution as he read, in the proceedings of 1851, nor *anything resembling it.*"[192]

On August 13 at Havana, where fistfights broke out among boisterous drunkards clogging the streets, Douglas delivered an intemperate speech in which he called Lincoln "a liar, a coward, a wretch and a sneak" and Trumbull "a liar and a wretch and a vagabond."[193] At Lewistown, Douglas denounced Lincoln and Trumbull as "liars, sneaks, wretches, cowards, villains and pickpockets." Asked why he used such strong language, Douglas replied "that Lincoln's course has been such as to leave him no other line of argument."[194] In Peoria on August 18, his abusive epithets for Lincoln and Trumbull—"infamous liar," "low rascal," "knave," and "Billingsgate orator"—caused a pro-Douglas farmer to observe: "His temper is so rough, you could grate a nutmeg on it."[195] From afar, the New York *Times* noted that Douglas's "envenomed" rhetoric demonstrated "how absurd was the hope indulged in some quarters of uniting the Republicans with the supporters of the Little Giant."[196] On August 31 at Joliet, Douglas abused Congressman and Congregational minister Owen Lovejoy for "wearing the clerical robe and uttering vulgarity and mendacity, slandering private character, [and] traducing honest men." Projecting his own flaws onto his opponents, he characterized Lincoln as a "man who lets go of principle . . . of stern integrity, and undertakes, by the aid of schemes, tricks and dodging, to get popularity in each locality."[197]

In September, Douglas's temper grew even worse. At Pontiac on September 2, he exploded in anger when asked a challenging question about a person's right to recover a fugitive slave who runs away from a slave territory to a free state. The questioner reported that the senator "looked at us as though he would take perfect delight in eating us up, or would derive exquisite pleasure in knocking the daylights out of us. Approaching us, with upraised hand and flashing eye, shaking his shaggy locks, and fairly trembling with rage, he answered: 'Yes, sir; he can be recaptured under the Fugitive Slave Law!' He then commenced a volley of billingsgate which would make a fishmonger blush, calling us an Abolitionist; that we were in the habit of going round lecturing in church basements, making abolition harangues, after the fashion of Lovejoy and other pincushion lecturers."[198] During a speech at Gillespie on October 16, David L. Phillips raised a question about the Little Giant's role in amending a bill that would have allowed the people of Kansas a fair chance to vote on any proposed constitution for that territory. Douglas "lost his dignity and self-respect, abused and blackguarded Mr. P.," calling "him a liar half a dozen times." An observer described the senator's behavior as "scandalous and galling in the extreme."[199]

The Little Giant, whom one Republican called a "drunken demagogue," may have been intoxicated during some of these speeches.[200] He drank and smoked so much that throat and liver problems combined to kill him at the age of forty-eight. During the 1858 campaign he "was drinking himself to death," according to Horace White.[201] In a dispatch from Havana, White remarked that it would be difficult "to give an adequate idea of the littleness, meanness and foulness of Douglas' harangue here," and attributed it to inebriation.[202] Another witness agreed, saying that Douglas "was very bitter; he shook his shaggy locks, rolled his eyes, stamped his feet, flourished his arms, pointed his fingers and gnashed his teeth."[203] The senator's friends reportedly "claimed as an excuse for his language that he was intoxicated at the time."[204] A reporter suspected the "unshaven and unshorn" senator was drunk at Carlinville on September 8 and at Centralia nine days later.[205] At Centralia, the reporter wrote: "I have never heard him commence a harangue so entirely out of temper as on this occasion. . . . In my hearing some one asked, 'Is he drunk,' to which a reply was made, 'No, he has quit drinking,' another voice adding irreverently, 'Yes, that's so, I've seen him quit more than a dozen times to-day.'"[206] Another spectator noted that many in the crowd "thought that Douglas was under the influence of liquor, as a sober man would hardly talk and act as he did."[207]

The Little Giant's private railcar was well stocked with liquor. An observer of the Quincy debate in October recalled that when Douglas arrived in that train, he "was well loaded with booze."[208] Carl Schurz observed Douglas there and later reported that "his face seemed a little puffy, and it was said that he had been drinking hard with some boon companions."[209] George B. McClellan, a pro-Douglas executive of the Illinois Central, traveled one day during the campaign with the Little Giant, to whom he had offered his private railcar. McClellan recalled seeing the senator "somewhat affected by the large amount of whiskey he had taken, & looking unkempt & sleepy." Douglas had "brought with him a number of his political henchmen with whom he was up all night drinking whiskey etc."[210]

Douglas's drinking had drawn notice long before the 1858 campaign. According to Herndon, in 1854 Douglas was "a little 'cocked'" when he interrupted Lincoln repeatedly during his speech at Springfield.[211] Two years thereafter, an attendee at a Douglas rally alleged that the Little Giant "was considerably drunk and made one of the most sophistical and deceitful speeches I ever listened to."[212]

In time, word of Douglas's tippling spread. George D. Prentice of the Louisville *Journal* said that "Douglas fails to improve—perhaps from his keeping too near 'the dipper.'"[213] The Quincy *Whig* on several occasions alluded to Douglas's alcohol consumption, remarking "there are stories of late inebrieties that might be told" and suggested that his confinement to his house in 1860 was related to health problems caused by excessive drinking.[214] Douglas was evidently drunk at the Freeport debate in late August 1858. Herndon reported in October 1858 that "Douglas is [as] *bloated* as I ever saw him: he drinks very hard indeed: his look is awful to me, when I compare him as he now looks with what he was in Feb[ruar]y 1858."[215] In 1859, a brakeman aboard an Illinois Central train observed the Little Giant consume so much whiskey that "he got in a stupor and sort of slid down between the seats." In Chicago he had to be carried off the cars.[216] Campaigning for president in 1860, he stormed late one night into William Henry Seward's railroad sleeping car and urged the New York senator to arise and address a crowd at Toledo. Charles Francis Adams, Jr., who along with his father was accompanying Seward, recorded in his diary that Douglas "had a bottle of whiskey with him, and, as he left the car, he stopped to take a drink; and, next morning, I was told he was plainly drunk."[217] (Henry Adams, perhaps based on what his father and brother told him, called the Little Giant "a drunkard.")[218] Others reported that Douglas was so intoxicated he required assistance to detrain. At that time an editor of the New York *Herald* wrote privately that Douglas "drinks hard."[219] In March 1861, only months before Douglas died, a Washington correspondent noted that the senator "drinks a good deal, and has been what the boys call 'tight' pretty often during the past winter."[220]

"Those who know him best," the Cincinnati *Commercial* noted of Douglas in 1860, "are impressed that he cannot live many years." Early in his career he had "acquired habits of drinking spirituous liquors. He probably found it next to impossible to avoid those habits, and perhaps did not look upon it as dangerous." In the newspaper's view, the Little Giant was more to be pitied than censured for succumbing to "the temptations that beset public men." The *Commercial* cited "illustrious examples before him, of the ruinous consequences of indulging in stimulants, to sustain overwrought brain and nerves, and flesh and blood, in the devouring excitements of contests involving the issues of political life and death."[221] Lincoln agreed with this analysis; he may have had the example of Douglas in mind when he told a student in his law office: "a large per cent of professional men abuse their stomachs by imprudence in drinking and eating, and in that way health is injured and ruined and life is shortened."[222]

At Havana on August 14, Lincoln subtly referred to Douglas's drinking habits. The day before, Lincoln remarked, the Little Giant had "said something about *fighting,* as though referring to a pugilistic encounter between him and myself." These remarks prompted one of Douglas's more enthusiastic supporters to remove his coat and volunteer "to take the job off Judge Douglas' hands, and fight Lincoln himself." But, Lincoln said, he would not accept the pointless challenge. "If my fighting Judge Douglas would not prove anything," he continued, "it would certainly prove nothing for me to fight his bottle-holder."[223] In mid-September, taking offense at Douglas's conduct in the Charleston debate, Lincoln said he was tempted to protest publicly that he "did not have to have his wife along to keep him sober."[224]

In fact, the beautiful, cultivated, tactful, well-bred Mrs. Douglas (née Adele Cutts, his second wife), a grandniece of Dolley Madison, did accompany her husband, much to the consternation of Republicans, who regarded her as an effective weapon in the senator's arsenal. Horace White said he had "never seen a more queenly face and figure" and did not doubt "that this attractive presence was very helpful to Judge Douglas."[225] Another journalist covering that campaign remembered her as "a most lovely and a queenly apparition. Indeed, it seemed to me that I had never seen a woman more beautiful in every way. Her tall figure was perfectly proportioned, and her every movement and gesture most graceful. She presented a marked contrast, in her youthful, blooming freshness and vivacity, to her small, dark, sombre husband. She appeared to be devoted to him, and certainly helped him no little in his political aspirations."[226] Wherever her husband spoke, she attended receptions. At such an event even a Republican editor, Charles L. Bernays, was so taken with her beauty that he became an admirer of her husband.

In late September, Lincoln gallantly agreed to escort Mrs. Douglas on the train from Sullivan to Danville. The Little Giant's schedule forced him to ride all night between those two towns; Lincoln was traveling the same route by day. To spare her the discomfort of a night journey, Lincoln offered to be her traveling companion. When the challenger arrived in Danville, he "firmly, yet kindly" told the Republican welcoming committee that he "had a lady in care whom he must first put in the hands of her waiting friends." He then led her to a cab and wished her a good evening. She later remarked that "Mr. Lincoln was a very agreeable and considerate escort."[227] Unlike Mrs. Douglas, Mary Lincoln stayed home during most of the campaign.

In late July and early August, Lincoln attended some of his opponent's afternoon speeches and responded in the evening. On July 27 Lincoln listened at Clinton, when Douglas finally answered Lincoln's conspiracy charge. "Unfounded and untrue," Douglas said; "I never exchanged a word with Chief Justice Taney or any other member of the Supreme Court about the Dred Scott decision in my life, either before or after it was rendered. I never exchanged a word with President Pierce on the subject . . . nor did I exchange a word with President Buchanan upon it until long after it was made." He menacingly warned that if Lincoln "resorts to this game after this explanation, he will get my answer in monosyllables."[228] When Douglas "said that no man could look him in the face and say that he ever denounced the U.S. Bank decision" of the Supreme Court, Lincoln stood and stared directly into Douglas's eyes. The Little Giant averted his gaze.[229] Tension mounted throughout Douglas's denunciatory speech, after which Lincoln "arose pale and trembling evidently wrought up to the highest pitch" and announced that he would reply in the evening at the courthouse.

There, by candlelight before a small crowd, Lincoln seemed "very much depressed, still smarting under the fierceness of the assault Douglas had made upon him." When a large contingent eventually appeared and filled the room to overflowing, he "began to cheer up and finally warmed himself into a very successful oratorical effort," during which he made "a withering allusion to the angelic temper, which Douglas had displayed in his speech," denied charges that he had voted against supplying U.S. troops in Mexico, reiterated arguments he had made at Springfield and Chicago, and in response to the Little Giant's assertion that he had never criticized the Supreme Court's ruling in the U.S. Bank case, "said he had heard Douglas as many as twenty times himself, and a thousand men all over the State would back him in this, both Democrats and Republicans."[230]

As he proceeded up the Illinois River in Douglas's wake, speaking at Beardstown, Havana, Bath, Lewistown, and Peoria, Lincoln seemed to be in high spirits. Many old Whig friends accompanied him, delighted to hear his stories and comments on the political scene. When Horace White asked why in his speeches "he did not oftener turn the laugh on Douglas," Lincoln "replied that he was too much in earnest, and that it was doubtful whether turning the laugh on anybody really gained any votes."[231] On the eve of the August 21 debate at Ottawa, Lincoln was once more urged to abandon his solemn style of oratory and to imitate the Ohio wit Thomas Corwin. He again refused, observing that the "subject is too serious & important."[232] His aim as an orator was simple: "I do not seek applause, nor to amuse the people, I want to convince them."[233]

White was struck by Lincoln's ability to say something new at each stop. "Many times," White recollected, "did I marvel to see him get on a platform at some out-of-the-way place and begin an entirely new speech, equal, in all respects, to any of the joint debates, and continue for two hours in a high strain of argumentative power and eloquence, without saying anything that I had heard before." In September he asked Lincoln about his ability to offer original remarks in almost every speech, whereas the Little Giant repeated himself over and over. Lincoln "replied that Douglas was not lacking in versatility, but that he had a theory that the popular sovereignty speech was the one to win on, and that the audiences whom he addressed would hear it only once and would never know whether he made the same speech elsewhere or not, and would never care." Lincoln, in contrast, "said that he could not repeat to-day what he had said yesterday. The subject kept enlarging and widening in his mind as he went on, and it was much easier to make a new speech than to repeat an old one."[234]

Lincoln took umbrage at Douglas's Beardstown speech in which the senator had deemed the conspiracy charge "an infamous lie." On August 12, showing "much agitation," Lincoln fired back: "it would be vastly more to the point for Judge Douglas to say he did *not* do some of these things, did *not* forge some of these links of overwhelming testimony, than to go vociferating about the country that possibly he may hint that somebody is a liar! [Deafening applause.] I repeat and renew, and shall continue to repeat and renew this 'charge' until he denies the evidence, and then I shall so fasten it upon him that it will cling to him as long as he lives."[235] A reporter noted that it "would be impossible for me to give your readers an idea of the energy and vehemence with which Lincoln uttered these words. It was the most terrible indictment I ever heard. Its effect was electrical. The vast audience gave three tremendous cheers when he pronounced the concluding sentence."[236] (A Democratic paper, on the other hand, alleged that Lincoln's auditors "received his niggerisms with disgust.")[237]

At Havana the following day, Lincoln arrived as Douglas was speaking. He did not proceed to the site where the Little Giant held forth, explaining to someone who suggested that he do so: "No, the Judge felt so 'put out' by my listening to him at Bloomington and Clinton, that I promised to let him alone for the rest of the canvass. I understand he is calling Trumbull and myself liars, and if he saw me in the crowd he might be so ashamed of himself as to omit the most vivid part of his argument."[238] He spoke later that day to a crowd much smaller than Douglas's. The following day at Bath, a town he had laid out as a surveyor decades earlier, Lincoln turned for support to admirers of Henry Clay, who had resoundingly condemned slavery. Lincoln contrasted those views with Douglas's indifference on the subject.

On August 17 at Lewistown, facing a Democratic transparency proclaiming "Lincoln declares the negro his equal," the challenger with unwonted "vehemence and force" denounced amoral neutrality on the slavery issue. The Little Giant, he said, "was the only statesman of any note or prominence in the country who had *never said to friend or enemy whether he believed human slavery in the abstract to be right or wrong.*"[239]

Also at Lewistown, Lincoln delivered an even more ringing apostrophe to signers of the Declaration of Independence than the one he had made in Springfield a month earlier. "In their enlightened belief, nothing stamped with the divine image and likeness was sent into the world to be trodden on, and degraded, and imbruted by its fellows. They grasped not only the whole race of man then living, but they reached forward and seized upon the farthest posterity. They erected a beacon to guide their children, and their children's children, and the countless myriads who should inhabit the earth in other ages. Wise statesmen as they were, they knew the tendency of prosperity to breed tyrants, and so they established these great self-evident truths, that when in the distant future some man, some faction, some interest, should set up the doctrine that none but rich men, or none but white men, or none but Anglo-Saxon white men, were entitled to life, liberty, and the pursuit of happiness, their posterity might look up again to the Declaration of Independence and take courage to renew the battle which their fathers began—so that truth, and justice, and mercy, and all the human and Christian virtues might not be extinguished from the land; so that no man would hereafter dare to limit and circumscribe the great principles on which the temple of liberty was being built." With "great earnestness," he told his audience: "if you have been taught doctrines conflicting with the great landmarks of the Declaration of Independence; if you have listened to suggestions which would take away from its grandeur, and mutilate the fair symmetry of its proportions; if you have been inclined to believe that all men are *not* created equal in those inalienable rights enumerated by our chart[er] of liberty, let me entreat you to come back. Return to the fountain whose waters spring close by the blood of the Revolution. Think nothing of me—take no thought for the political fate of any man whomsoever—but come back to the truths that are in the Declaration of Independence. You may do anything with me you choose, if you will but heed these sacred principles. You may not only defeat me for the Senate, but you may take me and put me to death. While pretending no indifference to earthly honors, I *do claim* to be actuated in this contest by something higher than an anxiety for office. I charge you to drop every paltry and insignificant thought for any man's success. It is nothing; I am nothing; Judge Douglas is nothing. *But do not destroy that immortal emblem of humanity—the Declaration of American Independence.*"[240]

Horace White reported that the "applause which followed these noble utterances rang far and wide through the pleasant village." White called Lincoln's effort "truly one of the finest efforts of public speaking I ever listened to."[241] A Massachusetts newspaper declared that Lincoln's peroration "ranks him at once among the foremost orators of the land."[242]

Although Lincoln told a friend, "[m]y recent experience shows that speaking at the same place the next day after D[ouglas] is the very thing—it is, in fact, a concluding speech on him," some Republicans frowned on such a strategy.[243] Farmers were reluctant to neglect their chores for two consecutive days. One of his strong supporters said that Lincoln should not allow Douglas to take advantage of him; the Little Giant persuaded friends to give him elaborate receptions and draw big crowds for a daytime speech, after which most of the audience departed. Thus, "Douglas takes the crowd & Lincoln the leavings."[244] At Lewistown, Lincoln only drew about 2,000, whereas Douglas had an audience of 3,000 the day before. At Havana on August 13, according to the Democratic press, Lincoln attracted only 659 people, compared with Douglas's 6,000 the preceding day. "Lincoln's speech was not up to his usual efforts," one Democratic correspondent alleged. "He is evidently discouraged. His ultra negroism being found to be disgustingly unpalatable to the masses."[245] The *Illinois State Register* ran similar accounts of his meeting at Clinton on July 27. After that speech, Lincoln reportedly said "that he would have to make his own appointments because Douglas, under present circumstances, has the crowd, and the people will not turn out in the evening to hear him reply. He is much disappointed at his reception in Clinton," where he only drew an audience of 250.[246]

Democrats were even more critical of Lincoln's tactics than were Republicans. The Chicago *Times* called Lincoln a "cringing, crawling, ... poor, desperate creature," who could not attract an audience on his own and therefore lurked "on the outskirts of Douglas' meetings, begging the people to come and hear him." Such conduct, the *Times* declared, was "mean, sneaking and disreputable!"[247] Richard T. Merrick of Chicago threatened to follow Lincoln and reply to his charges wherever he spoke. George B. McClellan thought Merrick's proposal "an excellent one." (McClellan praised Douglas, saying apropos of one of his debates with Lincoln: "Douglas' speech was compact, logical & powerful—Mr. Lincoln's disjointed, & rather a mass of anecdotes than of arguments. I did not think that there was any approach to equality in the oratorical powers of the two men.")[248]

Unsatisfied by the results of his rebuttals of Douglas, Republicans in Illinois and elsewhere urged Lincoln to challenge his opponent to debate. The New York *Tribune* suggested that the two candidates "speak together at some fifteen or twenty of the most important and widely accessible points throughout the State, and that the controversy will be prosecuted . . . at every county seat and considerable town."[249] The Chicago *Press and Tribune* said: "Let Mr. Douglas and Mr. Lincoln agree to canvass the State together, in the usual western style."[250]

On July 24, when Lincoln saw the published announcement of Douglas's appointments for August, he conferred with Norman B. Judd about debating his opponent. Judd, sensing that Lincoln had already determined to challenge the senator, said he thought it would be a good idea. Lincoln then wrote a letter for Judd to deliver to Douglas, formally proposing that they "divide time, and address the same audiences." (According to one account, Lincoln stated: "I will give him the length of my knife.")[251]

With great difficulty, Judd tracked Douglas down. When, after three days, Judd finally did catch up with him and presented Lincoln's note, the Little Giant angrily asked: "What do you come to me with such a thing as this for?"[252] He berated Judd for abandoning the Democratic Party. Ignoring the insults, Judd handed over Lincoln's challenge, which Douglas "angrily and emphatically declined to consider on the ground that it was a childish idea and that he would be belittling himself and dignifying Lincoln."[253] (Another reason for Douglas's hesitation was his respect for Lincoln's ability. As he told Joseph O. Glover, "I do not feel, between you and me, that I want to go into this debate. The whole country knows me and has me measured. Lincoln, as regards myself, is comparatively unknown, and if he gets the best of this debate, and I want to say he is the ablest man the Republicans have got, I shall lose everything and Lincoln will gain everything. Should I win, I shall gain but little.")[254] Judd warned Douglas that if he refused to debate, he would seem afraid of his rival.

It was a telling point; the Chicago *Press and Tribune* noted that "it has been justly held that the candidate who refused to speak in that way [i.e., in debates] had no better reason than cowardice for declining the challenge."[255] The Chicago *Times* asked why Lincoln had not issued the challenge earlier. It was a reasonable question, for as Douglas noted, the underdog stands to benefit more than the favorite in political debates.

Realizing that he could not afford to look cowardly, Douglas offered a counterproposal: noting that the Democratic State Central Committee had committed him to speak at party meetings throughout the state, he declined to share time with Lincoln at those occasions, but he would agree to debate in each of the state's nine congressional districts, except for the two where they had already in effect debated (i.e., Chicago and Springfield). In picking up the gage thus flung down, Douglas peevishly, and falsely, suggested that Lincoln was plotting to include a National Democratic candidate for the senate in the debates. Forwarding Douglas's response to Lincoln, Judd observed that it "is a clear dodge, but he has made the best case he could."[256] On July 29, protesting against the "unjust" insinuations of "attempted unfairness," Lincoln accepted Douglas's terms.[257]

The following day Douglas submitted a schedule for the debates: Ottawa (August 21), Freeport (August 27), Jonesboro (September 15), Charleston (September 18), Galesburg (October 7), Quincy (October 13), and Alton (October 15). Each debate would last three hours, evenly divided between the two candidates, with one opening for an hour, the other replying for an hour and a half, and the first speaker concluding with a half-hour rejoinder. Douglas would have the opening and closing speeches at the first, third, fifth, and seventh debates. Mildly protesting that this arrangement gave the Little Giant four openings and closes to his three, Lincoln accepted these conditions. He also pledged, "I shall be at no more of your exclusive meetings."[258]

Republicans belittled Douglas's offer. The *Illinois State Journal* complained that there were "about one hundred points in the State where the candidates . . . ought to have held discussions." The senator's excuse for confining the debates to seven sites "is a cowardly showing of the white feather," the *Journal* protested.[259] "The little dodger shirks, and backs out, except at half a dozen places which he himself selects!" exclaimed the Chicago *Press and Tribune*. Douglas's reply was so "cowardly and contemptible" that the editors surmised he "is afraid of 'Long Abe' on the stump" and "would rather go about the country like a strolling mountebank, with his cannon, to[a]dies and puffers, to shoot, cheer and blow for him than to stand up to the work with a full grown man to confront him." In 1840, Douglas had ridiculed William Henry Harrison for placing himself in the hands of a committee; now the Little Giant was using that same excuse.[260] The *Illinois State Register* countered: "The idea that a man who has crossed blades in the senate with the strongest intellects of the country, who has, as the champion of democratic principles in the senatorial arena, routed all opposition—that such a man dreads encounter with Mr. A. Lincoln is an absurdity that can be uttered by his organs only with a ghastly phiz."[261] Lincoln, the Chicago *Times* predicted, "will get enough of debate and discomfiture to last him the balance of his life."[262]

Throughout the country, eyes turned to Ottawa, where the candidates would inaugurate what one Illinois abolitionist regarded as "a contest for the advancement of the kingdom of Heaven or the kingdom of Satan—a contest for an advance or a retrograde in civilization."[263] The New York *Times* prophetically remarked: "The battle must be close, severe, and doubtful. That it will be well fought is certain, and its results will be both important and memorable."[264]

"A David Greater than the Democratic Goliath"
The Lincoln-Douglas Debates
(1858)

In 1860, the radical abolitionist Parker Pillsbury dismissed Lincoln as "the Kentucky clodhopper," scoffed at his antislavery record, and maintained there was "no essential difference" between him and Stephen A. Douglas.[1] In fact, the two Illinois rivals disagreed fundamentally about slavery, the Declaration of Independence, the Constitution, the role of the U.S. Supreme Court, racial equality, and American history. Their epic battle in 1858 threw into sharp relief not only those disagreements but also the stark difference in the combatants' fundamental character. In addition, as some sensed at the time, their debates proved to be a dress rehearsal for the presidential contest two years later. As Herndon accurately predicted, "the *Race* in Ills for 1858 & 9—for the Senatorial seat . . . will be hot—energetic—deadly; it will be broader—wider, and deeper in *principle* than the race in 1856."[2]

As the Little Giant and his challenger girded for battle, odds-makers would probably have favored Douglas, though he suffered a few potential handicaps, including the split in his party; the reluctance of some former Whigs to back a Democrat; the increasing population of the northern part of the state, where hostility to slavery was intense; and the hard times produced by the Panic of 1857, which the public blamed on the Democrats. Outweighing those disadvantages were the Little Giant's obvious strengths: he was much better known than Lincoln; his leadership in the struggle against the Lecompton Constitution had won respect among Illinoisans who had earlier lost faith in him because of the Kansas-Nebraska Act; his forceful personality endeared him to many; his party had long dominated the state's politics; his appeals to race prejudice resonated in Illinois, one of the most Negrophobic of the Free States; and his skills as a debater were legendary. In addition, the Illinois General Assembly, which would choose the senator, was malapportioned; the heavily Democratic southern counties of the state had more than their fair share of legislative seats, depriving the Republicans of six to ten votes that they would have had if a reapportionment had been undertaken based on the most recent census. The twenty-five-member state senate contained Democratic holdovers from some districts that now had Republican majorities.

Lincoln acknowledged that Douglas's eminence benefited the Democrats. "Senator Douglas is of world wide renown," he observed. "All the anxious politicians of his party, or who have been of his party for years past, have been looking upon him as a certainty, at no distant day, to be the President of the United States. They have seen in his round, jolly, fruitful face, postoffices, landoffices, marshalships, and cabinet appointments, chargeships and foreign missions, bursting and sprouting out in wonderful exuberance ready to be laid hold of by their greedy hands." Hoping for such patronage rewards, these politicos "rush about him, sustain him, and give him marches, triumphal entries, and receptions." Lincoln, on the other hand, had no such support: "nobody has ever expected me to be President. In my poor lean, lank, face, nobody has ever seen that any cabbages were sprouting out."[3]

Helping to make Douglas formidable in debate was his lack of scruples. As William Herndon told a friend in Massachusetts, Illinois Republicans faced "a clever villian. . . . Douglas is an ambitious and an unscrupulous man; he is the greatest liar in all America; he misrepresents Lincoln throughout, and our people *generally* are not logical enough to see the precise manner, point & issue of [the] deception."[4] In addition, Douglas's verbal dexterity and overweening self-assurance enabled him to impress audiences, even though he might be uttering non-sequiturs.

Lincoln possessed offsetting advantages: his party was comparatively unified; the appeal of the antislavery cause was waxing; the sincerity of his commitment to that cause was palpable and persuasive; he was an effective, seasoned debater with political skills honed over the past quarter of a century; his psychological maturity and paternal qualities predisposed men to regard him with the affection and trust bestowed on a wise father; his self-effacing modesty and keen sense of humor made him likable; and his reputation for integrity had won him an unusual measure of respect.

Nevertheless, some Republicans were nervous about the debates. The unpopularity of Lincoln's stands on the Mexican War and on racial issues, along with the opposition of prominent Eastern Republicans like Horace Greeley, whose New York *Tribune* was widely read in Illinois, boded ill. Shortly before the debates began, Lincoln asked Hiram W. Beckwith of Danville how the party leaders in his area felt. When told that they anticipated the contest "with deep concern," Lincoln at first looked pained but quickly changed his expression as he described two men about to fight: "one of them brags about what he means to do. He jumps high in the air, cracking his heels together, smites his fists, and wastes his breath trying to scare somebody." The "other fellow, he says not a word." His "arms are at his side, his fists are closely doubled up, his head is drawn to the shoulder, and his teeth are set firm together. He is saving his wind for the fight, and as sure as it comes off he will win it, or die a-trying."[5]

The Opening Debate

Anticipation of the debates was keen. When Lincoln and Douglas took the platform for their first meeting, at Ottawa, the crowd of over 10,000 doubled the population of that county seat. People flocked there on special trains from LaSalle, Peru, and Chicago (84 miles to the northeast); from less distant locales they poured in on horseback, on foot, on hayracks, and in wagons and carriages. Boats conveyed others along the Illinois and Michigan Canal, which passed through the town. Many came the night before the debate, quickly filling the hotels and private houses; latecomers were forced to camp wherever they could find space. A resident recalled that the "campfires that spread up and down the valley for a mile made it look as if an army was gathered."[6]

Like a conquering hero, Douglas arrived in a splendid carriage drawn by four horses and flanked by bands playing martial music and by several hundred supporters waving flags and banners. Adding to the din, cannons fired volleys, well-wishers cheered lustily, and street vendors noisily hawked their wares. Lincoln made a less grandiose entrance into town aboard a train full of supporters from Chicago. En route he seemed unruffled, and when asked about the upcoming debate, he "calmly and indifferently replied, that he was fully prepared."[7]

At the depot a large crowd holding aloft banners emblazoned with pro-Republican mottos greeted him: "Abe the Giant-Killer," "Edgar County for the Tall Sucker," "Illinois born under the Ordinance of '87."[8] His friend W. H. L. Wallace escorted him to the home of Mayor Joseph O. Glover, where he would spend the night. Because the weather had been unusually dry, so much dust was stirred up that the town looked like a huge smokehouse. Under a blazing sun, the audience jammed into the unshaded public square, where they stood patiently for three hours listening to the debaters. With difficulty the speakers and dignitaries made their way through the mass of humanity to reach the platform, which was so crowded that part of it collapsed.

Douglas opened the debates by repeating many of his earlier arguments, fiercely denying that he had conspired to nationalize slavery and charging that Lincoln favored racial equality. He underscored his points by furiously gesturing skyward, giving his head a shake, and moving forward like a springing panther.

Douglas's "sledge-hammer style" displeased some auditors, who thought him too "dogmatic" and "coarse in his expressions."[9] A local Republican paper reported that his "face was livid with rage and despair; he threw himself into contortions, shook his head, shook his fists; his whole body shook as with a palsy; his eyes protruded from their sockets; he raved like a mad bull. His voice at times descended to a demonized howl; and such looks as he gave his antagonist!"[10] A former admirer of Douglas found it "disgusting" to observe how "he shuns and avoids the real solid *matter and marrow* of the matter, avoids everything that looks like fair debate upon questions of national or even of State policy; how he quibbles, how he misrepresents, how he prevaricates; nay—it must be said—how he lies, how he panders to the lowest portions of the lowest classes, with slang, with coarse jokes, with ribaldry, with vile abuse."[11]

In his opening remarks, Douglas praised his opponent's character, then abruptly asked the audience: "are you in favor of conferring upon the negro the rights and privileges of citizenship? ["No, no."] Do you desire to strike out of our State Constitution that clause which keeps slaves and free negroes out of the State, and allow the free negro to flow in ["never"] and cover our prairies with his settlements? Do you desire to turn this beautiful State into a free negro colony ["no, no"], in order that when Missouri shall abolish slavery, she can send us these emancipated slaves to be-

come citizens and voters on an equality with you? ["Never, no."] If you desire negro
citizenship—if you desire them to come into the State and stay with white men—if
you desire to let them vote on an equality with yourselves—if you desire to make
them eligible to office—to have them serve on juries and judge of your rights—then
go with Mr. Lincoln and the Black Republicans in favor of negro citizenship. ["Never,
never."] For one, I am opposed to negro citizenship in any form. [Cheers.]"

(Instead of citing the threat posed by Missouri, some other Democrats pointed to
Connecticut, where the state House of Representatives had recently passed a bill to
enfranchise blacks. "This is republican policy where that party has full sweep," according to the *Illinois State Register.* "When seeking power, as in this state, they endeavor to cover up their real designs.—Let them once secure the power, and, as in
Connecticut, they will raise the negro to the political level of the native white." If
blacks were allowed to vote in Illinois, the Chicago *Times* predicted, thousands of
them "will drift into this State.")[12]

Blacks were hopelessly inferior, Douglas argued. Snidely he remarked, "I do not
question Mr. Lincoln's conscientious belief that the negro was made his equal, and
hence is his brother. [Laughter.] But, for my own part, I do not regard the negro as my
equal, and I positively deny that he is my brother, or any kin to me whatever. ["Never."
"Hit him again," and cheers.]" Citing history, he added: "I do not believe the Almighty ever intended the negro to be the equal of the white man. ["Never, never."] If
he did he has been a long time demonstrating the fact. [Laughter, cheers.] For six
thousand years the negro has been a race upon the earth, and during that whole six
thousand years—in all latitudes and climates wherever the negro has been—he has
been inferior to whatever race adjoined him. The fact is he belongs to an inferior race
and must occupy an inferior position. ["Good," "that's so," &c.]"[13]

Douglas may have said "nigger" instead of "Negro." The Quincy *Whig* sarcastically noted that the Little Giant's "elegant terms" included an accusation that Lincoln
espoused "the doctrine that '*niggers* were equal to white men.'" The *Whig* asked: "Isn't
this beautiful language to come from a United States Senator?"[14] A journalist who
interviewed Robert R. Hitt, the shorthand journalist who covered the debates for the
Chicago *Press and Tribune,* wrote that during the second debate, held at Freeport,
Owen Lovejoy became "thoroughly aroused by Douglas' reference to 'the nigger'—
Douglas said 'nigger' not 'negro' as the *Times* reported him on that occasion."[15]
Throughout the debate, "Douglas said 'nigger,'" though his "organ printed it 'negro.'"[16]
At Hillsboro, Douglas gave a speech in which "he uttered scarcely a sentence which
had not the word 'nigger' in it," according to the Chicago *Press and Tribune.*[17] In the
later Alton debate, a reporter had difficulty hearing the Little Giant, but could make
out some "emphatic words" like "nigger equality" and the Declaration of Independence was not made for "niggers."[18]

Douglas made several false allegations in addition to the charge that Lincoln favored social and political equality for blacks. He accused Lincoln and Trumbull of
having conspired in 1854 to break up the Whig and Democratic parties, with the former to succeed Shields in the senate the following year and the latter to take Douglas's seat in 1859. The Little Giant followed this falsehood with another, which would

significantly undermine his credibility: he charged that Lincoln had helped write an antislavery platform allegedly drawn up at Springfield in October 1854. Douglas read portions of what he wrongly identified as that document, calling for the repeal of the Fugitive Slave Act, the abolition of slavery in the District of Columbia, the elimination of the interstate slave trade, and a ban on the acquisition of more slave territory, among other things. He then posed seven interrogatories, asking if Lincoln agreed with that platform. He added that he would trot Lincoln down to Egypt and "bring him to his milk"—that is, confront him with the strong antislavery statements he made in northern Illinois.

Transcribing Douglas's remarks later, Robert R. Hitt discovered that the Little Giant was quoting a radical platform adopted in 1854 at Aurora, not the more moderate one endorsed at Springfield. Douglas later claimed that he had relied on an 1856 speech by Congressman Thomas L. Harris, who cited a resolution adopted by what he termed the "first State convention of the Black Republican party in Illinois."[19] (The day before the Ottawa debate, this resolution appeared in the *Illinois State Register,* which mistakenly stated that it had been written by a committee on which Lincoln had served.) In mid-August, Douglas had asked Harris where and when that convention was held. According to the Little Giant, the editor of the *Illinois State Register,* Charles H. Lanphier, who replied for the indisposed Harris, misinformed him, saying that it had occurred in Springfield in October 1854 and providing a clipping from the *Illinois State Register* containing the Aurora platform, misidentified as the Springfield platform. Republicans in 1854 had pointed out the *Register*'s gaffe. Leading Republican newspapers, like the Chicago *Journal* and *Democrat,* had opposed those Aurora resolutions.

When the Chicago *Press and Tribune* revealed Douglas's error, he recounted this tale and asked rhetorically at Galena on August 25, "Had I not abundant reason for supposing they *were* the Republican State platform of 1854?"[20] This was a lame excuse, for Douglas had made the same mistake in 1856 in a speech on the senate floor, where Trumbull set him straight. In October, Douglas repeated his explanation and scornfully declared, "it will not do for him [Lincoln] to charge forgery on Charles H. Lanphier or Thomas L. Harris. No man on earth who knows these men or Lincoln could believe Lincoln on oath against either of them. . . . Any man who attempts to make such charges as Mr. Lincoln has indulged in against them, only proclaims himself a slanderer."[21] The Chicago *Press and Tribune* scoffed at Douglas's "evasion of responsibility of his own act," which it called "mean and pitiful to the last degree, second only to the pusillanimity of trying to fasten it upon an absent friend."[22] Clearly, Douglas had not made an honest mistake, his protestations to the contrary notwithstanding.

Lanphier, who did not seem to resent Douglas's attempt to blame him for the error, insouciantly argued that it mattered little whether the Republicans at Aurora adopted a platform different from the Springfield platform, for they were all Republicans. This assertion was disingenuous, for the moderate platforms adopted by the Republican state conventions at Bloomington in 1856 and Springfield in 1858 were far more representative of the state party's views than the more radical ones adopted in 1854 by county conventions in northern Illinois.

Angry Republicans condemned Douglas's forgery as the "shameful" and "outrageous" act of a "little coward."[23] The *Illinois State Journal* pointed out that in 1854 some local *Democratic* conventions in northern Illinois had adopted resolutions endorsing the principle of "no more slave states" and calling for the abolition of the domestic slave trade and of slavery in the District of Columbia. It deemed the Little Giant's misrepresentation of the Springfield platform "an act that, in the ordinary business transactions of life, would consign its authors and abettors to . . . the society of thieves and blacklegs" and remarked that Douglas now wore "the brand of the forger upon his forehead."[24] The Chicago *Press and Tribune* indignantly observed that "Mr. Douglas knew that he basely, maliciously and willfully LIED. He not only lied circumstantially and wickedly; but he spent the first part of his speech in elaborating the lie with which he set out, and the entire latter part, in giving the lie application and effect. . . . Men of Illinois, here is your Senator! . . . Here is the man who is traversing the State from end to end in pursuit of votes, bellowing as he goes—'You lie! you lie!'"[25] The Chicago *Journal* expressed disbelief "that such wanton falsehoods will obtain for their author consideration from honorable men."[26]

Because the debates drew national attention, newspapers from other states joined the chorus of criticism. The Louisville *Journal* declared: "*Douglas has done a deed of shame*"; the "minuteness of detail" in his charge "utterly precluded *any idea that he was simply and innocently mistaken.*"[27] Chester P. Dewey of the New York *Evening Post* reported that "Douglas waded very deeply into the mire of mendacity" and concluded that his error "takes the very heart and core out of Douglas's Ottawa speech. It strips it to the very bone, and leaves only a hollow and baseless frame behind. . . . The very audacity of this charge gave Douglas this seeming advantage; that it put Lincoln on the explanatory and defensive, in regard to a series of resolutions which, whether passed at a 'one-horse meeting in Kane county' or at Springfield, he could know nothing about it, as he had no hand in making them; and it is asking too much, to require a politician to have at his tongue's end all the resolutions of four-year-old conventions."[28]

Douglas untruthfully implied that Lincoln was a drinker. In praising his challenger, the senator remarked: "I have known him for nearly twenty-five years. We had many points of sympathy when I first got acquainted with him. We were both comparatively boys—both struggling with poverty in a strange land for our support. I was an humble school teacher in the town of Winchester, and he a flourishing grocery [i.e., saloon] keeper in the town of Salem. [Laughter.] . . . He could beat any of the boys wrestling—could outrun them at a foot race—beat them at pitching quoits or tossing a copper, and could win more liquor than all the boys put together." (The *Times'* account said "ruin more liquor.")

Yet another misleading charge concerned Lincoln's record in Congress, where, Douglas said, the challenger "distinguished himself by his opposition to the Mexican war, taking the side of the common enemy, in time of war, against his own country. [Cheers and groans. That's true.]"

Lincoln fully expected the Little Giant's mendacity. He had told a friend the previous month, "Douglas will tell a lie to ten thousand people one day, even though he knows he may have to deny it to five thousand the next."[29] In October he stated flatly, "Douglas is a liar."[30] Two years later, when asked about the Little Giant's truthfulness, he replied: "Douglas don't tell as many lies as some men I have known. But I think he *keers* as little for the truth *for truth's sake,* as any man I ever saw."[31]

When Lincoln's turn to speak came, he responded to what he called "very gross and palpable" misrepresentations, which he treated as more amusing than provoking. As he spoke, he swept his arms so vigorously that he resembled a windmill. He thanked Douglas for calling him "a kind, amiable, and intelligent gentleman," a compliment that truly gratified him. "I was a little 'taken,' for it came from a great man. I was not very much accustomed to flattery, and it came the sweeter to me. I was rather like the Hoosier, with the gingerbread, when he said he reckoned he loved it better than any other man, and got less of it. [Roars of laughter.]" With more good humor Lincoln denied the charge that he and Trumbull had conspired to seize the senate seats and to destroy the Whig and Democratic parties. Because he did not recognize Douglas's mistake in attributing to the Springfield Republicans of 1854 the radicalism of the Aurora Republicans, he failed to call attention to it. Instead, he found himself on the defensive, protesting that he had not helped frame the "Springfield" platform.

As for his alleged saloon-keeping, Lincoln said Douglas "is awfully at fault about his early friend Lincoln being a 'grocery-keeper.' [Laughter.] I don't know as it would be a great sin if I had been, but he is mistaken. Lincoln never kept a grocery anywhere in the world. [Laughter.] It is true that Lincoln did work the latter part of one winter in a small still house, up at the head of a hollow. [Roars of laughter.]" He also asserted that Douglas was "grossly and altogether mistaken" in conveying "the idea that I withheld supplies from the soldiers who were fighting in the Mexican war, or did anything else to hinder the soldiers."

Shrewdly, Lincoln did not react to the charge that he "could win [or ruin] more liquor than all the boys put together." If he had done so, Douglas would have harped on the issue repeatedly, diverting the debate from the central issue of slavery expansion.

In defending his conspiracy charge against Douglas, Lincoln pointed out that five months earlier the Little Giant had arraigned the Buchanan administration for plotting with pro-Lecompton forces in Congress, as well as with the Washington *Union* and the authors of the Lecompton Constitution to make slavery national. If Lincoln had a "corrupt heart" for daring to state that Douglas had conspired to promote that same end, did not the Little Giant have an equally "corrupt heart" for daring to say that Buchanan et al. had done the same thing?

Lincoln rejected the charge of abolitionism and racial egalitarianism, quoting from his 1854 Peoria address to illustrate the point. "This is the whole of it," he said, "and anything that argues me into his idea of perfect social and political equality with the negro, is but a specious and fantastic arrangement of words, by which a man can prove a horse chestnut to be a chestnut horse. [Applause, laughter.]" He then elaborated: "I have no purpose directly or indirectly to interfere with the institution of slavery in the States where it exists. I believe I have no lawful right to do so, and I have no inclination to do so. I have no purpose to introduce political and social equality between the white and black races. There is a physical difference between the two, which in my judgment will probably forever forbid their living together upon the footing of perfect equality, and inasmuch as it becomes a necessity that there must be a difference, I, as well as Judge Douglas, am in favor of the race to which I belong, having the superior position. I have never said anything to the contrary, but I hold that notwithstanding all this, there is no reason in the world why the negro is not entitled to all the natural rights enumerated in the Declaration of Independence, the right to life, liberty, and the pursuit of happiness. [Applause, loud cheers.] I hold that he is as much entitled to these as the white man. I agree with Judge Douglas that he is not my equal in many respects—certainly not in color, perhaps not in moral or intellectual endowment. But in the right to eat the bread, without the leave of anybody else, which his own hand earns, *he is my equal and the equal of Judge Douglas and the equal of every living man.* ["Bully for you," "all right," great applause.]"

Eloquently, Lincoln gave his reasons for fearing that Douglas was paving the way for a second Dred Scott decision making it illegal for any state to exclude slavery. "In this and like communities," Lincoln argued, "public sentiment is everything. With public sentiment, nothing can fail; without it nothing can succeed. Consequently he who moulds public sentiment, goes deeper than he who enacts statutes or pronounces decisions. He makes statutes and decisions possible or impossible to be executed." As an influential party leader, Douglas had the power to shape public opinion significantly, and he was doing so by stating repeatedly that Supreme Court decisions must be obeyed without cavil, even though he himself had undermined the independence of the Illinois Supreme Court in 1841 when he helped engineer the legislative coup by which the court was packed in order to get it to reverse its decision in the Alexander P. Field controversy.[32] (Douglas had then been named a justice of the court.) So the Little Giant, a man traditionally contemptuous of the sacredness of court decisions, was helping persuade the public to abide docilely by any ruling handed down by the U.S. Supreme Court, presumably even if that body decided that no state could outlaw slavery.

Lincoln invoked the authority of Henry Clay, "my beau ideal of a statesman, the man for whom I fought all my humble life." That Kentuckian "once said of a class of men who would repress all tendencies to liberty and ultimate emancipation, that they must, if they would do this, go back to the era of our Independence, and muzzle the cannon which thunders its annual joyous return; they must blow out the moral lights around us; they must penetrate the human soul, and eradicate there the love of liberty; and then and not till then could they perpetuate slavery in this country! [Loud cheers.]" Douglas, Lincoln charged, was blowing out those candles, muzzling those cannons, and eradicating that love of liberty by proclaiming his indifference to the morality of slavery, by asserting that the black man "has nothing in the Declaration of Independence," and by stating he "cares not whether slavery is voted down or voted up." Once he persuaded the public to adopt his amoral attitude, "then it needs only the formality of the second Dred Scott decision which he endorses in advance, to make Slavery alike lawful in all the States—old as well as new, North as well as South."[33]

Enraged, Douglas sprang up to deliver his half-hour rejoinder. When he alleged that his challenger had met with the Republicans in Springfield in 1854 as they drafted their platform, Lincoln interrupted angrily to deny it. Republican committeemen silenced him, saying: "What are you making such a fuss for? Douglas didn't interrupt you, and can't you see that the people don't like it?" Douglas went on at length, asking Lincoln if he agreed with the Springfield (actually Aurora) platform of 1854 and denouncing his "miserable quibbles." He insisted that Lincoln was responsible for that platform, for he "was the leader of that party, and on the very day that he made his speech there in reply to me, preaching up the same doctrine of the Declaration of Independence that niggers were equal to white men—that very day this Republican Convention met there. ["Three cheers for Douglas."]" Passionately, the Little Giant rejected the conspiracy charge, calling it "an infamous lie." (Lincoln's face registered indignation at this point.) The senator further protested that "Mr. Lincoln has not character enough for integrity and truth, merely on his own *ipse dixit* to arraign President Buchanan and President Pierce, and the Judges of the Supreme Court, any one of whom would not be complimented if put on a level with Mr. Lincoln. ["Hit him again," three cheers, &c.]"[34]

At the close of the debate, half a dozen well-meaning supporters lifted Lincoln and carried him from the site. The Republican marshal had unwisely selected mostly short men for the job. The lanky challenger's head towered above his honor guard, but his feet dragged. Lincoln protested in vain, saying "Don't boys! Let me down!" but they did not do so until they reached Mayor Glover's house.[35] Recovering himself, he seemed pleased and, turning to one of the gang that had transported him, "said good naturedly 'never mind, never mind! I've get even with you, you rascal!'"[36]

The following day Lincoln described the Ottawa debate to a friend: "the fur flew some, and I am glad to know I am yet alive. There was a vast concourse of people—more than could [get] near enough to hear."[37]

Press reaction to the debate followed party lines. Democratic newspapers praised Douglas for exposing Lincoln's "nigger-loving propensities" and for showing that he himself was no "nigger worshipper."[38] The Milwaukee *News* declared that the Little Giant had put his opponent "on the defensive and kept him there."[39] The Chicago *Times* reported that Douglas's "excoriation of Lincoln was so severe, that the Republicans hung their heads in shame," while the Democrats "were loud in their vociferations."[40]

Douglas was delighted with the outcome, believing with some justice that he had Lincoln on the defensive, for the challenger had ducked the seven interrogatories and even if he were to answer them in the next debate, it would not undo the damage. An impartial judge would probably have awarded this first round to Douglas, whose aggressive style seemed to give him the whip hand.

An astute Douglas supporter thought Lincoln seemed to repudiate his "House Divided" and Chicago speeches and speculated on the reason why: "Lincoln has killed himself by his ultra Abolition-equality doctrine. His declaration that the negro is the equal of the white man, and that our laws should be uniform throughout the United States, has aroused the people," who "now see that such monstrous doctrines are repugnant to the genius and spirit of our institutions." So at Ottawa Lincoln was "endeavoring to shape a new course, by denying that the negro is the equal of the white man."[41] Though oversimplified, that conclusion is not far from the truth; Lincoln's comments in Ottawa about black equality sounded far different from his comments in his Chicago speech, in which he called for an end to "all this quibbling about this man and the other man, this race and that race and the other race being inferior." It is noteworthy that this disavowal of any intention to promote racial equality was delivered in northern Illinois, where abolitionist sentiment was far stronger than it was in the more Negrophobic central and southern parts of the state.

Not all Democrats were pleased, however. An enthusiastic Douglas supporter recalled that the Little Giant "had not made quite so convincing a speech as was expected" and that the challenger had bested him. "When Lincoln got up and said in his slow, frank style that when a fellow heard himself misrepresented a little, he felt ugly, but when he was misrepresented a good deal, it seemed funny, it was plain to see he had caught the crowd considerably better than did Douglass in his opening." Although Lincoln's "gestures were awfully awkward," they appeared "weighty." There was an obvious sincerity "that carried you with him. You could not help it, for he made you feel that he was so honest. When he got through, it was pretty clear that, in the mind of the crowd, he was ahead."[42] The Democratic *Post* in Providence Rhode Island, conceded that Douglas's speech "contains a little more of gall and wormwood . . . than we can heartily endorse."[43]

Illinois Republicans rejoiced over Lincoln's performance. Those at the debate concluded that "Douglas is 'a dead cock in the pit,'" and Republican leaders unable to attend expressed delight at the challenger's triumph.[44] L. D. Whiting in Bureau County told Lincoln that "in common with every Republican I have heard express himself, [I] think you in most respects proved yourself his [Douglas's] superior."[45] According to the Ottawa *Republican*, "[c]andid, intelligent men of all parties are free to say that Lincoln won the field—Douglas lost friends and lost votes by the exhibition he made of himself."[46] Herndon judged that "Lincoln whipped Douglas badly—very badly" and opined that "Douglas' forgery hurts him. . . . This fraud—this base forgery would kill '*Hell.*'"[47]

Republicans outside Illinois cheered the news. Schuyler Colfax of Indiana congratulated Lincoln for having "so signally triumphed."[48] From Ohio, Samuel Galloway wrote to John Locke Scripps, editor of the Chicago *Press and Tribune*, asking "who is this new man; he has completely worsted the little giant. You have a David greater than the Democratic Goliath or any other I ever saw."[49] The correspondent of the New York *Evening Post* informed his readers that Lincoln "is altogether a more fluent speaker than Douglas, and in all the arts of debate fully his equal. The Republicans of Illinois have chosen a champion worthy of their heartiest support, and fully equipped for the conflict with the great 'squatter Sovereign.'"[50] The New York *Tribune* said: "Of the two, Lincoln and Douglas, all partiality being left out of the question, we think Mr. Lincoln has decidedly the advantage. Not only are his doctrines truer and better than those of his antagonist, but he states them with more propriety, and with an infinitely better temper."[51]

Abolitionists, however, were disappointed. Theodore Parker objected to Lincoln's evasiveness, for he "did not meet the issue. He made a *technical evasion*; 'he had nothing to do with the Resolutions [adopted at Aurora] in question.' Suppose he had not, admit they were forged; still they were the vital questions, pertinent to the issue, & L[incoln] dodged them. That is not the way to fight the battle of Freedom."[52]

Some Republicans thought Lincoln had been excessively defensive. Herndon explained that his partner "is too much of a Kentucky gentleman to debate with Douglas; i e, he will not condescend to lie: he will not bend to expediency: he will not hug shams, and so he labors under a disadvantage."[53] Charles H. Ray implored Elihu B. Washburne, "When you see Abe at Freeport, for God's sake tell him to 'Charge Chester! Charge!' Do not let him keep on the defensive. Let him be fortified with his proofs and commence thus: 'I charge so and so, and prove it thus.' 'I charge so-and-so, and prove it thus!' and so on until the end of his hour, charging in every paragraph. Let him close the hour with a charge, and in his half hour following, let him pay no attention to Douglas' charges, but lump all his own together and fling them at his head, and end up by shrieking a loud note for Freedom! We must not be parrying all the while. We want the deadliest thrusts. Let us see blood flow every time he closes a sentence."[54]

Lincoln received similar advice from many quarters, including a Republican in Jacksonville who insisted that "Mercy to Douglas is treachery to the cause of Right and Humanity."[55] Henry C. Whitney told Lincoln that his friends "think that you ought not to treat him [Douglas] tenderly:—he is going to try to intimidate you:—you have got to treat him severely. . . . I don't of course mean that you ought to call him a *liar* or anything of that sort but that you ought to let him know that you are 'terribly in earnest.'"[56]

One reporter believed Lincoln had made it clear that he was in earnest. Chester P. Dewey of the New York *Evening Post*, in describing the Ottawa debate, said the Republican champion might be ugly in repose, but "stir him up, and the fire of his genius plays on every feature. His eye glows and sparkles, every lineament, now so ill formed, grows brilliant and expressive, and you have before you a man of rare power and of strong magnetic influence. He takes the people every time, and there is no getting away from his sturdy good sense, his unaffected sincerity, and the unceasing play of his good humor, which accompanies his close logic and smoothes the way to conviction."[57]

Dewey's Republican sympathies may have colored his assessment, but German-born Henry Villard, a pro-Douglas reporter and stump speaker, rendered a similar judgment. Villard recalled that the Little Giant was more polished, for he "commanded a strong, sonorous voice, a rapid, vigorous utterance, a telling play of countenance, impressive gestures, and all the other arts of the practised speaker." Lincoln, on the other hand, made a poor first impression, with his "lean, lank, indescribably gawky figure" and his "odd-featured, wrinkled, inexpressive, and altogether uncomely face." He "used singularly awkward, almost absurd, up-and-down and sidewise movements of his body to give emphasis to his arguments." Yet, Villard recollected, "the unprejudiced mind felt at once that, while there was on the one side a skilful dialectician and debater arguing a wrong and weak cause, there was on the other a thoroughly earnest and truthful man, inspired by sound convictions in consonance with the true spirit of American institutions. There was nothing in all Douglas's powerful effort that appealed to the higher instincts of human nature, while Lincoln always touched sympathetic chords. Lincoln's speech excited and sustained the enthusiasm of the audience to the end."[58]

Gustave Koerner similarly recalled that the "impetuous, denunciatory" Douglas "frequently lost his temper" but nevertheless "magnetized the big crowd by his audacity and supreme self-confidence. Lincoln impressed his audiences by his almost too extreme fairness, his always pure and elevated language, and his appeals to their higher nature. Douglas, on the contrary, roused the existing strong prejudices against the negro race to the highest pitch, and not unfrequently resorted to demagogism unworthy of his own great reputation as a statesman."[59]

Deliberate Garbling of Lincoln's Speeches

Casting even more doubt on Douglas's claim to statesmanship was the conduct of his organ, the Chicago *Times*, which ran a hopelessly garbled and ridiculous version of Lincoln's remarks at Ottawa. Hundreds of discrepancies exist between its version of the challenger's words and the version published in the *Press and Tribune*. The *Times's* account is briefer; occasionally, it amounts to gibberish. The *Press and Tribune* declared that a "more cowardly and knavish trick was never undertaken by a desperate politician," a trick which "betokens a meanness so despicable, a malignity so purely fiendish, and a nature so lost to honor that we know not where to look for a parallel."[60] Chester P. Dewey called it "altogether a shameful instance of the dishonorable warfare practiced by the Douglasites."[61]

Throughout the debates the Chicago *Times* and other Democratic papers persistently misreported Lincoln's remarks, eliciting fierce Republican protests. *The Democrat* of Galesburg, site of the fifth debate, complained that the *Times's* account of Lincoln's speech there contained "scarcely a correctly reported paragraph in the whole speech! Many sentences are dropped out which were absolutely necessary for the sense; many are transposed so as to read wrong end first; many are made to read exactly the opposite of the orator's intention." The paper counted over 180 errors in the *Times's* version.[62] The *Press and Tribune* concurred: "Not a paragraph has been fairly reported, from the commencement to the conclusion of his speech. Some of his finest passages are disemboweled, and chattering nonsense substituted in their stead. Wherever Lincoln made a 'hit,' the sentence containing it is blurred, and the point carefully eviscerated." The same paper protested that the *Times's* account of Lincoln's speech at Quincy was so "shockingly mutilated" as to be unrecognizable, while the reporting of the Alton debate made Lincoln sound "like a half-witted booby."[63]

The *Times's* shorthand reporter who deliberately mangled Lincoln's remarks was a disreputable character named Henry Binmore. Many years later Robert R. Hitt gave an interview stating that the "misrepresentation of Lincoln in the *Times* was in accordance with the purpose to make him appear ignorant and uncouth in language beside Douglas. Among the reporters it was well understood that the report of Lincoln for the *Times* was to be done in a slovenly manner, to carry out the Democratic estimate of Lincoln." James B. Sheridan, a shorthand expert for the Philadelphia *Press*, temporarily on assignment to the Chicago *Times*, "was above lending himself to such a dishonorable practice" and took down only Douglas's speeches. Sheridan "frequently talked privately about this treatment of Lincoln, but did not go further than to express his confidential opinion of it."[64] Because Sheridan refused to misrepresent Lincoln's words, the *Times* turned to the more pliant Binmore, of whom the *Press and Tribune* said: "If mutilating public discourses were a criminal offense, the scamp whom Douglas hires to report Lincoln's speeches would be a ripe subject for the Penitentiary."[65] Binmore had already been fired from the St. Louis *Missouri Republican* for lying. Hitt, who in July had teamed up with Binmore to report Lincoln and Douglas's Chicago speeches, expressed great contempt for him, calling him "seedy," "a complete little fop and fool" with "no common sense," a man "hard to get along with" and "always needy." On one occasion, Binmore "asked for the loan of a quarter," explaining that "he had nothing but a hundred-dollar check with him." Hitt confided to his diary, "I have . . . seldom known Binmore to tell the truth about his family." In addition, Hitt complained about Binmore's "fondness for telling stories about his connections, the amounts of money he has made and the familiarity of his acquaintance with every great man ever named in his presence." Hitt complained with some irritation that "[n]o land can be mentioned in his presence but he has been there and is perfectly familiar with the greatest men in the country." Understandably, Hitt had no faith in anything Binmore said.[66]

(Five years later, Binmore's misbehavior and deceit led to his dismissal from the army. While in the service he had introduced an "abandoned woman" as his wife, had refused to pay his laundry bills in Memphis, and had behaved shamefully in Cairo. He was arrested for drunkenness and disorderly conduct. In an appeal for mercy, he explained that he had married at the age of 18 against his parents' wishes, settled in New York, found no work, was evicted by a hard-hearted landlord, sired children, abandoned them and their mother, established a liaison with another woman, then led a vagabond existence, flitting from Utah to Nicaragua, "everywhere where excitement was to be found." After his expulsion from the service, Binmore returned to the Chicago *Times*, where his colleagues held him in contempt.)[67]

Binmore, it seems clear, would deliberately garble Lincoln's words if told to do so, and his colleague Sheridan confirmed that he did. Because Douglas frequently repeated himself, Hitt would cut and paste passages from the Little Giant's earlier speeches rather than take down his words in shorthand. On observing this, Sheridan quipped: "Hitt mucilates Douglas for the *Press and Tribune*, while [Binmore] mutilates Lincoln for the *Times*."[68] The *Times*'s claims for the "the high characters of our reporters of these debates" fit Sheridan but not Binmore.[69] Lincoln doubtless had Binmore in mind when referring to the *Times*'s "villainous reporters."[70]

Just who instructed Binmore to perform that mutilation is unclear. The *Press and Tribune* alleged that Douglas himself, with the assistance of two lawyers and Chicago *Times* editor James W. Sheahan, had dictated "interlineations, [and] mutilations, *destroying the sense and turning awry the grammar of his adversary!*" Binmore had "undoubtedly defaced and garbled" Lincoln's words at the "express orders" of Douglas. No hard evidence corroborates this charge, though the *Press and Tribune* alleged that Binmore had "offered to do for us, for pay, in behalf of Lincoln, what he is now doing for Douglas."[71] The Little Giant's lies about Lincoln's record, his claim that Lincoln had helped write the 1854 "Springfield" Republican platform, and his general unscrupulousness make it seem likely that either directly or indirectly Douglas commanded Binmore to misrepresent Lincoln.

Badly as the *Times* garbled Lincoln's words, a pamphlet version of the fourth debate (at Charleston) mangled them even worse. Published anonymously, it presented Douglas's speech in larger type than his opponent's. Probably issued by the Douglas campaign, it further strengthens the suspicion that the Little Giant was behind the misrepresentation of Lincoln's remarks. "Abraham Lincoln and His Doctrines," a similar pamphlet of badly mutilated excerpts from Lincoln's speeches, appeared without an imprint.

The *Times* denied all charges and alleged in return that "the Republicans have a candidate for the Senate of whose bad rhetoric and horrible jargon they are ashamed," and that "they called a council of 'literary' men to discuss, re-construct and re-write" Lincoln's words before allowing them to be published, for "they dare not allow Lincoln to go into print in his own dress." Those who heard Lincoln's speeches, said the *Times*, "must know that he cannot speak five grammatical sentences in succession."[72] The *Press and Tribune* retorted that everyone "who has ever heard Abraham Lincoln address the people . . . knows that he is forcible, agreeable and correct in his delivery, and that he never did and never can talk the nonsense which the *Times* attributes to him."[73]

Some of Douglas's supporters in Chicago acknowledged that the *Times* presented Lincoln's words inaccurately but ascribed "the mutilation entirely to the incompetency of the reporter." To the Chicago *Press and Tribune*, it seemed that "if this charge of incompetency were true, it is quite as dishonorable for Douglas to keep the man employed for the specific purpose of reporting his opponent, as it would be to compel a competent reporter to mutilate his speeches."[74]

For their part, the *Press and Tribune* editors may have lightly retouched the text of Lincoln's speeches, which an assistant named Larminie had transcribed from Hitt's notes. The primitive conditions under which reporters had to cover the debates necessitated at least some repair to their field notes, which the wind could blow. In addition, the small, crowded, unsteady tables on which their notes were taken could be jarred.

Whatever cosmetic surgery the editors at the *Press and Tribune* may have performed on Lincoln's text, however, they never inflicted nearly the damage to the record achieved by the carelessness, incapacity, and partisan malice of Henry Binmore and the *Times*.

Lincoln could be a difficult speaker to report because of his tendency to qualify his points. His sentences, according to Hitt, "were not finished and harmonious like those of Douglas but broken with endless explanation and qualifications and parentheses, which made it difficult to write or read it. Often he repeated what he had to say two or three times and each time qualified in some new way. His mind seems to be one of excessive caution and no statement that he makes will he suffer to go forth without a qualification that will prevent all misunderstanding, but which at the same time deprived the statement of its vigorous and independent tone."[75] Lincoln would, Hitt remembered, "dwell upon and emphasize several important words, perhaps in the middle of a sentence, and the rest of it would be spoken with great rapidity, and quickly followed by another sentence in the same manner, convincing to his hearers, but annoying and fatiguing to the reporters."[76] Horace White, who italicized the words Lincoln spoke with special emphasis, concurred, noting that Lincoln's "words did not flow in a rushing, unbroken stream like Douglas'. He sometimes stopped for repairs before finishing a sentence, especially at the beginning of a speech. After getting fairly started, and lubricated, as it were, he went on without any noticeable hesitation, but he never had the ease and grace and finish of his adversary."[77] A Democratic observer of the Ottawa debate noted the same pattern. Lincoln's speech there "was made up with such expressions as 'I think it is so,' 'I may be mistaken,' 'I guess it was done,' &c., &c. There were no straightforward assertions."[78]

Reporters also struggled with Lincoln's talking speed. Binmore's only defense for his inaccurate accounts was his inability to keep pace with Lincoln. On July 10, both Hitt and Binmore recorded Lincoln's speech at Chicago. Hitt noted in his journal that "so fast did his words follow each other that it was with the utmost difficulty that I could follow him and I was aware all the time that I was not writing my notes in such a neat and legible style." The following day, as he helped Binmore transcribe his shorthand notes, Hitt discovered that "there was much matter that Binmore had omitted in his report. These passages were just where I remember Lincoln spoke the fastest."[79] In old age, Binmore told an interviewer, "I never became a record-breaker. Two hundred words a minute for a short time was the best I could do."[80]

Lincoln may not have been surprised by the *Times*'s distortions. On August 12, he declared that he "would cheerfully allow any gentleman to report his speeches, but at the same time he would not be responsible for a perverted, distorted or patched up report which might appear in the Douglas prints."[81]

Second Debate: Freeport

Two days after the Ottawa event, Lincoln asked Ebenezer Peck and Norman B. Judd to meet him for consultation. "Douglas is propounding questions to me," he explained, "which perhaps it is not quite safe to wholly disregard. I have my view of the means to dispose of them." But he wanted his friends' advice.[82] The night before the second debate, at Freeport, Judd and Peck met with Lincoln at Macomb, where they arrived at 2 A.M. They awakened the candidate, who received them in a brief night shirt that struck his visitors as comical. When he read to them his proposed replies to Douglas's queries, Judd suggested modifications to suit the strong antislavery sentiment of northern Illinois. "But I couldn[']t stir him," Judd recalled. "He listened very patiently to both Peck and myself, but he wouldn't budge an inch from his well studied formulas."[83]

Earlier that day, Judd and Peck had conferred in Chicago with Joseph Medill, Martin Sweet, Stephen Hurlbut, and Herman Kreismann to discuss Lincoln's tactics. They recommended answers to Douglas's interrogatories and urged him to ask "a few ugly questions" of the Little Giant, including this fateful one: "What becomes of your vaunted popular Sovereignty in [the] Territories since the Dred Scott decision?"[84] Lincoln had already anticipated Douglas's reply to such a query. In late July, when Henry Asbury suggested that he pose that very question, Lincoln replied: "You shall have hard work to get him directly to the point whether a territorial Legislature has or has not the power to exclude slavery. But if you succeed in bringing him to it, though he will be compelled to say it possesses no such power; he will instantly take ground that slavery can not actually exist in the ter[r]itories, unless the people desire it, and so give it protective territorial legislation. If this offends the South he will let it offend them; as at all events he means to hold on to his chances in Illinois."[85]

Medill and his colleagues recommended that Lincoln put two other questions to Douglas: "Will you stand by the adjustment of the Kansas question on the basis of the English bill compromise?" and "Having given your acquiescence and sanction to the Dred Scott decision that destroys popular sovereignty in the Territories will you acquiesce in the other half of that decision when it comes to be applied to the States, by the same court?" Echoing many others, they also counseled Lincoln to be aggressive: "Don[']t act on the *defensive* at all. . . . [H]old Dug up as a traitor & conspirator a proslavery, bamboozling demagogue. . . . Above all things be bold, defiant and dogmatic. . . . Make short work of his nigger equality charges. . . . For once leave modesty aside. You are dealing with a bold, brazen, lying rascal & you must '*fight the devil with fire.*' . . . Be saucy with the 'Catiline' & permit no browbeating—in other words give him h[el]l."[86]

While drawing up the questions he intended to ask Douglas, Lincoln reviewed the Little Giant's speech at Bloomington, where he said (as Lincoln had predicted he would) that despite the Dred Scott decision, "slavery will never exist one day or one hour in any Territory against the unfriendly legislation of an unfriendly people. I care not how the Dred Scott decision may have settled the abstract question so far as the practical result is concerned."[87] So Lincoln knew how the senator would respond and wanted those answers published so that the entire country could read them. They might well undermine Douglas's support not only in the South but also among the pro-Buchanan forces in Illinois.

En route to Freeport, Douglas spoke in Galena, where a Republican journalist reported that he "dilated luxuriously for half an hour upon negro equality, amalgamation, marriages of black and white in Boston, and gave the African a general overhauling." He "grew even blacker in the face than usual as he said he was no kin to, and never meant to be kin to, the negro."[88]

On August 27, a crowd one-third larger than the one at Ottawa converged on Freeport, a Republican stronghold of 7,000 located 100 miles west of Chicago. Hoteliers and saloonkeepers blanched at the hordes demanding food and drink, and the streets were choked with visitors. Arriving by train the morning of the debate, Lincoln was greeted by cannons, bands, and cheering friends. He tried to find some privacy in his hotel, but his admirers demanded that he shake their hands. After lunch, he boarded a plain Conestoga wagon that conveyed him and a dozen salt-of-the-earth farmers to a nearby grove, where the speakers' platform had been erected. Lincoln sat on the rear of the wagon's box, his long legs sticking out, like "the skeleton of some greyhound."[89]

Lincoln's modest arrangements contrasted sharply with Douglas's regal entrance the previous night. The next morning, fearful that his customary triumphalism might offend the egalitarian sensibilities of Freeporters, the Little Giant abandoned plans to ride in a grand carriage drawn by white horses and instead walked to the debate site.

As Lincoln was about to open the debate on that cool, windy, cloudy afternoon, he was interrupted by William "Deacon" Bross of the Chicago *Press and Tribune,* who said: "Hold on, Lincoln. You can't speak yet. Hitt ain't here, and there is no use of your speaking unless the *Press and Tribune* has a report."[90] After delaying until the shorthand reporter was found, Lincoln rose and handed his shawl to E. W. Brewster with the remark, "There, Father Brewster, hold my clothes while I stone Stephen."[91] During Lincoln's opening speech, Douglas sat nearby puffing on a cigar, to the consternation of his immediate neighbors.

Lincoln began by answering the seven interrogatories Douglas had posed at Ottawa. He did not, he said, "stand pledged" to the unconditional repeal of the Fugitive Slave Act, nor to the admission of more Slave States into the Union, nor to admitting new states into the Union with a constitution approved by the people, nor to the abolition of slavery in the District of Columbia, nor to the abolition of the domestic slave trade. He did believe that Congress had a right and duty to prohibit slavery in all the territories, and he would oppose the admission of a new territory if it would "aggravate the slavery question among ourselves."

These remarks evidently did not sit well with some antislavery auditors, who, according to Henry Villard's report, "thought that by his seven answers Lincoln had repudiated the whole Republican creed." They "began to be restive, to grumble and otherwise express their displeasure in undertones." Villard observed that "these seven answers may still give Mr. Lincoln much trouble and we should not be surprised if the Republicans in Northern Illinois might label them 'Lincoln's seven deadly sins.'"[92]

After succinctly responding to Douglas, Lincoln elaborated on his answers. The Fugitive Slave Act, he said, "should have been framed so as to be free from some of the objections that pertain to it, without lessening its efficiency," but since that statute was not now a matter of controversy, he did not favor making it one. He "would be exceedingly sorry" to have to vote on the admission of a new Slave State, but he thought it highly unlikely that such an application from a territory would be made in the future if Congress prohibited slavery from entering the territory in the first place. He "would be exceedingly glad to see Congress abolish slavery in the District of Columbia, and, in the language of Henry Clay, 'sweep from our Capital that foul blot upon our nation.' [Loud applause.]" But he would favor such a step only if it were carried out in accordance with the provisions he had incorporated into his 1849 emancipation bill (gradualism, compensation for owners, and approval by a majority of the voters of the District). If Congress were to abolish the domestic slave trade, it should be done in accordance with those same provisions.

Having answered Douglas's questions, Lincoln read slowly and distinctly four questions to the Little Giant:

1. Would he favor the admission of Kansas if it had not the population called for in the English Bill compromise (i.e., 93,000)?
2. In light of the Dred Scott decision, could the inhabitants of a territory lawfully "exclude slavery from its limits prior to the formation of a State Constitution" if a citizen wished to bring slaves into that territory?
3. Would he support a second Dred Scott decision forbidding states to exclude slavery?
4. Would he support the acquisition of new territory "in disregard of how such acquisition may affect the nation on the slavery question?"

By far the most important question was the second, which placed Douglas in an awkward position. The senator would alienate Illinois voters if he stated that the Supreme Court's ruling forbade settlers from excluding slavery in the territories; yet, to maintain that the court's decision did not do so would antagonize the South. Lincoln told a friend, "If he sticks to the Dred Scott decision, he may lose the Senatorship; if he tries to get around it, he certainly loses the Presidency."[93] The question was not original with Lincoln. In July, a Quincy attorney had suggested it, and Republican newspapers had included it among several queries for the Little Giant. Two years earlier, Trumbull and other members of Congress had posed the same query to Douglas, who replied that it was up to the courts.

Lincoln scolded Douglas for confusing the radical Aurora Republican platform of 1854 with the more moderate one of the Springfield Republicans. Caustically he observed that the discovery of the Little Giant's error did not relieve Lincoln of anything, for he had participated in neither convention. "I am just as much responsible for the resolutions at [Aurora in] Kane county as those at Springfield, the amount of the responsibility being exactly nothing in either case; no more than there would be in regard to a set of resolutions passed in the moon. [Laughter and loud cheers.]" Douglas had not qualified his allegations but "stated them roundly as *being true.*" How could such an eminent man make such a mistake? When "we consider who Judge Douglas is—that he is a distinguished Senator of the United States—that he has served nearly twelve years as such—that his character is not at all limited as an ordinary Senator for the United States, but that his name has become of world-wide renown—it is *most extraordinary* that he should so far forget all the suggestions of justice to an adversary, or of prudence to himself, as to venture upon the assertion of that which the slightest investigation would have shown him to be wholly false. [Applause, cheers.]" Witheringly Lincoln speculated about the cause of such a blunder, emphasizing Douglas's amorality: "I can only account of his having done so upon the supposition that that evil genius which has attended him through his life, giving to him an apparent astonishing prosperity, such as to lead very many good men to doubt there being any advantage in virtue over vice—I say I can only account for it on the supposition that the evil genius has at last made up its mind to forsake him. [Continued cheers and laughter.]" How hypocritical of Douglas to make such a mistake when "he is in the habit, in almost all the speeches he makes, of charging falsehood upon his adversaries." In fact, he preferred to "stand upon his dignity and call people liars" rather than answer questions.

Lincoln betrayed annoyance at Douglas's condescending remarks about "an insignificant individual like Lincoln" daring to charge conspiracy against such eminent men as presidents, congressional leaders, and Supreme Court justices. Again Lincoln asked if it were not the case that Douglas had himself leveled a charge of conspiracy against Buchanan et al.[94]

As Douglas rose to reply, a melon hurled from the predominantly Republican crowd glanced off his shoulder. Unfazed, he answered Lincoln's interrogatories, which the challenger had written out and left on the podium. Douglas picked up the paper on which they appeared, read the questions aloud, and replied. In response to the first one, he asserted that he would support the admission of Kansas with a small population even if its voters rejected the Lecompton Constitution. (This angered the Buchanan administration, which regarded it as a betrayal of an earlier agreement. Promptly, more pro-Douglas officeholders in Illinois were fired.) After reciting the crucial second question, the Little Giant "threw down the slip of paper as if he was disposing of a most trifling matter" and offered what became known as the Freeport Doctrine, a proposition that he had made earlier (most notably in his June 1857 speech at Springfield and his addresses at Bloomington and Springfield in July 1858) but which now became much better known. The Dred Scott decision may have officially forbidden the people of a territory to exclude slavery, he said, but informally they could do so by refusing to pass "local police regulations" guaranteeing the rights of slaveholders. Slavery "cannot exist a day or an hour anywhere unless supported by local police regulations," which "can only be furnished by the local legislature. If the people of the Territory are opposed to slavery they will elect members to the legislature who will adopt unfriendly legislation to it."[95]

Douglas also argued that the judgment of the court regarding the power of Congress to prohibit slavery in the territories was *obiter dictum*—lacking the force of law. Presumably he held a similar view of the passage in Taney's majority decision, which stated that "if Congress itself cannot do this [i.e., prohibit slavery in the territories]—if it is beyond the powers conferred on the Federal Government—it will be admitted, we presume, that it could not authorize a territorial government to exercise them. It could confer no power on any local government, established by its authority, to violate the provisions of the Constitution."[96]

Douglas's answer, Lincoln knew, would sit well with Illinoisans but would startle and infuriate Southerners, who had been led to believe that the Little Giant's seemingly neutral popular sovereignty doctrine really favored the interests of slaveholders. The correspondent of the New York *Evening Post* accurately predicted that when Douglas's Freeport remarks "shall go forth to all the land, and be read by men of Georgia and South Carolina, their eyes will doubtless open."[97]

Indeed, as soon as they heard of it, Southern newspapers denounced the Freeport Doctrine, calling it "radically unsound," a "snare and a swindle, full of mean cunning, rank injustice, and insolence . . . more dangerous and fatal to the interests of the South than any ever advocated by the rankest abolitionist." It added "insult to injury, for it mocks and derides the just claim of the slaveholder" and constituted the "scurviest possible form of all possible heresies. . . . [William Lloyd] Garrison, with all his fanatical and demoniacal hatred of slavery, has never in his whole life uttered an opinion at once so insulting and injurious to the South." The Little Giant had earned "the contempt and abhorrence of honest men in all sections."[98] The Cincinnati *Gazette* asked Southerners "to consider this fresh and faithless conduct of a man who reported the Kansas Nebraska Bill for the purpose of cheating the North into his support, and thought he had purchased the vote of the South."[99] Douglas's presidential chances were doomed, the *Missouri Democrat* prophetically declared: "If his opposition to the Lecompton Constitution could be forgiven, his Freeport speech, equivocal as it is, would put him out of the ring."[100] The New York *Herald* exclaimed: "To this 'lame and impotent conclusion' has Judge Douglas' championship of the rights of the South come at last!" Could this possibly be "the feast to which the author of the Kansas-Nebraska bill invited the South?"[101] The Washington *Union* remarked that Douglas "boldly and unblushingly, repudiate[s] the Dred Scott decision."[102]

The Freeport Doctrine prompted the Democratic press to insist on a federal slave code for the territories. That cry was taken up by Southern senators, including James M. Mason of Virginia, a supporter of the Kansas-Nebraska Act, who angrily told Douglas: "You promised us bread, and you have given us a stone; you promised us a fish, and you have given us a serpent; we thought you had given us a substantial right; and you have given us the most evanescent shadow and delusion."[103] Senator Jefferson Davis of Mississippi called the Freeport Doctrine "worse than even the Wilmot Proviso."[104] Mississippi's other senator, Albert Gallatin Brown, also denounced it: "I would rather see the Democratic party sunk, never to be resurrected, than to see it successful only that one portion of it might practice a fraud on another."[105] Senators Clement C. Clay of Alabama and William M. Gwin of California echoed Brown.

Republicans pounced on the Freeport Doctrine. "Douglas' answer to Mr. Lincoln's question amounts to nothing more nor less than *Mob Law* to keep slavery out of the Territories, and the Dred Scottites cannot help seeing it," said the Chicago *Press and Tribune*. "What sort of 'police regulations' enable old [Milton] McGee, of Ruffian notoriety, to hold slaves in Kansas? According to Douglas, he holds them simply because his neighbors don't club him and his niggers out of the Territory!"[106] The *Missouri Democrat* called the Freeport Doctrine "the most odious embodiment of higher law," contemplating "an appeal from the Supreme Court, to 'tumultuous town meetings'—to use Douglas' own language," and "an ascription of sovereignty and supremacy to mobocracy."[107]

Although Lincoln was not the first to expose this weakness in Douglas's popular sovereignty doctrine, at Freeport he brought it fully into public consciousness. The debate with Lincoln "is drawing the attention of the whole country to that matter," observed the Washington *States*.[108] The Little Giant had not invented the notion that slavery could not exist in territories where settlers did not want it—Senators Alexander H. Stephens of Georgia, Lewis Cass of Michigan, Jefferson Davis of Mississippi,

and Jacob Collamer of Vermont, as well as Congressmen William A. Montgomery of
Pennsylvania, James L. Orr of South Carolina, and Samuel O. Peyton of Kentucky
had all expressed similar sentiments. But Douglas's clear statement of it at Freeport
both ruined his reputation in the South and widened the breach within the Illinois
Democracy.

In his rejoinder, Douglas continued to patronize Lincoln, sneering at his "miserable impositions," broadly implying that he was a "demagogue," contemptuously likening him to "a school boy" for feigning ignorance of the senator's stand on slavery in
the territories, and suggesting that Lincoln was a hypocrite who would fear to espouse opinions in southern Illinois that he voiced at Freeport. He ridiculed Lincoln's
intellect, saying of his four interrogatories: "He racked his brain so much in devising
these few questions that he exhausted himself, and has not strength enough to invent
another. [Laughter.]" Inaccurately, he stated that Lincoln had "been driven into obscurity" because of his "political sins" (i.e., his denunciation of the way President Polk
had led the United States into war with Mexico). Condescendingly, he said: "I don't
think there is much danger" of Lincoln's being elected. Douglas claimed that his
challenger had tried to deceive voters in 1854 by pretending to be a Whig while he was
secretly an abolitionist Republican. Appealing to the deep-seated racial prejudice of
white Illinoisans, the Little Giant predicted that as soon as Lincoln "can hold a council of his advisers, by getting [Congressman Owen] Lovejoy, and [Congressman John
F.] Farnsworth [Cheers], and [Congressman Joshua R.] Giddings, and Fred. Douglass together, he will then frame and propound the other interrogator[ies] ["Good,
good," &c. Renewed laughter, in which Mr. Lincoln feebly joined, saying that he
hoped with their aid to get seven questions, the number asked him by Judge Douglas,
and so make *conclusions* again.] I have no doubt you think they are all good men—good
Black Republicans. ["White, white."] I have reason to recollect that some people in
this country think that Fred. Douglass is a very good man. The last time I came here
to make a speech, while I was talking . . . I saw a carriage, and a magnificent one too,
drive up and take its position on the outside of the crowd, with a beautiful young lady
on the front seat, with a man and Fred. Douglass, the negro, on the back seat, and the
owner of the carriage in front driving the negro. [Laughter, cheers, cries of "Right,
what have you to say against it," &c.] I witnessed that here in your town." When a
member of the audience cried out, "What of it?" Douglas exclaimed: "What of it! All
I have to say is this, if you Black Republicans think that the negro ought to be on a
social equality with your wives and daughters, and ride in the carriage with the wife
while the master of the carriage drives the team, you have a perfect right to so do.
[Laughter; "Good, good," and cheers, mingled with shouting and cries of "White,
white."] I am told also that one of Fred. Douglass' kinsmen [evidently an allusion to
H. Ford Douglas, who was not related to Frederick Douglass], another rich black
negro, is now traveling this part of the State making speeches for his friend Mr. Lincoln, who is the champion of the black man's party. [Laughter; "White men, white
men," "what have you got to say against it." "That's right," &c.] All I have got to say
on that subject is this, that those of you who believe that the nigger is your equal, and
ought to be on an equality with you socially, politically and legally, have a right to

entertain those opinions, and of course will vote for Mr. Lincoln. ["Down with the negro," "no, no," &c.]"

Such crude race-baiting further diminished Douglas's claim to statesmanship. When he referred to "you Black Republicans," and audience members shouted "white, white," he contemptuously observed: "there was not a Democrat here vulgar enough to interrupt Mr. Lincoln when he was talking [Great applause and cries of "hurrah for Douglas"]. I know the shoe is pinching you when I am clinching Lincoln, and you are scared to death for the result. [Cheers.]" (A youngster in the crowd cried out in response, "Lincoln didn't use any such talk.")[109] Melodramatically, the Little Giant declared, "I have seen your mobs before and I defy your wrath. [These remarks were followed by considerable disturbance in the crowd, ending in a cheer.]" (Douglas uttered the word *black* with angry contempt. At first the crowd did not respond, but as he repeated the taunt, they replied by shouting out "white, white.")[110]

Republican newspapers denounced Douglas's racial demagoguery, asserting that he "deliberately insulted the audience, in order to provoke them to interrupt him, so that he might make capital for himself by the cry of persecution and unfairness."[111] The *Illinois State Journal* reported that Douglas's "platitudes about amalgamation and nigger equality—his only political stock in trade—were too old, too stupid to be listened to with patience."[112] The *Missouri Democrat* asked rhetorically, "How can there be negro equality, when the negro is intrinsically inferior to the child of Circassian blood? When Nature has made him inferior, how can a political party, if it were so insane as to attempt it, make him equal?"[113]

In dealing with the mistake he had made at Ottawa—confusing the Aurora platform of 1854 with the one adopted at Springfield—Douglas offered no apology but explained that he had obtained the document from the Springfield *Illinois State Register*. Refusing to acknowledge his error, he pledged to investigate the matter when he next visited the capital. He aggressively argued that it made little difference where the platform had been adopted. Alluding to Lincoln's 1847 "spot resolutions," he observed sarcastically, "Lincoln is great in the particular spots at which a thing is to be done." Instead of citing the state Republican platforms of 1856 or 1858, Douglas then read the platform the Republicans of the Freeport district had adopted when they chose their congressional candidate in 1854 and quoted resolutions introduced into the legislature in 1855. These he misleadingly used to illustrate Republican doctrine in 1858. Chastising Lincoln for his alleged failure to state clearly whether he would vote for the admission of new Slave States, Douglas boasted: "I have stood by my principles in fair weather and foul—in the sunshine and in the rain. I have defended the great principle of self-government here among you, when Northern sentiment ran in a torrent against it. [That is so.] I have defended the same great principle of self-government, when Southern sentiment came down with its avalanche upon me. I was not afraid of the test they put to me."

Douglas again denounced Lincoln's conspiracy charge as "an infamous lie." As for the contention that he had accused the Washington *Union*, President Buchanan, and the framers of the Lecompton Constitution of a conspiracy to nationalize slavery, Douglas maintained that he had criticized only the newspaper's editor, whom he called "that most corrupt of all corrupt men."[114] (How a conspiracy could be carried out by one man he did not explain.)

Elihu B. Washburne thought Douglas's speech "was not up to his usual standard. He was evidently embarrassed by the questions, and floundered in his replies."[115] The Dixon *Republican and Telegraph* found the Little Giant's language "coarse, blustering and insulting," while the Rockford *Republican* condemned the senator for his "Marat-like rant and invective."[116] One observer reported that Douglas "had evidently been drinking very strongly, it is said, of brandy."[117]

Henry Villard had only positive impressions of Douglas's speech, asserting that it "was undeniably one of the best and most brilliant of his life."[118] The independent Cincinnati *Commercial* said that never before had he appealed "with more skill to the prejudices of the white people against the African race, to the political self-righteousness of American citizens, or to the love of Conquest and Dominion, the passion of the extension of Territory and National and self-aggrandizement."[119]

Closing the debate, Lincoln expressed irritation at Douglas's habit of insulting his opponents. Contrasting his own restraint with the senator's intemperate oratory, Lincoln said, "in regard to Judge Douglas's declaration about the 'vulgarity and blackguardism' in the audience—that no such thing, as he says, was shown by any Democrat while I was speaking. Now, I only wish . . . to say, that while I was speaking, I used no 'vulgarity or blackguardism' toward any Democrat." He insisted that he had never attempted to conceal his opinions "nor tried to deceive any one in reference to them." He pointed out that the radical platform statements of northern Illinois Republicans in 1854 were moderated at the Bloomington Convention in 1856 to accommodate the downstate opponents of slavery. He emphatically promised to honor every plank in that platform and indignantly declared, "I hope to deal in all things fairly with Judge Douglas, and with the people of the State, in this contest. And if I should never be elected to any office, I trust I may go down with no stain of falsehood upon my reputation—notwithstanding the hard opinions Judge Douglas chooses to entertain of me."

In an evident allusion to the question of black citizenship rights, Lincoln urged the antislavery members of the audience to "waive minor differences on questions which either belong to the dead past or the distant future." He observed that he turned almost "with disgust" from Douglas's distortions of his "House Divided" speech and recommended that people read that address to "see whether it contains any of those 'bugaboos' which frighten Judge Douglas." He denied ducking the question about the admission of new Slave States, reiterating that he would vote to admit one in the highly unlikely event that such a question were ever to arise. He objected to the Little Giant's "working up these quibbles." At some length he quoted from Douglas's speech denouncing the editor of the Washington *Union* as well as President Buchanan and the framers of the Lecompton Constitution.[120]

A correspondent for the New York *Tribune*, who judged that Lincoln had made the "best impression," called him "an earnest, fluent speaker, with a very good command of language, and he run the Judge so hard that the latter quite lost his temper."[121] The New York *Times* declared that Lincoln's speech was "full of good hits," while the

Missouri Democrat praised his "[c]omprehensiveness, tact, temper, logic, and . . . most racy humor."[122]

Not all Republicans were pleased. Lincoln's continued defensiveness, according to Joseph Medill, might doom the party to defeat in November. Abolitionists expressed disappointment with his moderation. The Marengo *Press*, a Republican paper in McHenry County, disapproved of Lincoln's answer to Douglas's questions at Freeport. The *Press* asked: "Are such really his views? And are Douglas' much worse? If this is bringing Lincoln to his milk, why the Judge of course has done it; and it proves to be of a quality that some, at least, cannot get down. We think he must have been browsing quite too long in Egypt. Let him be kept till November, in a good Northern pasture. We think it would improve him."[123]

The Democratic press predictably ridiculed Lincoln. In the *New Yorker Staats-Zeitung*, Henry Villard portrayed him as "the apostle of the abolitionists, negro-amalgamationists, nativists, and all other conceivable—ists" and "a would-be statesman who adorns his speeches with platitudes, with ordinary, shopworn puns, and with a kind of crude backwoods humor," a man "who grounds his arguments in Bible quotations, and instead of appealing to the intelligence of his listeners merely tries to tickle their funny bones!"[124]

But by forcing Douglas to reiterate his "unfriendly legislation" doctrine and exposing his false accusation regarding the radical Aurora platform, Lincoln won the debate and regained the initiative he had lost at Ottawa.

In the three weeks before the third debate, both candidates stumped central Illinois, the Whig Belt where most of the 37,351 Fillmore voters of 1856 lived. With good reason, David Davis was especially worried about Tazewell County, which he visited at Lincoln's request. There he found "a *deadness* . . . that I have seen no where." Though he believed the county could be carried "by energy," in mid-August there was little enthusiasm, and Republicans were "generally dispirited." The main problem lay "with the charge of abolition at Lincoln. Lincoln is liked personally in the Co. better than any man in the state. It needs canvassing, active, thorough, old fashioned canvassing, to dissipate this charge." Davis arranged for Lincoln to speak in Tremont on August 30.[125]

At Bloomington on September 4, young Joseph Fifer, a future governor of Illinois, stood close to the speaker's stand and heard Leonard Swett introduce Lincoln, who began awkwardly. "His first sentence didn't seem to suit him," Fifer recalled, "and he came back to try it again." Fifer's brother whispered, "Swett is the better speaker; maybe he'd make a better Senator." But as so often happened, once Lincoln warmed up, he mesmerized his audience. "Every one had faces up to Lincoln with their attention riveted on him," Fifer recalled. "They looked as though they were hewn out of rock. They were sober and serious."[126]

A week later, Lincoln was unusually eloquent at a rally in Edwardsville, where his good friend Joseph Gillespie lived. Gillespie, one of the leading Fillmore supporters in 1856, now backed the Republicans. Lincoln sought to win other Fillmore men by appealing to their moral sense. Succinctly he noted that Republicans "consider slavery a moral, social and political wrong," whereas Democrats like Douglas "*do not* consider it either a moral, social or political wrong." Expanding on the theme, he added: "The Republican party . . . hold[s] that this government was instituted to secure the blessings of freedom, and that slavery is an unqualified evil to the negro, to the white man, to the soil, and to the State." Republicans "will use every constitutional method to prevent the evil from becoming larger and involving more negroes, more white men, more soil, and more States in its deplorable consequences." Arguments in favor of Douglas's popular sovereignty doctrine made sense only "if you admit that slavery is as good and as right as freedom," but "not one of them is worth a rush if you deny it."

Appealing to former Whigs, Lincoln quoted from Henry Clay's antislavery writings, including an 1849 letter in which the Great Compromiser said: "I know there are those who draw an argument in favor of slavery from the alleged intellectual inferiority of the black race. Whether this argument is founded in fact or not, I will not now stop to inquire, but merely say that if it proves anything at all, it proves too much. It proves that among the white races of the world any one might properly be enslaved by any other which had made greater advances in civilization. And, if this rule applies to nations there is no reason why it should not apply to individuals; and it might easily be proved that the wisest man in the world could rightfully reduce all other men and women to bondage."[127]

(In a memorandum probably written in the 1850s, Lincoln paraphrased Clay's argument, imagining a dialogue with a defender of slavery in which this question was addressed: "If A. can prove, however conclusively, that he may, of right, enslave B.—why may not B. snatch the same argument, and prove equally, that he may enslave A?—You say A. is white, and B. is black. It is *color*, then; the lighter, having the right to enslave the darker? Take care. By this rule, you are to be slave to the first man you meet, with a fairer skin than your own. You do not mean *color* exactly?—You mean the whites are *intellectually* the superiors of the blacks, and, therefore have the right to enslave them? Take care again. By this rule, you are to be slave to the first man you meet, with an intellect superior to your own. But, say you, it is a question of *interest;* and, if you can make it your *interest,* you have the right to enslave another. Very well. And if he can make it his interest, he has the right to enslave you.")[128]

Closing his Edwardsville address, Lincoln reflected on what the future might hold if Douglas's moral neutrality prevailed and a second Dred Scott decision were handed down: "Now, when by all these means you have succeeded in dehumanizing the negro; when you have put him down, and made it forever impossible for him to be but as the beasts of the field; when you have extinguished his soul, and placed him where the ray of hope is blown out in darkness like that which broods over the spirits of the damned; are you quite sure the demon which you have roused *will not turn and rend you?*" Rhetorically he asked, "What constitutes the bulwark of our own liberty and independence?" Not "our frowning battlements" or "bristling sea coasts," or "the guns of our war steamers," not even "the strength of our gallant and disciplined army." These assets "are not our reliance against a resumption of tyranny in our fair land," for they all "may be turned against our liberties, without making us stronger or weaker for the struggle." Instead "[o]ur reliance is in the *love of liberty* which God has planted in our bosoms. Our defense is in the preservation of the spirit which prizes liberty as the heritage of all men, in all lands, every where. Destroy this spirit, and you have planted the seeds of despotism around your own doors. Familiarize your-selves with the chains of bondage, and you are preparing your own limbs to wear them. Accustomed to trample on the rights of those around you, you have lost the genius of your own independence, and become the fit subjects of the first cunning tyrant who rises. And let me tell you, all these things are prepared for you with the logic of history, if the elections shall promise that the next Dred Scott decision and all future decisions will be quietly acquiesced in by the people."[129]

After this memorable address, Gillespie drove Lincoln to Highland, a German community on the road to his next scheduled appointment. There Gillespie "got the first inkling of the amazing popularity of Mr Lincoln among the Germans." The residents of Highland "were perfectly enraptured," Gillespie recalled. "The bare sight of the man threw them into extacies." The next day as the challenger and Gillespie continued on toward Greenville, Lincoln "said that he had but one serious charge to make against Douglass," namely, "that Douglass arrogated to himself a superiority on account of having a national reputation." He added: "I would not do that, if we oc-cupied each others places."[130]

On September 6, as Lincoln was approaching Monticello, a crowd came out to escort his carriage into town. When he saw Henry C. Whitney, he invited the young attorney to join him. "I'm mighty glad you are here," said the candidate. "I hate to be stared at, all by myself; I've been a great man such a mighty little time that I'm not used to it yet."[131]

That same day, Douglas, without evident irony, told a crowd at Jacksonville that his friends had chided him for being "too courteous by half to Lincoln" and that he "would show the lying, wooly-headed abolitionist how he would talk to him." Rhe-torically, he asked: "Have any of you an old father in Kentucky, or perhaps a mother in Virginia? Then don't let those dear ties be broken by a demagogue like Lincoln throwing bomb-shells across the Ohio at 'em!"[132] Two days later at Carlinville he characterized his opponents as "Yankees and intimates of niggers" and "miserable abolitionists" who were "unacquainted with the true courtesies of civilized life." He also boasted that "I am much like Gen. Jackson. He didn't understand Latin, neither do I; and when I was presented the Latin sheepskin making me L. L. D., I couldn't read it."[133] Of the pro-Buchanan Washington *Union* and its supporters, the Little Giant said: "I intend to expose their treachery, their treason and their infamy, in their coalition with abolitionists everywhere."[134] The Democratic press echoed Douglas's arguments, calling Lincoln "a red-hot abolitionist" who would, if chosen senator, "be the worst enemy of the Slave States to be found in that body."[135]

Third Debate: Jonesboro

In contrast to Ottawa and Freeport, the 800 residents of Jonesboro seemed indifferent to the senatorial debate in their town. Located 350 miles south of Chicago in the poorest, most backward, and most heavily Democratic part of the state, Jonesboro did little to welcome either the candidates or the 1,400 people who came to hear them, many traveling in dilapidated wagons drawn by stunted oxen. When trains arrived bearing Lincoln and Douglas, no one cheered them. On the morning of the debate, only one procession paraded through the streets, a pitiful delegation from Johnson County, made up of two yoke of steers and an upside-down banner inscribed "Stephen A. Douglas." A bystander remarked to Lincoln, "Do you see that? Here where Douglas holds sway is ignorance; up north where you are the champion we would find no such display of ignorance, we would see intelligence." Lincoln chuckled mildly but offered no reply.[136] The county was a hotbed of pro-Buchanan sentiment.

Conditions were far from ideal; the weather was hot, the railroads badly constructed, the country roads primitive, the taverns woeful, and food and lodging simply intolerable. Lincoln was fortunate enough to stay at the elegant home of David L. Phillips, the Republican candidate for Congress in that district. He arrived the night before the debate and sat on the porch observing Donati's comet, which he much admired.

After lunch on September 15, a desultory crowd ambled to the fairgrounds to attend the debate. While Douglas delivered the opening speech, Lincoln cut a comic figure, sitting in a low chair with his feet drawn in and his knees projecting toward the sky.

At Jonesboro, where Douglas had threatened to bring Lincoln "to his milk," the Little Giant once again stressed the race issue, for, as the challenger had been advised, "in Egypt there is little sympathy for the nigger."[137] Recounting the history of the birth of the Republican Party in 1854, the Little Giant alleged that in New York, antislavery forces had adopted a platform "every plank of which was as black as night, each one relating to the nigger, and not one referring to the interests of the white man." Republicans throughout the North followed suit, Douglas asserted. The leaders of that new party were "restless mortals and discontented politicians." In northern Illinois they "brought out men to canvass the State of the same complexion with their political creed, and hence you find Fred. Douglass, the negro, following Gen. Cass, the illustrious Senator from Michigan, and attempting to speak in behalf of Mr. Lincoln and Trumbull and abolitionism against that illustrious Senator. [Applause; renewed laughter.] Why they brought Fred. Douglass to meet me when I was addressing the people at Freeport as I am here, in a carriage with a white lady and her daughter in the carriage sitting by his side, and the owner of the carriage having the honor to drive the coach to convey the negro. [Applause. "Shame."]"

In addition to his usual arguments about "the negro," the "savage Indians," the "Feejee," the "Malay," and "any other inferior or degraded race," the senator introduced a new element into the debates: expansionism. Since 1843, Douglas had been calling for the annexation of Cuba. He told the Jonesboro audience that "our interests would be advanced by the acquisition of the island of Cuba. [Terrific applause.] When we get Cuba we must take it as we find it, and leave the people of Cuba to decide the question of slavery for themselves without the interference of the federal government, or of any other State in the Union." If other areas in the Western Hemisphere are to become part of the United States, "I will take them with slavery or without it, just as the people shall determine. ["That's good." "That's right," and cheers.]"[138]

(At Belleville on September 10, Douglas had expressed confidence about how voters in Cuba might act: "they will never turn loose a million free negroes to desolate that beautiful island."[139] Although he had not raised this point in previous debates, Douglas had asked at Joliet on August 31: "I want to know if when we take Cuba, Lincoln will oppose its becoming a part of the Territory of the United States 'unless slavery is first prohibited therein?'"[140] In December, Douglas would announce: "It is our destiny to have Cuba, and it is folly to debate the question. It naturally belongs to the American Continent.")[141]

At the beginning of Lincoln's reply, he said he was embarrassed by the evident preponderance of Democrats in the audience. When his backers let out a cheer, however, he felt reassured and launched his remarks good-naturedly. Initially, his high-pitched voice and awkward gestures failed to impress his auditors. One journalist noted that "he got around about as gracefully as a woman climbs a rail fence."[142] But as usual, his earnestness made the crowd forget his ungainly appearance.

Responding to the allegation that he and Trumbull had conspired to abolitionize the two parties, the exasperated Lincoln said: "I don't want any harsh language indulged in, but I do not know how to deal with this persistent insisting on a story that I know to be utterly without truth. It used to be the fashion amongst men that when a charge was made, some sort of proof was brought forward to establish it, and if no proof was found to exist, the charge was dropped. I don't know how to meet this kind of an argument. I don't want to have a fight with Judge Douglas, and I have no way of working an argument up into the consistency of a corn-cob and stopping his mouth with it at all. [Laughter and applause.] All I can do is, good-humoredly to say to that story about a bargain between Judge Trumbull and myself, *there is not a word of truth in it*. [Applause.]" Douglas had cited a speech by James Matheny about that alleged conspiracy, to which Lincoln replied: "I hope the Judge will pardon me for doubting the genuineness of this document since his production of those Springfield Resolutions at Ottawa." At this, the audience applauded loudly, disconcerting the cigar-puffing Douglas.

Lincoln devoted much of his time at Jonesboro to reading Democratic antislavery platforms and resolutions adopted in 1850 throughout northern Illinois. These documents were provided by Herndon, who acted as his partner's research assistant, plowing though old speeches, digging up statistics, and clipping articles from many newspapers.

Lincoln argued that if Douglas were justified in holding him responsible for radical resolutions endorsed by Republicans in Aurora and other northern Illinois towns, the Little Giant should also be held responsible for the 1850 documents he read. He even introduced resolutions adopted by Democrats in Douglas's home state of Vermont.

Lincoln denied the central tenet of Douglas's Freeport Doctrine, that slavery could not exist without "friendly legislation" to protect it. After all, he pointed out, Dred Scott had been held in slavery in Minnesota, which had no police regulations supporting slavery; in fact, Congress had explicitly forbidden slavery in that region. "It takes not only law but the *enforcement* of law to keep it out," he sensibly observed. He then chided the Little Giant for inconsistency. Before 1857, Douglas had maintained that the Supreme Court should decide whether the people of a territory could

exclude slavery; at Freeport (and on earlier occasions) he declared that the settlers in a
territory could make an end-run around the court and were not obliged to abide by its
explicit decision. Was not Douglas oath-bound to support laws protecting the right of
slaveholders to take their slaves into the territories, just as opponents of slavery like
Lincoln were honor-bound to support the Fugitive Slave Act, even though they found
it "distasteful"? Pointedly Lincoln asked how Douglas could swear to uphold the
Constitution and simultaneously "assist in legislation *intended to defeat that right?*"

Lincoln then posed a fifth interrogatory to Douglas, supplementing the ones he
had asked at Ottawa: "If the slaveholding citizens of a United States Territory should
need and demand Congressional legislation for the protection of their slave property
in such Territory, would you, as a member of Congress, vote for or against such legislation?" Lyman Trumbull had advised him to ask Douglas that question, anticipating
that the Little Giant would "answer promptly that Congress possessed no such power,
or that he was opposed to its exercise if it did." Prophetically, Trumbull argued that
such a response "would effectually use him up with the South & set the whole
pro-slavery Democracy against him."[143]

Lincoln's patience was tried beyond endurance by Douglas's August 31 speech at
Joliet, where the Little Giant alleged that at the close of the Ottawa debate his opponent was so frightened by the prospect of having to defend his views in Jonesboro
that it "made him tremble in the knees, so that he had to be carried from the
platform."[144] Indignantly, Lincoln expostulated: "I have really come to the conclusion
that I can explain it in no other way than by believing the Judge is crazy. [Renewed
laughter.]" When the senator asked, "Wasn't you carried off at Ottawa?" Lincoln exclaimed: "There! That is Douglas—just like him!" and denied that he *had* to be carried.[145] Again Lincoln asserted that when the Little Giant made that claim he "must
have been crazy and wholly out of his sober senses." (Perhaps Lincoln meant to imply
that Douglas was drunk. The Chicago *Press and Tribune* observed that the senator
presented "unaccountable falsehoods," which "no sober man could ever have uttered."[146]
Herndon commented that "Douglas is mad—is wild & sometimes I should judge
'half seas over.' [drunk]")[147] Lincoln denied that he feared speaking in Jonesboro.
"Why, I know this people better than he does. I was raised just a little east of here. I
am a part of this people." (The audience warmed up to him when he claimed to have
grown up nearby, even though Lincoln's boyhood home in Indiana was 140 miles
distant.) The Little Giant, Lincoln added, "has set about seriously trying to make the
impression that when we meet at different places I am literally in his clutches—that I
am a poor, helpless, decrepit mouse, and that I can do nothing at all. This is one of
the ways he has taken to create that impression. I don't know any other way to meet
it, except this. I don't want to quarrel with him—to call him a liar—but when I come
square up to him I don't know what else to call him. [Cheers and laughter.]"[148]

Lincoln ended his remarks ten minutes early, prompting Henry Villard to comment: "if he were a man of intelligence, of talent and political wit he could have
pressed a masterful speech into those ten minutes."[149] The Louisville *Journal* observed
that Lincoln's "searching, scathing, stunning" remarks "belong to what some one has
graphically styled the *tomahawking* species."[150]

In his rejoinder, Douglas protested that at Joliet he "in a playful manner" asserted that Lincoln had to be carried off from the platform at Ottawa. (An account in the Peoria *Transcript*, whose "nigger-worshipping proclivities" were condemned by the *Illinois State Register*, noted that this explanation left "the inference that he was probably drunk.")[151] In commenting on Lincoln's assertion that he had been raised nearby, Douglas accused him of dishonoring his parents: "I don't know that a native of Kentucky who was raised among slaves, and whose father and mother were nursed by slaves, is any more excusable when he comes to Illinois and turns Abolitionist, to slander the grave of his father and the institutions under which he was born and where his father and mother lived."

Responding to Lincoln's question about a federal slave code for the territories, the Little Giant declared that "there shall be non-interference, non-intervention by Congress in the States and Territories." Although this was a platitude that failed to address the question, the audience applauded lustily. As Trumbull had predicted, this stance would cost Douglas dearly, for, especially after Freeport, Southerners would interpret it as an affront to their section.[152]

An Illinois reporter thought Douglas's "delivery was remarkably tame."[153] The Little Giant's performance, according to Chester P. Dewey of the New York *Evening Post*, "was not marked by his usual ability, and the delivery was very bad—a sort of school boy monotone, with an especial *aplomb* on every emphatic syllable." On the other hand, Dewey thought Lincoln's speech "the best I have heard from him."[154] The following day Lincoln wrote that the meeting at Jonesboro "was not large; but, in other matters altogether respectable. I will venture to say that our friends were a little better satisfied with the result than our adversaries."[155] One such friend was Governor William H. Bissell, who told E. B. Washburne in late September that the Republican "cause is unquestionably gaining daily. . . . *Lincoln is doing well*. He has made much, *much* in Egypt. There is no mistake about it."[156]

But in fact, Lincoln's abbreviated Jonesboro speech was the lamest he made in the debates. His abuse of Douglas as a crazy liar was undignified, as was his remark about stuffing the Little Giant's mouth with a corncob. Moreover, his reading of documents was tedious, and his claim that he grew up nearby disingenuous.

At Centralia two days after the Jonesboro debate, the Little Giant, evidently drunk, delivered an ill-tempered "harangue" that "was particularly severe on the unfortunate odor of the black man." Douglas "asked if his audience wished to eat with, ride with, go to church with, travel with, and in other ways bring Congo odor into their nostrils and to their senses." He concluded that blacks were meant to be servants and averred that "*if God Almighty intended them for anything else, he was a long time bringing it about.*"[157] This prompted a Republican editor to ask, indignantly: "And what is the ground upon which he asks the support of freemen? It is nothing more nor less than his ability to kick a nigger. It is the staple of all his speeches, it is the great one idea of his Statesmanship! When it is urged that our Fathers expected, and took such action as they thought would cause, the ultimate extinction of Slavery, Douglas valiantly 'pitches into the nigger.' If he is reminded that Freedom is on grounds of public policy, preferable to Slavery, that Free Territory will prove immensely more valuable to the Union than Slave Territory, and that our public domain should be kept free for the European emigrants, and the white inhabitants of this country, he summons all his courage to his aid, shakes his shaggy locks, and amid the roar of his cannon, again pitches into the negro. He threshes the nigger in the fence, and the nigger in the field, the free nigger and the nigger slave, declares that he ought to be a slave, and says if it is otherwise the Almighty has been a long time in demonstrating it!"[158]

Lincoln also visited Centralia, attending the state fair with Henry C. Whitney and Jesse K. Dubois. The night before the next debate, to be held at Charleston, Whitney and Lincoln caught an Illinois Central train bound for that town. On board, local politicians pestered Lincoln so much that he could get no sleep. When Whitney asked a conductor if the candidate, in dire need of rest, could use the empty apartment car at the end of the train, he was refused. Whitney, who managed somehow to gain access to that car, was outraged that his friend should be treated so shabbily while Douglas traveled in a luxurious car on a special train. Bitterly Whitney recalled that "every interest of that Road and every employee was against Lincoln and for Douglas."[159] Republican newspapers made similar charges about other railroads.

Fourth Debate: Charleston

On September 18 the candidates clashed again, at Charleston, shire town of Coles County in east central Illinois, known as the "Buckle on the Corn Belt." From surrounding villages like Greasy Creek, Muddy Point, Dog Town, Pinhook, Bloody Hutton, and Goosenest Prairie (where Lincoln's stepmother resided and his father lay buried), some 12,000 people streamed in to hear the debate.

Chester P. Dewey of the New York *Evening Post* remarked that "I have seen and watched these other demonstrations, but have failed to notice the hot and fevered flush which has marked this one." Dewey painted a graphic picture of the debates in general: "It is astonishing how deep an interest in politics this people take. Over long, weary miles of hot and dusty prairie, the processions of eager partisans come—on foot, on horseback, in wagons drawn by horses or mules; men, women and children, old and young; the half sick, just out of the last 'shake'; children in arms, infants at the maternal fount, pushing on in clouds of dust beneath a blazing sun; settling down at the town where the meeting is, with hardly a chance for sitting, and even less opportunity for eating, waiting in anxious groups for hours at the places of speaking, talking, discussing, litigious, vociferous, while the roar of artillery, the music of bands, the waving of banners, the huzzas of the crowds, as delegation after delegation appears; the cry of pedlars vending all sorts of wares, from an infallible cure for 'augur' to a monster watermelon in slices to suit purchasers—combine to render the occasion one scene of confusion and commotion." At one o'clock, "a perfect rush is made for the grounds; a column of dust rising to the heavens and fairly deluging those who are hurrying on through it. Then the speakers come, with flags, and banners, and music, surrounded by cheering partizans. Their arrival at the ground and immediate approach to the stand is the signal for shouts that rend the heavens. They are introduced to the audience amid prolonged and enthusiastic cheers; they are interrupted by frequent applause, and they sit down finally amid the same uproarious demonstrations.

The audience sit or stand patiently throughout, and as the last word is spoken, make a break for their homes, first hunting up lost members of their families, gathering their scattered wagon loads together, and as the daylight fades away, entering again upon the broad prairies and slowly picking their way back 'to the place of beginning.'"160

Charleston was alive with this excitement. The badges, flags, bunting, and other campaign trappings were far more elaborate and numerous than they had been at previous debate sites. Among those banners was one emblazoned with a quotation from the Little Giant: "This government was made for white men—Douglas for life."161

On the hot, clear day of this fourth debate, Lincoln approached Charleston from nearby Matoon, accompanied by many of its residents, mostly of Northern origin. In the procession was a float carrying thirty-two young women, each representing a state of the Union, with a banner reading "Westward the star of Empire takes its way, The girls *link-on* to Lincoln, as their mothers did to Clay." In addition, a comely maiden on horseback carried a banner with the motto, "Kansas—I will be free." (Horace White thought her so attractive that "she would not remain free always.")162 Upon arriving, Lincoln was greeted by his friend H. P. H. Bromwell, who delivered a warm welcoming address. The challenger replied graciously, with special praise for the float bearing the young women, whom he likened to a "beautiful basket of flowers."163

Tension charged the air. As Lincoln and Douglas proceeded to the fairgrounds after lunch, the Little Giant erupted in anger at a banner showing Lincoln clubbing him to the ground. In a rage, he declared that he would not tolerate such an indignity. Petulantly, he added, "If I can't be treated with some respect, I'll get out of the procession."164

Lincoln had a better cause for complaint, for at 2:45 P.M., as he rose to speak, several Democrats pushed their way to the platform and unfurled a huge banner with a caricature of a white man, a black woman, and a black child, bearing the caption "Negro Equality." When Republican demands that it be removed were ignored, two men leapt from the platform and tore it down.

Lincoln had been warned that Negrophobia was intense in Coles County. His friend William M. Chambers, an influential American Party leader in Charleston, urged him to attack Douglas's "political inconsistencies and tergiversations" and give his audiences "less of the favouring of negro equality." Appeals for racial justice pleased neither Fillmore voters nor Republicans around Charleston.165 The town's leading Republican, Thomas A. Marshall, with whom Lincoln stayed, recommended that he tell Dr. Chambers that "as for negro equality in the sense in which the expression is used you neither believe in it nor desire it. You desire to offer no temptations to negroes to come among us or remain with us, and therefore you do not propose to confer upon them any further social or political rights than they are now entitled to."166 This counsel echoed what David Davis had told Lincoln about Tazewell County: "Among all the Kentuckians it is industriously circulated that, *you favor negro* equality. All the [Republican] Orators should distinctly & emphatically disavow *negro suffrage*—negro holding office, serving on juries, & the like."[167] In August, Jediah F. Alexander wrote from Greenville, 90 miles southwest of Charleston: "You must be full and explicit in explaining that. . . . the Republicans are not in favor of making the Blacks socially and politically equal with the Whites."[168] In July, the Republican district convention at Dixon in northern Illinois had adopted a resolution declaring that "the republican party has not held and does not hold to the political and social equality of the races or individually, and has re-affirmed and ever will re-affirm with the declaration of independence, the equality of all men of whatever race or color, in *natural right,* to life, liberty and the pursuit of happiness."[169] A Republican in Shawneetown declared that the only way his party could win was "to satisfy the people the republicans are not amalgamationists."[170]

In his opening remarks Lincoln showed that he had taken the advice of Chambers, Marshall, Davis, et al. to heart. "When I was at the hotel to-day," he began, "an elderly gentleman called upon me to know whether I was really in favor of producing a perfect equality between the negroes and white people. [Great laughter.]" Lincoln had not planned to address that subject, but since he was asked, he thought he "would occupy perhaps five minutes in saying something in regard to it." He declared bluntly: "I am not, nor ever have been, in favor of bringing about in any way the social and political equality of the white and black races [applause]; that I am not, nor ever have been, in favor of making voters or jurors of negroes, nor of qualifying them to hold office, nor to intermarry with white people; and I will say, in addition to this, that there is a physical difference between the white and black races which I believe will forever forbid the two races living together on terms of social and political equality. And inasmuch as they cannot so live, while they remain together there must be the position of superior and inferior, and I as much as any other man am in favor of having the superior position assigned to the white race."

Then Lincoln qualified this stark avowal: "I do not perceive that because the white man is to have the superior position the negro should be denied everything. I do not understand that because I do not want a negro woman for a slave I must necessarily want her for a wife. [Cheers and laughter.] My understanding is that I can just let her alone. I am now in my fiftieth year, and I certainly never had had a black woman for either a slave or a wife. So it seems to me quite possible for us to get along without making either slaves or wives of negroes. I will add to this that I have never seen, to my knowledge, a man, woman, or child who has been in favor of producing a perfect equality, social and political, between negroes and white men." Alluding to the Democratic vice-president in the late 1830's, a man who had sired children with a black mistress, Lincoln added: "I recollect of but one distinguished instance that I ever heard of so frequently as to be entirely satisfied of its correctness, and that is the case of Judge Douglas's old friend Colonel Richard M. Johnson. [Laughter and cheers.]"

Continuing in a satirical vein, Lincoln added that "I have never had the least apprehension that I or my friends would marry negroes if there was no law to keep them from it [laughter]; but as Judge Douglas and his friends seem to be in great apprehension that they might, if there were no law to keep them from it, [roars of laughter] I give him the most solemn pledge that I will to the very last stand by the law of this State, which forbids the marrying of white people with negroes. [Continued laughter and applause.]" In concluding his remarks on the subject of black citizenship, Lincoln observed that only state legislatures could alter "the social and political relations of negro and the white man," and "as I do not really apprehend the approach of any such thing myself, and as Judge Douglas seems to be in constant horror that some such danger is rapidly approaching, I propose as the best means to prevent it that the Judge be kept at home, and placed in the State Legislature to fight the measure. [Uproarious laughter and applause.]"

Lincoln devoted most of his opening speech to a repetition of Lyman Trumbull's accusation that Douglas had thwarted Georgia Senator Robert Toombs's proposed 1856 bill that would have allowed Kansas settlers to vote on the proposed state constitution. Thus, he argued, the Little Giant was no true friend of popular sovereignty, and his opposition to the Lecompton Constitution was hypocritical. Toombs's measure had been referred to Douglas's Committee on Territories, which removed the provision calling for submission of the constitution to the voters of Kansas. The issue resonated in Coles County; a Charlestonian told Douglas "that Toombs matter is a great bugaboo with the nigger party here."[171] Lincoln's friends advised him to attack Douglas for his evisceration of the Toombs bill. Mark Delahay reported to Lincoln that Trumbull's charge "hit the right c[h]ord, from the uneasiness & fluttering which is discoverable among the Douglas bolters." To criticize Douglas for altering the Toombs bill would compel the senator "to defend these charges and When ever he does you have got the 'Word on him.'"[172] "It is *true*," J. H. Jordan said of the accusation, "therefore *make him eat it.*"[173] Douglas's supporters in the Jacksonville area were "staggered" and "reeling" in part because of "Trumbull's charge in regard to popular sovereignty and the Toombs bill."[174] Newspapers devoted many columns to that issue.

Earlier in the campaign, Lincoln had not directly addressed the matter of the Toombs bill; he had simply vouched for Trumbull's honesty and integrity. This, in turn, prompted Douglas to hold Lincoln responsible for Trumbull's charge. At Charleston, Lincoln counterattacked, repeating Democratic Senator William Bigler's statement that a senatorial conference headed by Douglas had agreed to strike from Toombs's bill the provision for submitting the constitution to a vote of the Kansas settlers. As for Douglas's allegation that Trumbull "forges his evidence from beginning to end" Lincoln replied: "upon my own authority I say that it is not true. [Great cheers and laughter.]" The Toombs bill, Bigler's speech, and Douglas's own speech of December 9, 1857, were part of the public record, not forgeries. "I have always wanted to deal with every one I meet, candidly and honestly," Lincoln said. "If I have made any assertion not warranted by facts, and it is pointed out to me, I will withdraw it cheerfully. But I do not choose to see Judge Trumbull calumniated, and the evidence he has brought forward branded in general terms 'a forgery from beginning to end.'"[175]

Lew Wallace, who admired Douglas, initially thought Lincoln's opening remarks risible, but in time he changed his mind. "The pleasantry, the sincerity, the confidence, the amazingly original way of putting things, and the simple, unrestrained manner withal, were doing their perfect work; and then and there I dropped an old theory, that to be a speaker one must needs be graceful and handsome." Wallace found Douglas's reply disappointing. "His face was darkened by a deepening scowl, and he was angry," a sure sign that his opponent had the upper hand. "He spoke so gutturally, also, that it was difficult to understand him."[176]

Douglas began with a disingenuous boast: "I am glad to have gotten an answer from him on that proposition, to wit: the right of suffrage and holding office by ne-groes, for I have been trying to get him to answer that point during the whole time that the canvass has been going on." This was misleading; Lincoln had made his stand on that matter clear at Ottawa in their initial debate.

As for the Toombs bill, Douglas asked why Trumbull and Lincoln had not ob-jected in 1856, when that legislation was introduced and then modified. He chided Lincoln for devoting inordinate time to rehashing Trumbull's "vile charge," and as-serted that Pennsylvania Senator William Bigler had retracted his allegation. The senator further protested that a requirement for a popular referendum on the Lecomp-ton Constitution was implicit and that none of the statehood bills passed before 1856 stipulated that the constitution must be ratified by a vote of the people.

The Little Giant expressed contempt for the "petty, malicious assaults" made against him. Without evident irony he declared, "I despair ever to be elected to office by slandering my opponent and traducing other men [cheers]. Mr. Lincoln asks you to-day for your support in electing him to the Senate solely because he and Trumbull can slander me." While Lincoln had not mentioned his conspiracy theory, Douglas offered one of his own: "here is a conspiracy to carry an election by slander or not by fair means. Mr. Lincoln's speech this day is conclusive evidence of the fact." Scorn-fully he ridiculed his opponent for trying "to ride into office on Trumbull's back and Trumbull is going to carry him by falsehood into office." With disdain he added: "It won't do for Mr. Lincoln, in parading his calumny against me, to put Trumbull be-tween him and the odium and the responsibility that attaches to such calumny. I tell him that I am as ready to prosecute the endorser as the maker of a forged note. [Ap-plause; cheers.]" With a characteristic air of injured innocence, he voiced regret that he had to spend time on "these petty personal matters. It is unbecoming the dignity of a canvass for an office of the character for which we are candidates." He implied that he would now withdraw the compliments he had earlier paid Lincoln. "If there is anything personally disagreeable, unkind or disrespectful in these personalities, the sole responsibility is on Mr. Lincoln, Trumbull and their backers." Averring that he had "no charges to make against Mr. Lincoln," Douglas immediately thereafter said: "If Mr. Lincoln is a man of bad character, I leave it to you to find out. If his voting in the past was not satisfactory to you, I leave others to ascertain the fact, and if his course on the Mexican war was not in accordance with your opinions of patriotism and duty in defence of our country against a public enemy, I leave you to ascertain the fact. I have no assault to make against him."

The Little Giant again appealed to the Negrophobia of his audience by attacking Frederick Douglass. Four years earlier in northern Illinois, he recalled, "I passed Lin-coln's ally there, in the person of Fred. Douglass, the negro, preaching revolutionary principles, while Lincoln was discussing the same principles down here, and Trumbull a little further down attempting to elect members of the Legislature, and acting in harmony each with the other." At Chicago he observed an effort by "Lincoln's then associates and new supporters to put Fred. Douglass on the stand at a Democratic meeting, to reply to the illustrious Gen. Cass, when he was addressing the people there. ["Shame on them."] They had that same negro hunting me down, the same as they have a negro canvassing the principal counties of the North in behalf of Lincoln. ["Hit him again." "He's a disgrace to the white people," &c.]" Lincoln, said the Little Giant, knew that when they were debating at Freeport, "there was a distinguished colored gentleman there, [laughter] who made a speech that night and the night after, a short distance from Freeport, in favor of Lincoln, and showing how much interest his colored brethren felt in the success of their brother, Abraham Lincoln [Laughter]." Douglas then offered to read a speech by Frederick Douglass "in which he called upon all who were friends of negro equality and negro citizenship to rally as one man around Abraham Lincoln, as the chief embodiment of their principles, and by all means to defeat Stephen A. Douglas. [Laughter; "it can't be done."]"

(In fact, on August 2 at Poughkeepsie, New York, Frederick Douglass assailed the senator, quoted from Lincoln's "House Divided" speech, which he called "great," and thanked Lincoln and his party colleagues "because they have nobly upheld and made prominent the principles of the Republican Party in Illinois, which seemed about to be compromised and sacrificed at the very heart of Government." Democratic newspapers in Illinois found great significance in Douglass's endorsement of the "House Divided" speech, which showed "that Mr. Lincoln has reached the very top round of ultra abolitionism, where he now stands, side by side with Fred Douglass." They also asked ominous questions: "Can the white men of Illinois fail to see in this adoption of Mr. Lincoln's position as a text for a negro agitator's glorification speech, in favor of the equality of the races, the tendency of black republican policy to that end?" "Will you elect a man your Senator whose words fit so well the mouth of a negro?")[177]

To cheers from his supporters, Douglas thundered: "I say this Government was created on the white basis by white men for white men and their posterity forever, and should never be administered by any but white men. [Cheers.] I declare that a negro ought not to be a citizen whether imported into this country or born here, whether his parents were slave or not. It don't depend upon the question where he was born, or where his parents were placed, but it depends on the fact that the negro belongs to a race incapable of self-government, and for that reason ought not to be on an equality with the white man. [Immense applause.]" (In December, Douglas would tell an audience in New Orleans: "It is a law of humanity, a law of civilization, that whenever a man, or a race of men, show themselves incapable of managing their own affairs, they must consent to be governed by those who are capable of performing the duty. It is on this principle that you establish those institutions of charity, for the support of the blind, or the deaf and dumb, or the insane. In accordance with this principle, I assert that the negro race, under all circumstances, at all times and in all countries, has shown itself incapable of self-government.")[178]

The senator charged Lincoln with being inconsistent in the previous debate: "There were many white sentiments contained in Lincoln's speech down in Jonesboro, and I could not help contrasting them with the speeches of the same distinguished orator in the northern parts of the State." Douglas erred; while it was true that Lincoln in Egypt said he would be willing to admit new Slave States, he had said nothing different at Ottawa or Freeport. Instead of statements by his rival, the Little Giant cited utterances by Republican congressional candidates Owen Lovejoy, John Farnsworth, and E. B. Washburne, all of whom opposed admitting new Slave States.[179] (Farnsworth assured Lincoln that while he personally refused to support the admission of new Slave States, he was careful to "say that is not the position of the republican party.")[180] Obviously, Lincoln had not contradicted himself, and Douglas's argument did him little credit. If either candidate was guilty of talking one way in the northern part of the state and another way in the southern part, it was Douglas. At Freeport he deemphasized the significance of the Dred Scott ruling, calling it an "abstraction." In Egypt he spoke of it with much greater respect as "the supreme law of the land."[181] The Chicago *Press and Tribune* demanded that Douglas "be one thing or another, fish, flesh, or fowl, and not be dodging and skulking about, sometimes one thing, sometimes another, and sometimes both at once."[182]

Closing the debate, Lincoln denied that Douglas had ever asked him specifically about black citizenship rights and protested against the Little Giant's misinterpretation of his criticism of the Dred Scott decision. As for the charge that he espoused radical views in the north and conservatives ones in the south, Lincoln said: "*I dare him to point out any different between my speeches north and south.* [Great cheering.]" Defending his House Divided doctrine, Lincoln estimated that slavery might not be abolished any time soon. "I do not suppose that in the most peaceful way ultimate extinction would occur in less than a hundred years at least; but that it will occur in the best way for both races, in God's own good time, I have no doubt. [Applause.]"

Addressing Douglas's allusion to his record during the Mexican War, Lincoln grew angry, though he began moderately: "I don't want to be unjustly accused of dealing illiberally or unfairly with an adversary, either in court, or in a political canvass, or anywhere else. I would despise myself if I supposed myself ready to deal less liberally with an adversary than I was willing to be treated myself." He complained that Douglas "revives the old charge against me in reference to the Mexican war," even though "the more respectable papers of his own party throughout the State [like the *Illinois State Register* and the Matoon *Gazette*] have been compelled to take it back and acknowledge that it was a lie. [Continued and vociferous applause.]" He then turned to Congressman Orlando B. Ficklin, sitting on the platform. Lincoln astonished him by grabbing his coat collar and hauling him forward "as if he had been a kitten."[183] The astonished crowd burst out laughing. Lincoln explained to them: "I do not mean to do anything with Mr. Ficklin except to present his face and tell you that *he personally knows it to be a lie!*" Ficklin had served in Congress with Lincoln and could testify that the Representative from Springfield had always voted to supply the army. A Democrat who was hosting Douglas, Ficklin artfully dodged the question, merely stating that Lincoln had voted for the Ashmun amendment, declaring that the war had been unnecessarily and unconstitutionally commenced by President Polk.

In reviewing Douglas's charges, Lincoln compared his opponent to a cuttlefish, "a small species of fish that has no mode of defending itself when pursued except by throwing out a black fluid, which makes the water so dark the enemy cannot see it, and thus it escapes. [Roars of laughter.]" Insisting that Douglas had evaded the central question about his role in gutting the Toombs bill, Lincoln emphatically scolded the Little Giant: "*I suggest to him it will not avail him at all that he swells himself up, takes on dignity, and calls people liars.* [Great applause and laughter.]"[184]

During Lincoln's rejoinder, Douglas's friends on the platform grew so agitated and the senator was "so boisterously profane" that reporters could scarcely make out what the challenger was saying. Three times Robert R. Hitt asked the Douglasites to quiet down, and the correspondent of the Paris *Prairie Beacon News* was unable to hear Lincoln. Finally, Douglas, who had been nervously glancing at his watch, interrupted Lincoln, excitedly insisting that he had "overspoken his time two minutes now."[185] Lincoln replied, "I will quit when the Moderator so says."[186] A gentleman on the platform wryly told Lincoln, "Yes, Douglas has had enough; it is time you let up on him."[187]

The Chicago *Press and Tribune* was unusually enthusiastic about Lincoln's performance, particularly his reply to Douglas's remarks: "We regard this debate as the GREAT TRIUMPH of the campaign for the friends of Mr. Lincoln." As the newspaper observed, Douglas had demonstrated little more than an "uncommon fertility of quibbles, an opulence of sophistry, and a faculty of obscuring the issues."[188] The Charleston *Courier* remarked that Lincoln's riposte "was the most effectual and perpetual and incessant pouring of hot shot upon the head of Douglas that ever poor mortal was the victim of."[189] Chester P. Dewey wrote that the challenger's retort "was especially eloquent and convincing."[190]

Lincoln's friends were delighted. David Davis told him: "Your concluding speech on Douglass at Charleston was admirable."[191] Three days after the debate, Richard J. Oglesby reported that the challenger had scored "the most full and complete triumph . . . in the speeches, the crowds, the turnout and the sympathy, I have ever seen." Douglas "writhed and winced and at last left the stand in a bad humor."[192] Years later Oglesby still recalled the Charleston debate as "a day of triumph and glory. Douglas was manifestly tiring of that joint discussion. Lincoln, on the contrary, like a precious stone in the rough, was growing constantly brighter and more brilliant by the attrition of the contest. Douglas was petulant. Lincoln was calm, grave, and impressive."[193] Horace White remembered that "we all considered that our side had won a substantial victory. The Democrats seemed to be uneasy and dissatisfied, both during the debate and afterward."[194] To Hiram W. Beckwith, the final fifteen minutes of Lincoln's rejoinder constituted the turning point of the campaign: "his remorseless logic toppled pillar after pillar from the Senator's cunningly devised subterfuges. One could see the fabric tottering to its fall. Republicans saw it. The Democrats felt it. A panic among them began near the speakers stand and spread outward and onward over the great mass of upturned faces. . . . From this time on none doubted who was to be the winner in the fight."[195] One Democrat confessed that he had gone to Charleston expecting to see Douglas pulverize his opponent but came away from the debate "the most astonished squatter sovereign you ever saw. Who the — was Lincoln? What in thunder was the matter with Douglas? I was sick—very sick."[196]

The Paris *Prairie Beacon News* thought that reasonable persons must be convinced that Lincoln did not favor political and social equality for blacks. If they were not, the only way the candidate could persuade them would be if he were to "arm himself with a huge cleaver, and at the next meeting between himself and his competitor, with appropriate formality and due solemnity, kill at least one nigger." One listener, commenting on Lincoln's denial of charges that he favored racial amalgamation, said: "If they can't believe that, you might as well talk to stumps."[197]

The Democrats rushed into print a garbled version of the Charleston debate. A Republican in Naperville told Lincoln that "your speech is so badly mutilated that it is well calculated to work a great injury to yourself & our party's cause. . . . We look upon this here abouts as the most shameful and dishonest imposition & fraud, yet Committed by our unscrupable opponents."[198]

In Massachusetts, the Springfield *Republican* also deplored Douglas's tactics, though it had been sympathetic to him before the debate at Charleston. There, the *Republican* protested, the Little Giant had appealed to "the ignorance and prejudices of the people to sustain him in a coarse tirade against the blacks."[199] Similarly, the *Missouri Democrat* observed that Douglas "entertains but a poor opinion of the intellectual capacities of the people."[200]

Some abolitionists were disappointed in Lincoln's remarks about black citizenship. "Our standard bearer has faltered thus soon," lamented the Chicago *Congregational Herald*. "Lincoln deliberately, and with repetition, declared himself to be opposed to placing colored men on a political equality with white men. He made color and race the ground of political proscription. He forsook *principle,* and planted himself on *low prejudice.*" The editors declared that "[w]it, sharp repartee, readiness of speech, good humor, [and] effective stump oratory, amount to something; but they cannot compensate for moral cowardice, or ignorance of the first truths of liberty. . . . when he proscribes an entire class of the population, irrespective of intelligence or character, merely because of color and race, . . . he has fallen from a position which we can respect."[201] Disenchanted Republicans in northern Illinois allegedly schemed to replace Lincoln with Norman B. Judd as their senatorial candidate.

Democrats complained that Lincoln was two-faced on the slavery issue. Belying his radical talk was the bill he had planned to introduce in Congress nine years earlier, which contained a clause calling for the rendition of slaves fleeing to Washington. (In 1860, the radical abolitionist Wendell Phillips would criticize Lincoln on the same grounds.) Moreover, they argued plausibly, his statement at Charleston about black citizenship stood in marked contrast to the idealism of his Chicago speech.

In response to such criticism, the *National Anti-Slavery Standard* sensibly remarked that "a certain degree of anxiety to escape the odium of abolitionism is pardonable on the part of our Republican friends, especially in election times."[202]

Abolitionist Maria Chapman made a similar point to Lyman Trumbull, and Herndon told Theodore Parker: "Reformers must get so low—crawl along in the mud till a working majority *sticks*."[203]

Lincoln's rejoinder was in fact the turning point in the debate. Then he seemed to gain traction and to go on the offensive. In the next three debates he would best his opponent soundly.

Race

Other committed opponents of slavery, including congressmen, shared Lincoln's views on citizenship rights for blacks and expressed skepticism about racial equality. In 1859, Lincoln's old friend Joshua R. Giddings declared on the floor of the House: "We do not say the black man is, or shall be, the equal of the white man; or that he shall vote or hold office."[204] Eleven years earlier he had stated that slavery had been established because of "the physical and intellectual superiority of the whites over the colored race."[205] Although Congressman Owen Lovejoy hated slavery with a passion inspired by the murder of his abolitionist brother Elijah, he told a Chicago audience in 1860: "I know very well that the African race, as a race, is not equal to ours." He added that he also knew "that, in regard to the great overwhelming majority, the Government may be considered, in a certain sense, a Government for white men."[206] Lovejoy further insisted that the white and black races were not equal "in gracefulness of motion, or loveliness of feature; not in mental endowment, moral susceptibility, and emotional power; not socially equal; not of necessity politically equal."[207] In 1852, Horace Mann told the annual Convention of Freemen of Ohio: "The blacks as a race, I believe to be less aggressive and predatory than the whites, more forgiving, and *generally* not capable of the white man's tenacity and terribleness of revenge. In fine, I suppose the almost universal opinion to be, that in intellect the blacks are inferior to the whites."[208]

Antislavery senators shared these views. In 1860, William Henry Seward, one of the foremost opponents of the peculiar institution in the upper chamber, stated: "The great fact is now fully realized that the African race here is a foreign and feeble element like the Indians, incapable of assimilation" and "is a pitiful exotic unwisely and unnecessarily transplanted into our fields, and which it is unprofitable to cultivate at the cost of the desolation of the native vineyard."[209] Seward maintained that "the motive of those who have protested against the extension of slavery . . . always has . . . been, concern for the welfare of the white man," not "an unnatural sympathy with the negro."[210]

In 1859, another leading antislavery senator, Lyman Trumbull, voiced similar opinions: "When we say that all men are created equal, we do not mean that every man in organized society has the same rights. We do not tolerate that in Illinois. I know that there is a distinction between these two races because the Almighty himself has marked it upon their very faces; and, in my judgment, man cannot, by legislation or otherwise, produce a perfect equality between these two races, so that they will live happily together."[211] When asked if he would favor admitting Arizona as a state if it were "colonized and filled up with free colored people," Trumbull replied that he "did not believe these two races could live happily and pleasantly together, each enjoying equal rights, without one domineering over the other; therefore he advocated the policy of separating these races by adopting a system to rid the country of the black race, as it becomes free. He would say that he should not be prepared under the existing state of state of affairs to admit as a sovereign member of the Union, a community of negroes or Indians either."[212] In recommending that free blacks leave the country, he told Chicagoans: "I want to have nothing to do either with the free negro or the slave negro. We, the Republican party, are the white man's party. [Great applause.] . . . I would be glad to see this country relieved of them."[213]

Senator Henry Wilson of Massachusetts, another eminent opponent of slavery, told his colleagues during an 1860 debate on educating black children in the District of Columbia: "I do not believe in the equality of the African with the white race, mentally or physically, and I do not think morally."[214] "So far as mental or physical equality is concerned," Wilson said, "I believe the African race inferior to the white race."[215] "I have studied the negro character," declared one of Kentucky's foremost abolitionists, Cassius M. Clay. "They lack self reliance—we can make nothing out of them. God has made them for the sun and the banana!" Clay thought the country "must spew out the negro."[216] The New York *Tribune* asserted that it did not believe in "the *intellectual* equality of the Colored with the White man."[217] Similarly, a Republican campaigner in 1860 declared that his party was "not the nigger party. We are the white man's party. It's the Democrats who are the nigger party."[218] In September, Frank P. Blair, a leader of the antislavery forces in Missouri, told audiences in New York and Pennsylvania that the "Republican party is the white man's party, and will keep the Territories for white men."[219]

Although neither Lincoln nor Douglas was a racial egalitarian, they differed sharply on race. Lincoln let slip the term *nigger* far less often than his opponent, and when he did use the word, it was usually in a context suggesting that he was paraphrasing Democrats. Unlike Douglas, he never claimed that his party was the white man's party; he seldom argued that slavery should be contained primarily to preserve the territories for whites; he did not raise the race issue except in response to Douglas's race-baiting; and Lincoln's statements regarding black inferiority were much more guarded, mild, and tentative than Douglas's blatant assertions of white superiority.

The Mexican War Issue

Two days after the Charleston debate, Douglas virtually accused Lincoln of treason for his stand on the Mexican War:

"[D]uring the war, and after it was declared, and while the battles were being fought in Mexico, Lincoln took the side of the common enemy against his own country. He called Col. Ficklin forward on Saturday, as a witness about supplies, and drew him right up on the stand and said, 'come now, just tell them it is a lie.' 'Well, said Ficklin, I will tell them all I know about it. All I recollect is that you voted for Ashmun's resolutions declaring the war unconstitutional and unjust.' Lincoln replied, 'That is true, I did.' [Cries of "that's so."] Thus he acknowledged that he voted for a resolution declaring the Mexican war unconstitutional and unjust. [A voice—"That's enough; when did he do that?"] He did it after the war had begun, after the battles of Palo Alto, Resaca de la Palma, Monterey and Buena Vista had been fought. He did it when our army was in Mexico, ten thousand men combating an enemy 180,000 strong.—He did it at the time when the American army was in great peril of being destroyed. The enemy took that and other votes and Corwin's speech and published it in pamphlet form in Mexico, and distributed it all over the army to show that there was a Mexican party in America, hence if the army could stand out a little longer, if the guerrillas would keep murdering our soldiers, or poisoning them a little longer, the Mexican party in America would get the control and decide all questions in favor of Mexico. [A voice, "My God! That is worse than his abolitionism."] I say that his vote was sent to Mexico and circulated there at the head of the Mexican army as an evidence of the influence of the Mexicans in the American congress. [A voice—"I was there and saw it."] You may appeal to every soldier that was there for the truth of what I say, and I add that vote.—This record made by Lincoln and others and sent to Mexico to be circulated there, did more harm than the withholding of thousands of loads of supplies."[220]

At that point, Lincoln's friends, en route to their meeting, came by with their band and distracted Douglas's crowd. (Unaware that the senator had scheduled a speech for September 20 at Sullivan, Lincoln arranged to speak there that day. When he learned of the conflict, he told Douglas he would not attend his event and would postpone his own speech so as not to conflict with that of the Little Giant.) Indignant Democrats attacked the musicians, and blows were exchanged. Douglas charged that it "was a deliberate attempt on the part of his [Lincoln's] friends to break up a democratic meeting. It was started at the very time when I was making a point upon Mr. Lincoln, from which all of his friends shrunk in despair, and it was begun suddenly, in order to break off the chain of my argument. It was evidently a preconcerted plan and therefore I say that I am warranted under this state of facts in charging that Mr. Lincoln, as well as his friends, have been a party this day to break up this meeting, in order to prevent me from exposing his alliance with the abolitionists, and repelling the false charges which he made against me at Charleston, and to which I had no opportunity to reply at that place."[221] Republicans countered that Douglas's followers had been the aggressors, attacking their procession at the behest of the Little Giant.

At Springfield on October 20, Douglas repeated his charge about Lincoln's opposition to the Mexican War, alleging that his vote on the Ashmun resolution, along with the text of that document and Thomas Corwin's anti-war speech, "were all sent to Mexico and printed in the Mexican language, and read at the head of the Mexican army, to prove to them that there was Mexican party in the congress of the United States. . . . Lincoln's vote and Corwin's speech did more to encourage the Mexicans and the Mexican army than all of the soldiers that were brought into the field; they induced the Mexicans to hold out the longer, and the guerrillas to keep up their warfare on the roadside, and to poison our men, and to take the lives of our soldiers wherever and whenever they could."[222]

In the three weeks between the Charleston debate and the next one at Galesburg in early October, Lincoln spoke at Danville, Urbana, Jacksonville, Winchester, Pittsfield, Metamora, Pekin and Sullivan. In Jacksonville he encountered the president of Illinois College, Julian Sturtevant, who solicitously observed: "you must be having a weary time." Lincoln replied: "I am, and if it were not for one thing I would retire from the contest. I know that if Mr. Douglas' doctrine prevails it will not be fifteen years before Illinois itself will be a slave state."[223]

Lincoln, though tired, was not discouraged. In Danville, he attracted a huge, enthusiastic crowd under a banner proclaiming: "Free territory for white men."[224] A local newspaper described him unflatteringly as having "a sand-hill crane like body, surmounted by head which looks like a starved canvassed ham." But it acknowledged that he "talked away at least fifty percent of his ugliness" with "clear articulation" in a voice "shrill, and not a little harsh." The audience "seemed to be convinced, not charmed or captivated."[225] From that town Lincoln reported on September 23: "We had a fine and altogether satisfactory meeting here yesterday. . . . I believe we have got the gentleman [Douglas], unless they overcome us by fraudulent voting."[226]

Texts of Lincoln's speeches delivered between the Charleston and Galesburg debates have not survived, but notes evidently written at that time reveal what he may have said. In those jottings, he emphasized the danger that the moral indifference of Douglas and his allies posed to whites. Citing not only the Little Giant's speeches during the campaign but also editorials in the Richmond *Enquirer* and the New York *Day Book,* both of which endorsed the idea of white slavery, and the assertion by Senator John Pettit of Indiana that the Declaration of Independence was "a self-evident lie," Lincoln concluded that they were all "laboring at a common object," namely, "to deny the equality of men, and to assert the natural, moral, and religious right of one class to enslave another." Acknowledging that Douglas "does not draw the conclusion that the superiors ought to enslave the inferiors, he evidently wishes his hearers to draw that conclusion. He shirks the responsibility of pulling the house down, but he digs under it that it may fall of its own weight."[227]

In October, Douglas repeatedly accused Lincoln of favoring the interests of the unpopular Illinois Central Railroad over those of the people. Three months earlier, Henry C. Whitney had urged Lincoln to "turn the hatred of the people to the I. C. R. Rd. against Douglas," but Lincoln never did.[228] The senator understood the advantage of making his opponent appear a tool of the Illinois Central, which the previous year had gone into receivership and then foreclosed on 4,000 mortgages; it was also asking to be relieved of its tax obligation to the state. After denying that he had ever worked as an attorney for the company or recommended that it be exempted from state taxation, Douglas suggested that his listeners pose questions to the challenger: "Ask him whether he did not hire out to the Company, to make a good bargain for the Company, against the State; and ask him how much money he got for having induced the Legislature to reduce the per centage from fifteen to seven per cent; and then ask him whether he is not to-day in the pay of that Company, and whether he is not now living and getting his bread from that Company." He implied that Lincoln favored eliminating the 7 percent tax; and denounced anyone who favored such a step "as an enemy to the State of Illinois—as a traitor to her best interests."

The Little Giant further declared that, in the late 1840s, he had persuaded the senate to grant land to the state of Illinois, not directly to the Illinois Central, for promoting the growth of the rail network. But the House of Representatives, in which Lincoln then sat, defeated the measure. "We tried it over and again got beaten," he recalled, "and we never could pass that bill as long as Lincoln was there. Lincoln was then regarded as an abolitionist, making war upon the south, as a sectional man." He further implied that Lincoln was one of the lobbyists for the Illinois Central who managed to get the tax rate set at 7 percent, below what Douglas thought fair, and attacked Lincoln for receiving a $5,000 fee as payment for representing the company in the suit brought by McLean County, money that would be used "toward defraying his campaign expenses." Douglas added, "notwithstanding the enormous fee that Lincoln was paid, he is still the agent and attorney of that company. . . . I applied to the company not three weeks ago and ascertained that he is now in their employ-ment." Indignantly, he protested that "Lincoln and his friends might as well charge me with a conspiracy to murder my own children as to deprive the state of that [seven percent tax] fund."[229]

Lincoln, who had never charged Douglas with any impropriety involving the Illi-nois Central, denied supporting the elimination of the tax on that company, explained how he and Herndon won their large fee in the McLean County tax case, protested against the implication that he had "received any of the people's money" or was "on very cozy terms with the Railroad company," and urged his audience to ask candidates for the state legislature how they stood on taxing the Illinois Central.[230]

Douglas also alleged that Lincoln was on cozy terms with the pro-Buchanan Democrats: "He has control of that body of men who are active as the agents of Presidential aspirants in other States, and through patronage are trying to destroy the Democracy in this State. Lincoln knows that these men are all his allies, all his sup-porters and his only hope, and the only hope of the Republican party is in that unholy and unnatural alliance with these Federal officeholders, to break me down." Lincoln was thus part of "a combination for selfish and unworthy and malicious purposes to hunt me down."[231] This was an effective tactic, for, as a Philadelphia paper observed, the "negative strength of the Administration . . . is virtually with Lincoln, being bit-terly directed against Douglas, and instructed to defeat him, no matter who else may be elected. This is the hardest load Lincoln has to carry, for the suspicion of even in-direct and undesired aid from that quarter, is damaging."[232]

When Douglas charged that the Republicans had formed an "unholy alliance" with the Danites (i.e., pro-Buchanan forces), Lincoln disavowed "any contact with either wing of the Democratic party."[233] He did readily own that he was not cha-grined to see factions of the Democracy fighting each other. He jocularly alluded to a well-known story about a disenchanted wife observing her spouse wrestle with a bear; "Go it husband!—Go it, bear!" she exclaimed.[234] According to Herndon, Lincoln paid little attention to the seamier side of the campaign. But he was kept informed of the anti-Douglas Democrats' efforts. In early July, a Danite leader informed him that the National Democracy planned "to run in every County and District a National Democrat for each and every office," prompting Lincoln to remark, "If you do this the thing is settled—the battle is fought."[235] He may also have subsidized a Danite newspaper, the Springfield *State Democrat,* edited by James A. Clarkson. In September, Clarkson said that he "expected $500 of Mr. Lincoln in a day or two."[236]

Fifth Debate: Galesburg

On October 7, the fifth debate was held at Galesburg, a Republican town 175 miles southwest of Chicago. It drew the biggest crowd of the series, exceeding the turnout at Ottawa and Freeport by 2,000 or 3,000 and far outnumbering the 5,500 residents of the town. Abolitionism flourished at Knox College, where the debate took place on a platform adjacent to Old Main, the largest structure on campus. (To reach that platform, speakers and dignitaries had to enter the building, walk down a corridor, and then step through a window. After Lincoln did so, he quipped: "At last I have gone through . . . college.")[237] Although the sun was shining, cold temperatures and high winds made for a disagreeable day. Many banners were blown down, including one that proclaimed "Small-fisted Farmers, Mud Sills of Society, Greasy Mechanics, for A. Lincoln."[238] This banner alluded to a statement South Carolina Senator James H. Hammond had made about slaves the previous year: "In all social systems there must be a class to do the mean duties, to perform the drudgery of life. . . . It constitutes the very mud-sills of society."[239]

Because of a hoarse throat, Douglas had trouble projecting his rough voice and struggled to be heard in the wind. At Onarga on September 24 and at Kankakee the following day, he announced that he was suffering from a cold. A week later at Oquawka, he had trouble articulating words and sounded like a man with a swollen tongue. He referred to his opponent as "Misha Linka."[240]

Douglas opened the debate at Galesburg complaining about the Buchanan administration's efforts to defeat him through an "unholy and unnatural" alliance with the Republicans. Contemptuously he remarked that Lincoln had "no hope on earth," and "would never dream that he had a chance of success but for the aid that he is receiving from federal officers," who were acting "against me in revenge for my having defeated the Lecompton Constitution." In denouncing the Republican Party for its sectionalism, he asked: "What Republican from Massachusetts can visit the Old Dominion without leaving his principles behind him when he crosses Mason and Dixon's line?" Instead of criticizing the South for its intolerance, he blamed Northerners for holding views that Southerners disliked. (Earlier he had asserted that the "whole stock in trade of our opponents is an appeal to northern prejudice, northern interest and northern ambition against the southern states, southern people and southern rights.")[241]

Douglas asserted with some justification that Lincoln's speech in Chicago was far different from his opening statement at Charleston. He taunted the Republicans for using different names in different parts of the state; in southern and central Illinois they called themselves "Lincoln men" and the "Free Democracy" instead of using the more radical term, Republican. (An editor in Pekin had informed Lincoln, "You are stronger here than Republicanism and in all of our meetings instead of heading them 'Republican' I shall say 'Meeting of the friends of Lincoln.'" Thus "we can gain some thing from the old whigs, who may be wavering, and soften down the prejudices of others.")[242] Pointing out that the author and many of the signers of the Declaration of Independence owned slaves, Douglas asked how it could be inferred that they meant to include blacks in the proposition that "all men are created equal."[243]

Lincoln replied that Thomas Jefferson, though a slaveholder, had said that "he trembled for his country when he remembered that God was just." He challenged Douglas to "show that he, in all his life, ever uttered a sentiment at all akin to that of Jefferson." He also noted that no signers of the Declaration of Independence ever alleged that blacks were excluded from that document's statement that "all men are created equal."

In dealing with the charge that he spoke out of both sides of his mouth on the race issue, Lincoln ridiculed Douglas's logic: "[T]he Judge will have it that if we do not confess that there is a sort of inequality between the white and black races, which justifies us in making them slaves, we must, then, insist that there is a degree of equality that requires us to make them our wives." Lincoln reiterated that he would not interfere with slavery where it already existed, but "I have insisted that, in legislating for new countries, where it does not exist, there is no just rule other than that of moral and abstract right!" In the territories, he said, no one should be denied the right "to life, liberty, and the pursuit of happiness."

If the Republicans' inability to preach their doctrines in the South indicated that those doctrines were unsound, then would democracy itself be considered unsound because Douglas could not espouse it in Russia? "Is it the true test of the soundness of a doctrine, that in some places people won't let you proclaim it?" Was popular sovereignty unsound because Douglas had been unable defend it before a hostile crowd at Chicago in 1854? He challenged the Little Giant to discuss the state platform adopted by Republicans in 1858 rather than the county platforms of 1854.

The central issue dividing the parties, Lincoln maintained, was the morality of slavery. Douglas and his friends denied "that there is any wrong in slavery." The Republicans disagreed. "I confess myself as belonging to that class in the country who contemplate slavery as a moral, social, and political evil" and who "desire a policy that looks to the prevention of it as a wrong, and looks hopefully to the time when as a wrong it may come to an end."

As for the purported alliance between the Republican and the pro-Buchanan Democrats, Lincoln acknowledged that he had "no objection to the division in the Judge's party." Republicans viewed the internecine warfare among the Democrats the same way that Democrats had regarded the split between Frémont and Fillmore supporters in 1856.

Heatedly Lincoln attacked Douglas for the "fraud" and "absolute forgery" that he had introduced at the Ottawa debate. A month earlier the Little Giant had promised to look into the matter when next in the capital, but he had yet to issue any explanation of how the Aurora Republican platform was palmed off as the work of the Springfield anti-Nebraska conclave of 1854. In that year, both Douglas and Thomas

L. Harris used the Aurora document to discredit their opponents and then blamed the mistake on the editor of the Springfield *Register*, Charles Lanphier, who would not explain how his paper made the error. (Lanphier's paper had run a garbled version of Lincoln's 1857 speech on the Dred Scott case.) Since the *Register* had reported accurately most of the proceedings of the anti-Nebraskaites at Springfield, it was "absurd" to say that the substitution of the Aurora platform for the Springfield platform "was done by mistake." Clearly, Lanphier was responsible, but was he put up to it by Douglas or Harris, or both of them, who were in Springfield at the time of the anti-Nebraska meeting? The stratagem had worked in 1854, helping to defeat Congressman Richard Yates's bid for reelection; Harris revived it in 1856 to attack Congressman Jesse O. Norton, and Douglas made use of it to assail Lyman Trumbull; at Ottawa it was trotted out yet again to discredit Lincoln. The recycling of the original fraud reminded Lincoln of "the fisherman's wife, whose drowned husband was brought home with his body full of eels." When asked what to do with the corpse, she replied: "*Take the eels out and set him again.*" In the absence of an explanation from Douglas, Lincoln inferred that blame for the fraud could be equally divided among the Little Giant, Lanphier, and Harris.

Lincoln repeated his interrogatory about a second Dred Scott case forbidding states to outlaw slavery. Douglas, Lincoln said, had not answered the question but merely sneered at him for asking it. Citing the language of the majority opinion in *Dred Scott vs. Sandford*—"The right of property in a slave is distinctly and expressly affirmed in the Constitution"—Lincoln asked cogently why the court might not eventually rule that the supremacy clause of the Constitution would forbid Free States to continue making slavery illegal.

Lincoln empathically disagreed with Douglas that the Constitution recognized the right of property in slaves. He offered as "the opinion of one very humble man" his belief that the Dred Scott decision would not have been handed down if the Democrats had not won the presidential election of 1856. He felt that if that party retained its hold on the White House, a second Dred Scott decision was likely to follow. Paving the way for the new Dred Scott decision was Douglas's insistence that he "don't care whether Slavery is voted up or voted down," that "whoever wants Slavery has a right to have it," that "upon principles of equality it should be allowed to go everywhere," that "there is no inconsistency between free and slave institutions." Abandoning the conspiracy theory that he had put forward in his "House Divided" speech, Lincoln did not allege that Douglas was deliberately "preparing the way for making the institution of Slavery national," but insisted that the senator's actions had that effect even if he did not intend it. This represented a sensible modification of his earlier charge. The Little Giant's amoral neutrality on slavery "is penetrating the human soul, and eradicating the light of reason and the love of liberty."

Lincoln deplored Douglas's indifference to the status of slavery in newly acquired territory. "If Judge Douglas' policy upon this question succeeds, . . . the next thing will be a grab for the territory of poor Mexico, an invasion of the rich lands of South America, then the adjoining islands will follow, each one of which promises additional slave-fields." Since the struggle over slavery alone presented a threat to the

Union, Lincoln counseled that it would be unwise to acquire new territory that might intensify that struggle.[244]

When Douglas rose to reply, he seemed agitated as he paced the platform, shaking his fist in anger. He huffily dismissed Lincoln's charge of conspiracy against himself, Harris, and Lanphier. Approaching his rival, Douglas said: "I did not believe that there was an honest man in the State of Illinois who did not believe that it was an error I was led into innocently. . . . I do not believe that there is an honest man in the face of this State that don't abhor with disgust his insinuations of my complicity with that forgery, as he calls it." Brazenly, he maintained that the Aurora Republican platform of 1854 reflected the party's ideology throughout the state in 1858 (an assertion which was demonstrably untrue). With great vehemence he denounced Lincoln's stand on the Dred Scott decision and the finality of the Supreme Court's rulings.[245]

Even though the Chicago *Times* stated that "Lincoln limps, equivocates, and denies," Republicans were jubilant.[246] The *Illinois State Journal* noted that whereas Douglas at the beginning of the debate cycle had "entered upon the discussion with a grand flourish of trumpets from his followers, and from the name he has managed to acquire, they expected to see him literally 'swallow his adversary whole'," by the close of the Galesburg debate "what is their surprise and mortification to see him badly worsted at every encounter he undertakes with 'Old Abe.'"[247]

From afar, however, the debates began to appear excessively partisan. The New York *Herald* judged that the "controversy in Illinois between Douglas and Lincoln, on Kansas, the Kansas-Nebraska bill, Lecompton, popular sovereignty, Dred Scott, the Declaration of Independence, States rights and niggers in every style" had "degenerated into the merest twaddle upon quibbles, 'forgeries,' falsehoods, and mutual recriminations of the most vulgar sort."[248] The *Missouri Democrat* lamented that "the canvass has turned so much on personal issues" and blamed Douglas for that development. The Cincinnati *Commercial* leveled similar criticism, calling the antagonists "a pair of unscrupulous office-seekers" and "political pettifoggers" who "have insulted the people of Illinois and of the country, by the daily utterance . . . of the most transparent fallacies and the most vulgar personalities." That newspaper found "very little . . . that merits much attention, or that can be esteemed as of interest to the public, or calculated to add to the reputation of the parties. Few debates less dignified in their external manifestations, or containing so little that was worthy to be remembered, have fallen under our observation. . . . Falsehood and personal vituperation are among the most common of the offenses committed, upon one side at least, if not upon both."[249]

The *Commercial* was doubtless alluding to Douglas's tactics, for Lincoln had taken the moral high ground at Galesburg. Horace White thought Lincoln's speech there "the best of the series."[250] Indeed, it represented a considerable advance over the earlier debates in which the challenger had tended to stress his opposition to black citizenship and to accuse Douglas of conspiring to nationalize slavery. As he had done earlier at Lewistown and Edwardsville, Lincoln de-emphasized legal and historical arguments, which often involved logic-chopping and hair-splitting, in favor of broad moral appeals, which he would make even more eloquently in the final two debates.

Earlier he had often acted as if he were in court, scoring points before a jury and trying to win the specific trial of the moment; now he shed the role of lawyer for that of statesman and consistently spoke to the conscience and heart of his audience.

All the while Lincoln eschewed personal attacks. In late September a correspondent of the *Missouri Democrat* accurately noted that Lincoln "treats his opponent with a deference which the latter is incapable of reciprocating." More "than any other public man of the present time," Lincoln "infuses the milk of human kindness, and the frankness and courtesy of a gentleman of the old school into his discussions." Whereas he "says nothing calculated to wound the feelings of Douglas," the Little Giant "deals in exaggerated statements, glaring sophistries, and coarse, fierce declamation. Douglas has cast his fortunes on a sentiment—the antipathy of the white to the black race. . . . Whatever incidental topics he may treat, it will be found that the substance of his speeches in this canvass is an invocation of prejudice." Lincoln avoided "exaggeration or vindictiveness" and "acerbity of temper," while his opponent "has fallen into an impotent passion several times."[251]

Sixth Debate: Quincy

Less than a week after the Galesburg event, the candidates clashed again at Quincy, a Democratic stronghold where Douglas had lived for a time. On the train carrying him there, Lincoln shook hands with his fellow passengers, including Carl Schurz, a prominent German Republican orator. The challenger received Schurz "with an off-hand cordiality, like an old acquaintance." Schurz recalled that Lincoln "talked in so simple and familiar a strain, and his manner and homely phrase were so absolutely free from any semblance of self-consciousness or pretension to superiority, that I soon felt as if I had known him all my life and we had long been close friends."[252]

The crowd at Quincy was smaller than the one at Galesburg, though still large. The event began inauspiciously when the railing of the speakers' platform gave way, sending a dozen people crashing to the ground. Once order was restored, Lincoln delivered the opening speech. He showed no signs of fatigue but rather seemed energized by his extensive campaigning. Douglas, on the other hand, appeared tired. A reporter noted that "[b]ad whisky and the wear and tear of conscience have had their effect" on the Little Giant.[253]

Before getting to the heart of the dispute between the parties, Lincoln addressed Douglas's complaint about the use of "hard names" such as "forgery," "fraud," and "conspiracy." He insisted that the Little Giant had been the first to engage in personalities, starting at Bloomington in July, continuing at Ottawa in August, and at Galesburg in October. On those occasions Douglas had impeached his "veracity and candor." Therefore, Lincoln said, he had been forced to respond in kind, but he would abandon that tactic if Douglas would do the same. In response to the Little Giant's question as to whether he wished to "push this matter to the point of personal difficulty," Lincoln said no. The senator, he asserted, "did not make a mistake, in one of his early speeches, when he called me an 'amiable' man, though perhaps he did when he called me an 'intelligent' man. It really hurts me very much to suppose that I have wronged anybody on earth. I again tell him, no! I very much prefer, when this canvass shall be over, however it may result, that we at least part without any bitter recollections of personal difficulties."

At Galesburg, Douglas had charged that Lincoln was trying "to divert the public attention from the enormity of his revolutionary principles by getting into personal quarrels, impeaching my sincerity and integrity." In rebuttal, Lincoln repeated his understanding of the fundamental difference between the two parties, which, "reduced to its lowest terms, is no other than the difference between the men who think slavery a wrong and those who do not think it wrong. The Republican party think it wrong—we think it is a moral, a social and a political wrong." Yet, "in all the arguments sustaining the Democratic policy, and in that policy itself, there is a careful, studied exclusion of the idea that there is anything wrong in slavery." Douglas, said Lincoln, "has the high distinction, so far as I know, of never having said slavery is either right or wrong." Addressing Democrats, he asked: "You say it [slavery] is wrong; but don't you constantly object to anybody else saying so? Do you not constantly argue that this is not the right place to oppose it? You say it must not be opposed in the free States, because slavery is not there; it must not be opposed in the slave States, because it is there; it must not be opposed in politics, because that will make a fuss; it must not be opposed in the pulpit, because it is not religion. [Loud cheers.] Then where is the place to oppose it? There is no suitable place to oppose it. There is no place in the country to oppose this evil overspreading the continent, which you say yourself is coming."[254]

Stepping forward to respond, the weary Douglas managed to radiate supreme confidence. His haughty, contemptuous mien seemed to ask, "How dare anyone stand up against me?" Though his gestures were defiant, his hoarse voice was weak, carrying but a short distance. He spoke quite slowly, pausing after each word. Schurz recalled that his "sentences were well put together, his points strongly accentuated, his argumentation seemingly clear and plausible, his sophisms skillfully woven so as to throw the desired flood of darkness upon the subject and thus beguile the untutored mind, his appeals to prejudice unprincipled and reckless, but shrewdly aimed, and his invective vigorous and exceedingly trying to the temper of the assailed party."[255]

The Chicago *Times* reported that Lincoln behaved in a "most improper and ungentlemanly" fashion during Douglas's remarks. Sitting where his opponent could not see him, Lincoln would, "whenever a point was made against him," rudely "shake his head at the crowd, intimating that it was not true, and that they should place no reliance on what was said. This course was in direct violation of the rules of the debate, and was a mean trick, beneath the dignity of a man of honor."[256]

Curiously, Douglas devoted much of his rebuttal to a defense against charges leveled by the Buchanan administration's organ, the Washington *Union*. He also continued to attack Lincoln personally. Repeating his lame explanation of the Ottawa forgery, he insisted that Lincoln was a "slanderer" and denied the conspiracy charge yet again. Boastfully and insultingly, he compared himself to Lincoln: "[W]hen I make a mistake I correct it without being asked, as an honest man is bound to. When he makes a false charge, he sticks to it and never corrects it." Douglas again contrasted Lincoln's opening statement at Charleston ("I am not nor ever have been in favor of bringing about in any way, the social and political equality of the white and black races") and the conclusion of his Chicago speech ("let us discard all this quibbling about this man and the other man—this race and that race and the other race being inferior"). Addressing Lincoln's analysis of the Dred Scott decision, the Little Giant grew reminiscent: "When I used to practice law with Lincoln, I never knew him to get beat in a case in the world, that he did not get mad at the Judge and talk about appealing it (laughter). And when I got beat in the case, I generally thought the Court was wrong; but I never dreamed of going out of the court house and making a stump speech to the people against the Judges, merely because I found out that I didn't know the law as well as they did. (Great laughter.)" Touting popular sovereignty, Douglas declared that "it don't become Mr. Lincoln, or anybody else, to tell the people of Kentucky that they have no consciences—to tell them that they are living in a state of iniquity—to tell them that they are cherishing the institution to their bosom, in violation of the law of God. Better for him to adopt the doctrine of 'Judge not, lest ye be judged.'" Rather than caring about blacks, Douglas counseled Lincoln and other antislavery proponents to focus on "our own poor, and our own suffering, . . . before we go abroad to intermeddle with other people's business." Besides, he argued, Northerners "know nothing" of the condition of slaves.

The Little Giant denounced as inhumane Lincoln's plan to contain slavery. If the peculiar institution were bottled up in the states where it already existed, then "the natural increase will go on until the increase will be so plenty that they [the slaves] cannot live on the soil. He will hem them in until starvation awaits them. Thus he would "put slavery in the course of ultimate extinction." Although this argument was specious, Douglas did raise a question here on which Lincoln was vulnerable: just how would the containment of slavery necessarily lead to its demise? To be sure, if more Free States were admitted to the Union, the Slave States' power in Congress and the electoral college would wane, but the slave states would long be able to block a constitutional amendment abolishing the peculiar institution.[257]

With justice an auditor recalled that "Douglas was the demagogue all the way through. There was no trick of presentation that he did not use. He suppressed facts, twisted conclusions, and perverted history. He wriggled and turned and dodged; he appealed to prejudices."[258]

In his rejoinder, Lincoln ridiculed popular sovereignty as "*do nothing sovereignty*" and asked apropos of the Freeport Doctrine: "Has it not got down as thin as the homoeopathic soup that was made by boiling the shadow of a pigeon that had starved to death? [Roars of laughter and cheering.]" It was one of his more telling metaphors.

As for Douglas's complaint that Lincoln would not utter in downstate Illinois what he said in Chicago, the challenger cited his address on the Dred Scott case, delivered in Springfield the previous year, which contained "the substance of the Chicago speech." He once again protested against Douglas's contention that if people believed that blacks were incorporated in the statement that "all men are created equal" in the Declaration of Independence, they must therefore support racial intermarriage. "He can never be brought to understand that there is any middle ground on this subject. I have lived until my fiftieth year, and have never had a negro woman either for a slave or a wife, and I think I can live fifty centuries, for that matter, without having had one for either."

Lincoln disputed Douglas's boast that he had voluntarily come forward when he discovered the Ottawa forgery. In fact, Lincoln argued, it was only after the Republican press had exposed the fraud that Douglas acknowledged his error, an acknowledgment that he now sought to make a virtue, though the newspapers had made it a necessity.[259]

In Lincoln's speech, Carl Schurz detected flashes of "lofty moral inspiration; and all he said came out with the sympathetic persuasiveness of a thoroughly honest nature, which made the listener feel as if the speaker looked him straight in the eye and took him by the hand, saying: 'My friend, what I tell you is my earnest conviction, and, I have no doubt, at heart you think so yourself.'"[260]

The *Illinois State Journal* regarded the Quincy debate "as the most damaging to Douglas in the series. Lincoln carried the war into Africa, and came off with flying colors."[261] Many Iowans crossed the Mississippi River to hear the debate and returned favorably impressed with Lincoln. The Chicago *Times,* however, called Lincoln's effort "the lamest and most impotent attempt he has yet made to bolster up the false position he took at the outset of the fight."[262]

After the debate, Lincoln met at a hotel with the humorist David R. Locke, creator of the comic character Petroleum V. Nasby. Explaining that "I like to give my feet a chance to breathe," the candidate removed his boots. He said of a recently deceased Illinois politician, "If General _____ had known how big a funeral he would have had, he would have died years ago." Lincoln predicted that the Republicans would carry the state but that Douglas would retain his senate seat. "You can't overturn a pyramid," he said, "but you can undermine it; that's what I have been trying to do."[263]

Seventh Debate: Alton

Two days later the final debate took place at Alton, a sluggish town on the Mississippi River 25 miles north of St. Louis, where Lincoln and James Shields had once met for a duel and where a proslavery mob had killed Elijah Lovejoy. On the morning of the debate, Lincoln suggested to Gustave Koerner that they pay their respects to Mrs. Lincoln, who was attending a debate for the first time. As he introduced Koerner to his wife, Lincoln said: "Now, tell Mary what you think of our chances! She is rather dispirited." Koerner gave an optimistic prognostication, which was not shared by Lincoln, who seemed "a little despondent."[264]

Others also grew pessimistic as the election day approached. Salmon P. Chase reported from northern Illinois that it was not "certain that Lincoln will be elected: as it is possible that the Senate may be held by the Dems. & the House by the Republicans." If that were the case, the Senate Democrats could block Lincoln's election by refusing to go into joint session with the House Republicans.[265]

The Alton crowd of approximately 5,000 was smaller than usual because of the complacency of the population; because both men had spoken in that county earlier in the campaign; and because few believed that anything new would be said. The event was subdued, generating so little excitement that there was no procession.

When Douglas began his address, his bloated face, haggard appearance, and hoarse, barely audible voice shocked some auditors. He seemed exhausted and in a sour temper. At the outset, he lost his composure when Dr. Thomas M. Hope, a Buchanan Democrat and the editor of the Alton *Democratic Union,* asked him if territorial legislatures should pass laws protecting slavery. In reply, the enraged senator said "in a most violent manner if he [Hope] wished to help Republicans beat Democrats he could do so."[266] After brushing off Dr. Hope, the Little Giant, in addition to rehearsing earlier arguments, roasted President Buchanan. Douglas proudly declared that even though the Chief Executive had dismissed many of the senator's friends from their government posts, he "can never get me to abandon one iota of Democracy out of revenge or personal hostility to his course."[267]

Lincoln replied to Douglas in a clear, steady voice which showed no signs of wear and tear. One observer recalled that he spoke slowly and seemed "awkward and diffident" at first, but that, as he so often did, he warmed up until "his voice rang out in clearness, rose in strength, his tall form towered to its full height, and there came an outburst of inspiring eloquence and argument."[268] He finally got around to declaring "untrue" the Little Giant's repeated allegation that his primary objection to the Dred Scott decision was its denial of black citizenship rights. "I have done no such thing; and Judge Douglas' so persistently insisting that I have done so, has strongly impressed me with the belief of a predetermination on his part to misrepresent me." Emphatically he denounced Douglas's assertion that in 1855 nobody thought that blacks were included in the Declaration of Independence's statement that "all men were created equal." Lincoln said, "*I combat it* as having an evil tendency, if not an evil design. I combat it as having a tendency to dehumanize the negro, to take away from him the right of ever striving to be a man. I combat it as being one of the thousand things constantly done in these days to prepare the public mind to make property, and nothing but property, of the *negro in all the States of this Union.*"

To support his position, Lincoln quoted to the traditionally Whig crowd a passage from Henry Clay's reply to an abolitionist in 1842. The Great Compromiser had said of slavery: "I look upon it as a great evil, and deeply lament that we have derived it from the parental government, and from our ancestors. I wish every slave in the United States was in the country of his ancestors. But here they are, and the question is, how they can be best dealt with? If a state of nature existed, and we were about to lay the foundations of society, no man would be more strongly opposed than I should be, to incorporate the institution of slavery among its elements."[269]

With passionate eloquence, Lincoln effectively challenged Douglas's claims to statesmanship. The agitation over slavery expansion, he argued, could not be attributed to politicians' selfish desire for power; it had, after all, divided the largest Protestant churches (Methodist, Baptist, Presbyterian) into northern and southern wings, as well as the American Tract Society and, in Alton, the Unitarian church. Douglas urged people to stop talking about the slavery issue and to allow settlers in the territories decide the matter. "But where is the philosophy or statesmanship which assumes that you can quiet that disturbing element in our society which has disturbed us for more than half a century, which has been the only serious danger that has threatened our institutions . . . ? Is it not a false statesmanship that undertakes to build up a system of policy upon the basis of caring nothing about *the very thing that every body does care the most about?*—a thing which all experience has shown we care a very great deal about?" They were good questions.

Setting aside the moral aspect of the slavery controversy, Lincoln asserted that "I am still in favor of our new Territories being in such a condition that white men may find a home—may find some spot where they can better their condition; where they can settle upon new soil and better their condition in life. I am in favor of this, not merely . . . for our own people who are born amongst us, but as an outlet for *free white people everywhere,* the world over—in which Hans, and Baptiste, and Patrick, and all other men from all the world, may find new homes and better their conditions in life."

After this pragmatic point, Lincoln stressed the moral dimension of the antislavery cause in the most eloquent language of the campaign. He first dismissed accusations that he wanted "to make war between the free and slave States" or that he favored "introducing a perfect social and political equality between the white and black races." Those he considered "false issues" that Douglas had invented. "The real issue in this controversy—the one pressing upon every mind—is the sentiment on the part of one class that looks upon the institution of slavery as a wrong, and of another class that does not look upon it as a wrong. The sentiment that contemplates the institution of slavery in this country as a wrong is the sentiment of the Republican party. It is the sentiment around which all their actions, all their arguments, circle, from which all their propositions radiate. They look upon it as being a moral, social and political wrong; and while they contemplate it as such, they nevertheless have due regard for its actual existence among us, and the difficulties of getting rid of it in any satisfactory way and to all the constitutional obligations thrown about it." Yet the Republicans "insist that it should, as far as may be, *be treated* as a wrong, and one of the methods of treating it as a wrong is to *make provision that it shall grow no larger.* [Loud applause.]" Lincoln repeated an earlier injunction: "if there be a man amongst us who does not think that the institution of slavery is wrong in any one of these aspects of which I have spoken, he is misplaced, and ought not to be with us. And if there be a man amongst us who is so impatient of it as a wrong as to disregard its actual presence among us and the difficulty of getting rid of it suddenly in a satisfactory way, and to disregard the constitutional obligations thrown about it, that man is misplaced if he is on our platform."

The Democratic Party, by contrast, contains "all who positively assert that it [slavery] is right, and all who, like Judge Douglas, treat it as indifferent and do not say it is either right or wrong." The morality of slavery was the crux of the matter. Passionately he continued: "That is the real issue. That is the issue that will continue in this country when these poor tongues of Judge Douglas and myself shall be silent. It is the eternal struggle between these two principles—right and wrong—throughout the world. They are the two principles that have stood face to face from the beginning of time, and will ever continue to struggle. The one is the common right of humanity, and the other the 'divine right of kings.' It is the same principle in whatever shape it develops itself. It is the same spirit that says, 'You work and toil and earn bread, and I'll eat it.' [Loud applause.] No matter in what shape it comes, whether from the mouth of a king who seeks to bestride the people of his own nation and live by the fruit of their labor, or from one race of men as an apology for enslaving another race, it is the same tyrannical principle." (An auditor noted that the "melting pathos with which Mr. Lincoln said this and its effect on his audience cannot be described.")[270]

Optimistically Lincoln predicted that once the public became fully aware of this fundamental difference between the parties, and the opponents of slavery united, then "there will soon be an end" of the controversy, and that end will be the "ultimate extinction" of slavery. "Whenever the issue can be distinctly made, and all extraneous matter thrown out so that men can fairly see the real difference between the parties, this controversy will soon be settled, and it will be done peaceably too. There will be no war, no violence."

With unwonted heat, Lincoln denounced the Freeport Doctrine as "a *monstrous* sort of talk about the Constitution of the United States! [Great applause.] *There has never been as outlandish or lawless a doctrine from the mouth of any respectable man on earth.*" Logically, the notion that the people of a territory could in effect overrule the Supreme Court by "unfriendly legislation" was no different from the argument that the people of a state could effectively overrule the Fugitive Slave Act. Thus, Lincoln argued, "there is not such an Abolitionist in the nation as Douglas, after all. [Loud and enthusiastic applause.]"[271]

Douglas concluded the debates by once again attacking Lincoln's stand on the Mexican War. Replying to Lincoln's charge that the senator wanted slavery to continue indefinitely, Douglas declared: "I look forward to the time when each State shall be allowed to do as it pleases. If it chooses to keep slavery forever, it is its business, not ours. If it chooses to abolish [slavery,] very good, it is its business and not mine. I care more for the great principle of self-government—the right of the people to rule themselves— than I do for all the niggers in Christendom. [Cheers.] I would not dissolve this Union; I would not endanger its perpetuity; I would not blot out the great inalienable rights of the white man for all the niggers that ever existed."[272]

Evidently thinking that Lincoln's antislavery statements and the senator's reply would win friends for the Little Giant below the Mason Dixon line, one Douglas supporter issued a pamphlet version of the Alton debate and distributed it throughout the South by the thousands. Its introduction belittled Lincoln as an "artful dodger" and alleged that he sought to "palm himself off to the Whigs of Madison county as a friend of Henry Clay and no abolitionist, AND IS EXPOSED!"[273]

This final debate elicited little applause. The subdued response was curious, for, as one reporter noted, "in many respects it was the greatest discussion yet held."[274] It was certainly Lincoln's finest rhetorical hour. After the debate, while dining with several Republican leaders, he asked Lyman Trumbull, a resident of nearby Belleville, about the crowd's reaction. The senator replied "that public meetings in Madison County were usually undemonstrative, but he thought a favorable impression had been made." Then Mrs. Lincoln invited Horace White and Robert R. Hitt to spend a few days at her home in Springfield; Hitt tactfully declined, saying "that he would never call at her house until she lived in the White House. She laughed at the sugges-tion, and said there was not much prospect of such a residence very soon."[275]

Intervention by Outsiders

As the campaign heated up, prominent figures of both parties joined the fray. Feeling beleaguered after the Ottawa debate, Douglas wired Usher F. Linder: "For God's sake, Linder, come up into the Northern part of the State and help me. Every *dog* in the State is let loose after me—from the bull-dog Trumbull to the smallest canine quadruped that has a kennel in Illinois."[276] (When this telegram appeared in the newspapers, Linder acquired the sobriquet "For-God's-Sake Linder.") Rallying to Douglas were eminent Democrats like Vice-President John C. Breckinridge and Vir-ginia Governor Henry A. Wise, who wrote public letters urging his reelection, and former Senator James C. Jones of Tennessee, who stumped Illinois for the Little Giant. (Whatever help these men provided against Lincoln, their efforts severely undermined the pro-Buchanan candidates.) For his part, Lincoln was assisted by Lyman Trumbull, Richard J. Oglesby, Owen Lovejoy, William H. Herndon, and John M. Palmer, all of whom campaigned actively. ("I am out all the time at the school-houses & village churches where good can be done and where the 'big bugs' do not go," Herndon reported in October.)[277]

In addition, the 27-year-old black abolitionist H. Ford Douglas of Chicago made speeches on behalf of Lincoln, prompting the *Illinois State Register* to observe: "he spoke in one of the Ottawa churches, much to the edification and delight of his aboli-tion republican brethren, who seem in duty bound . . . to swallow every greasy nigger that comes along."[278] In Ottawa, Senator Douglas remarked that "[w]e heard a prominent Republican tell another the other day that Mr. Schlosser should have been kicked out of the court house for presuming that a Nigger was going to speak at the Free church, although the object of his address was to help Lincoln. Every fool knows that his speech would do Lincoln more harm than good."[279]

A small number of Republicans from outside Illinois assisted Lincoln. Among them were Governor Salmon P. Chase of Ohio and Congressman Frank Blair of Missouri. (Douglas charged Blair "with laboring to abolish slavery in Missouri, and to ship off the free blacks to Illinois," where they were "*to be made citizens and our equals!*")[280] In appealing to the German vote, Republicans also enjoyed the support of Carl Schurz of Wisconsin and others. "The black Republicans have a half dozen Ger-man hirelings traveling and spouting niggerism through this region," sneered the *Illi-nois State Register*.[281] Several nationally prominent Republicans, including Caleb B. Smith, Benjamin F. Wade, Cassius M. Clay, and Joseph Galloway, were invited to stump Illinois but declined. In 1859, Lincoln expressed gratitude to Chase for "being one of the very few distinguished men, whose sympathy we in Illinois did receive last year, of all those whose sympathy we thought we had reason to expect."[282] Although his letter to Chase seemed tinged with bitterness at the failure of more prominent Republicans to come to his aid, Lincoln had in June 1858 cautioned against "import-ing speakers from a distance and the like. They excite prejudice and close the avenues to sober reason."[283]

To offset the German Republican campaigners, Douglas hired Henry Villard, a native of Germany who delivered thirteen speeches and wrote dispatches for a New York newspaper belittling Lincoln. He told Douglas that he was "as enthusiastic & faithful a supporter of your political claims as any can be found anywhere in the State of Illinois." He eventually quit when Douglas failed to pay the promised fee.[284]

The eminent Whig, Kentucky Senator John J. Crittenden, widely regarded as Henry Clay's heir, provided by far the most significant outside intervention. Four days after the Alton debate, Lincoln's campaign suffered a grievous blow when T. Lyle Dickey publicly read a pro-Douglas letter he had received months earlier from Crittenden. Congressman Thomas L. Harris had informed the Little Giant that Crittenden "would write to any body—& give his views & wishes in your favor in any mode in which they would be most effective. If he will write a letter or come here & make a speech he will control 20,000 American or old line Whig votes in the center & south."[285] Hearing rumors that Crittenden favored Douglas's reelection and had agreed to write friends in Illinois saying so, Lincoln asked the Kentucky senator in early July if that was in fact the case and predicted that Crittenden's Illinois admirers would be "mortified exceedingly" by any such correspondence.[286] On July 29, Crittenden replied that he admired the Little Giant's opposition to the Lecompton Constitution and deplored his "persecution" by the Buchanan administration, and that he had so expressed himself to several men at Washington during the last session of Congress. Now he was besieged by Illinoisans, including Dickey, for confirmation of those discussions and would answer their requests honestly. He added that he had "no disposition for officious intermeddling" and that he "should be extremely sorry to give offence or cause mortification to you or any of my Illinois friends."[287] Three days later, Crittenden wrote Dickey recounting the praise he had bestowed upon Douglas in April and authorizing him to repeat what he had said.

Dickey kept the letter private until October 19, when he incorporated it into a speech denouncing Lincoln as an apostate from Clay's Whiggery. The Democrats cited that document as a conclusive reason why Old Line Whigs should not support Lincoln, though in fact it was hardly a ringing endorsement of Douglas's bid for reelection. Crittenden, in company with many Republicans, applauded the Little Giant's attack on the Lecompton Constitution, but that document had ceased being an issue when voters in Kansas decisively rejected it in August. (The Louisville *Journal*, edited by Crittenden's friend George D. Prentice, declared: "We hailed him [Douglas] with applause when he mounted the solid ground of constitutional justice, but we feel under no obligation to extol him when he plunges back into the mire of Democracy.")[288]

The *Illinois State Journal* fanned the fires of controversy by mistakenly suggesting that Dickey's Crittenden letter was a forgery and erroneously claiming that the Kentucky senator had written to a leading resident of Springfield expressing "himself heartily in favor of the triumph of the united opposition against Douglas, and bids them God speed in the good work."[289] The Springfield *Register* fired back that the "leading resident" was Lincoln himself, and denied that the letter supported the opposition to Douglas. "On the contrary," it stated, "that letter expresses no such thing, but gives Mr. Abraham Lincoln a cold bath. . . . Will Mr. Lincoln, through the *Journal,* trot out that letter?" Democrats asked Crittenden if he had written in support of Lincoln, to which he telegraphed a reply: "I have written no such letter."[290] This telegram was published in the *Missouri Republican* at the behest of Owen G. Cates of St. Louis, who had seen a copy of the letter from Crittenden to Lincoln. Cates complained to the editor of the *Missouri Republican* that Lincoln knew Crittenden's letter was being misrepresented, yet he remained silent. The Kentucky senator's telegram and Dickey's speech profoundly affected Old Line Whigs in central Illinois. Crittenden apologized to Lincoln, disclaiming any responsibility for the release of his letter to the press.

Compounding Lincoln's problems were pro-Douglas public letters from two other Kentuckians, Vice-President John C. Breckinridge and Congressman James B. Clay, son of Henry Clay. Moreover, James W. Singleton of Quincy, a former Whig but now a Democrat, reported that Lincoln had abandoned Clay in 1847 and worked hard to defeat his nomination for the presidency. Douglas, T. Lyle Dickey, and others repeated Singleton's accusation, and the Democratic press insisted that Lincoln had betrayed the principles of Clay. To counter this attack, Republican newspapers ran extracts of speeches by Clay and Lincoln, showing the similarity of their views on slavery, race, amalgamation, squatter sovereignty, and the Constitution.

The race issue continued to dog Lincoln in the closing days of the campaign. The Chicago *Times* spelled out eleven principles for which the Democratic Party stood; heading the list was the assertion that Illinois Democrats "affirm the original and essential inferiority of the negro." The *Times* declared that the election of Lincoln would disgrace Illinois. Rhetorically its editor asked voters, "Shall you by your want of zeal and inattention allow the Republicans to elect Abraham Lincoln, and send him, the advocate of negro equality and negro citizenship to the United States Senate, and thus forever put a blot upon the proud name of Illinois? Let Massachusetts, and Rhode Island, and Vermont, if they choose, send to the national councils men glorying in the profession of negro loving, negro equality, and negro citizenship doctrines, but must Illinois be brought to the shameful acknowledgment that her people, too, claim an equality for the negro with the white race, and claim for the negro all the political rights of the white man?" The *Times* denounced Lincoln for "shamelessly" promoting the "revolting" and "odious" principle of black equality.[291]

In an undated manuscript, perhaps written at that time, Lincoln exclaimed: "Negro equality! Fudge!! How long, in the government of a God, great enough to make and maintain this Universe, shall there continue knaves to vend, and fools to gulp, so low a piece of demagogueism as this."[292] On October 18, Lincoln gave to James N. Brown, a Republican candidate for the state legislature who expressed concern about the charges of black equality, a small notebook with clippings from his speeches dealing with black citizenship. In a cover letter, Lincoln reiterated that "I think the negro is included in the word 'men' used in the Declaration of Independence" but added that "it does not follow that social and political equality between the whites and blacks, *must* be incorporated, because slavery must *not*. The declaration does not so require."[293]

Lincoln often had to deal with hecklers, and he usually got the better of them. In Dallas City on October 23, one Tom Gates interrupted him with charges that he had lied. Lincoln asked him to rise and then blasted him severely. An observer remarked, "great God how Lincoln scored him. You could have heard the boys shout a mile."[294] In Clinton, when the crowd began to eject a heckler, Lincoln instructed them to stop: "No, don't throw him out. Let him stay and maybe he'll learn something."[295] When he spoke at Rushville, a Democratic town, he passed a group of socially prominent young women, some of whom had dark complexions. To taunt him for his antislavery views, one of them held up to Lincoln a black doll baby, prompting him to ask quietly: "Madam, are you the mother of that?"[296]

In Springfield, as Lincoln delivered his final speech of the long contest to a wildly enthusiastic crowd of 10,000, he was interrupted by a haughty man who rode close to the speaker's stand and shouted: "How would you like to sleep with a nigger?" Lincoln did not reply but simply stared at him in pity. Unnerved, the rider tried to leave, but the crowd restrained his horse and spat all over him. Some even removed tobacco chaws from their mouths and hurled them in his face.

After this episode, Lincoln sadly remarked that the "the contest has been painful to me." Alluding to Crittenden and Dickey, he told the Springfield audience that he and his allies "have been constantly accused of a purpose to destroy the union; and bespattered with every immaginable odious epithet; and some who were friends, as it were but yesterday[,] have made themselves most active in this. I have cultivated patience, and made no attempt at a retort." In a similar vein, he said: "I have meant to assail the motives of no party, or individual; and if I have, in any instance (of which I am not conscious) departed from my purpose, I regret it." As for the charges of disunionism, he protested that "I have labored *for,* and not *against* the Union. As I have not felt, so I have not expressed any harsh sentiment towards our Southern brethren. I have constantly declared, as I really believed, the only difference between them and us, is the difference of circumstances." Frankly he acknowledged his ambition but emphasized that he cared more for the success of the antislavery cause than he did for merely attaining power. "God knows how sincerely I prayed from the first that this field of ambition might not be opened. I claim no insensibility to political honors; but today could the Missouri restriction be restored, and the whole slavery question replaced on the old ground of 'toleration['] by necessity where it exists, with unyielding hostility to the spread of it, on principle, I would, in consideration, gladly agree, that Judge Douglas should never be *out,* and I never *in,* an office, so long as we both or either, live."[297] The *Illinois State Journal* called this peroration "one of the most eloquent appeals ever addressed to the American people."[298]

As election day drew near, the Chicago *Press and Tribune* reviewed Lincoln's conduct: "From first to last he has preserved his well-earned reputation for fairness, for honor and gentlemanly courtesy, and more than maintained his standing as a sagacious, far-seeing and profound statesman. Scorning the use of offensive personalities and the ordinary tricks of the stump, his efforts have been directed solely to the discussion of the legitimate issues of the campaign and the great fundamental principles on which our government is based."[299] Two years later the Springfield, Massachusetts, *Republican*, which originally had urged Illinois Republicans not to run a candidate against Douglas, said that the "judgment of all men of mind upon the Illinois canvass is in favor of Lincoln as against Douglas." Lincoln "handled Douglas as he would an eel—by main strength."[300]

Thanks to the rapid growth of the railroad network in Illinois, the campaign had been unusually extensive. Douglas traveled 5,227 miles in 100 days; in less than four months, Lincoln covered almost as much ground (350 miles by boat, 600 by carriage, and 3,400 by train). Excluding short responses, Lincoln by his own count gave sixty-three addresses; Douglas claimed that he delivered twice as many, though a journalist counted fifty-nine set speeches, seventeen brief responses to serenades, and thirty-seven replies to addresses of welcome. They both spoke in forty towns; Douglas addressed crowds at twenty-three sites where his opponent did not, and Lincoln did so in a dozen where the Little Giant did not.

Election Results

Prairie State voters trooped to the polls on November 2 to choose members of the General Assembly, a state treasurer, and a state superintendent of public instruction. "What a night next Tuesday will be all over the Union!" exclaimed the Burlington, Iowa, *State Gazette*, in excited anticipation. "The whole Nation is watching with the greatest possible anxiety for the result of that day. No State has ever fought so great a battle as that which Illinois is to fight on that day. Its result is big with the fate of our Government and the Union and the telegraph wires will be kept hot with it until the result is known all over the land."[301]

Like many of his party colleagues, Lincoln anticipated electoral fraud. To Norman B. Judd he expressed "a high degree of confidence that we shall succeed, if we are not over-run with fraudulent votes to a greater extent than usual." In Naples he had noticed several Irishmen dressed as railroad workers carrying carpetbags; he reported that hundreds of others were rumored to be leaving districts where their votes were superfluous in order to settle briefly in hotly contested counties. To thwart this so-called colonization of voters, Lincoln offered Judd "a bare suggestion"—namely, that where "there is a known body of these voters, could not a true man, of the '*detective*' class, be introduced among them in disguise, who could, at the nick of time, control their votes? Think this over. It would be a great thing, when this trick is attempted upon us, to have the saddle come up on the other horse."[302] It is not entirely clear what Lincoln intended; the "true man of the 'detective' class" that he mentioned was perhaps a distributor of bribes.

Many Republicans were willing to counter Democratic maneuvers with trickery of their own. In July 1857, O. M. Hatch, a close friend of Lincoln and the secretary of state in Illinois, wrote: "let us *colonize*—some four or five districts, and begin now—this fall—without fail—this must be done—and can be done, with money—and the end Justifies the means in this instance, certainly, in my Judgment—I have written this much after a talk with Mr Dubois & Herndon."[303] (Three years later, David Davis declared that "the Democracy are pipe laying for the Legislature" by "transferring Irish voters from the Northern part of the State into the doubtful districts. This can only be counteracted by like means on our behalf.")[304] Colonizing voters was a common electoral strategy in the 1850s, when registry laws were weak or nonexistent.

Some Republicans even contemplated violence. On election eve, Herndon explained to a Massachusetts correspondent that Illinois Republicans "have this question before us—'What shall we do? Shall we tamely submit to the Irish, or shall we rise and cut their throats?' If blood is shed in Ill[inoi]s to maintain the purity of the ballot box, and the rights of the popular will, do not be at all surprised."[305]

Reports of Democratic fraud abounded. A St. Louis newspaper claimed that hundreds of men were "being hired, publicly in our streets to go to Illinois, ostensibly to work on the Railroads, but really to vote for the Democratic candidates for the Legislature."[306] A resident of Princeton complained that "Irishmen are sent into the doubtful districts along the lines of railroads by the hundreds, with the intention, no doubt, of getting their votes into the ballot boxes if possible." He also warned that even if Republican candidates prevailed, Democratic clerks might certify their opponents as the victors, as they had done in two districts in 1856.[307] Chester P. Dewey reported in mid-October that a "gentle colonization of voters is going on, almost imperceptibly." A newcomer "is seen for a moment at a depot, and then merged in the general population of the region. Here and there a few Irishmen leave the [rail] cars, and either go to work upon railroads or seek employment in cutting corn among the farmers."[308] Governor Matteson, whose corruption would be exposed the following year, allegedly said that he had so arranged things that the Democrats would carry McLean, Sangamon, Madison, and Morgan counties, the swing districts where the outcome of the election would be determined. On election eve, David Davis told a friend: "Lincoln has made a magnificent canvass. There would be no doubt of Douglas defeat if it was not from the fact that he is colonizing Irish voters."[309] Herndon predicted that "there is nothing which can well defeat us but the elements, & the wandering roving robbing Irish, who have flooded over the State."[310]

When the votes were tallied, Lincoln's prediction to David R. Locke was borne out: the Republicans won the two statewide offices (by an average margin of 124,993 to 122,011—50.6% to 49.4%) but failed to gain control of the legislature. The election results are somewhat difficult to interpret with precision, but generally speaking Republican candidates for the Illinois House of Representatives won a total of 190,468, their Democratic opponents 166,374, and the Danites 9,951. If in fact all votes for Democratic legislative candidates were cast to indicate a preference for Douglas over Lincoln, and all Republican votes were deliberately cast to indicate a preference for Lincoln over Douglas, then the challenger beat the incumbent handily, winning 52 percent to the Little Giant's 45 percent. Similarly, in the twelve races for senate seats, Republican candidates won 54 percent of the votes cast. Obviously, many who voted in the legislative election failed to vote for the state treasurer or state superintendent of education. If, in 1858, U.S. senators had been popularly elected, Lincoln would have trounced Douglas.

But even under the prevailing system for choosing senators, Lincoln would have won if the legislature had been fairly apportioned. In the eight years following the 1850 census, upon which the legislative districts were created, the state's population had swollen, especially in the north. The Republican Party won 50 percent of the votes for statewide office but only 46 percent of legislative races, whereas Douglas's faction won 48 percent of the statewide vote and 54 percent of the legislature. According to the 1855 census, the forty House districts carried by the Democrats had a population of 606,278, and the thirty-three Republican districts had 699,840 inhabitants. In Madison County, where 4,300 votes were cast, the Democrats won by a margin of 200 and sent two Representatives to the General Assembly; in McLean County, where 4,900 votes were cast, the Republicans won by a majority of 600 and sent one member to the Illinois House. Adams County, where 6,000 votes were cast, went Democratic by a margin of 200 and sent two Representatives to the House; in the Republican counties of La Salle, Livingston, and Grundy, 11,000 votes were cast, yet only two members were sent to the House. Fulton County, with 5,500 votes, also had two legislators, while Cook, with nearly four times the voting population (19,000), had only four Representatives. Will County with 10,000 voters had just three Representatives. A switch of 400 votes in Sangamon and Madison counties would have given the Republicans a majority of the House and the ability to elect Lincoln. According to calculations made by the *Illinois State Journal,* if the legislature had been apportioned on a one-man one-vote basis, the Republicans would have elected forty-one Representatives and fourteen Senators, giving Lincoln the U.S. senate seat. The Little Giant clearly owed his victory to a malapportioned legislature.

Although the *Illinois State Register* was pleased that Douglas would be returned to the senate, it regretted that Republican candidates for the legislature had in the aggregate outpolled their Democratic rivals. The editors asserted that the "treachery of Danite officials" gave "niggerism this preponderance."[311] In races for the General Assembly, which Democrats already controlled going into the election, they did especially well in the counties that two years earlier had gone for Fillmore (or a combination of Fillmore and Frémont voters). They gained one senate seat (in the Madison-Bond-Montgomery district) and six House seats: two in Madison County, two in Sangamon County, one in Wabash and White counties combined, and one in Mason and Logan counties combined. In Morgan County, Lincoln had hoped that Richard Yates would run for the legislature, just as he had done to help Yates four years earlier; Yates, however, did not reciprocate.

The Republican margin of victory in the popular vote was considerably greater than Governor Bissell had enjoyed in 1856. It might have been even larger if Republicans in northern Illinois had turned out in greater numbers. There 5,000 to 10,000 party faithful did not bother to vote because of bad weather (election day was cold and raw) and because they rightly assumed that their legislative candidates would win easily. In addition, some labored under the false impression that Douglas had forever broken with the Democratic Party; others were influenced by the Eastern Republicans' support of the Little Giant.

With justice, Republicans also blamed apostate Old Line Whigs for the failure to capture the legislature. As they had done in the Frémont campaign, those Whigs balked, especially in Sangamon, Madison, Jersey, and Tazewell counties. David Davis, who was grieved "beyond measure," complained bitterly to Lincoln that the

"Pharisaical old Whigs in the Central counties, who are so much more righteous than other people, I can[']t talk about with any patience—The lever of Judge Dickey[']s influence has been felt—He drew the letter out of Mr Crittenden, & I think, in view of every thing, that it was perfectly outrageous in Mr Crittenden to have written any thing—. . . . It was very shameful in my opinion for Dickey, to have kept that letter from 1st Augt & then published it a week before the election."[312] (Lincoln also felt that Dickey's efforts had helped defeat him, but he bore no grudge.)

Illinois Republicans seethed with anger over the conduct of the Eastern leaders of their party, especially Seward and Greeley. The Chicago *Press and Tribune* ascribed Lincoln's defeat primarily to the intervention of Crittenden and the coolness of the East Coast Republicans, of whom it exclaimed: "every effort of our friends abroad was for our enemies at home!"[313] Indeed, the pro-Seward New York *Times* lauded Douglas on the eve of the election, and the New York *Tribune* acknowledged that its relative silence during the campaign "was damaging in a State where more people read this paper than any other."[314] Ebenezer Peck bitterly complained to Trumbull: "Now that Seward Greel[e]y & Co have contributed so much to our defeat, they may expect us, in the true christian spirit to return good for evil—but in this I fear they will find themselves mistaken. If the vote of Illinois can nominate another than Seward—I hope it will be so cast. The coals of fire, I would administer, will be designed to raise a severe blister."[315] John M. Palmer, agreeing that Lincoln was "betrayed by the eastern Republicans," suggested that in the future the antislavery forces in Illinois should just advocate "free homes for free white people."[316] The heartsick George W. Rives exclaimed: "I say D[am]n Greeley & Co.—they have done more harm to us in Ills. than all others beside not excepting the D[am]n Irish." Lincoln "is too good a man to be thus treated by these D[amned] Sons [of] bitches." John Tilson of Quincy echoed Rives and claimed that he could identify twenty "ardent Republicans" who "swear they never will vote for Wm. H. Seward." Among those twenty, Tilson probably counted his neighbor Jackson Grimshaw, who feared that "Seward will be forced on us for President. I can[']t work for him or any man that actively or quietly endorsed or aided Douglas."[317] To a friend in Massachusetts, Herndon complained that "Greeley has done us infinite harm." Republicans in the Prairie State "were like innocent fools waiting out here to hear Greeley open in his great Tribune: we expected that he would open the ball, but no signal boom came, and we grew restively cold, and our party slumbered as with a chill—a *bivouac* of death upon an iceberg."[318] David Davis told another Bay State resident that "Greeley & Truman Smith &c have thrown cold water on the election of Lincoln. Their conduct is shameful. . . . To think of Greeley taking no part in the contest."[319] Davis told Lincoln, "Some of you may forgive him [Crittenden], & Gov Seward & Mr Greeley, but I cannot."[320]

For their part, a few Republicans in the East were equally bitter about their party confreres in Illinois. Senator Henry Wilson of Massachusetts maintained that "the course of the Republicans in that state was a great political crime, that if they had supported him [Douglas], he would have ensured us the North as a unity & at the same time not been the leader—but now he can dictate terms."[321]

William Herndon offered a plausibly complex analysis of Lincoln's defeat: "We never got a smile or a word of encouragement outside of Ill[inoi]s from any quarter—during all this great canvass. The East was for Douglas *by silence.* This silence was terrible to us. . . . Crittenden wrote letters to Ill[inoi]s urging the Americans and old line whigs to go for Douglas, and so they went '*helter-skelter.*' Thousands of whigs dropt us just on the eve of the election, through the influence of Crittenden. . . . All the pro-slavery men, North as well as South, went to a man for Douglas. They threw into this State money, and men, and speakers. These forces & powers we were wholly denied by our Northern & Eastern friends. This cowed us somewhat." Herndon was especially indignant at the "hell-doomed Irish." He complained that "thousands of wild roving robbing bloated pock-marked Irish" were "imported upon us from Phila[delphia], N[ew] Y[ork], St. Louis, and other cities." No single cause defeated Lincoln; "it was the combination . . . that '*cleaned us out.*'" Herndon did emphasize, however, the critical importance of the southern-born Old Line Whigs, whom he described as "timid—shrinking, but good, men."[322]

The Chicago *Democrat* thought Crittenden's intervention more damaging than the attitude of the Eastern Republicans. "The Seward papers in New York and other places may have done us a little injury upon the popular vote, but the loss of no member of the legislature can be attributed to them. It was in the Old Whig and American portions of the State; it was among the Fillmore voters that Mr. Lincoln was slaughtered. The Republican papers there that made Senator Crittenden much stronger than he ever was before, and he was always strong among the emigrants from the slave States. He did all he could against Lincoln. Thus was Lincoln slain in Old Kentucky."[323]

Lincoln shared this view. Two days after the election, he told Crittenden: "The emotions of defeat, at the close of a struggle in which I felt more than a merely selfish interest, and to which defeat the use of your name contributed largely, are fresh upon me; but, even in this mood, I can not for a moment suspect you of anything dishonorable."[324] (The following year, Lincoln publicly described Crittenden as a man "I have always loved with an affection as tender and endearing as I have ever loved any man.")[325] To Anson G. Henry he complained that "nearly all the old exclusive silk-stocking whiggery is against us. I do not mean nearly all the old whig party; but nearly all of the nice exclusive sort. And why not? There has been nothing in politics since the Revolution so congenial to their nature, as the present position of the great democratic party."[326] Lincoln remarked that attorney William W. Danenhower was one of the very few prominent members of the American Party in Illinois who supported him.

Those "emotions of defeat" Lincoln spoke of were mixed. On January 7, he "good-naturedly" told a journalist "that he felt like the Kentucky boy, who, after having his finger squeezed pretty badly, felt 'too big to cry, and too badly hurt to laugh.'"[327] Years later he recalled that on the "dark, rainy, & gloomy" night when the election returns showed that the Democrats had won the legislature, he started to walk home. "The path had been worn hog-back & was slippering. My foot slipped from under me, knocking the other one out of the way, but I recovered myself & lit square: and I said to myself, *'It's a slip and not a fall.'*"[328] He told friends that even though he lost, he felt "ready for another fight," predicted that "it will all come out right in the end," and remarked: "Douglas has taken this trick, but the game is not played out."[329] Henry Villard, who called on Lincoln shortly after the election, reported that the defeat "did not seem to grate upon his mind. He was resigned. He knew that he had made a good fight—no matter what the result. His talk was cheerful. His wit and humor had not deserted him."[330]

But they did desert him on January 5, 1859, when the legislature formally reelected Douglas by a vote of 54 to 46, despite the Danites' attempts to prevent a quorum and thus leave the senate seat vacant. Later that day Henry C. Whitney found Lincoln alone in his office "gloomy as midnight . . . brooding over his ill-fortune." Whitney "never saw any man so radically and thoroughly depressed." Lincoln, "completely steeped in the bitter waters of hopeless despair," said "several times, with bitterness, 'I expect everybody to desert me.'"[331]

Lincoln did not commit such sentiments to paper; when writing to friends, he was stoic. In mid-November he told Norman B. Judd: "I am convalescent, and hoping these lines may find you in the same improving state of health. Doubtless you have suspected for some time that I entertained a personal wish for a term in the U.S. Senate; and had the suspicion taken the shape of a direct charge, I think I could not have truthfully denied it. But let the past as nothing be."[332] To his old friend Anson G. Henry he declared, "I am glad I made the late race. It gave me a hearing on the great and durable question of the age, which I could have had in no other way; and though I now sink out of view, and shall be forgotten, I believe I have made some marks which will tell for the cause of civil liberty long after I am gone."[333] (Henry assured him that he had not disappeared from sight and predicted that the people "will bear you on their memories untill the time comes for putting you in possession of their House at Washington.")[334] Three weeks later Lincoln wrote in a similar vein: "while I desired the result of the late canvass to have been different, I still regard it as an exceeding small matter. I think we have fairly entered upon a durable struggle as to whether this nation is to ultimately become all slave or all free, and though I fall early in the contest, it is nothing if I shall have contributed, in the least degree, to the final rightful result."[335]

Lincoln derived consolation from the history of the British movement to abolish the African slave trade. "I have never professed an indifference to the honors of official station," he wrote during the campaign, "and were I to do so now, I should only make myself ridiculous." But, he added, "I have never failed—do not now fail—to remember that in the republican cause there is a higher aim than that of mere office. I have not allowed myself to forget that the abolition of the Slave-trade by Great Britain, was agitated a hundred years before it was a final success; that the measure had it's open fire-eating opponents; it's stealthy 'don't care' opponents; it's dollar and cent opponents; it's inferior race opponents; its negro equality opponents; and its religion and good order opponents; that all these opponents got offices, and their adversaries got none. But I have also remembered that though they blazed, like tallow-candles for a century, at last they flickered in the socket, died out, stank in the dark for a brief season, and were remembered no more, even by the smell." But the champions of the movement to abolish the slave trade achieved enduring fame. "School-boys know that [William] Wilbe[r]force, and Granville Sharpe, helped that cause forward; but who can now name a single man who labored to retard it? Remembering these things I can not but regard it as possible that the higher object of this contest may not be completely attained within the term of my natural life. But I can not doubt either that it will come in due time. Even in this view, I am proud, in my passing speck of time, to contribute an humble mite to that glorious consummation, which my own poor eyes may not last to see."[336]

Lincoln was also confident that Douglas would eventually be crushed between the upper and nether millstones, for he could not continue to please both the South and the North. To Charles H. Ray, who said he was "feeling like h-ll," Lincoln wrote in late November: "Quit that. You will soon feel better. Another 'blow-up' is coming; and we shall have fun again. Douglas managed to be supported as the best instrument to *put down* and to *uphold* the slave power; but no ingenuity can long keep these antagonisms in harmony."[337] In 1860, Lincoln voiced similar amazement at another of Douglas's feats. More than any man he had ever known, the Little Giant "has the most audacity in maintaining an untenable position. Thus, in endeavoring to reconcile popular sovereignty and the Dred Scott decision, his argument, stripped of sophistry, is: 'It is legal to expel slavery from a territory where it legally exists.' And yet he has bamboozled thousands into believing him."[338]

What the Democratic press called "Mr. Lincoln's niggerism," which Douglas emphasized heavily, played a key role in the election. The Springfield *Illinois State Register,* the leading Democratic paper downstate, harped on the race question throughout the campaign. A typical example of its rhetoric appeared in a description of the menu for the Republicans of Sangamon County at a local convention. The choices, said the *Register,* consisted of "nigger in the soups, nigger in the substantials, nigger in the desert [*sic*]—Lincoln and nigger equality all through." On election eve, the *Register* proclaimed in extra large print: "PEOPLE OF SANGAMON REMEMBER, A VOTE FOR [Republican legislative candidates John] COOK AND [James N.] BROWN IS A VOTE FOR LINCOLN AND NEGRO EQUALITY." The next day that same journal warned readers: "Lincoln says that a negro is your equal."[339] On election day, the Chicago *Times* thrice proclaimed, in large capital letters: "A VOTE FOR THE REPUBLICAN CANDIDATES IS A VOTE TO CROWD WHITE LABORERS OUT OF, AND BRING NEGROES INTO THE CITY."[340] The town of Lincoln voted against its namesake because, as one resident put it, "We had too many honest incorruptable boys who did not nor would [not] believe a negro their equal."[341]

Partisans from both sides saw the role that racism played in the outcome. A Democrat in Prairie City reported that the coroner of Fulton County "has just held an inquest over the defunct Black Republican party, and . . . the verdict of the jury is 'died from a surfeit of negro wool.'"[342] Republicans in eastern Illinois allegedly complained that "in taking his stand in favor of negro equality, Mr. Lincoln has placed them in a false light before their people, and that he has given them a heavier load to carry than they can bear."[343] Douglas's victory prompted the *Register* to declare that Lincoln "has failed in the first open fight upon the proposition of negro equality."[344] Many Illinois voters evidently agreed with a journalist who wrote that Douglas, for all his faults, "is *sound on niggers*," especially when compared with Lincoln, "a crazy fanatic, who openly proclaims the equality of the black and white races, and advocates the abolishing of the Supreme Court for its decision in the Dred Scott Case."[345]

Leonard Swett ascribed Lincoln's defeat to the first ten lines of his "House Divided" speech, which were simply too radical for Moderates. That may have been true with German voters. A report prepared for Douglas indicated that while two-thirds of the state's Germans were nominally Republicans, they were "wavering and malcontent since . . . Mr. Lincoln's speeches and the disclosures of his past. He is evidently almost too much for them, and it will not take a superhuman labor to bring them over in squads."[346]

Douglas attracted voters who saw him as a martyr hounded by the leaders of his own party for standing on principle. From Springfield it was reported that "Douglas has made more friends out of the Lecomptonites on account of the proscription of his friends, than he could have hoped to have gained without. . . . It is very natural that one who is persecuted from within, and without, should excite the sympathies of all honest men."[347] The Chicago *Press and Tribune* plausibly speculated that "if the Administration had supported instead of opposing him, the Republicans would have carried the Legislature by a decided majority."[348] Many opponents of the Lecompton Constitution believed that Douglas's defeat would be regarded as a triumph for Buchanan.

Douglas prevailed in part because he outspent the Republicans by an astonishing amount. Lincoln said that the "whole expense of his campaign with Douglas did not exceed a few hundred dollars."[349] (In fact, the campaign cost more than that. After it was over, Judd begged Lincoln to help the state committee pay off $2,500 in bills.) The Little Giant's campaign cost approximately $50,000. In late October, the Peoria *Union* published copies of mortgages recently made by Douglas on his Chicago property amounting to $52,000. New York boss Fernando Wood was the main mortgagee. The Quincy *Whig and Republican* commented that with those funds, "Douglas expects to carry the election. He thinks that he can *buy* enough votes for that purpose. He pays for the puffs he gets in the newspapers. He carries around with him hirelings whose business it is to manufacture crowds and enthusiasm. The occupation of this toady is the same as that of the man who is hired to puff some quack medicine into notoriety: 'the greatest wonder of the age! one dose cures the most obdurate cases! certificates from some of the most distinguished clergymen, who have been miraculously saved through its instrumentality!' This is the way Douglas' hired quacks talk about him, and about what he is saying and doing in his perambulations through the State; and Douglas pays for the piping out of this $52,000. He carries a big cannon with him, to give him a puff wherever he goes, and he pays for that. He has somebody to go around and shoot it for him and *he* pays for that also. In fact, he has to throw his money right and left, and with a liberal hand, to keep up the little fictitious enthusiasm which has been manufactured by his creatures."[350]

During the canvass, when Lincoln's friend William H. Hanna, a Bloomington attorney, offered to give him $500, Lincoln replied: "I am not so poor as you suppose—don't want any money—don't know how to use money on such occasions—Can't do it & never will—though much obliged to you."[351] But in late June he did ask Alexander Campbell for financial assistance: "In 1856, you gave me authority to draw on you for any sum not exceeding five hundred dollars. I see clearly that such a privilege would be more available now than it was then. I am aware that times are tighter now than they were then. Please write me at all events; and whether you can now do anything or not, I shall continue grateful for the past."[352]

Some Republicans blamed Lincoln's defeat on mismanagement by Norman B. Judd, head of the party's state central committee. David Davis, who complained that Judd's "policy at the head of that Committee was unwise," thought that the central committee should have been based in Springfield "and composed of men of intellect and accustomed to a political campaign." In mid-August Davis was appalled to find that there was "no plan of a campaign yet laid down."[353] John Wentworth criticized Judd for making the committee too large and unwieldy and for convening it too infrequently. "The triumph of Douglass falls heavily upon me," Wentworth said, "& I feel as if he might have been beaten had the promptings of all political experience been followed."[354] Lincoln emphatically branded the charge "false and outrageous" but could not convince several party leaders that Judd was blameless.[355] In fact, Judd deserved credit for suggesting the debates, for Lincoln did so well that he gained a national reputation.

In the end, Douglas may have won simply because his forces worked harder than Lincoln's. From Galena, where the Democrats won handily, Elihu B. Washburne reported on election day that "such unheard-of efforts as have been made by the Douglas party are without parallel." Washburne confided to his wife: "I am utterly disgusted with politics and I have no desire ever to be at another election. Drunkenness, rowdyism, whiskey have been in the ascendant to-day."[356]

Lincoln had accomplished much in defeat. The Illinois Republican organization survived a fateful challenge, thanks largely to his efforts. A supporter congratulated him, saying, "I consider that your Campaign permanently established the Republican party."[357] Late in the canvass, Herndon speculated plausibly that "had we not organized the Republican forces in Ill[inoi]s this year, we should have been disorganized in 1860, and thrown into the great Traitor's arms—Douglas' arms; and *he* would have sold us to the Charleston Convention in 1860; or if he could not we would have been powerless, because *disorganized*. The whole People of all the U States may thank us in Ill[inoi]s."[358]

The Chicago *Press and Tribune* observed that Lincoln had gained "a splendid national reputation. Identified all his life long with the old Whig party, always in a minority in Illinois, his fine abilities and attainments have necessarily been confined to a very limited sphere. He entered upon the canvass with a reputation confined to his own State—he closed it with his name a household word wherever the principles he holds are honored, and with the respect of his opponents in all sections of the country." His speeches, the editor accurately predicted, "will become landmarks in our political history."[359]

The debates were shortly to become landmarks, for Lincoln, obviously believing that he had won those seven encounters, had the text of both his speeches and Douglas's published in book form. When that volume appeared early in 1860, it became a best seller and helped Lincoln secure the Republican presidential nomination. In the campaign that followed, the New York *Tribune* asked: "Did you ever hear a Douglas man urge or advise any candid inquirer to read the discussions between Messrs. Lincoln and Douglas?"[360] The published debates became a handbook for Republicans. The *Tribune* recommended that spokesmen for the party obtain "a copy of the Illinois Discussions between Lincoln and Douglas, and master the arguments, not on one side only, but on both sides of the great question."[361] Even some prominent Democrats conceded that Lincoln won the debates. In 1860, Caleb Cushing declared that "Lincoln is a much abler man than is generally supposed, even in his own party. In his canvass with Douglas he beat him in law, beat him in argument, and beat him in wit; and the published debates of that canvass will sustain this assertion."[362] In fact, it could plausibly be argued that Douglas prevailed in the debates at Ottawa and Jonesboro, that the Freeport and Charleston debates were a draw, and that Lincoln won the last three (Galesburg, Quincy, and Alton).

Other papers agreed with the *Press and Tribune,* including the Cincinnati *Commercial,* which proclaimed that the "reputation of Mr. Lincoln has gone all over the country. It is in extent, undoubtedly national. He has won high honors and made troops of friends."[363] The Ottawa *Republican* noted that Lincoln "has created for himself a national reputation that is both envied and deserved."[364] The Peoria *Message* declared that "[d]efeat works wonders with some men. It has made a hero of Abraham Lincoln." Similarly, the New York *Evening Post* observed that "[n]o man of this generation has grown more rapidly before the country than Mr. Lincoln in this canvass."[365] The *Iowa Citizen* judged that Lincoln "has linked himself to the fortunes of the Republicans by hooks of steel. The name of Lincoln will be a household word for years to come. He has a brilliant future."[366] According to the Rochester, New York, *Democrat,* "Lincoln has now a reputation as a statesman and orator, which eclipses that of Douglas as the sun does the twinklers of the sky."[367] In Indiana, the Greensburg *Republican* observed that Lincoln "has won for himself a fame that will never die," and the Indianapolis *Journal* called Lincoln "an able man, in close logical argument superior to Douglas himself, honest, tried, and true."[368] It is not surprising that the Springfield *Register* speculated with some astonishment: "If the Republican journals are to be taken as an index, Mr. Lincoln is to be made a presidential candidate upon the creed which he enunciated here in his June convention speech."[369]

Individuals concurred. Anson Miller declared that "Lincoln has made a brilliant canvass. He has achieved a National reputation and has gallantly & powerfully defended and sustained the Republican Cause. There is a future for him."[370] William Hanna and John H. Wickizer of Bloomington told Lincoln he had gained a national reputation greater than "that of S. A. Douglas, or any other Locofoco."[371] Another Bloomingtonian, David Davis, echoed his fellow townsmen: "You have made a noble canvass—(which, if unavailing in this State) has earned you a national reputation, & made you friends every where."[372] From Charleston arrived similar praise from H. P. H. Bromwell, with a prediction: "The way seems paved for the presidential victory of 1860," where Lincoln had "a chance upon a wider field to meet our enemies where they Cannot skulk behind gerrymandered District lines to deprive you of the fruits of honest victory."[373] Horace White offered Lincoln this consoling message: "I don't think it possible for you to feel more disappointed than I do, with this defeat, but your popular majority in the State will give *us* the privilege of naming our man on the national ticket in 1860—either President or Vice Pres't. *Then,* let me assure you, Abe Lincoln shall be an honored name before the American people. . . . I believe you have risen to a national reputation & position more rapidly than any other man who ever rose at all."[374] Dr. James Smith, pastor at the First Presbyterian Church of Springfield, consoled Lincoln by assuring him that the work he had performed would make him president one day. "If I am President," Lincoln replied, perhaps jocularly, "I will make you Consul at Dundee."[375] (Three years later he did precisely that.)

Lincoln was also gaining respect in the East. Chester P. Dewey of the New York *Evening Post* told him in late October, "I find that the N. Y. Republicans who were in love with Douglas, are rather more inclined to take a different view now. They find much to admire & praise in your conduct of the campaign & be assured that you have made hosts of warm friends at the East."[376] Another resident of the Empire State, John O. Johnson, reported that the debates had won Lincoln "golden opinions" and "*hosts* of friends here."[377] In the Portland, Maine, *Advertiser,* James G. Blaine observed that the debates secured for Lincoln "a wide-spread and most honorable reputation as a man of fine intellect, of ready and condensed power, and of chivalric and statesman-like bearing."[378] Horace Greeley declared that "the man who stumps a State with Stephen A. Douglas, and meets him, day after day, before the people, has got to be no fool. Many a man will make a better first speech than Douglas, but, giving and taking, back and forward, he is very sharp. . . . I don't believe we have got another man living who would have fought through that campaign so effectively and at the same time so good-naturedly as he did. . . . Lincoln went through with perfect good nature and entire suavity, and beat Stephen A. Douglas."[379]

Lincoln's admiring party colleagues began searching for a fitting next step, a leadership position that would both reward him and strengthen the Republican cause. One suggested that he run for the seat of Congressman Thomas Harris, who had died in November.

Others, however, began referring to Lincoln as presidential timber. George W. Rives said of the election results: "I am One of the Sickest men you ever Saw. I can Stand it as to myself but the thought of Lincoln's defeat is almost too much for me to Stand." Yet, he added, "We Must bear it—Now I am for Lincoln for the nomination for president in 1860."[380] The first known public suggestion that Lincoln should receive that nomination came from Israel Green, who had helped found the Republican Party in Ohio in 1854 and two years later served as a delegate to the party's national convention. Writing on November 6 to the Cincinnati *Gazette*, Green proposed Lincoln for president and John Pendleton Kennedy of Maryland as his running mate. Two days later, the *Illinois Gazette* of Lacon declared that Lincoln "should be the standard-bearer of the Republican party for the Presidency in 1860."[381] Soon thereafter the Chicago *Democrat* recommended that Illinois Republicans "present his name to the National Republican Convention, first for President, and next for Vice President."[382] In November and December, other papers, both in state (the *Illinois State Journal*, the *Illinois State Register*, the Olney *Times*, the Rockford *Republican*) and out of state (the New York *Herald*, the Reading, Pennsylvania, *Journal*), mentioned Lincoln as a potential presidential candidate. The following spring, when the editor of the *Central Illinois Gazette* in West Urbana suggested to him that he should seek the presidency, Lincoln modestly pooh-poohed the idea. The editor nonetheless endorsed him on May 4. In the summer of 1859, Josiah M. Lucas reported from Washington that "I have heard various prominent men lately freely express themselves to me, and in crowds also, that Lincoln is the best man that we have got to run for the next President."[383]

While the debates significantly improved Lincoln's chances for the presidency, they materially injured Douglas's. Disillusioned by the "Freeport heresy," and even more by the Little Giant's refusal to support the Lecompton Constitution and a federal slave code for the territories, Southerners turned on the senator; in December, his Democratic colleagues deposed him from the chairmanship of the Senate Committee on Territories. In 1860, the South refused to support his presidential bid for reasons spelled out by Louisiana Senator Judah P. Benjamin: "We accuse him of this, to wit: that having bargained with us upon a point upon which we were at issue [slavery in the territories], that it should be considered a judicial point; that he would abide the decision; that he would act under the decision, and consider it a doctrine of the party; that having said that to us here in the Senate, he went home, and under the stress of a local election, his knees gave way; his whole person trembled. His adversary stood upon principle and was beaten; and lo he is the candidate of the mighty party for the Presidency of the United States. The Senator from Illinois faltered. He got the prize for which he faltered, but lo, the grand prize of his ambition slips from his grasp because of his faltering which he paid as the price for the ignoble prize—ignoble under the circumstances under which he attained it."[384] The debate at Freeport, along with his opposition to the Lecompton Constitution, had wrecked Douglas's chances to become president.

The campaign against Lincoln diminished Douglas in the eyes of many Northerners, too. Horace Greeley, who had championed the senator's candidacy, said that Douglas's campaign "has stamped him first among county or ward politicians" and "has evinced a striking absence of the far higher qualities of statesmanship." His speeches lacked "the breadth of view, the dignity, the courtesy to his opponent" that mark the true statesman. "They are plainly addressed to an excited crowd at some railway station, and seem uttered in unconsciousness that the whole American People are virtually his deeply interested though not intensely excited auditors. They are volcanic and scathing, but lack the repose of conscious strength, the calmness of conscious right."[385]

Douglas's 1858 victory, then, came at ruinous cost. Hurt by his own tactics and language, he was irreversibly connected to a doctrine—popular sovereignty—whose time had come and gone. It no longer satisfied either North or South. He soon would suffer decline, defeat, and an early death.

In 1859, looking back on the race against Douglas, Lincoln took some pride in its results. "Slavery is doomed," he told David R. Locke, "and that within a few years. Even Judge Douglas admits it to be an evil, and an evil can't stand discussion. In discussing it we have taught a great many thousands of people to hate it who would had never given it a thought before. What kills the skunk is the publicity it gives itself. What a skunk wants to do is to keep snug under the barn—in the day-time, when men are around with shot-guns."[386]

With determination, Lincoln insisted that the "fight must go on. The cause of civil liberty must not be surrendered at the end of *one*, or even, one *hundred* defeats."[387] The future looked bright, for "the Republican star gradually rises higher everywhere."[388] He had "abiding faith that we shall beat them in the long run."[389] Perhaps that victory might even occur in the short run because, he predicted, "it is almost certain that we shall be far better organized for 1860 than ever before."[390] And so they were.

"That Presidential Grub Gnaws Deep"
Pursuing the Republican Nomination
(1859–1860)

In 1863, Lincoln reflected that "[n]o man knows, when that Presidential grub gets to gnawing at him, just how deep in it will get until he has tried it."[1] The grub began seriously gnawing at Lincoln after the 1858 campaign. His astute friend Joseph Gillespie believed that the debates with Douglas "first inspired him with the idea that he was above the average of mankind."[2] Though that was probably true, Lincoln dismissed any talk of the presidency. During the canvass with the Little Giant he told a reporter: "Mary insists . . . that I am going to be Senator and President of the United States, too." Then, "shaking all over with mirth at his wife's ambition," he exclaimed: "Just think of such a sucker as me as President!"[3] In December 1858, when his friend and ally Jesse W. Fell urged him to seek the Republican presidential nomination, he replied: "Oh, Fell, what's the use of talking of me for the presidency, whilst we have such men as Seward, Chase and others, who are so much better known to the people, and whose names are so intimately associated with the principles of the Republican party." When Fell persisted, arguing that Lincoln was more electable than Seward, Chase, and the others, Lincoln agreed: "I admit the force of much of what you say, and admit that I am ambitious, and would like to be President. I am not insensible to the compliment you pay me . . . *but there is no such good luck in store of me as the presidency.*"[4]

The following spring, when Republican editors planned to endorse him for president, he balked. "I must, in candor, say I do not think myself fit for the Presidency," he said. "I certainly am flattered, and gratified, that some partial friends think of me in that connection; but I really think it best for our cause that no concerted effort . . . should be made."[5] When William W. Dannehower told Lincoln that his name was being seriously considered by Republican leaders for the presidency, he laughingly replied: "Why, Danenhower, this shows how political parties are degenerating; you and I can remember when we thought no one was fit for the Presidency but 'Young Harry of the West,' [i.e., Henry Clay] and now you seem to be seriously considering me for that position. It's absurd."[6]

But it was not absurd, for the race for the nomination was wide open. Seward was the ostensible front-runner, but many thought him unelectable. Other men whose names were being tossed about—Salmon P. Chase, John McLean, Nathaniel P. Banks, Edward Bates, Lyman Trumbull, Jacob Collamer, Benjamin F. Wade, Henry Wilson—were all long shots at best. As an Indiana Republican noted in December 1858, "there is no *serious* talk of any one."[7]

Despite his modesty, between August 1859 and March 1860 Lincoln positioned himself for a presidential run by giving speeches and corresponding with party leaders in several states, among them Iowa, Ohio, Wisconsin, New York, Connecticut, Rhode Island, New Hampshire, and Kansas. At the same time, he labored to keep Republicans on a prudent middle course between the Scylla of Douglas's popular sovereignty and the Charybdis of radical abolitionism. Only thus could his party capture the White House. And only thus could a lesser-known Moderate like himself lead the ticket.

Lincoln took encouragement from the ever-widening rift in the Democratic Party over such issues as a federal slave code for the territories and the reopening of the African slave trade. To Herndon and others he said, in substance: "an explosion must come in the near future. Douglas is a great man in his way and has quite unlimited power over the great mass of his party, especially in the North. If he goes to the Charleston Convention [of the national Democratic Party in 1860], which he will do, he, in a kind of spirit of revenge, will split the Convention wide open and give it the devil; & right here is our future success or rather the glad hope of it." Herndon recalled that Lincoln "prayed for this state of affairs," for "he saw in it his opportunity and wisely played his line."[8]

Law Practice

Before turning his attention fully to politics, Lincoln had to restore his depleted bank account. Two weeks after the 1858 election, he told Norman B. Judd, "I have been on expences so long without earning any thing that I am absolutely without money now for even household purchases."[9] Worse still, he was expected to help pay off the party's $3,000 debt. He pledged $250 which, he said, "with what I have already paid . . . will exceed my subscription of five hundred dollars. This too, is exclusive of my ordinary expences during the campaign, all which being added to my loss of time and business, bears pretty heavily upon one no better off in world's goods than I; but as I had the post of honor, it is not for me to be over-nice."[10] He lamented that "this long struggle has been one of great pecuniary loss," so much so that he feared he would "go to the wall for bread and meat, if I neglect my business this year as well as last."[11]

As Lincoln grudgingly devoted himself once again to the law, he found it difficult to readjust to the routine of legal work. "Well," he told a friend, "I shall now have to get down to the practice. It is an easy matter to adjust a harvester to tall or short grain by raising or lowering the sickle, but it is not so easy to change our feelings and modes of expression to suit the stump or the bar."[12]

Lincoln was especially vexed to have to execute judgments by selling land. In the fall of 1858, Samuel C. Davis and Company of St. Louis, an excellent client whom Lincoln and Herndon had represented twenty-seven times in federal court, complained that the two lawyers had failed to collect money won in a judgment. Angrily Lincoln told his client that, as he had earlier explained, the money was to be raised by the sale of land owned by the defendant, that "under our law, the selling of land on execution is a delicate and dangerous, matter; that it could not be done safely, without a careful examination of titles; and also of the *value* of the property." To carry out this task "would require a canvass of half the State." When Davis and Company failed to give clear instructions about how to proceed, Lincoln and Herndon hired a young lawyer to conduct such a canvass. The results were forwarded with the request that Davis and Company state what they wanted done. The company did not answer. Lincoln heatedly declared: "My mind is made up. I will have no more to do with this class of business. I can do business in Court, but I can not, and will not follow executions all over the world. . . . I would not go through the same labor and vexation again for five hundred [dollars]." He told Davis and Company to turn the matter over to the attorney who had examined the titles.[13]

Other clients were also growing impatient with Lincoln & Herndon. Peter and Charles Ambos of the Columbus Machine Company expressed disappointment at Lincoln's neglect in pressing a claim. Exasperated by what he called an "annoyance" and a "disagreeable matter," Lincoln told Ambos in June 1859, "I would now very gladly surrender the charge of the case to anyone you would designate, without charging anything for the much trouble I have already had."[14] Samuel Galloway of Ohio assured Lincoln that Ambos and his colleagues, like most clients, were simply trying to make their lawyer a scapegoat.

In the late summer of 1859, Lincoln tried one of his few murder cases, defending Peachy Quinn Harrison, a grandson of his former political adversary, Peter Cartwright. Harrison allegedly stabbed to death a young attorney named Greek Crafton. Since both the Crafton and Harrison families were well-known in Sangamon County, the lengthy, complicated, and tedious trial became a *cause célèbre*. Herndon recalled that the case was "ably conducted on both sides; every inch of ground was contested, hotly fought . . . with feeling, fervor, and eloquence."[15]

Throughout the trial Lincoln was thwarted by adverse rulings from the bench. When he objected, citing authorities that clearly sustained his argument, the judge, Edward Y. Rice, overruled him. According to Herndon, Lincoln grew "so angry that he looked like Lucifer in an uncontrollable rage." Careful to stay "within the bounds of propriety just far enough to avoid a reprimand for contempt of court," he was "fired with indignation and spoke fiercely [and] strongly" against the ruling of the judge, whom "he pealed . . . from head to foot." He "had the crowd, the jury, the bar, in perfect sympathy and accord."[16]

The turning point of the trial came when Peter Cartwright testified that the dying Crafton told him that he forgave his killer and urged that Harrison not be held responsible. Cartwright's hearsay testimony, which amazingly was allowed to stand, helped sway the jury. In his closing speech, Lincoln urged the jurors to heed Cartwright's lachrymose account of Crafton's deathbed plea, which they did, finding Harrison innocent.

Combating Douglasism

Surveying the political landscape in late 1858, Lincoln saw his party still tempted to unite with Douglas. He anticipated that the Little Giant might once again bolt the

Democratic Party as he had done over the Lecompton Constitution; this time his rebellion might be against a federal slave code for the territories. The senator could, Lincoln thought, "claim that all Northern men shall make common cause in electing him President as the best means of breaking down the Slave power." If that should happen, Lincoln predicted, "the struggle in the whole North will be, as it was in Illinois last summer and fall, whether the Republican party can maintain it's identity, or be broken up to form the tail of Douglas's new kite." In December 1858, he bitterly remarked to Lyman Trumbull that "[s]ome of our great Republican doctors will then have a splendid chance to swallow the pills they so eagerly prescribed for us last Spring." But the idea was still foolish: "The truth is, the Republican principle can, in no wise live with Douglas; and it is arrant folly now, as it was last Spring, to waste time, and scatter labor already performed, in dallying with him."[17]

In January 1859, a Pennsylvanian called Lincoln's attention to a Republican editor who praised Douglas. In reply, Lincoln was emphatic: "All dallying with Douglas by Republicans, . . . is, at the very least, time, and labor lost," and those who do would live to regret their folly. The Little Giant and President Buchanan, for all their antagonism, both supported the Dred Scott decision, both remained indifferent to the moral wrong of slavery, both viewed the slavery issue as a matter of economics, and both accepted the principle that the peculiar institution must exist in the South. To support either of those Democrats "is simply to reach the same goal by only slightly different roads."[18]

Lincoln made the same point in March 1859, reminding a Republican audience in Chicago that the fight against slavery expansion was a struggle against slavery itself, indirect though it may be: "Never forget that we have before us this whole matter of the right or wrong of slavery in this Union, though the immediate question is as to its spreading out into new Territories and States." Let us not lower our standard, he counseled. "If we do not allow ourselves to be allured from the strict path of our duty by such a device as shifting our ground and throwing ourselves into the rear of a leader who denies our first principle, denies that there is an absolute wrong in the institution of slavery, then the future of the Republican cause is safe and victory is assured." All that was necessary was "to keep the faith, to remain steadfast to the right, to stand by your banner. Nothing should lead you to leave your guns. Stand together, ready, with match in hand."[19]

Lincoln cautioned the platform-writing Republicans of Kansas: "the only danger will be the temptation to lower the Republican Standard in order to gather recruits," either from Douglas's supporters or from his Southern opponents. Such a tactic "would open a gap through which more would pass *out* than pass *in*." The core Republican principle, he reminded them, was "preventing the *spread* and *nationalization* of Slavery. This object surrendered, the organization would go to pieces." If a coalition with Democrats could be formed by ignoring the slavery issue, "it will result in gaining no single electoral vote in the *South* and losing ev[e]ry one in the North."[20]

When American Party leader Nathan Sargent, Lincoln's former messmate at Mrs. Sprigg's boarding house in Washington, suggested that the Republicans coalesce with the Douglas Democrats on a platform opposing the resumption of the African slave trade and calling for "eternal hostility to the rotten democracy," Lincoln predicted that such an alliance might carry Maryland, but no other state. "Your platform proposes to allow the spread, and nationalization of slavery to proceed without let or hindrance, save only that it shall not receive supplies directly from Africa," he told Sargent. "Surely you do not seriously believe the Republicans can come to any such terms."[21]

In a public letter to Massachusetts Republicans, who were organizing a festival to honor the memory of Thomas Jefferson, Lincoln appealed in more idealistic terms. He argued that the current Democratic Party had deserted Jefferson by holding "the *liberty* of one man to be absolutely nothing, when in conflict with another man's right of *property*." Jefferson's Declaration of Independence framed "the definitions and axioms of free society," which were now disowned by Democrats, who refer to them as "glittering generalities," "self-evident lies," and principles applying "only to 'superior races.'" Such expressions "are identical in object and effect—the supplanting the principles of free government, and restoring those of classification, caste, and legitimacy. They would delight a convocation of crowned heads, plotting against the people. They are the vanguard—the miners, and sappers—of returning despotism. We must repulse them, or they will subjugate us." Forcefully he maintained that whoever "would *be* no slave, must consent to *have* no slave. Those who deny freedom to others, deserve it not for themselves; and, under a just God, can not long retain it." Jefferson should be revered for the "coolness, forecast, and capacity to introduce into a merely revolutionary document, an abstract truth, applicable to all men and all times, and so to embalm it there, that to-day, and in all coming days, it shall be a rebuke and a stumbling-block to the very harbingers of re-appearing tyranny and oppression."[22]

(Lincoln was a Jeffersonian only in his devotion to the principles of the Declaration of Independence and to the antislavery sentiment embodied in the Northwest Ordinance of 1787 and in Jefferson's remark about slavery, often quoted by Lincoln: "I tremble for my country when I reflect that God is just: that his justice cannot sleep for ever." Lincoln rejected Jefferson's agrarianism, his devotion to states rights, and his hostility to industrialization, urbanization, banks, and protective tariffs.)[23]

Impressed, the Springfield, Massachusetts, *Republican* said that "as a literary document" Lincoln's letter was "one of the most remarkable we ever met."[24] Another admirer was Lincoln's shrewd friend, Nathan M. Knapp, who detected in Lincoln's honoring of Jefferson "more of old '76 Republicanism" than any other Republican aspirant for the presidency displayed.[25]

If Republicans could keep their focus and avoid unseemly alliances, they still faced the difficulty of their own heterogeneity. As an Indiana politico put it, "Jack Falstaff never marched through Coventry with a more motl[e]y crowd than will be gathered under the Republican banner," including "Abolitionists died in the wool, know Nothings, [and] Maine Liquor Law [temperance] men."[26] The most ominous fault line in the new party was the barely suppressed antagonism between former Whigs and former Democrats. A southern Illinois Republican wrote in March 1860, "We have not forgotten our former party prejudices. And whigs and democrats retain altogether too much hostility against each other to be good Republicans."[27] When Trumbull informed him that John Wentworth was working to create ill-will between ex-Whigs and ex-Democrats (notably, between the Illinois senator and Lincoln), Lincoln felt he had to respond sharply. "Any effort," he told Trumbull, "to put enmity between you and me, is as idle as the wind." Promising to sustain Trumbull in his reelection bid in 1860, Lincoln played down concern over "the old democratic and whig elements of our party breaking into opposing factions. They certainly shall not, if I can prevent it."[28]

Yet another threat to Republican solidarity emerged in the spring of 1859 when the Massachusetts Legislature passed an amendment to the state constitution requiring immigrants to wait two years after naturalization before becoming eligible to vote or hold office. Germans throughout the country waxed indignant at the Bay State Republicans and demanded that the party repudiate the so-called two-years amendment. "You know we are powerless here without the Protestant foreign vote," Charles Henry Ray warned Massachusetts Governor Nathaniel P. Banks; "no party which cannot command it in the next Presidential election has the ghost of a chance of success." If the amendment were adopted, Ray said, Republicans would "go into the contest of 1860 with the certainty of defeat."[29] Lincoln bemoaned the shortsightedness of the Bay Staters: "Massachusetts republicans should have looked beyond their noses; and then they could not have failed to see that tilting against foreigners would ruin us in the whole North-West."[30]

When Theodore Canisius, the German-American editor of the Springfield *Illinois Staats-Anzeiger*, asked Lincoln to give his opinion of the Massachusetts amendment, he replied: "I am against its adoption in Illinois, or in any other place, where I have a right to oppose it." Tactfully disclaiming any authority to tell Massachusetts voters how they should behave, he nevertheless condemned the animus behind the two-years amendment. Because "the spirit of our institutions" is "to aim at the *elevation* of men I am opposed to whatever tends to *degrade* them. I have some little notoriety for commiserating the oppressed condition of the negro; and I should be strangely inconsistent if I could favor any project for curtailing the existing rights of *white men*, even though born in different lands, and speaking different languages from myself."

As for Canisius's query about whether Republicans should ally with other opponents of the Democrats (like Know-Nothings), Lincoln said: "I am for it, if it can be had on republican grounds; and I am not for it on any other terms. A fusion on any other terms . . . would lose the whole North, while the common enemy would still carry the whole South. The question of men is a different one. There are good patriotic men, and able statesmen, in the South whom I would cheerfully support, if they would now place themselves on republican ground. But I am against letting down the republican standard a hair's breadth."[31] Democrats complained of Lincoln's inconsistency in saying that he had no right to advise Massachusetts about her policies while simultaneously criticizing slavery in the fifteen states where it existed. In the Bay State, the Springfield *Republican* praised Lincoln's letter as "an apple of gold in a picture of silver."[32]

Lincoln did more than merely write to Canisius; in May 1859, in order to help secure the German vote, he bought a printing press and gave it to Canisius with the understanding that he would publish a German-language, pro-Republican paper in

Springfield through the election of 1860. Lincoln also encouraged friends to find subscribers for the *Staats-Anzeiger*. (Democrats alleged that Lincoln helped James Matheny establish a very different newspaper, the Springfield *American,* a "quasi American journal," which was to serve as "a bridge for old whigs to cross to black republicanism.")[33]

While counseling against the snare of nativism, Lincoln also combated the threat posed by radicalism. In Ohio, Republicans adopted a platform calling for the repeal of "the atrocious Fugitive Slave Law." Alarmed, Lincoln told Salmon P. Chase that their stand was "already damaging us here. I have no doubt that if that Plank be even *introduced* into the next Republican National convention, it will explode it. Once introduced, its supporters and it's opponents will quarrel irreconcilably. . . . I enter upon no argument one way or the other; but I assure you the cause of Republicanism is hopeless in Illinois, if it be in any way made responsible for that plank."[34] When Chase suggested that the Fugitive Slave Law was unconstitutional, Lincoln demurred, citing the Constitution's provision that fugitive slaves "shall be delivered up" and that Congress had the power to pass all laws "necessary and proper" to carry out its responsibilities. But, he added, that was irrelevant; the main point was that a platform calling for the repeal of the Fugitive Slave Act would jeopardize Republican unity.[35] (Lincoln also wished that Wisconsin Congressman C. C. Washburn had not denounced the proposed constitution of Oregon because of its clause excluding free blacks.)

Lincoln discouraged a flirtation with popular sovereignty by several Republicans, including Illinois Congressman William Kellogg, Ohio political leader Thomas Corwin, Massachusetts Congressman Eli Thayer, and the editors of the Chicago *Press and Tribune.* Lincoln warned that "no party can command respect which sustains this year, what it opposed last." Dalliance with the Little Giant's "humbug" enhanced its author's reputation and provided him bargaining chips to use in wooing Southern support, Lincoln argued. He also maintained that widespread acceptance of popular sovereignty would pave the way not only for nationalizing slavery but also for reviving the African slave trade. "Taking slaves into new ter[r]itories, and buying slaves in Africa, are identical things—identical *rights* or identical *wrongs*—and the argument which establishes one will establish the other. Try a thousand years for a sound reason why congress shall not hinder the people of Kansas from having slaves, and when you have found it, it will be an equally good one why congress should not hinder the people of Georgia from importing slaves from Africa."[36]

Turning to Indiana, Lincoln appealed to Congressmen Schuyler Colfax to avoid divisive issues that might split the party: "The point of danger is the temptation in different localities to '*platform*' for something which will be popular just there, but which, nevertheless, will be a firebrand elsewhere, and especially in a National convention." Everywhere, Lincoln counseled, "we should look beyond our noses; and at least say *nothing* on points where it is probable we shall disagree." He suggested that Colfax urge Hoosier Republicans to avoid "these apples of discord." Colfax agreed, though he acknowledged that uniting Conservatives and Radicals was a "great problem" and declared that whoever solved it was "worthier of fame than Napoleon."[37]

Through the winter, spring, and summer of 1859, Lincoln, pleading poverty, declined invitations to speak. In September, however, he agreed to make a brief swing through Ohio, where voters were about to elect a governor and legislators, who would in turn choose a U.S. senator. Douglas was already stumping for the Democratic cause there.

The Little Giant had just published in *Harper's Magazine* a lengthy, turgid, repetitious article, written with the help of historian George Bancroft, on "The Dividing Line between Federal and Local Authority: Popular Sovereignty in the Territories." The article in effect continued his debate with Lincoln and with Southerners who denounced the Freeport Doctrine. Inexplicably ignoring the Northwest Ordinance of 1787 and the Missouri Compromise of 1820, Douglas argued that historically the people of the territories had been empowered to regulate "all things affecting their internal polity—slavery not excepted" without congressional interference. This was a basic principle endorsed in the Compromise of 1850, which the major parties had accepted in 1852 and which the Supreme Court had upheld in the Dred Scott decision, as well as in the Kansas-Nebraska Act. Unaware of the crucial Supreme Court decision in *Barron vs. Baltimore* (1833), Douglas mistakenly argued that the Bill of Rights in the Constitution limited the power of the states as well as the federal government. After reading Douglas's article, Lincoln became aroused and burst into Milton Hay's law office and "without a salutation, said: 'This will never do. He puts the moral element out of this question. It won't stay out.'"[38]

On September 7 at Columbus, Douglas delivered a speech repeating arguments from the previous year's debates and summarizing his piece in *Harper's*. This constituted "the opening manifesto of the Presidential canvass," declared the New York *Times*, which carried it in full.[39] When Lincoln announced that he would reply to Douglas, the Cincinnati *Enquirer* observed that "the Illinois fight is to be gone over again in Ohio."[40] As he had done the previous year, Joseph Medill urged Lincoln to be aggressive: "Go in boldly, strike straight from the shoulder—hit *below* the belt as well as above, and kick like thunder."[41]

In a two-hour address at the Ohio capital on September 16, Lincoln took a gentler approach than the one Medill recommended. Calling Douglas's magazine article "the most maturely considered" of his opponent's "explanations explanatory of explanations explained," he challenged it on historical and constitutional grounds, citing the Northwest Ordinance of 1787. The contention that the Revolutionary generation adopted popular sovereignty in dealing with slavery, Lincoln said, "is as impudent and absurd as if a prosecuting attorney should stand up before a jury, and ask them to convict A as the murderer of B, while B was walking alive before them." Popular sovereignty, when boiled down to its essence, meant that "if one man chooses to make a slave of another man, neither that other man nor anybody else has a right to object." Similarly, he reduced the Freeport Doctrine to a simple proposition: "*a thing may be lawfully driven away from where it has a lawful right to be.*" The fundamental question, Lincoln maintained, was whether Douglas was correct in regarding slavery as a minor matter. "I suppose the institution of slavery really looks small to him. He is so put up by nature that a lash upon his back would hurt him, but a lash upon anybody else's back does not hurt him." The Little Giant's popular sovereignty doctrine would, he predicted, pave the way not only for a new Dred Scott decision but also for the re-opening of the African slave trade and for a federal slave code in the territories.[42]

Lincoln also dealt with the charge, made by the *Ohio Statesman,* that he sup-ported black voting rights. Quoting from his statements at Ottawa and Charleston in the debates of the previous year, he denied the allegation. (After the speech, David R. Locke asked him about his support for a ban on interracial marriage, to which he re-sponded: "The law means nothing. I shall never marry a negress, but I have no objec-tion to any one else doing so. If a white man wants to marry a negro woman, let him do it—*if the negro woman can stand it.*")[43]

The Chicago *Press and Tribune* praised Lincoln's "new and fatal discovery among the maze of Douglasisms," namely, that the Little Giant had "dropped the 'unfriendly legislation' dodge and commenced prating about the right to control slavery as other property. . . . It is patent as sunlight that Popular Sovereignty is abandoned by the great popular sovereign himself."[44] Frank Blair called Lincoln's speech "the most complete overthrow Mr Douglass ever received."[45]

That evening, Lincoln spoke briefly at the Columbus city hall, and the following day he delivered a version of his Columbus speech at Dayton, where the local Demo-cratic paper complimented him as "a very seductive reasoner."[46] (The Democratic *Ohio Statesman* of Columbus was less generous, declaring that Lincoln "is not a great man—very, very far from it," and calling his speech "very inferior.")[47] At Hamilton, Lincoln and his traveling companion, the diminutive Congressman John A. Gurley, stopped briefly to allow the Illinoisan to address a crowd, which was mightily amused by the appearance of such a tall man as Lincoln next to such a short man as Gurley. "'My friends,' said Lincoln, 'this is the long of it,' pointing to himself, then, laying his hand on Gurley's head, 'and this is the short of it.'"[48]

That night in a speech at Cincinnati, Lincoln aimed his remarks primarily at residents of his native Kentucky, just across the Ohio River. Some Republicans hoped that the visitor would "not give a too strictly partisan cast to his address,"[49] but Lin-coln candidly acknowledged at the outset that he was a "Black Republican." Republi-cans, he assured the Kentuckians, had no plans to invade the South or tamper with slavery there. "We mean to leave you alone, and in no way to interfere with your insti-tution, to abide by all and every compromise of the constitution, and, in a word, com-ing back to the original proposition, to treat you . . . according to the examples of those noble fathers—Washington, Jefferson, and Madison. We mean to remember that you are as good as we; that there is no difference between us other than the dif-ference of circumstances. We mean to recognise and bear in mind always that you have as good hearts in your bosoms as other people, or as we claim to have, and treat you accordingly. We mean to marry your girls when we have a chance—the white ones I mean—and I have the honor to inform you that I once did have a chance in that way." How would you Southerners react if the Republicans were to capture the White House, he asked. Would you secede? How would that help you? Will you go to war? You may well be at least as gallant and brave as Northerners, but you will none-theless lose because they outnumber you.

Turning from Kentucky back to Ohio, Lincoln appealed to its Republicans to support only those candidates who embraced the party's basic principle: unyielding opposition to the spread of slavery. In discussing the evils of slavery, Lincoln employed one of his favorite metaphors in a new form. "I hold that if there is any one thing that can be proved to be the will of God by external nature around us, without reference to revelation, it is the proposition that whatever any one man earns with his hands and by the sweat of his brow, he shall enjoy in peace. . . . God Almighty has given every man one mouth to be fed, and one pair of hands adapted to furnish food for that mouth, if anything can be proved to be the will of Heaven, it is proved by this fact, that that mouth is to be fed by those hands, without being interfered with by any other man. . . . I hold that if the Almighty had ever made a set of men that should do all the eating and none of the work, he would have made them with mouths only and no hands, and if he had ever made another class that he had intended should do all the work and none of the eating, he would have made them without mouths and with all hands. But inasmuch as he has not chosen to make man in that way, if anything is proved, it is that those hands and mouths are to be co-operative through life."

Lincoln defended the free labor system against critics who claimed that slaves were better off than hired laborers. Pointing to his own experience, he denied that a permanent laboring class existed in the North. Men like himself might start off with no capital and thus be forced to work for others, but in time they could, if they were industrious, accumulate capital and hire others to work for them. "In doing so they do not wrong the man they employ, for they find men who have not their own land to work upon, or shops to work in, and who are benefited by working for others, hired laborers, receiving their capital for it. Thus a few men that own capital, hire a few others, and these establish the relation of capital and labor rightfully. A relation of which I make no complaint." No man, he said, was locked into the position of hired laborer forever unless he sank into vice, fell victim to misfortune, or simply chose such a life. The free institutions of the country were designed to promote social and economic mobility. "This progress by which the poor, honest, industrious, and resolute man raises himself, that he may work on his own account, and hire somebody else, is that progress that human nature is entitled to, is that improvement in condition that is intended to be secured by those institutions under which we live, is the great principle for which this government was really formed. Our government was not established that one man might do with himself as he pleases, and with another man too."[50]

The Cincinnati *Commercial* reported that Lincoln's "strong and peculiar speech" had "commanded the attention of a large body of citizens for more than two hours. He was clear headed and plain spoken, and made his points with decided effect." The peculiar feature of his address was the speaker's "odd wit that takes the crowds immensely."[51] Moncure D. Conway, a prominent Unitarian minister, remembered the event vividly. Lincoln, he said, called to mind Robert Browning's "description of the German professor, 'Three parts sublime to one grotesque.'" His "face had a battered and bronzed look, without being hard. His nose was prominent and buttressed a strong and high forehead; his eyes were high-vaulted and had an expression of sadness;

his mouth and chin were too close together, the cheeks hollow." All in all, "Lincoln's appearance was not very attractive until one heard his voice, which possessed variety of expression, earnestness, and shrewdness in every tone. The charm of his manner was that he had no manner; he was simple, direct, humorous. He pleasantly repeated a mannerism of his opponent,—'This is what Douglas calls his gur-reat perrinciple.'"[52] Rutherford B. Hayes considered Lincoln an unusual speaker, "so calm, so undemonstrative, but nevertheless an orator of great merit." Comparing him to Kentucky Senator John J. Crittenden, Hayes added: "It is easy to contrast him after the manner of Plutarch, but his like has not been heard in these parts. His manner is more like Crittenden's, and his truth and candor are like what we admire in the Kentuckian, but his speech has greater logical force, greater warmth of feeling."[53] Hayes, who met with Lincoln and had a long chat, thought to himself: "Here is Henry Clay all over again."[54] Some newspapers ran excerpts of the speech and referred to its author as "Abe the Giant Killer."[55]

The Democratic press was less complimentary. "He makes no pretension to oratory or the graces of diction," observed the Cincinnati *Enquirer*, "but goes directly to his point, whatever it may be, bent upon uttering his thought, regardless of elegance or even system, as best he can." His pronunciation "puzzles the ear sometimes to determine whether he is speaking his own or a foreign tongue."[56]

Over 75,000 copies of Lincoln's Ohio speeches were distributed throughout the state. The following year, Douglas's friends sent reprints of the Cincinnati address to Southern Democrats to prove that the Little Giant was their friend because he was Lincoln's opponent. A correspondent of the Washington *Star* protested that "a more villainously abolition incendiary document than this same was never essayed to be scattered broadcast throughout a slaveholding State."[57]

The morning after his Cincinnati speech, Lincoln received a visitor at his hotel room who asked: "how would you feel if we nominated you for President?"[58] Many Ohioans were taken with such a possibility. Hours after Lincoln had spoken in Dayton, former Congressman Robert C. Schenck told a crowd that "if an honest, sensible man was wanted" to head the 1860 Republican national ticket, "it would be well to nominate the distinguished gentleman from Illinois." (Lincoln regarded Schenck's remarks "as the first suggestion of his name for that office before any large assembly, or on any public occasion.")[59]

During his visit, Ohioans reacted with surprised interest to their first look at the newly prominent "Old Abe" Lincoln from Illinois. A reporter covering the speech described him as "dark-visaged, angular, awkward, positive-looking," with "character written in his face and energy expressed in his every movement."[60] Another observed that "Lincoln is a dark complexioned man, of a very tall figure, and so exceedingly 'well preserved' that he would not be taken for more than thirty eight, though he is rising of fifty years of age."[61]

As Lincoln traveled nationally in the following year, the same reaction cropped up elsewhere. Simon P. Hanscom of the New York *Herald* remarked, "I do not see why people call him Old Abe. There is no appearance of age about the man, excepting the deeply indented wrinkles on his brow, and the furrow ploughed down his bare cheeks, hairless as an Indian's; you can hardly detect the presence of frost in his black, glossy hair." Another reporter concurred, saying that "he certainly has no appearance" of being fifty-one, for his black hair was "hardly touched with gray, and his eye is brighter than that of many of his juniors." A friend of Lincoln's protested that the sobriquet "Honest Old Abe" did not accurately describe the candidate: "The term 'old' is hardly as applicable as the epithet *honest,* for he is in the full vigor of life, with a powerful constitution, and no symptoms of decay, mental or physical."[62]

En route home, Lincoln stopped in Indianapolis to deliver a speech denying Douglas's claim that Indiana and other states in the Northwest were free not because of the 1787 Northwest Ordinance but because the soil and climate of that region were unsuited for plantation agriculture. Lincoln noted that parts of Indiana and Ohio lay south of the northern boundary of Kentucky, where slavery flourished, and that Illinois abutted Missouri, a Slave State whose soil and climate resembled those in the Prairie State. He also attacked Douglas's oft-repeated observation "that in all contests between the negro and the white man, he was for the white man, but that in all contests between the negro and the crocodile, he was for the negro." The Little Giant evidently meant to imply "that you are wronging the white man in some way or other, and that whoever is opposed to the negro being enslaved is in some way opposed to the white man." Lincoln said that "was not true. If there were any conflict between the white man and negro, he would be for the white man as much as Douglas. There was no such conflict. The mass of white men were injured by the effect of slave labor in the neighborhood of their own labor." Another implication of the Little Giant's remark was, Lincoln asserted, "that there is a conflict between the negro and the crocodile." Lincoln "did not think there was any such struggle. He supposed that if a crocodile . . . came across a white man, he would kill him if he could! And so he would a negro. The proposition amounted to something like this—as the negro is to the white man, so is the crocodile to the negro, and as the negro may treat the crocodile as a beast or reptile, so the white man may treat the negro as a beast or reptile."[63] A Democratic paper said of the speech that "for deep thought, historical research and biting criticism, it has not been equaled by any Republican orator in the West, or the East either."[64] A Republican auditor described Lincoln as "a plain commonsense man without much polish[.] Evidently a backwoods man."[65]

Back in Springfield, Lincoln penned a note to Salmon P. Chase expressing regret that they had been unable to meet during his brief foray into Ohio. Having warned Chase earlier to avoid radicalism, he now counseled Buckeyes to give no "encouragement to Douglasism. That ism is all which now stands in the way of an early and complete success of Republicanism; and nothing would help it or hurt us so much as for Ohio to go over or falter just now. You must, one and all, put your souls into the effort."[66]

On October 13, Lincoln rejoiced at the news that Republicans had won control of the Ohio Legislature, paving the way for the election of David Tod to replace Democrat George Pugh in the U.S. senate. The Republican gubernatorial candidate, William Dennison, bested his opponent by 13,000 votes. "Is not the election news glorious?" Lincoln asked rhetorically.[67] On October 15 in a speech at Springfield, he "referred to the recent glorious victories achieved by the Republicans in Ohio and other States as clearly indicative that the good old doctrines of the fathers of the Republic would yet again prevail."[68]

The Ohio result damaged Douglas. As a correspondent for the New York *Times* had observed shortly before the election, "[i]f the Democrats do not gain largely; nay, if they do not positively succeed, it will be proof positive in the minds of candid men that the Douglas dogma has brought no strength to the party, even in the Northwest."[69] The Chicago *Press and Tribune* was premature, however, in concluding that the "necessity of warring upon Douglas seems to be at an end. The October elections in Pennsylvania, Ohio, Iowa, Indiana and Minnesota, resulting in the overthrow of the Democracy, have, by destroying whatever remaining chances he may have had for the Charleston nomination, sealed his fate."[70] Lincoln's prospects, on the other hand, were enhanced. "We all think that your visit aided us," Samuel Galloway wrote him from Columbus, "and we are grateful for your services—You have secured a host of friends among Republicans—and the respect of the better portion of the Democracy." Galloway urged him to run for president: "Your visit to Ohio has excited an extensive interest in your favor." Though admiring Salmon P. Chase's "eminent abilities," Galloway believed that "his nomination as our Candidate for the Presidency would sink us," for he had aroused too much "embittered feeling."[71]

Lincoln clubs sprang up in the Buckeye State. On October 31, Charles H. Ray asked Lincoln: "Do you know that you are strongly talked of for the Presidency—for the Vice Presidency at least."[72] Less than a month later, the Paris, Illinois, *Beacon* noted that "there are a great many influential journals, not only in the west but also in the middle and eastern states, who have expressed themselves in favor" of Lincoln for president, a sentiment the *Beacon* endorsed.[73] William O. Stoddard of the *Central Illinois Gazette* in West Urbana, Illinois, followed suit. (Stoddard would later serve in the White House as an assistant to Lincoln's two personal secretaries.) In Baltimore, the German *Turnzeitung* declared that if "on the score of expediency we pass Mr. Seward by, then will Mr. Lincoln be the man."[74]

In November, Mark W. Delahay of Kansas advised Lincoln to "discard a little modesty and not distrust your own Powers, and *strike boldly* and for the next 6 months cease to be a modist man." He could win the presidential nomination, said Delahay, because William Henry Seward had been discredited by the setback New York Republicans just suffered at the polls; American Party supporters would like Lincoln's Whig antecedents; and his championship of the tariff over the years would please Pennsylvanians. "You have always distrusted your own ability too much," Delahay scolded. The "only advantage Douglas ever possessed over you was that of *impudence*."[75] Prophetically Delahay added: "this is the most *important period* of your political life."[76] Similarly, the perceptive Nathan M. Knapp wrote that Lincoln "has not known his own power—uneducated in youth, he has always been doubtful whether he was not pushing himself into situations to which he was unequal, and has often been startled at looking down from his own elevation, which by the way he acquired by what seemed to him no great effort, but a sort of natural, perhaps clumsy, step."[77]

The victorious Ohio Republicans wanted to publish the 1858 Lincoln-Douglas debates, which Lincoln had unsuccessfully attempted to bring out a year earlier in

Illinois. They regarded those debates and his Ohio speeches as "luminous and triumphant expositions of the doctrine of the Republican Party . . . of great practical service to the Republican party in the approaching Presidential contest."[78] On his September visit Lincoln had brought along a carefully assembled scrapbook containing the Chicago *Times*'s account of Douglas's speeches and the Chicago *Press and Tribune*'s version of his own remarks, as well as addresses each had delivered in Chicago, Bloomington, and Springfield. Lincoln evidently showed it to the Ohio Republican leaders with a view to having them publish it. He explained that he had made a "very few . . . small verbal corrections" in the text of his speeches and none in Douglas's. "It would be an unwarrantable liberty for us to change a word or a letter in his," he explained.[79] (Douglas later complained that his own stenographers had inaccurately reported his words.) Lincoln entrusted the scrapbook to young John G. Nicolay to deliver to Columbus, where the firm of Follett, Foster and Company, which had been lobbied by Samuel Galloway, agreed to publish the volume. Chase's friends, motivated by fear and envy, contrived to delay publication.[80] A week before the Republican national convention at Chicago, Lincoln received his first copies. The New York *Tribune* reported selling hundreds before mid-May. This 268-page volume would be circulated widely in the presidential campaign, during which Lincoln himself delivered no speeches, in keeping with the custom for presidential candidates. In August 1860, when asked his views on the issues of the day, he replied: "my published speeches contain nearly all I could willingly say."[81] During the canvass, Republicans taunted Democrats about the debate volume. "We took the speeches of both of them [Lincoln and Douglas] and sent them over the country as an electioneering document," said Cassius M. Clay of Kentucky. "And what do you Democrats do? You go away into some cellar and read them and then burn the book, lest any one else should see them."[82]

After a week back in Springfield, Lincoln departed for Wisconsin to fill three speaking engagements. In Milwaukee he delivered an ostensibly nonpolitical speech before the Wisconsin Agricultural Society attacking the proslavery argument and vindicating free labor. Candidly Lincoln told his audience that he presumed he was not expected to engage "in the mere flattery of farmers, as a class. My opinion of them is that, in proportion to numbers, they are neither better nor worse than other people. In the nature of things they are more numerous than any other class; and I believe there really are more attempts at flattering them than any other; the reason of which I cannot perceive, unless it be that they can cast more votes than any other." (Among other things, Lincoln's unwillingness to pander to farmers reflected his alienation from the world of his father.) After recommending steps to improve agricultural productivity, deploring "mammoth farms," and speculating on the possible introduction of "steam plows," Lincoln reiterated his analysis of the advantages of free labor and refuted what he called "the 'mud-sill' theory" propounded by Southerners like George Fitzhugh and James H. Hammond. Labor, he argued, "is prior to, and independent of, capital," for "capital is the fruit of labor" and therefore "labor is the superior—greatly the superior—of capital." The free labor system, in which the "prudent, penniless beginner in the world, labors for wages awhile, saves a surplus with which to buy tools or land, for himself; then labors on his own account another while, and at length hires another new beginner to help," is "the just and generous, and prosperous system, which opens the way for all—gives hope to all, and energy, and progress, and improvement of condition to all." He also extolled "cultivated thought" (i.e., education) that would help promote efficient agriculture.[83] The turnout at the fair was disappointingly small, both at this event and in the evening, when he was scheduled to speak from the balcony of a hotel. Seeing so few people assembled in the street, Lincoln sadly asked the local officials in charge of his visit, "we can't call that a crowd, can we?" He cheered up, however, when the organizers arranged for an impromptu address in the hotel lobby.[84] The next day at Beloit and Janesville, Lincoln resumed his overtly political campaigning with speeches repeating earlier arguments.

Having bolstered his reputation in the Midwest, Lincoln looked east, especially to Pennsylvania, one of the swing states that the Republicans needed to win in 1860. (In 1856, Frémont had lost Illinois, Indiana, Pennsylvania, and New Jersey.) Two Pennsylvanians were being mentioned for the presidency: Simon Cameron, the state's leading Republican politico, and Judge John M. Read of the state Supreme Court. Cameron's supporters insisted that only their man could carry the Keystone State, which was essential if the Republicans were to win the presidency. Cameron and Read, together with Massachusetts Governor Nathaniel P. Banks, who had become a household name in 1855–1856 when he won a protracted battle for the speakership of the U.S. House, approached Lincoln about possibly being their running mate. In late October, Joseph Medill reported this news to his preferred candidate, Salmon P. Chase. Medill added that those feelers "set Lincoln's friends to talking of him for the first place on the ticket, on the grounds that he is a stronger and more available man than either Cameron or Reed—even in Pa. We have had several visits from Pittsburg Harrisburg, Lancaster & Phila. to negotiate for C[ameron] or R[ead] with L[incoln]. A Pittsburger is here now."[85]

To one of Cameron's emissaries, Lincoln replied with uncharacteristic circumlocution: "It certainly is important to secure Pennsylvania for the Republicans, in the next presidential contest; and not unimportant to, also, secure Illinois. As to the ticket you name [Cameron and Lincoln], I shall be heartily for it, after it shall have been fairly nominated by a Republican national convention; and I cannot be committed to it before. For my single self, I have enlisted for the permanent success of the Republican cause; and, for this object, I shall labor faithfully in the ranks, unless, as I think not probable, the judgment of the party shall assign me a different position. If the Republicans of the great State of Pennsylvania, shall present Mr. Cameron as their candidate for the Presidency, such an indorsement of his fitness for the place, could scarcely be deemed insufficient. Still, as I would not like the *public* to know, so I would not like *myself* to know I had entered a combination with any man, to the prejudice of all others whose friends respectively may consider them preferable."[86]

When a Pennsylvanian asked him whether he supported protective tariffs (the "*all absorbing question*" in that state), Lincoln cautiously but candidly replied that he was "an old Henry Clay tariff whig. In old times I made more speeches on that subject, than on any other. I have not since changed my views. I believe yet, if we could have a moderate, carefully adjusted, protective tariff, so far acquiesced in, as to not be a perpetual subject of political strife, squabbles, charges, and uncertainties, it would be better for us. Still, it is my opinion that, just now, the revival of that question, will not advance the cause itself, or the man who revives it. I have not thought much upon the subject recently; but my general impression is, that the necessity for a protective tariff will, ere long, force it's old opponents to take it up; and then it's old friends can join in, and establish it on a more firm and durable basis. We, the old whigs, have been entirely beaten out on the tariff question; and we shall not be able to re-establish the policy, until the absence of it, shall have demonstrated the necessity for it, in the minds of men heretofore opposed to it."[87]

In December, Jesse W. Fell urged Lincoln to supply a Pennsylvania journalist with an autobiographical sketch. Lincoln complied, saying: "There is not much of it, for the reason, I suppose, that there is not much of me. If anything be made out of it, I wish it to be modest, and not to go beyond the material. If it were thought necessary to incorporate anything from any of my speeches, I suppose there would be no objection. Of course it must not appear to have been written by myself."[88] This brief document was forwarded to Joseph J. Lewis, who used it to write a long article about Lincoln that appeared in the *Chester County Times* of West Chester on February 11, 1860, and was widely copied in the Republican press. It described its subject as "a consistent and earnest tariff man from the first hour of his entering public life," a statement endearing Lincoln to Pennsylvanians.[89] Lincoln noted in his autobiographical piece that his formal schooling had been brief in boyhood and adolescence. He added modestly, "The little advance I now have upon this store of education, I have picked up from time to time under the pressure of necessity."[90] A year earlier, in conversation with a young clergyman, Lincoln had "remarked how much he felt the need of reading, and what a loss it was to a man not to have grown up among books."

"Men of force can get on pretty well without books," the cleric replied. "They do their own thinking, instead of adopting what other men think."

Lincoln agreed, but added that "books serve to show a man that those original thoughts of his aren't very new, after all."[91]

In October, Joseph Medill wrote to a Virginia editor, making a strong case for Lincoln as a candidate able to win the doubtful states, for he was a native of Kentucky, a long-time resident of Indiana, a Henry Clay supporter, and a protectionist. Rhetorically Medill asked, "Is there any man who could suit P[ennsylvani]a better? . . . On the hypothesis that the four [Northern] States lost by Frémont should name the candidate, has not 'Old Abe' more available points than any man yet named?"[92] In the columns of the Chicago *Press and Tribune* Medill kept Lincoln's name before the public throughout the fall and winter of 1859 and the spring of 1860.

Meanwhile, other papers mentioned Lincoln as a candidate for president or vice-president. One of the first to do so was the Aurora *Beacon*, which on November 10, 1859, said he "has every element of popularity and success." Lincoln proudly showed the editorial to his friends, who recalled that he was "very much pleased."[93]

Young Whitelaw Reid, who was to become one of the nation's premier journalists, suggested that Lincoln combined better than any other aspirant *the requisites of earnest Republicanism, fitness and availability.*[94] In January, the *Illinois State Journal* endorsed its fellow townsman enthusiastically as "a man for the times," a "conservative National Republican," and "a tower of strength to the party whose leader he is now regarded."[95]

The October electoral victories were sweet, but the Republicans' euphoria was short-lived. On October 16, abolitionist firebrand John Brown led an abortive raid on the federal arsenal at Harper's Ferry, Virginia, sending shock waves throughout the South. His goal was to seize arms and provide them to slaves for an uprising. Republicans feared that Brown's act might injure them at the polls. Newspapers throughout the South and Border States fumed that Brown's act was a logical consequence of Republican agitation over slavery. "We are damnably exercised here about the effect of Old Brown's wretched *fiasco* in Virginia, upon the Moral health of the Republican party!" exclaimed Charles H. Ray in Chicago. "The old idiot—The quicker they hang and get him out of the way, the better."[96] In Sangamon County, Lincoln worried that John M. Palmer, "a good and true man" and the Republican candidate running for the seat vacated by the death of Congressman Thomas L. Harris, was in trouble. Sure enough, on election day Palmer lost to Democrat John A. McClernand.[97] "I reckon the Harpers Ferry affair damaged Palmer somewhat," Lyman Trumbull speculated plausibly.[98]

That affair also damaged other Republicans, especially Radicals like William Henry Seward, the front-runner for the presidential nomination as of October. His service as governor of New York and senator from that state had earned him respect, especially in advanced antislavery circles. But he had acquired an unmerited reputation as an extremist for his declaration in 1850 that there was a "higher law" than the Constitution and for an 1858 speech in which he alluded to an "irrepressible conflict" between North and South, widely misrepresented as a call for civil war. That speech also irritated former Democrats in the Republican coalition, who resented Seward's implication that Jacksonian Democracy was always partial to slavery. Many Republicans thought of Seward as "a brilliant comet, with fiery tail and dragon claws, rushing through the political heavens to burn up" and destroy everything in its path.[99] "Since the Humbug insurrection at Harpers Ferry, I presume Mr Seward will not be urged," a Pennsylvanian told Lincoln.[100] The influential journalist James Shepherd Pike "had a very strong belief in Mr. Seward[']s nomination till since Mr. Brown visited Virginia. That little incident has thrown a new cloud over the presidential talk and I think obscured Mr. Seward[']s prospects not a little."[101] The raid severely hurt Seward's chances in Illinois in particular.

Aside from objections about radicalism, some frowned on Seward's transparent eagerness for the presidency. In the spring, Maine Senator William P. Fessenden said that the New Yorker, who "already puts on the airs of a President in his intercourse with friends," would "die if he is not nominated. He has forgotten every thing else, even that he is a Senator, & has duties as such." Seward's "friends appear so utterly indifferent to any result except his nomination, or any consequences which may follow that I am getting disgusted with the whole concern," Fessenden confided to his son.[102] Horace Greeley, who thought that John Brown's action "will probably help us to nominate a moderate man for Pres[iden]t," was convinced that an "Anti-Slavery man *per se* cannot be elected; but a Tariff, River-and-Harbor, Pacific Railroad, Free-Homestead man *may* succeed *although* he is Anti-Slavery."[103] To fill these qualifications, the *Tribune* editor favored Edward Bates, a colorless Missouri politician who was far too conservative for most Republicans. Bates also had suspect *bona fides* as a real Republican, for he had been a leader of the American Party in 1856. His prim personality led some to refer to him as "old Madame Bates."[104] Others deemed him "a man of very gentle, cordial nature, but not one of extraordinary brilliancy."[105] In Iowa, a Republican leader observed of the Missourian, "I go in for *electing*; but why go into the bowels of Niggerdom for a Candidate."[106] A Minnesotan warned that nominating "an old 'granny' like McLean or Bates will be a perfect wet blanket to all our zealous, working, reliable Republicans."[107]

The most obvious beneficiary of John Brown's raid was Lincoln, who seemed acceptably moderate compared to Seward and acceptably radical and energetic compared to Bates. In the late autumn, Lincoln expanded his political horizons westward with a visit to Kansas. Arriving at Elwood a week before the scheduled December 6 election in the Territory, he expressed relief that he was no longer in the Slave State of Missouri: "I am indeed delighted to be with you," he told his hosts. "I can now breathe freely."[108] He gave speeches there and at Troy, Doniphan, Atchison, and Leavenworth, all located in a heavily Democratic region. In Elwood, he spoke informally to a crowd at the local hotel, even though he was tired and somewhat ill. Alluding to the bloody history of the Kansas Territory over the past five years, he said that "both parties had been guilty of outrages" and that "he had his opinions as to the relative guilt of the parties, but he would not say who had been most to blame." Ultimate blame he put on the popular sovereignty doctrine itself. As for John Brown, who in 1856 had achieved notoriety in Kansas by cold-bloodedly murdering five settlers to retaliate for proslavery attacks, he observed: "We have a means provided for the expression of our belief in regard to Slavery—it is through the ballot box—the peaceful method provided by the Constitution." Referring to the October raid on Harper's Ferry, Lincoln continued: "John Brown has shown great courage, rare unselfishness. . . . But no man, North or South, can approve of violence or crime."[109]

Wrapped in a buffalo robe to protect him against fierce cold winds, Lincoln traveled to Troy, an unimpressive hamlet where he spoke to a meager crowd of forty. A journalist described the event: "With little gesticulation, and that little ungraceful, he began, not to declaim, but to talk. In a conversational tone, he argued the question of Slavery in the Territories, in the language of an average Ohio or New York farmer." He said that whenever "he heard a man avow his determination to adhere unswervingly to the principles of the Democratic party," he was reminded of a lad in Illinois busily plowing. When he asked his father where to strike the next furrow, he was told: "Steer for that yoke of oxen standing at the further end of the field." Just as the boy began to follow this instruction, the oxen started to move. The boy, in obedience to paternal instructions, followed them around the field and wound up plowing a circle rather than a line. A prominent slaveholder generously called Lincoln's speech "the most able" and the "most logical" address he had ever heard, even though he disagreed profoundly with its conclusions.[110]

On December 2, from a church pulpit at Atchison, Lincoln spoke of Southern threats to secede, declaring "that any attempt at secession would be treason." John J. Ingalls recalled that "none who heard him can forget the impressive majesty of his appearance as he drew himself up, and, leaning forward with his arms extended, until they seemed to reach across the small auditorium, said: 'If they attempt to put their threats into execution we will hang them as they have hanged old John Brown to-day.'"[111] After his speech, when told about a river in Nebraska called "Weeping Water," Lincoln made one of his cornier puns: "You remember the laughing water up in Minnesota, called Minnehaha. Now, I think, this should be Minneboohoo."[112] Later, in conversation with the pro-slavery leader Benjamin F. Stringfellow, Lincoln said: "one of the arguments you Democrats used to present why Kansas should be a slave State was that no one but a 'nigger' could turn up the tough prairie sod. Now, in my time I have broken many acres of prairie sod, and under this argument the question recurs whether I am a white man or a 'nigger.'"[113] (Stringfellow allegedly considered Lincoln's address "the greatest antislavery speech he ever heard.")[114]

The following day in Leavenworth, Lincoln again addressed the case of John Brown: "Old John Brown has just been executed for treason against a state. We cannot object, even though he agreed with us in thinking slavery wrong. That cannot excuse violence, bloodshed, and treason. It could avail him nothing that he might think himself right. So, if constitutionally we elect a [Republican] President, and therefore you undertake to destroy the Union, it will be our duty to deal with you as old John Brown has been dealt with. We shall try to do our duty. We hope and believe that in no section will a majority so act as to render such extreme measures necessary."[115] Still in Leavenworth two days later, he called any "attempt to identify the Republican party with the John Brown business" an "electioneering dodge." A reporter noted that in "Brown's hatred of slavery the speaker sympathized with him. But Brown's insurrectionary attempt he emphatically denounced. He believed the old man insane, and had yet to find the first Republican who endorsed the proposed insurrection." Slavery itself caused slave revolts, Lincoln maintained, and not outside agitation; the Nat Turner uprising of 1831 could hardly be blamed on the Republicans. He scotched the Democrats' complaint that Republicans would grant citizenship to blacks by arguing that the Democracy consisted of two elements, "original and unadulterated Democrats" and "Old line and *eminently* conservative Whigs." In two states that Democrats cited to prove their case against Republicans (New Hampshire and Massachusetts), laws enfranchising blacks were passed by Old Whigs and Democrats. The Wyandotte Constitution, framed by Kansas Republicans and ratified two months earlier, granted suffrage to whites only.[116]

Henry Villard, who had written so scathingly of Lincoln the year before, called this effort "the greatest address ever heard here."[117] Democrats objected to Lincoln's exclusive focus on slavery. "Is there no other issue in this wide country, but that of 'nigger'?" asked the Leavenworth *Herald*, which described the Illinoisan as "an imbecile old fogy of one idea; and this is—nigger, nigger, nigger."[118]

Although Kansas Republicans were overwhelmingly pro-Seward, some talked of Lincoln for president. At Leavenworth, Able Carter Wilder grabbed the speaker by the hand and announced, "Here comes the next President of the United States."[119] Wilder, along with Daniel Anthony (brother of feminist leader Susan B. Anthony) and William Tholen, spent a cold evening with Lincoln in a room with a stove but no wood. When they resorted to some thick Patent Office reports for fuel, one of his companions asked Lincoln: "when you become President will you sanction the burning of government reports by cold men in Kansas territory?" "Not only will I not sanction it, but I will cause legal action to be brought against the offenders," Lincoln jested.[120]

At dinner in the home of Mark Delahay, who had urged Lincoln to visit Kansas, the host announced to his half-dozen guests, "Gentlemen, I tell you Mr. Lincoln will be our next President." Lincoln replied, "Oh, Delahay, hush." Delahay protested: "I feel it, and I mean it."[121]

Lincoln remained in Kansas for the election on December 6. As he left Leavenworth for home, he seemed disappointed that the town's Democrats had increased their majority over the last election despite his two speeches there. A Kansan sought to comfort him with the assurance that the Democrats' margin of victory in Leavenworth County (1,404 to 997) would have been much larger "had he not aroused his sluggish, slumbering Abolition brethren."[122] Lincoln's efforts in frigid, primitive Kansas testified to his devotion to the Republican cause. As a resident of Leavenworth observed, few politicos would "have been forced to do the work in which Abraham Lincoln *volunteered*. In dead of Winter he left the comforts of an attractive home to couple his energies with those of a young people in a distant Territory battling for the RIGHT." Speaking at small towns before audiences no larger than 200, he "paid the kindest deference to all inquiries, and seemed gratified at any interruptions that indicated interest in his 'talk,' as he was pleased to term his able and eloquent efforts." Referring to those small crowds, he said: "I never stop to inquire as to the character or numbers of those likely to hear me. To accomplish a little good is more gratifying to me than to receive empty applause." He refused all offers of compensation, saying that the organizers' "satisfaction was more than a sufficient return for the little he had done."[123]

The Leavenworth *Times* sent Lincoln home with a verbal bouquet: "His short stay in Kansas has been full of significance. He has met a reception that would be extended to but few in the nation, and he has sown seed that cannot but be productive of great good."[124] But six months later those seeds did not sprout into votes at the Republican national convention, where every Kansas delegate supported Seward on all ballots. The more radical Republicans thought him too moderate, partly because his candidacy was championed by Delahay, who was identified with the conservative wing of the party. In March 1860, when asked for advice about where to settle, Lincoln told a friend: "If I went West, I think I would go to Kansas—to Leavenworth or Atchison. Both of these are, and will continue to be, fine growing places."[125]

Combating Factionalism

Returning to Illinois, Lincoln found himself drawn at once into a nasty quarrel between two leading Republicans, Norman B. Judd and Long John Wentworth, whose feud threatened the party's chances to carry the state in 1860. Wentworth, a spiteful marplot, accused Judd of behaving treacherously toward Lincoln by supporting Trumbull in the senatorial contest of 1854–1855, by bungling the campaign in 1858, and by championing Trumbull's presidential bid in 1860. He also charged that Judd had misspent party funds and abused his power as state chairman in order to boost his own chances for the gubernatorial nomination. (Other aspirants for the governorship included the bibulous Richard Yates, who was successful, and Leonard Swett. Judd lost in part because the quondam Whigs, who dominated the party, resented his failure to support Lincoln for senator in 1855.) When Lincoln's close friends like David Davis and William H. Herndon echoed Wentworth's charges, Judd grew angry. "I have slaved for L[incoln] . . . and that I should today be suffering amongst *his* friends by the charge of having cheated him, and he silent is an outrage that I am not disposed to submit to," he complained.[126]

On December 1, Judd wrote Lincoln protesting his failure to refute those allegations and asking him to write a vindication. Lincoln denied that he had neglected to combat such gossip and said that Judd's letter "has a tone of blame towards myself which I think is not quite just." After all, Lincoln observed, you did vote for Trumbull in 1855, though "I think, and have said a thousand times, that was no injustice to me." Lincoln added: "As to the charge of your intriguing for Trumbull against me, I believe as little of that as any other charge. . . . I do not understand Trumbull and myself to be rivals. You know I am pledged not to enter a struggle with him for the seat in the Senate now occupied by him; and yet I would rather have a full term in the Senate than in the Presidency."[127]

Wentworth's anger at Judd evidently spilled over onto Lincoln. Long John's newspaper, the Chicago *Democrat*, ignored Lincoln's Ohio speeches, though the *Press and Tribune* published them. David Davis urged Wentworth to run those addresses, explaining that in central Illinois, opponents of Judd "love Lincoln very much and wish to see him elevated." To achieve that elevation, he needed help, for his friends knew "that Lincoln has few of the qualities of a politician and that he cannot do much personally to advance his interests. They know him to be a guileless man and they think with many of the qualifications and talents for a statesman." Such friends were therefore upset with Wentworth for failing to publish Lincoln's September speeches.[128]

On December 14, Lincoln wrote a defense of Judd, full of praise but cautiously worded so as not to antagonize Wentworth: "I have been, and still am, very anxious to take no part between the many friends, all good and true, who are mentioned as candidates for a Republican Gubernatorial nomination; but I can not feel that my own honor is quite clear, if I remain silent, when I hear any one of them assailed about matters of which I believe I know more than his assailants." He authorized publication of the letter, which appeared in late January 1860.[129]

Lincoln took further steps as a peacemaker. When Judd threatened Wentworth with a libel suit, Long John asked Lincoln to represent him; he declined, offering instead to mediate the dispute. He suggested that Wentworth withdraw charges impugning Judd's character and state that "I have made no reflections upon Mr Judd, morally, socially, pecuniarily, professionally, and in no other way, save politically, and if I have used any language capable of different construction I have not intended it & now retract it."[130] At the February meeting of the Republican State Central Committee in Springfield, Lincoln vainly tried to get the two antagonists together, recommending that they stop their press attacks on each other. Judd complied, withdrawing his suit and supporting Wentworth's successful bid for the Chicago mayoralty. On the heels of that victory in March, Trumbull optimistically speculated that Wentworth's opposition to Judd "would cease since the magnanimous support he has just rec[eive]d from Mr. Judd's friends."[131] But in fact Long John, who resented Lincoln's attempt to please all parties, fought fiercely and successfully to deny Judd the gubernatorial nomination. David Davis found him "insane almost on the subject of Judd."[132] The vindication that Lincoln provided may have pleased Judd but, Lincoln ruefully remarked, "Some folks are pretty bitter towards me" on account of it, for they interpreted it as an endorsement of Judd's candidacy for the governorship.[133]

Boosting Lincoln's Candidacy

In late January 1860 at Springfield, Judd along with Lincoln attended a caucus of leading Republicans who wished to boost Lincoln's vice-presidential candidacy. Few of them thought he had a chance to head the national ticket, for, as Governor Bissell explained, "Lincoln is every thing that we can reasonably desire in a man, and a politician. Still, I do not suppose that many of our friends seriously expect to secure his nomination as candidate for the Presidency. In fact they would be very well satisfied, probably, if he could secure the 2d place on the ticket."[134] A Peoria Republican prophesied that with Lincoln as his vice-presidential running mate, Seward would be unbeatable. David Davis confided to a friend that he would like to see Lincoln nominated for president, but he assumed the party would choose either Bates or Seward. Some supporters believed it best to run Lincoln for governor in 1860, for the U.S. senate in 1864, and for president in 1868. Throughout southern Illinois, Lincoln's potential candidacy was regarded skeptically. Ben L. Wiley from Anna thought Lincoln "a good, amiable and talented gentleman, but is not in my opinion the man for the times."[135] Less flatteringly, A. M. Blackburn of Jerseyville insisted that Lincoln "will not do at all. He has been twice beaten for Congress—He is not available—Nor do I think he has talent or standing for the place. Why he is named I cannot see."[136] In March, Henry Barber, who chaired the Washington County Republican convention, said that "no one expects Lincoln to get the nomination."[137] Three months earlier, when Horace Greeley asked several leading Republicans in Quincy whom they supported for president, only one named Lincoln.

The foremost spirit at the January meeting in Springfield, Jackson Grimshaw, had been organizing Cameron-Lincoln clubs throughout Illinois and intended to win more backing for that effort. Judd reported that he "strongly opposed this action, saying the proper and only thing to do was to claim the Presidency for him [Lincoln] and nothing less."[138] Judd was evidently persuasive, for Grimshaw asked Lincoln "if his name might be used at once in Connection with the Coming Nomination and election." With "characteristic modesty," Lincoln responded by expressing doubt "whether he could get the Nomination even if he wished it and asked until the next morning to answer . . . whether his name might be announced as one who was to be a candidate for the office of President." Leonard Swett accosted him, saying: "Now, see here, Lincoln, this is outrageous. We are trying to get you nominated for the presidency, and you are working right against us. Now you must stop it, and give us a chance." Lincoln "laughed, and said it wasn't serious enough to make any fuss about, but he promised he wouldn't interfere if we were bound to put him forward." The following day he agreed to his friends' request, but when they inquired if they might push for his nomination as vice-president in case the presidential bid failed, he demurred, saying: "My name has been mentioned rather too prominently for the first place on the ticket for me to think of accepting the second."[139] In the spring of 1859, when Elijah M. Haines informed him that friends might be able to win him the second place on the national ticket, Lincoln had answered with a statement implying that the vice-presidency "was scarcely big enough for one who had aspired to a U.S. Senatorship."[140]

Mary Lincoln shared her husband's view of the vice-presidency. When he told a friend that Iowa delegates to the Chicago Convention would cast most of their votes for him as president and all of them for him as vice-president, "Mrs. Lincoln spoke up in a hard, bitter manner and said: 'If you can not have the first place, you shall not have the second.'"[141]

Having authorized friends to promote his candidacy, Lincoln sought to avoid offending his rivals or their supporters. On the evening of February 8, after the Republican State Central Committee had met, he conferred with Orville H. Browning, who opined that Edward Bates of Missouri would be the strongest Republican presidential candidate. Lincoln tactfully replied that "it is not improbable that by the time the National convention meets in Chicago he may be of [the] opinion that the very best thing that can be done will be to nominate Mr Bates." Browning added that Richard Yates and David L. Phillips "also think Mr Bates stronger in this State than any other man who has been named."[142] Yates was not the only resident of Jacksonville to favor Bates over Lincoln. One of them reported in December 1859 that "there is an almost unanimous feeling in this county *at present* in favor of Bates" and that the "movement in favor of Lincoln, which is strong at Springfield, finds no response at all here."[143] From Charleston, Lincoln's friend Thomas A. Marshall acknowledged that "Bates can get 100 votes in this county more than Lincoln can."[144]

Alarmed by his conversation with Browning, the next day Lincoln wrote to Judd: "I am not in a position where it would hurt much for me not to be nominated on the national ticket; but I am where it would hurt some for me to not get the Illinois delegates. What I expected when I wrote the letter [vindicating Judd] . . . is now happening. Your discomfited assailants are most bitter against me; and they will, for revenge upon me, lay to the Bates egg in the South, and to the Seward egg in the North, and go far towards squeezing me out in the middle with nothing. Can you not help me a little in this matter?"[145] Judd was willing to help in many ways. A week after Lincoln wrote him, the Chicago *Press and Tribune*, to which Judd had close ties, abandoned its neutrality and heartily endorsed Lincoln for president. The paper lauded him as "the peer of any man yet named," a "gentleman of unimpeachable purity in private life" and "great breadth and great acuteness of intellect," with "executive capacity," who was "more certain to carry Illinois and Indiana than any one else" and had political antecedents that would "commend him heartily to the support of Pennsylvania and New Jersey."[146] Shortly thereafter Judd asked Lincoln: "You saw what the Tribune said about you—was it satisfactory?"[147] In April 1860, Judd suggested to Lyman Trumbull that "a quiet combination between the delegates from New Jersey Indiana and Illinois be brought about—including Pennsylvania." Together they could stop Seward, but they must maintain a low profile. "It will not do to make a fight for delegates distinctly Lincoln," but he could get at least the unanimous backing of the Illinois delegation.[148] Judd and other friends of Lincoln thought it best not to promote his candidacy vigorously but rather to let the supporters of Seward, Chase, Bates, and Cameron fight among themselves; then at the proper time, when a strong push was to be made, he would face no embittered opponents.

Echoing the *Press and Tribune*'s editorial, a Washington dispatch dated February 20 by Joseph Medill speculated that Lincoln would be more electable than the conservative Bates or the radical Seward: "Does not common sense whisper in every man's ear that the middle ground is the ground of safety?" Medill heard "the name of Lincoln mentioned for President in Washington circles, ten times as often as it was one month ago. The more the politicians look over the field in search of an *available* [i.e., electable] candidate, the more they are convinced that 'Old Abe' is the man to win the race with. If the States of the Northwest shall unite upon him, and present his name to the Chicago Convention, there is a strong probability that he will receive the nomination, and as certain as he is nominated he will be President."[149]

This article angered Seward, who considered it insulting. He accused Medill of "going back" on him and of preferring the "prairie statesman," as he patronizingly referred to Lincoln. Seward boastfully told Medill "that he was the chief teacher of the principles of the Republican party before Lincoln was known other than as a country lawyer of Illinois."[150] Seward's men tried to thwart Lincoln's chances by puffing him for the vice presidency and by arguing that since both men were equally radical, the more prominent and long-serving Seward should be the presidential nominee.

When not quarrelling with Wentworth, Judd was busy trying to persuade the Republican National Committee, on which he sat, to hold the party's national convention in Chicago. It was Lincoln's good fortune to have a man like Judd aiding his cause. Known as a shrewd manager, he was genial, personable, and popular with the men who tended to the party machinery. Lincoln was more concerned about the timing than the location of convention. In mid-December, he told Judd that "some of our friends here, attach more consequence to getting the National convention in our State than I did, or do. Some of them made me promise to say so to you. As to the *time*, it must certainly be after the Charleston fandango [i.e., the Democratic national convention scheduled for April]; and I think, within bounds of reason, the later the better."[151] Judd found the National Committee divided: Seward's men wanted the convention held in New York, Chase's men argued for Cleveland, and supporters of

Bates insisted on St. Louis. Judd slyly suggested that because Illinois had no eminent candidate for the presidency, Chicago should be chosen as a neutral compromise site. Aided by George G. Fogg of New Hampshire, Judd on December 21 persuaded the committee to accept his proposal, thus improving Lincoln's chances for the nomination. "The friends of Lincoln are highly pleased with the selection of Chicago as the place for holding the Republican National Convention," reported the New York *Herald*. "Many of them now declare that his nomination is a foregone conclusion."[152] A newspaper in Iowa said that Chicago's designation as the convention site was "a stroke of policy . . . on the part of the friends of Lincoln which will doubtless place him upon the ticket for Vice-President."[153]

In February the committee rescheduled the opening of the convention, originally slated for June 13, to May 16 in order to allow more time for organizing the campaign. They believed that a whole month was "entirely too long to allow the enemy to be in the field without striking a blow."[154] Seward's Illinois supporters objected to moving the time of the convention, arguing that the proposal was designed to thwart the New York senator and improve the prospects of Chase and other potential nominees.

Cooper Union Speech

One day in October 1859, Lincoln rushed into his office brandishing an invitation to deliver a lecture at Plymouth Church in Brooklyn, where the renowned minister, Henry Ward Beecher, presided. The topic could be virtually anything. An organizer of the lecture series explained to William H. Bailhache, co-editor of the *Illinois State Journal,* that Lincoln "must come. We want to hear a speech from him, such a one as he delivered in Cincinnati [in September] would be perfectly satisfactory. He may speak on any subject . . . the utmost latitude may be observed."[155] With this opportunity Lincoln could, if successful, overcome Eastern skepticism about the wisdom of nominating an ill-educated "prairie statesman." Some of Lincoln's friends, however, urged him to decline, arguing "that the contrast of his sledge hammer style with the polished language of the best Eastern orators would be disastrous." Lincoln, who shared their misgivings, said: "I don't know whether I shall be adequate to the situation; I have never appeared before such an audience as may possibly assemble to hear me." But Bailhache maintained "that the people were weary of polished platitudes and many were ready and wishing for strong meat."[156] Seconding Bailhache was Herndon, who opined that he "could see the meaning of the move by the New York men, [and] *thought* it was a move against Seward."[157] In fact, a leading Chase operative, James A. Briggs, had extended the invitation, and Chase men, eager to stop Seward or any other rival of their hero, had earlier talked of boosting Lincoln as a way to head off a Bates movement. Seward was told that "Mr. Lincoln was brought to New York to divide your strength."[158]

Months later, Lincoln said that he had intended "to give a lecture on some other than a political subject, but as the time approached he could not find leisure to prepare a satisfactory discourse, and took up with politics, as being a topic with which he was more familiar."[159] So Lincoln proposed to Briggs that he give a political address toward the end of February. Because that was too late for the lecture series, the organizers approached the New York Republican Executive Committee, which showed no interest. Briggs offered to help underwrite Lincoln's appearance. Later, Briggs and his friends, fearing that they would not be able to cover expenses ($350), turned Lincoln's appearance over to the Young Men's Republican Union of New York. Anti-Seward forces in that organization—whose advisory board included the poet-editor William Cullen Bryant, William Curtis Noyes, Hamilton Fish, and Horace Greeley—were employing the Union as a forum to showcase alternative candidates to Seward. Frank Blair, who was championing Bates, and Cassius M. Clay, a long-shot presidential hopeful, had already addressed it.

In preparation for his New York appearance, Lincoln conducted thorough research in order to rebut Douglas's *Harper's Magazine* article. Assiduously he pored over his own copy of Jonathan Elliot's *Debates on the Adoption of the Federal Constitution* and at the Illinois State Library he consulted numerous volumes of political history and congressional proceedings. Despite his painstaking efforts, Lincoln left Springfield for New York with some trepidation, which his friends shared.

Accompanying Lincoln on the train journey were his neighbor, Mrs. Stephen Smith, and her baby, to whom Lincoln was quite devoted. She had been planning to visit her family in Philadelphia and, at Lincoln's suggestion, delayed her trip so that they could travel together. The infant, as a friend of the Smiths' reported, "satisfied something which he [Lincoln] was always shy about explaining." In Springfield he would often carry the youngster over his shoulder. On the way to New York, Lincoln seemed preoccupied, but whenever the train paused at stations, he would eagerly take up the child in his arms and walk him about the platform. He would then return to the car feeling refreshed and continue his introspective ruminations.[160]

En route from Philadelphia to New York, Lincoln was surprised to read in a newspaper that he would be speaking at the Cooper Institute in New York instead of the Plymouth Church in Brooklyn. Feeling the need to revise his speech to suit the New York audience, Lincoln devoted himself to that task. (Organizers of the event variously described that audience as New York's "better, but busier citizens" who "generally attend lectures and rarely ever attend political meetings," as "intelligent but inert individuals usually called 'respectable citizens,'" and as "the best sort of citizens.")[161] Lincoln turned down the offer of merchant Henry C. Bowen to stay at his home, explaining that "he was afraid he had made a mistake in accepting the call to New York, and feared his lecture would not prove a success. He said he would have to give his whole time to it, otherwise he was sure he would make a failure, in which case he would be very sorry for the young men who had kindly invited him." The following day, after the two men had attended services at Plymouth Church, Bowen repeated his offer of hospitality, and once again Lincoln declined, saying: "I am not going to make a failure at the Cooper Institute to-morrow night, if I can possibly help it. I am anxious to make a success of it on account of the young men who have so kindly invited me here. It is on my mind all the time. . . . Please excuse me and let me go to my room at the hotel, lock the door, and there think about my lecture."[162]

On Monday, February 27, the day of the speech, Lincoln's Illinois friend Mason Brayman, in New York on business, reported that he and Lincoln were lodging at the same hotel and had "spent much time together." At dinner that day, Lincoln "was waited upon by some admirers," to whom he introduced Brayman "as a Democrat, but one so good tempered that he and I could 'eat out of the same rack without a pole between us.'"[163] In the restaurant, Lincoln asked his waiter to translate the French menu. Even in English, the names of the dishes were unfamiliar to him. Finally, when beans were mentioned, "Lincoln's face brightened, and he made a quick gesture. 'Hold on there, bring me some of those—some beans. I know beans.'"[164] After their meal, Richard C. McCormick and George B. Lincoln called to take him sightseeing along Broadway. Their guest may have been startled by the hustle and bustle of Broadway, so different from Springfield. After this interlude, a New Jersey delegation called on Lincoln to ask him to campaign in their state. Brayman remarked to a friend, "you perceive the fame of *Ancient Abraham* has extended even into foreign lands."[165]

Later, members of the Young Men's Republican Union visited Lincoln, who was wearing a black suit so badly wrinkled that he apologized for his appearance. His guests considered him "the most unprepossessing public man" they had ever seen. Lincoln recalled that despite the bustle and attention, the day of the speech "was one of the loneliest days of his life." He "was perfectly conscious that the club committee who came to see him at the Astor House & took him around to see the sights, were over critical of his entire appearance." He felt the same way "when on the platform of the hall *before* he spoke."[166] When urged to supply newspapers with a copy of his remarks, Lincoln expressed doubt that any paper would want to publish them. He visited the studio of Mathew Brady, where he had a photograph (which he called his "shadow") taken. Brady found it difficult to pose his subject naturally. "When I got him before the camera," Brady remembered, "I asked him if I might not arrange his collar, and with that he began to pull it up. 'Ah,' said Lincoln, 'I see you want to shorten my neck.' 'That's just it,' I answered, and we both laughed."[167]

At Brady's gallery Lincoln met the worldly George Bancroft (who had helped Douglas write his *Harper's* article), a model of sophistication compared with the provincial Lincoln, who apologized frequently for his unfamiliarity with city ways. He told the eminent historian that he was on his way to New England to visit his son Robert who, he said, "already knows much more than his father."[168] (Robert was a student at Phillips Exeter Academy in New Hampshire.)

In urging its readers to attend Lincoln's speech, the New York *Tribune* praised the Illinoisan for his "clearness and candor of statement," his "chivalrous courtesy to opponents," and his "broad genial humor."[169] Fifteen hundred New Yorkers took the *Tribune*'s advice, packing the Cooper Institute. There William Cullen Bryant, the distinguished poet and editor, introduced Lincoln as "a gallant soldier of the political campaign of 1856" and the man who almost defeated Douglas in 1858. "I have only to pronounce his name to secure your profound attention." (Lincoln, a devotee of poetry, thought it "worth a visit from Springfield, Illinois, to New York to make the acquaintance of such a man as William Cullen Bryant.")[170]

As Lincoln awkwardly stepped to the podium, his ill-fitting clothing, self-conscious rusticity, and ungainly manner inspired pity in some members of the audience. His opening words, which he delivered in a Kentucky accent as he fiddled with his suspenders, grated on cultivated Eastern ears. (He addressed the chairman of the meeting as "Mr. Cheerman.") He spoke in a low, dull monotone, emphatically stressing his words. One auditor was led to think, "Old fellow, you won't do; it's all very well for the wild West, but this will never go down in New York."[171] After a few minutes, Lincoln straightened himself up and began gesturing with some grace. His voice gained in volume and clarity, filling the hall. The audience at first thought his manner quite peculiar but soon found themselves captivated by it. His face, which seemed lit from within, contorted expressively. Mason Brayman considered it "somewhat funny" that Lincoln's podium manner in New York differed so markedly from his style in Illinois. Brayman reported that he "was a little *straightened*" because he "was aware that much was expected of him, and that much significance was attached to his words; and he talked like a man who was aware that his *talk* would be *talked about* by all people on the morrow." Instead of speaking "in so familiar a way, walking up and down, swaying about, swinging his arms, bobbing forward, telling droll stories and laughing at them himself," Lincoln stood "stiff and straight, with his hands quiet, pronouncing sentence after sentence, in good telling english, with elaborate distinct-ness, though well condensed, and casting at each finished period, a timid, sidelong glance at the formidable array of Reporters who surrounded the table close at his el-bow, as if conscious, that after all the *world* was his audience, on whose ear his words would fall from the thousand multiplying tongues of the Press; and that for the time being, these little busy fellows were the arbiters of his fate."[172] Fearing that he might not be heard by everyone, Lincoln had arranged with Brayman that the latter would sit in the rear of the hall and if Lincoln's voice was not audible there, his friend would send a signal by lifting up his hat on his cane. That precaution proved unnecessary.

The opening portion of Lincoln's address contained an elaborate refutation of Douglas's article in *Harper's Magazine* on "The Dividing Line between Federal and Local Authority," though it was not mentioned by name. (Lincoln did, however, re-peatedly speak of the "line dividing local from Federal authority.") In a brilliant piece of historical research and analysis, he examined the views of the thirty-nine signers of the Constitution as manifested in votes on the Northwest Ordinances of 1784 and 1787, a 1789 bill enforcing the Northwest Ordinance of 1787, a 1798 bill forbidding the importation of slaves into the Mississippi Territory from abroad, an 1804 statute regu-lating slavery in the Louisiana Territory, and the Missouri Compromise of 1820. On those measures, twenty-three of the thirty-nine signers expressed an opinion through their votes; of those twenty-three, twenty-one indicated their belief that Congress could regulate slavery in the territories; two did not. Among the sixteen signers whose opinion could not be inferred from voting records were leading critics of slavery, in-cluding Benjamin Franklin, Alexander Hamilton, and Gouverneur Morris. The first Congress, which passed the Fifth and Tenth Amendments, cited by those who de-nied that Congress had the power to regulate slavery in the territories, also passed legislation implementing the Northwest Ordinance of 1787. If the men who passed those amendments really believed that the Constitution did not empower the federal government to regulate slavery in the territories, why would they have given effect to the Ordinance? It would be "presumptuous," nay "impudently absurd," to maintain that the authors of those statutes and amendments were acting inconsistently. Lincoln then chastised Douglas (without naming him) for "substituting falsehood and deception for truthful evidence and fair argument."

In the second section of his hour-and-a-half speech, Lincoln addressed Southern whites, who would not respond to Republicans except "to denounce us as reptiles" and men "no better than outlaws." Lincoln urged them to abandon their insults and to deal rationally with their opponents' arguments. Would you break up the Union if the Republicans won the 1860 election, he asked. Such a rule-or-ruin approach was unjustified, for Republicans were hardly depriving the South "of some right, plainly written down in the Constitution." Indignantly, he said of Southern threats to secede: "you will not abide the election of a Republican President! In that supposed event, you will destroy the Union; and then, you say, the great crime of having destroyed it will be upon us! That is cool. A highwayman holds a pistol to my ear, and mutters through his teeth, 'Stand and deliver, or I shall kill you, and then you will be a murderer!'" Lincoln denied that the Republican Party could be held responsible for John Brown's raid, which he likened to attempted assassinations of monarchs. "An enthusiast broods over the oppression of a people till he fancies himself commissioned by Heaven to liberate them. He ventures the attempt, which ends in little else than his own execution."

Lincoln directed the final segment of the speech to Republicans, urging them to remain patient in the face of Southern provocations. "It is exceedingly desirable that all parts of this great Confederacy shall be at peace, and in harmony, with one another," said Lincoln. "Let us Republicans do our part to have it so. Even though much provoked, let us do nothing through passion and ill temper. Even though the southern people will not so much as listen to us, let us calmly consider their demands, and yield to them if, in our deliberate view of our duty, we possibly can." But what would placate the Southerners? Only if we "cease to call slavery *wrong,* and join them in calling it *right.*" As proof, he cited Douglas's proposed statute virtually outlawing criticism of slavery. Southerners would eventually demand the repeal of Free State constitutions forbidding slavery, Lincoln predicted. Republicans must stand fast by their determination to halt the spread of the peculiar institution.

In a mighty crescendo, he concluded: "Let us be diverted by none of those sophistical contrivances wherewith we are so industriously plied and belabored—contrivances such as groping for some middle ground between the right and the wrong . . . —such as a policy of 'don't care' on a question about which all true men do care—such as Union appeals beseeching true Union men to yield to Disunionists, reversing the divine rule, and calling, not the sinners, but the righteous to repentance—such as invocations to Washington, imploring men to unsay what Washington said, and undo what Washington did. Neither let us be slandered from our duty by false accusations against us, nor frightened from it by menaces of destruction to the Government nor of dungeons to ourselves. Let us have faith that right makes might, and in that faith, let us, to the end, dare to do our duty as we understand it."[173]

This ringing conclusion touched off thunderous applause. One auditor shouted like a "wild Indian" and proclaimed Lincoln "the greatest man since St. Paul." Richard

C. McCormick of the New York *Evening Post* said he "never saw an audience more thoroughly carried away by an orator."[174] The "vast assemblage frequently rang with cheers and shouts of applause, which were prolonged and intensified at the close," reported the New York *Tribune*. Not since the era of Clay and Webster had a man "spoken to a larger assemblage of the intellect and mental culture of our City." Lincoln was "one of Nature's orators, using his rare powers solely and effectively to elucidate and to convince, though their inevitable effect is to delight and electrify as well." The printed version of the speech was eloquent, "yet the tones, the gestures, the kindling eye and the mirth-provoking look, defy the reporter's skill." No speaker "ever before made such an impression on his first appeal to a New-York audience." The *Tribune* called Lincoln's speech "probably the most systematic and complete defense yet made of the Republican position with regard to Slavery. We believe no speech has yet been made better calculated to win intelligent minds to our standard."[175]

William Cullen Bryant, who thought this address "was the best political speech he ever heard in his life," singled out for special praise Lincoln's analysis of the Founders' views on slavery expansion and his closing argument about the unreasonable demands of the "arrogant innovators" in the South. Though there was little new in the speech, Bryant remarked, "it is wonderful how much a truth gains by a certain mastery of clear and impressive statement."[176] Another poet, Edmund C. Stedman, wrote that "no public man has so ably commended himself to the respect of his hearers in a first appearance before the New York public. I heard a leading politician and able critic say, the next morning that it was by far the ablest effort made in the Cooper Institute since its erection two years ago. This is high praise, when 'tis remembered that such men as Cassius M. Clay and Thomas Corwin have spoken within its walls."[177]

Newspapers sang Lincoln's praises. "There was not a word in it of vulgar stump speaking—not a word of the 'spread eagle' style of oratory—not a word of claptrap," said the New York *Independent*; "it was straight-forward argument on the great questions of the times, and was as able as it was honest."[178] In Boston, Republican editors declared that the "completeness with which popular sovereignty and its progenitor were used up has rarely, if ever, been equaled" and praised Lincoln for being "clear in his style, with no pretensions to oratory, but apt and forcible."[179] Horace Greeley called it "the very best political address to which I ever listened—and I have heard some of Webster's grandest."[180] Several papers ran the full text of the speech. A Washington correspondent reported that "Republicans here, from all sections of the Union, are loud in their praises of Lincoln's magnificent speech in New York. It has stamped him as one of the leaders of the progressive thought of the age, and has caused his claims as a Presidential candidate to be fully discussed among many men who had not previously given them much consideration. A Senator, a well-known Seward man, said to me a few days since, 'I don't know but we shall have to nominate Lincoln at Chicago.'"[181]

Lincoln provided the New York *Tribune* with the manuscript of his speech and carefully examined the galleys with the proofreader, who threw away the document when he was finished. In September, a reprint was published with elaborate notes by Cephas Brainerd and Charles C. Nott, who ransacked every library in New York to identify Lincoln's sources. Nott offered a perceptive appraisal of the speech's scholarly merits: "No one who has not actually attempted to verify its details can understand the patient research and historical labor which it embodies. The history of our earlier politics is scattered through numerous journals, statutes, pamphlets, and letters; and these are defective in completeness and accuracy of statement, and in indices and tables of contents. Neither can any one who has not travelled over this precise ground appreciate the accuracy of every trivial detail, or the self-denying impartiality with which Mr. Lincoln has turned from the testimony of 'the Fathers,' on the general question of slavery, to present the single question which he discusses. From the first line to the last—from his premises to his conclusion, he travels with swift, unerring directness which no logician ever excelled—an argument complete and full, without the affectation of learning, and without the stiffness which usually accompanies dates and details. A single, easy, simple sentence of plain Anglo-Saxon words contains a chapter of history that, in some instances, has taken days of labor to verify and which must have cost the author months of investigation to acquire."[182] Lincoln declared that "no acts of his New York friends had pleased him so much" as this description of his speech.[183]

The Republican Congressional Document Committee mailed over 100,000 copies of that edition. Leaders of the New York Young Men's Republican Union of New York, which published the pamphlet, boasted that it was "the most elaborate and popular campaign document ever issued."[184]

The Democratic press was less enthusiastic. The New York *Herald* called Lincoln's speech a "hackneyed, illiterate composition" and "unmitigated trash, interlarded with coarse and clumsy jokes," and the Boston *Post* objected to Lincoln's alleged misrepresentation of James Madison's views.[185] The *Illinois State Register,* however, deemed the address "a more maturely conceived effort than any of his speeches during the Douglas campaign," though it criticized Lincoln for accepting a speaker's fee of $200.[186]

Lincoln's triumph at Cooper Institute unleashed a flood of speaking invitations from Republicans in New England, Pennsylvania, and New Jersey. He had originally intended to visit his son Robert at Phillips Exeter Academy in New Hampshire and then return to Springfield promptly but agreed to take to the stump in Rhode Island and Connecticut, where state elections were scheduled for April. The race in Connecticut was especially important, for Democrats believed that their popular candidate, Thomas Seymour, could capture the governorship, thus breaking the Republican hold on New England and inspiring Democrats everywhere. During the next two weeks Lincoln gave hastily scheduled addresses in Providence and Woonsocket, Rhode Island; Manchester, Exeter, Concord, and Dover, New Hampshire; and Hartford, New Haven, Bridgeport, Norwich, and Meriden, Connecticut. In the midst of that whirlwind tour, he complained to his wife: "I have been unable to escape this toil. If I had foreseen it I think I would not have come East at all. The speech at New-York, being within my calculation before I started, went off passably well, and gave me no trouble whatever. The difficulty was to make nine others, before reading audiences, who have already seen all my ideas in print."[187]

In most of his talks Lincoln repeated his Cooper Institute address, but in Connecticut he added a new element: a discussion of the laborers' right to strike. At Hartford on March 5, he attacked Douglas for condemning a strike by Massachusetts shoemakers. "I am glad to know that there is a system of labor where the laborer can strike if he wants to!" Lincoln exclaimed. "I would to God that such a system prevailed all over the world." If the encroachments of slavery were not resisted, "instead of *white* laborers who *can* strike, you'll soon have *black* laborers who *can't* strike."[188] The next day in New Haven he elaborated on his support of the right to strike and his faith in the free labor system, which left "each man free to acquire property as fast as he can. Some will get wealthy. I don't believe in a law to prevent a man from getting rich; it would do more harm than good. So while we do not propose any war upon capital, we do wish to allow the humblest man an equal chance to get rich with everybody else." Ringingly he declared "I want every man to have the chance—and I believe a black man is entitled to it—in which he *can* better his condition—when he may look forward and hope to be a hired laborer this year and next, work for himself afterward, and finally to hire men to work for him! That is the true system. Up here in New England, you have a soil that scarcely sprouts black-eyed beans, and yet where will you find wealthy men so wealthy, and poverty so rarely in extremity?"[189] A Yale professor of rhetoric found Lincoln's speech so impressive that he lectured his class on its merits, and a student from the South, who had come to jeer him, remarked at the close, "That fellow could shut up old Euclid himself, to say nothing of Steve Douglas."[190] Another undergraduate recalled that Lincoln "never paused for a word nor for an idea" and that he "gave a western intonation" to a few words.[191]

At Hartford, Lincoln decried the opposition's charge that Republicans had incited John Brown to raid Harper's Ferry. Scornfully he predicted that "if they think they are able to slander a woman into loving them, or a man into voting with them, they will learn better presently." Of white Southerners he sarcastically remarked: "If a slave runs away, they overlook the natural causes which impelled him to the act; do not remember the oppression or the lashes he received, but charge us with instigating him to flight. If he screams when whipped, they say it is not caused by the pains he suffers, but he screams because we instigate him to outcrying." Senator James M. Mason of Virginia, who wore homespun clothes to protest Northern criticism of slavery, received a blast of Lincoln's ridicule: "To carry out his idea, he ought to go *barefoot!* If that's the plan, they should begin at the *foundation,* and adopt the well known 'Georgia costume' of a shirt-collar and a pair of spurs!"[192] In the Connecticut capital, Lincoln's down-to-earth style and appearance pleased his audience, which regarded him as a true man of the people.

In New Haven, Lincoln chided Douglas for going "into hydrophobia and spasms of rage" when discussing Seward's "irrepressible conflict" speech. There Lincoln also used a homely metaphor that he had tried out a few days earlier in New Hampshire. In describing the danger presented by the expansion of slavery into the territories, he said: "If I saw a venomous snake crawling in the road, any man would say I might seize the nearest stick and kill it; but if I found that snake in bed with my children, that would be another question." To strike at the snake in the bed might injure the youngsters or provoke the snake to bite them. By the same token, "if I found it in bed with my neighbor's children, and I had bound myself by a solemn compact not to meddle with his children under any circumstances," then he would leave it alone. "But if there was a bed newly made up, to which the children were to be taken, and it was proposed to take a batch of young snakes and put them there with them, I take it no man would say there was any question how I ought to decide!"[193]

In Meriden, a heckler interrupted Lincoln, asking whether the Republicans would be able to inaugurate a president if they should win the November election. Lincoln replied, to the delight of his audience: "I reckon, friend, that if there are *votes* enough to elect a Republican President, there'll be *men* enough *to put him in.*"[194]

At another seat of learning—Exeter, New Hampshire (home to Phillips Exeter Academy)—Lincoln also impressed his audience. Many townspeople were highly educated, and the audience contained Lincoln's son, Robert, and his Academy school-mates. During his presentation Lincoln threw out questions; receiving no answers, he remarked, "You people here don't jaw back at a fellow as they do out West." Despite his unusual style, Lincoln captured his listeners, even those who had found his ap-pearance uncouth and his Western expressions peculiar. When Lincoln first took the stage, one boy whispered, "Don't you feel kind of sorry for Bob?" A girl remarked, "Isn't it too bad Bob's got such a homely father?" But after his speech, the students no longer pitied Robert; they took pride in his father. Lincoln had Robert with him on his next stops at Concord, Manchester, and Dover, where he continued to impress his audiences.[195]

On the rainy afternoon of March 1 in Concord, Lincoln spoke to a hastily as-sembled crowd, which included the influential journalist George G. Fogg, who de-spaired when he heard the speaker's halting and awkward opening remarks. Called aside briefly during the speech, Fogg was astonished when he returned to see the "hesitating and almost grotesque speaker commanding the audience by his tones and his gestures, and holding them as completely in his power as the graceful [Wendell] Phillips or the majestic [Daniel] Webster could have done."[196] Fogg's newspaper praised Lincoln's effort as "one of the ablest, most closely reasoned and eloquent speeches ever listened to in Concord."[197]

Calvin C. Webster was so impressed by Lincoln's oratory that he predicted: "That man will be the next president of the United States." When he made the same prophecy to Lincoln, the Illinoisan "replied that a good many men wanted to be president."[198] Sharing Webster's view was the New Hampshire State Republican chairman, Edward H. Rollins, who introduced Lincoln at the New Hampshire capi-tal. (A few weeks later Rollins would play a key role in the Republican national con-vention in Chicago as chairman of the New Hampshire delegation.) Rollins earnestly promoted Lincoln's candidacy after hearing him speak and predicted that if Lincoln were to campaign for three more weeks in the Granite State, the Republicans would carry the state with a majority of 10,000. When an abolitionist frequently interrupted Lincoln during his speech in Manchester, the audience tried to hush the man. Lincoln, however, said: "No! I *want* you to jaw back. This is the man I want to meet here. What did you say, sir?" By the end of the evening, his erstwhile heckler hurried to the platform to congratulate the speaker.[199] One journalist reported that "Lincoln exhibited less . . . energy than was expected."[200] He was doubtless fatigued, having given a talk in Concord that afternoon.

At Manchester, Mayor Frederick Smyth introduced Lincoln as the next president. After his talk, Lincoln skeptically asked Smyth if he meant his prediction seriously. The mayor replied that if Lincoln "had made the same impression in the other States where he had spoken that he made that day on the people of New Hampshire, he would certainly receive the presidential nomination." Lincoln replied, "No! No! That is impossible. Mr. Seward should and will receive the nomination. I do not believe that three States will vote for me in the convention." Earlier he had told Smyth that Seward's February 29 senate speech, in which the New Yorker sought to portray himself as a Moderate rather than a Radical, would make him the next president.[201] (In that address, the senator disclaimed any desire "to introduce negro equality," much to the dismay of abolitionists.)[202] Later, Smyth boasted to Lincoln that he was "the first man in N. Hampshire who advicated your nomination to the highest office in the world," and that he had "labored for more than a year to convince my Republican friends that you were the man for the times."[203]

In Rhode Island, even the editor of a Democratic paper called Lincoln's speech at Providence "the finest constitutional argument for a popular audience that I ever heard."[204] A Republican observed that Lincoln "made a decided hit & left a good impression" with his "plain, able and argumentative" address, which came "directly from the heart."[205] (Not everyone agreed. After the election, in which the Republicans suffered a reverse, a Bostonian claimed that Lincoln's speech in the Rhode Island capital "is the very reason that Providence has by such an overwhelming majority repudiated the party of which Mr. Lincoln is a leader.")[206]

On his return trip to Illinois, Lincoln stopped over in New York where, on Sunday, March 11, he attended Beecher's church with James A. Briggs. A gallery usher recalled that as Beecher spoke, "Lincoln's body swayed forward, his lips parted, and he seemed at length entirely unconscious of his surroundings—frequently giving vent to his satisfaction, at a well-put point or illustration, with a kind of involuntary Indian exclamation—'*ugh!*'—not audible beyond his immediate presence, but *very* expressive!"[207] Lincoln told the Rev. Dr. Henry M. Field of New York that "he thought there was not upon record, in ancient or modern biography, so *productive* a mind, as had been exhibited in the career of Henry Ward Beecher."[208]

Afterward, accompanied by Briggs and Hiram Barney, a pro-Chase lawyer, Lincoln visited the Five Points House of Industry School in one of the poorest districts of New York. When a teacher asked him to address the children, he at first declined, saying: "I am not used to speaking in religious meetings." At the youngsters' insistence, he finally spoke to them, saying "the way was open to every boy present, if honest, industrious, and persevering, to the attainment of a high and honorable position." When he tried to cut short his remarks, the lads clamored for more, and he obliged them.[209]

Lincoln found Barney quite impressive. Barney's sister-in-law, Julia Tappan, daughter of the philanthropic abolitionist Lewis Tappan, had tea with Lincoln and was at first put off by his "awkwardness of manner, homeliness of feature, and not over clean hands." But quickly she "forgot the disagreeable in admiration of his intelligence and heartiness and wit."[210]

Briggs had predicted that Seward, Chase, or Lincoln would win the Republican presidential nomination. (Mason Brayman reported that the "New-Yorkers really regard him [Lincoln] as one of the strongest of the Republicans—and treated him accordingly.")[211] Now Lincoln told Briggs that during his tour of New England, "several gentlemen made about the same remarks to me that you did . . . about the Presidency; they thought my chances were about equal to the best."[212]

By the time his Eastern tour ended, Lincoln had achieved a new stature and attracted a horde of presidential supporters. Among them was James G. Blaine, a rising star in the political firmament of Maine, who resolved to work for Lincoln's nomination. In New Haven, Lincoln was so impressive that the editor of the *Palladium*, James Babcock, endorsed him for the presidency and persuaded two delegates to the national convention to vote for him. In response, Lincoln told Babcock: "I do not envy the man who shall stand at the helm of this great Ship of State during the next four years."[213] After his talk in Norwich, Lincoln and local Republican leaders conferred at the Wauregan Hotel, where one gentleman suggested that their guest of honor might be a candidate for vice president. "Sir," interjected Amos W. Prentice, "we want him at the other end of the Avenue." This remark elicited long and loud applause.[214]

Connecticut journalist Gideon Welles, with whom Lincoln visited during his stay in Hartford, heaped praise on him: "This orator and lawyer has been caricatured. He is not Apollo, but he is not Caliban. He was made where the material for strong men is plenty, and his huge, tall frame is loosely thrown together. He is every way large, brain included, but his countenance shows intellect, generosity, great good nature, and keen discrimination. When he is called a great stump orator, people think of bellowing eloquence, and clownish stories. He is an effective speaker, because he is earnest, strong, honest, simple in style, and clear as crystal in his logic."[215] (Lincoln found Welles "one of the clearest headed men he had ever met" and a year later would name him secretary of the navy.)[216]

New England's most influential journal, the Springfield, Massachusetts, *Republican*, declared that Lincoln's "visit East has added greatly to his reputation among the republicans of this section, and they will be readily reconciled to any use of his name which the Chicago convention may propose in its selections for the national ticket."[217] An Illinois paper concurred: "The enthusiasm which his presence raised in the East is an earnest of that which would be excited by his nomination for the Presidency. There seems to be a strong feeling in favor of nominating Mr. Lincoln in case Douglas is the Democratic candidate; it being generally conceded that he is the strongest candidate against Douglas."[218] In Maine, the Machias *Republican* predicted that "Lincoln on the Republican Presidential ticket second, if not first, will give it strength and prestige all over the Union."[219] A pro-Seward lawyer in

Poughkeepsie speculated that Lincoln would do better than the New York senator not only in New Jersey, Pennsylvania, Indiana, and Illinois, but even in the Empire State. Lincoln, said this attorney, "is emphatically a man of the people, and he will run like a wild-cat."[220] Another New Yorker, who preferred Seward, admitted that Lincoln "would make the strongest Republican candidate." When visiting Springfield in the winter of 1860, this same man had asked a Douglas supporter what effect Lincoln's nomination would have on the Little Giant's chances. "*It would be devilish bad for us,*" came the reply.[221]

Lincoln's success encouraged his friends from Ohio. Samuel Galloway wrote, "I . . . congratulate you . . . You could not have ever anticipated a more cordial & favorable welcome than you received."[222] Lyman Trumbull concurred: "You made a great many friends by your Eastern trip. Have not heard a single man speak of your speeches but in the highest terms."[223] C. D. Hay told Lincoln: "I have been highly delighted at seeing the perfect success of your tour East. It is very evident that nothing has transpired recently to so much advance your interest and elevate you in the minds of the people, as that short trip."[224] Hay expressed regret that Lincoln had not spoken in Pennsylvania or New Jersey; indeed, it is curious that he turned down invitations from those swing states. En route to New York he was invited to meet with Simon Cameron and David Wilmot when stopping briefly in Philadelphia; he tried to avail himself of the offer but could not connect with them.

Also mysterious is Lincoln's decision to decline an invitation to address the Massachusetts Republican convention on March 7. Evidently, he believed that the Bay Staters were so strongly pro-Seward that he could win no support among them. In addition, the lack of a gubernatorial contest made a visit there less urgent than in other states holding elections that spring. Edward H. Rollins told him that the "Connecticut people need you more," for the party "is strong in Massachusetts & Connecticut is suffering."[225] (In the Nutmeg State, Republicans were in trouble because they were "stiff people who undertake to abolish niggers and lager beer at the same time," according to Herman Kreismann. Connecticut Germans resented the "foolish persecution of the lager beer saloons" by Republican prohibitionists.)[226]

When Lincoln departed New Hampshire, the Concord *Independent Democrat*, edited by George G. Fogg, said that the "blessings and hopes of many thousands who have seen and heard him for the first time, will go with him."[227] Fogg, a member of the Republican National Committee, would play an important role at the Chicago Convention a few weeks later.

A chorus of praise and optimism greeted Lincoln when he returned to Springfield in mid-March. "No inconsiderable portion of your fellow citizens in various portions of the country have expressed their preference for you as the candidate of the Republican party for the next Presidency," Milton Hay proudly told him on behalf of the capital's Republican Club. "There are those around you sir who have watched with manly interest and pride your upward march from obscurity to distinction. There are those here who know something of the obstacles which have lain in your pathway. . . . In the long list of those who have thus from humble beginnings won their way worthily to proud distinction there is not one can take precedence of the name of Abraham Lincoln." Since the dawn of the Republican movement in 1854, said Hay, Lincoln had demonstrated "statesmanship . . . well worthy of the Presidency itself."[228]

Probably travel-weary, Lincoln declined most invitations to speak, explaining that "I am not personally very prepossessing" and that potential audiences "have seen all my thoughts on paper."[229] One exception was a request from Republicans in Bloomington, where on April 10 he attacked popular sovereignty from a new angle. A bill criminalizing polygamy, which had passed the U.S. House five days earlier, prompted Lincoln to charge Illinois Democrats with hypocrisy. For Congress to outlaw polygamy in the Utah Territory would violate the principle of popular sovereignty, yet to allow it would be unpalatable to the voters of Illinois. Therefore, said Lincoln, Congressman John A. McClernand had proposed a compromise measure, which would have divided up Utah among other territories. But, asked Lincoln, "If you can put down polygamy in that way, why may you not thus put down slavery?" Lincoln "said he *supposed* that the friends of popular sovereignty would say—if they dared speak out—that *polygamy* was wrong and slavery right; and therefore one might thus be put down and the other not." To undermine thus the principle of popular sovereignty, Lincoln argued, would be like saying: "If I cannot rightfully murder a man, I may tie him to the tail of a kicking horse, and let him kick the man to death!"[230]

Girding for the Republican National Convention

Lincoln faced moral and practical dilemmas about using money to line up delegates to the Republican national convention. His ally Mark W. Delahay had complained to Lincoln that Seward spent freely to win support in Kansas and that "we, your friends, are all very poor" and hinted that "a very little money now would do us and you a vast deal of good." Lincoln would have none of it: "I can not enter the ring on the money basis—first, because in the main, it is wrong; and secondly, I have not, and can not get, the money." Yet, he added, "for certain objects, in a political contest, the use of some, is both right, and indispensable." So saying, he agreed to give Delahay $100 to enable him to attend the Chicago Convention, assuming that he would be chosen a delegate. When Delahay and all other Lincoln supporters in Kansas were defeated, Lincoln advised Delahay not to stir the Seward delegates "up to anger, but come along to the convention, & I will do as I said about expenses."[231] The following day, Lincoln told a correspondent who had proposed some scheme involving the expenditure of $10,000: "I could not raise ten thousand dollars if it would save me from the fate of John Brown. Nor have my friends, so far as I know, yet reached the point of staking any money on my chances of success."[232]

News that the Republicans won in Connecticut (though by a narrow margin) and in New Hampshire delighted Lincoln. He deemed the result in Rhode Island a "quasi defeat." The Republican gubernatorial candidate, Radical Seth Padelford, lost to the wealthy William Sprague, running as an independent. (The Democrats had fielded no candidate.) The political implications, Lincoln thought and others agreed, boded ill for Seward's nomination and well for his own, increasing his appetite for the ever-more-attainable nomination. To Lyman Trumbull, he confided on April 29,

"The taste *is* in my mouth a little."[233] He spelled out his strategy to a loyal booster, Samuel Galloway: "If I have any chance, it consists mainly in the fact that the *whole* opposition would vote for me if nominated. . . . My name is new in the field; and I suppose I am not the *first* choice of a very great many. Our policy, then, is to give no offence to others—leave them in a mood to come to us, if they shall be compelled to give up their first love. This, too, is dealing justly with all, and leaving us in a mood to support heartily whoever shall be nominated." Lincoln was particularly eager to avoid offending Chase, for "he gave us his sympathy in 1858, when scarcely any other distinguished man did."[234]

This strategy made sense, for the front-runners might well knock each other out of contention. In April, a supporter of dark horse John M. Read of Pennsylvania prophetically remarked that he had never seen "so many candidates before an 'opposition' convention with fair chances. The result it seems must not be in favor of either one of the three having the most strength now."[235] (Presumably he was referring to Seward, Bates, and Chase.) Lincoln worked hard to avoid offending other presidential aspirants, including Bates, Seward, and Cameron. When asked about their chances to carry Illinois, he tactfully observed that "Mr. Seward is the very best candidate we could have for the North of Illinois, and the very *worst* for the South of it. The estimate of Gov. Chase here is neither better nor worse than that of Seward, except that he is a newer man." Bates "would be the best man for the South of our State, and the worst for the North of it. If [75-year-old] Judge McLean was fifteen, or even ten years younger, I think he would be stronger than either, in our state, taken as a whole; but his great age, and the recollection of the deaths of Harrison and Taylor have, so far, prevented his being much spoken of here. I really believe we can carry the state for either of them, or for any one who may be nominated; but doubtless it would be easier to do it with some than with others."[236] More candidly, Lincoln told Trumbull: "I think neither Seward nor Bates can carry Illinois if Douglas shall be on the track; and that either of them can, if he shall not be. I rather think McLean could carry it with D. on or off," though McLean's age told against him. Seward's nomination would, Lincoln said, make it difficult to win the Illinois Legislature, though Seward and Bates were equally likely to carry the state.[237]

To reduce conflict within the state party, Lincoln urged Trumbull to "write no letters which can possibly be distorted into opposition, or quasi opposition to me. There are men on the constant watch for such things out of which to prejudice my peculiar friends against you. While I have no more suspicion of you than I have of my best friend living, I am kept in a constant struggle against suggestions of this sort. I have hesitated some to write this paragraph, lest you should suspect I do it for my own benefit, and not for yours; but on reflection I conclude you will not suspect me."[238] Wentworth and others were alleging that Trumbull angled to outstrip Lincoln in the race for the vice-presidential nomination. When Long John advised "You must do like Seward does—get a feller to run you," Lincoln replied that "events, and not a man's own exertions in his behalf, made presidents."[239] Wentworth spoke warmly of Lincoln but urged the nomination of Seward. Similarly, though expressing support for Lincoln, Trumbull favored McLean.

As the date for the Republican national convention (May 16) drew near, Lincoln expressed guarded optimism, predicting that only the Illinois delegation would unanimously support him, though Indiana "might not be difficult to get." In the other states, "I have not heard that any one makes any positive objection to me."[240] The clear implication was that if Seward did not win, Lincoln might well do so, especially since most delegates would support a candidate who could carry Illinois, Indiana, Pennsylvania, and New Jersey. The shrewd Mark W. Delahay had told him that Seward was unacceptably radical to delegates from those swing states; that Connecticut was also "a doubtful state" and therefore chary of Seward; that Ohio would go for any Republican and therefore Chase "can claim nothing in the way of availability"; that Bates was unacceptable to the Germans and to the Radicals and could not carry his own state; and that Cameron, known as a corrupt wheeler-dealer, was unable to win the nomination.[241]

Delahay's astute analysis was echoed by many of Lincoln's correspondents and jibed with his own understanding. Certainly, Cameron was weakened by doubts surrounding his character. His sobriquets—"The Great Winnebago Chief" and "Old Winnebago"—referred to his conduct in 1838 when he, acting as a claims commissioner, had allegedly cheated the Winnebago Indians by paying them $66,000 in wildcat currency, issued by his own Pennsylvania bank, which could not be cashed or used to purchase anything in their territory. One Pennsylvanian remarked acidly: "If Cameron had his deserts, he would be serving out a sentence in the penitentiary instead of serving in the U.S. Senate." A New York *Herald* correspondent called him "shrewd, unscrupulous and selfish."[242] Chase and Seward suffered from their prominence; having been in the spotlight for many years, they had made enemies. David Wilmot believed that Old Line Whigs would not back either of them, though they "would support other men of equally advanced republican positions, but who had not been held up before them for years, in so unfavorable a light."[243] That description fit Lincoln, who looked good by comparison, for he was, as Horace Greeley pointed out, "unencumbered by that weight of prejudice, and that still heavier responsibility for the sins of others, sure to be fastened upon the shoulders of every man who occupies for a long time the position of a political leader."[244]

Lincoln was also more likable than the vain, hyper-ambitious Chase and the arrogant, dictatorial Seward. Chase had antagonized many potential supporters. The militantly antislavery Congressman Joseph Root of Ohio said "Chase is too supremely selfish to be popular or to have any devoted personal friends among men of sense who know him thoroughly but this is not his worst misfortune. I will not say that he cannot distinguish between a sycophant and a friend but I will say that he ever preferred the former until every one of his [native?] political helpers that I know belongs to the class of cheats or nincompoops."[245] Justice John McLean of the Supreme Court deemed Chase "the most unprincipled man politically that I have ever known. He is selfish, beyond any other man."[246] Both Cameron and Chase were damaged by a lack of unanimity in their home state delegations. In addition, the overconfident Ohioan had ineptly organized his presidential bid, appointing no one to serve as his manager at Chicago, where his free trade views did not sit well with the crucial Pennsylvania delegation.

Complicating the picture was the stalemate reached by Democrats at their strife-torn national convention in Charleston, which opened on April 23 and adjourned on May 3 without choosing a candidate. Along with most other observers, Lincoln had expected Douglas to win there. (In 1859, when asked about Douglas's chances at Charleston, Lincoln replied: "Well, were it not for certain matters that I know transpired, which I regarded at one time among the impossibilities—I would say he stood no possible chance. I refer to the fact that in the Illinois contest with myself, he had the sympathy and support of Greeley, of Burlingame and Wilson of Massachusetts, and other leading Republicans; that at the same time he received the support of [Virginia Governor Henry A.] Wise and [Vice-President John C.] Breckinridge [of Kentucky], and other Southern men; that he took direct issue with the Administration, and secured, against all its power, 125,000 out of 130,000 Democratic votes cast in the State. A man that can bring such influences to bear with his own exertions, may play the d—l at Charleston.")[247] The Democrats were to reconvene in mid-June at Baltimore, when presumably they would finally name Douglas. In the meantime, the Republicans would be meeting in Chicago in mid-May without knowing for sure whom they would face. Since Lincoln was regarded as the strongest foe against Douglas, any uncertainty about the Little Giant's becoming the Democratic standard-bearer improved Seward's chances.

Meanwhile, conservative ex-Whigs, mostly pro-slavery Southerners, had met in Baltimore to form the Constitutional Union Party, which nominated a ticket of John Bell of Tennessee and Edward Everett of Massachusetts and adopted a platform calling simply for support of the Union and the Constitution and for the enforcement of the laws. They hoped to preempt the Republicans and force them to endorse their nominee. This move enhanced Lincoln's prospects, for it was feared that moderate Republicans might vote for Bell if the Chicago Convention chose a candidate viewed as an antislavery Radical, like Seward or Chase.

Illinois Republican Convention

Looking ahead hopefully, Lincoln predicted that he would receive unanimous support from the Illinois delegation to the coming national convention. He felt he could overcome both pro-Bates sentiment in the central and southern sections of the state and Seward support in the north. On May 9 and 10 at Decatur, 645 Republican delegates gathered in a hastily-erected structure to choose a gubernatorial candidate and adopt a platform. With John Moses and Nathan M. Knapp, Lincoln arrived a day before the convention and spent the night at the Junction House hotel, where Lincoln and Knapp shared a bed too short for them. After they retired for the night, they found that as soon as one tried to turn over, the other would wind up on the floor. After such an unceremonious ejection from the bed, Knapp exclaimed: "Well, Lincoln, I guess we shall have to reconstruct our platform!" Lincoln was so pleased with this witticism that he repeated it to many men the next day.[248]

Shortly after the convention opened, the tall, good-looking Richard J. Oglesby, a rising political star from Decatur who would eventually be elected governor of Illinois three times as well as U.S. senator, interrupted the proceedings by announcing: "I am informed that a distinguished citizen of Illinois, and one of whom Illinois ever delights to honor, is present, and I wish to move that this body invite him to a seat on the stand." The 3,000 onlookers and delegates who were jammed into the makeshift 900-seat convention center impatiently waited for this man to be identified. Oglesby teased the audience by refusing to name the "distinguished citizen" immediately. When he finally shouted, "Abraham Lincoln," the crowd roared its approval and tried to move Lincoln, who had been sitting in the rear of the hall, through the densely packed crowd to the stage. Because he was unable to penetrate the throng, they hoisted him up and passed him forward over the heads of the multitude. Scrambling and crawling over this uneasy surface, he finally reached the platform, where half a dozen delegates set him upright. "The cheering," reported an observer, "was like the roar of the sea. Hats were thrown up by the Chicago delegation, as if hats were no longer useful." Lincoln, who "rose bowing and blushing," appeared to be "one of the most diffident and worst plagued men I ever saw." With a smile, he thanked the crowd for its expression of esteem.[249]

After the aspirants for governor had been placed in nomination but before the voting began (in which Yates defeated Swett and Judd), Oglesby once again interrupted, announcing that "an old Democrat of Macon county . . . desired to make a contribution to the Convention." The crowd yelled, "Receive it!" Thereupon Lincoln's second cousin John Hanks, accompanied by a friend, entered the hall bearing two fence rails along with a placard identifying them thus: "Abraham Lincoln, The Rail Candidate for President in 1860. Two rails from a lot of 3,000 made in 1830 by Thos. Hanks and Abe Lincoln—whose father was the first pioneer of Macon County." (The sign painter was wrong about Hanks's first name and about Thomas Lincoln's status as an early settler in Illinois.) Oglesby's carefully-staged theatrical gesture, conjuring up images of the 1840 log-cabin-and-cider campaign, electrified the crowd, which whooped and hollered for over ten minutes. In response to those thunderous cheers and calls of "Lincoln," the candidate-to-be rose, examined the rails, then sheepishly told the crowd: "Well, gentlemen, I must confess I do not understand this: I don't think I know any more about it than you do." (This may have surprised some delegates, for the *Illinois State Journal* had the day before informed them that among "the sights which will greet your eyes will be a lot of rails, mauled . . . thirty years ago, by old Abe Lincoln and John Hanks.")[250] He added jocularly that the rails may have been hewn by him, "but whether they were or not, he had mauled many and many better ones since he had grown to manhood."[251] (Another witness recalled Lincoln's words slightly differently: "My old friend here, John Hanks, will remember I used to shirk splitting all the hard cuts. But if those two are honey locust rails, I have no doubt I cut and split *them*.")[252] Once again the crowd cheered Lincoln, whose sobriquet "the Rail-splitter" was born that day. Ardent Seward supporters realized immediately that their champion would not win the Illinois delegation.

(According to Noah Brooks, Lincoln "was not greatly pleased with the rail incident," for he disapproved of "stage tricks."[253] But he was, Brooks reported in 1863, rather proud of his rail-splitting talent. While visiting Union troops at the front, Lincoln noticed trees that they had chopped down. Scrutinizing the stumps, he said:

"That's a good job of felling; they have got some good axemen in this army, I see." When Brooks asked about his expertise in rail-splitting, the president replied: "I am not a bit anxious about my reputation in that line of business; but if there is any thing in this world that I am a judge of, it is of good felling of timber." He "explained minutely how a good job differed from a poor one, giving illustrations from the ugly stumps on either side.")[254]

Oglesby had been seeking ways to emphasize Lincoln's humble origins to justify something like Henry Clay's cognomen, "the mill boy of the slashes." A few days before the convention he had asked Hanks what Lincoln had done well as a young settler in Illinois. "Well, not much of any kind but dreaming," replied Hanks, "but he did help me split a lot of rails when we made a clearing twelve miles west of here." Intrigued, Oglesby urged Hanks to show him the spot. They rode out, identified some rails that Lincoln and Hanks may have split three decades earlier, and carried away two of them. When Oglesby proposed to some friends that the rails be introduced at the Decatur Convention, they told him to go ahead, for it could do no harm and might do some good. Oglesby was not the only Illinois Republican to think the rail-splitter image would help Lincoln. In March, Nathan M. Knapp had told a friend, "I want *Abe* to run; then I want a picture of him splitting rails on the Sangamon Bottom, with 50 cts per hundred marked on a chip placed in the fork of a tree nearby. I think it will win."[255]

The next day, when John M. Palmer introduced a resolution "that Abraham Lincoln is the first choice of Illinois for the Presidency, and that our delegates be instructed to use all honorable means for his nomination by the Chicago convention, and to cast their votes as a unit for him," Thomas J. Turner, the leading champion of Seward's candidacy, rose to object. Somewhat bitterly, Palmer asked if Turner were "so blind and deaf . . . that he cannot see and hear that this Convention is literally sitting on a volcano of its own enthusiasm for Abraham Lincoln, and just aching to give three cheers and a tiger for Old Abe?"[256] In response, the convention enthusiastically passed the resolution. Obviously moved by this tribute, Lincoln briefly expressed his heartfelt thanks.

The committee charged with selecting four at-large delegates sought Lincoln's advice. The previous day, he had indicated that he wanted David Davis and Norman B. Judd chosen. In keeping with Lincoln's wishes, both Davis, who was to act as Lincoln's manager at Chicago, and Judd were named at-large delegates. They did not particularly like each other but cooperated to promote Lincoln's candidacy. The two other at-large delegates, also selected by Lincoln, were Gustave Koerner, an obvious choice to please the crucial German vote, and Orville H. Browning, a Bates supporter with close ties to the Old Whigs. Lincoln ignored Davis's plea to have John Wentworth named a delegate. Some of Lincoln's friends, including Oglesby and Nathaniel G. Wilcox, objected that to appoint Browning would be "putting the child into the nurse[']s arms to be strangled." Lincoln replied, "I guess you had better let Browning go." He explained: "I know that old Browning is not for me . . . but it won't do to leave him out of the convention," for he "will do more harm on the outside than he could on the inside." Lincoln was "satisfied that Bates has no show. When Orville sees this he'll undoubtedly come over to me, and do us some good with the Bates men."[257] In the end, Browning did exactly that.

Of the eighteen delegates chosen by congressional district, a few were pro-Seward, but operating under the unit rule, all would vote for Lincoln. "Our delegation will stick to Lincoln as long as there is a chance to prevent Seward getting any votes from us at all," Herman Kreismann predicted.[258] Francis Lou and James M. Ruggles, delegates who were staying at the same Decatur hotel as Lincoln, invited him to accompany them to Chicago for the national convention. "I should like to go," Lincoln replied, "but possibly I am too much of a candidate to be there—and probably not enough to keep me away—on the whole I think I had best not go." Enthusiastically they declared, "as to that, Mr. Lincoln, we are going to nominate you," and boarded a train for the Windy City.[259]

Although the Illinoisans were prepared to work hard for Lincoln's nomination, they did not really expect him to win. It was widely assumed that they would cast a complimentary vote for him and then turn to some other candidate. Above all they wanted to stop Seward, whose nomination would make it impossible to win the legislature, which was to choose a U.S. senator in 1861. They dreaded the prospect of a Democrat replacing Trumbull. For all his recent successes and optimistic calculations, Lincoln shared the delegation's doubts about his chances at Chicago. He guessed that he might receive around 100 votes. "I have a notion that will be the high mark for me," he predicted.[260] In March, Henry C. Whitney told Lincoln that he could win the presidential nomination; in reply, Lincoln modestly brushed aside his friend's speculation, saying: "It is enough honor for me to be talked about, for it."[261] Around that time he speculated to a student in his law office, "I haven't a chance in a hundred."[262] To William Bross, who suggested he should be preparing his acceptance speech, Lincoln cautiously replied: "Well, it does look a little that way; but we can never be sure about such things."[263]

"The Most Available Presidential Candidate for Unadulterated Republicans"
The Chicago Convention
(May 1860)

In May 1859, Lincoln's friend Nathan M. Knapp prophetically called him "the most available" (i.e., the most electable) presidential candidate "for unadulterated Republicans."[1] The following January, when a former congressman from Indiana was told that Republicans should nominate William L. Dayton of New Jersey for president and Lincoln as his running mate, he replied: "I would like Lincoln & Dayton better than Dayton & Lincoln," for he favored "the most available" among the "decided straight out anti slavery men."[2]

By the time the Republican national convention met in the spring of 1860, that view had become so prevalent that the "Rail-splitter" was able to capture the Republican nomination, for of all the outspoken critics of slavery, he seemed to have the best chance of winning. But his success was not inevitable; he faced strong rivals, most notably William Henry Seward of New York, the odds-on favorite as the delegates gathered in Chicago.

Undermining Seward

Delegates began arriving in Chicago well before May 16, the official opening day of the Republican convention, and they were something to behold. The journalist Simon P. Hanscom remarked that of all the sights in the world, "the small politician at a National Convention is the most entertaining. Attired in solemn black, he stalks gloomily along, as if the fate of the nation rested on his shoulders. He affects the diplomatic, and pretends to be acquainted with the sundry terrible schemes which are hatching." Chicago itself "is a wonder to a stranger," with "its broad avenues, magnificent buildings, splendid shops, and fine private residences." There one could observe "all the good and the bad in our national character," all "our headlong haste to be rich—all our contempt of old forms and ceremonies—all our ridiculous parvenu affectation—all our real energy, enterprise and perseverance, opposed to which no difficulties are insurmountable."[3]

On May 12 Lincoln's operatives gathered in the Windy City where they had failed to secure hotel rooms ahead of time, so little did they think of their man's chances. After persuading some families to surrender their rooms in the Tremont House, they established headquarters there. Judge David Davis took command, ably assisted by attorneys from the Eighth Circuit, including Leonard Swett, Stephen T. Logan, Ward Hill Lamon, Samuel C. Parks, Clifton H. Moore, Lawrence Weldon, and Oliver Davis; by Lincoln's friends like Jesse W. Fell, Ozias M. Hatch, Ebenezer Peck, Richard J. Oglesby, Jackson Grimshaw, Nathan M. Knapp, Jesse K. Dubois, William Butler, John M. Palmer, Theodore Canisius, and Mark W. Delahay; and by Illinois delegates, notably Norman B. Judd, Gustave Koerner, Burton C. Cook, Richard Yates, and Orville H. Browning.

"If you will put yourself at my disposal day and night," Davis told them, "I believe Lincoln can be nominated."[4] The judge dispatched these troops in squads of two or three to lobby delegations. "No one ever thought of questioning Davis' right to send men hither and thither, nor to question his judgment," recalled Swett, who described the judge as "the most thorough manager of men I ever knew," a "born ruler," a "teacher of teachers, a man among men, a master of masters," one who "never faltered, never gave up, never made any mistakes."[5]

Their strategy was simple: first, stop Seward; next, line up about 100 delegates for Lincoln on the first ballot (233 were necessary to win); then make sure that he had more votes on the second ballot in order to gain momentum; finally, clinch the nomination on the third ballot. It was important not to get Lincoln out front too early, lest other candidates combine to stop him.

To effect this plan, Davis assigned handlers to work tactfully with the delegates, greeting them upon their arrival in Chicago, escorting them to their lodgings, and making sure that all their needs were met. These handlers engaged in no hard salesmanship but rather urged their charges to consider making Lincoln their second choice, if not their first. Many delegates not already pledged to Seward were cared for in this way. On May 14, Lincoln's operatives informed him that they were "dealing tenderly with delegates, taking them in detail, and making no fuss," and were "not pressing too hard your claims" and thus winning "friends every where."[6] To delegates favoring Seward, they quietly argued that the New Yorker, unlike Lincoln, could not carry the swing states—Illinois, Indiana, Pennsylvania, and New Jersey. (Some also included Connecticut and Rhode Island in that category.) Among the targets of this strategy were Bates supporters, led by Horace Greeley, who was serving as a delegate from Oregon as well as a Bates manager. The Lincoln men persuaded Bates's delegates to support the Rail-splitter as second choice, arguing that most westerners thought the party would surely lose the national election with Chase or Seward as its standard-bearer.

Their arguments were aptly summarized by Charles H. Ray, who told a pro-Chase delegate from Massachusetts: "We must win to extend ourselves into the border slave states, and to have in our hands the power to fill the places of the four judges of the Supreme Court who will die . . . before the next Presidential term expires. We can win with *Lincoln*, with Judge [John M.] Read, possibly with [William L.] Dayton or [Jacob] Collamer; but not with Seward." To be sure, Ray conceded, the New Yorker had "earned and now deserves the place." But, he asked rhetorically, "why on a point of gratitude, throw away a victory now within our grasp?" Of the electable men he listed, "Lincoln is the best," for he "is intensely radical on fundamental principles; but has never said an intemperate word," was sound on the tariff and homestead legislation, supported sensible internal improvements, was "a Southern man by birth and education," a "people[']s man," and "as true and as honest a man as ever lived." Nothing more could be asked of a candidate. "Why not go for him and make victory certain? Depend upon it, . . . we have no votes to throw away. We shall want every man." If Seward must be passed over, so be it.[7]

The only serious objection some delegates made to Lincoln was that he was as radical, and thus unelectable, as Seward. To combat that impression, Lincoln notified his operatives, "I agree with Seward in his 'Irrepressible Conflict,' but I do not endorse his 'Higher Law' doctrine."[8]

Davis and his allies worked doggedly to stop the Seward bandwagon. The challenge was daunting, for, as Ray noted, the senator had long been regarded as the leader of the party, richly deserving the nomination for his many contributions to the cause. He himself thought the nomination was his due. "Clamorous as crows," his operatives "went to Chicago with the joy, pride and self confidence of a bridegroom marching to his wedding feast," remarked the New York *Herald*.[9] They were led by the shrewd, calculating Thurlow Weed, known variously as "the Wizard of the Lobby," "Lord Thurlow," "the Richelieu of his party," and "the Dictator." An observer at the convention noted that Weed's "motions are as rapid as a rope-dancer's; his eye heretofore dull lights up with an expression both powerful and charming; he speaks quick and short and always in a low tone, smiling you into acquiescence, and looking you into conviction with his sincerity; he calls with his finger, and changes proceedings with a word. Marvellous is his power over man—indescribable it is felt, not seen; you act upon his convictions, not your own, and know not when or how the substitution was made."[10] Flush with money, accompanied by bands and celebrities (like the prizefighter Tom Hyer, whose presence caused some wags to jest about Seward's "Hyer law doctrine"), Weed and his allies sought to lend an air of inevitability to their candidate's nomination.

Some Seward backers were imposingly sophisticated, dressed in trim business suits. Others were more brash; the Cincinnati journalist Murat Halstead noted that they "can drink as much whiskey, swear as loud and long, sing as bad songs, and 'get up and howl' as ferociously as any crowd of Democrats. They are opposed as they say to being 'too d–d virtuous.' . . . They slap each other on the back with the emphasis of delight when they meet, and rip out 'How *are* you?' with a 'How are you hoss?' style, that would do honor to Old Kaintuck on a bust."[11] They had little use for Lincoln; Weed's assistant editor on the Albany *Evening Journal* acknowledged that Seward's friends "labored earnestly to prevent his [Lincoln's] nomination," for they "deemed him greatly the inferior, in every way, of their candidate. And they said so, kindly but with emphasis."[12] They were also imperious, insisting that their man had earned the nomination and threatening to bolt the party if he were passed over.

This threat tended to demoralize Seward's numerous but scattered opponents as the convention began, but fear that the New Yorker's backers might abandon the party was overmatched by fear that moderate and conservative Republicans in the Lower North would desert and vote for John Bell, nominee of the newly-formed Constitutional Union Party (composed mainly of conservative ex-Whigs) if Seward, with his Radical antislavery reputation, were named the party's standard-bearer. Conversely, some strong antislavery men were disenchanted with Seward's February 29 speech, in which he referred to the Slave States as "capital states" and the Free States as "labor states." The Sage of Auburn seemed to be backsliding from his earlier strong denunciation of slavery. A New Hampshireman asked, "Did Seward aim to appease the South by the obsequious use of new terms? It struck me so. I think he is *overanxious* to be President, and may have to 'wait for the wagon,' though his consummate abilities are everywhere acknowledged."[13] Seward's address reminded one critic of the modest Indiana maiden who "wouldn't swing in the garden any more 'kase 'taters had eyes!"[14] Lydia Maria Child warned a fellow abolitionist: "Beware how you endorse William H. Seward. He is no more to be trusted than Daniel Webster was. He is thoroughly unprincipled and selfish."[15] The indignation at all such Republican attempts to mollify Southerners was colorfully expressed by Herndon, who said they made him feel "ashamed that I am a Republican. I am like the little girl who accidentally shot off wind in company—she said 'I wish I was in "hell" a little while.'"[16]

Seward faced other objections. Nativists disliked his action as governor of New York twenty years earlier, when he recommended granting state money to Catholic schools. At Chicago, Thaddeus Stevens, a leading Pennsylvania Radical who championed the candidacy of John McLean, intoned repeatedly: "Pennsylvania will never vote for the man who favored the destruction of the common-school system in New York to gain the favor of Catholics and foreigners."[17] From Philadelphia came a warning that nativists "have engendered so thorough a prejudice against him [Seward], that a life-time [of] apologies and explanations of his acts and connexion with Bishop Hughes, of New York, and his favoring a division of the 'Public School fund with the Catholics' could not induce them to vote for him," and hence "it would be suicidal to nominate him for the Presidency." The nativists would prefer Bates or McLean, but "will not object to Fessenden, or Lincoln, or Dayton."[18] An Illinoisan at the convention reported that the "Americans or old Fillmore men were all opposed to Seward because, it is believed that if he does not work hard to get Catholic votes now, he *once* did."[19]

Charges of fiscal recklessness also hurt Seward. Some critics complained that he belonged to "the New York school of very expensive rulers" and that his "uniform votes for lavish expenditures" might "embarrass the argument against the extravagance if not the corruption of Pierce and Buchanan."[20] The New York *Evening Post* observed that no "rogue comes to Washington with a plausible device for spending the money obtained from the people . . . who does not find a friend and champion in Senator Seward."[21] In the eyes of George G. Fogg, Seward was a man who "has *always* distinguished himself by his willingness to squander the public moneys on any and every scheme of private emolument with which Congress has been approached."[22]

Republicans who hoped to capitalize on fresh revelations of corruption in the Buchanan administration, as documented by Pennsylvania Congressman John Covode's investigating committee and by the press, shied away from Seward. Fogg thought that Seward "won't steal, himself, but he don't care how much his friends steal."[23] The chief engineer of the Illinois and Michigan Canal noted that "a large number of influential Republicans in all the States opposed nominating Seward because his leading friends in his own State were believed to be *awfully corrupt*."[24] (Earlier that year, Weed had arranged for the passage of monopolistic legislation by the New York State Legislature offering street-railway builders sweetheart franchises to construct trolley lines in New York City. In turn the contractors provided kickbacks, which Weed planned to use in securing Seward's nomination and election.) Shortly after the convention, a delegate explained that "however honest and pure Seward may be" personally, the party would "have lost much, if not all the capital we have in this campaign in the extravagance and corruption of the Administration, had Seward been our candidate."[25]

It was perhaps unfair to hold Seward responsible for Weed's corrupt ways, but they tainted the senator in the eyes of many delegates nonetheless. Connecticut Senator James Dixon, who liked Seward personally, lamented that he was "surrounded by a corrupt set of rascals" and feared that "his administration would be the most corrupt the country has ever witnessed."[26] Even such an enthusiastic Seward supporter as Carl Schurz of Wisconsin was dismayed when he beheld Weed, a "tall man with his cold, impassive face, giving directions to a lot of henchmen, the looks and the talk and the demeanor of many of whom made me feel exceedingly uncomfortable."[27] Several delegates thought Weed "the devil incarnate," and "the most corrupt and dangerous politician in the United States."[28] A New Yorker declared, "We owe Mr. Seward everything; he founded the party, and built it up to greatness; our debt to him is incalculable; *but we won't pay it in hard cash to Thurlow Weed.*"[29]

On May 16, James G. Blaine wrote that Seward's men "assume an air of dictation which is at once unwarranted & offensive, & which I think will create a reaction."[30] A delegate protested that "the New Yorkers were there with money to corrupt, with bullies to intimidate and with houries to seduce."[31] (The previous year journalist Simon P. Hanscom had noted that there was "a threatening, bullying disposition, on the part of the Seward men" which, he predicted, "will do their favorite no sort of good.")[32] On May 15, it was reported that Sewardites "have plenty of money and are using it freely" and that the "rumor that money has been freely used to bring about the success of Seward has greatly damaged his prospects."[33] New York operatives asked delegates, "If you don't nominate Seward, where will you get your money?"[34] William Maxwell Evarts, a leading Wall Street lawyer and one of the most eloquent supporters of the Sage of Auburn, assured delegates that Seward could win because his friends in New York would freely spend money to elect their man in the key battleground state of Pennsylvania.

Such tactics backfired. Joshua Giddings told a fellow Radical that Seward's operatives "disgusted members by their constant assertions that they had the money to win his election, that they could buy up the doubtful states."[35] A month after the convention, a Boston journalist confided to a friend that "I was a Seward man and am now but. . . . I do not like Governor Seward[']s Albany friends. I believe them corrupt and I further believe that it was the fear that the Albany Regency with Weed at its head, and some tool of his at its tail would be the power behind the throne that really defeated Seward."[36]

New Yorkers who had observed the Seward machine in action were especially alarmed. Alluding to Weed's shady street railway deals, William Cullen Bryant reported from Manhattan that "the best men here— . . . think it an omen of what we may expect from Seward's administration."[37] Another New Yorker anticipated the demise of the Republican Party if Seward were nominated, for the public would not abide the "horde of political pirates and plunderers" in the retinue of the senator, who was "embarrassed by his obligations to them and complicities with them."[38] Wall Street lawyer and moderate Republican George Templeton Strong dreaded the prospect of Seward and Weed, "the most adroit of wire-pullers," with "their tail of profligate lobby men promoted from Albany to Washington."[39]

An Iowa delegate recalled that among "the influential considerations in making many of us fight Seward so hard at Chicago was the feeling that the forces of 'commercialism' and corrupt political rule would triumph by his election." Seward's men "'talked big' about the need of money in the approaching election and the sources they would control and tap. It was notorious at that time that Weed manipulated the Albany legislature to secure New York City franchises for coteries or cliques of his personal and political friends. He was regarded as the most potent political manager in the country. . . . One of the New Yorkers came up to me and said, 'It is absurd for you westerners to want to nominate an Illinois man or any other man than Seward. No man can carry Pennsylvania or Indiana unless he and his backers have plenty of the sinews of war.' I asked, 'What do you mean?' 'I mean money, of course,' he rejoined. 'Just so,' I retorted, 'and that is one of the reasons why we from Iowa and the West are afraid of you and are fighting you. You and your kind think you can purchase the election as you buy stocks. But you can't buy Iowa. We need a little money for ordinary campaign expenses but not to buy votes. . . . Mr. Seward must not be nominated. Not because we think he is personally bad or wants to do anything unrighteous, but because he could not control the forces that are back of him and that would work through him.'"[40]

Such objections were widely shared. William Curtis Noyes, a Seward organizer at Chicago, lamented that he and his allies "could not resist the charges made against the last Legislature on the score of corruption, etc., and it was mainly imputed to his [i.e., Seward's] friends."[41] Journalist James Shepherd Pike told Senator William P. Fessenden that Seward's votes in the senate formed "part of the hateful plundering policy that mocks & degrades New York politics & which is poisoning those of the federal gov[ernmen]t. We have got to make war on that policy & slay it or it will be the death of the republican party." To Pike it seemed "as though it was our luck to be cursed with leading men having one damned rascally weakness or [an]other. If he will vote with the thieving party it is deeply to be lamented for we all wish otherwise."[42] The only candidate who appeared to lack a "damned rascally weakness" was Lincoln, whose reputation as "Honest Old Abe" played a vital role in his eventual nomination and election.

The Seward forces tried to derail Lincoln's candidacy by promoting him for vice-president. On May 15, Lincoln's friend William Butler was approached by a Mr. Street of New York, along with Senator Preston King, a confidant of Thurlow Weed. Street pledged that if the Illinois delegation would agree to have Lincoln named as Seward's running mate, they would receive $100,000 for both the Illinois and Indiana campaigns. When David Davis learned that a similar offer was being made to New Jersey men if Dayton would run on a ticket with Seward, he became "greatly agitated" and along with John M. Palmer paid a visit to the Garden State delegation. There a solemn, elderly judge was urging that Lincoln be made Seward's running mate. Palmer told him: "you may nominate Mr. Lincoln for Vice-President if you please. But I want you to understand that there are 40,000 Democrats in Illinois who will support this ticket if you will give them an opportunity. We are not Whigs, and we never expect to be Whigs. We will never consent to support two old Whigs on this ticket. We are willing to vote for Mr. Lincoln with a Democrat on the ticket, but we will not consent to vote for two Whigs."

The judge indignantly asked Davis, "is it possible that party spirit so prevails in Illinois that Judge Palmer properly represents public opinion?"

"Oh," said Davis, feigning distress at Palmer's remarks, "oh, Judge, you can't account for the conduct of these old Locofocos."

"Will they do as Palmer says?"

"Certainly. There are 40,000 of them, and, as Palmer says, not one of them will vote for two Whigs."

When Palmer and Davis left, the New Jersey judge was enraged. Upon returning to the Tremont House, Palmer complained: "Davis, you are an infernal rascal to sit there and hear that man berate me as he did. You really seemed to encourage him."

In reply, Davis merely laughed heartily.[43]

The most potent stop-Seward activists were in the Indiana and Pennsylvania delegations. Their gubernatorial candidates (Henry S. Lane and Andrew G. Curtin, respectively) protested that if Seward were nominated, they would lose. (When Curtin warned Edward L. Pierce that Massachusetts's backing of Seward jeopardized the party's chances, Pierce retorted that the Pennsylvania governor could expect no hearing from the Bay State as long as his state supported Cameron.) The eloquent Lane mounted a table at Tremont House, swung a cane about his head, and in a trumpet-like voice threatened to withdraw his candidacy if Seward became the standard-bearer. The modest, unassuming Hoosier leader had already spurned an offer of financial assistance from Weed. The New York boss promised to send Lane sufficient money to guarantee his election as governor if he would have the Indiana delegation back the New Yorker. Lane replied indignantly that "there was neither money nor influence enough in their State" to induce him to change his mind.[44]

Curtin's efforts were equally effective, for he was highly persuasive in private conversations. Horace Greeley told a friend, "If you had seen the Pennsylvania delegation, and known how much money Weed had in hand, you would not have believed we could do so well as we did. Give Curtin thanks for that."[45]

Complicating Davis's task was the ever-troublesome John Wentworth. On the eve of the convention, Wentworth's paper, the Chicago *Democrat*, endorsed Seward. In addition, Long John lobbied key delegations on behalf of anyone but Lincoln. Evidently, he aspired to a cabinet post, which would be unattainable if a fellow Illinoisan became president. To counteract his efforts, Lincoln operatives had a critic follow in his wake denouncing him.

Winning Indiana

After helping to slow the Seward bandwagon, David Davis and his coterie turned their attention to the Indiana delegation, which at first seemed divided, with some members favoring Bates, others McLean, and still others Lincoln. Strengthening Lincoln's chances was his personal acquaintance with some Indiana delegates whom he knew from his court circuit practice in Illinois counties bordering the Hoosier State. Two such delegates were George K. Steele, who had visited Lincoln in the early spring and found him impressive, and Greencastle attorney Dillard C. Donnohue, who had no desire "to go to Chicago for the purpose of putting in nomination a man just for the fun of seeing him defeated."[46] Fearful of bucking the strong Bates tide in his part of the state, Steele, along with Donnohue, conferred with Lane; the three men thought it best to divide the delegation evenly between Bates and Lincoln. That represented an important first step in eroding the Missourian's support in the Hoosier ranks.

Shortly before the convention, Caleb B. Smith, head of the Indiana delegation, asked some of his colleagues about Bates's chances. Citing Bates's unpopularity among the Germans of Cincinnati, R. M. Moore replied that Bates stood no chance of winning but that Lincoln did. Other Hoosier leaders, like John D. Defrees, ostensibly supported Bates but thought of "bringing forward a man who has more 'running pints'."[47] In March, an Indiana congressman suggested that Lincoln could "by some exertion be nominated."[48]

Two other key delegates from western Indiana—James C. Veatch, chairman of the Judiciary Committee of the State House of Representatives, and Cyrus M. Allen, the speaker of that body—helped persuade the rest of the delegation to back Lincoln. In April, when Allen asked Lincoln who would be representing his interests at Chicago, he replied: "Our friend Dubois, and Judge David Davis, of Bloomington, one or both, will meet you at Chicago on the 12th. If you let [John Palmer] Usher & [William D.] Griswold of Terre-Haute know, I think they will co-operate with you."[49] Dubois was from the Illinois county across the river from Vincennes, where Allen lived. A week before the convention, Allen predicted that Lincoln would carry his congressional district by 2,000 votes but that Seward would probably lose it.

Instructed to vote for Bates if the Missourian seemed to have a chance, Veatch and Allen journeyed to St. Louis to confer with Bates's main supporters; en route they canvassed the situation thoroughly and concluded that Bates could not win the nomination. Veatch told Allen that he would vote for Lincoln, whom he had heard speak very effectively in 1844. Allen had also heard Lincoln sixteen years earlier and was impressed not only by his eloquence but also by the fact that he had spent his boyhood and adolescence in their region of Indiana. At St. Louis, they inferred that Bates's champions did not really expect their man to win and only put him forward in the hopes of securing a cabinet post. When Veatch and Allen reached Chicago, they worked hard to persuade their colleagues to support Lincoln.

Helping to win over the Hoosiers was the eloquence of Gustave Koerner. When he heard that Frank Blair and other Bates spokesmen were addressing the Indianans, he and Orville Browning hurried over to their conclave to speak on behalf of Lincoln. Blair had been arguing that Bates could carry Missouri and Maryland, thus cleansing the party of the taint of sectionalism. Koerner denied that Bates could win his home state against Douglas, and insisted Bates did not deserve the support of Germans because in 1856 he had presided at the Whig national convention, which had endorsed the Know-Nothing candidacy of Millard Fillmore. Moreover, Bates had backed Know-Nothings in St. Louis municipal elections. If Bates were the nominee, Koerner predicted, the Germans would place an independent ticket in the field. (On May 14 and 15, German leaders did meet at the Deutsches Haus in Chicago and threatened to bolt the party should Bates be nominated.) When Koerner mentioned Lincoln's name, the crowd applauded vigorously. Browning, who had once favored Bates, assured the Hoosiers that Lincoln was a good Whig who opposed nativism. He concluded his remarks with an electrifying paean to Lincoln. (In Illinois, Browning's oratorical gifts were regarded as second only to Edward D. Baker's.)

Bates's champions, Caleb B. Smith and John D. Defrees, reluctantly concluded that their man could not win. Henry S. Lane, who had at first backed McLean, then Bates, energetically lobbied for Lincoln once he understood that the Rail-splitter was the only one who could stop Seward. Other Hoosiers shared Lane's alarm at the prospect of an early Seward victory. To meet that threat, they agreed to vote unanimously for Lincoln or Cameron or McLean as long as any of one of them appeared capable of winning. (McLean was in fact out of the running.) There seemed to be a fair chance that the Indianans would support Cameron, until dissension within the Pennsylvania ranks, especially from delegates representing the western part of the state, cooled their enthusiasm.

With other alternatives to Seward rapidly fading, Veatch and Allen, with the able assistance of Dr. Eric Locke, managed to convince all but two of their colleagues to support Lincoln; one of the holdouts agreed to abstain, and the other they eventually won over. Bates's supporters came to the reluctant conclusion that defeating Seward required them to vote as a bloc for Lincoln. On the night of May 15, the Indianans decided to back Lincoln. From that point on they worked efficiently and actively, night and day, cooperating with the Illinoisans to promote Lincoln's candidacy. This was a key turning point, for it elevated the Rail-splitter above the status of a mere favorite son. Easterners were impressed by the united front presented by these two Midwestern swing states.

The offer of a cabinet post for their state may have persuaded some Indiana delegates to back Lincoln. David Davis allegedly promised that Lincoln would appoint Caleb B. Smith to head a department. The evidence supporting this hypothesis is contradictory, however. On the one hand, Davis flatly denied it. In September, he told Thomas H. Dudley: "Mr Lincoln is committed to no one on earth in relation to offices. He promised nothing to gain his nomination, and has promised nothing since. No one is authorized to speak for him."[50] Leonard Swett also insisted that "[n]o pledges have been made, no mortgages executed."[51] On May 21, Lincoln wrote Joshua Giddings: "It is indeed, most grateful to my feelings, that the responsible position assigned me, comes without conditions, save only such honorable ones as are fairly implied."[52] Ten days later he assured callers, "I . . . have made no pledges to any man and intend to make none."[53]

On the other hand, several people testified that Indiana was promised a cabinet seat. (In fact, Caleb B. Smith became Lincoln's first secretary of the interior.) One convention delegate, William T. Otto, a leading Indiana Republican who was to serve as Lincoln's assistant secretary of the interior, averred that Smith "made Judge Davis believe that the Indiana delegation would go to Seward unless Smith was promised a place in the cabinet; when the truth was that none of us cared for Smith, and after we got to Chicago and looked over the ground all were for Lincoln."[54] William P. Fishback, a law partner of Indiana's Republican state chairman, reported in January 1861: "There was a determination and a promise on the part of Mr Lincoln to give Mr. C. B. Smith a place in his *Cabinet*."[55] Medill recalled Charles Henry Ray saying, "We are going to have Indiana for Old Abe, sure," because "we promised them everything they asked. We promised to see Smith put in the cabinet."[56]

Such bargaining was standard procedure. Davis promised rewards to Know-Nothings as well as Hoosiers for their support. Returning to Springfield by train after the convention, Davis encountered A. M. Whitney, father of Lincoln's friend Henry C. Whitney and a leading Illinois Know-Nothing. In 1863, Whitney reminded Davis of that encounter: "I said to you that regardless of my own party I should support Mr L with whatever influence I had—that I had supported Fremont in '56 notwithstanding I received over 37,000 votes for Am[erican Party] Elector myself in the 3rd Con[gressional] Dist[rict]. You remarked that if Mr Lincoln was elected that I should be remembered and well taken care of and you said that in saying so that you spoke by *authority*."[57]

Lincoln was advised that deals must be cut if he were to win the nomination. On May 14, Charles Henry Ray told him that he should authorize friends like Judd, Davis, or himself to speak on his behalf, because a "pledge or two may be necessary when the pinch comes."[58] Similar advice reached Lincoln from Mark W. Delahay, who on May 17 wrote: "If we could tonight say to Ohio, Penna, Mass & Iowa—concentrate on you [Lincoln] . . . and your . . . representative men . . . may dispense whatever Patronage they respectively are . . . entitled to. . . . you would beyond doubt be nominated."[59] In January 1861, Jesse W. Fell recommended that Lincoln appoint men from Indiana and Pennsylvania to cabinet posts because "such a disposition of favors was a good deal spoken of at Chicago."[60] Herndon claimed that Davis had pledged a cabinet post to Smith. A delegate who helped lead the Bates forces recalled that "Judge Davis, Lamon, and Swett, traded off a cabinet position to Caleb Smith for our [nineteen] Indiana votes and another place in the cabinet to Simon Cameron for our [fifteen] Pennsylvania votes."[61]

Many years later, Davis reportedly acknowledged that he had made some dubious promises at the convention. He told Wirt Dexter, a leading Chicago attorney, that he and his allies won over delegates by "making promises to bring them into line. Sometimes the promises overlapped a little."

Dexter asked, "you must have prevaricated somewhat?"

"'PREVARICATED?' replied Davis in his high voice, raising his right hand . . . and gesturing towards Mr. Dexter, 'Prevaricated, Brother Dexter? We lied, lied like hell.'"[62]

In late November 1860, John D. Defrees, a prominent Hoosier Republican, warned Davis that the president-elect should not ignore Indiana when cabinet members were chosen, "considering some matters occurring at Chicago within your knowledge," which if revealed "would be unfortunate and might give great dissatisfaction."[63]

In all probability, Davis did not specify that a cabinet post would go to Smith but rather pledged that an Indianan would be named to some cabinet position and that he would personally urge Smith's appointment. Swett told his law partner, Peter S. Grosscup, that he and Davis had promised the Indiana delegation that a Hoosier would receive a cabinet post if they backed Lincoln for the nomination. After the November election, Davis did lobby vigorously on behalf of Smith, telling Lincoln: "No one rendered more efficient service from Indiana, at the Chicago Convention" than Smith. Absent "his active aid & co-operation, the Indiana delegation could not have been got as a Unit to go for you. And until we had got the Indiana delegation, entirely united, we could not properly appeal to the other delegations for votes."[64] In 1862, after Smith had proved a poor choice for secretary of the interior, Davis ruefully confessed to Swett: "We made a great mistake in urging [Smith] . . . for a cabinet appointment."[65]

It was also agreed that the rich merchant William P. Dole, a shrewd politician and delegate who had lived in Indiana and was then residing in Illinois, would become commissioner of Indian affairs. In 1861, Dole was appointed to that post.

When Lincoln's cabinet was finally selected, Francis Preston Blair, Sr., whose son Montgomery was picked as postmaster general, said the president "has suffered himself to be seduced by a grateful & unsuspicious heart into early commitments which he has had too much pride upon the point of honor involved in promises—although made by others—to revoke."[66]

The Platform

As the convention opened on Wednesday, May 16, the city was so overrun with visitors that some wound up sleeping atop tables in billiard parlors. Wielding the gavel as temporary chairman, David Wilmot of Pennsylvania impressed Orville Browning as "a dull, chuckel headed, booby looking man" who "makes a very poor presiding officer."[67] The convention hall, specially built of rough timber for the occasion, was called the Wigwam because it resembled an Indian longhouse. A large, clumsy, solid, barn-like structure, measuring 100 x 180 feet, with a capacity of 12,000 people, it was "decorated so completely with flags, banners, bunting, etc., that when filled it seemed a gorgeous pavilion aflame with color and all aflutter with pennants and streamers." The interior resembled a huge theater whose stage was reserved for delegates and journalists. The acoustics were such that an ordinary voice could easily be heard throughout the building.[68] An "overflowing heartiness and deep feeling pervaded the whole house," John G. Nicolay remembered. "The galleries were as watchful and earnest as the platform. There was something genuine, elemental, uncontrollable in the moods and manifestations of the vast audience."[69]

The first two days were devoted to routine business and to consideration of a platform that criticized attempts to limit the rights of immigrants; condemned disunionism, the popular sovereignty doctrine, and threats to reopen the African slave trade; upheld the right of states to regulate their own institutions; denounced the Buchanan administration's corruption, abuse of power, and support of the Lecompton Constitution; maintained that the normal condition of the territories was freedom; called for the immediate admission of Kansas as a Free State; and endorsed protective tariffs, internal improvements (including a Pacific railroad), and homestead legislation. The plank on corruption was emphatic: "That the people justly view with alarm the reckless extravagance which pervades every department of the Federal Government; that a return to rigid economy and accountability is indispensable to arrest the system of plunder of the public treasury by favored partisans; while the recent startling developments of fraud and corruption of the Federal metropolis, show that an entire change of administration is imperatively demanded."[70] The platform committee omitted any reference to the Declaration of Independence. When the doughty old abolitionist lion Joshua R. Giddings moved that a plank endorsing its principles be added, he was overruled. Angered, he stormed out of the Wigwam, whereupon young George William Curtis of New York made a stirring speech which reversed that action. Giddings came back radiant.

This platform, largely the handiwork of Horace Greeley, did not please everyone. Proponents of strong language on slavery extension were especially disgruntled at Greeley's determined effort to omit what he deemed "all needlessly offensive or irritating features—such as that concerning the 'twin relics of barbarism,' and the requirement that Congress shall positively prohibit Slavery in every Territory whether there be or be not a possibility of its going thither."[71] Eli Thayer claimed that Greeley had originally proposed to endorse the Wilmot Proviso. "I said," Thayer recalled, "it was nonsense now, and worse, to insert this in our Platform, since we had shown in the Kansas contest how free States could be made without it. As matters were, there could never be another slave State, and that it would be much wiser and safer to encourage the freedom-loving people of the North to trust in themselves and their own acts for the restriction of slavery, rather than in any act of Congress, which had always disappointed us." Greeley acquiesced, and the plank was adopted over the objections of some committee members, including George F. Talbot of Maine, George Boutwell of Massachusetts, and Carl Schurz of Wisconsin.[72] Abolitionists complained that "by omission at least," the platform "surrenders its old non-extension of slavery policy, and thus virtually endorses the 'popular sovereignty' doctrine."[73]

Pennsylvanians would probably have raised objections to the tepid, obscure tariff plank if the noise and confusion in the Wigwam had not made it inexpedient. That weak endorsement of protectionism, which Democrats scorned as "two-faced—Tariff & Free Trade," tried to placate Keystone State protectionists while offending no free-traders.

The fourteenth plank, which dealt with immigrants' rights and was intended as an antidote to the Massachusetts two-years amendment, angered the Bay State delegation, which railed against it vehemently. The Massachusetts men argued that "the insult offered the State by the 14th clause can only be wiped out by the nomination of Banks or Wade," while former members of the American Party protested "loudly against the submission of the Convention to the demands of the German leaders," saying "it will cost them Connecticut and Rhode Island."[74] This so-called Dutch plank was regarded in some circles as the result of "undue pandering to German fanaticism" partly because it had been written by two Germans—Carl Schurz and Gustave Koerner—over the objections of Eastern leaders like New Jersey's Thomas H. Dudley.[75] Radical Germans, on the other hand, dismissed it is a mere "plaster for this Massachusetts wound."[76]

But most delegates received the platform with enthusiasm, and those who objected went along in the interest of party harmony. When the announcement came that it had been unanimously adopted, multitudes in the Wigwam leapt to their feet, cheering, waving hats and handkerchiefs, and screaming at the top of their lungs for more than ten minutes. Murat Halstead thought that a "herd of buffaloes, or lions, could not have made a more tremendous roaring."[77]

A Republican newspaper called the plank condemning government corruption "the strongest practical point in the platform" and predicted that it would do more to unite the party than anything else. The paper rightly noted that there was "a feeling that corruptions have grown frightfully rank at Washington, and that it is high time that the honest masses should interfere. The great document of this canvass will not be the Kansas Committee report, but the Covode Committee report [on government corruption]; and the great watchword will be not antagonism to slavery, but 'honest Abe Lincoln.'"[78] Though exaggerated, there was much truth in this forecast. Slavery would dominate the campaign, but the corruption issue would induce many Know-Nothings and others who had shied away from the Republicans four years earlier to join them in 1860.

Winning Pennsylvania and New England

Meanwhile, behind the scenes, David Davis and his allies, having secured Indiana, turned their attention to Pennsylvania, whose favorite son candidate, Simon Cameron, would receive almost all the state's votes on the first ballot but stood no chance of winning the nomination. Illinois gained the Pennsylvanians' support with the material aid of John A. Andrew of Massachusetts. On the eve of the convention, a New England delegation led by Andrew made a proposition to their Keystone State counterparts. Though ideologically sympathetic to Seward, the New Englanders wanted above all to win in November and feared that the New Yorker could not do so; along with the rest of the convention delegates, they regarded Pennsylvania, New Jersey, Indiana, and Illinois as keys to victory. New Jersey, like Pennsylvania, was backing a favorite son, William L. Dayton, who was clearly unable to secure the nomination. Illinois and Indiana supported Lincoln. So Andrew proposed that the four swing states hold a joint caucus and try to unite on a candidate.

The four states' delegates met on May 17. Thomas Dudley of New Jersey, observing that no compromise candidate was emerging, successfully moved that a special committee of three members from each state recommend a standard-bearer. From Pennsylvania, Governor Andrew Reeder chose David Wilmot, B. Rush Peterkin, and Henry D. Moore, all of whom were Cameron backers. But half the delegation was poised to vote against Cameron, and those anti-Cameron men objected to Reeder's slate. To placate them, Moore stepped aside for William B. Mann, a rising boss of Philadelphia and a fierce critic of Cameron.

David Davis headed the Illinois contingent, Caleb B. Smith the Indianans, and Dudley the Jerseymen. That evening they all gathered in Wilmot's rooms, where for five hours they negotiated inconclusively. Around ten o'clock Horace Greeley dropped by, observed the deadlock, and telegraphed the New York *Tribune* that Seward would be nominated the next day.

After Greeley left, Dudley suggested that each delegation rank order its preferences. Indiana, Illinois, and New Jersey quickly determined that they could all agree on Lincoln. In Pennsylvania, Cameron topped the list, and McLean, who was championed by Thaddeus Stevens, came in second. Since neither Cameron nor McLean could win the nomination, the choice of the third name would determine how Pennsylvania would go after casting a complimentary vote for her native son. The contest between Lincoln and Bates for that crucial third spot was close, with the Illinoisan prevailing by a few votes after a tension-filled debate. Curtin and some of Cameron's supporters who favored the selection of Congressman John Hickman or John M. Read as vice-president swung the delegation to support Lincoln. (On the first day of the convention, there had been much talk of a Lincoln-Hickman ticket.)

That choice by the twelve-member committee proved a crucial and unexpected turning point. When Andrew learned of the decision, he "said he could not comprehend it."[79] The New Jersey and Pennsylvania men were unable to guarantee their states, but they promised to try. At 1 A.M. the Jerseymen met and agreed to support Lincoln after casting complimentary ballots for Dayton. The Pennsylvania delegation was scheduled to consider the committee's recommendation the next morning, as polling for the presidential nomination began.

That night, while the Sewardites complacently downed innumerable bottles of champagne in anticipation of their imminent triumph, Davis and his cohorts barely slept. Henry S. Lane, Caleb B. Smith, and George K. Steele lobbied furiously for Lincoln, especially among the Vermont and Virginia delegates. They broke Seward's momentum, undermining his support in the New England and Southern delegations. Lane repeatedly declared that Seward's nomination would be so injurious to his gubernatorial chances that he would quit rather than waste time and money on a futile campaign. Helping to persuade the Pennsylvanians were the heroic efforts of George

W. Lawrence of Maine, who boarded at the hotel where the Keystone State delegation was staying.

David Davis wanted to cut a deal with the Pennsylvanians, but the previous day Lincoln had sent a terse message via Edward L. Baker: *"Make no contracts that will bind me."*[80] According to Henry C. Whitney, Baker "related that when he read the note to the delegates and workers gathered at the Lincoln headquarters he was greeted with a burst of laughter." Davis, who guffawed louder than anyone, said: "Lincoln ain't here, and don't know what we have to meet, so we will go ahead, as if we hadn't heard from him, and he must ratify it."[81] Davis and Swett negotiated with the leading Cameron operatives, John P. Sanderson and Joseph Casey, deep into the night. Even before the convention met, Sanderson had predicted that Lincoln, unlike other contenders, might carry the Keystone State. In the wee hours of Friday morning, Cameron was allegedly offered a cabinet post in return for the votes of the Pennsylvania delegates. Cameron's representatives, wary because their counterparts had no authorization from Lincoln to act, were reassured that the Rail-splitter would never repudiate a promise they made.

Whitney's account of the Cameron bargain has been challenged, but it seems plausible in light of abundant reminiscent testimony. Swett described to a convention delegate "his labors with Cameron," the "promises he made Pennsylvania on behalf of Mr. Lincoln," and "the subsequent difficulty he encountered in persuading Mr. Lincoln to carry out the contracts, or 'bargains,' as Mr. Lincoln called them."[82] Swett also confided to his law partner that he had promised Cameron a cabinet appointment if Pennsylvania supported Lincoln on the second ballot. In 1875, Cameron informed an interviewer that when "Lincoln told me that he was more indebted to Judd than any other one man for his nomination, . . . I told him I thought Davis and Swett did more for him. They bought all my men—Casey and Sanderson and the rest of them. I was for Seward[.] I knew I couldn't be nominated but I wanted a complimentary vote from my own State. But Davis and the rest of them stole all my men. Seward accused me of having cheated him."[83]

Cameron's statement may have been disingenuous. To be sure, he had told Seward he would back him, but on May 10, Casey wrote Cameron (aka the Chief) from Chicago that if he could not be nominated, then the delegation would go for Seward "unless we are satisfied that we can do better for our State, by the arrangement we spoke of when I last saw you." That arrangement is unclear, but evidently Cameron was willing to abandon Seward if he could obtain a better deal for Pennsylvania and himself.[84] Seward's confidential friends were, according to Casey, "overbearing and refused to talk of any thing but his unconditional nomination."[85] Their cocky inflexibility may have cost Seward the nomination.

Norman B. Judd told his son about a deal that gave Cameron an unspecified cabinet post in exchange for Pennsylvania's votes. Alexander K. McClure of Pennsylvania, chairman of the Republican State Committee, testified that two cabinet posts, "one for Pennsylvania and one for Indiana, were positively promised by David Davis at an early period of the contest."[86] McClure added that the bargain with Pennsylvania was, in fact, unnecessary. Sanderson approached Swett and Davis with an offer to switch to Lincoln on the second ballot only *after* the delegation had already made Lincoln their third choice, thus guaranteeing that the Illinoisan would receive their support once Cameron had his complimentary vote. The deal specified that the Chief would have a cabinet post if a majority of the Pennsylvania congressional delegation backed him for it. McClure reported that Lincoln was unaware of the bargain until early 1861. Upon learning of it, Lincoln allegedly declared: "They have gambled me all around, bought and sold me a hundred times. I cannot begin to fill all the pledges made in my name."[87]

Contemporary evidence supports those various recollections. On May 21, the Philadelphia *Press* reported a rumor that Cameron had been promised the Treasury Department portfolio. A week after the convention, Swett informed Lincoln about assurances he had given to delegates at Chicago. He explained that on May 16, in an attempt to woo the Pennsylvanians, he had approached an intimate friend, John W. Shaffer of Freeport, Illinois, who supported Cameron and enjoyed the confidence of some Keystone State delegates. Reluctantly, Shaffer confided that Cameron's supporters would not back Lincoln as their second choice for fear that he might deny them a fair share of patronage; they suspected that Lincoln's allies would vindictively persuade him to shut them out because they had not supported the Rail-splitter early on. Encouraging them in this belief were eight Illinois delegates who, though pledged to Lincoln, actually preferred Seward. Those Illinoisans had been in discussions with both the Pennsylvania and New York delegations. After consulting with Davis, Swett tried to appease those eight men. As he told Lincoln, "I gave them the most solemn assurances I am capable of giving, that they should not only not be proscribed but that by-gones should be by-gones & they should be placed upon the same footing as if originally they had been your friends[.] After a general talk of all past grievances, which I answered as well as I could they agreed to go to the two delegations [Pennsylvania and New York] & try to get you as their second choice[.] From that time I have the fullest confidence they did labor honestly and effectively & I shall always believe it was through Shaffer we got the real friends of Cameron on that delegation."

Swett apologized for burdening Lincoln with this tale of wheeling and dealing: "Now of course it is unpleasant for me to write all this *stuff* & for you to read it[.] Of course I have never feared you would intentionally do anything unfair towards these men[.] I only mean to suggest the very delicate situation I am placed towards them so that you might cultivate them as much as possible[.] My position towards them is that *I agreed to hold myself personally responsible to them for general fairness, and agreed forever to forfeit their confidence if it were not done.*" After the November election, Swett informed Lincoln of other negotiations he had conducted at the convention: "The truth is, at Chicago we thought the Cameron influence was the controlling element & tried to procure that rather than the factions[.] The negotiations we had with them, so far as I can judge was one of the reasons, which induced the Cameron leaders to throw the bulk of that force to you."[88]

Letters by Joseph Casey shed light on what Swett and Davis may have pledged. Less than a week after the convention, Casey told Cameron that a virtually united

Pennsylvania delegation was able "to control & make the nomination. It was only done after every thing was arranged carefully & unconditionally in reference to your-self to our satisfaction. . . . Mr. Lincoln's confidential friend Hon. Leonard Swett, will be here [in Harrisburg] in a couple of weeks, & will bring with him assurances from Mr. Lincoln himself to you—&c."[89] (In fact, Swett did not go east during the campaign.) Five months later, Casey discussed patronage with Lincoln in Spring-field. Afterward, the Pennsylvanian wrote to Swett: "From some things that occurred when I was at Springfield, my mind has since been in doubt, as to whether Mr. Lin-coln has been made *fully acquainted* with the conversations and understandings had between you & Judge Davis on the one side, & myself, on the other, at the Tremont House, the night before the nomination." Casey said he had been compelled to reveal their agreement to Cameron's friends "to counteract other schemes, and overcome other inducements, proceeding from different quarters."[90] It is possible that Swett and Davis merely pledged that a Pennsylvanian would receive a cabinet post, but since that agreement had been struck with Cameron's spokesman, clearly the Chief would be that man.

In addition to these recollections and contemporary documents, common sense suggests that deals were made on Lincoln's behalf. Politicians strike bargains all the time, and there is little reason to doubt the conclusion of historian Paul M. Angle: "that understandings, no less effective because they were not explicit, existed, is cer-tain."[91]

Lincoln appointed Cameron and Smith to his cabinet; both proved inadequate.

In addition to slowing Seward's momentum and gaining Indiana's twenty-six votes and most of Pennsylvania's fifty-four (at least on the second ballot), Davis and his allies tried to bolster their strength at the very outset of the polling. They found key support in New England, the region which would lead off the roll call. Weed, Seward, and many delegates assumed that at least the northern part of that region was solidly behind the New Yorker. If Seward's support there proved weak at the opening stage of the first ballot, and Lincoln's stronger than anticipated, it might have a pro-found psychological effect.

Gideon Welles of Connecticut, a Chase partisan, rallied New Englanders against Seward. Ably assisting Lincoln's men in lining up New England support was Amos Tuck of New Hampshire, a militant opponent of slavery who had served in Congress with Lincoln. Weeks later, Tuck modestly told David Davis: "It was but a trifle that I did, in attempting early to carry our entire delegation for Lincoln, but that trifle is enough to give me sincere satisfaction in the belief that the nomination was the only fit and proper nomination we could have made."[92] Tuck had originally supported Chase, but as the convention approached, he switched his allegiance to Lincoln. On May 14, Tuck informed his quondam House colleague: "I am taking hold of hands with our N[ew] Eng[land] delegates, and find the prospect good for general co-operation. Be not misled by our first votes. It will be expedient not to strike at first, but to let the west make the first move. But we shall come in, 'on time.'"[93] Other New Hampshiremen, including George G. Fogg, William E. Chandler, and Nehe-miah Ordway, had long been working on Lincoln's behalf. Fogg boasted that "I had much more to do with the action of *our* delegation than any other man."[94] These pro-Lincoln New Englanders reflected public opinion back home, for, as a Granite State newspaper noted, "Mr. Lincoln's eastern tour last spring had given him popularity in N. H., and his sterling qualities were fully recognized."[95]

Swett, born and raised in Maine, lobbied his old friends from the Pine Tree State. He received help from George W. Lawrence, Governor Lot M. Morrill, Mark F. Wentworth, and James G. Blaine. On the train to Chicago, Blaine buttonholed Morrill, who remained noncommittal until arriving at the Windy City, whereupon he quickly became an ardent Lincoln man. Hannibal Hamlin, realizing that his favorite, John M. Read, had no chance, worked behind the scenes in Maine to keep the delegation from endorsing Seward. Davis and Swett told Lincoln that the Maine delegates at first "were apparently united for Govr Seward. We thought it important to break into the New England States, as much as we could, & that it was exceedingly important for us, as Maine led off, in the vote for President, & vice President, to have as much strength as possible from Maine." Lawrence and Governor Morrill won six votes for Lincoln on the first ballot.[96] The uncommitted Maine delegates wanted to support William P. Fessenden, but he expressed no interest. They then decided to go for Lincoln as long as he seemed viable. Helping persuade the Pine State contingent to support Lincoln was Orville Browning, who addressed it on May 15. Greeley, disappointed by his failure to line up support for Bates, called Maine and Massachusetts "the two worst behaved delegations in the Convention" and bemoaned the absence of his newspaper's top Washington reporter, James Shepherd Pike, who "ought to have been able to do something" with delegates from his native state of Maine.[97]

Also on May 15, Browning spoke to the New Hampshire delegates, many of whom were former Know-Nothings or Democrats and thus unenthusiastic about Seward. David Davis sent natives of Vermont, including Samuel C. Parks and Gurdon Hubbard, to angle for that state's ten votes, all of which were pledged to favorite son Jacob Collamer on the first ballot. Under the leadership of Gideon Welles, the Connecticut and Rhode Island forces, though not pro-Lincoln, agreed that they would cast no votes for Seward.

Massachusetts was presumed to be safely in Seward's camp, but the state convention refused to instruct the nineteen radical and seven moderate delegates to support him. The chairman of that convention's credentials committee told Charles Sumner: "A majority of our delegates, I fear, though elected as Seward men, & going to Chicago nominally to support him, really mean to cut his throat."[98] William Schouler explained that "Seward was not Strong in Massachusetts. He had many strong friends, but he had no especial hold upon the people. The truth is that there is a very strong American feeling in our Republican ranks and the old Puritan faith, so hostile to popery and priest craft, permeates our whole social system, and Seward has been regarded as 'a seeker after popularity, through the highways and byways of Popery and irishmen.'"[99] Delegation chairman John A. Andrew sympathized with Lincoln's cause, as did the influential editor of the Worcester *Spy*, Congressman John D. Baldwin. Lincoln also enjoyed the support of Charles O. Rogers, Josiah Dunham, Timothy Davis, and Timothy Winn, all of whom voted for the Illinoisan on each ballot.

Boston merchant Samuel Hooper also worked behind the scenes to thwart Seward and pave the way for Lincoln. Edward Lillie Pierce, who claimed that he "favored the nomination of Lincoln and quite early too," voted for him on the third ballot, along with thirteen others in addition to the original four backers.[100] National committeeman John Z. Goodrich of Stockbridge, a major fundraiser for the party, urged his fellow Bay Staters to support Lincoln.

David Davis's minions also trolled for votes in Southern state delegations (most notably Virginia and Kentucky) and in Midwestern states like Ohio (which was badly split among Salmon P. Chase, Benjamin F. Wade, and John McLean) and Iowa (where Lincoln's old friend Hawkins Taylor lived and was working hard for his candidacy). By the time the convention opened on May 16, Lincoln's operatives felt confident that they had secured about 100 votes for the initial ballot, with some reserves ready to be added on the second ballot (from Pennsylvania, Vermont, New Hampshire, and Delaware).

Victory

Most observers believed Seward had the nomination locked up. With remarkable prescience, the Chicago *Times* estimated that on the first ballot, the senator would command 172 votes. (He actually received 173½.) Less accurately, it predicted that Bates would get 100, Cameron 81, Lincoln 45, McLean 24, Banks 11, Chase 10, and Wade 5. Weed and his colleagues said "that if Seward is not the man, let the opposition bring forward a better candidate," and argued that since that opposition "cannot probably unite upon anybody else, their candidate must and should be nominated."[101] They were encouraged when the convention voted down a proposal requiring that a majority of the entire electoral college was needed to nominate a candidate. The defeated change, offered by an anti-Seward delegate from Massachusetts, would have stipulated that the winning candidate must secure 304 votes instead of 233.

Weed and his allies boasted that Seward's nomination was a sure thing. Thursday night, New York Congressman Elbridge G. Spaulding wired the senator: "Your friends are firm & confident that you will be nominated after a few ballots." E. D. Morgan echoed that sentiment: "We have no doubt of a favorable result tomorrow." The next morning other Seward lieutenants assured their man: "Everything indicates your nomination today sure."[102] Straw polls taken on trains pouring into Chicago showed overwhelming support for Seward. The night before the balloting began, champagne corks popped like firecrackers and bands played festive music at the New Yorker's headquarters. Murat Halstead reported that "every one of the forty thousand men in attendance upon the Chicago Convention will testify that at midnight of Thursday-Friday night, the universal impression was that Seward's success was certain."[103]

But that night, while Davis and his crew were busy securing the Pennsylvania delegation, anti-Seward New Yorkers, led by David Dudley Field, were also hard at work. A prominent lawyer, Field had persuaded four other anti-Seward residents of the Empire State to join him in Chicago to lobby against their senator. They shared Wall Street attorney George Templeton Strong's opinion that Seward was "an adroit, shifty, clever politician" who "has used anti-Masonry, law reform, the common school system, and anti-slavery as means to secure votes, without possessing an honest conviction in regard to any of them."[104]

Early on May 18, Illinois Congressman John Farnsworth accurately predicted that "Lincoln will be nominated." His reasoning was simple: "I think he is the second choice of everybody."[105]

The Sewardites planned to use mob psychology to convince delegates that their man's triumph was inevitable. A gigantic claque of Seward supporters was to infiltrate the Wigwam and stampede the convention with their enthusiasm. Weed imported hundreds of men, to be led by a uniformed band.

This move almost caught the Lincolnites by surprise. When they realized the magnitude of the crowd being assembled for Seward, they fired off urgent telegrams summoning Illinoisans and Hoosiers to Chicago. Alexander H. Conner, the pro-Lincoln Republican state chairman of Indiana, rounded up supporters of the Rail-splitter throughout the state and the next day led thousands of them to join forces with a like number of Illinoisans in the Windy City. As Swett reported: "After the first days we were aided by the arrival of at least 10,000 people from Central Illinois and Indiana."[106] Finding admission tickets for Lincoln's hordes proved a challenge. The quick-witted Conner obtained one ticket and persuaded a Chicago printer to run off 5,000 copies of it, which were evenly distributed between the Illinois and Indiana contingents. They were instructed to arrive at the Wigwam early on May 18, the day the nominee would be chosen.

That morning while the cocksure Seward forces marched across town, the Lincoln shouters were already streaming into the Wigwam, led by a leather-lunged Chicagoan and a Dr. Ames of Ottawa. Those two men organized cheering sections on opposite sides of the hall with orders to bellow when Lincoln's name was placed in nomination and again when it was seconded. After parading through the streets, the Sewardites were astounded to learn that they could not all enter the packed convention hall, even though they held tickets.

Also frustrating the Seward forces was the seating arrangement devised by Judd, who as a member of the Republican National Committee had been assigned that task. Because New York expected to have its man named, Judd logically gave it the place of honor, in front, to the right of speaker's rostrum. Then he surrounded it with solid Seward delegations, effectively shielding the New Yorkers from the undecided states. To the left he deployed Illinois and Indiana; opposite those two, and very close by, he seated Pennsylvania and Missouri.

Postponement of balloting until May 18 also thwarted the Sewardites. After the adoption of the platform on May 17, they were so confident that they insisted on commencing the roll call. The Lincolnites, needing more time to shore up their support, unsuccessfully moved to adjourn. If the voting had begun then, Seward may have won. But George Ashmun, president of the convention, announced that "the papers necessary for the purpose of keeping the tally are prepared, but are not yet at hand, but will be in a few minutes." The motion to adjourn was renewed, and even though few votes were actually cast for and against, Ashmun ruled that it had carried.

Seward's operatives, though disgusted by this decision, remained supremely confident.

The morning of May 18, well before the official opening hour, a flood of humanity surged toward the Wigwam, jamming the entrances badly. After the noisy 10,000 attendees managed to gain their places, an opening prayer silenced the hum of the crowd, but only temporarily. As the presiding officer read routine communications, it buzzed with excitement. Who could care about railroad excursions or addresses from associations when everyone was atingle to learn who would be nominated? When it was finally decided to begin voting, the impatient crowd applauded. But it was further frustrated when a debate arose over voting procedures. Mercifully, discussion of that matter was cut short, and Ashmun announced that nominations could now be made.

By the time Seward's name was placed in nomination, enough of his men had somehow gained admission to give such a deafening roar that Lincoln's operatives were taken aback. Once Ashmun managed to restore quiet, Norman B. Judd rose and emphatically nominated Lincoln. Then, said Swett, "our people tested their lungs. We beat them a little."[107] Though Ashmun banged his gavel and ordered silence, the audience, "like a wild colt with [the] bit between his teeth, rose above all cry of order, and again and again the irrepressible applause broke forth and resounded far and wide."[108] The spectators were electrified by this sudden, vehement outburst, none more so than Seward's forces, who "turned pale and looked wild."[109] But they rallied when their man's nomination was seconded and they outshouted the Lincolnites. "The effect was startling," reported Murat Halstead. "Hundreds of persons stopped their ears in pain. The shouting was absolutely frantic, shrill and wild. No Comanches, no panthers, ever struck a higher note, or gave to a scream more infernal intensity. Looking from the stage over the vast amphitheater nothing was to be seen below but thousands of hats—a black swarm of hats—flying with the velocity of hornets over a mass of human heads."[110]

The Lincoln forces responded at an even greater decibel level. "The idea of our Hoosiers and Suckers being outscreamed would have been as bad to them as the loss of their man," Swett remarked. So when Lincoln's name was seconded, 5,000 men and women jumped up and gave what Swett called a "wild yell" that "made soft whisper breathing of all that had preceded. No language can describe it. A thousand steam whistles, ten acres of hotel gongs, a tribe of Comanches, headed by a choice vanguard from pandemonium, might have mingled in the scene unnoticed."[111] Halstead varied the metaphor: "The uproar that followed was beyond description. Imagine all the hogs ever slaughtered in Cincinnati giving their death squeals together, a score of big steam whistles going together . . . and you can conceive something of the same nature." Enhancing the tumult was the stamping of feet so vigorous that it "made every plank and pillar in the building quiver." Seward's delegates sat silent "as the Lincoln *yawp* swelled into a wild hosanna of victory."[112] For five minutes the Lincolnites waved their hats, handkerchiefs, and arms, shouting and yelling "like savages."[113] A Seward man pessimistically remarked, "We may easily guess the result."[114]

At last polling began. The shouting duel continued throughout the first ballot, with the Lincolnites winning each round. Color drained from the faces of the Sewardites at the unexpected announcement that Maine, instead of going for their champion as a unit, awarded six votes to Lincoln. Following on the heels of that shocker came New Hampshire, which awarded seven votes to Lincoln and only one to Seward.

(At 10:30 the previous night, Weed allegedly had obtained the Granite State's promise to support his candidate. The Wizard of the Lobby had admonished them that if Seward were passed over, New York might not vote Republican in November. But the New Hampshire delegation shared the widely-held view that he could not carry the swing states and doubted that New York would go Democratic even if her favorite son were rejected. Shortly thereafter Andrew G. Curtin told the delegation that if Seward won the nomination, he would withdraw his candidacy for governor of Pennsylvania because having the senator at the head of the ticket would doom the party in his state. Amos Tuck, meanwhile, ably pleaded Lincoln's case to his fellow New Hampshiremen.)

With only two states polled, Seward had fallen behind in a region where he was supposedly dominant. Many New England delegates wept while acknowledging they had to desert Seward because of his inability to win Pennsylvania and Indiana. (Alexander K. McClure estimated that over one-third of the votes cast for Lincoln came from Seward admirers who abandoned him only because of his weakness in swing states.) Of the eighty-two New England delegates, Seward received a disappointing thirty-two to Lincoln's nineteen.

Another shock came when Virginia, a presumed Seward stronghold, cast fourteen votes for Lincoln and only eight for the senator. This was the crucial turning point on the first ballot, causing New Yorkers to despair. Greeley reported shortly after the convention that "Virginia had been regularly sold out; but the seller couldn't deliver. We had to rain red hot bolts on them, however, to keep the majority from going for Seward."[115] The chairman of that delegation thought Lincoln more likely to win than Seward because the Rail-splitter "was not a sectional man."[116] Kentucky also disappointed Weed, for it gave Seward only five of its twenty-three votes. (Cassius M. Clay explained to the senator that "it was difficult to get our delegation to vote for you, because the opposition press had taken the pains to single you out for denunciation: and because Chase was in continual communication . . . with our friends.")[117] A Sewardite lamented that the "old sinner F. P. Blair with his two cubs Frank and Montgomery were active and bitter against Seward and did us a good deal of harm with the delegates from Virginia, Kentucky etc. who were inclined to go with us in the beginning."[118]

As Lincoln's total increased, so too did the enthusiasm of his backers, who were ecstatic when the results were announced: Seward 173½ (only 3½ from the Lower North), Lincoln 102, Cameron 50½, Chase 49, Bates 48, with the rest scattering. The tally dealt a deathblow to Seward's chances, for clearly Lincoln, Cameron, Chase, and Bates could stop the New Yorker. The Empire State delegation "looked like a funeral procession."[119]

In Springfield, however, Lincoln received the news with some concern. When a friend observed, "that's a great deal better than we had any right to expect," he replied: "I don't like the looks of it; I imagine that about forty of those votes were cast for me by men who supposed they were bound to give me an empty compliment on the first ballot. They were cast, according to my figuring, by friends of Wade and Bates. If so if I lose them on the next ballot, the nomination will also be lost, for in the Convention as in every-day life, everybody is more or less anxious to help a man who is traveling down hill."[120]

Back in Chicago, the next ballot began. The third state to be called, Vermont, gave Lincoln all ten of its votes, igniting a spontaneous eruption of applause that the chairman had trouble checking. This significant gain of support that had previously gone to Jacob Collamer constituted "a blighting blow upon the Seward interest," Halstead reported. "The New Yorkers started as if an Orsini bomb had exploded."[121] One of them thought that Vermont's switch represented the turning of the tide, assuring Lincoln's victory. Weed later complained that "Greeley took possession of a perverted Delegation from Vermont," and the *Tribune* editor said it "was all we could do to hold Vermont by the most desperate exertions."[122] But the head of the Vermont delegation denied that Greeley had exercised much influence; rather, he said, the Green Mountaineers had listened to the pleas of the Hoosiers and Pennsylvanians, who begged them not to vote for Seward. Heeding that appeal, the Vermonters noted Lincoln's strength on the first ballot and decided to support him as the candidate most able to win in November. They liked Seward but feared he would lose; they also admired Cassius Clay, but he stood less of a chance than Seward. From Connecticut and Rhode Island, Lincoln picked up five more votes. He now topped Seward in New England, thirty-six to thirty-three.

Surprisingly, New Jersey gave Seward four votes, the remaining ten going to favorite son Dayton. Then came a stunning announcement; Pennsylvania cast forty-eight votes for Lincoln, a net gain of forty-four. That proved the clincher. In its wake, Delaware switched its six votes from Bates to Lincoln, whose count increased by three in both Kentucky and Iowa and by six in Ohio. (Bates's chief lobbyists, the Blairs, were staying at the home of Norman B. Judd, who doubtless urged them to support the Rail-splitter once their man faltered.) The second ballot totals were Seward 184½, Lincoln 181, Chase 42½, Bates 35, and the rest scattering. Seward had gained eleven, Lincoln seventy-nine.

This result cheered Lincoln. "I have no fault to find," he said, and added calmly, "I think the convention will nominate me on the next ballot."[123]

As voting resumed, the suspense was palpable. Throughout the Wigwam, delegates and spectators scribbled down the votes as they were cast. Lincoln's bandwagon rapidly gathered momentum. In Massachusetts he picked up four, in New Jersey eight, in Pennsylvania four, in Maryland nine, in Kentucky four, in Ohio fifteen, and in Oregon four, giving him a total of 231½, a scant one-and-a-half votes short of victory. Seward had slipped to 180, despite Weed's best efforts. During the balloting, a Bates operative urged Greeley "to hold on for Bates" for "he had just seen Mr. Weed, and, if no nomination should be made, there would be a strong rally of Seward's friends on Bates" during the next ballot.[124] But that desperate ploy was futile.

Suddenly the Wigwam grew profoundly silent. All talking and fluttering of fans ceased. In the stillness could be heard only pencils scratching and telegraph instruments clicking. Because the chairman had not yet announced the result, changes could still be made. Everybody looked around to see who would put Lincoln over the top. The chairman of the Ohio delegation, David K. Cartter, suddenly sprang upon his chair. A big, coarse, strong-willed man with shiny eyes, a speech impediment, and numerous smallpox scars, Cartter had just been told by Joseph Medill, "If you can throw the Ohio vote for Lincoln, Chase can have anything he wants." "H-how d-d'ye know?" asked Cartter. "I know, and you know I wouldn't say so if I didn't know. Ask Judge Davis. He holds the authority from Lincoln."[125]

Catching the attention of presiding officer George Ashmun, with whom he had served in Congress, Cartter won recognition and declared: "I rise (eh) Mr. Chairman (eh) to announce the change of four votes of Ohio from Mr. Chase to Mr. Lincoln."[126]

After a brief moment of stillness, the Wigwam erupted. One delegate smashed his hat on the head of a colleague, who did the same in return; they then hugged each other. Henry S. Lane also beat his silk topper on a fellow Hoosier's head, then waved it vigorously as he stood on a chair, silently grinning from ear to ear. John A. Andrew reported hearing "a peal of human voices, a grand chorus of exultation, the like of which has not been heard on earth since the morning stars first sang together, and the sons of God shouted for joy." Illinois delegates, who at first were so stunned that they sat still weeping for joy, recovered themselves, jumped up on their benches, and frantically waved hats and coats. Their contagious enthusiasm inspired neighboring delegations from Maine, Massachusetts, Ohio, and Connecticut to celebrate wildly. Soon the entire convention was caught up in the excitement as waves of applause rolled on and on. When it began to ebb, Andrew observed some old men with "quivering lips and streaming eyes, and hearts so full of joy they could not check their emotion" rise "in their seats to renew their cheers."[127] Atop the Wigwam, a cannon repeatedly fired announcements of the result to the immense crowd outside, which issued a roar "like the breaking up of the fountains of the great deep." It was so loud that the cannonade on the roof could not be heard in the hall.[128]

Amid this pandemonium, Thurlow Weed struggled to fight back tears. He was not alone. Several of his fellow delegates from the Empire State "cried like heart broken children." Others "sat like marble statues."[129] Finally, a sorrowful William M. Evarts mounted a table and with tears in his eyes graciously moved that the nomination be made unanimous. Other Seward supporters seconded the motion. Orville Browning responded with a speech on behalf of the Lincolnites, thus ending the morning session. Supporters of the Rail-splitter celebrated manically while Seward backers "were terribly stricken down," Halstead reported. "They were mortified beyond all expression, and walked thoughtfully and silently away from the slaughter house, more ashamed than embittered. They acquiesced in the nomination, but did not pretend to be pleased with it." It "was their funeral, and they would not make merry."[130]

Some New York delegates sneered at Lincoln's nomination, asking sourly: "What was it Webster said when Taylor was nominated?" (Daniel Webster had expressed scorn for the "illiterate frontier colonel," whom he thought unfit.)[131] Supporters of the Rail-splitter retorted: "What was the result of the [1848] election?"[132] When a Pennsylvania leader called on Thurlow Weed, he found the Wizard of the Lobby sulking.

He rudely declined to discuss the campaign. To Curtin, Weed said: "You have defeated the man who of all others was most revered by the people and wanted as President. You and Lane want to be elected, and to elect Lincoln you must elect yourselves."[133] Some especially angry New Yorkers swore they would rather back Jefferson Davis, Stephen A. Douglas, or any slavery supporter rather than "third rate, rail splitting Lincoln." At their headquarters, bets were made that the nominee would lose the Empire State by 20,000 votes. Some offered 50-to-1 odds that Douglas would be elected. Those mortified delegates were almost afraid to return to New York, for fear of encountering popular anger. As one of them prepared to leave Chicago, he joked that he would travel by night only, lest he be recognized. They cursed the most active operatives who had worked against their hero, especially Greeley, David Dudley Field, and Anson Burlingame. Seward champion James W. Nye almost came to blows with Burlingame. As soon as Lincoln won, Burlingame congratulated Field, exclaiming: "You have nominated Mr. Lincoln; now help us to nominate the 'bobbin boy' [N. P. Banks] for Vice-President!"[134]

Back in New York, some regarded Seward's defeat as poetic justice. Referring to the senator and his operatives, Hamilton Fish remarked that "[a]s he & they served others, so have he & they have been served. The little seeds that have been sown along the path way of twenty five years of ambition & selfishness, have just come to maturity & have overwhelmed the sower."[135]

At the Tremont House, Lincoln's operatives celebrated wildly, forming processions, drinking gallons of whiskey, and carrying rails through the streets. A journalist deemed them "the craziest men I ever saw. Their demonstrations were such as to defy competition from the inmates of any Lunatic Asylum. Screeches were made, embraces were exchanged, and songs were sung." From the hotel's roof, one hundred artillery rounds were fired.[136]

That afternoon the convention chose as Lincoln's running mate the affable and portly Maine Senator Hannibal Hamlin, a long-time opponent of slavery and close friend of Seward's lieutenant, Senator Preston King, who would have been nominated himself if he had wanted that honor. As a former Democrat, Hamlin lent both geographical and ideological balance to the ticket, but it would have made more sense to nominate someone from the swing state of Pennsylvania, where the outcome of the election was to be determined. To assuage the New Yorkers, Lincoln's managers offered them the vice-presidency, but none of them showed interest. They did, however, insist on having the power to name someone from another state. Cameron would have been an obvious choice, but the Sewardites, resentful at his failure to support their man, resolved that he would not receive that honor. The Seward people also blackballed Andrew Reeder, John Hickman, John M. Read, and all other Pennsylvanians. Angry at Massachusetts and Kentucky as well, they vetoed the candidacies of Cassius M. Clay, the crowd favorite, and Nathaniel P. Banks, Burlingame's favorite. Seward, like his operatives, was spiteful and seized opportunities to punish foes. Earlier he had dangled the vice-presidency before Frank Blair in return for his family's support, but the offer was spurned. Maine's delegates lobbied hard for Hamlin, suggesting to the New Yorkers that if they had no candidate for the second slot, the Maine senator should be glad to have their backing. Preston King agreed and successfully championed Hamlin's cause. After all the excitement culminating in Lincoln's nomination, the delegates paid little attention to the vice-presidential question.

Democrats ridiculed the swarthy Hamlin, alleging that "his blood is that of the Niggergee" and that he resembled "a free negro, more than any man living who claims to be a white man!"[137] When he first entered the Maine Legislature a decade earlier, he was known as "Negro Hamlin."[138] Some South Carolinians facetiously offered to purchase him. "A free nigger to preside in the United States Senate!" exclaimed an Alabamian. "How would Southern Senators like that? The humiliation and disgrace of the thing would certainly be something, but the smell would be awful."[139]

Some delegates believed Lincoln would have won at Chicago even if no bargains had been struck, because his debates with Douglas and his Cooper Union speech had won respect from all factions and because he was the only candidate with solid anti-slavery credentials who could carry the swing states. Although it is true that the delegates made the smart, rational choice, political conventions are not always ruled by reason. Without the able leadership of Davis and Judd, the support of their indefatigable operatives, the fortunate decision to hold the convention in Chicago, and the influence of the stentorian pro-Lincoln shouters, it is not at all unthinkable that Seward could have been the Republican nominee.

Reaction in Springfield

When news of Lincoln's victory reached Springfield, the bearer of the dispatch rushed into the office of the *Illinois State Journal*, where the candidate and a large crowd had been following events, and proposed three cheers "for Abraham Lincoln, the next President of the United States." After the huzzahing, Lincoln took the dispatch, read it, and said: "I must go home; there is a little short woman there that is more interested in this matter than I am." En route people stopped him on the street to offer congratulations. He thanked them and jokingly said: "you had better come and shake hands with me now that you have an oppertunity—for you do not know what influence this nomination may have on me. I am human, you Know."[140] Two years later, he "said that when he received the nomination he had forebodings as to the trouble which might ensue. This passed away for a resolution to abide the consequences, whatever they might be."[141]

Springfielders rejoiced wildly, dragging a cannon from the capitol to celebrate. Asked if it should fire one salute for each state or 100 salutes, Lincoln said: "I must begin my administration on the principle of retrenchment and economy. You had better fire but *one* gun for each state."[142] Lincoln banners of all varieties waved in the breeze, and church bells hailed the victory of the local hero. In the evening, townsfolk flocked to the statehouse to hear speeches and then marched to Eighth and Jackson Streets to serenade the nominee, who expressed his thanks "in a few good-humored and dignified words."[143] When the crowd rushed forward to shake his hand, Lincoln invited them into his modest home. One of the revelers streaming across the threshold shouted prophetically, "We'll give you a larger house on the fourth of next March!"[144]

"I Have Been Elected Mainly on the Cry 'Honest Old Abe'"

The Presidential Campaign
(May–November 1860)

Shortly after the Chicago Convention, Joshua Giddings assured Lincoln with "certain knowledge" that "your selection was made upon two grounds," first that "you are an *honest* man," and second that "you are not in the hands of corrupt or dishonest men."[1] Seward suffered by contrast, and some of the senator's backers acknowledged that they "must not blame the people of the United States for being afraid that the election of a leading New York politician to the Presidency would only displace the existing corruption at Washington by a new importation of venality and political knavery from Albany."[2] A New York delegate, former Lieutenant-Governor Henry R. Selden, declared that all the forces working against Seward would have been insufficient to defeat him "had not his opponents strengthened their arguments by allusion to the corruptions practiced at Albany during the past winter. No man entertained the idea that Mr Seward was connected with them, but it was charged that his friends were, and it was pretended that if elected the same practices would be transmitted to Washington."[3]

Hostility to corruption not only contributed to Lincoln's nomination in May, but it also helped clinch his victory in November. The public was fed up with steamship lobbies, land-grant bribery, hireling journalists, the spoils system, rigged political conventions, and cost overruns on government projects. At a New York ratification meeting, Horace Greeley introduced a resolution proclaiming that there were two irrepressible conflicts, one pitting freedom against slavery and the other, "not less vital," between "frugal government and honest administration" on the one hand and "wholesale executive corruption, and speculative jobbery" on the other.[4] Along with several other newspapers, the Cincinnati *Commercial* predicted that a Lincoln administration would be "honest, economical and capable."[5] William Cullen Bryant pledged that his New York *Evening Post* would do all it could to "turn out the present most corrupt of administrations, and install an honest administration in its stead."[6]

New Englanders stressed the corruption issue. Samuel Bowles of the Springfield, Massachusetts, *Republican* accurately prophesied that on "an issue likely to rival, if not to overshadow, that of the irrepressible negro—that of honesty, simplicity and economy in public affairs," Lincoln would run well, for "'Honest old Abe' will mean something serious, as well as prove a taking campaign cry."[7] Emphatically the Concord *New Hampshire Statesman* argued that Lincoln's lack of national political experience was "an element of strength," for it meant that he had not succumbed "to the gross corruptions so prevalent at Washington." The nation "is suffering for want of an incorruptible Chief Magistrate; a man who will indignantly crush out . . . and drive into perpetual exile the inexorable army of blood-suckers that hang around the democratic camp at Washington. This troop is Legion, and hover over the Treasury like Cossacks in the rear of the French army on its retreat from Moscow. . . . A change cannot be for the worse, and may be for the better; then let us have a change. Abraham Lincoln is 'honest, capable and friendly to the constitution.' Let us put him in [as] president, and drive all the treasury rats away."[8] In Connecticut, the Hartford *Courant* declared that "[o]ne of the strongest arguments in favor of the election of Lincoln to the Presidency is his HONESTY" and "old-fashioned integrity and firmness." The people "all want the government administrated with integrity and economy. We have tried two dishonest Administrations of the Democratic party. Let us try them no longer, but place the government in the hands of uncorrupted and uncorruptible men."[9]

After winning the presidency, Lincoln told a visitor, "[a]ll through the campaign my friends have been calling me 'Honest Old Abe,' and I have been elected mainly on that cry."[10] His reputation as an honest man was as important as his reputation as a foe of slavery.

National Reaction

As word of Lincoln's nomination spread throughout the North, jubilant Republicans set off fireworks, rang bells, ignited bonfires, illuminated buildings, erected rail fences, paraded by torchlight, cheered speakers, and fired cannons with the same high spirits that had characterized the boisterously successful Harrison campaign of 1840. An Illinois delegate freshly returned from the Chicago Convention predicted accurately that "the coming campaign will not be a whit behind that of [18]40 in point of enthusiasm."[11]

There was, in fact, a great deal of hoopla in the canvass, provided largely by Rail-splitter and Wide-Awake organizations, which led countless demonstrations. Wide-Awakes, groups of young Republican activists, made their debut in Connecticut that spring during the gubernatorial campaign. They were best known for nighttime parades, during which they carried tin torches on poles, which they deemed "rails."

Lincoln himself said he "was not particularly fond of show and parade, and personally did not care much for such demonstrations," though he acknowledged that the organizations were useful in turning out crowds for speakers and in providing opportunities for partisans to take an active role in the campaign.[12] "Principle composed only about ten per cent of our political contests," he told a New Yorker.[13] Sharing Lincoln's aversion to hoopla was New York attorney George Templeton Strong, who eventually voted for Lincoln, though not enthusiastically. A month after the convention he confided to his diary: "I am tired of this shameless clap-trap. The log-cabin hard-cider craze of 1840 seemed spontaneous. This hurrah about rails and rail-splitters seems a deliberate attempt to manufacture the same kind of furor by appealing to the shallowest prejudices of the lowest class."[14] Fellow New Yorker Hamilton Fish agreed, sarcastically exclaiming, "Hurrah for Lincoln & Hamlin!!!! . . . We want a log-splitter, not a hair splitter—a flatboatman, not a flat statesman. Log cabin—coon skins—hard cider—Old Abe & dark Ham—hurrah!"[15]

In Washington, Republican members of Congress received the news from Chicago "with great enthusiasm."[16] Senator William P. Fessenden of Maine, who had favored Ben Wade of Ohio for the presidency, reported that Lincoln's nomination "surprised us all, but, on the whole, has given general satisfaction to the Republicans, & frightened the democrats."[17] Wade himself said: "We are all safe if Old Abe is on the track." A Representative from Wade's state was reminded of a traveler in the Southwest who once asked a black man how distant a certain town was. "Well, sah," came the answer, "wid an oddinary hoss, it am 'bout sixteen mile; wid a right smarht nag, it 'ud be 'bout eight mile; but wid massa Jim's horse, you dar now!" Said the congressman: "So, with Seward we should have had a hard road to travel; with Ben Wade, we should have been pretty sure of winning the race, having no dead weights; but with Honest Old Abe, we're there now!"[18] Congressman Charles Francis Adams, who thought Seward deserved the nomination, expressed reservations about Lincoln. "I believe him honest and tolerably capable," he wrote, "but he has no experience and no business habits." Yet, Adams noted, many of his Republican colleagues in the House seemed delighted.[19]

Because all Republican factions could unite behind Lincoln, the party enjoyed a huge advantage over its badly divided rivals. Already the candidacy of the cold, reserved, colorless, 64-year-old Tennessee slaveholder and former senator, John Bell—standard-bearer of the new Constitutional Union Party, comprised mostly of Southern ex-Whigs—had weakened Democrats in the Upper South. (He was to win his own state plus Kentucky and Virginia.) When in June the Democratic national convention reassembled in Baltimore, Northern and Southern delegates continued the bitter fight that had begun at Charleston. Utterly unable to compromise, each section nominated its own candidate. Douglas won the endorsement of the Northern Democrats, while Vice-President John C. Breckinridge of Kentucky became the choice of the Southerners. With his opposition now backing three different candidates, Lincoln appeared to have an excellent chance.

Lincoln confidently believed that the Democrats could not reunite. He said their predicament reminded him of a story: "I once knew a good, sound churchman, whom we'll call Brown, who was on a committee to erect a bridge over a very dangerous and rapid river. Architect after architect failed, and at last Brown said he had a friend named Jones who had built several bridges and could build this. 'Let's have him in,' said the committee. In came Jones. 'Can you build this bridge, sir?' 'Yes,' replied Jones; 'I could build a bridge to the infernal regions, if necessary.' The sober committee were horrified, but when Jones retired, Brown thought it but fair to defend his

friend. 'I know Jones so well,' said he, 'and he is so honest a man and so good an architect that, if he states soberly and positively that he can build a bridge to Hades, why, I
believe it. But I have my doubts about the abutment on the infernal side.' So, when
politicians said they could harmonize the northern and southern wings of the Democracy, why, I believed them. But I had my doubts about the abutment on the southern
side."[20]

Republican newspapers rejoiced at the nomination of such an appealing and
unblemished candidate. One called him "just the man that this sorely swindled and
disgraced nation needs for President," for Lincoln "is a man of stainless purity—his
whole life is as spotless as the driven snow. He is no corruptionist, no trickster, no
time-server, but an honest, brave, straight-forward, able man, who will restore the
Government to the purity of practice and principle which characterized its early days
under the administrations of the Revolutionary patriots." A pro-Seward journal assured its readers that Lincoln was "no expediency candidate, but one who early embraced the Republican cause, has always labored consistently for its success, has,
from the beginning, stood, and stands now fair and square on its national and conservative platform." It was a cause for celebration that "a candidate is fixed upon who
has so many recommendations as Abraham Lincoln, whose character embraces so
many excellent qualities, and whose personal history gives him so strong a hold on
the good will of the people." He would attract voters "who float loosely between the
two parties." The convention had wisely picked two candidates "fresh from the
people, of broad and statesmanlike qualities, of unquestioned abilities, and of tried
patriotism."[21]

Northern Democrats countered that the "platform and the head of the ticket are
a shrewdly disguised, abolition whig move." Lincoln was, they sneered, "an obscure
lawyer, confessedly lacking the culture and capacity which are requisite to the creditable occupancy of the high office for which he has been nominated," an "extreme abolitionist of the revolutionary type," a "weak and unfit man for so high a place," a "third
rate country lawyer," an "uneducated man—a vulgar village politician, without any
experience worth mentioning in the practical duties of statesmanship," a "fourth rate
lecturer, who cannot speak good grammar," a "man whose only merit consists in splitting rails or splitting the sides of a village audience with his smutty stories," an "obscure partisan," a "bigot and extremist," and an "honest, well-meaning man of less
than average mental caliber . . . who is almost a monomaniac on the subject of negro
slavery" and who "is brim full of nigger."[22]

What the Republicans applauded as Lincoln's freshness the Democrats denounced
as an appalling lack of credentials. The Philadelphia *Evening Journal* complained that
his "record as a statesman is blank. He has done nothing whatever in any executive,
judicial, or legislative capacity, that should entitle him to public respect."[23] In the
opinion of a former colleague in the Illinois Whig Party, Lincoln's experience was
"only that which has been acquired in the worst governed State in the Union—he
himself being identified with its worst blunders and follies."[24] Another former ally,
Benjamin S. Edwards, publicly "asked what had Lincoln ever done to stamp him as a
statesman worthy to be at the head of a great nation like ours?"[25] The Albany *Atlas*

and Argus chastised the Republicans for nominating an obscure man who "represents no principle and no sentiment except hostility to Seward."[26]

Above all, Democrats objected to Lincoln as an antislavery Radical. Politically, "he is as rabid an abolitionist as John Brown himself, but without the old man's courage," jeered the New York *Herald*.[27] Citing Lincoln's 1837 vote against a resolution condemning abolitionists and his protest stating that slavery was based "on injustice and bad policy," the *Illinois State Register* said he "is as much an abolitionist as are [William Lloyd] Garrison, Gerrit Smith, or Wendell Phillips."[28] Democratic Congressman Charles Drake Martin of Ohio called Lincoln the originator of a "treasonable heresy," the irrepressible conflict doctrine.[29] Don Morrison of Illinois condemned him as a Kentucky abolitionist, "infinitely worse than a Yankee Abolitionist." To illustrate the candidate's devotion to the doctrine of racial equality, Morrison quoted passages from his Chicago speech of July 10, 1858:

- "I should like to know if taking this old Declaration of Independence, which declares that all men are equal upon principle and making exceptions to it where will it stop. If one man says it does not mean a negro, why not another say it does not mean some other man? If that declaration is not the truth, let us get the Statute book, in which we find it and tear it out!"
- "Let us discard all this quibbling about this man and the other man—this race and that race and the other race being inferior, and therefore they must be placed in an inferior position—discarding our standard that we have left us. Let us discard all these things, and unite as one people throughout this land, until we shall once more stand up declaring that all men are created equal."
- "I thank you for this most extensive audience you have furnished me to-night. I leave you, hoping that the lamp of liberty will burn in your bosoms until there shall no longer be a doubt that all men are created free and equal."[30]

Democrats also cited passages from Lincoln's 1854 Peoria address:

- "What I do say is, that no man is good enough to govern another man without the other's consent. I say this is the leading principle, the sheet anchor of republicanism."
- "I have quoted so much at this time merely to show that according to our ancient faith the just powers of governments are derived from the consent of the governed. Now the relation of slave and master is pro rata a total violation of this principle. The master not only governs the slave without his consent, but he governs him by a set of rules altogether different from those which he prescribes for himself. Allow all the governed an equal voice in the government, and that, and that only, is self-government."[31]

"In what speech of Seward are such violent sentiments as these set forth?" asked a correspondent of the New York *Herald*. "Where can anything be found to exceed them in the ferocious abolitionism of Phillips or Garrison?"[32] Democratic papers repeatedly cited Lincoln's "House Divided" speech and his 1854 Peoria address to prove that he was as devoted to the extermination of slavery as any abolitionist. They even falsely ascribed to him an 1856 speech calling for black suffrage in Illinois. As further proof of Lincoln's radicalism, it was alleged that he had subscribed funds to help John Brown in Kansas. (Lincoln had signed a document pledging financial aid to the "peaceful inhabitants of Kansas" who were being attacked by Missouri border-ruffians; the money was never collected.)[33]

The bitterest denunciations of Lincoln were flagrantly racist. John Cochrane of New York declared that the Republican standard-bearer and his party engrafted "negrology" onto "their political stock," producing thereby "its natural fruit—nigger—the eternal nigger. They ate nigger—they drank nigger—they (at least the amalgamationists) slept nigger. They saw him in their dreams—they saw him in their waking hours—all over, everywhere, they saw the sable gentleman." As for the choice of Lincoln, "When nominating a rail splitter for the Presidency they were really resolved that they saw a nigger in the fence."[34] The *Illinois State Register* claimed that if Lincoln won, "we shall have the nigger at the polls, the nigger on our juries, the nigger in the legislature."[35] The Cleveland *Campaign Plain Dealer* agreed: "Give black Republicanism the power, and they will leave no effort spared to reach that 'practical equality of all men,' which Mr. *Lincoln* tells us is the great 'central idea' to be 'labored for.' Successful, we shall have the nigger at the polls, the nigger on our juries, the nigger in the Legislature, in our public offices, and, with political power, it is but one step, with those who think with them, to concede them that social position which will realize the 'central idea' of a common mulattodom."[36]

In an attempt to undermine Lincoln's reputation for integrity, the Chicago *Times* accused him of illegally billing the federal government for three pairs of boots while he served in Congress. The charge was refuted by Josiah M. Lucas, Lincoln's friend who was serving as the postmaster of the U.S. House and had access to the expense records of the Thirtieth Congress.

Southern Democrats were even more contemptuous than their Northern counterparts, calling Lincoln the nominee of a "free-filth and wool-gathering Convention," a "recreant son of the South—a traitor to the mother that bore him," a "*nigger* in principle," "coarse, vulgar and uneducated," a "mere politician, of small calibre," and a "third rate Western lawyer."[37] A former governor of South Carolina told his wife that the Republicans "have selected a wretched backwoodsman, who have [*sic*] cleverness indeed but no cultivation; who is a fanatic in his policy and an agrarian in his practice. Nothing but ruin can follow in his trail."[38] The *Missouri Republican* asserted that Lincoln's nomination meant that "the 'irrepressible conflict' between the free and the slave States [is] to be kept up until the free States drive slavery out of all the slave States."[39] A letter in that paper charged that Lincoln "appears to think the only mission of the white man is to rescue, by any means, the negro from bondage." The doctrine of "the entire and complete 'equality of races'" has been "believed and proclaimed by him long, long before the rise of the Republican party." Although members of that party hesitated to commit themselves to racial equality openly, Lincoln understood that they "must and would, whenever they deemed they had sufficient strength, not only proclaim, but put into practical action" that radical doctrine. Lincoln was "a much more dangerous man than Mr. Seward," for he lacked "the sense and intellect of Mr. Seward; nor yet is he as wily or as politic as Seward; he is not such a statesman as Seward, nor has he Seward's suavity of manners nor breeding; nor is he as well versed in the practical working of our complex government; nor does he know just as well how far to go with safety, nor when to relax, lest their tension becoming too great, the cord should snap; but he has all of Seward's sectional ideas, and even more, and if in power would inevitably press them to their utmost."[40]

Southerners made dire predictions about the future under a Republican regime. "As soon as Lincoln is installed into office . . . he will wave his black plume Southward," speculated a Texas newspaper. "With the army and navy, and the fanatical North, he will invade us. He will issue his ukase, enfranchising the negroes, and arming them; he will confiscate property, and commend us to the mercy of torch and steel." The Richmond *Enquirer* accused Lincoln of wanting "to sink the proud Anglo-Saxon and other European races into one common level with the lowest races of mankind." The Montgomery, Alabama, *Mail* also emphasized the miscegenation theme: "If the North chooses to mullatoize itself, that is all right. . . . Let the North . . . be the home of the mixed race; and let the South be the home of the *white man,* proud of his race, and proud of his race's superiority! . . . If Lincoln and his free nigger outrider are elected, we must not submit. We must leave the North with its vile free-negroism, to shift for itself. . . . Southern men are *white men* and intend to *continue* such!"[41]

A few realistic Democrats understood that the Republicans had chosen well. A Georgia journalist, J. Henly Smith, thought that the Lincoln-Hamlin "ticket is a strong one" which "will get up such an amount of courage and effort on their part as will be hard to overcome."[42] A New Yorker sensibly pointed out to Stephen A. Douglas that Lincoln had an advantage because he "is little known except by the notoriety you gave him, & there are few prejudices against him."[43] The New Orleans *Crescent* praised Lincoln for having conducted the 1858 campaign "with distinguished ability" and said "no other man in the State was so capable as himself of encountering the intellectual 'giant' of the North-West. We regard this nomination as perhaps the strongest the Republican party could have made."[44] A Kentucky newspaper accurately predicted that there were "some things in the personal character and career of Mr. Lincoln, which will give him great popularity. . . . Born of humble parentage, and passing the years of his childhood, youth and early manhood amid the hardships of the backwoods of Kentucky, Indiana and Illinois, acquiring an education by his own labors as best he could, and gradually working his way to distinction, his life has been one well calculated to excite the admiration and sympathy of voters, most of whom are themselves working men. When to this is added the purity of his private life, the general recognition of which has given him, in his own State, the sobriquet of 'Honest Old Abe,' we are compelled to admit that the Chicago Convention has nominated the very hardest man to beat it could possibly have given us."[45]

Other Democrats agreed that Lincoln was the most formidable opponent the Republicans might have chosen. Douglas certainly thought so. When the results of the Chicago Convention reached Washington, he "repeatedly said . . . that the nomination of Mr. Lincoln was the strongest the republicans could have made."[46]

But some rejoiced at Lincoln's nomination because they thought he could be defeated. "Next to Seward, we have all earnestly desired Lincoln's nomination," a correspondent told Douglas. "You have beaten him once & will beat him more surely again." The editor of the Chicago *Times* considered Lincoln "weaker than any other candidate" before the Chicago Convention.[47]

Lincoln's nomination pleased many, though not all, militant opponents of slavery. Frederick Douglass called him "a man of unblemished private character" with "a cool well balanced head" and "great firmness of will," who "is perseveringly industrious," "one of the most frank, honest men in political life," and a "radical Republican . . . fully committed to the doctrine of the 'irrepressible conflict.'" During the campaign of 1858, Douglass remarked, Lincoln "came fully up to the highest mark of Republicanism, and he is a man of will and nerve, and will not back down from his own assertions. He is not a compromise candidate by any means."[48] Douglass would eventually support the Radical Abolitionist Party nominee, Gerrit Smith, but he hoped that the Republicans would win. "While I see . . . that the Republican party is far from an abolition party," he told an upstate New York audience, "I cannot fail to see also that the Republican party carries with it the anti-slavery sentiment of the North, and that a victory gained by it in the present canvass will be a victory gained by that sentiment over the wickedly aggressive pro-slavery sentiment of the country. . . . I sincerely hope for the triumph of that party."[49] In his autobiography, the black orator said that "[a]gainst both Douglas and Breckinridge, Abraham Lincoln proposed his grand historic doctrine of the power and duty of the National Government to prevent the spread and perpetuity to slavery. Into this contest I threw myself, with firmer faith and more ardent hope than ever before, and what I could do by pen or voice was done with a will."[50] John S. Rock of Boston, another black abolitionist, also supported Lincoln.

A week after the Chicago Convention, Joshua Giddings told his militantly antislavery son-in-law: "As to Lincoln I would trust him on the subject of slavery as soon as I would Chase or Seward. I have been well acquainted with him and think I understand his whole character. I know him to be *honest* and faithful." Seven months later, Giddings said of Lincoln: "I have no doubt that we did the best thing we could when we nominated him."[51] The New York *Independent,* which had urged the Republicans to choose a militant opponent of slavery like Seward, Chase, Charles Sumner, or Benjamin Wade, praised Lincoln as "a true man, a man of great ability, who has thoroughly studied the question of the times, a man honored and beloved by his fellow-citizens at home, and one who, if chosen President, will use all his power and official influence to re-establish the Constitution as our fathers made it."[52]

Female abolitionists also applauded Lincoln's nomination. Jane Grey Swisshelm deemed him "as much of an anti-Slavery man" as Seward and said that the Rail-splitter suited her "admirably."[53] Lydia Maria Child told Charles Sumner, "I don't place much reliance on any political party; but I am inclined to think this Mr. Lincoln . . . is an honest, independent man, and sincerely a friend to freedom. *One* thing makes me strongly inclined to like him and trust him. At a public meeting in Illinois, two years ago, in discussion with Stephen A. Douglass, he said, 'A negro is my equal; as good as I am.' Considering that Lincoln came from Kentucky, and that his adopted state, Illinois, is *very* pro-slavery, I think he was a brave man to entertain such a sentiment and announce it."[54]

Radical Republicans joined the pro-Lincoln chorus. Senator James R. Doolittle of Wisconsin rejoiced that by nominating Lincoln, he and his allies had created "a real Republican party . . . no old fogy or conservative party, but one that can march to the logic of Events and keep step with the Providence of God."[55] Another Midwestern Radical, Senator James W. Grimes of Iowa, was equally enthusiastic. "The nomination of Lincoln strikes the mass of the people with great favor," he told his wife. "He is universally regarded as a scrupulously honest man, and a genuine man of the people."[56]

Lincoln assured Wait Talcott, a leading Illinois abolitionist, that he sympathized with him. "I know you Talcotts are all strong abolitionists," said Lincoln, "and while I have had to be very careful in what I said I want you to understand that your opinions and wishes have produced a much stronger impression on my mind than you may think."[57]

Frederick Douglass's candidate, Gerrit Smith, publicly criticized Lincoln as too lukewarm an advocate of freedom, but privately he confided to Giddings: "Seward is a very able man. But so also is Lincoln—& he will, I have no doubt, get a greater vote than Seward would have got. I have read in the newspapers what Lincoln said so wisely and sublimely of the Declaration of Independence. I feel confident that he is in his heart an abolitionist." Though on principle Smith voted for no one who acknowledged the legality of slavery, he told Giddings that Lincoln's victory at the polls "will be regarded as an Abolition victory—not less so than if you yourself were elected President."[58] The Boston correspondent of the New York *Tribune* opined that Lincoln was "ahead of the Anti-Slavery sentiment of the Republican party, rather than behind it, and therefore to rally round and defend him will be to improve the political morals of the country."[59]

Some abolitionists were less enthusiastic. One protested that during the 1858 campaign Lincoln's "ground on the score of humanity towards the oppressed race was too low."[60] Gerrit Smith's party adopted a resolution proclaiming that "for Abolitionists to vote for a candidate like Abraham Lincoln, who stands ready to execute the accursed Fugitive Slave Law, to suppress insurrections among slaves, to admit new slave States, and to support the ostracism, socially and politically, of the black man of the North, is to give the lie to their professions, to expose their hypocrisy to the world, and to do what they can to put far off the day of the slave's deliverance."[61] The party's candidate for governor of New York, William Goodell, condescendingly remarked that if anyone supporting Lincoln called himself an abolitionist, "we know not how to vindicate the sincerity of his professions, except by entertaining a less elevated conception of his intelligence."[62] Goodell sneered that the Republicans had chosen the "most available, because the least known, the least prominent, the least distinguished or distinguishable among those to be selected from."[63] A leading member of the party in Ohio said Lincoln "ignores all the principles of humanity in the colored race, both free and slave; and as abolitionists claim the right to freedom of the one class, and political equality to the other, how can they be consistent, to say nothing of honest, in supporting such a man?"⁶⁴ Gerrit Smith's agent at his Oswego colony for free blacks scornfully remarked to those urging him to support the Republican ticket, "I should look beautiful voting for a President, who would be for sending the Marshal after me for helping fugitive slaves to Canada."⁶⁵ Equally contemptuous was an Illinois Radical who declared, "I hate the Lincoln party. I would as soon call Hell a paradise as to call the Lincoln Party a Republican Party."⁶⁶ Beriah Green, known as "abolition's axe," indignantly asked how any self-respecting opponent of slavery could possibly support a "craven wretch" like Lincoln: "He who goes for the Fugitive Slave bill of '50! Hasn't made up his mind that the interstate slave trade should be abolished! Is against negro equality! A *man* is not to be classified with men! . . . Is against the abolition of slavery in the District except on conditions which none but a damned cross between a knave and a fool could either impose or endure!"⁶⁷

Other abolitionists like Stephen S. Foster denounced the Republican standard-bearer as a man "who declared his willingness to be a slave-driver general." They also argued that "in voting for a slave-catching President, we do as truly endorse and sanction slave-catching as the non-extension policy which he advocates." Lincoln not only "stands ready to hunt slaves" but also "supports the ostracism, socially and politically, of the blacks at the North."⁶⁸ Parker Pillsbury told his fellow Radicals, "in voting for Abraham Lincoln, you as effectually vote for slavery as you would in voting for Stephen A. Douglas."⁶⁹ Swayed by Pillsbury, the Western Anti-Slavery Society denounced Lincoln for being "committed to every constitutional compromise for slavery ever claimed by Calhoun or conceded by Webster." The Republican party was not fit "to be entrusted with the interests of humanity and liberty."⁷⁰

Oliver Johnson, editor of the *National Anti-Slavery Standard*, organ of the American Anti-Slavery Society, criticized attacks on Lincoln by men like Pillsbury and Foster: "Instead of allowing for a fair margin for honest differences of opinion, and thus keeping on good terms with the better portion of the Republicans," the Western Society "has selected for special denunciation such men as Sumner, and thereby reduced itself needlessly & recklessly to a small faction of growlers, showing their teeth and snapping just where they should have been generous and conciliatory." Johnson thought it "utterly preposterous to deny that Lincoln's election will indicate growth in the right direction."⁷¹

H. Ford Douglas, an eloquent black abolitionist from Chicago, asked an antislavery gathering in Massachusetts "if any man can tell me the difference between the anti-slavery of Abraham Lincoln, and the anti-slavery of the old Whig party, or the anti-slavery of Henry Clay," who "was just as odious to the anti-slavery cause and anti-slavery men as ever was John C. Calhoun. . . . I do not believe in the anti-slavery of Abraham Lincoln, because he is on the side of this Slave Power." Douglas alleged that Lincoln in 1858 had refused his request to sign a petition calling for the repeal of Illinois's infamous black laws. He also complained that in 1849 Lincoln "introduced, on his own responsibility, a fugitive slave law for the District of Columbia."⁷²

Rising from the audience, Massachusetts Senator Henry Wilson challenged Douglas's version of that proposed 1849 statute. "Mr. Lincoln was born in Kentucky, a slave State, and went to Illinois, and living in a portion of that State which did not entertain the sentiments of this State [Massachusetts], and with a constituency living under what he called the Black Laws of Illinois, he went into Congress and proposed to make the District of Columbia free. I think that he should be honored for that and not misrepresented." Wilson passionately admonished the assembled opponents of slavery: "When you undertake to arraign men who, in the halls of Congress, before dominating majorities, in a city where public sentiment is against them, where the sneer and the profane word meet them at every step in the streets, are true to the right, I ask you when you deal with such men that you shall do them justice, and that if they have done good deeds and brave deeds, that you say it." Wilson declared that Lincoln was "ahead of the Anti-Slavery sentiment of the Republican party, rather than behind it." No one, Wilson added, "ever grew faster in intellectual stature than Mr. Lincoln, from the time he commenced the contest with Douglas till the day he received the Chicago nomination."[73]

In addition to Wilson, some other Radicals were willing to make allowances for Lincoln. Although the Pennsylvania Anti-Slavery Society chastised him for supporting the Fugitive Slave Act, for opposing citizenship rights for blacks, and for advocating a timid approach to abolition in the District of Columbia, it nevertheless acknowledged that "it is due to truth and candor to say that, as between him and his opponents, and on the issues involved in the present contest, the election of Abraham Lincoln will be a great and encouraging triumph."[74]

As the campaign wore on, H. Ford Douglas came to regard Lincoln more favorably, reasoning that even if there was little difference between Lincoln and Stephen A. Douglas, "there is in the Republican party a strong anti-slavery element. And though the party will do nothing for freedom now, that element will increase; and before long—I trust—springing up from the ruins of the Republican party will come a great anti-slavery party." So he endorsed Lincoln.[75] Another black abolitionist, John Mercer Langston of Ohio, also supported Lincoln even though he thought that the candidate's "ground on the score of humanity" was "too low" and "did him no honor."[76]

H. Ford Douglas was not the only Radical to criticize Lincoln's 1849 bill to abolish slavery in the District of Columbia. In May, the antislavery purist Wendell Phillips cited that legislation as justification for calling the Republican standard-bearer "the slave hound of Illinois," a "knave," a "huckster in politics," and "a county court lawyer, whose only recommendation was that, out of the emptiness of his past, lying newspapers could make him any character they pleased."[77] He paid Lincoln the dubious compliment of being candid: "I wish I could say of Mr. Lincoln, as I can of Giddings or Sumner, when I see him swearing to support the Constitution of the United States, 'I respect him so much that I do not believe he will do what he promises.'"[78] Curiously, Phillips compared Lincoln unfavorably to Seward because the latter had enunciated the "great philosophical principle" of the "irrepressible conflict" while the former "is merely known as the antagonist of Douglas."[79] Readers of Phillips's philippic were quick to point out that Lincoln's "House Divided" address clearly spelled out the same thesis as that of Seward's Rochester speech, delivered five months after the Rail-splitter's.

Phillips's attack did not go unchallenged. The Connecticut antislavery editor Joseph Hawley indignantly protested against it. "I know Mr. Lincoln; he is not quite up to my standard," Hawley told the Massachusetts abolitionist orator, "but he has always been ahead of his neighbors; he has fought gallantly, honorably and unselfishly." Phillips's criticism of Lincoln made Hawley feel "really insulted, grossly wronged." Applying such "savage epithets" to Lincoln was worthy of an irresponsible Radical like Parker Pillsbury, but not of a gentleman, Hawley declared.[80] A "highly esteemed friend and long-time supporter" of the New York *National Anti-Slavery Standard* called Phillips's attack a "calumny against Lincoln."[81] The New York *Tribune* also protested against Phillips's "calumnious," "unfounded," "reckless," and "unmanly" condemnation of Lincoln's proposal to abolish slavery in Washington; his strictures were a "gross misrepresentation" that constituted "a slander."[82]

A fellow Massachusetts abolitionist, Edward Lillie Pierce, gently but firmly disagreed with Phillips, describing Lincoln as "an able lawyer, a fair disputant and an honest man." Pierce asserted that "[f]ew public men of our time have in their discourses treated slavery as a wrong more logically and feelingly" than Lincoln. To be sure, he may have "a technical record in favor of legislation by Congress for the rendition of fugitive slaves," but so did Seward and John Quincy Adams. (The Albany *Evening Journal* echoed that point, stating that Lincoln's 1849 emancipation bill was "a project somewhat similar to those which were proposed by John Quincy Adams and Gov. Seward, and if there is any more reasonable and practicable way of legislating on the subject at all, we should like to hear it proposed.")[83] "Considering the community and associations among which he was reared & has lived," Pierce concluded, "I think Lincoln stands as well as they [Seward and Adams] do on record. And whatever may have been his technical record, I believe that 'he *himself is right*'!"[84]

In September, when antislavery Radicals gathered in Worcester, Massachusetts, to choose an alternative to Lincoln, Thomas Wentworth Higginson (who styled himself "a rather radical Republican") told the convention that "he was glad of the excellence of the Republican nominations for President and Governor [John A. Andrew], and intended, for himself, to go for them."[85] Charles Sumner, the most radical antislavery member of the U.S. senate, paid tribute to Lincoln as one "whose ability, so conspicuously shown in his own State, attracted at once the admiration of the whole country, whose character no breath has touched, and whose heart is large enough to embrace the broad Republic and all its people."[86] Other abolitionists supporting Lincoln included Henry B. Stanton, Elizur Wright, Theodore Tilton, Sydney Howard Gay, Moncure D. Conway, William H. Burleigh, John Jay, George Luther Stearns, Richard Hinton, John Wallace Hutchinson, and David Lee Child.

The conservative New York *Herald* predicted that Phillips's speech exposing "the inconsistency and insincerity of 'honest Abe'" would seriously hurt the candidate.[87] An Illinoisan reported that Radical Republicans in his state "find it very hard to support Lincoln, on account of his position on the fugitive slave law, slavery in the

District of Columbia, the admission of slave states, &c. They think he is not so good as the Chicago platform, and too much like his political progenitor, Henry Clay."[88]

Moderate and conservative Republicans were more uniformly enthusiastic about Lincoln. Senator James Dixon of Connecticut, who disapproved of Lincoln's "House Divided" speech, nevertheless said his was "as good a nomination as could have been made" and predicted that he would run well and "as a President he will be capable & incorruptible. . . . I know him well. He is a man of more than average talents—and as honest as the light of day."[89] Daniel Ullman, the Know-Nothing candidate for governor of New York in 1856, praised Lincoln as the true heir of Henry Clay. William L. Dayton of New Jersey declared that, except for slaveholders themselves, "he did not believe there was a man in the whole country more conservative in his views on the question of Slavery than Abraham Lincoln."[90]

Some Northern Democrats also had positive things to say. In New Hampshire they called Lincoln "a man of respectable character and talents" and complimented the Republicans on the "improvement they have made over 1856."[91] In neighboring Massachusetts, a Democratic paper remarked that Lincoln's nomination "is a strong one, and will be difficult to defeat, and those who flatter themselves that the Democrats are to walk over the Presidential course with ease will find themselves mistaken. The Convention at Chicago has given evidence of shrewdness, no less in the nomination of Mr. Lincoln than in the platform adopted, which is progressive without being ultra."[92]

Even some Southerners praised Lincoln. William L. Goggin, a prominent Virginia supporter of Bell, lauded his industry and character. George D. Prentice, editor of the Louisville *Journal,* described the Republican standard-bearer as "a genial, delightful, and high toned gentleman, whose pleasant hospitality we have enjoyed, and, although we think him in great error in some of his political opinions, we have as much confidence in his patriotism as we have in that of any man except ourselves."[93] A dispatch from Louisville stated that there Lincoln "is liked for his honesty and sincerity, his Democratic habits and manners, and his Henry Clay type of character."[94] The New Orleans *Bee* called Lincoln "a man of agreeable manners, a ready and forcible speaker, self-made and self-taught, and personally popular among the burly sons of the West."[95]

Douglas also spoke well of his opponent: "Lincoln and I have called each other some pretty hard names on the stump, but I'll do him justice. He is an honest, able and very popular man," a "very clever fellow; a kind-hearted, good-natured, amiable man. I have not the heart to say anything against Abe Lincoln; I have fought him so long that I have a respect for him. . . . I would not permit, without rebuke, any Democrat to say an unkind or disrespectful word about him."[96] To the Speaker of the U.S. House, the Little Giant stated: "I have competed with the most distinguished men in the country and I say the hardest man to beat I ever had to meet in combat, was Abraham Lincoln."[97] When it was speculated that the election might be thrown into the House of Representatives because no candidate would win a majority of the electoral votes, Douglas exclaimed: "By God, sir, the election shall never go into the House—before it shall go into the House, I will throw it over to Lincoln."[98]

Lincoln returned the compliment, saying that with Douglas "he has had personally only the most friendly relations, for, notwithstanding their public argumentative and political contests, there has never been any quarrel between them." For good measure he also praised John Bell as "an honorable, high-toned gentleman" and Breckinridge "as a man of considerable ability, who can make a scathing speech when occasion demands."[99]

Formal Notification

Lincoln was correct in assessing his wife's enthusiasm about the nomination. As the exceedingly ambitious Mary Lincoln and the rest of Springfield anxiously awaited news from the convention, she "said she thought she had more interest and concern in whom the Chicago convention nominated than her husband."[100] A Springfield clergyman believed that Mrs. Lincoln would be so puffed up with pride that she "ought to be sent to the cooper's and well secured against bursting with iron hoops."[101] Her childhood dream of becoming First Lady of the land was about to come true. (One Springfielder joked about Mrs. Lincoln's ambition, speculating that if Lincoln died before inauguration day, she "like another Boadicea, will repair to the 'White House' and assume the reins of government!")[102]

Mary Lincoln busily prepared for the arrival of the official delegation which would formally notify her husband of his nomination. Lincoln was not looking forward to the ceremony, which he thought unnecessary. To friends he complained "that he had no idea what to say to the gentlemen."[103]

Reaching the capital before the others was an advance party of that committee, including Ebenezer Peck, who suggested to some Springfielders that Mrs. Lincoln should be informed that her presence when the committee called would be inappropriate. Too timid to do so, the townsfolk replied: "Go up & tell her yourself."[104] When Peck and Gustave Koerner called at the Lincolns' house, they were taken aback by the sight of brandy decanters, champagne baskets and glasses, cakes, and sandwiches all spread out. (The alcoholic beverages had been provided by Lincoln's neighbors, who knew he was a teetotaler.) A black servant explained that the refreshments were for the committee. When Mrs. Lincoln came in and asked what Peck and Koerner thought of the repast she was providing for her guests, they replied that it was not advisable, for some of the committee members might be temperance men. She protested vigorously until Koerner finally instructed the black man to remove the refreshments. As he was doing so, she continued to argue. Overhearing the dispute, Lincoln entered the room and said: "Perhaps, Mary, these gentlemen are right. After all is over, we may see about it, and some may stay and have a good time."[105]

When the committee did call on the evening of May 19, Mrs. Lincoln swept into the parlor wearing a fancy low-neck dress. Lincoln, by contrast, looked anything but statesmanlike in his new but ill-fitting black suit. When the dignitaries arrived, he bowed awkwardly, evidently feeling ill-at-ease. One of the guests thought he resembled "an ungainly school-boy standing alone before a critical audience."[106] After George Ashmun, head of the delegation, briefly explained their mission, Lincoln replied that he was "[d]eeply, and even painfully sensible of the great responsibility which is inseparable from that honor—a responsibility which I could almost wish had fallen upon some one of the far more eminent men and experienced statesmen whose distinguished names were before the Convention." He promised to consider the proffered nomination carefully and reply soon in writing.[107]

Despite his initial awkwardness, Lincoln made a favorable impression on his visitors, most of whom felt completely at ease in his house. A Massachusetts member of the delegation thought "nothing could have been more elegant and appropriate" than Lincoln's brief response.[108] After the formalities, the host and guests chatted amiably for over an hour. George G. Fogg, secretary of the Republican National Committee, was impressed by "the unerring quickness with which he recognized every man whom he had, though ever so casually, met before, and the distinctness with which he recollected the time and place of such meeting."[109]

During the exchange of pleasantries, Lincoln asked William D. Kelley his height. When that Pennsylvania congressman replied 6 feet 3 inches, the candidate said he was 6 feet 4 inches. "Then," Kelley quipped, "Pennsylvania bows to Illinois. My dear man, for years my heart has been aching for a President that I could look up to, and I've found him at last in the land where we thought there was none but little giants."[110] (Months later, when Kelley asked Lincoln for permission to dedicate his two-volume treatise on international law to him, Lincoln consented as long as "the inscription may be in modest terms, not representing me as a man of great learning, or a very extraordinary one in any respect.")[111]

After leaving, the committee members expressed relief and gratification. Kelley declared: "Well, we might have done a more brilliant thing, but we could hardly have done a better thing."[112] A New Englander observed, "I was afraid I should meet a gigantic rail-splitter, with the manners of a flatboatman, and the ugliest face in creation; and he's a complete gentleman."[113]

Not everyone had such a positive impression of Lincoln. Edwin D. Morgan, shocked when the committee was greeted by Willie and Tad Lincoln looking like ragamuffins, came away especially skeptical. According to Carl Schurz, some committee members "could not quite conceal their misgivings as to how this single-minded man, this child of nature, would bear himself in the contact with the great world and in the face of the large and complicated problems, for grappling with which he had apparently so scant an equipment."[114]

Other Republicans shared that worry. Robert H. Morris of Chicago called Lincoln "honest, well-meaning & amiable," but with insufficient backbone. "In trying to please everybody he may fail to satisfy anybody.—From my own knowledge of the man I should say, if elected it will be very hard work for him to be President."[115] Connecticut Senator James Dixon, who had served in Congress with Lincoln, said privately, "I think he is rather credulous & unsuspecting, and may possibly be exposed to the craft & cunning of men, who professing honesty, may take advantage of him."[116] Perhaps the skeptics would have been reassured by the assessment of a Springfield Democrat, who argued that a man "engaged in political life so long as has been Mr. Lincoln, surrounded by all the temptation to rascality and sharp dealing of Western life, coming out unscathed, and with unblemished reputation for integrity must have not only a will, but one that is very determined."[117]

As he composed his acceptance letter, Lincoln heard from several leaders urging him to placate Know-Nothings by shying away from the platform's immigration provisions. Papers like the Boston *Atlas* and the Buffalo *Commercial Advertiser* deplored the so-called Dutch planks. E. B. Washburne warned that the "Pennsylvanians, of American proclivities, are somewhat troubled by the Anti-Know [Not]hing planks, and they have appealed to me to write you and suggest that in your letter of acceptance you say nothing about the platform, so they can support you, without committing themselves to those planks. I really think the suggestions are worth considering."[118] In Indiana, his old friend from congressional days, Richard W. Thompson, followed suit. Ignoring such counsel, Lincoln wrote a short formal letter of acceptance in which he endorsed the entire party platform: "The declaration of principles and sentiments, which accompanies your letter, meets my approval; and it shall be my care not to violate, or disregard it, in any part. Imploring the assistance of Divine Providence, and with due regard to the views and feelings of all who were represented in the convention; to the rights of all the states, and territories, and people of the nation; to the inviolability of the constitution, and the perpetual union, harmony, and prosperity of all, I am most happy to co-operate for the practical success of the principles declared by the convention."[119]

Placating the Losers

Lincoln's first task after his nomination was to placate the disgruntled losers at Chicago. Chase presented no problem; he quickly assured the candidate of his support. Lincoln graciously replied to the Ohio governor: "Holding myself the humblest of all whose names were before the convention, I feel in especial need of the assistance of all; and I am glad—very glad—of the indication that you stand ready. It is a great consolation that so nearly all . . . of those distinguished and able men, are already in high position to do service in the common cause."[120] Chase and his supporters thought Lincoln "honest & will no doubt be true to our principles," and that his nomination was "perhaps as good as under all the circumstances could have been expected & will no doubt succeed," for "he had the elements of popularity in him that would make him successful in the Campaign."[121] A pro-Chase congressman was relieved that "the Convention gave us men so unexceptionable."[122] Ex-Governor Chauncey F. Cleveland of Connecticut, however, did not go along; he told Chase that he was "disgusted with this Whig ingratitude," which led to the nomination of "the man who has done the least for the Party & the cause."[123]

Edward Bates and his followers were also happy to support Lincoln. Bates said the candidate was "[p]ersonally unexceptionable; his integrity unimpeached; his talents known and acknowledged; and his industry and moral courage fully proven. Politically, (aside from the negro question) all his antecedents are right—square up to the old Whig standard. And as to the negro question (which ought not to overrid[e] and subordinate all others) his doctrines, as laid down for use, are, in my judgment, substantially right."[124] From St. Louis, a Bates enthusiast wrote that "[o]ur friends accept the ticket cordially and will give it an earnest support."[125] On May 22, Frank Blair, who had served as Bates's campaign manager, heartily endorsed Lincoln.

To secure Bates's formal endorsement, Lincoln turned to Orville Browning. On May 21, David Davis and other Illinois Republican leaders urged the Quincy attorney to enlist Bates for active campaigning. When Browning visited St. Louis, Bates rejected as undignified the suggestion that he take the stump for Lincoln, although he admired the candidate's character and esteemed him highly. While he said he would "warmly and zealously support Mr Lincoln," he "wanted a little time for reflection." Three weeks later, Bates publicly lauded the candidate as "a sound, safe, national man" who "could not be sectional if he tried," and who "has earned a high reputation for truth, courage, candor, morals, and amiability."[126] In October, Bates wrote that he and Lincoln "are old acquaintances and friends. . . . We know each other very well, and I take pleasure in believing that our mutual confidence, which is of long standing, is not disturbed by any serious doubt."[127] Support from Bates and his followers helped offset Millard Fillmore's decision to endorse Bell, which disappointed Lincoln.

Cassius Clay of Kentucky, a very dark horse at the Chicago Convention, rejoiced that the delegates chose "two very good and available candidates" who would "make us an *honest* administration."[128]

Cameron, however, stayed aloof. At a ratification meeting in Harrisburg a week after the Chicago Convention, he praised Seward and rather perfunctorily endorsed Lincoln as a Republican who, "when demands have been made upon his zeal and patriotism, has borne himself bravely and honorably." But unlike Chase, he delayed a long while before congratulating the nominee personally. On August 1, he finally did so in a letter predicting that the Keystone State would go Republican in November. "We need no help here of any kind," he assured the candidate. Cameron's tardiness may have reflected his contempt for a man he considered his inferior. His letter was mailed only after he had met with David Davis and Thurlow Weed at Saratoga, New York, to discuss cabinet appointments under Lincoln. They agreed that Seward would be secretary of state (a foregone conclusion) and Cameron secretary of the treasury.[129]

Placating Seward's followers presented the most difficult challenge. They were "very much disappointed, & *very* cross" at the defeat of the man they considered "the greatest living statesman on the footstool of God."[130] An angry Seward backer spoke for many others when he announced that he would rather "the Republican party should be beaten with him [Seward] for [its] leader, than win with any other man."[131] A New Yorker reported that the "nominations have fallen like an iceberg upon us here, & some have already said in my hearing, that they will not support them."[132] Varying the image, another wrote that Lincoln's victory "comes over N. Y. and New England like a driving March storm over the rising July of our hopes. We may huzza to the nomination, but our hearts reproach us with the emptiness of the sound—a bride pronouncing the nuptial vow, while her heart is far away with another."[133] A similar feeling welled up in a devastated Rochester Republican, who said of himself and his friends, "If we vote for Lincoln, it will be purely a mechanical act. . . . Our zeal is quenched, our enthusiasm dead, our hearts are broken."[134] In the grudging support from Sewardites, one of them predicted, "there will be a lack of that spontaneous free spirit & consequently less of exertion & labor."[135] More bitterly, an Albany resident told Seward: "Let those who nominated Lincoln Elect Him. We are against him here."[136]

Lincoln's skimpy resumé caused a Philadelphian to ask Seward rhetorically: "What are the acquirements of Mr. Lincoln? Is he a man of varied accomplishments and long tried public experience? Is he what the President of the United States should be without exception—a pure, upright, firm, learned, classical, accomplished, dignified, and respected man? Where in the records of our National history is there one act to warrant, or by which he may claim, a Presidential nomination?" Scornfully, he predicted: "If we descend to nominate such men as Lincoln, we will have before long 5000 upstarts claiming the nomination."[137]

From the West a friend wrote Seward: "When I got the news, I felt as if I didn't want to have any thing more to do with white man's politics, and about ready to go out and live among the Potawattomies."[138] A Baltimore Republican denounced the "timidity" of the "'negrophobic' politicians" in the swing states who determined the outcome at Chicago.[139] The junior editor of Thurlow Weed's Albany *Evening Journal* sourly remarked that the outcome of the convention "is less a defeat of William H. Seward than a triumph of his personal enemies."[140] When Lincoln men lobbied Seward's supporters immediately after the convention, they were told: "Let us alone awhile; we will come into line after a little, but you must not crowd the mourners."[141]

At Chicago, as Lincoln's managers were discussing ways to deal with disgruntled Sewardites, the humorous James W. Nye of New York, a Seward delegate, dropped by and jocularly asked them to "please send an Illinois school-master to Albany to teach Thurlow Weed his political alphabet."[142] Similarly, when New York Congressman John B. Haskin was told that the Lincoln managers had spent no money to secure the nomination, he exclaimed: "You had better come down to Albany and teach us fellows something!"[143] Weed himself sent a Seward backer to suggest that Lincoln's men should visit him. Davis and Swett immediately hastened to Lord Thurlow's hotel, where he told them earnestly: "I hoped to make my friend, Mr. Seward, President, and I thought I could serve my country in so doing." Weed did not grow angry or complain about any person. Swett and Davis urged him to call on Lincoln before returning home.[144] The Dictator, as Weed was known in some circles, agreed to do so but thought it decorous to wait until the effects of the convention cooled. (Weed claimed that he accepted the invitation "very reluctantly.")[145] So he killed time by inspecting land he owned in Iowa and did some sightseeing on the prairies of Illinois where, he remarked sarcastically, "candidates for president grew, expanded and developed without the polishing aid of eastern refinement, and the aid of the educating influence of her colleges."[146]

On May 24, Weed finally met with Lincoln, who reported that his visitor "asked nothing of me, at all. He merely seemed to desire a chance of looking at me, keeping up a show of talk while he was at it. I believe he went away satisfied."[147] Seward's champion, he wrote, "showed no signs whatever of the intriguer" and assured the candidate that "N.Y. is safe, without condition."[148] He also let it be known that there was plenty of money to help fund the campaign.

During their five-hour conversation, Weed found Lincoln "sagacious and practical," with "so much good sense, such intuitive knowledge of human nature, and such familiarity with the virtues and infirmities of politicians," that he "became impressed very favorably with his fitness" for the presidency.[149] Two days after the meeting in Springfield, Weed's newspaper praised Lincoln warmly: "There is no more thorough or bolder Republican on the continent—not one of more sturdy integrity, or of more unflinching purpose." It predicted that backers of other candidates would soon "forget their disappointment" and added that "whoever holds to the extremest doctrines of undiluted Republicanism can find in Mr. Lincoln a fearless and an uncompromising exponent."[150]

Gideon Welles believed that Lord Thurlow "was somewhat presuming and officious" at this interview.[151] But Kansas Congressman Martin F. Conway, who met with the candidate on July 21, told Weed that Lincoln "expressed perfect confidence in you, and respect for your character. He attaches no importance whatever to the statements of your enemies. . . . He admires your caution in requesting him not to answer any letter you may write him."[152]

As for Seward himself, Weed counseled him that "a prompt and cheerful acquiescence in the Nomination . . . is not only wise, but a duty."[153] Seward's friend and New York delegate George M. Grier offered similar advice: "It would be best perhaps for your friends to keep their temper, and act wisely."[154] But the embittered, mortified, frustrated senator found it difficult to comply. Along with his neighbors and his aides, he had been poised to uncork champagne and fire off cannon salutes when the fateful telegram arrived at his Auburn home, where crowds of friends and well-wishers had gathered to celebrate. He felt humiliated "in the character of a leader deposed by my own party, in the hour of organization for decisive battle."[155] He said he was glad he did not keep a diary, for if he had done so there would be "recorded all my cursing and swearing on the 19th of May."[156]

Seward even contemplated quitting politics altogether. Before the Chicago Convention, he had heatedly declared to Joseph Medill that "if he was not nominated as the Republican candidate for President . . . he would shake the dust off his shoes, and retire from the service of an ungrateful party for the remainder of his days."[157] A week after the convention he informed Weed that he would leave public life in March 1861, when his senate term expired. (From Capitol Hill, William P. Fessenden reported a rumor that Seward "will not come back to W[ashington] but I hope he will not make himself ridiculous." If he "retires in a pet, it will end his political career.")[158] Seward's peevishness lasted throughout the summer. On June 26, he again wrote to Weed about his retirement plans: "If I can rightly and to the satisfaction of my friends remain at rest I want to do so. I am content to quit with the political world when it proposes to quit with me."[159]

Through the newspapers of both Weed and Henry J. Raymond, Seward indirectly quarreled with Greeley and let it be known that he probably would not actively campaign for the Republican ticket. Many other Sewardites also attacked Greeley, who they thought had single-handedly defeated their man out of spite. But a pro-Seward delegate from California protested that "the outcry against Mr. Greeley seems but a convenient vent for disappointed and selfish malignity." The Republicans at Chicago wanted to nominate a winner, and Seward simply did not fit that description.[160] Actually, Greeley had injured Lincoln's chances and inadvertently helped Seward; by championing Bates, the eccentric editor had delayed the unification of anti-Seward forces on the Rail-splitter.

Sewardites also criticized Governor E. D. Morgan, who as chairman of the Republican National Committee felt constrained to be neutral. They argued that if Morgan had warned delegates that New York might go Democratic if Seward were not nominated, then the senator could well have triumphed on the first ballot. It was further alleged that Morgan had joined other anti-Seward New Yorkers in maintaining that "the unfortunate associations which surround Seward will be carried to Washington, and the corruptions of the Albany Legislature and lobby be transferred to Congress."[161]

In late May, the press ran a cool, stiffly formal public letter from the Sage of Auburn, endorsing the party's platform and candidates without mentioning Lincoln by name. The following month, Seward wrote a similarly frosty reply to an invitation to speak in Michigan. Two months later, he expressed to a reporter little enthusiasm for the Republican standard-bearer: "Governor Seward had very little to say about Lincoln, further than that he should receive his support."[162] Seward did agree, however, to make a campaign speech in Chicago.

On May 21, a bitter, angry dispatch from the Windy City appeared in Weed's Albany newspaper complaining of a "spirit of envy and hate," "ingratitude," and "malignity" at the convention. "The sentiment which culminated in his [Seward's] rejection was chiefly manufactured by those whose dislike of the man was infinitely in advance of their love for his principles."[163] A week later that paper scouted reports that the senator lost because he was too radical for the battleground states: "the ready acceptance of Mr. Lincoln, whose Free Soil record is as ultra, and whose principles harmonise, exactly, with those of Gov. Seward, perplexes us. It may be all consistent and right, but we cannot understand it."[164]

Soon, however, Weed publicly backed Lincoln, explaining that the Sewardites could be reconciled to defeat because their hero had lost to the only competitor who commanded their respect. On June 7, Lord Thurlow told Leonard Swett: "but for the entire confidence reposed in Mr Lincoln, we would have collapsed in this State. Any nomination, other than Mr L's, instead of Seward, would have been fatal. As it is, we shall 'harness up the old team' and drive it through[.]"[165] Weed's newspaper spoke highly of Lincoln, calling him "an honest, devoted, fearless, true-hearted Republican."[166]

Other Sewardites followed Weed's example. On May 19, delegate George William Curtis confided to his wife that the convention had made "a good nomination. If Seward were impossible Lincoln was the man."[167] In Boston, William Schouler expressed confidence in the Rail-splitter: "The nominations at Chicago take well here and they will receive larger majorities in New England than Governor Seward would have done. I was a Seward man and am now but I think Lincoln and Hamlin are wise nominations."[168] Elsewhere in Massachusetts, William S. Robinson of the Springfield *Republican,* though deeply grieved by Seward's defeat, agreed that the "convention did the next best thing."[169] Two weeks after the convention, it was reported from the northwestern corner of the Bay State that people there "fall in with the nomination, and seem as a general thing to think it a good one. Some lamentations are heard for Seward but they grow less and less."[170]

Many New Yorkers held similar views. When word of Lincoln's nomination first reached Manhattan, the poet-stockbroker Edmund C. Stedman reported that Lincoln's Cooper Union speech "was quoted by hundreds, and to those who saw the man on the occasion of its delivery, no name could so effectually compensate for the withdrawal of Seward, as that of Abraham Lincoln."[171] John Bigelow regretted Seward's defeat but thought Lincoln's nomination "a very wise one, much wiser than I had hoped for." He explained to an English friend that the candidate "is not precisely the sort of man who would be regarded as entirely *a la mode* at your splendid European Courts, nor indeed is his general style and appearance beyond the reach of criticism in our Atlantic drawing rooms." He was "essentially a self made man and of a type to which Europe is as much a stranger as it is to the Mastodon." Nonetheless "he has a clear and eminently logical mind, a nice sense of truth and justice" as well as a superior "capacity of statement." Nothing in the candidate's background or in the way he won the nomination was "calculated to render Mr. S's friends indifferent to his success."[172] Another Seward supporter, E. G. Brooks, actually felt relief at the nomination: "Lincoln is so much better than I feared we shd. get that I am well satisfied. He is a strong straight out, *live man.* . . . I was afraid we shd. get Bates or some purely expediency candidate, resurrectionized and galvanized for the occasion."[173] Ex-governor Washington Hunt, a leader of New York's Whig Party, found that many Sewardites "feel sore & dissatisfied. But they are all sectional rep[ublican]s & can be nothing else, & will generally support Lincoln, believing that Mr. Seward will have full command of his adm[inistratio]n & will use it to secure the succession."[174]

Lincoln salved a lot of hurt feelings by reassuring New Yorkers that they would occupy honored places at the patronage trough. Congressman Elbridge G. Spaulding, a Weed lieutenant from Buffalo, requested a letter from David Davis containing a pledge to that effect. Lincoln drafted such a document for Davis's signature: "Since parting with you, I have had full, and frequent conversations with Mr. Lincoln. The substance of what he says is that he neither is nor will be, in advance of the election, committed to any man, clique, or faction; and that, in case the new administration shall devolve upon him, it will be his pleasure, and, in his view, the part of duty, and wisdom, to deal fairly with all. He thinks he will need the assistance of all; and that, even if he had friends to reward, or enemies to punish, as he has not, he could not afford to dispense with the best talent, nor to outrage the popular will in any locality."[175] This letter was emblematic of Lincoln's inclination to forgive and forget so that he could rally the party and enlist the best talent. To Carl Schurz, an ardent Sewardite at Chicago, Lincoln wrote: "I beg you to be assured that your having supported Gov. Seward, in preference to myself in the convention, is not even remembered by me for any practical purpose, or the slightest u[n]pleasant feeling. I go not back of the convention, to make distinction among its' members."[176]

When Swett asked permission to write a similar letter to Judge John W. Shaffer, reassuring the Seward and Cameron men to whom he had made pledges at Chicago, Lincoln cautiously assented, but stipulated: "do not let him know I have seen it." He instructed Swett to burn his letter, "not that there is any thing wrong in it; but because it is best not to be known that I write at all."[177]

In reality, even Seward's most disenchanted New York friends could not sit on their hands lest the Democrats win control of the state legislature and thus prevent their man's reelection to the senate.

Front Porch Campaign

Publishers scrambled to meet the great demand for information about the little-known Republican candidate, who at first was widely referred to as Abram. The most informative of the thirteen campaign lives that appeared in 1860 were by William Dean Howells, a young Ohio journalist who would later achieve literary fame, and by John Locke Scripps, editor of the Chicago *Press and Tribune* and a good friend of Lincoln.

For Howells, Scripps, and other authors, Lincoln prepared an autobiographical sketch, which, though brief, was longer than the one he had drafted in 1859 for Jesse W. Fell. In this political document he said little about slavery, other than to reproduce his 1837 resolution denouncing the peculiar institution as based on "injustice and bad policy" and assert that his views had not changed since then. He devoted much more space to his Mexican War stand, correctly assuming that the Democrats would once again attack his record on that conflict. In addition to relying on that autobiographical sketch, Scripps sought to interview Lincoln about his life. At first the candidate was reluctant to cooperate, telling his would-be biographer: "it is a great piece of folly to attempt to make anything out of my early life. It can all be condensed into a single sentence and that sentence you will find in Gray's Elegy: 'The short and simple annals of the poor.' That's my life, and that's all you or any one else can make of it.'"[178] Nevertheless, he told Scripps much about his life that was then incorporated into the campaign biography, making it virtually an autobiography. The busy editor hastily churned out ninety-six pages of copy, only to be instructed by his New York publisher (Horace Greeley's *Tribune*) to reduce it to thirty-two. After reluctantly making wholesale cuts, he apologized to Lincoln for the "sadly botched" final section, which was trimmed at the last minute. Amusingly, he instructed the candidate that if he had not read *Plutarch's Lives*, he should do so immediately, for the biography asserted that he had read it in his youth! Earlier Scripps had written a 4,000-word biographical sketch for the Chicago *Press and Tribune*, which he used as the basis for the campaign biography. In the latter he omitted a sentence that had appeared in the former: "A friend says that once, when in a towering rage in consequence of the efforts of certain parties to perpetrate a fraud on the State, he was heard to say 'They shan't do it, d—n 'em!'"[179] Evidently, it was thought advisable to play down Lincoln's formidable capacity for anger.

Like Scripps's biography, William Dean Howells's was enriched by interviews. They were conducted by a research assistant, James Quay Howard, who visited Springfield and talked briefly with Lincoln and at greater length with several of his friends. When the publisher, Follett and Foster of Columbus, Ohio (which had issued the Lincoln-Douglas debates earlier that year), advertised it as "authorized by Mr. Lincoln," the candidate protested vigorously. To Samuel Galloway he complained about Follett and Foster: "I have scarcely been so much astounded by anything, as by their public announcement that it is authorized by me." He had, he said, made himself "tiresome, if not hoarse, with repeating to Mr. Howard" that he "authorized nothing—would be responsible for nothing." He would not endorse a biography unless he thoroughly reviewed and corrected it, which he was then unable to do. He could not consistently obey the advice of all his "discreet friends" to make no public statements while simultaneously approving a campaign life for his opponents "to make points upon without end." If he were to do so, "the convention would have a right to reassemble" and name a different candidate.[180] To maintain deniability, Lincoln refused to read the manuscript of any campaign biography before its publication. He had his friends at the *Illinois State Journal* run a disclaimer and had letters of protest sent both to Howard and to Follett and Foster.

Lincoln himself wrote few letters that season, in part because friends urged him to remain silent lest he, like Henry Clay, ruin his presidential chances by seeming to modify earlier positions. James A. Briggs told him that "as the gallant 'Harry of the West' struck himself down by writing letters to *medlers*, I hope if any *Mourning owl politicians*, write you letters, asking your opinions, *you will let them wait for answers until the Jews are restored to their ancient Judea!*"[181]

Heeding the counsel of Briggs and several others, Lincoln turned aside urgent appeals to speak out, especially on slavery. He had a secretary reply to such requests with a form letter stating that friends had advised him "to write nothing whatever upon any point of political doctrine. They say his positions were well known when he was nominated, and that he must not now embarrass the canvass by undertaking to shift or modify them."[182] The New York *Times* argued that any statement Lincoln made during the campaign "would have been justly open to the suspicion of having been said for effect:—while it could not have been stronger or more directly to the point than what he has already and repeatedly said, at a time when his motives were not open to any such construction."[183]

This strategy did not sit well with all of Lincoln's correspondents, including Benjamin G. Wright, an Illinois Republican who told party confreres that he was leaving them because "the non-committalism of Mr. A. Lincoln makes it an imperative duty. Mr. Lincoln's right to pursue this policy is not questioned, but I do question its correctness, because it subverts our representative system of government."[184]

In dealing privately with requests for a clarification of his views, Lincoln seemed hypersensitive about appearing weak, timid, biddable, unmanly, or cowardly. When a Tennessean asked him to reassure the South that he would, if elected, not interfere with the peculiar institution, he gently but firmly declined: "in my judgment, it would do no good. I have already done this many—many, times; and it is in print, and open to all who will read, or heed. Those who will not read, or heed, what I have already publicly said, would not read, or heed, a repetition of it. 'If they hear not Moses and the prophets, neither will they be persuaded though one rose from the dead.'"[185]

Lincoln did, however, tell a visitor from Louisiana "that he would dispel the illusion existing at the South, that he would have to send men from the Free States to fill the offices, by assuring him that there would be found plenty of persons at the South glad enough to get them, and that he had already received four hundred letters from the slave states begging office, a large and considerable portion of which came from Louisiana."[186]

Protectionists nagged Lincoln for a public avowal of his tariff views. To James E. Harvey of Pennsylvania he explained that in 1844 he had served as an elector for Henry Clay and had sat on a committee that wrote a resolution favoring protective tariffs. But, he asked, "after all, was it really any more than the tariff plank of our present platform? And does not my acceptance pledge me to that? And am I at liberty to do more, if I were inclined?"[187] (Harvey's newspaper, the Philadelphia *North American and United States Gazette*, heaped praise on Lincoln's tariff stand.) When a gentleman with the improbable name of G. Yoke Tams made a blunt inquiry about tariffs, Lincoln patiently reiterated his support of the party platform. Then he added: "Now, if I were to publicly shift this position, by adding or subtracting anything, the convention would have the right, and probably would be inclined, to displace me as their candidate. And I feel confident that you, on reflection, would not wish me to give private assurances to be seen by some, and kept secret from others."[188] Lincoln appreciated the delicacy of the tariff issue. Early in the campaign he said that "the tariff subject must be touched lightly. My speeches in favor of a Protective Tariff would please Pennsylvania and offend W. C. Bryant in the same degree. It is like the case of three men who had nothing to cover them but a blanket only sufficient to cover two. When No 1 pulled it *on* himself he pulled it *off* No. 3."[189]

Just as he would not write about his views, Lincoln refused speaking invitations as well. The National Republican Campaign Committee told him that he should follow the traditional custom of staying quietly at home during the campaign lest he appear to be an undignified "stump candidate."[190]

(Ignoring that custom, Douglas busily campaigned around the country, denouncing Republicans and pro-secessionist Southerners alike, alleging that Congress had no constitutional power to exclude slavery from the territories, and insisting that settlers in the territories had as much right to govern themselves as the inhabitants of the states. Although political etiquette dictated that the office should seek the man rather than the man the office, the Little Giant protested to crowds that "I am not canvassing. I'm only showing you how you can preserve the integrity of the Union and Constitution by supporting this great principle of non-intervention."[191] He boasted that "Lincoln is under great obligations to me," for the Republicans "would never have dreamed of taking up Lincoln as a candidate for the Presidency, if I had not brought him into notice by beating him in Illinois."[192] The Rail-splitter also owed a debt of gratitude to the pro-Breckinridge forces, for, said Douglas, "if they had not bolted I would have beaten Lincoln in every State of the Union except Vermont and Massachusetts."[193] If Lincoln actually did win, Douglas pledged to help impeach and hang him "higher than Virginia hung John Brown" if he violated the Constitution or made "war upon the rights of any State or any section."[194] He also leveled criticism at Lincoln for his reluctance to speak out. "The Republicans have asked me a great many [questions], and got more answers than they wished they had. After answering their questions I have turned to them and asked them to propound the same questions to their own candidates. I said to a leading republican the other day, who asked me questions on the stand, that I would answer them unequivocally, and then would like to have him propound them to Lincoln. Why is this not done?"[195] Many condemned Douglas's unorthodox campaign tactics in the same fashion as did the *Illinois State Journal,* which scathingly remarked: "in the whole history of the country, no other candidate for the Presidency ever degraded himself by such a course as Mr. Douglas is now pursuing. No other candidate ever traveled about the country, delivering partisan harangues. . . . Mr. Douglas is doing what Mr. Lincoln would scorn to do. His regard for the proprieties of his position, as well as his confidence in the respect for the intelligence of the American people, alike forbid his entering into the campaign.")[196]

Only once did Lincoln depart from the strategy of public silence. On August 8, he attended a "monster meeting" in Springfield, where he delivered public remarks for the first and last time of the campaign. The event featured a number of prominent speakers, who, according to the local Democratic paper, "threw out an indescribable amount of gas on the nigger question."[197] Entering the fairgrounds, Lincoln was surprised when some members of the huge crowd rushed his carriage, removed him "almost violently," hoisted him onto their shoulders, and conveyed him to the speakers' platform. The onlookers cheered lustily for ten minutes, producing "a noise not unlike the roar of Niagara Falls."[198] When they finally quieted down, he briefly thanked them for their enthusiastic applause, which he interpreted as no tribute to himself personally but rather to the cause and party he represented. Taken aback by the tumultuous reception, Lincoln closed saying: "I came here, fellow citizens, expecting quiet, but as it seems, I am a great disturber of the peace. I wish you would allow me to depart."[199] After escaping on horseback, he remarked: "I was afraid of being caught and crushed in that crowd. The American people remind me of a flock of sheep."[200]

Lincoln spent most of his days in the state capitol, where he occupied the governor's office, which Yates used only when the legislature was in session. Measuring approximately 15 by 12 feet, and furnished with a sofa, a table, and a few armchairs, it could accommodate up to a dozen people comfortably. There was also a desk where his secretary, John G. Nicolay, worked. The industrious, efficient Nicolay was a 28-year-old, German-born journalist from Pike County who since 1857 had been clerking for Secretary of State Ozias M. Hatch. A week before the Chicago Convention, Nicolay had helped build support for Lincoln's candidacy by publishing an elaborate article comparing his record on slavery with Henry Clay's, arguing that they were very similar. He probably did so at the suggestion of the hopeful candidate, who may have written the piece himself. Since 1858, Nicolay had been contributing occasional articles to the *Missouri Democrat* of St. Louis; he filed a long report on the Chicago Convention for that newspaper. Shortly after his nomination, Lincoln told Hatch: "I wish I could find some young man to help me with my correspondence. It is getting so heavy I can't handle it. I can't afford to pay much, but the practice is worth something." When Hatch recommended Nicolay, Lincoln found it easy to accept the advice, for he regarded the young man as "entirely trust-worthy" and had often conversed and played chess with him in Hatch's office, which served as an informal Republican headquarters. Nicolay had hoped to be given the task of writing a campaign biography and was jealous when William Dean Howells was chosen. He was solaced when Lincoln hired him at $75 per month, for he vastly admired his employer, who served as a kind of surrogate father to the orphaned Nicolay.[201]

As time passed and the correspondence grew heavier, Nicolay required help. Milton Hay proposed that the committee covering Lincoln's extra expenses hire his young nephew, John Hay, saying that he had "great literary talent and great tact." The committee agreed to the suggestion, and the 23-year-old Hay, a suave, sophisticated graduate of Brown University with a touch of the poet and a reputation for "humorous gayety," began assisting Nicolay, who had been his school chum in Pittsfield.[202] Both young men later accompanied Lincoln to Washington, where they served as his private secretaries. During the campaign, Hay wrote occasional press dispatches under the pen name "Ecarte."

The secretary's desk was covered with innumerable letters and newspapers. Editors sent copies of their journals, all carefully marked up for the inspection of the president-elect, who ignored them. Also strewing the desktop were some of the hundreds of gifts and souvenirs people sent Lincoln. Among them were canes, axes, mauls, fragments of old rails that he had allegedly split and of the cabins where he had supposedly lived, pieces of furniture and surveyor's tools he had once owned, mementos of the Black Hawk War, wedges, pictures, books, and a chain of links ingeniously carved from a single piece of wood. The various tools became conversation pieces that Lincoln described to his city-based well-wishers, one of whom observed two steel wedges and asked, "Are those the wedges, Sir?" Lincoln replied: "These, Sir, are the identical wedges—that were sent to me about a week ago."[203] Upon receiving an elegant hat, he remarked to Mrs. Lincoln: "Well, wife, there is one thing likely to come out of this scrape, any how. We are going to have some *new clothes*!"[204]

At the governor's office Lincoln received politicians from around the country. He usually told them a story, said nothing significant, and sent them home happy. Uncomplainingly, he also met ordinary people who wished to see him. "I am a public man now," he said, "and I am the public's most obedient servant." He was especially happy to chat with old friends from his early days in the state. No matter how eminent a figure he was entertaining, Lincoln, when informed that such a caller sought an audience, would promptly excuse himself to offer his greetings and make his new guest comfortable. They would then reminisce about the old days. One such friend was an elderly gentleman who greeted him with the salutation "Mr. President."

"Not yet," said Lincoln. "We mustn't count our chickens before they are hatched, you know." "Well," said the caller, "maybe yourn aint quite hatched, but they're peepin' sure."

Lincoln's patience, affability, and dignity impressed his callers, including some Southerners who found to their surprise that their prejudices against him were unfounded. A Mississippian who had just emerged from a long conversation with Lincoln declared, "I am perfectly astonished. I expected to find a fierce and ignorant fanatic, but I find instead, not only an affable and genial gentleman, but a wise and moderate statesman. . . . Why, our whole southern people are deceived in regard to that man."[205] Another visitor reported that Lincoln "makes every one feel not only easy, but delighted and fascinated by his fine narratives, references and classical quotations. He does not pretend to be familiar with literature, though not many will be willing to enter a second time on literary themes with him, unless their minds be well stored."[206]

Some callers expressed concern for Lincoln's life, reminding him that his Whig predecessors, Harrison and Taylor, had both died in office. His only regular companion in the governor's office, John G. Nicolay, noted that it was "astonishing how the popular sympathy for Mr. Lincoln draws fearful forebodings from these two examples."[207]

Lincoln's office was overrun with all kinds of visitors virtually every day. He made no distinction between the great and the humble. "The flat-boatman and the statesman, the beggar and the millionaire, are treated with equal courtesy, and all heard with marvelous patience," a journalist observed. "Honors have not changed the manners of 'Honest Old Abe.'"[208] His old friend Orville Browning also found Lincoln bearing "his honors meekly." As they chatted freely and easily for an hour or two, the candidate told several amusing stories.[209]

Some visitors annoyed him, particularly office seekers, who flocked to Springfield from all parts of the country. Simon Hanscom observed wryly: "If these gentlemen do not get an opportunity of serving their country for the next four years, in positions where there is little work and much pay, you may depend upon it that it will not be for any want of blowing their own trumpets nor from any modesty in magnifying their own achievements."[210] Lincoln was keenly aware that many federal officials needed to be replaced. Hanscom noted that anyone "by conversing with Mr. Lincoln for a short time on national politics, will see that he is firm in the opinion that the whole government wants overhauling and cleaning out; that he is posted to an astonishing degree in the details of our government in all its departments."[211] When asked about the men he wanted to head those departments, he replied that "*after* his election he would form his own Cabinet."[212]

To escape patronage hounds, Lincoln occasionally carved out time to play with his children, Willie and Tad. While doing so one day that summer, he told a friend that "he was having a little season of relaxation with the boys, which he could not always enjoy now, as so many callers and so much correspondence occupied his time."[213]

In October, William Henry Seward, on a campaign swing through the Northwest, stopped briefly in Springfield. His trip was a curious one, for he spent most of his time in safe Republican states. Back in July, Lincoln had urged Seward to speak in Springfield, saying: "I shall be personally much gratified to meet him here."[214] But the Republican State Committee reportedly tried to keep the senator from visiting central and southern Illinois, where his reputation as an antislavery extremist made him unpopular. The *Illinois State Register*, which denounced the radicalism of Seward's speeches, claimed that the New Yorker spoke for Lincoln. But caution about inviting him was overcome by concern that Seward's failure to visit Springfield might be interpreted as evidence of hostility to Lincoln. So, at the last minute, the senator made a detour to see the man who had bested him for the Republican nomination. The Republicans of Springfield had only a two-hour notice of Seward's arrival but managed to turn out 1,500 people to greet him.

Instead of calling on Lincoln at his house or office, the haughty New Yorker allowed the candidate to come to the depot, make his way through the crowd, and climb aboard the train. The meeting was brief and awkward, for Lincoln seemed ill at ease and Seward was almost rude. A journalist noted that Lincoln's "manner to Mr. Seward was marked rather by deference and respect than cordiality, and Mr. Seward himself seemed to avoid friendly advances—a little unusual for him."[215] After introducing his traveling party to the candidate, Seward sat back down without speaking further with Lincoln. No sooner had he resumed his seat than he was summoned to address the crowd. Seemingly glad to have an excuse not to talk with Lincoln, he immediately repaired to the rear platform, where he told his audience: "The State of New York will give a generous and cheerful and effective support to your neighbor."

Afterward, Lincoln spoke briefly with his visitor, suggesting a point for him to incorporate into his upcoming Chicago address. Seward ignored the advice, later observing that he had already made that point in a previous speech. Lincoln then reminisced: "Twelve years ago you told me that this cause would be successful, and ever since I have believed that it would be. Even if it did not succeed now, my faith would not be shaken."[216] Seward's entire stopover in Springfield lasted no more than a quarter of an hour, during most of which he addressed the crowd. A mere five minutes were consumed in introductions and conversation.

Simon P. Hanscom, who witnessed this scene, was struck by "Seward's ill concealed dislike of Lincoln." After the senator left Springfield, he continued to snub Lincoln in his speeches. As Hanscom noted, "throughout Mr. Seward's grand ovation in the Northwest, he very rarely, and then only in the curtest manner, spoke of the republican candidate for the Presidency." Obviously, the senator's "heart was not in the cause of Lincoln and Hamlin. And so, while he talked of the irrepressible conflict, of the backwardness of slave communities, and of the present and prospective grandeur of the great West, he never attempted to inspire his hearers with any elevated idea of the talents or abilities of Mr. Lincoln."[217]

After Seward's opening address in Detroit, the New York *Journal of Commerce* remarked that he "is forced by circumstances to go forth on a speech-making mission, ostensibly in favor of his successful rival." But, as the paper observed of Seward's addresses, "Mr. Lincoln will get cold comfort from them, if that made at Detroit last evening, is to be the standard." Save for one paragraph, Seward's remarks contained "not the slightest allusion to the contest for the Presidency, or the most remote reference to Mr. Lincoln or the importance of his election."[218] In Chicago, Seward referred positively to John Brown and Elijah Lovejoy, but only mentioned Lincoln's name once. In the other fifteen speeches he delivered on his western tour, Seward ignored Lincoln in seven and only briefly alluded to him in the rest.

Hanscom's paper, the New York *Herald*, asserted that everybody "knows, and he [Seward] has never attempted to disguise it, that he is no admirer of the country lawyer of Illinois. . . . It is not unnatural that he would regard with disfavor, if not with some degree of contempt, a man who, without any special merit of his own, was taken from the subordinate ranks of the party and promoted over his head."[219] George G. Fogg assured Lincoln that the senator "has no more doubt of his measureless *superiority to you*, than of his existence. . . . He either *hates you* for being nominated over him at Chicago, or he contemptuously expects to make you 'play second fiddle' to all his schemes."[220] (Alluding to Seward's "enormous self-conceit," Horace Greeley once asked Schuyler Colfax, "Do *you* happen to know of his ever consulting and counseling with *any body* on terms of equality?")[221]

Seward long harbored resentment against Lincoln for defeating him at Chicago. In March 1861, when told that German-Americans would be disappointed if he, as secretary of state, did not have Carl Schurz appointed to a first-class foreign mission, Seward exploded in rage: "Disappointment! You speak to me of disappointment. To me, who was justly entitled to the Republican nomination for the presidency, and who had to stand aside and see it given to a little Illinois lawyer! You speak to me of disappointment!" He found it humiliating to be "*simply a clerk of the President!*"[222] (Two months later, Seward told his wife bitterly that he felt like "a chief reduced to a subordinate position, and surrounded with a guard, to see that I do not do too much for my country, lest some advantage may revert indirectly to my own fame." Seward worried a lot about his fame. With immense self-pity, he added that the "country so largely relying on my poor efforts to save it, had refused me the full measure of its confidence, needful to that end.")[223]

Lincoln had been advised not to accompany Seward to Chicago, lest he seem to be deferring to the senator or to be violating the rule that presidential candidates eschew overt campaigning. Fogg warned that "Seward is evidently making a sort of triumphal march through the Country, with a large army of retainers. I trust that he will help the Republican cause. But there is *one* man [i.e., Lincoln] who must not be seen at his chariot wheels."[224] Lincoln's Chicago friends opposed his visiting that city when Seward appeared there. Norman B. Judd, who in July had invited Seward to speak in Chicago, later criticized the Sage of Auburn's appearance there as a ploy to enhance John Wentworth's standing rather than to help Lincoln and Trumbull win their elections.

Democrats charged that "Mr. Seward was Captain and Lincoln was only Lieutenant" and that the senator "would keep [the rank of] Captain after Lincoln was elected."[225] The *Illinois State Register* argued that in a Lincoln administration, Seward "will be, *de facto*, President of the United States.—Mr. Lincoln will be but an automaton in the White House."[226]

Illinois was the only battleground state Seward visited, in part because some Republican leaders had strenuously objected to the senator's plans to campaign in their states, lest he frighten off moderate voters. His ally Henry J. Raymond had warned shortly after the Chicago Convention that New Yorkers believed "Pennsylvania, New-Jersey, Illinois and Indiana have taken upon themselves the main burden of the canvass, and New-York will feel that she has done her part if she succeeds in casting her electoral vote for the nominees of the Convention."[227] (In the immediate aftermath of Lincoln's nomination, Raymond had ordered the New York *Times* not to commit to the Rail-splitter.)

Unlike the imperious Seward, Carl Schurz called on Lincoln at his house during a swing through Illinois. As they discussed the campaign and laughed at some of its twists and turns, Lincoln's manner was so unpretentious that Schurz could scarcely realize that he was in the presence of a man likely to become president in a few months. Afterward Lincoln escorted his guest to the site where he was scheduled to speak. Because the July day was exceedingly hot, Lincoln shed his waistcoat and donned a linen duster, the back of which had large perspiration stains, making it resemble a map of the western hemisphere. He also wore an ancient, beat-up stovepipe hat. As the two men marched behind a brass band to the meeting place, Lincoln showed no signs of inflated ego but rather behaved as if nothing special had happened to him in the past few months. His neighbors waved and cheered, and he greeted them unself-consciously with his usual cordiality. He declined to sit on the platform where Schurz spoke, but instead took a seat in the front row. After listening to the impassioned young orator hold forth, Lincoln told him: "You are an awful fellow! I understand your power now!"[228] Like many others, Lincoln regarded Schurz as one of the foremost speakers in the country.

A prominent visitor to Springfield who did not call on Lincoln was the Prince of Wales, the future King Edward VII of England. Lincoln told Simon P. Hanscom that "he would like very much" to have met the heir-apparent to the British throne when he quietly passed through town on September 29. Lincoln stayed away as Springfielders welcomed the royal traveler because he worried about "having his motive misrepresented and a charge of immodesty brought against him." He explained: "Being thus situated and not able to take any lead in the matter, I remained here at the State House, where I met so many sovereigns [i.e., fellow citizens] during the day that really the Prince had come and gone before I knew it."[229]

None of Lincoln's many visitors was a client, because he had stopped practicing law, save for a handful of cases which he attended to in June. He said that he had pity for those clients because "the demands of his position made him an indifferent lawyer."[230]

Some callers were journalists, including an interviewer from the *Missouri Democrat*, who reported that the candidate's "health and spirits are excellent; and though not quite so embrowned as when canvassing the State with Mr. Douglas, he is less lean than usual, and certainly looks as though he would not easily wither and die, even in the hot bed of the President's house."[231] To another reporter, Lincoln expressed skepticism about the popularity of slavery among white Southerners. "Public opinion is not always private opinion," he noted, citing "Lamartine's account of the execution of Louis XVI., wherein it appeared that, although the leading revolutionists were publicly obliged to declare in favor of that deed, they were privately opposed to it. He said that it was the same with many people in the South; they were obliged to sustain slavery, although they secretly abhorred the institution." He regretted that Southerners misunderstood the Republicans' stand on slavery and expressed a wish to enlighten them.[232]

In addition to visitors, Lincoln sometimes chatted with Newton Bateman, state superintendent of education, whose office was adjacent to the one the candidate was using. One day Lincoln complained to Bateman about the politics of Springfield's clergymen. Informed that twenty of the town's twenty-three ministers opposed his election, he pointed to a Bible and remarked sadly: "These men well know that I am for freedom . . . and that my opponents are for slavery. They know this, and yet, with this book in their hands, in the light of which human bondage cannot live a moment, they are going to vote against me. I do not understand it at all."[233] It was rumored that Lincoln seldom attended his wife's church because its minister, John Howe Brown, favored Douglas.

Many years later, Nicolay explained that the "opposition of the Springfield clergy to his election was chiefly due to remarks about them. One careless remark I remember was widely quoted. An eminent clergyman was delivering a series of doctrinal discourses which had attracted considerable local attention. Although Lincoln was frequently invited, he would not be induced to attend them. He remarked that he wouldn't trust Brother———to construe the statutes of Illinois and much less the laws of God; that people who knew him wouldn't trust his advice on an ordinary business transaction because they didn't consider him competent; hence he didn't see why they did so in the most important of all human affairs, the salvation of their souls. These remarks were quoted widely and misrepresented, to Lincoln's injury. In those days people were not so liberal as now and anyone who criticized a parson was considered a skeptic."[234]

Following his nomination, Lincoln spoke to a journalist about his mail and callers, saying that "he liked to see his friends, and as to the letters, he took good care not to answer them." His most serious grievance, he declared, was with "the artists; he tried in vain to recognize himself in some 'Abraham Lincolns'" that were sent to him.[235]

Indeed, capturing Lincoln's image challenged even good artists. He jokingly explained that it was "impossible to get my graceful motions in—that's the reason why none of the pictures are like me!"[236] When told that none of the photographs accurately depicted him, he "laughingly suggested that it might not be desirable to have justice done to such forbidding features as his."[237] He did admire a photograph taken by Alexander Hesler in 1857; that likeness he deemed "a very true one; though my wife, and many others, do not. My impression is that their objection arises from the disordered condition of the hair. My judgment is worth nothing in these matters."[238] (The photographer had mussed Lincoln's hair to make him look more natural.) When a lithograph of this photo was rushed into print, Lincoln enjoyed telling friends that newsboys hawking it on city streets cried out: "'Ere's yer last picter of Old Abe! He'll look better when he gets his *hair* combed!"[239] (One day during the Civil War, while visiting the front, Lincoln asked to borrow a hairbrush. When the request was honored, he said: "I can't do anything with such a thing as that. It wouldn't go through my hair. Now, if you have anything you comb your horse's mane with, that might do.")[240]

Among the artists for whom Lincoln sat during the campaign were George Frederick Wright, Alban Jasper Conant, Thomas M. J. Johnston, J. Henry Brown, Jesse Atwood, Thomas Hicks, George P. A. Healy, and Charles A. Barry. A native of Boston, Barry was commissioned by Nathaniel P. Banks and John A. Andrew to do a crayon portrait of Lincoln. When Barry finished, Lincoln gestured toward the result and said: "Even my enemies must declare that to be a true likeness of Old Abe."[241] Of Hicks's oil portrait, he remarked: "It will give the people of the East a correct idea how I look at home. . . . I think the picture has a somewhat pleasanter expression than I usually have, but that, perhaps, is not an objection."[242] Orville Browning called it "an exact, life like likeness" and "a beautiful work of art. It is deeply imbued with the intellectual and spiritual, and I doubt whether any one ever succeeds in getting a better picture of the man."[243]

Lincoln was also pleased by J. Henry Brown's miniature portrait, which he deemed "an excellent one, so far as I can judge. To my unpracticed eye, it is without fault."[244] Nicolay, too, admired the portrait by Brown, who had been dispatched to Springfield by the wealthy Pennsylvania Republican leader, John M. Read. Brown explained to Nicolay that "the impression prevails East that Mr. Lincoln is very ugly—an impression which the published pictures of him of course all confirm." Read, however, "had an idea that it could hardly be so—but was bound to have a good-looking picture," and so ordered Brown "to make it good-looking whether the original would justify it or not." Thus, when Brown reached Springfield to carry out his commission, he had some forebodings, but "was very happy when on seeing him [Lincoln] he found that he was not at all such a man as had been represented."[245] Brown thought that there were "so many hard lines in his face that it becomes a mask to the inner man. His true character only shines out when in an animated conversation, or when telling an amusing tale." Lincoln's popularity impressed Brown, who was surprised to find that "even those opposed to him in politics speak of him in unqualified terms of praise."[246] Nicolay lauded Brown's portrait as "strikingly faithful and correct. It is, in my opinion, as perfect a likeness of him as could be made."[247] When he saw the engraving made from it, Nicolay told Brown: "I am highly gratified that Mr. Lincoln's friends will at length be enabled to obtain a good likeness of him."[248]

Mary Lincoln lauded Alban Jasper Conant's portrait of her husband: "That is excellent, that is the way he looks when he has his friends about him."[249] Lincoln found it "more satisfactory than any portrait of him that has been painted, probably, he says, because it makes a better-looking man of him than the others do."[250] (In 1864, when he was introduced to the Pennsylvania artist A. B. Sloanaker, who had reportedly painted "a most beautiful portrait" of him, Lincoln replied: "I presume, sir, in painting your beautiful portrait, you took your idea of me from my principles, and not from my person.")[251] Mrs. Lincoln also admired Healy's painting, though she "remarked that it gave Mr. Lincoln a graver expression than he usually wore."[252]

In fact, no artist did justice to Lincoln's face. As Nicolay observed many years later, "Lincoln's features were the despair of every artist who undertook his portrait." Nicolay recalled seeing "nearly a dozen, one after another, soon after the first nomination to the presidency, attempt the task. They put into their pictures the large rugged features, and strong prominent lines; they made measurements to obtain exact proportions; they 'petrified' some single look, but the picture remained hard and cold. Even before these paintings were finished it was plain to see that they were unsatisfactory to the artists themselves, and much more so to the intimate friends of the man; this was not he who smiled, spoke, laughed, charmed. The picture was to the man as the grain of sand to the mountain, as the dead to the living. Graphic art was powerless before a face that moved through a thousand delicate gradations of line and contour, light and shade, sparkle of the eye and curve of the lip, in the long gamut of expression from grave to gay, and back again from the rollicking jollity of laughter to that serious, far-away look that with prophetic intuitions beheld the awful panorama of war, and heard the cry of oppression and suffering. There are many pictures of Lincoln; there is no portrait of him."[253]

One of those pictures was taken by the Springfield photographer Christopher S. German in January 1861, just as Lincoln's new beard began to fill out. The candidate told a visitor that it "was in his judgment, and that of his friends, the best ever had."[254]

Artists enjoyed working with Lincoln. Thomas D. Jones, a sculptor for whom he sat in the winter after his election, wrote a friend that he was "astounded at the man's simplicity & modesty" and that he had spent "some very happy hours" with him. Jones described him as "a perfect child of nature—so fond of fun," one who "tells the best stories in the world, and more of them than any man I have ever met."[255] To his patron, J. Henry Brown reported that Lincoln "must be seen and known to be properly appreciated. Ten minutes after I was in his presence I felt as if I had known him for years," for "he has an easy frankness and charm of manner which made me comfortable and happy while in his presence."[256]

Wooing the Fillmore Supporters and the Protectionists

The election hinged on the Whig/American voters of 1856, especially in Indiana and Pennsylvania, where gubernatorial contests were to be held in October, and also in New York. Such voters might easily follow the lead of their 1856 candidate, Millard Fillmore, who supported John Bell. To prevent that from happening was Lincoln's greatest electoral challenge. To do so, he realized that he must win over men like "the great high priest of Know-nothingism," James O. Putnam, the postmaster at Fillmore's hometown of Buffalo and a close friend of the former president.[257] Putnam, said Lincoln, resembled Weed: "these men ask for just the same thing—fairness, and fairness only."[258] Putnam came to admire Lincoln vastly, calling him "one of the most remarkable speakers of English, living." For "logical eloquence, straight-forwardness, clearness of statement, sincerity that commands your admiration and assent, and a compact stren[g]th of argument," Lincoln was "infinitely superior to Douglas," he thought.[259] As for Bell, Putnam acknowledged that the Tennesseean "has the respect and confidence of every man of American antecedents, but of what earthly service can 20,000 or 30,000 votes be to him in New York?" Putnam deserted the Bell forces because "he saw no chance for them to carry the Northern States, and his only hope in defeating the Democratic party, and thereby promoting the interests of the country, was in a union with the Republicans upon the Chicago platform and nominees."[260] (As president, Lincoln was to name Putnam consul at Le Havre.)

In Putnam's hometown of Buffalo, the leading American Party newspaper detected in Lincoln qualities that the corrupt Republican legislature at Albany lacked: "Mr. Lincoln's nomination . . . guarantees executive honesty. It assures us that no bargains have been made, no greedy disposition of the spoils already accomplished. His principles are our principles. We only differ from Republicans in the relative importance attached to the Slavery issue and in having perhaps a larger faith in the final triumph of the right. Thus holding, thus satisfied of the honesty of the party with which we act, we are unreserved in our support of Lincoln and Hamlin."[261] Such admiration of Lincoln's honesty was characteristic of American Party members, who tended to blame corruption on immigrants. It proved to be a key factor in making Lincoln's election possible. Commenting on this endorsement, Washington Hunt, a leading conservative, said that the editor's view of Lincoln, "unsound and fallacious as it is, operates upon many persons who are disposed to follow the current and take refuge in what they consider a strong and prosperous party."[262] Other American Party members shared the belief that voting for Bell would be futile, while electing Lincoln would rebuke the hated Democrats and stem the tide of corruption.

Another American Party leader to be cultivated was David Davis's cousin, Henry Winter Davis of Maryland, who was so influential that the committee of twelve at the Chicago Convention had asked him to run for vice-president. He declined lest his candidacy ruin the ticket in the Northwest. Like many other Know-Nothings, he objected to the Republican platform's "Dutch plank" regarding immigration policy. Since the term *Republican* was poison in Maryland, Davis said he would support Bell there but hinted that he might be willing to stump for Lincoln in Pennsylvania and New Jersey. He thought "the Chicago nomination a wise one."[263]

Lincoln urged Richard W. Thompson, his friend from their days together in Congress and a leader of the Constitutional Union Party in Indiana, to "converse freely" with Davis.[264] Thompson did so. He also told Lincoln that while he might not vote Republican, he would work to block a Bell ticket in Indiana. (In 1856, Thompson had badly damaged the Republicans' chances in the Hoosier state by thwarting their attempts to fuse with the Americans; in return, he received a rich reward from the Democrats.) Thompson, whose influence with Midwestern Know-Nothings was considerable, assured them that the Rail-splitter could not "be led into ultraism by radical men" and that his administration "will be national." In choosing the Illinoisan over Seward, the delegates at Chicago "demonstrated to the country that the great body of the Republicans are conservative." Lincoln's "strength consists in his conservatism. His own principles are conservative." Thompson asked Lincoln if he could cite his 1849 vote against the Gott resolution (to end the slave trade in the District of Columbia) in order to allay the fears of conservatives. The candidate, fearful of alienating antislavery Radicals, replied: "If my record would hurt any, there is no hope that it will be over-looked; so that if friends can help any with it, they may as well do so. Of course, due caution and circumspection, will be used."[265] (A week later, Horace Greeley pointed to Lincoln's vote on the Gott resolution as proof of his conservatism.)

In July, when Thompson expressed a wish to meet with Lincoln, the candidate hesitated. Because Democratic papers had been accusing Lincoln of nativist proclivities (even charging falsely that he had attended a Know-Nothing lodge), he wished to do nothing that might lend credence to such allegations. So rather than invite Thompson to Springfield, he dispatched Nicolay to Indiana with instructions to ask what his old friend wanted to discuss and assure him that his motto was "Fairness to all," but to make no commitments. In mid-July Nicolay carried out this mission, finding that Thompson "sought only to be assured of the general 'fairness' to all elements giving Mr Lincoln their support, and that he did not even hint at any exaction or promise as being necessary to secure the 'Know Nothing' vote for the Republican ticket."[266]

Anxious about the influence of Know-Nothings in northern Illinois, Lincoln asked Thompson to write to John Wilson, an American Party leader in Chicago who had been a delegate to the Constitutional Union Party's convention. Thompson complied, and Wilson abandoned the Bell movement after its Illinois leaders tried to merge with the Douglasites. David Davis urged Lincoln to cultivate Wilson, which he did, making sure that the Chicagoan was invited to speak at a major Republican rally in Springfield.

More worrisome than Chicago nativists were those in Pennsylvania, which everyone agreed was a vitally important state. If the Democrats carried all the Slave States plus either California or Oregon, they could, with the addition of Pennsylvania, win the election. "We expect to have hard work in Pennsylvania, & in the Eastern part especially, where Mr. Bell has many friends, & the American element is Considerable in numbers," the influential journalist James E. Harvey told Lincoln immediately after the Chicago Convention.[267] Charles Leib advised Lincoln that the Dutch plank was "the only thing that causes the radical Americans in Penna. to even halt for an instant, and I trust and pray, that every time friends of yours will extend the 'Olive branch' to that party."[268] Schuyler Colfax also reported that there was "a little discontent in Eastern Pa. about the German plank."[269] From Washington, Elihu B. Washburne wrote that the "idea now prevails here that Pennsylvania is the battle ground, and that the locofocos will Stake all on that State. The American element of the State *we must have*, and it is wise to consider fully its importance."[270]

Lyman Trumbull sounded the alarm, too, complaining that the Dutch plank made John Bell more attractive to the Fillmore voters of 1856. The senator told Lincoln: "I wish our German friends could have been satisfied without such a resolution. Surely they were in no danger of an abridgement of their rights from any actions of the Republicans; but the thing is done, & we must now make the best of it."[271] Horace Greeley scolded Germans for their attempts at "dictation" and declared that any man "who votes in our election as an Irishman or German has no moral right to vote at all."[272]

In the end, Republican worries about Fillmore voters flocking to Bell proved unfounded. In June, an Indianan reported that many people "like Bell and Everett, but they say, as there is no chance for them, they will support Lincoln and Hamlin."[273] From the capital of New Jersey, a resident observed that Bell was "like a 'tinkling cymball,' an empty sound wherever it goes."[274] This reluctance to throw away their vote affected large numbers of Bell supporters above the Mason-Dixon line.

South of that line, Lincoln had little hope of winning electoral votes, partly because of John J. Crittenden's public warning that, although the Republican nominee was "an honest, worthy and patriotic man," nevertheless as "the Republicans' President" he "would be at least a terror to the South."[275] A former congressman (and future senator) from the Blue Grass State, Garrett Davis, called Lincoln "an honest man of fair ability" but found him unacceptable because "for some years past he has been possessed of but one idea—hostility to slavery."[276]

Lincoln had to win over protectionists as well as Know-Nothings in the Keystone State, whose Republican politicians said "you may cry nigger, nigger, as much as you please, only give us a chance to carry Pennsylvania by crying tariff."[277] From Chambersburg, state party chairman A. K. McClure informed Lincoln that in "the Eastern, Southern & Central counties especially, the Tariff will be the overshadowing question in this contest. . . . In these Tariff counties the *Conservative* element predominates."[278] Pennsylvanians had been hit hard by the Panic of 1857, which depressed iron and coal prices and threw thousands of men out of work. The unemployed blamed low tariff rates for their misery. Republican newspapers hammered away at the tariff issue incessantly. To counter that popular cry, Democrats appealed to racial prejudice, condemning the Republicans for their support of "niggerism and 'the Negro.'"[279]

At the Chicago Convention, Leonard Swett and David Davis had agreed to stump Pennsylvania and testify to Lincoln's soundness as a protectionist. John P. Sanderson urged that they pay special attention to the Keystone State, for Republicans there were in real danger. Similar appeals came from Joseph Casey and Joseph J. Lewis. Davis and Swett replied that they would rather remain in Illinois, but said they would go east if they must. McClure advised against the proposed visit, telling Lincoln the two Illinoisans "would be presumed to represent you, and with even the greatest care, might put us on the defensive in some respect."[280] McClure probably feared that Davis and Swett would be induced to side with the Cameron faction against the Curtin faction, which McClure supported. Lincoln grew alarmed about Pennsylvania when Joseph Casey warned that the Republican state committee, led by McClure, inspired little confidence. This led Lincoln to fear that Casey and other malcontents might "rebel, and make a dangerous explosion."[281] (They did, in fact, establish a separate state committee and packed it with Cameron supporters.)

Another problem in Pennsylvania was the lackluster campaigning of gubernatorial candidate Andrew G. Curtin. "We have been somewhat disappointed in Curtin as an efficient stumper and he really excites but little interest," reported Joseph J. Lewis from West Chester. But, Lewis noted, "there is a feeling that his success is of importance to Lincoln and that consideration helps Curtin greatly."[282]

Adding to Lincoln's alarm were reports that McClure had misused campaign funds. Joseph Medill recommended that some trustworthy Republican investigate the allegation. Lincoln concurred and reluctantly sent David Davis eastward with a letter introducing him as "my very good personal and political friend." Davis also carried "scraps" Lincoln had written in 1847 about the tariff.[283] (Pennsylvanians wanted to see the text of speeches Lincoln had delivered on protection during the 1840s, but because newspapers at that time did not carry full accounts of political addresses he had no texts of them.) When Davis showed the scraps to Cameron, the Pennsylvania boss called them "abundantly satisfactory."[284] Quite pleased with Davis's visit, Cameron agreed "to work earnestly."[285] To Cameron, Sanderson wrote that Davis "had seen enough to know that you were the power in the State, & that if McClure & his party would let you & your friends carry it, it would be done."[286] After consulting with several other leaders, including McClure, Davis confidently predicted to Lincoln, "You will be elected Presdt."[287] While in the East, the judge also visited New Jersey and met with Weed in New York.

Despite Davis's visit, internal strife continued to rage in the Keystone State. At the end of August, when John M. Pomeroy of Pennsylvania informed Lincoln about the feud between the Cameron and Curtin factions, the candidate replied: "I am slow to listen to criminations among friends, and never expose their quarrels on either side. My sincere wish is that both sides will allow by-gones to be by-gones, and look to the present & future only."[288]

Despite the factionalism in Pennsylvania, Lincoln was not discouraged about his prospects. With the Democrats split and the Constitutional Union Party weakening them further in the Border States, his election began to look more and more likely as autumn approached. One Republican predicted that Douglas would carry no states at all. As Charles Henry Ray told Lincoln, "it will do you no harm to begin to consider what shall be the quality and cut of your inaugural suit. It does not seem to me that you have anything else to do in the campaign."[289] Lincoln agreed. To his old friend Simeon Francis he wrote in August: "I hesitate to say it, but it really appears now, as if the success of the Republican ticket is inevitable. We have no reason to doubt any of the states which voted for Fremont. Add to these, Minnesota, Pennsylvania, and New-Jersey, and the thing is done. Minnesota is as sure as such a thing can be; while the democracy are so divided between Douglas and Breckenridge in Penn. & N.J. that they are scarcely less sure."[290]

Optimistic though Lincoln was, he shared Henry Wilson's belief that unglamorous organizational work deserved more attention than it was receiving. He told the Massachusetts senator that the "point you press—the importance of thorough organization—is felt, and appreciated by our friends everywhere. And yet it involves so much more of dry, and irksome labor, that most of them shrink from it—preferring parades, and shows, and monster meetings. I know not how this can be helped. I do what I can in my position, for organization; but it does not amount to so much as it should."[291] Part of that work may have included lending covert support to the Breckinridge forces. The *Illinois State Register* claimed that the Danites' successful effort to weaken Douglas by fielding a Breckinridge ticket in the Prairie

State "was got up under the immediate personal supervision of Mr. Lincoln and his state committee."[292]

Trumping the Race Card

Lincoln was publicly silent, working behind the scenes to combat Democratic criticism, especially the frequent charge that he and other Republicans favored social and political equality for blacks. Democrats believed that if they "would ignore the absurd quarrel raised upon the territorial question and resolve to fight the ensuing campaign upon new ground such as broadly, white man vs Negro," they "could not fail to win."[293] So they energetically played upon racial fears. Commenting on Lincoln's July 10, 1858 speech, the Chicago *Herald* observed: "This declaration of Mr. Lincoln unequivocally places the white man and negro on the same level. . . . This is the 'ultima thule' of national self-degradation. The naked, greasy, bandy-shanked, blubber-lipped, monkey-headed, muskrat-scented cannibals from Congo and Guinea can come here in hoards, and settle down upon terms of equality with the descendants of Alfred the Great, the Van Tromps, the Russells, the Washingtons, the Lafayettes, the Emmitts! Mr. Lincoln will have no quibbling about this matter. They are not only not born inferior; but he will have them assigned no inferior position. A race, which for five thousand years has fallen so low as to have almost lost the image of manhood, who eat human flesh and indulge in every horror of vice and infamy, and whose very persons offend every sense of civilized man, are to rank at once with the races which, from their virtue and inherent strength, have, after a conflict of a thousand years, won the brilliant civilization of the nineteenth century!"[294]

A St. Louis paper identified the central Republican principle as "negro equality." The party "seeks to confound the white and black races; and as it can never elevate the negro to the moral and intellectual level of the white, it can never bring about that promised equality save by dragging the whites down to the level of the blacks." The result would be "intellectual, moral and physical degradation of both whites and blacks."[295] That paper ran a satirical letter maintaining that Black Republicanism was the progeny of Abraham Lincoln and the "darkey" Hagar.[296]

The *Illinois State Register* described Lincoln's "detestable doctrines" thus: "the worthless negro of our state" must be placed "upon full social and political equality with you—to associate him with you at the ballot box, in your legislative halls, in your judiciary, and in your family circle, and finally, if that full equality which Lincoln claims is his right, should be brought about, to mingle the African with the blood of the whites, by intermarriage with your sisters and daughters." The *Register* claimed that Lincoln's policies would turn Illinois into "an asylum for the worthless free negro population of the whole valley of the Mississippi." Republican policy "must end in the Africanization of the slave states, and a gradual mingling of the races in the political control of the government."[297]

The New York *Herald* argued that the essential difference between the Republicans and Democrats was Republican insistence on "an equalization of the white and black races—which has never produced anything but bloodshed in other parts of the world, and which can only result in the subjugation or destruction of the numerically weaker race. There is no possibility of the black and the white existing harmoniously together in social and political equality," the paper warned. "Even the blacks and mulattoes cannot do it." The Republican doctrine of racial equality would lead to "anarchy, civil war, the rule of the military tyrant and the public robber," such as could be seen in Spanish America. The paper speculated that once emancipated, blacks would flee the South for the North, where they would become public charges, for "the negro South cannot support himself in a state of freedom." Rhetorically it asked readers, "Are you ready to divide you patrimony with the negro?"[298]

Not only Democratic newspapers but also the party's organizers and speakers stressed racial issues. In New York, the Second Ward Democratic Clubs drove a wagon through the streets of Manhattan carrying a huge transparency that depicted a boat with Lincoln in the bow waving a black flag labeled "Discord" and Horace Greeley in the stern, steering with his right hand and holding a copy of the *Tribune* in his left. Between them were a thick-lipped black male embracing a white girl, while a fellow black says, "Is looking at you, Sam," and Sam answers, "Yah, yah." Greeley remarks, "Colored folks have preference of state rooms"; and one of the passengers says, "Free Love and Free Niggers will certainly elect Old Abe if he (Lincoln) pilots us safe." Another wagon bore a transparency representing a black man grasping Greeley with one hand and Lincoln with the other. Beneath them was a caption: "The Almighty Nigger."[299] Other banners read:

> "Republican Principle—'The Negro better than the White Man,' Republican Practice—'Union of Black and White.'"
> What 'Free Negro Suffrage' Really Means—'Amalgamation in the Military. Amalgamation in the Fire Department. Amalgamation in the Social Circle.'"
> "No Negro Equality."
> "The Niggers of the North!"
> "Free Love, Free Niggers, and Free Women!"[300]

Another campaign sign displayed a cartoon of a huge black man above an inscription identifying him as "The successor of Abraham Lincoln in 1864."[301]

New York Congressman Theodore R. Westbrook told several hundred of his fellow Democrats that the "only argument advanced by the Republicans is 'Freedom, Freedom, Freedom—Darky, darky, darky.' Indeed, they have a darky for breakfast, darky for dinner, darky for supper, and darky for bed-fellows." Calling for a vote on what he termed "the nigger question," Westbrook declared: "down with the darky."[302] The New York *Morning Examiner* asked, "Shall Africans govern Americans? Are you ready for negro equality? Are you ready for assimilation? Both are Republican principles."[303]

Constitutional Unionists also appealed to race prejudice. "In the spirit of profound fanaticism," proclaimed John J. Crittenden of Kentucky, the Republicans "would destroy the white man in order that the black man might be free."[304]

Lincoln did not openly respond to race-baiting, but in September the *Illinois State Journal* published an anonymous contribution on race that he may well have written.

Headlined "Negro Equality and Amalgamation," it focused on the Douglas Democratic Party platform's call for the acquisition of Cuba. That policy, the author pointed out, did not square with the Little Giant's analysis of the Revolutionary fathers' attitude toward mixed races (that they wanted nothing to do with them).

Rather than write many such pieces, Lincoln left it to Republican orators and newspapers to rebut charges that he was a deep-dyed abolitionist, that he had been unpatriotic during the Mexican War, that he sought to provoke warfare between the sections, that he had betrayed Henry Clay, and that he favored equality for blacks.

In reply to such charges, Republican spokesmen sometimes echoed the Democrats' racism. Pointing to Maryland, Frank P. Blair noted that half its population lived in Baltimore but that the state legislature was dominated by rural areas where slaves were numerous. "Talbot County, where they had nothing but niggers and blackbirds," was represented by one state senator, as was the populous city of Baltimore. "The nigger representatives in Maryland have charge of the City of Baltimore, and have disfranchised it; the niggers vote down the white residents." Blair protested against the perversion of language whereby "the Republicans were called 'Black,' because their aim was to dignify free white labor, and sustain white men: and the Democracy called themselves white because they wished to cover the country with niggers, to the exclusion of white men." He urged laborers to "put the Government into the hands of Lincoln. He will respect the rights of the whites."[305]

The New York *Times* scoffed at charges that Republicans favored racial equality. Over 90 percent of the delegates to the Chicago Convention, the paper argued, would oppose "making negroes, in all respects, the political equals of whites,—of giving them the same rights of suffrage, the same right to office and the same political standing and consideration which belong to the white race. Nor is the proportion greater among their constituents." Pointing to the lack of political rights enjoyed by blacks in the Free States, the *Times* asked rhetorically, "how is the doctrine of negro equality to be 'forced upon the South' by the Republicans, when they scout and scorn it for the free negroes of the North?" Republicans do not "have any more love of the negro—any greater disposition to make sacrifices for his sake, or to waive their own rights and interests for the promotion of his welfare, than the rest of mankind, North and South." The Republican Party is "pretty thoroughly a white man's party."[306] The Indianapolis *Daily Journal* said it was absurd to charge "'nigger equality' against a party, the first cardinal principle of whose creed is, exclusion of Niggers from the Territories."[307]

In addition to attacking Lincoln's record and principles, Democrats also ridiculed him personally. According to the Manchester, New Hampshire, *Union Democrat,* he was "a stiff-necked, cold-blooded, calculating man, who keeps an eye to the main chance, and was never known to serve even his own party except as a means of personal advantage."[308] When opponents belittled Lincoln's appearance, origins, education, and even his nicknames, Congressman John Sherman of Ohio admitted that "Lincoln cannot be recommended as a parlor President, like Gen. Pierce, and is not as familiar with the etiquette of foreign courts, as Mr. Buchanan," but, Sherman insisted, "he is honest, faithful and capable. . . . He is far better for having lived a short time in Washington, for that city of politicians is not particularly celebrated for sound principles or rigid morals."[309]

Democrats also tried to show that Lincoln's relatives opposed his election, and they were not entirely wrong. In July, John Hanks published a 1,600-word letter countering rumors that he would not vote for his cousin, but in fact, he was the only member of the Hanks family who did support the Republican nominee. John's brother Charles criticized his account of Lincoln's life, which was widely reprinted. Asserting that he had known the candidate well as a young man, Charles scornfully called him "a wild harum scarum boy" and insisted that "jumping and wrestling were his only accomplishments. His laziness was the cause of many mortifications to me; for as I was an older boy than either Abe or John, I often had to do Abe's work at uncle's, when the family were sick . . . and Abe would be rollicking around the county neglecting them."[310] To rebut these allegations, Lincoln wrote a public letter pointing out that he had spent virtually no time with Charles Hanks in Indiana or Kentucky but had done so in Macon County in 1830–1831.

Lincoln composed another reminiscence responding to charges by John Hill, son of the New Salem merchant Samuel Hill, that he had betrayed the principles of Henry Clay. In a detailed rebuttal, which he left incomplete, Lincoln reviewed Hill's allegations and showed that his record as a state legislator and a congressman had been misrepresented.

Another misrepresentation which Lincoln took pains to challenge involved an attack on Jefferson that he had allegedly made in 1844. The language ascribed to Lincoln actually came from a hostile sketch of the Sage of Monticello written by a Scottish Tory, Thomas Hamilton. Insisting that his name not be used in any denials, the candidate authorized friends to denounce the misattribution. The *Illinois State Journal* did so in an editorial that Lincoln himself probably wrote: "This is a bold and deliberate forgery, whether originating with the Chicago *Times and Herald* or the Macomb *Eagle*. Mr. Lincoln never used any such language in any speech at any time. Throughout the whole of his political life, Mr. Lincoln has ever spoken of Mr. Jefferson in the most kindly and respectful manner, holding him up as one of the ablest statesmen of his own or any other age, and constantly referring to him as one of the greatest apostles of freedom and free labor. This is so well known that any attempt, by means of fraud or forgery, to create the contrary impression, can only react upon the desperate politicians who are parties to such disreputable tactics."[311]

In August, Lincoln told an interviewer from the New York *Herald* that when invited to visit his birthplace in Kentucky, he playfully asked if he would not be lynched if he were to accept. The *Herald's* report did not make his remark sound playful. Lincoln, said the paper, concluded "that the invitation was a trap laid by some designing person to inveigle him into a slave State for the purpose of doing violence to his person."[312] When Lincoln declined the invitation, Democrats attacked him as a coward. Douglas pounced on the report, telling an audience in Indiana how Kentuckians "regretted exceedingly that Lincoln was afraid to come to Kentucky to look after his mother." (Lincoln's mother was buried in Indiana, and his stepmother lived in Illinois.) "But I told them to have no uneasiness on that subject, for Lincoln was a friend of mine, and I never yet failed to do him an act of kindness when I had a chance; that while, perhaps, his principles would not allow him to visit the grave of his grandfather in the valley of Virginia, or his mother, in Kentucky, mine would allow me to go wherever the American flag waved over American soil. Hence I told them when I returned to Illinois I would call on my friend Lincoln and tell him I had visited his good old mother [in] Kentucky and that she was grieved to know that her son had forgotten the land of his birth; had proved false to the grave of his fathers; had joined her enemies, and was now preaching a crusade against the State that gave him birth."[313]

To Samuel Haycraft, who had invited Lincoln to visit Kentucky, he denied the *Herald* report: "I was not guilty of stating, or insinuating, a suspicion of any intended violence, deception, or other wrong, against me, by you, or any other Kentuckian."[314] Lincoln prepared a correction for the *Herald* to publish: "We have such assurance as satisfies us that our correspondent writing from Springfield, Ills., under date of Aug. 8—was mistaken in representing Mr. Lincoln as expressing a suspicion of a design to inveigle him into Kentucky for the purpose of doing him violence. Mr. Lincoln neither entertains, nor has intended to express any such suspicion." He asked George G. Fogg to persuade the *Herald*'s editor, James Gordon Bennett, to run the correction. Bennett replied that he would not do so unless Fogg would sign it or it could be datelined Springfield. Fogg advised Lincoln to drop the matter, and so he did, explaining: "Although it wrongs me, and annoys me some, I prefer to let it run it's course, to getting into the papers over my own name."[315]

Simon P. Hanscom of the *Herald* helped undo some of the damage created by his newspaper. He interviewed Lincoln and published the candidate's explanation of the Kentucky story, which resembled the denial he had penned for Fogg. According to Illinois Congressman William Kellogg, Hanscom was one of Lincoln's "warmest supporters" at the Chicago Convention and "well known to be a true and staunch republican" whose coverage of Congress for the *Herald* was fair and just to the party. "No man I am confident enjoys more of the confidence of the republicans here than he does," Kellogg told Lincoln, "and no man has done more than him to present Douglass in his true character before the American people, and to the utmost of his ability will he, I do know wage an unyielding warfare against [the] democracy in any of [its] phases."[316] Hanscom claimed that at Chicago he had "contributed somewhat . . . to remove the obstacles in the way of his [Lincoln's] nomination" and was one of the original members of a rail-splitter's club.[317] (Not everyone in the capital agreed with Kellogg. A Washington correspondent of the New York *Tribune* alleged that Hanscom "is known here, as one of the most unscrupulous & notorious of all the corrupt gang who infest this capital.")[318]

Hanscom visited Springfield, where he wrote two pro-Lincoln dispatches that ran in the *Herald* on October 20. The candidate evidently disliked the publicity that had been generated earlier that month by his brief meeting with Seward. To help put a positive gloss on that story, Hanscom (perhaps at Lincoln's urging) said that Seward should be honored "for his avoidance of even the semblance of hypocrisy." The brief stopover in Springfield "may be said the proof of Mr. Seward's regard for Lincoln."

On one hand, if the senator had failed to visit the party's standard-bearer, it "would surely be construed into an evidence of hostility against Lincoln." On the other hand, if the two men held a long conversation, "the same slanderous spirit might find in that fact 'confirmation as strong as proofs of holy writ' that Seward was negotiating for the State Department or for the mission to London." So the New Yorker decided to stop in the Illinois capital but to avoid any private consultation with Lincoln.[319]

Hanscom also sought to modify the out-and-out abolitionist image of Lincoln that the *Herald* had been portraying. He assured readers that Seward would "not hold a place in the next administration." Unlike the New York senator, Lincoln "rather inclines to follow a moderate, fair, constitutional course of policy. If you believe his own assurances, the most violent Southern fire-eater will find it difficult to question his patriotism or impartiality. He is a man of a rough, original turn of mind, and just such a man, it strikes me, as would, in the administration over which he should preside, show rather more obstinacy and self-will. . . . And such a man would not be likely to tolerate such a vizier as Wm H. Seward." "I found him eminently conservative," Hanscom added; "I have reason to know that because of the great ability he exhibited and the high national conservative position taken by him" in the 1858 campaign, "he was selected by the Chicago Convention as the standard bearer of the republican party. The platform adopted by that Convention is in harmony with the view expressed by Mr. Lincoln in his discussions with Douglas." On slavery, Lincoln's record "is not nearly so radical as some of the avowed doctrines of the democratic party" a few years earlier.[320]

Hanscom forwarded a copy of his handiwork to Lincoln with a cover note: "Of course you will find some things in it that will amuse you, but it had to be dished for peculiar appetites and in taking advantage of my opportunities and facilities I trust I have done you no injustice. At first I thought I would not publish the paragraph about your visit to Kentucky, but many of your best and most sagacious friends advised that it had better be done. . . . The editorial accompanying the letter is quite as important as the letter."[321] That editorial, in stark contrast to Bennett's earlier ones denouncing Lincoln as a dangerous Radical, referred to the candidate as "a conservative republican" who "contemplates no war upon the constitutional rights of slavery in the slave States," and predicted "that his general policy upon slavery will be to conciliate the South into submission instead of exasperating her people into open rebellion."[322]

During the Civil War, Hanscom would become Lincoln's favorite journalist. In 1863, the well-informed Noah Brooks, Washington correspondent of the Sacramento *Union*, asserted that Hanscom, "a pushing and persevering man, has managed to so ingratiate himself with the President that he has almost exclusive access to the office of the Executive, and there obtains from our good-natured Chief Magistrate such scanty items of news as he is willing to give out for publication."[323] Hanscom laid the foundations for his status as presidential insider during the 1860 campaign. Lincoln's cultivation of Hanscom was yet another example of his solicitude for the press and his subtle manipulation of it to ensure favorable coverage for him and his party.

The *Herald*'s new tune was indicative of a growing trend. By September the New York *Times* could observe that critics had abandoned their earlier attacks on Lincoln as a Radical. "It begins to be universally seen and felt, that Mr. Lincoln's position is eminently conservative, and that his election will by no means involve a triumph of the ultra Anti-Slavery element of the Northern and Eastern States."[324] Some Northern papers, however, still pictured him as a dangerous extremist. In September the *Illinois State Register* said: "Lincoln has the insane idea that he is a sort of second Messiah; that he is the man selected from all time to establish a new law, under which African slavery is to be abolished in the United States."[325]

Voters Cast Their Ballots

On August 6, a harbinger of things to come appeared in Missouri, where Frank Blair won election to the U.S. House on the Republican ticket, reversing the outcome of 1858. "I count that day as one of the happiest in my life," Lincoln said a few weeks later.[326]

The first gubernatorial election of the campaign occurred on September 10 in Maine, which Douglas's strategists regarded as vital and where the Little Giant had stumped. To counter his efforts, Republicans imported outside speakers, including Anson Burlingame, who proved especially effective. "The way Burlingame hits the crowds is astonishing," James Shepherd Pike reported. "Everybody thinks him angelic."[327] Lincoln felt some anxiety about the Pine Tree State when late in August he heard an allegation that Hannibal Hamlin predicted a Republican loss of two congressional seats and a narrow, 6,000-vote victory in the gubernatorial race. Lincoln wrote to his running mate that he was "annoyed some" by this news, especially since he had received optimistic reports from other Maine leaders. "Such a result as you seem to have predicted in Maine . . . would, I fear, put us on the down-hill track, lose us the State elections in Pennsylvania and Indiana, and probably ruin us on the main turn in November."[328] Hamlin promptly denied saying any such thing and accurately predicted a Republican landslide. Thanks in part to the popularity of gubernatorial candidate Israel Washburn, the party swept all six congressional races and won the governorship by more than 15,000 votes.

In Ohio, Indiana, and Pennsylvania state tickets were elected on October 9. Assured by Pennsylvanians that the Republican gubernatorial candidate would win easily, and with Ohio safely in hand, Lincoln advised that all efforts be focused on Indiana, where a fusion movement of the three opposition parties threatened Henry S. Lane's chances of capturing the governorship. In August, after stumping the Hoosier State for two weeks, Herman Kreismann of Chicago was pessimistic. "I have worked like a nigger," he reported. "I have been in the d[amnde]st holes worse than any places we have in Egypt. It was the first time many of them had ever heard anything about slavery etc." The Republicans in Indiana "are just four years behind us [Illinoisans] in organization and efficiency."[329] David Davis, who thought Indiana was "in great danger," urged Thurlow Weed and Edwin D. Morgan to send thousands of dollars for speakers and efforts to combat fraud.[330] Davis's old friend John Z. Goodrich of Massachusetts, a wealthy member of the Republican National Committee, swiftly provided the money. Goodrich visited Boston in September and raised $7,000 to counter Democratic "pipelaying" operations in Indiana.[331] Luckily for the Republicans, the leader of Indiana's Breckinridge forces, Jesse D. Bright, hated Douglas and spitefully threw his support to Lane. Exacerbating tension between the Democratic factions, the Little Giant unwisely abused Breckinridge and his followers during a swing through Indiana. In addition, Bell's supporters, headed by Lincoln's friend Richard W. Thompson, eventually decided to back the Republican gubernatorial candidate. On the eve of the October elections, Davis, who was heroically organizing the Lincoln campaign, told his son: "Tomorrow is the most important day in the history of the Country." Davis felt "uneasy, very, about the Indiana & Pennsylvania elections."[332]

Davis need not have worried, for Republicans triumphed in both states. Lane defeated his opponent 136,725 to 126,968 (52% to 48%), in part because during the final months of the campaign, the Republicans had taken Lincoln's counsel and flooded Indiana with money and speakers. As Lincoln had been advised, the Republicans did much better than usual in southwestern Indiana, where he grew up. In Pennsylvania, Democrats bemoaned the power of their opponents' emphasis on protectionism. One Democrat observed that "the Tariff possesses more interest to the working classes than the 'Nigger' question" and that "the Republicans, in their speeches say nothing of the nigger question, but all is made to turn on the Tariff."[333] Cameron noted that to his constituents, the tariff "is the great question of the day, it is our nigger."[334] Feuding within the Republican ranks, though worrisome to Lincoln, was far less bitter than it was among the Democrats. As a result, Andrew G. Curtin was elected governor by a vote of 262,403 to 230,239 (53% to 47%).

Predictably, Republicans did well in Ohio, one of their safe states, winning thirteen of the twenty-one congressional races and electing their candidate for the state supreme court by a 13,000 vote majority. In Cleveland, a party leader observed that "Old Abe has nothing left for himself to do but to put his affairs at home in order and get ready for the White House."[335]

Lincoln received the good news from the key October states with characteristic equanimity. On election night, while awaiting the returns in the capitol, he calmed his neighbors who feared the opposition might combine against him, saying "that he was not only morally convinced that the people of the North, East, and Northwest would teach the Fusionists a hard lesson, but that he had precise forecasts and reports from the best-informed men in Pennsylvania, New York, and Indiana showing that his election was beyond a doubt in those states." Favorable dispatches rolled in until finally, a little after midnight, the Republican victories seemed assured. As his friends whooped and hollered, Lincoln alone retained his composure. He permitted himself to rejoice only upon receipt of Cameron's telegram announcing the Pennsylvania result, which prompted him to remark: "Now Douglas might learn a lesson about what happens when one tries to get people opposed to slavery to vote for slavery. It is not my name, it is not my personality which has driven Douglas out of Indiana and Pennsylvania, it is the irresistible power of public opinion, which has broken with slavery."[336] When a crowd of well-wishers called at his home, he had his houseguest, Lyman Trumbull, address them.

On paper, Lincoln was more effusive, writing John M. Read: "We are indulging in much rejoicing over the late splendid victories in Pennsylvania, Indiana, and Ohio, which seem to foreshadow the certain success of the Republican cause in November."[337] Those victories, he told Seward, "have surpassed all expectation, even the most extravagant."[338] But approaching success also meant that he must soon cope with burdensome challenges. After visiting Springfield in mid-October, David Davis wrote his wife that "Lincoln looked as if he had a heavy responsibility resting on him. The cares & responsibilities of office will wear on him. . . . Politicians are gathering round Lincoln. The cormorants for office will be numerous & greedy." In contrast, Mary Lincoln "seemed in high feather" at her prospects, according to Davis. She was "not to my liking," he added. "I don[']t think she would ever mesmerise any one." His feelings were not unique, he said, for the "people of Springfield do not love Lincoln's wife as they do him." Davis's hope "that she will not give her husband any trouble" would prove vain.[339]

After the October triumphs, attention shifted to New York, which the Democrats strove to win and thus force the election into the U.S. House of Representatives. In August, Lincoln had told Weed, "I think there will be the most extraordinary effort ever made, to carry New-York for Douglas. . . . it will require close watching, and great effort on the other side."[340] His prediction seemed borne out later when the Bell, Breckinridge, and Douglas forces agreed on a unified slate of presidential electors. The fusionists spent lavishly, causing some alarm, for the overconfident Empire State Republicans had exported money to New Jersey and Delaware and could not match their opponents' last-minute outlays.

To improve the Republican chances of carrying New York, Joseph Medill had been trying since June to persuade James Gordon Bennett to moderate the New York *Herald*'s criticism of the Republican ticket. That paper initially dismissed Lincoln as "an uneducated man—a vulgar village politician, without any experience worth mentioning in the practical duties of statesmanship, and only noted for some very unpopular votes which he gave while a member of Congress." To compare "this illiterate Western boor" with Seward "is odious—it is Hyperion to a satyr."[341] After speaking twice with the crusty Bennett, Medill reported to Lincoln that the editor pledged "he would not treat you harshly," for he "thought you would make a very respectable President, if you kept out of the hands of the radicals." Bennett boasted to Medill that he and his fellow conservatives "could beat your man Lincoln, if we would unite, but I think it would be better for the country to let him be elected. I'll not be hard on him."[342] The *Herald* originally favored Breckinridge and later switched to support the fusion ticket of Bell-Douglas-Breckinridge electors.

Also lobbying Bennett on Lincoln's behalf was Simon Hanscom, who wrote the candidate in late October: "I had a long talk with Mr. Bennett, about you, after my return and he was pleased at the assurances I made him that you would persue a conservative course &c. &c. and said he would give you his support with the greatest pleasure, especially if you would make a clean sweep of the present corrupt office-holders."[343]

Though Illinois seemed safely in his column, Lincoln and the Republican National Committee worried that the legislature might go Democratic and thus jeopardize Trumbull's reelection. In August, it appeared likely that the Democrats would retain control of the General Assembly. John Wentworth, whom Caleb B. Smith described as "a man of great energy & a shrewd manager" but "unscrupulous and unreliable," complicated matters in Illinois by publishing radical antislavery editorials which Democrats cited as proof that Lincoln was an out-and-out abolitionist.[344] Joseph Medill warned Lincoln that Long John's plan "is to pretend that he is your devoted friend; that you are an ultra abolitionist who will if elected put down slavery in the South. . . . While he is thus stabbing you, he is deluding the more radical anti-slavery element into the belief that he is a sincere abolitionist."[345] To combat the deleterious effects of Wentworth's editorials, Medill wrote to newspapers in the East denouncing Long John, and the Chicago *Press and Tribune* regularly excoriated the mayor.

Because Wentworth's strategy would alienate voters in southern Illinois, outside speakers were dispatched to that region. When Robert C. Schenck, a "strong, terse and sometimes withering" orator from Ohio and a quondam Whig, offered his services, Lincoln accepted enthusiastically, telling him: "We really want you."[346] In October, Schenck and other Ohioans—including Donn Piatt, Samuel Galloway, Thomas Corwin, and David Cartter—stumped throughout lower Illinois, where they impressed local Republicans mightily.

Lincoln was also eager to have Republicans carry Springfield and Sangamon County for a change, partly for sentimental reasons but more importantly because Trumbull's election depended on it. (The senatorial district composed of Sangamon and Morgan counties would elect Republican William Jayne by a margin of seven votes, thus giving the Republicans a majority of one in the state senate.) When he asked a Republican running for some county office what steps were being taken to turn out the vote, the answer was so unsatisfactory that Lincoln spelled out a plan for generating the maximum number of Republican votes.

Fearing that a split in the Republican ranks in Vermilion County might cost the party a seat in the legislature, Lincoln urged the contending parties—William H. Fithian and Oscar F. Harmon—to patch up their quarrel. "To lose Trumbull's re-election next winter would be a great disaster," he wrote to Fithian. "Please do not let it fall upon us. I appeal to you because I can to no other, with so much confidence."[347] The plea worked; both aspirants withdrew in favor of a third candidate.

Secession Threats

After the Republican victories in Ohio, Indiana, and Pennsylvania, Southern threats of secession grew louder. The day after that electoral sweep, the Alabama fire-eater William L. Yancey announced that if Lincoln were to win and then "undertake to use Federal bayonets to coerce free and sovereign states in this Union," he would "fly to the standard of that state and give it the best assistance in my power."[348] A newspaper in Yancey's state said ominously: "Let the boys arm. Every one that can point a shot-gun or revolver should have one. Let every community supply itself with munitions, and store them safely. Abolitionism is at your doors, with torch and knife in hand!"[349] In mid-October, the pro-Breckinridge Richmond *Enquirer* lamented that "Virginia can no more prevent the dissolution of this Union after Lincoln's election, than she can prevent that election. She will be powerless to prevent civil war, with all its horrors."[350] A pro-Douglas newspaper in Georgia defiantly announced that "the south will never permit Abraham Lincoln to be President of the United States. This is a settled and sealed fact. It is the determination of all parties at the south. And let the consequences be what they may—whether the Potomac is crimsoned in human gore, and Pennsylvania avenue is paved ten fathoms in depth with mangled bodies, or whether the last vestige of Liberty is swept from the face of the American continent. The south, the loyal south, the constitutional south, will never submit to such humiliation and degradation as the inauguration of Abraham Lincoln."[351]

The South's reaction to Lincoln's impending victory puzzled Northerners, who regarded the Rail-splitter as a Moderate. As one observer noted, however, many Republicans "spurn indignantly the imputation of being Abolitionists when it is preferred against them, and yet they are ignorant of the characteristics of those whom the Southerners almost universally declare to be Abolitionists. The South do[es] not think it alone requires an incendiary, cut-throat, robber, assassin, or a nigger insurrectionist to be an Abolitionist. The moderate members of the Northern Republican party think it does. But the South insist[s] that Abolitionism consists in lesser evils than these; and those are the demands of the anti-slavery men of the North—demands they have been urging and presenting in the face of the South for years past—upon which the anti-slavery movement of the North is based, and which infuse into it much of its vitality, independent of the Territorial question."[352] To Southerners, Lincoln's call for the "ultimate extinction" of slavery conjured up visions of the bloody revolt in Haiti two generations earlier and Nat Turner's uprising in 1831.

As time went by, Lincoln received many warnings about Southern secession, but, like most Republicans, he failed to take them seriously. In August, he told John B. Fry: "The people of the South have too much of good sense, and good temper, to attempt the ruin of the government, rather than see it administered as it was administered by the men who made it. At least, so I hope and believe."[353] Southerners had so frequently raised the specter of secession that their threats had lost credibility. In 1859, the New York *Courier and Enquirer* observed that for almost five decades "a mere handful of ignorant, reckless and unprincipled men at the South, have, by bullying and threatening, governed the millions of educated and intelligent men of the North; simply because they are men of peace and busily engaged in moral industrial pursuits which do not encourage or foster restlessness and excitement."[354] Senator William Pitt Fessenden of Maine told his son, "All this vaporing about secession is nonsense, and nobody cares a button for it."[355] A Connecticut newspaper scoffed at the secessionist threat, calling it "an empty sham"; secessionists had "about as good a chance of succeeding as the lunatics in the Retreat at Hartford would have of capsizing the state of Connecticut into Long Island Sound. They are too few and too crazy."[356]

Secession threats aided Republicans, for Northern voters had grown tired of Southern intimidation and contempt for fair play. They had come to think of the typical Southerner as a Preston "Bully" Brooks, the cane-wielding South Carolina congressman who had bashed in the skull of Senator Charles Sumner four years earlier; just as Southerners regarded Brooks's tactic as a legitimate way to deal with political opponents, so they viewed disunion threats as a legitimate tactic in election campaigns. The Chicago *Press and Tribune* assured Southerners "that they entirely underestimate the character of the Northern people, and that their 'boo-boos' and their 'bug-a-boos,' instead of frightening any one, are really helping Lincoln." Free State residents "have become entirely satisfied that the only way to effectually stop this threat of disunion, is by the election of a Republican President."[357]

That fall, many Northerners did vote Republican to protest the South's arbitrary, high-handed behavior. On November 6, the New York *Tribune* exclaimed: "the repudiation of the Missouri Compact, the brutal bludgeoning of Charles Sumner, the wanton outrages that so long desolated Kansas, the infamous Lecompton outrage, and all the long series of plots and crimes by which Kansas and Nebraska were temporarily subjugated to Slavery, all come up for review To-Day!"[358] The *Tribune* declared that the South "is only semi-civilized. It may call itself republican; it may profess the abstract faith of Christianity; it may possess, to a certain limited degree, the arts of a cultivated people; it may live under some of the forms of enlightened society; but it wants that inherent moral sense, that accurate conception of social law, that intelligent submission to the purpose of civil government which mark the highest civilization. It is merely semi-barbarous in its spirit, savage in its instincts, reckless of human life and human rights, faithless in everything but brute force, unintelligent in its aims, and unscrupulous in the means with which it seeks to attain them."[359] The *Missouri Democrat* observed that the "north has habitually yielded, until we are supposed to be craven, and incapable of the manhood to defend our common rights or liberties. This system has been carried far enough, and it must stop."[360] William Cullen Bryant likened the South to "a spoiled child" and the federal government to "its foolishly indulgent nurse." Everything the South "asked for has been eagerly given it; more eagerly still if it cries after it; more eagerly still if it threatens to cut off its nurse's ears. The more we give it the louder it cries and the more furious its threats; and now we have Northern men writing long letters to persuade their readers that it will actually cut off its nurse's ears if we exercise the right of suffrage, and elect a President of our own choice, instead of giving it one of its own favorites."[361]

Democrats urged the public to defeat black equality. "Let voters remember Lincoln's famous declaration that it is dangerous to except one race from perfect equality; that if we deny it to the negro to-day, that denial will be used as a precedent for denying it to some other race to-morrow," warned the *Illinois State Register*. "Let the national policy of the republicans,—to admit negroes to a perfect equality with the whites, be considered, and let voters pause before they give their approval to any such policy." The editors predicted that slaves would rebel if the Republicans won. In Texas, the *Register* alleged hyperbolically, "This fever got so high that the election of Lincoln could not be waited for; something must be done, and done at once; so, acting under the impulse men and women poisoned the wells, servants poisoned the food of their master's family, laborers fired the dwellings, strong men used the assassin's knife, women seized helpless infants and brained them against trees, stalwart men seized the weak females of the whites, and after perpetrating outrages too horrible to relate, mutilated with fiendish cruelty the bodies they had so recently violated.

Mr. Abraham Lincoln this is the fruit of your teaching; this is the crop grown from the seed planted by you in your speeches of 1858–59."[362]

After the election, Lincoln addressed such allegations, maintaining "that some of the politicians of the South had falsely announced, during the recent campaign, that if he (Mr. Lincoln) was elected armed bands were formed in the North to go down there and liberate the slaves, and the most that he feared was, that an insurrectionary movement among the slaves would result from their own teachings."[363]

As Douglas stumped the country, he displayed true statesmanship by warning the South against disunion. Lincoln's election might constitute "a great national calamity," but he insisted that the South must abide by the result: "the election of any man . . . according to the provisions of the Constitution is no pretext for breaking up this Union." In New York, Douglas told a large audience, "I know him [Lincoln] well. . . . I have no word of unkindness or personal disrespect to utter concerning him, but I do believe that he holds political opinions which, if carried out, would be subversive of all the principles of the American Constitution." Yet "if Lincoln should be elected—which God in his mercy forbid [laughter]—he must be inaugurated according to the Constitution and the laws of the country, and I, as his foremost, strongest and irreconcilable opponent, will sustain him in the exercise of every Constitutional function [applause]."[364] Undermining his claim to statesmanship, however, was Douglas's continued race-baiting; he told a Rhode Island crowd "that he preferred clams to niggers" and at Baltimore he insisted that the U.S. government was "made by white men for white men, to be administered by white men, and by nobody else, forever."[365]

With the campaign drawing to a close, Lincoln became ever more confident. Two weeks before its conclusion, Benjamin Welch of New York met with him in Springfield and reported that "Lincoln was in excellent spirits, regarding his election as certain."[366] When asked how he could stand the pressure, he replied "that he should endeavor to sustain himself" at least until November 6.[367]

Victory in November

On election day, Springfield shed its customary tranquility as cannons boomed to herald the dawn. Augmenting their din were bands blaring from wagons drawn about the city to arouse the populace. Vociferous men loitering around the polls contributed their mite to the pandemonium. There was little violence, though the editor of the *Illinois State Register* was caned by a gentleman whom he had accused of lying.

That morning at the statehouse, Lincoln showed little concern as he received visitors while sitting in an armchair that dwarfed him. Among his callers were some Illinoisans who, having cast their ballots, wanted to see him in the flesh. Then came a few New Yorkers, who, Lincoln thought, should have remained home to vote. He told one resident of the Empire State that "he was afraid there were too many of us from New York that day." When that caller asked Lincoln whether the South would secede if the Republicans captured the White House, he "said they might make a little stir about it before [the inauguration], but if they waited until after his inauguration and for some overt act, *they would wait all their lives*."[368] When queried about rail-splitting, he showed how it had been performed when he was young and contrasted that technique with the method then employed, which he acknowledged was superior.

Lincoln had intended to vote late in the day to avoid crowds; in mid-afternoon, however, when told that there were few people at the polls, he decided to cast his ballot then. The day before he had been asked for whom he would vote. "Yates," he replied puckishly. When pressed how he would vote for president, he responded: "How vote? Well, undoubtedly like an Ohio elector of which I will tell you—by ballot."[369]

As Lincoln approached the courthouse, accompanied by Ozias M. Hatch and other friends, the crowd started shouting wildly and parted to allow him entrance to the polling place. They then followed him down the hall and up the stairs to the jam-packed courtroom, cheering him all the while. There the huzzaing grew ever louder. Even men handing out Douglas tickets joined in. An elderly gentleman with an armload of Democratic documents led several cheers for Lincoln. Before depositing his ballot, he cut off the names of the presidential electors so that he would not be voting for himself. One wag cried out, "You ought to vote for Douglas, Uncle Abe, he has done all he could for you."[370] As Lincoln made his way back to the statehouse, he passed through a screaming gauntlet of enthusiasts who grabbed his hands and his coat. Still others embraced him.

Lincoln spent the rest of the afternoon at the capitol, where he discussed not his own election prospects but those of local and state candidates. At one point, "he mentioned a candidate for the Legislature in one of these counties who he hoped would be elected, and he would be, Mr. Lincoln added, 'if he didn't find Abe Lincoln too heavy a load to carry on the same ticket.'" Later "he said that elections in this country were like 'big boils'—they caused a great deal of pain before they came to a head, but after the trouble was over the body was in better health than before. He hoped that the bitterness of the canvass would pass away 'as easily as the core of a boil.'"

When one of his friends mentioned the New York fusionists, Lincoln "remarked that they would probably get into such a row going up Salt River as to 'obstruct navigation' thereafter." To Ozias Hatch's observation "that it was lucky for him that women couldn't vote, otherwise the monstrous portraits of him which had been circulated during the canvass by friends would surely defeat him," Lincoln replied smilingly: "Hatch, I tell you there is a great deal more in that idea than you suppose," and "then related a story about a Presbyterian church in McLean County in Illinois holding a congregational meeting to vote a call to a pastor. The elders and deacons and principal men in the church had united in recommending a certain man, and it was supposed he would be called unanimously; but in an evil hour somebody got hold of the man's likeness and exhibited it to the sisters. They didn't like the wart he had on his nose, so they turned out in force and voted down the call."[371]

When a dispatch arrived from Charleston, South Carolina, expressing the wish that Lincoln would win because, if he did, the Palmetto State "would soon be free," Lincoln laughed as he remarked that several Southerners had written him to the same effect. He handed the message to Hatch, telling him "that the sender of it would bear watching."[372]

At about 7 P.M., the crowd at the statehouse flooded into the room where Lincoln awaited the returns. When someone suggested that they be cleared out, he immediately objected, saying "he had never done such a thing in his life and wouldn't commence now." Soon the room was jammed. The candidate remained cool and collected until a messenger arrived from the telegraph office; his face then betrayed a touch of anxiety. That first dispatch, from Decatur, showed a significant Republican gain over the previous election. It was greeted with shouts and taken from the governor's office to the assembly chamber as if it were a trophy. At 8 P.M. Lincoln was greatly pleased by a dispatch from Jacksonville indicating a 210-vote Republican gain.

An hour later Lincoln and some friends left the statehouse for the telegraph office to see the returns as they arrived. Fragmentary reports coming in from nearby counties were like tea leaves that Lincoln was able to read cannily. He was gleeful when news arrived from Saline County, where in 1856 Frémont had received one lone vote while Buchanan got nearly 2,000; but now three of the main precincts gave Lincoln a majority of nearly 200 over Douglas. Laughingly, he called the result "a tribute from Egypt to the success of our public school fund."

As the good news rolled in, Lincoln's friends and the telegraph operators could hardly contain their enthusiasm. The nominee himself, however, remained calm. A dispatch announcing that Lincoln had won by 2,500 votes in Chicago occasioned a thrill of elation. The candidate instructed: "Send it to the boys" in the statehouse. He was equally delighted with good news from St. Louis, where he bested Douglas by over 900 votes. When word from Pittsburgh arrived indicating that Lincoln had carried Allegheny County by 10,000 votes, he "remarked that this was better than expected."[373]

Soon returns arrived from more distant points. Lincoln betrayed some anxiety about the result in New York, "remarking that 'the news would come quick enough if it was good, and if bad, he was not in any hurry to hear it.'" Around 10:30, in response to a hopeful message from Thurlow Weed, Lincoln said "that the news was satisfactory so far, only it was not conclusive." Then returns from New Jersey showed that the Douglas-Bell-Breckinridge slate was doing surprisingly well. Offsetting this bad news were encouraging returns from New England. When word came in that Massachusetts had gone for him by 50,000, Lincoln called it "a clear case of the Dutch taking Holland."[374] As expected, he carried Pennsylvania easily, a result that he said could be accounted for "only on one supposition and that is that the Quakers voted."[375] (The Democrats had feared a large Quaker turnout in Philadelphia, a city that Lincoln won with 52% of the vote.) Worries about New York, however, persisted. Then, after hours of mostly positive news, returns began arriving from Democratic states. "Now we should get a few licks back," Lincoln remarked.[376]

As predictable results continued to roll in from the South, Lincoln and his friends took a break shortly after midnight, visiting the collation prepared by the women of Springfield, who lined up to kiss him on the cheek. He ruled that it would be "a form of coercion not prohibited by the Constitution or Congress," and submitted meekly to the friendly assault.

After partaking of the abundant refreshments, Lincoln and his companions returned to the telegraph office. There cheering news from New York thrilled Lincoln's companions, but he observed solemnly, "Not too fast, my friends. Not too fast, it may not be over yet." When even more favorable reports arrived Lincoln's friend and neighbor Jesse K. Dubois asked: "Well, Uncle Abe, are you satisfied now?" Lincoln replied with a smile, "Well, the agony is most over, and you will soon be able to go to bed."

When it was learned that Bell had carried Virginia, Lincoln "suggested that this was the most hopeful return for the peace of the country he had heard, and he hoped the majority was so large as to crush out the fire-eaters completely. He spoke with considerable emphasis and satisfaction about the strength shown for the conservative American ticket in the border States."[377]

Finally, when definitive word of his victory in New York arrived, Lincoln read the fateful dispatch with obvious pleasure. So did the crowd at the statehouse, where men cheered lustily, tossed their hats, and even rolled about on the floor in uncontrollable delight. Men dashed through the streets to inform the citizenry that Lincoln had won. The citizenry shouted from their houses, stores, roofs, and everywhere else. Some ran about singing "Ain't I glad I've joined the Republicans" over and over. The howling and cheering continued throughout the night; then, near dawn, a cannon was dragged out and fired a few times.

After accepting hearty congratulations, Lincoln prepared to leave. When a messenger announced that he had won Springfield by 69 votes, he abandoned his reserve and exuberantly let out an expression of joy that sounded like a cross between a cheer and a crow. Then he laughed contentedly, bade everyone good night, and returned home. (Though he won Springfield, he lost Sangamon County by 42 votes.)

Later, when serenaders called at Eighth and Jackson, Mrs. Lincoln reportedly "cursed—swore and held him back, so that it was with difficulty that he went out to meet the people."[378]

Several times the next day Lincoln told friends, "Well, boys, your troubles are over now, but mine have just commenced." As callers became more numerous, he held a regular levee, shaking the hands of all, including an elderly farmer who exclaimed, "Uncle Abe, I didn't vote for yer, but I am mighty glad yer elected just the same." Lincoln responded, "Well, my old friend, when a man has been tried and pronounced not guilty he hasn't any right to find fault with the jury."[379] David Davis reported from Springfield that "Mr. Lincoln seems as he always does. You would not think that he had been elevated to the highest office in the world."[380]

Lincoln made no formal response to his victory until a grand celebration took place in Springfield two weeks later. During that time he received advice to make a Union-saving address to appease Southern fire-eaters, but Joseph Medill insisted that "[w]e want no speech from Lincoln on the 20th on political questions. W[e] are content with the Republican platform, his letter of acceptance and his published speeches."[381] The capital was subdued, as if the populace needed time to recover from the great excitement of election night. Sobered by the Deep South's earnest preparations to secede, they postponed their celebration several times. It finally took place on November 20, when the city, overflowing with visitors, was brilliantly illuminated.

Although Lincoln won only 39.9 percent of the popular vote (far more than the 29% Douglas received), he took a solid majority of the electoral votes, 180 out of 303. He carried all the Free States except New Jersey, where the Bell, Breckinridge, and Douglas forces created a fusion ticket at the last moment and took 52.1 percent of the ballots cast. (But because some anti-Lincoln voters refused to go for the fusion slate, the Republicans took four of the state's seven electoral votes.) According to John Bigelow, "That little State, the property of a railroad company [the Camden and Amboy] which runs through it and twirls it around like a Skewer[,] voted against him because it has the misfortune to be inhabited by two men, each of whom wished to be Secretary of the Navy and hoped by making the State look insecure, to get an offer of terms."[382] Those men were William L. Dayton and William Pennington, former speaker of the U.S. House. Their lukewarm support of the ticket was widely criticized.

The Republicans triumphed because of their party's unity and the bitter split within the Democracy; because of the rapidly growing antislavery feeling in the North, where the Lecompton Constitution and the Dred Scott decision outraged many who had not voted Republican in 1856; because of the North's ever-intensifying resentment of what it perceived as Southern arrogance, high-handedness, and bullying; because Germans defected from the Democratic ranks; because the Republican economic program appealed both to farmers (with homestead legislation) and to manufacturers and workers (with tariffs) far more than the Democratic economic policies adopted in response to the Panic of 1857; because the rapidly improving economy blunted fears that businessmen had felt as they contemplated a Republican victory; and because of public disgust at the corruption of Democrats, most notably those in the Buchanan administration. Lincoln did especially well among younger voters, newly eligible voters, former nonvoters, rural residents, skilled laborers, members of the middle class, German Protestants, evangelical Protestants, native-born Americans, and most especially former Know-Nothings and Whig-Americans.

Correspondence, newspaper commentary, and other anecdotal sources suggest that Lincoln's victory was in part due to his character, biography, and public record. In July, John A. Kasson reported from Iowa: "I never talk to an audience of farmers without noticing the intense interest as they listen to the story of his early life & trials in making himself what he is,—the ablest & most eminent man in the West."[383] An Ohio farmer praised Lincoln as "a self-made man, who came up a-foot. We like his tact—we like his argumentative powers—we like his logic, and we like the whole man."[384] A resident of Champaign, Illinois, wrote that "[e]very man who is struggling to improve his fortune by honest toil and patient endeavor, feels that in Abraham Lincoln he has a generous and confiding friend, and dignified representative." Lifelong Democrats, he observed, "now find themselves irresistibly impelled by their reverence for the public virtues of Mr. Lincoln."[385] By choosing a candidate with such a humble background, Republicans demonstrated "that their hearts are with the people," said Frank Blair.[386] Lincoln "is the representative of the great idea of the Republican party—labor—free labor," Richard Yates told a crowd at Springfield. "The poor boy . . . can point to Abraham Lincoln, and straighten himself up and say, 'I have the same right and same opportunity to be President as any other boy.'"[387]

The rail-splitter image underscored that message. Throughout the campaign, Republicans emphasized rail-splitting in posters, transparencies, newspapers, rallies, cartoons, and oratory. The Breckinridge-Democratic candidate for governor of New York sneeringly asked "whether it would not be just as good reasoning to claim that a man ought to be made President of the United States because he had once carried a hod?"[388] Horace Greeley responded that the sobriquet *rail-splitter* "is merely an emphatic way of stating that he rose from the class of men stigmatized by slave-holding Senators as the 'mud-sills' of society." Since he advanced "from rail-splitting to be a prominent citizen of Illinois, and a candidate for the Presidency, there must be talent and capacity enough in him to qualify him for the discharge of the duties of that office. The main object, however, is an appeal . . . to the sympathy and the self-respect of that great body of voters who split rails or follow similar laborious employments."[389] According to the Milwaukee *Free Democrat*, "it is not because Abe Lincoln once mauled and split rails for a living that he thus takes hold of the popular heart, but because from the position of occupation of a common farm laborer he has ascended to the position of a probable President, without ever stooping to a mean thing or in any way tampering with his integrity."[390] The Houston *Telegraph* called Lincoln "the most dangerous politician in the Union—doubly dangerous from the fact of his popularity as a self-made man."[391]

In addition to his appealing biography, Lincoln's reputation as "Honest Abe" helped his cause immeasurably. Corruption in the Pierce and Buchanan administrations, as well as in state and local governments throughout the 1850s, had scandalized the nation. Many voters shared Indiana Congressman David Kilgore's desire "to see this *God forsaken Hell deserving* set of corrupt politicians turned out of office, and honest men put in their places."[392] The *Missouri Democrat* was sure that "the deep and just hatred of the corrupt and reckless National Democracy" would carry Lincoln to victory and stay "the waves of the deluge of corruption."[393] On election eve the New York *World* remarked that thousands "of intelligent men support the candidates of the republican party, not that they care a broken tobacco-pipe for the negro question, but because they see no other way to honest management at Washington. . . . If Mr. Lincoln's administration shall prove honest, economical and tranquillizing, they will be quite satisfied, though he should never once allude to free soil in any of his annual messages."[394] Similarly, the Springfield, Massachusetts, *Republican* noted that Democrats "cannot deny the demoralization that has come over the democratic party by its long lease of power, or the gross corruptions that have disgraced the recent administrations of the general government, and they think it will be a good thing to put the cormorants who have so long hung around the federal offices on a low diet for four years at least."[395] Joseph Medill asserted that "[w]e got Lincoln nominated on the *idea* of his honesty, and elected him by endorsing him as *honest Abe*."[396] Joshua R. Giddings, when asked by friends for his opinion of the candidate, said simply: "Lincoln is an honest man." Giddings clearly admired Lincoln's antislavery principles, but he chose to emphasize his integrity above his opposition to slavery, evidently thinking that it was a more salient consideration for voters.[397] The New York *Courier and Enquirer*, the Philadelphia *North American and*

United States Gazette, and the New York *Times* all agreed that the corruption issue
was the dominant one for many voters.

After the election, a Republican congressman told Lincoln that nothing "did
more to secure the enthusiasm and unanimity in your favor than the general impression and belief of the corruption of the present administration and the confident belief that your character and history afforded the best guarantee of a change for the
better."[398] New York Congressman Francis E. Spinner asserted that "[l]arge numbers
of true men, from all parties, joined our standard because of the corruptions of the
national administration."[399] Republican Senator James W. Grimes of Iowa said that
the Republican "triumph was achieved more because of Lincoln[']s reputed honesty
& the known corruptions of the Democrats" than because of "the negro question."[400]
A leading Democrat, August Belmont, concurred: "The country at large had become
disgusted with the misrule of Mr. Buchanan, and the corruption which disgraced his
Administration. The Democratic party was made answerable for his misdeeds." Belmont noted that the anti-corruption backlash "was particularly strong in the rural
districts."[401] A prominent New York Democrat complained that "our rural people, like
those of New England, are so thoroughly & generally anti-Slavery that they will support Lincoln in an almost compact mass—& so they would do if they knew disunion
would be the result."[402] (Democrats did well in urban areas. Though receiving 55% of
all votes in the North, Lincoln won a majority in only four of its eleven cities with a
population of 50,000 or more.) A New Englander assured John J. Crittenden that
"[m]ultitudes of us voted the republican ticket because we wanted *honesty* to displace
corruption."[403] A case in point was the economist David A. Wells, who said: "I voted
for Mr. Lincoln, not because I hated slavery, or thought it a sin, or wished in any way
to do my neighbor a wrong,—but because I was disgusted with the present Administration, & wished for a change."[404]

Lincoln himself interpreted his election as a rebuke to corruptionists. During an
interview in June, he "spoke with great freedom of corruption in high places. He regarded it as the bane of our American politics; and said he could not respect, either as
a man or a politician, one who bribed or was bribed." The New York journalist to
whom he said this remarked, "I wish the thousands of people in my own State who
loathe corrupt practices could have heard and seen Mr. Lincoln's indignant denunciation of venality in high places. I can now understand how the epithet of 'Honest Abraham Lincoln' has come to be so universally applied to him by the Great West."[405]

Essential to Lincoln's victory were the Fillmore supporters of 1856, especially in
Pennsylvania, New York, and the Midwest. Bell won only 78,000 Northern votes,
whereas Fillmore had received 395,000 four years earlier. The Fillmoreites, who had
shied away from the Republicans in 1856 because of the party's radicalism on slavery
and race, regarded Lincoln's antislavery views as acceptably moderate. They also favored protectionism and other economic measures endorsed by the Chicago Convention, and they appreciated the Republicans' willingness to enact nativist legislation in
several states and to share patronage plums with Know-Nothings. In addition, they
hated corruption, not just among immigrants, but also among the cynical native politicians who manipulated the immigrant vote. Moreover, the Know-Nothings did not

want to waste their votes on Bell, who had no chance of winning, nor did they want to throw the election into the House. Know-Nothings like Richard W. Thompson feared that if the election were to be settled in Congress, Democrat Joseph Lane (Breckinridge's running mate and widely regarded as a disunionist) seemed likely to win the presidency. Some nativists voted Republican simply because they would do anything to defeat the hated Democrats. This exasperated a leading ex-Whig, Washington Hunt, who complained that in New York "a portion of the old Whigs, who are still inclined to be national, could not be induced to cooperate heartily with the democrats. They could not be made to realize the full danger to the country from a sectional election."[406] Anti-Catholic bigots feared that Douglas's Catholic wife might persuade him to become a tool of the Pope. These were voters whom Seward probably could not have won. Many delegates at the Chicago Convention regarded the Sage of Auburn as unelectable; the returns suggested that they were right.

The outcome of the election pleased some Radicals, including Frederick Douglass, who exulted: "For fifty years the country has taken the law from the lips of an exacting, haughty and imperious slave oligarchy. . . . Lincoln's election has vitiated their authority, and broken their power" and "has demonstrated the possibility of electing, if not an Abolitionist, as least [a man with] an anti-slavery reputation to the Presidency."[407] Salmon P. Chase acknowledged that Lincoln "may not be so radical as some would wish" but predicted that he "will never surrender our principles."[408] Wendell Phillips was less charitable, charging that the president-elect was "hardly an anti-slavery man" and that he "believes a negro may walk where he wishes, eat what he earns, read what he can, and associate with any other who is exactly the same shade of black he is. That is all he can grant."[409] Responding to such criticism, the Springfield, Massachusetts, *Republican* dismissed Phillips as a crank and "a political Ishmaelite whose hand is against every man."[410]

At the opposite end of the political spectrum, Southern fire-eaters prepared to carry out their secession threats. Well before the election, South Carolina, Alabama, and Mississippi had provided that in case of a Republican victory, they would hold conventions to determine their response. On November 10, the Palmetto State Legislature unanimously authorized a secession convention to be elected three weeks later. Georgia and the five Gulf States rapidly followed suit. When the New York *Herald* predicted that "Lincoln's troubles will begin on the first day after his election," for the "selection of his cabinet will sow the bitterest discord among his supporters," it was only partially correct.[411] Lincoln faced the daunting challenge of uniting not only his young party but also the nation; and yet he would be unable to exercise power for four long, frustrating months, during which seven Slave States pulled out of the Union and others seemed likely to join them.

It is no wonder that Lincoln remarked upon learning of his triumph, "I feel a great responsibility. God help me, God help me."[412] The weight of that new responsibility kept him awake that night. He told a friend that though "much fatigued and exhausted he got but little rest." The next morning, he "rose early, oppressed with the overwhelming responsibility that was upon him and which he had not before fully realized."[413]

17

"I Will Suffer Death Before I Will Consent to Any Concession or Compromise"
President-elect in Springfield
(1860–1861)

During the four months separating his election from his inauguration, Lincoln faced the daunting challenge of Southern secession. Although he would not officially take office until March 1861, his party looked to him for guidance. Like most Republicans, he was startled when the Cotton States made good their supposedly idle threats to withdraw from the Union. Should they be allowed to go in peace? Should they be forcibly resisted? Should they be conciliated or appeased? What compromise measures might preserve national unity without sacrificing the party's principles?

Radicals like Michigan Senator Zachariah Chandler believed all would be well if only Lincoln would "'Stand like an Anvil when the sparks fall thick & fast, a fiery shower,'" but some Republicans feared that he would not do so.[1] (Chandler was quoting, somewhat inaccurately, a poem by George Washington Doane.) A few days after the election, Charles Francis Adams viewed Southern threats to secede as a means "to frighten Mr Lincoln at the outset, and to compel him to declare himself in opposition to the principles of the party that has elected him." Adams confessed that he awaited the president-elect's reaction "with some misgivings," for "the swarms that surround Mr Lincoln are by no means the best."[2]

Adams need not have worried, for Lincoln sided with the "stiff-backed" Republicans in rejecting any concession of basic principle, just as he had rebuffed those Eastern Republicans who two years earlier had supported the reelection of Douglas. Secession would not be tolerated, nor would slavery be allowed to expand into the territories. "By no act or complicity of mine, shall the Republican party become a *mere sucked egg, all shell & no principle* in it," he told a visitor in January 1861.[3] If it meant war, then so be it. He remarked to an Illinois Republican leader, "we have got plenty of corn & pork and it wouldn't be exactly brave for us to leave this question to be settled by posterity."[4]

To Thomas Hutchinson, who informed Lincoln that he and his fellow Kentuckians would support the secessionists if coercion were employed against them, the president-elect emphatically replied: "If Kentucky means to say that if the federal government undertakes to recapture the southern forts and collect the revenue and war ensues, she will unite with the South, let her prepare for war."[5] Thus, it was no surprise that Lincoln's friends and allies like Horace White considered him "quite belligerent."[6] Herndon called his law partner "Jackson redivivus" and assured Wendell Phillips that "Lincoln has a superior will—good common sense, and moral, as well as physical courage." The president-elect would "make a grave yard of the South, if rebellion or treason lifts its head: he will execute the laws, as against Treason & Rebellion." His Republican convictions were as "as firm . . . as the rocks [*sic*] of Gibraltar." To be sure, on "questions of *economy—policy—calculation—* . . . & dollars you can rule him; but on the questions of Justice—Right—Liberty he rules himself."[7] Lincoln repeatedly told Herndon "that rather than back down—rather than concede to traitors, his soul might go back to God from the wings of the Capitol."[8]

Lincoln's firmness was rooted in a profound self-respect that forbade knuckling under to what he perceived as extortionate bullying. He insisted that "he did not wish to *pay* for being inaugurated."[9] In addition, his hatred of slavery and his unwillingness to abandon the principle of majority rule made him reluctant to appease disunionists. Moreover, if secession were tolerated, the nation and the idea for which it stood—that ordinary people should have a significant voice in their governance and be allowed to advance socially and economically as far as their talent, virtue, industry, and ability allowed—would be discredited. Practical political considerations also influenced his thinking, for he could ill afford to alienate the many Republicans opposed to any abandonment of the party's platform.

Answering Mail and Receiving Visitors

Immediately after the election, Lincoln was inundated with mail. His assistant personal secretary, John Hay, reported that Lincoln "reads letters constantly—at home—in the street—among his friends. I believe he is strongly tempted in church."[10] The sculptor Thomas D. Jones, who executed a bust of Lincoln in Springfield that winter, told a friend that the president-elect "generally opened about seventy letters every morning in my [hotel] room. He *read* all the *short* ones—laid all of the long ones aside. One morning he opened a letter of ten or twelve pages folio—he immediately returned it into the envelope—saying—'That man ought to be sent to the Penitentiary, or lunatic assylum.'"[11] Henry Villard, stationed in Springfield by the New York *Herald* and the Cincinnati *Commercial* to cover the president-elect, observed that "Lincoln's correspondence would offer a most abundant source of knowledge to the student of human nature." The mail, which "emanates from representatives of all grades of society," included "grave effusions of statesmen," poetic tributes, "disinterested advice of patriots," "able editorials" clipped from innumerable journals, "wretched wood-cut representations of his surroundings," volumes from "speculative booksellers," inventors' circulars and samples, "well calculated, wheedling praises" from "the expectant politician," "[e]xuberant wide awake enthusiasm," as well as "the meaningless commonplaces of scribblers from mere curiosity." Nicolay often called his boss's attention to "[f]emale forwardness and inquisitiveness." More ominously, letters arrived

from impulsive Southerners containing "senseless fulminations, and, in a few instances, disgraceful threats and indecent drawings."[12]

Indecent language also appeared in some missives, including one from A. G.
Frick: "if you don't Resign we are going to put a spider in your dumpling and play the
Devil with you you god or mighty god dam sundde of a bit[c]h go to hell and kiss my
Ass suck my prick and call my Bolics your uncle Dick goddam a fool and goddam
Abe Lincoln who would like you goddam you excuse me for using such hard words
with you but you need it you are nothing but a goddam Black nigger."[13] Many others
urged Lincoln to resign. An anonymous correspondent, signing himself "Hand of
God against you," cursed Lincoln: "May the hand of the devil strike you down before
long— You are destroying the country. Damn you — every breath you take."[14] (From
South Carolina, Mrs. Lincoln received a picture of her husband with a rope about his
neck, his feet in manacles, and his back coated with tar and feathers.) Such threats did
not bother Lincoln. To suggestions that he resign, he replied that "it will do no good
to put him out of the way" for vice-president-elect Hannibal Hamlin "has plenty of
backbone" and "plenty of *Pluck*."[15]

To carve out time to answer his more polite letters as well as to formulate a
Southern policy, to consider cabinet appointments, and to compose his inaugural address, Lincoln restricted public visits to two hours in the morning and two and a half
in the afternoon. (He usually arose before dawn, breakfasted around 7 A.M., arrived at
the office by 8, and read mail and held private interviews till 10.) A typical reception
began with the crowd making its way up the stairs of the statehouse to the governor's
room, which continued to be available to Lincoln throughout November and December. (Thereafter he used a room in the nearby Johnson's Building.) Upon reaching
their destination, callers were greeted by the president-elect, who shook hands with
the leader of the delegation and heartily announced, "Get in, all of you." Fewer than
twenty could comfortably be accommodated. After informal introductions, he genially launched a conversation. Villard reported that in "this respect he displays more
than ordinary talent and practice. Although he is naturally more listened than talked
to, he does not allow a pause to become protracted. He is never at a loss as to subjects
that please the different classes of visitors, and there is a certain quaintness and originality about all he has to say, so that one cannot help feeling interested. His 'talk' is
not brilliant. His phrases are not ceremoniously set, but pervaded by a humorousness,
and, at times, a grotesque joviality, that will always please. I think it would be hard to
find one who tells better jokes, enjoys them better and laughs oftener, than Abraham
Lincoln." Some of the jokes, Villard informed his readers, "are rather crude, both as
to form and substance. But they are regularly to the point, and hence never come
short of effect."[16] (In his memoirs, Villard offered a less favorable assessment of Lincoln's humor: "I could not take a real personal liking to the man" because of his vulgar
taste: "the coarser the joke, the lower the anecdote, and the more risky the story, the
more he enjoyed them.")[17]

All sorts of people availed themselves of the opportunity to call on the
president-elect. Some men wore mud-caked brogans and hickory shirts, others elegant broadcloth and linen garments. Most women were attired in their Sunday best.

Not all visitors behaved well. Churls with their hats on and pants tucked into their boots and reeking of the barnyard would puff away on malodorous cigars while staring at Lincoln as if he were an object in a museum. Occasionally, a few rural folk would elbow their way through the crowd, announce their names, shake Lincoln's hand, and promptly retreat.

Those receptions were fittingly democratic. Lincoln showed no signs of self-importance, remaining ever the kind, good-natured, affable neighbor that he had been since his arrival in Springfield twenty-three years earlier. All visitors, even the most irksome and annoying, received a cordial greeting. He made no distinction between rich and poor, though he did show an unusually strong affection for friends from his early days in Illinois. He genially set every guest at ease, joking, answering questions, and reminiscing. Should strangers seem awkward and abashed, he strove to make them feel comfortable. He would sometimes take a break to confer with Nicolay at a corner table strewn with books and newspapers. After an interview in late December, one Eastern merchant described the president-elect as "perfectly cool," "very discreet of remark," and "thoroughly '*posted*'" about "the entire history of our Government—with all persons of note that from time to time have been connected with it—with all that surrounds him *now*!"[18]

Another caller asked the president-elect to explain how Southerners could, with a straight face, argue that they were as entitled to carry slaves into the western territories as Northerners were to carry any form of property there. "Do you not see," replied Lincoln, "that the South is right from her point of view? We northerners, if we go into the territories, are able to live without slaves, but the southerners are not. The southerner is not a perfect human being without his negro. . . . There is an old proverb: 'Clothes make the man;' but it is also true that 'Negroes make the man.'"[19]

Many callers sought jobs. "These office-seekers are a curse to this country," he told a Canadian visitor early in the Civil War. "No sooner was my election certain, than I became the prey of hundreds of hungry, persistent applicants for office, whose highest ambition it is to feed at the government crib."[20] In Springfield, would-be civil servants met with frustration, for he gently but firmly refused to make any commitments. By January, job hunters had learned that they would incur his displeasure if they pestered him. He told a young friend, who informally asked for a land office post, "that he would forget such requests of his friends, unless the person himself or some friend would present their claims at the proper time & place."[21]

Secession of the Lower South

That winter the nation trembled at the prospect of secession and the possibility of war. Between December and February, seven states of the Deep South, fearing that Lincoln's victory would lead to emancipation and social chaos, withdrew from the Union amid cries of "nigger equality," "abolitionism," "*Black* Republicanism," "spaniel submissionists," "buck niggers and our daughters," "equality in the territories," and "equal rights."[22] According to an Arkansasan, many Southerners "have been taught that Lincoln intends to use every means to instigate revolt among the slaves; that the Republicans are organized into military companies, and intend to march against the South under the leadership of Giddings, Seward & Co., to cut the throat of every white man, distribute the white females among the negroes, and to carry off each man for himself an ebony beauty to ornament and grace his home in the North; that northern white men are more impressed by the charms of a dark, rich hue, than by their pale faced beauties at home."[23]

Fear of slave revolts had long pervaded the South, especially in the areas where blacks were most numerous, and that fear intensified dramatically after John Brown's raid on Harper's Ferry in 1859. A perceived upsurge of slave insubordination frightened slaveholders and led them to favor secession. In September 1860, Congressman Lawrence Keitt of South Carolina, which had proportionally the largest black population in the country (57%), told a friend: "See—poison in the wells in Texas and fire for the Houses in Alabama—Our negroes are being enlisted in politics—With poison and fire how can we stand it? If Northern men get access to our negro[e]s to advise poison and the torch we must prevent it at every hazard."[24] A newspaper in Keitt's state warned: "The midnight glare of the incendiary's torch will illuminate the country from one end to the other; while pillage, violence, murder, poisons and rape will fill the air with the demoniac revelry of all the passions of an ignorant, semi-barbarous race, urged to madness by the licentious teachings of our Northern brethren. A war of races—a war of extermination—must arise, like that which took place in St. Domingo." Northerners "cannot, or will not, understand this state of things," complained the editor.[25] When asked, "Do you desire the millions of negro population of the South, to be set free among us, to stalk abroad in the land, following the dictates of their own natural instincts, committing depredations, rapine, and murder upon the whites?" residents of the Cotton States replied "NO!"[26]

To prevent such mayhem, slavery and white supremacy must be maintained by seceding from the Union. On November 16, 1860, the Augusta, Georgia, *Constitutionalist* said that the South regarded the American flag as "the emblem of a gigantic power, soon to pass into the hands of that sworn enemy, and knows that African slavery, though panoplied by the Federal Government, is doomed to a war of extermination. All the powers of a Government which has so long sheltered it will be turned to its destruction. The only hope for its preservation, therefore, is out of the Union."[27] When the Deep South formed the Confederate States of America in February 1861, the vice president of that new entity, Alexander H. Stephens of Georgia, asserted that its "foundations are laid, its corner-stone rests upon the great truth that the negro is not equal to the white man; that slavery—subordination to the superior race—is his natural and normal condition. This, our new government, is the first, in the history of the world, based upon this great physical, philosophical, and moral truth." Jefferson and the other Founding Fathers had written the Declaration of Independence and the Constitution "upon the assumption of the equality of races. This was an error."[28] Stephens and many others maintained that white liberty required black slavery. At his state's secession convention Congressman Keitt declared, "I am willing in this issue to rest disunion upon the question of slavery. It is the great central point from which we are now seceding."[29] In Texas, the secession convention issued a Declaration of Causes condemning the Republicans as a party "based upon the unnatural feeling of hostility to these Southern States and their beneficent and patriarchal system of African slav-ery, proclaiming the debasing doctrine of the equality of all men, irrespective of race or color—a doctrine at war with nature, in opposition to the experience of mankind, and in violation of the plainest revelations of the Divine Law."[30]

Southerners thought it unmanly to bow to the Republicans' refusal to allow them to take their slaves into the western territories. In midsummer 1860, John Bell had predicted that "the whole South, in 30 days after the election of 'Lincoln,' would feel his election to be an *insult* to them."[31] They must have equal rights! They would not tolerate second-class citizenship! Too long had they endured criticism of their section and its peculiar institution! "To deny us the right and privilege [of taking slaves into the territories] would be to deny us equality in the Union and would be a wrong and a degradation to which a high spirited people should not submit," declared a group of Mississippians in 1859.[32] (Slaves comprised 55% of the Magnolia State's population.) In 1850, the state's junior senator, Jefferson Davis, told his legislative colleagues that Southerners would become "an inferior class, a degraded class in the Union" if they were forbidden to take their slaves into the territories.[33] In urging secession, a Georgia editor in 1860 exhorted his neighbors: "Let us act like men. Let us be equals."[34] "We were not born to be mastered, nor to submit to inferior position," cried a Virginia newspaper.[35]

Secessionists would rather destroy the government than submit to it if it forbade them equal rights in the territories. That prohibition they termed, in the words of fire-eating William L. Yancey, "discrimination as degrading as it is injurious to the slaveholding states."[36] James H. Hammond of South Carolina favored secession rather than "submitting to gross insult."[37] A Texas editor exclaimed, "The North has gone overwhelmingly for NEGRO EQUALITY and SOUTHERN VASSALAGE! Southern men, will you SUBMIT to the DEGRADATION?"[38]

The Deep South sent commissioners to proselytize in the Upper South and the Border States. An Alabama secession commissioner, trying to persuade Kentucky to leave the Union, called Lincoln's election "the last and crowning act of insult and outrage upon the people of the South." He dramatically predicted that if the Repub-licans carried out their announced policies "and the South submits, degradation and ruin must overwhelm alike all classes of citizens in the Southern States. The slave-holder and non-slave-holder must ultimately share the same fate; all be degraded to a position of equality with free negroes, stand side by side with them at the polls, and fraternize in all the social relations of life. . . . What Southern man, be he slave-holder or non-slave-holder, can without indignation and horror contemplate the triumph of negro equality, and see his own sons and daughters in the not distant future associat-ing with free negroes upon terms of political and social equality, and the white man stripped by the heaven-daring hand of fanaticism of that title to superiority over the black race which God himself has bestowed? . . . Can Southern men submit to such degradation and ruin?"[39]

A congressman from Alabama, where 45 percent of the residents were bondsmen, told a friend that he would "rather die a freeman than live a slave to Black Republi-canism" and would either "be an equal, or a corpse."[40] Robert Barnwell of South

Carolina predicted that white Southerners "must become a degraded people" if slavery were not "upheld as a political institution essential to the preservation of our civilization."[41] A fellow South Carolinian, William Porcher Miles, declared that accepting restrictions on slavery expansion would put the "seal of inferiority" on Southerners and brand them "as those who from perverse moral obliquity are not entitled to the enjoyment of full participation in the common goods and property of the Republic."[42] Echoing him was Texas Senator Louis T. Wigfall, who told his Northern colleagues: "You denounce us, degrade us, deride us, tell us . . . that we are degraded, that we are not your equals."[43] An Alabamian observed that accepting restrictions on slavery expansion was tantamount to admitting "that a free citizen of Massachusetts was a better man and entitled to more privileges than a free citizen of Alabama." He asked the voters of his state: "Will you submit to be bridled and saddled and rode under whip and spur," or instead demand to be treated in accordance with "the great doctrine of *Equality*: Opposition to ascendancy in any form, either of classes, by way of monopolies, or of sections, by means of robbery."[44] Alexander H. Stephens issued a public letter alleging that any exclusion of slavery from the territories "would be in direct violation of the rights of the Southern people to an equal participation" in those lands "and in open derogation of the equality between the states of the South and the North which should never [be] surrendered by the South."[45]

The South took offense at several other criticisms. In 1850, an Alabama newspaper protested against "the unwillingness of Northern men to sit around the same altars with Southern men—the denunciations of us by the press and the people of the North—the false slanders circulated in their periodicals and reviews—the rending of churches for a theoretical sentiment, and then appropriating to their use what they sanctimoniously call the price of blood." These slights "have alienated the two sections of a common country, and would alone, at some future day, terminate in a dissolution of the union."[46] The South's hurt feelings were illustrated by a New Orleans editor, who proclaimed that his region "has been moved to resistance chiefly . . . by the popular dogma in the free States that slavery is a crime in the sight of GOD. . . . The South in the eyes of the North, is degraded and unworthy, because of the institution of servitude."[47] A fellow Louisianan, Senator Judah P. Benjamin, denounced "the incessant attack of the Republicans, not simply on the interests, but on the feelings and sensibilities of a high-spirited people by the most insulting language, and the most offensive epithets."[48] Mississippi Governor John Jones Pettus declared that Republicans "attempted to *degrade us* in the estimation of other nations by denouncing us as barbarians, pirates, and robbers, unfit associates for Christian or civilized men."[49]

The South also feared losing power. Strong though the desire to attain power may have been, the dread of having it taken away was stronger still, especially if that loss imperiled slavery. Charles Francis Adams believed that the "question is one of *power*. And nothing short of a surrender of everything gained by the election will avail." The secessionists "want to continue to rule." Their "true grievance and the only one is the loss of power."[50] Another diarist, Sidney George Fisher of Philadelphia, concurred: "The southern people are arrogant and self-willed. They have been accustomed generally to govern the country, always to have large influence in the government. They cannot bear to lose power, and to submit to the control of the North."[51] The New York *Tribune* argued that the great complaints of the South included the "loss of sixty years' monopoly of the Government, its military and civil offices" and "the loss of prestige and power by the old political parties, and their humiliated leaders."[52]

As members of a traditional society, Southerners resented the modernizing Northerners, whose watchwords were "improvement" and "progress." Below the Mason-Dixon line, new economic, social, intellectual, and cultural trends enjoyed little favor; innovation and reform, highly prized in the North, were suspect in the South. The Southern revolt against the Union represents, among other things, a chapter in the long history of traditionalist resistance to modernization. "We are an agricultural people," a leading secessionist, Senator Louis T. Wigfall, explained to an English visitor; "we are a primitive but a civilized people. We have no cities—we don't want them. We have no literature—we don't need any yet. We have no press—we are glad of it."[53]

Secessionists scoffed at Stephen A. Douglas and others who argued that Lincoln could do little harm because his party did not control Congress. They replied that Republicans would sooner or later dominate the House of Representatives and eventually the senate and the Supreme Court; in the meantime, the new administration could undermine slavery with its power of appointment. Congressman Henry W. Hilliard of Alabama explained that it "is not any apprehension of aggressive action on the part of the incoming administration which rouses the southern people to resistance, but it is the demonstration which Mr Lincoln's election by such overwhelming majorities affords, of the supremacy of a sentiment hostile to slavery in the non-slaveholding states of the Union."[54] A reapportionment of the House based on the 1860 census would give the North almost two-thirds of the seats in that chamber. Even a Unionist journal like the New Orleans *Picayune* alleged that the Republicans "will be the most moderate of national men in their professions, without abating a jot of the ultimate purpose of forcing the extinction of slavery. . . . It is for these future, progressing, insidious, fatal results, more than from an 'overt act' of direct oppression, that the triumph of Black Republicanism . . . is to be profoundly deprecated by every Southern man of every shade of party opinion."[55]

Some slaveholders feared that Lincoln would appoint local nonslaveholders to office and thus create a Republican Party in the South threatening Democratic hegemony. "The prospective development of a Republican party among the non-slaveholding whites of the South. . . . is the great grievance," said the New York *Tribune*. Poorer farmers and artisans might combine to displace the planter elite.[56] But divisions among whites in the Deep South were minor compared with their overwhelming agreement on the need to protect slavery and white supremacy at all costs.

Skepticism about Secession Threats

On election night, when the first ominous rumblings of secession reached Springfield—in the form of a report that South Carolina Senators James Chesnut and

James H. Hammond had resigned their seats—it alarmed most of Lincoln's friends but not him. "There are plenty left," he remarked, alluding to the other sixty-four senators. "A little while ago I saw a couple of shooting stars fall down, hissing and sputtering. Plenty left for many a bright night."[57] Soon thereafter, Elihu B. Washburne found Lincoln "in fine spirits and excellent health, and quite undisturbed by the blustering of the disunionists and traitors."[58] An Ohio journalist recalled that the president-elect "considered the movement [in the] South as a sort of political game of bluff, gotten up by politicians, and meant solely to frighten the North. He believed that when the leaders saw their efforts in that direction [i.e., of secession] were unavailing, the tumult would subside." Lincoln predicted that they "won't give up the offices. Were it believed that vacant places could be had at the North Pole, the road there would be lined with dead Virginians."[59] In September he had stated that there were "no real disunionists in the country."[60] He told his law partner that "he could not in his heart believe that the South designed the overthrow of the Government."[61] On election eve, Lincoln explained to a Washingtonian "that in his part of the country, when a man came among them they were in the habit of giving him a fair trial." That "was all he desired from the South," which "had always professed to be law-abiding and constitution-loving; placing their reliance on the constitution and the laws." As president, he would make sure that "these should be sustained to the fullest extent."[62] The following month, when a visitor asked whether Lincoln thought the Southern states would secede, he expressed doubt: "I do not think they will. A number from different sections of the South pass through here daily, and all that call appear pleasant and seem to go away apparently satisfied, and if they only give me an opportunity I will convince them that I do not wish to interfere with them in any way, but protect them in everything that they are entitled to." With eyes flashing, he added a caveat: "If they do [secede], the question will be [posed], and it must be settled come what may."[63] To a Tennesseean he declared that "to execute the laws is all that I shall attempt to do. *This, however, I will do, no matter how much force may be required.*"[64]

   Lincoln's optimism rested not only on the information derived from visitors and newspapers but also on his interpretation of the election results. In the Slave States, John C. Breckinridge, whose candidacy was widely interpreted as pro-secession (although the nominee himself repudiated disunionism), received only 44 percent of the vote. Together, Bell and Douglas, who opposed secession, won 110,000 more Southern votes than Breckinridge. Bell carried Virginia with 44 percent of the ballots cast, Tennessee with 48 percent, Kentucky with 45 percent, and nearly won North Carolina with 47 percent, Maryland with 45.15 percent (to Breckinridge's 45.92%), and Missouri with 35.3 percent (to Douglas's 35.5%). In those states, as Henry Adams colorfully put it, old Whigs "had grown up to despise a Democrat as the meanest and most despicable of creatures" and "had been taught in the semi-barbarous school of southern barbecues and stump harangues, gouging and pistol shooting, to hate and abhor the very word Democrat with a bitterness unknown to the quieter and more law-abiding northerners." For them, "the idea of submitting finally and hopelessly to the Democratic rule, was not to be endured."[65]

In the months following the election, Lincoln took heart from the strong Unionist sentiment in the Upper South states of Virginia, North Carolina, Arkansas, and Tennessee, as well as the Border States of Kentucky, Missouri, Delaware, and Maryland, where slaves were less numerous and Whiggish sentiments and organizations more persistent than they were in the Deep South. The white population of the Slave States was pretty evenly divided among the Deep South (2,629,000), the Upper South (2,828,000), and the Border States (2,589,000.) Unionists doubted that economic benefits were to be gained by joining a Southern confederacy, regarded leading secessionists as delusional conspirators irresponsibly frightening their neighbors, feared that Southern misunderstanding of Northern intentions might lead to hostilities, and thought that the Republicans could end that misunderstanding. A few of these men, including Andrew Johnson of Tennessee, were Unconditional Unionists, whose loyalty to the nation depended on no concessions by the Republicans; most of them were Conditional Unionists, who would eschew secession as long as the federal government took no aggressive action against the seceders and as long as the Republicans demonstrated sufficient willingness to compromise.

Lincoln was not unrealistic in imagining that the Upper South and Border States might remain in the Union. After all, the Deep South had threatened to secede in 1832–1833, in 1850–1851, and yet again in 1856; as recently as 1859–1860, secessionists in South Carolina, Alabama, and Mississippi had failed to win support for disunion. William B. Campbell, ex-governor of Tennessee, warned hotheads in the Lower South that secession was "unwise and impolitic" because it would hasten "the ruin and overthrow of negro slavery" and put at risk "the freedom and liberty of the white man." Campbell, who blamed cynical politicians for frightening the Deep South into secession, predicted that Kentucky and Tennessee could not be "dragged into a rebellion that their whole population utterly disapproved."[66] A Louisianan expressed puzzlement at the Upper South's reluctance to join the Cotton States in seceding: "Is it not strange, when the border states suffer so much more from Northern fanaticism, from actual loss in their property, and these same states equally interested in slavery, that a feeling of antagonism to the North, should be so much stronger [in the Deep South]."[67] The highly respected legal scholar Bartholomew F. Moore of North Carolina predicted that secession would intensify antislavery agitation, extinguish Southern claims to the western territories, dash hopes of expansion into the Caribbean and Central America, and cause a hemorrhage of runaway slaves.

Some North Carolina Unionists feared that their state, after an initial reluctance to follow their immediate neighbor's lead, would ultimately secede. "*We* the Union men will make a firm resistance," predicted Thomas K. Thomas, "but the bad element in our State will overcome us—sooner or later."[68]

Lincoln assumed that reasonable people understood that nothing had occurred, including his election, to justify secession. The Southern grievance most often cited was insufficiently rigorous enforcement of the Fugitive Slave Act. But very few slaves escaped from the South; in 1860, there were only 803 runaways, constituting less than one-fiftieth of 1 percent of the slave population, and most of those fled from the Border States, not the Deep South, where disunionist sentiment prevailed. Privately,

Southerners acknowledged that in practical terms, a Northern state's Personal Liberty Bill, designed to hinder enforcement of the Fugitive Slave Act, was insignificant. To them the psychological cost was greater than the economic. "The loss of property is felt, the loss of honor is felt still more," said influential Virginia Senator James M. Mason.[69]

Lincoln pointed out to a group of Kentuckians that during the nullification controversy of 1832–1833, "the South made a special complaint against a law of recent origin [i.e., the tariff of 1828]—*Now* they had no new law—or new interpretation of [an] old law to complain of—no specialty whatever, nothing but the naked desire to go out of the Union."[70] If secessionists were to await passage of such a statute before acting, or for any other "aggressive" action, "they would never go out of the Union," he predicted.[71]

Many Northerners shared Lincoln's skepticism about the prospects of Southern secession. In September, Seward had declared that "the slave power. . . . rails now with a feeble voice, instead of thundering as it did in our ears for twenty or thirty years past. With a feeble and muttering voice they cry out that they will tear the Union to pieces. They complain that if we will not surrender our principles, and our system, and our right, being a majority, to rule, and if we will not accept their system and such rulers as they will give us, they will go out of the Union. 'Who's afraid?' Nobody's afraid."[72] Long John Wentworth called the secession threat "the old game which has been used time and time again to scare the North into submission to Southern demands and Southern tyranny."[73] John Bigelow advised an English friend that the South's threats were uttered "with the faint hope of frightening Lincoln into a modification of the Republican policy and the concession of a Cabinet Minister to the Fire Eaters."[74] In 1856, James Buchanan had observed to a fellow Democrat: "We have so often cried 'wolf,' that now, when the wolf is at the door, it is difficult to make the people believe it."[75]

Northerners tended to regard secessionists as spoiled children in need of discipline. "Our stock of quieting sugar plums, in the shape of compromises, is about exhausted, and the fretful child is as insubordinate as ever," remarked the Evansville, Indiana, *Journal* scornfully. If "the little rebel" (South Carolina) did not calm down but remained "insubordinate," then "a well-administered spanking may be productive of good."[76] Another Hoosier recommended that the Palmetto State be "*sunk out of sight*—and a *dead Sea* cover the *place where she stood.*"[77] William M. Reynolds, president of Illinois University, felt that it was "not now a question whether the South shall extend negro slavery down to the Isthmus, but whether the freemen of the North are to be mere vassals & tools to register their decrees."[78]

Appeasement Proposals

Not everyone in the North agreed with this assessment. Commercial interests in New York eagerly sought to appease the South, lest they suffer economically. In the month after the election, as legislatures in the Deep South authorized secession conventions, some influential Republican editors in New York, including Henry J. Raymond, James Watson Webb, and Thurlow Weed, recommended conciliatory gestures. On

November 14, Raymond urged Congress to compensate slaveholders for runaways escaping to the North; later he recommended repealing of Personal Liberty Laws, toughening enforcement of the Fugitive Slave Act, and allowing slavery to expand. Webb's New York *Courier and Enquirer* endorsed the restoration of the Missouri Compromise line. Weed also ran editorials questioning the need for Personal Liberty Laws and asking "why not restore the Missouri Compromise Line? That secured to the South all Territory adapted, by Soil and Climate, to its 'peculiar institution.'"[79] Weed doubtless spoke for Seward, who had consulted with him on November 15.

Radical Republicans frowned on Weed's proposals. After interviewing Lord Thurlow, a Connecticut journalist described him as "the most dangerous foe to Liberty that lives in the country. He is either scared to death or a bought traitor.... Seward is a Jesuit. He will keep his record tolerably clean—probably, but is hand & glove with Weed of course, & I sincerely believe secretly encourages a compromise though they will not give it that name. They call it making up *a good record* against secession. They do not expect to prevent secession."[80]

In response to such compromise trial balloons, Lincoln expressed surprise that "*any* Republican could think, for a moment, of abandoning in the hour of victory, though in the face of danger, every point involved in the recent contest."[81] When a Virginia newspaper argued that he should quiet the Southerners' fears by letting them take bondsmen into the territories, Lincoln said he was reminded of a little girl who wanted to go outside and play. Her mother refused permission. When the youngster begged and whined insistently, she exhausted the patience of her mother, who gave the child a sound thrashing. "Now, Ma, I can certainly run out," exclaimed the girl.[82] From Springfield, Henry Villard reported that the "true motives of the voluntary backsliding of certain New York journals are ... well understood out here. The throbs of Wall street are known to have produced certain sudden pangs of contrition. But Mr. Lincoln is above bulling and bearing. Although conservative in his intentions, and anxious to render constitutional justice to all sections of the country, he is possessed of too much nobleness and sense of duty to quail before threats and lawlessness. He knows well enough that the first step backward on his part, or that of his supporters, will be followed by a corresponding advance on the part of the cotton rebels, and he knows that for every inch yielded, a foot will be demanded."[83]

Those journalistic peace feelers ignited a debate that exacerbated tension within the Republican Party between the Conservatives, who favored some kind of compromise, and the "stiff-backed" Radicals, who believed that "[t]o be frightened by threats of war, & bloodshed is the part of children."[84] A leading Radical, Pennsylvania Congressman Thaddeus Stevens, said: "I do not blame the gentlemen from the South ... for the language of intimidation, for using this threat of rending God's creation from the turret to the foundation. All this is right in them, for they have tried it fifty times, and fifty times they have found weak and recreant tremblers in the North who have been affected by it, and who have acted from those intimidations."[85] In Congress's upper chamber, Henry Wilson of Massachusetts echoed that view, arguing that disunion threats had been able to "startle and appal[l] the timid, make the servility of the servile still more abject, [and] rouse the selfish instincts of ... nerveless conservatism."[86] Two weeks after the election, Horace Greeley declared that most Southerners had no desire to break up the Union: "They simply mean to bully the Free States into concessions which they can exult over as neutralizing the election of Lincoln."[87] The Chicago *Tribune* also suspected that secessionists were bluffing and predicted that when they finally realized that the North could not be browbeaten into compromising its principles, "they will probably return to their fealty to the Union."[88]

Some stiff-backs did not quail at the prospect of war. "Without a little blood-letting, this Union will not, in my estimation, be worth a rush," wrote Michigan Senator Zachariah Chandler in February.[89] Chandler had earlier insisted that "we are men of *Peace* but will *whip* disunionists into Subjection, the moment the first overt act of treason is perpetrated. *Halters* & not compromizes are now needed & like certain very pungent medicines, *a very little will answer.*"[90] He would "rather see every master in South Carolina hanged & *Charleston burned,* than to see one line from Mr Lincoln to appease them in advance of his inaugural."[91] A leading Republican activist in Freeport, Illinois, told his congressman that if a "collision *must* come, let it; if blood must flow, it is better that it should, better, ten fould better that a million lives be sacrificed . . . than self government and free society be an admitted failure."[92] To Frank Blair, it seemed that "we must either accept the Southern slaveholders as our masters or dispute the point on the field of battle, and for my part I do not hesitate to embrace the last alternative. Their arrogance has become intolerable."[93]

Gustave Koerner asserted that the "spilling of blood in a civil war often cements a better Union. History is full of such examples."[94] Koerner told Lincoln that if the South seceded, "he should call into the field at once several hundred thousand militia" and pointed out that when a few cantons of Switzerland had recently seceded and mustered 40,000 troops, the government had met the challenge with 100,000 soldiers, whose numbers overawed the disunionists and led to a bloodless restoration of national unity.[95] In central Illinois, William Herndon reported that the watchword was: "War bloody and exterminating rather than secession or Disunion."[96] In 1857, Herndon had written that if "the South will tap the dinner gong and call the wild, bony, quick, brave Peoples to a feast of civil war, and make this land quiver and ring from center to circumference,—then I can but say,—'the quicker the better.'"[97]

In December, Iowa Senator James W. Grimes predicted that "war of a most bitter and sanguinary character will be sure to follow in a short time. . . . This is certainly deplorable, but there is no help for it. No reasonable concession will satisfy the rebels."[98] In Indiana, the Terre Haute *Wabash Express* believed that "if this Union is not worth fighting for, it is not worth having." When South Carolina seceded, Hoosier Republicans were urged to "'whip her into the traces' if she commits any 'overt act.' The 'appeal' of gun powder and cold steel is the kind to make to disunion traitors."[99] Said the *Indiana American,* "we are heartily tired of having this [secession] threat stare us in the face evermore. If nothing but blood will prevent it, let it flow."[100] An Ohio Democrat announced that he would rather "see a Civil war, a Fratricidal war, engaged in and fought out than to see the government converted into a supple pro-slavery bloodhound."[101]

Less sanguinary Moderates disagreed about which concessions to offer the South. Some were out-and-out appeasers, willing to abandon the Chicago platform by allowing slavery to expand into the territories. On December 18, the chief spokesman for this approach, John J. Crittenden of Kentucky, the 72-year-old Nestor of the U.S. senate, introduced a comprehensive package of six irrevocable constitutional amendments and four supplementary resolutions. They included a variation on Weed's suggestion that the Missouri Compromise line be extended to California; under Crittenden's plan, slavery would be protected south of 36° 30' during the territorial stage, and any further states would be admitted to the Union with or without slavery as its people saw fit. This would apply to existing territories and to any that might be acquired later. Other amendments stipulated that Congress could not abolish slavery in federal facilities; nor could it do so in Washington without the consent of the voters, without compensation to owners, and as long as the peculiar institution persisted in Virginia and Maryland; nor could Congress outlaw the interstate slave trade or the transportation of slaves across state lines; owners whose slaves successfully fled to the North would be compensated for their losses; and finally, no future amendments could undo these protections for slavery. Of the ten items in the package, only one was a concession to the antislavery forces.

Most Republicans understandably thought this represented "no compromise at all, but a total surrender of every principle for which the Republicans and Douglas Democrats contended, in connexion with the subject of slavery, during the last Presidential canvass," as an Indiana newspaper put it.[102] Iowa Senator James W. Grimes thought the Crittenden Compromise asked Republicans "to surrender all of our cherished ideas on the subject of slavery, and agree, in effect, to provide a slave code for the Territories south of 36° 30' and for the Mexican provinces, as soon as they shall be brought within our jurisdiction. It is demanded of us that we shall consent to change the Constitution into a genuine pro-slavery instrument, and to convert the Government into a great slave-breeding, slavery-extending empire."[103] (In fact, Southern expansionists in the 1850s had dreamed of establishing a Caribbean slave empire and undertook freebooting missions to carry out that scheme.) Grimes's colleague Charles Sumner said that his Massachusetts constituents would rather "see their State sink below the sea & become a sandbank before they would adopt those propositions."[104] One of those constituents, Henry Adams, opined that Crittenden "does not seem to suppose that the North has any honor" and suggested that Republicans with a modicum of self-respect could well view the Kentuckian's compromise proposal as insulting.[105] Other Bay State residents called the Crittenden Compromise a "scheme of abominations" to which "no true Republican can accede" and which "would result in accepting all of Mexico and Central America as Slave States."[106] Alexander K. McClure predicted to a fellow Republican that the "Crittenden proposition would demoralize us utterly. . . . Even the Border States seem determined to humiliate the Republican forces. They come with proffers of peace but with the condition annexed that we must incorporate into the Constitution a political platform against which *four-fifths* of the people voted in November last; and they all come with secession as their alternative if we fail to accede."[107] Another Pennsylvanian observed that the

Crittenden plan "is a virtual declaration of a purpose to filibuster for the acquisition of more territory, with the direct design of extending slavery. The Republicans will under no circumstances agree to this exaction, come what may."[108] It was "outrageous to foist on the country demands never made during the late election," fulminated Maryland Congressman Henry Winter Davis.[109]

Some Moderates were conciliators rather than appeasers, favoring less drastic measures such as the repeal of Personal Liberty Laws, compensation to slaveowners for runaways, tougher enforcement of the Fugitive Slave Act, a constitutional convention to deal with the crisis, patrols along the border between Free and Slave States to discourage runaways, admittance of the territories to the Union immediately, a ban on the acquisition of more land, and guarantees of both the security of slavery where it already existed and the preservation of the internal slave trade.

Lincoln, like most of his Northern constituents-to-be, sympathized with the hard-liners rather than with the appeasers or the conciliators. Though accommodating by nature, he stubbornly refused to be bullied. Truculent Southerners and timid Northerners could not make him submit to what he considered unreasonable demands. According to a journalist who interviewed him on November 13, Lincoln believed that his election "is only a public pretext for what has long been preparing;" that Southern hotheads had been plotting secession for years and were looking for a convenient excuse to carry out their plans; "that his position on all questions of public concern—all which affect the Slavery question nearly or remotely—is so well known that no declaration of his would change treasonable purposes already announced, and that a reiteration of views which are patent to all men who have sought to know them, would be an evidence of timidity which he does not feel, and of which he would have no man suspect him."[110] He shared the opinion of a Kentucky friend who told him that the "Hotspurs of the South will no doubt try a while to kick up a dust, but sober second thoughts may calm them down into a decent acquiescence to the choice of the Nation."[111] To make possible that sober second thought, those Hotspurs must be firmly resisted.

The day before the election, Lincoln rejected the appeal of the prosperous Connecticut businessman and former Whig Henry S. Sanford to "reassure the men honestly alarmed" about the threat to the Union. "There are no such men," Lincoln replied bluntly. He had, said he, "thought much about it—it is the trick by which the South breaks down every Northern man—I would go to Washington without the support of the men who supported me and were my friends before [the] election. I would be as powerless as a block of buckeye wood." When Sanford persisted, Lincoln added: "The honest man (you talk of honest men) will look at our platform and what I have said—there they will find everything I could now say or which they would ask me to say.—all I could say would be but repetition. Having told them all these things ten times already would they believe the eleventh declaration[?] Let us be practical—there are many general terms afloat such as 'conservatism'— 'enforcement of the irrepressible conflict at the point of the bayonet'—'hostility to the South &c'—all of which mean nothing without definition. What then could I say to allay their fears, if they will not define what particular act or acts they fear from me or my friends?" When Sanford handed him letters from anxious merchants, Lincoln snapped: "[I] recognize them as a sett of liars and knaves." Sanford then pointed out that Southerners were taking steps to arm themselves. "The North does not fear invasion from the Sl[ave] S[tates]—and we of the North certainly have no desire and never had to invade the South," Lincoln insisted with some heat. "If I shall begin to yield to these threats—If I begin dallying with them, the men who have elected me, if I shall be elected, would give me up before my inauguration—and the South seeing it, would deliberately kick me out." His first duty, Lincoln explained, "would be to stand by the men who elected me."[112] Sanford, "convinced that no right of the South will be imperilled" in a Lincoln administration, assured William C. Rives that the Rail-splitter's speeches contained nothing that the Virginia Unionist "would have objected to in 1856" and that the "nigger question" would be solved without bloodshed.[113]

Another resident of Connecticut, Lincoln's former colleague in the U.S. House, Truman Smith, joined Sanford in urging that Lincoln issue a statement placating the South. But the president-elect declined, stressing that he must maintain his self-respect and succumb to no demands that he appease unreasonable Southerners. "It is with the most profound appreciation of your motive, and highest respect for your judgment too, that I feel constrained, for the present, at least, to make no declaration for the public," he tactfully told Smith on November 10. "I could say nothing which I have not already said, and which is in print, and open for the inspection of all. To press a repetition of this upon those who *have* listened, is useless; to press it upon those who have *refused* to listen, and still refuse, would be wanting in self-respect, and would have an appearance of sycophancy and timidity, which would excite the contempt of good men, and encourage bad ones to clamor the more loudly. I am not insensible to any commercial or financial depression that may exist; but nothing is to be gained by fawning around the '*respectable scoundrels*' who got it up. Let them go to work and repair the mischief of their own making; and then perhaps they will be less greedy to do the like again."[114]

To an interviewer, Lincoln again emphasized his desire to maintain his self-respect while confronting bullies: "I know the justness of my intentions and the utter groundlessness of the pretended fears of the men who are filling the country with their clamor. If I go into the Presidency, they will find me as I am on record—nothing less, nothing more. My declarations have been made to the world without reservation. They have been often repeated; and now, self-respect demands of me and the party that has elected me that when threatened I should be silent."[115] Other Republicans expressed similar views. Lincoln's friend Thomas Marshall of Coles County told his fellow state senators, "I cherish this Union as dearly as any man in this chamber," but, he insisted, "there is something dearer than even the Union—there is something dearer even than peace—it is *manhood*—it is principle."[116]

On November 16, Lincoln explained to visitors that "[m]y own impression is, at present, (leaving myself room to modify the opinion, if upon a further investigation I should see fit to do so), that this government possesses both the authority and the power to maintain its own integrity;" but, he added, that was "not the ugly point of this matter. The ugly point is the necessity of keeping the government together by force, as ours should be a government of fraternity."[117] When Judge Daniel Breck of Kentucky, a distant relative of Mrs. Lincoln, urged him to appoint conservatives to office and shun "obnoxious men" like Seward and Cassius M. Clay, Lincoln challenged him to identify a speech in which Seward "had ever spoken menacingly of the South." He also "said that so far as he knew not one single prominent public Republican had justly made himself obnoxious to the South by anything he had said or done, and that they had only become so because the Southern politicians had so persistently bespotted and bespattered every northern man by their misrepresentations to rob them of what strength they might otherwise have[.]" Lincoln told Breck that the Kentuckian was in effect suggesting "that the Republicans should now again surrender the Government into the hands of the men they had just conquered." [118] Rhetorically he asked: "Does any man think that I will take to my bosom an enemy?" Breck concluded that the president-elect "was rather *ultra* in the Republican faith."[119]

That same day, in a sharply worded letter to a Democratic editor, Lincoln criticized Southern distortions of his views: "Please pardon me for suggesting that if the papers, like yours, which heretofore have persistently garbled, and misrepresented what I have said, will now fully and fairly place it before their readers, there can be no further misunderstanding. I beg you to believe me sincere when I declare I do not say this in a spirit of complaint or resentment; but that I urge it as the true cure for any real uneasiness in the country that my course may be other than conservative. The Republican newspapers now, and for some time past, are and have been republishing copious extracts from my many published speeches, which would at once reach the whole public if your class of papers would also publish them. I am not at liberty to shift my ground—that is out of the question. If I thought a *repetition* would do any good I would make it. But my judgment is it would do positive harm. The secessionists, *per se* believing they had alarmed me, would clamor all the louder."[120] In December, Lincoln gave Thurlow Weed his views on secession: "my opinion is that no state can, in any way lawfully, get out of the Union, without the consent of the others; and that it is the duty of the President, and other government functionaries to run the machine as it is."[121]

During his first month as president-elect, Lincoln fended off appeals to placate the South by pointing out that he would not be officially chosen until December 5. "My time not having arrived," he told a visitor in mid-November, "I am content to receive all possible light on the subject, and glad to be out of the ring."[122] He was following the policy of "masterly inactivity" recommended by several advisors and Republican editors. Because "Mr. Lincoln is nothing beyond a private American citizen at this time," the *Ohio State Journal* argued on November 14 that it would be manifestly inappropriate for him to issue unofficial proclamations.[123] Joseph Medill spoke for many Republicans when he insisted that Lincoln's letter of acceptance and published speeches, along with the party's platform, were sufficient: "There are a class of d[amne]d fools or knaves who want him to make a 'union saving speech'—in other words to *set down* to conciliate the disunionists and fire-eaters. He must keep his feet out of all such wolf traps."[124]

On November 20, during the jubilation in Springfield, Lincoln spoke publicly for the first time since the election. His tone was far more conciliatory than the one he had used in dealing with Truman Smith, Henry S. Sanford, and others. A torch-light procession of Wide Awakes led an exultant crowd to his house, where they shouted themselves hoarse. Distinctly and emphatically, he told them: "I thank you, in common with all those who have thought fit, by their votes, to endorse the republican cause. [Applause.] I rejoice with you in the success which has so far attended that cause. [Applause.] Yet in all our rejoicings let us neither express nor cherish any harsh feelings towards any citizen who by his vote has differed with us. [Loud cheering.] Let us at all times remember that all American citizens are brothers of a common country, and should dwell together in the bonds of fraternal feeling. [Immense applause.]"[125]

Although these vague remarks offered little to reassure the South, Lincoln penned a more explicit statement, which Lyman Trumbull incorporated into his speech that same day in Springfield. The president-elect had been urged to have a surrogate like Trumbull deliver such a message; a Tennessee merchant had advised him that secessionists in South Carolina "are sending their emisaries all over the South, and the people are made to believe that the Republicans are intending to emancipate the ignorant negroes by force. If some of your friends, (like Trumbull), would make a declaration that you were eminently conservative it would do no harm, but we at the South could use it to combat our political disunion antagonists."[126] Others seconded that suggestion.

In his speech, Trumbull spoke the following words written by Lincoln: "I have labored in, and for, the Republican organization with entire confidence that whenever it shall be in power, each and all of the States will be left in as complete control of their own affairs respectively, and at as perfect liberty to choose, and employ, their own means of protecting property, and preserving peace and order within their respective limits, as they have ever been under any administration. Those who have voted for Mr. Lincoln, have expected, and still expect this; and they would not have voted for him had they expected otherwise. I regard it as extremely fortunate for the peace of the whole country, that this point, upon which the Republicans have been so long, and so persistently misrepresented, is now to be brought to a practical test, and placed beyond the possibility of doubt. Disunionists *per se,* are now in hot haste to get out of the Union, precisely because they perceive they can not, much longer, maintain apprehension among the Southern people that their homes, and firesides, and lives, are to be endangered by the action of the Federal Government. With such 'Now, or never' is the maxim." Naively, Lincoln added this closing thought: "I am rather glad of this military preparation in the South. It will enable the people the more easily to suppress any uprisings there, which their misrepresentations of purposes may have encouraged."[127]

The press identified Lincoln as the author of these sentiments, and the public reaction confirmed his view that he should remain silent. Although Republican journals praised the speech, opposition papers did not. To Henry J. Raymond, editor of the New York *Times,* Lincoln explained: "On the 20th. inst. Senator Trumbull made a short speech which I suppose you have both seen and approved. Has a single newspaper, heretofore against us, urged that speech [upon its readers] with a purpose to quiet public anxiety? Not one, so far as I know. On the contrary the Boston Courier, and its' class, hold me responsible for the speech, and endeavor to inflame the North with the belief that it foreshadows an abandonment of Republican ground by the incoming administration; while the Washington Constitution, and its' class hold the same speech up to the South as an open declaration of war against them. This is just as I expected, and just what would happen with any declaration I could make. These political fiends are not half sick enough yet. 'Party malice' and not 'public good' possesses them entirely. 'They seek a sign, and no sign shall be given them.'"[128]

According to Henry Villard, the South's reaction to Trumbull's speech convinced people in Springfield (presumably including Lincoln) that "disunion has been determined upon, and that it will be accomplished at all hazards." Almost all residents of the Illinois capital "have made up their minds to the certainty of the secession of South Carolina, and their apprehensions now centre in the question whether she will be followed by any other of the restive states. The ineffectiveness of Trumbull's effort precludes the probability of another definition of Mr. Lincoln's executive intentions in advance of the inaugural. A repetition of the attempt to pacify the South by mere words, without the additional guarantee of official acts, it is believed would prove equally fruitless, and perhaps be construed into a sign of fear and weakness."[129]

Criticizing Lincoln's silence, Democrats sneered that he was "nothing but a weak, prejudiced local politician" from "a retired country village in the interior of Illinois," a man of little understanding, "surrounded constantly by venal flatterers and breathing but one atmosphere . . . that created by the extreme and fanatical portion of his party."[130] In the draft of a speech he did not deliver, Lincoln explained his refusal to issue a public statement about the crisis: "During the present winter it has been greatly pressed upon me by many patriotic citizens . . . that I could in my position, by a word, restore peace to the country. But what word? I have many words already before the public; and my position was given me on the faith of those words. Is the desired word to be confirmatory of these; or must it be contradictory to them? If the former, it is useless repe[ti]tion; if the latter, it is dishonorable and treacherous. Again, it is urged as if the word must be spoken before the fourth of March. Why? Is the speaking the word a 'sine qua non' to the inaugeration? Is there a Bell-man, a Breckinridge-man, or a Douglas man, who would tolerate his own candidate to make such terms, had he been elected? Who amongst you would not die by the proposition, that your candidate, being elected, should be inaugerated, solely on the conditions of the constitution, and laws, or not at all." Lincoln denied that his silence was "a matter of mere personal honor."[131]

Lincoln's unwillingness to make a public declaration may have been a mistake. Such a document might have allayed fears in the Upper South and Border States and predisposed them to remain in the Union when hostilities broke out. But it might also have wrecked the Republican coalition and doomed his administration to failure before it began.

Lincoln did not issue formal statements before leaving Springfield in February, but he did make his views known in other ways. He sometimes spoke about the crisis with visitors, who then leaked his remarks to the press. "He receives all with winning affability, converses freely upon political topics, [and] does not hesitate to express his opinions thereon," according to one report.[132] But he would often qualify his remarks by saying that he hoped his callers "would bear in mind that he was not speaking as President, or for the President, but only exercising the privilege of talking which belonged to him, in common with private citizens." He also possessed "the faculty of checking and turning conversation, when it seems to be taking a direction not likely to suit him, and of barring by his mere manner rising inquiries which ought not to be put."[133]

Lincoln occasionally let his guard down. When a visitor speculated that disunionists would seize Washington before his inauguration if they were not appeased, he replied: "I will suffer death before I will consent or will advise my friends to consent to any concession or compromise which looks like buying the privilege of taking possession of this government to which we have a constitutional right; because, whatever I might think of the merit of the various propositions before Congress, I should regard any concession in the face of menace the destruction of the government itself, and a consent on all hands that our system shall be brought down to a level with the existing disorganized state of affairs in Mexico."[134] This strong statement was widely published by Northern newspapers, including the Chicago *Tribune* and the New York *Tribune,* both of which ran it daily below their mastheads. To a Missourian who urged him to support a "backdown declaration," Lincoln replied with emphasis that he "would sooner go out into his backyard & hang himself."[135] On February 8, making yet another allusion to suicide, he answered an old friend who asked him if he would stand by his 1858 speeches, by the Chicago platform, and by the Constitution: "I will die before I will depart from any of those things under threats made by traitors and secessionists under arms, defying the government. I can go out to my barn and hang myself for the good of my country; but to stultify myself, my party, the people, to buy from the traitors for the people what are the people's rights and dues, thus demoralizing the government and the Union, I shall never do it—*no, never.*" The friend to whom he made these remarks noted that Lincoln had "a dominant, ruling will on questions pertaining to the right, the just and the true."[136]

Lincoln also used journalists to broadcast his views. From November to February, Henry Villard of the New York *Herald* and Cincinnati *Commercial* reported almost daily from Springfield, often describing the opinion of "Springfield" or "the men at the capitol," which doubtless reflected the president-elect's thinking. Villard's dispatches were extensively reprinted. In addition, Lincoln continued his decades-long habit of writing for the Springfield *Illinois State Journal,* widely regarded as his mouthpiece. Major newspapers like the New York *Tribune* quoted the *Journal*'s editorials as an indicator of Lincoln's intentions. Lincoln occasionally granted formal interviews in which he discussed public affairs. His assistant personal secretary, John Hay, wrote anonymous dispatches for the *Missouri Democrat* reporting Lincoln's views.

As he followed events in the South, Lincoln conscientiously searched for precedents to guide him in shaping his response. According to Villard, Lincoln "is at all times surrounded by piles of standard works, to which constant reference is made. His strong desire for full and reliable information on all current topics renders it especially regretful to him, that circumstances debar him from obtaining anything but ex parte statements as to the progress of events in the South."[137]

Lincoln's imperfect sources of information about South Carolina cheered him up shortly before the state's secession convention met on December 17. He told a visitor he thought that "things have reached their worst point in the South, and they are likely to mend in the future. If it be true, as reported, that the South Carolinians do not intend to resist the collection of the revenue, after they ordain secession, there need be no collision with the federal government. The Union may still be maintained. The greatest inconvenience will arise from the want of federal courts; as with the present feeling, judges, marshals, and other officers could not be obtained." With moderation and good humor, he added that the charges the South made against the North "were so indefinite that they could not be regarded as sound. If they were well-defined, they could be fairly and successfully met. But they are so vague, that they cannot be long maintained by reasoning men even in the Southern States." He expressed some irritation with the New York *Tribune* and other newspapers which recommended that the erring sisters be allowed to depart in peace; such advice, said he, "was having a bad effect in some of the border States, especially in Missouri, where there was danger that it might alienate some of the best friends of the cause." There and in "some other States, where Republicanism has just begun to grow, and where there is still a strong pro-slavery party to contend with, there can be no advantage in taunting and bantering the South." Republican leaders in such areas "had urged him to use his influence with the journals referred to, and induce them to desist from their present tone towards the South." His caller reported that Lincoln "did not say he had promised to do this, and I only gathered from his manner and language that he would prefer to see the bantering tone abandoned." He had formed his opinion of the situation at the South, he cautioned, "after much study and thought; they were his views at the present time but were of course liable to be modified by his more mature judgment, after further information and further study of the progress of events."[138]

When news reached Springfield that South Carolina had officially seceded on December 20, it profoundly shook nearly everyone with the notable exception of Lincoln, who rather coolly quipped that "he would henceforth look for 'foreign inland news' in his dailies." Henry Villard concluded that "[t]imidity is evidently no element of his moral composition" and that "there are dormant qualities in 'Old Abe' which occasion will draw forth, develope and remind people to a certain degree of the characteristics of 'Old Hickory.'"[139] Herman Kreismann also thought Lincoln had "the notion of playing General Jackson."[140]

That fateful December day the *Illinois State Journal* ran a bellicose editorial that was thought to reflect Lincoln's views. South Carolina, it declared, "cannot get out of this Union until she conquers the Government. The revenues must be collected at her ports, and any resistance on her part will lead to war." A violation of the laws would compel the president to act. "The laws of the United States must be executed—the President has no discretionary power on the subject—his duty is emphatically pronounced in the Constitution. Mr. Lincoln will perform that duty. Disunion, by armed force, is TREASON, and treason must and will be put down at all hazards." Secessionists should understand that "the Republican party, that the great North, aided by hundreds of thousands of patriotic men in the slave States, have determined to preserve the Union—peaceably if they can, forcibly if they must."[141] The *Journal* ran equally strong editorials in the following weeks.

This should have come as no surprise, for the *Journal* had been publishing similar commentary for over a month and quoting the anti-secession speeches that Lincoln had delivered in Kansas a year earlier, including his statement that "if constitutionally we elect a President, and therefore you undertake to destroy the Union, it will be our duty to deal with you as old John Brown was dealt with. We can only do our duty."[142] One of the most prescient and hard-hitting editorials appeared on December 18 (probably by Lincoln), arguing that the Cotton States girded for war because "they know that the friends of Union and this Government will not yield up everything to an insolent, treasonable slave power without a struggle." Once the secessionists have defied the law, "the work of death will begin" and the North will be united against the South's rule-or-ruin stance. "We do not like to contemplate the results of civil war, but if the secessionists are determined to bring it about, it may be well enough to look it in the face." The first result would be "the total overthrow of slavery." Fugitive slaves from the Border States, which probably would not secede, will escape in droves to the North. Slaves in the Gulf States would rise up against their masters. "Who will say that an African Garibaldi may not even now be awaiting, with plan and arms prepared, the approaching hour? Burning dwellings—outraged, murdered wives and children, is a horrible, heart-rending picture. Yet to it we would direct the gaze of the madmen who are leading the Cotton States into rebellion against the best Government the world has ever witnessed." Through secession, Southerners would achieve nothing "but war and all the evils resulting from it." They "cannot gain peace nor security—they cannot gain territory—they cannot recover fugitives—they cannot blow out the moral lights that guide the Northern mind, and repress all sympathy for struggling bondsmen." Europe would not aid the secessionists. Territories would not be opened to them. The Fugitive Slave Act would not be enforced. "The North may lose much in life and property, but she will preserve the Government, and win the applause and admiration of the world."[143]

Events in Georgia strengthened Lincoln's hope that South Carolina's example would not be imitated. The disunionist governor of the Peach State, Joseph E. Brown, met stiff resistance from prominent leaders like Alexander H. Stephens, Herschel V. Johnson, and Benjamin H. Hill. Lincoln read Stephens's November 14 pro-Union speech before the Georgia Legislature with pleasure and requested a copy from its author. Stephens, who had been a friend and ally of Lincoln during his term in the House over a decade earlier, argued that since the Democrats would control Congress,

Lincoln could do little harm; that his mere election was no justification for rash action; and that secession should not be undertaken unless the federal government committed an aggressive act. Lincoln commented that "Mr. Stephens is a great man—he's a man that can get up a blaze whenever he's a mind to—his speech has got up a great blaze in Georgia—I never could get up a blaze more than once or twice in my life."[144] Privately, Stephens expressed admiration for Lincoln: "In point of merit as a man I have no doubt Lincoln is just as good, safe and sound a man as Mr. Buchanan, and would administer the Government so far as he is individually concerned just as safely for the South and as honestly and faithfully *in every particular.* I know the man well. He is not a bad man. He will make as good a President as Fillmore did and better too in my opinion. He has a great deal more practical common sense."[145] On November 30, Lincoln was "reported to have said that the best item of news he had received since the 6th of November was that of Mr. Stephens' election as delegate to the Georgia State Convention."[146] If that convention were to reject secession, the disunionist movement might collapse elsewhere. In December, Lincoln asked Stephens: "Do the people of the South really entertain fears that a Republican administration would, *directly, or indirectly,* interfere with their slaves, or with them, about their slaves? If they do, I wish to assure you, as once a friend, and still, I hope, not an enemy, that there is no cause for such fears. The South would be in no more danger in this respect, than it was in the days of Washington. I suppose, however, this does not meet the case. You think slavery is *right* and ought to be extended; while we think it is *wrong* and ought to be restricted. That I suppose is the rub. It certainly is the only substantial difference between us."[147]

Secessionists agreed, for they denounced the doctrines of the Republican Party rather than Lincoln himself. "There are no objections to him as a man, or as a citizen of the North," remarked James Henley Thornwell of the Presbyterian Theological Seminary in South Carolina. "He is probably entitled, in the private relations of life, to all the commendations which his friends have bestowed upon him."[148] Similarly, a leading North Carolina Unionist wrote: "It is not Lincoln—so far as he is concerned, he is taken but little in the account. There is but little bitterness of feeling against him individually. So far from it, he is regarded as neither a dangerous or a bad man. We have no fears, that he is going to attempt any great outrage upon us. We rather suppose his purpose will be to conciliate. But it is . . . the *fundamental idea,* that underlies the whole movement of his nomination, the canvass, & his election. It is the declaration of unceasing warfare against slavery as an institution, as enunciated by the Representative men of the party—the Sewards, & Wades, & Wilsons & Chases, & Sumners &c. &c. We Southern people, being warm-hearted, and candid, & impetuous if you please, are also confiding & credulous. When men of high position assert any thing seriously, we believe they are in earnest. And when the men who lead & direct the Republican party tell us, that they do not intend to pause in their work, till they have driven slavery off the American Continent—when Wilson tells us that the election of Lincoln has placed *our* necks under *their* heels—& Sumner tells us that Lincoln's election involves a change in the policy of the government—when we are thus notified beforehand, that we may expect a still more relentless war upon our property—I say when we see this, our people think it is time to have this dispute settled."[149]

Responses to Secession in Washington—Buchanan and Seward

In December, the nation turned its eyes toward Washington where Buchanan and Congress would confront the gathering storm. Lincoln felt quite anxious as he awaited the president's annual message. The weak, vacillating Old Public Functionary, as Buchanan was called, disappointed Lincoln and most other Northerners by proclaiming that, although secession was unconstitutional, the federal government could do nothing legally to stop it. The lame-duck president denounced the antislavery movement and blamed the crisis on the "long-continued and intemperate interference of the Northern people with the question of slavery in the Southern States."[150]

Lincoln was incensed at Buchanan's ascription of blame for the crisis to the anti-slavery forces rather than to the Southern fire-eaters. The *Illinois State Journal* denounced "the weak and delusive argument of Mr. Buchanan and his Attorney-General, that to execute the laws within a State is to 'coerce a State,' and that to protect the property of the United States from plunder and preserve the national flag from dishonor, is to 'make war on a sovereign State.' We would restore words to their honest use, and have the truth shine out that a State cannot secede, nor by any act of its Legislature or Convention, oust the Government of its jurisdiction; nor change its own relation or the relation of its citizens to the Government one jot or tittle; but if aggrieved must seek the remedy in the manner prescribed by the Constitution for its own amendment."[151]

When Buchanan's message was referred to a special House committee consisting of one member from each of the thirty-three states, Lincoln's fear of a split between radical and conservative Republicans grew. Such a committee, he thought, was too big and comprised of too many diverse elements. He was right; the committee, which wrangled throughout the winter, failed to reach a consensus. On December 13, its Republican members divided eight to eight on a motion acknowledging that the South's complaints were justified. The next day, Illinois Congressman William Kellogg assured the committee that Lincoln had no desire to touch slavery where it existed by law; that he supported the repeal of unconstitutional Personal Liberty Laws; and that he favored a just enforcement of the Fugitive Slave Act. To the delight of Democrats, Kellogg promised to introduce a measure providing that territories would be admitted to the Union with or without slavery in accordance with the wishes of their inhabitants. Along with Committee Chairman Thomas Corwin and Iowa Representative Samuel R. Curtis, Kellogg—but not Lincoln—had become an appeaser willing to abandon the Chicago Platform and adopt Stephen A. Douglas's popular sovereignty nostrum.

Dominating Congress that winter, Seward maneuvered desperately to keep the Union from breaking apart before Lincoln's inauguration. The senator viewed himself as a well-informed realist who must somehow save the nation from fire-eaters in the Deep South and naïve stiff-back Republicans like Lincoln who failed to understand the gravity of the crisis. He paid lip service to upholding the party's principles while urging his colleagues "to practice reticence and kindness."[152] Meanwhile, behind the scenes, he maneuvered to win concessions that might placate the South even if they violated the Chicago Platform. Privately (but not publicly), he supported the Critten-den Compromise. When James Barbour, a prominent Virginia Unionist, told him "frankly that nothing materially less than the Crittenden compromise" would sat-isfy the Old Dominion, Seward replied: "I am of your opinion that nothing short of that will allay the excitement, and therefore I will favor it substantially."[153] Seward was delighted to learn that the House Committee of Thirty-Three would contain pro-compromise Representatives, including his chief ally in the lower chamber, Charles Francis Adams. On December 18, the U.S. senate established a Committee of Thirteen, akin to the House Committee of Thirty-Three, and named Seward a member.

Alarmed by the ferocity of Deep South secessionists, many Republicans joined Seward in favoring conciliation. On December 5, North Carolina Representative John A. Gilmer reported that "the anxiety here from all quarters (except the Southern *fire eaters*) to preserve the Union, is intense. In fact the North seems inclined to yield everything to preserve the Union."[154] Gilmer exaggerated. To be sure, moves to intro-duce a Force Bill were squelched, but it remained unclear what further gestures the North was willing to make. Many appealed for sectional calm in vague terms. A con-stituent told John Sherman of Ohio that "the great mass desire the preservation of the Union, if that be possible without too great a sacrifice of principles."[155] How should "too great a sacrifice of principles" be defined? The Moderates looked to Lincoln for guidance. Congressman Elbridge G. Spaulding told Weed that if the president-elect would "lead off on some reasonable and practicable plan it would have great weight and decide the course of many who are now passive and in doubt as what should be done."[156] A Democratic member of the House Committee of Thirty-Three who fa-vored Weed's proposal to extend the Missouri Compromise line to California (allow-ing slavery to expand below the latitude of 36° 30') said, "Lincoln must soar above party ties & party fealty."[157]

Pressure by Lincoln to Resist Appeasement

In mid-December, the House committee almost adopted Weed's scheme, but it failed thanks largely to Lincoln's behind-the-scenes intervention. Believing Weed's plan contained "too great a sacrifice of principles," Lincoln adamantly opposed it. Slavery, he insisted, must not be allowed to expand. Twelve years earlier, he, along with the overwhelming majority of Northern congressmen, had voted against extending the Missouri Compromise line to the Pacific coast. In 1859, he had told Republicans: "Never forget that we have before us this whole matter of the right or wrong of slavery in this Union, though the immediate question is as to its spreading out into new Ter-ritories and States."[158] The symbolic significance of the issue of slavery in the territo-ries as well as its practical implications dominated Lincoln's thinking in the winter of 1860–1861. On December 6, he wrote to Congressman Kellogg, Illinois's representa-tive on the Committee of Thirty-Three, who had asked him for guidance: "Entertain no proposition for a compromise in regard to the *extension* of slavery. The instant you do, they have us under again; all our labor is lost, and sooner or later must be done over. Douglas is sure to be again trying to bring in his 'Pop. Sov.' Have none of it. The tug has to come & better now than later. You know I think the fugitive slave clause of the constitution ought to be enforced—to put it on the mildest form, ought not to be resisted."[159] (He assured a Kentucky Democrat that the Fugitive Slave Law "will be better administered under my Administration than it ever has been under that of my predecessors.")[160] Two days thereafter Lincoln urged Congressman E. B. Washburne to "[p]revent, as far as possible, any of our friends from demoralizing themselves, and our cause, by entertaining propositions for compromise of any sort, on 'slavery exten-tion.' There is no possible compromise upon it, but which puts us under again, and leaves all our work to do over again. Whether it be a Mo. line, or Eli Thayer's Pop. Sov. it is all the same. Let either be done, & immediately filibustering and extending slavery recommences. On that point hold firm, as with a chain of steel."[161] On De-cember 10, Lincoln wrote Trumbull in the same vein: "Let there be no compromise on the question of *extending* slavery. If there be, all our labor is lost, and, ere long, must be done again. The dangerous ground—that into which some of our friends have a hankering to run—is Pop. Sov. Have none of it. Stand firm. The tug has to come, & better now, than any time hereafter."[162] A week later he reiterated to Trumbull his firm stance: "If any of our friends do prove false, and fix up a compromise on the ter-ritorial question, I am for fighting again."[163] The following day he told John D. De-frees of Indiana: "I am sorry any republican inclines to dally with Pop. Sov. of any sort. It acknowledges that slavery has equal rights with liberty, and surrenders all we have contended for. Once fastened on us as a settled policy, filibustering for all South of us, and making slave states of it, follows in spite of us, with an early Supreme court decision, holding our free-state constitutions to be unconstitutional."[164] When Penn-sylvania Governor-elect Andrew G. Curtin asked his advice about what to say in his inaugural address, Lincoln counseled that he should make clear "without passion, threat, or appearance of boasting, but nevertheless, with firmness, the purpose of yourself, and your State to maintain the Union at all hazzards."[165]

These letters were private, but the public learned of Lincoln's firmness from news-paper reports suggesting that he would not be intimidated by the prospect of war. On December 12, the New York *Herald* spoke of his hard-line position. Intimate friends, evidently reflecting his views, declared "that peaceable secession was a matter of abso-lute impossibility." They asserted "that even though coercion were not employed by the federal government, a conflict would be made inevitable by the improbability of an agreement upon the terms of the separation between the two sections of the country. Secession and civil war were evidently thought contemporaneous contingencies by the parties in question. Reconciliation on the basis of Northern concessions was scouted with much vehemence; although aggression was deprecated, collision was confidently predicted." At the same time, Lincoln "took no pains to conceal his indignation" at reports that Western merchants were being molested by Southern mobs.[166]

Editorials in the *Illinois State Journal*, widely viewed as reflecting Lincoln's opin-ion, also rejected appeasement. "We feel indignant, sometimes," said the *Journal* on

December 17, "when we hear timid Republicans counseling an abandonment, in part, of Republican grounds. We are asking for nothing that is not clearly right. We have done nothing wrong—we have nothing to apologize for—nothing to take back, as a party. We have fought a hard battle—we have come out victorious, and shall we now call back the routed, flying enemy, and basely surrender all that we have gained? Never!"[167] (Henry Villard called this editorial proof of Lincoln's "growing mettle.")[168]

No concession would satisfy the South, Lincoln argued. "Give them Personal Liberty bills & they will pull in the slack, hold on & insist on the border state Compromise—give them that, they'll again pull in the slack & demand Crit[tenden]'s Compr[omise]—that pulled in, they will want all that So[uth] Carolina asks."[169] Lincoln's pessimism was well founded: it is not clear that any compromise was possible. A New York Republican observed that "Lincoln was right . . . when he said in his Cooper Institute speech that the *only* thing that will satisfy them at all is for us to *think* as they do about slavery and *act* accordingly. This we *cannot* do—if we pretended to do it they would give us no credit for sincerity & would be right in not doing it. If any *less* is offered it only subjects [us] to the disgrace of failure."[170] A congressman from Vermont concurred, predicting that nothing "short of legalizing and introducing slavery in the North would satisfy" the Cotton States.[171] On December 13, before serious efforts to avert civil war were undertaken in Washington, thirty Southern members of Congress stated that "argument is exhausted. All hope of relief in the Union, through the agency of committees, Congressional legislation, or constitutional amendments, is extinguished. . . . We are satisfied the honor, safety, and independence of the Southern people are to be found only in a Southern Confederacy."[172] That same day, Alabama Congressman David Clopton wrote in a similar vein to a friend: "The argument is exhausted, further remonstrance is dishonorable, hesitation is dangerous, delay is submission, 'to your tents, O Israel!' and let the God of battles decide the issue."[173] These deeply held convictions made it unlikely that concessions of any kind would have persuaded the Deep South to return voluntarily.

While privately refusing to support the Crittenden Compromise, Lincoln continued to balk at issuing a public statement. When catechized by North Carolina Congressman John A. Gilmer, a strong Unionist, he replied: "Is it desired that I shall shift the ground upon which I have been elected? I can not do it. You need only to acquaint yourself with that ground, and press it on the attention of the South. It is all in print and easy of access. May I be pardoned if I ask whether even you have ever attempted to procure the reading of the Republican platform, or my speeches, by the Southern people? If not, what reason have I to expect that any additional production of mine would meet a better fate? It would make me appear as if I repented for the crime of having been elected, and was anxious to apologize and beg forgiveness. To so represent me, would be the principal use made of any letter I might now thrust upon the public. My old record cannot be so used; and that is precisely the reason that some new declaration is so much sought." He assured Gilmer that he had "no thought of recommending the abolition of slavery in the District of Columbia, nor the slave trade among the slave states." Even if he "were to make such recommendation, it is quite clear Congress would not follow it." He would not employ slaves in arsenals and dockyards, nor would he use political litmus tests in appointing officials in areas of the South with few Republicans. In sum, he concluded, "I never have been, am not now, and probably never shall be, in a mood of harassing the people, either North or South. On the territorial question, I am inflexible. . . . On that, there is a difference between you and us; and it is the only substantial difference. You think slavery is right and ought to be extended; we think it is wrong and ought to be restricted. For this, neither has any just occasion to be angry with the other." He claimed that he had never read any of the Personal Liberty Laws, but he pledged that he would be glad to see their repeal if they violated the Constitution. Yet he "could hardly be justified, as a citizen of Illinois, or as President of the United States, to recommend the repeal of a statute of Vermont, or South Carolina."[174]

Lincoln was doubtless correct in thinking that no statement would placate the Deep South. The editors of the Charleston *Mercury* had announced that even if he were "to come out and declare that he held sacred every right of the South, with respect to African slavery, no one should believe him; and, if he was believed, his professions should not have the least influence on the course of the South."[175]

Lincoln's legendary patience wore thin as disunionists continued to misrepresent him. He declared that the South "has eyes but does not see, and ears but does not hear."[176] William C. Smedes, president of the Southern Railroad Company of Mississippi, claimed that the president-elect "holds the black man to be the equal of the white," "stigmatizes our whole people as immoral & unchristian," and made "infamous & unpatriotic avowals . . . on the presentation of a pitcher by some free negroes to Gov: Chase of Ohio." When Henry J. Raymond forwarded these allegations, Lincoln replied heatedly: "What a very mad-man your correspondent, Smedes is. Mr. Lincoln is not pledged to the ultimate extinctinction of slavery; does not hold the black man to be the equal of the white, unqualifiedly as Mr. S. states it; and never did stigmatize their white people as immoral & unchristian; and Mr. S. can not prove one of his assertions true. Mr. S. seems sensitive on the questions of morals and christianity. What does he think of a man who makes charges against another which he does not know to be true, and could easily learn to be false? As to the pitcher story, it is a forgery out and out. I never made but one speech in Cincinnati. . . . I have never yet seen Gov. Chase. I was never in a meeting of negroes in my life; and never saw a pitcher presented by anybody to anybody."[177]

Lincoln told another Mississippian, E. D. Ray, that "if the Southern States concluded upon a contingent secession, that is, upon awaiting aggressive acts on the part of his Administration, they would never go out of the Union."[178] The president-elect handed Ray a copy of his 1858 debates with Douglas and assured him: "You will find that the only difference between you and me is, that I think slavery wrong, and you think it right; that I am opposed to its extension, while you advocate it; and that as to the security of the institution and the protection of slave property in the States where it has a lawful existence, you will find it as great under my administration as it ever was under that of Mr. Buchanan." When Lincoln expressed the hope that Southerners were not fearful that he would hurt them, Ray replied: "No we ain't."[179] Yet another caller from the Magnolia State came away from an interview with the president-elect admitting that "the idea of 'raw head and bloody bones'—the beast with 'seven heads and ten horns' at once passed from his mind." He wished all his people could see Lincoln, for the "mere sight of him would drive secession out of the heart of every honest Southerner."[180] Similarly, a muscular Virginian declared after an interview, "Lincoln is a fine man; he will never intentionally harm any one."[181] To an Illinois Democrat born in the Old Dominion, Lincoln expressed "cordial sentiments toward the people of Virginia."[182] When a South Carolina woman exclaimed to him, "you look, act, and speak like a humane, kind and benevolent man!" he asked in reply: "Did you take me for a savage, madam?"[183]

Resisting the Crittenden Compromise

Back in Washington, Seward, sensing that his original strategy was not working, decided to take the offensive. Fertile in expedients, he dispatched Weed to Springfield to lobby the president-elect on behalf of the Crittenden Compromise. Perhaps Lincoln could yet be persuaded to back the Kentucky senator's solution to the sectional crisis. Lord Thurlow pressured Lincoln to support the Crittenden plan, which the Albany *Evening Journal* was touting. That paper had just reiterated its call for the extension of the Missouri Compromise line and declared that it was "*almost* prepared to say, that Territories may be safely left to take care of themselves; and that, when they contain a Population which . . . entitles them to a Representative in Congress, they may come into the Union with State Governments of their own framing."[184] In Albany it was believed that this editorial reflected Seward's views, for as the senator himself once remarked: "Seward is Weed and Weed is Seward. What I do, Weed approves. What he says, I endorse. We are one."[185] Seward made no attempt to dissociate himself from Weed's editorial, which the president-elect termed "a heavy broadside." Lincoln told its author: "You have opened your fire at a critical moment, aiming at friends and foes alike. It will do some good or much mischief. Will the Republicans in New York sustain you in this view of the question?" Weed said he would press his case even if it remained unpopular. Lincoln optimistically replied "that while there were some loud threats and much muttering in the cotton States, he hoped that by wisdom and forbearance the danger of serious trouble might be averted, as such dangers had been in former times."[186] He strenuously rejected the proposal to restore the Missouri Compromise line, and he then gave Weed the following resolutions to pass along to Seward for submission to Congress:

> That the fugitive slave clause of the Constitution ought to be enforced by a
>   law of Congress, with efficient provisions for that object, not obliging
>   private persons to assist in it's execution, but punishing all who resist it,
>   and with the usual safeguards to liberty, securing free men against
>   being surrendered as slaves
> That all state laws, if there be such, really, or apparently, in conflict with
>   such law of Congress, ought to be repealed; and no opposition to the
>   execution of such law of Congress ought to be made
> That the Federal Union must be preserved.

Lincoln felt that these resolutions "would do much good, if introduced and unanamously supported by our friends."[187] Weed was instructed to show them to Senators

Hamlin and Trumbull and, if they approved, to have them introduced in Congress.

Another visitor to Springfield in late December urged Lincoln to endorse the Crittenden Compromise. Duff Green, a prominent Democrat who had served in Andrew Jackson's kitchen cabinet and whose wife was distantly related to Mary Todd Lincoln, traveled to Illinois to persuade the president-elect to lobby Congress on behalf of the Kentucky senator's plan, which was languishing without his support. Green first spoke with President Buchanan, who suggested that he enlist Lincoln's aid. On December 28, Green and Lincoln conversed at length; the president-elect said of the Crittenden resolutions "that he believed that the adoption of the [Missouri Compromise] line proposed would quiet *for the present* the agitation of the Slavery question, but believed it would be renewed by the seizure and attempted annexation of Mexico.—He said that the real question at issue between the North & the South, was Slavery 'propagandism' and that upon that issue the republican party was opposed to the South and that he was with his own party; that he had been elected by that party and intended to sustain his party in good faith, but added that the question of the Amendments to the Constitution and the questions submitted by Mr. Crittenden, belonged to the people & States in legislatures or Conventions & that he would be inclined not only to acquiesce, but give full force and effect to their will thus expressed." Green proposed that Lincoln write him a letter referring the measure to the attention of the states.[188]

Lincoln did prepare such a document, in which he bluntly declared: "I do not desire any amendment of the Constitution. Recognizing, however, that questions of such amendment rightfully belong to the American People, I should not feel justified, nor inclined, to withhold from them, if I could, a fair opportunity of expressing their will thereon, through either of the modes prescribed in the instrument. In addition I declare that the maintainance inviolate of the rights of the States, and especially the right of each state to order and control its own domestic institutions according to its own judgment exclusively, is essential to that balance of powers on which the perfection, and endurance of our political fabric depends—and I denounce the lawless invasion, by armed force, of the soil of any State or Territory, no matter under what pretext, as the gravest of crimes. I am greatly averse to writing anything for the public at this time; and I consent to the publication of this, only upon the condition that six of the twelve United States Senators for the States of Georgia, Alabama, Mississippi, Louisiana, Florida, and Texas shall sign their names to what is written on this sheet below my name, and allow the whole to be published together."[189] Instead of giving this document to Green, Lincoln sent it to Trumbull with instructions to pass it on to Green only if it seemed likely to do no harm. Trumbull evidently decided not to forward it.

Others, including Edward Bates and a wealthy New York businessman and Republican activist, James H. van Alen, also pressed Lincoln to back the Crittenden Compromise. In a speech that he penned sometime before February 12 but did not deliver, Lincoln explained why he rejected that advice: "I so refused, not from any party wantonness, nor from any indifference to the troubles of the country. I thought

such refusal was demanded by the view that if, when a Chief Magistrate is constitutionally elected, he cannot be inaugurated till he betrays those who elected him, by
breaking his pledges, and surrendering to those who tried and failed to defeat him at
the polls, this government and all popular government is already at an end. Demands
for such surrender, once recognized, are without limit, as to nature, extent and repetition. They break the only bond of faith between public and public servant; and they
distinctly set the minority over the majority. I presume there is not a man in America,
(and there ought not to be one) who opposed my election, who would, for a moment,
tolerate his own candidate in such surrender, had he been successful in the election.
In such case they would all see, that such surrender would not be merely the ruin of a
man, or a party; but, as a precedent, would be the ruin of the government itself. I do
not deny the possibility that the people may err in an election; but if they do, the true
cure is in the next election; and not in the treachery of the party elected."[190]

In January, Crittenden attempted to have the senate approve his plan even without the endorsement of the Committee of Thirteen, which had turned it down on
December 22. He tacked on two constitutional amendments suggested by Stephen A.
Douglas: that free blacks in the states and territories be denied the right to vote or
hold office and that free blacks be colonized to Africa or South America at federal
expense. (Why the Little Giant made those proposals is unclear, for Southerners did
not want them. It suggests that the racist demagoguery he had long practiced may
have reflected his true personal feelings. It is noteworthy that in supporting the Crittenden Compromise, Douglas abandoned popular sovereignty, an indication that his
devotion to principle was shallow.) Crittenden moved that this altered version of his
plan be submitted to a national plebiscite. When Pennsylvania Congressman James
T. Hale suggested to Lincoln a compromise like Crittenden's revised proposal, he
patiently explained why he opposed extending the Missouri Compromise line: "We
have just carried an election on principles fairly stated to the people. Now we are told
in advance, the government shall be broken up, unless we surrender to those we have
beaten, before we take the offices. In this they are either attempting to play upon us,
or they are in dead earnest. Either way, if we surrender, it is the end of us, and of the
government. They will repeat the experiment upon us *ad libitum*. A year will not pass,
till we shall have to take Cuba as a condition upon which they will stay in the Union.
They now have the Constitution, under which we have lived over seventy years, and
acts of Congress of their own framing, with no prospect of their being changed; and
they can never have a more shallow pretext for breaking up the government, or ex-
torting a compromise, than now. There is, in my judgment, but one compromise
which would really settle the slavery question, and that would be a prohibition against
acquiring any more territory."[191]

Many Republicans shared Lincoln's belief that slaveholders fully intended to have
the country expand southwards and that Northern Democrats supported them. William J. Gregg of Paris, Illinois, predicted that if the Crittenden Compromise were
adopted, "the democracy in company with the disunionists will commence their filibustering for the acquisition of Cuba, Mexico, South America etc."[192] Throughout the
1850s, Douglas had been calling for the annexation of Cuba, and in 1854 the Ostend

Manifesto—which warned Spain that if she did not sell that island to the United States, Americans had every right to seize it—made clear that he was not alone. The Democratic Party supported the acquisition of Cuba and an aggressive Caribbean foreign policy. "*We* shall have an empire sufficiently large for *our* purposes and for empire during the next hundred years," predicted the Charleston *Mercury.* "In the meantime, we shall colonize Texas throughout, and Chihuahua [Mexico] and a few more good Southern States. We shall have all the Gulf country when once we have shaken ourselves free of the Puritans." A Georgia editor scouted the argument that the Confederacy's expansion southward could be thwarted by Indians, Spaniards, blacks, or Creoles, "for the dominant race will supplant all others, and slavery will expand South to Brazil, and from her till stopped by snow. It may be an evil, but like cholera, no power can check it but frost."[193] Lincoln's argument was no mere straw man but reflected his genuine belief that to accept the Crittenden Compromise would strengthen the expansionists' hand, with potentially dire consequences for the cause of freedom.

Lincoln's emphatic opposition to the Crittenden Compromise was partly responsible for its defeat in the Committee of Thirteen on December 22 and in the senate on January 16. On the day of the first vote, Charles Francis Adams observed that the "declarations coming almost openly from Mr Lincoln have had the effect of perfectly consolidating the Republicans."[194] Senator Henry Wilson reported that some congressional Republicans "are weak; most of them are firm. Lincoln's firmness helps our weak ones."[195]

It was one of Lincoln's most fateful decisions, for the Kentucky senator's scheme, though fraught with many practical problems and silent on the constitutionality of secession and the right of a legally-elected president to govern, represented the best hope of placating the Upper South and thus possibly averting war, though it was a forlorn hope at best, given Southern intransigence. The House Committee of Thirty-Three might have approved Crittenden's plan, which Conditional Unionists of the Upper South regarded as the bare minimum for remaining in the Union, if the Democrats had not insisted that slavery be protected south of the 36° 30′ line in all future acquisitions as well as in territory already belonging to the United States. Though senate Republicans rejected the compromise, it still could have passed the upper house on January 16 if three of the six Southern senators in attendance had voted for it instead of abstaining. Similarly, on December 22 if two abstaining Democratic senators on the Committee of Thirteen had voted for the compromise, it would have received the endorsement of that body. In light of these facts, Duff Green's allegation that the Civil War was the result of Lincoln's refusal to back the Crittenden Compromise hardly seems warranted.

Stiff-backed Republicans cheered Lincoln's course. Carl Schurz told his wife that the president-elect "stands firm as an oak" and that "his determination has communicated itself to the timid members of the party."[196] After visiting Springfield in early January, Indiana Congressman George W. Julian reported that he was "quite captivated" by Lincoln. "He is *right*," Julian told a friend. "His backbone is pronounced good by the best judges."[197] Julian's father-in-law, the old antislavery warhorse Joshua Giddings, came away from an interview with the president-elect convinced that "he intends doing *right* and will act according to the dictates of his conscience" and "in the most perfect good faith endeavor to carry out the doctrines of the Republican platform."[198] Missouri Congressman Frank Blair met with Lincoln and said that he was "as firm as the rock of ages" and that he "will live up to the principles on which he was elected."[199] The leading senate Radical, Charles Sumner, was optimistic about defeating compromise proposals because "Lincoln stands firm. *I know it*."[200] Sumner's ally and future biographer, Edward L. Pierce, rejoiced "to learn that Lincoln is stiffening the backs of our men."[201] Not every Radical agreed. Charles Henry Ray, who called Lincoln "patriotic and honest," nonetheless thought that "more *iron* would do him no harm."[202]

Lincoln could not be aware that his rejection of the Crittenden plan would necessarily help pave the road to war. He believed that if he were conciliatory on all matters other than slavery expansion and secession, the Upper South and the Border States would remain in the Union and that the Deep South, after a sober second thought, might return to the fold. In retrospect, that seems like wishful thinking, but it was not unreasonable, given the size of the Bell and Douglas vote in the South and other indications that disunionism enjoyed only limited popularity there. On April 6, the eminent author John Pendleton Kennedy of Baltimore observed that "there is great reason to doubt, if the people of Louisiana, or Texas or Georgia are actually in favor of the secession." Moreover, he noted, Unionism prevailed in northern Alabama, Arkansas, and the Border States. The South Carolina secession ordinance had not been submitted to the voters for ratification; the same held true for five of the six other Cotton states—Florida, Alabama, Mississippi, Georgia, and Louisiana—which followed suit that winter. (Texas was the sole exception.) In February the voters of Virginia, North Carolina, Arkansas, and Tennessee decisively rejected secession. In Kentucky, Delaware, Maryland, and Missouri, disunion efforts also fizzled. Even in the Deep South, Unionism was hardly extinct. In January, Georgia's immediate secessionists barely won a majority of the votes cast; in the subsequent convention, they carried a crucial motion by the narrow margin of 166 to 130. In Louisiana and Alabama, disunionist candidates did not win by landslides. In fact, fair plebiscites in those three states may well have revealed that immediate secessionists were in the minority. Lincoln said that it "was probably true" that the Louisiana secession ordinance "was adopted against the will of a majority of the people."[203] (It should be borne in mind, however, that the "cooperationists," those who resisted secession on a state-by-state basis rather than collectively, were not necessarily Unionists but moderate rather than radical secessionists.) It was widely believed that many secessionists had no intention of leaving the Union permanently but simply wanted to strengthen their bargaining position in negotiations with the North, hoping to extort concessions through a temporary withdrawal.

If Lincoln overestimated the depth and extent of Southern Unionism, secessionists underestimated Northern resolve to resist their scheme. Misleading them were conservative newspapers like the Detroit *Free Press*, which that winter warned Republicans that "if the refusal to repeal the personal liberty laws shall be persisted in, and if there shall not be a change in the present seeming purpose to yield to no accommodation of national difficulties, and if troops shall be raised in the North to march against the people of the South, a fire in the rear will be opened on such troops which will either stop their march altogether or wonderfully accelerate it."[204] Ohio Congressman Clement L. Vallandigham declared that he would shoulder arms to fend off an attack on his state but not to invade the South. After hostilities began, the New Orleans *Bee* acknowledged that such reassurances "completely deceived" thousands of Southerners. "There is no doubt whatever," said the editors, "that an opinion prevailed among us that if Lincoln should attempt to make war upon the South, the conservative element in the North would overwhelm his administration, and by timely diversions would extend aid and succor to us."[205]

Lincoln may have anticipated that war would follow the rejection of the Crittenden Compromise, but he might also have reckoned that the Upper South and Border States would assist in putting down Cotton State rebels. An editorial in the *Illinois State Journal,* perhaps by the president-elect, argued that the Deep South had different economic interests from the other Slave States. Secession "would certainly render the recapture of fugitive slaves utterly impossible when they had once crossed the northern border," and thus "slave property would at once become a hundred fold more precarious than it is now," especially in those states close to the Ohio River and the Mason-Dixon line. Moreover, the Upper South and the Border States had reason to fear that the Cotton States might reopen the African slave trade, thus drastically reducing the price of their most lucrative export, slaves. "We are of opinion, therefore, that it will be entirely safe for the Free States, who are perfectly united in their attachment to the Union and the Constitution as it is, to abide by that, make no alterations in it, and no compromise of its principles. We also incline to the belief that the great body of the border Slave States are pretty much of the same opinion, and at all events, doubtful whether they would gain anything by tinkering at the Constitution. If the Cotton States are not satisfied with this, as it appears they are not, and persist in their mad schemes of secession—the General Government will of course have to do its duty, and see that the Constitution and laws are faithfully observed in South Carolina as well as in Massachusetts. And if any extra force is needed for this purpose, we think that the border Slave States, whose tranquility and interests are more imperiled than those of any other part of the country, are just as likely to furnish it as any other part of the Union."[206]

By the same token, many Southerners misjudged Northern economic divisions. The New Orleans *Bee* pointed out that there "were not wanting among us . . . numbers of shrewd and experienced citizens who calculated largely on the commercial ties and identity of interests between the South and West, and who believed that ultimately Ohio, Indiana, and other States in that quarter would be glad to unite their destinies with those of a Southern Confederacy."[207] This view was not entirely confined to the South. An Ohio legislator predicted that his state and its neighbors "will never consent that the mouth of the Miss. River shall be held by a foreign power. In case of a rupture between the Slave and free States All our pecuniary interests will drive us in Ohio with the South. We cannot afford to pay Tariff[s] to keep up eastern manufacturers alone."[208]

Others argued that economic considerations would impel Midwesterners to crush any Southern rebellion. An Illinois Democratic congressman boldly declared that he would prefer "war for five hundred years, rather than the exclusion of the people of the Upper Mississippi from the unshackled navigation of that river to its mouth."[209]

Lincoln doubtless shared the widespread, misguided belief that if war broke out, it would be short and relatively bloodless.

"What If I Appoint Cameron, Whose Very Name Stinks in the Nostrils of the People for His Corruption?"

Cabinet-Making in Springfield
(1860–1861)

As he struggled with the thorny problem of secession, Lincoln faced a related challenge: selecting a cabinet. Should he take a Southerner from either the Democratic or Constitutional Unionist parties? Many Republican conciliators urged him to appoint at least one of them to his cabinet. He was not averse to the suggestion, telling Herndon "that he wanted to give the South, by way of placation, a place in his cabinet; that a fair division of the country entitled the Southern States to a reasonable representation there."[1] But who? Among the Republicans, should he select only ex-Whigs, or should he form a coalition government including ex-Democrats? Should he favor the Conservatives, the Moderates, or the Radicals? The day after the election he had tentatively chosen his department chiefs, but six weeks later he complained that "the making of a cabinet, now that he had it to do, was by no means as easy as he had supposed." He believed "that while the population of the country had immensely increased, really great men were scarcer than they used to be."[2]

Throughout the long weeks from the election until his departure from Springfield in February 1861, callers besieged Lincoln offering advice about the cabinet. As one of them observed, "he is troubled," for "every name he mentions in connection with [the] Cabinet brings to Springfield an army of Patriotic Individuals protesting against this or that man[']s appointment."[3] To his old friend, Illinois attorney Joseph Gillespie, Lincoln expressed the desire to "take all you lawyers down there with me, Democrats and Republicans alike, and make a Cabinet out of you. I believe I could construct one that would save the country, for then I would know every man and where he would fit. I tell you, there are some Illinois Democrats, whom I know well, that I would rather trust than a Republican I would have to learn, for I'll have no time to study the lesson."[4]

Lincoln, unlike many executives, had no fear of surrounding himself with strong-willed subordinates who might overshadow him. When advised not to appoint Salmon P. Chase to a cabinet post because the Ohioan regarded himself as "a great deal bigger" than the president-elect, Lincoln asked: "Well, do you know of any other men who think they are bigger than I am? I want to put them all in my cabinet."[5] He included every major competitor at the Chicago Convention in his cabinet, a decision that required unusual self-confidence, a quality misunderstood by some, including his assistant personal secretary, John Hay. Deeming modesty "the most fatal and most unsympathetic of vices" and the "bane of genius, the chain-and-ball of enterprise," Hay argued that it was "absurd to call him a modest man."[6] But Hay was projecting onto his boss his own immodesty. Lincoln was, in fact, both remarkably modest and self-confident, and he had no need to surround himself with sycophants dependent on him for political preferment. Instead he chose men with strong personalities, large egos, and politically significant followings whose support was necessary for the administration's success.

Initial Appointments

Seward's stature as a leading exponent of Republican principles virtually guaranteed that he would be named secretary of state. Though physically unprepossessing, he had a powerful personality and a keen intellect. His small body contrasted with his enormous head, which featured deep-set eyes, a huge Roman nose, a wide, deep forehead, and a receding chin. Henry Adams limned him memorably as "a slouching, slender figure" with "a head like a wise macaw; a beaked nose; shaggy eyebrows; unorderly hair and clothes; hoarse voice; offhand manner; free talk, and perpetual cigar."[7] He charmed friend and foe alike. One of his bitterest enemies in the Lincoln administration, Montgomery Blair, called him "a kindly man in his social relations" who "had a warm and sympathetic feeling for all that pertained to his domestic life." Blair "always found his society attractive" because of the "freshness and heartiness in his manner" and his humorous conversation.[8] William Howard Russell of the London *Times* deemed Seward "a subtle, quick man, rejoicing in power" and "fond of badinage, bursting with the importance of state mysteries."[9] Although he got off to a rocky start with Lincoln, the two men became close friends. The president valued Seward's wit, charm, bonhomie, and competence.

Lincoln offered Seward the State Department portfolio on December 8 after some elaborate preliminary maneuvering. Weed attempted to inveigle the president-elect into calling on the senator at his Auburn home, just as William Henry Harrison before his inauguration in 1841 had conferred with Henry Clay at Clay's Kentucky estate. When Lincoln refused to follow Harrison's example, Weed tried to persuade him to meet with Seward in Chicago; Lincoln rejected that proposal as well.

Lincoln may have been reluctant to meet in Chicago because he wanted to avoid a repetition of the disagreeable experience he had had there in late November while discussing cabinet appointments with Hannibal Hamlin. Chicago's local elite had ridiculed him and his wife for their unsophisticated ways, and when he was back in Springfield, he complained about the social whirl he had endured in the metropolis. Henry Villard reported from the Illinois capital that Lincoln's description "of the dinner and other parties, and the Sunday school meetings he had to attend—of the crowds of [the] curious that importuned him at all hours of the day, of the public levees he was obliged to hold, &c., &c., was graphic. It seems that instead of enjoying rest and relief, as expected, he was even more molested than in this place. If people only knew his holy horror of public ovations, they would probably treat him more sparingly. To be lugged around from place to place to satisfy the curiosity of the populace, is a doubtful mode of bestowing honor and rendering homage, &c. Mr. Lincoln's experience at Chicago in this respect will probably deter him from undertaking another journey previous to his final departure for Washington City."[10]

Although Lincoln found the Chicago ordeal disagreeable, he nonetheless treated callers there with his usual courtesy. When the eminent Presbyterian pastor Theodore L. Cuyler visited him at his hotel, he enjoyed a hospitable reception. "His manner is exceedingly genial," Cuyler wrote. "He grasped my hand warmly—put me at ease by a cordial recognition."[11]

In Chicago, amid all the distractions (including office-seekers who fastened on to him like ticks to a dog), Lincoln managed to accomplish his primary goal of launching the cabinet search in consultation with Hamlin, who had earlier met with Weed. At that time Weed had argued that Seward deserved the State Department portfolio but predicted he would decline it. Lincoln instructed Hamlin to divine Seward's true intentions. (At Lincoln's request, Hamlin burned the president-elect's letters about this project.) Lincoln wanted to appoint the New Yorker because of "his ability, his integrity, and his commanding influence, and fitness for the place." He also considered it "a matter of duty to the party, and to Mr. Seward[']s many and strong friends, while at the same time it accorded perfectly with his own personal inclinations—notwithstanding some opposition on the part of sincere and warm friends."[12] Seward did indeed enjoy great prestige, not only among Republicans but also among Northern Democrats.

But opposition to Seward was strong. Especially hostile were the Barnburners (ex-Democrats in New York who opposed slavery more vehemently than did most ex-Whigs). When Trumbull reported that many anticorruption leaders in New York objected to the Sage of Auburn, Lincoln said that he regretted "exceedingly the anxiety of our friends in New-York," but it seemed that "the sentiment in that state which sent a united delegation to Chicago in favor of Gov. S[eward] ought not, and must not be snubbed, as it would be by the omission to offer Gov. S. a place in the cabinet. I will, myself, take care of the question of 'corrupt jobs' and see that justice is done to all."[13]

On December 8, Lincoln sent Hamlin two letters to deliver to Seward, one a brief, formal offer of the State Department portfolio, the other a longer, more personal appeal. After consulting with Trumbull, the Maine senator called on Seward in Washington. Seward began the interview protesting, perhaps sincerely, that "he was tired of public life," that he "intended to resign his seat or decline a reelection and retire," and that "there was no place in the gift of the President which he would be willing to take." Hamlin then presented the letters offering Seward the State Department post. In them, Lincoln tactfully stated that "Rumors have got into the newspapers to the effect that the [State] Department . . . would be tendered you, as a compliment, and with the expectation that you would decline it. I beg you to be assured that I have said nothing to justify these rumors. On the contrary, it has been my purpose, from the day of the nomination at Chicago, to assign you, by your leave, this place in the administration. I have delayed so long to communicate that purpose, in deference to what appeared to me to be a proper caution in the case. Nothing has been developed to change my view in the premises; and I now offer you the place, in the hope that you will accept it, and with the belief that your position in the public eye, your integrity, ability, learning, and great experience, all combine to render it an appointment pre-eminently fit to be made."[14] This letter seems to have reflected Lincoln's true feelings.

Seward, whose extensive travels abroad and service on the Senate Foreign Relations Committee prepared him well for the job, responded cautiously: "This is remarkable, Mr. Hamlin. I will consider the matter, and, in accordance with Mr. Lincoln's request give him my decision at the earliest practicable moment."[15] Seward delayed responding in the hopes that Weed's late-December mission to Springfield regarding the Crittenden Compromise might succeed.

Having failed to win Lincoln's backing for the Crittenden Compromise, Seward hoped to persuade him to appoint conciliators rather than stiff-backs to the cabinet. Like Seward, Weed believed that if the tariff were reduced and patronage were given to Southern Unionists promptly, a Union Party would emerge in the Upper South which would defeat the secessionists within two years. Weed recalled that at their December 20 meeting, Lincoln told him "that he supposed I had had some experience in cabinet-making; that he had a job on hand, and as he had never learned that trade, he was disposed to avail himself of the suggestions of friends." Weed replied that he would be glad to help. Lincoln stated that "he had, even before the result of the election was known, assuming the probability of success, fixed upon the two leading members of his cabinet," namely, Seward and Chase. The president-elect remarked that "aside from their long experience in public affairs, and their eminent fitness, they were prominently before the people and the convention as competitors for the presidency, each having higher claims than his own for the place which he was to occupy." Lincoln added that he would probably name Gideon Welles, Simon Cameron, Montgomery Blair, and Norman B. Judd as their colleagues. Weed strongly objected to the stiff-backed Montgomery Blair, arguing "that the Blair blood was troublesome, and traced evidence of this back to the time of General Jackson." Lincoln "replied that he must have some one from the Border States, and Montgomery Blair seemed to possess more of this element than any other available person, because he lived in Maryland, and Frank, his brother, in Missouri." Lord Thurlow suggested that if a Southerner was to be appointed, Henry Winter Davis of Baltimore or John A. Gilmer of North Carolina would be preferable to Blair. Weed also objected to Gideon Welles of Connecticut, prompting Lincoln to explain that he had authorized Hamlin to pick New England's representative in the cabinet, and Hamlin had recommended the Connecticut editor, who had served effectively in the Navy Department under Polk. When discussing Simon Cameron, Weed was less free than he had been in speaking of the others. He had kind things to say about the Chief (as Cameron was often called) but thought him better suited for some post other than treasury secretary.

When Weed recommended that at least two Southerners outside the Republican ranks be chosen, Lincoln "inquired whether . . . they could be trusted, adding that he did not quite like to hear Southern journals and Southern speakers insisting that there must be no 'coercion;' that while he had no disposition to coerce anybody, yet after he had taken an oath to execute the laws, he should not care to see them violated." (Most Southerners interpreted as "coercion" any attempt to enforce the law, collect customs duties, retain control of federal facilities, or retake facilities already seized.) Weed suggested that men from the Upper South be taken. Somewhat skeptically, Lincoln said: "Well, let us have the names of your white crows, such ones as you think fit for the cabinet." The Wizard of the Lobby proposed John Minor Botts, John A. Gilmer, and Henry Winter Davis. But, Lincoln asked, what if he appointed Southerners whose states subsequently left the Union? Could "their men remain in the cabinet? Or, if they remained, of what use would they be to the government?"[16]

(Those were good questions. Henry Winter Davis feared that if North Carolina seceded, Gilmer as a cabinet member would "be too timid to remain or to act."[17] If Lincoln had appointed Gilmer, he would have been mightily embarrassed by that gentleman's conduct when war finally came. On April 17, Gilmer wrote to Stephen A. Douglas: "may the God of battles *crush to the earth and consign to eternal perdition,* Mr. Lincoln, his cabinet and 'aiders and abettors,' in this cruel, needless, *corrupt betrayal* of the conservative men of the South. We would have saved the country, but for the fatuity and cowardice of this infernal Administration. . . . I hope you will not aid or countenance so detestable a *parvenue.*")[18]

Although Weed left Springfield "with an extra large flea in his ear," he praised Lincoln as "capable in the largest sense of the term. He has read much and thought much, of Government, 'inwardly digesting' its theory and principles. His mind is at once philosophical and practical. He sees all who go there, hears all they have to say, talks freely with everybody, reads whatever is written to him; but thinks and acts by himself and for himself."[19] Swett, who was present at the interview, remarked that Weed and the president-elect "'took to each other' from that very day they met, and their relations grew gradually more agreeable and friendly."[20]

When Seward learned of this conversation, he was displeased, telling a friend that the ideologically diverse cabinet envisioned by Lincoln "was not such a cabinet as he had hoped to see, and it placed him in great embarrassment what to do. If he declined [to serve in the cabinet], could he assign the true reason for it, which was the want of support in it?"[21] Disappointed by his failure to win Lincoln's backing for compromise or the appointment of a cabinet to his liking, Seward had to decide whether to reject the State Department portfolio and champion Crittenden's scheme and a conciliatory cabinet or to accept the cabinet post and find some other way to placate the South. On December 28, he chose the latter course. (James Watson Webb believed that Seward had planned to turn down the offer and instead to serve as minister to Great Britain, but that the secession of the Lower South led him to change his mind.)

Seward told his wife grandiloquently: "I will try to save freedom and my country." As that statement indicates, he had a massive savior complex, streaked with self-pity. (In August 1861, he asserted that "there has not been a day since last January, that I could, safely for the Government, have been absent." The following year he told Thurlow Weed, "I am doing all I am capable of doing to save our country" and wrote his daughter: "Some one has to exert an influence to prevent the war from running into social conflict; and battles being given up for indiscriminate butchery. I hope and trust that I may succeed in doing this."[22] Four years later he peevishly complained "that he had saved the country & nobody mentioned him while they went mad over Farragut & Grant!")[23]

When word of Seward's appointment leaked out, Trumbull reported to Lincoln that it "is acquiesced in by all our friends. Some wish it was not so, but regard it rather as a necessity and are not disposed to complain."[24] One who wished it was not so was George G. Fogg, who backed Chase for the State Department post. Fogg assured Lincoln that Seward "has not the nerve for the present crisis. He would bring a clamor with him at the outset, and would be a source of weakness in every emergency which required courage and action. He is a *talker*, and only *that* in *quiet times*."[25] (After speaking with the president-elect, Fogg concluded that he "is anxious to do exactly right, and is likely to do so in the main," but "lacks knowledge of *men*, and especially of politicians and place-hunters.")[26]

For colleagues in the cabinet, Seward desired former Whigs who would support a policy of conciliation, not former Democrats like Judd, Welles, and Blair, who favored a hard line in dealing with secessionists. So the Sage of Auburn recommended to Lincoln the appointment of Randall Hunt of Louisiana, Robert E. Scott of Virginia, and either John A. Gilmer or Kenneth Rayner of North Carolina.

Lincoln chose to approach the cheerful, likeable Gilmer, for he was the only one of those mentioned by Seward and Weed who currently held office and also lived south of the Border States. (Curiously, Lincoln evidently did not consider asking Andrew Johnson, though he told some Virginians who suggested the Tennessee senator for the cabinet, "I have no idea Mr Johnson would accept Such a position, His course is truly *noble* but just as is to be expected from a man possessing such a heart as his.")[27] Gilmer, one of the few Southerners to vote against the Lecompton Constitution, had attained some stature as the American Party's gubernatorial candidate in 1856, the Southern Opposition's nominee for Speaker of the U.S. House in the winter of 1859–1860, and the chairman of the House Committee on Elections. His only obvious drawback was an affiliation with nativism. "Our german friends might not be quite satisfied with his appointment," Lincoln told Seward, "but I think we could appease them."[28] So he invited Gilmer to Springfield, without revealing his purpose. "Such a visit would I apprehend not be useful to either of us, or the country," Gilmer replied, unaware that he was being considered for the cabinet.[29] Upon returning to Washington after the Christmas recess, Gilmer was accosted by Weed and Seward, who urged him to accept a cabinet appointment. The North Carolinian agreed to think it over. (He eventually declined because of "Lincoln's determination to appoint *one* gentleman to the Cabinet." That gentleman was either Chase or Blair.)[30]

Meanwhile, Lincoln had been sounding out other Southern leaders. He sent a feeler to another Tarheel, William A. Graham, who expressed no interest. He also tried to recruit James Guthrie of Kentucky, Franklin Pierce's secretary of the treasury. Not wanting to approach the 68-year-old resident of Louisville directly, Lincoln asked Joshua Speed to confer with his fellow townsman. When Speed did so, Guthrie, after affirming his strong Unionism, said: "I am old and don't want the position."[31]

Frustrated in these bids, Lincoln published an unsigned query in the *Illinois State Journal* on December 12: "We see such frequent allusion to a supposed purpose on the part of Mr. Lincoln to call into his cabinet two or three Southern gentlemen, from the parties opposed to him politically, that we are prompted to ask a few questions.

"1st. Is it known that any such gentleman of character, would accept a place in the cabinet?

"2—If yea, on what terms? Does he surrender to Mr. Lincoln, or Mr. Lincoln to him, on the political difference between them? Or do they enter upon the administration in open opposition to each other?"[32]

The *Journal* also quoted an apposite passage from Lincoln's "House Divided" speech of 1858: "Our cause, then, must be intrusted to, and conducted by, *its own undoubted friends*."[33] To Frank Blair, Lincoln stated that "he could hardly maintain his self respect" if he were to appoint a Southern opponent to his cabinet, asserting that "he considered such a course an admission that the Republican party was incapable of governing the country & would be a rebuke by him to those who had voted for him."[34] He told Joshua Speed that he hesitated to name men from the Deep South for fear that "they might decline, with insulting letters still further inflaming the public mind."[35]

Lincoln next turned to a Southern Republican two years younger than Guthrie, Edward Bates of Missouri, whom he described as "an excellent Christian Gentleman" and an unrivaled authority on the legal writings of the eminent jurist, Sir Edward Coke.[36] At first the president-elect intended to call on him at his St. Louis home, but when Bates learned of this plan, he insisted on visiting Springfield. When the two men met there on December 15, Lincoln told his guest "that since the day of the Chicago nomination it had been his purpose, in case of success . . . to tender him one of the places in his cabinet." He had delayed making the offer "to be enabled to act with caution, and in view of all the circumstances of the case." Lincoln added that he did not wish to saddle Bates "with one of the drudgery offices," but could not name him to the premier cabinet post, secretary of state, for that was earmarked for Seward. (If Seward turned it down, however, Bates might get that coveted post. Some believed that the Missourian would be better able to bring harmony to cabinet councils than anyone else.) Therefore, Lincoln "would offer him, what he supposed would be the most congenial [post] and for which he was certainly in every way qualified, viz: the Attorney Generalship."

Bates replied that he had declined a similar offer from Millard Fillmore in 1850, but now that the nation "was in trouble and danger," he "felt it his duty to sacrifice his personal inclinations, and if he would, to contribute his labor and influence to the restoration of peace in, and the preservation of his country." After expressing his pleasure, Lincoln asked Bates "to examine very thoroughly, and make himself familiar with the constitution and the laws relating to the question of secession, so as to be prepared to give a definite opinion upon the various aspects of the question." In addition, he requested the Missourian to inquire into the legality of Southern attempts to censor the mails. Lincoln "feared some trouble from this question. It was well understood by intelligent men, that the perfect and unrestrained freedom of speech and the press which exists at the North, was practically incompatible with the existing institutions at the South, and he feared that Radical Republicans at the North might claim at the hands of the new Administration the enforcement of the right, and endeavor to make the mail the means of thrusting upon the South matter which even their conservative and well-meaning men might deem inimical and dangerous." This was a curious statement, implying that Lincoln would condone censorship.

Bates promised to look into the question and condemned "the present practice, which permitted petty postmasters to examine and burn everything they pleased." Yet "he foresaw the practical difficulty of enforcing the law at every cross-road." Bates indicated that he was "inflexibly opposed to secession, and strongly in favor of maintaining the government by force if necessary." He asserted that "he is a man of peace, and will defer fighting as long as possible; but that if forced to do so against his will, he has made it a rule *never to fire blank cartridges*."[37]

Upon returning to St. Louis, Bates wrote Lincoln suggesting that his appointment be made public. Accordingly, Lincoln penned a brief statement for the *Missouri Democrat* announcing that Bates would be named to a cabinet post yet to be determined; it ran on December 21. This news failed to placate those wishing to reassure most Southerners, for Bates was too prominent an antislavery Republican and he hailed from a Border State. Radical Republicans also objected to Bates's conservatism. Calling him a "fossil of the Silurian era—red sandstone, at least," Joseph Medill snorted that he "should never have been quarried out of the rocks in which he was imbedded."[38]

The Cameron Dilemma

Causing Lincoln even more difficulty than finding Southerners for his cabinet was his quest for a Pennsylvanian acceptable to the party. Since he had already named two of his rivals at Chicago (Seward and Bates), it seemed logical to pick Cameron. And that is what he did—and undid—and then did again.

Cameron's operatives went to work immediately after the election. Joseph Casey, accompanied by Pittsburgh newspaper editor Russell Errett, called on Lincoln. To Casey's surprise, the president seemed ignorant of the pledges made at Chicago. On November 27, Casey complained about it to Leonard Swett, who was exasperated by Lincoln's reluctance to appoint Cameron. David Davis recommended that Casey and Errett solicit letters from leading Pennsylvania Republicans to bolster Cameron's chances. They took his advice, and in late November and throughout December, Lincoln received an avalanche of pro-Cameron mail. In addition, Pennsylvanians traveled to Springfield to lobby on behalf of the Chief. In December, Hannibal Hamlin told Lincoln: "I do not believe *one man* can be found amongst all our friends in the Senate who will not say it will be ruinous to ap[poin]t Cameron—Whatever *all* the politicians in P[ennsylvani]a may say, and I understand he has about all, my own opinion is clear it *will not do,* embarrassing as it may be some other man should be taken—It would be better to take no one from P[ennsylvani]a, or some other man—[James] Meredith or Judge [John M.] Reed."[39] But the president-elect received few anti-Cameron letters, for Cameron's opponents were complacent. As Alexander K. McClure recalled, "no one outside a small circle of Cameron's friends, dreamed of Lincoln calling him to the Cabinet. Lincoln's character for honesty was considered a complete guarantee against such a suicidal act."[40] Lincoln prepared a summary of all correspondence on the subject, which heavily favored Cameron. He also composed a short, lawerly memorandum on allegations that Cameron had bought his senate seat and had bribed members of a convention.

On December 5, the president-elect summoned David Wilmot to discuss Pennsylvania appointments. That veteran antislavery champion said he would comply as soon as he could and added that "[m]y mind has rather inclined to Gen. Cameron as the man; but it cannot be concealed that he is very objectionable to a large portion of the Republicans of this State. In the main, his opponents are our most reliable men. Gen. Cameron however is a man of unquestioned ability in his way, and of great power as a politician in this State. He has tact and knowledge of men, and is very successful in dealing with them. It would hardly do to make an appointment very obnoxious to him. I have sometimes thought it might be as well in view of our quarrels to pass over our State in the Cabinet appointments."[41] On Christmas Eve, Wilmot finally arrived in Springfield, where he had a long talk with Lincoln.

Five days later Cameron himself appeared in the Illinois capital. He had been urged by friends to visit Springfield but was too proud to go on his own initiative. In December, Leonard Swett, while en route to Washington to serve as Lincoln's eyes and ears, stopped over in Harrisburg, where he invited Cameron to confer with the president-elect. It is not clear whether Lincoln had authorized Swett to do so, although Swett said he did. Joseph Medill heard from "the highest authority" that David Davis had urged Swett to invite Cameron to Springfield, and that "Swett accompanied by his delectable friend Charley Wilson, went out to Cameron's house and assured him that L. desired to see him at Springfield for the purpose of making him Sec of Treasury."[42] Months later, Lincoln complained that Davis had a "way of making a man do a thing whether he wants to or not."[43] George G. Fogg asserted that during "the summer and fall a bargain was struck between Weed and Cameron, with Seward to become secretary of state and the Winnebago Chief secretary of the treasury. Cameron went to Albany and then to Saratoga, where he spent several days with the intriguers," including Davis. "Cameron subsequently tried to get an invitation that fall to Springfield, but Lincoln would not give it. This annoyed the clique. After the election, Swett . . . was sent, or came, East to feel the public pulse. . . . Swett was seized by Weed and Company, open rooms and liquors were furnished by the New York junto, and his intimacy with Lincoln was magnified. Cameron took him to his estate Lochiel and feasted him. Here the desire of Cameron to go to Springfield was made known to Swett, who took it upon himself to extend an invitation in Mr. Lincoln's name."[44] Elihu B. Washburne, who regarded Swett as a tool in the hands of Weed and Seward, wrote to Lincoln on January 7: "Great commotion and excitements exist to-day in our ranks in regard to a *Compromise* that is supposed to be hatching by the Weed-Seward dynasty. Weed is here and the great object now is to obtain your acquiescence in the scheme & sell out and degrade the republicans. Leonard Swett is the agent to be employed to get you into it. He is acting under the direction of Weed, and it is said writes a letter to you dictated by Weed."[45] In mid-January, Herman Kreismann reported from Washington that "Swett is still here but looks quite chopfallen. His Cameron intrigue has proved very disastrous." (Swett was convinced that Cameron would reject a cabinet post.) "Lincoln ought to have a confidential and discreet man—not a damn fool like Swett—here to keep him posted and watch all the schemes and intrigues going on."[46] From the capital, Joseph Medill similarly complained that "Swett has been carrying rather too much sail here—acting the part of envoy extraordinary and magnifying his *status*."[47] Swett shared Weed's view that "Lincoln's whole theory of uniting the elements of our party by coupling in a cabinet rival chiefs is a very bad one."[48]

Cameron, who held Lincoln in contempt, adopted a coy approach. He later asserted that "I told Swett I didn't want to go—and before I went I made Swett write it down what I was wanted for."[49] On December 30, to the surprise of everyone in Springfield, Cameron, accompanied by his operative John P. Sanderson, arrived there. Cameron had two long conversations with Lincoln, who expressed concern about which post to offer his visitor. If it were the treasury portfolio, which Cameron wanted, what should Chase receive? As a prominent Republican leader, Chase held an undeniable claim to a high cabinet position.

"Let him have the War Department," said Cameron.

"Would you accept that job?" Lincoln asked,

"I am not seeking for any position, and I would not decline of course what I had recommended to another," came the reply.[50]

"What about Seward?" asked Lincoln, who seemed to be uncertain whether the New Yorker would join the cabinet. The president-elect had told Bates that if Seward refused his offer, "that would excite bad feeling, and lead to a dangerous if not fatal rupture of the party."[51]

Cameron responded, "you needn't hesitate on that score," for Seward "will be sure to accept."[52]

Afterward, as Cameron prepared to leave town, the president-elect handed him a letter: "I think fit to notify you now, that by your permission, I shall, at the proper time, nominate you to the U.S. Senate, for confirmation as Secretary of the Treasury, or as Secretary of War—which of the two, I have not yet definitely decided. Please answer at your own earliest convenience."[53]

Cameron triumphantly shared this document with friends and leaked it to the press, causing E. B. Washburne to complain to Lincoln that the Pennsylvania boss "has acted the fool completely—showing round your letter offering the place to him to any body and every body as a child would show a toy."[54] When the news arrived in Washington, Cameron's enemies exploded in wrath, swamping Lincoln and his political friends with protests.

Remarkably, over the years Cameron had alienated three Democratic presidents who had once been his friends. Andrew Jackson said he was "not to be trusted by any one in any way" and called him "a renegade politi[ci]an" and "a Bankrupt in politics . . . who got elected senator by selling himself to the whiggs."[55] James K. Polk referred to Cameron as "a managing, tricky man in whom no reliance is to be placed. He professes to be a Democrat, but he has his own personal and sinister purposes to effect."[56] In 1850 James Buchanan, with whom Cameron had been close for two decades, called the Winnebago Chief a "scamp" and predicted that if "the base conduct of Cameron towards myself could be known throughout Pennsylvania, this would floor him."[57]

Republican senators were indignant over the proposed appointment; one of them was so upset that he wept. As Kingsley Bingham of Michigan observed, "Lincoln don't want a thief in his cabinet, to have charge of the Treasury."[58] Hamlin predicted "that Lincoln's administration will be more odious than Buchanan's if Abe goes on in the way he has set out" and urged that an "earnest expression should go to Lincoln from all hands."[59] Maine Senator William Pitt Fessenden told Lincoln: "I have been associated with him [Cameron], during this and the preceding Congress, on the Committee of Finance, and consider him utterly incompetent to discharge the duties of a Cabinet officer, in any position. Such is also the opinion of other Senators in whom you would place confidence. My belief is . . . that there are not three members of the Senate, on our side, to whom the appointment referred to would not be a matter of deep regret."[60] Trumbull, who was "struck speechless with amazement" and "absolutely prostrated," informed the president-elect that "Cameron is very generally regarded as a trading unreliable politician," that he "has not the confidence of our best men," and that many Pennsylvania congressmen "came rushing to me in regard to it greatly excited & declaring openly that it would be the ruin of the party in the State, & take away all the benefit which the party expected to gain by purifying the government."[61] One of those Keystone State congressmen, surprised by the selection of Cameron, speculated that Seward "must have counseled it."[62] Cameron's appointment would, Trumbull predicted, "be fatal to the administration."[63]

A disgusted Joseph Medill exclaimed, "by God! we are sold to the Philistines." Paraphrasing Stephen A. Douglas's remarks about Buchanan, Medill expostulated: "We made Abe and by G— we can *unmake* him."[64] He concluded that the president-elect "had fallen into the toils of the Weed gang, and has not the moral courage or firmness to rise superior to their meshes."[65] Horace White threatened to bolt the Republican Party if Cameron went into the cabinet. "I can stand a good deal of 'pizen' in a political way but I can't stand that," he declared. "The principle with which Cameron entered public life was to pocket everything that came within his reach, & he is too old a dog to learn new tricks." White felt that he could "not belong to a party which places thieves in the charge of the most important public interests."[66]

Bayard Taylor denounced Cameron as "a perfectly unscrupulous man" and predicted that "his appointment would give the new Administration an unfavorable *prestige*."[67] John D. Defrees, who feared that it would "be fatal to us" if Lincoln chose men "whose appointment would be regarded by the public as a 'license to steal,'" reported from Washington in mid-January that word of Cameron's selection "is received here with astonishment and almost universal execration. The Democracy sneer at us and say 'talk no more about honesty and fraud and corruption.' His name is but another name for all that is dishonest. His venality is not dignified with brains. He is really a very small affair. Mr. Lincoln will be compelled to relieve himself of the blunder, else his administration will be odious at the start."[68]

On New Years Day, Elihu B. Washburne told the president-elect that the "report which has reached here this morning that Cameron is going into your cabinet, has created intense excitement and consternation among *all* of our friends here. I trust in God, it is not so. It is impossible to give reasons in this letter, but I am constrained to say, should the report prove true, it would do more than almost anything else to impair confidence in your administration. The best and strongest men in the Senate, & upon whom you must rely for support, are appalled at the apparent probability of the report being true. *I speak what I know.*—All say you must have greatest, the wisest, the purest men in your cabinet without regard to location—men whose very names challenge the confidence of the country."[69] To Charles H. Ray, Washburne was even more emphatic: "Dismay reigns among our republican friends at the capitol." Word of Cameron's appointment "has literally appalled our best men and created a most painful impression that our victory has turned to ashes, and that Lincoln is a failure. Never have I seen men feel such indignation and chagrin as has attended this appointment."[70]

Other congressmen agreed with Washburne. Among the indignant Representatives from Pennsylvania was John P. Verree, who warned Lincoln that "the selection of Senator Cameron *for any position* in your cabinet will not only cause a feeling of deep disappointment here and throughout the state but will surround your administration with a quiet and undefined feeling of fear and suspicion of future investigations."[71] Congressman Edward Joy Morris of Philadelphia told the president-elect that "Cameron has but few superiors" as a "political intriguer," for "he resorts to artifices, which men of a nicer sense of principle would spurn." By promising "the same office to many different persons, he has troops of deluded followers who eventually become his implacable enemies from the deception practised on them." Cameron "is famous for subsidizing newspaper correspondents, and working up a public opinion in his favor, which has no real existence. This he is doing now."[72] Another Philadelphian, Representative William D. Kelley, warned Lincoln that there was such a "general doubt" about Cameron's "integrity in political matters" that his "appointment would taint your administration with suspicion, and would necessarily destroy our party in this state."[73] Equally disenchanted lawmakers from the Keystone State included Galusha Grow, Thaddeus Stevens, John Covode, Chapin Hall, Benjamin F. Junkin, John Hickman, William Millward, and Robert McKnight. They and other leading Pennsylvania Republicans protested that Cameron's appointment "will sow the seeds of discord demoralization and dissolution in the party in that State."[74]

Discontent in Washington was matched by indignation in New York, where reform Republicans denounced the Cameron appointment, saying that they felt like "victims of misplaced confidence," "betrayed and sold out to the Forty thieves," "taken in and done for." In frustration they cursed the appointment, saying "D—n Illinois."[75] On January 3, William Cullen Bryant protested to Lincoln that "Cameron has the reputation of being concerned in some of the worst intrigues of the democratic party a few years back. His name suggests to every honest Republican in this State no other than disgusting associations, and they will expect nothing from him when in office but a repetition of such transactions. At present those who favor his appointment, in this State, are the men who last winter seduced our legislature into that shamefully corrupt course by which it was disgraced."[76] James van Alen explained to Lincoln that Cameron's "reputation as one of the most corrupt men of the old Democratic and the new Republican Party is so fixed, that to stamp your Cabinet with his name would be to start your Adm[istration] under obstacles which even your acknowledged purity of character could not remove. Pennsylvanians, ambitious of his place in the Senate, or expectants of treasury pap, may advise you to [take] such a step, but the honest & intelligent & disinterested members of our Party with whom the name of Simon Cameron is a synonym of corruption will stand aghast at such an app[ointment]t & will feel that they have already lost the long-coveted fruits of a victory for which they have fought so long, so faithfully, [and] so patriotically."[77]

Alarmed by both the volume and tenor of these complaints, Lincoln asked the economist and publisher Henry C. Carey of Philadelphia what Cameron had done to earn such an unsavory reputation. In reply, Carey offered nineteen telling reasons why Cameron should not be given a seat in the cabinet, emphasizing his intellectual as well as ethical shortcomings.

When Alexander K. McClure heard of Cameron's visit to Springfield, he fired off a long, damning protest to Lincoln stating that the "movement to place Gen C in your Cabinet emanates from himself. He is its master spirit—its life & soul, & he personally directs it[.] I speak advisedly on this point[.] His most trusted friends have on various occasions proposed terms to me, directly from Gen C. himself, involving honors & emoluments, in consideration of which I was asked to join in the effort to make him one of your constitutional advisers. It is within my personal knowledge that the appointments within your gift, and contracts *ad infinitum,* to come from the different departments, have been offered from man to man, by Gen C in person & through his friends." McClure begged Lincoln not to appoint Cameron lest the Pennsylvania Republican party be destroyed.

In response to this heartfelt plea, Lincoln invited McClure to Illinois for a consultation. There, on January 3, they met for four hours. McClure was disappointed with his first glimpse of the president-elect, who was "illy clad" and "ungraceful in movement." As the visitor made his case, Lincoln listened patiently, asking questions now and then but indulging in no humor. McClure felt as though he were making his appeal "to a sphinx."[78] After presenting remonstrances from leaders like Governor Curtin, David Wilmot, Thaddeus Stevens, and others, McClure urged Lincoln to appoint either Wilmot or Stevens to his cabinet, but not "mere subjects of Cameron" like James Pollock or Andrew Reeder. (Lincoln had indirectly expressed an interest in Pollock, his messmate from his days in Congress.) "I put it squarely to Lincoln," McClure reported, "why such an appointment could not be made. I told him also that if there were insuperable objections I was entitled to know them as he had appealed to me most earnestly to help him to reconcile matters in our State. He finally answered that Gen C. would *not* consent to any other appointment than himself in Penna. My answer was—that I considered that fact the strongest evidence that he was unfit for the trust in a political sense." The president-elect told McClure "that to revoke C's appointment now" would disgrace the Chief, "hence his painful anxiety & hesitation." At first, Lincoln was skeptical, for he had been told that McClure "was waging a *personal* war" on Cameron, but by the time he left, McClure felt he had established his credibility.[79] Lincoln assured him that he would reconsider the plan to appoint Cameron and would inform McClure of his decision within twenty-four hours. He did so, asking for specific charges against Cameron along with proof to substantiate them. McClure said he would rather not play the role of "an individual prosecutor of Cameron." The main objection to the Chief was not so much public corruption as "notorious incompetency."[80]

But Lincoln did not wait for evidence. Stunned by the hostile reaction to the appointment, he regretted that his friends had failed to inform him more explicitly and candidly about the Chief. But how could they have done so? As Joseph Medill maintained, Lincoln had "consulted nobody—not one original friend, not one honest man."[81] The president-elect had alienated some senators by failing to ask their advice. In late January, Seward complained that "Mr L has undertaken his Cabinet without consulting me. For the present I shall be content to leave the responsibility on his own broad shoulders."[82]

On January 3 the president-elect wrote Cameron asking him to retract his acceptance of a cabinet post. "Since seeing you things have developed which make it impossible for me to take you into the cabinet. You will say this comes of an interview with McClure; and this is partly, but not wholly true. The more potent matter is wholly outside of Pennsylvania; and yet I am not at liberty to specify it. Enough that it appears to me to be sufficient. And now I suggest that you write me declining the appointment, in which case I do not object to its being known that it was tendered you. Better do this at once, before things so change, that you can not honorably decline, and I be compelled to openly recall the tender. No person living knows, or has an intimation that I write this letter. P.S. Telegraph, me instantly, on receipt of this, saying 'All right.'"[83]

Hurt and embarrassed, Cameron sent no such telegram or letter; he had already resigned his senate seat and was thus out of office. From Washington, Trumbull reported to Lincoln that "Cameron is behaving very badly about the tender of an appointment. It was very injudicious for him to be exhibiting your letter about as he did, & after the receipt of your second letter he talked very badly—said to me that he would not then go into the cabinet, but that he would not decline by which I suppose he meant that he would embarrass you all he could, & he made a good many other remarks which I do not choose to repeat; but showing to me that he is wholly unfit for the place."[84]

Lincoln scrambled to find a way to soothe Cameron's wounded feelings. He told Trumbull that the Treasury Department portfolio could not be reoffered to Cameron, for that must go to Chase, whose "ability, firmness, and purity of character, produce the propriety." Moreover, Chase's appointment was necessary for political reasons: "he alone can reconcile Mr. Bryant, and his class, to the appointment of Gov. S[eward] to the State Department." Chase's selection, however, would not suit the Pennsylvania protectionists, who deplored his free trade views. To placate the Pennsylvanians, something must be done for Cameron. Perhaps he might be given the War Department portfolio, which he would accept, but "then comes the fierce opposition to his having any Department, threatening even to send charges into the Senate to procure his rejection by that body." (How Lincoln knew that Cameron would accept the War Department portfolio is not clear. There is some evidence suggesting that the Chief wrote to the president-elect agreeing to accept the War Department and recommending Charles Francis Adams for the Treasury Department.) Perhaps Cameron could be returned to the senate. His recently chosen successor, David Wilmot, might be inveigled into stepping aside for Cameron if he were given "a respectable, and reasonably lucrative place abroad." Patronage plums could be used to sweeten the deal: "let Gen. C's friends be, with entire fairness, cared for in Pennsylvania, and elsewhere."[85]

That compromise suggestion went nowhere. On January 6, Lincoln, in obvious distress, consulted with his old friends Gustave Koerner and Norman B. Judd. "I am in a quandary," he explained. "Pennsylvania is entitled to a cabinet office. But whom shall I appoint?"

"Not Cameron," they replied.

"But whom else?" he asked.

They suggested Reeder and Wilmot, but he responded: "Oh, they have no show. There has been delegation after delegation from Pennsylvania, hundreds of letters, and the cry is, 'Cameron, Cameron!' Besides, you know I have already fixed on Chase, Seward and Bates, my competitors at the convention. The Pennsylvania people say: 'If you leave out Cameron you disgrace him.' Is there not something in that?"

Koerner insisted that "Cameron cannot be trusted; he has the reputation of being a tricky and corrupt politician."

"I know, I know," said Lincoln, "but can I get along if that State should oppose my administration?" Judd and Koerner presciently warned that he would have cause to regret Cameron's appointment.[86]

Lincoln thought his old messmate from Mrs. Sprigg's boarding house, James Pollock, might be an acceptable compromise candidate. Pollock had served as governor of Pennsylvania from 1855 to 1858. The Rev. Dr. William M. Reynolds, president of Illinois University, with whom Lincoln spoke about political developments, informed Pennsylvania Congressman Edward McPherson that the president-elect "is anxious to have a representative of Penn^a in his Administration. But he is *determined not to take part* in a war of personal factions in Pa. The opposition to Mr. Cameron appears to be very bitter. Would Ex-Governor *Pollock* be acceptable to Pennsylvania generally?"[87] That suggestion produced no results. (Lincoln eventually appointed Pollock director of the Philadelphia mint.) Pollock informed Lincoln that "he should regard it as exceedingly disastrous to the Republican party of P[ennsylvani]a if Gen Cameron should not be appointed."[88]

George G. Fogg denounced Cameron roundly not only as corrupt and unprincipled, but also as stupid and dismissive of Lincoln. Fogg spoke bluntly to the president-elect: "Nearly every Republican Senator who has had the opportunity to *know* him, pronounces him *intellectually* incompetent for the proper discharge of the duties of a Cabinet officer. Besides, he has indulged in expressions of contempt for you personally, which should render his official connection with you an impossibility. No matter what communications have passed, you *cannot,* without sacrificing your own personal respect, and without losing, at the start, the confidence of all the *honest* men in the country, appoint him."[89] Fogg's friend, New Hampshire Congressman Mason Tappan, reported from Washington that Lincoln's announcement of cabinet choices "is creating heart-burning, and many of our folks here are particularly down on Cameron."[90]

Cameron's supporters and opponents continued to bombard the president-elect with affidavits, letters, and petitions. Five of McClure's fellow townsmen wrote Lincoln alleging that McClure was corrupt and that Lincoln should not rely on his judgment regarding Cameron. John P. Sanderson returned to Springfield bearing the suggestion that Lincoln retract his abrupt January 3 letter to Cameron and replace it with a gentler missive. Eager to apply some salve to the wounds he had unintentionally inflicted, Lincoln wrote to Cameron on January 13: "When you were here about the last of December, I handed you a letter saying I should at the proper time, nominate you to the Senate for a place in the cabinet. It is due to you, and to truth, for me to say you were here by my invitation, and not upon any suggestion of your own. You have not, as yet, signified to me, whether you would accept the appointment; and, with much pain, I now say to you, that you will relieve me from great embarrassment by allowing me to recall the offer. This springs from an unexpected complication; and not from any change of my view as to the ability or faithfulness with which you would discharge the duties of the place." Lincoln assured Cameron that on January 3 he had written "under great anxiety" and had "intended no offence." He suggested that the Chief should destroy or return that hurtful letter. Tactfully, the president-elect added, "I say to you now I have not doubted that you would perform the duties of a Department ably and faithfully. Nor have I for a moment intended to ostracise your friends. If I should make a cabinet appointment for Penn. before I reach Washington, I will not do so without consulting you, and giving all the weight to your views and wishes which I consistently can. This I have always intended."[91]

In Springfield, Charles Henry Ray of the Chicago *Press and Tribune* also lobbied against Cameron. He told E. B. Washburne that Lincoln "regrets what has passed and would gladly see an avenue of escape. But the poor man has been run down by Pennsylvania politicians, most of whom are candidates for the Senate, and each of whom hopes to squat in Cameron's place. Among them Dave Wilmot is conspicuous. He is the man who did it. Bah! They are all a set of cowardly tricksters, and seem to have combined to carry off spoils. But it is not too late. I have sent for Mr. Bryant and

Geo. Opdyke, and if they will come out and tell him the truth, the bad thing may be defeated—to our loss in Pennsylvania, no doubt, but to Lincoln's infinite credit in the nation."[92]

In mid-January, responding to Ray's appeal, Opdyke, Hiram Barney, and Judge John T. Hogeboom of New York visited Lincoln, who told them he had decided not to name any more cabinet members until he reached Washington. (Four days earlier he had written Seward, "I shall have trouble with every other Northern cabinet appointment—so much so that I shall have to defer them as long as possible, to avoid being teased to insanity to make changes.")[93] Barney and his colleagues, who denounced Cameron and praised Chase, tried to dissuade Lincoln from appointing the Chief, but Lincoln would not budge. He wanted and expected to name Chase to head the Treasury Department, but he feared that appointment would offend Pennsylvania, and therefore he would wait until the situation in the Keystone State was settled. He thought Chase should be willing to let the matter stand "till he can be named without embarrassment; he was counting on Chase's patriotism."[94] These New Yorkers warned that if men like Weed, Cameron, and Caleb B. Smith "got the reins, there is nothing left but a disgraceful compromise with the South, and afterward a reconstruction of the Radical Democratic party in all the free States; that the Administration thus manned cannot command the confidence of the country."[95] (Privately, Lincoln confided to Barney that he had offered Cameron the post of secretary of war and promised Henry Lane that he would appoint Caleb B. Smith secretary of the interior.)

George G. Fogg sent Lincoln a similar message: "if the policy of Seward & Cameron is allowed to prevail—if their utter abandonment of the principles of the Chicago platform shall receive even your tacit sanction, your administration will, at the start, be cut off from the sympathy and confidence of a large majority of the Republican members of the Senate, and from *all* the honest and earnest masses who *believe* in the principles for which they cast their votes."[96]

To counter such pressure, pro-Cameron forces entrained for Illinois. Despite his extreme reluctance to visit Springfield uninvited, Weed, at Seward's urging, headed west to lobby on Cameron's behalf. But his train broke down, and he returned to Albany. Stricken by illness, Leonard Swett was also unable to reach his home state to champion Cameron. But Pennsylvania Congressman James K. Moorhead and Alexander Cummings, one of Cameron's operatives, were able to get through. On January 20, they were met in Springfield by David Davis, who was eager to have Cameron appointed. (Davis was irritated by the delay in naming both the Chief and Caleb B. Smith to cabinet posts.) In an interview, Lincoln, according to Moorhead, "was very much opposed to appointing Cameron, and expressed himself very emphatically." The president-elect, insisting that he had won the election because of his reputation as Honest Old Abe, heatedly asked: "What will be thought now if the first thing I do is to appoint C[ameron], whose very name stinks in the nostrils of the people for his corruption?" That same day, Lyman Trumbull explained why Cameron had so many endorsers like Moorhead: "He is a great manager, & by his schemes has for the moment created an apparent public sentiment in Pa. in his favor. Many of the persons who are most strenuously urging his appointment are doubtless doing so in anticipation of a compensation." Trumbull urged Lincoln to "put Chase into the Cabinet & leave Cameron out, even at the risk of a rupture with the latter; but I am satisfied he can be got along with. He is an exacting man, but in the end will put up with what he can get."[97]

When Lincoln asked Congressman Albert Gallatin Riddle about Cameron, the Ohioan answered that "he was a mystery, that his influence in Pennsylvania seemed out of all proportion to his ability, but that he was a wonderful manager." Lincoln "replied that he had the same impression of him."[98]

On January 24, Lincoln told a group of pro-Cameron Philadelphians that he had devoted much thought to constructing a cabinet and that he would like to appoint Cameron because he had been a Democrat while Bates and Seward were former Whigs. Moreover, he had been assured that Cameron was "eminently fitted for the position which his friends desire him to fill, and that his appointment would give great satisfaction to Pennsylvania." But, he added, the Chief's "opponents charge him with corruption in obtaining contracts, and contend that if he is appointed he will use the patronage of his office for his own private gain." Lincoln said he would have the charges investigated, and in the unlikely event that they were proven true, Cameron would not be appointed, for cabinet ministers "must be, as far as possible, like Caesar's wife, pure and above suspicion, of unblemished reputation, and undoubted integrity." If, on the other hand, the charges were disproved, then Cameron would be named to the cabinet. Lincoln closed with an ominous warning: "If, after he has been appointed, I should be deceived by subsequent transactions of a disreputable character, the *responsibility will rest upon you gentlemen of Pennsylvania who have so strongly presented his claims to my consideration.*"[99]

To help clarify matters, Lincoln asked his troubleshooter Leonard Swett to visit Harrisburg. There Swett interviewed Cameron supporters and detractors, including McClure, who told him that the president-elect must abandon Cameron and support the Lancaster congressman, Thaddeus Stevens, for leading politicians of Pennsylvania were backing Stevens. Swett "expressed great *amazement* at the information, altho he admitted that he had seen Cameron just before leaving Washington. He said that Cameron was positively averse to the appointment of any one but himself from Penna." Swett added that if Pennsylvanians "did not accede to Cameron," they "would be without a representative & that Chase would have the Treasury." According to McClure, Swett was "thoroughly in the Cameron interest, and exhausted himself while here to frighten us by the danger of an unsound Tariff man in the Treasury."[100]

Torn by conflicting advice and reluctant to appoint a spoilsman to his cabinet, Lincoln was, as Herndon told Trumbull, "in a fix. Cameron's appointment to an office in his Cabinet bothers him. If Lincoln do[es] appoint Cameron he gets a fight on his hands, and if he do[es] not he gets a quarrel deep-abiding, & lasting. . . . Poor Lincoln! God help him!"[101] In early February, Lincoln said that the question of Cameron's appointment had given him "more trouble than anything that he had yet to encounter," including the secession of the Lower South. He would, once he was in Washington, ask the Republican senators their candid opinion of the Chief.[102]

The Case of Chase

The struggle over Chase's appointment pitted Lincoln against Seward in a battle to determine who would dominate the cabinet. When Seward's appointment as secretary of state was announced, Weed's paper was quick to dub him the "Premier" of the cabinet.[103] George G. Fogg warned the president-elect that "Seward would insist on being *master* of the administration, and would utterly scorn the idea of playing a subordinate part. He has no more doubt of his measureless *superiority to you,* than of his existence. And this has been apparent from the day when Mr. Weed so magnificently announced that Mr. S[eward] had 'accepted the *premiership* in Mr. Lincoln's Cabinet.' That very term 'premiership' told the whole story—that Mr. Lincoln had selected his 'prime minister,' and was henceforth to be *subject* to *his* policy, just as the queen or king of England is subject to the policy of the ministry." Seward "contemptuously expects to make you 'play second fiddle' to all his schemes, and those of Weed too."[104] Francis P. Blair Sr. thought Seward would try to undermine Lincoln in order to win the presidency in 1864. The New Yorker, in Blair's view, "has the most eager restless ambition for power of any man I have known and Weed the greediest maw for the spoils of Govt. The last is the Jackall of the first. Neither can wait 8 years for the consummation of their hopes."[105]

Seward and Weed's first scheme was to dominate the cabinet by packing it with former Whigs who would defer to the senator and agree with him that the South ought to be conciliated and the slavery issue deemphasized. Chase was anathema to the Albany duo because he espoused radical antislavery views and fought against the appeasement of secessionists; moreover, he had a strong personality and would challenge Seward for leadership. From late December, when he accepted the State Department portfolio, until inauguration day in March, Seward, with the help of his *fidus Achates* Weed, lobbied against Chase and for Cameron. To reconcile these contending forces would severely tax Lincoln's patience and statesmanship.

On December 31, the day he offered Cameron a cabinet post, Lincoln summoned Chase with great urgency: "In these troublous times, I would much like a conference with you. Please visit me here at once."[106] The president-elect had received strong recommendations for the Ohioan from William Cullen Bryant, George G. Fogg, Joseph Medill, Elihu B. Washburne, Amos Tuck, Owen Lovejoy, John F. Farnsworth, John P. Hale, and other Radicals who considered Chase an essential counterbalance to Seward. Amos Tuck assured Lincoln that without Chase, "I fear too much of the N. York flavor will be attributed to the administration, and its patronage."[107] Joshua Giddings urged Lincoln to appoint not only Chase but also two other Radicals to the cabinet.

Both protectionists and moderate Republicans objected to Chase. Former Ohio Congressman Columbus Delano presciently warned that Chase "will use his place first and chiefly to promote his own ambition. His past history justifies this opinion; and he will, probably, become an embarrassing element in Mr. Lincoln's cabinet, as well as an embarrassing element in any fair adjustment of our national troubles."[108] Other Ohioans called Chase a "supremely selfish" and "very vindictive" political intriguer. Congressman Benjamin Stanton described him as "specially obnoxious to the Conservative Republicans of Ohio. His antecedents . . . are of the most extreme character—a Birney man in 1844, a Van Buren man in 1848 and a Hale man in 1852, no man has done so much to break down the Old Whig party of Ohio."[109]

On Friday, January 4, Ohio Governor (and Senator-elect) Chase arrived in Springfield, where he spent two days. Lincoln began their first interview by thanking him for his help in the 1858 campaign against Douglas. Indeed, the president-elect felt "under obligations for his services" in that contest.[110] Lincoln made his guest a peculiar offer: "I have done with you what I would not perhaps have ventured to do with any other man in the country—sent for you to ask you whether you will accept the appointment of Secretary of the Treasury, without, however, being exactly prepared to offer it to you."[111] The problem was "mainly the uncertainty whether the app[ointment]t w[oul]d be satisfactory to Pennsylvania." The hyper-ambitious Chase replied that he was not eager for a cabinet post, especially a subordinate one, and would prefer to keep the senate seat which he was to occupy beginning in March. But he coyly promised to think over the possibility of heading the Treasury Department, and Lincoln pledged to write him more definitely soon. Chase said their conversations "were entirely free & unreserved" and that he had "every reason to be satisfied with the personal confidence which Mr. Lincoln manifested in me."[112]

The two men admired each other. Lincoln said of Chase: "take him all in all he is the foremost man in the party."[113] He regarded the governor "as the Moses that brought us out of the land of bondage, but he had not been as lucky as some of us in reaching the promised land. I esteem him highly, very highly."[114] Chase, he declared, was "the ablest & best man in America" and "about one hundred and fifty to any other man's hundred."[115] In time, Lincoln would come to think less highly of the opportunistic, stately, vain, self-important, egotistical, Machiavellian, humorless, cold, industrious, priggish, and imperious Ohioan.

Chase prized Lincoln's "clearsightedness, uprightness, fidelity to the principles he represents, & firm resolve to administer the Government in the most patriotic spirit" and called him "a genuine patriot of the old school" who "loves the Country & the Union with the devotion of a son." Although Lincoln "may not be so radical as some would wish," he was nonetheless in Chase's view "perfectly sincere" and could be counted on to "never surrender our principles or seek to abase our standard."[116]

But much as he admired Lincoln, Chase resented his failure to offer him the treasury portfolio unconditionally. His feelings were badly hurt. If the president-elect "had thought fit to tender me the Treasury Department with the same considerate respect which was manifested towards Mr. Seward and Mr. Bates I might have felt under a pretty strong obligation to . . . accept it," he complained.[117] Rhetorically, he asked the New York abolitionist John Jay: "Would you be willing to take charge of a broken-down department, as a member of a cabinet with which you could not be sure of six months agreement, and enslave yourself to the most toilsome drudgery almost without respite for four years, exchanging a position from which you could speak freely to the country during half the year and during the other half retire to books, travel or friends for one you could not speak at all except through a report and where no leisure is to be expected?" But, Chase said, if the offer were repeated, "I shall consider all the wishes so flatteringly if not kindly expressed, and if really satisfied that I ought to take the post I shall. But I do not now see on what grounds I could be so satisfied."[118] Clearly, he was being disingenuous, for behind the scenes he was urging George Opdyke and others to lobby on his behalf for the cabinet post.

The Case of Caleb B. Smith

Alarmed by the Seward and Bates appointments, Chase feared that ex-Whigs would dominate the cabinet; he regarded Cameron, though nominally a former Democrat, as a tool of Seward. When rumor suggested that another former Whig, Caleb B. Smith of Indiana, would be appointed, he protested to Lincoln that the Hoosier's ethics were suspect. The 52-year-old Smith had been president of a Cincinnati railroad company that went bankrupt in 1857; he had also served on the Mexican Claims Commission, whose actions "stunk in the nostrils of the American people."[119] According to Joseph Medill, "Chase regards Smith with aversion on account of his notoriously corrupt conduct as Commissioner on Mexican claims. The Gardiner claim was a sample of the way he did business. His action as President of a Railroad is reported to have been shamefully dishonest."[120]

(The Mexican Claims Commission, established by the 1848 Treaty of Guadalupe-Hidalgo, awarded George A. Gardiner $428,000 for a silver mine he allegedly lost to the Mexicans, even though the claim was transparently fraudulent. After his conviction on a forgery charge, Gardiner committed suicide. Ohio Senator Thomas Corwin, who served as an attorney before the Commission—on which his cousin Robert G. Corwin sat—bought a share of the claim. Smith helped guarantee the $22,500 loan that Corwin used to buy his share, which yielded him a profit of $20,000.)

Joseph Medill viewed the short, overweight, ingratiating Smith as "a doughface," a "cipher on the right hand of the Seward integer," a "fugitive slave law-Southern 'Constitutional guarantee' fanatic, and a hater of free principles."[121] Chase's organ, the Cincinnati *Commercial*, ridiculed Smith as a "poor businessman" with a "total want of administrative ability" who could not meet the Jeffersonian qualifications of "being honest and capable."[122] Schuyler Colfax warned that "Smith's Soap Factory, Mexican Claim Commission, and Railroad management at Cincinnati are ugly matters for Lincoln to get over."[123] A leading Indianapolis Republican called Smith a "debauched corrupt politician."[124] Josiah M. Lucas informed Lincoln that word of "the appointment of Smith, has awakened the reminiscences of Galphinism and Gardnerism. You remember that Smith, [former Whig Senator George] Evans of Maine &c, composed that celebrated *Board* on Mexican indemnities, who passed sundry claims that the country, with general acclaim pronounced against—whilst the skirts of the Board were by many believed to be unclean."[125]

(Heirs of George Galphin, an eighteenth-century Indian trader, claimed that the United States owed them money that had been promised to Galphin. In 1848, Congress appropriated $44,000 to honor the claim. The heirs then insisted that they were owed interest on that amount dating back to the Colonial era—$191,000. The lawyer representing the Galphin heirs, George Crawford, was to receive half of the amount awarded. Crawford, then secretary of war, won the case for his client thanks to opinions written by his fellow cabinet members, Attorney General Reverdy Johnson and Treasury Secretary William Meredith.)

Some considered Smith intellectually ill-equipped for a cabinet post. Henry Villard, who deplored his "incompetency" and "worse than mediocrity," reported that the "mental caliber of that choice of the Hoosier politicians seems to be thought altogether inadequate to a creditable performance of the duties of the Secretary of the Interior." Smith's "only real qualification," he sneered, "is a stentorian voice."[126] While conceding that Smith was a superior stump speaker, John D. Defrees predicted he would be "worthless as a Cabinet officer."[127] Smith was also derided as a "fossil." James C. Veatch, a key delegate to the Chicago Convention who had actively supported Lincoln, told the president-elect that the Buchanan administration "shows most clearly of how little value in times of peril are these old gentlemen of the past generation."[128]

In light of such criticism, Lincoln hesitated to name Smith to the cabinet, but at the same time he felt grateful to Smith for helping him win both the presidential nomination and the election. Shortly after the Chicago Convention, he wrote Smith saying: "I am, indeed, much indebted to Indiana; and, as my home friends tell me, much to you personally."[129] In late January 1861, Lincoln spoke of the recent campaign, "dwelling especially on the eloquence and ability" of Smith, "who had, in his opinion, rendered him more effective service than any other public speaker."[130] David Davis encouraged Lincoln in this belief. "Mr Smith is an able man," the judge told the president-elect in November. "He has worked harder in the canvass this year than any man in Indiana—No one rendered more efficient service from Indiana, at the Chicago Convention than he did." Davis, who had promised Indiana a place in the cabinet (and perhaps specified that it would go to Smith), added that "Indiana, as you have assured me, will receive a cabinet appointment from you—but I do not know who you have thought of for the position— . . . I should really be gratified—if Caleb B. Smith could receive the appointment."[131]

Smith's principal Indiana competitor was Congressman Schuyler Colfax of South Bend. Although Henry Villard speculated that the president-elect's "deep grudge against Colfax ever since the latter's advocacy of Douglas's claims to reelection in 1858" would prevent the congressman's elevation to the cabinet, Lincoln denied harboring any such resentment.[132] In December, when Indiana Republican leaders called at Springfield to lobby for Smith, they suggested that Colfax "was a man of detail and too inexperienced" and "that his reputation and claims were manufactured by newspaper scribblers." Lincoln replied that he "could only say that he saw no insuperable objections to Indiana's having a man [in the cabinet], nor to Smith being that man."[133] Others, including George G. Fogg, were less confident of Colfax's ability. Maine Governor Israel Washburn objected to his cabinet candidacy, asserting that "it would be most disgraceful for that flunkey & trifler to be in any white man's company."[134]

The financially strapped Smith eagerly sought the post. One Hoosier, alluding to Smith's personal problems, asked Lincoln if Smith "can not manage his own affairs," then "how can he manage Government affairs?"[135] The Radical George W. Julian protested against the conservative Smith, arguing that "[n]o man's record as a business man & financier for the past twenty years & more is so uniformly & consistently bad, & this is too well known to allow his appointment to the post in question to be regarded as even tolerable by the country."[136]

To offset such criticism, Smith skillfully organized a letter-writing campaign which swelled Lincoln's mail bag. Colfax complained that "Smith has been guilty of the meanness of writing himself into my district and other portions of the North, saying that Lincoln wants to appoint him, but does not wish to offend Northern Indiana which all seems for me; and urging them to get signatures privately to a recommendation for him and send them to Springfield. I could have had thousands all over the state if I had descended to this kind of electioneering."[137] Smith was "moving every appliance possible, promising patronage & electioneering, all of which I will not do," Colfax observed.[138] When Cyrus Allen called on Lincoln to endorse Colfax, the president-elect said that no pro-Colfax delegations had lobbied him and that he therefore supposed Colfax did not enjoy widespread support. In fact, Colfax was unwilling to engage in an all-out lobbying effort, though he did work behind the scenes to win newspaper endorsements. "I don't believe in any Committee of my friends *from Ind[iana]* going to Springfield," he said. "Let Smith's friends bore Mr. Lincoln that way if they will." In early January, when he became convinced that Smith had defeated him, Colfax explained the likely outcome: "Smith[']s persistent electioneering & his friends, with my refusal to pledge offices & follow his example has done it. . . . Mr Lincoln said last week that with the troubles before us I could not be spared from Congress—that a new & untried man would fill my place [in the House] . . . & that Smith had nothing, while I was in office." He added that he felt it would do Colfax "no service" to take him from his House seat to serve in the cabinet.[139] (In 1862, Colfax would turn down a cabinet offer because he feared that a Democrat would capture his seat in the House, which almost did happen.)

Foremost among Smith's backers were Seward and Weed, aided by David Davis and Leonard Swett. In December and January, Swett reported from Washington that he was doing all he could for Smith. He worked closely with Seward, informing Lincoln that Seward believed that the cabinet should be ideologically homogeneous. Lincoln's desire to have a heterogeneous cabinet was "all very well for fair-weather times," but not in a period of crisis like the one they faced. Therefore, he recommended former Whigs like Smith.[140] A week later Swett told the president-elect that Colfax was widely regarded as "a clever fellow but a gun of too small bore" and that Smith "is very well spoken of[.]"[141] Even his supporters conceded that Colfax "is not a great man."[142] Smith argued that Colfax enjoyed support only in northern Indiana and that Colfax's backers there regarded Smith as their second choice.

In addition to Colfax, Smith faced competition from Norman B. Judd, whose candidacy was championed by former Democrats like Lyman Trumbull, Gustave Koerner, Ebenezer Peck, Joseph Medill, and the Blairs. Fierce opposition came from

Illinois ex-Whigs like Richard Yates, Leonard Swett, William Kellogg, and David Davis, who could not forgive Judd for his unwillingness to support Lincoln for senator in 1855. Lincoln, ever magnanimous, would have liked to appoint Judd but feared such a move would alienate too many allies. He told Gideon Welles "that he had, personally a stronger desire that Judd should be associated with him in the administration than any one else but he was from Illinois."[143] He acknowledged that although "he never had a truer friend" than Judd and "there was no one in whom he placed greater confidence," still the appointment of a fellow Illinoisan would embarrass him.[144] He had only seven cabinet positions to fill and wished to use them to strengthen the Republican Party in key states like Indiana, Ohio, Pennsylvania, and New York, as well as important regions like the South and New England; Illinois did not need a representative in the cabinet, for it already had one in the White House. Lincoln told a delegation of Judd's supporters "that if his occupancy of the office of President could not command the undivided loyalty of Illinois, a dozen Cabinet officers could not do it, adding that he had never doubted the loyalty of his own State, and that it was the border States which were the objects of his greatest solicitude."[145] The battle over Judd, which raged throughout January, greatly distressed Lincoln, who doubtless recalled the howl of protest raised when Buchanan named an attorney general (Jeremiah Black) from his own state of Pennsylvania.

Lincoln reluctantly passed over Judd, who in disgust told a friend that he would wash his hands "of politics and politicians. It requires more philosophy than I have got to do the drudgery and take only the kick and cuffs."[146] Leonard Swett informed Ward Hill Lamon that he could tell Caleb Smith "that it was through the Illinois fight and judge Davis that Judd went out and he went in."[147] As a consolation prize, Lincoln offered Judd the lucrative post of minister to Prussia, which he accepted.

The Case of Gideon Welles

Lincoln delegated to Hannibal Hamlin the choice of a New Englander for the cabinet. Two days after the election, the president-elect invited his running mate to confer with him in Chicago, where in late November they discussed cabinet matters at some length. After asking the vice-president-elect to negotiate with Seward, Lincoln mentioned some possible nominees for the Navy Department portfolio, including Charles Francis Adams and Nathaniel P. Banks of Massachusetts, Gideon Welles of Connecticut, and Amos Tuck of New Hampshire.

As Hamlin proceeded to carry out his assignments, Lincoln met with Thurlow Weed on December 20 and expressed partiality for Welles, a former Democrat who edited the Hartford *Evening Press*. Weed ridiculed the bearded, bewigged leader of the Connecticut Republicans, facetiously suggesting that Lincoln could, while traveling to Washington for his inauguration, stop at an eastern seaport, buy a ship's figurehead, "to be adorned with an elaborate wig and luxuriant whiskers, and transfer it from the prow of a ship to entrance of the Navy Department." It would, Weed jibed, "be quite as serviceable" as Welles and cheaper.

"Oh," replied Lincoln, "'wooden midshipmen' answer very well in novels, but we must have a live secretary of the navy."[148]

The president-elect complained that Weed had been "very intrusive and importunate on this subject," being "strongly opposed" to the entry into the cabinet of Welles or any other former Democrat, with the exception of Cameron. In addition to disliking Welles's Democratic antecedents, Weed resented him for having opposed Seward at the Chicago Convention. But Weed's pressure backfired, only strengthening Lincoln's inclination to appoint Welles.

(Before leaving Albany for Springfield, Weed allegedly told a Lincoln supporter: "Had Seward been nominated and elected it was my intention to have taken a foreign mission and gone abroad to avoid the charge that I would unduly influence Seward. But you beat him. You nominated a man whom you supposed was beyond my influence or control. Now G-d damn you I am going to show you who will influence Lincoln, who will go in his cabinet, who will shape his policy, who will control his patronage. If any of you can wield more influence over *your man* Lincoln than me, please to send me word when it is done, and I'll send you a receipt.")[149]

On Christmas Eve, Lincoln instructed Hamlin to recommend "a man of Democratic antecedents from New England." The president-elect explained that he could not "get a fair share" of the Democratic element in the cabinet without appointing a Democrat from that region. "This," said Lincoln, "stands in the way of Mr. Adams." (Adams, happy to continue serving in Congress, had no desire for a cabinet post.) He suggested Banks, Welles, or Tuck and asked which of them the New England congressional delegation preferred. "Or shall I decide for myself?"[150] (From the day after the election he had intended to appoint Welles but wished to give Hamlin a chance to voice his opinion.) By this time, Lincoln had decided on two former Whigs (Seward and Bates), and was leaning toward one more (Smith) and three ex-Democrats (Chase, Montgomery Blair, and Cameron). If he picked one more former Democrat, at cabinet meetings the number of ex-Whigs (including himself) would equal that of ex-Democrats. Therefore Adams, a former Whig, was out of the picture, despite Weed and Seward's entreaties. Amos Tuck, who was glad to receive the well-remunerated post of naval officer of the port of Boston, modestly recommended Welles as the best choice for New England.

When Lincoln praised Banks as a capable administrator with a national reputation, Hamlin disagreed, calling the Bobbin Boy a "trimmer in politics."[151] Massachusetts Governor John A. Andrew denounced Banks's "relations to 'Know Nothingism,' his non-commitalism on any matter of principle in the face of any danger, & his willingness to make everything a subject of doubt by his logomachy of sounding and double meaning phrases."[152] Banks, who had served three terms as governor of Massachusetts and one term as speaker of the U.S. House of Representatives, would remain a viable candidate, despite such disapproval. He enjoyed strong support from influential Massachusetts businessmen as well as the New York *Herald*.

Banks's eligibility for the New England seat, however, was compromised in the summer of 1860 when he accepted the presidency of the Illinois Central Railroad and agreed to move to Chicago. Lincoln told a friend of Banks that if the former governor had "remained in New England there would have been no second man thought of," that Banks's "name was in the first list that he ever made, that previous to his own election he did not feel at liberty to make any suggestion" about Banks's move to Illinois, "but that the change put it out of his power to do what he should otherwise at once have done without a suggestion from any one."[153] In February 1861, Lincoln told friends of the former governor, "I like your man Banks, and have tried to find a place for him in my Cabinet, but I am afraid I shall not quite fetch it."[154]

That left Welles as the front-runner. Months earlier he had impressed Lincoln during his campaign visit to Hartford, and the president-elect knew of the helpful role Welles had played at the Chicago Convention. The Connecticut editor also had strong backing from Hamlin, Horace Greeley, John A. Andrew, Henry B. Stanton, Edwin D. Morgan, George G. Fogg, Edward Lillie Pierce, E. S. Cleveland, Congressman John Dennison Baldwin, and Senators Henry Wilson, James Dixon, and Preston King. As Welles recalled, King, who had been a close friend for two decades, "was most earnest and emphatic in favor of my appointment, and was sleepless and unremitting in thwarting and defeating the intrigues of Weed and others against me."[155] Lincoln, fearing that Welles might be too radical an opponent of the Fugitive Slave Act, had Hamlin investigate that matter; the vice-president-to-be interviewed Connecticut Senator James Dixon, who vouched for Welles's soundness on the issue. Hamlin also elicited a letter from Welles explaining that while he deplored that law, wanted it reformed, and thought that states rather than the federal government should assume the responsibility of carrying it out, he nevertheless supported its enforcement. Swett spoke highly of Welles. Thus, when Lincoln, who was persuaded of Welles's obvious suitability for the position, left Springfield for Washington in mid-February, the Connecticut Republican stood the best chance of occupying the New England seat in the cabinet.

Maryland in the Cabinet

Eager to keep the Upper South and Border States in the Union, Lincoln resolved to appoint a Marylander to his cabinet. "The propriety of giving a Cabinet appointment to that State is very generally recognized," said the New York *Times*.[156] The two leading candidates were Montgomery Blair, the scholarly, quarrelsome, socially awkward West Point graduate and son of the long-time political insider Francis P. Blair Sr., and Whig-American Congressman Henry Winter Davis, the combative, self-righteous, vain cousin of David Davis. Blair had support from influential senators like Trumbull, Hamlin, Preston King, Zachariah Chandler, and Benjamin F. Wade; Ohioans like Congressman John A. Gurley and Governor-elect William Dennison; New Hampshire Governor Ichabod Goodwin; John C. Frémont; and some leading Maryland Republicans. But Weed and Seward supported Davis and opposed Blair because he was a former Democrat who, along with his father and brother, had worked hard at Chicago to defeat Seward. Radicals in the Free State, however, opposed both Blair and Davis in favor of Judge William L. Marshall. On Christmas Eve, Lincoln told Trumbull that he expected "to be able to offer Mr. Blair a place in the cabinet; but I can not, as yet, be committed on the matter, to any extent whatever."[157]

Henry Winter Davis, who enjoyed the backing of Indianans like Governor-elect Henry S. Lane and John D. Defrees as well as leading New York newspapers and dozens of his colleagues in the U.S. House, had alienated some Maryland Republicans by campaigning for Bell in the presidential election. Congressman John Covode warned Lincoln that "Davis has scarcely enough of firmness for the times," while Frank Blair complained that Davis "is not a Republican and has no sympathy with our party."[158] Davis himself refused to lobby on his own behalf, arguing that "Mr. Lincoln must be left *free* & keep himself free—or he will make shipwreck of himself and the Govt."[159]

Seward as Dictator for Defense

Lincoln postponed a final decision on the five unfilled cabinet positions until he could meet with congressional leaders in person. He also delayed his trip to Washington. Many people, including Seward, feared, with some reason, that disunionists were plotting to disrupt the count of the electoral vote and seize the capital. When Seward urged him to come to Washington early, Lincoln declined, explaining that in his view the inauguration "is not the most dangerous point for us. Our adversaries have us more clearly at disadvantage, on the second Wednesday of February, when the [electoral college] votes should be officially counted [in Congress]. If the two Houses refuse to meet at all, or meet without a quorum of each, where shall we be? I do not think that this counting is constitutionally essential to the election; but how are we to proceed in absence of it?"[160] So he determined to remain in Springfield until February 11, when he would begin a circuitous, two-week train journey to the capital. He understandably feared that after reaching Washington "he could have no time to himself."[161]

Since Lincoln was not at the center of power during the crucial weeks when the Cotton States were pulling out of the Union, Seward took it upon himself to keep the country intact at least until inauguration day. To those urging him to back the Crittenden Compromise, Seward replied that it would be politically suicidal and insisted that "you must let me save the Union in my own way."[162] He viewed himself as indispensable; if he were away from Washington for only three days, he predicted, "this Administration, the Congress, and the District would fall into consternation and despair. I am the only *hopeful, calm, conciliatory* person here."[163] He asserted that "the majority of those around him were determined to pull the house down & he was determined not to let them."[164] Both Buchanan and Lincoln, he crowed, "unite in devolving on me the responsibility of averting . . . disasters."[165] He had, he said, "assumed a sort of dictatorship for defense."[166] He envisioned his role as that of commander-in-chief; in mid-January he told his wife: "I hope what I have done will bring some good fruits, and, in any case, clear my own conscience of responsibility, if, indeed, I am to engage in conducting a war against a portion of the American people."[167] Henry Adams regarded Seward as the "virtual ruler of this country."[168] Adams's father agreed, writing in mid-January that "Seward is even now the guiding hand at the helm."[169] When Seward spoke in favor of conciliation, the public assumed that he reflected Lincoln's views. But, as the president-elect told a visitor in early February, "Seward made all his speeches without consulting him."[170] Instead of acting as Lincoln's agent, the senator served as an independent negotiator between the president-elect and representatives of the Upper South and the Border States, whose loyalty was essential for the preservation of the Union.

Seward calculated that time would heal the sectional wounds. According to his friend Lord Lyons, the British minister to the United States, "Mr. Seward's real view of the state of the country appears to be, that if bloodshed can be avoided until the new Government is installed, the Seceding States will in no long time return to the Confederation. He has unbounded confidence in his own skill in managing the American people. . . . He thinks that in a few months the evils and hardships produced by Secession will become intolerably grievous to the Southern States; that they will be completely reassured as to the intentions of the Administration; and that the conservative element which is now kept under the surface by violent pressure of the Secessionists, will emerge with irresistible force. From all these causes he confidently expects that when elections . . . are held in the Southern States in November next, the Union Parties will have a clear majority, and will bring the Seceding States back into the Confederation. He then hopes to place himself at the head of a strong Union party, having extensive ramifications both in the North and in the South, and to make Union or Disunion not Freedom or Slavery the watchword of political parties."[171]

In late December, Seward introduced four resolutions in the Committee of Thirteen, but they were not the ones that Lincoln had asked Weed to pass along to him with the recommendation that "that you substantially adopt his views."[172] Unlike the president-elect, Seward called for a guarantee of slavery in the states where it already existed. Moreover, he failed to include Lincoln's affirmation that the Union must be preserved, as well as his support for federal enforcement of the fugitive slave provision of the Constitution and his suggestion that private citizens be exempted from the requirement to assist slave catchers. Seward reported to the president-elect that his Republican colleagues on the Committee of Thirteen, along with Senators Trumbull and Fessenden, objected to Lincoln's resolutions because "the ground has already been covered" and that they "would divide our friends, not only in the Committee, but in Congress," many of whom believed that the rendition of fugitive slaves was a state and not a federal responsibility.[173] (Hamlin, who had been asked to pass judgment on the resolutions, found them unobjectionable.) But Seward, like his boss-to-be, did reject any concession on slavery expansion, which the South was demanding. (The territorial question lay at the heart of the Crittenden Compromise and its toned-down variant, the Border State plan.) Thus any hopes of compromise seemed doomed in the senate.

The House devised an alternative to the Crittenden and Border State panaceas. On December 20, Henry Winter Davis metaphorically fired "a cannon shot clear through the line" with a proposal to admit the New Mexico Territory, thus finessing the vexed question of slavery in territories south of 36° 30'.[174] (In 1859 the residents of New Mexico had adopted a slave code, but in the future they might frame a constitution outlawing slavery.) Davis's suggestion was taken up by the House Committee of Thirty-Three, where some Southerners, "starting as if a bomb-shell had fallen among them," quickly rejected it.[175] Not deterred, Chairman Thomas Corwin and another influential member, Charles Francis Adams (known as the "Archbishop of Antislavery"), bundled it with a constitutional amendment guaranteeing the security of slavery in the states where it already existed. Seward, who was a close friend of Adams and a frequent caller at his house, probably persuaded the Massachusetts congressman to introduce this amendment, which may well have been written by the New Yorker himself. Believing that the slavery issue had been "substantially settled by the late election," Adams took the lead in championing this package, which antislavery militants denounced as the work of a traitor to the cause.[176]

In the Committee of Thirty-Three, nine of fifteen Republicans voting supported the admission of New Mexico with the understanding that it might become a Slave State. They argued that even if it did so, it was so huge that no more such states would enter the Union. One opponent, who believed that "*Peon* Slavery" in New Mexico was "worse than African Slavery," bitterly remarked that the Republicans would for their efforts "only get nicely b[ull]shit."[177] While Southern hotheads were vexed, Southern Moderates were temporarily placated by this compromise, which demonstrated that the North could offer something positive instead of merely objecting to the Crittenden and Border State plans. The New York *Tribune*'s James Shepherd Pike observed that the New Mexico Compromise provided Southern Moderates "a temporary holding-ground during the height of the Secession storm."[178] Iowa Senator James Harlan considered it "the only practical measure that could be adopted with honor by the Republicans."[179] For the time being at least, the Upper South would not cast its lot with the Cotton States. Adams and Seward had achieved their short-term goal, driving a wedge between the Upper South and the Lower South and buying time to allow for the inauguration of Lincoln with most Slave States still in the Union. Throughout January and into February, Congress tried valiantly to blend the Border State and the Davis-Adams-Corwin schemes.

Meanwhile, Seward publicly championed a different plan. In a major speech on January 12, he shocked Radical Republicans by urging immediate concessions to keep the Upper South in the Union and offering a long-range proposal to settle outstanding differences between the sections. When Seward spoke, the atmosphere in the senate chamber, packed with 2,000 spectators, was tense. Three days earlier, South Carolina authorities had fired on an unarmed ship, the *Star of the West*, laden with supplies for the Fort Sumter garrison, forcing the vessel to abandon its mission. This news had deeply disturbed Lincoln and many other Northerners. The nation seemed to teeter on the brink of war. Could Seward keep the peace? After extolling the advantages of the Union for all sections, including the South, the senator, in conciliatory tones, endorsed the creation of two huge new states, one slave and one free, out of the existing western territories; a constitutional amendment guaranteeing slavery where it already existed; a modification of the Fugitive Slave Act exempting bystanders from any role in the pursuit of runaways; and a law forbidding invasions of one state by residents of another. He also recommended a cooling-off period of two or three years, to be followed by a national constitutional convention.

"It is the speech of an adroit politician rather than of a great statesman," wrote New York Congressman Charles B. Sedgwick; it afforded "skulking ground for those who wish to dodge and compromise," seemed to offer a reward "for rascality and treachery," and "has hurt Seward and shaken the confidence of many of his strongest friends."[180] The editor of the Washington *Constitution* asserted that "Seward's speech fell like a pall over the entire community. When he finished speaking all hope seemed to have fled, and even Mr. Crittenden despaired."[181] The leading Radical in the U.S. House, Thaddeus Stevens, confessed himself "mortified and discouraged" by Seward's backsliding.[182] It was reported that while "practical men, smarting under the return of the Star of the West, think it not strong, too cool, too calm," Radicals "feel that it yields too much" and "are suspicious of one who will yield so much to evil."[183]

Although Lincoln was allegedly "not overpleased with Seward's speech," he told the senator that it "is well received here [in Springfield], and, I think, is doing good all over the country."[184] The *Illinois State Journal* praised the address, noting that a constitutional convention "will take *time,* and time is all that is necessary to cure the secession fever." Seward, said the editors, "thinks that time will settle the matter—that reason will return, and secession will die."[185] Lincoln shared that view, as John Hay reported in the *Missouri Democrat:* "I have reason to believe that he coincides with Gov. Seward in favoring a convention of the people to suggest amendments to the Constitution. Conscious of nothing in his acts or sentiments which should justly excite alarm, he will insist upon his quiet inauguration, without further assurances on his part; but when once at the head of the nation, those who are laboring for peace with singleness of heart, will never find their plans balked by any factious opposition from him."[186]

Although the reaction to Seward's address was generally positive, the New Yorker knew that he must win over Lincoln for any compromise. To this end, he enlisted the aid of Illinois Congressman William Kellogg, who visited Springfield on January 20. To Kellogg's appeal for concessions on the territorial issue, Lincoln emphatically replied that he would endorse no measure betraying the Chicago Platform, but he did indicate that if the American people wished to call a convention dealing with Southern grievances, he would not object. During his meeting with Kellogg, Lincoln received a dispatch from Trumbull urging him to do nothing until he received letters that the senator was forwarding from Washington. The president-elect informed Kellogg that he would honor Trumbull's request and then write to Seward explaining his position on compromise measures.

Frustrated yet again, Seward sank into depression. In late January, he warned Lincoln that compromise was necessary to prevent the Upper South from seceding: "The appeals from the Union men in the Border states for something of concession or compromise are very painful since they say that without it those states must all go with the tide, and your administration must begin with the free states, meeting all the Southern states in a hostile confederacy. Chance might render the separation perpetual. Disunion has been contemplated and discussed so long there that they have become frightfully familiar with it, and even such men as Mr Scott and William C. Rives are so far disunionists as to think that they would have the right and be wise—in going if we will not execute new guaranties which would be abhorrent in the North. It is almost in vain that I tell them to wait, let us have a truce on slavery, put our issue on Disunion and seek remedies for ultimate griefs in a constitutional question." Seward predicted that "you are to meet a hostile armed confederacy when you commence—You must reduce it by force or conciliation— The resort to force would very soon be denounced by the North, although so many are anxious for a fray. The North will not consent to a long civil war—A large portion, much the largest portion of the Republican party are reckless now of the crisis before us—and compromise or concession though as a means of averting dissolution is intolerable to them. They believe that either it will not come at all, or be less disastrous than I think it will be—For my own part I think that we must collect the revenues—regain the forts in the gulf and, if need be maintain ourselves here—But that every thought that we think ought to be conciliatory forbearing and patient, and so open the way for the rising of a Union Party in the seceding states which will bring them back into the Union."[187]

Seward's admonition was well taken, for he accurately gauged Southern public opinion. But, ironically, he misjudged the mood in his own section. The North, he feared, would shatter into bickering factions once war broke out, making it impossible to restore the Union by force; hence everything must be done to prevent hostilities. Lincoln may have overestimated the depth and extent of Southern Unionism, but he understood Northern opinion better than Seward did.

Despite Seward's desperate plea, Lincoln refused to budge on the central issue. On February 1, reiterating his earlier opposition to compromise, he told the New Yorker that "on the territorial question—that is, the question of extending slavery under the national auspices,—I am inflexible. I am for no compromise which *assists* or *permits* the extension of the institution on soil owned by the nation. And any trick by which the nation is to acquire territory, and then allow some local authority to spread slavery over it, is as obnoxious as any other. I take it that to effect some such result as this, and to put us again on the high-road to a slave empire is the object of all these proposed compromises. I am against it." Changing his tone, Lincoln closed with a startling concession: "As to fugitive slaves, District of Columbia, slave trade among the slave states, and whatever springs of necessity from the fact that the institution is amongst us, I care but little, so that what is done be comely, and not altogether outrageous. Nor do I care much about New-Mexico, if further extension were hedged against."[188]

Lincoln's rather casual statement about New Mexico represented a momentous policy shift. Three weeks earlier Villard had reported that the president-elect "does not approve of the advocacy by certain Republican Congressmen of the scheme of admitting New Mexico as a state with its territorial slave code unimpaired. His faith in the Chicago dogma of the right of Congressional prohibition of slavery in the territories is as firm as ever."[189] Soon thereafter Lincoln softened his opposition to compromise, telling a group of visitors who inquired about plans to restore the 36° 30' line "that although the recent presidential election was a verdict of the people in favor of freedom upon all the territories, yet personally he would be willing, for the sake of the Union, to divide the territory we now own by that line, if in the judgment of the nation it would save the Union and restore harmony. But whether the acquisition of territory hereafter would not re-open the question and renew the strife, was a question to be thought of and in some way provided against." When asked if he would recommend the repeal of Personal Liberty Laws, he "replied that he had never read one of them, but that if they were of the character ascribed to them by Southern men, they certainly ought to be repealed. Whether as President of the United States he ought to interfere with State legislation by Presidential recommendation, required more thought than he had yet given the subject." As for the right of holding slaves in federal dockyards and arsenals, he said "the subject has not entered my mind." Unconvincingly, he also denied that he had given any thought to the abolition of slavery in the nation's capital. He added that it "was sometimes better for a man to pay a debt he did not owe, or to lose a demand which was a just one, than to go to law about it."[190]

On January 24, the *Illinois State Journal* seemed to endorse the admission of New Mexico with its slave code: "if the Southern people fear or believe that the Republican party are opposed to the admission of any more slave States, we are willing that it should be made the law or the Constitution that Territories applying for admission into the Union, shall be admitted with or without slavery, as the people of such Territory, so applying, shall determine."[191] But, the paper counseled, any concession should be accompanied by a demand that the Slave States explicitly renounce the doctrine of secession. A few days earlier Lincoln reportedly told a prominent Illinois politician that the Border States' propositions "would only be worth noticing in case a proposition for a Constitutional amendment requiring the consent of two-thirds of all the States to any additional acquisitions of territory, should be incorporated."[192]

There were other indications that Lincoln would support compromise measures. In November, a Mississippi planter who spoke with him reported that the president-elect "was opposed to any interference with slavery in the states, or with the inter-state slave trade; that he was opposed to abolishing or interfering with slavery in the district of Columbia; and that he was only opposed to its extension in the territories, but added, 'that was only an opinion of his.'" As for appointing postmasters and other federal officials in South Carolina if it seceded, he "stated that if no one would accept office in that state, of course they could receive no benefits from the government, and the whole expenses for the distribution of the mails would devolve on her own citizens."[193] In late January, the *Illinois State Journal* spoke of the North's wish for peace: "There is no intention in the loyal states to invade and conquer the states which have rebelled. They might undoubtedly be subdued by the superior force of the United States, but their forcible subjugation would answer no good end. All that is contemplated is to make them obey the laws relating to foreign intercourse."[194] The *Illinois State Register* marveled at the *Journal*'s abrupt turn away from confrontation toward conciliation.

It is difficult to know why Lincoln shifted his stance on New Mexico. Perhaps he believed that slavery could never take root in that huge territory, which included the later state of Arizona as well as New Mexico. The 1860 census showed that no slaves lived there.

Lincoln's change of heart could perhaps have averted bloodshed if Seward had exploited it and if Southern Unionists had accepted the New Mexico scheme. Radicals viewed that as the most dangerous compromise proposal, for it might pass. But nothing came of it, for Seward failed to act on Lincoln's new position regarding New Mexico statehood. Curiously, Henry Adams later wrote that Seward, Adams, Davis, John Sherman, and other Republican conciliators lobbied hard for the New Mexico plan but were unsuccessful because "the mass of the party hesitated, and turned for the decisive word to the final authority at Springfield. The word did not come."[195] But in fact it did come.

Seward's behavior is one of the great mysteries of the secession crisis. If he had informed House and Senate Republicans that Lincoln supported the New Mexico Compromise, they would not have lamented, as John Sherman did on February 9, that "we are powerless here because we don't know *what Lincoln wants*. As he is to have the Executive power we can't go further than he approves. He communicates nothing even to his friends here & so we drift along."[196] (Two weeks earlier Henry Adams observed, "Lincoln's position is not known, but his course up to this time has shown his utter ignorance of the right way to act, so far as his appointments go. It is said, too, here [in Washington], that he is not a strong man.")[197]

Perhaps Seward feared that Southern Moderates would accept nothing less than a guarantee that slavery be allowed to expand into territory south of 36° 30'. He had good reason to think so, for when the New Mexico Compromise was before the House Committee of Thirty-Three, only two Southern members supported it. But in late January, James Shepherd Pike reported from Washington: "it is now believed that the Secession movement can be arrested there [in Virginia and Kentucky] on the basis of Mr. Adams's proposition."[198] A month later, the Washington correspondent of the New York *Times* asserted that the only thing necessary "to secure the loyalty of the Border States, and pave the way for the adjustment of our sectional differences, is the passage of an Enabling act for New-Mexico, authorizing that Territory to form a State Government." He thought such a measure involved no surrender of principle and would pass.[199] On March 1, Democrats supported New Mexico statehood, voting 45–39 against a motion to table a bill granting it. Seward had allegedly been telling stiff-backs that he only paid lip service to schemes like the New Mexico Compromise and "*had no idea of bringing them forward*" since "there were not *three* men on our side in the Senate who would support them."[200] But surely if Lincoln's approval had been made known, many Republicans would have backed a measure that he and Charles Francis Adams championed. On December 29, nine of the fifteen Republicans on the Committee of Thirty-Three had voted for it. Seward missed a potential opportunity to effect genuine compromise, for a majority of his party colleagues seemed willing to accept the New Mexico scheme. Lincoln did not again raise the New Mexico plan, which was before the House throughout February. On March 1 the Representatives shelved it, with Republicans voting in favor of the motion to table, 76–26.

The stunning victories achieved by antisecessionists in Virginia and Tennessee elections in early February led Henry Winter Davis to crow that there the "back of the revolution is broken."[201] (In Virginia, far more Moderates won election to a secession convention than did secessionists; in Tennessee, voters rejected a proposal to hold a secession convention.) With this turn of events, Seward may well have felt that his job was over and that he could calmly await Lincoln's arrival without further efforts on behalf of compromise. "At least," said he, "the danger of conflict, here or elsewhere, before the 4th of March, has been averted. Time has been gained."[202] On February 8, Henry Adams reported that "Seward is in high spirits and chuckles himself hoarse with his stories. He says it's all right. We shall keep the border states, and in three months or thereabouts, if we hold off, the Unionists and Disunionists will have their hands on each others throats in the cotton states. The storm is weathered."[203] Adams later observed that with the Unionist landslide victory in Virginia, "the country began to wake from its despair. Slowly the great ship seemed to right itself, broken and water-logged it is true, but not wrecked."[204] Varying that metaphor, Seward wrote his wife in mid-February as Lincoln's train wended its circuitous way toward the capital: "I am, at last, out of direct responsibility. I have brought the ship off the sands, and am ready to resign the helm into the hands of the Captain whom the people have chosen."[205] Seward deserves credit, for he, with the help of Charles Francis Adams and Henry Winter Davis, among others, had managed to keep the Upper South in the Union, at least temporarily.

Not every supporter of compromise thought highly of Seward. When the influential William C. Rives of Virginia, a former senator and minister to France, conferred with him in January, he was dismayed at the New Yorker's assertion that his "irrepressible conflict" rhetoric was "intended for effect at home, and not designed to reach the ears of the South." Rives regarded Seward as "a very small man, relying exclusively upon political maneuvering & without the least pretension to true & manly statesmanship."[206] If Seward had been able to work with Rives, the cause of compromise would have been greatly strengthened.

Others questioned Seward's statesmanship. Charles Sumner, who was to chair the Senate Foreign Relations Committee throughout the Civil War, called him "only a cunning contriver of little plots" and "not a true man." Sumner had good reason to conclude that the New Yorker "was not frank and straightforward."[207] Jefferson Davis was scandalized when Seward told him that his appeals on behalf of blacks "are potent to affect the rank and file of the North." When Davis asked if he never spoke "from conviction alone," the New Yorker replied: "Nev–er."[208] Montgomery Blair thought Seward "a most unsafe public man." Reminiscing after the Civil War, Blair called Seward "the personification of old Polonius' politician who 'by indirection found direction out.'" Nobody, Blair asserted, "has ever associated long with him, who has not heard him recount by the hour his successful political strategy." To Seward, politics was nothing more than "a harmless game for power." Blair could not forget how shocked he was when the senator confided "that he was the man who put Archy Dixon . . . up to moving the repeal of the Missouri Compromise," thus ruining Dixon's reputation.[209] James Lyons, a leading member of the Virginia bar and a prominent Whig, was equally scandalized when Seward told him that he had argued against the annexation of Texas on constitutional grounds only because it would become a Slave State. "If you had given us free territory every man of us would have voted for Texas," he later acknowledged insouciantly, causing Lyons to write Seward off "as a man destitute of all public principle."[210] The Russian minister to the United States, Edouard Stoeckl, was disgusted with Seward, whom he described as an arrogant, vain, small-time politician, and poseur who would listen to advice from no one. Similarly, George G. Fogg was appalled by Seward's "insolent refusal to even *consult* on the measures to be adopted" and by the "the lordly bearing" that he maintained "towards *all* the Republican members of the Senate."[211]

Old Gentlemen's Convention

By early February, Seward may have felt that the initiative for compromise could now be assumed by the Peace Conference, which Virginia had summoned to meet in Washington. He hoped that the conclave, which opened on February 4, would last for weeks and thus postpone any violent sectional clash. All states were invited to send delegates to consider a peaceful solution to the crisis, based on a variation of the Crittenden Compromise.

When the invitation to send delegates to the Peace Conference arrived at Springfield, Lincoln suggested that the legislature take no immediate action. Employing morbid imagery yet again, he said "that he would rather be hung by the neck till he was dead on the steps of the Capitol, before he would buy or beg a peaceful inauguration."[212] The *Illinois State Journal* was equally emphatic: "She [Virginia] says to us, 'unless you see fit to comply with our terms, we will lead our people to the commission of treason, and compel you to coerce us to obedience to the laws.' She proposes to us that we should adopt the Breckinridge platform as a basis of settlement. Not only this; but she insists that in all territory that may hereafter be acquired, slavery shall be protected by constitutional amendment. That is the proposition. And we can scarcely consider it with that degree of patience its importance would seem to demand. The character of the proposition can find a parallel only in the demand, that Mr. Lincoln, having been constitutionally elected, shall resign, and allow tra[i]tors and rebels to fill the offices, which the people have decided, shall be filled by Republicans the next four years. . . . We do not like the idea of *buying* the right to control the offices which the people have given the Republicans." To all Southern states urging compromise and concession, the *Journal* declared, "we are not aware of having done any wrong to them or their people," and "we do not propose to make either concession or compromise—if in doing so we are required to yield up any essential principle of Republican faith."[213]

Lincoln submitted draft resolutions to his friends calling for the governor to appoint representatives to the Peace Conference and making it clear that such action was not to be construed as endorsing any form of the Crittenden Compromise. In addition, the delegates were to be guided by instructions from the legislature. When Norman B. Judd advised that it would be premature to submit those resolutions to the General Assembly, Lincoln agreed. After Ohio and New York decided to send delegates, the Illinois Legislature followed suit, passing Lincoln's resolutions in order to help keep weak-kneed appeasers from dominating the convention. To that end, Governor Richard Yates chose five Republicans as delegates: Stephen T. Logan, former

Lieutenant-Governor Gustave Koerner, Burton C. Cook, ex-Congressman Thomas J. Turner, and ex-Governor John Wood, most of whom were Lincoln's friends. Koerner, thinking no good could come of the conclave, declined and recommended that John M. Palmer be named in his stead. Yates took that advice. When Lincoln received a protest against the appointment of Turner, who allegedly had "neither ability or respectability," he replied that he "did not think any objection to Turner of enough importance to have a squabble over."[214] The president-elect told Orville H. Browning that "no good results would follow the border State Convention . . . but evil rather, as increased excitement would follow when it broke up without having accomplished any thing," and that "no concession by the free States short of a surrender of every thing worth preserving, and contending for would satisfy the South, and that Crittenden's proposed amendment to the Constitution in the form proposed ought not to be made."[215]

In fact, the Peace Conference deliberated for weeks before recommending a variation on the Crittenden Compromise, which Congress rejected. During their deliberations, Republican leaders in Washington awaited Lincoln's arrival impatiently. An Indiana delegate to the Peace Conference explained that he and his fellow Republicans "have thus far done all in our power to procrastinate, and shall continue to do so, in order to remain in Session until after the 4th of March, for after the inauguration we shall have an honest fearless man at the helm, and will soon know whether the honest masses of the People desire to preserve and perpetuate our Government."[216]

Struggling with cabinet selections and compromise schemes, Lincoln suffered agony as Buchanan allowed the Cotton States to seize federal forts, arsenals, custom houses, post offices, and courthouses. In late December, upon hearing a rumor that the president would surrender Fort Moultrie in Charleston harbor, Lincoln snapped: "If that is true, they ought to hang him!"[217] A visitor reported that Lincoln's "Kentucky blood is up, he means *fight*. He says he has not yet had time to examine the list of vessels in our navy suitable for the purpose, but he intends to use them *all* if necessary, for blockading the ports in every seceding State, & the Army to garrison every fort on the coast, from Savannah to New Orleans."[218] He intended to preserve "the integrity of the Union if it costs blood enough to fill Charleston harbor," according to Horace White.[219]

Lincoln's anger was widely shared in the North, where the secessionists' takeover of U.S. government facilities was regarded as outrageous theft on a massive scale. Such wholesale robbery undermined support for compromise measures. Even before the Gulf States had seceded, the North was, according to a New Yorker, "fast being consolidated in opposition to the rumored attempts of the South to take possession of public property."[220] The secession of South Carolina was offensive enough to Northerners; but when the Palmetto State then seized federal property, it caused even greater indignation. In referring to this "sad blunder" by the disunionists, John Pendleton Kennedy of Maryland observed on February 10: "It is treason, and an indignity to the Sovereignty of the United States. That incident alone has changed the temper of the whole North. It has done very much the same thing here [in Maryland]. The hauling down of our glorious Stars and Stripes . . . has awakened a volume of ardor in favor of the Union which might otherwise have slept."[221] In New York, John A. Dix observed the same phenomenon. If the secessionists had behaved peaceably, the North probably would have acquiesced, but, recalled Dix, "the forcible seizure of arsenals, mints, revenue-cutters, and other property of the common government, . . . aroused a feeling of exasperation which nothing but the arbitrament of arms could overcome."[222]

Worried about Southern forts, Lincoln turned to Winfield Scott, the highest ranking officer in the U.S. Army. In late October, the general had recommended to him that all unmanned or undermanned U.S. forts be garrisoned, and he expressed the hope that a moderate but firm policy would thwart the secessionists. Lincoln thanked Scott and instructed E. B. Washburne to tell him "to be as well prepared as he can to either *hold*, or *retake*, the forts, as the case may require, at, and after the inaugeration."[223] On December 21, he wrote Francis P. Blair Sr. that "if the forts shall be given up before the inauguration, the General must retake them afterwards."[224] Five days later, Major Robert Anderson caused a sensation when he abandoned Fort Moultrie, which he rightly feared the secessionists would overrun, and moved his troops to Fort Sumter in the middle of Charleston harbor, a site far less vulnerable to attack. Hard-liners in the North cheered this bold action. Assessing events in the Palmetto State, Lincoln allegedly said "that the laws must be enforced, that the general government can do nothing else till the people consent to release that State from her allegiance to the government." He approved Anderson's conduct "in the most emphatic terms" and indicated that if "Buchanan should dismiss Major Anderson he would be reinstated the moment Mr. Lincoln comes into power, and probably promoted; and if not dismissed [by Buchanan], he would be cordially sustained by the incoming administration."[225]

Anticipating that violence might disrupt his inauguration, Lincoln asked Simon Cameron to consult with General Scott about assuring a safe inauguration. The Chief replied that "I have seen Genl. Scott, who bids me say he will be glad to act under your orders, in all ways to preserve the Union. He says Mr Buchanan, at last, has called on him to see that order shall be preserved at the inauguration in this District. That, for this purpose, he has ordered here 2 companies of flying artillery; and that he will organize the militia—and have himself *sworn in as a constable.* The old warrior is roused, and he will be equal to the occasion."[226] On January 4, Scott assured Lincoln that all would be well: "The President elect may rely, with confidence, on Genl. S's utmost exertions in the service of his country (the *Union*) both before & after the approaching inauguration."[227]

Perhaps because the general hailed from Virginia, Lincoln felt the need for further reassurance of his trustworthiness and loyalty. So the president-elect dispatched Thomas S. Mather, adjutant general of Illinois, to consult with him. In the capital, Old Fuss and Feathers urged Mather to tell Lincoln that "I shall expect him to come on to Washington as soon as he is ready. Say to him also that, when once here, I shall consider myself responsible for his safety. If necessary, I shall plant cannon at both ends of Pennsylvania Avenue, and if any of the Maryland or Virginia gentlemen who have become so threatening and troublesome of late show their heads or even venture to raise a finger, I shall blow them to hell!"[228] This report ended Lincoln's doubts about Scott, whose arrangements for the inauguration enjoyed the president-elect's full confidence.

Composing the Inaugural Address

By late January, Lincoln was devoting much time to his inaugural address and to the speeches he would deliver en route to Washington. To concentrate on that task and avoid distracting visits, he squirreled himself away in a small, little-used room in the store owned by his brother-in-law, Clark M. Smith, who provided a table and chair, the only furniture available to Lincoln there. He also took refuge in the hotel room of Thomas D. Jones, a Cincinnati sculptor who was executing a bust of the president-elect.

Herndon recalled that in late January, Lincoln "informed me that he was ready to begin the preparation of his inaugural address. He had, aside from his law books and the few gilded volumes that ornamented the centre-table in his parlor at home, comparatively no library. He never seemed to care to own or collect books. On the other hand I had a very respectable collection, and was adding to it every day. To my library Lincoln very frequently had access. When, therefore, he began on his inaugural speech he told me what works he intended to consult. I looked for a long list, but when he went over it I was greatly surprised. He asked me to furnish him with Henry Clay's great speech delivered in 1850; Andrew Jackson's proclamation against Nullification; and a copy of the Constitution." Herndon also supplied a copy of George Washington's farewell address. With these few books and documents at his fingertips, Lincoln secluded himself at Smith's store and drafted his inaugural.[229]

An editorial in the *Illinois State Journal*, perhaps written by Lincoln, quoted President Jackson's January 16, 1833, message to Congress attacking the nullification doctrine: "The right of the people of a single state to absolve themselves at will, and without the consent of the other States, from their most solemn obligations, and hazard the liberties and happiness of the millions composing this union, *cannot be* acknowledged. Such authority is believed to be utterly repugnant both to the principles upon which the general government is constituted, and to the objects which it was expressly formed to attain. . . . While a forbearing spirit may, and I trust will, be exercised toward the errors of our brethren in a particular quarter, duty to the rest of the Union demands that *open and organized resistance to the laws should not be executed with impunity.*"[230]

In late December, Lincoln was reportedly given to quoting Henry Clay's 1850 speech regarding South Carolina's threatened secession: "I should deplore as much as any man living or dead that armies should be raised against the authority of the Union, either by individuals or States. But after all that has occurred, if any one State, or a portion of the people of any State, choose to place themselves in military array against the government of the Union, I am for trying the strength of the government. I am for ascertaining whether we have a government or not—practical, efficient, ca-

pable of maintaining its authority and upholding the powers and interests which belong to a government. Now, sir, am I to be alarmed or dissuaded from any such course
by intimations of spilling blood? If blood is to be spilled, by whose fault will it be?
Upon this supposition I maintain it will be the fault of those who raise the standard
of disunion and endeavor to prostrate the government. And, sir, when that is done, so
long as it pleases God to give me a vote to express my sentiment, and an arm, weak
and enfeebled as it may be by age, that voice and that arm will be on the side of my
country, for the support of the general authority, and for the maintenance of the powers of this Union." If "the standard should be raised of open resistance to the union,
and constitution and the laws, what is to be done? There can be but one possible answer: the power, the authority and dignity of the government ought to be maintained,
and resistance put down at every hazard. . . . the moment a daring hand is raised to
resist, by force, the execution of the laws, the duty of enforcing them arises, and if the
conflict which may ensue should lead to civil war, the resisting party, having begun it,
will be responsible for all the consequences."[231] This stern rejection of secession would
characterize Lincoln's inaugural.

At Lincoln's request, William Bailhache of the *Illinois State Journal* secretly
printed a few copies of the inaugural address and kept them under lock and key. Before leaving Springfield, Lincoln showed one copy to a firm opponent of appeasing
the South, Carl Schurz, who approved its insistence that the revenues be collected,
that federal facilities be retaken, and that the laws be enforced.

In preparation for his departure, Lincoln "with his characteristic dutifulness"
rented out his house, sold his furniture, threw an elaborate farewell party, visited his
stepmother, reminisced with old friends, and arranged his itinerary.[232] The day he left,
after roping the trunks that had been packed by his servant Mariah Vance, he affixed
simple identification tags to them: A. Lincoln White House Washington, D.C.

On January 30 he took affectionate leave of his stepmother, Sarah Bush Lincoln,
whom he saw at Farmington near Charleston, where she was living with Augustus
H. Chapman. He had asked Lincoln to visit her: "She is getting somewhat childish
and is very uneasy about you fearing some of your political opponents will kill you.
She is very anxious to see you once more."[233]

Lincoln was also affectionate with Herndon when he said good-bye. "Billy," he
asked on the eve of his departure for Washington, "how long have we been together?"

"Over sixteen years."

"We've never had a cross word during all that time, have we?"

"No, indeed we have not."

After reminiscing about various cases, Lincoln pointed to the firm's signboard
outside the office and said, "Let it hang there undisturbed. Give our clients to understand that the election of a President makes no change in the firm of Lincoln and
Herndon. If I live I'm coming back some time, and then we'll go right on practicing
law as if nothing had ever happened."[234] (Herndon told Caroline Dall a different version of this farewell: "I will have no other partner while you live Bill, if you keep
straight.")[235]

As a parting gift, Lincoln offered Herndon his books. Overhearing him, Mary Lincoln sharply asked: "Abraham, are you going to give away everything we have got?" He replied: "Mary, if you will attend to your business, I will attend to mine."[236]

When Republican legislatures and governors throughout the North urged him to speak in their cities as he made his way to the nation's capital, Lincoln remarked that if he were accept them all, "he would not get to Washington until the Inauguration was over."[237] He did agree, however, to make addresses in Indiana, Ohio, New York, Pennsylvania, and New Jersey.

Eager to take the reins of government, Lincoln looked on with dismay as Buchanan failed to resist the takeover of federal facilities in seceding states, or to try regaining them once they were seized, or to dispatch the navy to collect revenues at Southern ports, or to call for volunteers to uphold the Union. The president-elect lamented to his old friend Joseph Gillespie on New Year's Day 1861 that "every hour adds to the difficulties I am called upon to meet, and the present Administration does nothing to check the tendency toward dissolution. I, who have been called to meet this awful responsibility, am compelled to remain here, doing nothing to avert it or lessen its force when it comes to me." Speaking with more bitterness than Gillespie ever heard him express, Lincoln added: "It is not of myself that I complain. But every day adds to the difficulty of the situation and makes the outlook for the country more gloomy. Secession is being fostered, rather than repressed, and if the doctrine meets with general acceptance in the border States it will be a great blow to the Government." His plight reminded Lincoln of a law case that he and Gillespie had once tried: "I suppose you will never forget that trial down in Montgomery County where the lawyer associated with you gave away the whole case in his opening speech. I saw you signaling to him, but you couldn't stop him. Now that's just the way with me and Buchanan. He is giving away the case and I have nothing to say and can't stop him."[238]

A few days thereafter a friend reported that Lincoln "has a world of responsibility & seems to feel it & to be oppressed by it. He looks care worn & more haggard & stooped than I ever saw him."[239] Gustave Koerner, who also noted that Lincoln "looks care worn," thought that "no man was ever in this country placed in a more perplexing and trying situation, than he is."[240] The sculptor Thomas Jones observed that in late January, "a deep-seated melancholy seemed to take possession of his soul."[241]

Lincoln grew exasperated with congressional Republicans as well as with Buchanan. On February 4, the senate passed a bill organizing the Colorado Territory with no provision excluding slavery. A short while later, similar legislation was adopted for Nevada and Dakota. "It seems to me," Lincoln told Gillespie, "that Douglas got the best of it at the election last fall. I am left to face an empty treasury and a great rebellion, while my own party endorses his popular sovereignty idea and applies it in legislation." As he was about to leave for Washington, he said to his old friend: "I only wish I could have got there to lock the door before the horse was stolen."[242]

On February 11, Lincoln boarded a train that would take him to the nation's capital where he would try to keep other horses—the eight Slave States in the border region and the Upper South—from being stolen. Just before the train pulled out, he delivered a brief farewell to Springfield, one of the most affecting of his prose masterpieces. In the immediately preceding days, he seemed sad at the prospect of leaving old friends. That morning, he spent half an hour at the small, dingy depot shaking hands with innumerable well-wishers. He was so deeply moved that he could hardly speak. The mood was solemn and anxious as he mounted the platform of the train's rear car. There, a friend noted, his "breast heaved with emotion and he could scarcely command his feelings sufficiently to commence."[243] Briefly he surveyed the large crowd, consisting of Republicans and Democrats alike, as the cold wind blew a combination of snow and rain into their faces. Only the locomotive's steady hiss broke the silence.

Trembling with suppressed emotion and radiating profound sadness, he slowly and distinctly delivered his eloquent remarks: "My friends—No one, not in my situation, can appreciate my feeling of sadness at this parting. To this place, and the kindness of these people, I owe every thing. Here I have lived a quarter of a century, and have passed from a young to an old man. Here my children have been born, and one is buried. I now leave, not knowing when, or whether ever, I may return, with a task before me greater than that which rested upon Washington. Without the assistance of that Divine Being, who ever attended him, I cannot succeed. With that assistance I cannot fail. Trusting in Him, who can go with me, and remain with you and be every where for good, let us confidently hope that all will yet be well. To His care commending you, as I hope in your prayers you will commend me, I bid you an affectionate farewell."[244]

"We will do it; we will do it," responded many in the crowd, who, like the speaker, had tears in their eyes.[245] An editor of the *Illinois State Journal* called it "a most impressive scene. We have known Mr. Lincoln for many years; we have heard him speak upon a hundred different occasions; but we never saw him so profoundly affected, nor did he ever utter an address which seemed to us so full of simple and touching eloquence, so exactly adapted to the occasion, so worthy of the man and the hour. Although it was raining fast when he began to speak, every hat was lifted, and every head bent forward to catch the last words of the departing chief."[246] The New York *World* commented that nothing "could have been more appropriate and touching," while the Chicago *Press and Tribune* accurately predicted that it "will become a part of the national history."[247] Lincoln's friend, Chicago Congressman Isaac N. Arnold, told his House colleagues that there was "not a more simple, touching, and beautiful speech in the English language."[248] After Lincoln took leave of his family and entered the car, the crowd gave three cheers and then stood silent as the train slowly pulled away.

NOTES

List of Abbreviations

AL MSS DLC: Abraham Lincoln Papers, Library of Congress

CSmH: Huntington Library, San Marino, California

DLC: Library of Congress

HI: Herndon's Informants

H-W MSS DLC: Herndon-Weik Papers, Library of Congress

ICHi: Chicago History Museum

IHi: Abraham Lincoln Presidential Library and Museum, Springfield

InU: Indiana University

LMF: Lincoln Museum, Fort Wayne

MHi: Massachusetts Historical Society

RPB: Brown University

Author's Note

1. Nevins to Benjamin P. Thomas, New York, 10 Dec. 1951, Thomas Papers, Lincoln Presidential Library, Springfield.

2. Sandburg to F. Lauriston Bullard, Herbert, Michigan, 10 May 1940, carbon copy, Barrett-Sandburg Papers, Newberry Library, Chicago. On Bullard's criticism, see Joseph E. George, Jr., "F. Lauriston Bullard as a Lincoln Scholar" (Ph.D. dissertation, Boston University, 1959), 28–42.

3. John W. Starr, *The Dual Personality of Abraham Lincoln: A Brief Psychological Study* (privately printed, 1928), 5.

4. Morison to Beveridge, Oxford [England], 15 June 1925, Beveridge Papers, Library of Congress.

5. Nathaniel W. Stephenson to Albert J. Beveridge, New Haven, Connecticut, 23 June 1926, Beveridge Papers, Library of Congress.

6. Allen G. Bogue, "Historians and Radical Republicans: A Meaning for Today," *Journal of American History* 70 (1983): 29.

7. Speech by Frederick Douglass at New York's Cooper Union, 1 June 1865, manuscript in the Douglass Papers, Library of Congress.

8. Norton to George William Curtis, Shady Hill, 10 December 1863, Sara Norton and M. A. DeWolfe Howe, eds., *Letter of Charles Eliot Norton* (2 vols.; Boston: Houghton Mifflin, 1913), 1:266.

Chapter 1. "I Have Seen a Good Deal of the Back Side of This World"

1. Lincoln to James Madison Cutts Jr., Washington, 26 Oct. 1863, Roy P. Basler et al., eds., *Collected Works of Abraham Lincoln* [hereafter *CWL*] (8 vols. plus index; New Brunswick, NJ: Rutgers University Press, 1953–1955), 6:538.

2. James Grant Wilson, "Recollections of Lincoln," *Putnam's Magazine* 5 (Feb. 1909):515.

3. Lincoln to Jesse Lincoln, Springfield, 1 Apr. 1854, *CWL*, 2:217.

4. William Dean Howells, *Life of Abraham Lincoln*, ed. Harry E. Pratt (Springfield, IL: Abraham Lincoln Association, 1938, facsimile of the 1860 edition with emendations made by Lincoln), 30.

5. William H. Herndon, "Nancy Hanks," notes written in Greencastle, Indiana, ca. 20 Aug. 1887, H-W MSS DLC; Jesse W. Weik, *The Real Lincoln: A Portrait*, ed. Michael Burlingame (1922; Lincoln: University of Nebraska Press, 2002), 37–38.

6. William E. Barton's notes of an interview with Mrs. Ben Hardin Helm, Lexington, Kentucky, 11 Mar. 1921, Barton Papers, University of Chicago.

7. Edgar K. Webb, "Lincoln's Birthplace to Be Made a National Park," unidentified

clipping, 1905, reference files of the Abraham Lincoln Association, "Romance" folder, IHi.

8. Dennis Hanks, quoted in an unidentified clipping, LMF.

9. Otis M. Mather, "Thomas Lincoln in Larue County, Kentucky," talk given 26 June 1937, p. 2, Mather Papers, Filson Club, Louisville, Kentucky.

10. George T. Balch, recalling the words of his father, George B. Balch, paraphrased in Dr. W. H. Doak, Martinsville, Illinois, to his nephew, Dr. W. D. Ewing of Cambridge, Ohio, [1 Feb. 1923], Terre Haute, Indiana, *Star,* 11 Feb. 1923.

11. Henry C. Whitney, manuscript version of *Lincoln the Citizen,* p. 24, Lincoln Memorial University, Harrogate, Tennessee. This passage was omitted from the published edition of the biography (Henry C. Whitney, *Lincoln the Citizen,* vol. 1 of *A Life of Lincoln,* ed. Marion Mills Miller [2 vols.; New York: Baker and Taylor, 1908]). The words quoted by Whitney are from Henry Clay's description of his own paternal inheritance.

12. Samuel Haycraft to Herndon, Elizabethtown, Kentucky, [June 1865], Douglas L. Wilson and Rodney O. Davis, eds., *Herndon's Informants: Letters, Interviews, and Statements about Abraham Lincoln* [hereafter *HI*] (Urbana: University of Illinois Press, 1998), 67; Jack Peck (b. 1800), interviewed by Harvey H. Smith in 1888, Harvey H. Smith, *Lincoln and the Lincolns* (New York: Pioneer Publications, 1931), 168; the Rev. Mr. Thomas Goodwin, in Walter B. Stevens, *A Reporter's Lincoln,* ed. Michael Burlingame (1916; Lincoln: University of Nebraska Press, 1998), 167; Janesville, Illinois, correspondence, 30 May 1880, Chicago *Chronicle,* n.d., copied in *La Porte Weekly Herald* (Indiana), 27 [?] Oct. 1921, clipping, LMF; George B. Balch, "The Father of Abraham Lincoln," manuscript pasted into a copy of Francis Fisher Browne, *The Every-Day Life of Abraham Lincoln,* Lilly Library, InU.

13. Dennis F. Hanks, interview with Erastus Wright, Chicago, 8 June 1865, *HI,* 28.

14. Balch, "The Father of Abraham Lincoln."

15. William Bender Wilson, "A Glimpse of the United States Military Telegraph Corps, and of Abraham Lincoln" (pamphlet; Philadelphia: Holmburg, [1889]), 18–19.

16. William G. Greene to Herndon, Tallula, Illinois, 20 Dec. 1865, *HI,* 145; Greene interviewed by George A. Pierce, dispatch dated "on the cars," 12 Apr., Chicago *Inter-Ocean,* 30 Apr. 1881.

17. John J. Hall in Eleanor Gridley, *The Story of Abraham Lincoln, or The Journey from the Log Cabin to the White House* (n.p.: Juvenile Publishing Co., 1900), 62.

18. Balch, recalling the words of his father, Terre Haute, Indiana, *Star,* 11 Feb. 1923.

19. Marcy Gordon Bodine of Western Illinois University, "Story of the Lincolns of Hancock County," paper delivered before the Illinois State Historical Society, published in the Macomb, Illinois, *Journal,* 12 Feb. 1955.

20. James S. Pirtle, summarizing the testimony of his father, who was a neighbor of Mordecai's in Kentucky. James S. Pirtle to Joshua F. Speed, Louisville, Nov. 1877 [no day of the month indicated], Joseph Gillespie Papers, ICHi.

21. A. R. Simmons to William E. Barton, Colchester, Illinois, 7 Mar. 1923, Barton Papers, University of Chicago.

22. Bernice V. Lovely to W. A. Evans, Colchester, Illinois, 21 Apr. 1921, and Lovely to William E. Barton, Colchester, Illinois, 14 May 1922, Barton Papers, University of Chicago.

23. William H. Townsend, *Lincoln and the Bluegrass: Slavery and Civil War in Kentucky* (Lexington: University of Kentucky Press, 1955), 19.

24. Hancock County Court, "Verdict of Jury in the Matter of Mary Jane Lincoln Alleged to Be Insane," 17 May 1867, Illinois State Archives, in Joshua Wolf Shenk, *Lincoln's Melancholy: How Depression Challenged a President and Fueled His Greatness* (Boston: Houghton Mifflin, 2005), 247.

25. E. R. Burba to Herndon, Hodgenville, Kentucky, 31 Mar. 1866, *HI,* 240; Balch, recalling the words of his father George B.

Balch, Terre Haute, Indiana, *Star,* 11 Feb. 1923; "Abraham Lincoln's Boyhood," anonymous manuscript written on the stationery of the Spencer County Assessor's Office, assessor Bartley Inco, 189_, copy, Francis Marion Van Natter Papers, Vincennes University; Samuel Haycraft, quoted in Elizabethtown correspondence, n.d., Louisville *Courier Journal,* n.d. [ca. 1886], clipping, Lincoln Scrapbook, Rare Book Room, DLC.

26. Dennis Hanks to Herndon (interview), Chicago, 13 June 1865, *HI,* 37; Augustus H. Chapman's statement for Herndon, [before 8 Sept. 1865], ibid., 97.

27. Gridley, *Story of Lincoln,* 61–62.

28. George Tuthill Borrett, *Out West: Letters from Canada and the United States* (London: J. E. Adlard, 1865), 253 (letter dated "on board the Kangaroo," Nov. 1864).

29. Notes for a law lecture, [1 July 1850?], *CWL,* 2:81.

30. Gridley, *Story of Lincoln,* 48, 45.

31. Wayne C. Temple, "Thomas and Abraham Lincoln as Farmers" (pamphlet; Racine, Wisconsin: Lincoln Fellowship of Wisconsin, 1996), passim; Kenneth J. Winkle, *The Young Eagle: The Rise of Abraham Lincoln* (Dallas, TX: Taylor, 2001), 143–144.

32. Balch, "The Father of Abraham Lincoln;" Balch, interview with Jesse W. Weik, [1886?], *HI,* 597.

33. Nathaniel Grigsby, interview with Herndon, Gentryville, Indiana, 12 Sept. 1865, *HI,* 113.

34. Recollections of William E. Grigsby, recounted by his great granddaughter, Elizabeth Decker of Arizona, memorandum on the Grigsby family, Lincoln Boyhood National Memorial, Lincoln City, Indiana.

35. Robert Mitchell Thompson, interviewed in the Louisville *Times,* clipping, ca. 1891, William H. Townsend Papers, University of Kentucky, Lexington.

36. Interview with Austin Gollaher by J. C. M., Hodgenville correspondence, 23 Mar., Cincinnati *Tribune,* 24 Mar. 1895; Joseph Davis Armstrong, undated article in the Oakland City, Indiana, *Enterprise,* copy, Francis Marion

Van Natter Papers, Vincennes University; "Abraham Lincoln's Boyhood," anonymous manuscript written on the stationery of the Spencer County (Indiana) Assessor's Office, Assessor Bartley Inco, 189_, copy, ibid.

37. Greene to Herndon, Tallulah, Illinois, 29 May 1865, *HI,* 12; Greene interviewed by George A. Pierce, dispatch dated "on the cars," 12 Apr., Chicago *Inter-Ocean,* 30 Apr. 1881; Francis F. Browne, *The Every-Day Life of Abraham Lincoln* (New York: N. D. Thompson, 1886), 87; Whitney, *Lincoln the Citizen,* 74.

38. William Henry Perrin, *The History of Coles County, Illinois* (Chicago: Lebaron & Co., 1879), 422.

39. Arthur E. Morgan, "New Light on Lincoln's Boyhood," *Atlantic Monthly* 125 (Feb. 1920):213.

40. Dennis F. Hanks to Herndon (interview), Chicago, 13 June 1865, *HI,* 39.

41. John Mack Faragher, *Sugar Creek: Life on the Illinois Prairie* (New Haven, CT: Yale University Press, 1986), 97.

42. Francis Grierson, *The Valley of Shadows: Sangamon Sketches,* ed. Robert Bray (1909; Urbana: University of Illinois Press, 1990), 44.

43. Lincoln to John D. Johnston, Washington, 24 Dec. 1848, and Shelbyville, Illinois, 4 Nov. 1851, *CWL,* 2:16, 111; William H. Herndon to a clergyman in New York, Springfield, 24 Nov. 1882, Washington *Post,* 4 Feb. 1883.

44. Autobiograpy enclosed in Lincoln to Jesse W. Fell, Springfield, 20 Dec. 1859, *CWL,* 3:511; autobiography written for John L. Scripps, [ca. June 1860], ibid., 4:61.

45. Dennis Hanks in Robert McIntyre, "Lincoln's Friend," Charleston, Illinois, *Courier,* n.d; Paris, Illinois, *Gazette,* n.d., Chicago *Tribune,* 30 May 1885; Dennis F. Hanks to Herndon, n.p., 26 Jan. 1866, *HI,* 176.

46. Augustus H. Chapman to Herndon, Charleston, Illinois, 28 Sept. 1865, *HI,* 134.

47. Lincoln to John D. Johnston, Springfield, 12 Jan. 1851, *CWL,* 2:97.

48. Usher F. Linder, *Reminiscences of the Early Bench and Bar of Illinois* (Chicago: Chicago Legal News, 1879), 38.

49. William H. Herndon to Ward Hill Lamon, Springfield, 25 Feb. 1870, Lamon Papers, CSmH.

50. Caroline Dall to James Freeman Clarke, Chicago, 1 Nov. 1866, Dall Papers, Bryn Mawr College.

51. Ward Hill Lamon, *The Life of Abraham Lincoln: From His Birth to His Inauguration as President* (Boston: J. R. Osgood, 1872), 40n.

52. Dennis Hanks to Herndon (interview), Chicago, 13 June 1865, *HI*, 39; Amanda Hanks Poorman, "New Stories about the Great Emancipator," St. Louis *Post-Dispatch*, 26 May 1901.

53. Notes of Arthur E. Morgan's interview with Nancy Davidson, half-sister of Sophie Hanks's son James LeGrande, Feb. 1909, Morgan Papers, DLC.

54. "Notes on Arthur E. Morgan's first trip—Jasper [Arkansas, Feb. 1909]," Morgan Papers, DLC.

55. Undated questionnaire filled out for Arthur E. Morgan by Dr. James LeGrande, Morgan Papers, DLC.

56. Dennis Hanks to Herndon (interview), Chicago, 13 June 1865, *HI*, 41.

57. William G. Greene in Whitney, *Lincoln the Citizen*, 75; Browne, *Every-Day Life of Lincoln*, 88.

58. John Hanks to Jesse W. Weik, Linkville, Oregon, 12 June 1887, *HI*, 615; Dennis F. Hanks, interview with Jesse W. Weik, [1886?], ibid., 598; Nathaniel Grigsby, interview with Herndon, Gentryville, Indiana, 12 Sept. 1865, ibid., 113, 111; Augustus H. Chapman's statement for Herndon, [before 8 Sept. 1865], ibid., 97; John Hanks, interview with John Miles, Decatur, Illinois, 25 May 1865, ibid., 5; Elinor Peck's reminiscences of Nancy Hanks as recounted by her daughter-in-law, Mrs. Henry B. Peck (née Catherine Smith, 1827–1909), the daughter of Dr. William B. Smith, in Harvey H. Smith, *Lincoln and the Lincolns* (New York: Pioneer Publications 1931), 11–12; Samuel Haycraft to John B. Helm, Elizabethtown, Kentucky, 5 July 1865, and to

Herndon, Elizabethtown, Kentucky, [June 1865], *HI*, 84, 67; Henry Brooner, paraphrased in David Turnham to Herndon, Dale, Indiana, 19 Nov. 1866, ibid., 403; John Hanks, interview with Herndon, [1865–1866], ibid., 454; Nathaniel Grigsby, interview with Herndon, Gentryville, Indiana, 12 Sept. 1865, ibid., 113.

59. J. Edward Murr, "Some Pertinent Observations Concerning 'Abe Lincoln—The Hoosier,'" 5, unpublished typescript, Murr Papers, DePauw University, Greencastle, Indiana.

60. Herndon to Ward Hill Lamon, Springfield, 25 Feb. 1870, Lamon Papers, CSmH; Herndon to John W. Wartman, Springfield, 19 Feb. 1870, copy, Southwestern Indiana Historical Society Papers, Evansville Central Library.

61. Dennis F. Hanks to Herndon (interview), Chicago, 13 June 1865, *HI*, 37.

62. Nathaniel Grigsby, interview with Herndon, Gentryville, Indiana, 12 Sept. 1865, *HI*, 113.

63. Dennis Hanks to Herndon (interview), Chicago, 13 June 1865, *HI*, 40.

64. Undated letter by Charlotte Spear Hobart Vawter to the editor of the Indianapolis *Journal*, Indianapolis *Journal*, n.d., copied in the Louisville *Courier-Journal*, 20 Feb. 1874, in *HI*, 585.

65. Reminiscences of Pamelia Cowherd (b. 1804), in an 1885 interview, Smith, *Lincoln and the Lincolns*, 151; William H. Herndon to Jesse W. Weik, Springfield, 10 Oct. 1888, H-W MSS DLC.

66. Elinor Peck's reminiscences of Nancy Hanks, recounted by her daughter-in-law, Catherine (Mrs. Henry) Peck (b. 1826), the daughter of Billy Smith, in Smith, *Lincoln and the Lincolns*, 76.

67. J. Edward Murr to Albert J. Beveridge, [New Albany, Indiana, 21 Nov. 1924], Beveridge Papers, DLC.

68. Brown to Reuben T. Durrett, Louisville, Kentucky, 12 May 1886, Durrett Personal Papers, University of Chicago.

69. John B. Helm to Herndon, n.p., 1 Aug. 1865, *HI*, 82; Presley Nevil Haycraft to John B. Helm, 19 July 1865, ibid., 86.

70. Herndon to Charles H. Hart, Springfield, 28 Dec. 1866, Hart Papers, CSmH.

71. Herndon to Jesse W. Weik, Springfield, 19 Jan. 1886, H-W MSS DLC.

72. Linder, *Reminiscences of the Early Bench and Bar*, 39.

73. This is based on research done by John Y. Ewing of Louisville. Ida N. Pendleton to Ida Tarbell, Hartford, Kentucky, 17 June 1896, Tarbell Papers, Allegheny College.

74. Mrs. William Maffitt Smith (1814–1902), who claimed to be related to Nancy Hanks Lincoln through her mother (Jane Gray), interviewed by Harvey H. Smith in 1889, in Smith, *Lincoln and the Lincolns*, 219, 71.

75. Herndon to Truman H. Bartlett, Springfield, Oct. 1887, Bartlett Papers, MHi.

76. Herndon to Ward Hill Lamon, Springfield, 25 Feb. 1870, Lamon Papers, CSmH; Herndon, "Nancy Hanks," memo written in Greencastle, Indiana, ca. 20 Aug. 1887, H-W MSS DLC.

77. Herndon told this to Caroline Dall in 1866. Dall, "Journal of a tour through Illinois, Wisconsin and Ohio, Oct. & Nov. 1866," entry for 29 Oct. 1866, Dall Papers, Bryn Mawr College.

78. Murr to Noble L. Moore, New Albany, Indiana, 17 Aug. 1942, Murr Papers, Indiana Division, Indiana State Library, Indianapolis.

79. Herndon to Charles H. Hart, Springfield, 28 Dec. 1866, Hart Papers, CSmH; Herndon to Lamon, Springfield, 25 Feb. 1870, Lamon Papers, ibid.

80. David Turnham, interview with Herndon, 15 Sept. 1865, *HI*, 122.

81. Herndon to Ward Hill Lamon, Springfield, 6 Mar. 1870, Lamon Papers, CSmH.

82. Herndon to Charles H. Hart, Springfield, 2 Mar. 1867, Hart Papers, CSmH.

83. Herndon, "Nancy Hanks," notes written in Greencastle, Indiana, ca. 20 Aug. 1887, H-W MSS DLC.

84. Scripps to Herndon, Chicago, 24 June 1865, *HI*, 57.

85. Lincoln to Mrs. Orville H. Browning, Springfield, 1 Apr. 1838, *CWL*, 1:118.

86. "Conversation with Redmond Grigsby, Sr., July 17, 1904," in Charles F. Brown's notebook, copy, Francis Marion Van Natter Papers, Vincennes University.

87. Cincinnati *Commercial*, n.d., copied in the New York *Evening Post*, 8 July 1865.

88. Eliza W. Farnham, *Life in Prairie Land* (New York: Harper & Brothers, 1846), 65–66.

89. Quoted in William E. Wilson, "'There I Grew Up,'" *American Heritage* 17 (Oct. 1966):102.

90. Interview with Jack Peck (b. 1800), 1888, in Smith, *Lincoln and the Lincolns*, 170–171.

91. William H. Herndon and Jesse W. Weik, *Herndon's Lincoln*, ed. Douglas L. Wilson and Rodney O. Davis (1889; Urbana: University of Illinois Press, 2006), 33.

92. John L. Scripps to Herndon, Chicago, 24 June 1865, *HI*, 57.

93. Leonard Swett in Allen Thorndike Rice, ed., *Reminiscences of Abraham Lincoln by Distinguished Men of His Time* (New York: North American Review, 1886), 457.

94. Lincoln to Andrew Johnston, Springfield, 6 Sept. 1846, *CWL*, 1:384.

95. After returning to Springfield following his travels in the East during the late winter of 1860, Lincoln told this to a friend named Jim (probably James Matheny), who in turn related it to Edward Eggleston. Browne, *Every-Day Life of Abraham Lincoln*, 323.

96. E. R. Burba to Herndon, Hodgenville, Kentucky, 31 Mar. 1866, *HI*, 240; Usher F. Linder, speech before the Chicago Bar Association, 17 Apr. 1865, Washington *Sunday Chronicle*, 23 Apr. 1865.

97. Louisville *Courier-Journal*, 11 Sept. 1895; interview with Austin Gollaher by J. C. M., Hodgenville correspondence, 23 Mar. 1895, Cincinnati *Tribune*, 24 Mar. 1895; Gollaher paraphrased in J. M. Atherton to Otis M. Mather, 20 June 1924, copy, enclosed in Mather to Albert J. Beveridge, Hodgenville, Kentucky, 24 July 1924, Beveridge Papers, DLC.

98. A Mrs. Rathbone, paraphrased in the Louisville correspondence of the *Enquirer* [Cincinnati?], 10 Feb. [1911? or 1912], clipping headlined "Governor Willson to Leave for Hodgenville, Ky.," clipping collection, LMF.

99. Dennis Hanks to Herndon, 26 Jan. 1866, *HI,* 176.

100. Paris, Illinois, correspondence, 21 Oct., Roanoke, Illinois, *Times,* 12 Nov. 1892, clipping collection, LMF.

101. Maude Jennings Cryderman (daughter of Josiah and Elizabeth Crawford) to Mrs. Calder Ehrmann, Tipton, Indiana, 4 Mar. 1928, John E. Iglehart Papers, Indiana Historical Society, Indianapolis.

102. Presley Nevil Haycraft to John B. Helm, n.p., 19 July 1865, *HI,* 87; John Pitcher, paraphrased in Oliver C. Terry to Jesse W. Weik, Mt. Vernon, Indiana, 14 July 1888, and [?] July 1888, ibid., 658–659, 662–663.

103. Reminiscences of Mrs. Annie Heibach, daughter of James L. Grant, San Francisco *Call,* 16 Feb. 1896.

104. Mrs. Bartley Inco (née Nancy Grigsby), in a talk given 20 June 1916, Grandview, Indiana, *Monitor,* 20 Sept. 1934; Carrie Grigsby, wife of Reuben Grigsby's grandson, in a roundtable discussion in Gentryville, n.d., paraphrased in Arietta F. Bullock, "Jonesboro in 1830," 19, typescript of a paper delivered to the Southwestern Indiana Historical Society, 1938, Bullock Papers, Indiana Historical Society, Indianapolis.

105. John W. Wartmann's talk, 20 June 1916, Evansville *Courier,* n.d., in "Sarah Lincoln Grigsby, Remarks of Hon. Charles Lieb, of Indiana, in the House of Representatives, June 28, 1916," *Congressional Record,* 64th Congress, 1st Session, vol. 53, part 10, p. 10177.

106. Joseph Blackford in the New York *Evening Post,* 11 Feb. 1911.

107. Murr, "He Knew Lincoln's Neighbors," Bess V. Ehrmann, *The Missing Chapter in the Life of Abraham Lincoln* (Chicago: Walter M. Hill, 1938), 92–93.

108. Murr, "Lincoln in Indiana," *Indiana Magazine of History* 14 (1918):13.

109. Joseph D. Armstrong, "History of Spencer County," in *An Illustrated Historical Atlas of Spencer County, Indiana* (Philadelphia: D. J. Lake, 1879), 13.

110. Harriet A. Chapman to Herndon, Charleston, Illinois, 10 Dec. 1866, *HI,* 512–513.

111. Joseph Gillespie to Herndon, Edwardsville, Illinois, 31 Jan. 1866, *HI,* 185.

112. The Reverend Mr. Noyes M. Miner, "Personal Reminiscences of Lincoln," manuscript, IHi.

113. Clark, "The Kentucky Influence on the Life of Abraham Lincoln" (pamphlet; Address at Annual Meeting of the Lincoln Fellowship of Wisconsin, Madison, 13 Feb. 1961; Historical Bulletin No. 20, 1963), 4.

114. Edgar K. Webb, "Lincoln's Birthplace to Be Made a National Park," unidentified clipping, 1905, Abraham Lincoln Association reference files, "Romance" folder, IHi; Richard A. Creal to Herndon, Larue County, Kentucky, 12 Mar. 1866, *HI,* 228.

115. J. J. Wright, M.D., to Ida Tarbell, Emporia, Kansas, 18 Apr. 1896, Ida M. Tarbell Papers, Allegheny College.

116. John G. Nicolay and John Hay, *Abraham Lincoln: A History* (10 vols.; New York: Century, 1890), 1:27.

117. E. R. Burba to Herndon, Hodgenville, Kentucky, 31 Mar. 1866, *HI,* 241.

118. Alexander Sympson told this to Henry Clay Whitney. Whitney, *Life on the Circuit,* ed. Angle, 37.

119. Charles Friend to Herndon, Sonora, Kentucky, 20 Aug. 1889, *HI,* 676.

120. Whitney, *Lincoln the Citizen,* 22.

121. Samuel Haycraft to Herndon, Elizabethtown, Kentucky, [June 1865], *HI,* 67.

122. Austin Gollaher interviewed by J. C. M., Hodgenville correspondence, 23 Mar., Cincinnati *Tribune,* 24 Mar. 1895.

123. Autobiography written for Jesse W. Fell, 20 Dec. 1859, *CWL,* 3:511.

124. Mrs. Susie Yeager to James M. Yeager, 1890, New York *Tribune,* 26 Dec. 1897.

125. Howells, *Life of Lincoln,* ed. Pratt, 20.

126. Dennis Hanks, interview with Herndon, Chicago, 13 June 1865, *HI*, 39.

127. William E. Barton to Robert Todd Lincoln, n.p., 15 Mar. 1919, copy, Barton Papers, University of Chicago.

128. Interview with Fields Elkin, Elizabethtown, Kentucky, 21 June 1922, conducted by Louis A. Warren, copy, Lincoln files, "David Elkins" folder, Lincoln Museum, Lincoln Memorial University, Harrogate, Tennessee.

129. John Locke Scripps, *Life of Abraham Lincoln*, ed. Roy P. Basler and Lloyd A. Dunlap (1860; Bloomington: Indiana University Press, 1961), 37–38.

130. Andrew R. L. Cayton, *Frontier Indiana* (Bloomington: Indiana University Press, 1996), 272.

131. John Badollet, quoted in Cayton, *Frontier Indiana*, 265.

132. William Makepeace Thayer, *The Pioneer Boy and How He Became President* (Boston: Walker, Wise, 1863), 79.

133. Autobiography written for John Locke Scripps, [ca. June 1860], *CWL*, 4:61–62.

134. Dennis Hanks to Herndon (interview), Chicago, 13 June 1865, *HI*, 36.

135. Burba to Herndon, Hodgenville, 31 Mar. and 25 May 1866, *HI*, 240, 257.

136. Scripps, *Life of Lincoln*, ed. Basler and Dunlap, 29.

137. Dennis Hanks, interview with Herndon, Charleston, 8 Sept. 1865, *HI*, 103–104.

138. Reminiscence by an unidentified native of Kentucky, Springfield, Illinois, correspondence by Henry Villard, 29 Nov., New York *Herald*, 4 Dec. 1860.

139. Sarah Bush Lincoln, interview with Herndon, Charleston, 8 Sept. 1865, *HI*, 106.

Chapter 2. "I Used to Be a Slave"

1. Elias Pym Fordham, *Personal Narrative of Travels in Virginia, Maryland, Pennsylvania, Ohio, Indiana, Kentucky; and of a Residence in the Illinois Territory: 1817–1818* (Cleveland: Arthur H. Clark, 1906), 96.

2. Dennis Hanks to Herndon, 12 Mar. 1866, and Augustus H. Chapman, statement for Herndon, [before 8 Sept. 1865], Douglas L. Wilson and Rodney O. Davis, eds., *Herndon's Informants: Letters, Interviews, and Statements about Abraham Lincoln* [hereafter *HI*] (Urbana: University of Illinois Press, 1998), 229, 98.

3. J. Edward Murr, "The Wilderness Years of Abraham Lincoln," 125–126, unpublished typescript, Murr Papers, DePauw University, Greencastle, Indiana.

4. Autobiography written for Jesse W. Fell, 20 Dec. 1859, Roy P. Basler et al., eds., *Collected Works of Abraham Lincoln* [hereafter *CWL*] (8 vols. plus index; New Brunswick, NJ: Rutgers University Press, 1953–1955), 3:511; autobiography written for John Locke Scripps, [c. June 1860], ibid., 4:62.

5. Lincoln to Andrew Johnston, Tremont, Illinois, 18 Apr. 1846, *CWL*, 1:378; "The Bear Hunt," ca. 6 Sept.1846, ibid., 1:386.

6. *CWL*, 4:62.

7. Augustus H. Chapman, statement to Herndon, [before 8 Sept. 1865], *HI*, 98.

8. Dennis Hanks, interview with Herndon, Charleston, Illinois *HI*, 8 Sept. 1865, 105.

9. David Turnham to Herndon, Dale, Indiana, 21 Feb. 1866, *HI*, 217.

10. Dennis Hanks to Herndon, 6 Jan. 1866, *HI*, 154.

11. Herndon to Joseph Smith Fowler, Springfield, 18 Feb. 1887, Herndon Papers, IHi; Herndon to Cyrus O. Poole, Springfield, 5 Jan. 1886, and Herndon, "Lincoln's Superstition," H-W MSS DCL.

12. Lincoln to Joshua F. Speed, Springfield, 4 July 1842, *CWL*, 1:289.

13. Henry C. Whitney, "Lincoln a Fatalist," Rockport, Indiana, *Journal*, 11 Feb. 1898.

14. Autobiography written for John Locke Scripps, [ca. June 1860], *CWL*, 4:62.

15. Herndon to Ward Hill Lamon, Springfield, 6 Mar. 1870, Lamon Papers, CSmH.

16. William Faux, *Memorable Days in America: Being a Journal of a Tour to the United*

States (London: W. Simpkin and R. Marshall, 1823), Reuben Gold Thwaites, ed., *Early Western Travels, 1748–1846: A Series of Annotated Reprints of Some of the Best and Rarest Contemporary Volumes of Travel, Descriptive of the Aborigines and Social and Economic Conditions in the Middle and Far West, during the Period of Early American Settlement* (32 vols.; Cleveland: Arthur H. Clark, 1904–1907), II:226.

17. Dennis Hanks to Herndon (interview), Chicago, 13 June 1865, *HI*, 40.

18. Lincoln to Fanny McCullough, Washington, 23 Dec. 1862, *CWL*, 6:16–17.

19. Jesse W. Weik, *The Real Lincoln: A Portrait*, ed. Michael Burlingame (1922; Lincoln: University of Nebraska Press, 2002), 293.

20. William H. Townsend, *Lincoln and the Bluegrass: Slavery and Civil War in Kentucky* (Lexington: University of Kentucky Press, 1955), 136.

21. Nathaniel Grigsby, interview with Herndon, Gentryville, Indiana, 12 Sept. 1865, *HI*, 113.

22. Interview with Gollaher by J. C. M., Hodgenville correspondence, 23 Mar., Cincinnati *Tribune*, 24 Mar. 1895.

23. Felix Brown, "Depression and Childhood Bereavement," *Journal of Mental Science* 107 (1962):770.

24. Address by Clarence W. Bell in Mattoon, Illinois, 11 Feb. 1931, in the Lerna, Illinois, *Eagle*, 27 Feb. 1931.

25. Unidentified clipping in Dennis Hanks Dowling's scrapbook, quoted in William F. Sullivan, "Tales of Lincoln's Early Life," Paris, Illinois, *News*, 14 Feb. 1922; address by Clarence W. Bell in Mattoon, Illinois, 11 Feb. 1931, in the Lerna, Illinois, *Eagle*, 27 Feb. 1931.

26. John B. Helm to Herndon, 1 Aug. 1865, *HI*, 82.

27. Herndon to Jesse W. Weik, Springfield, 19 Jan. 1886, H-W MSS DLC.

28. Samuel Haycraft to John B. Helm, Elizabethtown, 5 July 1865; Presley Nevil Haycraft to John B. Helm, 19 July 1865; Samuel Haycraft to Herndon, Elizabethtown, [June 1865], *HI*, 85, 87, 68; Samuel Haycraft's reminiscences, as told to John W. Cunningham, pastor of the Elizabethtown circuit of the Louisville conference of the Methodist Church South (1865–1866), St. Louis *Globe Democrat*, 13 Feb. 1897; Samuel Haycraft's reminiscences, unidentified clipping from the *Indianapolis Star*, datelined Evansville, 12 Feb. [no year indicated], Eleanor Gridley clipping collection, owned by Charles Hand of Paris, Illinois; Samuel Haycraft's reminiscences, Decatur, Illinois, *Magnet*, 28 Apr. 1869, copied in the *Shelby County Leader*, 3 July 1902; Samuel Haycraft quoted in Elizabethtown correspondence, n.d., Louisville *Commercial*, [ca. 1886], Lincoln Scrapbook, p. 10, Rare Book Room, DLC; William E. Barton, *The Life of Abraham Lincoln* (2 vols.; Indianapolis, IN: Bobbs-Merrill, 1925), 1:117n; Whitney, *Lincoln the Citizen*, manuscript, 47, Lincoln Memorial University, Harrogate, Tennessee; Whitney, *Lincoln the Citizen*, 35; *Lincoln Lore*, no. 1592 (Oct. 1970), 1–4.

29. Sarah Bush Lincoln, interview with Herndon, near Charleston, Illinois, 8 Sept. 1865, *HI*, 106.

30. Dennis Hanks to Herndon (interview), Chicago, 13 June 1865, *HI*, 41.

31. Augustus H. Chapman, statement for Herndon, [before 8 Sept. 1865], *HI*, 99.

32. Sarah Bush Lincoln, interview with Herndon, near Charleston, Illinois, 8 Sept. 1865, *HI*, 108.

33. Walter B. Stevens, "Recollections of Lincoln," St. Louis *Globe-Democrat*, 24 Jan. 1909, magazine section, p. 3.

34. Augustus H. Chapman, statement for Herndon, [before 8 Sept. 1865], *HI*, 99.

35. William H. Herndon and Jesse W. Weik, *Herndon's Lincoln*, ed. Douglas L. Wilson and Rodney O. Davis (1889; Urbana: University of Illinois Press, 2006), 35n.

36. Sarah Bush Lincoln, interview with Herndon, near Charleston, Illinois, 8 Sept. 1865, *HI*, 108.

37. Interview with Sarah Bush Lincoln, Tuscola, Illinois, *Journal*, n.d., copied in the Bloomington *Pantagraph*, 17 Dec. 1867.

38. Augustus H. Chapman, statement for Herndon, [before 8 Sept. 1865], *HI*, 99; Chapman to Herndon, Charleston, Illinois, 8 Oct. 1865, ibid., 136.

39. Joshua Speed, *Reminiscences of Abraham Lincoln and Notes of a Visit to California: Two Lectures* (Louisville, KY: John P. Morton, 1884), 36–37.

40. Herndon to Caroline Dall, Springfield, 8 Jan. 1867, Dall Papers, MHi.

41. Dr. James LeGrande, paraphrasing remarks he heard from his mother, Sophie Hanks, in an undated interview with Arthur E. Morgan, Morgan Papers, DLC.

42. John Cunningham (b. 1828) of Mattoon, Illinois, unidentified clipping, in Carl Sandburg, *Lincoln Collector: The Story of Oliver R. Barrett's Great Private Collection* (New York: Harcourt, Brace, 1950), 88; Charles H. Coleman, *Abraham Lincoln and Coles County, Illinois* (New Brunswick, NJ: Scarecrow Press, 1955), 60.

43. Interview with Sara Bush Lincoln, Tuscola, Illinois, *Journal*, n.d., copied in the Bloomington *Pantagraph*, 17 Dec. 1867.

44. Amanda Poorman, daughter of Dennis Hanks, "New Stories about the Great Emancipator," St. Louis *Post-Dispatch*, 26 May 1901.

45. Augustus H. Chapman to Herndon, Charleston, Illinois, 8 Oct. 1865, *HI*, 137; Henry C. Whitney, *Life on the Circuit with Lincoln*, ed. Paul M. Angle (1892; Caldwell, ID: Caxton Printers, 1940), 46.

46. Rockport, Indiana, correspondence, 21 Dec., Chicago *Times-Herald*, 22 Dec. 1895.

47. Lincoln to John D. Johnston, Washington, 24 Dec. 1848, *CWL*, 2:16.

48. Dennis Hanks to Herndon, 26 Jan. 1866, *HI*, 176.

49. Brief autobiography, [15?] June 1858, *CWL*, 2:459.

50. Eulogy on Henry Clay, 6 July 1852, *CWL*, 2:124.

51. Autobiography written for Jesse W. Fell, 20 Dec. 1859, *CWL*, 3:511.

52. Autobiography written for John Locke Scripps, [ca. June 1860], *CWL*, 4:62.

53. *CWL*, 1:1 (dated [1824–1826]).

54. George Cary Eggleston, *The First of the Hoosiers: Reminiscences of Edward Eggleston* (Philadelphia: Drexel Biddle, 1903), 34.

55. Unidentified source, quoted in D. D. Banta, "The Early Schools of Indiana—Third Installment," *Indiana Magazine of History* 2 (1906): 136.

56. Herndon to Jesse W. Weik, Springfield, 21 Oct. 1885, H-W MSS DLC.

57. Henry J. Raymond, *The Life and Public Services of Abraham Lincoln* (New York: Derby and Miller, 1865), 21.

58. William Riley McLaren, "Reminiscences of Pioneer Life in Illinois," quoted in John Mack Faragher, *Sugar Creek: Life on the Illinois Frontier* (New Haven: Yale University Press, 1986), 153.

59. Charleston, Illinois, *Plaindealer*, Feb. 1892, photocopy, Abraham Lincoln Association reference files, folder marked "Coles County," IHi.

60. Matilda Johnston Moore, interview with Herndon, near Charleston, Illinois, 8 Sept. 1865, *HI*, 109.

61. Mary Owens Vineyard to Herndon, Weston, Missouri, 22 July 1866, *HI*, 262.

62. John Wickizer to Herndon, Chicago, 25 Nov. 1866, *HI*, 424.

63. Speed, *Reminiscences of Lincoln*, 25–26.

64. Article by Andrew M. Sweeney, Indianapolis *Star*, 12 Mar. 1933.

65. Edward Eggleston, *The Hoosier Schoolmaster* (New York: Grosset & Dunlap, 1913), 131n.

66. Ibid., 54; Benjamin Brown French to Mrs. Catherine J. Wells, Washington, 3 June 1862, French Family Papers, DLC.

67. Albert Blair, in Walter B. Stevens, *A Reporter's Lincoln*, ed. Michael Burlingame (1916; Lincoln: University of Nebraska Press, 1998), 97.

68. "Robert Livingston Stanton's Lincoln," ed. Dwight L. Smith, *Lincoln Herald* 76 (1974):174.

69. Joshua Speed, statement for Herndon, [by 1882], *HI*, 589.

70. Leonard Swett's address at the dedication of Augustus St. Gaudens's statue of

Lincoln in Chicago, Chicago *Times,* 23 Oct. 1887.

71. Mrs. Allen Gentry (née Anna Caroline Roby), interview with Herndon, Rockport, Indiana, 17 Sept. 1865, *HI,* 132.

72. Robert McIntyre, "Lincoln's Friend," Charleston, Illinois, *Courier,* n.d., Paris, Illinois, *Gazette,* n.d., Chicago *Tribune,* 30 May 1885.

73. Wilson and Davis, eds., *Herndon's Lincoln,* 28n.

74. Ibid., 29; William Wood, interview with Herndon, 15 Sept. 1865, *HI,* 124.

75. John Hanks, interview with Herndon, [1865–1866], *HI,* 454.

76. Sarah Bush Lincoln, interview with Herndon, near Charleston, Illinois, 8 Sept. 1865, *HI,* 107.

77. Elizabeth Crawford, interview with Herndon, 16 Sept. 1865, *HI,* 126; Elizabeth Crawford to Herndon, 4 Jan. 1866, ibid., 151.

78. Leonard Swett in Rice, ed., *Reminiscences of Lincoln,* 459; Elizabeth Crawford to Herndon, 7 Sept. 1866, *HI,* 335.

79. *CWL,* 3:362–363.

80. John Locke Scripps, *Life of Abraham Lincoln,* ed. Roy P. Basler and Lloyd A. Dunlap (1860; Bloomington: Indiana University Press, 1961), 29, 30–31.

81. Mentor Graham, interview with Herndon, [1865–1866], *HI,* 450.

82. Oakland City, Indiana, *Enterprise,* n.d., copied in the Indianapolis *Journal,* copied in a clipping marked "Times," 27 Aug. 1899, Lincoln scrapbooks, vol. 2, InU.

83. J. Rowan Herndon to Herndon, Quincy, Illinois, 28 May 1865, *HI,* 7.

84. Herndon, quoting Lincoln, in Weik, *Real Lincoln,* ed. Burlingame, 22.

85. Definition of democracy, [1 Aug. 1858?], *CWL,* 2:532.

86. Laurence Sterne, "Liberty and Slavery," in William Scott, *Lessons in Elocution or a Selection of Pieces in Prose and Verse for the Improvement of Youth in Reading and Speaking* (Lancaster, PA: Robert Bailey, 1805), 212–213.

87. Sarah Bush Lincoln, interview with Herndon, near Charleston, Illinois, 8 Sept. 1865, *HI,* 107.

88. John P. Gulliver, "A Talk with Abraham Lincoln," New York *Independent,* 1 Sept. 1864.

89. Joseph Nicholas Barker, "What I Remember of Abraham Lincoln," undated manuscript, Lincoln Collection, Chicago History Museum.

90. Jacques Barzun, *From Dawn to Decadence: 500 Years of Western Cultural Life, 1500 to the Present* (New York: HarperCollins, 2000), 27–28.

91. John Langdon Kaine, "Lincoln as a Boy Knew Him," *Century Magazine* 85 (Feb. 1913): 557; reply to loyal colored people of Baltimore upon presentation of a Bible, 7 Sept. 1864, *CWL,* 7:542.

92. Speed, *Reminiscences of Lincoln,* 32–33.

93. Noah Brooks, "Personal Recollections of Abraham Lincoln," *Harper's New Monthly Magazine,* July 1865, in Michael Burlingame, ed., *Lincoln Observed: Civil War Dispatches of Noah Brooks* (Baltimore, MD: Johns Hopkins University Press, 1998), 219.

94. Anna L. Boyden, *Echoes from Hospital and White House: A Record of Mrs. Rebecca R. Pomroy's Experiences in War-Times* (Boston: Lothrop, 1884), 62.

95. *CWL,* 4:169.

96. Lincoln to Speed, Springfield, 4 July 1842, *CWL,* 1:289.

97. *CWL,* 2:141.

98. Ibid., 2:467.

99. F. B. Carpenter, *Six Months at the White House with Abraham Lincoln: The Story of a Picture* (New York: Hurd and Houghton, 1866), 230.

100. Ibid., 246.

101. *CWL,* 4:239.

102. Ibid., 1:411; 7:368; 8:155, 333.

103. Ibid. 7:368, 8:333.

104. Ibid., 8:333.

105. Ibid., 1:315; 2:461.

106. Statement of Andrew H. Goodpasture, Petersburg, Illinois, 31 Mar. 1869, *HI,* 573.

107. *CWL*, 1:115, 4:194.

108. Ibid., 4:130.

109. Ibid., 7:368.

110. Lincoln paraphrased Jesus thus: "By the fruit the tree is to be known. An evil tree can not bring forth good fruit." Lincoln to Williamson Durley, Springfield, 3 Oct. 1845, *CWL*, 1:347.

111. Lincoln to Henry J. Raymond, 28 Nov. 1860, *CWL*, 4:146.

112. Lincoln paraphrased Jesus thus: "out of the abundance of his heart, his mouth will continue to speak." *CWL*, 2:271.

113. *CWL*, 2:501.

114. Dennis Hanks, interview with Herndon, Charleston, Illinois, 8 Sept. 1865, *HI*, 106; Robert McIntyre, "Lincoln's Friend," Charleston, Illinois, *Courier*, n.d., Paris, Illinois, *Gazette*, n.d., Chicago *Tribune*, 30 May 1885.

115. Sarah Bush Lincoln, interview with Herndon, near Charleston, Illinois, 8 Sept. 1865, *HI*, 107.

116. Albert Hale to Theron Baldwin, Springfield, 15 June 1860, in Michael Burlingame, ed., *An Oral History of Abraham Lincoln: John G. Nicolay's Interviews and Essays* (Carbondale: Southern Illinois University Press, 1996), 97.

117. Eggleston, *Hoosier Schoolmaster*, 84–85.

118. William E. Barton, *The Soul of Abraham Lincoln* (New York: George H. Doran, 1920), 48.

119. In 1888, John J. Hall, son of Matilda Johnston Moore, reported this to John E. Remsburg. Remsburg, *Abraham Lincoln: Was He a Christian?* (New York: Truth Seeker Company, 1893), 197.

120. Wilson and Davis, eds., *Herndon's Lincoln*, 62.

121. [D. W. Dow], Peoria, Illinois, n.d., to the editor, "Editor's Drawer," *Harper's New Monthly Magazine*, June 1875, 155–156.

122. George Tuthill Borrett, *Letters from Canada and the United States* (London: J. E. Adlard, 1865), 254 (letter dated "on board the Kangaroo," Nov. 1864).

123. Mary Todd Lincoln, interview with Herndon, [Sept. 1866], *HI*, 358, 360.

124. Leonard W. Volk, "The Lincoln Life-Mask and How It Was Made," *Century Magazine* 23 (Dec. 1881):226.

125. Sarah Bush Lincoln, interview with Herndon, near Charleston, Illinois, 8 Sept. 1865, *HI*, 108.

126. Clara Stillwell, "A Few Lincoln-in-Indiana Stories," typescript, 3, Lincoln Papers, Lilly Library, InU.

127. Polly Richardson Egnew, in J. Edward Murr, "Lincoln in Indiana," *Indiana Magazine of History* 14 (1918):57.

128. Jane L. Mosby (daughter of Elizabeth Wood) to Anna C. O'Flynn, Grandview, Indiana, 8 Mar. 1896, O'Flynn Papers, Vincennes University.

129. T. Hardy Masterson, "Lincoln's Life in Indiana," Rockport, Indiana, *Journal*, 12 Feb. 1897; interview with Tuley's grandniece, Mrs. Louisa K. Barr, St. Paul, Minnesota, *Pioneer Press*, 12 Feb. 1925; Nora Bender, granddaughter of Elizabeth Tuley, to Laura Wright, Chrisney, Indiana, 16 Aug. 1926, copy, and C. E. Jones to Nora Bender, Wichita, Kansas, 28 Jan. 1926, copy, Francis Marion Van Natter Papers, Vincennes University; interviews with Elizabeth Tuley, Evansville *Courier and Journal*, 12 Feb. 1928, and Rockport, Indiana, correspondence, 21 Dec., Chicago *Times-Herald*, 22 Dec. 1895.

130. Eli Grigsby, second interview with Francis Marion Van Natter, Gentryville, Indiana, 12 Dec. 1935, Van Natter Papers, Vincennes University.

131. Statement of Mrs. Allen Gentry (née Anna Caroline Roby), Rockport, Indiana, 17 Sept. 1865, *HI*, 131.

132. Dr. James LeGrande's answers to a questionnaire, [ca. 1909], Arthur E. Morgan Papers, DLC.

133. Sara Bush Lincoln, interview with Herndon, near Charleston, Illinois, 8 Sept. 1865, *HI*, 108.

134. John Hanks, interview with Herndon, [1865–1866], *HI*, 455.

135. Dennis Hanks, interview with Herndon, Charleston, Illinois, 8 Sept. 1865, *HI*, 105; Hanks quoted in the Charleston, Illinois, correspondence, 24 July [1891], Chicago *Republic*, undated clipping, LMF; Dennis Franklin Johnston, son of John D. Johnston, paraphrasing what his father told him, Los Angeles *Times*, 12 Feb. 1929, part 2.

136. Reminiscences of John E. Roll, Chicago *Times-Herald*, 25 Aug. 1895.

137. Green B. Taylor, interview with Herndon, 16 Sept. 1865, *HI*, 129–130; S. Grant Johnson, "Abraham Lincoln," Dale, Indiana, *Weekly Reporter*, 18 Feb. 1944.

138. Wilson and Davis, eds., *Herndon's Lincoln*, 51.

139. William D. Kelley, in Allen Thorndike Rice, ed., *Reminiscences of Abraham Lincoln by Distinguished Men of His Time* (New York: North American Review, 1888), 280.

140. William Makepeace Thayer, *The Pioneer Boy and How He Became President* (Boston: Walker, Wise, 1863), 205.

141. E. Grant Gentry, recalling what his grandmother, Anna Caroline Roby Gentry, wife of Allen Gentry, had told him, in Francis Marion Van Natter's notes of two interviews (dated 21 Jan. and 10 Feb. 1936), and an affidavit dated Rockport, 5 Sept. 1936, and notes of an interview with his sisters Anna, Hannah, and Rose, Rockport, 21 Jan. 1936, Van Natter Papers, Vincennes University.

142. Frances Trollope, *Domestic Manners of the Americans* (1832; New York: Dodd, Mead, 1901), 22–23.

143. William Wood, interview with Herndon, 15 Sept. 1865, *HI*, 124.

144. John B. Rowbotham to Herndon, Cincinnati, 24 June 1865, *HI*, 56.

145. Augustus H. Chapman, statement for Herndon, [before 8 Sept. 1865], *HI*, 102.

146. John Romine, statement to Herndon, Lincoln Farm, Indiana, 14 Sept. 1865, *HI*, 118.

147. An unidentified resident of Charleston, quoted in Alonzo Hilton Davis, "Lincoln's Goose Nest Home," *Century Magazine*, Sept. 1892, 798–799.

148. Volney Hickox, "Lincoln at Home," *Illinois State Journal* (Springfield), 15 Oct. 1874.

149. Matilda Johnston Moore, interview with Herndon, near Charleston, Illinois, 8 Sept. 1865, *HI*, 109.

150. Sarah Bush Lincoln, interview with Herndon, near Charleston, Illinois, 8 Sept. 1865, *HI*, 106–107.

151. Francis Marion Van Natter, *Lincoln's Boyhood: A Chronicle of His Indiana Years* (Washington, DC: Public Affairs Press, 1963), 36.

152. Elizabeth Crawford, interview with Herndon, 16 Sept. 1865, *HI*, 127.

153. Notes of Anna C. O'Flynn's interview with Joseph Gentry, ca. 1895, Anna C. O'Flynn Papers, Vincennes University.

154. James LeGrande, recalling the words of his mother, undated memo, Arthur E. Morgan Papers, DLC.

155. Joseph C. Richardson, interview with Herndon, [14? Sept. 1865], *HI*, 119.

156. Interview with Joseph C. Richardson, correspondence dated "down the Ohio and round about," 10 Sept., Chicago *Tribune*, 21 Sept. 1890, p. 25.

157. Mrs. Eli Grigsby, wife of Sarah Lincoln Grigsby's great nephew, was asked if the relatively prosperous Grigsbys looked down on Sarah as the child of a poor family. "'Well,' she answered hesitantly, 'Sally was hired help and you know how you'd feel about that.'" Indianapolis *Star*, 11 Feb. 1940.

158. "Young Abe in Indiana," correspondence dated "down the Ohio and round about," 10 Sept., Chicago *Tribune*, 21 Sept. 1890, p. 25.

159. Redmond Grigsby in the Lincoln City, Indiana, correspondence, 1 Oct. [1902], Evansville *Journal News*, clipping, LMF Rockport, Indiana, correspondence, 21 Dec., Chicago *Times Herald*, 22 Dec. 1895.

160. Whitney, *Lincoln the Citizen*, 36.

161. Joseph C. Richardson, interview with Herndon, [14? Sept. 1865], *HI*, 119–120.

162. Nathaniel Grigsby, interview with Herndon, Gentryville, Indiana, 12 Sept. 1865, *HI*, 114.

163. Joseph C. Richardson, interview with Herndon, [14? Sept. 1865], *HI,* 120.

164. Elizabeth Crawford, interview with Herndon, 16 Sept. 1865, and letter to Herndon, 4 Jan. 1866, *HI,* 127, 152.

165. James Gentry, interview, correspondence dated "down the Ohio and round about," 10 Sept., Chicago *Tribune,* 21 Sept. 1890, p. 25.

166. Green B. Taylor, interview with Herndon, 16 Sept. 1865, *HI,* 130; Nathaniel Grigsby, interview with Herndon, Gentryville, Indiana, 12 Sept. 1865, ibid., 114.

167. Clara Stillwell, "A Few Lincoln-in-Indiana Stories," typescript, pp. 4–5, Lincoln Papers, Lilly Library, InU.

168. Whitney, *Lincoln the Citizen,* 43.

169. Unidentified clipping in Dennis Hanks Dowling's scrapbook, quoted in William F. Sullivan, "Tales of Lincoln's Early Life," Paris, Illinois, *News,* 14 Feb. 1922.

170. Horace White to Jesse W. Weik, New York, 14 Dec. 1913, in Weik, *Real Lincoln,* ed. Burlingame, 382.

171. Nathaniel Grigsby, interview with Herndon, Gentryville, Indiana, 12 Sept. 1865, *HI,* 112.

172. Enclosure in T. Hardy Masterson to George H. Honig, Kennett, Missouri, 21 Oct. 1927, copy, Papers of the Southwestern Indiana Historical Society, Willard Library, Evansville.

173. Dennis Hanks to Herndon, 27 Dec. 1865, *HI,* 147.

174. J. Rowan Herndon to Herndon, Quincy, Illinois, 3 July 1865, *HI,* 69.

175. Nathaniel Grigsby interview with Herndon, Gentryville, Indiana, 16 Sept. 1865, *HI,* 128.

176. Dennis Hanks to Herndon (interview), Chicago, 13 June 1865, *HI,* 42, 39; Dennis Hanks, interview with Herndon, Charleston, Illinois, 8 Sept. 1865, ibid., 105.

177. John Rust, recalling what Green Taylor told him in 1865, Grandview, Indiana, *Monitor,* 25 Oct. 1928; Green B. Taylor, interview with Herndon, 16 Sept.

1865, *HI,* 130; Anna C. O'Flynn, "The Environments of Abraham Lincoln in Indiana: The Best Witnesses," talk delivered to the Southwestern Indiana Historical Society, 17 Nov. 1925, copy, Southwestern Indiana Historical Society Papers, Willard Library, Evansville.

178. James W. Wartmann to Herndon, Rockport, Indiana, 21 July 1865, *HI,* 79; John W. Lamar, interview with Anna C. O'Flynn, 1895, Ida M. Tarbell Papers, Allegheny College.

179. Church records, entry for 10 Jan. 1830, Louis A. Warren, *Lincoln's Youth: Indiana Years, 1816–1830* (Indianapolis: Indiana Historical Society, 1959), 207.

180. Van Natter, *Lincoln's Boyhood,* 152; Andrew W. Sweeney's reminiscences of conversations with Grigsby, Indianapolis *Star,* 16 Apr. 1933.

181. Jesse K. Dubois, interview with Herndon, 1 Dec. 1888, *HI,* 718–719.

182. Whitney, *Lincoln the Citizen,* 62–63.

183. George Close, interview with James Q. Howard, [May 1860], AL MSS DLC.

184. Reminiscences of Robert Warnick, Decatur *Review,* 22 Mar. 1903.

185. Whitney, *Lincoln the Citizen,* p. 86, manuscript at Lincoln Memorial University, Harrogate, Tennessee. This passage does not appear in the published version of Whitney's biography.

186. William Butler, interview with John G. Nicolay, Springfield, 13 June 1875, in Burlingame, ed., *Oral History of Lincoln,* 20.

187. George Close, interview with James Q. Howard, [May 1860], AL MSS DLC.

188. John Hanks, interview with Herndon, [1865–1866], *HI,* 456.

189. Whitney, *Lincoln the Citizen,* 67.

190. William C. Smith, in Joseph Stevens, *History of Macon County, Illinois* (Philadelphia: Brink, McDonough, 1880), 145.

191. John J. Hall, paraphrased in Dr. W. H. Doak, Martinsville, Illinois, to his nephew, Dr. W. D. Ewing of Cambridge, Ohio, [1 Feb. 1923], Terre Haute, Indiana, *Star,* 11 Feb. 1923.

192. Horace Greeley, *Recollections of a Busy Life* (New York: J. B. Ford, 1869), 60.

193. Mary Todd Lincoln quoting her husband, interview with Herndon, [Sept. 1866], *HI,* 359.

Chapter 3. "Separated from His Father, He Studied English Grammar"

1. Lincoln to Herndon, Washington, 10 July 1848, in Roy P. Basler et al., eds., *Collected Works of Abraham Lincoln* [hereafter *CWL*] (8 vols. plus index; New Brunswick, NJ: Rutgers University Press, 1953–1955), 1:497.

2. Lincoln to Martin S. Morris, Springfield, 26 Mar. 1843, *CWL,* 1:320.

3. Mentor Graham to Herndon (interview), Petersburg, Illinois, 29 May 1865, Douglas L. Wilson and Rodney O. Davis, eds., *Herndon's Informants: Letters, Interviews, and Statements about Abraham Lincoln* [hereafter *HI*] (Urbana: University of Illinois Press, 1998), 9; Hardin Bale to Herndon (interview), Petersburg, Illinois, 29 May 1865, ibid., 13.

4. Charles Maltby, *The Life and Public Services of Abraham Lincoln* (Stockton, CA: Daily Independent Steam Print, 1884), 25.

5. John E. Roll interviewed in the Chicago *Times-Herald,* 25 Aug. 1895.

6. Caleb Carman to Herndon, Petersburg, Illinois, 30 Nov. 1866, *HI,* 429; Carman to Osborn H. Oldroyd, Petersburg, 2 Apr. 1882, Carman Papers, IHi.

7. Clawson Lacy in Volney Hickox, "Lincoln at Home," *Illinois State Journal* (Springfield), 15 Oct. 1874.

8. Caleb Carman to Herndon, Petersburg, Illinois, 30 Nov. 1866, *HI,* 429.

9. Clark E. Carr, *My Day and Generation* (Chicago: McClurg, 1908), 107.

10. Caleb Carman, interview with Herndon, Petersburg, 12 Oct. 1866, *HI,* 373.

11. Clawson Lacy in Volney Hickox, "Lincoln at Home," *Illinois State Journal* (Springfield), 15 Oct. 1874.

12. Henry E. Dummer, interview with Herndon, [1865–1866], *HI,* 442.

13. Henry C. Whitney to Herndon, Chicago, 17 Sept. 1887, *HI,* 644.

14. Bledsoe, review of Ward Hill Lamon's biography of Lincoln, *Southern Review* 12 (Apr. 1873):347.

15. Ellis's undated statement, enclosed in Ellis to Herndon, Moro, Illinois, 23 Jan. 1866, *HI,* 171, 174.

16. William Herndon, "A Story of Lincoln or a Story which he loved to tell," H-W MSS DLC, in Paul M. Zall, ed., *Abe Lincoln Laughing: Humorous Anecdotes from Original Sources by and about Abraham Lincoln* (Berkeley: University of California Press, 1982), 100–101.

17. John B. Weber to Herndon, Pawnee, Illinois, 5 Nov. 1866, *HI,* 396.

18. Scrapbook, pp. 45, 47, George Alfred Townsend Papers, DLC.

19. Caleb Carman to Herndon, Petersburg, Illinois, 30 Nov. 1866, *HI,* 429.

20. Ellis's undated statement, enclosed in Ellis to Herndon, Moro, Illinois 23 Jan. 1866, *HI,* 173.

21. Herndon to "Mr. Noyes," Chinquapin Hill, Illinois, 4 Feb. 1874, Herndon Papers, IHi.

22. Swett to Herndon, Chicago, 17 Jan. 1866, *HI,* 165–166.

23. Herndon interviewed by George Alfred Townsend, Springfield correspondence, 25 Jan., New York *Tribune,* 15 Feb. 1867.

24. William Schouler, "Political and Personal Recollections, Number Eight," Boston *Journal,* 18 Mar. 1870.

25. Springfield correspondence, 4 Sept., New York *Evening Post,* 8 Sept. 1860.

26. Henry Onstot witnessed this scene. Onstot quoted in Erastus Wright to Josiah G. Holland, Springfield, 10 July 1865, Holland Papers, New York Public Library.

27. Coleman Smoot to Herndon, Petersburg, Illinois, 7 May 1866, *HI,* 254.

28. *CWL,* 4:64; John Hanks to Herndon (interview), Chicago, 13 June 1865, *HI,* 44.

29. John Hanks interview with Herndon [1865–1866], *HI,* 457.

30. Herndon to Isaac N. Arnold, 21 Oct. 1882, in Arnold, *The Life of Abraham Lincoln* (Chicago: A. C. McClurg, 1884), 31n.

31. Autobiography written for John Locke Scripps, [ca. June 1860], *CWL*, 4:64.

32. Caleb Carman to Herndon, Petersburg, Illinois, 30 Nov. 1866, *HI*, 429.

33. William H. Herndon interview, Springfield correspondence by V. H., July 1867, Cincinnati *Commercial*, 25 July 1867.

34. *Illinois State Journal* (Springfield), 21 Aug. 1879.

35. Thomas S. Edwards, interviewed by John Hay, Sept. 1860, Michael Burlingame, ed., *Lincoln's Journalist: John Hay's Anonymous Writings for the Press, 1860–1864* (Carbondale: Southern Illinois University Press, 1998), 10.

36. John Mack Faragher, *Sugar Creek: Life on the Illinois Frontier* (New Haven: Yale University Press, 1986), 112–113.

37. Charles James Fox Clarke to his mother, Mrs. Mary Clarke, New Salem, 3 Aug. 1834, Clarke Papers, IHi.

38. T. G. Onstot, *Pioneers of Menard and Mason Counties* (Forest City, IL: T. G. Onstot, 1902), 219, 157.

39. Stephen A. Douglas to Julius N. Granger, Jacksonville, 11 Mar. 1834, Robert W. Johannsen, ed., *The Letters of Stephen A. Douglas* (Urbana: University of Illinois Press, 1961), 5.

40. Sarah M. Worthington, "Stories of Pioneer Mothers in Illinois," manuscript, IHi, quoted in Faragher, *Sugar Creek,* 114.

41. William Brown to Jeremiah Brown Jr., Dillon, Illinois, 20 Apr. 1830, typed copy, Jesse W. Fell Papers, DLC.

42. Charles James Fox Clarke to Hollis J. Clarke, New Salem, 15 Mar. 1835, photocopy, Clarke Papers, IHi.

43. Temperance Address, delivered in Springfield, 22 Feb. 1842, *CWL*, 1:274.

44. Robert D. Miller, *Past and Present of Menard County, Illinois* (Chicago: Clarke, 1905), 43.

45. Onstot, *Pioneers of Menard and Mason Counties,* 121.

46. Douglas to Gehazi Granger, Jacksonville, 9 Nov. 1835, Johannsen, ed., *Letters of Douglas,* 21.

47. Allen to Eleazar Baldwin, New Salem, 5 May 1832, typed copy in the New Salem Museum, copied in "John Allen Residence," p. 31, typescript in the Sangamon Valley Collection, Lincoln Public Library, Springfield.

48. William G. Greene to Herndon, Tallula, Illinois, 29 May 1865, *HI*, 11.

49. Henry C. Whitney, *Lincoln the Citizen,* vol. 1 of *A Life of Lincoln,* ed. Marion Mills Miller (2 vols.; New York: Baker and Taylor, 1908), 80.

50. Autobiography written for John Locke Scripps, [ca. June 1860], *CWL*, 4:64.

51. Thomas P. Reep, *Lincoln at New Salem* (Chicago: Old Salem Lincoln League, 1927), 21.

52. Mentor Graham to Herndon (interview), Petersburg, Illinois, 29 May 1865, *HI*, 9.

53. Royal Clary, interview with Herndon, [Oct. 1866?], *HI*, 370.

54. Close, interview with James Q. Howard, [May 1860], AL MSS DLC.

55. William G. Greene to Herndon (interview), Elm Wood, Illinois, 30 May 1865, *HI*, 17–18.

56. "Stories of Lincoln, Reminiscences Missed by His Biographers Gathered in the 'Old Salem' Region," unidentified clipping, LMF.

57. Havana correspondence, 14 Dec. 1865, Chicago *Republican*, n.d., copied in the Belleville *Advocate,* 5 Jan. 1866.

58. Harvey Lee Ross, *Lincoln's First Years in Illinois,* ed. Rufus Rockwell Wilson (1889; Elmira, NY: Primavera Press, 1946), 5.

59. Reep, *Lincoln at New Salem,* 55.

60. Greene interviewed by Adolph Bristol, Tallula, Illinois, correspondence, 29 Oct., Chicago *Inter-Ocean,* 4 Nov. 1876; George Kirby paraphrased in Paul Hull, "Another Lincoln Tale," New York *Mail and Express,* 1 Feb. 1896, p. 11; Greene, interviewed by George A. Pierce, correspondence dated "on the cars," 12 Apr., Chicago *Inter-Ocean,* 30 Apr. 1881; Greene to Herndon, 11 June 1865, *HI*, 33;

Whitney, *Lincoln the Citizen*, 85–86; William Makepeace Thayer, *The Pioneer Boy and How He Became President* (Boston: Walker, Wise, 1863), 249–253.

61. Thomas S. Edwards, interviewed by John Hay, Sept. 1860, Burlingame, ed., *Lincoln's Journalist*, 10.

62. Russell Godbey, interview with Herndon, [1865–1866], *HI*, 449.

63. Reminiscences of Uncle Johnny Potter, Washington correspondence by Walter B. Stevens, 17 Dec., St. Louis *Globe-Democrat*, 20 Dec. 1888.

64. John Todd Stuart's interview with James Q. Howard, [May 1860], copy in John G. Nicolay's hand, John Hay Papers, RPB.

65. Henry McHenry, interview with Herndon, Petersburg, Illinois, 29 May 1865, *HI*, 14.

66. Reminiscences of John Watkins, paraphrased by Thomas P. Reep, based on an interview conducted by Reep in 1890, in Reep's interview with Joseph F. Booton, Petersburg, Illinois, 18 Oct. 1934, typescript, pp. 19–21, IHi.

67. Autobiography written for John L. Scripps, [ca. June 1860], *CWL*, 4:62.

68. Graham to Herndon (interview), Petersburg, Illinois, 29 May 1865, *HI*, 10.

69. Robert H. Browne, *Abraham Lincoln and the Men of His Time* (2 vols.; Cincinnati: Jennings and Pye, 1901), 1:159.

70. Interview with Nancy Rutledge Prewitt, conducted by Margaret Flindt, Fairfield, Iowa, correspondence, 10 Feb., Chicago *Inter-Ocean*, 12 Feb. 1899.

71. William G. Greene interviewed by Paul Hull, "Another Lincoln Tale," New York *Mail and Express*, 1 Feb. 1896, p. 11.

72. J. B. Turner to his wife, Washington, 19 Sept. 1862, in Mary Turner Carriel, *The Life of Jonathan Baldwin Turner* (Urbana: University of Illinois Press, 1961), 250–251.

73. Jason Duncan to Herndon, [late 1866–early 1867], *HI*, 539.

74. [Cornelius A. Runkle's reminiscences] in Noah Brooks, *Abraham Lincoln and the*

Downfall of American Slavery (New York: Putnam's, 1894), 186.

75. George S. Coe's recollections in E. J. Edwards, "President Lincoln and 'Fee-nance," St. Louis *Globe-Democrat*, 27 May 1910; E. D. Keyes, *Fifty Years' Observations of Men and Events, Civil and Military* (New York: Charles Scribner's Sons, 1884), 383; George Templeton Strong, *Diary of the Civil War, 1860–1865*, ed. Allan Nevins (New York: Macmillan, 1962), 188, 204 (entries for 23 Oct. 1861 and 29 Jan. 1862).

76. Henry Clay Whitney, *Life on the Circuit with Lincoln*, ed. Paul M. Angle (1892; Caldwell, ID: Caxton Printers, 1940), 185.

77. Chicago *Times*, 29 Aug. 1858.

78. George B. McClellan to Mary Ellen McClellan, Washington, 21 Nov. 1861, Stephen W. Sears, ed., *The Civil War Papers of George B. McClellan: Selected Correspondence, 1860–1865* (New York: Ticknor & Fields, 1989), 137.

79. Whitney, *Life on the Circuit with Lincoln*, ed. Angle, 46.

80. Sue E. Onstot to James R. B. Van Cleave, Forest City, Illinois, 17 Mar. 1909, Harry E. Pratt Papers, University of Illinois; reminiscences of R. Johnson Onstott, Bloomington, Illinois, *Pantagraph*, 6 Feb. 1909.

81. George Tuthill Borrett, *Letters from Canada and the United States* (London: J. E. Adlard, 1865), 254–255 (letter dated "on board the Kangaroo," Nov. 1864).

82. John Hay, "Life in the White House in the Time of Lincoln," in Michael Burlingame, ed., *At Lincoln's Side: John Hay's Civil War Correspondence and Selected Writings* (Carbondale: Southern Illinois University Press, 2000), 137–138.

83. John McNamar to Herndon, Petersburg, Illinois, 25 Nov. 1866, *HI*, 421.

84. Lincoln to James H. Hackett, Washington, 17 Aug. 1863, *CWL*, 6:392.

85. Whitney, *Life on the Circuit*, ed. Angle, 121.

86. Robert B. Rutledge, son of James Rutledge, to Herndon, [ca. 1 Nov. 1866], *HI*, 384–385.

87. Wayne C. Temple, ed., "Lincoln and the Burners at New Salem," *Lincoln Herald* 67 (1965):68–69.

88. Records of the Rock Creek Lyceum, copy, Fern Nance Pond Papers, Menard County Historical Museum, Petersburg, Illinois.

89. Stephen A. Douglas to Julius N. Granger, Jacksonville, 24 May 1835, Johannsen, ed., *Letters of Douglas*, 19.

90. Greene, who alleged this was the only time he ever heard Lincoln swear, told the story to Henry C. Whitney. Whitney, *Lincoln the Citizen*, 96.

91. Autobiography enclosed in Lincoln to Jesse W. Fell, Springfield, 20 Dec. 1859, *CWL*, 3:512.

92. Benjamin F. Irwin to Herndon, Pleasant Plains, Illinois, 22 Sept. 1866, *HI*, 353.

93. William Cullen Bryant to his wife, Jacksonville, Illinois, 19 June 1832, in Bryant, *Prose Writings*, ed. Parke Godwin (2 vols.; New York: Appleton, 1889), 2:20.

94. Wilson and Davis, eds., *Herndon's Lincoln*, 70.

95. Ben: Perley Poore in Allen Thorndike Rice, ed., *Reminiscences of Abraham Lincoln by Distinguished Men of His Time* (New York: North American Review, 1888), 218–219.

96. William Miller?, statement for Herndon, Sept. 1866, *HI*, 362.

97. Royal Clary interview with Herndon, [Oct. 1866?], *HI*, 372.

98. Wilson and Davis, eds., *Herndon's Lincoln*, 73.

99. Francis Fisher Brown, *The Every-Day Life of Abraham Lincoln* (New York: N. D. Thompson, 1886), 107.

100. Letter by "Scrutatok," New York, 4 July, New York *Herald*, 9 July 1860.

101. George M. Harrison to Herndon, Richland, Illinois, 29 Jan. 1867, *HI*, 555.

102. John Todd Stuart, interview with Herndon, [1865–1866], *HI*, 481.

103. John Todd Stuart, interview with John G. Nicolay, 23 June 1875, Michael Burlingame, ed., *An Oral History of Abraham Lincoln: John G. Nicolay's Interviews and Essays* (Carbondale: Southern Illinois University Press, 1996), 8.

104. John Todd Stuart, interview with James Q. Howard, [May 1860], copy in the hand of John G. Nicolay, John Hay Papers, RPB; Stuart, interview with John G. Nicolay, 23 June 1875, Burlingame, ed., *Oral History of Lincoln*, 8–9.

105. William Greene to Herndon (interview), Elm Wood, Illinois, 30 May 1865, *HI*, 19.

106. John F. Snyder to Frank E. Stevens, Virginia, Illinois, 1 Apr. and 28 Mar. 1916, Frank E. Stevens Papers, IHi.

107. Greene to Herndon (interview), Elm Wood, Illinois, 30 May 1865, *HI*, 18–19.

108. Reminiscences of a conversation held at Lincoln's Springfield home on 8 Aug. 1860, with Risdon M. Moore, in Moore, "Mr. Lincoln as a Wrestler," *Transactions of the Illinois State Historical Society* 9 (1904):434.

109. William G. Greene to Herndon (interview), Elm Wood, Illinois, 30 May 1865, *HI*, 19; Greene's recollections, dated Tallula, 1882, in Osborn H. Oldroyd, *The Lincoln Memorial: Album-Immortelles* (New York: G. W. Carleton, 1883), 517; Greene, interviewed by George A. Pierce, correspondence dated "on the cars," 12 Apr., Chicago *Inter-Ocean*, 30 Apr. 1881; Whitney, *Lincoln the Citizen*, 97–98; Moore, "Lincoln as a Wrestler," 433–434.

110. William G. Greene, interviewed by George A. Pierce, correspondence dated "on the cars," 12 Apr., Chicago *Inter-Ocean*, 30 Apr. 1881.

111. Joseph Gillespie to Isaac N. Arnold, Edwardsville, Illinois, 6 Sept. 1881, in Isaac N. Arnold, "Abraham Lincoln: A Paper Read before the Royal Historical Society, London, June 16, 1881" (pamphlet; Chicago: Fergus, 1881), 194a-b.

112. Ben: Perley Poore in Rice, ed., *Reminiscences of Lincoln*, 219.

113. James Grant Wilson, "Recollections of Lincoln," *Putnam's Magazine* 5 (Feb. 1909):516.

114. Speech in the House of Representatives, 27 July 1848, *CWL*, 1:509–510.

115. Robert B. Rutledge to Herndon, [c. 1 Nov. 1866], *HI*, 385.

116. Whitney, *Life on the Circuit*, ed. Angle, 56.

117. Quoted in Michael F. Holt, *The Rise and Fall of the American Whig Party: Jacksonian Politics and the Onset of the Civil War* (New York: Oxford University Press, 1999), 67.

118. New York *Tribune*, 29 Nov. 1845, quoted in Holt, *Rise and Fall of the Whig Party*, 70.

119. New York *Tribune*, 2 June 1848, in William R. Brock, *Parties and Political Conscience: American Dilemmas, 1840–1850* (Millwood, NY: KTO Press, 1979), 12.

120. Fragment on government, [1 July 1854?], *CWL*, 2:220. This dating is probably inaccurate; in all likelihood, it was composed in the 1840s.

121. *CWL*, 1:5–9.

122. *CWL*, 2:126.

123. *Illinois State Journal* (Springfield), 5 Nov. 1864.

124. J. Rowan Herndon to William H. Herndon, 28 May 1865, *HI*, 7. I have modernized the spelling and punctuation in this quote.

125. Henry McHenry, interview with Herndon, Petersburg, Illinois, 29 May 1865, *HI*, 15.

126. S. T. Logan, interviewed by John G. Nicolay, Springfield, 6 July 1875, Burlingame, ed., *Oral History of Lincoln*, 35.

127. Whitney, *Lincoln the Citizen*, 100.

128. J. Rowan Herndon to William H. Herndon, Quincy, Illinois, 28 May 1865, *HI*, 7. I have modernized spelling and punctuation in this quote.

129. Autobiography enclosed in Lincoln to Jesse W. Fell, Springfield, 20 Dec. 1859, *CWL*, 3:512.

130. Matheny told this to Henry Clay Whitney. Whitney, *Life on the Circuit*, ed. Angle, 56.

131. John Todd Stuart, interview with John G. Nicolay, Springfield, 23 June 1875, Burlingame, ed., *Oral History of Lincoln*, 10.

132. Greene, interview with J. W. S., Chicago *Tribune*, n.d., copied in the *Petersburg Observer* (Illinois), 23 Aug. 1884; Greene, interviewed by George A. Pierce, correspondence dated "on the cars," 12 Apr., Chicago *Inter-Ocean*, 30 Apr. 1881.

133. *CWL*, 3:16.

134. Autobiography written for John Locke Scripps, [ca. June 1860], *CWL*, 4:65.

135. Leonard Swett in Rice, ed., *Reminiscences of Lincoln*, 465–466; Herndon interviewed by George Alfred Townsend, Springfield correspondence, 25 Jan., New York *Tribune*, 15 Feb. 1867.

136. Bloomington *Leader*, n.d., copied in the *Illinois State Journal* (Springfield), 2 Mar. 1870.

137. George J. Barrett, interview with Herndon, [1865–1866], *HI*, 436.

138. Autobiography written for John Locke Scripps, [ca. June 1860], *CWL*, 4:65.

139. Lincoln to George C. Spears, [1 July 1834], *CWL*, 1:25.

140. James Miles, interview with Herndon, [1865–1866], *HI*, 473.

141. [Anson G.] H[enry] to the editor of the Portland *Oregonian*, Lafayette, Oregon, 16 July 1860, copied in an unidentified newspaper clipping, Nicolay-Hay Papers, IHi; Bernice Babcock, "Postmaster Abe Lincoln," undated clipping, Emanuel Hertz Scrapbooks, DLC.

142. James Short to Herndon, Petersburg, Illinois, 7 July 1865, *HI*, 74.

143. Reminiscences of George B. Lincoln, *The Caledonian* (St. Johnsbury, Vermont), 23 Oct. 1890.

144. John Moore Fisk, interview with Herndon, 18 Feb. 1887, *HI*, 715.

145. Reep, *Lincoln at New Salem*, 62.

146. Greene's interview with James Q. Howard, [ca. May 1860], AL MSS DLC.

147. Henry McHenry, interview with Herndon, [1866], *HI*, 534.

148. Undated letter by Chandler's daughter, Mrs. S. L. B. Chandler, in Josephine Craven Chandler, "New Salem: Early Chapter

in Lincoln's Life," *Journal of the Illinois State Historical Society* 22 (1930): 546–548.

149. Henry McHenry, interview with Herndon, Petersburg, Illinois, 29 May 1865, *HI*, 15.

150. A Mr. Maguire, quoted in the Chicago *Times-Herald*, 22 Sept. 1895.

151. Van Bergen, interview with John G. Nicolay, Springfield, 7 July 1875, Burlingame, ed., *Oral History of Lincoln*, 33.

152. Elizabeth Abell to Herndon, 15 Feb. 1867, *HI*, 557.

153. James Short to Herndon, Petersburg, Illinois, 7 July 1865, *HI*, 74; Reep, *Lincoln at New Salem*, 65.

154. John Todd Stuart, interview with John G. Nicolay, Springfield, 23 June 1875, Burlingame, ed., *Oral History of Lincoln*, 11.

155. "Hints to Emigrants," *Illinois Monthly Magazine*, quoted in the *Sangamo Journal*, 9 Feb. 1832.

156. J. R. Herndon to William Herndon, Quincy, Illinois, 27 May 1865, *HI*, 6–8, 103.

157. Maltby, *Lincoln*, 44.

158. Vienna Camron Lyster, daughter of John M. Camron, interviewed in the Los Angles *Times*, 2 October 1904; undated statement by Martha C. Camron (Mrs. Noah McCuistion), in Julia A. Drake, *Flame o' Dawn: The Story of Reverend John M. Camron, Who Boarded Lincoln at New Salem* (New York: Vantage, 1959), 209.

159. Fell to Ward Hill Lamon, Normal, Illinois, 26 Sept. 1870, Jeremiah S. Black Papers, DLC.

160. Herndon to Ward Hill Lamon, Springfield, 25 Feb. 1870, Lamon Papers, CSmH.

161. Bledsoe, review of Ward Hill Lamon's biography of Lincoln, *Southern Review* 12 (Apr. 1873):354.

162. Parthena Hill, interview with Walter B. Stevens, 1886, in Stevens, *A Reporter's Lincoln*, ed. Burlingame, 12.

163. Dr. James LeGrande (paraphrasing remarks he heard from his mother, Sophie Hanks), undated interview with Arthur E. Morgan, Morgan Papers, DLC.

164. The Rev. Mr. L. R. Cronkhite, "The Church Lincoln Didn't Join," *The Christian Century*, 6 Feb. 1935, p. 170.

165. Henry C. Deming, *Eulogy of Abraham Lincoln* (Hartford: A. N. Clark, 1865), 42.

166. Dillard C. Donnohue, interview with Jesse W. Weik, 13 Feb. 1887, *HI*, 602.

167. Matheny, interview with Herndon, 3 May 1866, *HI*, 251.

168. Reminiscences of Cornelius Cole, *Illinois State Register* (Springfield), 5 Feb. 1923.

169. Hawkins Taylor, "Early Reminiscences," Peoria *Weekly Journal*, 1895, copied in Emma Siggins White, *Genealogy of the Descendants of John Walker of Wigton, Scotland* ([Kansas City, MO]: Press of Tiernan-Dart Printing Company, 1902), 430.

170. Leonard Swett in Rice, ed., *Reminiscences of Lincoln*, 466.

171. Ninian W. Edwards, interview with Herndon, [1865–1866], *HI*, 446.

Chapter 4. "A Napoleon of Astuteness and Political Finesse"

1. Abner Y. Ellis to Herndon, Moro, Illinois, 6 Dec. 1866; enclosure by Abner Y. Ellis in Ellis to Herndon, Moro, Illinois, 23 Jan. 1866, in Douglas L. Wilson and Rodney O. Davis, eds., *Herndon's Informants: Letters, Interviews, and Statements about Abraham Lincoln* [hereafter *HI*] (Urbana: University of Illinois Press, 1998), 501, 173.

2. James McGrady Rutledge, quoted in Ida M. Tarbell, *The Early Life of Abraham Lincoln* (New York: McClure, 1896), 200.

3. Thomas P. Reep, *Lincoln at New Salem* (Chicago: Old Salem Lincoln League, 1927), 81.

4. Baker's speech in the U.S. Senate, 3 Jan. 1861, *Congressional Globe*, 36th Congress, 2nd Session, 238.

5. J. Rowan Herndon to Herndon, Quincy, Illinois, 3 July 1865, *HI*, 69; I have standardized the spelling and punctuation of this passage.

6. A. Y. Ellis, statement for Herndon, enclosed in Ellis to Herndon, Moro, Illinois, 23 Jan. 1866, *HI*, 173. I have standardized the spelling and punctuation of this passage.

7. Frederick Trevor Hill, *Lincoln the Lawyer* (New York: Century, 1906), 24.

8. Blackstone, *Commentaries on the Laws of England* (4th ed.; Dublin: John Exshaw, 1771), 1:33.

9. Richard H. Beach of New York City in *History of Sangamon County* (Chicago: Interstate Publishing, 1881), 183.

10. L. M. Greene, interview with James Q. Howard, [May 1860], AL MSS DLC.

11. Gibson W. Harris, "My Recollections of Abraham Lincoln," *Woman's Home Companion*, Nov. 1903, p. 10.

12. Herndon, "Lincoln the Lawyer," H-W MSS DLC.

13. Caroline Owsley Brown, "Springfield Society Before the Civil War," *Journal of the Illinois State Historical Society* 15 (1922):490.

14. Herndon to Jesse W. Weik, Springfield, 10 Dec. 1885, H-W MSS DLC.

15. *Illinois State Register* (Springfield), 14 May, 3 Sept., and 9 July 1841.

16. Autobiography written for John Locke Scripps, [ca. June 1860], in Roy P. Basler et al., eds., *Collected Works of Abraham Lincoln* [hereafter *CWL*] (8 vols. plus index; New Brunswick, NJ: Rutgers University Press, 1953–1955), 4:65.

17. Brown, "Springfield Society Before the Civil War," 490.

18. Jesse W. Fell to David Davis, Normal, Illinois, 15 Dec. 1885, *Illinois State Journal* (Springfield), 14 Jan. 1886; David Davis, address to the Illinois State Bar Association, 13 Jan. 1886, Bloomington, Illinois, *Pantagraph*, 6 Feb. 1886.

19. Alban Jasper Conant, "My Acquaintance with Abraham Lincoln" (pamphlet; New York: De Vinne Press, 1893), 172.

20. Allen B. Clough to Andrew Clough, Tolono, Illinois, 16 Nov. 1859, Clough Papers, ICHi.

21. Joseph Story to T. Kennedy, Cambridge, 15 May 1844, in William W. Story, *Life and Letters of Joseph Story* (2 vols.; Boston: C.C. Little and J. Brown, 1851), 2:486.

22. Josiah Quincy, *An Address Delivered at the Dedication of the Dane Law College in Harvard University, October 23, 1832* (Cambridge, MA: Metcalf, 1832), 17.

23. Lincoln to John M. Brockman, Springfield, 25 Sept. 1860, *CWL*, 4:121.

24. Lincoln to James T. Thornton, Springfield, 2 Dec. 1858, *CWL*, 3:344.

25. Lincoln to Isham Reavis, Springfield, 5 Nov. 1855, *CWL*, 2:327.

26. Lincoln to George C. Latham, Springfield, 22 July 1860, *CWL*, 4:87.

27. Parthena Hill, interview with Walter B. Stevens, 1886, Stevens, *A Reporter's Lincoln*, ed. Michael Burlingame (1916; Lincoln: University of Nebraska Press, 1998), 9.

28. Paul Hull, "Lincoln as a Wrestler," New York *Mail and Express*, 11 Jan. 1896, p. 11; Stephen T. Logan, interviewed by John G. Nicolay, Springfield, 6 July 1875, in Michael Burlingame, ed., *An Oral History of Abraham Lincoln: John G. Nicolay's Interviews and Essays* (Carbondale: Southern Illinois University Press, 1996), 35.

29. Russell Godbey, interview with Herndon, [1865–1866], *HI*, 450.

30. Henry McHenry, interview with James Q. Howard, [May 1860], AL MSS DLC.

31. New York *Herald Tribune*, 27 July 1926, 5.

32. Herndon, quoted in Volney Hickox, "Lincoln at Home," *Illinois State Journal* (Springfield), 15 Oct. 1874.

33. John Dean Caton, *Early Bench and Bar of Illinois* (Chicago: Chicago Legal News, 1893), 170–171.

34. Coleman Smoot to Herndon, Petersburg, Illinois, 7 May 1866, *HI*, 254.

35. Jesse K. Dubois, interview with Nicolay, Springfield, 4 July 1875, Burlingame, ed., *Oral*

History of Lincoln, 30; Leonard Swett to Herndon, Chicago, 15 Jan. 1866, *HI*, 160.

36. Dr. James C. Finley to Joseph Duncan, Jacksonville, 27 May 1834, Duncan-Putnam Family Papers, Putnam Museum, Davenport, Iowa.

37. Joseph Gillespie's appendix to Usher F. Linder, *Reminiscences of the Early Bench and Bar of Illinois* (Chicago: Chicago Legal News, 1879), 401.

38. "A lobby member" to the editor, 31 Dec. 1840, Quincy *Whig*, 16 Jan. 1841.

39. John G. Nicolay to John Hay, Washington, 29 Jan. 1864, in Michael Burlingame, ed., *With Lincoln in the White House: Letters, Memoranda, and Other Writings of John G. Nicolay, 1860–1865* (Carbondale: Southern Illinois University Press, 2000), 125; Milton Hay to John Hay, Springfield, 8 Feb. 1887, John Hay Papers, RPB.

40. Davis to William P. Walker, Bloomington, Illinois, 16 Nov. 1840, Springfield, 2 Mar. 1844 and 25 June 1847, David Davis Papers, IHi.

41. Anna Paschall Hannum, ed., *A Quaker Forty-Niner: The Adventures of Charles Edward Pancoast on the American Frontier* (Philadelphia: University of Pennsylvania Press, 1930), 50.

42. Thomas Ford, *A History of Illinois from Its Commencement as a State in 1818 to 1847* (Chicago: S. C. Eriggs, 1854), 282, 286.

43. Paul Simon, *Lincoln's Preparation for Greatness: The Illinois Legislative Years* (Norman: University of Oklahoma Press, 1965), 23.

44. John J. Hardin to Sarah Hardin, Vandalia, Illinois, 14 Dec. 1836, Hardin Family Papers, ICHi; Joseph Duncan to Elizabeth Caldwell Smith Duncan, Vandalia, 18 Dec. 1836, Duncan-Putnam Family Papers, Putnam Museum, Davenport, Iowa.

45. Frederick Hollman, "Autobiographical Sketch," photocopy of an unpublished manuscript, dated Platteville, Wisconsin, 1870, p. 21, Evans Public Library, Vandalia.

46. David Jewett Baker of Kaskaskia to Elias Kent Kane, Vandalia, 1 Dec. 1834, copy made by Elizabeth Duncan Putnam, Duncan-Putnam Family Papers, Putnam Museum, Davenport, Iowa.

47. Sarah Smith Hardin to John J. Hardin, Jacksonville, 19 Feb. 1839, Hardin Family Papers, ICHi.

48. Lemuel H. Smith to John J. Hardin, Shelbyville, 2 Mar. 1837, Hardin Family Papers, ICHi.

49. James Stuart, *Three Years in North America* (2 vols.; Edinburgh: R. Cadell, 1833), 2:227.

50. Browning, interview with John G. Nicolay, Springfield, 17 June 1875, Burlingame, ed., *Oral History of Lincoln*, 3–4.

51. Lincoln, John J. Hardin, E. B. Webb, and John Dawson to Mrs. Browning, [Springfield, 11 Dec. 1839], *CWL*, 1:156.

52. Ford, *History of Illinois from Its Commencement as a State in 1818 to 1847*, 304.

53. Ibid., 90, 288–89.

54. William H. Fithian to Amos Williams, Vandalia, 26 Jan. 1835, Springfield, 2 Dec. 1839, Woodbury Collection, Illinois Historical Survey, University of Illinois, Urbana-Champaign, in Donald G. Richter, *Lincoln: Twenty Years on the Eastern Prairie* (Mattoon, IL: United Graphics, 1999), 16, 33.

55. Chicago *Democrat*, n.d., quoted in the *Illinois State Register* (Springfield), 23 Apr. 1841.

56. Caton, *Early Bench and Bar of Illinois*, 231.

57. John T. Stuart, interview with Herndon, [1865–1866], *HI*, 481.

58. William H. Herndon and Jesse W. Weik, *Herndon's Lincoln*, ed. Douglas L. Wilson and Rodney O. Davis (1889; Urbana: University of Illinois Press, 2006), 227.

59. Andy Van Meter, *Always My Friend: A History of the State Journal-Register and Springfield* (Springfield, IL: Copley Press, 1981), 109.

60. Douglas L. Wilson, *Honor's Voice: The Transformation of Abraham Lincoln* (New York: Alfred A. Knopf, 1998), 302.

61. *Illinois State Register* (Springfield), 25 July 1840.

62. *Sangamo Journal,* 31 Jan. 1835.

63. *CWL,* 1:31.

64. Joshua F. Speed, interview with Herndon, [1865–1866], *HI,* 476.

65. Harry E. Pratt, "Lincoln and the Division of Sangamon County," *Journal of the Illinois State Historical Society* 47 (1954):400.

66. Stuart, interview with Herndon, [1865–1866], *HI,* 481.

67. John Moses, *Illinois, Historical and Statistical* (2 vols.; Chicago: Fergus, 1889), 1:403–404.

68. Linder, *Reminiscences,* 37, 40; speech of Linder before the bar of Chicago, 17 Apr. 1865, Washington *Sunday Chronicle,* 23 Apr. 1865.

69. Dubois, interview with John G. Nicolay, Springfield, 4 July 1875, Burlingame, ed., *Oral History of Lincoln,* 31.

70. John Locke Scripps, *Life of Abraham Lincoln,* ed. Roy P. Basler and Lloyd A. Dunlap (1860; Bloomington: Indiana University Press, 1961), 68–69.

71. Abner Y. Ellis to Herndon, Moro, Illinois, 6 Dec. 1866, *HI,* 501.

72. Fred R. Jeliff, "The Lincoln-Douglas Debate," Galesburg *Republican-Register,* 10 Oct. 1896.

73. Vienna Camron, quoted in H. Donald Winkler, *The Women in Lincoln's Life* (Nashville, TN: Rutledge Hill Press, 2001), 47.

74. Havana correspondence, 14 Dec. 1865, Chicago *Republican,* n.d., copied in the Belleville *Advocate,* 5 Jan. 1866.

75. Jason Duncan to Herndon, [late 1866–early 1867], *HI,* 541.

76. Nathaniel W. Branson to Herndon, Petersburg, Illinois, 3 Aug. 1865, *HI,* 91.

77. Statement by Ellis, enclosed in Ellis to Herndon, Moro, Illinois, 23 Jan. 1866, *HI,* 170.

78. Interview with Susan Reid Boyce, Calistoga, California, correspondence, 22 May 1897, San Francisco *Call,* n.d., copied in *Iowa State Register* (Des Moines), 6 June 1897.

79. William E. Connelley, p. 3 of a commentary on chapter six of the first volume of Albert J. Beveridge's biography of Lincoln, memo enclosed in Connelley to Beveridge, [Topeka, Kansas], 7 Dec. 1925, copy, Beveridge Papers, IHi.

80. Interview with Mrs. Alexander R. McKee (née Martinette Hardin), Marietta Holdstock Brown, "A Romance of Lincoln," clipping identified as "Indianapolis, January 1896," LMF.

81. Art Wells, "Incident Shaped Lincoln's Future," unidentified clipping, "Childhood and Youth—Illinois" folder, LMF.

82. Mrs. [H. K.?] Rule of Tallula, Illinois, quoted in George A. Pierce's dispatch dated "on the cars," 15 Apr., Chicago *Inter-Ocean,* 16 Apr. 1881.

83. William Butler, interview with John G. Nicolay, Springfield, 13 June 1875, Burlingame, ed., *Oral History of Lincoln,* 19.

84. John Q. Spears, grandson of Mary Spears, undated interview with Herndon, *HI,* 705.

85. Charles Maltby, *The Life and Public Services of Abraham Lincoln* (Stockton, CA: Daily Independent Steam Print, 1884), 28.

86. Havana, Illinois, correspondence, 14 Dec. 1865, Chicago *Republican,* n.d., copied in the Belleville *Advocate,* 5 Jan. 1866.

87. Reminiscences of E. J. Rutledge, nephew of Ann Rutledge, Ottumwa, Iowa, *Courier,* n.d., typed copy, clipping collection, LMF.

88. William G. Greene, interview with Herndon, Elm Wood, Illinois, 30 May 1865, *HI,* 21; John McNamar to G. U. Miles, 5 May 1866, ibid., 253.

89. Ida M. Tarbell, *The Early Life of Abraham Lincoln* (New York: McClure, 1896), 211, 217.

90. William G. Greene, interview with Herndon, Elm Wood, Illinois, 30 May 1865, *HI,* 21.

91. Isaac Cogdal, interview with Herndon, [1865–1866], *HI,* 440.

92. Mrs. Samuel Hill, in Laura Isabelle Osborne Nance, *A Piece of Time (In Lincoln*

Country), ed. Georgia Goodwin Creager (n.p.: n.p., n.d. [ca. 1967]), 26.

93. Henry B. Rankin, *Personal Recollections of Abraham Lincoln* (New York: G. P. Putnam's Sons, 1916) 69–70.

94. Nance, *A Piece of Time,* 26.

95. Interview with Mrs. Josephine Chandler by Malvina Lindsay, Washington *Post,* 7 July 1937.

96. Interview with Nancy Rutledge Prewitt, conducted by Margaret Flindt, Fairfield, Iowa, correspondence, 10 Feb., Chicago *Inter-Ocean,* 12 Feb. 1899.

97. Sarah Rutledge Saunders, interview with Katherine Wheeler, *Chicago Tribune Magazine,* 22 Feb. 1922; undated statement by Sarah Rutledge Saunders, enclosed in J. R. Saunders (her daughter) to Mary Saunders, Sisquoc, California, 14 May 1919, Saunders Papers, IHi; interview with Nancy Rutledge Prewitt, conducted by Margaret Flindt, Fairfield, Iowa, correspondence, 10 Feb., Chicago *Inter-Ocean,* 12 Feb. 1899; interview with Nancy Rutledge Prewitt, conducted by E. E. Sparks, Los Angeles *Times,* 14 Feb. 1897.

98. Henry McHenry to Herndon, Petersburg, Illinois, 8 Jan. 1866, *HI,* 155–156.

99. William G. Greene, interview with Herndon, Elm Wood, Illinois, 30 May 1865, *HI,* 21.

100. Greene in an 1887 interview, Paul Hull, "Another Lincoln Tale," New York *Mail and Express,* 15 Feb. 1896, p. 16.

101. Elizabeth Abell to Herndon, n.p., 15 Feb. 1867, *HI,* 556–557.

102. Eliza Armstrong Smith, daughter of Hannah Armstrong, Springfield correspondence, 9 Sept., Lerna, Illinois, *Eagle,* 19 Sept. 1930.

103. George U. Miles to Herndon, Petersburg, Illinois, 23 Mar. 1866, *HI,* 236.

104. John Hill to Ida M. Tarbell, Columbus, Georgia, 6 and 17 Feb. 1896, Tarbell Papers, Allegheny College.

105. Eliza Armstrong Smith, daughter of Hannah Armstrong, Springfield correspon-

dence, 9 Sept., Lerna, Illinois, *Eagle,* 19 Sept. 1930.

106. "Stories of Lincoln: Reminiscences Missed by His Biographers Gathered in the 'Old Salem' Region," unidentified clipping, LMF.

107. Mentor Graham, interview with Herndon, 2 Apr. 1866, *HI,* 243.

108. Robert L. Wilson to Herndon, Sterling, Illinois, 10 Feb. 1866, *HI,* 205.

109. Cogdal, interview with Herndon, [1865–1866], *HI,* 440.

110. Matthew Marsh to George M. Marsh, New Salem, 17 Sept. 1835, Lincoln Papers, Addendum 1, DLC.

111. Lincoln to Speed, Springfield, 13 Feb. 1842, *CWL,* 1:269–270.

112. Graham to Herndon, Petersburg, Illinois, 29 May 1865, *HI,* 11.

113. Cogdal, interview with Herndon [1865–1866], *HI,* 441.

114. *Sangamo Journal,* 23 June 1838.

115. Douglas L. Wilson, *Lincoln Before Washington: New Perspectives on the Illinois Years* (Urbana: University of Illinois Press, 1997), 63, 66.

116. Reminiscences of Col. L. H. Waters, Kansas City *Star,* 10 Feb. 1907.

117. Letter to the editor of the *Sangamo Journal,* [New Salem], 13 June 1836, *CWL,* 1:48.

118. John Woods, *Two Years' Residence on the English Prairie of Illinois,* ed. Paul M. Angle (1822; Chicago: Lakeside Press, 1968), 175.

119. Thomas F. Gossett, *Race: The History of an Idea in America* (New York: Oxford University Press, 1997), 59, 63.

120. Jesse W. Weik, *The Real Lincoln: A Portrait,* ed. Michael Burlingame (1922; Lincoln: University of Nebraska Press, 2002), 70.

121. Herndon to Jesse W. Weik, Springfield, 23 Jan. 1890, H-W MSS DLC.

122. Helen Ruth Reed, "A Prophecy Lincoln Made," Boston *Herald,* 9 Feb. 1930.

123. James Matheny, quoted in Weik, *Real Lincoln,* ed. Burlingame, 71.

124. Stevens, *A Reporter's Lincoln*, ed. Burlingame, 7.

125. *CWL*, 1:48.

126. Henry C. Whitney, *Lincoln the Citizen*, vol. 1 of *A Life of Lincoln*, ed. Marion Mills Miller (2 vols.; New York: Baker and Taylor, 1908), 127.

127. Lincoln to Allen, New Salem, 21 June 1836, *CWL*, 1:48–49.

128. Undated handbill [ca. July 1836], *CWL*, 8:429.

129. Vandalia correspondence, 26 and 27 Dec. 1835, *Sangamo Journal,* 2 Jan. 1836.

130. Joshua Speed, statement for Herndon, [by 1882], *HI*, 589.

131. Account of the meeting by "Up to the Hub," *Sangamo Journal*, 16 July 1836.

132. Linder, *Reminiscences*, 280.

133. Scripps, *Life of Lincoln*, ed. Basler and Dunlap, 73–74.

134. Johnny Blubberhead to "My inesteemable friend," Springfield, 17 Feb., *Sangamo Journal,* 20 Feb. 1836.

135. B. Willis to Artemas Hale, 26 Dec. 1834, IHi, quoted in Simon, *Lincoln's Preparation for Greatness*, 19.

136. Johnny Blubberhead to "My Dear Friend," Springfield, 29 [*sic*] Feb., *Sangamo Journal*, 27 Feb. 1836.

137. Letter by "May," Washington, 13 Feb., *Sangamo Journal,* 19 Mar. 1836.

138. Letter dated Springfield, 9 Apr., *Sangamo Journal,* 30 Apr. 1836.

139. *Sangamo Journal,* 7 Nov. 1835.

140. Ibid., 3 Sept. 1836.

141. Vandalia correspondence, 6 Jan., *Sangamo Journal*, 16 Jan. 1836.

142. Letter dated Washington, 27 Apr., *Sangamo Journal,* 4 June 1836.

143. *Sangamo Journal,* 4 June 1836.

144. Anonymous letter from North Fork, 4 June, *Sangamo Journal,* 11 June 1836.

145. Letter dated Springfield, 14 June, *Sangamo Journal,* 18 June 1836.

146. Letter dated Springfield, 23 June, *Sangamo Journal,* 25 June 1836.

147. Letter from a Democrat, Lick Creek, 2 July, *Sangamo Journal,* 9 July 1836.

148. Van Buren to Junius Amis et al., 4 Mar. 1836, quoted in William G. Shade, "'The Most Delicate and Exciting Topics': Martin Van Buren, Slavery, and the Election of 1836," *Journal of the Early Republic* 18 (1998):478.

149. *Sangamo Journal,* 2 and 16 Jan. 1836 (dispatches of 26 Dec. and 6 Jan.).

150. Letter dated Springfield, 23 Mar., *Sangamo Journal,* 2 Apr. 1836.

151. Undated letter by "Spoon River," *Sangamo Journal,* 11 June 1836.

152. *Sangamo Journal,* 2 Jan. 1836 (dispatches of 26 and 27 Dec.).

153. Springfield *Republican*, n.d., quoted in the *Sangamo Journal,* 16 Jan. 1836.

154. *Sangamo Journal,* 16 Jan. 1836 (dispatch of 7 Jan.).

155. Ibid., 19 Dec. 1835 (dispatch of 14 Dec.).

156. Ibid., 19 Dec. 1835 (dispatch of 13 Dec.).

157. Ibid., 2 Jan. 1836 (dispatch of 26 Dec. 1835).

158. Ibid., 19 Dec. 1835 (dispatch of 13 Dec.) and 16 Jan. 1836 (dispatch of 7 Jan.).

159. Herndon's recollection of a story he heard Lincoln tell often, n.d., H-W MSS DLC.

160. Robert L. Wilson to Herndon, Sterling, Illinois, 10 Feb. 1866, *HI*, 202–205.

161. John Hill to Ida M. Tarbell, Columbus, Georgia, 4 Apr. and 17 Feb. 1896, Tarbell Papers, Allegheny College.

162. Bledsoe, review of Ward Hill Lamon's biography of Lincoln, *Southern Review* 12 (Apr. 1873): 333–334.

163. Thomas J. Nance to Catherine Nance, Springfield, 19 Dec. 1839, Fern Nance Pond, ed., "Letters of an Illinois Legislator: 1839–1840," *Abraham Lincoln Quarterly* 5 (1949):42.

164. William Herndon to C. O. Poole, Springfield, 5 Jan. 1886, H-W MSS DLC.

165. Whitney, *Lincoln the Citizen*, 140.

166. Lincoln to Mary Owens, Vandalia, 13 Dec. 1836, *CWL*, 1:54–55.

167. *Illinois State Register* (Vandalia), 12 Dec. 1836.

168. Speech of 11 Jan. 1837, *CWL*, 1:61–69.

169. Ibid., 1:69.

170. "The Difference," *Sangamo Journal*, 13 Oct. 1838.

171. "Seat of Government," by "The People," *Sangamo Journal*, 1 June 1833.

172. Chester A. Loomis, *A Journey on Horseback through the Great West in 1825* (Bath, NY: Plaindealer Press, n.d.), unpaginated (entries for 4 and 5 July).

173. William Oliver, *Eight Months in Illinois* (Newcastle upon Tyne: William Andrew Mitchell, 1843), 99–100.

174. Stevens, *A Reporter's Lincoln*, ed. Burlingame, 14.

175. Samuel D. Lockwood to Mary V. Nash Lockwood, Vandalia, 15 Dec. 1836, Lockwood Papers, IHi.

176. Stuart, interview with John G. Nicolay, Springfield, 24 June 1875, Burlingame, ed., *Oral History of Lincoln*, 13.

177. Recollections of Benjamin F. Lee (1817–1916) as told to a Mr. Goad, Vandalia *Union*, 28 Dec. 1916.

178. "An Observer," *Illinois State Register* (Vandalia), 22 Dec. 1837; "Spectator" to the editor of the Vandalia *Free Press*, 23 Dec. 1837, copied ibid., 2 Mar. 1838.

179. *Sangamo Journal*, 1 July 1837.

180. Hardin to the editor, 15 Dec., Jacksonville *Patriot*, 22 Dec. 1836, copied in the *Illinois State Register* (Vandalia), 30 Dec. 1836.

181. Hardin to Sarah Smith Hardin, Vandalia, 14 Dec. 1836 and 26 Feb. 1837, Hardin Family Papers, ICHi.

182. David Davis to William P. Walker, Bloomington, 26 Jan. 1839, Davis Papers, IHi.

183. Springfield correspondence by G., 18 Dec., Alton *Telegraph*, 28 Dec. 1839.

184. John Reynolds, *My Own Times, Embracing Also the History of My Life* (Chicago: Fergus, 1879), 324.

185. Ford, *History of Illinois*, 186–187.

186. Speech of 20 June 1848 in the U.S. House of Representatives, *CWL*, 1:488–489.

187. John F. Snyder, *Adam W. Snyder and His Period in Illinois History, 1817–1842* (2nd ed., rev.; Virginia, IL: E. Needham, 1906), 200.

188. Dubois, interview with John G. Nicolay, Springfield, 4 July 1875, Burlingame, ed., *Oral History of Lincoln*, 31.

189. Wilson to Herndon, Sterling, Illinois, 10 Feb. 1866, *HI*, 204.

190. Representative John Hogan of Madison County, paraphrasing the charges of the system's opponents, speech in the House, 30 Jan., Alton *Telegraph*, 10 May 1837.

191. Whitney, *Lincoln the Citizen*, 131–132.

192. *House Journal*, 1836–1837, 702.

193. Dubois, interview with John G. Nicolay, Springfield, 4 July 1875, Burlingame, ed., *Oral History of Lincoln*, 30.

194. Henry C. Whitney, *Lincoln the Citizen*, manuscript version, 174, Lincoln Memorial University, Harrogate, Tennessee. This passage was omitted from the published edition of Whitney's biography.

195. Walker in the Jacksonville *Gazette and News*, n.d., copied in the *Sangamo Journal*, 20 May 1837.

196. "The Internal Improvements System," Jacksonville *Illinoisan*, 10 Feb. 1838.

197. *Congressional Globe*, 28th Congress, 1st Session, Appendix, 236 (17 Jan. 1844).

198. Letter by Ewing, 9 July, in "The Seat of Government," *Sangamo Journal*, 21 July 1838.

199. Linder, *Reminiscences*, 62.

200. Statement made at a public meeting, Vandalia, 7 July, *Illinois State Register* (Vandalia), 20 July 1838.

201. Statement by a committee headed by N. M. McCurdy, Vandalia, July 1838, *Illinois State Register* (Vandalia), 10 Aug. 1838.

202. Letter by "Oregon," *Illinois State Register* (Springfield), 22 Sept. 1843.

203. "Removal of the Seat of Government," Alton *Telegraph & Democratic Review*, 24 May 1845.

204. "Internal Improvements, No. VI," by E[dson] H[arkness], Peoria *Register and North-Western Gazette*, 8 Sept. 1838.

205. Vandalia *Free Press*, 21 Feb. 1839, in *CWL*, 1:144.

206. "Mr. Lincoln," *Illinois State Register* (Vandalia), 5 Apr. 1839.

207. *Sangamo Journal*, 29 July 1837.

208. Wilson to Herndon, Sterling, Illinois, 10 Feb. 1866, *HI*, 206.

209. *Sangamo Journal*, 29 July 1837.

210. Harry E. Pratt, ed., *Lincoln: 1809–1839* (Springfield, IL: Abraham Lincoln Association, 1941), liii.

211. Joshua Speed, interview with Herndon, [1865–1866], *HI*, 475.

212. William Butler, interview with John G. Nicolay, Springfield, 13 June 1875, Burlingame, ed., *Oral History of Lincoln*, 21.

213. Logan, interview with John G. Nicolay, Springfield, 6 July 1875, Burlingame, ed., *Oral History of Lincoln*, 37.

214. Linder, *Reminiscences*, 61.

215. Vandalia correspondence by "Illinois," 23 Feb., *Sangamo Journal*, 4 Mar. 1837.

216. Linder, *Reminiscences*, 59–60.

217. Ford, *History of Illinois*, 187.

218. Ibid., 222.

219. Stuart to John J. Hardin, Washington, 24 Jan. 1843, Hardin Family Papers, ICHi.

220. Springfield correspondence by Henry Villard, 29 Nov., New York *Herald*, 4 Dec. 1860.

221. *House Journal*, 1836–1837, 241–244.

222. *CWL*, 1:75

223. *Illinois State Journal* (Springfield), 25 Aug. 1860.

224. Duncan to Gideon Blackburn, Jacksonville, 12 Dec. 1837, Julia Duncan Kirby, "Biographical Sketch of Joseph Duncan, Fifth Governor of Illinois" (pamphlet; Fergus Historical Series, no. 29; Chicago: Fergus, 1888), 50–51.

225. Clay to Calvin Colton, Lexington, 2 Sept. 1843 and to John Sloane, Lexington, 27 Oct. 1843, James F. Hopkins et al., eds., *The Papers of Henry Clay* (11 vols.; Lexington: University Press of Kentucky, 1959–1992), 9:852, 874.

226. Paul Revere Frothingham, *Edward Everett: Orator and Statesman* (Boston: Houghton Mifflin, 1925), 132.

227. Albany *Argus*, 7 Jan. 1837, quoted in Lorman Ratner, *Powder Keg: Northern Opposition to the Antislavery Movement, 1831–1840* (New York: Basic Books, 1968), 72; Marcy, message of 5 Jan. 1836, quoted in Ivor Debenham Spencer, *The Victor and the Spoils: A Life of William L. Marcy* (Providence, RI: Brown University Press, 1959), 104.

228. *Sangamo Journal*, 28 Oct. 1837.

229. Van Meter, *Always My Friend*, 30.

230. *Illinois State Journal* (Springfield), 19 Oct. 1854.

231. E. M. to Messrs. Leavitt and Alden, Morgan County, Illinois, 22 June, *Emancipator and Weekly Chronicle* (Boston), 16 July 1845.

232. *Our Constitution* (Urbana), 16 Aug. 1856.

233. *CWL*, 2:492

234. Parks to Herndon, Lincoln, Illinois, 25 Mar. 1866, *HI*, 239.

235. Ralph Hoyt, "Personal Reminiscences of Abraham Lincoln," unidentified clipping [15 Apr. 1900], Lincoln Shrine, A. K. Smiley Public Library, Redlands, California.

236. Lincoln to A. G. Hodges, Washington, 4 Apr. 1864, *CWL*, 281.

237. Robert H. Browne, *Abraham Lincoln and the Men of His Time* (2 vols.; Cincinnati: Jennings and Pye, 1901), 1:285.

238. Reminiscences of John E. Roll, in John Linden Roll, "Sangamo Town," *Journal of the Illinois State Historical Society* 19 (1926–1927): 159.

239. Autobiography written for John Locke Scripps, [ca. June 1860], *CWL*, 4:65.

240. *House Journal*, 1836–1837, 241–242 (12 Jan. 1837).

241. Merton Dillon, *Elijah P. Lovejoy, Abolitionist Editor* (Urbana: University of Illinois Press, 1961), 47.

242. Clay's speech delivered in Lexington, Kentucky, 13 Nov. 1847, Hopkins, ed., *Papers of Clay*, 10:372.

243. Speech at Vincennes, Indiana, quoted in *The Old Soldier* (Springfield, Illinois), 2 Mar. 1840.

244. *Illinois State Register* (Springfield), 15 Apr. 1854.

245. *Right and Wrong in Boston,* no. 2, 53, quoted in Gilbert Hobbs Barnes, *The Antislavery Impulse, 1830–1844* (1933; New York: Harcourt Brace & World, 1964), 25.

246. "Declaration of Sentiments," written for the American Antislavery Society in 1833, quoted in William Lee Miller, *Arguing about Slavery: The Great Battle in the United States Congress* (New York: Knopf, 1996), 71; *The Liberator* (Boston), 11:191, quoted in Wendell Phillips Garrison et al., *William Lloyd Garrison, 1805–1879: The Story of His Life Told by His Children* (4 vols.; New York: Century, 1885–1889), 1:410, 3:32–33.

247. *The Letters of William Lloyd Garrison,* ed. Walter M. Merrill (6 vols.; Cambridge, MA: Belknap Press of Harvard University Press, 1971–1981), 1:249; *The Liberator* (Boston), 3 Feb. 1843.

248. *The Liberator* (Boston), 1 Jan. 1831.

249. *CWL,* 1:271–279; William D. Kelley to the editor of the New York *Tribune,* Philadelphia, 23 Sept. 1885, in William D. Kelley, *Lincoln and Stanton* (New York: G. P. Putnam's Sons, 1885), 86; Michael Burlingame and John R. Turner Ettlinger, eds., *Inside Lincoln's White House: The Complete Civil War Diary of John Hay* (Carbondale: Southern Illinois University Press, 1997), 216 (entry for 1 July 1864).

250. Dillon, *Lovejoy,* 40–41.

251. *Shepherd of the Valley* (St. Louis), 28 Feb. 1834, in "Elijah P. Lovejoy As an Anti-Catholic," *Records of the American Catholic Historical Society of Philadelphia* 62 (1951):174 (no author given).

252. Eulogy on Henry Clay, 6 July 1852, *CWL,* 2:130.

Chapter 5. "We Must Fight the Devil with Fire"

1. Patrick Shirreff, *A Tour through North America; Together with a Comprehensive View of the Canadas and the United States as Adapted for Agricultural Emigration* (Edinburgh: Oliver & Boyd, 1835), 242; James Stuart, *Three Years in North America* (2 vols.; New York: J. and J. Harper, 1833), 2:224;

Springfield correspondence, 21 June, Utica, New York, *Herald,* 27 June, copied in the New York *Tribune,* 9 July 1860; excerpts from an unpublished autobiography by William Henry, brother of Anson G. Henry, enclosed in Harry S. Douglas to Carl Sandburg, Arcade, New York, 12 Feb. 1955, Abraham Lincoln Association reference files, IHi.

2. William Cullen Bryant to his wife, Jacksonville, Illinois, 12 and 19 June 1832, in Parke Godwin, ed., *Prose Writings of William Cullen Bryant* (2 vols.; New York: D. Appleton, 1889), 2:13–14, 16.

3. John Moses, *Illinois, Historical and Statistical* (2 vols.; Chicago: Fergus, 1889), 1:431–432.

4. Miriam Morrison Worthington, ed., "Diary of Anna R. Morrison, Wife of Isaac L. Morrison," *Journal of the Illinois State Historical Society* 7 (1914): 43 (entry for 13 Dec. 1840).

5. Elizabeth Lushbaugh Capps, "Early Recollections of Abraham Lincoln," Abraham Lincoln Association reference files, "Reminiscences" folder, IHi.

6. Clinton L. Conkling, *Illinois State Journal* (Springfield), 13 Feb. 1919.

7. George R. Weber, "Good-Bye," *Old Settlers Telephone* (Springfield), n.d., clipping, LMF; "Mentor" in the *Sangamo Journal,* 1 Apr. 1847.

8. Letter by "Chicago," Springfield, 7 Oct., Chicago *Daily Times,* 12 Oct. 1858.

9. Dispatch by "Traveler," Springfield, 6 Dec., Chicago *Times,* n.d., copied in the *Illinois State Journal* (Springfield), 15 Dec. 1856; John Lewis Peyton, *Over the Alleghenies and Across the Prairies: Personal Recollections of the Far West, One and Twenty Years Ago* (London: Simpkin, Marshall, 1869), 300.

10. Springfield correspondence, 26 Nov., Cincinnati *Commercial,* n.d., copied in the *Missouri Democrat* (St. Louis), 4 Dec. 1860.

11. Hezekiah Morse Wead diary, 31 Aug. 1847, IHi.

12. John Hay to Nora Perry, Springfield, 20 May 1859, John Hay Papers, RPB.

13. James Caird, *Prairie Farming in America, with Notes by the Way on Canada and the United States* (New York: D. Appleton, 1859), 65.

14. John Hay to Charles G. Halpine, Washington, 22 Nov. 1863, Michael Burlingame, ed., *At Lincoln's Side: John Hay's Civil War Correspondence and Selected Writings* (Carbondale: Southern Illinois University Press, 2000), 68.

15. Lincoln to Mary Owens, Springfield, 7 May 1837, Roy P. Basler et al., eds., *Collected Works of Abraham Lincoln* [hereafter *CWL*] (8 vols. plus index; New Brunswick, NJ: Rutgers University Press, 1953–1955), 1:78–79.

16. William Butler, interview with John G. Nicolay, [June 1875], Michael Burlingame, ed., *An Oral History of Abraham Lincoln: John G. Nicolay's Interviews and Essays* (Carbondale: Southern Illinois University Press, 1996), 22–23.

17. Stephen A. Douglas to Julius N. Granger, Jacksonville, 9 May 1835, Robert W. Johannsen, ed., *The Letters of Stephen A. Douglas* (Urbana: University of Illinois Press, 1961), 15.

18. Speed's recollections, 1882, Osborn H. Oldroyd, *The Lincoln Memorial: Album Immortelles* (New York: G. W. Carleton, 1883), 146; Joshua Speed, *Reminiscences of Abraham Lincoln and Notes of a Visit to California: Two Lectures* (Louisville, KY: John P. Morton, 1884), 21–22; statement Speed made "some years" before his death in 1882, quoted in a Washington letter, n.d., to the Louisville *Courier-Journal*, copied in the Bloomington *Pantagraph*, 17 Jan. 1884.

19. Complaint of plaintiff in the suit of *Hawthorn vs. Woolridge*, 1 July 1836, Martha L. Benner, Cullom Davis et al., eds., *The Law Practice of Abraham Lincoln: Complete Documentary Edition*, DVD-ROM (Urbana: University of Illinois Press, 2000) [hereafter *LPAL*], case file #03504.

20. Fragment: Notes of a Law Lecture, [1 July 1850?], *CWL*, 2:81.

21. Robert McIntyre, "Lincoln's Friend," Charleston, Illinois, *Courier*, n.d., Paris,

Illinois, *Gazette*, n.d., Chicago *Tribune*, 30 May 1885.

22. Stephen T. Logan, interviewed by John G. Nicolay, Springfield, 6 July 1875, Burlingame, ed., *Oral History of Lincoln*, 39; Milton Hay, interview with Nicolay, Springfield, 4 July 1875, ibid., 27.

23. *Illinois Republican*, n.d., copied in the *Sangamo Journal*, 17 June 1837.

24. Undated letter by "Springfield," *Sangamo Journal*, 10 June 1837.

25. *Sangamo Journal*, 15 July 1837.

26. Ibid., 5 Aug. 1837.

27. *Illinois State Register* (Vandalia), 29 Sept. 1837, 25 May 1838.

28. Andy Van Meter, *Always My Friend: A History of the State Journal-Register and Springfield* (Springfield, IL: Copley Press, 1981), 64.

29. First Reply to James Adams, 6 Sept. 1837, *CWL*, 1:95–100.

30. "An Old Settler—No. 1," *Sangamo Journal*, 7 Oct. 1837.

31. Second Reply to James Adams, 18 Oct. 1837, *CWL*, 1:101–106.

32. *Sangamo Journal*, 12 May 1838.

33. Unsigned letter purportedly by a Democratic politician (doubtless John Calhoun) to Reuben Whitney, Springfield, 3 May 1837, *Sangamo Journal*, 13 May 1837.

34. Unsigned letter purportedly by a Democratic politician (doubtless John Calhoun) to [Reuben Whitney?], Springfield, 1 June, *Sangamo Journal*, 3 June 1837.

35. Usher F. Linder, *Reminiscences of the Early Bench and Bar of Illinois* (Chicago: Chicago Legal News, 1879), 62–64.

36. David Davis to William P. Walker, Bloomington, Illinois, 1 July 1837 and 19 Jan. 1840, David Davis Papers, IHi.

37. Samuel D. Marshall to Henry Eddy, Springfield, 19 Dec. 1839, Eddy Papers, IHi.

38. John Pearson to James W. Stephenson, Joliet, Illinois, 8 Jan. 1838 (misfiled 1834), Stephenson Papers, IHi.

39. Letters of 25 Apr. and 7 May, *Sangamo Journal*, 26 May 1838.

40. *Sangamo Journal,* 16 June 1838.

41. David Davis, memorial address at services for John Todd Stuart, 13 Jan. 1886, Bloomington, Illinois, *Pantagraph,* 6 Feb. 1886.

42. *Sangamo Journal,* 13 Jan. 1838; Douglas to Simeon Francis, 26 Jan. 1838, enclosed in Douglas to George Weber, Springfield, 30 Jan. 1838, in Johannsen, ed., *Letters of Douglas,* 52.

43. Conservative No. 2, *Sangamo Journal,* 27 Jan. 1838; Conservative No. 2, addendum, *Sangamo Journal,* 3 Feb. 1838.

44. Columbia, South Carolina, *Southern Times,* 28 Aug. 1835, quoted in David Grimsted, *American Mobbing, 1828–1861: Toward Civil War* (New York: Oxford University Press, 1998), 3.

45. Speech in the Illinois House of Representatives, 11 Jan. 1837, *CWL,* 1:69.

46. Address before the Young Men's Lyceum of Springfield, Illinois, 27 Jan. 1838, *CWL,* 1:113–114.

47. Lincoln to William A. Minshall, Springfield, 7 Dec. 1837, *CWL,* 1:107.

48. Alton *Telegraph and Democratic Review,* n.d., quoted in John Michael Rozett, "The Social Bases of Party Conflict in the Age of Jackson: Individual Voting Behavior in Greene County Illinois, 1838–48" (Ph.D. dissertation, University of Michigan, 1974), 43.

49. William H. Herndon and Jesse W. Weik, *Herndon's Lincoln,* ed. Douglas L. Wilson and Rodney O. Davis (1889; Urbana: University of Illinois Press, 2006), 126; Henry Clay Whitney, *Life on the Circuit with Lincoln,* ed. Paul M. Angle (1892; Caldwell, ID: Caxton Printers, 1940), 12.

50. Albert Taylor Bledsoe, review of Ward Hill Lamon's biography of Lincoln, *Southern Review* 12 (Apr. 1873): 334.

51. Michael Burlingame and John R. Turner Ettlinger, eds., *Inside Lincoln's White House: The Complete Civil War Diary of John Hay* (Carbondale: Southern Illinois University Press, 1997), 26 (entry for 12 Oct. 1861).

52. Edwin Wlipple, ed., *The Great Speeches and Orations of Daniel Webster* (Boston: Little, Brown, 1889), 135.

53. *CWL,* 1:108–115.

54. *Sangamo Journal,* 5 Dec. 1835.

55. *CWL,* 1:111, 110, 109.

56. Conservative No. 3, *Sangamo Journal,* 10 Feb. 1838.

57. Lincoln to John Todd Stuart, Springfield, 1 Mar. 1840, *CWL,* 1:206.

58. Lincoln to Jesse W. Fell, n.p., [23 July 1838], *CWL,* 1:120.

59. Letter by Ewing, 9 July 1838, in "The Seat of Government," *Sangamo Journal,* 21 July 1838.

60. Lincoln to John Todd Stuart, Vandalia, 14 Feb. 1839, *CWL,* 1:143.

61. John J. Hardin to his wife, Vandalia, 21 Feb. 1839, Hardin Family Papers, ICHi.

62. *House Journal,* 1838–1839, 98–100.

63. Remarks in Illinois Legislature, 8 Dec. 1838, *CWL,* 1:123.

64. Report and Resolutions, 17 Jan. 1839, *CWL,* 1:135.

65. *Illinois State Register* (Springfield), 8 Jan. 1840.

66. *Sangamo Journal,* 1 Nov. 1839.

67. Lincoln to William S. Wait, Vandalia, 2 Mar. 1839, *CWL,* 1:148.

68. Thomas J. Nance to Catherine Nance, Springfield, 23 Jan. 1840, Fern Nance Pond, ed., "Letters of an Illinois Legislator: 1839–1840," *Abraham Lincoln Quarterly* 5 (1949):417.

69. David Davis to William P. Walker, Bloomington, 18 Mar. 1839, David Davis Papers, IHi.

70. Letter dated 6 Sept. 1838, *Sangamo Journal,* 15 Sept. 1838.

71. *Sangamo Journal,* 16 Feb. 1839.

72. John G. Nicolay interviewed in "Lincoln in Early Life, Colonel Nicolay's Reminiscences," Washington correspondence by C., Chicago *Herald,* 4 Dec. 1887.

73. Lincoln to Butler, Vandalia, 26 Jan. 1839, *CWL,* 1:139–140.

74. Baker to Butler, Vandalia, 26 Jan. 1839, *CWL,* 1:138.

75. Lincoln to Butler, Vandalia, 1 Feb. 1839, *CWL,* 1:141.

76. *House Journal*, 1838–1839, p. 171 (5 Jan. 1839).

77. Remarks of 5 Jan. 1839, *CWL*, 1:126.

78. *House Journal*, 1838–1839, p. 323 (1 Feb. 1839).

79. Paul M. Angle, *"Here I Have Lived": A History of Lincoln's Springfield, 1821–1865* (Springfield: Abraham Lincoln Association, 1935), 90–91.

80. Remarks made on 30 Jan. 1840, *CWL*, 1:201.

81. *Illinois State Register* (Springfield), 8 Jan. 1840.

82. Remarks made on 22 Jan. 1840, *CWL*, 1:196.

83. Lincoln to John Todd Stuart, Springfield, 23 Dec. 1839, *CWL*, 1:159.

84. Lincoln to John Stuart, Springfield, 20 Jan. 1840, *CWL*, 1:184.

85. Clinton L. Conkling, "Movement for a Third Capital," in Newton Bateman and Paul Selby, eds., *Historical Encyclopedia of Illinois*, vol. II, part 1 (Chicago: Munsell, 1912), 646–647.

86. Thomas Ford, *History of Illinois from Its Commencement as a State in 1818 to 1847* (Chicago: S. C. Griggs, 1854), 139.

87. David Davis to John J. Hardin, Bloomington, Illinois, 1 June 1839, Hardin Family Papers, ICHi.

88. Communication to the readers of *The Old Soldier*, 28 Feb. 1840, *CWL*, 1:205.

89. *Sangamo Journal*, 3 Nov. 1838.

90. Ibid., 26 May 1838.

91. Anthony Banning Norton, *The Great Revolution of 1840: Reminiscences of the Log Cabin and Hard Cider Campaign* (Mt. Vernon, OH: A. B. Norton, 1888), 10.

92. Thomas Elder, paraphrased in Richard Smith Elliott, *Notes Taken in Sixty Years* (St. Louis: Studley, 1883), 121; C. Davis in Holt, *Rise and Fall of the Whig Party*, 105.

93. Circular to the readers of *The Old Soldier*, 28 Feb. 1840, *CWL*, 1:205.

94. Bledsoe's review of Ward Hill Lamon's biography of Lincoln, *Southern Review* 12 (Apr. 1873):360–361.

95. J. S. Buckingham, *The Eastern and Western States of America* (3 vols.; London: Fisher, 1842), 3:285.

96. M. Bradley to Thurlow Weed, 29 Aug. 1839, quoted in Holt, *Rise and Fall of the Whig Party*, 101.

97. Linder, *Reminiscences*, 136.

98. Lincoln to Stuart, Springfield, 20 Jan. 1840, *CWL*, 1:184.

99. *Illinois State Register* (Springfield), 23 Nov. 1839.

100. Joseph Gillespie to Herndon, Edwardsville, Illinois, 31 Jan. 1866, Douglas L. Wilson and Rodney O. Davis, eds., *Herndon's Informants: Letters, Interviews, and Statements about Abraham Lincoln* [hereafter *HI*] (Urbana: University of Illinois Press, 1998), 181.

101. He said this in 1856. Speech of "Judge Park" (perhaps Samuel C. Parks) at a banquet in Joliet, Illinois, Washington *Post*, 1 Apr. 1883.

102. Henry C. Whitney, *Lincoln the Citizen*, vol. 1 of *A Life of Lincoln*, ed. Marion Mills Miller (2 vols.; New York: Baker and Taylor, 1908), 145.

103. "To the Public," Illinois State Register (Springfield), 3 Apr. 1840; John B. Weber, interview with Herndon, [ca. 1 Nov. 1866], *HI*, 389.

104. Linder, *Reminiscences*, 249.

105. Joseph Gillespie to Herndon, Edwardsville, Illinois, 31 Jan. 1866, *HI*, 181.

106. *CWL*, 1:158.

107. Lincoln to John Todd Stuart, Springfield, 23 Dec. 1839, *CWL*, 1:159.

108. *CWL*, 1:159–179.

109. Speed, *Reminiscences of Lincoln*, 25.

110. Speed to Herndon, Louisville, 6 Dec. 1866, *HI*, 499.

111. "Oration of John M. Palmer, Delivered at Galesburg, Ill., October 7, 1896," in *Personal Recollections of John M. Palmer: The Story of an Earnest Life* (Cincinnati: Clarke, 1901), 604–605.

112. *Illinois State Register* (Springfield), 8 Feb. 1840.

113. Ibid., 27 Mar. 1840; Springfield correspondence by Virginius [George T. M. Davis], 7 Dec., Alton *Telegraph*, 12 Dec. 1840.

114. John F. Snyder, *Adam W. Snyder and His Period in Illinois History, 1817–1842* (2nd ed., rev.; Virginia, IL: E. Needham, 1906), 341.

115. Field to Henry Eddy, Springfield, 17 Aug. 1840, Eddy Papers, IHi; Logan Hay, "Lincoln One Hundred Years Ago," *Abraham Lincoln Quarterly* 1 (1940):89–90; Linder, *Reminiscences*, 206–207.

116. Belleville *Advocate*, 29 Aug. 1840.

117. Elihu B. Washburne, "Abraham Lincoln, His Personal History and Public Record, Speech delivered in the U.S. House of Representatives, May 29, 1860," pamphlet ed. (1860), 2; Washburne in Allen Thorndike Rice, ed., *Reminiscences of Abraham Lincoln by Distinguished Men of His Time* (New York: North American Review, 1888), 9–10.

118. John Hay, "Colonel Baker" (1861) in Burlingame, ed., *At Lincoln's Side*, 155–156.

119. Reminiscences of Anthony Thornton, Chicago *Tribune*, 12 Feb. 1900.

120. *Masonic Trowel* (Springfield), 15 May 1865, p. 70.

121. Thomas J. McCormack, ed., *Memoirs of Gustave Koerner, 1809–1896* (2 vols.; Cedar Rapids, IA: Torch Press, 1909), 1:443–444.

122. Alton *Telegraph*, 11 Apr. 1840.

123. *Illinois State Register* (Springfield), 17 July and 25 Jan. 1840.

124. *Old Hickory* (Springfield), 24 Feb. 1840; *Old Hickory*, n.d., copied in the *Illinois State Register* Springfield, 21 Feb. 1840, in Johannsen, ed., *Letters of Douglas*, 79.

125. *Illinois State Register* (Springfield), 12 June 1840, in Johannsen, ed., *Letters of Douglas*, 84.

126. John A. Chesnut, letter in the *Sangamo Journal*, 8 May 1840.

127. Reminiscences of Abram Brokaw, Bloomington *Pantagraph*, 18 Feb. 1903.

128. Tremont correspondence, 4 May, *Sangamo Journal*, 15 May 1840; *Illinois State Register* (Springfield), 29 May 1840.

129. Ward Hill Lamon to Lincoln, Bloomington, Illinois, 17 Aug. 1860, AL MSS DLC.

130. James H. Matheny, interview with Herndon, [1865–1866], *HI*, 471.

131. Ibid.

132. *Great Western* (Belleville), 18 Apr. 1840.

133. *Sangamo Journal*, 3 July 1840.

134. John M. Scott, "Lincoln on the Stump and at the Bar," enclosed in Scott to Ida Tarbell, Bloomington, Illinois, 14 Aug. 1895, Tarbell Papers, Allegheny College.

135. Response to a serenade, 10 Nov. 1864, *CWL*, 8:101.

136. David Davis, quoted in Willard L. King, *Lincoln's Manager: David Davis* (Cambridge, MA: Harvard University Press, 1960), 38; Albert Taylor Bledsoe, review of Ward Hill Lamon's biography of Lincoln, *Southern Review* 12 (Apr. 1873): 332–333.

137. *Illinois State Register* (Springfield), 24 July 1840.

138. Wilson and Davis, eds., *Herndon's Lincoln*, 128; J. McCan Davis to Ida Tarbell, Springfield, Illinois, 11 Mar. 1895, copy, J. G. Randall Papers, DLC; Whitney, *Lincoln the Citizen*, 143.

139. Ninian W. Edwards, interview with Herndon, [1865–1866], *HI*, 447.

140. James H. Matheny, interview with Herndon, [1865–1866], *HI*, 472.

141. McCormack, ed., *Memoirs of Gustave Koerner*, 1:443.

142. Belleville *Advocate*, 18 Apr. 1840.

143. Letter by an unidentified correspondent, Waterloo, Illinois, 26 Aug., *Illinois State Register* (Springfield), 4 Sept. 1840; Belleville *Advocate*, 29 Aug. 1840.

144. Letter by "Patriot," Mt. Vernon, Illinois, 3 Oct., *Illinois State Register* (Springfield), 16 Oct. 1840.

145. Quincy *Whig*, 23 May 1840.

146. Letter by "Patriot," Mt. Vernon, Illinois, 3 Oct., *Illinois State Register* (Springfield), 16 Oct. 1840.

147. Letter by an unidentified correspondent, Equality, Illinois, 14 Sept., *Illinois State Register* (Springfield), 25 Sept. 1840.

148. Judge William H. Stickney of Chicago related this story in a letter to the Palatine, Illinois, *Enterprise,* n.d., copied in the *Illinois State Journal* (Springfield), 13 Feb. 1884.

149. Andrew J. Galloway's reminiscences, Chicago *Tribune,* 12 Feb. 1900.

150. Letter by "Patriot," Mt. Vernon, Illinois, 3 Oct., *Illinois State Register* (Springfield), 16 Oct. 1840.

151. Gibson W. Harris, "My Recollections of Abraham Lincoln," *Women's Home Companion,* Nov. 1903, p. 10.

152. J. A. Powell to the editor of *The Century,* copy, and Powell to John G. Nicolay, Homer, Illinois, 11 Feb. 1889, both in the Nicolay Papers, DLC.

153. Lincoln to William G. Anderson, Lawrenceville, 31 Oct. 1840, *CWL,* 1:211.

154. Letter by "A Looker-on," Clinton County, Illinois, 23 Oct. *Sangamo Journal,* 8 Nov. 1839.

155. "An Old Jackson Man," Nos. I, II, III, IV, VII, *Sangamo Journal,* 6 and 13 Mar., 10 Apr. 1840.

156. "Son of an Old Ranger" to the editor, Macoupin County, 20 Feb., *The Old Soldier,* 1 Apr. 1840.

157. *Sangamo Journal,* 27 Mar. 1840.

158. William G. Green, interview with James Q. Howard, [May 1860], AL MSS DLC.

159. "A Citizen," *Sangamo Journal,* 3 and 10 July 1840.

160. Herndon to "Fellow Citizens," Springfield, 14 July 1840, *Illinois State Register* (Springfield), 17 July 1840.

161. "Quiz" [Archer Herndon] to Van Buren, Springfield, 14 July, *Sangamo Journal,* 17 July 1840.

162. Davis to William P. Walker, Bloomington, Illinois, 16 Nov. 1840, David Davis Papers, IHi.

163. Joshua Speed, interview with Herndon, [1865–1866], *HI,* 475.

164. Edward H. Thayer, quoted in Thomas Dale Logan, "Lincoln, the Early Temperance Reformer," *The Christian Century,* 13 Feb. 1909, p. 152.

165. Lincoln to Stuart, Springfield, 1 Mar. 1840, *CWL,* 1:206.

166. Nance to John Taylor, Rock Creek, 30 Jan. 1838, Records of the Auditor's Office, Springfield Land Office, Illinois State Archives, Springfield.

167. *Sangamo Journal,* 14 Apr. 1838.

168. Lincoln to John Todd Stuart, Springfield, 26 Mar. 1840, *CWL,* 1:208.

169. Anson G. Henry to John J. Hardin, Springfield, 11 Nov. 1843, Hardin Family Papers, ICHi.

170. T[homas] D[rummond] to the editor, Springfield, 19 Dec., *Rock River Express* (Rockford), 26 Dec. 1840.

171. William H. Fithian to Amos Williams, Springfield, 12 Dec. 1840, Woodbury Collection, Illinois Historical Survey, University of Illinois, in Donald G. Richter, *Lincoln: Twenty Years on the Eastern Prairie* (Mattoon, IL: United Graphics, 1999), 40.

172. Springfield correspondence by Virginius [George T. M. Davis], 4 Jan., Alton *Telegraph,* 16 Jan. 1841.

173. Springfield correspondence, 11 June, New York *Herald,* 26 June 1860.

174. Reminiscences of John A. McClernand, Chicago *Tribune,* 12 Feb. 1900.

175. *Illinois State Register* (Springfield), 11 Dec. 1840.

176. Lucian P. Sanger to Augustus A. Evans, Springfield, 5 Dec. 1840, Augustus A. Evans Papers, Missouri Historical Society.

177. *Illinois State Register* (Springfield), 16 Feb. 1844.

178. Joseph Gillespie to Herndon, Edwardsville, Illinois, 31 Jan. 1866, *HI,* 188.

179. Springfield correspondence by "Pompey," 4 Dec., Peoria *Register and North-Western Gazette,* 11 Dec. 1840.

180. Adam W. Snyder to Gustave Koerner, Springfield, 21 Feb. 1841, John Francis Snyder Papers, IHi.

181. Adam W. Snyder to Gustave Koerner, Springfield, 6 Feb. 1841, John Francis Snyder Papers, IHi.

182. James Harvey Ralston to "Dear Sir," Springfield, 30 Jan. 1841, Ralston Papers, IHi.

183. John J. Hardin to John Todd Stuart, Springfield, 20 Jan. 1841, Hardin Family Papers, ICHi.

184. Stuart to John J. Hardin, Washington, 30 Jan. 1841, Hardin Family Papers, ICHi.

185. William H. Fithian to Amos Williams, Springfield, 29 Dec. 1840, Woodbury Collection, Illinois Historical Survey, University of Illinois, Urbana-Champaign, in Richter, *Lincoln: Twenty Years on the Eastern Prairie*, 40.

186. Rodney O. Davis, "Illinois Legislators and Jacksonian Democracy, 1834–1841" (Ph.D. dissertation, University of Iowa, 1966), 288–292; "The Case Stated," by "a member of the House," *Sangamo Journal*, 5 Feb. 1841.

187. *Sangamo Journal*, 12 Feb. 1841; letter dated Springfield, 13 Feb., ibid., 19 Feb. 1841.

188. Protest dated 26 Feb. 1841, *CWL*, 1:244–249.

189. Remarks made on 26 Feb. 1841, in *CWL*, 1:244.

190. James C. Conkling in Francis Fisher Browne, *The Every-Day Life of Abraham Lincoln* (New York: N. D. Thompson, 1886), 171.

191. *Illinois State Register* (Springfield), 12 Mar. 1841, in *CWL*, 1:244n.

192. Clark E. Carr, *The Illini: A Story of the Prairies* (Chicago: McClurg, 1904), 148.

193. Koerner, *Memoirs*, 1:480.

194. *Northwestern Gazette and Galena Advertiser*, 17 Feb. 1841, in *CWL*, 1:237–238.

195. Springfield correspondence by "A Member of the Lobby," 23 Dec. 1840, Quincy *Whig*, 9 Jan. 1841.

196. Henderson's reminiscences, Omaha *Daily Bee*, 9 Feb. 1896.

197. Editorial copied in the *Sangamo Journal*, 15 Oct. 1841.

198. Alton *Telegraph* quoted in *Lincoln Day by Day*, 1:164 (entry for 20 July 1841).

199. *Sangamo Journal*, 12 Nov. 1841.

200. Ibid., 15 Oct. 1842.

201. Herndon to Ward Hill Lamon, 25 Feb. 1870, Lamon Papers, CSmH.

202. Lyman Trumbull to Walter Trumbull, n.p., n.d., in Horace White, *The Life of Lyman Trumbull* (Boston: Houghton Mifflin, 1913), 427.

203. Samuel C. Parks, *The Geat Trial of the Nineteenth Century* (Kansas City, MO: Hudson-Kimberly, 1900), 141.

204. Bledsoe, review of Ward Hill Lamon's biography of Lincoln, *Southern Review* 12 (Apr. 1873):364.

Chapter 6. "It Would Just Kill Me to Marry Mary Todd"

1. William H. Herndon to Truman Bartlett, Springfield, 22 Sept. 1887, Bartlett Papers, Massachusetts Historical Society; Michael Burlingame, *The Inner World of Abraham Lincoln* (Urbana: University of Illinois Press, 1994), 268.

2. Caleb Carman to Herndon, Petersburg, Illinois, 12 Oct. 1866, Douglas L. Wilson and Rodney O. Davis, eds., *Herndon's Informants: Letters, Interviews, and Statements about Abraham Lincoln* [hereafter *HI*] (Urbana: University of Illinois Press, 1998), 374; Lynn McNulty Greene to Herndon, Avon, Illinois, 3 May 1866, ibid., 250; statement by Benjamin R. Vineyard, enclosed in Vineyard to Jesse W. Weik, St. Joseph, Missouri, 14 Mar. 1887, ibid., 609–610; Mary Owens Vineyard to Herndon, Weston, Missouri, 23 May and 6 Aug. 1866, ibid., 256, 265; Johnson Gaines Green, interview with Herndon, [1866], ibid., 530; Esther Summers Bale, interview with Herndon, [1866], ibid., 527; William G. Greene to Herndon, Tallula, Illinois, 23 Jan. 1866, ibid., 175; Mentor Graham, interview with Herndon, 2 Apr. 1866, ibid., 243.

3. Mary Owens to Thomas J. Nance, Green City, Kentucky, 11 Apr. 1835, Fern Nance Pond, ed., "New Salem Community Activities:

Documents," *Journal of the Illinois State Historical Society* 48 (1955):100–101.

4. Lincoln to Mrs. Orville H. Browning, Springfield, 1 Apr. 1838, in Roy P. Basler et al., eds., *Collected Works of Abraham Lincoln* [hereafter *CWL*] (8 vols. plus index; New Brunswick, NJ: Rutgers University Press, 1953–1955), 1:117.

5. Mary Owens Vineyard to Herndon, Weston, Missouri, 22 July and 23 May 1866, *HI*, 263, 256.

6. Parthena Hill, interview with Walter B. Stevens, 1886, in Stevens, *A Reporter's Lincoln*, ed. Michael Burlingame (1916; Lincoln: University of Nebraska Press, 1998), 9.

7. Lincoln to Mrs. O. H. Browning, Springfield, 1 Apr. 1838, *CWL*, 1:117–119.

8. Lincoln to Mary Owens, Vandalia, 13 Dec. 1836, *CWL*, 1:54–55.

9. Parthena Hill, interview with Walter B. Stevens, 1886, in Stevens, *A Reporter's Lincoln*, ed. Burlingame, 10.

10. Mary Owens Vineyard to Herndon, Weston, Missouri, 23 May 1866, *HI*, 256.

11. Mary Owens Vineyard to Herndon, Weston, Missouri, 22 July 1866, *HI*, 262.

12. Johnson Gaines Greene, interview with Herndon, [1866], *HI*, 531; William G. Greene to Herndon, Tallula, Illinois, 23 Jan. 1866, *HI*, 175; William G. Greene in George A. Pierce, "Lincoln's Love," dispatch dated "on the cars," 16 Apr., Chicago *Inter-Ocean*, 23 Apr. 1881. Pierce has Greene quoting Mary Owens speaking in an ungrammatical, unsophisticated fashion. Her son protested, maintaining that she spoke like the well-educated woman that she was. Because Mary Owens claimed she had a good education and because her letters are perfectly grammatical and many others testified to her intelligence and refinement, I have recast Pierce's words to make her language suit her known character and background. Benjamin R. Vineyard to Jesse W. Weik, St. Joseph, Missouri, 13 Jan. 1887, *HI*, 599.

13. L. M. Greene to Herndon, Avon, Illinois, 30 July 1865, *HI*, 81.

14. Johnson Gaines Green interview with Herndon, [1866], *HI*, 530–531.

15. Lincoln to Mary Owens, Springfield, 7 May 1837, *CWL*, 1:78.

16. Lincoln to Mary Owens, Springfield, 16 Aug. 1837, *CWL*, 1:94.

17. Mary Owens Vineyard to Herndon, Weston, Missouri, 22 July 1866, *HI*, 263.

18. Harold D. Lasswell, *Power and Personality* (New York: W. W. Norton, 1948), 38, 39. A prominent Washington journalist who observed the political world from 1961 to 1999 wrote that the typical successful public figure in the capital longed to be "a praised person," a desire formed in childhood. Meg Greenfield, *Washington* (New York: Public Affairs, 2001), 32. In a study of highly ambitious entrepreneurs, Orvis F. Collins and his colleagues found that many of their subjects had in childhood either lost a parent or suffered from other forms of emotional abandonment. Collins et al., *The Enterprising Man* (East Lansing: Michigan State University Press, 1964), 54–56.

19. Lasswell, *Power and Personality*, 50. An unusually prominent business executive, Jim Barksdale, told an interviewer who asked him why he worked hard even though he had far more money than he could ever need: "I am very conscious of coming from the South. I know that people laugh at the southern accent. I know of many successful people with hardscrabble backgrounds. Many of us are driven to overcome what we came from." The media mogul Ted Turner "has attributed his relentless ambition to a 'latent inferiority complex' based on his childhood inability to satisfy a demanding father . . . in the middle of a speech, Turner held up a copy of a business magazine with his face on the cover and called out, 'Is this enough for you, dad?'" Dinesh D'Souza, *The Virtue of Prosperity: Finding Values in an Age of Techno-Affluence* (New York: The Free Press, 2000), 107–108.

20. Scripps to William Herndon, Chicago, 24 June 1865, *HI*, 57.

21. Autobiography written for John L. Scripps, [ca. June 1860], *CWL*, 4:61, 62.

22. Brief autobiography, [15?] June 1858, *CWL*, 2:459.

23. Stephen T. Logan, interview with John G. Nicolay, Springfield, 6 July 1875, Michael Burlingame, ed., *An Oral History of Abraham Lincoln: John G. Nicolay's Interviews and Essays* (Carbondale: Southern Illinois University Press, 1996), 38.

24. Stephen Fiske, "When Lincoln Was First Inaugurated," *Ladies' Home Journal* 14 (Mar. 1897):8.

25. "A Talk with Abraham Lincoln," John P. Gulliver, New York *Independent*, 1 Sept. 1864.

26. Autobiographical sketch enclosed in Lincoln to Jesse W. Fell, Springfield, 20 Dec. 1859, *CWL*, 3:511.

27. This story was told many times to Lawrence B. Stringer by Col. Robert B. Latham, a founder of the town, to whom Lincoln made the remark. Stringer, "The Lincoln Town," unpublished essay, 11, Stringer Papers, IHi.

28. *CWL*, 1:8–9, 320.

29. Hall to William E. Barton, Worcester, Massachusetts, 3 Oct. 1922, in a scrapbook marked "The Life of Lincoln, Vol. 2," Barton Papers, University of Chicago.

30. *CWL*, 1:8.

31. Burlingame, *Inner World of Lincoln*, 236–257.

32. Lincoln to Speed, Springfield, 25 Feb. 1842, *CWL*, 1:281.

33. Henry C. Whitney, *Life on the Circuit with Lincoln*, ed. Paul M. Angle (1892; Caldwell, ID: Caxton, 1940), 411.

34. Mrs. Elizabeth L. Norris (née Humphreys) to Emilie Todd Helm, Garden City, Kansas, 28 Sept. 1895, Elizabeth L. Norris Papers, IHi; Sarah Rickard, sister of Mrs. William Butler, interviewed by Nellie Crandall Sanford, Kansas City *Star*, 10 Feb. 1907. Mrs. Norris was the niece of Elizabeth Humphreys Todd and lived with the Todds while attending school in Lexington. She and Mary were good friends.

35. Octavia Roberts Corneau, "My Townsman—Abraham Lincoln," 9, typescript

of a talk given to the Lincoln Group of Boston, 18 Nov. 1939, Abraham Lincoln Association Reference Files, "Reminiscences," folder 5, IHi.

36. James C. Conkling to Mercy Levering, Springfield, 21 Sept. 1840, Conkling Papers, IHi.

37. Mary Edwards Raymond, *Some Incidents in the Life of Mrs. Benjamin S. Edwards* (n.p., 1909), 11–12.

38. Elizabeth Todd Edwards, interview with Herndon, [1865–1866], *HI*, 443.

39. Ninian W. Edwards, interview with Herndon, [1865–1866], *HI*, 446; Katherine Helm, *The True Story of Mary, Wife of Lincoln* (New York: Harper, 1928), 62–63.

40. Lincoln to Mary Owens, Springfield, 7 May 1837, *CWL*, 1:78.

41. Herndon to Ward Hill Lamon, Springfield, 6 Mar. 1870, Lamon Papers, CSmH.

42. Reminiscences of Catherine Bergen Jones, daughter of the Reverend Mr. John G. Bergen, who founded the first Presbyterian Church in Springfield, in Eugenia Jones Hunt, *My Personal Recollections of Abraham and Mary Todd Lincoln*, ed. Helen A. Moser (Peoria, IL: Helen A. Moser, 1966), 5.

43. Reminiscences of Elizabeth Harmon, Vermilion County Museum, in Donald G. Richter, *Lincoln: Twenty Years on the Eastern Prairie* (Mattoon, IL: United Graphics, 1999), 225.

44. Mrs. Charles Ridgely (née Jane Maria Barret, 1836–1922), who attended the Jacksonville party, told this story to Caroline Owsley Brown. Brown, "Springfield Society Before the Civil War," [Edwards Brown Jr.], *Rewarding Years Recalled* (privately published, 1973), 35–36. This is a fuller version of Mrs. Brown's article, originally written for the "Anti-Rust Club," than the one of the same title published in *Journal of the Illinois State Historical Society* 15 (1922).

45. Helm, *Mary, Wife of Lincoln*, 80–81, 83.

46. Mrs. John Lyman Child, interviewed by Katherine Pope, "Memories of Lincoln's Day," Streator, Illinois, *Independent Times*,

clipping [1920], Emanuel Hertz Scrapbooks, vol. 9, p. 2235, DLC.

47. Emilie Todd Helm, interview with Jesse W. Weik, 22 Mar. 1887, *HI,* 612.

48. Norman F. Boas, "Unpublished Manuscripts: Recollections of Mary Todd Lincoln by Her Sister Emilie Todd Helm; An Invitation to a Lincoln Party," *Manuscripts* 43 (Winter 1991):25.

49. Harriet A. Chapman, interview with Jesse W. Weik, [1886–1887], *HI,* 646.

50. Douglas Wilson, *Honor's Voice: The Transformation of Abraham Lincoln* (New York: Alfred A. Knopf, 1998), 213–230. I have relied heavily on Wilson's persuasive account, based on a careful, sensitive analysis of the confusing evidence about the courtship.

51. Elizabeth and Ninian W. Edwards, interview with Herndon, 27 July 1887, *HI,* 623.

52. Joshua F. Speed, interview with Herndon, [1865–1866], *HI,* 474.

53. Orville H. Browning, interview with John G. Nicolay, Springfield, 17 June 1875, Burlingame, ed., *Oral History of Lincoln,* 2.

54. Sarah Rickard interviewed by Nellie Crandall Sanford, Kansas City *Star,* 10 Feb. 1907.

55. Herndon to Jesse W. Weik, Springfield, 11 Jan. 1889, H-W MSS DLC. Herndon claimed that Joshua Speed informed him of this collusion.

56. Notes of a conversation with Mrs. Benjamin S. Edwards, 1895, "Lincoln Marriage" folder, Ida M. Tarbell Papers, Allegheny College.

57. Reminiscences of H. M. Powel, Taylorville, Illinois, *Semi-Weekly Breeze,* 12 Feb. 1909. As a youth of 12 and 13, Powel (b. 1839) recalled, he was hired to spend the night at the Lincoln home while Lincoln was away on business. From the summer of 1851 to the fall of 1853, Powel said, he often visited the Lincolns. His father was Richard Powel (1801–1875), born in Pennsylvania and living in Parkersburg, Virginia, in September 1851, when he moved his family to Springfield, where they lived until 1853, when they settled in Taylorville. *Portrait and Biographical Record of Christian County, Illinois* (Chicago: Lake City, 1893), 286.

58. William H. Herndon and Jesse W. Weik, *Herndon's Lincoln,* ed. Douglas L. Wilson and Rodney O. Davis (1889; Urbana: University of Illinois Press, 2006), 134.

59. Mary Lincoln to Abram Wakeman, Washington, 30 Jan. [1865], in Justin G. Turner and Linda Levitt Turner, eds., *Mary Todd Lincoln: Her Life and Letters* (New York: Alfred A. Knopf, 1972), 200.

60. Mary Todd Lincoln to Eliza Stuart Steele, Chicago, May [23, 1871], Turner and Turner, eds., *Mary Todd Lincoln,* 588.

61. William H. Townsend, *Lincoln and His Wife's Home Town* (Indianapolis, IN: Bobbs-Merrill, 1929), 46; Jean Baker, *Mary Todd Lincoln: A Biography* (New York: W. W. Norton, 1987), 24, 28–32, 330–332, 333; Charles B. Strozier, *Lincoln's Quest for Union: Public and Private Meanings* (New York: Basic Books, 1982), 72–73. Mary Lincoln's letters say almost nothing about her father, mother, or stepmother.

62. Wilson and Davis, eds., *Herndon's Lincoln,* 133, quoting a statement given by Mrs. Edwards on 3 Aug. 1887.

63. Deposition in the case of George R. C. *Todd vs. Elizabeth L. Todd et al.,* regarding the estate of Robert S. Todd, in Townsend, *Lincoln and His Wife's Home Town,* 229.

64. Stephen Berry, *House of Abraham: Lincoln and the Todds, A Family Divided by War* (Boston: Houghton Mifflin, 2007), 6–12.

65. Mary Lincoln to Elizabeth Keckley, Chicago, 29 Oct. [1867], Turner and Turner, eds., *Mary Todd Lincoln,* 447.

66. E[lizabeth] Humphreys Norris to Emilie [Todd Helm], Garden City, Kansas, 28 Sept. 1895, photostat, J. G. Randall Papers, DLC.

67. Mary Lincoln to her husband, Lexington, May 1848, Turner and Turner, eds., *Mary Todd Lincoln,* 37.

68. Berry, *House of Abraham,* 52–156.

69. Noyes W. Miner, "Mrs. Abraham Lincoln: A Vindication," 2–3, manuscript, Small Collection 1052, folder 1, IHi.

70. Elizabeth Keckley, *Behind the Scenes; or, Thirty Years a Slave and Four Years in the White House* (New York: G. W. Carleton, 1868), 135–136.

71. Berry, *House of Abraham*, 92.

72. James C. Conkling to Mercy Levering, Springfield, 7 Mar. 1841, Carl Sandburg and Paul M. Angle, *Mary Lincoln: Wife and Widow* (New York: Harcourt, Brace, 1932), 180–181.

73. Laura Catherine Redden Searing, writing under the pen name Howard Glyndon, "The Truth about Mrs. Lincoln," *The Independent* (New York), 10 Aug. 1882. Another female journalist also found her essentially childish. Mary Clemmer [Ames], *Ten Years in Washington; or, Inside Life and Scenes in Our National Capital as a Woman Sees Them* (Hartford, CT: Hartford Publishing Co., 1882), 236–242.

74. Helen Nicolay, *Personal Traits of Abraham Lincoln* (New York: Century, 1912), 205.

75. Browning, interview with John G. Nicolay, Springfield, 17 June 1875, Burlingame, ed., *Oral History of Lincoln*, 3, 1.

76. Helm, *Mary, Wife of Lincoln*, 32.

77. Berry, *House of Abraham*, 99–100.

78. Albert S. Edwards to S. M. Inglis, Springfield, 20 Feb. 1897, Small Collection 923, IHi.

79. Jason Emerson, *The Madness of Mary Lincoln* (Carbondale: Southern Illinois University Press, 2007), contains much new information about Mrs. Lincoln's incarceration and her release. See also Mark E. Neely and R. Gerald McMurtry, eds., *The Insanity File* (Carbondale: Southern Illinois University Press, 1986).

80. Davis told this to Orville Hickman Browning in 1873. Browning diary, 3 July 1873, IHi.

81. Davis to Adeline Burr, 19 July 1882, Adeline Ellery Burr Davis Green Papers,

Duke University. I am grateful to Jason Emerson for calling this document to my attention.

82. Berry, *House of Abraham*, 41–42, 188–190.

83. W. A. Evans, *Mrs. Abraham Lincoln: A Study of Her Personality and Her Influence on Lincoln* (New York: Alfred A. Knopf, 1932), 49–50.

84. Testimony of Captain C. W. Brant, in *Report on the Treatment of Prisoners of War by the Rebel Authorities during the War of the Rebellion*, Serial Set #1391, House Report #45, 40th Congress, 3rd Session (Washington, DC, 1869), 1086.

85. See Berry, *House of Abraham*, 83–91.

86. William H. Townsend to Harry E. Pratt, n.p., 22 Mar. 1954, carbon copy, Townsend Papers, IHi. See also Berry, *House of Abraham*, 61–63, 182–183.

87. Evans, *Mrs. Abraham Lincoln*, 47–48; Temple, *From Skeptic to Prophet*, 421; Berry, *House of Abraham*, 173–174.

88. Jessie Palmer Weber to Albert J. Beveridge, Springfield, 23 Mar. 1925, Beveridge Papers, DLC; Albert J. Beveridge to [William E. Barton], Beverly Farms, Massachusetts, 4 Jan. 1926, Lincoln Collection, RPB.

89. Mary Lincoln to Elizabeth Todd Grimsley, Washington, 29 Sept. 1861, in Turner and Turner, eds., *Mary Todd Lincoln*, 105.

90. Evans, *Mrs. Abraham Lincoln*, 47.

91. Elizabeth Edwards to Robert Todd Lincoln, Springfield, 13 Aug. 1875, Insanity File, Robert Todd Lincoln Papers, IHi.

92. Mrs. William H. Bailhache (née Ada Brayman) to Truman Bartlett, Coronado, Colorado, 4 July 1912, Truman Bartlett Papers, Boston University.

93. That trustee was Christopher Columbus Brown. "Condemnation Proceedings to Acquire More State House Land," manuscript dated 3 Apr. 1878, State House File, Illinois State Archives, Springfield, cited in Temple, *From Skeptic to Prophet*, 384. An 1878 map shows a plot of land across

from the state capitol owned by "Christopher C. Brown trustee of Julia C. Baker." Wayne C. Temple, "Alfred Henry Piquenard: Architect of Illinois' Sixth Capitol," in Mark W. Sorenson, ed., *Capitol Centennial Papers: Papers Prepared for the Centennial Observation of the Completion of the Illinois State Capitol, 1988* (Springfield: Illinois State Archives, 1990), 24.

94. Mary Lincoln to Mercy Levering Conkling, 19 Nov. [1864], Turner and Turner, eds., *Mary Todd Lincoln,* 187.

95. Octavia Roberts Corneau (Mrs. Barton Corneau), "My Townsman—Abraham Lincoln," typescript of a talk given to the Lincoln Group of Boston, 18 Nov. 1939, 17, Abraham Lincoln Association Reference Files, "Reminiscences" folder 5; Octavia Roberts, "'We All Knew Abr'ham,'" 29.

96. Elodie Todd to Nathaniel Dawson, 23 May, 23 July, 21 June 1861, Dawson Papers, Southern Historical Collection, University of North Carolina at Chapel Hill, in Berry, *House of Abraham,* xi, 128.

97. Temple, *From Skeptic to Prophet,* 384.

98. Robert Todd Lincoln to George N. Black, Augusta, Georgia, 20 Mar. 1906, Robert T. Lincoln Papers, IHi.

99. "Brief account of Lincoln's courtship & marriage," undated typescript marked "From Ms. in [Oliver] Barrett Collection—S. C. Parks," Carl Sandburg Papers, University of Illinois.

100. Mary Lincoln to Josiah G. Holland, Chicago, 4 Dec. 1865, and to James Smith, [Marienbad, 8 June 1870], Turner and Turner, eds., *Mary Todd Lincoln,* 293, 566.

101. Elizabeth Edwards, interview with Herndon, [1865–1866], *HI,* 443.

102. Ninian Edwards, interview with Herndon, [1865–1866] *HI,* 446.

103. Herndon to Henry C. Whitney, Springfield, 16 Apr. 1887, H-W MSS DLC.

104. Whitney to Herndon, Chicago, 4 July 1887, *HI,* 621.

105. On Matilda Edwards and Lincoln, see Wilson, *Honor's Voice,* 219–242, and "Abraham Lincoln and 'That Fatal First of January,'" in Douglas L. Wilson, *Lincoln Before Washington: New Perspectives on the Illinois Years* (Urbana: University of Illinois Press, 1997), 99–132; J. Bennett Nolan, "Of a Tomb in the Reading Cemetery and the Long Shadow of Abraham Lincoln," *Pennsylvania History* 19 (July 1952): 262–306; Orville H. Browning, interview with Nicolay, Springfield, 17 June 1875, Burlingame, ed., *Oral History of Lincoln,* 1; Harry O. Knerr, two essays, both entitled "Abraham Lincoln and Matilda Edwards," enclosed in Knerr to Ida M. Tarbell, Allentown, 26 Oct. 1936, Ida M. Tarbell Papers, Allegheny College; Allentown (Pennsylvania) *Morning Call,* 9 Feb. 1936; Herndon to Ward Hill Lamon, Springfield, 25 Feb. 1870, Lamon Papers, CSmH; Jane D. Bell to Anne Bell, Springfield, 27 Jan. 1841, copy, Lincoln files, "Wife" folder, Lincoln Memorial University, Harrogate, Tennessee; Albert S. Edwards in Stevens, *A Reporter's Lincoln,* ed. Burlingame, 113; Octavia Roberts, "'We All Knew Abr'ham,'" 27; William O. Stoddard, *Abraham Lincoln: The True Story of a Great Life* (New York: Ford, Howard, & Hulbert, 1884), 122. Mrs. Nicholas H. Ridgely (née Jane Huntington), a leader of Springfield society in Lincoln's day, told her granddaughter, Octavia Roberts Corneau, "that it was common report that Lincoln had fallen in love with Matilda Edwards." There "was never the least doubt in her mind that this was the case, and she left the story to her daughters." Octavia Roberts Corneau, "My Townsman—Abraham Lincoln," typescript of a talk given to the Lincoln Group of Boston, 18 Nov. 1939, Abraham Lincoln Association reference files, "Reminiscences" folder 5, p. 11, IHi; Octavia Roberts Corneau, "The Road of Remembrance," unpublished manuscript, 119, Corneau Papers, IHi. Matilda Edwards's niece told Mrs. Corneau that "It is an undisputed fact that Lincoln was in love with her. She never cared for him." Virginia Quigley to [Octavia Roberts] Corneau, Alton, Illinois, 13 July [1939?], F. Lauriston Bullard Papers, Boston University. In the Edwards's family tradition it was

reported that "Lincoln was very anxious to marry into the Edwards family because of their political influence, but his attempts to court the Edwards girls were rudely repulsed." Edward M. Quigley to J. G. Randall, Louisville, Kentucky, 7 Feb. 1950, Randall Papers, DLC.

Lincoln had earlier been smitten by a beautiful girl. In August 1827, it is reported, he was captivated by the beauty of Julia Evans in Princeton, Indiana. John M. Lockwood to Jesse W. Weik, Mount Vernon, Indiana, 4 Jan. 1896, and two letters to Mr. J. A. Stuart of Indianapolis, dated Princeton, Indiana, 25 and 26 Jan. 1909, one from an unknown correspondent and the other from "Hastings," in Jesse W. Weik, *The Real Lincoln: A Portrait*, ed. Michael Burlingame (1922; Lincoln: University of Nebraska Press, 2002), 365–367.

106. Brown, "Springfield Society," 33–34.

107. Alice Edwards Quigley to "Dear Sir," Alton, Illinois, 22 Mar. 1935, Allentown, Pennsylvania, *Morning Call,* 9 Feb. 1936; Virginia Quigley to [Octavia Roberts] Corneau, Alton, Illinois, 13 July [1939?], F. Lauriston Bullard Papers, Boston University; Orville H. Browning, interview with John G. Nicolay, Springfield, 17 June 1875, Burlingame, ed., *Oral History of Lincoln,* 1; Albert S. Edwards, in Stevens, *A Reporter's Lincoln,* ed. Burlingame, 113.

108. *Berks and Schuylkill Journal,* 8 Feb. 1851, quoted in Nolan, "Of a Tomb in the Reading Cemetery," 292.

109. James C. Conkling to Mercy Levering, Springfield, 7 Mar. 1841, Sandburg and Angle, *Mary Lincoln,* 180.

110. Jane Hamilton Daviess Bell to Anne Bell, Springfield, 27 Jan. 1841, copy, Lincoln files, "Wife" folder, Lincoln Memorial University, Harrogate, Tennessee. Mrs. Benjamin S. Edwards recalled that Lincoln "was deeply in love with Matilda Edwards." Mrs. Benjamin S. Edwards to Ida M. Tarbell, Springfield, 8 Oct. 1895, copy, Ida M. Tarbell Papers, Allegheny College. Orville H.

Browning thought that "Lincoln became very much attached" to Matilda Edwards and "finally fell desperately in love with her." Browning, interview with John G. Nicolay, Springfield, 17 June 1875, Burlingame, ed., *Oral History of Lincoln,* 2. Alice Edwards Quigley, a niece of Matilda Edwards, told an interviewer: "Undoubtedly Lincoln was in love with Mathilda Edwards, although she never cared for him." Octavia Roberts Corneau, "My Townsman—Abraham Lincoln," typescript of a talk given to the Lincoln Group of Boston, 18 Nov. 1939, 11, Abraham Lincoln Association Reference Files, "Reminiscences" folder 5. See also Virginia Quigley to [Octavia Roberts] Corneau, Alton, 13 July [1939?], F. Lauriston Bullard Papers, Boston University.

111. Elizabeth Todd Edwards, interview with Herndon, [1865–1866], *HI,* 444. Matilda Edwards may not have been entirely truthful with Elizabeth Edwards. A niece of one of Mary Todd's sisters said it "was always known in our family . . . that Mr. Lincoln courted Matilda Edwards, a fact which for many reasons she divulged only to her nearest and dearest." Horace Green, "New Cases of Women's Influence Over Lincoln," New York *Times,* 11 Feb. 1923, section 8, p. 1.

112. Interview with Hardin's sister, Mrs. Alexander R. McKee (née Martinette Hardin), "A Romance of Lincoln," clipping identified as "Indianapolis, January 1896," LMF. Hardin also shared this story with another of his sisters, Lucy Jane, whose son-in-law informed a journalist that "some have questioned whether he [Lincoln] ever wanted to marry Mary Todd. He was in love with her cousin," Matilda Edwards. Unidentified newspaper article by Frank G. Carpenter, [1891], LMF. Carpenter's source was Judge Daniel H. Solomon of Iowa, whose wife (née Elizabeth Hardin at Jacksonville in 1839) was the daughter of John J. Hardin's sister, Lucy Jane. Another of Mary's cousins, Elizabeth Grimsley, thought Lincoln "doubted whether he was responding as fully as a manly generous nature" should to Mary Todd; his

feeling for her "had not the overmastering depth of an early love." Mrs. Grimsley to Ida Tarbell, Springfield, 9 Mar. 1895, copy, Ida M. Tarbell Papers, Allegheny College. Despite all this evidence, some have questioned whether Lincoln ever loved Matilda Edwards. See, for example, David Herbert Donald, *Lincoln* (New York: Simon & Schuster, 1995), 84–87.

113. Sarah Rickard, sister of Mrs. Butler, interviewed by Nellie Crandall Sanford, Kansas City *Star,* 10 Feb. 1907.

114. Speed, interview with Herndon, [1865–1866], *HI,* 474–477. Later Speed wrote, "a gloom came over him till his friends were alarmed for his life." Joshua F. Speed, *Reminiscences of Abraham Lincoln and Notes of a Visit to California: Two Lectures* (Louisville, KY: John P. Morton, 1884), 39. According to Orville H. Browning, Lincoln "told Miss Todd that he loved Matilda Edwards." Browning, interview with John G. Nicolay, Springfield, 17 June 1875, Burlingame, ed., *Oral History of Lincoln,* 2. Browning added that Mary "had very bitter feelings towards her rival." But if she did, those feelings did not last long, for in April 1842 Mary Todd invited Matilda Edwards to visit her in Springfield. Letter from Matilda Edwards to her brother Nelson, n.d., quoted in Randall, *Lincoln's Courtship,* 163. Matilda Edwards died childless in 1851 at the age of 29.

115. Mary Lincoln to Josiah G. Holland, Chicago, 4 Dec. 1865, Turner and Turner, eds., *Mary Todd Lincoln,* 293.

116. Elizabeth Todd Edwards, interview with Herndon, [1865–1866], *HI,* 444.

117. Ninian Edwards, interview with Herndon, 22 Sept. 1865, *HI,* 133. Edwards's wife Elizabeth also described Lincoln in the month of January 1841 as "crazy." Elizabeth Todd Edwards, interview with Herndon, [1865–1866], ibid., 443. It is possible that Lincoln suffered two separate attacks, one in late November or early December and the other in January. Wilson, *Honor's Voice* 233–264; Joshua Wolf Shenk, *Lincoln's*

Melancholy: How Depression Challenged a President and Fueled His Greatness (Boston: Houghton Mifflin, 2005) 50–58.

118. Letter from Jacksonville, 22 Jan. 1841, quoted in *CWL,* 1:229n. Basler mistakenly identifies the author as "Martin McKee" instead of Martinette Hardin McKee.

119. Jane D. Bell to Anne Bell, Springfield, 27 Jan. 1841, copy, Lincoln files, "Wife" folder, Lincoln Memorial University, Harrogate, Tennessee.

120. James H. Matheny, interview with Herndon, 3 May 1866, *HI,* 251; Orville H. Browning, interview with John G. Nicolay, Springfield, 17 June 1875, Burlingame, ed., *Oral History of Lincoln,* 1–2. Mrs. William Butler confided to her sister that Lincoln was tormented by "the thought that he had treated Mary badly, knowing that she loved him and that he did not love her." This caused him "an agony of remorse." Sarah Rickard, sister of Mrs. Butler, interviewed by Nellie Crandall Sanford, Kansas City *Star,* 10 Feb. 1907. Jane D. Bell reported on 27 Jan. 1841 that "It seems he had addressed Mary Todd and she accepted him and they had been engaged some time when a Miss Edwards of Alton came here, and he fell desperately in love with her and found he was not so much attached to Mary as he thought." Jane D. Bell to Anne Bell, Springfield, 27 Jan. 1841, copy, Lincoln files, "Wife" folder, Lincoln Memorial University, Harrogate, Tennessee.

121. James H. Matheny, interview with Herndon, 3 May 1866, *HI,* 251. Speed wrote, "a gloom came over him till his friends were alarmed for his life." Joshua F. Speed, *Reminiscences of Abraham Lincoln and Notes of a Visit to California: Two Lectures* (Louisville, KY: John P. Morton, 1884), 39.

122. Speed, interview with Herndon, [1865–1866], *HI,* 474–475.

123. Speed, *Reminiscences of Lincoln,* 39; Speed to Herndon, Louisville, 7 Feb. and 13 Sept. 1866, *HI,* 197, 337. The extant files of the *Sangamo Journal* for 1841 contain no poem about suicide. Herndon alleged that when he

searched that file, he discovered that someone had clipped excerpts from an issue of the paper. He guessed that Lincoln or someone acting at his instigation had excised the poem. Herndon to Ward Hill Lamon, Springfield, 25 Feb. 1870, Lamon Papers, CSmH. In 1899, J. McCan Davis also searched the 1841 file of the *Sangamo Journal*, which he found incomplete but which contained no issue from which anything had been clipped. J. McCan Davis, "Lincoln's Poem on 'Suicide,'" memo dated Springfield, 5 June 1899, Ida M. Tarbell Papers, Smith College. A similar search in 1997 of the microfilmed version of the paper revealed no issue with a portion clipped out. On 15 Aug. 1838, however, the *Sangamo Journal* ran an unsigned poem titled "The Suicide's Soliloquy," which may have been by Lincoln.

124. Thornton told this story to his brother, who in turn related it to his son. Frank Norbury to Logan Hay, 26 Dec. 1936, copy, Abraham Lincoln Association Reference Files, folder "Historical Data, K–N," IHi. Norbury said that this episode took place in Vandalia, but Thornton served in the legislature between 1840 and 1842, after the capital had moved from Vandalia to Springfield.

125. Lincoln to Stuart, Springfield, 20, 23 Jan. 1841, *CWL*, 1:228–229.

126. Remarks in the legislature, 8 Jan. 1841, *CWL*, 1:226.

127. Speech in the Illinois Legislature concerning apportionment, [9 Jan. 1841?], *CWL*, 1:228.

128. James C. Conkling to Mercy Levering, Springfield, 24 Jan. 1841, Conkling Papers, IHi.

129. Chicago *Tribune*, 12 Feb. 1900.

130. Sarah Hardin to John J. Hardin, [Jacksonville], 26 Jan. 1841, Hardin Family Papers, ICHi.

131. Turner R. King, interview with Herndon, [1865–1866], *HI*, 464.

132. Conkling to Mercy Levering, Springfield, 7 Mar. 1841, Sandburg and Angle, *Mary Lincoln*, 180.

133. *Memorials of the Life and Character of Stephen T. Logan* (Springfield, IL: H. W. Rokker, 1882), 16–17.

134. *Sangamo Journal*, 13 Apr. 1843.

135. Hay, "Colonel Baker," *Harper's New Monthly Magazine*, 24 (Dec. 1861), in Michael Burlingame, ed., *At Lincoln's Side: John Hay's Civil War Correspondence and Selected Writings* (Carbondale: Southern Illinois University Press, 2000), 154.

136. *Sangamo Journal* (Springfield), 13 Apr. 1843.

137. Hezekiah Morse Wead diary, 15 July 1847, IHi.

138. Ibid.

139. Herndon, "Character of Lincoln," 437–438; Herndon, "Lincoln the Lawyer," H-W MSS DLC.

140. Logan, interview with John G. Nicolay, Springfield, 6 July 1875, Burlingame, ed., *Oral History of Lincoln*, 37.

141. Herndon, "Analysis of the Character of Abraham Lincoln," 431.

142. *Memorials of Logan*, 38–39.

143. Linder, *Reminiscences*, 155.

144. Reminiscences of R. R. Hitt, in Otis B. Goodall, "Hon. Robert Roberts Hitt," *The Phonographic Magazine* 7 (1 June 1893): 206–207; *Illinois State Journal* (Springfield), 19 July 1880.

145. Lincoln's endorsement, dated 26 Mar. 1862, on a letter by Logan, Springfield, 13 Jan. 1862, Gilder-Lehrman Collection, New-York Historical Society.

146. Mary Todd to Mercy Levering, Springfield, June 1841, Turner and Turner, eds., *Mary Lincoln*, 27.

147. Interview with Mrs. Alexander R. McKee (née Martinette Hardin), Marietta Holdstock Brown, "A Romance of Lincoln," clipping identified as "Indianapolis, January 1896," LMF.

148. Sarah A. Rickard Barret to Herndon, 12 Aug. 1888, *HI*, 665.

149. William E. Barton, memorandum of a conversation in Springfield with Mrs. Charles Ridgely, [1921], Barton Papers, University of Chicago.

150. Address by James Speed at Cincinnati, 4 May 1887, Speed Family Papers, Filson Club, Louisville, Kentucky.

151. John Gilmer Speed, "Lincoln's Hesitancy to Marry," *Ladies' Home Journal* 12 (Oct. 1895):2.

152. Lincoln to Mary Speed, Bloomington, Illinois, 27 Sept. 1841, *CWL*, 1:261.

153. Joshua Speed to Mary L. Speed, Springfield, 31 Oct. 1841, Speed Family Papers, Filson Club, Louisville, Kentucky.

154. Lincoln to Speed, Springfield, 3 Feb. 1842, *CWL*, 1:268.

155. Lincoln to Speed, Springfield, 5 Oct. 1842, *CWL*, 1:303.

156. Lincoln to Speed, n.p., [3 Jan.? 1842], *CWL*, 1:266.

157. Lincoln to Speed, Springfield, 3 Feb. 1842, *CWL*, 1:268.

158. Lincoln to Speed, Springfield, 13 Feb. 1842, *CWL*, 269–270.

159. Lincoln to Speed, Springfield, 25 Feb. *CWL*, 1:280.

160. Lincoln to Speed, Springfield, 27 Mar. 1842, *CWL*, 1:282. January 1 is customarily thought to be the day on which Lincoln broke his engagement to Mary Todd, but Douglas L. Wilson has shown that this is most improbable. Wilson, *Honor's Voice*, 231–255.

161. Lincoln to Speed, Springfield, 4 July 1842, *CWL*, 1:289. In the Book of Exodus (14:13), Moses tells the Israelites as Pharaoh's army closed in on them: "Fear ye not, stand still, and see the salvation of the Lord, which he will show to you today."

162. Chicago *Press and Tribune*, n.d., copied in the *Illinois State Journal* (Springfield), 27 Apr. 1860.

163. Mel T. Cook to Jesse W. Weik, New Brunswick, NJ, 4 Mar. 1923, Weik Papers, IHi.

164. The "Rebecca" letter, 27 Aug. 1842, *CWL*, 1:295–296.

165. Shields to Lincoln, Tremont, IL, 17 Sept. 1842, *CWL*, 1:299n. Most Lincoln biographers have asserted that Lincoln was protecting Mary Todd, who had allegedly written the Rebecca letter that so offended Shields. They were seemingly justified, for she, in a somewhat garbled account, said that Lincoln had done so. Mary Todd Lincoln to Mary Jane Welles, Chicago, 6 Dec. 1865, and to Francis B. Carpenter, Chicago, 8 Dec. 1865, in Turner and Turner, eds., *Mary Lincoln*, 295, 299. But Douglas L. Wilson has demonstrated that Mary Todd's version of events could not be accurate. Wilson, *Honor's Voice*, 265–283. After the three Rebecca letters appeared, Mary Todd did compose some verses signed "Cathleen," published two weeks after the abusive second Rebecca letter. Julia Jayne's husband "never understood that the Shields duel had any thing to do with hastening the marriage" of Lincoln and Mary Todd. Lyman Trumbull to Jesse W. Weik, Chicago, 17 Apr. 1895, Weik, *Real Lincoln*, ed. Burlingame, 378.

166. Koerner, undated letter to *The Century Magazine* 33 (Oct. 1887):974.

167. Undated article by Col. Thomas Bangs Thorpe, reproduced in another undated article, clipping collection, LMF.

168. Merryman to the editor, Springfield, 8 Oct., *Sangamo Journal*, 14 Oct. 1842.

169. I. M. Short, *Abraham Lincoln: Early Days in Illinois: Reminiscences of Different Persons Who Became Eminent in American History* (Kansas City, MO: Simpson Publishing Company, 1927), 35–37.

170. Lincoln to Shields, Tremont, 17 Sept. 1842, *CWL*, 1:299.

171. Bledsoe, "Reminiscences of Abraham Lincoln," *Alexandria Gazette* (Virginia), 8 Nov. 1876.

172. Ibid.

173. Sophie Bledsoe Herrick, letter to *The Century Magazine*, Mar. 1892, 796.

174. Linder, *Reminiscences*, 66–67.

175. Reminiscences of Josiah M. Lucas, Chicago *Journal*, n.d, copied in the Washington *Post*, 22 Aug. 1882.

176. Undated article by Col. Thomas Bangs Thorpe, reproduced in another undated article, clipping collection, LMF.

177. This description of the near-duel is based on the eyewitness accounts by William G. Souther, a reporter for the Alton *Telegraph*. See H. G. McPike, "The Lincoln-Shields Duel," *The Magazine of History* 4 (1906):145–147; Topeka correspondence of the Kansas City *Journal*, n.d., copied in the New York *Tribune*, 25 May 1896; Topeka correspondence, 11 May, Chicago *Tribune*, 12 May 1896; and Stevens, *A Reporter's Lincoln*, ed. Burlingame, 15–20.

178. Quoted in Lincoln's memo of duel instructions for E. H. Merryman, [19 Sept. 1842], *CWL*, 1:301.

179. *Illinois State Register* (Springfield), 4 Nov. 1842, 30 June, 11 and 18 Aug. 1843; letter by "Loco," Jacksonville, 7 Oct., ibid., 20 Oct. 1843.

180. Shawneetown *Illinois Republican*, 8 Oct. 1842, reprinted in *Springhouse* 14 (1998):16.

181. Shawneetown *Illinois Republican*, 3 Nov. 1842, reprinted ibid., 17.

182. *Alton Daily Telegraph & Democratic Review*, 1 Oct. 1842.

183. Jacksonville *Illinoisan*, n.d., copied in the Chicago *Weekly Democrat*, 8 Oct. 1842.

184. George W. Meeker to Lyman Trumbull, Chicago, 29 Sept. 1842, Illinois State Archives, copied on the Web site of the Abraham Lincoln Historical Digitization Project, Northern Illinois University.

185. Lincoln to Martin S. Morris, Springfield, 26 Mar. 1843, *CWL*, 1:320.

186. Milton Hay to Thomas Venmun, Springfield, 16 Jan. [18]92, Milton Hay Papers, IHi.

187. F. B. Carpenter, *Six Months at the White House with Abraham Lincoln: The Story of a Picture* (New York: Hurd and Houghton, 1867), 305.

188. Mary Todd Lincoln to Mary Jane Welles, Chicago, 6 Dec. 1865, Turner and Turner, eds., *Mary Todd Lincoln*, 296.

189. Whitney, *Life on the Circuit*, ed. Angle, 58.

190. Wilson and Davis, eds., *Herndon's Lincoln*, 146.

191. Mary V. Stuart, undated interview with Ida Tarbell, Tarbell Papers, quoted in Wilson, *Honor's Voice*, 285–286; reminiscences of Christopher C. Brown, Chicago *Times-Herald*, 25 Aug. 1895. Ninian and Elizabeth Todd Edwards told Herndon that "[a]fter the match was broken off between Mary and Lincoln Mrs Francis shrewdly got them together. Doct. Henry who admired and loved Mr. Lincoln had much to do in getting Mary and Lincoln together again." Elizabeth and Ninian W. Edwards, interview with Herndon, 27 July 1887, *HI*, 623. Leigh Kimball, who lived with the Edwards family, "said he frequently took Miss Mary Todd to the house of Mr. Simeon Francis to meet Mr. Lincoln." Brown, "Springfield Society," 35. The great-grandniece of Simeon Francis, who married Eliza Rumsey of New London, Connecticut, in 1820, reported a similar tradition. Katherine M. Goodloe to Katherine Helm, Rio Vista, California, 18 May 1928, William H. Townsend Papers, University of Kentucky, Lexington. Mrs. Francis refused Herndon's request for a statement about the Lincolns. Mrs. Francis to Herndon, Portland, Oregon, 10 Aug. 1887, *HI*, 624. Most biographers have credited Simeon Francis and his wife with facilitating the rapprochement. Douglas L. Wilson has shown that the Hardins were more responsible for that development; see Wilson, *Honor's Voice*, 281–284.

192. Sarah Rickard interviewed by Nellie Crandall Sanford, Kansas City *Star*, 10 Feb. 1907.

193. Elizabeth Todd Edwards, interview with Herndon, [1865–1866], *HI*, 444.

194. Lincoln to Speed, Springfield, 5 Oct. 1842, *CWL*, 1:303.

195. Speed's friend, W. H. McKnight, reporting what Speed had told him, in McKnight to Ida M. Tarbell, Louisville, 1 Feb. 1909, Louisville *Courier-Journal*, n.d., clipping collection, LMF.

196. Caroline Owsley Brown, quoting Elizabeth Edwards, in "Springfield Society before the Civil War," [Brown], *Rewarding Years Recalled*, 34. This is a fuller version of Mrs. Brown's article, originally written for the

"Anti-Rust Club," than the one published in *Journal of the Illinois State Historical Society* 15 (1922). See also Helm, *Mary, Wife of Lincoln,* 94.

197. Betsy Davis, a relative of Dr. Dresser, in Corneau, "Road of Remembrance," 120.

198. Elizabeth Todd Edwards, interview with Herndon, [1865–1866], *HI,* 444.

199. Albert S. Edwards, in Stevens, *A Reporter's Lincoln,* ed. Burlingame, 116. The bride recalled that her sister "gave us quite a big wedding" and that her sister Elizabeth "wanted to give her [Mary Todd] a big wedding." On 12 May 1839, Frances was married to William S. Wallace. Chicago *Times Herald,* 25 Aug. 1895.

200. Helm, *Mary, Wife of Lincoln,* 94; Mrs. Benjamin S. Edwards's reminiscences, Chicago *Tribune,* 12 Feb. 1900; Albert S. Edwards in Stevens, *A Reporter's Lincoln,* ed. Burlingame, 117; Weik, *Real Lincoln,* ed. Burlingame, 60–61. According to Albert S. Edwards, Lincoln said that he and Mary planned to wed at the home of Simeon Francis.

201. Frances Todd Wallace, quoted in Eugenia Jones Hunt, *My Personal Recollections of Abraham and Mary Todd Lincoln* (Peoria, IL: H. A. Moser, 1966), 8.

202. Brown, "Springfield Society Before the Civil War," 34.

203. Raymond, *Incidents in the Life of Mrs. Benjamin S. Edwards,* 14–15; letter by Mrs. Benjamin S. Edwards, n.d., unidentified clipping, LMF; reminiscences of Mrs. Edwards's niece, Mrs. H. D. Ames, Washington *Post,* 13 Feb. 1929. See also T. G. Onstot, *Pioneers of Menard and Mason Counties* (Peoria, IL: J. W. Franks and Sons, 1902), 36; Dorothy Meserve Kunhardt, "An Old Lady's Lincoln Memories," *Life,* 9 Feb. 1959, 57. Mary Lincoln's sister-in-law witnessed the scene and described it much later to Octavia Roberts. Roberts, "Our Townsman: Pictures of Lincoln as a Friend and Neighbor," *Collier's,* 12 Feb. 1909, 17, 24.

204. James H. Matheny, quoted in Weik, *Real Lincoln,* ed. Burlingame, 61–62; Linder,

Reminiscences, 73; James H. Matheny, interview with Jesse W. Weik, Springfield, 21 Aug. 1888, *HI,* 665.

205. Lincoln to Samuel D. Marshall, Springfield, 11 Nov. 1842, *CWL,* 1:305.

206. *Battle Axe, and Political Reformer* (Winchester, IL), 19 Nov. 1842, in Thomas F. Schwartz, "'—in short, he is *married!*': A Contemporary Newspaper Account," *For the People: A Newsletter of the Abraham Lincoln Association* (Winter 1999), 4. The quoted verse is from Shakespeare's *Richard III.*

207. Lincoln to Joshua Speed, Springfield, 18 May 1843, *CWL,* 1:325.

208. Mrs. B. S. Edwards to Ida Tarbell, Springfield, 8 Oct. 1895, Ida M. Tarbell Papers, Allegheny College.

209. Ida Tarbell to T. A. Frank Jones, n.p., 12 Dec. 1922, copy, Tarbell Papers, Allegheny College.

210. Eleanor Gridley to W. A. Evans, n.p., 4 June 1932, copy, Gridley Papers, ICHi. Mrs. Gridley believed that "LOVE is the essence of kindness, compassion, tenderness, thoughtfulness, [and] consideration."

211. Corneau, "The Road of Remembrance," 118. Albert J. Beveridge doubted that Lincoln "really 'loved'" Mary Todd. Beveridge to William E. Barton, Indianapolis, 24 Jan. 1927, Lincoln Collection, RPB.

212. John S. Bradford, in Weik, *Real Lincoln,* ed. Burlingame, 99.

213. Mary Lincoln to Emilie Todd Helm, Springfield, 20 Sept. [1857], in Turner and Turner, eds., *Mary Todd Lincoln,* 50.

214. Remarks at Bloomington, 21 Nov. 1860, *CWL,* 4:143–144.

215. *Frank Leslie's Illustrated Newspaper,* 8 Dec. 1860.

216. Herndon, "Lincoln and Mary Todd," manuscript, H-W MSS DLC.

217. Speed, interview with Herndon, [1865–1866], *HI,* 475.

218. Browning, interview with John G. Nicolay, Springfield, 17 June 1875, Burlingame, ed., *Oral History of Lincoln,* 2.

219. William J. Butler, grandson of William Butler, in the *Illinois State Journal* (Springfield), 28 Feb. 1937.

220. John Todd Stuart, interview with Herndon, [late June 1865], *HI*, 64.

221. Note by Jesse W. Weik, n.d., memo book no. 2, box 2, Weik Papers, IHi. In the Herndon-Weik biography of Lincoln, the authors speculated that because "Lincoln was inordinately ambitious," it was therefore "natural that he should seek by marriage in an influential family to establish strong connections and at the same time foster his political fortunes." Wilson and Davis, ed., *Herndon's Lincoln*, 132.

222. Lincoln to Martin S. Morris, Springfield, 26 Mar. 1843, *CWL*, 1:320.

223. Matheny, interview with Herndon, 3 May 1866, *HI*, 215. Herndon's notes of his interview with Matheny contain this further explanation: "Said it was Concocted & planned by the Edwards family." It is not clear whether Matheny is paraphrasing what Lincoln told him or offering his own speculation about why Lincoln felt "driven" into wedding Mary Todd.

224. Lincoln allegedly told this to Speed Butler, son of William Butler. William J. Butler, grandson of William Butler, *Illinois State Journal* (Springfield), 28 Feb. 1937. See also Salome Butler, daughter of William Butler, in Roberts, "'We All Knew Abr'ham,'" 28, and in Hunt, *My Personal Recollections of Abraham and Mary Todd Lincoln*, 10; statement by Speed Butler to Lincoln Dubois, in a questionnaire filled out by Dubois, 15 June 1924, enclosed in Lincoln Dubois to Albert J. Beveridge, 15 June 1924, Beveridge Papers, DLC.

225. Temple, *Lincoln: From Skeptic to Prophet*, 27–28.

226. Matheny, interview with Herndon, 3 May 1866, *HI*, 251.

227. Herndon to Charles H. Hart, Springfield, 12 Dec. 1866, Hart Papers, CSmH.

228. These activities are detailed in Michael Burlingame, "Mary Todd Lincoln's Unethical Conduct as First Lady," in Burlingame, ed., *At Lincoln's Side*, 185–203, based

in part on long-suppressed passages from the diary of Orville Hickman Browning, which were made public in 1994. See also David Rankin Barbee's untitled essay on Mrs. Lincoln's misconduct, Barbee Papers, Georgetown University. Barbee was an indefatigable researcher who turned up abundant evidence in newspapers, manuscripts, archives, and the *Congressional Record*.

229. Hodder to Albert J. Beveridge, Lawrence, Kansas, 30 May 1925, Beveridge Papers, DLC. In this letter, Hodder speculated "that Mary captured him and that he finally married her from an exaggerated sense of justice."

230. E. B. Webb to John J. Hardin, Springfield, 6 Jan. 1842, Hardin Family Papers, ICHi.

231. Mary Todd to Mercy Ann Levering, Springfield, June 1841, Turner and Turner, eds., *Mary Todd Lincoln*, 26.

232. Herndon told this to Caroline Dall in the fall of 1866, according to Dall's "Journal of a tour through Illinois, Wisconsin and Ohio, Oct. & Nov. 1866," entry for 29 Oct. 1866, Dall Papers, Bryn Mawr College. Helen R. Deese, who is editing Dall's journal for publication, believes that its entries are not contemporary but were written three decades later, based on notes taken in 1866 and no longer extant. Douglas L. Wilson, "Keeping Lincoln's Secrets," *The Atlantic Monthly*, May 2000, 84.

233. William Jayne to Herndon, Springfield, 17 Aug. 1887, *HI*, 624–625.

234. Helm, *Mary, Wife of Lincoln*, 84.

235. James Gourley, interview with Herndon, [1865–1866], *HI*, 453. As this reminiscence suggests, it is possible that Mary Lincoln was unfaithful to her husband. In 1866 Caroline Dall apparently saw evidence in Herndon's memorandum books (no longer extant) that indicated as much. Wilson, "Keeping Lincoln's Secrets," 88. See also Burlingame, *Inner World of Lincoln*, 291–292.

236. David Davis, interview with Herndon, 20 Sept. 1866, *HI*, 350. No credible contemporary evidence suggests that Lincoln was

homosexual or bisexual. On that subject, see David Herbert Donald, *"We Are Lincoln Men": Abraham Lincoln and His Friends* (New York: Simon and Schuster, 2003), 35–38, 140–146; Michael Burlingame, "Afterword" in C. A. Tripp, *The Intimate World of Abraham Lincoln* (New York: Free Press, 2005). 225–238.

237. Herndon to Jesse W. Weik, Springfield, 23 Jan. 1890 and Jan. 1891, and Herndon to James H. Wilson, n.p., 23 Sept. 1889, H-W MSS DLC. Herndon went on to say that Lincoln suspected that he had contracted syphilis. Some writers have speculated that Mary Todd Lincoln contracted that disease from her husband and died of it. The best evidence suggests, however, that she died of diabetes. Norbert Hirschhorn and Robert G. Feldman, "Mary Lincoln's Final Illness: A Medical and Historical Reappraisal," *Journal of the History of Medicine* 54 (1999):511–542.

238. Herndon to Jesse W. Weik, Springfield, 5 Jan. 1889, H-W MSS DLC. Douglas L. Wilson sensibly observed that these "stories of overnight encounters on the road with young women" were "probably based on real incidents," though they "may have been colored by the familiar genre of stories about 'the farmer's daughter.'" Wilson, "Keeping Lincoln's Secrets," 81.

239. N. W. Branson to Herndon, Petersburg, Illinois, 3 Aug. 1865, *HI*, 90.

240. Henry C. Whitney to Herndon, 23 June 1887, *HI*, 617.

241. C. C. Brown, interview with Herndon, [1865–1866], *HI*, 438. Lincoln had attended Brown's wedding. "Autobiography of Christopher C. Brown," in [Brown], *Rewarding Years Recalled*, 14.

242. *CWL*, 3:360.

243. Herndon's account in Caroline Dall, "Journal of a tour through Illinois, Wisconsin and Ohio, Oct. & Nov. 1866," entry for 29 Oct. 1866, Dall Papers, Bryn Mawr College.

244. Herndon to Jesse W. Weik, Springfield, 10 Dec. 1885, H-W MSS DLC. Abner Y. Ellis said that Lincoln "had no desire for strange woman[.] I never heard him speak of any *particular Woman* with disrespect though he had Many opportunities for doing so while in Company with J[oshua] F. S[peed] and Wm B[utler] two old rats in that way." A. Y. Ellis, statement for Herndon, enclosed in Ellis to Herndon, Moro, Illinois, 23 Jan. 1866, *HI*, 171.

245. Speed, interview with Herndon, 5 Jan. 1889, *HI*, 719; Herndon added, "Lincoln went out of the house, bidding the girl good evening and went to the store of Speed, saying nothing. Speed asked no questions and so the matter rested a day or so. Speed had occasion to go and see the girl in a few days, and she told him just what was said and done between herself & Lincoln and Speed told me the story and I have no doubt of its truthfulness."

246. Hannah Armstrong, interview with Herndon, [1866], *HI*, 527.

247. John Hill to Herndon, Petersburg, Illinois, 6 June 1865, *HI*, 23. Hill asserted that "I have this from W. G. Greene & others as the truth."

248. Herndon to Jesse W. Weik, Springfield, Jan. 1891, H-W MSS DLC.

249. Colfax told this story to Franz Mueller. "Lincoln and Colfax," reminiscences by Mueller, enclosed in Mueller to Ida Tarbell, Spokane, 13 Feb. 1896, Ida M. Tarbell Papers, Allegheny College.

250. John Hay to John G. Nicolay, Washington, 20 June 1864, Burlingame, ed., *At Lincoln's Side*, 85.

251. Reminiscences of a Dr. Hatch, Washington correspondence by Frank G. Carpenter, 8 Apr., Cleveland *Leader*, 9 Apr. 1884.

252. Lincoln told this to James A. Briggs, a Cleveland attorney and businessman who served as the Ohio state agent in New York and was a Republican Party leader and orator. Cincinnati *Commercial*, n.d., copied in the Belleville, Illinois, *Advocate*, 8 June 1866, copied in the card catalogue of Lincolniana, microform division, IHi. It was reprinted with

the wrong date (8 July 1866, a day on which the weekly paper was not published) in *The Journal of the Illinois State Historical Society* 32 (1939):399. Lincoln commended Briggs to the attention of William Henry Seward, saying "I know James A. Briggs, and believe him to be an excellent man." Lincoln to Seward, Washington, 11 Aug. 1862, *CWL*, 5:367.

253. Adam Badeau, *Grant in Peace: From Appomattox to Mount McGregor; A Personal Memoir* (Hartford, CT: S. S. Scranton, 1887), 357.

254. Herndon to Jesse W. Weik, Springfield, 16 Jan. 1886, H-W MSS DLC.

255. Herndon to Horace White, Springfield, 13 Feb. 1891, White Papers, IHi.

256. Herndon to Jesse W. Weik, Springfield, 8, 15, 16 Jan. 1886, H-W MSS DLC.

257. John Hay to John G. Nicolay, Washington, 5 and 9 Apr. 1862, in Burlingame, ed., *At Lincoln's Side*, 19–20; John G. Nicolay to John Hay, Washington, 29 Jan. 1864, in Michael Burlingame, ed., *With Lincoln in the White House: Letters, Memoranda, and Other Writings of John G. Nicolay, 1860–1865* (Carbondale: Southern Illinois University Press, 2000), 125; Dr. Stone paraphrased in the manuscript diary of General John Meredith Read Jr., quoted in Old Hickory Book Shop (New York) catalogue, n.d., clipping in the Lincoln files, "Wife" folder, Lincoln Memorial University, Harrogate, Tennessee; Benjamin Brown French to his son Frank, Washington, 9 July 1865, French Family Papers, DLC.

258. James H. Matheny, interview with Herndon, 3 May 1866, *HI*, 251. Matheny had heard stories about Mrs. Lincoln from the "Butler girls," presumably the daughters of William Butler, at whose Springfield home Lincoln had boarded for years before his wedding. Ibid.

259. Undated statement by Gourley in Weik, *Real Lincoln*, ed. Burlingame, 121–122. A Pennsylvania-born boot and shoemaker, Gourley (1810?–1876) lived for several years at the corner of Jackson and Ninth Streets, one block from the Lincolns' house.

260. Reminiscences of Page Eaton, Utica *Herald*, n.d., copied in the Belvedere, Illinois, *Standard*, 14 Apr. 1868. Eaton's life is summarized in Wayne C. Temple, "Builder of Lincoln's Home: Page Eaton" (pamphlet; Harrogate, TN: Lincoln Memorial University Press, 1962), 1–3. Eaton lived at the south end of Fifth Street in 1855.

261. Judge Anthony Thornton heard Peter Van Bergen state this. Judge Thornton interviewed by Jesse W. Weik, Shelbyville, 18 June 1895, Weik, *Real Lincoln*, ed. Burlingame, 375.

262. Emilie Todd Helm, interview with William H. Townsend, 27 Dec. 1922, Townsend Papers, University of Kentucky, Lexington. On another occasion, Mrs. Helm said that Mary "had a high temper, and perhaps did not always have it under control." Helm, *Mary, Wife of Lincoln*, 110.

263. Harriet Hanks Chapman in Weik, *Real Lincoln*, ed. Burlingame, 94; Mrs. John A. Logan, *Thirty Years in Washington; or, Life and Scenes in Our National Capital* (Hartford, CT: A. D. Worthington, 1901), 646.

264. Interview with Mrs. Alexander R. McKee (née Martinette Hardin), Marietta Holdstock Brown, "A Romance of Lincoln," clipping identified as "Indianapolis, January 1896," LMF.

265. Eleanor Gridley to Honore Morrow, n.p., 30 Jan. 1932, copy, Gridley Papers, ICHi.

266. Corneau, "Road of Remembrance," 118; Octavia Roberts, *Lincoln in Illinois* (Boston: Houghton Mifflin, 1918), 53.

267. Reminiscences of Mrs. Cecelia McConnell, who in 1856, at the age of 18, went to Springfield to live with her aunt and uncle. Buffalo *Courier-Express*, 11 Aug. 1929, section 9, p. 2.

268. Ida M. Andrews to Jesse W. Weik, Indianapolis, 8 Jan. 1917, Weik, *Real Lincoln*, ed. Burlingame, 318. Mrs. Andrews was a daughter of Leaton and a niece of Matheny.

269. Statement of Robert Williams, Bloomington, Illinois, 9 Feb. 1923, William E. Barton Papers, University of Chicago.

270. Mrs. Jacob M. Early observed this scene. Judith Peterson, "Secret of an Unhappy Incident," *Illinois Junior Historian* 5 (Feb. 1952): 91. The author heard this story from her grandmother's cousin, Beulah Miles Wood. Miss Peterson was the great-great-great granddaughter of George U. Miles, who married Catherine Rickard Early after her first husband, Jacob Early, was murdered. Mrs. Early was the sister of Mrs. William Butler, at whose home Lincoln boarded from 1837 to 1842. In 1840, Lincoln became guardian *ad litem* of Mrs. Early's two young sons. Seven years later he represented her in a chancery suit. Harry E. Pratt, "Abraham Lincoln's First Murder Trial," *Journal of the Illinois State Historical Society* 37 (1944):248–249.

271. Mrs. Early often told this story to her nephew Jimmy Miles, who in turn related it to Dale Carnegie. Carnegie, *Lincoln the Unknown* (New York: Century, 1932), 72. Louis A. Warren, commenting on Mary Lincoln's reputation for having "a quick temper and a sharp tongue," said that "[p]ossibly she threw coffee at Lincoln and drove him out of the house with a broom and probably he deserved it." *Lincoln Lore*, no. 15 Feb. 1937.

272. Thurlow Weed observed this outburst. Alvan F. Sanborn, ed., *Reminiscences of Richard Lathers: Sixty Years of a Busy Life in South Carolina, Massachusetts and New York* (New York: Grafton Press, 1907), 184.

273. Margaret Ryan, interview with Jesse W. Weik, 27 Oct. 1886, *HI*, 597; Herndon to Jesse W. Weik, Springfield, 23 Jan. 1886, H-W MSS DLC.

274. Dubois, undated interview with Jesse W. Weik, *HI*, 692.

275. Thomas Stackpole, the White House steward, told this to Ward Hill Lamon. Lamon, interview with Herndon, [1865–1866], *HI*, 467.

276. Mrs. Hillary A. Gobin (née Clara Leaton [1854–1941]) to Albert J. Beveridge, South Bend, Indiana, 17 May 1923, Beveridge Papers, DLC. Mrs. Gobin's father, James Leaton, pastor of the Methodist Church in

Springfield (1858–1859), lived with his family at Fifth and Monroe Streets, five blocks from the Lincolns' house. In 1895 she became the second wife of Dr. Gobin, president of DePauw University and a Methodist minister. She had previously been married to Harry Lincoln Beals (1864–1893). Material on Mrs. Gobin can be found in the Hillary A. Gobin Papers, folder 8, DePauw University, Greencastle, Indiana.

277. Stephen Whitehurst, interview with Herndon, [1885–1889], *HI*, 722. Whitehurst had heard this story from a man named Barrett, who allegedly observed the episode in 1856 or 1857. This Barrett was probably John H. Barrett, deputy assessor of Sangamon County, who lived on Jackson Street, between Third and Fourth Streets, near the Lincolns.

278. Mrs. George Carleton Beal (née Lizzie De Crastos in 1856) quoted in the New York *Times*, 6 Feb. 1938; *Commonweal*, 2 Mar. 1932, 494.

279. In 1950, Christiana Bertram said that "many years ago I met two people who had been neighbors of the Lincolns in Springfield" who shared this story with her. Christiana Bertram, letter to the editor of the *New York Times Sunday Magazine*, Tenafly, NJ, n.d., issue of 5 Mar. 1950.

280. Margaret Ryan, interview with Jesse W. Weik, 27 Oct. 1886, *HI*, 597.

281. Turner R. King, interview with Herndon, McLain Station, Illinois, [1865–1866], *HI*, 465. As a congressman, Lincoln helped King obtain the post of register of the Springfield land office. As president, he appointed him collector of internal revenue for the Eighth District of Illinois. Ibid., 758.

282. Herndon to Caroline H. Dall, Springfield, 28 Jan. 1862, Dall Papers, MHi. Herndon had just returned from a visit to Washington, where he saw Lincoln.

283. Paul M. Angle, "Notes of Interview with Mrs. Fanny Grimsley, July 27, 1926," enclosed in Angle to William E. Barton, Springfield, 10 Jan. 1927, William E. Barton

Papers, University of Chicago. A life-long resident of Springfield, Mary Frances Burch Grimsley (1846–1927) was the wife of William P. Grimsley and the daughter of William S. Burch, who lived across Eighth Street from the Lincolns. "Philip Dingle," age 5, appears in the 1850 census of Sangamon County. The 1860 census for Sangamon County lists Phillip Dinkell living in the Lincoln household as a servant. Military records show German-born Philip Dinkle, age 18, on the rolls of the Union army in 1862–1863. He died of consumption in 1865. *Illinois State Journal* (Springfield), 27 Oct. 1865. His widowed mother, Barbara Dinkel, lived a block and a half from the Lincolns, on Edwards Street between Eighth and Ninth, according to the 1860–1861 Springfield City Directory. Wayne C. Temple, *By Square & Compass: Saga of the Lincoln's Home* (Mahomet, IL: Mayhaven, 2002), 132–133; George J. Dinkel to Lincoln, Memphis, 28 May 1864, AL MSS DLC.

284. James H. Matheny, undated interview with Jesse W. Weik, *HI,* 667n.; Matheny, interview with Herndon, Jan. 1887, ibid., 713–714; Herndon to Weik, Springfield, Jan. 1887, H-W MSS DLC; Roland W. Diller's recollections of Matheny's story, in Paul Hull, "Lincoln in Springfield," New York *Mail and Express,* 8 Feb. 1896, p. 15. There is some confusion about the miller's last name. In the 1850 Sangamon County census, a miller named Jacob Tiger is listed. He was 27 and born in Ohio. In the files of the Sangamon Valley Collection at Springfield's Lincoln Public Library is a patent deed dated 4 Dec. 1865 showing that Jacob Tiger of Springfield purchased an interest in a patent for certain improvements in hominy mills. An advertisement in the 1866 Springfield City Directory identifies Jacob Tiger as the proprietor of Phoenix Mills, formerly Grimsley's Mills, corner Tenth and Madison. Jesse W. Weik claimed that the miller's name was actually Taggart. Weik, memorandum book, Weik Papers, IHi. No such person is listed in the Springfield census or city directory. Giving no

reasons for his conclusion or any evidence to support it, David Donald dismissed this story as both a "malicious rumor" and "a joke." David Donald, *Lincoln's Herndon* (New York: Alfred A. Knopf, 1948), 304.

285. Josiah P. Kent, interview with Jesse W. Weik, Springfield, 21 Nov. 1916, Weik, *Real Lincoln,* ed. Burlingame, 363; reminiscences of Olivia Leidig Whiteman (Mrs. James M.), Vandalia, Illinois, correspondence, 4 Feb., New York *Herald,* 10 Feb. 1929, section 3, p. 4. Josiah Kent is listed as a 13-year-old in the 1860 Federal Census of Sangamon County. His father Jesse was a carriage maker and carpenter. The Kents lived five houses north of the Lincolns on the same side of Eighth Street in the same block. Mrs. Whiteman was born in Vandalia; after her parents died when she was young, she was raised by her aunt, Julia Ann Sprigg (Mrs. John C.), who lived on Eighth Street between Jackson and Edwards Streets, half a block from the Lincoln house. Mary Lincoln was quite fond of Mrs. Sprigg. See her letter of 29 May [1862] to Mrs. Sprigg in Turner and Turner, eds., *Mary Todd Lincoln,* 127–128. Olivia Leidig said she was "in the Lincoln home often." Interview with William E. Barton, Vandalia, 10 Apr. 1923, Barton Papers, University of Chicago.

286. Mrs. Benjamin S. Edwards in Stevens, *A Reporter's Lincoln,* ed. Burlingame, 162.

287. Lincoln to Speed, Springfield, 22 Oct. 1846, *CWL,* 1:391. Ruth Painter Randall's claim that "the Lincolns did not spank their children" is clearly wrong. Randall, *Lincoln's Animal Friends* (Boston: Little, Brown, 1958), 89. Also wrong is Jean Baker's similar assertion. Jean Baker, *Mary Todd Lincoln: A Biography* (New York: W. W. Norton, 1987), 122.

288. Margaret Ryan, interview with Jesse W. Weik, 27 Oct. 1886, *HI,* 597.

289. Frank Edwards, "A Few Facts along the Lincoln Way," typescript enclosed in Mrs. Jacob H. Stoner to William E. Barton, Waynesboro, Pennsylvania, 21 July 1930,

uncatalogued material, box 10, folder 180, Barton Papers, University of Chicago. A 6-month-old Francis Edwards is listed in the 1850 Sangamon County census. His father was William Edwards.

290. Undated interview with Elizabeth Edwards by Jesse W. Weik, Weik, *Real Lincoln,* ed. Burlingame, 355. Many children endured corporal punishment in mid-nineteenth-century Illinois. George Perrin Davis, son of David Davis, recalled that when he was 8 years old, he once amused himself by heating and bending a poker in the fireplace. "Whether or not my mother whipped me afterwards I don't remember, but it was very likely, as it was the custom in those days." George Perrin Davis to [Jesse W. Weik], n.p., n.d., ibid., 350.

291. Anna Eastman Jackson, quoted in A. Longfellow Fiske, "A Neighbor of Lincoln," *Commonweal,* 2 Mar. 1932, 494. In 1860, Anna H. Eastman (1842–1920) appears in the Sangamon County Federal Census as living with her sister, mother, and father, Asa Eastman (1804–1888), a prosperous miller and native of Maine. He was known as "the grain and flour king" of central Illinois. Joseph Wallace, *Past and Present of the City of Springfield and Sangamon County, Illinois* (Chicago: S. J. Clarke, 1904), 823; John Mack Faragher, *Sugar Creek: Life on the Illinois Frontier* (New Haven, CT: Yale University Press, 1986), 175–176. The Springfield City Directory for 1855 gives the Eastmans' address as the corner of Eighth and Edwards, one block from the Lincolns' house. Anna Eastman married James M. Johnson of St. Louis. After his death, she returned to Springfield.

292. Walter Graves to Ida M. Tarbell, Salina, Kansas, 18 Aug. 1929, Tarbell Papers, Allegheny College.

293. Harriet A. Chapman to Herndon, Charleston, Illinois, 21 Nov. 1866, *HI,* 407.

294. Reminiscences of Thomas Stackpole, *Illinois State Journal* (Springfield), 20 June 1865. Mary Lincoln denied this story,

claiming that her children never had such shoes. "It is a new story—that in my life I have ever whipped a child—In the first place *they,* never required it, a gentle, loving word, was all sufficient with them—and if I have erred, it has been, in being too indulgent." Mary Lincoln to Alexander Williamson, Chicago, 15 June 1865, Turner and Turner, eds., *Mary Todd Lincoln,* 251. In light of other evidence of her violent temper and child-beating, this denial is unconvincing. Moreover, mothers have traditionally been more likely to abuse their children than their fathers have been. Murray A. Straus, Richard J. Gelles, Suzanne K. Steinmetz, *Behind Closed Doors: Violence in the American Family* (Newbury Park, CA: Sage Publications, 1988), 65–72, 212–218.

295. Reminiscences of Mrs. Mary Virginia Pinkerton Thompson, in Frazier Hunt, "The Little Girl Who Sat on Lincoln's Lap," *Good Housekeeping,* Feb. 1931, 17.

296. Herndon to Jesse W. Weik, Springfield, 16 Jan. 1886, H-W MSS DLC.

297. Reminiscences of Page Eaton, Utica *Herald,* n.d., copied in the Belvidere, Illinois, *Standard,* 14 Apr. 1868.

298. Herndon told this to Caroline Dall in the fall of 1866, according to Dall's "Journal of a tour through Illinois, Wisconsin and Ohio, Oct. & Nov. 1866," entry for 29 Oct. 1866, Dall Papers, Bryn Mawr College.

299. Victor Kutchin to the editor of the New York *Times,* Green Lake, Wisconsin, 21 Aug., New York *Times,* 26 Aug. 1934; see also ibid., 29 July 1934. Kutchin was a close friend of Mason Brayman, to whom Lincoln entrusted the couch when he left Springfield in 1861. Brayman in turn gave it to Kutchin.

300. In the mid-to-late 1880s, David Bigelow Parker was told this by "an elderly man" who was a fellow passenger aboard a train. That gentleman heard the story from an old friend in Ohio. David Bigelow Parker, *A Chautauqua Boy in '61* (Boston: Small, Maynard, 1912), 47–48.

301. Josiah P. Kent, in Weik, *Real Lincoln,* ed. Burlingame, 126, 362–363.

302. Herndon to Isaac N. Arnold, Springfield, 24 Oct. [18]83, Lincoln Collection, ICHi.

303. Stevens, *A Reporter's Lincoln*, ed. Burlingame, 119.

304. Fiske, "A Neighbor of Lincoln," 494.

305. In 1950, Christiana Bertram said that "many years ago I met two people who had been neighbors of the Lincolns in Springfield" who shared this story with her. Christiana Bertram, letter to the editor of the *New York Times Sunday Magazine,* Tenafly, NJ, n.d., issue of 5 Mar. 1950.

306. Eleanor Gridley, *The Story of Abraham Lincoln; or, The Journey from the Log Cabin to the White House* (Chicago: Monarch, 1902), 167.

307. Pascal P. Enos, interview with Herndon, [1865–1866], *HI,* 449. Ellis was postmaster of Springfield from 1849 to 1853.

308. The carpenter's story was reported by Mary Todd Melvin Dewing (b. 1861), a neighbor whose family was close to the Lincolns. "A Child Neighbor's Memories of Springfield," *Christian Science Monitor,* 12 Feb. 1925. Samuel Houston Melvin, who lived with his family one block from the Lincolns at Eighth and Market Streets, evidently became Lincoln's druggist in late 1860. Temple, *From Skeptic to Prophet,* 97–101.

309. Reminiscences of Mary Scott Uda, New York *Herald Tribune,* 7 Feb. 1926. The writer stated that her Kentucky-born father, an old-line Whig and a prominent physician, was friendly with Lincoln.

310. John B. Brownlow to Henry B. Rankin, Knoxville, Tennessee, 2 Sept. 1920, Rankin Papers, IHi. As a member of the U.S. Senate Committee on Pensions, Brownlow's father, William G. Brownlow, heard the testimony, which was never published.

311. Decatur, Illinois, *Herald,* 7 Feb. 1909. In 1860, Sarah B. Corneau, age 37, is listed in the federal census for Sangamon County. The 1855 Springfield City Directory indicates that her household, headed by Stephen A. Corneau, deputy clerk of the county court, resided at the corner of Eighth and Adams Streets, three blocks from the Lincolns' house.

312. Photocopy of an unidentified clipping from a Springfield newspaper, [ca. Apr. 1930], in the author's possession. Mrs. DeSouza (1840–1932) lived in Springfield from 1856 till her death. According to her obituary, she "was employed by the Lincolns for several months. After Lincoln received the nomination for president, Mrs. DeSouza was kept busy making beautiful clothes for Mrs. Lincoln." *Illinois State Journal* (Springfield), 31 Aug. 1932. Charlotte K. Rodrigues married Manuel DeSouza on 26 Mar. 1860. *Illinois State Journal* (Springfield), 27 Mar. 1860. Mrs. De Souza told Octavia Roberts Corneau that Mrs. Lincoln would "stand no sassy talk." Octavia Roberts Corneau, "My Townsman—Abraham Lincoln," typescript of a talk given to the Lincoln Group of Boston, 18 Nov. 1939, 14, Abraham Lincoln Association reference files, "Reminiscences," folder 5, IHi.

313. William E. Walter to Carl Sandburg, New York, 11 Jan. 1940, Sandburg Papers, University of Illinois. Born in England in 1847, Jane King was the daughter of the merchant William King (b. 1818), who settled in Springfield in the 1850s, residing at Seventh and Jackson Streets, one block from the Lincolns. Her son said her hatred of Mrs. Lincoln "lived with her until her death" in 1917. The 1860 census refers to her as Jennie.

314. Edward H. House to Edmund C. Stedman, 10 July 1883, quoted in James L. Huffman, *A Yankee in Meiji Japan: The Crusading Journalist Edward H. House* (Lanham, MD: Rowman & Littlefield, 2003), 189.

315. Herndon to Jesse W. Weik, Springfield, 8 Jan. 1886, H-W MSS DLC; Milton Hay to his wife, Springfield, 6 Apr. [1862], Stuart-Hay Papers, IHi.

316. John Jay Janney, "Talking with the President: Four Interviews with Abraham Lincoln," *Civil War Times Illustrated* 26 (1987):35.

317. Archibald L. Bowen, "A. Lincoln: His House," *Lincoln Centennial Association Papers*, 1925, 63.

318. Reminiscences of Mary Scott Uda, recounting a story told by her mother, New York *Herald Tribune*, 7 Feb. 1926. The trip could well have been the one taken by the Lincolns to Washington in 1847 or to New York a decade later.

319. Eleanor Gridley to W. A. Evans, n.p., 4 June 1932, copy, Gridley Papers, ICHi.

320. Herndon to Jesse W. Weik, Springfield, 1 Dec. 1885, H-W MSS DLC.

321. Thomas L. D. Johnston, interview with Herndon, [1866], *HI*, 532. In 1851, Lincoln told his stepbrother that Johnston's adolescent son, Abraham, was welcome to stay at his house in Springfield: "I understand he wants to live with me so that he can go to school, and get a fair start in the world, which I very much wish him to have." He promised that "[w]hen I reach home, if I can make it convenient to take him, I will take him." Lincoln to John D. Johnston, Shelbyville, 9 Nov. 1851, *CWL*, 2:112. See also Charles H. Coleman, *Abraham Lincoln and Coles County, Illinois* (New Brunswick, NJ: Scarecrow Press, 1955), 70–71.

322. Albert A. North, paraphrased in Herndon to Jesse W. Weik, Springfield, 9 Jan. 1886, H-W MSS DLC. Born in 1825 in Pennsylvania, North was a physician who served as justice of the peace in Capitol Township, Sangamon County, from 1885 to 1889. I am grateful to Dr. Wayne C. Temple of the Illinois State Archives for information about North. Herndon thought the young man's name was Charles Lewis. He was, Herndon said, "somehow a nephew of Mrs. Lincoln or probably other relative."

323. Harriet Chapman, interview with Jesse W. Weik (1886–1887), *HI*, 646.

324. Charles Arnold told this to Benjamin Franklin Stoneberger who in turn told it to Dr. W. A. Evans. Evans, *Mrs. Abraham Lincoln,* 130. Charles E. Arnold (1808–1888), who lived across the street from the Lincolns'

house from 1849 to 1869, served as treasurer of Sangamon County and later as its sheriff. Stoneberger (1853–1939), who had conversations with Lincolns' neighbors, was the son of William and Josephine Stoneberger. The family appears in the Springfield City Directory for the first time in 1863. They lived on North Fifth Street through the 1870s and 1880s. B. F. Stoneberger, who was in the candy business in Springfield, died in Chicago. *Illinois State Journal* (Springfield), 18 Apr. 1939. His sister married Osborn Oldroyd (1842–1930), who lived in the Lincoln home from 1883 to 1893.

325. Mary Lincoln to Emilie Todd Helm, Springfield, 20 Sept. [1857], in Turner and Turner, eds., *Mary Todd Lincoln,* 50.

326. Reminiscences of McCoy in an unidentified newspaper clipping, dated 12 Feb. 1901, Lincoln Scrapbooks, 3:40, Judd Stewart Collection, CSmH. This McCoy was perhaps Joseph Geiting McCoy (1837–1915), a prominent cattle dealer who was born in Sangamon County on Spring Creek, 10 miles west of Springfield. He attended Knox College (1857–1858) and married Sarah Epler of Pleasant Plains in 1861. They lived for a time near Springfield. After the Civil War McCoy moved to Kansas, where he achieved prominence in business and politics. See the introduction to Ralph P. Bieber's edition of McCoy's *Historic Sketches of the Cattle Trade of the West and Southwest* (1874; Glendale, CA: A. H. Clark, 1940), 17–68.

327. Reminiscences of William T. Baker (b. 1828), *Illinois State Journal* (Springfield), 18 Jan. 1909. Baker was born in Kentucky in 1828; shortly thereafter his family moved to central Illinois, where his father, James Baker, served in the Black Hawk War with Lincoln in Captain Jacob Early's company. The Baker family settled in Mt. Pulaski. See Stevens, *A Reporter's Lincoln*, ed. Burlingame, 123–127.

328. Preston H. Bailhache, "Recollections of a Springfield Doctor," *Journal of the Illinois State Historical Society* 47 (1954): 60. Bailhache

(1835–1919) lived in Springfield from 1857 to 1861 and cared for the Lincolns' children when his partner, Dr. William S. Wallace, was unavailable.

329. Henry B. Stanton, *Random Recollections* (New York: Harper and Brothers, 1887), 221.

330. Pascal P. Enos, interview with Herndon, [1865–1866], *HI*, 448–449.

331. Mrs. John A. Logan in the New York *Evening Sun*, 12 Feb. 1912.

332. Fragment of the manuscript of Helm, *Mary, Wife of Lincoln*, William H. Townsend Papers, University of Kentucky, Lexington. This passage was not included in the published version of the biography.

333. Harriet A. Chapman to Herndon, Charleston, Illinois, 10 Dec. 1866, *HI*, 512. Milton Hay reported that Mary Lincoln "was of very saving habits." Ibid., 729.

334. Undated interview with Elizabeth Edwards by Jesse W. Weik, Weik, *Real Lincoln*, ed. Burlingame, 355. Paraphrasing what James H. Matheny told him about Mrs. Lincoln, Weik wrote that she "loved fine clothes, but in other respects she was close and in no sense extravagant." Ibid., 91.

335. Herndon to Jesse W. Weik, Springfield, 5 Feb. 1887 and 10 Oct. 1888, H-W MSS DLC.

336. Gibson William Harris, "My Recollections of Abraham Lincoln," *Woman's Home Companion*, Jan. 1904, p. 15.

337. Elizabeth Edwards, interview with Herndon, [1865–1866], *HI*, 445. This servant may have been Mariah Drake. See Weik, *Real Lincoln*, ed. Burlingame, 100, and Josiah Kent, interview with Weik, 21 Nov. 1916, ibid., 363.

338. Margaret Ryan, interview with Jesse Weik, 27 Oct. 1886, *HI*, 597.

339. John F. Mendosa to James R. B. Van Cleve, Springfield, 2 July 1908, reference files of the Abraham Lincoln Association, "Reminiscences," folder 3, IHi.

340. Henry Haynie in "Success," n.d., *Youth's Companion*, 1 Sept. 1898.

341. Carpenter, *Six Months in the White House*, 273–274.

342. Whitney, *Life on the Circuit*, ed. Angle, 184.

343. Isaac N. Arnold, *The History of Abraham Lincoln, and the Overthrow of Slavery* (Chicago: Clarke, 1866), 503.

344. Nathan W. MacChesney, *Abraham Lincoln: The Tribute of a Century, 1809–1909* (Chicago: McClurg, 1910), 300.

345. John McNamar, paraphrased in Volney Hickox, "Lincoln at Home," *Illinois State Journal* (Springfield), 15 Oct. 1874.

346. Hay to his wife, Springfield, 9 Apr. 1862, Stuart-Hay Papers, IHi.

347. Margaret Ryan, interview with Jesse W. Weik, 27 Oct. 1886, *HI*, 596–597.

348. Judge George W. Murray heard this story from Herndon, his law partner during the year 1884. Murray's statement for William E. Barton, 21 Apr. 1920, Barton Papers, University of Chicago. See also G. W. Murray to Albert J. Beveridge, Springfield, 9 June 1923, Beveridge Papers, DLC. A similar account of this event can be found in Sandburg and Angle, *Mary Lincoln*, 70–71. Born in 1839 in Ohio, Murray moved to Springfield in 1874 and was elected a judge of Sangamon County in 1890, after having served in the lower house of the Illinois General Assembly. It is not surprising that Lincoln seldom turned on his wife. Social scientists have interviewed battered husbands who do not retaliate against their spouses and report that there are several reasons for their passivity: "The first, based on chivalry, considers any man who would stoop to hit a woman to be a bully. The second, usually based on experience, is a recognition of the severe damage which a man could do to a woman. . . . A final reason expressed by these beaten men is perhaps a self-serving one. The combination of crying out in pain during the beating and having the wife see the injuries, which often take several weeks to heal, raise the wife's level of guilt which the husbands consider to be a form of punishment."

Suzanne K. Steinmetz, "The Battered Husband Syndrome," *Victimology* 2 (1977):507.

349. Fred I. Dean to Ida M. Tarbell, Washington, 7 Jan. 1900, Tarbell Papers, Smith College. Dean claimed that he had "several talks" with Herndon "upon the subject, & he fully agreed with my views." Dean to Tarbell, 19 Dec. 1899, ibid. Dean's parents, Frederick S. and Harriet Dean, moved from Bloomington to Springfield in 1841. Eight years later, they purchased from Peter Van Bergen a lot across from the Lincoln house, and the following year they bought part of an adjacent lot from Lincoln. Dean's father either died or abandoned the family in the early 1850s, and his wife ran a school until her son, Frederick Irwin Dean (b. 1832), committed her, at the age of 56, to the Jacksonville insane asylum in 1860. She died three days after entering that institution. Dean to Tarbell, Washington, 7 Jan. 1900, ibid.; Fischer-Wisnosky Architects Inc., Historical Structure Report, Dean House (HS-13) (draft, 1990, Sangamon Valley Collection, Lincoln Public Library, Springfield), pp. 2.1–2.5.

350. Helm, *Mary, Wife of Lincoln*, 120.

351. James Gourley, interview with Herndon, [1865–1866], *HI*, 452.

352. Fred I. Dean to Ida M. Tarbell, Washington, DC, 7 Jan. 1900, Tarbell Papers, Smith College.

353. Weik, *Real Lincoln*, ed. Burlingame, 123.

354. Taylorville *Semi-Weekly Breeze*, 12 Feb. 1909.

355. Elizabeth Lushbaugh Capps, interview with Hannah Hinsdale, clipping dated Yakima, Washington, 2 Feb. [1929?], Lincoln Shrine, A. K. Smiley Library, Redlands, California. Mrs. Capps's father, Thomas P. Lushbaugh, a merchant in partnership with David Spear, had built a house directly across Eighth Street from the one that the Lincolns bought. Soon after the Lushbauhs took up residence in their new home, the Lincolns moved into the house opposite them. In 1840,

Lushbaugh helped organize the first Grand Lodge of Odd Fellows in Springfield. In 1862, his daughter Elizabeth married Charles R. Capps, who had been born in Springfield in 1841. The Lushbaugh family lived in Springfield for approximately six years before moving to Mt. Pulaski (Logan County) in 1846. *History of Sangamon County* (Chicago: Interstate Publishing, 1881), 622; John Carroll Power, *History of the Early Settlers of Sangamon County, Illinois* (Springfield, IL: Edwin A. Wilson, 1876), 186.

356. Elizabeth A. Capps, "My Early Recollections of Abraham Lincoln," reference files of the Abraham Lincoln Association, "Reminiscences," folder 1, IHi.

357. Reminiscences of Mrs. Cecelia McConnell, who in 1856, at the age of 18, went to Springfield to live with her aunt and uncle. *Buffalo Courier-Express*, 11 Aug. 1929, section 9, p. 2. Her uncle witnessed the peddler telling the story to Lincoln.

358. John B. Weber, interview with Herndon, Pawnee, Illinois, [ca. 1 Nov. 1866], *HI*, 389. Weber (1810–1889) was a cabinetmaker who in 1841 became copyist of land records for the state of Illinois, a post he held until 1849. Sheriff of the county from 1854 to 1856, he lived on Eighth Street between Jackson and Edwards Streets, less than a block from the Lincolns' house.

359. Herndon to C. O. Poole, Springfield, 5 Jan. 1886, H-W MSS DLC.

360. John Todd Stuart, interview with Herndon, [late June 1865], *HI*, 63.

361. Bradwell's statement to Ida Tarbell, memo marked "Lincoln—Items," folder "Mary Todd Lincoln," Ida M. Tarbell Papers, Allegheny College. Bradwell (1828–1897), a county judge in Chicago, was the husband of Myra Bradwell, an attorney who represented Mary Lincoln in her successful attempt to win release from a mental hospital in 1875.

362. Charles Arnold, quoted by B. F. Stoneberger, in Evans, *Mrs. Lincoln*, 155.

363. Elizabeth Todd Edwards, interview with Herndon, 27 July 1887, *HI*, 623.

364. John H. Littlefield interviewed by C. D. B., Brooklyn *Eagle*, 16 Oct. 1887.

365. Herndon to Jesse W. Weik, Springfield, 12 Jan. 1886, H-W MSS DLC.

366. Letter by Mary Todd quoted from memory by Mrs. William Preston (née Mary Wickliffe) in a dispatch to the Philadelphia *Times* from White Sulphur Springs, Virginia, [ca. 1882], copy, William H. Townsend Papers, University of Kentucky, Lexington. In an undated clipping in the William H. Townsend Papers in the Lincoln Presidential Library, Springfield, it is alleged that the "story of Mrs. Lincoln writing, when a young girl, a letter in which she expressed a determination to become the wife of a President, is confirmed by the production of the document, now in the possession of General Preston, of Lexington, Ky. It was addressed to a daughter of Governor Wickliffe, and contained a playful description of the gawky young Lincoln, to whom she was betrothed." Townsend Papers, box 1 1/2, folder marked "May–Aug. 1954," IHi. Lincoln wrote Mrs. Preston in 1862, saying: "Your despatch to Mrs. L. received yesterday. She is not well. Owing to her early and strong friendship for you, I would gladly oblige you, but I can not absolutely do it." Lincoln to Mrs. Margaret Preston, Washington, 21 Aug. 1862, *CWL*, 5:386.

367. Ward Hill Lamon, *Recollections of Abraham Lincoln, 1847–1865*, ed. Dorothy Lamon Teillard (2nd ed.; Washington, DC: Privately published, 1911), 21. Cf. John. Bittinger's similar account in Mahlon T. Dolman, "With Lincoln Every Night," *National Magazine* 29 (Feb. 1909):524.

368. Thomas J. Pickett in the Peoria *Weekly Republican*, 22 Feb. 1856; Thomas L. Harris to Charles Lanphier, Washington, 7 Mar. [1856], Lanphier Papers, IHi.

369. Reminiscences of Olivia Leidig Whiteman, Vandalia, Illinois, correspondence, 4 Feb., New York *Herald*, 10 Feb. 1929, section 3, p. 4.

370. Milton Hay, interview with George Alfred Townsend, Cincinnati *Inquirer*, 26 Aug.

1883; Hay, quoted in Weik, *Real Lincoln*, ed. Burlingame, 91.

371. Speed told this to John Todd Stuart. Stuart, interview with Herndon, [late June 1865], *HI*, 63.

372. Wilson and Davis, eds., *Herndon's Lincoln*, 262–263. Herndon, David Davis, and James Matheny agreed that if Lincoln had married a more amiable woman, in all probability "he would have been satisfied with the modest emoluments of a country lawyer's practice . . . and buried in the delights of an inviting and happy home." Weik, *Real Lincoln*, ed. Burlingame, 90. See also Herndon quoted by Hardin W. Masters, Portland, Maine, *Sunday Telegram*, 16 July 1922, p. 30, and Le Grand Cannon to Herndon, near Burlington, Vermont, 7 Oct. [1889], *HI*, 678–679.

373. Hardin W. Masters, "Lincoln's Last Law Partner, William H. Herndon, As I Knew Him," typescript, p. 7, Albert J. Beveridge Papers, DLC.

374. Carl Schurz, *Abraham Lincoln: An Essay* (Boston: Houghton Mifflin, 1891), 19.

375. Carl Schurz, interview with Ida Tarbell, 6 Nov. 1897, Tarbell Papers, Allegheny College.

Chapter 7. "I Have Got the Preacher by the Balls"

1. John Hay, "Colonel Baker," *Harper's New Monthly Magazine* 24 (Dec. 1861), and "The Heroic Age in Washington," a lecture given in the early 1870s, in Michael Burlingame, ed., *At Lincoln's Side: John Hay's Civil War Correspondence and Selected Writings* (Carbondale: Southern Illinois University Press, 2000), 122, 154, 158; Hay, Washington correspondence, 22 Oct., *Missouri Republican* (St. Louis), 27 Oct. 1861, in Michael Burlingame, ed., *Lincoln's Journalist: John Hay's Anonymous Writings for the Press; 1860–1864* (Carbondale: Southern Illinois University Press, 1998), 123.

2. Charles H. Ray to Thomas Ford, 25 Aug. 1845, Governor's Correspondence, Illinois State Archives, quoted in Gayle Anderson Braden, "The Public Career of Edward

Dickinson Baker" (Ph.D. dissertation, Vanderbilt University, 1960), 50; William Herndon, "Analysis of the Character of Abraham Lincoln," lecture delivered on 26 Dec. 1865 at Springfield, *Abraham Lincoln Quarterly* 1 (Dec. 1941):437.

3. David Davis to [William P. Walker], Springfield, Illinois, 25 June 1847, David Davis Papers, IHi.

4. Joshua F. Speed to Lincoln, [Frankfort, Kentucky], 13 Feb. 1849, AL MSS DLC.

5. Logan, interview with John G. Nicolay, Springfield, 6 July 1875, Michael Burlingame, ed., *An Oral History of Abraham Lincoln: John G. Nicolay's Interviews and Essays* (Carbondale: Southern Illinois University Press, 1996), 37, 38.

6. Isaac Jones Wistar, *Autobiography of Isaac Jones Wistar, 1827–1905* (2 vols.; Philadelphia: Wistar Institute, 1914), 1:303–304.

7. Chicago *Democrat*, n.d., copied in the *Illinois State Register* (Vandalia), 18 May 1838.

8. Elizabeth J. Grimsley to John Todd Stuart, Washington, 8 May 1861, Grimsley Papers, IHi.

9. David Davis to Julius Rockwell, Bloomington, Illinois, 17 Dec. 1845, Davis Papers, DLC.

10. Elizabeth Caldwell Smith Duncan, biographical sketch of Hardin, [1866], manuscript in the Duncan-Putnam Family Papers, Putnam Museum, Davenport, Iowa.

11. Washington correspondence, 2 Jan. 1894, Boston *Herald*, n.d., clipping, LMF.

12. William Brown to Jeremiah Brown Jr., Delevan, 25 Dec. 1843, typed copy, Jesse W. Fell Papers, DLC; David Davis to Julius Rockwell, Bloomington, Illinois, 14 May 1844, Davis Papers, DLC.

13. Speech in Congress, 27 July 1848, Roy P. Basler et al., eds., *Collected Works of Abraham Lincoln* [hereafter *CWL*] (8 vols. plus an index; New Brunswick, NJ: Rutgers University Press, 1953–1955), 1:515; Lincoln to Robert Boal, Springfield, 7 Jan. 1846, and to B. F. James, Springfield, 14 Jan. 1846, ibid., 1:353, 354.

14. Lincoln to Richard S. Thomas, Springfield, 14 Feb. 1843, *CWL*, 1:307.

15. Campaign circular, 4 Mar. 1843, *CWL*, 1:309–318.

16. *Illinois State Register* (Springfield), 17 Mar. 1843.

17. Abner Y. Ellis to Herndon, Moro, IL, 14 Feb. 1866, *HI*, 211; Lincoln to Martin M. Morris, Springfield, 26 Mar. 1843, *CWL*, 1:320.

18. James H. Matheny, interview with Herndon, 3 May 1866, *HI*, 251.

19. *CWL*, 1:273, 278.

20. William H. Herndon and Jesse W. Weik, *Herndon's Lincoln*, ed. Douglas L. Wilson and Rodney O. Davis (1889; Urbana: University of Illinois Press, 2006), 166.

21. Lawrence Beaumont Stringer, "From the Sangamon to the Potomac: More Light on Abraham Lincoln," typescript of an unpublished manuscript, p. 131, Edgar Dewitt Jones Papers, Detroit Public Library. Stringer's informant was Colonel Charles H. Miller, who witnessed the trial, which took place in Logan County.

22. Lincoln to Joshua Speed, Springfield, 24 Mar. 1843, *CWL*, 1:319; *Sangamo Journal*, 13 Apr. 1843.

23. Lincoln to Morris, Springfield, 26 Mar. 1843, *CWL*, 1:320–321.

24. Donald W. Riddle, *Lincoln Runs for Congress* (New Brunswick, NJ: Rutgers University Press, 1948), 69–70; Lincoln to Morris, Springfield, 26 Mar. 1843, *CWL*, 1:320–321.

25. George U. Miles, interview with Herndon, 9 Oct. 1866, *HI*, 368.

26. John Bennett to Hardin, Petersburg, 25 Apr. 1843, Hardin Family Papers, ICHi. William G. Spears, sheriff of Menard County, told Hardin that Baker won twenty-one or twenty-two votes at a meeting, which Hardin's friends virtually boycotted. Offsetting that poll was the vote at a muster in Clary's Grove, where Spears drafted a set of instructions for the delegates to the Pekin Convention. Only one signer favored Baker, while twenty-five to thirty favored Hardin. Spears to Hardin, Petersburg, Illinois, 24 Apr. 1843, ibid.

27. *Illinois State Register* (Springfield), 5 May 1843. See also "Another case of shuffling," ibid., 21 July 1843.

28. J.M. Ruggles, "Reminiscences of the Pekin Convention and of Abraham Lincoln" Tarbell Papers, Allegheny College.

29. Lincoln to Joshua Speed, Springfield, 18 May 1843, *CWL,* 1:325.

30. Francis to Hardin, Springfield, 11 May 1843, Hardin Family Papers, ICHi.

31. Reminiscences of Dr. A. W. French, Chicago *Times-Herald,* 25 Aug. 1895.

32. Sophia Bledsoe Herrick, "Personal Recollections of My Father and Mr. Lincoln and Mr. Davis," Rufus Rockwell Wilson, ed., *Intimate Memories of Lincoln* (Elmira, NY: Primavera Press, 1945), 61 (originally published in the *Methodist Review Quarterly* of Nashville, Oct. 1915); Sophia Bledsoe Herrick, Bledsoe Family History, typescript of excerpts made by David Rankin Barbee, Albert Taylor Bledsoe Papers, University of Virginia.

33. Effie Sparks, "Stories of Abraham Lincoln," manuscript, Ida M. Tarbell Papers, Allegheny College, 23–24.

34. Paraphrased remarks of Mrs. John Bradford, a Springfield neighbor of the Lincolns, to Ida Tarbell, memo in "Mary Todd Lincoln" folder, Ida M. Tarbell Papers, Allegheny College; Mrs. John S. Bradford, quoted by Judith Bradner, in Walter B. Stevens, *A Reporter's Lincoln,* ed. Michael Burlingame (1916; Lincoln: University of Nebraska Press, 1998), 94. John S. Bradford, a partner in the bookstore-cum-drugstore called Bradford and Johnson, lived at Jackson and Walnut Streets, several blocks from the Lincolns' house. In the 1860 census he was listed as 45 years old and his wife, identified as A. W. Bradford, was 42.

35. "Anecdotes of Mrs. Lincoln," by "a neighbor of the family at the time of President Lincoln's funeral," quoted in *The News* (no city indicated), ca. 17 July 1882, unidentified clipping, LMF.

36. Mrs. Sina Wilbourn, interviewed by Bond P. Geddes, Omaha *Daily News,* 24 Jan.

1909. In 1842, Illinois-born Sina Henderson wed Robert W. Wilbourn in Sangamon County.

37. Boston *Courier,* n.d., quoted in the *Campaign Atlas and Bee* (Boston), 1 Sept. 1860.

38. Harriet Hanks Chapman, interviewed by Jesse W. Weik, Charleston, Illinois, 16 Oct. 1914, Jesse W. Weik, *The Real Lincoln: A Portrait,* ed. Michael Burlingame (1922; Lincoln: University of Nebraska Press, 2002), 328.

39. Reminiscences of Page Eaton, Belvedere, Illinois, *Standard,* 14 Apr. 1868.

40. Reminiscences of an old settler in Springfield, unidentified newspaper clipping, quoted in a memo in the John J. Duff Papers, box 1, folder 5, IHi.

41. Mrs. Mary Gaughan of 146 Cornelia Street, Springfield, quoted in "Lincoln's Domestic Life," unidentified clipping, LMF.

42. Elizabeth Todd Grimsley, "Six Months in the White House," *Journal of the Illinois State Historical Society* 19 (1926–1927): 54.

43. Elizabeth Lushbaugh Capps, "Early Recollections of Abraham Lincoln," reference files of the Abraham Lincoln Association, "Reminiscences," folder 1, IHi; Elizabeth Capps, interview with Hannah Hinsdale, clipping dated Yakima, Washington, 2 Feb. [1929?], Lincoln Shrine, A. K. Smiley Library, Redlands, California.

44. Richardson quoted by William R. Morrison, in the reminiscences of Secretary of Agriculture J. Sterling Morton of Nebraska, in an undated article by Alfred Henry Lewis, copied from *Human Life,* June [no year given], clipping collection, LMF. This reminiscence dates from 1895.

45. Interview with John A. Sylvester, *Sangamo Monitor* (Springfield), 5 Apr. 1893, in Wayne C. Temple, *By Square & Compass: Saga of the Lincoln Home* (revised ed.; Mahomet, IL: Mayhaven Publishing, 2002), 274–275. Sylvester was a workman who helped add the second story to the house in 1856. Wilkinson lived directly

across the street from the Lincoln
house.

46. Reminiscences of Mrs. John S. Bradford, recorded in Eugenia Jones Hunt, "When
Mrs. Abe Called Lincoln 'You Old Fool,'" Chicago *Tribune*, 8 Feb. 1931. Mrs. Hunt, whose
father was Albert Jones, a friend and colleague
of Lincoln at the bar, commented sarcastically:
"Mrs. Lincoln, we knew, was cultured and used
choice diction." See also Eugenia Jones Hunt,
*My Personal Recollections of Abraham Lincoln and
Mary Todd Lincoln*, ed. Helen A. Moser
(Peoria, IL: Helen A. Moser, 1966), 26. Shortly
after Lincoln's death, James Gourley told
William Herndon a similar story. *HI*, 452.

47. Interview with John A. Sylvester,
Sangamo Monitor (Springfield), 5 Apr. 1893, in
Temple, *By Square & Compass*, 275.

48. Mrs. John Todd Stuart to her daughter
Bettie, [Springfield], 3 Apr. [1856], Stuart-Hay
Family Papers, IHi.

49. Elizabeth Irons Folsom, "New Stories
of Abraham Lincoln," *The American Magazine*,
July 1923, 47.

50. Reminiscences of John E. Roll, Chicago
Tribune, 12 Feb. 1900.

51. The assistant superintendent of
Springfield's schools, Jacob C. Thompson
reported this. Article by Louis J. Humphrey,
dated Springfield, 12 Feb., unidentified
clipping, LMF.

52. Albert Stevenson Edwards, "The
Lincoln Home," *Blue Book of the State of Illinois*,
ed. James A. Rose (Springfield, IL: Phillips
Bros., 1908), 510.

53. Thomas E. Talmadge to Paul M. Angle,
Chicago, 9 Sept. 1930, Abraham Lincoln
Association research files, folder "Home
(Springfield)," IHi.

54. Frances Todd Wallace, interview with
Herndon, [1865–1866], *HI*, 486.

55. Weik, *Real Lincoln*, ed. Burlingame,
120–121.

56. Springfield correspondence, 11 June,
New York *Herald*, 26 June 1860.

57. Herndon to Isaac N. Arnold, Springfield, 24 Oct. [18]83, Lincoln Collection, ICHi.

58. Henry C. Whitney, *Lincoln the Citizen*,
vol. 1 of *A Life of Lincoln*, ed. Marion Mills
Miller (2 vols.; New York: Baker & Taylor,
1908), 189.

59. Wilson and Davis, eds., *Herndon's
Lincoln*, 194.

60. Davis interview with Herndon, 20
Sept. 1866, *HI*, 349.

61. Herndon to Jesse W. Weik, Springfield,
24 Feb. 1887, H-W MSS DLC.

62. Leonard Swett to Josiah H. Drum-
mond, 27 May 1860, Portland, Maine,
Evening Express, n.d., copied in the New York
Sun, 26 July 1891. Swett said that in addition
to Lincoln and himself, only Ward Hill
Lamon and David Davis attended all sessions
on the circuit. Swett, lecture on Lincoln,
Chicago *Times*, 21 Feb. 1876.

63. Herndon to Jesse W. Weik, Springfield, 7 Dec. 1875, Lincoln Collection, RPB.

64. Mrs. Norman B. Judd, undated
interview with Ida Tarbell, Ida M. Tarbell
Papers, Allegheny College.

65. Palmer to his wife, Carrollton, Illinois,
16 Apr. 1852, Palmer Papers, IHi.

66. Yates to his wife, Washington, 1 Jan.
1852, Richard Yates and Catharine Yates
Pickering, *Richard Yates: Civil War Governor*,
ed. John H. Krenkel (Danville, IL: Interstate
Printers, 1966), 77. Cf. same to same, Washington, 25 Jan. and 17 July 1852, 18 and 19 Dec.
1853, ibid., 79, 83, 88–90.

67. Browning to Eliza Caldwell Browning,
Lower Blue Licks, Kentucky, 24 July 1844,
Ricks Collection, IHi.

68. Eliza Browning to Ann Browning, 9
Oct. 1838, in Maurice G. Baxter, *Orville H.
Browning: Lincoln's Friend and Critic* (Bloom-
ington: Indiana University Press, 1957), 13.

69. Jesse W. Fell to Hester V. Fell,
Washington, 22 June 1841, Fell Papers, DLC.

70. David Davis to Sarah Walker Davis,
Clinton, Illinois, 12 Oct. 1860, Davis Papers,
ICHi.

71. Mary Lincoln to Myra Bradwell,
Springfield, 7 July 1876, copy, Robert Todd
Lincoln Papers, DLC.

72. Willard L. King to Ruth Painter Randall, Chicago, 21 Sept. 1953, J. G. Randall Papers, DLC.

73. Davis to his wife, Pekin, 8 May 1854, in Willard King, *Lincoln's Manager, David Davis* (Cambridge, MA: Harvard University Press, 1960), 94.

74. Robert Todd Lincoln to J. G. Holland, Chicago, 6 June 1865, Robert Todd Lincoln Papers, DLC.

75. Lincoln to Samuel Caldwell, Springfield, 27 May 1858, Roy P. Basler and Christian O. Basler, eds., *Collected Works of Abraham Lincoln: Second Supplement, 1848–1865* (New Brunswick, NJ: Rutgers University Press, 1990), 14.

76. The Rev. Mr. Albert Hale to the Rev. Mr. Theron Baldwin, Springfield, 31 May 1860, Burlingame, ed., *Oral History of Lincoln*, 95.

77. Statement of James Gourley, [1865–1866], *HI*, 453.

78. Leonard Volk in Wilson, ed., *Intimate Memories of Lincoln*, 243.

79. Eulogy on Clay, 6 July 1852, *CWL*, 1:121–130.

80. Beverly C. Sandrin to James B. Clay, 20 Feb. 1844, T. J. Clay Papers, quoted in Michael Holt, *The Rise and Fall of the Whig Party: Jacksonian Politics and the Onset of the Civil War* (New York: Oxford University Press, 1999), 162.

81. Speech of 22 May 1844, in Springfield, *CWL*, 1:337.

82. David Davis to Julius Rockwell, Bloomington, Illinois, 14 May 1844, Davis Papers, DLC.

83. Herndon to Ward Hill Lamon, Springfield, 6 Mar. 1870, Lamon Papers, CSmH; Wilson and Davis, eds., *Herndon's Lincoln*, 84.

84. David Davis to Julius Rockwell, Bloomington, Illinois, 18 Feb. 1858, Davis Papers, DLC.

85. Anson G. Henry to John J. Hardin, Springfield, 25 Mar. 1844, Hardin Family Papers, ICHi.

86. James Gourley, interview with Herndon, [1865–1866], *HI*, 451–452.

87. John B. Weber, interview with Herndon, Pawnee, Illinois, [ca. 1 Nov. 1866], *HI*, 388.

88. *Illinois State Register* (Springfield), 19 Apr. 1844.

89. Letter by "J. R. D." *Illinois State Register* (Springfield), 12 Apr. 1844.

90. Milton Hay to John Hay, Springfield, 8 Feb. 1887, John Hay Papers, RPB.

91. Fell to James R. Doolittle, Bloomington, Illinois, 4 Mar. 1873, reproduced in a pamphlet, "Autobiography of Abraham Lincoln," p. 7, copy in the Fell Papers, DLC.

92. David Davis to William P. Walker, Decatur, Illinois, 4 May 1844, David Davis Papers, IHi.

93. Speech of 1 Mar. 1844, *CWL*, 1:334.

94. Debates with John Calhoun and Alfred W. Cavarly, 20–25 Mar. 1844, *CWL*, 1:334.

95. Peoria *Register*, 14 Apr. 1844; Peoria *Democratic Press*, 17 Apr. 1844; [Thomas J. Pickett], "Anecdotes of Lincoln," Rock Island, Illinois, *Weekly Register*, 30 May 1860.

96. J[eriah] B[onham], "Recollections of Abraham Lincoln," Chicago *Tribune*, 5 May 1895; Jeriah Bonham, *Fifty Years' Recollections* (Peoria, IL: J. W. Franks & Sons, 1883), 159–160.

97. [Thomas J. Pickett], "Anecdotes of Lincoln," Rock Island, Illinois, *Weekly Register*, 30 May 1860; Thomas J. Pickett's recollections in the Lincoln, Nebraska, *Daily State Journal*, 12 Apr. 1881, Wilson, ed., *Intimate Memories of Lincoln*, 190–191; Enoch P. Sloan to the editor, Peoria *Daily Transcript*, 21 Apr. 1881; Jonathan K. Cooper to the same editor, ibid., 23 Apr. 1881.

98. Lincoln to James E. Harvey, [Springfield], 2 Oct. 1860, *CWL*, 4:125.

99. *Sangamo Journal*, 2 May 1844.

100. Resolutions, 12 June 1844, *CWL*, 1:337–338. Robert W. Johannsen stated that in 1844 Lincoln "was said to be one of the supporters of the nativist movement." No evidence suggests that Lincoln in fact

sympathized with or supported nativists. To the contrary, surviving evidence indicates that he opposed them and their principles. Robert W. Johannsen, *Stephen A. Douglas* (New York: Oxford University Press, 1973), 151.

101. *Illinois State Register* (Springfield), 21 June 1844.

102. *Sangamo Journal,* 4 July 1844.

103. George H. Honig, "Abe Lincoln and the Cosmic Ray," p. 12, typescript dated 11 Aug. 1947, Honig Papers, Willard Library, Evansville, Indiana.

104. Rockport *Herald,* 1 Nov. 1844, copied in the Grandview *Monitor,* 24 Oct. 1934.

105. T. Hardy Masterson, "Lincoln's Life in Indiana," Rockport, Indiana, *Journal,* 12 Feb. 1897.

106. Josiah G. Holland, *The Life of Abraham Lincoln* (Springfield, MA: Gurdon Bill, 1866), 94; John G. Nicolay and John Hay, *Abraham Lincoln: A History* (10 vols.; New York: Century, 1890), 1:235.

107. David Davis to Julius Rockwell, Bloomington, Illinois, 17 Dec. 1845, Davis Papers, DLC.

108. Lincoln to Williamson Durely, Springfield, 3 Oct. 1845, *CWL,* 1:347.

109. John W. Bunn quoted in "Memorandum dictated this 13th day of December 1917 by Clinton L. Conkling," Weik, *Real Lincoln,* ed. Burlingame, 337.

110. Herndon to Theodore Parker, Springfield, 24 Nov. 1858, Herndon-Parker Papers, University of Iowa.

111. Herndon to Caroline Dall, Springfield, 30 Dec. 1866, Dall Papers, MHi; Herndon in conversation with Caroline Dall in the fall of 1866, recorded in Dall's "Journal of a tour through Illinois, Wisconsin and Ohio, Oct. & Nov. 1866," entry for 29 Oct. 1866, Dall Papers, Bryn Mawr College.

112. Herndon to Jesse Weik, Springfield, 24 Feb. 1887, H-W MSS DLC.

113. William E. Barton's notes of an interview with Clinton L. Conkling, Springfield, 9 Mar. 1920, Barton Papers, University of Chicago.

114. Mrs. William Bailhache, wife of the co-owner of the *Illinois State Journal,* told this to Truman H. Bartlett. Truman Bartlett to Charles L. McLellan, Chocorua, New Hampshire, 6 Oct. 1908, Lincoln Collection, RPB.

115. Herndon told this to Caroline Dall in 1866. Dall, "Journal of a tour through Illinois, Wisconsin and Ohio, Oct. & Nov. 1866," entry for 29 Oct. 1866, Dall Papers, Bryn Mawr College.

116. Herndon, "Analysis of the Character of Lincoln," 417; Herndon to Francis B. Carpenter, Springfield, 11 Dec. 1866, H-W MSS DLC; Herndon to Caroline Dall, Springfield, 28 Oct. 1866, Dall Papers, MHi.

117. David Donald, *Lincoln's Herndon* (New York: Alfred A. Knopf, 1948), 13–14, 65–71, 129.

118. Herndon, "Analysis of the Character of Lincoln," 411–412.

119. Reminiscences of John H. Littlefield, in "Abe Lincoln's Wisdom," unidentified clipping, LMF; Littlefield's lecture, "Personal Recollections of Abraham Lincoln," 2 Dec. 1875, Brooklyn *Daily Eagle,* 3 Dec. 1875.

120. Herndon interviewed in Volney Hickox, "Lincoln at Home," *Illinois State Journal* (Springfield), 15 Oct. 1874.

121. Herndon's account in Caroline Dall, "Journal of a tour through Illinois, Wisconsin and Ohio, Oct. & Nov. 1866," entry for 29 Oct. 1866, Dall Papers, Bryn Mawr College.

122. Lincoln to Benjamin F. James, Springfield, 9 Dec. 1845, Roy P. Basler, ed., *Collected Works of Abraham Lincoln, 1832–1865, First Supplement* (Westport, CT: Greenwood Press, 1974), 9.

123. Lincoln to Benjamin F. James, Springfield, 17 Nov. 1845, *CWL,* 1:349.

124. Ford paraphrased in Robert Boal to Hardin, Lacon, 10 Jan. 1846, Hardin Family Papers, ICHi.

125. Lincoln to Hardin, Springfield, 7 Feb. 1846, *CWL,* 1:363.

126. Harris, "My Recollections of Abraham Lincoln," *Woman's Home Companion,* Dec. 1903, p. 15.

127. Franklin T. King to Herndon, Kumler, Illinois, 12 Sept. 1890, *HI,* 700.

128. Lincoln to Williamson Durley, Springfield, 3 Oct. 1845, *CWL,* 1:348.

129. Lincoln to Boal, Springfield, 7 Jan. 1846, *CWL,* 1:353.

130. Robert Boal to Hardin, Lacon, 10 Jan. 1846, Hardin Family Papers, ICHi.

131. Donald W. Riddle, *Lincoln Runs for Congress* (New Brunswick, NJ: Rutgers University Press, 1948), 93.

132. *Tazewell Whig,* 21 Feb. 1846, in Paul Findley, *A. Lincoln: The Crucible of Congress* (New York: Crown, 1979), 31.

133. Ira J. Fenn to Hardin, Lacon, 23 Jan. 1846, Hardin Family Papers, ICHi.

134. Thompson to Hardin, Pekin, 12 Jan. 1846, Hardin Family Papers, ICHi.

135. Morrison to Hardin, Tremont, 2 Feb. 1846, Hardin Family Papers, ICHi.

136. Hardin to Stephen A. Douglas, Jacksonville, 5 Feb. 1846, Douglas Papers, University of Chicago.

137. Lincoln to B. F. James, Springfield, 16 Jan. 1846, *CWL,* 1:355–356.

138. Lincoln to Hardin, Springfield, 19 Jan. 1846, *CWL,* 1:356–357.

139. Lincoln to Hardin Springfield 7 Feb. 1846, *CWL,* 1:360–365.

140. Lincoln to Benjamin F. James, Springfield, 6 Dec. 1845, Basler, ed., *Collected Works of Lincoln, First Supplement,* 9.

141. Harris, "My Recollections of Abraham Lincoln," *Woman's Home Companion,* Dec. 1903, p. 15.

142. *Sangamo Journal,* 26 Feb. 1846.

143. Riddle, *Lincoln Runs for Congress,* 124–125, 127.

144. Hardin to the voters of the Seventh Congressional District, Jacksonville, 16 Feb. 1846, *Sangamo Journal,* 26 Feb. 1846.

145. Stephen T. Logan, interview with Herndon, [1865–1866], *HI,* 468.

146. James H. Matheny, interview with Herndon, [1865–1866], *HI,* 471.

147. *Sangamo Journal,* 26 Feb. 1846.

148. Hardin to Simeon Francis, Jacksonville, 20 Feb. 1846, *Illinois Gazette* (Lacon), 28 Feb. 1846.

149. David Davis to [William P. Walker], Springfield, 25 June 1847, David Davis Papers, IHi.

150. "The Journal & Mr. Calhoun," *Illinois State Register* (Springfield), 15 Jan. 1846.

151. Robert Bray, *Peter Cartwright: Legendary Frontier Preacher* (Urbana: University of Illinois Press, 2005), 159.

152. T. G. Onstot, *Pioneers of Menard and Mason Counties* (Forest City, IL: Onstot, 1902), 112, 103.

153. Wilson and Davis, eds., *Herndon's Lincoln,* 172.

154. James Gourley, interview with Herndon, [1865–1866], *HI,* 452.

155. Speech in Lacon, 18 July 1846, *The Illinois Gazette* (Lacon), 25 July 1846.

156. Lincoln to Durley, Springfield, 3 Oct. 1845, *CWL,* 1:347–348.

157. *Illinois State Register* (Springfield), 16 July 1858, 31 May 1860.

158. *Sangamo Journal,* 4 June 1846.

159. Speech in the House, 12 Jan. 1848, *CWL,* 1:432.

160. Autobiography written for John L. Scripps, [ca. June 1860], *CWL,* 4:66.

161. *Illinois State Register* (Springfield), 8 May 1846.

162. Ibid., 10 July 1846.

163. Shelby Cullom, in Walter B. Stevens, *A Reporter's Lincoln,* ed. Michael Burlingame (1916; Lincoln: University of Nebraska Press, 1998), 154.

164. Springfield correspondence, [11 July 1847], for the Boston *Courier,* in J. H. Buckingham, "Illinois as Lincoln Knew It: A Boston Reporter's Record of a Trip in 1847," ed. Harry E. Pratt (pamphlet; Springfield, IL, 1938), 33–34.

165. Joshua Speed, quoting Lincoln, in Helen Nicolay, *Personal Traits of Abraham Lincoln* (New York: Century, 1912), 110–111.

166. Michael Burlingame and John R. Turner Ettlinger, eds., *Inside Lincoln's*

White House: The Complete Civil War Diary of John Hay (Carbondale: Southern Illinois University Press, 1997), 243 (entry for 8 Nov. 1864).

167. Boal to Richard Yates, Lacon, 25 Aug. 1850, Yates Papers, IHi.

168. Julian M. Sturtevant Jr., quoting his father, Julian M. Sturtevant in a letter to William E. Barton, Cleveland, 2 Aug. 1919, Barton Papers, University of Chicago.

169. Lawrence B. Stringer's unpublished biography of Lincoln, written ca. 1927, p. 92, IHi.

170. Handbill, "To the Voters of the Seventh Congressional District," 31 July 1846, *CWL*, 1:382.

171. "D." to Allen Ford, n.d., *Illinois Gazette* (Lacon), 22 Aug. 1846.

172. John Todd Stuart, interview with Herndon, [by 2 Mar. 1870], *HI,* 576.

173. James H. Matheny, interview with Herndon, [by 2 Mar. 1870], *HI,* 576.

174. Herndon to Ward Hill Lamon, Springfield, 25 Feb. 1870, Lamon Papers, CSmH.

175. J. Otis Humphrey to I. W. Read, n.p., 9 Mar. 1892, copy, Paul Angle Papers, ICHi.

176. Green Caruthers, a fellow boarder at Springfield's Globe Tavern, in John E. Remsburg, *Abraham Lincoln: Was He a Christian?* (New York: Truth Seeker Company, 1893), 200.

177. Bledsoe, review of Ward Hill Lamon's biography of Lincoln, *Southern Review* 12 (Apr. 1873):354.

178. Gillespie to Herndon, Edwardsville, 8 Dec. 1866, *HI,* 506.

179. *Illinois Gazette* (Lacon), 15 Aug. 1846.

180. *Illinois State Register* (Springfield), 7 Aug. 1846, 28 July 1848.

181. Judge Samuel Treat, statement for Herndon, [1865–1866], *HI,* 483.

182. Israel W. Crosby to the voters of the Seventh Congressional District, Springfield, 11 January, *Illinois State Journal* (Springfield), 15 Jan. 1847.

183. Lincoln to Speed, Springfield, 22 Oct. 1846, *CWL,* 1:391.

184. Lincoln to Andrew Johnston, Tremont, 18 Apr. 1846, and Springfield, 25 Feb. 1847, *CWL,* 1:378, 392. The poems can be found ibid., 1:367–369, 378–379, 385–389.

185. Lincoln to Andrew Johnston, Springfield, 25 Feb. 1847, *CWL,* 1:392.

186. Lincoln to Andrew Johnson, Tremont, 18 Apr. 1846, *CWL,* 1:378.

187. Ward Hill Lamon, *Recollections of Abraham Lincoln, 1847–1865,* ed. Dorothy Lamon Teillard (2nd ed.; Washington, DC: published by the author, 1911), 166.

188. *CWL,* 1:367–368.

189. Ibid., 1:1.

190. Wilson and Davis, eds., *Herndon's Lincoln,* 201–202.

191. Elizabeth Crawford to Herndon, 21 Feb. 1866, *HI,* 215–216.

192. Lamon, *Reminiscences of Lincoln,* 150.

193. Francis B. Carpenter, *Six Months at the White House with Abraham Lincoln: The Story of Picture* (New York: Hurd and Houghton, 1866), 59.

194. Benjamin Brown French, *Witness to the Young Republic: A Yankee's Journal, 1828–1870,* ed. Donald B. Cole and John J. McDonough (Hanover, NH: University Press of New England, 1989), 532 (entry for 24 Feb. 1867).

195. Howard K. Beale and Alan W. Brownsword, eds., *Diary of Gideon Welles, Secretary of the Navy under Lincoln and Johnson* (3 vols.; New York: W. W. Norton, 1960), 2:26 (entry for 9 May 1864).

196. *CWL,* 1:385–386.

197. Herndon to Jesse W. Weik, Springfield, 2 Jan. 1882, H-W MSS DLC.

198. Reminiscences of William P. Wood, Washington *Sunday Gazette,* 16 Jan. 1887.

199. *CWL,* 7:368.

200. Ibid., 1:412.

201. Speech at Chicago, 10 July 1858, *CWL,* 2:500, 493.

202. New York *Weekly Tribune,* 17 July 1848.

203. Pittsburgh *Journal* n.d., copied in the New York *Tribune,* 7 June 1860.

204. Reminiscences of E. B. McCagg, *Chicago Tribune*, 12, February 1900.

205. *Missouri Daily Republican* (St. Louis), 12 July 1847.

206. Allen Thorndike Rice, ed., *Reminiscences of Abraham Lincoln by Distinguished Men of His Time* (New York: North American Review, 1886), 16.

207. Cincinnati *Commercial*, 17 Sept. 1859, in *Abraham Lincoln: A Press Portrait*, ed. Herbert Mitgang (Chicago: Quadrangle Books, 1971), 137.

208. Springfield correspondence, 6 Nov., New York *Tribune*, 10 Nov. 1860.

209. Springfield correspondence, 4 Sept., New York *Evening Post*, 8 Sept. 1860.

210. Letter from an unidentified "man of high position," Springfield, 4 June 1860, New York *Tribune*, 11 June 1860.

211. William Wood, interview with Herndon, 15 Sept. 1865, *HI*, 124.

212. "Lincoln in Massachusetts," unidentified clipping, LMF.

213. Gibson William Harris, "My Recollections of Abraham Lincoln," *Woman's Home Companion*, Dec. 1903, p. 15.

214. Lincoln to Herndon, Washington, 10 July 1848, *CWL*, 1:497.

215. Robert H. Browne, *Abraham Lincoln and the Men of His Time* (2 vols.; Cincinnati: Jennings and Pye, 1901), 1:86.

216. Janet Jennings in *Abraham Lincoln, Tributes from His Associates: Reminiscences of Soldiers, Statesmen and Citizens*, ed. William Hayes Ward (New York: Thomas Y. Crowell, 1895), 237–238.

217. Reminiscences of R. H. Osborne, "Lincoln with His People," Lerna, Illinois, *Weekly Eagle*, Lincoln anniversary issue, Feb. 1928, broadside, William E. Barton Papers, uncatalogued addendum, box 7, folder 129, University of Chicago.

218. E. J. Edwards, quoting the conductor, Gilbert Finch, then retired and living in Connecticut, New York *Times*, 24 Jan. 1909.

219. "A Story of Long Ago," *The Sunday Sun* (Matoon, Illinois), 24 Aug. 1884; Jesse W. Weik, "Lincoln and the Matson Negroes: A Vista into the Fugitive-Slave Days," *Arena* 17 (Apr. 1897):753.

220. Duncan T. McIntyre, "Matson Slave Trial," Oakland (Illinois) *Herald*, 17 July 1896.

221. Hiram Rutherford, *On the Illinois Frontier; Dr. Hiram Rutherford, 1840–1848,* ed. Willene and George Hendrick (Carbondale: Southern Illinois University Press, 1981), 137; Hiram Rutherford, interview with Jesse W. Weik, Oakland, Illinois, [3?] Apr. 1892, Weik, *Real Lincoln*, ed. Burlingame, 372.

222. Orlando B. Ficklin, "Gen. Usher F. Linder," Charleston, Illinois, *Courier*, 15 Jan. 1885, copied in the Tuscola, Illinois, *Review*, 7 Sept. 1922.

223. Duncan T. McIntyre, "Lincoln and the Matson Slave Case," *Illinois Law Review* 1 (1906–1907):390–391.

224. Ficklin's recollection, in Weik, "Lincoln and the Matson Negroes," 757.

225. Ficklin, "Gen. Usher F. Linder."

226. "In the Matter of Jane, a Woman of Color," *Western Law Journal* 5:205–206, quoted in Mark E. Steiner, *An Honest Calling: The Law Practice of Abraham Lincoln* (DeKalb: Northern Illinois University Press, 2006), 121.

227. S. S. Ball, *Report on the Condition and Prospects of the Republic of Liberia; Made to the Tenth Annual Meeting of the Colored Baptist Association* (Alton, IL: Telegraph Office, 1848), quoted in Paul M. Angle, "Aftermath of the Matson Slave Case," *Abraham Lincoln Quarterly* 3 (1944):148.

228. Albert A. Woldman, *Lawyer Lincoln* (Boston: Houghton Mifflin, 1937), 56; John J. Duff, *A. Lincoln: Prairie Lawyer* (New York: Holt, Rinehart and Winston, 1960), 144; Paul M. Angle's comment in his edition of Henry C. Whitney, *Life on the Circuit with Lincoln*, 315n4.

229. George Sharswood, *An Essay on Professional Ethics* (2nd ed.; Philadelphia: Johnson, 1860), 27.

230. David Dudley Field, "The Study and Practice of the Law," *United States Magazine and Democratic Review* 14 (1844):347.

231. Reminiscences of George Edmunds, Chicago *Journal*, 12 Feb. 1909.

232. David Davis to William P. Walker, 31 Dec. 1844, in Harry Edward Pratt, "David Davis, 1815–1886" (Ph.D. dissertation, University of Illinois, 1930), 34.

233. Davis to Lincoln, Bloomington, 21 Feb. 1849, AL MSS DLC.

234. Davis, speech of 4 July 1881, quoted in Pratt, "David Davis," 21.

235. F. of Circleville, Ohio, "The Profession of the Law," *Western Law Journal* 7 (1849):110, 111, 98, 103.

236. John W. Bunn, statement for Jesse W. Weik, in Weik, *Real Lincoln*, ed. Burlingame, 198.

237. Katherine Helm, *The True Story of Mary, Wife of Lincoln* (New York: Harper, 1928), 101–102.

238. Herndon to Jesse Weik, Springfield, 18 Feb. 1887, H-W MSS DLC.

239. Herndon, "Analysis of the Character of Lincoln," 417–418.

240. Mary Todd Lincoln, interview with Herndon, [Sept. 1866], *HI*, 359.

241. Reminiscences of Annie Lanphier Walters, Chicago *Examiner*, 13 Feb. 1909.

242. Lincoln to Speed, Springfield, 18 May 1843, *CWL*, 1:325.

243. Robert Smith Todd to Ninian W. Edwards, Lexington, 13 Mar. 1844, *Journal of the Illinois State Historical Society* 72 (1979):275.

244. Todd to Ninian Edwards, Dec. 1844, quoted by Albert S. Edwards, nephew of Mary Todd Lincoln, in Stevens, *A Reporter's Lincoln*, ed. Burlingame, 118.

245. William H. Townsend, *Lincoln and the Bluegrass: Slavery and Civil War in Kentucky* (Lexington: University of Kentucky Press, 1955), 136–137.

246. Emilie Todd Helm, in Helm, *Mary, Wife of Lincoln*, 101; William E. Barton, memorandum of a conversation with Emilie Todd Helm, 6 Mar. 1921, William H. Townsend Papers, University of Kentucky, Lexington.

247. Townsend, *Lincoln and the Bluegrass*, 136.

248. *Lexington Observer & Reporter*, 3 Nov. 1847, in Townsend, *Lincoln and the Bluegrass*, 129.

249. Clay, speech in Lexington, 13 Nov. 1847, Robert Seager and James F. Hopkins, eds., *The Papers of Henry Clay* (10 vols.; Lexington: University of Kentucky Press, 1959–1991), 10:364, 370–371, 372.

250. David Davis to his wife, Springfield, 8 Aug. 1847, David Davis Papers, ICHi.

Chapter 8. "A Strong but Judicious Enemy to Slavery"

1. Mrs. Winfield Scott, speaking in 1855, quoted in Marian Gouverneur, *As I Remember: Recollections of American Society during the Nineteenth Century* (New York: D. Appleton, 1911), 170.

2. Lady Emmeline Stuart Wortley, *Travels in the United States, etc. during 1849 and 1850* (New York: Harper & Brothers, 1851), 83.

3. Charles Dickens, *American Notes* (New York: Harper & Brothers, 1842), 44, 45.

4. Anthony Trollope, *North America* (New York: Harper & Brothers, 1862), 301–302.

5. Alexander MacKay, *The Western World, or, Travels in the United States in 1846–47* (3 vols.; London: Richard Bentley, 1850), 3:177.

6. Adolphe Fourier de Bacourt to an unidentified correspondent, Washington, [July 1840], in Bacourt, *Souvenirs of a Diplomat: Private Letters from America during the Administrations of Presidents Van Buren, Harrison, and Tyler* (New York: Holt, 1885), 72.

7. Washington correspondence by Ben: Perley Poore, 3 Mar., Boston *Atlas*, 10 Mar. 1848.

8. Mark Ron Powers, *Mark Twain: A Life* (New York: Free Press, 2005), 67.

9. Carl Schurz to his wife, Washington, 15 Mar. 1854, Frederic Bancroft, ed., *Speeches, Correspondence and Political Papers of Carl Schurz* (6 vols.; New York: G. P. Putnam's, 1913), 1:9.

10. Carl Schurz, *The Reminiscences of Carl Schurz* (3 vols.; New York: McClure, 1907–1908), 2:20.

11. Mary Abigail Dodge to an unidentified correspondent, Washington, 14 Dec. 1858, in Dodge, *Gail Hamilton's Life in Letters* (2 vols.; Boston: Lee and Shepard, 1901), 1:203.

12. Samuel D. Boyd to "dear cousin," Martinsburg, [Illinois], 8 Aug. 1849, IHi.

13. Jesse W. Fell to Hester V. Fell, Washington, 27 June 1841, Fell Papers, DLC.

14. Wade to his wife, Washington, 29 Dec. 1851, Wade Papers, DLC.

15. Rufus Rockwell Wilson, *Washington: The Capital City, and Its Part in the History of the Nation* (2 vols.; Philadelphia; J. B. Lippincott, 1901), 2:66–67.

16. Mary Elizabeth Wilson Sherwood, *An Epistle to Posterity, Being Rambling Recollections of Many Years of My Life* (New York: Harper & Brothers, 1897), 48–49, 56.

17. "Washington Life," Washington *News*, 12 Apr. 1851.

18. MacKay, *Western World*, 1:181, 179.

19. T. D. Weld to Angelina G. Weld, Washington, 1, 2 Jan., 9 Feb. 1842, Gilbert H. Barnes and Dwight L. Dumond, eds., *Letters of Theodore Dwight Weld, Angelina Grimke Weld, and Sarah Grimke, 1822–1844* (2 vols.; Washington, DC: American Historical Association, 1934), 2:883, 885, 914.

20. Lincoln to Caleb B. Smith, Washington, 31 May 1861, Roy P. Basler et al., eds., *Collected Works of Abraham Lincoln* [hereafter *CWL*] (8 vols. plus index; New Brunswick, NJ: Rutgers University Press, 1953–1955), 4:391; Mary Lincoln to Caleb B. Smith, [Washington, 31 May 1861], Justin G. Turner and Linda Levitt Turner, eds., *Mary Todd Lincoln: Her Life and Letters* (New York: Alfred A. Knopf, 1972), 87.

21. Theodore Dwight Weld to Angelina G. Weld, Washington, 27 Dec. 1842, Barnes and Dumond, eds., *Letters of Weld*, 2:947.

22. *Illinois State Register* (Springfield), 21 Sept. 1855; Theodore Dwight Weld to Angelina Grimke Weld, Washington, 1 Jan. 1842, Barnes and Dumond, eds., *Letters of Weld*, 2:883; Benjamin Brown French, *Witness to the Young Republic: A Yankee's Journal, 1828–1870*, ed. Donald B. Cole and John J. McDonough (Hanover, NH: University Press, of New England, 1989), 208 (entry for 21 Jan. 1849); Giddings to his son Addison, Washington, 27 Dec. 1840, quoted in Richard W. Solberg, "Joshua Giddings: Politician and Idealist" (Ph.D. dissertation, University of Chicago, 1952), 149.

23. Washington correspondence, 21 Feb., New York *Tribune*, 22 Feb. 1859.

24. Samuel C. Busey, *Personal Reminiscences and Recollections of Forty-Six Years' Membership in the Medical Society of the District of Columbia, and Residence in This City* (Washington, DC: Dornan, 1895), 26.

25. Nathan Sargent, *Public Men and Events in the United States from the Commencement of Mr. Monroe's Administration in 1817 to the Close of Mr. Fillmore's Administration in 1853* (2 vols.; Philadelphia: Lippincott, 1875), 2:331.

26. James Pollock, "Lincoln & Douglas," undated manuscript, Lincoln Papers, RPB.

27. Giddings diary, 18 Jan. 1849, Ohio Historical Society, Columbus.

28. Busey, *Reminiscences*, 28, 25.

29. Ben: Perely Poore in Allen Thorndike Rice, ed., *Reminiscences of Abraham Lincoln by Distinguished Men of His Time* (New York: North American Review, 1888), 218.

30. David Rankin Barbee to Stephen I. Gilchrist, Washington, n.d., copy, William H. Townsend Papers, University of Kentucky.

31. Hampton to Lincoln, Pittsburgh, 30 Mar. 1849, AL MSS DLC.

32. Letter by J. A., Washington, 30 May, *Illinois State Journal* (Springfield), 22 June 1848.

33. Washington correspondence by X, 13 Dec., New York *Tribune*, 15 Dec. 1848.

34. Elizabeth P. Peabody to Horace Mann, Jr. n.p., [mid-Feb. 1865], in Arlin Turner, ed., "Elizabeth Peabody Visits

Lincoln, February 1865," *New England Quarterly* 48 (1975):119.

35. Charles H. Brainard, "Reminiscences of Abraham Lincoln," *Youth's Companion*, 9 Dec. 1880, 435–436.

36. John J. Hardin to [David Allen Smith], Washington, 23 Jan. 1844, Hardin Family Papers, ICHi.

37. Dickens, *American Notes*, 63, 65.

38. Horace Greeley to O. A. Bowe, Washington, 28 Feb. 1849, Greeley Papers, DLC.

39. Horace Greeley, Washington correspondence, 12 Dec., New York *Tribune*, 15 Dec. 1843.

40. Lincoln to Mary Todd Lincoln, Washington, 16 Apr. 1848, *CWL*, 1:465.

41. Giddings to Laura Waters Giddings, Washington, 18 June 1848, Giddings Papers, Ohio Historical Society, Columbus.

42. Yates to Catherine Geers Yates, Washington, 2 Jan. 1854, Richard Yates and Catharine Yates Pickering, *Richard Yates: Civil War Governor*, ed. John H. Krenkel (Danville, IL: Interstate Printers, 1966), 90.

43. John J. Hardin to [David Allen Smith], Washington, 12 Jan. 1844, Hardin Family Papers, ICHi.

44. *Congressional Globe*, 30th Congress, 1st Session, 17 (9 Dec. 1847).

45. William L. Goggin of Virginia, quoted in the New York *Tribune*, 4 Sept. 1860.

46. Letter by Mrs. Herediah Horsford, [ca. December 1847?] in Paul Findley, *A. Lincoln: The Crucible of Congress* (New York: Crown, 1979), 97.

47. Washington correspondence, n.d., Maysville, Kentucky, *Eagle*, n.d., copied in the *Indiana State Journal* (Indianapolis), weekly ed., 30 Apr. 1849.

48. Horace Greeley, Washington correspondence, 12 Dec., New York *Tribune*, 15 Dec. 1843.

49. Hugo Reid, *Sketches in North America with Some Account of Congress and the Slavery Question* (London: Green, Longman, & Roberts, 1861), 87.

50. Artemas Hale to his wife, Washington, 6 Feb. 1848, Hale Papers, William L. Clements Library, University of Michigan.

51. John J. Hardin to Eliza Caldwell Browning, Washington, 26 Dec. 1843, Orville H. Browning Papers, IHi; Baker to an unidentified legal client, 9 Dec. 1845, quoted in Gayle Anderson Braden, "The Public Career of Edward Dickinson Baker" (Ph.D. dissertation, Vanderbilt University, 1960), 100.

52. Washington correspondence by T[homas] M. B[rewer], 8 Mar. [Apr.], Boston *Atlas*, 13 Apr. 1848.

53. Amos Tuck, *Autobiographical Memoir of Amos Tuck* (n.p., 1902), 83–84.

54. Lincoln to Herndon, Washington, 13 Dec. 1847, *CWL*, 1:420.

55. *The National Era* (Washington), 3 Feb. 1848. House rules adopted in the early 1840s permitted speeches of no more than an hour's length. Often members would write out their speeches, inserting into the *Congressional Globe* not only the words uttered on the floor but also the words they were unable to deliver because of time constraints. Remarks of Congressman James Pollock of Pennsylvania, *Congressional Globe*, 30th Congress, 1st Session, 44 (18 Dec. 1847).

56. *Congressional Globe*, 30th Congress, 1st Session, 109 (5 Jan. 1848).

57. Washington correspondence by "Sigma," 8 Jan., *Illinois State Register* (Springfield), 21 Jan. 1848.

58. *Congressional Globe*, 30th Congress, 1st Session, Appendix, 1 (7 Dec. 1847).

59. Resolutions, 22 Dec. 1847, *CWL*, 1:420–422.

60. *Congressional Globe*, 30th Congress, 1st Session, 229 (24 Jan. 1848).

61. Washington correspondence by "Potomac," 22 Dec. 1847, Baltimore *Patriot*, n.d., copied in the Chicago *Journal*, 6 Jan. 1848.

62. *Rockford Forum*, 19 Jan. 1848; Quincy *Whig*, n.d, copied in the *Illinois State Register* (Springfield), 14 Jan. 1848.

63. Belleville *Times*, n.d., copied in the *Illinois State Register* (Springfield), 14 Jan. 1848.

64. *Illinois Globe* (Charleston), n.d., copied in the *Illinois State Register* (Springfield), 14 Jan. 1848.

65. *Free Trader* (Ottawa), n.d., copied in the Belleville *Advocate*, 2 Feb. 1848.

66. C. H. Lanphier to John A. McClernand, Springfield, 16 Jan. 1848, McClernand Papers, IHi.

67. *Illinois State Register* (Springfield), 14 Jan. 1848.

68. Chicago *Times*, n.d., copied in the *Illinois State Register* (Springfield), 26 June 1858.

69. *Congressional Globe,* 30th Congress, 1st Session, 95 (3 Jan. 1848).

70. *Illinois State Register* (Springfield), 21 Jan. 1848.

71. Lincoln to Horace Greeley, Washington, 27 June 1848, *CWL,* 1:494.

72. Speech of 12 Jan. 1848, *CWL,* 1:431–442.

73. Chicago *Tribune,* 12 Feb. 1900.

74. R. W. Thompson, "Abraham Lincoln," undated manuscript, 15, R. W. Thompson Papers, IHi.

75. Lincoln to Herndon, Washington, 8 Jan. 1848, *CWL,* 1:430.

76. Henry Clay Whitney, *Life on the Circuit with Lincoln,* ed. Paul M. Angle (1892; Caldwell, ID: Caxton Printers, 1940), 60.

77. Reminiscences of Samuel Lowry, in Horace Lowry to Ida Tarbell, n.d., Tarbell Papers, Allegheny College.

78. Washington correspondence by W. S., 12 Jan., Boston *Atlas,* 15 Jan. 1848.

79. Thompson, "Abraham Lincoln," undated manuscript, R. W. Thompson Papers, IHi.

80. Washington correspondence, 12 Jan., Baltimore *American,* 13 Jan. 1848.

81. Quincy *Whig,* 2 Feb. 1848.

82. *Congressional Globe,* 30th Congress, 1st Session, Appendix, 246 (18 Jan. 1848).

83. Ibid., 192–196 (18 Jan. 1848).

84. Ibid., Appendix, 108 (19 Jan. 1848).

85. Ibid., 289 (2 Feb. 1848).

86. Washington correspondence by Oliver, 12 Jan., New York *Evening Post* (weekly ed.), 20 Jan. 1848.

87. *Illinois State Register* (Springfield), 14 Apr. 1848.

88. Marshall *Illinoisan,* n.d., reporting a meeting held on 29 Jan. 1848, copied in the Ottawa *Free Trader,* 23 July 1858; *Illinois State Register* (Springfield), 18 Feb. 1848, 14 July 1858, 3 Oct. 1860.

89. *Illinois State Register* (Springfield), 10 Mar. 1848.

90. Belleville *Advocate,* 6 Jan. 1848, 14 June 1849.

91. Lincoln to Herndon, Washington, 1 Feb. 1848, *CWL,* 1:446–447.

92. Lincoln to Linder, Washington, 22 Mar. 1848, *CWL,* 1:457.

93. Lincoln to Herndon, Washington, 15 Feb. 1848, *CWL,* 1:451–452.

94. Lincoln to John M. Peck, Washington, 21 May 1848, *CWL,* 1:473.

95. Chicago *Journal,* n.d., quoted in the *Illinois State Register* (Springfield), 6 Nov. 1846.

96. Herndon to Jesse W. Weik, Springfield, 11 Feb. 1887, H-W MSS DLC.

97. Speech of 27 July 1848, *CWL,* 1:501–516.

98. Frank L. Owsley to Albert J. Beveridge, Nashville, Tennessee, 14 Apr. 1925, Beveridge Papers, DLC.

99. Birchall to Thomas Ewing, Springfield, 6 June 1849, Records of the Department of the Interior, Appointments Division, Central Office Appointment Papers, 1849–1907, box 32, Record Group 48, National Archives, College Park, Maryland.

100. *Illinois Gazette* (Lacon), 15 Apr. 1848.

101. Lincoln to Herndon, Washington, 8 Jan. 1848, *CWL,* 1:430–431.

102. Lawrence B. Stringer, unpublished biography of Lincoln, written ca. 1927, 157, IHi.

103. "A Day at the White House," Baltimore *American and Commercial Advertiser,* 23 Mar. 1865.

104. David Davis to Julius Rockwell, Bloomington, 7 Dec. 1848, Davis Papers, IHi.

105. Logan, interview with Herndon, [1865–1866], Douglas L. Wilson and Rodney O. Davis, eds., *Herndon's Informants: Letters, Interviews, and Statements about Abraham Lincoln* [hereafter *HI*] (Urbana: University of Illinois Press, 1998), 468.

106. Lincoln to Schouler, Washington, 28 Aug. 1848, *CWL,* 1:518–519.

107. David Davis, interview with Herndon, 20 Sept. 1866, *HI,* 348.

108. *Illinois State Journal* (Springfield), 24 Sept. 1850.

109. Ibid., 19 July 1880.

110. Herndon to Jesse W. Weik, Springfield, 11 Feb. 1887, H-W MSS DLC.

111. Peter Menard to Lincoln, Tremont, 4 Apr. 1849, AL MSS DLC; Herndon to Weik, Springfield, 15 Jan. 1886, H-W MSS DLC.

112. Hezekiah Morse Wead diary, 15 July 1847, IHi.

113. Thomas Harris to Charles Lanphier, Washington, 12 Aug. 1850, Lanphier Papers, IHi.

114. James Shields to Augustus C. French, Quincy, 13 Aug. 1848, French Papers, IHi.

115. Springfield correspondence by Ecarte (John Hay), 20 Nov., Missouri *Democrat* (St. Louis), 22 Nov. 1860.

116. Nathan M. Knapp to Ozias M. Hatch, Winchester, Illinois, 3 Sept. [1859], Hatch Papers, IHi.

117. *Illinois State Register* (Springfield), n.d., quoted in Jack Nortrup, "Richard Yates: Civil War Governor of Illinois" (Ph.D. dissertation, University of Illinois, 1960), 126.

118. Lincoln to Henry C. Whitney, Springfield, 7 June 1855, *CWL,* 2:313.

119. Washington correspondence, 22 June, New York *Journal of Commerce,* 24 June 1848.

120. Julius Rockwell to Lucy F. Rockwell, Washington, 19 Jan. 1848, typescript, Rockwell Papers, Lenox Public Library, Lenox, Massachusetts.

121. Thomas Butler King to Winfield Scott, 15 Feb. 1845, draft, King Papers, quoted in Michael Holt, *The Rise and Fall of the Whig Party: Jacksonian Politics and the Onset of the Civil War* (New York: Oxford University Press, 1999), 262.

122. George Ashmun to Daniel Webster, Springfield, Massachusetts, 14 June 1847, Charles M. Wiltse et al., eds., *The Papers of Daniel Webster, Correspondence* (7 vols.; Hanover, NH: University Press of New England, 1974–1986), 6:235–236.

123. Julius Rockwell to William P. Walker, Washington, 7 Jan. 1848, typescript, Rockwell Papers, Lenox Public Library, Lenox, Massachusetts.

124. Thomas Brewer to William Schouler, Roxbury, Massachusetts, 7 Jan. 1848, Schouler Papers, MHi.

125. Silas Noble to E. B. Washburne, Dixon, Illinois, 13 Mar. 1848, Washburne Papers, DLC.

126. Hardin to Joseph Gillespie, Washington, 7 Dec. 1844, Gillespie Papers, IHi.

127. Speech by Singleton in Jacksonville in 1858, quoted in the Lincoln, Illinois, correspondence, 4 June 1860, *Missouri Republican* (St. Louis), 7 June 1860, and in the Jacksonville correspondence, n.d., *Missouri Republican* (St. Louis), n.d., copied in the *Illinois State Register* (Springfield), 24 Sept. 1858.

128. Osborn H. Oldroyd, ed., *The Lincoln Memorial: Album-Immortelles* (Boston: D. L. Guernsey, 1882), 241.

129. Lincoln to Herndon, Washington, 2 Feb. 1848, *CWL,* 1:448.

130. *Congressional Globe,* 30th Congress, 1st Session, Appendix, 163 (2 Feb. 1848).

131. Lincoln to the Taylor Committee, Washington, 9 Feb. 1848, *CWL,* 1:449.

132. Lincoln to Thomas S. Flournoy, Washington, 17 Feb. 1848, and Lincoln to Jesse Lynch, Washington, 10 Apr. 1848, *CWL,* 1:452, 463.

133. Lincoln to Archibald Williams, Washington, 30 April 1848, and Lincoln to Silas Noble, Washington, 25 May 1848, *CWL*, 1:468, 474.

134. Caleb B. Smith to Allen Hamilton, 15 Feb. 1848, Hamilton Papers, quoted in Holt, *Rise and Fall of the Whig Party*, 273.

135. Fragment: What General Taylor Ought to Say, [Mar.?] 1848, *CWL*, 1:454.

136. Lincoln to Linder, Washington, 22 Mar. 1848, *CWL*, 1:457–458.

137. Giddings, speech before the New Hampshire House of Representatives, 26 June 1847, *Illinois State Register* (Springfield), 12 Aug. 1847.

138. Columbus Delano to Joshua R. Giddings, 25 May 1847, quoted in John H. Schroeder, *Mr. Polk's War: American Opposition and Dissent, 1846–1848* (Madison: University of Wisconsin Press, 1973), 135.

139. Greeley to Schuyler Colfax, New York, 3 Apr. 1848, Greeley Papers, New York Public Library.

140. Holt, *Rise and Fall of the Whig Party*, 317.

141. Detroit *Free Press*, 11 July 1848, quoted in Joseph G. Rayback, *Free Soil: The Election of 1848* (Lexington: University Press of Kentucky, 1971), 204.

142. Holt, *Rise and Fall of the Whig Party*, 329.

143. Lincoln to Herndon, Washington, 12 June 1848, *CWL*, 1:476–477.

144. Greeley to Colfax, n.p., n.d., copy of excerpt, Allan Nevins Papers, Columbia University.

145. Speech of 10 June 1848, *CWL*, 1:475–476.

146. Washington correspondence, 20 June, New York *Tribune*, 22 June 1848.

147. *CWL*, 1:501–516.

148. Washington correspondence by "Independent," 27 July, Philadelphia *North American and U.S. Gazette*, 29 July 1848; Baltimore *American*, n.d., copied in the *Illinois State Journal* (Springfield), 13 Aug. 1848.

149. Ben: Perley Poore in Allen Thorndike Rice, ed., *Reminiscences of Abraham Lincoln by Distinguished Men of His Time* (New York: North American Review, 1888), 221.

150. Hannibal Hamlin quoted by his grandson, Charles E. Hamlin, in Charles E. Hamlin, "Lincoln, the Man of Method," undated manuscript, Hamlin Family Papers, University of Maine.

151. Lincoln to Herndon, Washington, 22 June and 10 July 1848, *CWL*, 1:491, 497.

152. Chicago *Weekly Democrat*, 26 Sept. 1848.

153. William H. Howe to Roger Sherman Baldwin Jr., 25 July 1848, quoted in Holt, *Rise and Fall of the Whig Party*, 333.

154. Wilson to Joshua R. Giddings, 6 Feb. 1847, Giddings Papers, quoted in Reinhard H. Luthin, "Abraham Lincoln and the Massachusetts Whigs in 1848," *New England Quarterly* 14 (1941):623; Holt, *Rise and Fall of the Whig Party*, 326; Henry Wilson, *History of the Rise and Fall of the Slave Power in America* (2 vols.; Boston: Houghton Mifflin, 1872), 2:136.

155. "The Free Soil Whigs of Massachusetts," New York *Evening Post* (weekly ed.), 19 Oct. 1848.

156. Solomon Lincoln to Artemas Hale, Hingham, 2 Mar. 1848, Freehold, New Jersey, *Transcript*, 6 Mar. 1931.

157. *CWL*, 2:1–5.

158. Springfield, Massachusetts, *Republican*, 14 Sept. 1848.

159. Henry J. Gardner, statement for Edward L. Pierce, [Feb.–May 1890], *HI*, 699; *CWL*, 2:1–2.

160. [William Schouler], Worcester correspondence, 13 Sept., Boston *Atlas*, 13 Sept. 1848; *CWL*, 2:1–5.

161. Zephaniah W. Pease, ed., *The Diary of Samuel Rodman: A New Bedford Chronicle of Thirty-Seven Years, 1821–1859* (New Bedford, MA: Reynolds, 1927), 287 (entry for 15 Sept. 1848); New Bedford *Mercury*, in Richard J. Hinton, *Life and Public Services of Hon. Abraham Lincoln* (Boston: Thayer and Eldridgo, 1860), 26.

162. Boston *Herald*, 16 Sept. 1848, quoted in William F. Hanna, *Abraham among the Yankees: Abraham Lincoln's 1848 Visit to*

Massachusetts (Taunton, MA: Old Colony Historical Society, 1983), 50.

163. Samuel P. Hadley, "Recollections of Lincoln in Lowell in 1848," in Frederick W. Coburn, *History of Lowell and Its People* (3 vols.; New York: Lewis Historical Co., 1920), 1:235–236.

164. Letter by "Templeton" [George Harris Monroe], Boston Highlands, 22 Apr., Boston *Sunday Herald*, 26 Apr. 1885; "Lincoln in Massachusetts," unidentified newspaper article by Monroe, clipping collection, LMF.

165. Norfolk *Democrat*, 22 Sept. 1848, in Walter Austin, *Tale of a Dedham Tavern: History of the Norfolk Hotel* (Cambridge: Riverside Press, 1912), 146, 64; Robert Barton, "Lincoln Visited Dedham Just 100 Years Ago," typescript, Barton Papers, University of Illinois.

166. Taunton *Old Colony Republican*, 23 Sept. 1848, quoted in Sheldon H. Harris, "Abraham Lincoln Stumps a Yankee Audience," *New England Quarterly* 38 (1965):230.

167. Boston *Chronotype*, n.d., copied in the *Illinois State Register* (Springfield), 13 Oct. 1848.

168. "Abraham Lincoln at Union Hall," Taunton *Bristol County Democrat*, 29 Sept. 1848.

169. Boston *Journal*, n.d., copied in the New York *Tribune*, 25 Sept. 1848.

170. Francis B. Carpenter, "A Day with Governor Seward at Auburn," July 1870, Seward Papers, University of Rochester.

171. Frederick W. Seward, *Seward at Washington as Senator and Secretary of State: A Memoir of His Life, with Selections from His Letters* (2 vols; New York: Derby and Miller, 1891), 1:180.

172. Chicago correspondence, 1 Oct., New York *Herald*, 2 Oct. 1860.

173. Hamlin told this to C. J. Prescott. Reminiscences of C. J. Prescott, "Hamlin" folder, Ida M. Tarbell Papers, Allegheny College.

174. Pierce, statement for Herndon, [1887?], *HI*, 691.

175. *CWL*, 2:14.

176. Joseph Fifer, interview with Carl Sandburg, 1923, memo, Carl Sandburg Papers, University of Illinois.

177. Wilson, *Rise and Fall of the Slave Power*, 2:190–191.

178. Interview with Ficklin, *The Classmate: A Paper for Young People* (Cincinnati), 6 Feb. 1926.

179. Washington correspondence, 22 Dec. 1847, Chicago *Daily Democrat*, 4 Jan. 1848.

180. Lincoln voted with the 87–70 minority against tabling a petition calling for this measure. *House Journal*, 30th Congress, 1st Session, 167–168 (30 Dec. 1847).

181. Wentworth to Edmund S. Kimberly, 26 June 1848, quoted in Don E. Fehrenbacher, *Chicago Giant: A Biography of "Long John" Wentworth* (Madison, WI: American History Research Center, 1957), 79.

182. Horace Mann to Mary Mann, Washington, 18 and 29 July 1848, Horace Mann Papers, MHi.

183. Washington correspondence by [John] B[rown], 13 Aug., New York *Evening Post* (weekly ed.), 24 Aug. 1848.

184. Horace Mann to Mary Mann, Washington, 11 and 13 Aug. 1848, Horace Mann Papers, MHi.

185. Horace Mann to his wife, Washington, 1 May 1848, Horace Mann Papers, MHi.

186. John Randolph, quoted in Don E. Fehrenbacher, *The Slaveholding Republic: An Account of the United States Government's Relations to Slavery*, ed. Ward M. McAfee (New York: Oxford University Press, 2001), 67.

187. *CWL*, 2:253.

188. E. S. Abdy, *Journal of a Residence and Tour of the United States of North America, from April, 1833, to October, 1834* (3 vols.; London: John Murray, 1835), 2:96–97.

189. Horace Mann to Samuel Gridley Howe, Washington, 22 Apr. 1848, Horace Mann Papers, MHi.

190. Palfrey to Charles Francis Adams, Washington, 13 Dec. 1848, Adams Papers, MHi.

191. William Schouler, Washington correspondence, 26 Dec., Boston *Atlas,* 29 Dec. 1848.

192. Joshua Giddings to Charles Sumner, Washington, 22 Dec., 1848, Sumner Papers, Harvard University; Joshua R. Giddings, *History of the Rebellion: Its Authors and Causes* (New York: Follett, Foster, 1864), 286–288.

193. *House Journal,* 30th Congress, 2nd Session, 132 (21 Dec. 1848).

194. *Congressional Globe,* 30th Congress, 2nd Session, Appendix, 214 (10 Jan. 1849).

195. Washington correspondence, 26 Jan., Boston *Atlas,* 29 Jan. 1849.

196. Remarks of Robert M. McLane of Maryland, *Congressional Globe,* 30th Congress, 1st Session, 202 (19 Jan. 1848).

197. Horace Greeley, "Greeley's Estimate of Lincoln," *The Century Magazine,* July 1891, 374; George W. Julian, *The Life of Joshua R. Giddings* (Chicago: McClurg, 1892), 261.

198. *The Liberator* (Boston), 9 Feb. 1849.

199. *CWL,* 2:20–22.

200. James Quay Howard's notes of an interview with Lincoln, [May 1860], AL MSS DLC.

201. Washington correspondence, 2 Feb., New York *Herald,* 6 Feb. 1849.

202. *The Liberator* (Boston), 13 July 1860.

203. Giddings diary, 8 and 11 Jan. 1849, Ohio Historical Society, Columbus.

204. *National Era* (Washington), 28 Dec. 1848.

205. *Albany Patriot,* 22 Mar. and 24 May 1848, and *Anti-Slavery Reporter,* 1 May 1853, quoted in Stanley Harrold, *Subversives: Antislavery Community in Washington, D.C., 1828–1865* (Baton Rouge: Louisiana State University Press, 2003), 102—103.

206. "Greeley's Estimate of Lincoln," 374.

207. Baltimore *Sun,* n.d., copied in *The National Era* (Washington), 4 Jan. 1849.

208. [John Wentworth], Washington correspondence, 22 Dec. 1847, Chicago *Daily Democrat,* 4 Jan. 1848.

209. Speech at Peoria, 16 Oct. 1854, *CWL,* 2:260.

210. William Bissell to Joseph Gillespie, Washington, 19 Apr. 1850, Joseph Gillespie Papers, IHi.

211. Washington correspondence by "Athenian," 10 Jan., Boston *Atlas,* 15 Jan. 1849.

212. Washington correspondence, 2 Feb., New York *Herald,* 6 Feb. 1849.

213. Winthrop to John H. Clifford, Washington, 20 Jan. 1849, and to his son Robert, Washington, 18 Feb. 1849, Winthrop Papers, MHi.

214. *The Liberator* (Boston), 30 June 1860.

215. Giddings to Phillips, Jefferson, Ohio, 30 July 1860, Ashtabula, Ohio, *Sentinel,* n.d., copied in *The Liberator* (Boston), 24 Aug. 1860.

216. Herndon to Sydney Howard Gay, Springfield, 10 Aug. 1860, Gay Papers, Columbia University.

217. Washington correspondence by C. B. A., 20 Sept. 1849, New York *Tribune,* 22 Sept. 1849.

218. Speech of 22 May 1860 at Oberlin, Ohio, Springfield (Massachusetts) *Republican,* 28 May 1860.

219. Horace Mann to Charles Sumner, Washington, 27 Feb. 1849, Horace Mann Papers, MHi.

220. Horace Mann to his wife, Washington, 4 Mar. 1849, Horace Mann Papers, MHi.

221. Washington correspondence, n.d., Maysville, Kentucky, *Eagle,* n.d., copied in the *Indiana State Journal* (Indianapolis), weekly ed., 30 Apr. 1849.

222. Robert T. Scott to Reuben Chapman, 5 Mar. 1849, quoted in Holt, *Rise and Fall of the Whig Party,* 390.

223. Giddings to Charles Sumner, Jefferson, Ohio, 30 Mar. 1849, Sumner Papers, Harvard University.

224. Horace Mann to his wife, Washington, 17 Feb. 1849, Horace Mann Papers, MHi.

225. Giddings, *A History of the Rebellion: Its Authors and Causes* (Cleveland: Follet, Foster, 1864), 299.

226. Peter Menard to Lincoln, Tremont, 4 Apr. 1849, AL MSS DLC.

227. Crittenden to John M. Clayton, Frankfort, 13 Mar. 1849, Clayton Papers, DLC.

228. Philo H. Thompson to Lincoln, Pekin, 23 Apr. 1849, AL MSS DLC; David Davis to [William P. Walker], Bloomington, Illinois, 14 Mar. 1853, David Davis Papers, IHi.

229. Lincoln to George W. Rives, Springfield, 7 May 1849, *CWL*, 2:46.

230. William H. Herndon and Jesse W. Weik, *Herndon's Lincoln,* ed. Douglas L. Wilson and Rodney O. Davis (1889; Urbana: University of Illinois Press, 2006), 85.

231. Orville [Paddock?] to his sister, Springfield, 12 June 1849, Paddock Family Papers, Missouri Historical Society.

232. Rives to O. M. Hatch, Paris, Illinois, 10 Nov. 1858, Hatch Papers, IHi.

233. William H. Chandler to Elisha Embree, Evansville, Indiana, 3 Feb. 1849, Embree Papers, Manuscripts Department, Indiana Division, Indiana State Library, Indianapolis.

234. Lincoln to Thomas Ewing, Springfield, 3 June 1849, *CWL*, 2:52.

235. Barrett to Thomas Ewing, Springfield, 6 May 1849, copy, Ewing Papers, DLC.

236. Herndon to Jesse W. Weik, Springfield, 15 Jan. 1886, H-W MSS DLC;

237. Barrett to Ewing, Springfield, 6 May 1849, copy, Ewing Papers, DLC.

238. Lincoln to Thompson, Springfield, 25 Apr. 1849, *CWL*, 2:44.

239. Copy of a petition signed by P. H. Thompson and 138 others, Pekin, 1 May 1849, AL MSS DLC.

240. Lincoln to Thomas Ewing, Springfield, 10 May 1849, *CWL*, 2:46–47.

241. Lincoln to Speed, Washington, 20 Feb. 1849, *CWL*, 2:28–29.

242. John F. Snyder, "Col. Don Morrison," unpublished biographical sketch, p. 24, Snyder Papers, IHi.

243. Lincoln to Speed, Washington, 20 Feb. 1849, *CWL*, 2:29.

244. Lincoln's letter is quoted in Cyrus Edwards to Justin Butterfield, Woodlawn, Illinois, 11 June 1849, Records of the Department of the Interior, Appointments Division, Central Office Appointment Papers, 1849–1907, box 32, Record Group 48, National Archives, College Park, Maryland.

245. Lincoln to Davis, Washington, 12 Feb. 1849, Roy P. Basler, ed., *Collected Works of Lincoln, First Supplement* (Westport, CT: Greenwood Press, 1973), 14.

246. Butterfield to Caleb B. Smith, Chicago, 28 May 1849, Smith Papers, DLC.

247. Lincoln to William B. Warren and others, Springfield, 7 Apr. 1849, *CWL*, 2:41.

248. Cyrus Edwards to Justin Butterfield, Woodlawn, Illinois, 11 June 1849, Records of the Department of the Interior, Appointments Division, Central Office Appointment Papers, 1849–1907, box 32, Record Group 48, National Archives, College Park, Maryland.

249. Michael Burlingame and John R. Turner Ettlinger, eds., *Inside Lincoln's White House: The Complete Civil War Diary of John Hay* (Carbondale: Southern Illinois University Press, 1997), 73 (entry for 13 Aug. 1863).

250. Lucas to Lincoln, Washington, 12 Apr. 1849, AL MSS DLC.

251. Butterfield to Caleb B. Smith, Lasalle, Illinois, 5 June 1849, Smith Papers, DLC; Richard M. Young to Lincoln, Washington, 7 May 1849, AL MSS DLC.

252. Henderson to Lincoln, Washington, 13 and 18 May 1849, AL MSS DLC.

253. Butterfield to Caleb B. Smith, Lasalle, 5 June 1849, Smith Papers, DLC.

254. Butterfield to Caleb B. Smith, Chicago, [1?] June 1849, Smith Papers, DLC.

255. Butterfield to Caleb B. Smith, Chicago, 28 May 1849, Smith Papers, DLC.

256. Thomas Mather to William Mather, Springfield, 19 May 1849, Records of the Department of the Interior, Appointments Division, Central Office Appointment Papers,

1849–1907, box 32, Record Group 48, National Archives, College Park, Maryland.

257. Lincoln to Lucas, Springfield, 25 April 1849, *CWL*, 2: 43–44.

258. Lincoln to Preston, Springfield, 16 May 1849, *CWL*, 2:49.

259. Lincoln to Embree, Springfield, 25 May 1849, *CWL*, 2:51; Lincoln to Thomas Ewing, Springfield, 9 July 1849, Roy P. Basler and Christian O. Basler, eds., *The Collected Works of Abraham Lincoln: Second Supplement, 1848–1865* (New Brunswick, NJ: Rutgers University Press, 1990), 3–4.

260. A. G. Henry to Joseph Gillespie, Springfield, 2 June 1849, Joseph Gillespie Papers, IHi; Henry to David Davis, Springfield, 2 June 1849, Davis Papers, ibid.

261. Josiah M. Lucas to Lincoln, Washington, 15 Apr. 1849, AL MSS DLC.

262. Josiah M. Lueas to Lincoln, Washington, 10 May 1849, AL MSS DLC.

263. Josiah M. Lucas to Anson G. Henry, Washington, 22 May 1849, AL MSS DLC.

264. Ben E. Green to Lincoln, Washington, 29 May 1849, AL MSS, DLC.

265. *Illinois Gazette* (Lacon), 9 June 1849.

266. Butterfield to Caleb B. Smith, Springfield, 6 June 1849, Smith Papers, DLC; petition dated 6 June 1849, Records of the Department of the Interior, Appointments Division, Central Office Appointment Papers, 1849–1907, box 32, Record Group 48, National Archives, College Park, Maryland.

267. Undated petition, Records of the Department of the Interior, Appointments Division, Central Office Appointment Papers, 1849–1907, box 32, Record Group 48, National Archives, College Park, Maryland.

268. Butterfield to Caleb B. Smith, Springfield, 6 June 1849, Smith Papers, DLC; Anson G. Henry to Lincoln, Springfield, 11 June 1849, AL MSS DLC.

269. Butterfield to J. J. Brown, Springfield, 7 June 1849, Records of the Department of the Interior, Appointments Division, Central

Office Appointment Papers, 1849–1907, box 32, Record Group 48, National Archives, College Park, Maryland.

270. Herndon to Jesse W. Weik, Springfield, 11 Feb. 1887, H-W MSS DLC.

271. Herndon to Jesse W. Weik, Springfield, 8 and 15 Jan. 1886, H-W MSS DLC. Cf. Weik to Albert J. Beveridge, Larchmont, New York, 4 Feb. 1926, Beveridge Papers, DLC.

272. Butterfield to J. J. Brown, Springfield, 7 June 1849, Records of the Department of the Interior, Appointments Division, Central Office Appointment Papers, 1849–1907, box 32, Record Group 48, National Archives, College Park, Maryland.

273. Levi Davis to Butterfield, Springfield, 9 June 1849, Records of the Department of the Interior, Appointments Division, Central Office Appointment Papers, 1849–1907, box 32, Record Group 48, National Archives, College Park, Maryland.

274. William H. Herndon to Jesse W. Weik, Springfield, 8 Jan. 1886, H-W MSS DLC.

275. Memorandum to Taylor, [15?] June 1849, *CWL*, 2:54.

276. Butterfield to Hunter, Chicago, 4 June 1849, Records of the Department of the Interior, Appointments Division, Central Office Appointment Papers, 1849–1907, box 32, Record Group 48, National Archives, College Park, Maryland.

277. Lucas to Zachary Taylor, Washington, 6 June 1849, Department of Archives and Manuscripts, Louisiana State University, copy of a typescript, Small Manuscript Collections, DLC.

278. Wilcox told this to Joseph H. Barrett, who recorded the reminiscence in 1865. "Lincoln and the Land Office," memo by William E. Barton, Barton Papers, box 6, folder 94, University of Chicago.

279. Chicago *Journal,* 12 June 1849.

280. Francis F. Browne, *The Every-Day Life of Abraham Lincoln* (2nd ed.; Chicago: Browne & Howell, 1913), 107.

281. Lincoln to Gillespie, Springfield, 13 July 1849, *CWL*, 2:58.

282. "Mr. Butterfield," *Illinois State Journal* (Springfield), 20 Nov. 1850.

283. "*For your sake* I pledge a word which has never failed that I will bury the hatchet with Lincoln, and be ready to exert all my influence for the promotion of your views, *whatever they may be.*" Cyrus Edwards to Joseph Gillespie, Woodlawn, Illinois, 4 July 1860, copy, Ida M. Tarbell Papers, Allegheny College.

284. Lincoln to David Davis, Springfield, 6 July 1849, Basler, ed., *Collected Works of Lincoln, First Supplement*, 16.

285. Lincoln to Gillespie, Springfield, 13 July 1849, *CWL*, 2:59.

286. Washburne to Caleb B. Smith, Galena, Illinois, 17 Nov. 1849, Smith Papers, DLC.

287. Giddings to Wendell Phillips, Jefferson, Ohio, 30 July 1860, Ashtabula *Sentinel*, n.d., copied in *The Liberator* (Boston), 24 Aug. 1860.

288. *The National Era* (Washington), 21 Dec. 1848.

289. E. Harriman to Millard Fillmore, Washington, 2 Dec. 1850, Records of the Department of the Interior, Appointments Division, Central Office Appointment Papers, 1849–1907, box 32, Record Group 48, National Archives, College Park, Maryland.

290. Washington correspondence, 2 Aug., New York *Herald*, 4 Aug. 1850.

291. A document headed "Applications" listing all letters in support of candidates for the Commissionership of the General Land Office in 1849, National Archives; Lincoln to Ewing, Springfield, 9 July 1849, Basler and Basler, eds., *Collected Works of Lincoln, Second Supplement*, 3–4.

292. Lincoln to John Addison, Springfield, 9 Aug. 1849, *CWL*, 2:91–92.

293. Lincoln to Clayton, Springfield, 28 July 1850, *CWL*, 2:60.

294. *CWL*, 2:83–90.

295. Unidentified Massachusetts politician (probably John Alley) to Josiah G. Holland, Washington, 8 Aug. 1865, Holland Papers, New York Public Library.

296. Allen C. Clark, *Abraham Lincoln in the National Capital* (Washington, DC: W. F. Roberts, 1925), 6.

297. William Henry Milburn, *Ten Years of Preacher-Life: Chapters from an Autobiography* (New York: Derby and Jackson, 1859), 166.

298. John Cook's undated reminiscences, Lincoln Centennial Association Papers, IHi; Cook's reminiscences, *Illinois State Journal* (Springfield), 8 Feb. 1909.

299. Arthur P. Rugg, "Abraham Lincoln in Worcester," Worcester Society of Antiquity, *Proceedings*, 25 (1910): 5–7.

300. David Davis to Lincoln, Taylorville, 6 June 1849, AL MSS DLC.

301. Lyman D. Stickney to Elisha Embree, New Harmony, Indiana, 7 Sept. 1849, Embree Papers, Indiana Division, Manuscripts Department, Indiana State Library, Indianapolis.

302. Linder to Joseph Gillespie, Charleston, Illinois, 14 Jan. 1850, Gillespie Papers, IHi; *Illinois State Register* (Springfield), 15 Nov. 1849.

303. Elihu B. Washburne to Caleb B. Smith, aboard a Mississippi River steamboat, 15 Nov. 1849, Smith Papers, DLC.

304. Lincoln to the editor of the Chicago *Journal*, Springfield, 21 Nov. 1849, *CWL*, 2:68.

305. Stuart, interviewed by John G. Nicolay, Springfield, 24 June 1875, Burlingame, ed., *Oral History of Lincoln*, 15.

306. Noah Brooks, *Abraham Lincoln and the Downfall of American Slavery* (New York: G. P. Putnam's Sons, 1894), 116.

307. Statement dated 1866 by Nathaniel G. Wilcox, in Joseph H. Barrett, *Abraham Lincoln and His Presidency* (2 vols.; Cincinnati: Robert Clarke, 1904), 1:108.

308. R. W. Thompson, "Abraham Lincoln," undated manuscript, p. 15, R. W. Thompson Papers, IHi.

Chapter 9. "I was Losing Interest in Politics"

1. [John M. Scott], "Lincoln on the Stump and at the Bar," undated typescript enclosed in Scott to Ida Tarbell, Bloomington, Illinois, 14 Aug. 1895, Tarbell Papers, Allegheny College.

2. Robert H. Browne, *Abraham Lincoln and the Men of His Time* (2 vols.; Cincinnati: Jennings and Pye, 1901), 1:285.

3. Roy P. Basler et al., eds., *The Collected Works of Abraham Lincoln* [herafter cited as *CWL*] (8 vols. plus index; New Brunswick, NJ: Rutgers University Press, 1953–1955), 3:512, 4:67.

4. Henry C. Whitney, *Life on the Circuit with Lincoln*, ed. Paul M. Angle (1892; Caldwell, ID: Caxton Printers, 1940), 404.

5. Notes for a law lecture, Roy P. Basler, ed., *Collected Works of Lincoln, First Supplement* (Westport, CT: Greenwood Press, 1973), 19.

6. F. of Circleville, Ohio, "The Profession of the Law," *Western Law Journal* 7 (1849):109.

7. Gibson William Harris, "My Recollections of Abraham Lincoln," *Woman's Home Companion*, Dec. 1903, p. 15.

8. Herndon to Wendell Phillips, Springfield, 12 May 1857, Phillips Papers, Harvard University.

9. Herndon to Ward Hill Lamon, Springfield, 6 Mar. 1870, Lamon Papers, CSmH.

10. Herndon "Lincoln's Ingratitude," H-W MSS DLC.

11. Herndon, to Caroline Dall, Springfield, 28 Oct. 1866, Dall Papers, MHi.

12. Jesse W. Weik, *The Real Lincoln: A Portrait*, ed. Michael Burlingame (1922; Lincoln: University of Nebraska Press, 2002), 301.

13. Lincoln to William Martin, Springfield 6 Mar. 1851, *CWL*, 2:102.

14. Clipping dated Wichita, Kansas, 12 Feb. 1958, from an unidentified newspaper, LMF.

15. William H. Herndon, "Analysis of the Character of Abraham Lincoln," lecture delivered at Springfield, 26 Dec. 1865, *Abraham Lincoln Quarterly* 1 (1941): 428.

16. Harris, "My Recollections of Abraham Lincoln," *Woman's Home Companion*, Jan. 1904, p. 14.

17. Herndon, "Analysis of the Character of Lincoln," 427.

18. Mrs. James Judson Lord in Walter B. Stevens, *A Reporter's Lincoln*, ed. Michael Burlingame (1916; Lincoln: University of Nebraska Press, 1998), 188; Dr. James Judson Lord, interview with Herndon, [1865–1866], Douglas L. Wilson and Rodney O. Davis, eds., *Herndon's Informants: Letters, Interviews and Statements about Abraham Lincoln* [hereafter cited as *HI*] (Urbana: University of Illinois Press, 1998), 469.

19. Herndon, "Analysis of the Character of Lincoln," 427–428.

20. John H. Littlefield in *Everywhere*, Feb. 1902, copied in the Los Angeles *Times*, 9 Mar. 1902.

21. Lincoln to Abram Bale, Springfield, 22 Feb. 1850, *CWL*, 2:76.

22. Lincoln to Haden Keeling, Springfield, 3 Mar. 1859, *CWL*, 3:371.

23. Harris, "My Recollections of Abraham Lincoln," *Woman's Home Companion*, Jan. 1904, p. 14.

24. Ibid., p. 15.

25. Lawrence Beaumont Stringer, "From the Sangamon to the Potomac: More Light on Abraham Lincoln," typescript of an unpublished manuscript, p. 95, Edgar Dewitt Jones Papers, Detroit Public Library.

26. Pleading by Lincoln in case of *Beatty et ux. vs. Miller et ux.* (1845), Martha L. Benner and Cullom Davis, eds., *The Law Practice of Abraham Lincoln: Complete Documentary Edition* [hereafter cited as *LPAL*] (Champaign: University of Illinois Press, 2000), case file #02643.

27. Narratio, p. 5, in *Martin vs. Underwood* (1857–1858), *LPAL*, case file #01953.

28. Declaration in *Cantrall vs. Prim* (1849), *LPAL*, case file #03010.

29. *Mitchell et ux. vs. Mitchell* (1852), *LPAL*, case file #00673.

30. Declaration in *Torrance vs. Galloway* (1847–1848), *LPAL*, case file #01595.

31. Plea in *Thompson vs. Henline* (1851–1852), *LPAL*, case file #01689; plea in *Davidson vs. McGhilton* (1852), *LPAL*, case file #01753.

32. Declaration in *Patterson et ux. vs. Edwards et ux.* (1843–1844), *LPAL*, case file #00804.

33. Lawrence Weldon, "Reminiscences of Lincoln as a Lawyer," in William Hayes Ward, ed., *Abraham Lincoln, Tributes from His Associates: Reminiscences of Soldiers, Statesmen, and Citizens* (New York: Thomas Y. Crowell, 1895), 246.

34. *Fithian vs. Casseday* (1851), case file #01891, *LPAL*; Willard L. King, *Lincoln's Manager: David Davis* (Cambridge, MA: Harvard University Press, 1960), 81–82; Donald G. Richter, *Lincoln: Twenty Years on the Eastern Prairie* (Mattoon, IL: United Graphics, 1999), 98–110.

35. David Ross Locke, in Allen Thorndike Rice, ed., *Reminiscences of Abraham Lincoln by Distinguished Men of His Time* (New York: North American Review, 1888), 451.

36. Affidavit of 20 Oct. 1838 by Rogers, in the handwriting of Lincoln, *Rogers vs. Rogers* (1838–1839), *LPAL*, case file #04460.

37. Grant Goodrich to Herndon, Chicago, 9 Dec. 1866, *HI*, 510.

38. *Cowls vs. Cowls* (1845–1846), *LPAL*, case file #01617; Dennis E. Suttles, "'For the Well-Being of the Child': The Law and Childhood," in Daniel W. Stowell, ed., *In Tender Consideration: Women, Families, and the Law in Abraham Lincoln's Illinois* (Urbana: University of Illinois Press, 2002), 54–56; Dan W. Bannister, *Lincoln and the Illinois Supreme Court* (Springfield, IL: n.p., 1995), 134.

39. Harris, "My Recollections of Abraham Lincoln," *Woman's Home Companion*, Dec. 1903, p. 15.

40. Herndon, "Analysis of the Character of Abraham Lincoln," 430.

41. Linder to Joseph Gillespie, Chicago, 8 Aug. 1867, Gillespie Papers, ICHi.

42. Isaac N. Arnold, "Reminiscences of the Illinois-Bar Forty Years Ago: Lincoln and Douglas as Orators and Lawyers," paper read before the Bar Association of the State of Illinois, Springfield, 7 Jan. 1881 (pamphlet; Chicago: Fergus, 1881), 20, 22.

43. Hiram W. Beckwith, "Lincoln: Personal Recollections of Him, His Contemporaries and Law Practice in Eastern Illinois," Chicago *Tribune*, 29 Dec. 1895.

44. Henry C. Whitney, *Lincoln the Citizen*, vol. 1 of *A Life of Lincoln*, ed. Marion Mills Miller (2 vols.; New York: Baker & Taylor, 1908), 173; Whitney, *Life on the Circuit*, ed. Angle, 235.

45. Stevens, *A Reporter's Lincoln*, ed. Burlingame, 163; S. Wesley Martin, quoted in Charles Washington Moores, "Abraham Lincoln, Lawyer," *Indiana Historical Society Publications* 7 (1922):502.

46. Lecture by Swett, delivered in Chicago, 20 Feb. 1876, Chicago *Times*, 21 Feb. 1876.

47. James S. Ewing, speech at Bloomington, 12 Feb. 1909, in Isaac N. Phillips, *Abraham Lincoln by Some Men Who Knew Him*, ed. Paul M. Angle (1910; Chicago: Americana House, 1950), 39.

48. Scott, "Lincoln on the Stump and at the Bar."

49. Milton Hay interviewed by John G. Nicolay, Springfield, 4 July 1875, in Michael Burlingame, ed., *An Oral History of Abraham Lincoln: John G. Nicolay's Interviews and Essays* (Carbondale: Southern Illinois University Press, 1996), 27.

50. Scott, "Lincoln on the Stump and at the Bar."

51. Beckwith, "Lincoln: Personal Recollections of Him, His Contemporaries and Law Practice in Eastern Illinois."

52. Paul M. Zall, ed., *Abe Lincoln Laughing: Humorous Anecdotes from Original Sources by and about Abraham Lincoln* (Berkeley: University of California Press, 1982), 118–119; Whitney, *Life on the Circuit*, ed. Angle, 179.

53. Beckwith, "Lincoln: Personal Recollections of Him, His Contemporaries and Law Practice in Eastern Illinois."

54. Felix Ryan of Lincoln, Illinois, and John Strong of Atlanta, Illinois, quoted in Moores, "Abraham Lincoln, Lawyer," 509.

55. Herndon to Truman Bartlett, Springfield, 19 July 1887, Bartlett Papers, MHi.

56. Anonymous manuscript, n. d., doubtless by James C. Robinson, Ida Tarbell Papers, Allegheny College.

57. Letter by Charles Monroe Chase, Chicago, 6 June 1859, in the *DeKalb County Sentinel*, n.d., typed copy, J. G. Randall Papers, DLC.

58. "May Term of the Urbana Court," *Illinois Citizen* (Danville), 29 May 1850.

59. David Davis, interview with Herndon, 19 Sept. 1866, *HI*, 347

60. Logan interviewed by John G. Nicolay, Springfield, 6 July 1875, in Burlingame, ed., *Oral History Abraham Lincoln*, 39.

61. Samuel C. Parks to Herndon, Lincoln, Illinois, 25 Mar. 1866, *HI*, 238–239; Stringer, "From the Sangamon to the Potomac," 114.

62. Ratcliffe Hicks, letter to *The Century Magazine*, New York, 10 Nov. 1893, *The Century Magazine* 47 (Feb. 1894):638.

63. Gillespie to Herndon, Edwardsville, 31 Jan. 1866, *HI*, 182; *Buckmaster for the Use of Dedham vs. Beems and Archer*, *LPAL*, case file #02075.

64. Whitney, *Lincoln the Citizen*, 174.

65. Draft of Lincoln's public letter to Erastus Corning et al., Washington, [12 June 1863], AL MSS DLC.

66. Frederick T. Hill, *Lincoln the Lawyer* (New York: Century, 1906), 181.

67. Judge Owen T. Reeves in Stevens, *A Reporter's Lincoln*, ed. Burlingame, 49.

68. Swett, "An Old Friend's Recollections of David Davis," Chicago *Mail*, n.d., copied in the St. Louis *Globe-Democrat*, 27 June 1888.

69. John T. Lillard, son-in-law of Davis, to Harry E. Pratt, Bloomington, 4 Dec. 1929, in Harry E. Pratt, "David Davis, 1851–1886" (Ph.D. dissertation, University of Illinois, 1930), 58n.

70. "Court and Bar," Clinton *Transcript*, n.d., copied in the Bloomington *Pantagraph*, 12 October 1858, quoted in Lavern Marshall Hamand, "Ward Hill Lamon: Lincoln's 'Particular Friend'" (Ph.D. dissertation, University of Illinois, 1949), 74.

71. Whitney, *Life on the Circuit*, ed. Angle, 77.

72. Usher F. Linder, *Reminiscences of the Early Bench and Bar of Illinois* (Chicago: Chicago Legal News, 1879), 182–183. The text reads "difference he showed," doubtless a misprint for "deference he showed."

73. Herndon to Mrs. Leonard Swett, Springfield, 20 and 22 Feb. 1890, Swett Papers, IHi.

74. Urbana *Clarion*, 29 Oct. 1859, in Pratt, "Davis," 61.

75. Whitney, *Lincoln the Citizen*, 191–192.

76. Charles Henry Davis journal, 7 May 1864, in Charles Henry Davis, *Life of Charles Henry Davis, Rear Admiral, 1807–1877* (Boston: Houghton Mifflin, 1899), 303.

77. *Our Constitution* (Urbana), 18 Apr. 1857.

78. *Vermilion County Press* (Danville), 5 May 1859, in Richter, *Lincoln: Twenty Years on the Eastern Prairie*, 230.

79. Whitney, *Life on the Circuit*, ed. Angle, 62–63.

80. David Davis to William P. Walker, Bloomington, 16 Nov. 1840, Davis Papers, IHi.

81. David Davis to Julius Rockwell, Bloomington, Illinois, 14 May 1844, Davis Papers, DLC.

82. Leonard Sweet's speech, "The Life of Lincoln," delivered at the dedication of the St. Gaudens statue of Lincoln in Chicago, Chicago *Times*, 23 Oct. 1887; T. W. S. Kidd, lecture given in Washington, in Washington correspondence by Frank G. Carpenter, 14 Jan., Cleveland *Leader*, n.d. [probably 1883], clipping in scrapbook, Frank G. Carpenter Papers, DLC.

83. King, *Davis*, 77, 75, 82, 85, 78; David Davis to Julius Rockwell, Bloomington, Illinois, 14 May 1844, Davis Papers, DLC.

84. Clark E. Carr, *The Illini: A Story of the Prairies* (Chicago: McClurg, 1912), 47.

85. Herndon to Isaac N. Arnold, Springfield, 24 Oct. 1883, Herndon Collection, ICHi.

86. David Davis, interview with Herndon, 20 Sept. 1866, *HI*, 350.

87. Carl Sandburg, *Abraham Lincoln: The Prairie Years* (2 vols.; New York: Harcourt, Brace, 1926), 2:297.

88. David Davis, interview with Herndon, 20 Sept. 1866, *HI*, 349.

89. Lecture by Swett, delivered in Chicago, 20 Feb. 1876, Chicago *Times*, 21 Feb. 1876.

90. Whitney, *Life on the Circuit*, ed. Angle, 63.

91. Linder, "Reminiscences of the Late President Lincoln," Washington *Sunday Chronicle*, 23 Apr. 1865.

92. "Personal Reminiscences of the Late Abraham Lincoln by a contributor to the 'Bulletin,'" San Francisco *Daily Evening Bulletin*, 22 Apr. 1865.

93. Herndon to Isaac N. Arnold, Springfield, 24 Oct. 1883, Herndon Collection, ICHi.

94. Gibson W. Harris to George Williams, Springfield, 31 Oct. 1846, in Roger D. Bridges, ed., "Three Letters from a Lincoln Law Student," *Journal of the Illinois State Historical Society* 66 (1973):87.

95. John Dean Caton, *Early Bench and Bar of Illinois* (Chicago: Chicago Legal News, 1893), 185, 228.

96. J. D. Wickizer to Herndon, Chicago, 25 Nov. 1866, *HI*, 424; lecture by Swett, delivered in Chicago, 20 Feb. 1876, Chicago *Times*, 21 Feb. 1876.

97. Lecture by Swett, delivered in Chicago, 20 Feb. 1876, Chicago *Times*, 21 Feb. 1876; Whitney, *Life on the Circuit*, ed. Angle, 181.

98. T. W. S. Kidd, "Town Crier," Ida Tarbell Papers, Allegheny College.

99. Richard Price Morgan, address at Pontiac, Illinois, 12 Feb. 1909, in Phillips, *Lincoln by Some Men Who Knew Him*, ed. Angle, 71–72.

100. Whitney, *Lincoln the Citizen*, 175.

101. Gibson William Harris, "My Recollections of Abraham Lincoln," *Woman's Home Companion*, Jan. 1904, p. 13.

102. David Davis, "Memorial Address on Hon. John T. Stuart," quoted in Pratt, "Davis," 52.

103. Linder to Lincoln, Chicago, 26 Mar. 1864, AL MSS DLC.

104. Joseph Gillespie's introduction to Linder, *Reminiscences*, 18.

105. Williams to Justin Butterfield, Springfield, 10 Dec. 1849, Records of the Department of the Interior, Appointments Division, Central Office Appointment Papers, 1849–1907, box 32, Record Group 48, National Archives, College Park, Maryland.

106. Whitney, *Life on the Circuit*, ed. Angle, 196; Linder, *Reminiscences*, 239.

107. Benjamin P. Thomas, *Abraham Lincoln: A Biography* (New York: Alfred A. Knopf, 1952), 59.

108. Linder, *Reminiscences*, 238.

109. "May Term of the Urbana Court," *Illinois Citizen* (Danville), 29 May 1850; Aurora Hunt, *Kirby Benedict, Frontier Federal Judge* (Glendale, CA: Arthur H. Clarke, 1961), 44–47; Linder, *Reminiscences*, 201, 203.

110. Ralph Emerson Twitchell, *Old Santa Fe: The Story of New Mexico's Ancient Capital* (Santa Fe: Santa Fe Mexican Press, 1925), 351.

111. Danville *Independent*, 15 May 1856, quoted in Hamand, "Ward Hill Lamon," 50.

112. Thomas J. McCormick, ed., *Memoirs of Gustave Koerner, 1809–1896* (2 vols.; Cedar Rapids, IA: Torch Press, 1909), 2:540.

113. Scott, "Lincoln on the Stump and at the Bar."

114. Whitney, *Life on the Circuit*, ed. Angle, 85–88.

115. Richard Yates to Schuyler Colfax, Springfield, 9 Feb.1861, Abraham Lincoln Collection, Beinecke Library, Yale University;

Leonard Swett in "Our New York Letter," New York correspondence, 6 Feb. *Indiana Journal* (Indianapolis), 10 Feb. 1879; "Court and Bar," Clinton *Transcript*, n.d., copied in the Bloomington *Pantagraph*, 12 Oct. 1858, quoted in Hamand, "Ward Hill Lamon," 74.

116. Ward Hill Lamon, *Recollections of Abraham Lincoln, 1847–1865*, ed. Dorothy Lamon Teillard (2nd ed.; Washington, DC: privately printed, 1911), 17.

117. Ibid., 18–19.

118. Weldon, "Reminiscences of Lincoln as a Lawyer," 246.

119. Lincoln to George P. Floyd, Springfield, 21 Feb. 1856, *CWL*, 2:332–333.

120. Moores, "Abraham Lincoln, Lawyer," 520–521.

121. "More of Old Abe's Peculiarities," New York *Daily News*, 16 Nov. 1861.

122. Basler, ed., *Collected Works of Lincoln, First Supplement*, 20.

123. Lincoln to Andrew McCallen, Springfield, 4 July 1851, *CWL*, 2:106.

124. *CWL*, 4:62.

125. William H. Herndon and Jesse W. Weik, *Herndon's Lincoln*, ed. Douglas L. Wilson and Rodney O. Davis (1889; Urbana: University of Illinois Press, 2006), 194.

126. Whitney, *Lincoln the Citizen*, 182–183.

127. Lincoln to Mason Brayman, Springfield, 31 Mar. 1854, in William D. Beard, "Lincoln and the Illinois Central Railroad," *Lincoln Herald* 92 (1990):16.

128. Herndon to Mrs. Leonard Swett, Springfield, 22 Feb. 1890, Swett Papers, IHi.

129. *CWL*, 2:459; *LPAL*, case file #02160.

130. *LPAL*, case file #02489.

131. Dan W. Bannister, *Lincoln and the Illinois Supreme Court* (Springfield IL: n.p., 1995), 78.

132. John B. Thomas to Thompson R. Webber, "at home," 15 Sept. 1853, John W. Starr, *Lincoln and the Railroads: A Biographical Study* (New York: Dodd, Mead, 1927), 61.

133. Starr, *Lincoln and the Railroads*, 69.

134. Rock Island Railroad, "Seventieth Anniversary Brochure" (1922), p. 19, quoted in John J. Duff, *A. Lincoln: Prairie Lawyer* (New York: Rinehart, 1960), 129; L. O. Leonard, "The Founders and Builders of the Rock Island: Article 3, Abraham Lincoln," *Rock Island Magazine*, Feb. 1926, p. 5.

135. Colonel Peter A. Dey, an engineer on the Mississippi and Missouri Railroad, in Hill, *Lincoln the Lawyer*, 260–261n.

136. Grant Goodrich to William H. Herndon, Chicago, 9 Dec. 1866, *HI*, 511.

137. Reminiscences of Wells H. Blodgett, Ida M. Tarbell, *The Life of Abraham Lincoln* (2 vols.; New York: McClure, Phillips, 1902), 1:276.

138. Albert A. Woldman, *Lawyer Lincoln* (Boston: Houghton Mifflin, 1936), 164.

139. Bannister, *Lincoln and the Illinois Supreme Court*, 57.

140. Davis to Julius Rockwell, Bloomington, 10 Feb. 1841, David Davis Papers, IHi.

141. Whitney, *Life on the Circuit*, ed. Angle, 234.

142. Grant Goodrich to Herndon, Chicago, 9 Dec. 1866, *HI*, 510.

143. Harding's recollections in Robert Henry Parkinson, "The Patent Case that Lifted Lincoln into a Presidential Candidate," *Abraham Lincoln Quarterly* 4 (1946): 113–115.

144. William B. H. Dowse to Albert J. Beveridge, Boston, 16 Oct. 1925, Beveridge Papers, DLC.

145. Duff, *A. Lincoln: Prairie Lawyer,* 323; Donn Piatt in Benjamin P. Thomas and Harold M. Hyman, *Stanton: The Life and Times of Lincoln's Secretary of War* (New York: Alfred A. Knopf, 1962), 66; Benjamin Rush Cowen, *Abraham Lincoln: An Appreciation by One Who Knew Him* (Cincinnati: Robert Clarke, 1909), 10–12.

146. William B. H. Dowse to Albert J. Beveridge, Boston, 10 Oct. 1925, Beveridge Papers, DLC.

147. Report of a statement by Harding, n.d., typescript, Ida M. Tarbell Papers, Allegheny College.

148. W. M. Dickson, "Abraham Lincoln at Cincinnati," *Harper's New Monthly Magazine* 69 (June 1884):62.

149. Matheny in an unidentified newspaper clipping, Pasfield Scrapbook, IHi, quoted in Duff, *A. Lincoln, Prairie Lawyer*, 81–82.

150. Thomas Ford, *History of Illinois from Its Commencement as a State in 1818 to 1847*, ed. Rodney O. Davis (1854; Urbana: University of Illinois Press, 1995) 55.

151. *People vs. Goings* (1859), case file #01800, *LPAL*; John A. Lupton, "A. Lincoln, Esquire: The Evolution of a Lawyer," in Allen D. Spiegel, *A. Lincoln, Esquire: A Shrewd, Sophisticated Lawyer in His Time* (Macon, GA: Mercer University Press, 2002), 41.

152. Whitney to Herndon, Chicago, 27 Aug. 1887, *HI*, 632–633; Whitney, statement for Herndon, [1887?], ibid., 650.

153. Thomas S. Edwards, interviewed by John Hay, Sept. 1860, Michael Burlingame, ed., *Lincoln's Journalist: John Hay's Anonymous Writings for the Press, 1860–1864* (Carbondale: Southern Illinois University Press, 1998), 11.

154. J. N. Gridley, "Lincoln's Defense of Duff Armstrong: The Story of the Trial and the Celebrated Almanac" (pamphlet; Illinois State Historical Society, 1910), 21.

155. Tarbell, *Lincoln*, 1:272.

156. Milton Logan, interviewed in a dispatch datelined Boone, Iowa, 5 Sept. [1905], unidentified clipping, LMF.

157. John T. Brady in Gridley, "Lincoln's Defense of Duff Armstrong," 19.

158. Allen T. Lucas to Albert J. Beveridge, Chandlerville, Illinois, 2 Oct. 1925, Beveridge Papers, DLC.

159. Document #20690, jury instructions, *People vs. Armstrong*, case file #00800, *LPAL*.

160. Brady in Gridley, "Lincoln's Defense of Duff Armstrong," 20.

161. Milton Logan, interviewed in a dispatch datelined Boone, Iowa, 5 Sept. [1905], unidentified clipping, LMF.

162. Duff Armstrong, interviewed by J. McCan Davis, Los Angeles *Times*, 7 June 1896.

163. "Thrilling Episode in the Life of 'Abe Lincoln,'" Cleveland *Leader*, n.d., copied in the *Independent Democrat* (Concord, NH), 7 June 1860.

164. Brady in Gridley, "Lincoln's Defense of Duff Armstrong," 20.

165. J. Henry Shaw to Herndon, Beardstown, 22 Aug. and 5 Sept. 1866, *HI*, 316, 333; J. Henry Shaw in Gridley, "Lincoln's Defense of Duff Armstrong," 20.

166. William Walker to Herndon, Havana, 3 June 1865, *HI*, 22–23.

167. James Harriott, undated interview with Herndon, *HI*, 704.

168. Brady in Gridley, "Lincoln's Defense of Duff Armstrong," 19.

169. Hannah Armstrong, interview with Herndon, [1866], *HI*, 526.

170. "Interesting Story of Lincoln's Defense of Duff Armstrong," based on reminiscences of Duff's brother A. P. Armstrong, *Daily Illinoisan-Star* (Beardstown), 12 Feb. 1916.

171. Gibson William Harris, "My Recollections of Abraham Lincoln," *Woman's Home Companion*, Nov. 1903, p. 11.

172. Hill, *Lincoln the Lawyer*, 186–187.

173. "Joe Blackburn and Mr. Lincoln," undated clipping from the Chicago *News*, LMF.

174. "A Helping Hand," unidentified clipping, LMF.

175. Lawrence Weldon, "Reminiscences of Lincoln as a Lawyer," in William Hayes Ward, ed., *Abraham Lincoln: Tributes from His Associates* (New York: Thomas Y. Crowell, 1895), 241.

176. Jesse W. Weik, "A Law Student's Recollection of Abraham Lincoln," *The Outlook* (1911), 312–313.

177. Gibson William Harris, "My Recollections of Abraham Lincoln," *Woman's Home Companion*, Dec. 1903, p. 15.

178. R. R. Hitt, Journal, 274, Hitt Papers, DLC. The date for this entry is unclear, but probably sometime between Nov. 1860 and Feb. 1861.

179. Joseph Medill to Lincoln, Washington, 18 Dec. 1860, AL MSS DLC.

180. Whitney, *Lincoln the Citizen*, 177.

181. Declaration in *Regnier vs. Cabot and Taylor*, *LPAL*, case file #00158; Samuel C. Parks to Herndon, Lincoln, Illinois, 25 Mar. 1866, *HI*, 239.

182. Scott, "Lincoln on the Stump and at the Bar."

183. Whitney to Herndon, Chicago, 27 Aug. 1887, *HI*, 630.

184. Reminiscences of Adlai E. Stevenson, in Hill, *Lincoln the Lawyer*, 219.

185. *Pacific Commercial Advertiser*, n.d., copied in the New York *Sun*, 29 May 1908.

186. Wilson and Davis, eds., *Herndon's Lincoln*, 213; David Davis, interview with Herndon, 20 Sept. 1866, *HI*, 350.

187. Herndon to Weik, Springfield, 12 Nov. 1885, H-W MSS DLC.

188. Lincoln's amended bill in *Todd vs. Ware*, case file #5877, *LPAL*.

189. Herndon, "Analysis of the Character of Abraham Lincoln," 432–433.

190. Thomas Wesley Shastid, paraphrased in Thomas Hall Shastid, *My Second Life: An Autobiography* (Ann Arbor, MI: George Wahr, 1944), 62n.

191. Whitney, *Lincoln the Citizen*, 176.

192. Henry McHenry to Herndon, Petersburg, Illinois, 29 May 1865, *HI*, 15.

193. George M. Angell's reminiscences, in an undated clipping marked "originally in the Crickfield Bros. Papers," reminiscence files, folder 7, Abraham Lincoln Association files, IHi.

194. Reminiscences of a juror, George Minier, 1882, in Osborn H. Oldroyd, ed., *Lincoln Memorial: Album-Immortelles* (New York: G. W. Carleton, 1883), 188–189; Arnold, *Lincoln*, 85-87.

195. Lecture by Swett, delivered in Chicago, 20 Feb. 1876, Chicago *Times*, 21 Feb. 1876.

196. Whitney, *Lincoln the Citizen*, 179.

197. Undated memo by J. S. S., William E. Barton Papers, University of Chicago.

198. Reminiscences of Lawrence Weldon, in Hill, *Lincoln the Lawyer*, 215.

199. Kidd, "Town Crier," Ida Tarbell Papers, Allegheny College.

200. Lincoln told this story sometime during the Civil War, probably in 1863. Michael Burlingame and John R. Turner Ettlinger, eds., *Inside Lincoln's White House: The Complete Civil War Diary of John Hay* (Carbondale: Southern Illinois University Press, 1997), 77 (entry for [July–August 1863]).

201. Reminiscences of Henry Rickel, Cedar Rapids, Iowa, *Evening Gazette*, 6 Feb. 1909.

202. Newton Bateman, *Abraham Lincoln: An Address* (Galesburg, IL: Cadmus Club, 1899), 11–13.

203. Reminiscences of Hon. J. G. Gest, Xenia, Ohio, *Torchlight*, n.d., copied in the New York *Times*, 27 Feb. 1888.

204. Stringer, "From the Sangamon to the Potomac," 129.

205. Joseph Gillespie to Herndon, Edwardsville, 31 Jan. 1866, *HI*, 187.

206. Lawrence Weldon in Hill, *Lincoln the Lawyer*, 190.

207. Wilson and Davis, eds., *Herndon's Lincoln*, 216; William H. Somers to James R. B. Van Cleve, 7 Dec. 1908, in Pratt, "Judge Lincoln," 36; King, *Davis*, 95–97.

208. Herndon, "Lincoln the Lawyer," in Emanuel Hertz, ed., *The Hidden Lincoln: From the Letters and Papers of William H. Herndon* (New York: Viking, 1938), 428.

209. Allen B. Clough to Andrew Clough, Tolono, Illinois, 21 Aug. 1860, Clough Papers, ICHi.

210. Elliott B. Herndon, statement for William H. Herndon, [1865–1866], *HI*, 459–460.

211. Chicago *Journal*, 12 Feb. 1909.

212. Lawrence Weldon in Rice, ed., *Reminiscences of Lincoln*, 200.

213. Gibson William Harris, "My Recollections of Abraham Lincoln," *Woman's Home Companion*, Dec. 1903, p. 15.

214. Herndon to Weik, Springfield, 18 Feb. 1887, H-W MSS DLC.

215. Gibson William Harris, "My Recollections of Abraham Lincoln," *Woman's Home Companion*, Jan. 1904, p. 13.

216. Whitney to Herndon, n.p., 23 June 1887, *HI*, 616.

217. Mason Brayman quoted in an undated memorandum by his daughter, Mrs. Mary Brayman Gowdy, Ida Tarbell Papers, Allegheny College.

218. Wilson and Davis eds., *Herndon's Lincoln*, 210; Herndon to Weik, Chicago, 9 Dec. 1886, H-W MSS DLC.

219. *CWL*, 8:424.

220. Lincoln to Richard S. Thomas, Springfield, 27 June 1850, *CWL*, 2:80.

221. Lincoln to Alexander, n. p., [13 June 1854], *CWL*, 2:218–219.

222. Affidavit dated 9 Feb. 1846, in John P. Frank, *Lincoln as a Lawyer* (Urbana: University of Illinois Press, 1961), 18.

223. Quoted in Nelson G. Edwards to William E. Barton, Lexington, Virginia, 15 Jan. 1927, Barton Papers, University of Chicago.

224. Lincoln to Levi Davis, Springfield, 15 Mar. 1838, *CWL*, 1:116.

225. Schuyler Colfax in Rice, ed., *Reminiscences of Lincoln*, 333–334.

226. Weldon, "Reminiscences of Lincoln as a Lawyer," 241–242.

227. Letter by Charles Monroe Chase, Chicago, 6 June 1859, in the *DeKalb County Sentinel*, n.d., typed copy, J. G. Randall Papers, DLC.

228. Whitney, *Life on the Circuit*, ed. Angle, 235.

229. "Personal Reminiscences of the Late Abraham Lincoln by a Contributor to the 'Bulletin,'" San Francisco *Daily Evening Bulletin*, 22 Apr. 1865

230. Ann M. Scanlon, "Dun & Bradstreet's Credit Rating of Abraham Lincoln," *Lincoln Herald* 77 (1975):124.

231. Thurlow Weed Barnes, *Life of Thurlow Weed Including His Autobiography and a Memoir* (2 vols.; Boston: Houghton Mifflin, 1884), 1:610–611.

232. Titian J. Coffey in Rice, ed., *Reminiscences of Lincoln*, 240.

233. "Personal Reminiscences of the Late Abraham Lincoln by a Contributor to the 'Bulletin,'" San Francisco *Daily Evening Bulletin*, 22 Apr. 1865.

234. *CWL*, 2:132.

235. Ibid., 4:67.

236. Speech of 14 and 26 Aug. 1852, *CWL*, 2:135–157.

237. *Our Constitution* (Urbana), 4 July 1857.

238. John G. Nicolay, "Abraham Lincoln," speech of 14 Apr. 1894, Nicolay Papers, DLC.

239. Herndon to Jesse W. Weik, Springfield, 7, 10 Jan. 1886, H-W MSS DLC.

240. Fragment on Douglas, [Dec. 1856?], *CWL*, 2:382–383.

241. Notes for a law lecture, Basler, ed., *Collected Works of Lincoln, First Supplement*, 18.

242. Herndon to Jesse W. Weik, [Springfield], 15 Dec. 1886, in Hertz, ed., *Hidden Lincoln*, 113.

243. Herndon, "Facts Illustrative of Mr. Lincoln's Patriotism and Statesmanship," lecture given in Springfield, 24 Jan. 1866, *Abraham Lincoln Quarterly* 3 (1944–1945): 188–189.

244. Speed to Herndon, Louisville, 7 Feb. 1866, *HI*, 197.

245. Lucy Harmon McPherson, *Life and Letters of Oscar Fitzalan Harmon* (Trenton, NJ: MacCrellish & Quigley, 1914), 11.

246. Ibid.

247. Mary Todd Lincoln to James Smith, Marienbad, 8 June 1870, Justin G. Turner and Linda Levitt Turner, eds., *Mary Todd Lincoln: Her Life and Letters* (New York: Alfred A. Knopf, 1972), 567–568.

248. Lincoln to John D. Johnston, Springfield, 12 Jan. 1851, *CWL*, 2:97.

249. Emerson's journal, entry for 31 Jan. 1862, in Louis P. Masur, ed., *The Real War Will Never Get in the Books: Selections from Writers during the Civil War* (New York: Oxford University Press, 1993), 127.

250. Herndon, "Lincoln Individually," H-W MSS DLC.

251. Joshua Speed, *Reminiscences of Abraham Lincoln and Notes of a Visit to California: Two Lectures* (Louisville, KY: John P. Morton, 1884), 34.

252. Speed to Herndon, Louisville, 6 Dec. 1866, *HI*, 499.

253. Nathan M. Knapp to O. M. Hatch, Winchester, Illinois, 12 May 1859, Hatch Papers, IHi.

254. Forney interviewed in the Washington *Evening Star*, 27 June 1891.

255. David Dixon Porter, *Incidents and Anecdotes of the Civil War* (New York: Appleton, 1885), 283.

256. John H. Littlefield, "Recollections of One Who Studied Law with Lincoln," in Ward, ed., *Abraham Lincoln, Tributes from His Associates*, 204–205.

257. A document in Gillespie's papers, quoted in Josephine G. Pricket, "Joseph Gillespie," *Transactions of the Illinois State Historical Society for the Year 1912* (publication no. 17 of the Illinois State Historical Library), 108.

258. Henry C. Whitney, "Abraham Lincoln: A Study from Life," *Arena* 19 (1898):466.

259. Reminiscences of James A. Connolly, Peoria, Illinois, *Journal*, 11 Feb. 1910.

260. Reminiscences of Peter van Duchene, Milwaukee *Free Press*, 3 Feb. 1909.

261. Swisshelm in Oldroyd, ed., *Lincoln Memorial*, 413.

262. E. J. Edwards, quoting the conductor, Gilbert Finch, then retired and residing in Connecticut, New York *Times*, 24 Jan. 1909.

263. Noah Brooks, "Personal Recollections of Abraham Lincoln," *Harper's New Monthly Magazine*, July 1865, in Michael Burlingame, ed., *Lincoln Observed: Civil War Dispatches of Noah Brooks* (Baltimore, MD: Johns Hopkins University Press, 1998), 211.

264. Undated statement by a Dr. Parker, in John G. Nicolay's hand, Nicolay-Hay Papers, IHi.

Chapter 10. "Aroused as He Had Never Been Before"

1. Autobiography written for John Locke Scripps [ca. June 1860], Roy P. Basler et al., eds., *Collected Works of Abraham Lincoln* [hereafter *CWL*] (8 vols. plus index; New Brunswick, NJ: Rutgers University Press, 1953–1955), 4:67.

2. Mrs. Archibald Dixon, *History of Missouri Compromise and Slavery in American Politics: A True History of the Missouri Compromise and Its Repeal, and of African Slavery as a Factor in American Politics* [hereafter *True History*](2nd ed.; Cincinnati: Clarke, 1903), 445.

3. George G. Fogg to Elihu B. Washburne, Exeter, New Hampshire, 18 Mar. 1854, Israel Washburn Papers, DLC.

4. David M. Potter, *The Impending Crisis, 1848–1861,* ed. Don E. Fehrenbacher (New York: Harper & Row, 1976), 163.

5. New York *Tribune*, 10 May 1854.

6. William Henry Seward to Frances A. Seward, 19 Feb. 1854, in Frederic W. Seward, *William H. Seward; An Autobiography from 1801 to 1834, with a Memoir of His Life, and Selections from His Letters* (3 vols.; New York: Derby and Miller, 1891), 2:222.

7. Charles Henry Ray to Elihu B. Washburne, Galena, 14 Feb. 1854, Washburne Papers, DLC.

8. Douglas, speech at Pontiac, Illinois, 2 Sept. 1858, in Paul M. Angle, ed., *Created Equal? The Complete Lincoln-Douglas Debates of 1858* (Chicago: University of Chicago Press, 1958), 180.

9. Speech at Peoria, 16 Oct. 1854, *CWL*, 2:282.

10. Undated reminiscences of A. W. French, Ida M. Tarbell Papers, Allegheny College.

11. *Illinois State Journal* (Springfield), 27 July 1854.

12. David Davis to Julius Rockwell, Bloomington, Illinois, 15 July 1854, Davis Papers, IHi.

13. New York *Tribune,* 10 May 1854.

14. Stephen L. Hansen, *The Making of the Third Party System: Voters and Parties in Illinois, 1850–1876* (Ann Arbor, MI: UMI Research Press, 1980), 50.

15. Quincy *Herald,* 12 Sept. 1854.

16. Ibid., 16 Sept. 1854.

17. Chicago *Times,* n.d., copied in the Joliet *Signal,* 17 Oct. 1854.

18. Pittsfield *Union,* ca. 27 Sept. 1854, quoted in *The Free Press* (Pittsfield, IL), 28 Sept. 1854.

19. Arthur C. Cole, ed., *The Constitutional Debates of 1847* (vol. 14, Illinois Historical Collections; Springfield: Illinois State Historical Library, 1919), 216–217.

20. Chicago *Times,* 2 Aug. 1861, 2 Oct. 1858.

21. Springfield correspondence, 4 Jan., New York *Tribune,* 13 Jan. 1855.

22. *Illinois State Journal* (Springfield), 22 Mar. 1862.

23. Chicago *Tribune,* 12 Aug. 1861.

24. Chicago *Herald,* 18 Apr., 31 May, 7 June 1860.

25. Lincoln, Illinois, correspondence, 16 Aug., *Illinois State Register* (Springfield), 17 Aug. 1860; Dayton, Ohio, newspapers, mid-Sept. 1863, quoted in Frank L. Klement, *The Limits of Dissent: Clement L. Vallandigham and the Civil War* (Lexington: University Press of Kentucky, 1970), 247.

26. George W. Julian, *Political Recollections, 1840 to 1872* (Chicago: Jansen, McClurg, 1884), 115; G. W. Julian, *Speeches on Political Questions* (New York: Hurd and Houghton, 1872), 127.

27. William Wick, *Congressional Globe,* 29th Congress, 2nd Session, appendix, 159 (2 Feb. 1847).

28. Howe to William P. Fessenden, 28 Aug. 1864, Howe Papers, Historical Society of Wisconsin, quoted in Hans L. Trefousse, *The Radical Republicans: Lincoln's Vanguard for*

Racial Justice (New York: Alfred A. Knopf, 1969), 31; Kenneth M. Stampp, *America in 1857: A Nation on the Brink* (New York: Oxford University Press, 1990) 133.

29. *Ohio Patriot,* n.d., quoted in the Athens *Messenger,* 26 June 1857, in Richard H. Sewell, *Ballots for Freedom: Antislavery Politics in the United States, 1837–1860* (New York: Oxford University Press, 1976), 322.

30. Cincinnati *Commercial,* 3 Sept. 1858.

31. *Congressional Globe,* 36th Congress, 1st Session, appendix, 155 (7 Mar. 1860), in Trefousse, *Radical Republicans,* 30.

32. *Missouri Democrat,* 4 Apr. 1857, copied in the New York *Tribune,* 10 Apr. 1857.

33. New York *Tribune,* 29 Feb. 1860.

34. Greeley, "Christianity and Color," *The Independent* (New York), 20 Sept. 1860.

35. New York *Tribune,* 22 Sept. 1855.

36. Ibid., 3 Aug. 1857.

37. Theodore Parker to a Miss Hunt, 16 Nov. 1857, Octavius Brooks Frothingham, *Theodore Parker: A Biography* (Boston: Osgood, 1874), 467.

38. Theodore Parker, *The Present Aspect of Slavery in America and the Immediate Duty of the North* (Boston: Bela Marsh, 1858), 5.

39. Theodore Parker, *John Brown's Expedition in a Letter from Theodore Parker, at Rome, to Francis Jackson, Boston,* in Frances Power Cobbe, ed., *The Collected Works of Theodore Parker: Containing His Theological, Polemical, and Critical Writings, Sermons, Speeches, and Addresses, and Literary Miscellanies* (12 vols.; London: Trubner, 1863–1865), 12:173.

40. Channing paraphrased in William Lloyd Garrison to Lewis Tappan, Brooklyn, Connecticut, 17 Dec. 1835, in Walter M. Merrill, ed., *The Letters of William Lloyd Garrison* (6 vols.; Cambridge, MA: Belknap Press of Harvard University Press, 1971–1981), 1:581.

41. Nathaniel Paul, speech to the Albany Anti-Slavery Convention, 1 Mar. 1838, *Friend of Man,* 14 Mar. 1838, quoted in Jane H. Pease and William H. Pease, *They Who Would Be*

Free: Blacks' Search for Freedom, 1830–1861 (New York: Atheneum, 1974), 84.

42. William H. Herndon to John A. McClernand, Springfield, 8 Dec. 1859, McClernand Papers, IHi.

43. *The National Era* (Washington), 2 June 1853.

44. New York *Journal of Commerce*, 26 Oct. 1860.

45. Louis Agassiz to Samuel G. Howe, [Nahant], 10 Aug. 1863, in Elizabeth Cary Agassiz, ed., *Louis Agassiz: His Life and Correspondence* (2 vols.; Boston: Houghton Mifflin, 1893), 2:605–607.

46. Turner, *The Three Great Races of Men: Their Origin, Character and Destiny with Special Regard to the Present Conditions and Future Destiny of the Black Race in the United States* (Springfield, IL: Bailhache & Baker, 1861), 38, 47.

47. Bayard Taylor, lecture on "Man and Climate," quoted in the Cleveland *Plain Dealer*, 12 Jan. 1861, in Howard Cecil Perkins, ed., *Northern Editorials on Secession* (2 vols.; New York: D. Appleton-Century, 1942), 1:489.

48. "Speech of Gov. Chase at Sandusky, Ohio, August 25, 1859," clipping, box 17, Chase Papers, Historical Society of Pennsylvania, in Eric Foner, *Free Soil, Free Labor, Free Men: The Ideology of the Republican Party before the Civil War* (New York: Oxford University Press, 1995), 264.

49. Springfield (Massachusetts) *Republican*, 6 Oct. 1858.

50. Editorials quoted in Kenneth M. Stampp, "Race, Slavery, and the Republican Party of the 1850s," in Stampp, *The Imperiled Union: Essays on the Background of the Civil War* (New York: Oxford University Press, 1980), 109.

51. New York *Tribune*, 6 Mar. 1860.

52. Greeley quoted in *The Liberator* (Boston), 5 Oct. 1860.

53. "Shall the Territories be Africanized," speech of James Harlan, 4 Jan. 1860, quoted in William L. Barney, *The Road to Secession: A New Perspective on the Old South* (New York: Praeger, 1972), 124–125.

54. Alfred Caldwell, speech in Richmond to a convention of Whigs and others opposed to the Democrats, Wheeling, Virginia, *Intelligencer*, 7 Feb. 1859, quoted in Patricia P. Hicken, "Antislavery in Virginia, 1831–1861" (Ph.D. dissertation, University of Virginia, 1968), 723.

55. *Illinois State Chronicle* (Decatur), 17 June 1858.

56. William Cary to Elihu B. Washburne, Galena, 16 May 1858, Washburne Papers, DLC.

57. *Illinois State Journal* (Springfield), 15 July 1857.

58. Quoted in Stampp, "Race, Slavery, and the Republican Party," 109–110.

59. Chicago *Tribune*, 14 Mar. 1863.

60. *The Free Press* (Pittsfield, IL), 31 July 1856.

61. *Illinois Journal* (Springfield), 24 Mar. 1854.

62. Ibid., 11 Sept. 1854, *CWL*, 2:229–230.

63. Henry W. Hilliard, *Politics and Pen Pictures at Home and Abroad* (New York: G. P. Putnam's Sons, 1892), 129.

64. A Massachusetts editor quoted in Gerald M. Capers, *Stephen A. Douglas: Defender of the Union* (Boston: Little, Brown, 1959), 13–14.

65. James L. Huston, *Stephen A. Douglas and the Dilemmas of Democratic Equality* (Lanham, MD: Rowman and Littlefield, 2006), 8.

66. John W. Forney, *Anecdotes of Public Men* (2 vols.; New York: Harper & Brothers, 1873–1881), 1:146–147.

67. John Russell Young's autobiography, manuscript, Young Papers, DLC.

68. *The Reminiscences of Carl Schurz* (3 vols.; New York: McClure, 1907–1908), 2:30–31.

69. John Russell Young's autobiography, manuscript, Young Papers, DLC; New York *Tribune*, 6 Sept. 1866.

70. Horace White, "The Lincoln and Douglas Debates: An Address before the Chicago Historical Society, February 17, 1914" (pamphlet; Chicago: University of Chicago Press, 1914), 8.

71. Springfield, Massachusetts, *Republican,* 30 June 1860.

72. Schurz, *Reminiscences,* 2:30–32.

73. Washington correspondence by James Shepherd Pike, 4 Mar., New York *Tribune,* 7 Mar. 1854.

74. Robert W. Johannsen, *Stephen A. Douglas* (New York: Oxford University Press, 1973), 503.

75. Chicago correspondence, 1 Sept., New York *Tribune,* 9 Sept. 1860.

76. Washington correspondence, 4 Mar., New York *Tribune,* 7 Mar. 1854; Glyndon G. Van Deusen, *William Henry Seward* (New York: Oxford University Press, 1967), 153.

77. Godkin, dispatch of 13 July 1858, Rollo Ogden, ed., *Life and Letters of Edwin Lawrence Godkin* (2 vols.; New York: Macmillan, 1907), 1:178.

78. Speech at Richmond, Virginia, 9 July 1852, copy, George Fort Milton Papers, DLC.

79. Charles Francis Adams, ed., *Memoirs of John Quincy Adams, Comprising Portions of His Diary from 1795 to 1848* (12 vols.; Philadelphia: J. B. Lippincott, 1874–1877), 11:510–511 (diary entry for 14 Feb. 1844).

80. Boston correspondence by "Warrington" [William Stevens Robinson], 19 July, Springfield, Massachusetts, *Republican,* 20 July 1860.

81. Springfield, Massachusetts, *Republican,* 30 June 1860.

82. Isaac N. Arnold, remarks in the House of Representatives, Washington *Chronicle,* 21 Mar. 1864.

83. Isaac N. Arnold, "Reminiscences of the Illinois Bar Forty Years Ago: Lincoln and Douglas as Orators and Lawyers" (pamphlet; Chicago: Fergus, 1881), 20, in John M. Palmer, *The Bench and Bar of Illinois: Historical and Reminiscent* (2 vols: Chicago: Lewis, 1899), 1:177.

84. Horace White, "Abraham Lincoln's Rise to Greatness," New York *Evening Post,* 13 Feb. 1909.

85. William M. Dickson, "Abraham Lincoln at Cincinnati," *Harper's New Monthly Magazine* 69 (June 1884):64.

86. Speech at Chicago, 27 Oct. 1854, *CWL,* 2:283.

87. Washington correspondence by Harriet Beecher Stowe, n.d., New York *Independent,* 1 May 1856.

88. Archibald Dixon to Henry S. Foote, 1 Oct. 1858, in Mrs. Archibald Dixon, *True History,* 445.

89. Yates's speech in Springfield, 20 Nov. 1860, *Illinois State Journal* (Springfield), 22 Nov. 1860.

90. Recollections of Paul Selby, in Francis Fisher Browne, *The Every-Day Life of Abraham Lincoln* (2nd ed.; New York: G. P. Putnam's Sons, 1913), 160.

91. Robert L. Wilson to Elihu B. Washburne, Chicago, 19 Sept. 1854, Washburne Papers, DLC.

92. Lincoln to John M. Palmer, Springfield, 7 Sept. 1854, *CWL,* 2:228.

93. R. H. Ballinger's reminiscences, Seattle *Post-Intelligencer,* n.d., copied in the Los Angeles *Times,* 20 June 1894.

94. Speech at Springfield 9 Sept. 1854, *CWL,* 2:229.

95. Lincoln to Speed, Springfield, 24 Aug. 1855, *CWL,* 2:323.

96. David Davis to Julius Rockwell, Bloomington, Illinois, 27 Dec. 1855, Davis Papers, DLC.

97. Statement by Jayne, 15 Aug. 1866, Douglas L. Wilson and Rodney O. Davis, eds., *Herndon's Informants: Letters, Interviews, and Statements about Abraham Lincoln* [hereafter *HI*] (Urbana: University of Illinois Press, 1998), 266.

98. Henry C. Whitney, *Lincoln the Citizen,* vol. 1 of *A Life of Lincoln,* ed. Marion Mills Miller (2 vols. New York: Baker and Taylor, 1908), 150.

99. Lincoln to Elihu N. Powell, Springfield, 27 Nov. 1854, *CWL,* 2:289.

100. James S. Ewing, speech at the banquet of the Illinois Schoolmasters' Club, Bloomington, Illinois, 12 Feb. 1909, in Isaac N. Phillips, *Abraham Lincoln, by Some Men Who Knew Him,* ed. Paul M. Angle (1910; Chicago: Americana House, 1950), 44.

101. Francis Lynde Stetson to Horace White, New York, 7 Dec. 1908, in Horace White, *The Life of Lyman Trumbull* (Boston: Houghton Mifflin, 1913), 40n.

102. James S. Ewing, in Walter B. Stevens, *A Reporter's Lincoln*, ed. Michael Burlingame (1916; Lincoln: University of Nebraska Press, 1998), 60.

103. Carl Sandburg, *Abraham Lincoln: The Prairie Years* (2 vols.; New York: Harcourt, Brace, 1926), 2:11.

104. Jacob Thompson to Albert J. Beveridge, Springfield, 15 Feb. 1927, Beveridge Papers, DLC.

105. Leonard Bacon, *Slavery Discussed in Occasional Essays, from 1833 to 1846* (New York: Baker and Scribner, 1846), x.

106. Lincoln to Albert G. Hodges, Washington, 4 April 1864, *CWL,* 7:281.

107. Dr. James Miner, "Abraham Lincoln: Personal Reminiscences of the Martyr-Emancipator as He Appeared in the Memorable Campaign of 1854 and in His Subsequent Career," undated typescript, reference files of the Abraham Lincoln Association, IHi.

108. Springfield correspondence by W., 4 Oct., Chicago *Democrat,* 9 Oct. 1854.

109. Collinsville, Illinois, correspondence by W., 15 June, New York *Tribune,* 26 June 1858; Springfield correspondence by W., 4 Oct., Chicago *Journal,* 9 Oct. 1854.

110. Springfield correspondence by W., 4 Oct., Chicago *Journal,* 9 Oct. 1854.

111. Douglas, senate speech of 9 Dec. 1857, Robert W. Johannsen, ed., *The Letters of Stephen A. Douglas* (Urbana: University of Illinois Press, 1961), xxvi.

112. Johannsen, *Douglas,* 446.

113. Cassius M. Clay in Allen Thorndike Rice, ed., *Reminiscences of Abraham Lincoln by Distinguished Men of His Time* (New York: North American Review, 1886), 297.

114. Ward Hill Lamon, *Recollections of Abraham Lincoln, 1847–1865,* ed. Dorothy Lamon Teillard (2nd ed.; Washington, DC: Published by the editor, 1911), 15.

115. Robert H. Browne, *Abraham Lincoln and the Men of His Time* (2 vols.; Cincinnati: Jennings and Pye, 1901), 1:517; Alonzo J. Grover's reminiscences in Browne, *Every-Day Life of Lincoln,* 2nd ed., 249.

116. Letter by Zebina Eastman, unidentified clipping, Eastman Scrapbook, ICHi.

117. Samuel Willard, "Personal Reminiscences of Life in Illinois, 1830 to 1850," *Transactions of the Illinois State Historical Society* 11 (1906):86.

118. Lincoln to Joshua F. Speed, Springfield, 24 Aug. 1855, *CWL,* 2:320.

119. John W. Bunn, statement made to Jesse W. Weik, in Jesse W. Weik, *The Real Lincoln: A Portrait,* ed. Michael Burlingame (1922; Lincoln: University of Nebraska Press, 2002), 198.

120. William Herndon and Jesse W. Weik, *Herndon's Lincoln,* ed. Douglas L. Wilson and Rodney O. Davis (1889; Urbana: University of Illinois Press, 2006), 232–233.

121. Lincoln took notes on Douglas's speech and may have here rendered his words more accurately than the Peoria *Daily Union,* which reported that the Little Giant said: "They [settlers in Kansas] were permitted to legislate upon every subject affecting the white man, but were to be told that they had not sufficient intelligence to legislate for the black man." Peoria *Daily Union,* 24 Oct. 1854, in B. C. Bryner, *Abraham Lincoln in Peoria, Illinois* (2nd ed.; Peoria, IL: Lincoln Historical Publishing Company, 1926), 155–156.

122. Chicago *Tribune,* 30 May 1857.

123. Springfield correspondence by W., 4 Oct., Chicago *Democrat,* 9 Oct. 1854.

124. *CWL,* 2:247–276.

125. Autobiography written for John Locke Scripps [ca. June 1860], ibid., 4:67.

126. *Illinois State Register* (Springfield), 28 Sept. 1854.

127. Horace White, "Abraham Lincoln in 1854," *Transactions of the Illinois State Historical Society, 1908* (Springfield: Illinois State Journal, 1909), 10; White in William H. Herndon and Jesse W. Weik, *Lincoln's*

Herndon, ed. Douglas L. Wilson and Rodney O. Davis (1889; Urbana: University of Illinois Press, 2006), 388–389.

128. Springfield correspondence by W., 4 Oct. 1854, Chicago *Journal,* 9 Oct. 1854.

129. White, *Life of Trumbull,* 39.

130. *Illinois State Journal* (Springfield), 10 Oct. 1854; Wilson and Davis, eds., *Herndon's Lincoln,* 227–228.

131. "Personal Reminiscences of the Late Abraham Lincoln by a contributor to the 'Bulletin,'" San Francisco *Daily Evening Bulletin,* 22 Apr. 1865; *Illinois State Register* (Springfield), 6 Oct. 1854; Springfield correspondence by W., 4 Oct., Chicago *Democrat,* 9 Oct. 1854.

132. *Illinois State Register* (Springfield), 16, 9 Oct. 1854.

133. "Personal Reminiscences of the Late Abraham Lincoln, by a contributor to the 'Bulletin,'" San Francisco *Bulletin,* 22 Apr. 1865.

134. Ward H. Lamon, *The Life of Abraham Lincoln from His Birth to His Inauguration as President* (ghostwritten by Chauncey Black; Boston: J. R. Osgood, 1872), 354.

135. Robert Boal's undated reminiscence, Bryner, *Lincoln in Peoria,* 33–34.

136. *CWL,* 2:276–283.

137. Peoria *Press,* 21 Oct. 1854.

138. Peoria *Republican,* 20 Oct. 1854.

139. Wilson and Davis, eds., *Herndon's Lincoln,* 230.

140. Henry C. Whitney, *Life on the Circuit with Lincoln,* ed. Paul M. Angle (1892; Caldwell, ID: Caxton, 1940), 54, 55.

141. Joliet *Signal,* 14 Nov. 1854, in Arthur Charles Cole, *The Era of the Civil War, 1848–1870* (vol. 3 of *The Centennial History of Illinois,* ed. Clarence Walworth Alvord; Springfield: Illinois Centennial Commission, 1919), 133.

142. New York *Tribune,* 10 Nov. 1854.

143. Palmer to Lyman Trumbull, Carlinville, 11 Jan. 1856, Trumbull Papers, DLC.

144. Lincoln to Richard J. Oglesby, Springfield, 8 Sept. 1854, Roy P. Basler, ed., *Collected Works of Abraham Lincoln, First*

Supplement, 1832–1865 (Westport, CT: Greenwood Press, 1973), 24.

145. Springfield correspondence, 7 Oct., Chicago *Journal,* 12 Oct. 1854.

146. George Gage to Lincoln, McHenry, 4 Oct. 1854, AL MSS DLC. Lincoln's letter to Gage is not extant.

147. Whitney, *Life on the Circuit,* ed. Angle, 149, and "Abraham Lincoln: A Study from Life," *Arena* 19 (Apr. 1898):479–480.

148. Lincoln to Judd, Springfield, 9 Dec. 1859, *CWL,* 3:505.

149. Lincoln's remarks to General Benjamin Welch, memorandum by John G. Nicolay, Springfield, 25 Oct. 1860, Michael Burlingame, ed., *With Lincoln in the White House: Letters, Memoranda, and Other Writings of John G. Nicolay, 1860–1865* (Carbondale: Southern Illinois University Press, 2000), 7.

150. Horace White to Lincoln, Springfield, 25 Oct. 1854, AL MSS DLC.

151. Richard L. Wilson to Lincoln, Chicago, 20 Oct. 1854, ibid.

152. Randolph to Lincoln, Macomb, 29 Sept. 1854, ibid.

153. Jonas to Lincoln, Quincy, 16 Sept. 1854, ibid.

154. Wilson and Davis, eds., *Herndon's Lincoln,* 231.

155. Lincoln to Hoyt, Clinton, 10 Nov. 1854, *CWL,* 2:286.

156. Lincoln to Scammon, Clinton, 10 Nov. 1854, Basler, ed., *Collected Works of Lincoln, First Supplement,* 25.

157. Lincoln to Harding, Clinton, 11 Nov. 1854, *CWL,* 2:286.

158. Lincoln to Henderson, Springfield, 27 Nov. 1854, ibid., 2:288.

159. Lincoln to Joseph Gillespie, Springfield, 1 Dec. 1854, ibid., 2:290.

160. Shields to Lanphier, Belleville, 30 Dec. 1854, Lanphier Papers, IHi.

161. Lawrence B. Stringer, unpublished biography of Lincoln, 160, IHi.

162. David Davis to Lincoln, Bloomington, 27 Dec. 1854, AL MSS DLC.

163. Aurora *Guardian,* 11 Jan. 1855.

164. Rock River *Democrat,* 9 Jan. 1855.

165. Charles H. Ray to Elihu B. Washburne, Chicago, 29 Dec. 1854, Washburne Papers, DLC.

166. Lincoln to Ichabod Codding, Springfield, 27 Nov. 1854, *CWL,* 2:288.

167. Chicago *Free West,* 30 Nov. 1854.

168. Ibid., 14 Dec. 1854.

169. Joliet *Signal,* 19 Dec. 1854.

170. Lincoln to Washburne, Springfield, 11 and 14 Dec. 1854, *CWL,* 2:293.

171. Eastman to Washburne, Chicago, 14 Dec. 1854, Washburne Papers, DLC.

172. Anson S. Miller to Washburne, Rockford, 18 Dec. 1854, ibid.

173. Washburne to Lincoln, Washington, 19 Dec. 1854, AL MSS DLC; Washburne to Eastman, Washington, 19 Dec. 1854, Eastman Papers, ICHi.

174. Herndon to Eastman, Springfield, 6 Feb. 1866, copy, Albert J. Beveridge Papers, DLC.

175. Herndon to Caroline Dall, Springfield, 3 Jan. 1867 [misdated 1866], Dall Papers, Massachusetts Historical Society.

176. Zebina Eastman to Herndon, Bristol, England, 2 Jan. 1866, *HI,* 149–150.

177. Charles H. Ray to Elihu B. Washburne, North Norwich, New York, 16 and 24 Dec. 1854, Washburne Papers, DLC.

178. Washburne to Lincoln, [Washington], 21 Dec. 1854, AL MSS DLC.

179. Washburne to Lincoln, Washington, 17 January 1855, ibid.

180. Charles H. Ray to Elihu B. Washburne, Springfield, 12 Jan. 1855, Washburne Papers, DLC.

181. *CWL,* 2:301.

182. Jesse O. Norton to Lincoln, Washington, 20 Dec. 1854, 20 Jan. 1855, AL MSS DLC.

183. Reminiscences of Thomas J. Henderson, typescript, p. 10, Ida M. Tarbell Papers, Allegheny College.

184. Washburne to Lincoln, Washington, 26 Dec. 1854, AL MSS DLC.

185. Abraham Smith to Lincoln, Ridge Farm, Illinois, 31 May 1858, ibid.

186. Washburne to Lincoln, Washington, 12 Dec. 1854, ibid.

187. Lincoln to Washburne, Springfield, 19 Dec. 1854, *CWL,* 2:295.

188. Lincoln to Norton, Springfield, 16 Feb. 1855, Roy P. Basler and Christian O. Basler, eds., *Collected Works of Abraham Lincoln: Second Supplement, 1848–1865* (New Brunswick, NJ: Rutgers University Press, 1990), 9.

189. Washburne to Zebina Eastman, Washington, 19 Dec. 1854, Eastman Papers, ICHi.

190. Lincoln to Thomas J. Henderson, Springfield, 15 Dec. 1854, *CWL,* 2:293–294.

191. Yates to Lincoln, Washington, 22 Dec. 1854, AL MSS DLC.

192. Joliet *Signal,* 9 Jan. 1855.

193. Reminiscences of Elijah M. Haines in Francis Fisher Browne, *The Every-Day Life of Abraham Lincoln* (2nd ed.; New York: G. P. Putnam's Sons, 1913), 163.

194. Douglas to James W. Sheahan, Washington, 18 Dec. 1854 and 6 Feb. 1855, Johannsen, ed., *Letters of Douglas,* 333.

195. Shields to Charles Lanphier, Washington, 12 Jan. 1855, Lanphier Papers, IHi.

196. J. W. Sheahan to Charles Lanphier, Chicago, 17 Jan. 1855, ibid.

197. Allen to Trumbull, Alton, 19 Jan., 14 June 1866, Trumbull Papers, DLC.

198. Quincy *Whig,* n.d., copied in the Chicago *Tribune,* 23 Feb. 1855.

199. Chicago *Daily Democrat,* 6 Feb. 1855.

200. Lincoln to Washburne, Springfield, 9 Feb. 1855, *CWL,* 2:305.

201. Charles H. Ray to Elihu Washburne, Springfield, 12 Jan. 1855, Washburne Papers, DLC.

202. Mary N. Stuart to Elizabeth T. Stuart, Springfield, 28 Jan. 1855, Stuart-Hay Papers, IHi.

203. Richard J. Oglesby to Richard Yates, Decatur, 27 Jan. 1855, Yates Papers, IHi.

204. John M. Palmer to his wife, Springfield, 31 Jan. 1855, Palmer Papers, IHi.

205. Clark E. Carr, *The Illini: A Story of The Prairies*, (Chicago: McClurg, 1905), 176.

206. Thomas Ford, *A History of Illinois: From its Commencement as a State in 1818 to 1847*, ed. Rodney O. Davis (1854; Urbana: University of Illinois Press, 1995), 272–273.

207. Gustave Koerner to John D. Caton, Vandalia, 17 Aug. 1846, Caton Papers, DLC.

208. Lincoln to Yates, Springfield, 14 Jan. 1855, Basler, ed., *Collected Works of Lincoln, First Supplement*, 26.

209. Springfield correspondence, [8 Feb. 1855], Chicago *Tribune*, 13 Feb. 1855.

210. Chicago *Weekly Democrat*, 11 Aug. 1855.

211. Lincoln to Jesse O. Norton, Springfield, 16 Feb. 1855, Basler and Basler, eds., *Collected Works of Lincoln, Second Supplement*, 10.

212. New York *Tribune*, 9 Feb. 1855.

213. Chicago *Free West*, 15 Feb. 1855.

214. Chicago *Tribune*, 9 Feb. 1855.

215. Lincoln to Washburne, Springfield, 9 Feb. 1855, *CWL*, 2:306.

216. Lyman Trumbull to Salmon P. Chase, Alton, 23 Mar. 1855, Chase Papers, Historical Society of Pennsylvania.

217. Johannsen, *Douglas*, 464.

218. Chicago *Democratic Press*, n.d., copied in the Chicago *Tribune*, 10 Feb. 1855.

219. Lincoln to William H. Henderson, Springfield, 21 Feb. 1855, *CWL*, 2:306–307.

220. Herndon, "Lincoln's Ambition," H-W MSS DLC.

221. E. B. Washburne, "Abraham Lincoln in Illinois," *North American Review*, 1885, 316.

222. Joseph C. Howell to Yates, Springfield, 11 Feb. 1855, Yates Papers, IHi.

223. LeRoy H. Fischer, ed., "Samuel C. Parks's Reminiscences of Abraham Lincoln," *Lincoln Herald* 68 (Spring 1966):11.

224. Gillespie to [M. D. Hardin], Edwardsville, 22 Apr. 1880, Hardin Family Papers, ICHi.

225. Washington correspondence, 30 Sept. [1892?], Chicago *Evening Post*, clipping in the Lincoln Collection, Vertical File, "Reminiscences," folder 3, IHi.

226. White, *Trumbull*, 45.

227. R. E. Hoyt reported that Lincoln said this while riding on a train between Springfield and Decatur. Unidentified letter, probably in a newspaper, Chicago, 4 Oct. [no year indicated], copy of a fragment, Trumbull Papers, IHi.

228. Fischer, ed., "Parks's Reminiscences of Lincoln," 11.

229. Frank G. Carpenter, "From Plowboy to Senator: Shelby Cullom Talks of His Career," Chicago *Sunday Times-Herald*, 3 Nov. 1895, p. 47.

230. Whitney, *Life on the Circuit*, ed. Angle, 150.

231. Parks's statement for Herndon, [1866], *HI*, 538.

232. Speech of James Matheny in the fall of 1856, Chicago *Weekly Times*, 1 July 1858.

233. David Davis to Julius Rockwell, Bloomington, Illinois, 4 Mar. 1855, Davis Papers, DLC.

234. *Illinois State Register*, n.d., copied in the Ottawa *Free Trader*, 17 Feb. 1855; *Illinois State Journal* (Springfield), 13 Feb. 1855.

235. Abraham Smith to Lincoln, Ridge Farm, Illinois, 31 May 1858, AL MSS DLC.

236. Gillespie to Lincoln, Edwardsville, 6 June 1856, H-W MSS DLC.

237. Jean Baker, *Mary Todd Lincoln: A Biography* (New York: W. W. Norton, 1987), 150; Mary Lincoln to Leonard Swett, n.p., 12 Jan. [1867], in Justin G. Turner and Linda Levitt Turner, eds., *Mary Todd Lincoln: Her Life and Letters* (New York: Alfred A. Knopf, 1972), 406; Anson G. Henry to his wife, [Washington], [18?] Feb. 1863, in Charles B. Strozier, *Lincoln's Quest for Union: Public and Private Meanings* (New York: Basic Books, 1982), 76.

238. Julia Jayne Trumbull to Lyman Trumbull, Springfield, 14 Apr. and 5 May 1856, Trumbull Family Papers, IHi.

239. Julia Trumbull to Lyman Trumbull, Chicago, 12 Aug. 1860, Trumbull Family Papers, William L. Clements Library, University of Michigan; Mrs. Norman B. Judd, undated interview with Ida Tarbell, Ida M. Tarbell Papers, Allegheny College.

240. Mary Lincoln to Anson G. Henry, Chicago, 26 July 1865, Turner and Turner, eds., *Mary Todd Lincoln,* 264.

241. Norman B. Judd interviewed by John G. Nicolay, Washington, 28 Feb. 1876, Burlingame, ed., *Oral History of Lincoln,* 45–46.

242. John H. Bryant to Lyman Trumbull, Princeton, Illinois, 12 Feb. 1857, Trumbull Papers, DLC.

243. Washington correspondence, 30 Sept. [1892?], Chicago *Evening Post,* undated clipping in the Lincoln Collection, Vertical File, "Reminiscences," folder 3, IHi.

244. Oglesby to Herndon, Springfield, 5 Jan. 1866, *HI,* 153.

Chapter 11. "Unite with Us, and Help Us to Triumph"

1. Lincoln to Joshua Speed, Springfield, 24 Aug. 1855, Roy P. Basler et al., eds., *Collected Works of Abraham Lincoln* [hereafter *CWL*] (8 vols. plus index; New Brunswick, NJ: Rutgers University Press, 1953–1955), 2:322–323.

2. David Davis to Julius Rockwell, Bloomington, Illinois, 27 Dec. 1855, Davis Papers, DLC.

3. *Illinois State Journal* (Springfield), 23 Nov. 1855.

4. Lincoln to Lovejoy, Springfield, 11 Aug. 1855, *CWL,* 2:316–317.

5. Lyman Trumbull to Owen Lovejoy, Alton, 20 Aug. 1855, Trumbull Family Papers, IHi.

6. Giddings to Lincoln, Peoria, 18 Sept. 1855, H-W MSS DLC.

7. Lincoln to George Robertson, Springfield, 15 Aug, 1855, *CWL,* 2:317–318.

8. Lincoln to Speed, Springfield, 24 Aug. 1855, *CWL,* 2:320-322.

9. Samuel M. Hitt to David Davis, 4 Nov. 1855, in Willard King, *Lincoln's Manager: David Davis* (Cambridge, MA: Harvard University Press, 1960), 109.

10. David Davis to Julius Rockwell, Bloomington, Illinois, 27 Dec. 1855, Davis Papers, DLC.

11. Choate to Charles Eames, Boston, 29 June 1855, in Samuel Gilman Brown, ed., *The Works of Rufus Choate* (2 vols.; Boston: Little, Brown 1862), 1:196.

12. *Pike County Free Press* (Pittsfield), 20 Dec. 1855.

13. Paul Selby to Richard Yates, Jacksonville, 14 Feb. 1856, Yates Papers, IHi.

14. *Pike County Free Press* (Pittsfield), 16 Jan. 1856.

15. Tyler Anbinder, *Nativism and Slavery: The Northern Know Nothings and the Politics of the 1850s* (New York: Oxford University Press, 1992), 227.

16. Charles H. Ray to Lyman Trumbull, Chicago, 21 Mar. 1856, Trumbull Papers, DLC.

17. Charles H. Ray to Elihu B. Washburne, Chicago, 4 May [1856] Washburne Papers, DLC.

18. Frank I. Herriott to Albert J. Beveridge, Des Moines, Iowa, 14 Dec. 1922, Beveridge Papers, DLC.

19. Schneider in Ezra M. Prince, ed., *Bloomington, Illinois, Republican Convention, May 29, 1856 (Transactions of the McLean County Historical Society,* vol. 3 [Bloomington: Pantagraph, 1900]), 90.

20. For the full text of the platform, see Otto R. Kyle, *Lincoln in Decatur* (New York: Vantage Press, 1957), 139–142.

21. Schneider in Prince, ed., *Bloomington Convention,* 90.

22. Ida M. Tarbell, *The Life of Abraham Lincoln* (2 vols.; New York: McClure, Phillips, 1902), 1:291.

23. *Illinois State Chronicle* (Decatur), 28 Feb. 1856; Benjamin F. Shaw in Prince, ed., *Bloomington Convention,* 68.

24. Paul Selby in Tarbell, *Life of Lincoln,* 1:291.

25. John Wentworth to Lincoln, Chicago, 21 Oct. 1856, H-W MSS DLC.

26. New York *Herald,* 19 Sept. 1860, in Howard Cecil Perkins, ed., *Northern Editorials on Secession* (2 vols.; New York: D. Appleton-Century, 1942), 1:36.

27. *Illinois State Journal* (Springfield), 25 Feb. 1856.

28. [John M. Scott], "Lincoln on the Stump and at the Bar," enclosed in Scott to Ida M. Tarbell, Bloomington, 14 Aug. 1895, Tarbell Papers, Allegheny College.

29. Herndon to Trumbull, Springfield, 24 Apr. 1856, Trumbull Papers, DLC.

30. Washburne to Yates, Washington, 2 Apr. 1856, Richard Yates and Catherine Yates Pickering, *Richard Yates, Civil War Governor,* ed. John H. Krenkel (Danville, IL: Interstate Printers, 1966), 116.

31. Bissell to Trumbull, Belleville, 5 May 1856, Trumbull Papers, DLC.

32. Herndon to Trumbull, Springfield, 20 May 1856, ibid.

33. Brown to Lyman Trumbull, Alton, 12 May 1856, ibid.

34. J. O. Cunningham, "Some Recollections of Abraham Lincoln: Delivered before the Firelands Pioneer Association, at Norwalk, Ohio, July 4, 1907, and reprinted from the Pioneer of Dec. 1909" (pamphlet), 6.

35. J. O. Cunningham, "The Bloomington Convention of 1856 and Those Who Participated in It," *Transactions of the Illinois State Historical Society* 10 (1905):104.

36. John Locke Scripps, *Life of Abraham Lincoln,* ed. Roy P. Basler and Lloyd Dunlap (1860; Bloomington: University of Indiana Press, 1961), 121.

37. Henry Clay Whitney, *Life on the Circuit with Lincoln,* ed. Paul M. Angle (1892; Caldwell, ID: Caxton Printers, 1940), 92; Whitney, *Lincoln the Citizen,* vol. 1 of *A Life of Lincoln,* ed. Marion Mills Miller, (2 vols.; New York: Baker and Taylor, 1908), 259.

38. Whitney, *Lincoln the Citizen,* 260.

39. Prince, ed., *Bloomington Convention,* 160–161.

40. Whitney, *Lincoln the Citizen,* 260–261.

41. Prince, ed., *Bloomington Convention,* 160–161.

42. Ibid., 94.

43. Alton *Weekly Courier,* 5 June 1856, in *CWL,* 2:341.

44. Richmond *Enquirer,* n.d., copied in the *Illinois State Journal* (Springfield), 16 Oct. 1858.

45. Belleville *Weekly Advocate,* 4 June 1856.

46. Bloomington correspondence, 29 May, Chicago *Democratic Press,* 31 May 1856, in Prince, ed., *Bloomington Convention,* 174.

47. Bloomington *Pantagraph,* 4 June 1856.

48. Prince, ed., *Bloomington Convention,* 81; Thomas J. Henderson to Ida M. Tarbell, 12 Sept. 1895, Tarbell Papers, Allegheny College; Henderson's reminiscences in the Los Angeles *Times,* 9 Feb. 1896.

49. William Pitt Kellogg, "The Recollections of William Pitt Kellogg," ed. Paul M. Angle, *Abraham Lincoln Quarterly* 3 (1945):323; Cunningham, "Recollections of Lincoln," 8.

50. Scott, "Lincoln on the Stump and at the Bar."

51. Medill to the editor of *McClure's Magazine,* Chicago, 15 May 1896, *McClure's Magazine,* 7 (June–Oct. 1896):322.

52. Peoria *Sunday Star,* 1 Mar. 1908.

53. Whitney, *Lincoln the Citizen,* 261.

54. *CWL,* 2:344.

55. Lincoln to Lyman Trumbull, Springfield, 7 June 1856, ibid., 2:343.

56. John M. Palmer, ed., *The Bench and Bar of Illinois: Historical and Reminiscent* (2 vols.; Chicago: Lewis Publishing Co., 1899), 1:3.

57. Lincoln to Lyman Trumbull, Springfield, 7 June 1856, *CWL,* 2:342–343.

58. Browning to Trumbull, Quincy, 19 May 1856, Trumbull Papers, DLC.

59. Trumbull to Lincoln, Washington, 15 June 1856, Trumbull Family Papers, IHi.

60. *Proceedings of the First Three Republican National Conventions of 1856, 1860 and 1864* (Minneapolis: Charles W. Johnson, 1893), 61–63.

61. H. [Murat Halstead], *Cincinnati Commercial,* 23 June 1856.

62. *Proceedings of the First Three Republican National Conventions,* 62.

63. Quoted in *CWL,* 2:346.

64. O. B. Ficklin, interview with William Melvin McConnell, *The Classmate: A Paper for Young People* (Cincinnati), 6 Feb. 1926.

65. Jesse W. Weik, "Lincoln's Vote for Vice-President in the Philadelphia Convention of 1856," *Century Magazine,* June 1908, 187.

66. Henry C. Whitney, statement for Herndon, [Nov. 1866], Douglas L. Wilson and Rodney O. Davis, eds., *Herndon's Informants: Letters, Interviews, and Statements about Abraham Lincoln* [hereafter *HI*] (Urbana: University of Illinois Press, 1998), 406; Whitney, *Life on the Circuit*, ed. Angle, 97.

67. Chicago *Daily Democrat*, 26 June 1856.

68. Ottawa *Republican*, 4 July 1856, in C. C. Tisler and Aleita G. Tisler, "Lincoln Was Here for Another Go at Douglas" (pamphlet; Jackson, TN: McCowat-Mercer Press, 1958), 23.

69. *Illinois Republican*, n.d., copied in the Albany *Evening Journal*, 1 May 1860.

70. Lincoln to Davis, Springfield, 7 July 1856, Roy P. Basler, ed., *Collected Works of Lincoln, First Supplement* (Westport, CT: Greenwood Press, 1973), 27; Edward Magdol, *Owen Lovejoy: Abolitionist in Congress* (New Brunswick, NJ: Rutgers University Press, 1967), 157.

71. David Davis to Dickey, Bloomington, 18 July 1856, Isabel Wallace, ed., *Life and Letters of General W. H. L. Wallace* (Chicago: R. R. Donnelley, 1909), 74–75.

72. Gillespie to Lincoln, Edwardsville, 6 June 1856, H-W MSS DLC.

73. John Hawes to Lincoln, Eminence, 15 Sept. 1856, ibid.

74. John M. Palmer to Norman B. Judd, Carlinville, 6 Aug. 1856, Lincoln Collection, RPB.

75. William Pickering to Lyman Trumbull, Albion, 6 June 1856, Trumbull Papers, DLC.

76. Benjamin S. Edwards to Lyman Trumbull, Springfield, 24 July 1856, ibid.

77. *CWL*, 2:349–353.

78. Clark E. Carr, *My Day and Generation* (Chicago: McClurg, 1908), 274–275.

79. Marysville, California, *Appeal*, 4 Nov. 1860.

80. Speech in Vandalia, 23 Sept. 1856, Chicago *Democratic Press*, 27 Sept. 1856, in *CWL*, 2:377–378.

81. Denver *Tribune*, 18 May 1879.

82. Homer H. Cooper, "The Lincoln-Thornton Debate, 1856, Shelbyville,

Illinois," *Journal of the Illinois State Historical Society* 10 (1917): 104, 106.

83. *Illinois State Register* (Springfield), 19 Aug. 1856, in *CWL*, 2:359.

84. Newton Bateman and Paul Selby, *Historical Encyclopedia of Illinois and History of Shelby County* (Chicago: Munsell, 1910), 786.

85. *CWL*, 2:361–366.

86. Kalamazoo *Gazette*, n.d., copied in the Grand Rapids *Daily Enquirer*, 1 Sept. 1856, *Michigan Magazine of History* 5 (1921):287–288.

87. Dickey to Ward Hill Lamon, Ottawa, 5 June 1871, Jeremiah S. Black Papers, DLC.

88. *Illinois State Register* (Springfield), 4 Sept. 1856, in *CWL*, 2:366–368.

89. *The Illinois Sentinel* (Jacksonville), 12 Sept. 1856, ibid., 2:373.

90. John B. Turner to Lincoln, Springfield, 9 Sept. 1856, H-W MSS DLC.

91. Herndon to Lyman Trumbull, Springfield, 11 Aug. 1856, Trumbull Papers, DLC.

92. Lincoln to Trumbull, Springfield, 11 Aug. 1856, *CWL*, 2:360.

93. George T. Brown to Lyman Trumbull, Alton, 28 July 1856, Trumbull Papers, DLC.

94. Richard Yates to Trumbull, Jacksonville, 3 Aug. 1856, ibid.

95. Yates to Lincoln, Jacksonville, 18 Sept. 1856, H-W MSS DLC,

96. Joseph Medill to Lincoln, Chicago, 9 Aug. 1860, AL MSS DLC.

97. Herndon to Wendell Phillips, Springfield, 28 Sept. 1856, Phillips Papers, Harvard University.

98. Lincoln to John Bennett, Springfield, 4 Aug. 1856, *CWL*, 2:358.

99. Form letter dated Springfield, 8 Sept. 1856, ibid., 2:374.

100. Lincoln to Jesse A. Pickrell, Springfield, 15 Sept. 1856, Roy P. Basler and Christian O. Basler, eds., *Collected Works of Abraham Lincoln: Second Supplement, 1848–1865* (New Brunswick, NJ: Rutgers University Press, 1990), 12.

101. Ezra M. Prince, "A Day with Abraham Lincoln," H-W MSS DLC.

102. Lincoln to Robert S. Boal, Springfield, 14 Sept. 1856, *CWL*, 2:375.

103. Ottawa *Free Trader*, n.d., in Tisler and Tisler, "Lincoln Was Here," 21.

104. Belleville *Weekly Advocate*, 22 Oct. 1856, in *CWL*, 2:380.

105. Koerner, *Memoirs*, 2:33.

106. J. L. D. Morrison to Douglas, Belleville, 16 Apr. 1856, Douglas Papers, in Mildred C. Stoler, "The Democratic Element in the New Republican Party in Illinois, 1856–1860," *Papers in Illinois History and Transactions for the Year 1942* (Springfield: Illinois State Historical Society, 1944):42.

107. Lincoln to Ray, Bloomington, 13 Sept. 1856, Basler, ed., *Collected Works of Lincoln, First Supplement*, 27–28.

108. Joliet *Signal*, 14 Oct. 1856.

109. *Illinois State Register* (Springfield), 13 Oct. 1856.

110. *Our Constitution* (Urbana), 24 July 1856.

111. "Empire Club Song," *The Campaign Democrat* (New York), 30 July 1856.

112. Herndon to Theodore Parker, Springfield, 12 Nov. 1856, Herndon-Parker Papers, University of Iowa.

113. Notes for a speech at Chicago, 28 Feb. 1857, *CWL*, 2:390–391.

114. Speech in Chicago, 10 Dec. 1856, ibid., 2:385.

115. Letter by B., Chicago, 11 Dec., *Illinois State Journal* (Springfield), 13 Dec. 1856.

116. Brooks, "Personal Reminiscences of Abraham Lincoln," *Scribner's Monthly*, 15 (Feb. 1878):562.

117. Herndon to Theodore Parker, Springfield, 8 Apr. 1857, Herndon-Parker Papers, University of Iowa.

118. Reminiscences of Henry G. Little, given in June 1886, recorded in a memorandum dated Chicago, 20 Dec. 1886, by John A. Jameson, Nicolay Papers, DLC; Little, "Personal Recollections of Abraham Lincoln," undated typescript of excerpts, J. G. Randall Papers, DLC.

119. Lincoln to James W. Grimes, Springfield, [ca. 17] Aug. 1857, *CWL*, 2:413.

120. William H. Herndon, "Analysis of the Character of Abraham Lincoln," lecture delivered in Springfield, 26 Dec. 1865, *Abraham Lincoln Quarterly* 1 (1941): 429.

121. "One of Lincoln's Fees," an article from the *Illinois State Journal* (Springfield), n.d., typed copy, box 47, Illinois Central Railroad Archives, Newberry Library, Chicago.

122. Jesse W. Weik, *The Real Lincoln: A Portrait*, ed. Michael Burlingame (1922; Lincoln: University of Nebraska Press, 2002), 153.

123. James F. Joy, undated clipping from the Chicago *Tribune*, "New Stories of Lincoln," LMF.

124. Weik, *Real Lincoln*, ed. Burlingame, 153–154.

125. Lincoln to James Steele and Charles Summers, Springfield, 12 Feb. 1857, *CWL*, 2:389.

126. Capen to John G. Drennan, 6 Apr. 1906, in Albert J. Beveridge, *Abraham Lincoln, 1809–1858* (2 vols.; Boston: Houghton Mifflin, 1928), 1:589n.

127. W. H. Bradley to E. B. Washburne, Chicago, 11 July 1862, Washburne Papers, DLC.

128. *CWL*, 2:397–398.

129. Douglas to McClellan, 26 Jan. 1861, in Stephen W. Sears, *George B. McClellan: The Young Napoleon* (New York: Ticknor and Fields, 1988), 59–60.

130. John W. Starr, *Lincoln and the Railroads: A Biographical Study* (New York: Dodd, Mead, 1927), 76.

131. Ebenezer Lane to Osborn, Chicago, 14 Aug. 1857, Illinois Central Railroad Archives, box 94, Newberry Library, Chicago.

132. Douglas's speech at Oquawka, 4 Oct. 1858, Oquawka correspondence, 4 Oct., *Missouri Democrat* (St. Louis), 9 Oct. 1858.

133. Speech at Carthage, Illinois, 22 Oct. 1858, *CWL*, 3:331.

134. Weik, *Real Lincoln*, ed. Burlingame, 155, 194.

135. Whitney, *Life on the Circuit*, ed. Angle, 237–238.

136. Springfield correspondence, 4 Sept., New York *Evening Post*, 8 Sept. 1860.

137. Mary Lincoln to Emilie Todd Helm, Springfield, 20 Sept. [1857], Justin G. Turner and Linda Levitt Turner, eds., *Mary Todd Lincoln: Her Life and Letters* (New York: Alfred A. Knopf, 1972), 50.

138. Fragment on Niagara Falls, [ca. 25–30 Sept. 1848], *CWL,* 2:10–11.

139. *Illinois State Journal* (Springfield), 1 Jan. 1857.

140. Chicago *Tribune,* 10 Apr. 1857.

141. Speech of 12 June, New York *Herald,* 3 July 1857; Springfield correspondence by William Herndon, 23 June 1857, Chicago *Tribune,* n.d., clipping enclosed in Herndon to Wendell Phillips, Springfield, 29 June 1857, Phillips Papers, Harvard University.

142. Robert W. Johannsen, *Stephen A. Douglas* (New York: Oxford University Press, 1973), 501.

143. Speech in Springfield, 26 June 1857, *CWL,* 2:398–410.

144. *Southern Illinoisan,* n.d., copied in the *Illinois State Journal* (Springfield), 16 July 1857.

145. [William Herndon], Springfield correspondence, 27 June 1857, Chicago *Tribune,* n.d., clipping enclosed in Herndon to Wendell Phillips, Springfield, 4 July 1857, Phillips Papers, Harvard University.

146. Herndon to Wendell Phillips, Springfield, 29 June 1857, Phillips Papers, Harvard University; Herndon to Theodore Parker, Springfield, 29 June 1857, Herndon-Parker Papers, University of Iowa.

147. Gustave Koerner to Lyman Trumbull, Belleville, 4 July 1857, Trumbull Papers, DLC.

148. New York *Times,* 4 July 1857.

149. Springfield correspondence, 30 June, New York *Tribune,* 6 July 1857.

150. Statement by J. M. Sturtevant, Jacksonville, 1882, in Osborn H. Oldroyd, ed., *The Lincoln Memorial: Album-Immortelles* (New York: G. W. Carleton, 1883), 274.

151. *CWL,* 2:382–383.

Chapter 12. "A House Divided"

1. Lincoln to Jediah F. Alexander, Springfield, 15 May 1858, Roy P. Basler et al., eds., *Collected Works of Abraham Lincoln* [hereafter *CWL*] (8 vols. plus index; New Brunswick, NJ: Rutgers University Press, 1953–1955), 2:446.

2. Bancroft's oration, delivered in New York on 20 Nov. 1854, in Bancroft, *Literary and Historical Miscellanies* (New York: Harper & Brothers, 1857), 481–517.

3. Henry C. Whitney, *Life on Circuit with Lincoln,* ed. Paul M. Angle (1892; Caldwell, ID: Caxton Printers, 1940), 209.

4. *CWL,* 2:437–442; 3:356–363.

5. "Gus" to Mary P. Christian, Pontiac, Illinois, 28 Jan. 1860, Harry E. Pratt, ed., *Concerning Mr. Lincoln, in which Abraham Lincoln Is Pictured As He Appeared to Letter Writers of His Time* (Springfield, IL: Abraham Lincoln Association, 1944), 21.

6. Lincoln to John M. Carson, Springfield, 7 Apr. 1860, *CWL,* 4:39.

7. Herndon to Jesse W. Weik, Springfield, 21 Feb. 1891, H-W MSS DLC; Herndon to Ward Hill Lamon, Springfield, 6 Mar. 1870, Lamon Papers, CSmH.

8. Charles Henry Ray to Lyman Trumbull, Chicago, 24 Nov. 1857, Trumbull Papers, DLC; Douglas, speech in Milwaukee, New York *Evening Post,* 19 Oct. 1860.

9. G. C. Lanphere to Douglas, Galesburg, 24 Dec. 1857, Douglas Papers, University of Chicago.

10. James Williams to Douglas, Belvidere, 26 Jan. 1858, ibid.

11. Lincoln to Lyman Trumbull, Chicago, 30 Nov. 1857, *CWL,* 2:427; Peoria *Transcript,* n.d., copied in the *Illinois State Register* (Springfield), 25 Feb., copied in the *Illinois State Journal* (Springfield), 26 Feb. 1858.

12. Lincoln to Trumbull, Chicago, 30 Nov. 1857, *CWL,* 2:427.

13. Trumbull to Lincoln, Washington, 5 Dec. 1857, Trumbull Family Papers, IHi.

14. New York *Tribune,* 17 May 1858; Robert W. Johannsen, *Stephen A. Douglas* (New York: Oxford University Press, 1973), 632.

15. Greeley to Schuyler Colfax, New York, 5 Feb., 6, 17 May, 2 June 1858, Greeley Papers, New York Public Library; Greeley to Franklin

Newhall, Ann Arbor, Michigan, 8 Jan. 1859, copy, Greeley Papers, DLC.

16. John O. Johnson to Horace Greeley, Springfield, 6 May 1858, Greeley Papers, DLC.

17. New York *Times*, 5 Mar. 1858.

18. Springfield (Massachusetts) *Republican*, 18 June 1858, 15 Mar. 1860; George S. Merriam, *The Life and Times of Samuel Bowles* (2 vols.; New York: Century, 1885), 1:232–245.

19. Quoted by William Kellogg, 13 Mar. 1860, *Congressional Globe*, 36th Congress, 1st Session, appendix, 160.

20. Lincoln to Charles Henry Ray, Springfield, 27 June 1858, Col. Robert R. McCormick Research Center, Wheaton, Illinois; Chicago *Press and Tribune*, 21 Apr., copied in the *Illinois State Journal* (Springfield), 23 Apr. 1858.

21. Lincoln to Trumbull, Bloomington, 28 Dec. 1857, *CWL*, 2:430.

22. Lyman Trumbull to John M. Palmer, Washington, 14 Dec. 1857, quoted in George Thomas Palmer, *A Conscientious Turncoat: The Story of John M. Palmer* (New Haven, CT: Yale University Press, 1941), 50.

23. Trumbull to Lincoln, Washington, 25 Dec. 1857, Trumbull Family Papers, IHi.

24. Trumbull to Lincoln, Washington, 3 Jan. 1858, AL MSS DLC.

25. William Schouler to S. P. Chase, Washington, 23 Mar. 1858, Chase Papers, Historical Society of Pennsylvania.

26. Wentworth to Lincoln, Chicago, 19 Apr. 1858, AL MSS DLC.

27. Chicago *Press and Tribune*, 17 Mar. 1860.

28. Herndon to E. B. Washburne, Springfield, 10 Apr. 1858, Washburne Papers, DLC.

29. Ray to Trumbull, Chicago, 18 Dec. 1857, Lyman Trumbull Papers, DLC.

30. Hatch to Lyman Trumbull, Springfield, 14 Jan. 1858, Trumbull Papers, DLC.

31. Ray to Trumbull, Chicago, 9 Mar. 1858, ibid.

32. Washburne to Herndon, Washington, 28 Apr. 1858, Washburn Family Papers, Washburn Memorial Library, Norlands, Maine.

33. Lincoln to Washburne, Urbana, 26 Apr. 1858, *CWL*, 2:444.

34. Lincoln to Jediah F. Alexander, Springfield, 15 May 1858, ibid., 2:446–447.

35. *Illinois State Journal* (Springfield), 12 Jan. 1858.

36. Pascal P. Enos to Henry Wilson, Springfield, 12 Apr. 1858, P. P. Enos Papers, IHi.

37. Lincoln to Hatch, Lincoln, 24 Mar. 1858, Roy P. Basler, ed., *Collected Works of Lincoln, First Supplement, 1832–1865* (Westport, CT: Greenwood Press, 1974), 29.

38. Lincoln to Samuel Galloway, Springfield, 28 July 1859, *CWL*, 3:394.

39. Speech of 12 June 1857 in Springfield, New York, *Herald*, 3 July 1857.

40. Speech delivered to a deputation of Germans in Chicago, New York *Times*, 6 and 12 Aug. 1858.

41. Jacksonville *Sentinel*, 16 Oct. 1857, quoted in *CWL*, 2:449n.

42. Chicago *Daily Democratic Press*, 12 Nov. 1857, quoted ibid.

43. The draft of a speech, *CWL*, 2:248–254. The editors of Lincoln's *Collected Works* think this document may have been a speech delivered at Edwardsville on May 18, or that it may have been written several weeks earlier. It seems likely that it was in fact composed soon after Douglas's speech of 9 Dec. 1857. Don E. Fehrenbacher, *Prelude to Greatness: Lincoln in the 1850's* (Stanford, CA: Stanford University Press, 1962), 89–94.

44. Chicago *Press and Tribune*, 19 Mar. and 10 July 1858.

45. Dubois to Trumbull, Springfield, 8 Apr. 1858, Lyman Trumbull Papers, DLC.

46. *Illinois State Journal* (Springfield), 19 Apr. 1858.

47. Clinton *Central Transcript*, 4 June and 9 July 1858.

48. Dixon *Republican and Telegraph*, in Fehrenbacher, *Prelude to Greatness*, 61.

49. Charles Henry Ray to E. B. Washburne, Chicago, [15 Apr. 1858?], Washburne Papers, DLC.

50. Gustave Koerner to O. M. Hatch, Belleville, 20 Apr. 1858, Hatch Papers, IHi.

51. "A Republican" to the editor, Chicago, [18?] May, New York *Tribune,* 27 May 1858.

52. Palmer to Lyman Trumbull, Carlinville, 25 May 1858, Trumbull Papers, DLC.

53. Chicago *Democrat,* 8 May 1858.

54. Chicago *Times,* n.d, copied in the *Illinois State Register* (Springfield), 21 May 1858.

55. *Illinois State Register* (Springfield), 21 May 1858.

56. Lincoln to Wilson, Springfield, 1 June 1858, *CWL,* 2:457.

57. Herndon to Theodore Parker, Springfield, 23 Aug. 1858, Herndon-Parker Papers, University of Iowa.

58. Herndon to Jesse W. Weik, Springfield, 23 Dec. 1885, H-W MSS DLC.

59. Herndon to Lincoln, Boston, 24 Mar. 1858, ibid.; Herndon to Theodore Parker, Springfield, 31 Aug. 1858, Herndon-Parker Papers, University of Iowa.

60. Herndon to Greeley, Springfield, 8 Apr. and 20 July 1858, Greeley Papers, New York Public Library.

61. George E. Baker, ed., *The Works of William H. Seward* (5 vols.; Boston: Houghton Mifflin, 1888), 4:596.

62. Baker to Lincoln, Chicago, 6 Sept. 1858, copy in Lincoln's hand, AL MSS DLC.

63. Lincoln to Charles L. Wilson, Springfield, 1 June 1858, *CWL,* 2:457.

64. Lincoln to Whitney, Springfield, 18 Dec. 1857, *CWL,* 2:429.

65. Judd to Lyman Trumbull, Chicago, 19 Apr. 1858, Trumbull Papers, DLC.

66. Lincoln to Stephen A. Hurlbut, Springfield, 1 June 1858, *CWL,* 2:456.

67. Herndon to Charles Sumner, Springfield, 24 Apr. 1858, Sumner Papers, Harvard University; Herndon to Theodore Parker, Springfield, 27 Apr. 1858, Herndon-Parker Papers, University of Iowa; Herndon to Trumbull, Springfield, 24 Apr. 1858, Lyman Trumbull Papers, DLC.

68. Lincoln to E. B. Washburne, Urbana, 26 Apr. 1858, *CWL,* 2:444.

69. Herndon to Charles Sumner, Springfield, 24 Apr. 1858, Sumner Papers, Harvard University.

70. Lincoln to Samuel Wilkinson, Springfield, 10 June 1858, *CWL,* 2:458.

71. Lincoln to Lyman Trumbull, Springfield, 23 June 1858, ibid., 2:471–472.

72. Herndon to Trumbull, Springfield, 19 Feb. 1858, Lyman Trumbull Papers, DLC.

73. Herndon to Trumbull, Springfield, 24 June, 8 July 1858, ibid.

74. *Illinois State Register* (Springfield), 29 Oct. 1858.

75. Josh Whitmore to W. H. L. Wallace, Pontiac, 5 June 1858, Isabel Wallace, *Life and Letters of General W. H. L. Wallace* (Chicago: R. R. Donnelley, 1909), 82–83.

76. Lincoln to Lovejoy, Springfield, 8 Mar. 1858, *CWL,* 2:435.

77. Lincoln to Lamon, Springfield, 11 June 1858, ibid., 2:458.

78. "A Republican" to the editor of the Chicago *Press and Tribune,* Bloomington, 8 June 1858, Basler, ed., *Collected Works of Lincoln, First Supplement,* 31.

79. Henry C. Whitney, *Life on the Circuit with Lincoln,* ed. Paul M. Angle (1892; Caldwell, Idaho: Caxton, 1940), 411.

80. Clifton H. Moore to Lincoln, Clinton, 10 Aug. 1858, AL MSS DLC.

81. Dickey to Lincoln, Ottawa, 19 Nov. 1854, ibid.

82. Lincoln to Washburne, Springfield, 15 May 1858, *CWL,* 2:447.

83. Lincoln to Josiah M. Lucas, Springfield, 10 May 1858, ibid., 2:445.

84. Lincoln to Washburne, Springfield, 27 May 1858, ibid., 2:455.

85. *Illinois State Journal* (Springfield), 17 June 1858; Bloomington *Pantagraph,* n.d., in Ida M. Tarbell, *The Life of Abraham Lincoln* (2 vols.; New York: McClure, 1902), 1:305.

86. Bloomington *Pantagraph,* n.d., quoted ibid., 1:304–305.

87. Chicago *Press and Tribune*, 14 June 1858, copied in the *Illinois State Journal* (Springfield), 16 June 1858.

88. Herndon to Weik, Springfield, 1 Jan. 1886, H-W MSS DLC.

89. Charles M. Wiltse, ed., *The Papers of Daniel Webster: Speeches and Formal Writings* (2 vols.; Hanover, NH: University Press of New England, 1986), 1:287.

90. Chicago *Times*, n.d., copied in the *Illinois State Register* (Springfield), 26 June 1858; Pittsfield *Democrat*, n.d., copied in the Quincy *Daily Herald*, 20 July 1858; Beardstown correspondence, 11 Aug. 1858, Chicago *Times*, n.d., in Paul M. Angle, ed., *Created Equal? The Complete Lincoln-Douglas Debates of 1858* (Chicago: University of Chicago Press, 1958), 92.

91. Wiltse, ed., *Speeches of Webster*, 1:347.

92. *CWL*, 2:461–469.

93. Joseph Gillespie to William Herndon, Edwardsville, 31 Jan. 1866, *HI*, 183.

94. Cincinnati speech, 17 Sept. 1859, *CWL*, 3:451.

95. Richmond *Enquirer*, 6 May 1856.

96. Richmond *Enquirer*, n.d., quoted in J. to the editor, n.d., *Illinois State Journal* (Springfield), 13 Oct. 1858.

97. New York *Evening Post*, 11 Mar. 1864.

98. Quoted in Arthur C. Cole, "Lincoln's House Divided Speech: Did It Reflect a Doctrine of Class Struggle?" (pamphlet; Chicago: University of Chicago Press, 1923), 33.

99. Jackson *Mississippian*, 20 Oct. 1854, copied in the Alton *Weekly Courier*, 30 Nov. 1854, ibid.

100. Goodell, "What They Would Do If They Could," December 1835, quoted in Jonathan A. Glickstein, "The Chattelization of Northern Whites: An Evolving Abolitionist Warning," *American Nineteenth Century History* 4 (2003):48.

101. Russell B. Nye, *Fettered Freedom: Civil Liberties and the Slavery Controversy, 1830–1860* (East Lansing: Michigan State University Press, 1963), 287.

102. Concord *Independent Democrat*, 29 Apr. 1847, quoted in Catherine Newbold, "The Antislavery Background of the Principal State Department Appointees in the Lincoln Administration" (Ph.D. dissertation, University of Michigan, 1962), 211.

103. Speech of 30 Oct. 1854, John W. Blassingame, ed., *The Frederick Douglass Papers, Series One: Speeches, Debates, and Interviews* (5 vols.; New Haven, CT: Yale University Press, 1979–1992), 2:544.

104. Speech of February 18 in New York, New York *Tribune*, 20 Feb. 1854.

105. *Congressional Globe*, 33rd Congress, 1st session, appendix, 764 (speech of 25 May 1854).

106. Theodore Parker, "A Sermon on the Dangers which Threaten the Rights of Man in America, Preached at the Music Hall, on Sunday, July 2, 1854" (pamphlet; Boston: Benjamin B. Mussey, 1854), 31.

107. New York *Tribune*, 1854, quoted in Henry Luther Stoddard, *Horace Greeley: Printer, Editor, Crusader* (New York: G. P. Putnam's Sons, 1946), 165.

108. Herndon to Wendell Phillips, Springfield, 9 Mar. 1857, Phillips Papers, Harvard University.

109. Washington correspondence by James Shepherd Pike, 28 May and 18 Dec. 1856, New York *Tribune*, 2 June and 20 Dec. 1856.

110. George F. Talbot to Pike, 5 Feb. 1857, in Robert Franklin Durden, *James Shepherd Pike: Republicanism and the American Negro, 1850–1882* (Durham, NC: Duke University Press, 1957), 28.

111. Speech at Rochester, New York, 25 Oct. 1858, in Frederic Bancroft, *The Life of William H. Seward* (2 vols.; New York: Harper & Brothers, 1900), 1:458-459.

112. *The Works of Daniel Webster* (6 vols.; Boston: Little, Brown, 1853), 2:546.

113. John Parrish, *Remarks on the Slavery of the Black People, Addressed to the Citizens of the United States, Particularly to Those Who Are in Legislative or Executive Stations in the General or State Governments, and also to Such Individuals as Hold Them in Bondage* (Philadelphia: Kimber, Conrad, 1806), 9.

114. Letter dated 25 Mar. 1852, *Anti-Slavery Standard*, n.d., quoted in Allan Nevins, *The Ordeal of the Union* (2 vols.; New York: Charles Scribner's Sons, 1947), 2:78.

115. Parker, "Sermon on the Dangers which Threaten the Rights of Man," 27.

116. Edward B. Bryan, *The Rightful Remedy: Addressed to Slaveholders of the South* (Charleston, SC: Walker & James, 1850), 111.

117. Wendell Phillips Garrison and Francis Jackson Garrison, *William Lloyd Garrison, 1805–1879: The Story of His Life, Told by His Children* (4 vols.; New York: Century, 1889), 3:420.

118. Stowe, "An Appeal to the Women of the Free States of America on the Present Crisis in Our Country," New York *Tribune*, 20 Feb. 1854.

119. Theodore Parker to Gerrit Smith, Rome, Italy, 16 Feb. 1860, May Anti-Slavery Manuscript Collection, Cornell University.

120. Lyman Trumbull, speech in Chicago, 7 Aug. 1858, *National Era* (Washington), 2 Sept. 1858.

121. Fragment: Notes for Speeches, [ca. 21 Aug. 1858], *CWL*, 2:548–549.

122. *Illinois State Journal* (Springfield), 18 June 1858.

123. Burlington *Free Press*, 26 June 1858, in William Francis Hanna, "Abraham Lincoln and the New England Press, 1858–1860" (Ph.D. dissertation, Boston College, 1980), 17.

124. Herndon to Theodore Parker, Springfield, 8 July 1858, Herndon-Parker Papers, University of Iowa.

125. New Orleans *Delta*, n.d., copied in the Chicago *Press and Tribune*, 5 July 1858.

126. New York *Tribune*, 24 June and 12 July 1858.

127. [Greeley] to [Joseph Medill?], New York, 24 July 1858, copy in Lincoln's hand, AL MSS DLC.

128. Albany *Evening Journal*, 6 June 1860.

129. W. P. Boyd to John J. Crittenden, Bloomington, 17 July 1858, Crittenden Papers, DLC.

130. "Samuel C. Parks's Reminiscences of Abraham Lincoln," ed. Le Roy H. Fischer, *Lincoln Herald* 68 (1966):11–12.

131. Leonard Swett to Herndon, Chicago, 17 Jan. 1866, *HI*, 163.

132. Page proofs of an undated interview with White, White Papers, IHi.

133. John Locke Scripps to Lincoln, Chicago, 22 June 1858, AL MSS DLC.

134. Lincoln to John L. Scripps, Springfield, 23 June 1858, *CWL*, 2:471.

135. Chicago *Times*, 23 June 1858.

136. Freeport *Weekly Bulletin*, 26 Aug. 1858; *Illinois State Register* (Springfield), 26, 28 and 29 June 1858, 30 July 1860.

137. Medill to Lincoln, Chicago, 23 June 1858; Whitney to Lincoln, Chicago, 23 June 1858; O. R. Winters to Lincoln, Marion, 3 Sept. 1858, AL MSS DLC.

138. Lincoln to Medill, Springfield, 25 June 1858, *CWL*, 2:473–474.

139. Chicago *Press and Tribune*, 14 July 1858.

140. *Illinois State Journal* (Springfield), 25 June 1858; Alton *Courier*, 3 July 1858.

141. Springfield correspondence, 21 June, Utica, New York, *Herald*, 27 June 1860, copied in the New York *Tribune*, 9 July 1860.

142. Lincoln to Trumbull, Springfield, 23 June 1858, *CWL*, 2:472.

143. Herndon to Trumbull, Springfield, 8 July 1858, Lyman Trumbull Papers, DLC.

144. Ezra Prince, "A Day and a Night with Abraham Lincoln," p. 10, H-W MSS DLC.

145. John W. Forney, *Anecdotes of Public Men* (2 vols.; New York: Harper & Brothers, 1881), 2:179.

146. William Dickson, "A Leaf from the Unwritten History of the Rebellion," draft, William Dickson Papers, William L. Clements Library, University of Michigan.

147. Chicago *Press and Tribune*, 17 July 1858.

148. John R. Ridge to Douglas, Marysville, California, 19 Sept. 1858, Douglas Papers, University of Chicago.

149. Douglas's speech in Angle, ed., *Created Equal?*, 12–25.

150. Chicago *Press and Tribune*, 21, 12 and 15 July 1858.

151. Lincoln to Gustave Koerner, Springfield, 15 July 1858, *CWL*, 2:502.

152. Chicago *Press and Tribune*, 12 July 1858.

153. Reminiscences of a Dr. [William K. ?] McElfresh, *Western Christian Advocate* (Cincinnati), n.d., copied in the *Weekly Journal* (Jacksonville), 3 July 1901.

154. Reminiscences of Francis A. Eastman, Chicago *Journal*, 12 Feb. 1909.

155. Letter by "A Republican," Chicago, 14 July 1858, Chicago *Press and Tribune*, 16 July 1858.

156. Percy Coe Eggleston, *Lincoln in New England* (New London, CT: Tudor Press, 1943), 21.

157. *CWL*, 2:484–502.

158. New York *Tribune*, 15 and 16 July 1858; New York *Times*, 16 July 1858; New York *Herald*, 14 and 16 July 1858; Bangor *Courier*, 27 July 1858, in Hanna, "Lincoln and the New England Press," 19.

159. Elgin *Gazette*, n.d., copied in the *Illinois State Register* (Springfield), 8 Oct. 1858.

160. Abraham Smith to Lincoln, Ridge Farm, Illinois, 20 July 1858, AL MSS DLC.

161. Chicago *Journal*, 12 July 1858.

162. Chicago *Press and Tribune*, 12 July 1858.

163. Joseph Medill to Lincoln, Chicago, 10 Sept. 1859, AL MSS DLC.

164. *Illinois State Register* (Springfield), 14 July 1858.

165. Chicago *Weekly Times*, 15, 22 July, 12 Aug. 1858.

166. Boston *Courier*, n.d., copied ibid., 22 July 1858.

167. Madison, Wisconsin, *Argus*, n.d., copied ibid., 22 July 1858.

168. Timothy D. Lincoln to Lincoln, Cincinnati, 17 July 1858, AL MSS DLC.

169. Ray to Lincoln, Norwich, New York, 27 July 1858, ibid.

170. John Mathers to Lincoln, Jacksonville, 19 July 1858, ibid.

171. Judd to Trumbull, Chicago, 16 July 1858, Lyman Trumbull Papers, DLC.

172. *The Reminiscences of Carl Schurz* (3 vols.; New York: McClure, 1907–1908), 2:90–91.

173. Chicago *Press and Tribune*, 11 Oct. 1858.

174. Ward Hill Lamon, *Recollections of Abraham Lincoln, 1847–1865*, ed. Dorothy Lamon Teillard (2nd ed.; Washington, DC: privately published, 1911), 22.

175. *Political Debates between Abraham Lincoln and Stephen A. Douglas* (Cleveland: Burrows Brothers, 1894), 39, 37.

176. Bloomington *Pantagraph*, 17 July 1858.

177. Douglas's speech at Springfield, 17 July 1858, in Angle, ed., *Created Equal?*, 62–65, and in the *Indiana State Sentinel* (Indianapolis), 22 July 1858.

178. Chicago *Journal*, 22 July 1858.

179. *CWL*, 2:504–521.

180. Unsigned, undated article "for the Register," *Illinois State Register* (Springfield), 28 July 1858.

181. Letter by "Sangamon," Springfield, 19 July 1858, Chicago *Press and Tribune*, 20 July 1858.

182. *Illinois State Journal* (Springfield), 19 and 20 July 1858.

183. Springfield correspondence, 21 July, Alton *Weekly Courier*, 29 July 1858.

184. Lincoln to Gustave Koerner, Springfield, 6 August 1858, Roy P. Basler and Christian O. Basler, eds., *Collected Works of Abraham Lincoln, Second Supplement* (New Brunswick, NJ: Rutgers University Press, 1990), 16; Lincoln to Daniel A. Cheever, Springfield, 11 Aug. 1858, *CWL*, 8:415.

185. Louisville *Journal*, 24 Aug. 1858, copied in the *Illinois State Journal* (Springfield), 30 Aug. 1858.

186. Louisville *Democrat*, n.d., copied in the *Indiana State Sentinel* (Indianapolis), 8 Sept. 1858.

187. J. H. Jordan to Lincoln, Cincinnati, 25 July 1858, AL MSS DLC.

188. Greeley to Joseph Medill, New York, 24 July 1858, John G. Nicolay and John Hay, *Abraham Lincoln: A History* (10 vols.; New York: Century, 1890), 2:140–141n.

189. *Illinois State Register* (Springfield), 22, 23 July 1858.

190. Fragment on pro-slavery theology, [11 Oct. 1858?], *CWL*, 3:204–205.

191. Lincoln to Charles H. Fisher, Springfield, 27 Aug. 1860, *CWL*, 4:101.

192. [Henry Binmore], Beardstown correspondence, 11 Aug., *Missouri Republican* (St. Louis), 16 Aug. 1858; Beardstown correspondence, 10 Aug., Chicago *Weekly Times*, 19 Aug. 1858; *Illinois State Journal* (Springfield), 17 Aug. 1858; Chicago *Press and Tribune*, 18 Aug. 1858; Beardstown correspondence by T., 11 Aug. 1858, Chicago *Press and Tribune*, 16 Aug. 1858.

193. Havana correspondence, 13 Aug., Chicago *Press and Tribune*, 20 Aug. 1858; Havana correspondence, 14 Aug., and Bath correspondence, 12 Aug., *Illinois State Journal* (Springfield), 20 and 21 Aug. 1858.

194. Lewistown correspondence, 16 Aug., Chicago *Press and Tribune*, 19 Aug. 1858.

195. Peoria *Democratic Union*, n.d., quoted in the *Illinois State Journal* (Springfield), 23 Aug. 1858; Peoria correspondence, 18 Aug., Chicago *Press and Tribune*, weekly edition, 26 Aug. 1858; Peoria correspondence, 18 Aug., *Illinois State Journal* (Springfield), 23 Aug. 1858.

196. New York *Times*, 19 Aug. 1858.

197. Speech at Joliet, 31 Aug. 1858, *Missouri Republican* (St. Louis), 10 Sept. 1858.

198. Galena *Weekly Northwestern Gazette*, 14 Sept. 1858.

199. Letter by an unidentified correspondent, Gillespie, Illinois, 16 Oct. 1858, Alton *Courier*, n.d., copied in the *Missouri Democrat* (St. Louis), 20 Oct. 1858.

200. C. D. Hay to Lyman Trumbull, Burnt Prairie, Illinois, 10 July 1857, Lyman Trumbull Papers, DLC.

201. White to Jesse W. Weik, New York, 14 Dec. 1913, in Jesse W. Weik, *The Real Lincoln: A Portrait*, ed. Michael Burlingame (1922; Lincoln: University of Nebraska Press, 2002), 382.

202. Havana correspondence, 13 Aug. 1858, Chicago *Press and Tribune*, 20 Aug. 1858.

203. Bath correspondence, 16 Aug., Chicago *Press and Tribune*, 21 Aug. 1858.

204. Thomas G. Lowry, *Personal Reminiscences of Abraham Lincoln* (London: privately printed, 1910), 12.

205. Carlinville correspondence, 8 Sept., Chicago *Press and Tribune*, 11 Sept. 1858.

206. Centralia correspondence, 17 Sept., Chicago *Press and Tribune*, 20 Sept. 1858.

207. "Douglas at Centralia," by "one who was there," Chicago *Press and Tribune*, 21 Sept. 1858.

208. D. B. Spencer to an unidentified correspondent, Ruskin, Florida, 2 Aug. 1929, Leonard Crunelle, *Freeport's Lincoln* (Freeport, IL: Lincoln-Douglas Society, 1929), 152.

209. Schurz, *Reminiscences*, 2:94.

210. McClellan, draft of his autobiography, *McClellan's Own Story*, p. 16, McClellan Papers, DLC. The published version of this story is sanitized. *McClellan's Own Story* (New York: Webster, 1887), 36.

211. Herndon to Weik, Springfield, 24 Sept. 1890, H-W MSS DLC.

212. Theodore Parker to John P. Hale, Galesburg, 21 Oct. 1856, in John Weiss, *Life and Correspondence of Theodore Parker* (2 vols.; New York: Appleton, 1864): 2:187, and John White Chadwick, *Theodore Parker, Preacher and Reformer* (Boston: Houghton Mifflin, 1901), 331.

213. Louisville *Journal*, n.d., copied in the Chicago *Daily Times*, 2 Oct. 1858.

214. Quincy *Whig*, n.d., quoted in the Quincy *Herald*, n.d., copied in the *Illinois State Register* (Springfield), 4 June 1860.

215. Herndon to Theodore Parker, Springfield, 4 Oct. 1858, Herndon-Parker Papers, University of Iowa.

216. Benjamin F. Smith, "Memories of Lincoln and Douglas," undated typescript, William E. Barton Papers, University of Chicago; Walter B. Stevens, *A Reporter's Lincoln*, ed. Michael Burlingame (1916; Lincoln: University of Nebraska Press, 1998), 31.

217. Charles Francis Adams, undated diary entry, quoted in Adams, *Charles Francis Adams, 1835–1915: An Autobiography* (Boston: Houghton Mifflin, 1916), 66.

218. Henry Adams to Charles Francis Adams, Jr., Washington. 13 Feb. 1861, J. C. Levenson et al., eds., *The Letters of Henry Adams* (6 vols.; Cambridge, MA: Harvard University Press, 1982–1988), 1:231.

219. W. O. Bartlett to N. P. Banks, Washington, 4 May 1860, Banks Papers, DLC.

220. Washington correspondence, 20 Mar., Springfield (Massachusetts) *Republican,* 22 Mar. 1861.

221. Cincinnati *Commercial,* 31 May and 2 June 1860.

222. Charles S. Zane, "Lincoln as I Knew Him," *Sunset* 29 (Oct. 1912), reprinted in the *Journal of the Illinois State Historical Society* 14 (1921–1922):79.

223. *CWL,* 2:541–542.

224. Dillard C. Donnohue, interview with Jesse Weik, 13 Feb. 1887, *HI,* 602.

225. Wilson and Davis, eds., *Herndon's Lincoln,* 396.

226. Henry Villard, *Memoirs of Henry Villard, Journalist and Financier: 1838–1900* (2 vols.; Boston: Houghton Mifflin, 1904), 1:92.

227. Hiram W. Beckwith, "Lincoln: Personal Recollections of Him, His Contemporaries and Law Practice in Eastern Illinois," Chicago *Tribune,* 29 Dec. 1895.

228. Clinton correspondence, 27 July, Chicago *Weekly Times,* 5 Aug. 1858; Clinton correspondence, 27 July, *Illinois State Register* (Springfield), 30 July 1858; *Our Constitution* (Urbana), 7 Aug. 1858; Carthage *Republican,* 5 Aug. 1858.

229. Springfield correspondence, 2 Aug., Chicago *Press and Tribune,* 4 Aug. 1858.

230. Henry S. Green, interviewed by John G. Nicolay, Springfield, July 1875, Michael Burlingame, ed., *An Oral History of Abraham Lincoln: John G. Nicolay's Interviews and Essays* (Carbondale: Southern Illinois University Press, 1996) 32–33; speech at Clinton, 27 July 1858, *CWL,* 2:525–527; Chicago *Times,* 30 July 1858, in Angle, ed., *Created Equal?,* 85; Springfield correspondence, 2 Aug., Chicago *Press and Tribune,* 4 Aug. 1858.

231. White in Wilson and Davis, eds., *Herndon's Lincoln,* 395.

232. Ezra M. Prince to Truman H. Bartlett, Bloomington, 17 Sept. 1907, Bartlett Papers, Boston University.

233. Isaac N. Arnold, "Reminiscences of the Illinois-bar Forty Years Ago: Lincoln and Douglas as Orators and Lawyers, Paper Read before the Bar Association of the State of Illinois, Springfield, 7 January 1881" (pamphlet; Chicago: Fergus, 1881), 26.

234. White in Wilson and Davis, eds., *Herndon's Lincoln,* 391–392.

235. Thomas Lowry, *Personal Reminiscences of Abraham Lincoln* (London: Chiswick Press, 1910), *Reminiscences,* 12; *CWL,* 2:541.

236. Beardstown correspondence, 11 August, Chicago *Press and Tribune,* 16 Aug. 1858.

237. *Illinois State Register* (Springfield), 17 Aug. 1858.

238. Chicago *Press and Tribune,* weekly edition, 26 Aug. 1858.

239. Lewistown correspondence, 17 Aug. 1858, *Illinois State Journal* (Springfield), 21 Aug. 1858; speech at Lewistown, 17 Aug. 1858, *CWL,* 2:545.

240. *CWL,* 2:546–547.

241. Lewistown correspondence, 17 Aug., Chicago *Press and Tribune,* 21 Aug. 1858.

242. Lowell, Massachusetts, *Journal and Courier,* 30 Aug. 1858, Edwin Erle Sparks, ed., *The Lincoln-Douglas Debates of 1858* (Collections of the Illinois State Historical Library, vol. 3; Lincoln Series, vol. 1; Springfield: Illinois State Historical Library, 1908), 518.

243. Lincoln to William Fithian, Bloomington, 3 Sept. 1858, *CWL,* 3:84.

244. W. J. Usrey to Lincoln, Decatur, 19 July 1858, AL MSS DLC.

245. Letter by R., Havana, n.d., *Illinois State Register* (Springfield), 19 Aug. 1858.

246. Decatur correspondence, 27 and 28 July, Chicago *Weekly Times,* 5 Aug. 1858.

247. Chicago *Times,* 30 July 1858, Sparks, ed., *Lincoln-Douglas Debates,* 56.

248. Draft of McClellan's memoirs, quoted in Stephen W. Sears, *George B. McClellan: The Young Napoleon* (New York: Ticknor and Fields, 1988), 59.

249. New York *Tribune*, 12 July 1858.

250. Chicago *Press and Tribune* 22 July 1858, in Albert J. Beveridge, *Abraham Lincoln, 1809–1858* (2 vols.; Boston: Houghton Mifflin, 1928), 2:629.

251. Memo by Nicolay, citing no source, box 9, Nicolay Papers, DLC.

252. Norman B. Judd interviewed by John G. Nicolay, Washington, 28 Feb. 1876, Burlingame, ed., *Oral History of Lincoln*, 44–45.

253. Judd's son Edward, recalling a story he heard his father tell many times, Seattle *Post-Intelligencer*, 6 Feb. 1916.

254. Undated interview with Henry T. Glover, of Chicago, a son of Joseph O. Glover, Ida M. Tarbell Papers, Allegheny College.

255. Chicago *Press and Tribune*, 26 July 1858.

256. Judd to Lincoln, Chicago, 27 July 1858, AL MSS DLC.

257. Lincoln to Douglas, Springfield, 29 July 1858, *CWL*, 2:528.

258. Ibid., 2:530.

259. *Illinois State Journal* (Springfield), 3 Aug., 31 July 1858.

260. Chicago *Press and Tribune*, 28 and 29 July 1858.

261. *Illinois State Register* (Springfield), 31 July 1858.

262. Chicago *Times*, n.d., copied in the *Illionis State Register* (Springfield), 29 July 1858, in Sparks, ed., *Lincoln-Douglas Debates*, 375.

263. Abraham Smith to Lincoln, Ridge Farm, Illinois, 20 July 1858, AL MSS DLC.

264. New York *Times*, 13 July 1858.

Chapter 13. "A David Greater than the Democratic Goliath"

1. Pillsbury, speech at Framingham, Massachusetts, 4 July 1860, *The Liberator* (Boston), 20 July 1860.

2. Herndon to William Lloyd Garrison, Springfield, 29 May 1858, Garrison Papers, Boston Public Library.

3. Speech given in Springfield, 17 July 1858, Roy P. Basler et al., eds., *Collected Works of Abraham Lincoln* [hereafter *CWL*] (8 vols. plus index; New Brunswick, NJ: Rutgers University Press, 1953–1955), 2:506.

4. Herndon to Theodore Parker, Springfield, 24 July 1858, Herndon-Parker Papers, University of Iowa.

5. Ida M. Tarbell, *The Life of Abraham Lincoln* (2 vols.; New York: McClure, 1902), 1:308–309.

6. Recollections of George Beatty, undated manuscript, Ida M. Tarbell Papers, Allegheny College.

7. Henry C. Whitney, *Life on the Circuit with Lincoln*, ed. Paul M. Angle (1892; Caldwell, ID: Caxton Press, 1940), 408.

8. Chicago correspondence, 23 Aug., New York *Evening Post*, 27 Aug. 1858; Tarbell, *Lincoln* 1:313–314.

9. Charles W. Marsh, *Recollections, 1837–1910* (Chicago: Farm Implement News Company, 1910), 74.

10. Ottawa *Republican*, 28 Aug. 1858.

11. Letter from "Sandwich," De Kalb County, n.d., Chicago *Press and Tribune*, 26 Aug. 1858.

12. *Illinois State Register* (Springfield), 28 June, 30 July 1858; Chicago *Weekly Times*, 5 Aug. 1858.

13. Chicago *Press and Tribune*, 23 Aug. 1858. I have used the *Press and Tribune*'s version of the debates rather than that of the Chicago *Times* because the latter deliberately garbled Lincoln's words and applied cosmetic changes to Douglas's. Michael Burlingame, "The Accuracy of Newspaper Accounts of the 1858 Lincoln-Douglas Debates," in Walter B. Stevens, *A Reporter's Lincoln*, ed. Michael Burlingame (1916; Lincoln: University of Nebraska Press, 1998), 229–236. The audience responses are taken from both newspapers.

14. Quincy *Whig*, 26 Aug. 1858.

15. Stevens, *A Reporter's Lincoln*, ed. Burlingame, 75.

16. Ibid., 85.

17. Hillsboro correspondence, 2 Aug., Chicago *Press and Tribune*, 7 Aug. 1858.

18. Alton correspondence, 15 Oct., New York *Tribune* (semiweekly ed.), 26 Oct. 1858, in

Edwin Erle Sparks, ed., *The Lincoln-Douglas Debates of 1858* (Collections of the Illinois State Historical Library, vol. 3; Lincoln Series, vol. 1; Springfield, IL: Illinois State Historical Library, 1908), 504.

19. *Congressional Globe*, 34th Congress, 1st Session, Appendix, 1274 (9 Aug. 1856).

20. Douglas's speech at Galena, 25 Aug. 1858, quoted in the Galena correspondence, 25 Aug. 1858, Chicago *Press and Tribune*, 27 Aug. 1858.

21. Douglas in the debate at Quincy, 13 Oct. 1858, Chicago *Press and Tribune*, 15 Oct. 1858.

22. Chicago *Press and Tribune*, 27 Aug. 1858.

23. Charles Henry Ray to E. B. Washburne, n.p., n.d. [filed at the end of 1858], Washburne Papers, DLC.

24. *Illinois State Journal* (Springfield), 9 Sept., 25 and 26 Aug. 1858.

25. Chicago *Press and Tribune*, 23 and 27 Aug. 1858.

26. Chicago *Journal*, 23 Aug. 1858.

27. Louisville *Journal*, n.d., copied in the Chicago *Press and Tribune*, 28 Aug. 1858.

28. Chicago correspondence, 23 Aug., New York *Evening Post*, 27 Aug. 1858.

29. Jesse W. Weik, *The Real Lincoln: A Portrait*, ed. Michael Burlingame (1922; Lincoln: University of Nebraska Press, 2002), 231.

30. Thomas J. Henderson, interview with Ida M. Tarbell, 15 July 1895, Tarbell Papers, Allegheny College.

31. Walcott Hamlin to John Hay, Amherst, Massachusetts, 17 Mar. 1887, Nicolay-Hay Papers, IHi.

32. See above, Chapter Five.

33. *CWL*, 3:12–30.

34. Chicago *Press and Tribune*, 23 Aug. 1858.

35. Ottawa correspondence, n.d., Chicago *Times*, n.d., copied in the Jacksonville *Sentinel*, 27 Aug. 1858.

36. Richard Hughes, undated statement, Ida M. Tarbell Papers, Allegheny College.

37. Lincoln to Joseph O. Cunningham, Ottawa, 22 Aug. 1858, *CWL*, 3:37.

38. Freeport correspondence, 27 Aug., *Missouri Republican* (St. Louis), 31 Aug. 1858; Boston *Courier*, 23 and 24 Aug. 1858, in William Francis Hanna, "Abraham Lincoln and the New England Press, 1858–1860" (Ph. D. dissertation, Boston College, 1980), 24.

39. Milwaukee *News*, n.d., copied in the Chicago *Weekly Times*, 2 Sept. 1858.

40. Chicago *Times*, 22 Aug. 1858, in Sparks, ed., *Lincoln-Douglas Debates*, 142.

41. Philadelphia *Press*, 26 Aug. 1858.

42. Recollections of George Beatty, undated manuscript, Ida M. Tarbell Papers, Allegheny College.

43. Providence *Post*, 25 Aug. 1858, in Hanna, "Lincoln and the New England Press," 25.

44. Chicago *Journal*, 23 Aug. 1858.

45. L. D. Whiting to Lincoln, Tiskilwa, 23 Aug. 1858, AL MSS DLC.

46. Ottawa *Republican*, 28 Aug. 1858.

47. Herndon to Richard Yates, Springfield, 26 Aug. 1858, Richard Yates and Catherine Yates Pickering, *Richard Yates: Civil War Governor*, ed. John H. Krenkel (Danville, IL: Interstate Printers, 1966), 132–133.

48. Schuyler Colfax to Lincoln, Oxford, Indiana, 25 Aug. 1858, AL MSS DLC.

49. R. R. Hitt to Horace White, Washington, 10 Dec. 1892, White Papers, IHi.

50. Chicago correspondence, 23 Aug., New York *Evening Post*, 27 Aug. 1858.

51. New York *Tribune*, 27 Aug., quoted in the Galena *Weekly Northwest Gazette*, 7 Sept. 1858.

52. Theodore Parker to William H. Herndon, Boston, 9 Sept. 1858, Herndon-Parker Papers, University of Iowa.

53. Herndon to Theodore Parker, Springfield, 23 Aug. 1858, Herndon-Parker Papers, University of Iowa.

54. Ray to Washburne, n.p., n.d., [filed at the end of 1858], Washburne Papers, DLC.

55. B. Lewis to Lincoln, Jacksonville, 25 Aug. 1858, AL MSS DLC.

56. Henry C. Whitney to Lincoln, Chicago, 26 Aug. 1858, ibid.

57. Chicago correspondence, 23 Aug., New York *Evening Post*, 27 Aug. 1858.

58. Henry Villard, *Memoirs of Henry Villard, Journalist and Financier: 1838–1900* (2 vols.; Boston: Houghton Mifflin, 1904), 1:92–93.

59. Thomas J. McCormack, ed., *Memoirs of Gustave Koerner, 1809–1896* (2 vols.; Cedar Rapids, IA: Torch Press, 1909), 2:63.

60. Chicago *Press and Tribune,* 24 and 28 Aug. 1858.

61. Chicago correspondence, 24 Aug., New York *Evening Post,* 28 Aug. 1858

62. Galesburg *Democrat,* 13 Oct. 1858, in Sparks, ed., *Lincoln-Douglas Debates,* 83–84.

63. Chicago *Press and Tribune,* 11, 16, 18, 19 Oct. 1858.

64. Stevens, *A Reporter's Lincoln,* ed. Burlingame, 77.

65. Chicago *Press and Tribune,* 11 Oct. 1858.

66. Hitt, journal entry for 28 July 1858, Hitt Papers, DLC.

67. Benjamin P. Thomas, ed., *Three Years with Grant: As Recalled by War Correspondent Sylvanus Cadwallader* (New York: Alfred A. Knopf, 1955), 130; Special Orders 526, Washington, 27 Nov. 1863; Binmore to Stephen Hurlbut, Memphis, n.d. [ca. 14 July 1863], Record Group 94, Entry 158, Office of the Adjutant General, Staff Papers, box 5, file for Henry Binmore, National Archives, Washington.

68. Stevens, *A Reporter's Lincoln,* ed. Burlingame, 78.

69. Chicago *Daily Times,* 12, 16 Oct. 1858.

70. Lincoln to Martin P. Sweet, Centralia, 16 Sept. 1858, *CWL,* 3:144.

71. Chicago *Press and Tribune,* 24, 26 Aug., 11, 13, 16, 18 Oct. 1858.

72. Chicago *Weekly Times,* 26 Aug., 2 Sept. 1858.

73. Chicago *Press and Tribune,* 16 Oct. 1858.

74. Ibid., 13 Oct. 1858.

75. Hitt, journal entry for 23 July 1858, Hitt Papers, DLC.

76. Charles S. West, "The Lincoln-Douglas Debates," part 1, *Phonographic Magazine* (Cincinnati), 15 Nov. 1896, 346.

77. Horace White, "The Lincoln and Douglas Debates: An Address before the Chicago Historical Society, February 17, 1914" (pamphlet; Chicago: University of Chicago Press, 1914), 20.

78. Henry Villard in the Philadelphia *Press,* 26 Aug. 1858.

79. Hitt's journal, entry for 23 July 1858, Hitt Papers, DLC.

80. Unidentified clipping from a Kansas City newspaper, reference files of the Abraham Lincoln Association, IHi.

81. Beardstown correspondence, 11 Aug., Chicago *Press and Tribune,* 16 Aug. 1858.

82. Lincoln to Peck, Henry, 23 Aug. 1858, Roy P. Basler, ed., *Collected Works of Abraham Lincoln, First Supplement, 1832–1865* (Westport, CT: Greenwood Press, 1974), 32–33.

83. Norman B. Judd interviewed by John G. Nicolay, Washington, 28 Feb. 1876, Michael Burlingame, ed., *An Oral History of Abraham Lincoln: John G. Nicolay's Interviews and Essays* (Carbondale: Southern Illinois University Press, 1996), 45.

84. Joseph Medill to Lincoln, n.p. [27 Aug. 1858], AL MSS DLC.

85. Lincoln to Asbury, Springfield, 31 July 1858, *CWL,* 2:530.

86. Medill to Lincoln, n.p., [27 Aug. 1858], AL MSS DLC.

87. James W. Sheahan, *The Life of Stephen A. Douglas* (New York: Harper & Brothers, 1860), 424.

88. Galena correspondence, 25 Aug., New York *Evening Post,* 1 Sept. 1858.

89. Freeport *Weekly Bulletin,* 2 Sept. 1858.

90. Chicago *Times,* 29 Aug. 1858, Sparks, ed., *Lincoln-Douglas Debates,* 189.

91. Undated statement by William Bross, enclosed in Bross to John Hay and John G. Nicolay, Chicago, 31 Dec. 1886, Nicolay Papers, DLC.

92. *New Yorker Staats-Zeitung,* 4 Sept. 1858.

93. Koerner, *Memoirs,* 2:64–65.

94. *CWL,* 3:39–49.

95. Chicago *Press and Tribune,* 30 August 1858.

96. Don E. Fehrenbacher, *The Dred Scott Case: Its Significance in American Law and*

Politics (New York: Oxford University Press, 1978), 379.

97. Chicago correspondence, 2 Sept., New York *Evening Post,* 7 Sept. 1858.

98. Wilmington, North Carolina, *Journal,* n.d., in Sparks, ed., *Lincoln-Douglas Debates,* 526; Louisville *Journal,* n.d., copied in the Chicago *Press and Tribune,* 4 Sept. 1858 and in the *Illinois State Journal* (Springfield), 4 Oct. 1858; Memphis *Avalanche,* 8 Sept. 1858 and 2 July 1859, in Fehrenbacher, *The Dred Scott Case,* 513, 705.

99. Cincinnati Gazette, n.d., copied in the Chicago *Press and Tribune,* 10 Sept. 1858.

100. *Missouri Democrat* (St. Louis), 11 Sept. 1858.

101. Robert W. Johannsen, *Stephen A. Douglas* (New York: Oxford University Press, 1973), 670.

102. Washington *Union,* 4 Sept. 1858, in Sparks, ed., *Lincoln-Douglas Debates,* 522–523.

103. Johannsen, *Douglas,* 695.

104. Davis, speech at Vicksburg, n.d., quoted in the *Illinois State Journal* (Springfield), 29 Nov. 1858.

105. Brown, speech in the senate, *Congressional Globe,* 35th Congress, 2nd Session, 1243 (23 Feb. 1859).

106. Carlinville correspondence by "Upper Egyptian," 31 Aug. 1858, Chicago *Press and Tribune,* 3 Sept. 1858.

107. *Missouri Democrat* (St. Louis), 15 Sept. 1858.

108. *The States* (Washington, DC), 9 Oct. 1858.

109. Stephen A. Forbes to Charles Beneulyn Johnson, Urbana, 27 Mar. 1917, in Charles Beneulyn Johnson, *Illinois in the Fifties, or A Decade of Development, 1851–1860* (Champaign, IL: Flanigan-Pearson, 1918), 166.

110. Chicago *Press and Tribune,* 30 Aug. 1858.

111. Chicago correspondence, 1 Sept., New York *Tribune,* 9 Sept. 1858.

112. Freeport correspondence, 27 Aug., *Illinois State Journal* (Springfield), 30 Aug. 1858.

113. *Missouri Democrat* (St. Louis), 22 Sept. 1858.

114. Chicago *Press and Tribune* 30 Aug. 1858.

115. Washburne in Allen Thorndike Rice, ed., *Reminiscences of Abraham Lincoln by Distinguished Men of His Time* (New York: North American Review, 1886), 27.

116. Dixon *Republican and Telegraph,* 2 Sept. 1858; Rockford *Republican,* 2 Sept. 1858.

117. Seymour D. Thompson, "Lincoln and Douglas: The Great Freeport Debate," *American Law Review* 39 (1905):173.

118. *New Yorker Staats-Zeitung,* 4 Sept. 1858.

119. Cincinnati *Commercial,* 1 Sept. 1858.

120. *CWL,* 3:70–76.

121. Chicago correspondence, 1 Sept., New York *Tribune,* 9 Sept. 1858.

122. New York *Times,* 9 Sept. 1858; *Missouri Democrat* (St. Louis), 3 Sept. 1858.

123. Marengo *Press,* n.d., copied in the Freeport *Weekly Bulletin,* 30 Sept. 1858.

124. [Henry Villard], "Douglas und Lincoln, Die dritte Discussion zu Jonesboro, Ill., am 15. Sept." *New-Yorker Staats-Zeitung,* 22 Sept. 1858, and "Der Verlauf der Kampagne," Illinois, 9 Sept. 1858, ibid., 16 Sept. 1858.

125. David Davis to O. M. Hatch, Springfield and Bloomington, 18 Aug. 1858, *For the People: A Newsletter of the Abraham Lincoln Association* 4, no. 3 (Autumn 2002):6–7.

126. Joseph Fifer, interview with Carl Sandburg, Bloomington, 1923, Sandburg Papers, University of Illinois; speech of Joseph Fifer, 4 Dec. 1935, Bloomington *Pantagraph,* 5 Dec. 1935, in Sherman Day Wakefield, *How Lincoln Became President: The Part Played by Bloomington, Illinois and Certain of Its Citizens in Preparing Him for the Presidency and Securing His Nomination and Election* (New York: Wilson-Erickson, 1936), 89–90.

127. *CWL,* 3:92–93. This passage from Clay's works, in slightly different language, appeared in the Great Compromiser's public letter to Richard Pindell, New Orleans, 17 Feb. 1849, in Melba Porter Hay and Carol Reardon,

eds., *Candidate, Compromiser, Elder Statesman, 1844–1852* (vol. 10 of *The Papers of Henry Clay*; Lexington: University Press of Kentucky, 1991), 575.

128. Fragment on slavery [July 1, 1854?], *CWL*, 2:222–223. The date is a guess that may be years off.

129. Ibid., 3:95–96.

130. Undated memorandum by Gillespie, Gillespie Papers, IHi.

131. Whitney, *Life on the Circuit*, ed. Angle, 59.

132. Jacksonville correspondence, 6 Sept., *Illinois State Journal* (Springfield), 8 Sept. 1858.

133. Carlinville correspondence, 8 Sept., *Illinois State Journal* (Springfield), 10 Sept. 1858.

134. Douglas, speech at Paris, Illinois, 31 July, *Illinois State Register* (Springfield), 4 Aug. 1858.

135. *Missouri Republican* (St. Louis), 7 Sept. 1858.

136. Amy Davis Winship, *My Life Story* (Boston: Richard G. Badger, 1920), 101.

137. Sydney Spring to Lincoln, Grayville, 8 Sept. 1858, AL MSS DLC.

138. Chicago *Press and Tribune*, 17 Sept. 1858.

139. Richmond *South*, n.d., quoted in the New York *Evening Post*, 21 Sept. 1858.

140. Speech at Joliet, 31 Aug., *Missouri Republican* (St. Louis), 10 Sept. 1858.

141. "Speeches of Senator S. A. Douglas on the Occasion of His Public Receptions by the Citizens of New Orleans, Philadelphia, and Baltimore" (pamphlet; Washington: Lemuel Towers, 1860), 9 (speech of 6 Dec. 1858 at New Orleans).

142. Frank M. Daulton, who covered the debates for the Quincy *Herald*, quoted in the Macon, Missouri, correspondence, 26 Nov., New York *Sun*, 27 Nov. 1904.

143. Trumbull to Lincoln, St. Louis, 14 Sept. 1858, AL MSS DLC.

144. Joliet speech, 31 Aug., *Missouri Republican* (St. Louis), 9 Sept. 1858.

145. Jonesboro correspondence, 15 Sept., New York *Evening Post*, 20 Sept. 1858.

146. Chicago *Press and Tribune*, 17 Sept. 1858.

147. William H. Herndon to Theodore Parker, Springfield, 2 Sept. 1858, Herndon-Parker Papers, University of Iowa.

148. *CWL*, 3:116–135.

149. [Henry Villard], "Douglas und Lincoln, Die dritte Discussion zu Jonesboro, Ill., am 15. Sept." *New Yorker Staats-Zeitung*, 22 Sept. 1858.

150. Louisville *Journal*, n.d., copied in the *Illinois State Journal* (Springfield), 4 Oct. 1858.

151. *Illinois State Register* (Springfield), 28 Oct. 1858; Peoria *Transcript*, 20 Sept. 1858, Sparks, ed., *Lincoln-Douglas Debates*, 263.

152. Chicago *Press and Tribune*, 17 Sept. 1858.

153. Galesburg *Semi-Weekly Democrat*, 18 Sept. 1858.

154. Jonesboro correspondence, 15 Sept., New York *Evening Post*, 20 Sept. 1858.

155. Lincoln to Joseph Gillespie, Centralia, 16 Sept. 1858, Roy P. Basler and Christian O. Basler, eds., *Collected Works of Abraham Lincoln, Second Supplement* (New Brunswick, NJ: Rutgers University Press, 1990), 16.

156. Bissell to E. B. Washburne, Springfield, 23 Sept. 1858, Washburne Papers, DLC.

157. Centralia correspondence, 17 Sept., Chicago *Press and Tribune*, 20 Sept. 1858.

158. Galena *Weekly Northwest Gazette*, 5 Oct. 1858.

159. Whitney, statement for Herndon [Nov. 1866?], Douglas L. Wilson and Rodney O. Davis, eds., *Herndon's Informants: Letters, Interviews, and Statements about Abraham Lincoln* [hereafter *HI*] (Urbana: University of Illinois Press, 1998), 406.

160. Charleston correspondence, 18 Sept., New York *Evening Post*, 25 Sept. 1858.

161. Chicago *Times*, 21 Sept. 1858, Sparks, ed., *Lincoln-Douglas Debates*, 312.

162. Horace White in William H. Herndon and Jesse W. Weik, *Herndon's Lincoln*, ed. Douglas L. Wilson and Rodney O. Davis (1889; Urbana: University of Illinois Press, 2006), 406.

163. Chicago *Press and Tribune*, 21 Sept. 1858.

164. Charleston *Courier*, 22 Sept. 1858.

165. W. M. Chambers to Lincoln, Charleston, 22 July 1858, AL MSS DLC.

166. Thomas A. Marshall to Lincoln, Charleston, 22 July 1858, ibid.

167. David Davis to Lincoln, Bloomington, 3 Aug. 1858, ibid.

168. Jediah F. Alexander to Lincoln, Greenville, 5 Aug. 1858, ibid.

169. *Illinois State Register* (Springfield), 31 July 1858.

170. Orville Sexton to Lyman Trumbull, Shawneetown, 25 Sept. 1857, Trumbull Papers, DLC.

171. J. J. Brown to Douglas, Charleston, 26 Aug. 1858, typed copy, George Fort Milton Papers, DLC.

172. Delahay to Lincoln, Alton, 13 Aug. 1858, AL MSS DLC.

173. J. H. Jordan to Lincoln, Cincinnati, 24 Aug. 1858, ibid.

174. B. Lewis to Lincoln, Jacksonville, 25 Aug. 1858, ibid.

175. *CWL* 3:145–158.

176. Lew Wallace, *Lew Wallace: An Autobiography* (2 vols.; New York: Harper & Brothers, 1906), 1:254, 255.

177. John W. Blassingame et al., eds., *The Frederick Douglass Papers, Series 1: Speeches, Debates, and Interviews* (5 vols.; New Haven, CT: Yale University Press, 1979–1991), 3:233–237; *Illinois State Register* (Springfield), 7 Aug. 1858; Chicago *Weekly Times*, 12 Aug. 1858; Jacksonville *Sentinel*, 20 Aug. 1858.

178. "Speeches of Senator S. A. Douglas on the Occasion of His Public Receptions," 5 (speech of 6 Dec. 1858 at New Orleans).

179. Chicago *Press and Tribune*, 21 Sept. 1858.

180. Farnsworth to Lincoln, Chicago, 20 Sept. 1858, AL MSS DLC.

181. Jonesboro correspondence, 15 Sept., New York *Evening Post*, 20 Sept. 1858.

182. Chicago *Press and Tribune*, 7 Sept. 1858.

183. Ward Hill Lamon, *Recollections of Abraham Lincoln, 1847–1865*, ed. Dorothy Lamon Teillard (2nd ed.; Washington, DC: privately published, 1911), 24.

184. *CWL*, 3:178–201.

185. Chicago *Press and Tribune*, 21 Sept. 1858; Paris *Prairie Beacon News*, 24 Sept. 1858.

186. Undated statement by Hiram W. Beckwith, Ida M. Tarbell Papers, Allegheny College.

187. Francis Fisher Browne, *The Every-Day Life of Abraham Lincoln* (New York: N. D. Thompson, 1886), 287.

188. Chicago *Press and Tribune*, 21 and 23 Sept. 1858.

189. Charleston *Courier*, 22 Sept. 1858.

190. Charleston correspondence, 18 Sept., New York *Evening Post*, 25 Sept. 1858.

191. Davis to Lincoln, Lincoln, Illinois, 25 Sept. 1858, AL MSS DLC.

192. Oglesby to Sheridan Wait, 21 Sept. 1858, Otto Kyle, *Abraham Lincoln in Decatur* (New York: Vantage, 1957), 98.

193. Oglesby to Isaac N. Arnold, Lincoln, Illinois, 7 Mar. 1883, in Charles H. Coleman, *Abraham Lincoln and Coles County, Illinois* (New Brunswick, NJ: Scarecrow Press, 1955), 182.

194. Horace White in *Herndon's Lincoln*, ed. Wilson and Davis, 406.

195. Undated statement by Hiram W. Beckwith, Ida M. Tarbell Papers, Allegheny College.

196. Whitney, *Life on the Circuit*, ed. Angle, 410.

197. Paris *Prairie Beacon News*, n.d., copied in the *Missouri Democrat* (St. Louis), 16 Sept. 1858; *Illinois State Chronicle*, 9 Sept., copied in the *Missouri Democrat* (St. Louis), 16 Sept. 1858.

198. James G. Wright to Lincoln, Naperville, 11 Oct. 1858, AL MSS DLC.

199. Springfield *Republican*, 4 Oct. 1858, in Hanna, "Lincoln and the New England Press," 30.

200. *Missouri Democrat* (St. Louis), 22 Sept. 1858.

201. Chicago *Congregational Herald*, [30 Sept.], copied in the Chicago *Daily Times*, 9 Oct. 1858.

202. *The National Anti-Slavery Standard* (New York), 17 Nov. 1860.

203. Herndon to Parker, Springfield, 23 Nov. 1858. Herndon-Parker Papers, University of Iowa.

204. *Congressional Globe*, 35th Congress, 2nd Session, 346 (12 Jan. 1859).

205. Oliver Dyer, *Phonographic Report of the Proceedings of the National Free Soil Convention* (New York, 1848), 9, in Eric Foner, "Politics and Prejudice: The Free Soil Party and the Negro, 1849–1852," *Journal of Negro History* 50 (1965):242.

206. Lovejoy, speech in Chicago, 15 Oct. 1860, *The Liberator* (Boston), 9 Nov. 1860.

207. Speech of Feb. 1859, in William F. Moore and Jane Ann Moore, eds., *His Brother's Blood: Owen Lovejoy, Speeches and Writings, 1838–1864* (Urbana: University of Illinois Press, 2004), 177.

208. George Allen Hubbell, *Horace Mann: Educator, Patriot, and Reformer* (Philadelphia: Fell, 1910), 267.

209. Seward, "The National Divergence and Return," speech of 4 Sept. 1860, in George E. Baker, ed., *The Works of William Henry Seward* (5 vols.; Boston: Houghton Mifflin 1884–1887), 4:317.

210. Ibid., 312.

211. *Congressional Globe*, 36th Congress, 1st Session, 58–59 (8 Dec. 1859).

212. Unidentified clipping attached to a letter from Charles Taintor, Jr., to Trumbull, [Jackson, Michigan], Dec. 1859, Trumbull Family Papers, IHi.

213. Speech of Lyman Trumbull in Chicago, 7 Aug. 1858, *National Era* (Washington), 2 Sept. 1858.

214. *Congressional Globe*, 36th Congress, 1st Session, 1685 (12 Apr. 1860).

215. Foner, "Politics and Prejudice," 249.

216. Clay to the editor of the New York *World*, n.p., 19 Feb. 1861, Richard W. Thompson Collection, LMF.

217. New York *Tribune*, 26 Sept. 1857.

218. Speech of Samuel Carey of Cincinnati, Cincinnati *Commercial*, n.d., copied in the *Illinois State Journal* (Springfield), 10 Sept. 1860.

219. New York *Times*, 27, 28 June 1860.

220. Sullivan correspondence, 20 September, *Illinois State Register* (Springfield), 28 Sept. 1858.

221. Sullivan correspondence, 20 Sept., Chicago *Times*, 24 Sept. 1858, in Paul M. Angle, ed., *Created Equal? The Complete Lincoln-Douglas Debates of 1858* (Chicago: University of Chicago Press, 1958), 276–280; Sullivan correspondence, 20 Sept., *Illinois State Register* (Springfield), 28 Sept. 1858; Sullivan correspondence, 20 Sept., Chicago *Press and Tribune*, 25 Sept. 1858; Sullivan correspondence, 20 Sept., *Missouri Republican* (St. Louis), 23 Sept. 1858; Chicago *Weekly Times*, 30 Sept. 1858.

222. Douglas, speech at Springfield, 20 Oct., *Illinois State Register* (Springfield), 22 Oct. 1858.

223. Julian M. Sturtevant, *An Autobiography* (New York: F. J. Revell Company, 1896), 292.

224. *Vermilion County Press* (Danville), 29 Sept. 1858, in Donald G. Richter, *Lincoln: Twenty Years on the Eastern Prairie* (Mattoon, IL: United Graphics, 1999), 213.

225. *Lafayette Daily Courier*, 23 Sept. 1858, quoted ibid., 216.

226. Lincoln to Norman B. Judd, Danville, 23 Sept. 1858, *CWL*, 3:202.

227. Fragment: Notes for Speeches, [1 Oct. 1858?], ibid., 3:205.

228. Whitney to Lincoln, Chicago, 7 Aug. 1858, AL MSS DLC.

229. Douglas's speech at Oquawka, 4 Oct. 1858, Oquawka correspondence, 4 Oct., *Missouri Democrat* (St. Louis), 9 Oct. 1858; Douglas's speech at Springfield, 20 Oct., *Illinois State Register* (Springfield), 29 Oct. 1858; Douglas's speech at Henry, 29 Sept., summarized in the Chicago *Journal*, 5 Oct. 1858.

230. Speech at Carthage, 22 Oct. 1858, *CWL*, 3:206, 330–331.

231. Speech at Danville, 22 Sept. 1858, Danville correspondence, 22 Sept., *Missouri Republican* (St. Louis), 27 Sept. 1858.

232. Philadelphia *North American and United States Gazette,* 15 Oct., copied in the *Missouri Democrat* (St. Louis), 19 Oct. 1858.

233. Herndon to Trumbull, Springfield, 24 June 1858, Trumbull Papers, DLC.

234. Paul M. Zall, ed., *Abe Lincoln Laughing: Humorous Anecdotes from Original Sources by and about Abraham Lincoln* (Berkeley: University of California Press, 1982), 20.

235. William Herndon to Lyman Trumbull, Springfield, 24 June, 8 July 1858, Trumbull Papers, DLC.

236. A. Sherman to Ozias Hatch, Springfield, 27 Sept. 1858, Hatch Papers, IHi, quoted in Rodney O. Davis, "Dr. Charles Leib: Lincoln's Mole?" *Journal of the Abraham Lincoln Association* 24 (2003):23.

237. Stewart W. McClelland, "A. Lincoln, LL.D." *Lincoln Herald* 41, no. 3 (May 1939):3.

238. Chicago *Press and Tribune,* 9 Oct. 1858; Galesburg *Democrat,* 9 Oct. 1858, Sparks, ed., *Lincoln-Douglas Debates,* 372–373.

239. *Congressional Globe,* 35th Congress, 1st Session, 962 (7 Dec. 1857).

240. Onarga correspondence, 24 Sept., Chicago *Weekly Times,* 30 Sept. 1858; *Journal de l'Illinois,* 1 Oct., copied in the Chicago *Press and Tribune,* 8 Oct. 1858; Oquawka *Plaindealer,* n.d., copied in the Chicago *Journal,* 16 Oct. 1858.

241. Douglas's speech in Springfield, 5 Sept., *Illinois State Register* (Springfield), 6 Sept. 1858.

242. Thomas J. Pickett to Lincoln, Pekin, 3 Aug. 1858, AL MSS DLC.

243. Chicago *Press and Tribune,* 8 Oct. 1858.

244. *CWL,* 3:220–235.

245. Chicago *Press and Tribune,* 8 Oct. 1858.

246. Chicago *Daily Times,* 9 Oct. 1858.

247. *Illinois State Journal* (Springfield), 12 Oct. 1858.

248. New York *Herald,* 13 Oct. 1858.

249. Cincinnati *Commercial,* 23, 25 Sept. 1858.

250. Horace White in *Herndon's Lincoln,* ed. Wilson and Davis, 407.

251. St. Louis correspondence, 29 Sept., *Missouri Democrat* (St. Louis), 30 Sept. 1858.

252. *The Reminiscences of Carl Schurz* (3 vols.; New York: McClure, 1907–1908), 2:91.

253. Quincy correspondence, 13 Oct. *Missouri Democrat* (St. Louis), 15 Oct. 1858, in Sparks, ed., *Lincoln-Douglas Debates,* 443.

254. *CWL,* 3: 245–257.

255. Schurz, *Reminiscences,* 2:95.

256. Chicago *Daily Times,* 17 Oct. 1858.

257. Chicago *Press and Tribune,* 15 Oct. 1858.

258. David R. Locke in Rice, ed., *Reminiscences of Lincoln,* 444.

259. *CWL,* 3: 275–283.

260. Schurz, *Reminiscences,* 2:96.

261. *Illinois State Journal* (Springfield), 18 Oct. 1858.

262. Chicago *Daily Times,* 17 Oct. 1858.

263. David R. Locke in Rice, ed., *Reminiscences of Lincoln,* 441–443.

264. Koerner, *Memoirs,* 2:66–67.

265. Salmon P. Chase to Kate Chase, Warren, Illinois, 28 Oct. 1858, Chase Papers, Historical Society of Pennsylvania.

266. Isaac H. Sturgeon to John F. Snyder, St. Louis, 5 May 1860, John F. Snyder Papers, Missouri Historical Society; Isaac H. Sturgeon to James Buchanan, St. Louis, 6 Sept. 1860, Buchanan Papers, Historical Society of Pennsylvania.

267. Chicago *Press and Tribune,* 18 Oct. 1858.

268. J[eriah] B[onham], "Recollections of Abraham Lincoln," Chicago *Tribune,* 12 May 1895; Jeriah Bonham, *Fifty Years' Recollections* (Peoria, IL: J. W. Franks & Sons, 1883), 175–176.

269. Speech in Richmond, Indiana, 1 Oct. 1842, in Robert Seager et al., eds., *The Papers of Henry Clay* (10 vols.; Lexington: University of Kentucky Press, 1959–1991), 9:779.

270. Jonathan Birch, in Weik, *Real Lincoln,* ed. Burlingame, 201.

271. *CWL,* 3:297–318.

272. Chicago *Press and Tribune,* 18 Oct. 1858.

273. "The Campaign in Illinois, Last Joint Debate, Douglas and Lincoln at Alton, Illinois" (pamphlet; Washington, DC: Lemuel Towers, 1858).

274. Springfield correspondence, 18 Oct., New York *Evening Post*, 20 Oct. 1858.

275. Reminiscences of John Hitt, in Stevens, *A Reporter's Lincoln*, ed. Burlingame, 59.

276. Douglas to Linder, [Aug. 1858], telegram, Robert W. Johannsen, ed., *The Letters of Stephen A. Douglas* (Urbana: University of Illinois Press, 1961), 427.

277. William H. Herndon to Theodore Parker, Springfield, 3 Oct. 1858, Herndon-Parker Papers, University of Iowa.

278. *Illinois State Register* (Springfield), 27 Sept. 1858.

279. Ottawa *Little Giant*, 22 Sept. 1858, in C. C. Tisler and Aleita G. Tisler, "Lincoln Was Here for Another Go at Douglas" (pamphlet; Jackson, TN: McCowat-Mercer Press, 1958), 52.

280. Jacksonville correspondence, 6, 7 Sept., Chicago *Press and Tribune*, 9, 13 Sept. 1858.

281. *Illinois State Register* (Springfield), n.d., quoted in the *Illinois State Journal* (Springfield), 21 Oct. 1858.

282. Lincoln to Chase, Springfield, 30 Apr. 1859, *CWL*, 3:378.

283. Lincoln to Andrew McCallen, Springfield, 19 June 1858, ibid., 2:469.

284. H. Villardt to Douglas, Chicago, 24 Aug. 1858, Douglas Papers, University of Chicago. I am indebted to Professor Allen C. Guelzo for calling this letter to my attention.

285. Harris to Douglas, Springfield, 7 July 1858, ibid.

286. Lincoln to Crittenden, Springfield, 7 July 1858, *CWL*, 2:484.

287. Crittenden to Lincoln, Frankfort, 29 July 1858, AL MSS DLC.

288. Louisville *Journal*, 26 Oct., copied in the Chicago *Press and Tribune*, 27 Oct. 1858.

289. *Illinois State Journal* (Springfield), 25 and 29 Oct. 1858.

290. *Illinois State Register* (Springfield), 26 Oct. 1858; William H. Townsend, *Lincoln and the Bluegrass: Slavery and Civil War in Kentucky* (Lexington: University of Kentucky Press, 1955), 235–236.

291. Chicago *Times*, n.d., copied in the *Indiana State Sentinel*, Indianapolis, 13 Nov. 1858; Chicago *Daily Times*, 2 Oct. 1858; Chicago *Weekly Times*, 30 Sept. 1858.

292. Fragments: notes for speeches [ca. Sept. 1859?], *CWL*, 3:399.

293. Lincoln to James N. Brown, Springfield, 18 Oct. 1858, ibid., 3:327–328.

294. Alexander Sympson to John C. Bagby, Carthage, 25 Oct. 1858, Bagby Papers, IHi.

295. Lawrence Beaumont Stringer, "From the Sangamon to the Potomac: More Light on Abraham Lincoln," typescript of an unpublished manuscript, p. 134, Edgar Dewitt Jones Papers, Detroit Public Library.

296. Thomas Lowry, *Personal Reminiscences of Abraham Lincoln* (London: Privately printed, 1910), 15; Chicago *Press and Tribune*, 23 Oct. 1858.

297. Speech at Springfield, 30 Oct. 1858, *CWL*, 3:334.

298. *Illinois State Journal* (Springfield), 1 Nov. 1858.

299. Chicago *Press and Tribune*, 29 Oct. 1858.

300. George S. Merriam, *The Life and Times of Samuel Bowles* (2 vols.; New York: Century, 1885), 1:240.

301. Burlington, Iowa, *Gazette* 29 Oct. 1858, in Sparks, *Lincoln-Douglas Debates*, 533.

302. Lincoln to Judd, Rushville, 20 Oct. 1858, *CWL*, 3:329–330.

303. O. M. Hatch to Lyman Trumbull, Springfield, 13 July 1857, Trumbull Papers, DLC.

304. David Davis to E. D. Morgan, Bloomington, 22 Sept. 1860, Edwin D. Morgan Papers, New York State Library, Albany.

305. Herndon to Theodore Parker, Springfield, 30 Oct. 1858, Herndon-Parker Papers, University of Iowa.

306. *Missouri Democrat* (St. Louis), 22 Oct. 1858.

307. Princeton correspondence, 18 Oct., New York *Evening Post*, 21 Oct. 1858.

308. Springfield correspondence, 18 Oct., ibid., 20 Oct. 1858.

309. David Davis to Julius Rockwell, Danville, 26 Oct. 1858, Davis Papers, DLC.

310. William H. Herndon to Theodore Parker, Springfield, 30 Oct. 1858, Herndon-Parker Papers, University of Iowa.

311. *Illinois State Register* (Springfield), 9 Nov. 1858.

312. David Davis to Lincoln, Danville, 7 Nov. 1858, AL MSS DLC; David Davis to George Perrin Davis, Danville, 7 Nov. 1858, Davis Papers, IHi; Davis to Julius Rockwell, Danville, 26 Oct. 1858, Davis Papers, DLC.

313. Chicago *Press and Tribune*, 5, 17 Nov. 1858.

314. New York *Times*, 25 October 1858; New York *Tribune*, 24 May 1860.

315. Ebenezer Peck to Lyman Trumbull, Chicago, 22 Nov. 1858, Trumbull Papers, DLC.

316. Palmer to Trumbull, n. d., quoted in Palmer, *Conscientious Turncoat*, 54–55.

317. G. W. Rives to O. M. Hatch, Paris, Illinois, 5 and 10 Nov. 1858; Jackson Grimshaw to O. M. Hatch, Quincy, 14 Nov. 1858; John Tillson to O. M. Hatch, Quincy, 15 Nov. 1858, Hatch Papers, IHi.

318. William H. Herndon to Theodore Parker, Springfield, 11, 25 Sept. 1858, Herndon-Parker Papers, University of Iowa.

319. Davis to Julius Rockwell, Danville, 26 Oct. 1858, Davis Papers, DLC.

320. David Davis to Lincoln, Danville, 7 Nov. 1858, AL MSS DLC.

321. E. L. Pierce to Salmon P. Chase, Milton, Massachusetts, 5 Nov. 1858, Chase Papers, DLC.

322. Herndon to Theodore Parker, Springfield, 31 Aug., 26 Oct., 8 Nov. 1858, Herndon-Parker Papers, University of Iowa; Herndon to Lyman Trumbull, Springfield, 8 Nov. 1858, Trumbull Papers, DLC.

323. Chicago *Democrat,* n.d., copied in the *Illinois State Journal* (Springfield), 13 Nov. 1858.

324. Lincoln to Crittenden, Springfield, 4 Nov. 1858, *CWL*, 3:335–336.

325. Speech at Cincinnati, 17 Sept. 1859, ibid., 3:452.

326. Lincoln to Anson G. Henry, Springfield, 19 Nov. 1858, ibid., 3:339.

327. Springfield correspondence, 7 Jan., Cincinnati *Commercial*, 12 Jan. 1859.

328. Michael Burlingame and John R. Turner Ettlinger, eds., *Inside Lincoln's White House: The Complete Civil War Diary of John Hay* (Carbondale: Southern Illinois University Press, 1997), 244 (entry for 8 Nov. 1864).

329. Reminiscences of Bushrod E. Hoppin, typescript dated Apr. 1921, Lincoln Collection, Watkinson Library, Trinity College, Hartford, Connecticut; Shelby M. Cullom, interviewed by Frank G. Carpenter, Washington *Evening Star*, [3 Nov.] 1895, clipping in scrapbook, Frank G. Carpenter Papers, DLC; Charles S. Zane, "Lincoln as I Knew Him," *Sunset Magazine* 29 (Oct. 1912): 430–438, reprinted in the *Journal of the Illinois State Historical Society* 14 (1921–1922):79–80.

330. Springfield correspondence, 26 Nov., New York *Herald*, 1 Dec. 1860.

331. Whitney, *Life on the Circuit*, ed. Angle, 51, 411.

332. Lincoln to Judd, Springfield, 15 Nov. 1858, Basler, ed., *Collected Works of Lincoln, First Supplement*, 34.

333. Lincoln to Anson G. Henry, Springfield, 19 Nov. 1858, *CWL*, 3:339.

334. Anson G. Henry to Lincoln, Lafayette, Oregon, 16 Feb. 1859, AL MSS DLC.

335. Lincoln to H. D. Sharpe, Springfield, 8 Dec. 1858, *CWL*, 3:344.

336. Fragment on the struggle against slavery [c. July, 1858], ibid., 2:482.

337. Lincoln to Charles H. Ray, Springfield, 20 Nov. 1858, ibid., 3:342.

338. Springfield correspondence, 21 June, Utica, New York, *Herald*, 27 June 1860, copied in the New York *Tribune*, 9 July 1860.

339. *Illinois State Register* (Springfield), 6 Aug., 1, 2 Nov. 1858.

340. Chicago *Daily Times,* 2 Nov. 1858.

341. W. D. Wyatt to Douglas, Lincoln, 8 Nov. 1858, Douglas Papers, University of Chicago.

342. Charles Sweney to Douglas, Prairie City, Illinois, 11 Nov. 1858, ibid.

343. Paris, Illinois, correspondence, 31 July, *Illinois State Register* (Springfield), 4 Aug. 1858.

344. *Illinois State Register* (Springfield), 28 Aug., 9 Nov. 1858.

345. J. Henly Smith to Alexander H. Stephens, Washington, 3 Aug. 1858, Stephens Papers, DLC, quoted in Fehrenbacher, *Dred Scott Case,* 497.

346. Louis Didier, undated memo [ca. Aug. 1858], "A Report to the Honorable S. A. Douglas, U.S.S., on the German Press and German politics in the State of Illinois," Douglas Papers, University of Chicago.

347. Springfield correspondence, 11 Oct., *Missouri Republican* (St. Louis), 13 Oct. 1858.

348. Chicago *Press and Tribune,* 5 Nov. 1858.

349. Springfield correspondence, 21 June, Utica, New York, *Herald,* 27 June 1860, copied in the New York *Tribune,* 9 July 1860.

350. Quincy *Whig & Republican,* n.d., copied in the Dixon *Republican and Telegraph,* 28 Oct. 1858.

351. William H. Hanna, interview with Herndon, [1865–1866], *HI,* 459.

352. Lincoln to Campbell, Springfield, 25 June 1858, *CWL,* 2:473.

353. David Davis to O. M. Hatch, Springfield and Bloomington, 18 Aug. 1858, *For the People: A Newsletter of the Abraham Lincoln Association* 4, no. 3 (Autumn 2002):6–7.

354. John Wentworth to David Davis, n.d., quoted in Davis to Lincoln, Bloomington, 1 Jan. [1859, misdated 1858 by Davis], AL MSS DLC.

355. Lincoln to Judd, Springfield, 9 Dec. 1859, *CWL,* 3:505.

356. E. B. Washburne to Adele Washburne, Galena, 2 Nov. 1858, Washburn Family Papers, Washburn Memorial Library, Norlands, Maine.

357. H. S. Thomas to Lincoln, Vermont, Illinois, 29 Jan. 1859, AL MSS DLC.

358. Herndon to Theodore Parker, Springfield, 25 Sept., 23, 24 Nov. 1858, Herndon-Parker Papers, University of Iowa.

359. Chicago *Press and Tribune,* 29 Oct. and 10 Nov. 1858.

360. New York *Tribune,* 20 Aug. 1860.

361. New York *Tribune,* 29 May 1860.

362. Ibid., 18 Aug. 1860.

363. Cincinnati *Commercial,* 29 Oct. 1858.

364. Ottawa *Republican,* 13 Nov. 1858.

365. Sparks, ed., *Lincoln-Douglas Debates,* 582; New York *Evening Post,* 18 Oct. 1858.

366. *Iowa Citizen* (Des Moines), 17 Nov. 1858, in F. I. Herriott, *Iowa and Abraham Lincoln: Being an Account of the Presidential Discussion and Party Preliminaries in Iowa, 1856–1860* (Des Moines: n.p., 1911), 73.

367. Rochester *Democrat,* 10 Nov. 1858, in Sparks, ed., *Lincoln-Douglas Debates,* 583.

368. Greensburg, Indiana, *Decatur Republican,* 26 Nov. 1858, quoted in Elmer Duane Elbert, "Southern Indiana Politics on the Eve of the Civil War, 1858–1861" (Ph.D. dissertation, Indiana University, 1967), 73; Indianapolis *Journal,* 5 Nov. 1858.

369. *Illinois State Register* (Springfield), 1 Dec. 1858.

370. Anson Miller to E. B. Washburne, Rockford, 5 Nov. 1858, Washburne Papers, DLC.

371. William H. Hanna and John Wickizer to Lincoln, Bloomington, 5 Nov. 1858, AL MSS DLC.

372. David Davis to Lincoln, Danville, 7 Nov. 1858, ibid.

373. Bromwell to Lincoln, Charleston, 5 Nov. 1858, ibid.

374. White to Lincoln, Chicago, 5 Nov. 1858, ibid.

375. Robert Todd Lincoln to Isaac Markens, Manchester, Vermont, 4 Nov. 1917, Paul M.

Angle, ed., *A Portrait of Abraham Lincoln in Letters by His Oldest Son* (Chicago: Chicago Historical Society, 1968), 47.

376. Chester P. Dewey to Lincoln, Rochester, New York, 30 Oct. 1858, AL MSS DLC.

377. John O. Johnson to Ozias M. Hatch, New York, 17 Feb. 1860, Hatch Papers, IHi.

378. Portland *Advertiser,* 18 Nov., copied in the Alton *Courier,* 30 Nov. 1858.

379. Speech by Greeley, 22 May, New York *Tribune,* 23 May 1860.

380. Rives to Ozias M. Hatch, 5 and 10 Nov. 1858, Hatch Papers, IHi.

381. *Illinois Gazette* (Lacon), 8 Nov. 1858, in J[eriah] B[onham], "Recollections of Abraham Lincoln," Chicago *Tribune,* 12 May 1895.

382. Chicago *Daily Democrat,* 11 Nov. 1858, Sparks, ed., *Lincoln-Douglas Debates,* 588.

383. Josiah M. Lucas to O. M. Hatch, Washington, July [1859, no day of the month indicated], Hatch Papers, IHi.

384. *Congressional Globe,* 36th Congress, 1st Session, 2241 (22 May 1860).

385. New York *Tribune,* 5 Nov. 1858.

386. David R. Locke in Rice, ed., *Reminiscences of Lincoln,* 447.

387. Lincoln to Henry Asbury, Springfield, 19 Nov. 1858, *CWL,* 3:339.

388. Lincoln to Salmon P. Chase, Springfield, 30 Apr. 1859, ibid., 3:378,

389. Lincoln to Alexander Sympson, Springfield, 12 Dec. 1858, ibid., 3:346.

390. Lincoln to Lyman Trumbull, Springfield, 29 Jan. 1859, ibid., 3:351.

Chapter 14. "That Presidential Grub Gnaws Deep"

1. Comment made to J. Russell Jones, in "Lincoln and Grant in 1863," statement of Jones to J. McCan Davis, 10 Dec. 1898, typescript, Ida M. Tarbell Papers, Allegheny College.

2. Joseph Gillespie to [Martin Hardin], Edwardsville, 22 Apr. 1880, Hardin Family Papers, ICHi.

3. Henry Villard, *Memoirs of Henry Villard, Journalist and Financier: 1838–1900* (2 vols.; Boston: Houghton Mifflin, 1904), 1:96.

4. Jesse W. Fell in Osborn H. Oldroyd, ed., *The Lincoln Memorial: Album-Immortelles* (New York: G. W. Carleton, 1882), 474–476.

5. Lincoln to Thomas J. Pickett, Springfield, 16 Apr. 1859, Roy P. Basler et al., eds., *Collected Works of Abraham Lincoln* [hereafter *CWL*] (8 vols. plus index; New Brunswick, NJ: Rutgers University Press, 1953–1955), 3:377.

6. Seth Eyland [David Edward Cronin], *The Evolution of a Life* (New York: S. W. Green's Son, 1884), 293.

7. Schuyler Colfax to Charles M. Heaton, Sr., Washington, 20 Dec. 1858, Colfax Papers, Northern Indiana Center for History, South Bend.

8. Herndon to Horace White, Springfield, 25 Apr. 1890, White Papers, IHi.

9. Lincoln to Judd, Springfield, 16 Nov. 1858, *CWL,* 3:337.

10. Ibid.

11. Lincoln to Mark W. Delahay, Springfield, 16 Mar. 1860, ibid., 4:32; Lincoln to Hawkins Taylor, Springfield, 6 Sept. 1859, ibid., 3:400.

12. Charles S. Zane, "Lincoln As I Knew Him," *Sunset, the Pacific Monthly* 29 (Oct. 1912): 432.

13. Lincoln to Samuel C. Davis and Company, Springfield, 17 and 20 Nov. 1858, *CWL,* 3:338, and Roy P. Basler, ed., *Collected Works of Abraham Lincoln, First Supplement, 1832–1865* (Westport, CT: Greenwood Press, 1973), 35.

14. Lincoln to Samuel Galloway, Springfield, 27 July 1859; Lincoln to Charles Ambos, Springfield, 21 June 1859, *CWL,* 3:393, 387.

15. William Herndon to Jesse W. Weik, Springfield, 20 Nov. 1885, H-W MSS DLC.

16. William H. Herndon's interview with George Alfred Townsend, Springfield correspondence, 25 Jan., New York *Tribune,* 15 Feb. 1867; Herndon, "Analysis of the Character of Abraham Lincoln," lecture delivered at Springfield, 26 Dec. 1865, *Abraham Lincoln Quarterly* 1 (1941):429; William Herndon to Jesse W. Weik, Springfield, 20 Nov. 1885, H-W MSS DLC; William H. Herndon and

Jesse W. Weik, *Herndon's Lincoln,* ed. Douglas L. Wilson and Rodney O. Davis (1889; Urbana: University of Illinois Press, 2006), 205.

17. Lincoln to Lyman Trumbull, Springfield, 11 Dec. 1858, *CWL,* 3:345.

18. Lincoln to W. H. Wells, Springfield, 8 Jan. 1859, ibid., 3:349.

19. Speech in Chicago, 1 Mar. 1859, ibid., 3:369–370.

20. Lincoln to Mark W. Delahay, Springfield, 14 May 1859, ibid., 3:379.

21. Lincoln to Nathan Sargent, Springfield, 23 June 1859, ibid., 3:388.

22. Lincoln to Henry L. Pierce and others, Springfield, 6 Apr. 1859, ibid., 3:375–376.

23. The quote comes from Jefferson's only book, *Notes on the State of Virginia,* ed. Merrill D. Peterson (1781–1782; New York: Library of America, 1984), 289.

24. Springfield (Massachusetts) *Republican,* 13 July 1860.

25. Nathan M. Knapp to O. M. Hatch, Winchester, Illinois, 12 May 1859, Hatch Papers, IHi.

26. John Law to Richard W. Thompson, Evansville, 27 Feb. 1860, Richard W. Thompson Collection, LMF.

27. John Olney to Lyman Trumbull, Shawneetown, 12 Mar. 1860, Trumbull Papers, DLC.

28. Lincoln to Trumbull, Springfield, 3 Feb. 1859, *CWL,* 3:355–356.

29. Ray to N. P. Banks, Chicago, 2 Apr. [1859], Banks Papers, DLC.

30. Lincoln to Schuyler Colfax, Springfield, 6 July 1859, *CWL,* 3:391.

31. Lincoln to Canisius, Springfield, 17 May 1859, ibid., 3:380.

32. Springfield (Massachusetts) *Republican,* 13 July 1860.

33. *Illinois State Register* (Springfield), 26 June 1858.

34. Lincoln to Chase, Springfield, 9 June 1859, *CWL,* 3:384.

35. Lincoln to Chase, Springfield, 20 June 1859, ibid., 3:386.

36. Lincoln to Samuel Galloway, Springfield, 28 July 1858, ibid., 3:394–395.

37. Lincoln to Colfax, Springfield, 6 July 1859, ibid., 3:390–391; Colfax to Lincoln, South Bend, Indiana, 14 July 1859, AL MSS DLC.

38. John Hay, "The Heroic Age in Washington," lecture of 1871, in Michael Burlingame, ed., *At Lincoln's Side: John Hay's Civil War Correspondence and Selected Writings* (Carbondale: Southern Illinois University Press, 2000), 116.

39. New York *Times,* 8, 9 Sept. 1859.

40. Cincinnati *Enquirer,* 11 Sept. 1859.

41. Medill to Lincoln, Chicago, 10 Sept. 1859, AL MSS DLC.

42. Speech at Columbus, *CWL,* 3:400–425.

43. David R. Locke in Allen Thorndike Rice, ed., *Reminiscences of Abraham Lincoln by Distinguished Men of His Time* (New York: North American Review, 1886), 446–447.

44. Chicago *Press and Tribune,* 19 Sept. 1859.

45. Francis P. Blair, Jr., to Lincoln, St. Louis, 18 Oct. 1859, AL MSS DLC.

46. Dayton *Daily Empire,* 19 Sept. 1859, in John H. Cramer, "Lincoln in Ohio," *The Ohio State Archaeological and Historical Quarterly* 54 (1945):155.

47. *Ohio Statesman* (Columbus), 17 Sept. 1859.

48. Bert S. Bartlow and William H. Todhunter, *Centennial History of Butler County, Ohio* ([n. p.]: B. F. Bowen, 1905), 123.

49. Rutherford B. Hayes to A. P. Russell, Cincinnati, 14 Sept. 1859, Whelpley Collection, Cincinnati Historical Society.

50. Basler, ed., *Collected Works of Lincoln, First Supplement,* 44–45.

51. Cincinnati *Commercial,* 19, 17 Sept. 1859.

52. Moncure D. Conway, *Autobiography: Memories and Experiences* (2 vols.; Boston: Houghton Mifflin, 1904), 1:317.

53. Charles Richard Williams, *The Life of Rutherford Birchard Hayes, Nineteenth President of the United States* (2 vols.; Boston: Houghton Mifflin, 1914), 1:111.

54. Hayes, "Our Two Greatest Presidents," interview, ca. 1892, in Ari Hoogenboom, *Rutherford B. Hayes: Warrior and President* (Lawrence: University Press of Kansas, 1995), 108–109.

55. Josiah M. Lucas to O. M. Hatch, Washington, 7 Oct. 1859, Hatch Papers, IHi.

56. Cincinnati *Enquirer*, 18 Sept. 1859, in Herbert Mitgang, ed., *Abraham Lincoln: A Press Portrait* (Chicago: Quadrangle Books, 1971), 140.

57. *Illinois State Journal* (Springfield), 12 Mar. 1860.

58. J. H. Jordan to Lincoln, Cincinnati, 4 July 1861, AL MSS DLC.

59. Whitelaw Reid, *Ohio in the War: Her Statesmen, Her Generals, and Soldiers* (2 vols.; Cincinnati: Moore, Wilstach & Baldwin, 1868), 1:727

60. Cincinnati *Enquirer*, 18 Sept., quoted in the Cincinnati *Commercial*, 19 Sept. 1859.

61. Cincinnati *Commercial*, 17 Sept. 1859.

62. Springfield correspondence, 16 Oct., New York *Herald*, 20 Oct. 1860; Springfield correspondence, 6 Nov., New York *Tribune*, 10 Nov. 1860; letter by a Springfield resident to a prominent Philadelphian, Springfield, 4 June 1860, ibid., 11 June 1860.

63. *CWL*, 3:470.

64. Indianapolis *Daily State Sentinel*, 26 Sept. 1859, quoted in Elmer Duane Elbert, "Southern Indiana Politics on the Eve of the Civil War, 1858–1861" (Ph.D. dissertation, Indiana University, 1967), 103–104.

65. Gayle Thornbrough, ed., *The Diary of Calvin Fletcher* (8 vols.; Indianapolis: Indiana Historical Society, 1972–1981), 6:412 (entry for 19 Sept. 1859).

66. Lincoln to Chase, Springfield, 21 Sept. 1859, *CWL*, 3:471.

67. Lincoln to Mark W. Delahay, Springfield, 17 Oct. 1859, ibid., 3:490.

68. Ibid., 3:489.

69. Correspondence dated The Beeches, Ohio, 22 Sept., New York *Times*, 4 Oct. 1859.

70. Chicago *Press and Tribune*, 19 Oct. 1859.

71. Galloway to Lincoln, Columbus, 13 Oct. 1859, AL MSS DLC.

72. Charles H. Ray to Lincoln, Chicago, [20 Oct. 1859], ibid.

73. Paris, Illinois, *Beacon*, 30 Nov. 1859, in Donald G. Richter, *Lincoln: Twenty Years on the Eastern Prairie* (Mattoon, IL: United Graphics, 1999), 241–242.

74. Baltimore *Turnzeitung*, n.d., copied in the Chicago *Press and Tribune*, 2 May 1860.

75. Mark W. Delahay to Lincoln, Leavenworth, Kansas, 14 Nov. 1859, AL MSS DLC.

76. Delahay to Lincoln, Leavenworth, Kansas, 15 Nov. 1859, ibid.

77. Nathan M. Knapp to O. M. Hatch, n.p., 12 May 1859, Hatch Papers, IHi.

78. Republican Party of Ohio to Lincoln, Columbus, 7 Dec. 1859, and George M. Parsons et al. to Lincoln, Columbus, 7 Dec. 1859, AL MSS DLC.

79. Lincoln to George M. Parsons et al., Springfield, 19 Dec. 1859, and to James W. Sheahan, Springfield, 24 Jan. 1860, *CWL*, 3:510, 515.

80. Samuel Galloway to Lincoln, Columbus, 24 Jan. 1860; Richard P. L. Baber to Lincoln, Columbus 25 Jan. 1860, AL MSS DLC.

81. Lincoln to T. Apolion Cheney, Springfield, 14 Aug. 1860, *CWL.*, 4:93.

82. New York *Times*, 13 July 1860.

83. Speech of 30 September 1859, *CWL*, 3:471–482.

84. Reminiscences of Charles Caverno, dated Mar. 1902, typescript, William E. Barton Papers, University of Chicago; Henry J. Peterson, "Lincoln at the Wisconsin State Fair as Recalled by John W. Hoyt," *Lincoln Herald* 51, no. 4 (December 1949):6–10.

85. Medill to Chase, Chicago, 30 Oct. 1859, Chase Papers, Historical Society of Pennsylvania.

86. Lincoln to William E. Frazer, Springfield, 1 Nov. 1859, *CWL*, 3:491.

87. William M. Reynolds to Lincoln, Lancaster, Pennsylvania, 25 July 1860, AL MSS DLC; Lincoln to Edward Wallace, Clinton, 11 Oct. 1859, *CWL*, 3:487.

88. Lincoln to Jesse W. Fell, Springfield, 20 Dec. 1859, *CWL*, 3:511.

89. Lewis to Fell, West Chester, 30 Jan. 1860, Fell Papers, DLC; West Chester *Chester County Times,* 11 Feb. 1860.

90. *CWL,* 3:511.

91. Undated article in the New York *Tribune, The Pennsylvania School Journal* (Lancaster) 46 (Jan. 1898) 309-310.

92. Joseph Medill to Archibald W. Campbell, 30 Oct. 1859, Wheeling (West Virginia) *Register,* 1 May 1932.

93. J. Wainwright Ray to John G. Nicolay, Washington, 18 Oct. 1886, Nicolay Papers, DLC.

94. Xenia, Ohio, *News,* n.d., copied in the *Illinois State Journal* (Springfield), 28 Mar. 1860.

95. *Illinois State Journal* (Springfield), 14 Jan. 1860.

96. Ray to Lincoln, Chicago, [20 Oct. 1859], AL MSS DLC.

97. Lincoln to P. Quinn Harrison and to Jesse A. Pickrell, Springfield, 3 Nov. 1859, *CWL,* 3:492, 493.

98. Trumbull to Lincoln, Washington, 23 Nov. 1859, AL MSS DLC.

99. Jacob R. Freese to Seward, Trenton, New Jersey, 30 Apr. 1860, Thurlow Weed Papers, University of Rochester.

100. William E. Frazer to Lincoln, Cookstown, Pennsylvania, 12 Nov. 1859, AL MSS DLC.

101. James Shepherd Pike to Israel Washburn, New York, 29 Jan. 1860, Washburn Family Papers, Washburn Memorial Library, Norlands, Maine.

102. William P. Fessenden to Elizabeth Warriner, Washington, 16 Mar. and 1 Apr. 1860, and to his son William, Washington, 19 Mar. 1860, Fessenden Family Papers, Bowdoin College.

103. Horace Greeley to Schuyler Colfax, New York, 24 Oct. 1859, Greeley Papers, New York Public Library; Greeley to Mrs. Rebekah M. Whipple, [Apr. 1860], in Jeter Allen Isely, *Horace Greeley and the Republican Party, 1853–1861: A Study of the New York Tribune* (Princeton, NJ: Princeton University Press, 1947), 266.

104. New York *Herald,* 16 May 1860.

105. Charles A. Dana, *Recollections of the Civil War: With the Leaders at Washington and in the Field in the Sixties* (New York: D. Appleton, 1898), 171.

106. Fitz-Henry Warren to James Shepherd Pike, Burlington, Iowa, 2 and 20 Feb. 1860, Pike Papers, University of Maine.

107. George A. Nourse to Lyman Trumbull, St. Paul, 13 May 1860, Trumbull Papers, DLC.

108. Leavenworth, Kansas, correspondence, 18 Aug., New York *Tribune,* 30 Aug. 1860.

109. Speech at Elwood, 30 Nov. or 1 Dec. 1859, *CWL,* 3:496.

110. Albert D. Richardson, *The Secret Service: The Field, the Dungeon, and the Escape* (Hartford, CT: American, 1866), 314-315; Fred W. Brinkerhoff, "The Kansas Tour of Lincoln the Candidate," *Kansas Historical Quarterly* 13 (1944–1945):305.

111. Reminiscences of Senator John Ingalls, Washington *Post,* 29 June 1890.

112. "Humors of the Day," *Harper's Weekly,* 28 Apr. 1860.

113. John James Ingalls, "A Forgotten Chapter of History: Abraham Lincoln in Kansas in 1859," New York *Sun,* 31 May 1891.

114. Daniel Webster Wilder to George W. Martin, 22 Apr. 1902, in *Kansas State Historical Society Transactions* 7 (1901–1902): 536–537n.

115. *CWL,* 3:502.

116. Ibid., 3:503.

117. Villard's dispatch quoted in A. B. MacDonald, "Lincoln Gave His 'Most Important Speech' in Kansas," Kansas City *Star,* 10 Feb. 1929.

118. Leavenworth *Weekly Herald,* 10 Dec. 1859.

119. Unidentified clipping, reproducing the Washington correspondence by Ward Burlingame, n.d., Kansas City *Star,* [18 May 1893?], LMF.

120. "Early Days of a War Eagle," reminiscences of Daniel Anthony, Kansas City *Star,* 23 Feb. 1902.

121. Mary E. Delahay, "Judge Mark W. Delahay," typescript, p. 5, William E. Barton Papers, University of Illinois.

122. St. Joseph correspondence by William H. Gill, 8 Dec., Leavenworth *Weekly Herald*, 10 Dec. 1859.

123. Leavenworth, Kansas, correspondence, 18 Aug., New York *Tribune*, 30 Aug. 1860.

124. Leavenworth *Times*, 7 Dec. 1859, copied in the Leavenworth, Kansas, correspondence, 18 Aug., New York *Tribune*, 30 Aug. 1860.

125. Lincoln to James W. Somers, Springfield, 17 Mar. 1860, *CWL*, 4:33.

126. Judd to Lyman Trumbull, Chicago, 1 and 6 Dec. 1859, Trumbull Papers, DLC.

127. Lincoln to Judd, Springfield, 9 Dec. 1859, *CWL*, 3:505.

128. David Davis to [John Wentworth], Bloomington, 25 Sept. 1859, Ozias M. Hatch Papers, IHi.

129. Lincoln to George W. Dole, Gurdon S. Hubbard, and William H. Brown, Springfield, 14 Dec. 1859, *CWL*, 3:508.

130. Roy P. Basler and Christian O. Basler, eds., *Collected Works of Abraham Lincoln, Second Supplement* (New Brunswick, NJ: Rutgers University Press, 1990), 19.

131. Trumbull to Lincoln, Washington, 26 Mar. 1860, AL MSS DLC.

132. David Davis to Lincoln, Danville, 5 May 1860, ibid.

133. Lincoln to Judd, Springfield, 5 Feb. 1860, *CWL*, 3:516.

134. William H. Bissell to Salmon P. Chase, Springfield, 4 Feb. 1860, Chase Papers, DLC.

135. Wiley to Lyman Trumbull, Anna, 10 Jan. 1860, Trumbull Papers, DLC.

136. A. M. Blackburn to Lyman Trumbull, Jerseyville, 3 Feb. 1860, ibid.

137. Henry Barber to Lyman Trumbull, Osborn, 5 Mar. 1860, ibid.

138. Judd, interview with John G. Nicolay, Washington, 28 Feb. 1876, Michael Burlingame, ed., *An Oral History of Abraham Lincoln: John G. Nicolay's Interviews and Essays* (Carbondale: Southern Illinois University Press, 1996), 46.

139. Reminiscences of Swett in New York correspondence by "Jerome," 6 Feb., *Indiana Journal* (Indianapolis), 10 Feb. 1879; Jackson Grimshaw to William H. Herndon, Quincy, 28 Apr. 1866, Douglas L. Wilson and Rodney O. Davis, eds., *Herndon's Informants: Letters, Interviews, and Statements about Abraham Lincoln* [hereafter *HI*] (Urbana: University of Illinois Press, 1998), 247; reminiscences of Thomas J. Henderson, Princeton, Illinois, 28 Oct. 1895, Ida M. Tarbell Papers, Allegheny College.

140. Reminiscences of E. M. Haines, in Francis Fisher Browne, *The Every-Day Life of Abraham Lincoln* (New York: N. D. Thompson, 1886), 327.

141. Hawkins Taylor, "Early Reminiscences," Peoria *Weekly Journal*, 1895, in Emma Siggins White, *Genealogy of the Descendants of John Walker of Wigton, Scotland* ([Kansas City, Mo.]: Tiernan-Dart, 1902), in Rufus Rockwell Wilson, ed., *Intimate Memories of Lincoln* (Elmira, NY: Primavera, 1945), 11.

142. Theodore Calvin Pease and James G. Randall, eds., *The Diary of Orville Hickman Browning* (2 vols.; Springfield: Illinois State Historical Library, 1925–1933), 1:395 (entry for 8 Feb. 1860).

143. H. J. Atkins to Lyman Trumbull, Jacksonville, 28 Dec. 1859, Trumbull Papers, DLC.

144. Marshall to Lyman Trumbull, Charleston, 17 Feb. 1860, ibid.

145. Lincoln to Judd, Springfield, 9 Feb. 1860, *CWL*, 3:517.

146. Chicago *Press and Tribune*, 16 Feb. 1860.

147. Judd to Lincoln, Chicago, 21 Feb. 1860, AL MSS DLC.

148. Judd to Trumbull, Chicago, 2 Apr. 1860, Trumbull Papers, DLC.

149. Washington correspondence, 20 Feb., Chicago *Press and Tribune*, 27 Feb. 1860.

150. Joseph Medill to Frederic Bancroft, n.p., 18 Feb. 1896, Frederic Bancroft, *The Life of*

William H. Seward (2 vols.; New York: Harper and Brothers, 1900), 1:531n.

151. Lincoln to Judd, Springfield, 14 Dec. 1859, *CWL*, 3:509.

152. Chicago correspondence, n.d., New York *Herald*, n.d., copied in the *Illinois State Journal* (Springfield), 18 Jan. 1860.

153. *Sioux City Register*, 31 Dec. 1859.

154. John Law to Richard W. Thompson, Evansville, 27 Feb. 1860, Richard W. Thompson Collection, LMF.

155. S. M. Pettingill to William H. Bailhache, New York, 12 Oct. 1859, Lincoln Collection, RPB.

156. Lawrence Weldon, in Rice, ed., *Reminiscences of Lincoln*, 207; William H. Bailhache to John Hay, Los Angeles, 4 Apr. 1887, copy, Hay Papers, DLC.

157. Herndon to Ward Hill Lamon, Springfield, 6 Mar. 1870, Lamon Papers, CSmH.

158. Thurlow Weed Barnes, *Memoir of Thurlow Weed* (Boston: Houghton Mifflin, 1884), 269.

159. Springfield correspondence, 4 Sept., New York *Evening Post*, 8 Sept. 1860.

160. Interview with Mrs. Stephen Smith, Bloomington *Pantagraph*, 19 Feb. 1895; Elizabeth Irons Folsom, "New Stories of Abraham Lincoln," *The American Magazine* 96 (July 1923):47, 120–122.

161. Charles C. Nott to Lincoln, New York, 9 Feb. 1860, AL MSS DLC, and to John P. Hale, New York, 8 Mar. 1860, Hale Papers, New Hampshire Historical Society; Richard C. McCormick's reminiscences, New York, 29 Apr., New York *Evening Post*, 3 May 1865; Cephas Brainerd to N. P. Banks, New York, 2 Mar. 1860, Banks Papers, DLC.

162. Bowen in William Hayes Ward, *Abraham Lincoln, Tributes from His Associates: Reminiscences of Soldiers, Statesmen, and Citizens* (New York: Thomas Y. Crowell, 1895), 28; interview with Stephen M. Griswold in "Lincoln at Plymouth," unidentified, undated newspaper clipping, LMF.

163. Mason Brayman to W. H. Bailhache, New York, 27 Feb. 1860, Lincoln Collection, ICHi.

164. Undated reminiscences of Mrs. Theodore Gowdy (nèe Mary Brayman), daughter of Mason Brayman, Ida M. Tarbell Papers, Allegheny College; undated, unidentified newspaper clipping, Lincoln Scrap Books, Judd Stewart Collection, CSmH.

165. Mason Brayman to W. H. Bailhache, New York, 27 Feb. 1860, Lincoln Collection, ICHi.

166. Truman H. Bartlett to Charles L. McLellan, Chocorua, New Hampshire, 26 Aug. 1908, Lincoln Collection, RPB.

167. Roy Meredith, *Mr. Lincoln's Camera Man, Mathew B. Brady* (New York: Scribner's, 1946), 59.

168. Richard C. McCormick's reminiscences, New York, 29 Apr., New York *Evening Post*, 3 May 1865.

169. New York *Tribune*, 25 Feb. 1860.

170. James A. Briggs in the New York *Evening Post*, 16 Aug. 1867.

171. [Cornelius A. Runkle's reminiscences in] Noah Brooks, *Abraham Lincoln and the Downfall of American Slavery* (New York: Putnam's, 1894), 186.

172. Mason Brayman to William Bailhache, New York, 28 Feb. 1860, Bailhache-Brayman Papers, IHi.

173. *CWL*, 3:522–550.

174. [Cornelius A. Runkle's reminiscences in] Brooks, *Lincoln and the Downfall of American Slavery*, 187; Richard C. McCormick's reminiscences, New York, 29 Apr., New York *Evening Post*, 3 May 1865

175. New York *Tribune*, 28 Feb., 6 Mar. 1860.

176. John Bigelow to William Hargreaves, New York, 30 July 1860, Bigelow Papers, New York Public Library; New York *Evening Post*, 28 Feb. 1860; Charles H. Brown, *William Cullen Bryant* (New York: Scribner, 1971), 419.

177. New York correspondence by "Launcelot," 3 Mar. 1860, *Press and Tribune*, n.d., clipping in scrapbook # 11, Edmund C. Stedman Papers, Columbia University.

178. New York *Independent*, n.d., copied in the Chicago *Press and Tribune*, 4 June 1860.

179. Boston *Atlas and Daily Bee,* 29 Feb. 1860; Boston *Journal,* 29 Feb. 1860, in William Francis Hanna, "Abraham Lincoln and the New England Press, 1858–1860" (Ph.D. dissertation, Boston College, 1980), 47–48.

180. Horace Greeley "Greeley's Estimate of Lincoln: An Unpublished Address by Horace Greeley," *Century Magazine* 42 (July 1891):373.

181. Washington correspondence, n.d., Rock Island, Illinois, *Register,* n.d., copied in the *Illinois State Journal* (Springfield), 26 Mar. 1860.

182. Charles C. Nott and Cephas Brainerd, eds., "The Address of the Hon. Abraham Lincoln: In Vindication of the Policy of the Framers of the Constitution and the Principles of the Republican Party, Delivered at Cooper Institute, February 27th, 1860" (pamphlet; New York: G. F. Nesbitt, 1860), reproduced in George Haven Putnam, *Abraham Lincoln: The People's Leader in the Struggle for National Existence* (New York: G. P. Putnam's Sons, 1909), 233–288 (quote appears on 233–234).

183. Richard C. McCormick's reminiscences, New York, 29 Apr., New York *Evening Post,* 3 May 1865.

184. Charles T. Rodgers et al. to Lincoln, n.p., 26 Sept. 1864, AL MSS DLC.

185. New York *Herald,* 19 May 1860; Boston *Post,* n.d., copied in the Chicago *Daily Times,* 4 Mar. 1860.

186. *Illinois State Register* (Springfield), 3 and 19 Mar. 1860.

187. Lincoln to Mary Todd Lincoln, Exeter, New Hampshire, 4 Mar. 1860, Basler, ed., *Collected Works of Lincoln, First Supplement,* 49.

188. *CWL,* 4:7, 12.

189. Ibid., 4:25.

190. "A Talk with Abraham Lincoln," Rev. John P. Gulliver, New York *Independent,* 1 Sept. 1864; reminiscences of Edward Goodman Holden, Chicago *Tribune,* 12 Feb. 1900.

191. Reminiscences of Alfred Hemenway, enclosed in Hemenway to Albert J. Beveridge, Boston, 11 Nov. 1925, Beveridge Papers, DLC.

192. Speech at Hartford, 5 Mar. 1860, *CWL,* 4:7, 8, 12.

193. Speech of 6 Mar. 1860, ibid., 4:23, 18.

194. John P. Bartlett to the editor, n.d., *Century Magazine* 54 (July 1897):475.

195. Stevens, *A Reporter's Lincoln,* ed. Burlingame, 55, 96.

196. F. B. Sanborn, *Recollections of Seventy Years* (2 vols.; Boston: R.G. Badger, 1909), 1:25.

197. Concord *Independent Democrat,* 8 Mar. 1860.

198. Henry McFarland, *Sixty Years in Concord and Elsewhere: Personal Recollections of Henry McFarland, 1831–1891* (Concord, NH: Rumford Press, 1899), 204.

199. Ben: Perley Poore and F. B. Eaton, *Sketches of the Life and Public Services of Frederick Smyth of New Hampshire* (Manchester, NH: John B. Clarke, 1885), 99.

200. Manchester *American,* 2 Mar. 1860, quoted in Lucy Lowden, "The People's Party: the 'Heirs of Jackson' and the Rise of the Republican Party in New Hampshire, 1845–1860" (M.A. thesis, Western Illinois University, 1971), 91.

201. Poore and Eaton, *Smyth,* 100.

202. Theodore Tilton to Wendell Phillips, New York, 1 Mar. 1860, Phillips Papers, Harvard University.

203. Frederick Smyth to Lincoln, 5 Nov. 1860, Smyth Letterbooks, New Hampshire Historical Society, quoted in Lowden, "The People's Party," 90.

204. James B. Angell, *The Reminiscences of James Burrill Angell* (New York: Longmans, Green, 1912), 117.

205. G. W. Jackson to James F. Simmons, Providence, 2 Mar. 1860, James F. Simmons Papers, DLC.

206. John W. Mahan to Stephen A. Douglas, Boston, 10 Apr. 1860, Douglas Papers, University of Chicago.

207. Francis B. Carpenter, *The Inner Life of Abraham Lincoln: Six Months at the White House* (New York: Hurd and Houghton, 1867), 135.

208. Ibid.

209. *Monthly Record of the Five Points House of Industry* 8 (May 1865):1–3; "Lincoln Among

the Children," New York *Tribune*, 30 May 1860; Patrick McCarty and several other boys enrolled in the charity school at the Five Points House of Industry to Lincoln, New York, 16 Oct. 1863, AL MSS DLC; Edward Eggleston in Browne, *Every-Day Life of Lincoln*, 322–323; F. Lauriston Bullard, "When Lincoln Was Taken for 'a Western Clergyman,'" *Lincoln Herald* 46 (1944):23–25.

210. Julia Tappan to William Barney, New York, 25 Mar. 1860, in James N. Adams, "Lincoln and Hiram Barney," *Journal of the Ilinois State Historical Society* 50 (1957):347.

211. Mason Brayman to William Bailhache, New York, 28 Feb. 1860, Bailhache-Brayman Papers, IHi.

212. Briggs in the New York *Evening Post*, 16 Aug. 1867.

213. Babcock to Lincoln, New Haven, 22 Feb. 1864, AL MSS DLC.

214. Charles E. Dyer to John G. Nicolay, Norwich, Connecticut, 26 Aug. 1887, Nicolay Papers, DLC.

215. Hartford *Evening Press*, 6 Mar. 1860, in Hanna, "Lincoln and the New England Press," 75.

216. James F. Babcock to Gideon Welles, New Haven, 3 Feb. 1868, Abraham Lincoln Collection, Beinecke Library, Yale University.

217. Springfield (Massachusetts) *Republican*, 3 Mar. 1860.

218. *Menard Index* (Petersburg), n.d., copied in the Chicago *Press and Tribune*, 28 Mar. 1860.

219. Machias, Maine, *Republican*, n.d., copied in the *Illinois State Journal* (Springfield), 19 Mar. 1860.

220. Chicago *Press and Tribune*, 21 Mar. 1860.

221. Letter by L. B. G. [George B. Lincoln], Sandovel, Illinois, 9 Jan. 1860, Chicago *Press and Tribune*, 12 Jan. 1860.

222. Galloway to Lincoln, Columbus, 15 Mar. 1860, AL MSS DLC.

223. Trumbull to Lincoln, Washington, 26 Mar. 1860, ibid.

224. C. D. Hay to Lincoln, Newton, Illinois, 27 Mar. 1860, ibid.

225. Rollins to Lincoln, Concord, New Hampshire, 2 Mar. 1860, ibid.

226. Herman Kreismann to E. B. Washburne, Hartford, 30 Mar. 1860, Washburne Papers, DLC.

227. Concord *Independent Democrat*, 8 Mar. 1860.

228. *Journal of the Illinois State Historical Society*, 44–45 (1951–52): 171.

229. Lincoln to T. C. Moore, Springfield, 1 May 1860, Basler, ed., *Collected Works of Lincoln, First Supplement*, 53.

230. *CWL*, 4:41–42.

231. Delahay to Lincoln, Lawrence, Kansas, 17 Feb. 1860, and Leavenworth, Kansas, 7 Apr. 1860, AL MSS DLC; Lincoln to Delahay, Springfield, 16 Mar. and 14 Apr. 1860, *CWL*, 4:32, 44.

232. Lincoln to E. Stafford, Springfield, 17 Mar. 1860, *CWL*, 4:33.

233. Lincoln to Trumbull, Springfield, 29 Apr. 1860, ibid., 4:45.

234. Lincoln to Galloway, Chicago, 24 Mar. 1860, ibid., 4:34.

235. Henry C. Baird to John M. Read, Philadelphia, 23 Apr. 1860, Lincoln Collection, RPB.

236. Lincoln to Richard M. Corwine, Springfield, 6 Apr. 1860, *CWL*, 4:36.

237. Lincoln to Trumbull, Springfield, 29 Apr. 1860, ibid., 4:45–46.

238. Ibid.

239. Michael Burlingame and John R. Turner Ettlinger, eds., *Inside Lincoln's White House: The Complete Civil War Diary of John Hay* (Carbondale: Southern Illinois University Press, 1997), 26 (entry for 17 Oct. 1861); Whitney, *Life on the Circuit*, ed. Angle, 153.

240. Lincoln to Richard M. Corwine, Springfield, 2 May 1860, *CWL*, 4:47-48.

241. Delahay to Lincoln, Leavenworth, Kansas, 26 Mar. 1860, AL MSS DLC.

242. John A. Morton to Richard W. Thompson, n.p., 26 Mar. 1860, Thompson Papers, LMF; Washington correspondence, 1 Aug., New York *Herald*, 9 Aug. 1859.

243. Wilmot to Lincoln, Towanda, Pennsylvania, 11 July 1860, AL MSS DLC.

244. New York *Tribune,* 23 May 1860.

245. Joseph M. Root to Joshua R. Giddings, Sandusky, Ohio, 26 May 1860, Giddings Papers, Ohio Historical Society.

246. McLean to John Teesdale, Lake Pepin, Minnesota, 3 Sept. 1859, in William Salter, ed., "Letters of John McLean to John Teesdale," *The Biblioteca Sacra* 56 (1899):740.

247. St. Joseph correspondence by Gill, 8 Dec., Leavenworth *Weekly Herald,* 10 Dec. 1859.

248. Moses's reminiscences, Winchester, Illinois, *Independent,* n.d., copied in the *Illinois State Journal* (Springfield), 27 Oct. 1879.

249. Indianapolis correspondence by Charles A. Page, 30 Apr. 1865, in Charles A. Page, *Letters of a War Correspondent,* ed. James R. Gilmore (Boston: L. C. Page, 1899), 376; Mark A. Plummer, *Lincoln's Rail-Splitter: Governor Richard J. Oglesby* (Urbana: University of Illinois Press, 2001), 41–42; Johnson to William Herndon, [1865–1866], *HI,* 462–463; "Viator" to the editors, Decatur, 4 May, *Illinois State Journal* (Springfield), 7 May 1860.

250. "Viator" to the editors, Decatur, 4 May, *Illinois State Journal* (Springfield), 7 May 1860.

251. *CWL,* 4:48.

252. "Republican History, Some Reminiscences of the Decatur Convention of 1860," *Illinois State Journal* (Springfield), 26 May 1879.

253. Brooks, *Lincoln and the Downfall of American Slavery,* 184.

254. Noah Brooks, "Personal Recollections of Abraham Lincoln," *Harper's New Monthly Magazine,* July 1865, in Michael Burlingame, ed., *Lincoln Observed: Civil War Dispatches of Noah Brooks* (Baltimore, MD: Johns Hopkins University Press, 1998), 213–214.

255. N. M. Knapp to Ozias M. Hatch, Winchester, Illinois, 12 Mar. 1860, Hatch Papers, IHi.

256. Chicago *Herald,* 12 May 1860.

257. Henry Asbury to K. K. Jones, Quincy, Illinois, 2 Oct. 1882, copy, files of the Abraham Lincoln Association, IHi; Ida Tarbell to John S. Phillips, Bloomington, Illinois, 16 Nov. 1922, recounting a conversation with Oglesby's friend Joseph Fifer, Tarbell Papers, Allegheny College; Nathaniel G. Wilcox to Lincoln, Frederick, Illinois, 6 June 1864, AL MSS DLC; obituary of David Davis, Chicago *Times,* 27 June 1886.

258. Kreismann to E. B. Washburne, Chicago, 13 May 1860, Washburne Papers, DLC.

259. J. M. Ruggles, "Reminiscences of the Pekin Convention and of Abraham Lincoln," undated manuscript, Ida Tarbell Papers, Allegheny College.

260. "Lincoln at the Decatur Convention," speech by Richard Price Morgan, delivered in Pontiac, Illinois, 12 Dec. 1909, in Isaac N. Phillips, ed., *Abraham Lincoln by Some Men Who Knew Him* (Bloomington IL: Pantagraph, 1910), 94.

261. Whitney, *Life on the Circuit,* ed. Angle, 102.

262. Reminiscences of John H. Littlefield, *Every Where,* Feb. 1902, in Joseph Fort Newton, *Lincoln and Herndon* (Cedar Rapids, IA: Torch Press, 1910), 251.

263. William Bross to John G. Nicolay, Chicago, 25 Jan. 1887, Nicolay Papers, DLC.

Chapter 15. "The Most Available Presidential Candidate for Unadulterated Republicans"

1. Nathan M. Knapp to O. M. Hatch, Winchester, Illinois, 12 May 1859, Hatch Papers, IHi.

2. William Cumback to William Penn Clarke, Greensburgh, Indiana, 28 Jan., 2 Apr. 1860, Clarke Papers, State Historical Society of Iowa, Des Moines.

3. Chicago correspondence by Simon P. Hanscom, 15 May, New York *Herald,* 19 May 1860.

4. Leonard Swett to the editor, Chicago, 13 July, Chicago *Tribune,* 14 July 1878.

5. Swett's reminiscences, Chicago *Mail,* n.d., copied in the St. Louis *Globe-Democrat,* 27 June 1888.

6. Knapp to Lincoln, Chicago, 14 May 1860, and Delahay to Lincoln, Chicago, 14 May 1860, AL MSS DLC.

7. Charles Henry Ray to Edward Lillie Pierce, Chicago, [Apr. 1860], Pierce Papers, Harvard University.

8. Roy P. Basler et al., eds., *Collected Works of Abraham Lincoln* [hereafter *CWL*] (8 vols. plus index; New Brunswick, NJ: Rutgers University Press, 1953–1955), 4:50.

9. New York *Herald,* 22 May 1860.

10. Chicago correspondence by Samuel Bowles, 16 May, Springfield (Massachusetts) *Republican,* 19 May 1860.

11. Chicago correspondence, 17 May, Cincinnati *Commercial,* 19 and 21 May 1860.

12. Chicago correspondence by G[eorge] D[awson], 19 May, Albany *Evening Journal,* 21 May 1860, copied in the New York *Herald,* 23 May 1860.

13. Oliver Pillsbury to Mason W. Tappan, Henniker, 16 Apr. 1860, Mason Tappan Papers, New Hampshire Historical Society.

14. Russell Hinckley to his brother, Belleville, 28 Mar. 1860, Lyman Trumbull Papers, DLC.

15. Child to John Greenleaf Whittier, n.p., n.d., in Helene Gilbert Baer, *The Heart Is Like Heaven: The Life of Lydia Maria Child* (Philadelphia: University of Pennsylvania Press, 1964), 260.

16. Herndon to Theodore Parker, Springfield, 15 Dec. 1859, Herndon-Parker Papers, University of Iowa.

17. Reminiscences of Galusha Grow in Frederic Bancroft, *The Life of William H. Seward* (2 vols.; New York: Harper and Brothers, 1900), 1:535n.

18. E. G. Waterhouse to William P. Fessenden, Philadelphia, 18 Apr. 1860, Fessenden Papers, Western Reserve Historical Society, Cleveland.

19. William Gooding to William H. Swift, Lockport, Illinois, 11 June 1860, typed copy of an extract, Lincoln Collection, ICHi.

20. Washington correspondence by James Shepherd Pike, 20 May, New York *Tribune,* 22 May 1860; Joseph R. Hawley, "The Work at Chicago—Gossip and Speculations," Hartford *Evening Press,* 23 May 1860.

21. New York *Evening Post,* 11 May 1855, quoted in Mark W. Summers, *The Plundering Generation: Corruption and the Crisis of the Union, 1849–1861* (New York: Oxford University Press, 1987), 230–231.

22. George G. Fogg to Lincoln, Washington, 2 Feb. 1861, draft, Fogg Papers, New Hampshire Historical Society.

23. William James Stillman, *The Autobiography of a Journalist* (2 vols.; Boston: Houghton Mifflin, 1901), 1:374.

24. William Gooding to William H. Swift, Lockport, Illinois, 11 June 1860, typed copy of an extract, Lincoln Collection, ICHi.

25. Charles C. Nourse to James Harlan, Des Moines, 6 June 1860, in Frank I. Herriot, "Memories of the Chicago Convention of 1860," *Annals of Iowa* 12 (Oct. 1920): pamphlet ed., 19.

26. Dixon to Gideon Welles, Hartford, 27 Apr. 1860, Welles Papers, DLC.

27. *The Reminiscences of Carl Schurz* (3 vols.; New York: McClure, 1907–1908), 2:178.

28. Chicago correspondence by Samuel Bowles, 16 May, Springfield (Massachusetts) *Republican,* 19 May 1860; Chicago correspondence, 30 May, New York *Herald,* 19 June 1860.

29. Buffalo *Commercial Advertiser,* n.d., copied in the New York *Times,* 21 May 1860.

30. James G. Blaine to William Pitt Fessenden, Chicago, 16 May 1860, Fessenden Family Papers, Bowdoin College.

31. Henry P. Scholte to Seward, Cincinnati, 19 May 1860, Seward Papers, University of Rochester.

32. Simon P. Hanscom to N. P. Banks, Washington, 7 January 1859, Banks Papers, DLC.

33. Herman Kreismann to E. B. Washburne, Chicago, 15 May 1860, Washburne Papers, DLC; Manchester, New Hampshire,

Mirror, 16 May 1860, quoted in Lucy Lowden, "The People's Party: the 'Heirs of Jackson' and the Rise of the Republican Party in New Hampshire, 1845–1860" (M.A. thesis, Western Illinois University, 1971), 108.

34. Horace Greeley, "Last Week at Chicago," New York *Tribune*, 22 May 1860.

35. Joshua Giddings to George W. Julian, Jefferson, Ohio, 25 May 1860, Giddings-Julian Papers, DLC.

36. William Schouler to Israel Washburn, Boston, 14 June 1860, Washburn Family Papers, Washburn Memorial Library, Norlands, Maine.

37. Bryant to John Bigelow, New York, 20 Feb. 1860, John Bigelow, *Retrospections of an Active Life* (5 vols.; New York: Baker & Taylor, 1909–1913), 1:253.

38. Hiram Barney to Salmon P. Chase, New York, 3 Apr. 1860, Chase Papers, Historical Society of Pennsylvania.

39. Allan Nevins and Milton Halsey Thomas, eds., *The Diary of George Templeton Strong, 1835–1875* (4 vols.; New York: Macmillan, 1952), 3:27, 42 (entries for 16 May and 14 Sept. 1860).

40. Charles C. Nourse, delegate from Iowa, interviewed by Frank I. Herriot, Des Moines, 26 Apr. and 12 May 1907, in Herriot, "Memories of the Chicago Convention of 1860," 15–16.

41. William Curtis Noyes to Francis Lieber, n.p., n.d., Lieber Papers, CSmH.

42. Pike to William Pitt Fessenden, New York, 9 Apr. 1858, Pike Papers, DLC.

43. John M. Palmer, statement made to J. McCan Davis, 1897, in Ida M. Tarbell, *The Life of Abraham Lincoln* (4 vols.; New York: Lincoln History Society, 1903), 2:145.

44. Mrs. Henry S. Lane to Alexander K. McClure, n.p., 16 Sept. 1891, in McClure, *Abraham Lincoln and Men of War-Times* (Philadelphia: Times, 1892), 31n.

45. Greeley to James Shepherd Pike, New York, 21 May 1860, Pike Papers, University of Maine.

46. Dillard C. Donnohue to Daniel D. Pratt, Greencastle, Indiana, 31 Mar. 1860, Pratt Papers, Indiana State Library, Indianapolis.

47. John D. Defrees to Henry S. Lane, Washington, 19 Jan. 1860, Lane Papers, InU.

48. James Wilson to Henry S. Lane, Washington, 11 Mar. 1860, Lane Papers, InU.

49. Lincoln to Allen, Springfield, 1 May 1860, *CWL*, 4:46–47.

50. Davis to Thomas H. Dudley, Bloomington, 1 Sept. 1860, Dudley Papers, CSmH.

51. Leonard Swett to Josiah H. Drummond, 27 May 1860, Portland, Maine, *Evening Express*, n.d., copied in the New York *Sun*, 26 July 1891.

52. *CWL*, 4:51.

53. Albert Hale to Theron Baldwin, Springfield, 31 May 1860, in Michael Burlingame, ed., *An Oral History of Abraham Lincoln: John G. Nicolay's Interviews and Essays* (Carbondale: Southern Illinois University Press, 1996), 96.

54. Matilda Gresham, *Life of Walter Quintin Gresham, 1832–1895* (2 vols.; Chicago: Rand, McNally, 1919), 1:110–111.

55. Fishback to his brother Tip, Indianapolis, 19 Jan. 1861, photostatic copy, Miscellaneous Manuscripts, Indiana State Library, Indianapolis.

56. Interview with Medill by George Alfred Townsend on the eve of the Republican national convention of 1888, reproduced in the Chicago *Tribune*, 7 Feb. 1909.

57. A. M. Whitney to David Davis, Chicago, 1 Aug. 1863, Davis Papers, IHi.

58. Ray to Lincoln, Chicago, 14 May 1860, AL MSS DLC.

59. Delahay to Lincoln, Chicago, 17 May 1860, ibid.

60. Fell to Lincoln, Bloomington, 2 Jan. 1861, ibid.

61. Charles Gibson, typescript of an autobiography, p. 40, Gibson Papers, Missouri Historical Society.

62. Memorandum by Kellogg Fairbank, Chicago, 7 Apr. 1926, enclosed in Janet

Fairbank to Albert J. Beveridge, New York, 9 Apr. [1926], Beveridge Papers, DLC.

63. Defrees to David Davis, 26 Nov. 1860, Davis Papers, IHi, in Richard J. Thomas, "Caleb B. Smith: Whig Orator and Politician—Lincoln's Secretary of Interior" (Ph.D. dissertation, Indiana University, 1969), 163.

64. Davis to Lincoln, Danville, Illinois, 19 Nov. 1860, AL MSS DLC.

65. Davis to Swett, 26 Nov. 1862, in Willard King, *Lincoln's Manager, David Davis* (Cambridge, MA: Harvard University Press, 1960), 204.

66. Blair to Martin Van Buren, Silver Spring, 7 Mar. 1861, Van Buren Papers, microfilm ed.

67. Theodore Calvin Pease and James G. Randall, eds., *The Diary of Orville Hickman Browning* (2 vols.; Springfield: Illinois State Historical Library, 1925–1933), 1:407 (entry for 16 May 1860).

68. Isaac H. Bromley, "Historic Moments: The Nomination of Lincoln," *Scribner's Magazine* 14 (November 1893): 647.

69. John G. Nicolay and John Hay, *Abraham Lincoln: A History* (10 vols.; New York: Century 1890), 2:266.

70. *Proceedings of the First Three Republican National Conventions of 1856, 1860 and 1864* (Minneapolis: Charles W. Johnson, 1893), 131–133.

71. Card by Greeley, New York, 20 Feb., New York *Tribune,* 20 Feb. 1861.

72. Eli Thayer to Franklin P. Rice, Worcester, Massachusetts, 16 Dec. 1893, Eli Thayer Papers, RPB; Franklin P. Rice, typescript of an unpublished biography of Eli Thayer, chapter 30, pp. 1–10, Rice Papers, DLC; reminiscences of Thayer, Topeka, Kansas, *Commonwealth,* 24 Aug. 1888.

73. *The Liberator* (Boston), 25 May 1860.

74. Chicago correspondence by Joseph Howard, 17 May, New York *Times,* 18 May 1860; Boston correspondence, 28 May, New York *Herald,* 2 June 1860; Boston *Atlas and Bee,* n.d., copied in the New York *Herald,* 26 May 1860.

75. Chicago correspondence, 17 May, New York *Tribune,* 18 May 1860; Amos Tuck to Carl Schurz, Exeter, New Hampshire, 7 Sept. 1860, and Thomas H. Dudley to Schurz, Camden, New Jersey, 24 Aug. 1860, Carl Schurz Papers, DLC; Thomas J. McCormack, ed., *Memoirs of Gustave Koerner, 1809–1896* (2 vols.; Cedar Rapids, IA: Torch Press, 1909), 2:87.

76. *Der Westbote* (Columbus, Ohio), n.d., in Carl Wittke, *The German-Language Press in America* (Lexington: University of Kentucky Press, 1957), 145.

77. Chicago correspondence by Murat Halstead, 17 May 1860, Cincinnati *Commercial,* 21 May 1860.

78. New York *World,* n.d., copied in *The Liberator* (Boston), 13 July 1860.

79. Charles Albright to James C. Conklin[g], Mauch Chunk, Pennsylvania, 12 Nov. 1860, AL MSS DLC.

80. *CWL,* 4:50.

81. Jesse W. Weik, "Indiana at 1860 G. O. P. Convention in Chicago," undated clipping from the Indianapolis *Sunday Star,* LMF; Henry Clay Whitney, *Lincoln the Citizen,* vol. 1 of *A Life of Lincoln,* ed. Marion Mills Miller (2 vols.; New York: Baker and Taylor, 1908), 289.

82. Reminiscences of Richard S. Tuthill, Chicago *Times,* 9 June 1889.

83. Cameron, interview with Nicolay, Washington, 20 Feb. 1875, Burlingame, ed., *Oral History of Lincoln,* 43.

84. Joseph Casey to Cameron, Chicago, 10 May 1860, Cameron Papers, DLC.

85. Joseph Casey to Simon Cameron, Harrisburg, 23 May 1860, Cameron Papers, Dauphin County Historical Society, Harrisburg.

86. McClure, *Lincoln and Men of War-Times,* 79.

87. O. J. Hollister, *Life of Schuyler Colfax* (New York: Funk & Wagnalls, 1886), 147n.

88. Swett to Lincoln, [Bloomington], 25 May, 30 Nov. 1860, AL MSS DLC.

89. Casey to Cameron, Harrisburg, 23 May 1860, Cameron Papers, Dauphin County Historical Society, Harrisburg.

90. Casey to Swett, Harrisburg, 27 Nov. 1860, AL MSS DLC.

91. Whitney, *Life on the Circuit*, ed. Angle, 101n.

92. Amos Tuck to David Davis, Exeter, New Hampshire, 26 Aug. 1860, Davis Papers, IHi.

93. Amos Tuck to Lincoln, Chicago, 14 May 1860, AL MSS DLC.

94. George G. Fogg to William Butler, Washington, 13 Dec. 1860, Butler Papers, ICHi.

95. *Coos Republican* (Lancaster, NH), 29 May 1860.

96. David Davis and Leonard Swett to Lincoln, Danville, Illinois, 22 Nov. 1860, State Department Records, file for George W. Lawrence, Applications and Recommendations, 1861–1869, Record Group 59, M 650, National Archives.

97. Greeley to Schuyler Colfax, New York, 26 May 1860, Greeley Papers, New York Public Library.

98. Frank W. Bird to Charles Sumner, East Walpole, 3 Apr. 1860, Sumner Papers, Harvard University.

99. William Schouler to Lincoln, Boston, 21 May 1860, AL MSS DLC.

100. Pierce to Charles H. Ray, Boston, 4 Jan. 1861, Ray Papers, CSmH; memorandum of votes cast in the convention, John A. Andrew Papers, Massachusetts Historical Society; statement of Pierce, [Dec. 1889], *HI*, 683–684; William H. Herndon to E. L. Pierce, Springfield, 18 Feb. 1861, Pierce Papers, Harvard University.

101. Chicago correspondence, n.d., Boston *Journal*, 14 May, copied in the Springfield (Massachusetts) *Republican*, 15 May 1860; Chicago correspondence, 14 May, New York *Tribune*, 15 May 1860; Chicago correspondence by Simon Hanscom, 13 May, New York *Herald*, 16 May 1860.

102. Spaulding to Seward, Chicago, 17 May 1860, telegram; Morgan to Seward, Chicago, 17 May 1860, telegram; Preston King, William M. Evarts, and Richard M.

Blatchford to Seward, Chicago, 18 May 1860, telegram, Seward Papers, University of Rochester.

103. Murat Halstead's report in the Cincinnati *Commercial*, 21 May 1860.

104. Allan Nevins and Milton Halsey Thomas, eds., *The Diary of George Templeton Strong, 1835–1875* (4 vols.; New York: Macmillan, 1952), 3:282 (entry for 21 Dec. 1862).

105. Farnsworth to E. B. Washburne, Chicago, 18 May 1860, telegram, E. B. Washburne Papers, DLC.

106. Swett to Josiah H. Drummond, 27 May 1860, Portland, Maine, *Evening Express*, n.d., copied in the New York *Sun*, 26 July 1891.

107. Ibid.

108. Chicago correspondence by Joseph Howard, 18 May, New York *Times*, 21 May 1860.

109. Chicago *Herald*, 19 May 1860.

110. Murat Halstead's report in the Cincinnati *Commercial*, 21 May 1860.

111. Leonard Swett to Josiah H. Drummond, 27 May 1860, Portland, Maine, *Evening Express*, n.d., copied in the New York *Sun*, 26 July 1891.

112. Murat Halstead's report in the Cincinnati *Commercial*, 21 May 1860.

113. Chicago *Herald*, 19 May 1860.

114. Eustice Noyes, quoted in "Doctor Agnew's Notes on Governor Morgan," in Edwin D. Morgan, *Recollections for My Family* (New York: Scribner's, 1938), 22.

115. Greeley to James Shepherd Pike, New York, 21 May 1860, Pike Papers, University of Maine.

116. Alfred Caldwell, quoted in Reinhard H. Luthin, *The First Lincoln Campaign* (Cambridge, MA: Harvard University Press, 1944), 160.

117. Clay to Seward, n.p., 21 May 1860, Seward Papers, University of Rochester.

118. A. S. Murray to Israel Washburn, Gorham, 25 May 1860, Gaillard Hunt, *Israel, Elihu and Cadwallader Washburn: A Chapter in American Biography* (New York: Macmillan, 1925), 72.

119. Chicago correspondence by Simon Hanscom, 18 May, New York *Herald,* 19 May 1860.

120. Letter by a former employee of the editorial department of the *Illinois State Journal* to the editors of the *Missouri Democrat* (St. Louis), St. Louis, 20 May 1865, *Missouri Democrat,* n.d., copied in the *Illinois State Journal* (Springfield), 8 June 1865.

121. Murat Halstead's report in the Cincinnati *Commercial,* 21 May 1860.

122. Weed to Seward, Davenport, Iowa, 20 May 1860, Seward Papers, University of Rochester; Greeley to James Shepherd Pike, New York, 21 May 1860, Pike Papers, University of Maine.

123. Letter by a former employee of the editorial department of the *Illinois State Journal* to the editors of the *Missouri Democrat* (St. Louis), St. Louis, 20 May 1865, *Missouri Democrat,* n.d., copied in the *Illinois State Journal* (Springfield), 8 June 1865; Charles S. Zane, "Lincoln As I Knew Him," *Sunset* 29 (Oct. 1912), reprinted in the *Journal of the Illinois State Historical Society* 14 (1921–1922):82.

124. New York *Tribune,* 24 May 1860.

125. Murat Halstead's report in the Cincinnati *Commercial,* 21 May 1860; Chicago correspondence, 11 Mar. 1895, by Newton Macmillan (interview with Medill), Chicago *Tribune,* 14 Apr. 1895; Howard K. Beale and Alan W. Brownsword, eds., *Diary of Gideon Welles, Secretary of the Navy under Lincoln and Johnson* (3 vols.; New York: W.W. Norton, 1960), 2:359.

126. Interview with Cartter, Frank G. Carpenter, Washington correspondence of *The Press,* (no city indicated), 14 Aug. (no year indicated), clipping, LMF; Murat Halstead's report in the Cincinnati *Commercial,* 21 May 1860.

127. John A. Andrew, speech of 25 May 1860 in Faneuil Hall, Chicago *Press and Tribune,* 30 May 1860.

128. Murat Halstead's report in the Cincinnati *Commercial,* 21 May 1860.

129. Chicago correspondence by Simon Hanscom, 18 May, New York *Herald,* 19 May 1860.

130. Murat Halstead's report in the Cincinnati *Commercial,* 21 May 1860.

131. Allan Nevins, *The Ordeal of the Union* (2 vols.; New York: Charles Scribner's Sons, 1947), 1:195.

132. Chicago correspondence by Joseph Howard, 18 May, New York *Times,* 19 May 1860.

133. Curtin to A. K. McClure, n.p., 18 Aug. 1891, in McClure, *Lincoln and Men of War-Times,* 41n.

134. Henry M. Field, *The Life of David Dudley Field* (New York: Charles Scribner's Sons, 1898), 139.

135. Hamilton Fish to Lt. Henry A. Wise, New York, 24 May 1860, letterbooks, Fish Papers, DLC.

136. Chicago dispatch by B., 18 May, *Illinois State Journal* (Springfield), 19 May 1860; Murat Halstead's report in the Cincinnati *Commercial,* 21 May 1860.

137. William G. Brownlow in the Knoxville, Tennessee, *Whig,* n.d., copied in the New York *Tribune,* 29 May 1860.

138. Chicago correspondence, 30 May, New York *Herald,* 19 June 1860.

139. Carrollton *West Alabamian,* 19 Sept. 1860, quoted in Donald E. Reynolds, *Editors Make War: Southern Newspapers in the Secession Crisis* (Nashville, TN: Vanderbilt University Press, 1970), 58.

140. Letter by a former employee of the editorial department of the *Illinois State Journal* (Springfield) to the editors of the *Missouri Democrat* (St. Louis), St. Louis, 20 May 1865, *Missouri Democrat,* n.d., copied in the *Illinois State Journal* (Springfield), 8 June 1865; *Central Illinois Gazette,* 23 May 1860; Charles S. Zane, statement for Herndon, [1865–1866], *HI,* 492; Zane, "Lincoln as I Knew Him," 82–83.

141. John A. Dahlgren diary, copy, Nicolay Papers, DLC (entry for 19 Apr. 1862).

142. New York *Times,* 8 June 1860.

143. Springfield correspondence by John Hay, 21 May, Providence, Rhode Island, *Journal,* 26 May 1860, Michael Burlingame, ed., *Lincoln's Journalist: John Hay's Anonymous Writings for the Press, 1860–1864* (Carbondale: Southern Illinois University Press, 1998), 2.

144. Paul M. Angle, *"Here I Have Lived:" A History of Lincoln's Springfield* (Springfield, IL.: Abraham Lincoln Association, 1935), 237.

Chapter 16. "I Have Been Elected Mainly on the Cry 'Honest Old Abe'"

1. Giddings to Lincoln, Chicago, 19 May 1860, AL MSS DLC.

2. *The Independent* (New York), 24 May 1860.

3. Speech at Rochester, n.d., quoted in the Springfield (Massachusetts) *Republican,* 5 June 1860.

4. New York *Times,* 28 May 1860.

5. Cincinnati *Commercial,* 19 May 1860.

6. Charles H. Brown, *William Cullen Bryant* (New York: Scribner, 1971), 418.

7. Chicago correspondence by Samuel Bowles, 16 May, Springfield (Massachusetts) *Republican,* 19 May 1860; "Abraham Lincoln as a Candidate," ibid., 26 May 1860.

8. Concord *New Hampshire Statesman,* 26 May, 14 July 1860, in Lex Renda, *Running on the Record: Civil War-Era Politics in New Hampshire* (Charlottesville: University Press of Virginia, 1997), 91–92.

9. Hartford *Courant,* 24 May 1860.

10. J. K. Moorhead, interview with John G. Nicolay, Washington, 12 and 13 May 1880, Michael Burlingame, ed., *An Oral History of Abraham Lincoln: John G. Nicolay's Interviews and Essays* (Carbondale: Southern Illinois University Press, 1996), 41.

11. A. L. Chetlain to Elihu B. Washburne, Galena, 23 May 1860, Elihu B. Washburne Papers, DLC.

12. Springfield correspondence, 4 Sept., New York *Evening Post,* 8 Sept. 1860.

13. Albany correspondence, 18 Feb., New York *Herald,* 19 Feb. 1861.

14. Allan Nevins and Milton Halsey Thomas, eds., *The Diary of George Templeton Strong, 1835–1875* (4 vols.; New York: Macmillan, 1952), 3:33 (entry for 16 June 1860).

15. Hamilton Fish to Lt. Henry A. Wise, New York, 24 May 1860, letterbooks, Fish Papers, DLC.

16. Schuyler Colfax to Charles M. Heaton, Washington, 21 May 1860, Colfax Papers, Northern Indiana Center for History, South Bend.

17. William P. Fessenden to Elizabeth Warriner, Washington, 20 and 27 May 1860, Fessenden Family Papers, Bowdoin College.

18. Washington correspondence, 18 and 19 May, Chicago *Press and Tribune,* 23 and 24 May 1860.

19. Charles Francis Adams, diary entry for 18 May 1860, Adams Family Papers, MHi.

20. Springfield correspondence by Henry Villard, Cincinnati *Commercial,* n.d., copied in the New York *Times,* 27 Dec. 1860.

21. The New Haven *Palladium,* New York *Courier and Enquirer,* Boston *Atlas and Bee,* and New York *Evening Post,* all quoted in "Voice of the Republican Press," Albany *Evening Journal,* 22 May 1860.

22. Washington *Constitution,* 6 Sept. 1860, in Howard Cecil Perkins, ed., *Northern Editorials on Secession* (2 vols.; New York: D. Appleton, 1942), 1:34; Chicago *Herald,* 21 May 1860; New York *Herald,* 19, 22, and 30 May, 28 Aug., 6 and 8 Sept. 1860; Washington *Constitution,* n.d., copied in the Albany *Evening Journal,* 23 May 1860; Boston *Courier,* n.d., quoted in the New York *Tribune,* 24 May 1860; *Freeman's Journal* (New York), 26 May 1860; Hartford *Times,* n.d., quoted in the Hartford *Courant,* 23 May 1860.

23. Philadelphia *Evening Journal,* n.d., copied in the New York *Tribune,* 24 May 1860.

24. An "old gentleman residing in this city [Chicago] who was a companion of Lincoln in all the early political struggles of the State," interviewed by a correspondent of the New York *Herald,* Chicago correspondence, 30 May, New York *Herald,* 19 June 1860.

25. New York *Herald*, 22 May 1860.

26. Quoted in Hans L. Trefousse, *First Among Equals: Abraham Lincoln's Reputation during His Administration* (New York: Fordham University Press, 2005), 4.

27. New York *Herald*, 22 May 1860.

28. *Illinois State Register* (Springfield), 24 Aug. 1860.

29. *Congressional Globe*, 36th Congress, 2nd Session, Appendix, 334 (19 May 1860).

30. Speech of J. L. D. Morrison, 2 June 1860, *Missouri Republican* (St. Louis), 4 June 1860.

31. *Illinois State Register* (Springfield), 19 Sept. 1860.

32. Chicago correspondence, 12 June, New York *Herald*, 26 June 1860.

33. *Illinois State Register* (Springfield), 28 July 1860.

34. John Cochrane, speech in New York, 8 Oct., New York *Times*, 9 Oct. 1860.

35. *Illinois State Register* (Springfield), 17 July, 22 Aug. 1860.

36. *Campaign Plain Dealer* (Cleveland), 1 Sept. 1860.

37. Charleston, South Carolina, *Courier*, n.d., quoted in the New York *Tribune*, 23 May 1860; Augusta *Dispatch*, n.d., copied in the New York *Herald*, 8 June 1860; Newberry, South Carolina, *Rising Sun*, n.d., quoted in Manisha Sinha, *The Counterrevolution of Slavery: Politics and Ideology in Antebellum South Carolina* (Chapel Hill: University of North Carolina Press, 2000), 229; Newbern, North Carolina, *Weekly Progress*, 29 May 1860, quoted in Donald E. Reynolds, *Editors Make War: Southern Newspapers in the Secession Crisis* (Nashville, TN: Vanderbilt University Press, 1970), 57–58; John Rutherford to "My dear Hawkeley," Richmond, 19 Dec. 1860, Rutherford Papers, Duke University, typescript, Allan Nevins Papers, Columbia University.

38. John L. Manning to his wife, 29 May 1860, quoted in Steven A. Channing, *Crisis of Fear: Secession in South Carolina* (New York: W. W. Norton, 1974), 230.

39. *Missouri Republican* (St. Louis), 22 May 1860.

40. Letter by "National Democrat," n.p., n.d., *Missouri Republican* (St. Louis), 1 June 1860.

41. Corsicana (Texas) *Navarro Express*, 2 June 1860; Richmond *Enquirer*, 17 Aug. 1860; Montgomery *Weekly Mail*, 26 Oct. 1860, all quoted in Reynolds, *Editors Make War*, 58–59, 124, 125–126.

42. J. Henly Smith to Alexander H. Stephens, Washington, 19 May 1860, Stephens Papers, DLC.

43. H. G. Warner to Douglas, Rochester Bank, New York, 19 May 1860, Douglas Papers, University of Chicago.

44. New Orleans *Crescent*, n.d., copied in the New York *Tribune*, 28 May 1860.

45. Paris, Kentucky, *Citizen*, n.d., copied in the *Illinois State Journal* (Springfield), 2 June 1860.

46. Washington correspondence, 18 May, New York *Herald*, 19 May 1860.

47. J. G. Wright to Douglas, Chicago, 18 May 1860, and G. W. Sheahan to Douglas, Chicago, 21 May 1860, Douglas Papers, University of Chicago.

48. *Douglass's Monthly* 3 (June 1860):276.

49. Speech at Geneva, New York, 1 Aug. 1860, John W. Blassingame, ed., *The Frederick Douglass Papers, Series One: Speeches, Debates, and Interviews* (5 vols.; New Haven, CT: Yale University Press, 1979–1992), 3:381–382.

50. *The Life and Times of Frederick Douglass* (Hartford, CT: Park Publishing Co., 1881), 399.

51. Giddings to George W. Julian, Jefferson, [Ohio], 25 May 1860, Giddings-Julian Papers, DLC; Giddings to John Allison, Jefferson, Ohio, 25 Dec. 1860, AL MSS DLC.

52. *The Independent* (New York), 10 and 24 May 1860.

53. Saint Cloud (Minnesota) *Democrat*, 31 May 1860, in Sylvia D. Hoffert, *Jane Grey Swisshelm: An Unconventional Life, 1815–1884* (Chapel Hill: University of North Carolina Press, 2004), 124.

54. Child to Sumner, Wayland, 27 May 1860, *Lydia Maria Child: Selected Letters, 1817–1880,* ed. Milton Meltzer and Patricia G. Holland (Amherst: University of Massachusetts Press, 1982), 352.

55. James R. Doolittle to his wife, 29 May and 26 June 1860, Doolittle Papers, in William Ernest Smith, *The Francis Preston Blair Family in Politics* (2 vols.; New York: Macmillan, 1933), 1:485.

56. Grimes to his wife, Washington, 4 June 1860, William Salter, *The Life of James W. Grimes, Governor of Iowa, 1854–1858, A Senator of the United States, 1859–1869* (New York: D. Appleton, 1876), 128.

57. Ralph Emerson, "Mr. & Mrs. Ralph Emerson's Personal Recollections of Abraham Lincoln" (pamphlet; Rockford, IL: privately printed, 1909), 13.

58. Gerrit Smith to Giddings, Peterboro, New York, 2 June 1860, Giddings Papers, Ohio Historical Society.

59. Boston correspondence, 7 July, New York *Tribune,* 9 July 1860.

60. Charles Grandison Finney in the *Oberlin Evangelist,* 1860, quoted in Allen C. Guelzo, *Abraham Lincoln: Redeemer President* (Grand Rapids: William B. Eerdmans, 2002), 246.

61. *The Liberator* (Boston), 7 Sept. 1860.

62. *Principia,* 2 June 1860, in James M. McPherson, *The Struggle for Equality: Abolitionists and the Negro in the Civil War and Reconstruction* (Princeton, NJ: Princeton University Press, 1964), 17.

63. *Principia,* 26 May 1860, in M. Leon Perkal, "William Goodell: A Life of Reform" (Ph.D. dissertation, City University of New York, 1972), 297.

64. W. A. Hunter to William Goodell, 13 June 1860, in *Principia,* 21 July 1860, in McPherson, *Struggle for Equality,* 17.

65. John B. Edwards to Gerrit Smith, 11 July 1860, in Ralph Volney Harlow, *Gerrit Smith: Philanthropist and Reformer* (New York: Russell and Russell, 1939), 427.

66. John W. [Windham?] to Gerrit Smith, Lexington, Illinois, 25 Aug. 1860, William Lloyd Garrison Papers, Boston Public Library.

67. Green to Elizur Wright, n.p., n.d., in Philip G. Wright and Elizabeth Q. Wright, *Elizur Wright, the Father of Life Insurance* (Chicago: University of Chicago Press, 1937), 212.

68. Stephen S. Foster in *The Liberator* (Boston), 15 June 1860; C[harles] A. H[ammond] to Frederick Douglass, n.p., n.d., *Douglass's Monthly* 3 (Oct. 1860):343.

69. Parker Pillsbury, speech at Framingham, Massachusetts, 4 July 1860, *The Liberator* (Boston), 20 July 1860.

70. *National Anti-Slavery Standard,* 13 Oct. 1860.

71. Johnson to J. Miller McKim, n.p., 8 Nov. and 11 Oct. 1860, Samuel J. May Anti-Slavery Manuscript Collection, Cornell University.

72. H. Ford Douglas, speech at Framingham, Massachusetts, 4 July 1860, *The Liberator* (Boston), 13 July 1860;

73. Ibid.; New York *Herald,* 8 July 1860; Boston correspondence, 7 July, New York *Tribune,* 9 July 1860.

74. Annual report of the Pennsylvania Anti-Slavery Society, quoted in the New York *Herald,* 30 Oct. 1860.

75. Speech of 23 Sept. 1860, in Salem, Ohio, in C. Peter Ripley, ed., *The Black Abolitionist Papers* (5 vols.; Chapel Hill: University of North Carolina Press, 1985–1992), 5:91.

76. William Cheek and Aimee Lee Cheek, *John Mercer Langston and the Fight for Black Freedom, 1829–65* (Urbana: University of Illinois Press, 1989), 370.

77. New York *Times,* 8 June 1860; Wendell Phillips, speech of 30 May 1860 in Boston, *The Liberator* (Boston), 8 June 1860. For more on Phillips's criticism, see Chapter 8 of the present volume.

78. New York *Times,* 4 Sept. 1860.

79. Wendell Phillips, speech of 30 May 1860 in Boston, *The Liberator* (Boston), 8 June 1860.

80. Joseph Hawley to Wendell Phillips, Hartford, 17 July 1860, fragment of a draft, Hawley Papers, DLC.

81. New York *National Anti-Slavery Standard*, 11 Aug. 1860.

82. New York *Tribune*, 4, 18 July 1860.

83. Albany *Evening Journal*, 5 June 1860.

84. Pierce to Phillips, Boston, 25 Oct. 1860, Phillips Papers, Harvard University.

85. Higginson to Charles Francis Adams, Worcester, 22 Dec. 1860, Adams Family Papers; *The Liberator* (Boston), 28 Sept. 1860; Tilden G. Edelstein, *Strange Enthusiasm: A Life of Thomas Wentworth Higginson* (New Haven, CT: Yale University Press, 1968), 239.

86. *The Works of Charles Sumner* (15 vols.; Boston: Lee and Shepard, 1874–1883), 5:225.

87. New York *Herald*, 17 July 1860.

88. Letter by "an intelligent gentleman in Illinois," n.d., n.p., in *The Liberator* (Boston), n.d., copied in the New York *World*, 8 Aug. 1860.

89. Dixon to Gideon Welles, Washington, 1 and 25 May 1860, Welles Papers, DLC.

90. Speech by Dayton in New York, 19 Sept., New York *Times*, 20 Sept. 1860.

91. Manchester *Union Democrat*, 22 May 1860.

92. Boston *Herald*, n.d., copied in the Concord, New Hampshire, *Independent Democrat*, 24 May 1860.

93. Louisville *Journal*, n.d., copied in the Cincinnati *Commercial*, 11 June 1860.

94. Louisville correspondence by "Pontiac," 26 May, New York *Times*, 2 June 1860.

95. New Orleans *Bee*, n.d., copied in the *Illinois State Journal* (Springfield), 13 June 1860.

96. Washington correspondence, 20 May, New York *Evening Post*, 21 May 1860; speech at Manchester, New Hampshire, Cincinnati *Commercial*, 8 Aug. 1860.

97. William Pennington, speech at Jersey City, 9 Aug., *Illinois State Journal* (Springfield), 16 Aug. 1860.

98. Alfred E. Lewis to an unidentified correspondent, Philadelphia, 23 July 1860, Raleigh, North Carolina, *Standard*, n.d., copied in the New York *Times*, 28 Oct. 1860.

99. Springfield correspondence, 4 Sept., New York *Evening Post*, 8 Sept. 1860.

100. Reminiscences of John H. Littlefield in "Abe Lincoln's Wisdom," unidentified clipping, LMF.

101. Albert Hale to Theron Baldwin, Springfield, 31 May 1860, in Burlingame, ed., *Oral History of Lincoln*, 155–156.

102. Henry Quigley to John A. McClernand, Springfield, 8 Dec. 1860, McClernand Papers, IHi.

103. Roland W. Diller's recollections, in Paul Hull, "Lincoln in Springfield," New York *Mail and Express*, 8 Feb. 1896, p. 15

104. Interview with John Bunn, [15 Oct. 1914?], Jesse W. Weik, *The Real Lincoln: A Portrait*, ed. Michael Burlingame (1922; Lincoln: University of Nebraska Press, 2002), 319.

105. Thomas J. McCormack, ed., *Memoirs of Gustave Koerner, 1809–1896* (2 vols.; Cedar Rapids, IA: Torch Press, 1909), 2:94.

106. Charles C. Coffin in Allen Thorndike Rice, ed., *Reminiscences of Abraham Lincoln by Distinguished Men of His Time* (New York: North American Review, 1886), 168.

107. Roy P. Basler et al., eds., *Collected Works of Abraham Lincoln* [hereafter *CWL*] (8 vols. plus index; New Brunswick, NJ: Rutgers University Press, 1953–1955), 4:51.

108. George Boutwell said this to Newton Bateman. Bateman, *Abraham Lincoln: An Address* (Galesburg, IL: Cadmus Club, 1899), 29.

109. Springfield correspondence by G. G. F., 21 May, *Independent Democrat* (Concord, NH), 31 May 1860.

110. Springfield correspondence, 19 May, Chicago *Journal*, 22 May 1860.

111. Lincoln to Kelley, Springfield, 13 Oct. 1860, *CWL*, 4:127.

112. *The Reminiscences of Carl Schurz* (3 vols.; New York: McClure, 1907–1908), 2:188.

113. Springfield correspondence, 19 May, Chicago *Journal*, 22 May 1860.

114. Schurz, *Reminiscences*, 2:188–189.

115. Robert H. Morris to Hamilton Fish, Chicago, 21 May 1860, Fish Papers, DLC.

116. Dixon to Gideon Welles, Washington, 1 and 25 May 1860, Welles Papers, DLC.

117. Letter by an unidentified author to "Rev. and Dear Sir," Springfield, 24 Oct., New York *Times,* 6 Nov. 1860.

118. E. B. Washburne to Lincoln, Washington, 20 May 1860, AL MSS DLC.

119. Lincoln to George Ashmun, Springfield, 23 May 1860, *CWL,* 4:52.

120. Lincoln to Chase, Springfield, 26 May 1860, ibid., 4:53.

121. Chase to Wade, Cincinnati, 21 Nov. 1860, Wade Papers, DLC; Robert Hosea to Chase, Chicago, 18 May 1860, Thomas Spooner to Chase, Reading, Ohio, 21 May 1860, and David Taylor to Chase, Bryan, Ohio, 22 May 1860, Chase Papers, DLC.

122. John A. Bingham to Chase, Washington, 2 June 1860, Chase Papers, DLC.

123. Cleveland to Chase, Hampton, 28 May 1860, ibid.

124. Howard K. Beale, ed., *The Diary of Edward Bates, 1859–1866* (Annual Report of the American Historical Association for 1930, vol. 4; Washington, DC: U.S. Government Printing Office, 1933), 131 (entry for 19 May 1860).

125. Henry T. Mudd to John G. Nicolay, St. Louis, 23 May 1860, Nicolay Papers, DLC.

126. Browing to O. M. Hatch, Carthage, 1 June 1860, Hatch Papers, IHi; Bates to Browning, St. Louis, 11 June 1860, *Missouri Democrat* (St. Louis), 19 June 1860.

127. Bates to Worthington G. Snethen, St. Louis, 27 Oct. 1860, William Henry Seward Papers, University of Rochester.

128. Cassius M. Clay to William C. Bryant, White Hall, Kentucky, 22 May 1860, Bryant-Godwin Papers, New York Public Library.

129. Harrisburg correspondence, 25 May, Philadelphia *Press,* 26 May 1860; Cameron to Lincoln, Lochiel, 1 Aug. 1860, AL MSS DLC.

130. Hamilton Fish to Lt. Henry A. Wise, New York, 24 May 1860, letterbooks, Fish Papers, DLC; Oliver B. Peirce to Thurlow Weed, Rome, New York, 27 Aug. 1860, Weed Papers, University of Rochester.

131. C. S. Henry to Charles Sumner, Newburgh, New York, 20 May 1860, Sumner Papers, Harvard University.

132. Clark B. Wheeler to Seward, New York, 25 May 1860, Seward Papers, University of Rochester.

133. O[liver] B. Peirce to Seward, Rome, New York, 25 May 1860, ibid.; Oliver B. Peirce to Thurlow Weed, Rome, New York, 27 Aug. 1860, Weed Papers, University of Rochester.

134. Henry A. Bloss to Seward, Rochester, 18 May 1860, Seward Papers, University of Rochester.

135. John L. Cunningham to Thurlow Weed, Essex, New York, 2 Aug. 1860, Weed Papers, University of Rochester.

136. Gilbert C. Davidson to Seward, Albany, 18 May 1860, telegram, Seward Papers, University of Rochester.

137. Frank M. Coxe to Seward, Philadelphia, 22 May 1860, ibid.

138. Frederick W. Seward, *Seward at Washington as Senator and Secretary of State* (2 vols.; New York: Derby and Miller, 1891), 1:453.

139. Worthington G. Snethen to Seward, Baltimore, 20 May 1860, Seward Papers, University of Rochester.

140. Chicago correspondence by G[eorge] D[awson], 19 May, Albany *Evening Journal,* 21 May 1860.

141. Correspondence by Joseph Howard from the Steamboat *Metropolitan* on the Mississippi River, 20 May, New York *Times,* 25 May 1860.

142. Isaac N. Arnold, *The Life of Abraham Lincoln* (Chicago: Jansen, McClurg, 1885), 168.

143. John M. Palmer, interviewed by J. McCan Davis, undated typescript, Ida Tarbell Papers, Allegheny College.

144. Thurlow Weed Barnes, *Life of Thurlow Weed Including His Autobiography and a Memoir* (2 vols.; Boston: Houghton Mifflin, 1884), 2:292.

145. Weed to the Lincoln Club of New York, 12 Feb. 1879, ibid., 2:296.

146. Jeriah Bonham, *Fifty Years' Recollections* (Peoria, IL: J. W. Franks & Sons, 1883), 182.

147. Lincoln to David Davis, Springfield, 26 May 1860, Roy P. Basler and Christian O. Basler, eds., *Collected Works of Abraham Lincoln, Second Supplement* (New Brunswick, NJ: Rutgers University Press, 1990), 20.

148. Lincoln to Trumbull, Springfield, 5 June 1860, *CWL*, 4:71.

149. Barnes, *Weed Autobiography*, 2:603.

150. Albany *Evening Journal*, 26, 23 May 1860.

151. Gideon Welles, "Recollections in regard to the Formation of Mr Lincoln's Cabinet," undated manuscript, Abraham Lincoln Collection, Beinecke Library, Yale University.

152. Martin Franklin Conway to Weed, Springfield, Illinois, 22 July 1860, Weed Papers, University of Rochester.

153. Weed to Seward, Davenport, Iowa, 20 May 1860, Seward Papers, University of Rochester.

154. George M. Grier to Seward, Chicago, 18 May 1860, Seward Papers, University of Rochester.

155. Seward to his wife, Washington, 30 May 1860, Seward, *Seward at Washington,* 1:454.

156. *Charles Francis Adams, 1835–1915: An Autobiography* (Boston: Houghton Mifflin, 1916), 69.

157. Joseph Medill to Frederic Bancroft, n.p., 18 Feb. 1898, Frederic Bancroft, *The Life of William H. Seward* (2 vols.; New York: Harper and Brothers, 1900), 1:531n.

158. William P. Fessenden to his son William, Washington, 19 May 1860, and to Elizabeth Warriner, Washington, 20 May 1860, Fessenden Family Papers, Bowdoin College.

159. Seward to Weed, Auburn, 26 June 1860, Weed Papers, University of Rochester.

160. A. A. S[argent] to the editor, New York, 28 May 1860, New York *Tribune,* 29 May 1860.

161. James Watson Webb to Thurlow Weed, n.p., 28 June 1860, James Watson Webb Papers, Yale University; James Watson Webb in the New York *Courier and Enquirer,* 25 May, copied in the New York *Herald,* 27 May 1860.

162. Auburn, New York, correspondence, 23 Aug., New York *Herald,* 27 Aug. 1860.

163. Chicago correspondence by G[eorge] D[awson], 19 May, Albany *Evening Journal,* 21 May 1860.

164. Ibid., 28 May 1860.

165. Weed to Swett, Albany, 7 June 1860, David Davis Papers, IHi.

166. Albany *Evening Journal,* 20 July 1860.

167. George William Curtis to Anna Shaw Curtis, Chicago, 19 May 1860, Curtis Papers, Harvard University.

168. William Schouler to Israel Washburn, Boston, 14 June 1860, Washburn Family Papers, Washburn Memorial Library, Norlands, Maine.

169. William S. Robinson to his nephew, n.p., n.d., in William S. Robinson, *"War-rington" Pen-Portraits: A Collection of Personal and Political Reminiscences* (Boston: Lee and Shepard, 1877), 91.

170. William P. Porter to Henry L. Dawes, North Adams, 29 May 1860, Dawes Papers, DLC.

171. New York correspondence by "Lance-lot," 31 May, *Press and Tribune,* n.d., clipping in scrapbook # 11, Edmund C. Stedman Papers, Columbia University.

172. John Bigelow to William Hargreaves, New York, 17 June, 30 July 1860, Bigelow Papers, New York Public Library.

173. E. G. Brooks to Israel Washburn, New York, 7 June 1860, Gaillard Hunt, *Israel, Elihu and Cadwallader Washburn: A Chapter in American Biography* (New York: Macmillan, 1925), 73.

174. Washington Hunt to John Bell, Lockport, New York, 24 May 1860, John Bell Papers, DLC.

175. Lincoln to Davis, Springfield, 26 May 1860, Roy P. Basler, ed., *Collected Works of*

Abraham Lincoln, First Supplement, 1832–1865 (Westport, CT: Greenwood Press, 1973), 54.

176. Lincoln to Schurz, Springfield, 18 June 1860, *CWL*, 4:78.

177. Lincoln to Swett, Springfield, 26 and 30 May 1860, ibid., 4:55, 57.

178. Scripps to Herndon, Chicago, 24 June 1865, Douglas L. Wilson and Rodney O. Davis, eds., *Herndon's Informants: Letters, Interviews, and Statements about Abraham Lincoln* [hereafter *HI*] (Urbana: University of Illinois Press, 1998), 57.

179. "Lincoln as He Is," Chicago *Press and Tribune*, 23 May 1860.

180. Lincoln to Samuel Galloway, Springfield, 19 June 1860, *CWL*, 4:79–80.

181. James A. Briggs to Lincoln, New York, 25 May 1860, AL MSS DLC.

182. *CWL*, 4:60.

183. New York *Times*, 5 Nov. 1860.

184. Benjamin G. Wright to the editor, n.p., n.d., Rock Island *Weekly Register*, n.d., copied in the Rock Island *Argus*, n.d., copied in the *Illinois State Register* (Springfield), 20 Aug. 1860.

185. Lincoln to William S. Speer, Springfield, 23 Oct. 1860, *CWL*, 4:130.

186. New Orleans *Louisianian*, n.d., copied in the Chicago *Press and Tribune*, 3 Nov. 1860.

187. Lincoln to James E. Harvey, Springfield, 2 Oct. 1860, *CWL*, 4:125.

188. Lincoln to G. Yoke Tams, Springfield, 22 Sept. 1860, ibid., 4:119.

189. James Quay Howard's notes of an interview with Lincoln, ca. May 1860, AL MSS DLC.

190. George G. Fogg to Lincoln, New York, 18 Aug. 1860, AL MSS DLC.

191. Norwich, Connecticut, *Bulletin*, [22 Aug. 1860], copied in the New York *World*, 27 Aug. 1860.

192. Douglas's speech in Fort Wayne, Indiana, Washington *States and Union*, 10 Oct. 1860.

193. Ibid.

194. Douglas's speech at Baltimore, Washington *States and Union*, 8 Sept. 1860.

195. Speech in Chicago, 5 Oct., *Illinois State Register* (Springfield), 8 Oct. 1860.

196. *Illinois State Journal* (Springfield), 24 and 30 July 1860.

197. *Illinois State Register* (Springfield), 9 Aug. 1860.

198. *Illinois State Journal* (Springfield), 9 Aug. 1860; Springfield correspondence, 9 Aug., New York *Herald*, 14 Aug. 1860.

199. Springfield correspondence, 8 Aug., Cincinnati *Gazette*, n.d., copied in the New York *Courier and Enquirer*, 13 Aug. 1860.

200. Letter by Goyne S. Pennington, Pittsfield, Illinois, 7 July 1910, *Pike County Democrat* (Pittsfield), 29 July 1910.

201. Michael Burlingame, ed., *With Lincoln in the White House: Letters, Memoranda, and Other Writings of John G. Nicolay, 1860–1865* (Carbondale: Southern Illinois University Press, 2000), xv-xvi.

202. John W. Bunn to Weik, Springfield, 20 July 1916, in Weik, *Real Lincoln*, ed. Burlingame, 321; Michael Burlingame, ed., *At Lincoln's Side: John Hay's Civil War Correspondence and Selected Writings* (Carbondale: Southern Illinois University Press, 2000), xviii.

203. Springfield correspondence, 7 Nov., New York *Tribune*, 12 Nov. 1860.

204. Francis B. Carpenter, *The Inner Life of Abraham Lincoln: Six Months at the White House* (New York: Hurd and Houghton, 1867), 113.

205. Bateman, *Lincoln*, 16–23; Bateman, interview with Ida Tarbell, 22 Jan. 1895, Tarbell Papers, Allegheny College.

206. Letter by "tourist," n.p., n.d., *Missouri Democrat* (St. Louis), 26 July 1860.

207. Memorandum by Nicolay, 16 Oct. 1860, Burlingame, ed., *With Lincoln in the White House*, 6–7.

208. Springfield correspondence, 28 Jan., New York *Evening Post*, 1 Feb. 1861.

209. Theodore Calvin Pease and James G. Randall, eds., *The Diary of Orville Hickman Browning* (2 vols.; Springfield: Illinois State

Historical Library, 1925–1933), 1:415 (entry for 12 June 1860).

210. Springfield correspondence, 16 Oct., New York *Herald*, 20 Oct. 1860.

211. Springfield correspondence, 1 Oct., ibid.

212. New York *Daily News*, 20 Aug. 1860.

213. Bonham, *Fifty Years' Recollections*, 183.

214. Endorsement dated 21 July 1861, on John Wood et al. to Seward, Springfield, 21 July 1861, *CWL*, 4:86.

215. Chicago correspondence, 1 Oct., New York *Herald*, 2 Oct. 1860.

216. Chicago correspondence, 1 Oct., Albany *Evening Journal*, 2 Oct. 1860.

217. Springfield correspondence, 16 Oct., New York *Herald*, 20 Oct. 1860.

218. New York *Journal of Commerce*, 5 Sept. 1860.

219. New York *Herald*, 18 Oct. 1860.

220. Fogg to Lincoln, Washington, 5 Feb. 1861, AL MSS DLC.

221. Greeley to Schuyler Colfax, New York, 5 Feb. 1858, Greeley Papers, New York Public Library.

222. Seward said this to Congressman John F. Potter of Wisconsin. Schurz, *Reminiscences*, 2:221–222; Potter's account, given in 1867 to George B. Lincoln, in George B. Lincoln to Gideon Welles, Riverdale, New Jersey, 25 Apr. 1874, in "New Light on the Seward-Welles-Lincoln Controversy," *Lincoln Lore* #1718 (Apr. 1981): 3.

223. Seward to his wife, Washington, 17 May 1861, 1:575.

224. Fogg to Norman B. Judd, New York, 11 Sept. 1860, AL MSS DLC.

225. Leslie Coombs, speech in New York, 24 Oct., New York *Times*, 25 Oct. 1860.

226. *Illinois State Register* (Springfield), 25 May 1860.

227. Letter dated Auburn, 22 May, New York *Times*, 24 May 1860.

228. Schurz to his wife, Alton, 25 July 1860, Frederic Bancroft, ed., *Speeches, Correspondence and Political Papers of Carl Schurz* (6 vols.; New York: G.P. Putnam's Sons, 1913), 1:120–121.

229. Springfield correspondence, 1 Oct., New York *Herald*, 20 Oct. 1860.

230. Springfield correspondence, 21 June, Utica, New York, *Herald*, 27 June 1860, copied in the New York *Tribune*, 9 July 1860.

231. Chicago correspondence, 22 Sept., *Missouri Democrat* (St. Louis), 25 Sept. 1860.

232. Springfield correspondence, 8 Aug., New York *Herald*, 13 Aug. 1860.

233. Josiah G. Holland, *The Life of Abraham Lincoln* (Springfield, MA: Gurdon Bill, 1866), 236–237.

234. Edgar De Witt Jones, *Lincoln and the Preachers* (New York: Harper, 1948), 181.

235. Springfield correspondence, 21 June 1860, Utica, New York, *Herald*, 27 June 1860, copied in the New York *Tribune*, 9 July 1860.

236. Springfield correspondence by J. L., Aug. 1860 [no day of the month indicated], Philadelphia *North American and United States Gazette*, 22 Aug. 1860.

237. Richard C. McCormick's reminiscences, New York, 29 Apr., New York *Evening Post*, 3 May 1865.

238. Lincoln to James F. Babcock, Springfield, 13 Sept. 1860, *CWL*, 4:114.

239. Albert B. Chandler in *Harper's Monthly* 32 (Feb. 1866):405.

240. Le Grand B. Cannon, *Personal Reminiscences of the Rebellion, 1861–1866* (New York: Burr Printing House, 1895), 169.

241. Barry's reminiscences, Boston *Transcript*, 1902, in Rufus Rockwell Wilson, *Lincoln in Portraiture* (New York: Press of the Pioneers, 1935), 92.

242. Thomas Hicks in Rice, ed., *Reminiscences of Lincoln*, 602.

243. Pease and Randall, eds., *Browning Diary*, 1:415 (entry for 13 June 1860).

244. Lincoln to John M. Read, Springfield, 27 Aug. 1860, *CWL*, 4:102.

245. Nicolay to Therena Bates, Springfield, 26 Aug. 1860, Burlingame, ed., *With Lincoln in the White House*, 5.

246. Brown, diary entry for 26 Aug. 1860, in *McClure's Magazine*, 1896, 400.

247. Nicolay to John M. Read, Springfield, 27 Aug. 1860, Burlingame, ed., *With Lincoln in the White House*, 5.

248. Nicolay to Brown, Springfield, 5 Oct. 1860, Ibid., 6.

249. Alban Jasper Conant, "A Portrait Painter's Reminiscences of Lincoln," *McClure's Magazine* 32 (Mar. 1909):515.

250. Springfield correspondence, 4 Sept., New York *Evening Post*, 8 Sept. 1860.

251. Washington *Republican*, n.d., copied in the New York *Evening Post*, 27 June 1865.

252. Springfield correspondence by W., 14 Nov., Philadelphia *Evening Bulletin*, 21 Nov. 1860.

253. Nicolay, "Lincoln's Personal Appearance," *Century Magazine*, Oct. 1891, 933.

254. Richard C. McCormick's reminiscences, New York, 29 Apr., New York *Evening Post*, 3 May 1865.

255. Thomas D. Jones to [William Linn McMillen], Springfield, 30 Dec. 1860 and 11 Feb. 1861, Lincoln Collection, Lilly Library, InU.

256. Brown to John M. Read, Springfield, 16 Aug. 1860, Read Family Papers, DLC.

257. Albany *Argus*, 15 Sept. 1860, in Richard J. Carwardine, *Evangelicals and Politics in Antebellum America* (New Haven, CT: Yale University Press, 1993), 430n90.

258. Lincoln to Leonard Swett, Springfield, 30 May 1860, *CWL*, 4:57.

259. Putnam to Leonard Swett, n.p., n.d., copy in Lincoln's hand of an enclosure in Swett to Lincoln, n.p., [July 1860], AL MSS DLC.

260. Letter by Putnam to the Republicans of Wyoming, New York, n.d., Albany *Evening Journal*, 12 July 1860; speech by Putnam at Fredonia, New York, New York *Tribune*, 5 June 1860.

261. Buffalo *Commercial Advertiser*, n.d., copied in the New York *Tribune*, 6 June 1860.

262. Washington Hunt to John Bell, Lockport, 24 May 1860, John Bell Papers, DLC.

263. Henry Winter Davis to David Davis, [Baltimore, June 1860], David Davis Papers, IHi.

264. Lincoln to Richard W. Thompson, Springfield, 18 June 1860, *CWL*, 4:79

265. Lincoln to Richard W. Thompson, Springfield, 10 July 1860, ibid., 4:82–83.

266. Nicolay, "Lincoln in the Campaign of 1860," in Burlingame, ed., *Oral History of Lincoln*, 94–95.

267. James E. Harvey to Lincoln, Washington, 21 May 1860, AL MSS DLC.

268. Charles Leib to Lincoln, Chicago, 6 June 1860, ibid.

269. Schuyler Colfax to Lincoln, Washington, 26 May 1860, ibid.

270. Washburne to Lincoln, Washington, 20 May 1860, ibid.

271. Trumbull to Lincoln, Washington, 22 May 1860, ibid.

272. Carl Wittke, *Refugees of Revolution: The German Forty-Eighters in America* (Philadelphia: University of Pennsylvania Press, 1952), 214.

273. Unidentified correspondent in Washington, Indiana, undated letter, quoted in the *Missouri Democrat* (St. Louis), 25 June 1860.

274. B. O. Tyler to Henry L. Dawes, Trenton, 14 June 1860, Dawes Papers, DLC.

275. Crittenden's speeches of 2 Aug. and 30 Oct., Louisville correspondence, 2 Aug., New York *Times*, 8 Aug. 1860, Cincinnati *Commercial*, 31 Oct. 1860.

276. Davis to an unidentified correspondent, n.p., n.d., New York *World*, 24 July 1860.

277. Harrisburg correspondence, 6 Sept., New York *Herald*, 13 Sept. 1859.

278. A. K. McClure to Lincoln, Chambersburg, 16 June 1860, AL MSS DLC.

279. Philadelphia *Pennsylvanian*, 14 May 1860, quoted in Robert L. Bloom, "Newspaper Opinion in the State Election of 1860," *Pennsylvania History* 28 (1961):352.

280. McClure to Lincoln, Chambersburg, 2 July 1860, AL MSS DLC.

281. Lincoln to Swett, Springfield, 16 July 1860, *CWL*, 4:84.

282. Joseph J. Lewis to Jesse W. Fell, West Chester, 25 Sept. 1860, Fell Papers, DLC.

283. Lincoln to whom it may concern, Springfield, 2 Aug. 1860, Basler, ed., *Collected Works of Lincoln, First Supplement,* 58; Lincoln to Simon Cameron, Springfield, 6 Aug. 1860, *CWL,* 4:91.

284. Davis to Lincoln, Harrisburg, 5 Aug. 1860, AL MSS DLC.

285. Weed to Lincoln, Albany, 13 Aug. 1860, ibid.

286. Sanderson to Cameron, Philadelphia, 18 Aug. 1860, Cameron Papers, Dauphin County Historical Society, Harrisburg.

287. Davis to Lincoln, Scranton, Pennsylvania, 12 Aug. 1860, AL MSS DLC.

288. Lincoln to John Pomeroy, Springfield, 31 Aug. 1860, *CWL,* 4:103.

289. Charles Henry Ray to Lincoln, Chicago, 27 June 1860, AL MSS DLC.

290. Lincoln to Francis, Springfield, 4 Aug. 1860, *CWL,* 4:90.

291. Lincoln to Henry Wilson, Springfield, 1 Sept. 1860, *CWL,* 4:109.

292. *Illinois State Register* (Springfield), 13 July 1860.

293. R. J. Haldeman to Thomas H. Seymour, Harrisburg, 22 May 1860, Thomas H. Seymour Papers, Connecticut Historical Society.

294. Chicago *Herald,* 17 July 1860.

295. *Missouri Republican* (St. Louis), 3 Aug., 12 Sept. 1860.

296. "Isaac" to the editor, Independence, Missouri, 23 June 1860, ibid., 27 June 1860.

297. *Illinois State Register* (Springfield), 2 Aug., 14, 28 Sept. 1860.

298. New York *Herald,* 5, 18, and 19 Sept., 5 Nov. 1860.

299. New York *Daily News,* copied in the New York *Tribune,* 25 Oct. 1860.

300. New York *Express,* n.d., copied in *The Liberator* (Boston), 2 Nov. 1860.

301. New York *World,* 25 Oct. 1860.

302. New York *Tribune,* n.d., quoted in *The Liberator* (Boston), 9 Nov. 1860.

303. New York *Morning Examiner,* 31 Oct. 1860.

304. Crittenden, speech of 25 Oct. 1860, Boston *Courier,* 3 Nov. 1860, quoted in John V. Mering, "The Slave-State Constitutional Unionists and the Politics of Consensus," *Journal of Southern History* 43 (1977):405.

305. New York *Times,* 27, 28 June 1860.

306. New York *Times,* 28 Aug. 1860.

307. Indianapolis *Daily Journal,* quoted in Emma Lou Thornbrough, *Indiana in the Civil War Era, 1850–1880* (Indianapolis: Indiana Historical Bureau, 1965), 92–93.

308. Manchester, New Hampshire, *Union Democrat,* 22 May 1860.

309. Speech of John Sherman at Chadd's Ford, Pennsylvania, Chicago *Press and Tribune,* 17 Sept. 1860.

310. Undated letter by Charles Hanks to the editor of the *Decatur Magnet,* copied in the Rockport, Indiana, *Democrat,* 11 Aug. 1860.

311. *Illinois State Journal* (Springfield), 6 Sept. 1860.

312. Springfield correspondence, 8 Aug., New York *Herald,* 13 Aug. 1860.

313. Douglas's speech in Fort Wayne, Indiana, Washington *States and Union,* 10 Oct. 1860.

314. Lincoln to Haycraft, Springfield, 16 Aug. 1860, *CWL,* 4:97.

315. Enclosure in Lincoln to George G. Fogg, Springfield, 16 Aug. 1860; Lincoln to Fogg, Springfield, 29 Aug. 1860, ibid., 4:96–97, 102.

316. William Kellogg to Lincoln, Washington, 26 May 1860, AL MSS DLC.

317. Simon P. Hanscom to William Kellogg, Washington, 26 May 1860, AL MSS DLC.

318. James E. Harvey to John G. Nicolay, Washington, 25 Nov. 1860, AL MSS DLC.

319. Springfield correspondence, 16 Oct., New York *Herald,* 20 Oct. 1860.

320. Springfield correspondence, 1 Oct., New York *Herald,* 20 Oct. 1860.

321. Hanscom to Lincoln, Boston, 24 Oct. 1860, AL MSS DLC.

322. New York *Herald*, 20 Oct. 1860.

323. Washington correspondence, 14 Oct., Sacramento *Daily Union,* 7 Nov. 1863, in Michael Burlingame, ed., *Lincoln Observed: Civil War Dispatches of Noah Brooks* (Baltimore, MD: Johns Hopkins University Press, 1998), 69–70.

324. New York *Times,* 4 Sept. 1860.

325. *Illinois State Register* (Springfield), 29 Sept. 1860.

326. Springfield correspondence, 10 Oct., St. Louis *Anzeiger des Westens,* 15 Oct. 1860, in *Germans for a Free Missouri: Translations from the St. Louis Radical Press, 1857–1862,* selected and translated by Steven Rowan (Columbia: University of Missouri Press, 1983), 130.

327. Pike to William P. Fessenden, Calais, 2 Sept. [1860], Pike Papers, DLC.

328. Lincoln to Hamlin, Springfield, 4 Sept. 1860, *CWL,* 4:110.

329. Herman Kreismann to Elihu B. Washburne, Chicago, 3 Sept. 1860, Elihu B. Washburne Papers, DLC; Herman Kreismann to Lyman Trumbull, Chicago, 30 Aug. 1860, Trumbull Papers, DLC.

330. David Davis to Thurlow Weed, Bloomington, 24 Aug., 1860 Barnes, *Life of Weed,* 2: 299–300; David Davis to Thurlow Weed, Bloomington, 11 Sept. 1860, Weed Papers, University of Rochester; David Davis to E. D. Morgan, Bloomington, 22 Sept. 1860, and Indianapolis, 28 Sept. 1860, Edwin D. Morgan Papers, New York State Library, Albany.

331. John Z. Goodrich to Lincoln, Boston, 16 Mar. 1865, AL MSS DLC.

332. Willard King, *Lincoln's Manager: David Davis* (Cambridge, MA: Harvard University Press, 1960), 158.

333. Judge William L. Helfenstein to Stephen A. Douglas, New York, 31 July 1860, Douglas Papers, University of Chicago.

334. Pittsburgh *Gazette,* 24 May 1860, quoted in I. F. Boughter, "Western Pennsylvania and the Morrill Tariff," *Western Pennsylvania Historical Magazine* 6 (1923):118.

335. John Coon to Benjamin F. Wade, Cleveland, 13 Oct. 1860, Wade Papers, DLC.

336. Springfield correspondence, 10 Oct., St. Louis *Anzeiger des Westens,* 15 Oct. 1860, in Rowan, ed., *Germans for a Free Missouri,* 130–131.

337. Lincoln to Read, Springfield, 13 Oct. 1860, *CWL,* 4:127.

338. Lincoln to Seward, Springfield, 12 Oct. 1860, ibid., 4:127.

339. David Davis to his wife, Urbana, 15, 18 Oct. 1860, Davis Papers, IHi.

340. Lincoln to Weed, Springfield, 17 Aug. 1860, *CWL,* 4:98.

341. New York *Herald,* 22, 23 May, 21 July 1860.

342. Medill to Lincoln, Chicago, 5 July 1860, AL MSS DLC.

343. Hanscom to Lincoln, Boston, 24 Oct. 1860, ibid.

344. Caleb B. Smith to Cassius M. Clay, Indianapolis, 22 Apr. 1860, Clay Papers, Lincoln Memorial University, in the *Lincoln Herald* 45, no. 3 (Oct. 1943):35.

345. Medill to Lincoln, Chicago, 9 Aug. 1860, AL MSS DLC.

346. Indianapolis correspondence by Charles A. Page, 30 Apr. 1865, in Charles A. Page, *Letters of a War Correspondent,* ed. James R. Gilmore (Boston: L. C. Page, 1899), 375; Lincoln to Schenck, Springfield, 23 Aug. 1860, *CWL,* 4:100.

347. Lincoln to Fithian, Springfield, 15 Aug. 1860, *CWL,* 4:95.

348. Speech of Yancey at the Cooper Institute, 10 Oct. 1860, in Emerson D. Fite, *The Presidential Campaign of 1860* (New York: Macmillan, 1911), 327.

349. Montgomery *Mail,* n.d., copied in the New York *Tribune,* 22 Oct. 1860.

350. Richmond *Enquirer,* semiweekly ed., 16 Oct. 1860.

351. Atlanta *Southern Confederacy,* n.d., copied in the *Illinois State Democrat,* 19 Sept. 1860.

352. Undated, unidentified correspondence, quoted in the Lancaster correspondence, *Pennsylvania Statesman* (Harrisburg), 27 Oct. 1860.

353. Lincoln to John B. Fry, Springfield, 15 Aug. 1860, *CWL*, 4:95.

354. New York *Courier and Enquirer*, 7 Nov. 1859, copied in the New York *Journal of Commerce*, 3 Nov. 1860.

355. William Pitt Fessenden to Samuel Fessenden, Washington, 5 Jan. [1861—misdated 1860], Fessenden Family Papers, Bowdoin College.

356. Hartford *Evening Press*, 26 Oct. 1860, in Howard Cecil Perkins, ed., *Northern Editorials on Secession* (2 vols.; New York: D. Appleton-Century, 1942), 1:65.

357. Chicago *Press and Tribune*, 17 Oct. 1860.

358. New York *Tribune*, 6 Nov. 1860.

359. New York *Tribune*, 25 Feb. 1861.

360. *Missouri Democrat* (St. Louis), 30 Oct. 1860.

361. William Cullen Bryant II, ed., *Power for Sanity: Selected Editorials of William Cullen Bryant* (New York: Fordham University Press, 1994), 380.

362. *Illinois State Register* (Springfield), 11, 10, 4 Sept. 1860.

363. New York *Herald*, 16 Nov. 1860.

364. Douglas's speech at Jones' Wood, New York, 12 Sept., New York *World*, 13 Sept. 1860.

365. *Louisiana Signal*, 22 Sept. 1860; Douglas's speech at Baltimore, Washington *States and Union*, 8 Sept. 1860.

366. Welch to George G. Fogg, Lafayette, Indiana, 25 Oct. 1860, Fogg Papers, New Hampshire Historical Society.

367. Springfield correspondence, 6 Nov., New York *Tribune*, 10 Nov. 1860.

368. Springfield correspondence by A. C. C., 7 Nov., *Independent Democrat* (Concord, NH), 22 Nov. 1860.

369. Springfield correspondence, 6 Nov., New York *Tribune*, 7 and 10 Nov. 1860.

370. Springfield correspondence by [Samuel R.] W[eed], 6 Nov., *Missouri Democrat* (St. Louis), 7 Nov. 1860.

371. Samuel R. Weed, "Hearing the Returns with Mr. Lincoln," New York *Times Magazine*, 14 Feb. 1932 (written in the 1880s).

372. Ibid.

373. Springfield correspondence by [Samuel R.] W[eed], 7 Nov., *Missouri Democrat* (St. Louis), 8 Nov. 1860.

374. Weed, "Hearing the Returns with Mr. Lincoln."

375. George W. Brinkerhoff to Edward McPherson, Springfield, 19 Nov. 1860, McPherson Papers, DLC.

376. Springfield correspondence, 7 Nov., New York *Tribune*, 8 and 12 Nov. 1860.

377. Springfield correspondence, 7 Nov., New York *Tribune*, 8 and 12 Nov. 1860; Weed, "Hearing the Returns with Mr. Lincoln;" Springfield correspondence by [Samuel R.] W[eed], 7 Nov., *Missouri Democrat* (St. Louis), 8 Nov. 1860.

378. Herndon's account in Caroline Dall, "Journal of a Tour through Illinois, Wisconsin and Ohio, Oct. & Nov. 1866," entry for 29 Oct. 1866, Dall Papers, Bryn Mawr College.

379. Weed, "Hearing the Returns with Mr. Lincoln."

380. King, *Davis*, 161.

381. Joseph Medill to O. M. Hatch, Chicago, 16 Nov. 1860, copy, Hatch Papers, IHi.

382. John Bigelow to William Hargreaves, New York, 10 Nov. 1860, Bigelow Papers, New York Public Library. In New Jersey, the fusion ticket received 62,801 votes to Lincoln's 58,234.

383. John A. Kasson to Horace Greeley, Des Moines, Iowa, 1 July 1860, Greeley Papers, New York Public Library.

384. A letter from "an intelligent and substantial farmer in Union County, Ohio," New York *Tribune*, 6 June 1860.

385. Letter by "Sangamon," Champaign County, 25 May 1860, Chicago *Press and Tribune*, 30 May 1860.

386. Speech of F. P. Blair, Jr., St. Louis, 22 May 1860, New York *Times*, 26 May 1860.

387. Speech of Richard Yates, Springfield, 7 June, New York *Tribune,* 20 June 1860.

388. Speech by James T. Brady, 24 Sept., quoted in the New York *Tribune,* 27 Sept. 1860.

389. New York *Tribune,* 11 June 1860.

390. Milwaukee *Free Democrat,* n.d., copied in the New York *Tribune,* 26 May 1860.

391. Houston *Telegraph,* n.d., copied in the Springfield, Massachusetts, *Republican,* 13 June 1860.

392. David Kilgore to Richard W. Thompson, Indianapolis, 5 Sept. 1860, Richard W. Thompson Collection, LMF.

393. *Missouri Democrat* (St. Louis), 22, 21 May 1860.

394. New York *World,* 23 Oct. 1860.

395. Springfield, Massachusetts, *Republican,* 27 Sept. 1860.

396. Joseph Medill to Horace White, Washington, 4 Jan. 1861, Charles Henry Ray Papers, CSmH.

397. Giddings to Lincoln, Chicago, 19 May 1860, Tarbell, *Life of Lincoln,* 2:162.

398. John P. Verree to Lincoln, Washington, 1 Jan. 1861, AL MSS DLC.

399. Francis E. Spinner to Salmon P. Chase, Washington, 22 Jan. 1861, Chase Papers, DLC.

400. Grimes to Lyman Trumbull, Burlington, Iowa, 13 Nov. 1860, Trumbull Papers, DLC.

401. August Belmont to John Forsyth, New York, 22 Nov. 1860, in *Letters, Speeches and Addresses of August Belmont* (privately printed, 1890), 24.

402. Henry S. Randall to Caleb Cushing, Cortland Village, New York, 3 Nov. 1860, Cushing Papers, DLC.

403. James H. Reed to Crittenden, Greenwich, Connecticut, 17 Jan. 1861, Crittenden Papers, DLC.

404. David A. Wells to Andrew Johnson, Troy, New York, 29 Dec. 1860, Johnson Papers, DLC.

405. Springfield correspondence, 21 June, Utica, New York, *Herald,* 27 June 1860, copied in the New York *Tribune,* 9 July 1860.

406. Washington Hunt to John Bell, Lockport, 21 Nov. 1860, John Bell Papers, DLC.

407. *Douglass's Monthly* 3 (Dec. 1860):370.

408. Chase to George W. Julian, Columbus, 15 Dec. 1860, Giddings-Julian Papers, DLC.

409. Wendell Phillips, speech in Boston, 7 Nov. 1860, Boston *Atlas and Bee,* n.d., copied in the *National Anti-Slavery Standard* (New York), 17 Nov. 1860.

410. Springfield (Massachusetts) *Republican,* 13 July 1860.

411. New York *Herald,* 30 June 1860.

412. Statement by Frederic W. Sutton, the son of the mayor of Springfield, Evanston, Illinois, 7 Apr. 1926, copy enclosed in Oliver R. Barrett to Albert J. Beveridge, Chicago, 17 June 1926, Beveridge Papers, DLC.

413. Gideon Welles, "Recollections in regard to the Formation of Mr Lincoln's Cabinet," undated manuscript, Abraham Lincoln Collection, Beinecke Library, Yale University.

Chapter 17. "I Will Suffer Death Before I Will Consent to Any Concession or Compromise"

1. Zachariah Chandler to Lyman Trumbull, Detroit, 13 Nov. 1860, Trumbull Family Papers, IHi.

2. Charles Francis Adams diary, 11 Nov. 1860, Adams Family Papers, MHi.

3. George Sumner to John A. Andrew, Springfield, 21 Jan. 1861, Andrew Papers, MHi.

4. Herman Kreismann to E. B. Washburne, Washington, 27 Dec. 1860, Washburne Papers, DLC.

5. Louisville *Courier-Journal,* 11 Feb., copied in the Cincinnati *Enquirer,* n.d., copied in the *Illinois State Register* (Springfield), 13 Feb. 1861.

6. Herman Kreismann to E. B. Washburne, Washington, 27 Dec. 1860, Washburne Papers, DLC.

7. Herndon to Wendell Phillips, Springfield, 28 Dec. 1860, 12 Jan. 1861, and 1 Feb. 1861, Phillips Papers, Harvard University.

8. Herndon to Samuel Sewall, Springfield, 1 Feb. 1861, copy, William Lloyd Garrison Papers, Boston Public Library.

9. George Sumner to John A. Andrew, Springfield, 21 Jan. 1861, Andrew Papers, MHi.

10. Springfield correspondence by Hay, 9 Jan., *Missouri Democrat* (St. Louis), 11 Jan. 1861, Michael Burlingame, ed., *Lincoln's Journalist: John Hay's Anonymous Writings for the Press, 1860–1864* (Carbondale: Southern Illinois University Press, 1998), 18.

11. Thomas D. Jones to [William Linn McMillen], Springfield, 11 Feb. 1861, Lincoln Collection, Lilly Library, InU.

12. Springfield correspondence by Henry Villard, 26 Nov., New York *Herald*, 1 Dec. 1860.

13. Mr. A. G. Frick to Lincoln, n.p., 14 Feb. 1861, Lincoln Collection, ICHi.

14. Anonymous to Lincoln, n.p., 20 Feb. 1861, ibid.

15. Hawkins Taylor to Benjamin F. Wade, Keokuk, Iowa, 25 Dec. 1860, Wade Papers, DLC.

16. Springfield correspondence by Henry Villard, 17 Nov., 10 Dec., New York *Herald*, 22 Nov., 15 Dec. 1860; 19 Nov., Cincinnati *Commercial*, 21 Nov. 1860.

17. Henry Villard, *Memoirs of Henry Villard, Journalist and Financier: 1838–1900* (2 vols.; Boston: Houghton Mifflin, 1904), 1:93–94.

18. George B. Lincoln to Schuyler Colfax, Chicago, 29 Dec. 1860, Lincoln Collection, RPB.

19. Interview in an unidentified Western German newspaper, copied in the Springfield (Massachusetts) *Republican*, 28 Feb. 1861.

20. Alexander Milton Ross, *Recollections and Experiences of an Abolitionist, from 1855 to 1865* (Toronto: Rowsell and Hutchinson, 1875), 139.

21. George M. Brinkerhoff to Edward McPherson, Springfield, 30 Jan. 1861, McPherson Papers, DLC.

22. William S. Spear to Lyman Trumbull, Shelbyville, Tennessee, 16 Jan. 1861, Lyman Trumbull Papers, DLC.

23. *Illinois State Journal* (Springfield), 14 Dec. 1860.

24. Keitt to James Hammond, 10 Sept. 1860, in Stephen A. Channing, *Crisis of Fear:*

Secession in South Carolina (New York: Simon and Schuster, 1970), 269.

25. Charleston *Mercury*, 28 Jan. 1864.

26. Salisbury, North Carolina, *Banner*, 19 Feb. 1861, in Daniel W. Crofts, *Reluctant Confederates: Upper South Unionists in the Secession Crisis* (Chapel Hill: University of North Carolina Press, 1989), 94.

27. Dwight Lowell Dumond, ed., *Southern Editorials on Secession* (New York: Century, 1931), 242.

28. Alexander H. Stephens, speech delivered in Savannah, Georgia, 21 Mar. 1861, in Henry Cleveland, *Alexander H. Stephens, in Public and Private with Letters and Speeches, Before, During, and Since the War* (Philadelphia: National Publishing, 1866), 722.

29. Keitt quoted in Hans L. Trefousse, *The Radical Republicans: Lincoln's Vanguard for Racial Justice* (New York: Alfred A. Knopf, 1969), 166.

30. "A Declaration of the Causes which Impel the State of Texas to Secede from the Federal Union," in Ernest William Winkler, ed., *Journal of the Secession Convention of Texas, 1861* (Austin, TX: Austin Printing Company, 1912), 63.

31. John Bell to Alexander Robinson Boteler, 30 July 1860, quoted in Joseph Howard Parks, *John Bell of Tennessee* (Baton Rouge: Louisiana State University Press, 1950), 365.

32. *Weekly Democratic Advocate* [no town indicated], 5 May 1859, in Christopher H. Olsen, *Political Culture and Secession in Mississippi: Masculinity, Honor, and the Antiparty Tradition, 1830–1860* (New York: Oxford University Press, 2000), 183.

33. Jefferson Davis, speech of 13 Feb. 1850, in Dunbar Rowland, ed., *Jefferson Davis, Constitutionalist: His Letters, Papers and Speeches* (10 vols.; Jackson, Mississippi Department of Archives and History, 1923), 1:266.

34. Columbus *Times*, quoted in Anthony Gene Carey, *Politics, Slavery, and the Union in Antebellum Georgia* (Athens: University of Georgia Press, 1997), 239.

35. *Clark County Journal*, Virginia, 9 Nov., quoted in the New York *Tribune*, 13 Nov. 1860.

36. Clarence Phillips Denman, *The Secession Movement in Alabama* (Montgomery: Alabama State Dept. of Archives and History, 1933), 8.

37. Manisha Sinha, *The Counterrevolution of Slavery: Politics and Ideology in Antebellum South Carolina* (Chapel Hill: University of North Carolina Press, 2000), 232.

38. Corsicana *Navarro Express*, 16 Nov. 1860, quoted in Billy D. Ledbetter, "Slavery, Fear, and Disunion in the Lone Star State: Texans' Attitudes toward Secession and the Union, 1846–1861" (Ph.D. dissertation, North Texas State University, 1972), 284.

39. Stephen F. Hale to Beriah Magoffin, Frankfort, Kentucky, 27 Dec. 1860, in Charles B. Dew, *Apostles of Disunion: Southern Secession Commissioners and the Causes of the Civil War* (Charlottesville: University Press of Virginia, 2001), 96, 98–99.

40. David Clopton to C. C. Clay, 13 Dec. 1860, Clay Papers, Duke University, quoted in William J. Cooper, Jr., "The Politics of Slavery Affirmed: The South and the Secession Crisis," in *The Southern Enigma: Essays on Race, Class, and Folk Culture*, ed. Walter J. Fraser, Jr. and Winfred B. Moore, Jr. (Westport, CT: Greenwood Press, 1983), 204.

41. Barnwell to R. B. Rhett, 1 Nov. 1844, in Channing, *Crisis of Fear*, 66.

42. William Porcher Miles, *Oration Delivered Before the Fourth of July Association* (Charleston, SC, 1849), quoted in Eric H. Walther, *The Fire-Eaters* (Baton Rouge: Louisiana State University Press, 1992), 274.

43. *Congressional Globe,* 36th Congress, 2nd Session, 74, 667, quoted ibid., 179.

44. "Burleigh," in the Montgomery *Advertiser,* 25 June 1851, in J. Mills Thornton, *Politics and Power in a Slave Society: Alabama, 1800–1860* (Baton Rouge: Louisiana State University Press, 1978), 58.

45. Ulrich Bonnell Phillips, ed., *The Correspondence of Robert Toombs, Alexander H. Stephens, and Howell Cobb* (1913; New York: Da Capo Press, 1970), 118.

46. *Jackson County Democrat,* n.d., copied in the Montgomery *Advertiser,* 2 Oct. 1850, in Thornton, *Politics and Power in a Slave Society,* 220.

47. New Orleans *Bee,* 10 Dec. 1860, in Dumond, ed., *Southern Editorials,* 315–316.

48. *Congressional Globe,* 36th Congress, 2nd Session, 212 (31 Dec. 1860).

49. Pettus, speech to Mississippi Legislature, 26 Nov. 1860, in Edward Mayes, *Lucius Q.C. Lamer: His Life, Times, and Speeches, 1825–1893* (Nashville: Methodist Episcopal Church, 1896), 88.

50. Charles Francis Adams to E. Farnsworth, Washington, 9 Dec. 1860, letterbook copies, Adams Family Papers, MHi; Adams to Richard Henry Dana, Washington, 23 Dec. 1860, Dana Family Papers, MHi.

51. *A Philadelphia Perspective: The Diary of Sidney George Fisher Covering the Years, 1834–1871,* ed. Nicholas B. Wainwright (2 vols.; Philadelphia: Historical Society of Pennsylvania, 1967), 1:371 (entry for 25 Nov. 1860).

52. New York *Tribune,* 26 Feb. 1861.

53. William Howard Russell, *My Diary North and South* (New York: Harper and Brothers, 1863), 71 (entry for 8 May 1861).

54. Letter by Hilliard, n.p., n.d., quoted in the Springfield, Massachusetts, *Republican,* 1 Jan. 1861.

55. New Orleans *Picayune,* 8 Sept. 1860, quoted in Donald E. Reynolds, *Editors Make War: Southern Newspapers in the Secession Crisis* (Nashville, TN: Vanderbilt University Press, 1970), 214–215.

56. New York *Tribune,* 26 Feb. 1861.

57. Article by the New York *Tribune*'s correspondent, E. H. House, New York *Sun,* undated clipping, [probably 1883], LMF.

58. Elihu B. Washburne to his wife, [Galena], 14 Nov. 1860, Washburn Family Papers, Washburn Memorial Library, Norlands, Maine.

59. Donn Piatt, *Memories of the Men Who Saved the Union* (New York: Belford, Clarke, 1887), 30.

60. Springfield correspondence, 4 Sept., New York *Evening Post*, 8 Sept. 1860.

61. William H. Herndon and Jesse W. Weik, *Herndon's Lincoln*, ed. Douglas L. Wilson and Rodney O. Davis (1889; Urbana: University of Illinois Press, 2006), 284.

62. A lumber merchant of Washington in the Washington *Star*, n.d., copied in the New York *Evening Post*, 15 Nov. 1860.

63. David M. Swarr to John G. Nicolay and John Hay, Lancaster, Pennsylvania, 1 Nov. 1886, Nicolay Papers, DLC.

64. *Reminiscences of Parmenas Taylor Turnley, from the Cradle to Three Score and Ten* (Chicago: Donohue & Henneberry, 1892), 10.

65. Henry Adams, *The Great Secession Winter of 1860–61, and Other Essays*, ed. George Hochfield (New York: Sagamore Press, 1958), 15.

66. William B. Campbell to A. C. Beard, 15 Mar. 1861, quoted in Crofts, *Reluctant Confederates*, xvi.

67. William M. Clark to Lewis Thompson, 10 Jan. 1861, quoted ibid.

68. Thomas K. Thomas to Henry C. Carey, Louisburg, 3 Nov. 1860, Carey Papers in the Gardiner Collection, Historical Society of Pennsylvania.

69. Mason's speech in the U. S. Senate, *Congressional Globe*, 36th Congress, 2nd Session, 56 (11 Dec. 1860).

70. Thomas B. Webster, Jr., to John Sherman, St. Louis, 15 Nov. 1860, Sherman Papers, DLC.

71. Springfield correspondence by Henry Villard, 20 Dec., Cincinnati *Commercial*, 24 Dec. 1860.

72. George E. Baker, ed., *The Works of William H. Seward* (5 vols.; Boston: Houghton, Mifflin, 1884), 4:344.

73. Chicago *Democrat*, 27 July 1860, copied in the New York *Herald*, 1 Aug. 1860.

74. John Bigelow to William Hargraves, New York, 10 Nov. 1860, Bigelow Papers, New York Public Library.

75. James Buchanan to Nahum Capen, Wheatland, 27 Aug. 1856, in John Bassett Moore, ed., *The Works of James Buchanan*

(12 vols.; Philadelphia: J. B. Lippincott, 1908–1911), 2:180.

76. Evansville *Daily Journal*, 13 Nov. 1860, quoted in Elmer Duane Elbert, "Southern Indiana Politics on the Eve of the Civil War, 1858–1861" (Ph.D. dissertation, Indiana University, 1967), 164.

77. George B. Lincoln to Schuyler Colfax, Chicago, 29 Dec. 1860, Lincoln Collection, RPB.

78. William M. Reynolds to Edward McPherson, Springfield, 12 Feb. 1861, McPherson Papers, DLC.

79. Albany *Evening Journal*, 19 and 24 Nov. 1860.

80. Joseph R. Hawley to his father, Washington, 7 Jan. 1861, Hawley Papers, DLC.

81. George G. Fogg to Horace Greeley, St. Louis, 1 Dec. 1860, Greeley Papers, DLC.

82. Springfield correspondence by Gustave Koerner, 18 Nov. 1860, St. Louis *Westliche Post*, n.d., in Thomas J. McCormack, ed., *Memoirs of Gustave Koerner, 1809–1896* (2 vols.; Cedar Rapids, IA: Torch Press, 1909), 2:105.

83. Springfield correspondence by Henry Villard, Cincinnati *Commercial*, n.d., copied in the New York *Evening Post*, 17 Dec. 1860.

84. Richard C. Parsons to John Sherman, Cleveland, 12 Dec. 1860, John Sherman Papers, DLC.

85. *Congressional Globe*, 36th Congress, 1st Session, 24 (6 Dec. 1859).

86. Ibid., 572 (25 Jan. 1860).

87. New York *Tribune*, 20 Nov. 1860.

88. Chicago *Tribune*, 27 Nov. 1860.

89. Chandler to Austin Blair, Washington, 11 Feb. 1861, *Congressional Globe*, 36th Congress, 2nd Session, 1247 (27 Feb. 1861).

90. Z. Chandler to James Watson Webb, Washington, 20 Feb. 1858, James Watson Webb Papers, Yale University.

91. Z. Chandler to Lyman Trumbull, Detroit, 13 Nov. 1860, Trumbull Family Papers, IHi.

92. Smith D. Atkins to Elihu B. Washburne, Rockford, Illinois, 15 Feb. 1861, Washburne Papers, DLC.

93. Frank Blair to [Montgomery Blair], 23 Nov. 1860, Blair Papers, Princeton University.

94. Gustave Koerner to Lyman Trumbull, Belleville, 10 Dec. 1860, Trumbull Papers, DLC.

95. Koerner, *Memoirs*, 2:108–109.

96. Herndon to Lyman Trumbull, Springfield, 21 Dec. 1860, Trumbull Papers, DLC.

97. Herndon to Theodore Parker, Springfield, 10 Mar. 1857, Herndon-Parker Papers, University of Iowa.

98. Grimes to his wife, Washington, 16 Dec. 1860, in William Salter, *The Life of James W. Grimes, Governor of Iowa, 1854–1858, A Senator of the United States, 1859–1869* (New York: Appleton, 1876), 132.

99. Elbert, "Southern Indiana Politics on the Eve of the Civil War," 164–165.

100. Indianapolis *Indiana American,* 21 Nov. 1860, in Howard Cecil Perkins, ed., *Northern Editorials on Secession* (2 vols.; New York: D. Appleton-Century, 1942), 1:97.

101. John Haywood to S. S. Cox, Westerville, Ohio, 2 Jan. 1861, Cox Papers, RPB.

102. Evansville, Indiana, *Daily Journal,* 12 Feb. 1861.

103. Grimes to Samuel J. Kirkwood, Washington, 28 Jan. 1861, in Salter, *Grimes,* 133–134.

104. Charles Sumner to John A. Andrew, Washington, 3 Feb. 1861, Andrew Papers, MHi.

105. Washington correspondence, 7 Jan., Boston *Daily Advertiser,* 11 Jan. 1861.

106. James A. Dix to N. P. Banks, Boston, 15 Feb. 1861, and George S. Boutwell to Banks, Washington, 22 Feb. 1861, Banks Papers, DLC.

107. A. K. McClure to Edward McPherson, Harrisburg, 27 Feb. [1861], Edward McPherson Papers, DLC.

108. Washington correspondence by "Independent" (James E. Harvey), 26 Dec., Philadelphia *North American and United States Gazette,* 27 Dec. 1860.

109. Henry Winter Davis to Samuel Francis Du Pont, [Washington], 19 Jan. 1861, transcript, S. F. Du Pont Papers, Hagley Museum, Wilmington, Delaware.

110. Interview with Lincoln, Springfield correspondence, 14 Nov., New York *Evening Post,* 19 Nov. 1860.

111. Samuel Haycraft to Lincoln, Elizabethtown, Kentucky, 9 Nov. 1860, AL MSS DLC.

112. Memorandum by John G. Nicolay, Springfield, 5 Nov. 1860, Michael Burlingame, ed., *With Lincoln in the White House: Letters, Memoranda, and Other Writings of John G. Nicolay, 1860–1865* (Carbondale: Southern Illinois University Press, 2000), 7–8.

113. Sanford to William C. Rives, n.p., n.d., draft, Sanford Papers, Sanford, Florida, quoted in Joseph A. Fry, *Henry S. Sanford: Diplomacy and Business in Nineteenth-Century America* (Reno: University of Nevada Press, 1982), 31.

114. Lincoln to Smith, Springfield, 10 Nov. 1860, Roy P. Basler et al., eds., *Collected Works of Abraham Lincoln [hereafter CWL]* (8 vols. plus index; New Brunswick, NJ: Rutgers University Press, 1953–1955), 4:138.

115. Springfield correspondence, 14 Nov., New York *Evening Post,* 19 Nov. 1860.

116. Thomas Marshall, speech in the Illinois Senate, 1 Feb., *Illinois State Register* (Springfield), 5 Feb. 1861.

117. John G. Nicolay, memorandum, 15 Nov. 1860, Burlingame, ed., *With Lincoln in the White House,* 10.

118. John G. Nicolay, memorandum, 16 Nov. 1860, ibid., 10–11.

119. George Robertson to John J. Crittenden, Lexington, Kentucky, 16 Dec. 1860, Crittenden Papers, DLC.

120. Lincoln to Nathaniel P. Paschall, Springfield, 16 Nov. 1860, *CWL,* 4:140.

121. Lincoln to Thurlow Weed, Springfield, 17 Dec. 1860, ibid., 4:154.

122. Springfield correspondence by Henry Villard, 19 Nov., New York *Herald,* 20 Nov. 1860.

123. *Ohio State Journal* (Columbus), 14 Nov. 1860.

124. Medill to Ozias M. Hatch, Chicago, 16 Nov. 1860, Hatch Papers, IHi.

125. Springfield correspondence by Henry Villard, 20 Nov., New York *Herald,* 21 Nov. and 4 Dec. 1860.

126. L. F. Holbrook to Lincoln, New York, 12 Nov. 1860, AL MSS DLC.

127. *CWL,* 4:141–142.

128. Lincoln to Raymond, Springfield, 28 Nov. 1860, ibid., 4:145–146.

129. Springfield correspondence by Henry Villard, 1 Dec., New York *Herald,* 6 Dec. 1860.

130. Cincinnati *Enquirer,* 10 Apr. 1861, 27 Dec. 1860, quoted in John Thomas Hubbell, "The Northern Democracy and the Crisis of Disunion, 1860–1861" (Ph.D. dissertation, University of Illinois, 1969), 234, 233.

131. Fragment of a speech intended for Kentuckians, ca. 12 Feb. 1861, *CWL,* 4:200–201.

132. Springfield correspondence, 3 Nov., New York *World,* n.d., copied in the Philadelphia *Evening Bulletin,* 8 Nov. 1860.

133. *Missouri Democrat* (St. Louis), 8 Jan. 1861.

134. *CWL,* 4:175–176.

135. George Sumner to John A. Andrew, Springfield, 21 Jan. 1861, Andrew Papers, MHi.

136. Springfield correspondence by "Illinois," 8 Feb., Boston *Atlas and Bee,* 13 Feb. 1861.

137. Springfield correspondence by Henry Villard, 7 Dec., New York *Herald,* 15 Dec. 1860.

138. Chicago correspondence by G. P., 14 Dec., Philadelphia *Evening Bulletin,* 17 Dec. 1860.

139. Springfield correspondence by Henry Villard, 7, 20 Dec., New York *Herald,* 15, 25 Dec. 1860, and Springfield correspondence by Henry Villard, 20 Dec., Cincinnati *Commercial,* 26 Dec. 1860.

140. Herman Kreismann to Edward Lillie Pierce, Washington, 11 Jan. 1861, E. L. Pierce Papers, Harvard University.

141. *Illinois State Journal* (Springfield), 20 Dec. 1860.

142. Ibid., 12, 13, 15, 16, 17, 26, 29 Nov.; 7, 11, 14, 15, 17, 18, 19, 20 Dec. 1860; 13 Jan. 1861.

143. *Illinois State Journal* (Springfield), 18 Dec. 1860.

144. Linton Stephens to Alexander H. Stephens, Sparta, Georgia, 8 Feb. 1861, Alexander H. Stephens Papers, Manhattanville College, Purchase, New York.

145. Stephens to J. Henly Smith, Crawfordsville, [Georgia], 10 July 1860, in Ulrich B. Phillips, ed., *The Correspondence of Robert Toombs, Alexander H. Stephens, and Howell Cobb* (Annual Report of the American Historical Association for the Year 1911; 2 vols.; Washington, DC: Smithsonian Institution Press, 1913), 2:487.

146. Springfield correspondence by Henry Villard, 30 Nov., New York *Herald,* 1 Dec. 1860.

147. Lincoln to Stephens, Springfield, 22 Dec. 1860, *CWL,* 4:160.

148. Thornwell, "The State of the Country" (pamphlet; New Orleans: True Witness and Sentinel Office, 1861), in Jon L. Wakelyn, ed., *Southern Pamphlets on Secession, November 1860–April 1861* (Chapel Hill: University of North Carolina Press, 1996), 162.

149. Kenneth Rayner to Caleb Cushing, Raleigh, 9 Dec. 1860, Cushing Papers, DLC.

150. James D. Richardson, ed., *A Compilation of the Messages and Papers of the Presidents, 1789–1897* (10 vols.; Washington, DC: U.S. Government Printing Office, 1896–1899), 5:626.

151. *Illinois State Journal* (Springfield), 22 Jan. 1861.

152. Seward to his wife, Washington, 7 Dec. 1860, Frederick W. Seward, *Seward at Washington as Senator and Secretary of State: A Memoir of His Life, with Selections from His Letters* (2 vols.; New York: Derby and Miller, 1891), 1:480.

153. James Barbour to Frederic Bancroft, 24 Aug. 1893, Frederic Bancroft, *The Life of William H. Seward* (2 vols.; New York: Harper and Brothers, 1900), 2:32n.

154. Gilmer to W. A. Graham, 5 Dec. 1860, in Patrick Michael Sowle, "The Conciliatory Republicans during the Winter of Secession" (Ph.D. dissertation, Duke University, 1963), 52.

155. [J. Beatty?] to Sherman, 23 Dec. 1860, quoted ibid., 73.

156. Spaulding to Weed, Washington, 22 Dec. 1860, Weed Papers, University of Rochester.

157. John S. Phelps to Samuel Treat, Washington, 18 Dec. 1860, Treat Papers, Missouri Historical Society.

158. *CWL*, 3:369.

159. Lincoln to Kellogg, Springfield, 11 Dec. 1860, ibid., 4:150.

160. Reminiscences of A. H. Markland, New York *Tribune*, 2 Aug. 1885.

161. Lincoln to E. B. Washburne, Springfield, 13 Dec. 1860, *CWL*, 4:151.

162. Lincoln to Trumbull, Springfield, 10 Dec. 1860, ibid., 4:149–150.

163. Lincoln to Lyman Trumbull, Springfield, 17 Dec. 1860, ibid., 4:153.

164. Lincoln to John. D. Defrees, Springfield, 18 Dec. 1860, ibid., 4:155.

165. Lincoln to Curtin, Springfield, 21 Dec. 1860, ibid., 4:158.

166. Springfield correspondence by Henry Villard, 12 Dec., New York *Herald*, 17 Dec. 1860.

167. *Illinois State Journal* (Springfield), 17 Dec. 1860.

168. Springfield correspondence by Henry Villard, 17 Dec., New York *Herald*, 21 Dec. 1860.

169. George Sumner to John A. Andrew, Springfield, 21 Jan. 1861, Andrew Papers, MHi.

170. E. Peshine Smith to Henry C. Carey, Rochester, 16 Dec. 1860, Henry C. Carey Papers in the Edward Carey Gardiner Collection, Historical Society of Pennsylvania.

171. Justin S. Morrill to his wife, Washington, 7 Dec. 1860, Morrill Papers, DLC.

172. Edward McPherson, ed., *The Political History of the United States of America During the Great Rebellion* (2nd ed.; Washington, DC: Philp & Solomons, 1865), 37.

173. David Clopton to Clement C. Clay, 13 Dec. 1860, in Clement Eaton, *A History of the Southern Confederacy* (New York: Macmillan, 1954), 12.

174. Lincoln to John A. Gilmer, Springfield, 15 Dec. 1860, *CWL*, 4:151–152.

175. Charleston *Mercury*, 13 Oct. 1860.

176. Springfield correspondence by Henry Villard, 11 Dec., New York *Herald*, 15 Dec. 1860.

177. Lincoln to H. J. Raymond, Springfield, 18 Dec. 1860, *CWL*, 4:156.

178. Springfield correspondence by Henry Villard, 19 Dec., New York *Herald*, 24 Dec. 1860.

179. Springfield correspondence by Henry Villard., 20 Dec., Cincinnati *Commercial*, 24 Dec. 1860.

180. *Illinois State Journal* (Springfield), 25 Jan. 1861.

181. Springfield correspondence, 28 Jan., New York *Evening Post*, 1 Feb. 1861.

182. Herring Chrisman to William C. Rives, Springfield, 7 Feb. 1861, Rives Papers, DLC.

183. Isaac N. Arnold, *The History of Abraham Lincoln and the Overthrow of Slavery* (Chicago: Clarke, 1866), 184.

184. Albany *Evening Journal*, 17 Dec. 1860.

185. Gideon Welles, *Lincoln and Seward* (New York: Sheldon, 1874), 23.

186. Weed, *Autobiography*, 604–605.

187. Springfield correspondence, 20 Dec., New York *World*, 21 Dec. 1860; Springfield correspondence by Henry Villard, 20 Dec., New York *Herald*, 21 Dec. 1860; Lincoln to Trumbull, Springfield, 21 Dec. 1860, *CWL*, 4:158.

188. Green to Buchanan, Springfield, 28 Dec. 1860, Buchanan Papers, Historical Society of Pennsylvania.

189. Lincoln to Duff Green, Springfield, 28 Dec. 1860, *CWL*, 4:162–163.

190. Ibid., 4:200–201.

191. Lincoln to James T. Hale, Springfield, 11 Jan. 1861, ibid., 4:172.

192. W. J. Gregg to Lyman Trumbull, Paris, Illinois, 6 Feb. 1861, Trumbull Papers, DLC.

193. Charleston *Mercury* and the Augusta *Constitutionalist*, quoted in William L. Barney,

The *Secessionist Impulse: Alabama and Mississippi in 1860* (Princeton: Princeton University Press, 1974), 202.

194. Charles Francis Adams diary, 22 Dec. 1861, Adams Family Papers, MHi.

195. Henry Wilson to William S. Robinson, Washington, 16 Dec. 1860, in William S. Robinson, *"Warrington" Pen-Portraits: A Collection of Personal and Political Reminiscences* (Boston: Lee and Shepard, 1877), 93.

196. Schurz to his wife, Boston, 24 Dec. 1860, Frederic Bancroft, ed., *Speeches, Correspondence and Political Papers of Carl Schurz* (6 vols.; New York: G.P. Putnam's Sons, 1913), 1:177.

197. Julian to S. S. Boyd, n.p., n.d. [Jan. 1861], Julian Papers, Indiana State Library, Indianapolis.

198. Giddings to George W. Julian, Jefferson, Ohio, 14 Dec. 1860, Giddings-Julian Papers, DLC; Giddings to Gerrit Smith, Jefferson, Ohio, 29 Dec. 1860, Smith Papers, Syracuse University.

199. Frank Blair to Montgomery Blair, St. Louis, 14 Feb. 1861, Blair Family Papers, DLC.

200. Sumner to Joseph R. Hawley, Washington, 31 Jan. 1861, Hawley Papers, DLC.

201. Edward L. Pierce to Sumner, Boston, 31 Dec. 1860, Sumner Papers, Harvard University.

202. Ray to John A. Andrew, Springfield, 17 Jan. 1861, Andrew Papers, MHi.

203. Lincoln to Cuthbert Bullitt, Washington, 28 July 1862, *CWL*, 5:344.

204. Detroit *Free Press*, 29 Jan. 1861, quoted in Hubbell, "Northern Democracy and the Crisis of Disunion," 103.

205. New Orleans *Bee*, n.d., copied in the Cleveland *Plain Dealer*, 9 May 1861, quoted ibid., 197.

206. "The Border Slave States and the Cotton States," *Illinois State Journal* (Springfield), 24 Dec. 1860.

207. New Orleans *Bee*, n.d., copied in the Cleveland *Plain Dealer*, 9 May 1861, quoted in Hubbell, "Northern Democracy and the Crisis of Disunion," 198.

208. George S. Converse to S. S. Cox, Columbus, 9 Jan. 1861, Cox Papers, RPB.

209. John A. McClernand to S. S. Cox, Cairo, 4 Dec. 1861, ibid.

Chapter 18. "What If I Appoint Cameron, Whose Very Name Stinks in the Nostrils of the People for His Corruption?"

1. William H. Herndon and Jesse W. Weik, *Herndon's Lincoln*, ed. Douglas L. Wilson and Rodney O. Davis (1889; Urbana: University of Illinois Press, 2006), 284.

2. Thurlow Weed Barnes, *Life of Thurlow Weed Including His Autobiography and a Memoir* (2 vols.; Boston: Houghton Mifflin, 1884), 1:605–606.

3. J. W. Shaffer to Elihu B. Washburne, Freeport, 29 Jan. 1861, Washburne Papers, DLC.

4. "Lincoln's Time of Agony," reminiscences of Joseph Gillespie, Springfield correspondence, 2 Feb., New York *Tribune*, 5 Feb. 1888.

5. John W. Bunn to Isaac N. Phillips, Springfield, 8 Nov. 1910, in Isaac N. Phillips, ed., *Abraham Lincoln by Some Men Who Knew Him* (Bloomington, IL: Pantagraph, 1910), 163–164.

6. Hay to John G. Nicolay, Warsaw, Illinois, 22 Nov. 1872; Hay to Charles Hay, Paris, 9 Sept. 1866, letterpress copy, both in the Hay Papers, RPB; Hay to William H. Herndon, Paris, 5 Sept. 1866, in Michael Burlingame, ed., *At Lincoln's Side: John Hay's Civil War Correspondence and Selected Writings* (Carbondale: Southern Illinois University Press, 2000), 110.

7. Henry Adams, *The Education of Henry Adams* (Boston: Houghton Mifflin, 1918), 104.

8. Montgomery Blair to Gideon Welles, Washington, 17 May 1873, Welles Papers, DLC.

9. William Howard Russell, *My Diary North and South* (Boston: T. O. H. P. Burnham, 1863), 34.

10. Springfield correspondence by Henry Villard, 28 Nov., New York *Herald,* 2 Dec. 1860; Springfield correspondence by Henry Villard, 28 Nov., Cincinnati *Commercial,* 1 Dec. 1860.

11. T. L. Cuyler to the editor of the *Evangelist,* n.d., copied in the *Ohio State Journal* (Columbus), 20 Dec. 1860.

12. Springfield correspondence by Henry Villard, 26 Nov., Cincinnati *Commercial,* n.d., copied in the *Missouri Democrat* (St. Louis), 4 Dec. 1860; John G. Nicolay, memorandum of a conversation between Lincoln and Edward Bates, 15 Dec. 1860, Michael Burlingame, ed., *With Lincoln in the White House: Letters, Memoranda, and Other Writings of John G. Nicolay, 1860–1865* (Carbondale: Southern Illinois University Press, 2000), 18.

13. Lincoln to Trumbull, Springfield, 8 Dec. 1860, Roy P. Basler et al., eds., *Collected Works of Abraham Lincoln* [hereafter *CWL*] (8 vols. plus index; New Brunswick, NJ: Rutgers University Press, 1953–1955), 4:149.

14. Lincoln to Seward, Springfield, 8 Dec. 1860, ibid., 4:148.

15. Howard Carroll, *Twelve Americans: Their Lives and Times* (New York: Harper & Brothers, 1883), 154.

16. Barnes, *Weed Autobiography,* 1:605–606, 611; 2:294.

17. Henry Winter Davis to Samuel Francis Du Pont, [Washington], 20 Feb. 1861, transcript, S. F. Du Pont Papers, Hagley Museum.

18. Gilmer to Douglas, Greensboro, 17 Apr. 1861, Douglas Papers, University of Chicago.

19. Herman Kreismann to E. B. Washburne, Washington, 27 Dec. 1860, Washburne Papers, DLC; Albany *Evening Journal,* 24 Dec. 1860.

20. Leonard Swett to the editor, Chicago, 13 July, Chicago *Tribune,* 14 July 1878.

21. Charles Francis Adams diary, 27 Dec. 1861, Adams Family Papers, MHi.

22. Seward to his wife, [Washington], 28 Dec. 1860, 10 Aug. 1861, and to his daughter, 21 August 1862, Frederick W. Seward, *Seward at Washington as Senator and Secretary of State: A Memoir of His Life, with Selections from His Letters* (2 vols.; New York: Derby and Miller, 1891), 1:487, 610, 2:124; Seward to Weed, Washington, 22 Jan. 1862, Weed Papers, University of Rochester.

23. Seward told this to a New York Democrat. Henry Winter Davis to S. F. Du Pont, [Washington], 15 Jan. 1865, transcript, Du Pont Papers, Hagley Museum.

24. Trumbull to Lincoln, Washington, 20 Jan. 1861, AL MSS DLC.

25. Fogg to Lincoln, Washington, 13 Dec. 1860, ibid.

26. Fogg to E. D. Morgan, New York, 8 Feb. 1861, Edwin D. Morgan Papers, New York State Library, Albany.

27. J. Warren Bell to Andrew Johnson, Springfield, 16 Feb. 1861, LeRoy P. Graf and Ralph W. Haskins, eds., *The Papers of Andrew Johnson* (16 vols.; Knoxville: University of Tennessee Press, 1967–2000), 4:291.

28. Lincoln to Seward, Springfield, 29 Dec. 1860, *CWL,* 4:164.

29. Gilmer to Lincoln, Greensboro, 29 Dec. 1860, AL MSS DLC.

30. David Davis to Gideon Welles, Bloomington, Illinois, 27 July 1872, Abraham Lincoln Collection, Beinecke Library, Yale University; Henry Winter Davis to Samuel Francis Du Pont, [Washington], [Feb. or Mar. 1861], transcript, S. F. Du Pont Papers, Hagley Museum.

31. Joshua Speed, interview with Herndon, [1865–1866], Douglas L. Wilson and Rodney O. Davis, eds., *Herndon's Informants: Letters, Interviews, and Statements about Abraham Lincoln* [hereafter *HI*] (Urbana: University of Illinois Press, 1998), 475.

32. *CWL,* 4:150.

33. *Illinois State Journal* (Springfield), 17 Dec. 1860.

34. Frank Blair to Montgomery Blair, St. Louis, n.d. [15 Dec. 1860], Blair and Lee Family Papers, Princeton University.

35. Joshua Speed to Gideon Welles, Louisville, 8 Aug. 1872, Abraham Lincoln Collection, Beinecke Library, Yale University.

36. Charles H. Ambler, *Francis H. Pierpont, Union War Governor of Virginia and Father of West Virginia* (Chapel Hill: University of North Carolina Press, 1937), 157.

37. John G. Nicolay, memorandum, 15 Dec. 1860, Burlingame, ed., *With Lincoln in the White House*, 17–19; Silas Noble to E. B. Washburne, Springfield, 17 Dec. 1860, Washburne Papers, DLC.

38. Medill to Colfax, ca. Dec. 1862, in O. J. Hollister, *Life of Schuyler Colfax* (New York: Funk & Wagnalls, 1886), 200.

39. Hannibal Hamlin to Lincoln, Hampden, Maine, 27 Dec. 1860, AL MSS DLC.

40. McClure to Ward Hill Lamon, Philadelphia, 8 May 1871, Jeremiah Black Papers, DLC.

41. David Wilmot to Lincoln, Towanda, Pennsylvania, 12 Dec. 1860, AL MSS DLC.

42. Medill to Charles Henry Ray, Washington, 13 Jan. 1861, Ray Papers, CSmH.

43. Henry C. Whitney to Herndon, n.p., 23 June 1887, *HI*, 620.

44. Gideon Welles, "Recollections in regard to the Formation of Mr Lincoln's Cabinet," undated manuscript, Abraham Lincoln Collection, Beinecke Library, Yale University.

45. Elihu B. Washburne to Lincoln, Washington, 7 Jan. 1861, AL MSS DLC.

46. Kreismann to Charles H. Ray, Washington, 16 Jan. 1861, Ray Papers CSmH.

47. Medill to Charles H. Ray, Washington, 13 Jan. 1861, ibid.

48. Swett to David Davis, Washington, 1 Jan. 1861, Davis Papers, IHi.

49. Cameron, interview with John G. Nicolay, 20 Feb. 1875, Michael Burlingame, ed., *An Oral History of Abraham Lincoln: John G. Nicolay's Interviews and Essays* (Carbondale: Southern Illinois University Press, 1996), 42.

50. Memorandum of S. W. Crawford's conversation with Cameron, Bedford Springs, Pennsylvania, July 1883, typescript, S. W. Crawford Papers, IHi.

51. Howard K. Beale, ed., *The Diary of Edward Bates, 1859–1866* (Annual Report of the American Historical Association for 1930, vol. 4; Washington, D.C: U.S. Government Printing Office, 1933), 164 (entry for 16 Dec. 1860).

52. Cameron, interview with John G. Nicolay, 20 Feb. 1875, Burlingame, ed., *Oral History of Lincoln*, 42.

53. *CWL*, 4:168.

54. Elihu B. Washburne to Lincoln, Washington, 10 Jan. 1861, AL MSS DLC.

55. Jackson to Francis P. Blair, Hermitage, 7 and 9 Apr. 1845, in John Spencer Bassett, ed., *Correspondence of Andrew Jackson* (7 vols.; Washington, DC: Carnegie Institution of Washington, 1926–1935), 6:395, 397.

56. *The Diary of James K. Polk during His Presidency, 1845–1849*, ed. Milo Milton Quaif (4 vols.; Chicago: A. C. McClurg, 1910), 1:426 (entry for 25 May 1846).

57. Buchanan to Jefferson Davis, Wheatland, 16 Mar. 1850, and to William R. King, Wheatland, 20 Mar. 1850, John Bassett Moore, ed., *The Works of James Buchanan, Comprising His Speeches, State Papers, and Private Correspondence* (12 vols.; Philadelphia: J. B. Lippincott, 1908–1911) 8:373, 376.

58. Joseph Medill to Lincoln, Washington, 18 Dec. 1860, AL MSS DLC.

59. Hamlin to William P. Fessenden, n.p., n.d., paraphrased in Joseph Medill to Horace White, Washington, 4 Jan. 1861, and Elihu B. Washburne to Charles H. Ray, Washington, 2 Jan. 1861, Ray Papers, CSmH; Hamlin to Lyman Trumbull, Hampden, Maine, 27 Dec. 1860, Trumbull Papers, DLC.

60. Fessenden to Lincoln, Washington, 20 Jan. 1861, AL MSS DLC.

61. Trumbull to Lincoln, Washington, 3 and 20 Jan. 1861, ibid.; Trumbull to David Dudley Field, Washington, 3 Jan. 1861, copy, Trumbull Family Papers, IHi.

62. John Covode to Samuel Galloway, Washington, 3 Jan. 1861, Galloway Papers, Ohio Historical Society.

63. Trumbull to Norman B. Judd, Washington, 18 Jan. 1861, Lincoln Collection, RPB.

64. Medill to Horace White, Washington, 4 Jan. 1861, Charles H. Ray Papers, CSmH; Medill to Scripps and Ray, Washington, 6 Jan. 1861, ibid.

65. Medill to Charles H. Ray, Washington, 13 Jan. 1861, ibid.

66. Horace White to Charles H. Ray, n.p., n.d., ibid. White to Lyman Trumbull, Chicago, 10 Jan. 1861, Trumbull Papers, DLC; White to E. B. Washburne, Chicago, 5 Jan. 1861, Washburne Papers, DLC.

67. Bayard Taylor to Horace Greeley, Kennett Square, Pennsylvania, 10 Nov. 1860, Greeley Papers, New York Public Library.

68. John D. Defrees to David Davis, Indianapolis, 26 Nov. 1860, Davis Papers, IHi; John D. Defrees to Henry S. Lane, Washington, 18 Jan. 1861, typed copy, Lane Papers, InU.

69. Elihu B. Washburne to Lincoln, Washington, 1 Jan. 1861, AL MSS DLC.

70. Washburne to Charles H. Ray, Washington, 2 Jan. 1861, Ray Papers, CSmH.

71. John P. Verree to Lincoln, Washington, 1 Jan. 1861, AL MSS DLC.

72. Edward Joy Morris to Lincoln, Washington, 5 Jan. 1861, ibid.

73. William D. Kelley to Lincoln, Philadelphia, 7 Jan. 1861, ibid.

74. Medill to Horace White, Washington, 4 Jan. 1861, Charles H. Ray Papers, CSmH.

75. Ibid. 4.

76. William C. Bryant to Lincoln, New York, 4 Jan. 1861, AL MSS DLC.

77. James H. van Alen to Lincoln, New York, 5 Jan. 1861, ibid.

78. McClure to Lincoln, Harrisburg, 29 Dec. 1860, AL MSS DLC; Alexander K. McClure, *Our Presidents and How We Make Them* (New York: Harper & Brothers, 1900), 178–179.

79. McClure to Thaddeus Stevens, Harrisburg, 10 Jan. [1861], Stevens Papers, DLC.

80. McClure to Ward Hill Lamon, Philadelphia, 8 May 1871, Jeremiah Black Papers, DLC; Alexander K. McClure, *Abraham Lincoln and Men of War-Times* (Philadelphia: Times, 1892), 157.

81. Medill to Horace White, Washington, 4 Jan. 1861, Charles H. Ray Papers, CSmH.

82. Seward to Weed, Washington, 21 Jan. 1861, Weed Papers, University of Rochester.

83. Lincoln to Simon Cameron, Springfield, 3 Jan. 1861, *CWL*, 4:170.

84. Trumbull to Lincoln, Washington, 20 Jan. 1861, AL MSS DLC.

85. Lincoln to Lyman Trumbull, Springfield, 7 Jan. 1861, *CWL*, 4:171.

86. Thomas J. McCormack, ed., *Memoirs of Gustave Koerner, 1809–1896* (2 vols.; Cedar Rapids, IA: Torch Press, 1909), 2:114.

87. Reynolds to McPherson, Springfield, 12 Jan. 1861, McPherson Papers, DLC.

88. Caleb B. Smith to David Davis, Washington, 5 Feb. 1861, David Davis Papers, IHi.

89. Fogg to Lincoln, Washington, 5 Feb. 1861, AL MSS DLC.

90. Tappan to Fogg, Washington, 5 Jan. 1861, Tappan Papers, New Hampshire Historical Society.

91. Lincoln to Cameron, Springfield, 13 Jan. 1861, enclosing a letter backdated 3 Jan. 1861, *CWL*, 4:174.

92. Ray to Washburne, n.p., Thursday [ca. 10 Jan. 1861], filed at the end of 1861, Elihu B. Washburne Papers, DLC.

93. Lincoln to Seward, Springfield, 12 Jan. 1861, *CWL*, 4:173.

94. Barney to William Cullen Bryant, Chicago, 17 Jan. 1861, Bryant-Godwin Papers, New York Public Library.

95. C. H. Ray to E. B. Washburne, Springfield, Illinois, 16 Jan. 1861, Washburne Papers, DLC; C. H. Ray to Lyman Trumbull, Springfield, Illinois, 16 Jan. [1861], Trumbull Papers, DLC.

96. Fogg to Lincoln, Washington, 2 Feb. 1861, draft, Fogg Papers, New Hampshire Historical Society.

97. Moorhead interview with Nicolay, Washington, 12–13 May 1880, in Burlingame, ed., *Oral History of Lincoln*, 41; Trumbull to Lincoln, Washington, 20 Jan. 1861, AL MSS DLC.

98. A. G. Riddle, *Recollections of War Times: Reminiscences of Men and Events in Washington, 1860–1865* (New York: G. P. Putnam's Sons, 1895), 179.

99. *CWL*, 4:180–181.

100. McClure to Thaddeus Stevens, Harrisburg, 21 Jan. [1861], Stevens Papers, DLC.

101. Herndon to Lyman Trumbull, Springfield, 27 Jan. 1861, Trumbull Papers, DLC.

102. William Butler to Lyman Trumbull, Springfield, 7 Feb. 1861, Trumbull Papers, DLC; William Larimer to Cameron, Pittsburgh, 6 Feb. 1861, Cameron Papers, DLC.

103. Albany *Evening Journal*, 9 Jan. 1861.

104. Fogg to Lincoln, Washington, 5 Feb. 1861, AL MSS DLC.

105. Blair to Mrs. Norman B. Judd, Silver Spring, Maryland, 20 Jan. 1861, Lincoln Collection, RPB.

106. *CWL*, 4:168.

107. Amos Tuck to Lincoln, Exeter, New Hampshire, 14 Jan. 1861, AL MSS DLC.

108. John D. Defrees to David Davis, Washington, 18 Jan. 1861, ibid.

109. William M. Wilson to Lincoln, Drake County, Ohio, 19 Jan. 1861; Benjamin Stanton to Lincoln, Washington, 12 Jan. 1861., ibid.

110. David Davis paraphrased in Jonathan Renick to Benjamin F. Wade, Circleville, Ohio, 17 Feb. 1861, Wade Papers, DLC.

111. J. W. Schuckers, *The Life and Public Services of Salmon Portland Chase* (New York: D. Appleton, 1874), 201.

112. Chase to James Shepherd Pike, Columbus, 10 Jan. 1861, Pike Papers, University of Maine.

113. C. H. Ray to E. B. Washburne, Springfield, 7 Jan. 1861, Elihu B. Washburne Papers, DLC.

114. Thomas D. Jones to William Linn McMillen, Springfield, 30 Dec. 1860, Lincoln Collection, Lilly Library, InU.

115. Hiram Barney to William Cullen Bryant, Chicago, 17 Jan. 1861, Bryant-Godwin Papers, New York Public Library; George S. Boutwell, *Reminiscences of Sixty Years in Public Affairs* (2 vols.; New York: McClure, Phillips, 1902), 1:275.

116. Chase to N. P. Banks, Springfield, 7 Jan. 1861 [misdated 1860], Abraham Lincoln Collection, Beinecke Library, Yale University; Chase to James T. Worthington, Columbus, 14 Jan. 1861, Lincoln Collection, RPB; Chase to Joshua Giddings, Columbus, 15 Dec. 1860, Giddings-Julian Papers, DLC.

117. Chase to Lizzie Pike, Columbus, 27 Jan. 1861, James S. Pike Papers, University of Maine.

118. Chase to John Jay, Columbus, 16 Jan. 1861, Jay Family Papers, Columbia University.

119. Washington correspondence by "Potomac," 21 Mar., Baltimore *Exchange*, 23 Mar. 1861.

120. Medill to Charles H. Ray, Washington, 13 Jan. 1861, Ray Papers, CSmH.

121. Medill to Colfax, ca. December 1862, in Hollister, *Colfax*, 200; Medill to E. B. Washburne, Chicago, 13 Jan. 1862, Washburne Papers, DLC.

122. Cincinnati *Commercial*, 7, 8, 12, 18 Jan. 1861.

123. Schuyler Colfax to [Alfred] Wheeler, [Washington], 11 Jan. 1861, Forest H. Sweet, manuscript dealer, list no. 89, clipping from an undated catalogue, David Rankin Barbee Papers, Georgetown University.

124. Gayle Thornbrough et al., eds., *The Diary of Calvin Fletcher* (7 vols.; Indianapolis: Indiana Historical Society, 1972–1981), 7:49 (entry for 19 Feb. 1861).

125. Josiah M. Lucas to Lincoln, Washington, 10 Jan. 1861, AL MSS DLC.

126. Springfield correspondence by Henry Villard, 10 Jan., Cincinnati *Commercial*, 14 Jan. 1861; Springfield correspondence by Henry Villard, 29 Dec. 1860, 12 Jan. 1861, New York *Herald*, 3, 18 Jan. 1861.

127. John D. Defrees to David Davis, Indianapolis, 26 Nov. 1860, Davis Papers, IHi.

128. James C. Veatch to Lincoln, Indianapolis, 18 Feb. 1861, AL MSS DLC.

129. Lincoln to Smith, Springfield, 26 May 1860, *CWL,* 4:55.

130. Jesse W. Weik, *The Real Lincoln: A Portrait,* ed. Michael Burlingame (1922; Lincoln: University of Nebraska Press, 2002), 294.

131. David Davis to Lincoln, Danville, 19 Nov. 1860, AL MSS DLC.

132. Springfield correspondence by Henry Villard, 31 Jan., New York *Herald,* 7 Feb. 1861.

133. John G. Nicolay, memorandum, 11 Dec. 1860, Burlingame, ed., *With Lincoln in the White House,* 15.

134. Israel Washburn to Elihu B. Washburne, Boston, 9 Feb. 1861, Washburn Papers, Washburn Family Library, Norlands, Maine.

135. W. M. Winslow to Lincoln, Muncie, 9 Jan. 1861, AL MSS DLC.

136. George W. Julian to Lincoln, n.p., 23 Jan. 1861, ibid.

137. Colfax to [Alfred] Wheeler, [Washington], 11 Jan. 1861, Forest H. Sweet, manuscript dealer, list no. 89, clipping from an undated catalogue, David Rankin Barbee Papers, Georgetown University.

138. Colfax to George Washburn, Washington, 26 Dec. 1860, George Washburn Papers, Western Reserve Historical Society, Cleveland.

139. Colfax to Charles M. Heaton, Washington, 12, 27 Dec. 1860, 8 Jan., 7, 16 Feb. 1861, Colfax Papers, Northern Indiana Center for History, South Bend.

140. Swett to Lincoln, Washington, 31 Dec. 1860, AL MSS DLC.

141. Swett to Lincoln, Washington 5 Jan. 1861, ibid.

142. Richard C. Parsons to John Sherman, Cleveland, 12 Dec. 1860, John Sherman Papers, DLC.

143. Undated memo by Welles, Lincoln's Cabinet Collection, LMF.

144. Summary of a letter from William Butler, who had spoken with Lincoln, to Judd, n.p., n.d., in Judd to Lyman Trumbull, Chicago, 3 Jan. 1861, Trumbull Papers, DLC.

145. "Lincoln's Time of Agony," reminiscences of Joseph Gillespie, Springfield correspondence, 2 Feb., New York *Tribune,* 5 Feb. 1888.

146. Judd to Lyman Trumbull, Chicago, 24 Dec. 1860, Trumbull Papers, DLC.

147. Swett to Lamon, Bloomington, 7 Apr. 1861, Ward Hill Lamon, *Recollections of Abraham Lincoln, 1847–1865,* ed. Dorothy Lamon Teillard (2nd ed.; Washington, DC: Privately published, 1911), 318.

148. Barnes, *Autobiography of Weed,* 611.

149. Joseph Medill to Norman B. Judd, Washington, 20 Jan. 1861, Medill Papers, ICHi.

150. *CWL,* 4:161.

151. Charles Eugene Hamlin, *The Life and Times of Hannibal Hamlin* (Cambridge, MA: Riverside Press, 1899), 370.

152. Andrew to Lincoln, Boston, 20 Jan. 1861, copy, Andrew Papers, MHi.

153. George S. Boutwell to Banks, Boston, 8 Mar. 1861, Banks Papers, IHi.

154. Reminiscences of George B. Loring, New York *Tribune,* 9 Aug. 1885.

155. Gideon Welles, "Recollections in Regard to the Formation of Mr Lincoln's Cabinet," undated manuscript, Abraham Lincoln Collection, Beinecke Library, Yale University.

156. Washington correspondence, 11 Feb., New York *Times,* 12 Feb. 1861.

157. Lincoln to Lyman Trumbull, Springfield, 24 Dec. 1860, *CWL,* 4:162.

158. John Covode to Lincoln, Washington, 16 Jan. 1861, AL MSS DLC; Frank Blair to Henry L. Dawes, St. Louis, 9 Feb. 1861, Dawes Papers, DLC.

159. Henry Winter Davis to Samuel Francis du Pont, [Washington], 20 Feb. 1861, transcript, S. F. Du Pont Papers, Hagley Museum, Wilmington, Delaware.

160. Lincoln to Seward, Springfield, 3 Jan. 1861, *CWL,* 4:170.

161. Preston King to John Bigelow, Washington, 21 Dec. 1860, John Bigelow, *Retrospections of an Active Life* (5 vols.; New York: Baker & Taylor, 1909–1913), 1:318.

162. Washington correspondence by Henry Adams, 31 Jan., Boston *Daily Advertiser,* 2 Feb. 1861.

163. Seward to his wife, Washington, 18 Jan. 1861, Seward, *Seward at Washington,* 1:497.

164. Charles Francis Adams, Jr., to Richard Henry Dana, 28 Feb. 1861, Dana Papers, MHi.

165. Seward to his wife, Washington, 23 Jan. 1861, Seward, *Seward at Washington,* 1:497.

166. Seward to his wife, Washington, 3 Jan. 1861, ibid., 1:491.

167. Seward to his wife, Washington, 13 Jan. 1861, ibid., 1:496.

168. Henry Adams to Charles Francis Adams, Jr., Washington, 17 Jan. 1861, J. C. Levenson, ed., *Letters of Henry Adams* (6 vols.; Cambridge, MA: Harvard University Press, 1982–1988), 1:223.

169. Charles Francis Adams diary, 15 Jan. 1861, Adams Family Papers, MHi.

170. Carl Schurz to his wife, Springfield, 9 Feb. 1861, Joseph Schafer, ed., *Intimate Letters of Carl Schurz, 1841–1869* (Madison: State Historical Society of Wisconsin, 1928), 247.

171. Lyons to John Russell, Washington, 4 Feb. 1861, James J. Barnes and Patience P. Barnes, eds., *The American Civil War Through British Eyes: Dispatches from British Diplomats* (Kent, Ohio: Kent State University Press, 2003), 28.

172. Weed to Seward, Albany, 9 Jan. 1861, Seward Papers, University of Rochester.

173. Seward to Lincoln, Washington, 26 Dec. 1860, AL MSS DLC.

174. Charles Francis Adams diary, 21 Dec. 1860, Adams Family Papers, MHi.

175. Henry Adams, *The Great Secession Winter of 1860–61, and Other Essays,* ed. George Hochfield (New York: Sagamore Press, 1958), 18.

176. Adams to Richard Henry Dana, Washington, 9 Feb. 1861, Dana Papers, MHi.

177. Mason Tappan to George G. Fogg, Washington, 30 Dec. 1860, Tappan Papers, New Hampshire Historical Society.

178. Washington correspondence, 7 Jan., New York *Tribune,* 9 Jan. 1861.

179. James Harlan to William Penn Clarke, Washington, 26 Jan. 1861, Clarke Papers, State Historical Society of Iowa, Des Moines.

180. Charles B. Sedgwick to Israel Washburn, Washington, 25 Jan. 1861, Gaillard Hunt, *Israel, Elihu and Cadwallader Washburn: A Chapter in American Biography* (New York: Macmillan, 1925), 91–92.

181. William M. Browne to S. L. M. Barlow, Washington 14 Jan. 1861, Barlow Papers, CSmH.

182. Stevens to Chase, Washington, 3 Feb. 1861, Beverly Wilson Palmer, ed., *The Selected Papers of Thaddeus Stevens* (2 vols.; Pittsburgh: University of Pittsburgh Press, 1997–1998), 1:200.

183. Mrs. George Schuyler to [Henry W. Bellows], n. p., n.d., Bellow Papers, MHi.

184. George G. Fogg to Gideon Welles, Cincinnati, 27 Jan. 1861, Welles Papers, IHi; Lincoln to Seward, Springfield, 19 Jan. 1861, *CWL,* 4:176.

185. *Illinois State Journal* (Springfield), 6 Feb. 1861.

186. Springfield correspondence, 19 Jan., *Missouri Democrat* (St. Louis), 21 Jan. 1861, in Michael Burlingame, ed., *Lincoln's Journalist: John Hay's Anonymous Writings for the Press, 1860–1864* (Carbondale: Southern Illinois University Press, 1998), 19.

187. Seward to Lincoln, Washington, 27 Jan. 1861, AL MSS DLC.

188. Lincoln to Seward, Springfield, 1 Feb. 1861, *CWL,* 4:183.

189. Springfield correspondence by Henry Villard, 6 Jan., New York *Herald,* 10 Jan. 1861.

190. *Missouri Democrat* (St. Louis), 8 Jan. 1861.

191. *Illinois State Journal* (Springfield), 24 Jan. 1861.

192. Springfield correspondence by Henry Villard, 21, 26 Jan., Cincinnati *Commercial,* 25,

29 Jan. 1861; Springfield correspondence by Henry Villard, 22 Jan., New York *Herald,* 23 Jan. 1861.

193. Chattanooga *Gazette,* n.d., copied in the New York *World,* 28 Nov. 1860.

194. *Illinois State Journal* (Springfield), n.d., quoted in the *Illinois State Register* (Springfield), 1 Feb. 1861.

195. Adams, *Secession Winter,* 25.

196. Sherman to Frank Blair, Washington, 9 Feb. 1861, Blair Papers, DLC.

197. Henry Adams to Charles Francis Adams, Jr., Washington, 24 Jan. 1861, in Levenson, ed., *Letters of Henry Adams,* 1:225.

198. Washington correspondence by James Shepherd Pike, 24 Jan., New York *Tribune,* 26 Jan. 1861.

199. Washington correspondence by Observer, 27 Feb., New York *Times,* 1 Mar. 1861.

200. Charles Sumner to John A. Andrew, Washington, 18 Jan. 1861, Andrew Papers, MHi.

201. Henry Winter Davis to Samuel Francis Du Pont, [Washington], 14 Feb. 1861, transcript, S. F. Du Pont Papers, Hagley Museum, Wilmington, Delaware.

202. Undated letter in Seward, *Seward at Washington,* 1:502.

203. Henry Adams to Charles Francis Adams, Jr., Washington, 8 Feb. 1861, in Levenson, ed., *Letters of Henry Adams,* 1:230.

204. Adams, *Secession Winter,* 24.

205. Seward to his wife, [Washington, 15 Feb. 1861], Seward, *Seward at Washington,* 1:505.

206. William C. Rives to William C. Rives, Jr., 27 Jan. 1861, W. C. Rives Papers, DLC.

207. David Donald, *Charles Sumner and the Rights of Man* (New York: Alfred A. Knopf, 1970), 20.

208. Varina Davis, *Jefferson Davis, Ex-President of the Confederate States of America: A Memoir by His Wife* (New York: Belford, 1890), 581.

209. Montgomery Blair to Gideon Welles, Washington, 17 May 1873, Welles Papers, DLC.

210. James Lyons to Allen B. Magruder, White Sulphur Springs, West Virginia, 21 Aug. 1875, *Southern Historical Society Papers* 7:354–355.

211. Fogg to Lincoln, Washington, 2 Feb. 1861, draft, Fogg Papers, New Hampshire Historical Society.

212. William Jayne to Lyman Trumbull, Springfield, 28 Jan. 1861, Trumbull Papers, DLC.

213. *Illinois State Journal* (Springfield), 30 Jan. 1861.

214. William Jayne to Lyman Trumbull, Springfield, 2 Feb. 1861, Trumbull Papers, DLC.

215. Theodore Calvin Pease and James G. Randall, eds., *The Diary of Orville Hickman Browning* (2 vols.; Springfield: Illinois State Historical Library, 1925–1933), 1:453 (entry for 9 Feb. 1861).

216. Godlove Orth to Oliver P. Morton, Washington, 21 Feb. 1861, William Dudley Foulke Papers, Indiana State Library, Indianapolis.

217. John G. Nicolay, memorandum, 22 Dec. 1860, Burlingame, ed., *With Lincoln in the White House,* 21.

218. J[ames] H. v[an] A[len] to Horace Greeley, St. Louis, 21 Dec. 1860, Greeley Papers, New York Public Library.

219. Horace White to Edward L. Pierce, n.p., n.d., quoted in Pierce to Charles Sumner, Boston, 3 Jan. 1861, Sumner Papers, Harvard University.

220. Sidney Webster to Caleb Cushing, New York, 5 Jan. 1861, Caleb Cushing Papers, DLC.

221. John Pendleton Kennedy to Phillips C. Pendleton, Baltimore, 10 Feb. 1861, copy, Kennedy Letterbooks, Enoch Pratt Free Library, Baltimore.

222. Morgan Dix, ed., *Memoirs of John Adams Dix* (2 vols.; New York: Harper & Brothers, 1883) 1:345.

223. Lincoln to E. B. Washburne, Springfield, 21 Dec. 1860, *CWL,* 4:159.

224. Lincoln to F. P. Blair Sr., Springfield, 21 Dec. 1860, ibid., 4:157.

225. Washington correspondence, 6 Jan., New York *Herald,* 7 Jan. 1861.

226. Simon Cameron to Lincoln, Washington, 3 Jan. 1861, AL MSS DLC.

227. Scott to Lincoln, Washington, 4 Jan. 1861, ibid.

228. Jesse W. Weik, "How Lincoln Was Convinced of General Scott's Loyalty," *Century Magazine,* Feb. 1911, 594.

229. Wilson and Davis, eds., *Herndon's Lincoln,* 286–287.

230. *Illinois State Journal* (Springfield), 25 Dec. 1860.

231. Springfield correspondence by Henry Villard, 23 Dec., New York *Herald,* 27 Dec. 1860.

232. Springfield correspondence by T. W., 7 Feb., *Missouri Democrat* (St. Louis), 8 Feb. 1861.

233. A. H. Chapman to Lincoln, Charleston, Illinois, 3 Jan. 1861, National Archives, Washington, DC.

234. Wilson and Davis, eds., *Herndon's Lincoln,* 289–290.

235. Dall, "Journal of a tour through Illinois, Wisconsin and Ohio, Oct. & Nov. 1866," entry for 29 Oct. 1866, Dall Papers, Bryn Mawr College.

236. Elhanan J. Searle, a student in the Lincoln-Herndon law office, observed this episode, which his son, Judge Charles J. Searle, recounted to Joseph B. Oakleaf. Oakleaf memorandum, 14 Feb. 1925, Oakleaf Papers, InU.

237. Nathan Allen diary, entry for 1 Feb. 1861, Missouri Historical Society.

238. "Lincoln's Time of Agony," reminiscences of Joseph Gillespie, Springfield correspondence, 2 Feb., New York *Tribune,* 5 Feb. 1888.

239. W. H. L. Wallace to his wife Ann, Springfield, 11 Jan. 1861, Wallace-Dickey Papers, IHi.

240. Koerner to Lyman Trumbull, Belleville, 21 Jan. 1861, Trumbull Papers, DLC.

241. Jones's recollections in Cincinnati *Commercial,* 18 Oct. 1871, in John G. Nicolay, "Lincoln's Personal Appearance," *Century Magazine* 42 (1891): 933.

242. "Lincoln's Time of Agony," reminiscences of Joseph Gillespie, Springfield correspondence, 2 Feb., New York *Tribune,* 5 Feb. 1888.

243. James C. Conkling to Clinton L. Conkling, Springfield, 12 February 1861, in Pratt ed., *Concerning Mr. Lincoln,* 50.

244. *CWL,* 4:190.

245. Springfield correspondence, 11 February, New York *Tribune,* 12 February 1861.

246. *Illinois State Journal* (Springfield), 12 February 1861.

247. New York *World,* 12 February 1861; Chicago *Press and Tribune,* 23 February 1861.

248. *Congressional Globe,* 38th Congress, 1st session, 1198 (19 March 1864).

INDEX

Entries for newspapers may appear under the newspaper's title or the place of publication.

Lincoln, Abraham (AL): Law Practice (*cont'd.*)
—in Springfield: between 1849-1854, 309–62;
between 1858-1860, 559–77; anger, 348–51;
appellate lawyer, 334–41; clients, 132–37,
311–13, 349–50; divorce cases, 314–15; duel,
137–38, 190–94; Graham as mentor, 65–66,
77, 101; income from service fees, 132–33,
332–34, 339, 435–38; judge and lobbyist,
351–52; junior partners, 311; law partnership
with Herndon, 89, 229–30, 311, 318–21,
333–34, 338, 560; law partnership with
Logan, 184–89, 317, 333, 341; law partnership
with Stuart, 62, 131–35, 351; libel and slander
cases, 313–14; license to practice law, 131; life
on circuit, 132–37, 186–87, 222–24, 322–32;
mentors, 62, 65–66, 77, 89, 95–97, 101,
346–48; murder cases, 341–46; negligence,
355; offices, 310–11, 354–55; patent cases,
339–41, 444; railroad cases, 334–41, 437–38;
reputation, 352–57; start, 128–29; Stuart as
mentor, 62, 89, 95–97, 116, 347; trial lawyer,
315–22
Marriage and Domestic Life:
—general, 168; Browne officiated, 195; after
ceremony, 196; death conversations, 196;
move to Washington, 253–56; practical
advantages of, 197; speculations about, 196;
wedding party, 194–95
—as parent: care of children, 219; indulgent, 254
—relations with MTL: ambitions, 211–12, 213;
applied for pension, 206; bad temper, 201–3,
206, 210–11; domestic chores, 219–20; harsh
discipline of children, 203–4; "home was
hell," 222–24; in-laws, 207; left house in
search of peace and quiet, 204–7, 208; life at
Globe Tavern, 218–20; after marriage,
200–201; money matters, 207–8; not a good
cook or hostess, 208; penuriousness, 208–9;
physically abused AL, 203; Springfield
house, 218, 220–24, 253, 339–40
New Salem Years, 52; attended debating
society meetings, 65–66; boatman, 52–57, 59,
66–67; humorist and jack-of-all-trades,
52–57, 60, 82–83; self-education, 62–67;
sewed eyes of hogs, 56; sight of slavery at
New Orleans, 56–57
—Black Hawk War: conducted spy missions
during, 68; enlistment of, 67; friendships and
social life of, 68–69, 79–80, 89; popularity
of, 69–70; reenlistments of, 68; route home
after discharge by, 71; service in, 67–71;
tours, 67–68; witnessed horrors during,
67–68
—merchant and storekeeper, 57; in business
with Berry, 75–77; clerked for Offutt, 58,
59–62, 66, 76; free time, 61; indebtedness,
76–77; liquor sales, 76; popularity, 60; room

and board, 76–77; warehousing business,
66–67
—postmaster and surveyor: appointment and
accounts as postmaster, 77–78; completed
surveys, 80–81; creditor's judgment against,
81; delivered letters, 78; duties, 77–78; hired
as surveyor's assistant, 78–79; lodging, 80–81;
neglected duties, 101; personal finances,
78–79, 81; surveyor's duties, 79
Poetry:
—about Grigsby, W., 46–47; *Charity* (Cowper),
255–56; *The Cotter's Saturday Night* (Burns),
65; *Elegant Extracts, or Useful and Entertaining Passages from the Best English Authors and
Translations* (Bryant), 255; *Elegy Written in
a Country Church Yard* (Gray), 65; *Essay on
Man* (Pope), 41, 64; *The Fire-Worshippers*
(Moore), 246; *The Grave* (Blair), 255; *Holy
Willie's Prayer* (Burns), 84; *The Inquiry*
(Mackay), 243–44; *Lara* (Byron), 65; *The Last
Leaf* (Holmes), 245; *Little Eddie*, 359; Little
Pigeon Creek, 23; *Mortality* (Knox), 241; *My
Childhood Home I See Again*, 241–42; in New
Salem, 64–65; personal, 241–43, 246–47; *On
Receipt of my Mother's Picture* (Cowper), 26;
Thanatopsis (Bryant), 255
Politics:
—debates, 63–64, 65–66; 1840 presidential
debates, 149–52; with Calhoun, 225–26,
375–76; with Douglas, S.A., 337, 491–92,
568–71; first Douglas, S.A.'s (Ottawa), 63,
484, 486–97; second Douglas, S.A.'s
(Freeport), 484, 500–511; third Douglas,
S.A.'s (Jonesboro), 484, 511–16; fourth
Douglas, S.A.'s (Charleston), 484, 516–25;
fifth Douglas, S.A.'s (Galesburg), 484,
530–34; sixth Douglas, S.A.'s (Quincy), 484,
534–37; seventh Douglas, S.A.'s (Alton), 484,
537–45; garbling of, 497–500; with May,
226–27; pro-tariff, 225–27; religion, 238–39;
slavery, 260, 376–90
—legislation and platforms: 1832 platform, 97;
1837 special legislative session, 113–14,
137–38; 1838-1840, 138–67; 1840 special
legislative session, 161–65; appetite for,
88–89; Bank of Illinois, 113–14; Bank of the
United States, 96, 150–52; Dred Scott
decision, 438–42, 464; economic issues,
247–49; education, 72; freshman legislator,
92–97; Illinois and Michigan Canal
construction, 82, 96, 101–3, 111, 137, 147,
164–65, 309–10, 397; immigration, 227–28;
internal improvement bill, 72, 114–22,
143–45, 147–48; jurisdiction of justices of
peace, 95; land proposals, 144–45; New
Salem county divisions, 81–82, 145–46;
opposition to improve breed of cattle, 103;